ST. JAMES ENCYCLOPEDIA OF
POPULARCULTURE

ST. JAMES ENCYCLOPEDIA OF
POPULARCULTURE

VOLUME 2: E-J

EDITORS: Tom Pendergast   Sara Pendergast

with an introduction by Jim Cullen

ST. JAMES PRESS

AN IMPRINT OF THE GALE GROUP

DETROIT • SAN FRANCISCO • LONDON
BOSTON • WOODBRIDGE, CT

Tom Pendergast, Sara Pendergast, *Editors*

Michael J. Tyrkus, *Project Coordinator*

Laura Standley Berger, Joann Cerrito, Dave Collins,
Steve Cusack, Nicolet V. Elert, Miranda Ferrara, Jamie FitzGerald,
Kristin Hart, Laura S. Kryhoski, Margaret Mazurkiewicz
St. James Press Staff

Peter M. Gareffa, *Managing Editor, St. James Press*

Maria Franklin, *Permissions Manager*
Kimberly F. Smilay, *Permissions Specialist*
Kelly A. Quin, *Permissions Associate*
Erin Bealmear, Sandy Gore, *Permissions Assistants*
Mary Grimes, Leitha Etheridge-Sims, *Image Catalogers*

Mary Beth Trimper, *Composition Manager*
Dorothy Maki, *Manufacturing Manager*
Wendy Blurton, *Senior Buyer*

Cynthia Baldwin, *Product Design Manager*
Martha Schiebold, *Graphic Artist*

Randy Bassett, *Image Database Supervisor*
Robert Duncan, Michael Logusz, *Imaging Specialists*
Pamela A. Reed, *Imaging Coordinator*

Library of Congress Cataloging-in-Publication Data
St. James Encyclopedia of Popular Culture / with an introduction by Jim Cullen; editors,
Tom Pendergast and Sara Pendergast.
    p. cm.
    Includes bibliographical references and index.
    ISBN 1-558-62400-7 (set) — ISBN 1-558-62401-5 (v.1) — ISBN 1-558-62402-3 (v.2) —
    ISBN 1-558-62403-1 (v.3) — ISBN 1-558-62404-x (v.4) — ISBN 1-558-62405-8 (v. 5)
    1. United States—Civilization—20th century—Encyclopedias. 2. Popular culture—United
States—History—20th century—Encyclopedias. I. Pendergast, Tom. II. Pendergast, Sara.
E169.1.S764 1999
973.9 21—dc21   99-046540

Printed in the United States of America

St. James Press is an imprint of Gale Group
Gale Group and Design is a trademark used herein under license

10 9 8 7 6 5 4 3

CONTENTS

EDITOR'S NOTE

Thirty some years ago Ray Browne and several of his colleagues provided a forum for the academic study of popular culture by forming first the *Journal of Popular Culture* and later the Popular Culture Association and the Center for the Study of Popular Culture at Bowling Green State University. Twenty some years ago Thomas Inge thought the field of popular culture studies well enough established to put together the first edition of his *Handbook of Popular Culture*. In the years since, scholars and educators from many disciplines have published enough books, gathered enough conferences, and gained enough institutional clout to make popular culture studies one of the richest fields of academic study at the close of the twentieth century. Thirty, twenty, in some places even ten years ago, to study popular culture was to be something of a pariah; today, the study of popular culture is accepted and even respected in departments of history, literature, communications, sociology, film studies, etc. throughout the United States and throughout the world, and not only in universities, but in increasing numbers of high schools. Thomas Inge wrote in the introduction to the second edition of his *Handbook*: "The serious and systematic study of popular culture may be the most significant and potentially useful of the trends in academic research and teaching in the last half of this century in the United States."[2] It is to this thriving field of study that we hope to contribute with the *St. James Encyclopedia of Popular Culture*.

The *St. James Encyclopedia of Popular Culture* includes over 2,700 essays on all elements of popular culture in the United States in the twentieth century. But what is "popular culture?" Academics have offered a number of answers over the years. Historians Norman F. Cantor and Michael S. Werthman suggested that "popular culture may be seen as all those things man does and all those artifacts he creates for their own sake, all that diverts his mind and body from the sad business of life."[1] Michael Bell argues that:

> At its simplest popular culture is the culture of mass appeal. A creation is popular when it is created to respond to the experiences and values of the majority, when it is produced in such a way that the majority have easy access to it, and when it can be understood and interpreted by that majority without the aid of special knowledge or experience.[3]

While tremendously useful, both of these definitions tend to exclude more than they embrace. Was the hot dog created for its own sake, as a diversion? Probably not, but we've included an essay on it in this collection. Were the works of Sigmund Freud in any way shaped for the majority? No, but Freud's ideas—borrowed, twisted, and reinterpreted—have shaped novels, films, and common speech in ways too diffuse to ignore. Thus we have included an essay on Freud's impact on popular culture. Our desire to bring together the greatest number of cultural phenomena impacting American culture in this century has led us to prefer Ray Browne's rather broader early definition of popular culture as "all the experiences in life shared by people in common, generally though not necessarily disseminated by the mass media."[4]

Coverage

In order to amass a list of those cultural phenomena that were widely disseminated and experienced by people in relatively unmediated form we asked a number of scholars, teachers, librarians, and archivists to serve as advisors. Each of our 20 advisors provided us with a list of over 200 topics from their field of specialty that they considered important enough to merit an essay; several of our advisors provided us with lists much longer than that. Their collective lists numbered nearly 4,000 potential essay topics, and we winnowed this list down to the number that is now gathered in this collection. We sought balance (but not equal coverage) between the major areas of popular culture: film; music; print culture; social life; sports; television and radio; and art and perfomance (which includes theatre, dance, stand-up comedy, and other live performance). For those interested, the breakdown of coverage is as follows: social life, 23 percent (a category which covers everything from foodways to fashion, holidays to hairstyles); music, 16 percent; print culture, 16 percent; film, 15 percent; television and radio, 14 percent; sports, 10 percent; and art and performance, 6 percent. A variety of considerations led us to skew the coverage of the book in favor of the second half of the century. The massive popularity of television and recorded music, the mass-marketing of popular fiction, and the national attention given to professional sports are historical factors contributing to the emphasis on post-World War II culture, but we have also considered the needs of high school and undergraduate users in distributing entries in this way.

The Entries

The entries in this volume vary in length from brief (75 to 150-word) introductions to the topic to in-depth 3,000-word explorations. No matter the length, we have asked our contributors to do two things in each entry: to describe the topic and to analyze its significance in and relevance to American popular culture. While we hope that users will find the basic factual information they need concerning the topic in an entry, it was even more important to us that each user gain some perspective on the cultural context in which the topic has importance. Thus the entry on MTV, for example, chronicles the channel's rise to world popularity, but also analyzes the relationship between MTV, youth culture, and consumerism. The entry on John Ford, while tracing the outlines of the film director's long career, assesses the impact Ford's films have had on the film Western and on Americans' very perceptions of the West. Given the brevity of the entries, we chose to emphasize analysis of a topic's contribution to popular culture over a full presentation of biographical/historical information. The entry on World War I, for example, offers an analysis of how the war was understood in popular film, print culture, and propaganda rather than a blow-by-blow description of the actual military conflict.

Entries are accompanied by a list of further readings. These readings are meant to provide the user with readily accessible sources that provide more information on the specific topic. As befits a multimedia age, these "further readings" come not just from books and magazines, but also from albums, liner notes, films, videos, and web sites. Users of the Internet know well the perils of trusting the information found on the World Wide Web; there are as yet few filters to help browsers sift the useful from the absurd. We cited web sites when they provided information that was unavailable in any other known form and when our reasonable efforts to determine the veracity of the information led us to believe that the information provided was valid and useful. We have occasionally provided links to "official" web sites of performers or organizations, for the same reason that we provide citations to autobiographies. All web links cited were accurate as of the date indicated in the citation.

Organization and Indexing

Entries are arranged alphabetically by the name under which the topic is best known. For topics which might reasonably be sought out under differing names, we have provided in-text cross references. For example, a user seeking an entry on Huddie Ledbetter will be referred to the entry on Leadbelly, and a user seeking an entry on Larry Flynt will be referred to the entry on *Hustler* magazine. Far more powerful than the cross references, however, are the indexes provided in the fifth volume of the collection. The general index is by far the most powerful, for it leads the user searching for information on Humphrey Bogart, for example, to the entries on Lauren Bacall, *Casablanca, The Maltese Falcon, The African Queen,* and several other entries that contain substantive information about Bogie. Equally powerful is the subject index, a list of categories under which we listed all pertinent entries. Consulting the subject index listing for Sex Symbols, for example, will lead the user to entries on Marilyn Monroe, the Varga Girl, *Playboy* magazine, David Cassidy, Mae West, and a long entry on the Sex Symbol, among others. Finally, a time index, organized by decades, provides a list of the entries that concern each decade of the twentieth century. Those entries that concern nineteenth-century topics are indexed by the first decade of the twentieth century.

We encourage readers to use the indexes to discover the fascinating intertwinings that have made the development of popular culture in the twentieth century such a vital field of study. Using the indexes, it is possible to uncover the story of how the American humor that was first made popular on the vaudeville stage evolved into first the radio comedies that entertained so many Americans during the Depression and War years and later the sitcoms that have kept Americans glued to their television screens for the last 50 years. That story is here, in the entries on Vaudeville, the Sitcom, *Amos 'n' Andy,* and the many other programs and comedians that have defined this tradition. A teacher who wishes students to uncover the similarities between sitcoms of the 1950s, 1960s, 1970s, 1980s, and 1990s might well ask the students to use this collection to begin their research into such comedies. Similarly, a teacher who asks students to explore the cross-pollination between musical genres will find that the indexes reveal the mixing of "race music," rhythm and blues, gospel, soul, and rock 'n' roll. It is hoped that this collection will be of particular use to those instructors of high school and undergraduate courses who challenge their students to discover the real cultural complexity of the music, films, magazines, and television shows that they take for granted. This collection should also be of use to those more advanced scholars who are beginning new research into an area of popular culture or who are looking for some context in which to place their existing research.

Acknowledgments

The *St. James Encyclopedia of Popular Culture* represents the work of hundreds of people, and we owe our thanks to all of them. We have had the privilege of working with 20 advisors whose experience, knowledge, and wisdom have truly helped shape the contents of this collection. Each of our advisors helped us to discover hidden corners of popular culture that we would not have considered on our own, and the breadth of coverage in this collection is a tribute to their collective knowledge. Several of our advisors deserve special thanks: Paul Buhle, George Carney, B. Lee Cooper, Jerome Klinkowitz, and Ron Simon all showed an extraordinary level of commitment and helpfulness.

It has been a pleasure to work with the nearly 450 contributors to this collection; we've appreciated their expertise, their professionalism, and their good humor. Several of our contributors deserve special mention for the quality of their contributions to this collection: Jacob Appel, Tim Berg, Pat Broeske, Richard Digby-Junger, Jeffrey Escoffier, Bryan Garman, Tina Gianoulis, Milton Goldin, Ian Gordon, Ron Goulart, Justin Gustainis, Preston Jones, Robyn Karney, Deborah Mix, Leonard Moore, Edward Moran, Victoria Price, Bob Schnakenberg, Steven Schneider, Charles Shindo, Robert Sickels, Wendy Woloson, and Brad Wright. Our team of copyeditors helped us bring a uniformity of presentation to the writings of this mass of contributors, and spotted and corrected innumerable small errors. Heidi Hagen, Robyn Karney, Edward Moran, and Tim Seul deserve special thanks for the quality and quantity of their work; we truly couldn't have done it without them. The contributors and copyeditors provided us with the material to build this collection, but it has been the editors' responsibility to ensure its accuracy and reliability. We welcome any corrections and comments; please write to: The Editors, *St. James Encyclopedia of Popular Culture,* St. James Press, 27500 Drake Road, Farmington Hills, MI 48331-3535.

Gathering the photos for this collection was an enormous task, and we were helped immeasurably by the knowledgeable and efficient staff at several photo agencies. We'd like to thank Marcia Schiff at AP/Wide World Photos; Eric Young at Archive Photos; and Kevin Rettig at Corbis Images. Lisa Hartjens of ImageFinders, Inc. also helped us acquire a number of photos.

We would like to thank Shelly Andrews, Anne Boyd, Melissa Doig, Tina Gianoulis, Heidi Hagen, Robyn Karney, Edward Moran, Victoria Price, Rebecca Saulsbury, Tim Seul, and Mark Swartz for their careful copyediting of the entries.

At the St. James Press, we'd like to thank Mike Tyrkus for his good humor and efficiency in helping us see this project to completion; Peter Gareffa for his usual wise and benevolent leadership; Janice Jorgensen for helping us shape this project at the beginning; the permissions department for smiling as we piled the photos on; and the staff at the St. James Press for their careful proofreading and for all their work in turning so many computer files into the volumes you see today.

Finally, we'd like to thank Lee Van Wormer for his sage management advice and our children, Conrad and Louisa, for their warm morning cuddles and for the delightful artwork that adorns our office walls.

—Tom Pendergast and Sara Pendergast,
Editors

NOTES

1. Cantor, Norman F. and Michael S. Werthman. *The History of Popular Culture to 1815.* New York, Macmillan, 1968, xxiv.
2. Inge, M. Thomas, editor. *Handbook of American Popular Culture.* 2nd edition. Westport, Connecticut, Greenwood Press, 1989, xxiii.
3. Bell, Michael. "The Study of Popular Culture," in *Concise Histories of American Popular Culture,* ed. Inge, M. Thomas. Westport, Connecticut, Greenwood Press, 1982, 443.
4. Browne, Ray B. *Popular Culture and the Expanding Consciousness.* New York, Wiley, 1973, 6.

INTRODUCTION

The Art of Everyday Life

Sometimes, when I'm wandering in an art museum looking at the relics of an ancient civilization, I find myself wondering how a future society would represent a defunct American culture. What objects would be chosen—or would survive—to be placed on display? Would I agree with a curator's choices? Were I to choose the items that some future American Museum of Art should exhibit to represent twentieth-century American culture, here are some I would name: an Elvis Presley record; a Currier & Ives print; a movie still from *Casablanca*. To put it a different way, my priority would *not* be to exhibit fragments of an urban cathedral, a painted landscape, or a formal costume. I wouldn't deny such objects could be important artifacts of American culture, or that they belong in a gallery. But in my avowedly biased opinion, the most vivid documents of American life—the documents that embody its possibilities and limits—are typically found in its popular culture.

Popular culture, of course, is not an American invention, and it has a vibrant life in many contemporary societies. But in few, if any, of those societies has it been as central to a notion of national character at home as well as abroad. For better or worse, it is through icons like McDonald's (the quintessential American cuisine), the Western (a uniquely American narrative genre), and Oprah Winfrey (a classic late-twentieth century embodiment of the American Dream) that this society is known—and is likely to be remembered.

It has sometimes been remarked that unlike nations whose identities are rooted in geography, religion, language, blood, or history, the United States was founded on a democratic ideal—a notion of life, liberty, and the pursuit of happiness elaborated in the Declaration of Independence. That ideal has been notoriously difficult to realize, and one need only take a cursory look at many aspects of American life—its justice system, electoral politics, residential patterns, labor force, et. al.—to see how far short it has fallen.

American popular culture is a special case. To be sure, it evinces plenty of the defects apparent in other areas of our national life, among them blatant racism and crass commercialism. If nothing else, such flaws can be taken as evidence of just how truly representative it is. There is nevertheless an openness and vitality about pop culture—its appeal across demographic lines; its interplay of individual voices and shared communal experience; the relatively low access barriers for people otherwise marginalized in U.S. society—that give it real legitimacy as the art of democracy. Like it or hate it, few dispute its centrality.

This sense of openness and inclusion—as well as the affection and scorn it generated—has been apparent from the very beginning. In the prologue of the 1787 play *The Contrast* (whose title referred to the disparity between sturdy republican ideals and effete monarchical dissipation), American playwright Royall Tyler invoked a cultural sensibility where "proud titles of 'My Lord! Your Grace/To the humble 'Mr.' and plain 'Sir' give place." Tyler, a Harvard graduate, Revolutionary War officer, and Chief Justice of the Vermont Supreme Court, was in some sense an unlikely prophet of popular culture. But the sensibility he voiced—notably in his beloved character Jonathon, a prototype for characters from Davy Crockett to John Wayne—proved durable for centuries to come.

For much of early American history, however, artists and critics continued to define aesthetic success on European terms, typically invoking elite ideals of order, balance, and civilization. It was largely taken for granted that the most talented practitioners of fine arts, such as painters Benjamin West and John Singleton Copley, would have to go abroad to train, produce, and exhibit their most important work. To the extent that newer cultural forms—like the novel, whose very name suggests its place in late eighteenth- and early nineteenth-century western civilization—were noted at all, it was usually in disparaging terms. This was especially true of novels written and read by women, such as Susanna Rowson's widely read *Charlotte Temple* (1791). Sermons against novels were common; Harvard devoted its principal commencement address in 1803 to the dangers of fiction.

The industrialization of the United States has long been considered a watershed development in many realms of American life, and popular culture is no exception. Indeed, its importance is suggested in the very definition of popular culture coined by cultural historian Lawrence Levine: "the folklore of industrial society." Industrialization allowed the mass-reproduction and dissemination of formerly local traditions, stories, and art forms across the continent, greatly intensifying the spread—and development—of culture by, for, and of the people. At a time when North America remained geographically and politically fragmented, magazines, sheet music, dime novels, lithographs, and other print media stitched it together.

This culture had a characteristic pattern. Alexis de Tocqueville devoted 11 chapters of his classic 1835-40 masterpiece *Democracy in America* to the art, literature, and language of the United States, arguing that they reflected a democratic ethos that required new standards of evaluation. ''The inhabitants of the United States have, at present, properly speaking, no literature,'' he wrote. This judgment, he made clear, arose from a definition of literature that came from aristocratic societies like his own. In its stead, he explained, Americans sought books ''which may be easily procured, quickly read, and which require no learned researches to be understood. They ask for beauties self-proffered and easily enjoyed; above all they must have what is unexpected and new.'' As in so many other ways, this description of American literature, which paralleled what Tocqueville saw in other arts, proved not only vivid but prophetic.

The paradox of American democracy, of course, is that the freedom Euro-Americans endlessly celebrated co-existed with—some might say depended on—the enslavement of African Americans. It is therefore one of the great ironies of popular culture that the contributions of black culture (a term here meant to encompass African, American, and amalgamations between the two) proved so decisive. In another sense, however, it seems entirely appropriate that popular culture, which has always skewed its orientation toward the lower end of a demographic spectrum, would draw on the most marginalized groups in American society. It is, in any event, difficult to imagine that U.S. popular culture would have had anywhere near the vitality and influence it has without slave stories, song, and dance. To cite merely one example: every American musical idiom from country music to rap has drawn on, if not actually *rested* upon, African-American cultural foundations, whether in its use of the banjo (originally an African instrument) or its emphasis on the beat (drumming was an important form of slave communication). This heritage has often been overlooked, disparaged, and even satirized. The most notable example of such racism was the minstrel show, a wildly popular nineteenth century form of theater in which white actors blackened their faces with burnt cork and mocked slave life. Yet even the most savage parodies could not help but reveal an engagement with, and even a secret admiration for, the cultural world the African Americans made in conditions of severe adversity, whether on plantations, tenant farms, or in ghettoes.

Meanwhile, the accelerating pace of technological innovation began having a dramatic impact on the form as well as the content of popular culture. The first major landmark was the development of photography in the mid-nineteenth century. At first a mechanically complex and thus inaccessible medium, it quickly captured American imaginations, particularly by capturing the drama and horror of the Civil War. The subsequent proliferation of family portraits, postcards, and pictures in metropolitan newspapers began a process of orienting popular culture around visual imagery that continues unabated to this day.

In the closing decades of the nineteenth century, sound recording, radio transmission, and motion pictures were all developed in rapid succession. But it would not be until well after 1900 that their potential as popular cultural media would be fully exploited and recognizable in a modern sense (radio, for example, was originally developed and valued for its nautical and military applications). Still, even if it was not entirely clear how, many people at the time believed these new media would have a tremendous impact on American life, and they were embraced with unusual ardor by those Americans, particularly immigrants, who were able to appreciate the pleasures and possibilities afforded by movies, records, and radio.

Many of the patterns established during the advent of these media repeated themselves as new ones evolved. The Internet, for example, was also first developed for its military applications, and for all the rapidity of its development in the 1990s, it remains unclear just how its use will be structured. Though the World Wide Web has shown tremendous promise as a commercial enterprise, it still lacks the kind of programming—like *Amos 'n' Andy* in radio, or *I Love Lucy* in television—that transformed both into truly mass media of art and entertainment. Television, for its part, has long been the medium of a rising middle class of immigrants and their children, in terms of the figures who have exploited its possibilities (from RCA executive David Sarnoff to stars like Jackie Gleason); the new genres it created (from the miniseries to the situation-comedy); and the audiences (from urban Jews to suburban Irish Catholics) who adopted them with enthusiasm.

For much of this century, the mass appeal of popular culture has been viewed as a problem. ''What is the jass [*sic*] music, and therefore the jass band?'' asked an irritated New Orleans writer in 1918. ''As well as ask why the dime novel or the grease-dripping doughnut. All are manifestations of a low stream in man's taste that has not come out in civilization's wash.'' However one may feel about this contemptuous dismissal of jazz, now viewed as one of the great achievements of American civilization, this writer was clearly correct to suggest the demographic, technological, and cultural links between the ''lower'' sorts of people in American life, the media they used, and forms of expression that were often presumed guilty until proven innocent.

Indeed, because education and research have traditionally been considered the province of the ''higher'' sorts of people in American life, popular culture was not considered a subject that should even be discussed, much less studied. Nevertheless, there have always been those willing to continue what might be termed the ''Tocquevillian'' tradition of treating popular culture with intellectual seriousness and respect (if not always approval). In his 1924 book *The Seven Lively Arts* and in much of his journalism, critic Gilbert Seldes found in silent movies, cartoons, and pop music themes and motifs fully worthy of sustained exploration. Amid the worldwide crisis of the 1930s and 1940s, folklorist Constance Rourke limned the origins of an indigenous popular culture in books like *American Humor* (1931) and *The Roots of American Culture* (1942). And with the rise of the Cold War underlining the differences between democratic and totalitarian societies, sociologists David Riesman and Reuel Denny evaluated the social currents animating popular culture in Denny's *The Astonished Muse* (1957), for which Riesman, who showed a particular interest in popular music, wrote the introduction.

European scholars were also pivotal in shaping the field. Johan Huizinga's *Homo Ludens* (1938), Roland Barthes's *Mythologies* (1957), and Antonio Gramsci's prison letters (written in the 1920s and 1930s but not published until the 1970s) have proved among the most influential works in defining the boundaries, strategies, and meanings of popular culture. While none of these works focused on American popular culture specifically, their focus on the jetsam and flotsam of daily life since the medieval period proved enormously suggestive in an American context.

It has only been at the end of the twentieth century, however, that the study of popular culture has come into its own in its own right. To a great extent, this development is a legacy of the 1960s. The end of a formal system of racial segregation; the impact of affirmative action and government-funded financial aid; and the end of single-sex education at many long-established universities dramatically transformed the composition of student bodies and faculties. These developments in turn, began having an impact on the nature and parameters of academic study. While one should not exaggerate the impact of these developments—either in terms of their numbers or their effect on an academy that in some ways has simply replaced older forms of insularity and complacency with new ones—it nevertheless seems fair to say that a bona fide democratization of higher education occurred in the last third of the twentieth century, paving the way for the creation of a formal scholarly infrastructure for popular culture.

Once again, it was foreign scholars who were pivotal in the elaboration of this infrastructure. The work of Raymond Williams, Stuart Hall, and others at Britain's Centre for Contemporary Cultural Studies in the 1950s and 1960s drew on Marxist and psychoanalytic ideas to explain, and in many cases justify, the importance of popular culture. Though not always specifically concerned with popular culture, a panoply of French theorists—particularly Jacques Derrida, Louis Althusser, and Michel Foucault—also proved highly influential. At its best, this scholarship illuminated unexamined assumptions and highly revealing (and in many cases, damning) patterns in the most seemingly ordinary documents. At its worst, it lapsed into an arcane jargon that belied the directness of popular culture and suggested an elitist disdain toward the audiences it presumably sought to understand.

Like their European counterparts, American scholars of popular culture have come from a variety of disciplines. Many were trained in literature, among them Henry Nash Smith, whose *Virgin Land* (1950) pioneered the study of the Western, and Leslie Fiedler, who applied critical talents first developed to study classic American literature to popular fiction like *Gone with the Wind*. But much important work in the field has also been done by historians, particularly social historians who began their careers by focusing on labor history but became increasingly interested in the ways American workers spent their free time. Following the tradition of the great British historian E. P. Thompson, scholars such as Herbert Gutman and Lawrence Levine have uncovered and described the art and leisure practices of African Americans in particular with flair and insight. Feminist scholars of a variety of stripes (and sexual orientations) have supplied a great deal of the intellectual energy in the study of popular culture, among them Ann Douglas, Carroll Smith-Rosenberg, and Jane Tompkins. Indeed, the strongly interdisciplinary flavor of popular culture scholarship—along with the rise of institutions like the Popular Press and the Popular Culture Association, both based at Bowling Green University—suggests the way the field has been at the forefront of an ongoing process of redrawing disciplinary boundaries in the humanities.

By the 1980s, the stream of scholarship on popular culture had become a flood. In the 1990s, the field became less of a quixotic enterprise than a growing presence in the educational curriculum as a whole. Courses devoted to the subject, whether housed in communications programs or in traditional academic departments, have become increasingly common in colleges and universities—and, perhaps more importantly, have become integrated into the fabric of basic surveys of history, literature, and other fields. Political scientists, librarians, and curators have begun to consider it part of their domain.

For most of us, though, popular culture is not something we have to self-consciously seek out or think about. Indeed, its very omnipresence makes it easy to take for granted as transparent (and permanent). That's why trips to museums—or encyclopedias like this one—are so useful and important. In pausing to think about the art of everyday life, we can begin to see just how unusual, and valuable, it really is.

—Jim Cullen

FURTHER READING:

Barthes, Roland. *Mythologies.* Translated by Annette Lavers. 1957. Reprint, New York, The Noonday Press, 1972.

Cullen, Jim. *The Art of Democracy: A Concise History of Popular Culture in the United States.* New York, Monthly Review Press, 1996.

Fiske, John. *Understanding Popular Culture.* Boston, Unwin/Hyman, 1989.

Levine, Lawrence. *The Unpredictable Past: Explorations in American Cultural History.* New York, Oxford University Press, 1993.

Storey, John. *An Introductory Guide to Cultural Theory and Popular Culture.* Athens, University of Georgia Press, 1993.

Susman, Warren. *Culture as History: The Transformation of American Society in the Twentieth Century.* New York, Pantheon, 1984.

ADVISORS

Frances R. Aparicio
University of Michigan

Paul Buhle
Brown University

George O. Carney
Oklahoma State University

B. Lee Cooper
University of Great Falls

Corey K. Creekmur
University of Iowa

Joshua Gamson
Yale University

Jerome Klinkowitz
University of Northern Iowa

Richard Martin
Metropolitan Museum of Art
Columbia University
New York University

Lawrence E. Mintz
University of Maryland
Art Gliner Center for Humor Studies

Troy Paino
Winona State University

Grace Palladino
University of Maryland

Lauren Rabinovitz
University of Iowa

T. V. Reed
Washington State University

William L. Schurk
Bowling Green State University

Alison M. Scott
Bowling Green State University

Randall W. Scott
Michigan State University Libraries

Ron Simon
Museum of Television & Radio
Columbia University

Erin Smith
University of Texas at Dallas

June Sochen
Northeastern Illinois University

Colby Vargas
New Trier High School

CONTRIBUTORS

Nathan Abrams
Frederick Luis Aldama
Roberto Alvarez
Byron Anderson
Carly Andrews
Jacob M. Appel
Tim Arnold
Paul Ashdown
Bernardo Alexander Attias
Frederick J. Augustyn, Jr.

Beatriz Badikian
Michael Baers
Neal Baker
S. K. Bane
Samantha Barbas
Allen Barksdale
Pauline Bartel
Bob Batchelor
Vance Bell
Samuel I. Bellman
James R. Belpedio
Courtney Bennett
Timothy Berg
Lisa Bergeron-Duncan
Daniel Bernardi
R. Thomas Berner
Charlie Bevis
Lara Bickell
Sam Binkley
Brian Black
Liza Black
Bethany Blankenship
Rebecca Blustein
Aniko Bodroghkozy
Gregory Bond
Martyn Bone
Austin Booth
Gerry Bowler
Anne Boyd
Marlena E. Bremseth
Carol Brennan
Tony Brewer
Deborah Broderson
Michael Brody
Pat H. Broeske
Robert J. Brown
Sharon Brown
Craig Bunch
Stephen Burnett
Gary Burns
Margaret Burns

Manuel V. Cabrera, Jr.
Ross B. Care

Gerald Carpenter
Anthony Cast
Rafaela Castro
Jason Chambers
Chris Chandler
Michael K. Chapman
Roger Chapman
Lloyd Chiasson, Jr.
Ann M. Ciasullo
Dylan Clark
Frank Clark
Randy Clark
Craig T. Cobane
Dan Coffey
Adam Max Cohen
Toby I. Cohen
Susann Cokal
Jeffrey W. Coker
Charles A. Coletta, Jr.
Michael R. Collings
Willie Collins
Mia L. Consalvo
Douglas Cooke
ViBrina Coronado
Robert C. Cottrell
Corey K. Creekmur
Richard C. Crepeau
Jim Cullen
Susan Curtis

Glyn Davis
Janet M. Davis
Pamala S. Deane
S. Renee Dechert
John Deitrick
Gordon Neal Diem, D.A.
Richard Digby-Junger
Laurie DiMauro
John J. Doherty
Thurston Domina
Jon Griffin Donlon
Simon Donner
Randy Duncan
Stephen Duncombe
Eugenia Griffith DuPell
Stephanie Dyer

Rob Edelman
Geoff Edgers
Jessie L. Embry
Jeffrey Escoffier
Cindy Peters Evans
Sean Evans
William A. Everett

Alyssa Falwell
Richard Feinberg
G. Allen Finchum
S. Naomi Finkelstein
Dennis Fischer
Bill Freind
Bianca Freire-Medeiros
Shaun Frentner
James Friedman
Adrienne Furness

Paul Gaffney
Milton Gaither
Joan Gajadhar
Catherine C. Galley
Caitlin L. Gannon
Sandra Garcia-Myers
Bryan Garman
Eva Marie Garroutte
Frances Gateward
Jason George
Tina Gianoulis
James R. Giles
Milton Goldin
Ilene Goldman
Matthew Mulligan Goldstein
Dave Goldweber
Ian Gordon
W. Terrence Gordon
Ron Goulart
Paul Grainge
Brian Granger
Anna Hunt Graves
Steve Graves
Jill A. Gregg
Benjamin Griffith
Perry Grossman
Justin Gustainis
Dale Allen Gyure

Kristine J. Ha
Elizabeth Haas
Ray Haberski, Jr.
Jeanne Lynn Hall
Steve Hanson
Jacqueline Anne Hatton
Chris Haven
Ethan Hay
Jeet Heer
Andrew R. Heinze
Mary Hess
Joshua Hirsch
David L. Hixson
Scott W. Hoffman
Briavel Holcomb

Peter C. Holloran
David Holloway
Karen Hovde
Kevin Howley
Nick Humez

Judy L. Isaksen

Jennifer Jankauskas
E. V. Johanningmeier
Patrick Joncs
Patrick Jones
Preston Neal Jones
Mark Joseph
Thomas Judd

Peter Kalliney
Nicolás Kanellos
Robyn Karney
Stephen Keane
James D. Keeline
Max Kellerman
Ken Kempcke
Stephen C. Kenny
Stephen Kercher
Matt Kerr
M. Alison Kibler
Kimberley H. Kidd
Matthew A. Killmeier
Jason King
Jon Klinkowitz
Leah Konicki
Steven Kotok
Robert Kuhlken
Andrew J. Kunka
Audrey Kupferberg
Petra Kuppers

Emma Lambert
Christina Lane
Kevin Lause
Nadine-Rae Leavell
Christopher A. Lee
Michele Lellouche
Robin Lent
Joan Leotta
Richard Levine
Drew Limsky
Daniel Lindley
Joyce Linehan
Margaret Litton
James H. Lloyd
David Lonergan
Eric Longley
Rick Lott
Bennett Lovett-Graff
Denise Lowe

Debra M. Lucas
Karen Lurie
Michael A. Lutes
James Lyons
John F. Lyons

Steve Macek
Alison Macor
David Marc
Robin Markowitz
Tilney L. Marsh
Richard Martin
Sara Martin
Linda A. Martindale
Kevin Mattson
Randall McClure
Allison McCracken
Jennifer Davis McDaid
Jason McEntee
Cheryl S. McGrath
Daryna McKeand
Jacquelyn Y. McLendon
Kembrew McLeod
Josephine A. McQuail
Alex Medeiros
Brad Melton
Myra Mendible
Jeff Merron
Thomas J. Mertz
Nathan R. Meyer
Jonathan Middlebrook
Andre Millard
Jeffrey S. Miller
Karen Miller
P. Andrew Miller
Dorothy Jane Mills
Andrew Milner
Deborah M. Mix
Nickianne Moody
Richard L. Moody
Charles F. Moore
Leonard N. Moore
Dan Moos
Robert A. Morace
Edward Moran
Barry Morris
Michael J. Murphy
Jennifer A. Murray
Susan Murray
Pierre-Damien Mvuyekure

Michael Najjar
Ilana Nash
Mary Lou Nemanic
Scott Newman
Joan Nicks
Martin F. Norden
Justin Nordstrom
Anna Notaro

William F. O'Connor
Paul O'Hara
Angela O'Neal
Christopher D. O'Shea
Lolly Ockerstrom
Kerry Owens
Marc Oxoby

D. Byron Painter
Henri-Dominique Paratte
Leslie Paris
Jay Parrent
Felicity Paxton
Sara Pendergast
Tom Pendergast
Jana Pendragon
Geoff Peterson
Kurt W. Peterson
Emily Pettigrew
Daniel J. Philippon
S. J. Philo
Allene Phy-Olsen
Ed Piacentino
Jürgen Pieters
Paul F. P. Pogue
Mark B. Pohlad
Fernando Porta
Michael L. Posner
John A. Price
Victoria Price
Luca Prono
Elizabeth Purdy
Christian L. Pyle

Jessy Randall
Taly Ravid
Belinda S. Ray
Ivan Raykoff
Wendy Wick Reaves
James E. Reibman
Yolanda Retter
Tracy J. Revels
Wylene Rholetter
Tad Richards
Robert B. Ridinger
Jeff Ritter
Thomas Robertson
Arthur Robinson
Todd Anthony Rosa
Ava Rose
Chris Routledge
Abhijit Roy
Adrienne Russell
Dennis Russell

Lisa Jo Sagolla
Frank A. Salamone
Joe Sutliff Sanders

Andrew Sargent
Julie Scelfo
Elizabeth D. Schafer
Louis Scheeder
James Schiff
Robert E. Schnakenberg
Steven Schneider
Kelly Schrum
Christine Scodari
Ann Sears
E. M. I. Sefcovic
Eric J. Segal
Carol A. Senf
Tim Seul
Alexander Shashko
Michele S. Shauf
Taylor Shaw
Anne Sheehan
Steven T. Sheehan
Pamela Shelton
Sandra Sherman
Charles J. Shindo
Mike Shupp
Robert C. Sickels
C. Kenyon Silvey
Ron Simon
Philip Simpson
Rosemarie Skaine
Ryan R. Sloane
Jeannette Sloniowski
Cheryl A. Smith

Kyle Smith
John Smolenski
Irvin D. Solomon
Geri Speace
Andrew Spieldenner
tova stabin
Scott Stabler
Jon Sterngrass
Roger W. Stump
Bob Sullivan
Lauren Ann Supance
Marc R. Sykes

Midori Takagi
Candida Taylor
Scott Thill
Robert Thompson
Stephen L. Thompson
Rosemarie Garland Thomson
Jan Todd
Terry Todd
John Tomasic
Warren Tormey
Grant Tracey
David Trevino
Marcella Bush Trevino
Scott Tribble
Tom Trinchera
Nicholas A. Turse

Anthony Ubelhor
Daryl Umberger

Rob Van Kranenburg
Robert VanWynsberghe
Colby Vargas

Sue Walker
Lori C. Walters
Nancy Lan-Jy Wang
Adam Wathen
Laural Weintraub
Jon Weisberger
David B. Welky
Christopher W. Wells
Celia White
Christopher S. Wilson
David B. Wilson
Kristi M. Wilson
Jeff Wiltse
Wendy Woloson
David E. Woodward
Bradford W. Wright

Sharon Yablon
Daniel Francis Yezbick
Stephen D. Youngkin

Kristal Brent Zook

LIST OF ENTRIES

Bara, Theda
Baraka, Amiri
Barbecue
Barber, Red
Barbershop Quartets
Barbie
Barker, Clive
Barkley, Charles
Barney and Friends
Barney Miller
Barry, Dave
Barry, Lynda
Barrymore, John
Barton, Bruce
Baryshnikov, Mikhail
Baseball
Baseball Cards
Basie, Count
Basketball
Bathhouses
Batman
Baum, L. Frank
Bay, Mel
Bay of Pigs Invasion
Baywatch
Bazooka Joe
Beach Boys, The
Beach, Rex
Beanie Babies
Beastie Boys, The
Beat Generation
Beatles, The
Beatty, Warren
Beau Geste
Beauty Queens
Beavers, Louise
Beavis and Butthead
Bee Gees, The
Beer
Beiderbecke, Bix
Belafonte, Harry
Bell Telephone Hour, The
Bellbottoms
Belushi, John
Ben Casey
Bench, Johnny
Benchley, Robert
Ben-Hur
Benneton
Bennett, Tony
Benny Hill Show, The
Benny, Jack
Bergen, Candice
Bergen, Edgar
Bergman, Ingmar
Bergman, Ingrid
Berkeley, Busby
Berle, Milton
Berlin, Irving
Bernhard, Sandra

Bernstein, Leonard
Berra, Yogi
Berry, Chuck
Best Years of Our Lives, The
Bestsellers
Better Homes and Gardens
Betty Boop
Betty Crocker
Beulah
Beverly Hillbillies, The
Beverly Hills 90210
Bewitched
Bicycling
Big Apple, The
Big Bands
Big Bopper
Big Little Books
Big Sleep, The
Bigfoot
Bilingual Education
Billboards
Bionic Woman, The
Bird, Larry
Birkenstocks
Birth of a Nation, The
Birthing Practices
Black, Clint
Black Mask
Black Panthers
Black Sabbath
Black Sox Scandal
Blackboard Jungle, The
Blackface Minstrelsy
Blacklisting
Blade Runner
Blades, Ruben
Blanc, Mel
Bland, Bobby Blue
Blass, Bill
Blaxploitation Films
Blob, The
Blockbusters
Blondie (comic strip)
Blondie (rock band)
Bloom County
Blount, Roy, Jr.
Blue Velvet
Blueboy
Bluegrass
Blues
Blues Brothers, The
Blume, Judy
Bly, Robert
Board Games
Boat People
Bob and Ray
Bobbsey Twins, The
Bobby Socks
Bochco, Steven
Body Decoration

Bodybuilding
Bogart, Humphrey
Bok, Edward
Bomb, The
Bombeck, Erma
Bon Jovi
Bonanza
Bonnie and Clyde
Booker T. and the MG's
Book-of-the-Month Club
Boone, Pat
Borge, Victor
Borscht Belt
Boston Celtics, The
Boston Garden
Boston Marathon
Boston Strangler
Boston Symphony Orchestra, The
Bouton, Jim
Bow, Clara
Bowie, David
Bowling
Boxing
Boy Scouts of America
Bra
Bradbury, Ray
Bradley, Bill
Bradshaw, Terry
Brady Bunch, The
Brand, Max
Brando, Marlon
Brat Pack
Brautigan, Richard
Breakfast at Tiffany's
Breakfast Club, The
Breast Implants
Brenda Starr
Brice, Fanny
Brideshead Revisited
Bridge
Bridge on the River Kwai, The
Bridges of Madison County, The
Brill Building
Bringing Up Baby
Brinkley, David
British Invasion
Broadway
Brokaw, Tom
Bronson, Charles
Brooklyn Dodgers, The
Brooks, Garth
Brooks, Gwendolyn
Brooks, James L.
Brooks, Louise
Brooks, Mel
Brothers, Dr. Joyce
Brown, James
Brown, Jim
Brown, Les

Pittsburgh Steelers, The
Pizza
Place in the Sun, A
Planet of the Apes
Plastic
Plastic Surgery
Plath, Sylvia
Platoon
Playboy
Playgirl
Playhouse 90
Pogo
Pointer Sisters, The
Poitier, Sidney
Polio
Political Bosses
Political Correctness
Pollock, Jackson
Polyester
Pop Art
Pop, Iggy
Pop Music
Pope, The
Popeye
Popsicles
Popular Mechanics
Popular Psychology
Pornography
Porter, Cole
Postcards
Postman Always Rings Twice, The
Postmodernism
Potter, Dennis
Powell, Dick
Powell, William
Prang, Louis
Preminger, Otto
Preppy
Presley, Elvis
Price Is Right, The
Price, Reynolds
Price, Vincent
Pride, Charley
Prince
Prince, Hal
Prinze, Freddie
Prisoner, The
Professional Football
Prohibition
Prom
Promise Keepers
Protest Groups
Prozac
Pryor, Richard
Psychedelia
Psychics
Psycho
PTA/PTO (Parent Teacher Association/Organization)

Public Enemy
Public Libraries
Public Television (PBS)
Puente, Tito
Pulp Fiction
Pulp Magazines
Punisher, The
Punk
Pynchon, Thomas

Quayle, Dan
Queen, Ellery
Queen for a Day
Queen Latifah
Queer Nation
Quiz Show Scandals

Race Music
Race Riots
Radio
Radio Drama
Radner, Gilda
Raft, George
Raggedy Ann and Raggedy Andy
Raging Bull
Ragni, Gerome, and James Rado
Raiders of the Lost Ark
Rainey, Gertrude ''Ma''
Rains, Claude
Raitt, Bonnie
Rambo
Ramones, The
Ranch House
Rand, Sally
Rap/Hip Hop
Rather, Dan
Reader's Digest
Reagan, Ronald
Real World, The
Reality Television
Rear Window
Rebel without a Cause
Recycling
Red Scare
Redbook
Redding, Otis
Redford, Robert
Reed, Donna
Reed, Ishmael
Reed, Lou
Reese, Pee Wee
Reeves, Steve
Reggae
Reiner, Carl
Religious Right
R.E.M.
Remington, Frederic
Reno, Don

Renoir, Jean
Replacements, The
Retro Fashion
Reynolds, Burt
Rhythm and Blues
Rice, Grantland
Rice, Jerry
Rich, Charlie
Rigby, Cathy
Riggs, Bobby
Riley, Pat
Ringling Bros., Barnum & Bailey Circus
Ripken, Cal, Jr.
Ripley's Believe It Or Not
Rivera, Chita
Rivera, Diego
Rivera, Geraldo
Rivers, Joan
Rizzuto, Phil
Road Rage
Road Runner and Wile E. Coyote
Robbins, Tom
Roberts, Jake "The Snake"
Roberts, Julia
Roberts, Nora
Robertson, Oscar
Robertson, Pat
Robeson, Kenneth
Robeson, Paul
Robinson, Edward G.
Robinson, Frank
Robinson, Jackie
Robinson, Smokey
Robinson, Sugar Ray
Rock and Roll
Rock, Chris
Rock Climbing
Rockefeller Family
Rockettes, The
Rockne, Knute
Rockwell, Norman
Rocky
Rocky and Bullwinkle
Rocky Horror Picture Show, The
Roddenberry, Gene
Rodeo
Rodgers and Hammerstein
Rodgers and Hart
Rodgers, Jimmie
Rodman, Dennis
Rodriguez, Chi Chi
Roe v. Wade
Rogers, Kenny
Rogers, Roy
Rogers, Will
Rolle, Esther
Roller Coasters

E

Eames, Charles (1907-1978), and Ray (1916-1988)

The husband and wife team of Charles and Ray Eames created a multitude of artistic works in various fields from the 1940s to the 1970s. Charles Eames was trained as an architect; Ray (Kaiser) was an artist. After their marriage in 1941, they formed an unparalleled design team. Together the Eames' designed stage and film sets, furniture, exhibitions, interiors, houses, multimedia presentations, short films, graphic designs, industrial products, and books. Their greatest impact may have come from their work in two particular areas—architecture and furniture. The Eames' two Case Study Houses (1945-1950) with Eero Saarinen, Incorporated, prefabricated elements into a simple rectangular box; the houses became internationally famous as premier examples of domestic modernism. The Eames' furniture work evolved out of a series of experiments with molded plywood done for the Navy during World War II. "Eames Chairs" were widely praised in the 1940s and 1950s for their curving plywood forms, light weight, simplicity, and inexpensive price; they were also widely imitated.

—Dale Allen Gyure

FURTHER READING:

Albrecht, Donald, editor. *The Work of Charles and Ray Eames: A Legacy of Invention.* New York, Harry N. Abrams, 1997.

Kirkham, Pat. *Charles and Ray Eames: Designers of the Twentieth Century.* Cambridge and London, Cambridge University Press, 1995.

Neuhart, John and Marilyn, with Ray Eames. *Eames Design: The Office of Charles and Ray Eames 1941-1978.* New York, Harry N. Abrams, 1989.

Earth Day

Inspired by anti-war "teach-ins" and the activist culture of the late 1960s, United States Senator Gaylord Nelson of Wisconsin organized the first Earth Day on April 22, 1970, to raise awareness of environmental issues and elevate the state of the environment into mainstream political discourse. Rachel Carson's book, *Silent Spring* (1962), examined why there were increasing levels of smog in the nation's cities, and focused attention on environmental disasters such as the Santa Barbara oil spill (1969) and the fire on Cleveland's Cuyahoga River due to oil and chemical pollution (1969), and gave rise to local groups of concerned citizens and activists. Enlightening photographs of the Earth taken by astronauts underscored the fact that we inhabit a finite system, small in comparison with the vastness of the solar system, and changed the way people visualized the planet. On that first Earth Day, an estimated 20 million people participated in peaceful demonstrations, lectures, and celebrations all across the country—10,000 grade schools and high schools, 2,000 colleges, and 1,000 communities were involved. Extensive media coverage of the events succeeded in alerting people to the deteriorating condition of the environment and increased the influence of environmental groups on government and industry. For many, Earth Day 1970 radically altered the image of nature and how society should treat it, and marked the beginning of the modern environmental movement.

The dramatic rise in citizen awareness after Earth Day made pollution a major news story. Programs on pollution appeared on television, newspapers hired environmental reporters, advertisements stressed the ecological qualities of products, and books and magazines addressed the protection of nature. Within months of the original Earth Day, the Environmental Protection Agency was created. The Clean Air Act, the Clean Water Act, and several other important environmental laws were passed in the early 1970s. Politicians spoke out on ecological issues in their campaigns and speeches. Companies that violated pollution laws were taken to court, and membership in many environmental groups doubled and tripled. The construction of nuclear power plants in the United States halted in 1978. Many experienced activists, trained in the anti-war, civil rights, and women's movements, used civil disobedience to combat polluters. Subsequent Earth Days continued to put pressure on government and industry to act responsibly toward the environment.

Along with some environmental organizations, Earth Day lost steam during the pro-environmental Carter administration, as people perceived that ecological problems were being addressed. Some conservation efforts also prompted an angry backlash by conservative groups. During the 1980s, the Reagan and Bush administrations systematically dismantled many environmental laws. When Reagan named the imprudent and insensitive James Watt to the position of Secretary of the Interior, however, environmental organizations became rejuvenized and their membership rolls increased. In 1989, the editors of *Time* magazine abandoned their tradition of featuring a man or woman of the year in favor of featuring "The Endangered Planet." In reaction to such environmental concerns as global warming and the depletion of the ozone layer, and such eco-disasters as Bhopal, Chernobyl, and the Exxon Valdez oil spill, organizers of Earth Day intensified their efforts on the twentieth anniversary in 1990.

In 1990, Earth Day turned global. On April 22, Earth Day united more people concerned about a single cause than any other event in the history of the world—139 nations participated. The *New York Times* reported that 200 million people took part in the largest grassroots demonstration in history. More than one million people gathered in Central Park to hear speakers and entertainers, and more than 200,000 people assembled in front of the United States Capitol to listen to music and speeches.

The environmental movement is one of the most successful and enduring reform movements of the twentieth century. A majority of Americans now believe that the poor quality of the environment is one of our most serious national problems. Millions of families take for granted the policy of reduce, reuse, and recycle. While all environmental accomplishments since 1970 cannot be directly attributed to Earth Day, it has succeeded in transforming a fairly specialized interest into a pervasive, popular one, and has made ecological consciousness part of the American value system.

—Ken Kempcke

FURTHER READING:

Cahn, Robert, and Patricia Cahn. "Did Earth Day Change the World?" *Environment.* September, 1990, 16-42.

Devall, Bill. "Twenty-Five Years since Earth Day." *Humboldt Journal of Social Relations.* Vol. 21, No.1, 1995, 15-34.

Dunlap, Riley, and Angela Mertig. "The Evolution of the U.S. Environmental Movement from 1970 to 1990: An Overview." *Society and Natural Resources.* Vol. 4, No. 3, 209-18.

Gilbert, Bil. "Earth Day plus 20, and Counting." *Smithsonian.* April, 1990, 46-52.

Hayes, Denis. "Earth Day 1990: Threshold of the Green Decade." *World Policy Journal.* Vol. 7, No. 2, 1990, 289-304.

Earth Shoes

When the Earth Shoe was brought to America in 1970, its advertising campaign promised to bring wearers closer to nature. With "negative" heels that sat lower than the front, Earth Shoes claimed to offer wearers a more natural posture, closer to aboriginal human locomotion. The shoes were a startling multi-million dollar success for two reasons. First, the back-to-nature promise of Earth Shoes resonated with members of the burgeoning environmental movement. Second, the boxy appearance of the shoe was viewed as an antifashion statement; as such, it was a social statement favoring simplicity over image, substance over style. In time the square, broad shape of the Earth Shoe was emulated in a wide range of other shoes; for a few years its look became a hallmark style of the 1970s.

—Dylan Clark

FURTHER READING:

Kennedy, Pagan. *Platforms: A Microwaved Cultural Chronicle of the 1970s.* New York, St. Martin's, 1994.

Lauer, Jeanette C. *Fashion Power: The Meaning of Fashion in American Society.* Englewood Cliffs, New Jersey, Prentice-Hall, 1981.

Lofaro, Lina. "The Fate of the Earth Shoe." *Time.* May 1, 1995, 32.

Trasko, Mary. *Heavenly Soles: Extraordinary Twentieth Century Shoes.* New York, Abbeyville Press, 1989.

Eastman Kodak Company
See Kodak

Eastwood, Clint (1930—)

In the course of a career that, by the late 1990s, had spanned almost half-a-century, Clint Eastwood rose from obscure bit-part movie actor to America's number one box-office star, became a producer for his own highly successful company, Malpaso, and established himself as a film director of some accomplishment. He is often compared with Gary Cooper—both men have been frequently

Clint Eastwood

and accurately identified as long, lean, and laconic—but Eastwood's dark good looks and granite-like persona, often self-mocking under a cloak of grim impassivity, are very different from the earlier icon whose career ended as Eastwood's began.

Eastwood's own iconic associations are, most famously, the cheroot-chewing Man With No Name, poncho-clad, unkempt, and unshaven as he goes about his bloody business; he is also Harry Callahan, dark avenger of the San Francisco police force, clean-cut and neatly suited as he goes about even bloodier business. His true significance in the history of Hollywood filmmaking, however, attaches to the fact that, as both director and actor, he breathed new life into a dying American art form, the Western. Finally, with *Unforgiven* (1992), Clint Eastwood subverted the myth of this historic canon, inverting his own practiced characterization to transmit a moral message for a modern age. His now reluctant avenging gunslinger was Harry Callahan or, more appropriately, Josey Wales, grown weary of violence—a capitulation that, perhaps, paved the way for Frank Horrigan protecting the American president (*In the Line of Fire,* 1993) or, further expanding his range, Robert Kincaid surrendering to a woman's love (*The Bridges of Madison County,* 1995).

Born in San Francisco on May 31, 1930, Clinton Eastwood Jr. passed an itinerant, Depression-hit childhood with schooling to match. After high school, he earned his keep variously logging wood, stoking furnaces, and pumping gas before joining the army for four years, where he coached athletics and swimming. Subsequently, he briefly attended Los Angeles City College, where he met his first wife, Maggie Johnson (the mother of his actress daughter, Alison). In 1955, on the strength of his looks and physique, Eastwood was signed to a $75-a-week contract—dropped after eighteen months—by Universal Studios, one of a standard, low-paid intake of good-looking men whose screen potential studios neglected to nurture. For four years he passed unnoticed in a string of parts, ranging from tiny to small, in ten or so largely forgotten films beginning with *Revenge of the Creature* (1955), ending with *Lafayette Escadrille* (1958) and taking in along the way the Rock Hudson vehicle *Never Say Goodbye* (1956) and his first (and some say worst) excursion into cowboy territory, *Ambush at Cimarron Pass* (1958).

During this time, Eastwood supplemented his income with odd jobs until he was cast in a new TV Western series of uncertain future. In the event, *Rawhide* ran for eight seasons from 1959-1966 and Rowdy Yates, played by Eastwood, became a familiar figure to followers of the series. More importantly, he was noticed by the Italian director Sergio Leone, offered a part in Italy, and found himself launched as The Man With No Name in *A Fistful of Dollars/ Per un Pugno di Dollari* (1964). The film emerged from a genre newly popular in Italy during the 1960s that mined the ore of American cowboy films in a peculiarly bloody way and came to be known as spaghetti Westerns. *A Fistful of Dollars,* given a facelift by the presence of an American actor-hero and Leone's particular facility with celluloid violence, was astonishingly successful and two sequels—*For a Few Dollars More/Per Qualche Dollari in piu* and *The Good, The Bad and the Ugly/Il Buono il Brutto il Cattivo*—both starring Eastwood, followed in 1966 and 1967, bringing Leone a fortune and an invitation to Hollywood and catapulting Clint Eastwood to international stardom.

The first two of the Leone trilogy were released in America in 1967; the third followed a year later. The silent, detached, guncomfortable bounty hunter of the films returned to America, set up his Malpaso production company and, in a lucrative deal with United Artists, relaunched himself on home soil with *Hang 'em High* (1968), an unashamed attempt to emulate the noisy gore of his Italian vehicles, in which the newly-minted star, saved from a lynching and appointed as a deputy sheriff, grimly sets out to take revenge on nine men. The film was slick, violent, and not particularly good but, coinciding as it did with the popularity of the spaghetti Westerns, it established Eastwood with the cinema-going public and, indeed, with hindsight, one detects the first seeds of the avenging angel—or devil—which would come to mark his more serious and ambitious mid-period Westerns.

When the box-office top ten list was issued in 1968, the cowboy star was in at number five, having begun his association with director Don Siegel in *Coogan's Bluff* (1968). This "urban Western" let Eastwood loose in Manhattan as an Arizona sheriff whose methods clash with those of Lee J. Cobb's city detective. It was an explosive crime melodrama with Eastwood seen, for the first time, in modern clothes and minus his hat. Attempts to broaden his range in 1969 took him to World War II in *Where Eagles Dare* and back to the Gold Rush days in the musical *Paint Your Wagon*. The first was a soldiering potboiler, the second a visually attractive failure, but neither dented his popular image. He retained his number five position and, by 1970, after the crude war film *Kelly's Heroes* and *Two Mules for Sister Sara*, in which he reverted to cowboy hat and five o'clock shadow to play a taciturn mercenary protecting a supposed nun (Shirley MacLaine) from rapists, he rose to number two.

Nineteen seventy-one was a key year in Eastwood's career. Displaying the business acumen and Midas touch that would in time make many millions of dollars for Malpaso, he rejoined director Don Siegel for *Dirty Harry,* bringing to the disillusioned Harry Callahan

the same implacable qualities that had been displayed in his cowboy roles. The film is uncompromisingly brutal and raised questions in certain quarters as to its morality, perceived by some as favoring the vigilante methods of the ultra-conservative Right. A closer look confirms that it is, rather, a protest against messy loopholes in law enforcement. The moral message or otherwise aside, however, the film was monumentally successful, catering to audiences' taste for psychopathic serial killers and tough anti-heroes, and was followed by four increasingly formulaic and cynical sequels over the next 16 years.

More importantly for the long term, 1971 brought Eastwood's directing debut, *Play Misty for Me.* As he would continue to do in all but a couple of his self-directed films, he cast himself in the lead, here as a radio disc jockey who becomes the obsessive object of a murderously psychotic fan's infatuation. The film demonstrated that he had learned much from Siegel—it was taut, tense, entertaining, and very beautifully photographed in Carmel and Monterey. From 1971 to 1998, Clint Eastwood made 31 feature films, directing 18 of them and producing several. While bent, successfully, on proving he was not just a pretty face and a fine figure of a man, he veered alarmingly between the ambitious, the worthwhile, and the purely commercial. In the last category his intelligent judgment sometimes faltered, badly with the nonsensical tedium of *The Eiger Sanction* (1975); and although his screen presence only grew more charismatic with age— the body startlingly well-preserved, the seamed face topped by graying hair increasingly handsome—he made a number of films that were essentially worthless retreads of familiar ground (e.g. *The Gauntlet,* 1977, *City Heat,* 1994, *The Rookie,* 1990, and *A Perfect World,* 1993, in all of which he played cops of one sort or another).

At the same time, he experimented, not always successfully, with material that, in the context of his recognized *oeuvre,* was distinctly off the wall as in *Every Which Way but Loose* (1978), in which he crossed the country accompanied by an orangutan won in a bet. There was, however, a wistful sweetness about the small-scale *Honkytonk Man* (1982), in which he directed himself as an aging alcoholic country singer and allowed himself to play guitar and sing to touching effect.

During the 1980s, Eastwood the actor retained his superstar status, undamaged by the tabloid headline-making scandal of his affair with actress Sondra Locke, for whom he left his wife of 27 years. Indeed, he seemed to rise above gossip and escape mockery, despite court cases—Locke sued him, he sued the *National Enquirer*—and a liaison with actress Frances Fisher that produced a child, only for him to leave and marry Dina Ruiz in 1986, becoming a father for the fourth time. Eastwood the director, meanwhile, his best work yet to come, was held in increasing esteem by his peers, who acknowledged his unshowy professionalism. As early as 1980 the Museum of Modern Art in New York held a retrospective of his films; in 1985 he was given a retrospective at the elite Cinematheque Francaise in Paris and made a Chevalier des Arts et Lettres by the French government. From 1986-1988 he served as the elected mayor of his beloved Carmel, where Malpaso is based. Also during the decade, he made *Pale Rider* (1985) which, with *High Plains Drifter* (1972) and *The Outlaw Josey Wales* (1976), form a trio of classic Westerns, spare in execution against an epic landscape, in all of which the actor played the mysterious loner pitting himself against dark forces and giving no quarter.

Long a jazz aficionado (he played jazz piano in *In the Line of Fire*), in 1988 Eastwood made, as director only, *Bird,* a biopic of Charlie Parker (played by Forest Whitaker). Somewhat restrained and over-long—a recurring weakness of his more ambitious films—it was nevertheless lovingly crafted and raised his status as a serious director. He had his failures, too: the public did not respond to *White Hunter, Black Heart* (1990), an interesting faction about the making of *The African Queen,* while he was unable to find the key to capturing on film John Berendt's enthralling Savannah odyssey, *Midnight in the Garden of Good and Evil* (1997).

As the first century of the Hollywood film approached its end, Clint Eastwood had, however, earned universal respect and admiration for his achievements. The holder of four Academy Awards (including Best picture and Director) for *Unforgiven,* and presenting himself in public with gravitas and impeccably groomed dignity, he had become the elder statesman of the industry's creative arm, a position that was, as David Thomson put it, "rendered fitting by his majesty."

—Robyn Karney

FURTHER READING:

Locke, Sondra. *The Good, The Bad and the Very Ugly: A Hollywood Journey.* New York, William Morrow, 1997.

Schickel, Richard. *Clint Eastwood: A Biography.* New York, Alfred A. Knopf, 1996.

Thompson, Douglas. *Clint Eastwood, Sexual Cowboy.* London, Smith Griffin, 1992.

Thomson, David. *A Biographical Dictionary of Film.* New York, Alfred A. Knopf Inc., 1994.

Zmijewsky, Boris, and Lee Pfeiffer. *The Films of Clint Eastwood.* New York, Citadel Press, 1993.

Easy Rider

With *Easy Rider,* writers and co-stars Peter Fonda and Dennis Hopper captured in a popular medium many of the ideals of the youthful "counterculture" circa 1969. *Easy Rider* presented both the hedonism of drug use and the sober idealism of the hippy commune. The film also used a hip coterie of cutting-edge rock groups to articulate its indictment of conformist American culture. However, *Easy Rider*'s continuing cultural resonance and filmic influence also owes much to its evocation of more traditional myths of American identity.

Dennis Hopper came to prominence for his precocious performance in an earlier film about youthful rebellion, *Rebel without a Cause* (1955). After appearing again with James Dean in *Giant* (1956), Hopper became a proto-hippy drop-out from the Hollywood system, smoking pot and eating peyote in preference to making mainstream movies. In 1967, Hopper acted with his friend Peter Fonda, scion of Hollywood icon Henry, in *The Trip.* Director Roger Corman refused to spend time or money on pivotal scenes concerning LSD "trips," so Hopper and Fonda shot the scene themselves at their own expense, garnering valuable experience and ideas for their future masterpiece. *The Trip* was co-written by Jack Nicholson, who in the same period scripted another avant-garde psychedelic film, *Head* (featuring the

previously strait-laced Monkees), and starred in *Hells' Angels on Wheels,* an excruciating attempt at combining two types of cultural rebels—bikers and drug-taking hipsters—in one film. Fonda and Hopper worked on two more motorcycle movies—the high-grossing *Wild Angels* and *The Glory Stompers* respectively—before reuniting as co-writers (with Terry Southern, author of *Candy*) and co-stars (with Nicholson) for what Hopper called "another bike film. But a *different* one."

Easy Rider was "different" because, unlike *Hells' Angels on Wheels,* it successfully infused the "bike film" genre with the psychedelic surrealism of *The Trip* to produce a movie which could viably claim to reflect the ethics and aesthetics of contemporary youth culture. The film begins with two bikers, Wyatt/Captain America (Fonda) and Billy (Hopper), receiving payment for their role as middlemen in a cocaine deal, before setting off for Mardi Gras in New Orleans. The narrative thereafter is deliberately loose, but essentially focuses on the bikers' heroic will to freedom from the moral strictures of American society, which Wyatt and Billy periodically encounter from assorted, prejudiced provincials. When Billy complains that "All we represent to them, man, is somebody needs a haircut," alcoholic ACLU lawyer George Hanson (Nicholson), who joins the bikers' odyssey in Texas, explains that: "What you represent to them is freedom. . . . It's real hard to be free when you're bought and sold in the marketplace. . . . They're not free. . . . Then they're gonna get real busy killin' and maimin' to prove to you that they are." *Easy Rider*'s clarion call to "freedom" was also expressed by the titles of soundtrack songs such as "Born to Be Wild" (Steppenwolf) and "Wasn't Born to Follow" (The Byrds). This utilization of rock 'n' roll, the most popular mode of expression for youth culture in the late 1960s, was inspired. In *Village Voice,* Robert Christgau enthused: "*Easy Rider* is a double rarity . . . not only does it use rock successfully, it also treats the youth drop-out thing successfully. You can't have one without the other."

However, like its literary, beat generation antecedent, Jack Kerouac's *On the Road, Easy Rider* also tapped into older American notions of liberty and individualism. That the heroes' names echo Wyatt Earp and Billy the Kid is no accident. Billy and Wyatt move from the urbanized, un-Wild West to the Deep South reclaiming rural America (lovingly filmed by director of photography Laszlo Kovacs) as a frontier. Early in *Easy Rider,* Wyatt and Billy stop at a ranch, and an elaborate comparison is constructed between the rancher's horses and the bikers' machines. *Easy Rider* evinces some unease as to whether being perpetually on the road, astride a product of modern technology, is the most satisfactory form of "freedom." Wyatt lauds the rancher: "It's not every man who can live off the land. Do your own thing in your own time." Here, the free man is no less than Thomas Jefferson's ideal, the yeoman farmer. The hippy commune which Wyatt and Billy later visit is a countercultural reconstruction of this agrarian ideal: disillusioned young urbanites ("All cities are the same" says one) going back to the garden, even if this Eden is the desert landscape of the Southwest. As Frederick Tuten observed in 1969, "the commune scene is at the center of the film's nostalgic values." *Easy Rider*'s "nostalgia for a still beautiful America" (Tuten), and for a pre-urban, pre-capitalist American hero, is apparent in the doom-laden climax of the movie. While Billy rejoices "We're rich. . . . You go for the big money and you're free," his brooding compadre insists "We blew it." For Wyatt, the tainted cash gained from the cocaine deal has not facilitated liberty. Finally, even Wyatt and Billy have been "bought and sold in the marketplace," just like

Peter Fonda in a scene from the film *Easy Rider*.

the stereotypical Southern rednecks who murder the outlaws in the movie's final scene.

As well as projecting Jack Nicholson from art-house obscurity to Hollywood stardom, *Easy Rider* was extremely influential in establishing the road movie as the modern paradigm of the frontier freedom fable. *Vanishing Point* (1971) replaced *Easy Rider*'s pot fumes with amphetamine-fuelled paranoia appropriate to the decline of the hippy dream, while *Badlands* (1973) and *Natural Born Killers* (1994) both combined *Easy Rider*'s legacy with that of another neo-Western counterculture allegory, *Bonnie and Clyde*. *Thelma and Louise* (1991) went some way to revising the insidious sexism of *Easy Rider* and the genre in general, but in attempting to reveal ''the vanishing face of America'' (director Ridley Scott), this ''feminist road movie'' retained the convention of the hero(in)es' gloriously tragic demise.

—Martyn Bone

FURTHER READING:

Dalton, Stephen. ''Endless Highway.'' *Uncut.* September 1998, 30-35.

Hardin, Nancy, and Marilyn Schlossberg. *Easy Rider: Original Screenplay by Peter Fonda, Dennis Hopper, and Terry Southern Plus Stills, Interviews, and Articles.* New York, Signet, 1969.

Ebbets Field

From 1913 to 1957 Ebbets Field was the home to major league baseball's Brooklyn Dodgers. The venue was considered by many to be the heart and soul of Brooklyn, New York, but it is arguable that at no other point in sports history has there been an environment in which the players, the fans, and the ballpark were so intertwined. Ebbets Field, in all its baseball glory, gave Americans much to celebrate about the game that so closely mirrored the aspirations of their society. Ebbets Field stood as a symbol for the unique character of Brooklyn—a city not only with a baseball team, but one with an independent identity, different to the other boroughs of New York. The ballpark provided a setting in which everyone in the ethnically and racially diverse community of Brooklyn could come together on an equal footing. The electric environment of the Dodgers and their home ground helped maintain that interracial unity for the better part of the first half of the twentieth century. At Ebbets Field, the Dodgers and their fans pulled together in a common cause: the establishment of a baseball tradition in Brooklyn that would best reflect the identity of the people and the culture of the borough.

Charlie Ebbets, the owner of the Dodgers from 1898 to 1925, moved the team to the new venue, which he named after himself, after their old ballpark, Washington Park, became too crowded. Ebbets

Ebbets Field during the 1956 World Series.

Field opened on April 9, 1913, with a seating capacity of 25,000. In later years the stadium came to hold over 30,000 people. Renovations transformed the park over the years from a pitcher's to a hitter's stadium. The park was small, but it was acceptable to Brooklyn because it was very comfortable. When Dodger fans went to the stadium to see a game, the experience was made additionally interesting by the many different types of characters who were rooting for the team. The "Dodger Sym-phony," for example, was made up of five fanatical fans who danced and played in the stands and on top of the dugout. Before each game, fans lined up along the railing to shake the hands and acquire autographs of the players. The players and fans had a personal relationship that was unique to major league baseball. The Dodger fans loved their team because the Dodger players symbolized the working class ethos prevalent in Brooklyn society at the time; the fans could identify with the players and respect their efforts.

There were several milestones reached at Ebbets Field that affected major league baseball and American popular culture. The first ever televised major league baseball game was played at Ebbets Field on August 26, 1939 when Brooklyn met the Cincinnati Reds in

the first game of a Saturday afternoon doubleheader. Televised by NBC, the contest paved the way for the regular TV transmission of sport programs in later decades. The second milestone witnessed at this ballpark was more significant. On April 15, 1947, Jackie Robinson became the first African-American to play in a major league game, thus breaking the color barrier that baseball had been forced to adopt back in the 1880s. The Dodgers became the first integrated team in major league baseball, thanks to their innovative president and general manager, Branch Rickey. Soon, the sport would truly become interracial, with many African American players admitted to the major leagues. It was appropriate that Ebbets Field, a park that was already known for its ethnic and racial diversity among the fans, should have pioneered integration on the field.

Winning was as important to Dodger fans as it was to fans of other teams, but Dodger fans also supported their team through many losing seasons. Still, the Dodgers did win nine National League pennants and secured the World Series title, for the only time in their history, in 1955. The people of Brooklyn did much celebrating after that championship, acknowledging their team's star quality as they had always done, but this time giving them a victory parade. But their joy was short-lived. After the 1957 season, the Dodgers left Brooklyn and Ebbets Field for Los Angeles, where greater profits could be made. It was not an issue of attendance, for the Dodgers had always drawn well, but one that revolved around new financial opportunities on the West Coast. When the Dodgers left, the heart of Brooklyn departed with them and things were never the same again for the borough. Sadly, Ebbets Field, which had signified the ideal of what an American ballpark should be—a place of true community on the field and off—was demolished in 1960.

—David Treviño

FURTHER READING:

Golenbock, Peter. *Bums, An Oral History of the Brooklyn Dodgers.* New York, Putnam, 1984.

Kahn, Roger. *The Boys of Summer.* New York, Harper and Row, 1972.

McNeil, William. *The Dodgers Encyclopedia.* Champaign, IL, Sports Publishing, 1997.

Prince, Carl. *Brooklyn's Dodgers: The Bums, the Borough, and the Best of Baseball.* Oxford, Oxford University Press, 1996.

Ebert, Roger

See Siskel and Ebert

Ebony

In 1945, John H. Johnson conceived of a new magazine showing positive photographs of African Americans. The result was *Ebony,* the most successful African American publication in history, with a one-time circulation of more than two million and a pass-around readership of nine million. Building on the success of *Ebony,* Johnson went on to make privately-held Johnson Publishing Co. one of the five largest Black-owned businesses in the United States. With its sister magazines, including *Jet,* a Johnson publication reached one out of every two African-American adults by the end of the twentieth century, a saturation rate few other publishers could match. Johnson was one of the richest men in the United States and perhaps the most influential African American to ever live even though readers have not always been able to relate to the image of Blacks as presented in *Ebony.*

The first African American magazines, like Black newspapers, were born during the period of agitation against slavery that led in part to the Civil War. Titles such as the *Mirror of Liberty* and *National Reformer* were linked to abolitionism, but the French language *L'Album Litteraire, Journal des Jeunes Gens,* and *Les Canelles* and the American *Anglo-African Magazine* treated literature and other political issues as well. New Black magazines began appearing after the war and emancipation. Some of the more successful post-bellum titles that spoke to the conditions of their readers were *Southern Workman, African Methodist Episcopal Church Review, Colored American Magazine,* and *Voice of the Negro.* In the early twentieth century, the NAACP's *Crisis* briefly attracted more than one hundred thousand readers. It was joined by the *Messenger, Journal of Negro History, Opportunity, Journal of Negro Education, Phylon,* and

Ebony **founder John H. Johnson with his daughter, 1992.**

others. But none of these publications could boast of sustained mass circulation. They were read and supported by relatively small numbers of the better educated, upper-class Blacks. The vast majority of literate middle and lower-class Blacks read nationally-circulated newspapers like the *Negro World, Chicago Defender,* and *Pittsburgh Courier* before World War II.

John Harold Johnson was born into poverty in rural Arkansas City, Arkansas, on January 19, 1918. His father was killed in a sawmill accident when he was eight years old and his mother remarried in 1927. The curriculum for black students in the segregated Mississippi River town of Arkansas City stopped at the eighth grade, so Johnson and his family became part of the early twentieth-century Black diaspora to the North and migrated to Chicago in 1933, in part because of the World's Fair there. Johnson became an honor student at DuSable High School. At a convocation, he delivered a speech heard by Harry H. Pace, president of the Supreme Liberty Life Insurance Company, a company that sold to Blacks who would not have been otherwise able to get life insurance.

Pace had encouraged a number of talented young Blacks, including singer and actor Paul Robeson, and gave Johnson a part-time job at his insurance company so Johnson could attend the University of Chicago. Johnson's interests were in the business world however, and he dropped out of college to marry and work full time for Pace's insurance company. Among Johnson's duties was to collect news and information about African Americans and prepare a weekly digest for Pace, loosely based on the format of the popular *Reader's Digest.* Johnson reasoned that such a Black digest could be marketed, and sought a $500 bank loan in late 1942. The only collateral that he could offer was some new furniture that he had helped his mother buy. She considered his offer, but refused to give an answer until she had prayed on the matter. Without an answer a week later, Johnson offered to pray with her, as his 1989 autobiography relates. A few days later, check in hand, *Negro Digest* was born and reached $50,000 in sales within a year.

With the end of World War II in 1945, Johnson predicted that returning Black veterans would need a new magazine to help them cope with the racism back home. He was particularly concerned by how the White mainstream press portrayed African Americans. No notice was given of Black births, education, marriages, achievements, or even deaths in daily newspapers. Only when a Black committed a crime were names and photographs published. "We believed in 1945 that Black Americans needed positive images to fulfill their potential," Johnson wrote. "We believed then—and we believe now—that you have to change images before you can change acts and institutions." Johnson also recognized that the great Black and White magazines of words, *Time, Reader's Digest, Saturday Evening Post,* and his own *Negro Digest,* had reached their peak and were giving way to what he called the "blitzkrieg of the photograph." *Life,* a weekly magazine founded by Henry Luce in 1936, and *Look,* which first appeared in 1937, featured full page pictures by the leading photographers of the day and developed massive circulations. Johnson believed that the photographic magazines of the 1940s, including his monthly *Ebony,* accomplished what television did in the following decades, "opened new windows in the mind and brought us face to face with the multicolored possibilities of man and woman."

The first issue of *Ebony* appeared on November 1, 1945, sold for 25 cents, and featured a black-and-white photograph of seven boys, six White and one Black, from a New York City settlement house on its front cover. Inside were articles on novelist Richard Wright, a Black businessman who went from "slave to banker," and the first appearance of a regular feature, a photo-editorial, on post-war unemployment. The magazine was not an instant success. Johnson was eager to imitate the success of *Life,* which devoted a significant portion of each weekly issue to the activities of rich, famous, and glamorous people. Johnson sought to emphasize the more glamorous aspects of African-American life, in contrast to the negative tone of *Negro Digest,* so he concentrated on Black accomplishments in the worlds of entertainment and business. His elitist perspective did not always represent the aspirations of middle and lower-class Blacks, who bought the magazine for escapism rather than inspiration. Black press historian Walter C. Daniel observed that the early *Ebony* advanced a two-society portrait of American life, one Black and another White. "*Ebony* extracted a journalism model and economic clout from one and used these to propel the accomplishments and aspirations of the other without the encumbrances of philanthropy that had obligated almost every previous black institution," Daniel wrote. Still, *Life* and *Look* had much the same rose colored perspective as *Ebony,* and did not begin to promote actively more serious photojournalism, at least on their covers, until the 1950s and 1960s.

Before the first issue, Johnson had announced that he would not accept any advertising until *Ebony* had achieved a circulation of 100,000 copies. The first issue sold 50,000 copies but Johnson had to wait until May 1946 before accepting his first ad. He wanted to publish full page four-color ads like *Life* and *Look,* but most Black companies could not afford the cost. Johnson wrote to the chief executives of large corporations trying to convince them to consider Black as well as White publications for their advertising. He struck pay dirt with Eugene F. MacDonald, the CEO of the Chicago-based

Zenith Corporation. MacDonald was a former arctic explorer and personal friend of Matthew Henson, a Black man who was one of the first to step on the North Pole. Zenith was not the first White owned company to advertise in Black publication. Wrigley's gum and Bayer Aspirin had advertised in the *Negro World* in the 1920s. But a long term contract with Zenith opened doors to other White corporations and insured *Ebony*'s continued profitability as its circulation grew. Over its history, *Ebony* meant prestige to its advertisers even as the magazine was criticized for an excess of alcoholic beverage ads and the use of lighter hued Black models.

Along with profiles of celebrities and businessmen, *Ebony* provided reliable news on the battle against segregation and the rise of the Civil Rights movement during the 1950s and 1960s. Johnson's pictorial editorials praised student activism and condemned so-called Uncle Tom faculty and administrators in traditional African-American colleges and universities. *Ebony* presented news and analysis on the rise of nationalism among former African colonies, including biographical sketches of diplomatic and government officials in the new nations and the representatives they sent to the United States and United Nations. A 1953 photograph of Harry Belafonte with actors Janet Leigh and Tony Curtis was the first time a Black person was seen with two Whites on the cover of a U.S. magazine. Rev. Dr. Martin Luther King, Jr., published an article on a visit to India in *Ebony* and contributed a regular question and answer column, "Advice for Living By." *Ebony* photographer Moneta Sleet, Jr., became the first Black male to be awarded a Pulitzer Prize in 1969.

Johnson openly endorsed political candidates in *Ebony,* beginning with Harry Truman in 1948, in contrast to the more politically obtuse *Life.* He encouraged Blacks to think of politics in economic rather than racial terms, but remained a Democrat through the years, supporting Adlai Stevenson over Dwight Eisenhower, who had justified the Army's Jim Crowism during World War II. Johnson supported John F. Kennedy in 1960, and an *Ebony* writer predicted that Kennedy would support liberal race legislation in Congress, a promise fulfilled by Lyndon Johnson in 1964 and 1965. Johnson has met with every subsequent president, including his home state governor, Bill Clinton.

Ebony's bicentennial issue in 1976 presented "200 Years of Black Trials and Triumphs," an overview of African American history. On the occasion of its 35th anniversary in 1980, *Ebony* claimed a total readership of over six million readers. *Ebony* celebrated its 50th anniversary in 1995 with Johnson's daughter, Linda Johnson Rice, as president and chief operating officer. The issue featured "50 Who Have Changed America," a list of prominent Blacks including Rosa Parks, Michael Jordan, Colin L. Powell, and Oprah Winfrey. Johnson, written about and honored more than any living Black journalist, began the issue by observing "institutions, corporations, magazines, principalities have lived and died since Nov. 1, 1945, and *Ebony* is still here, and still No. 1" and repeated his favorite saying, "the only failure is failing to try." *Ebony* remains his living legacy to that end.

—Richard Digby-Junger

FURTHER READING:

Daniel, Walter C. *Black Journals of the United States.* Westport, Connecticut, Greenwood Press, 1982, 159-64.

"The *Ebony* Story." *Ebony.* November, 1995, 80-7.

Johnson, John H., and Lerone Bennett, Jr. *Succeeding Against the Odds*. New York, Warner Books, 1989.

Leslie, Michael. ''Slow Fade to ?: Advertising in *Ebony* Magazine.'' *Journalism and Mass Communication Quarterly*. Summer 1995, 426-35.

Pride, Armistead S., and Clint C. Wilson, II. *A History of the Black Press*. Washington, D.C., Howard University Press, 1997, 251-52.

Wilson, Clint C., II. *Black Journalists in Paradox*. Westport, Connecticut, Greenwood Press, 1991.

Wolseley, Roland E. *The Black Press, U.S.A.* 2nd ed. Ames, Iowa, Iowa State University Press, 1990, 85-9, 142-44, 321-24.

EC Comics

EC Comics was arguably the most innovative and controversial company in the history of mainstream comic-book publishing. Although EC thrived for only half-a-decade in the early 1950s, it accounted for a body of comic-book work that shook up the industry and has continued to influence popular culture artists ever since. EC's publications featured some of the cleverest writing and most accomplished artwork ever to appear in comic books, and attracted a fanatically enthusiastic following; but they also provoked harsh criticism from those who charged that they degraded the morals of the nation's youth. Whatever might be said of EC's comic books, they certainly left few readers disinterested.

EC began in 1946 as a company called Educational Comics. Its founder, Max C. Gaines, was one of the original entrepreneurs responsible for the development of comic-book magazines. In 1947 his son William M. Gaines inherited the company and soon thereafter embarked upon a new editorial direction for the line. Keeping the imprint EC, the younger Gaines changed the company's full name to Entertaining Comics in 1950 and launched a series of new titles promoted as EC's ''New Trend'' comic-books. These titles eventually included three horror comics called *Tales from the Crypt, The Vault of Horror,* and *The Haunt of Fear*; the crime titles *Crime SuspenStories* and *Shock SuspenStories*; the science-fiction series *Weird Fantasy* and *Weird Science*; the war comics *Two-Fisted Tales* and *Frontline Combat,* and a humor comic called *Mad.*

The New Trend titles were different from anything that had come before them. All featured quality artwork—some of the most innovative and accomplished ever seen in the medium, and writing that, while often crude, was still far more sophisticated than the norm for comic books. William Gaines and his chief collaborator, Al Feldstein, wrote most of the stories for the horror, crime, and science-fiction titles, and they obviously enjoyed their work. As Feldstein later explained, ''We always wrote to our level.'' They aimed the stories at adolescents and young adults, although their audience doubtless included many children as well. The stories commonly incorporated such ''adult'' themes as murder, revenge, lust, psychosis, political intrigue, and scathing satire.

An alternative, irreverent, and even confrontational perspective on American Cold War culture informed the stories in EC comics, which criticized, satirized, and subverted prevailing values, conventions, and institutions. At a time when the mass entertainment industry in general remained captive to conservative financial and political concerns, such social criticism was seldom to be found in popular media offerings, and EC comic books rank collectively as perhaps the most subversive work produced for profit by an entertainment enterprise during the McCarthy era.

The war comics, published concurrently with the Korean War, qualified as the first truly anti-war comic books ever produced. Harvey Kurtzman wrote and drew many of these, bringing to them both his penchant for historical accuracy and his gift for irony. In Kurtzman's hands, historical stories, ranging from Julius Caesar to the Battle of Little Big Horn to the atomic bombing of Hiroshima, became parables on the dangers inherent in military authority and the utter futility and horror of war—weighty material for comic-books.

In their science-fiction and crime titles, Gaines and Feldstein often attacked such social ills as racism and bigotry, and even dared to point the finger at McCarthyism. *Shock SuspenStories* in particular was a vehicle for realistic and damning portrayals of the violence and injustice inflicted upon African Americans, Jews, and Latinos. No other comic book even began to approach this kind of social commentary, and few contemporary movies or television series did so either.

Under the editorial direction of Harvey Kurtzman, *Mad* became the first and best satirical comic book ever published. Besides mocking many of the conventions, institutions, and icons held dear by mainstream America, *Mad* also took aim at its own competition with devastating parodies of such inviting targets as *Superman, Batman,* and *Archie*. This irreverence branded EC as a maverick within the comic-book industry, a distinction that Gaines welcomed.

EC became best known, however, for its horror comic books. Titles such as *Tales from the Crypt* offered readers some of the most grotesque and grisly images available in mass culture. To say that violence and murder were commonplace in these comics, hardly begins to do justice to stories wherein people were chopped to pieces, ground into pulp, deep-fried, and even eaten. One infamous story, called ''Foul Play,'' ended with a baseball team murdering a rival player, disemboweling his corpse, and playing a baseball game with his body parts. There was usually a tongue-in-cheek quality about these atrocities, as evidenced by the ghoulish narrators who introduced and concluded each tale with gallows humor and bad puns. Husbands murdered wives, wives murdered husbands, parents abused their children, and children rose up to murder their parents. Stories like these sold over half-a-million copies per issue and found a revealingly large audience within a society dominated elsewhere by images of affluence and vapid suburban conformity. They also made EC the most controversial publisher in the business and the one most vulnerable to the charges of the industry's critics. It was, therefore perhaps unsurprising that EC was unable to survive the crisis that engulfed the comic-book industry in 1954-55.

In 1954, Gaines testified before the U.S. Senate Subcommittee that was investigating the alleged influence of crime and horror comic books on juvenile delinquency. At one point he found himself in an absurd (and often recounted) debate with Senator Estes Kefauver over the artistic merits of an EC horror comic with an image of a severed head on the cover. When Gaines' competitors formed the Comics Magazine Association of America and adopted the self-censoring Comics Code, he initially refused to join the organization. He subsequently capitulated, but nervous distributors nevertheless refused to handle the EC publications, code-approved or not. In 1955 Gaines canceled the entire EC line except for *Mad*, which then enjoyed a long run of success in a black-and-white magazine format.

Long after its demise as a comic-book publisher, EC's influence remained evident. Successive generations of comic-book creators drew inspiration from the imaginative ideas of EC's writers and artists. Hard Rock acts such as Alice Cooper and Rob Zombie incorporated EC's grotesque world view into their own musical tributes to American junk culture, while horror novelist Stephen King has cited EC as a profound early influence on his imagination; he paid tribute to their horror titles in his 1982 movie *Creepshow*. Many of EC's crime and horror stories have been adapted into the successful live-action anthology series *Tales from the Crypt* on the HBO and Fox networks, and the original comic books themselves continue to be reprinted and sold in comic-book stores in the 1990s. As an exemplar of mass entertainment of the most inspired, gutsy, and irreverent sort, EC's place in comic-book immortality is assured.

—Bradford W. Wright

FURTHER READING:

Barker, Martin. A Haunt of Fears: The Strange History of the British Horror Comics

Campaign. London, Pluto Press, 1984.

Benton, Mike. *Horror Comics: The Illustrated History.* Dallas, Taylor Publishing, 1991.

The Complete EC Library. West Plains, Missouri, Russ Cochran, 1979-87.

Jacobs, Frank. *The Mad World of William M. Gaines.* Secaucus, NJ, Lyle Stuart, 1972.

Eckstine, Billy (1914-1993)

Although he was best known after 1948 as a singer of popular ballads, Pittsburgh-born Billy Eckstine was a standout jazz singer from 1939-43 with Earl Hines' Band and best known for his bluesy recording of "Jelly, Jelly." He also led a jazz orchestra in the mid-forties that was many years ahead of its time. During the transitional bebop era, Eckstine assembled such cutting-edge jazz stars as trumpeters Dizzy Gillespie and Miles Davis, saxophonists Charlie Parker and Dexter Gordon, and Art Blakey on drums. He also gave a start to Sarah Vaughan, one of the most innovative of jazz singers. Unfortunately, the Eckstine Band was so poorly recorded that no evidence remains of its extraordinary music.

—Benjamin Griffith

FURTHER READING:

Balliett, Whitney. *American Musicians.* New York, Oxford Press, 1986.

Simon, George T. *The Big Bands.* New York, MacMillan, 1974.

Eco-Terrorism

In the latter decades of the twentieth century, terrorist activity expanded into an ever-present threat in the United States of America and elsewhere, penetrating the fabric of national consciousness much as the specter of Communism had done during the Cold War years. Generally perpetrated by political and religio-political fanatics, terrorism has, however, developed a new and significant strain, perceived to have noble aims but intended, nonetheless, to wreak domestic havoc. The Federal Bureau of Investigation defines terrorism as "the unlawful use of force or violence against persons or property to intimidate or coerce a government, the civilian population, or any segment thereof, in furtherance of political or social objectives." The term "eco-terrorism" (or ecoterrorism) refers to two different kinds of terrorism: (1) terrorism intended to hinder activities considered harmful to the environment, and (2) terrorism intended to damage the environment of an enemy.

In February 1991, when Iraqi troops retreated from Kuwait during the Gulf War, they set more than 600 wells in the Greater Burgan oilfield on fire, a deed that has been referred to as "the world's worst act of eco-terrorism." Most popular cultural references to eco-terrorism, however, refer not to this second form of terrorism but to the first, which intends to preserve the environment, not harm it. Used in this manner, eco-terrorism is a highly contested term. Ron Arnold, a leader of the anti-environmental "Wise Use" movement, argues for a broad definition of eco-terrorism that includes almost every crime committed on behalf of the environment, even acts of civil disobedience. Many environmentalists, however, passionately disagree with this usage, preferring to distinguish between "eco-sabotage" (an assault on inanimate objects) and terrorism (an assault on living things). The environmentalist David Brower, for instance, has argued that the real terrorists are those who pollute and despoil the earth, not those who seek to protect it.

This distinction between violence toward property and violence toward living things reflects the influence of "deep ecology," a philosophy upon which much radical environmental action has been based. In 1973, the Norwegian Arne Naess distinguished between what he called "shallow ecology" (or human-centered environmentalism) and "deep ecology" (or earth-centered environmentalism). A central component of deep ecology, according to Naess, is the idea of "Self-realization," in which the "Self" is understood to include not just the individual consciousness, but all of human and non-human nature. Some environmentalists, therefore, argue that eco-sabotage cannot be labeled terrorism, because from this perspective it is actually an act of self-defense.

The roots of eco-sabotage or eco-terrorism can be traced back to the early nineteenth century, when bands of English craftsmen known as Luddites destroyed the textile machinery that was rendering their skills increasingly redundant. Generally masked and operating at night, the Luddites claimed to be led by Ned Ludd, an apparently mythical figure whom many modern eco-saboteurs have taken as their namesake. Henry David Thoreau, though by no means an eco-terrorist, has also been cited as a forerunner of the radical environmental movement. In *A Week on the Concord and Merrimack Rivers* (1849), Thoreau mourned the inability of shad to bypass the Billerica Dam in the Concord River. "I for one am with thee," Thoreau wrote of the fish, "and who knows what may avail a crow-bar against that Billerica Dam?"

Modern eco-terrorism came into being after the first Earth Day, held in 1970, when a handful of environmentalists in the United States began using force to achieve their political goals. In Arizona, the "Arizona Phantom" tore up railroad tracks and disabled equipment in an attempt to stop construction of a coal mine in the desert highlands. A group of college-age boys calling themselves the "Eco-Raiders" burned billboards, disabled bulldozers, and vandalized development projects in and around Tucson, causing over half a million dollars of damage. In Illinois, a man going by the name of "The Fox" plugged drainage pipes, capped factory smokestacks, and dumped industrial waste from a U.S. Steel plant into the office of the company's chief executive. In Michigan, the ''Billboard Bandits'' cut down roadside signs with chainsaws, and in Minnesota, a group of farmers calling themselves the ''Bolt Weevils'' disabled 14 electrical towers that were part of a high-voltage power line being built across the prairie.

These early eco-radicals may have been encouraged by the founding in 1971 of the environmental group Greenpeace, which advocated non-violent direct action against high-profile targets. They may also have been influenced by the publication of several books, including *The Anarchist Cookbook* (1971), by William Powell; *Ecotage!* (1972), edited by Sam Love and David Obst; and *The Monkey Wrench Gang* (1976), by Edward Abbey, a novel about four ''ecoteurs'' who roam the Southwestern United States blowing up bridges and vandalizing bulldozers in the name of environmental protection.

The Monkey Wrench Gang not only gave the activity of eco-sabotage its popular moniker (''monkeywrenching''), it also inspired the formation of the environmental group most closely associated with eco-terrorism in the popular imagination—Earth First! Founded in 1980 by Dave Foreman and other disenchanted activists, Earth First! took as its motto the phrase ''No Compromise in Defense of Mother Earth,'' and its journal served as a clearinghouse for monkeywrenching tactics, though the group never officially advocated the practice. In 1985, however, Foreman edited the first of several editions of *Ecodefense: A Field Guide to Monkeywrenching*, which contained instructions for such actions as how to spike trees, close roads, and burn machinery. By 1990, monkeywrenching was estimated to be costing business and industry from $20 to $25 million a year, had spawned federal legislation against tree-spiking, and had caught the attention of the FBI, Scotland Yard, and other intelligence organizations.

Whether incidents of eco-terrorism are increasing or decreasing in frequency is unclear, due in part to the elastic nature of the term itself. Opponents of eco-terrorism point to incidents such as the October 1998 burning of a Vail, Colorado, ski resort as evidence that eco-terrorism is on the rise. The arson, which caused some $12 million in damage, was attributed to the Earth Liberation Front, a radical environmental group, working to prevent the expansion of the ski resort into one of the last known habitats of the lynx. Author David Helvarg, however, contends that radical environmentalists have become less likely to resort to monkeywrenching tactics and more likely to employ civil disobedience to achieve their goals. Similarly, he claims that environmentalists are more likely to be victims of violence than to act violently. In 1998, for instance, David Chain, an Earth First! protestor, was killed by a tree felled by a Pacific Lumber logger in Humboldt County, California.

Whatever the future of eco-terrorism, its appearance in such films as Terry Gilliam's *12 Monkeys,* novels such as Tom Clancy's *Rainbow Six,* and such computer games as Eidos Interactive's *Final Fantasy VII,* suggests that this highly contested term has quite clearly hit a nerve.

—Daniel J. Philippon

FURTHER READING:

Abbey, Edward. *The Monkey Wrench Gang.* New York, Avon, 1976.

Arnold, Ron. *Ecoterror: The Violent Agenda to Save Nature: The World of the Unabomber.* Bellevue, Washington, Free Enterprise Press, 1997.

Foreman, Dave, editor. *Ecodefense: A Field Guide to Monkeywrenching.* 2nd ed. Tucson, Ned Ludd Books, 1985.

Helvarg, David. *The War against the Greens: The ''Wise-Use'' Movement, the New Right, and Anti-environmental Violence.* San Francisco, Sierra Club Books, 1994.

Lee, Martha F. *Earth First! Environmental Apocalypse.* New York, Syracuse University Press, 1995.

Manes, Christopher. *Green Rage: Radical Environmentalism and the Unmaking of Civilization.* Boston, Little, Brown, 1990.

Eddy, Duane (1938—)

Known for his ''twangy'' guitar sound, Duane Eddy was a leading rock and roll instrumentalist, with fifteen Top 40 hits between 1958 and 1963. Born in upstate New York, Eddy moved to Arizona at the age of thirteen. He was an early experimenter with natural sources of echo and reverberation, which resulted in the ''twangy'' sound that quickly became his trademark. Eddy recorded on the Jamie label through 1961, and moved to the more prestigious RCA Victor label for his last few records in 1962 and 1963.

His popularity and good looks led to a few supporting roles in motion pictures such as *Because They're Young* (for which he also performed the main theme song), along with a custom line of Duane Eddy signature guitars. There was an excessive similarity inherent in the various songs Eddy recorded, and only two ever reached the major success of the Top Ten. Those were ''Rebel Rouser'' in 1958 and ''Forty Miles of Bad Road'' in 1959.

—David Lonergan

FURTHER READING:

Stambler, Irwin. *The Encyclopedia of Pop, Rock and Soul,* revised edition. New York, St. Martin's Press, 1989.

Eddy, Mary Baker (1821-1910)

Mary Baker Eddy is regarded as one of the most influential women in American history. In 1992 the Women's National Book Association recognized her *Science and Health* as one of the 75 books by women ''whose words have changed the world.'' In 1995 she was elected into the National Women's Hall of Fame as the only American woman to have founded a religion recognized worldwide.

Eddy was born the sixth child of a Puritan family outside of Concord, New Hampshire on July 16, 1821. As a child she was extremely frail and suffered from persistent illnesses. In 1843, Eddy married her first husband, Major George Washington Glover, who died of yellow fever six months after their marriage, leaving her penniless and 5 months pregnant. Once born, her son was taken from her and given to a couple who had just lost twins. In 1853, Eddy married her second husband Daniel Patterson, a Baptist dentist. Since her health was persistently in decline, she began to investigate many ''mind over matter'' theories that were popular at the time. She even went so far as to consult a psychic healer in 1862.

Mary Baker Eddy

Eddy's struggle with illness lasted until her epiphany experience on February 4, 1866. Eddy was bedridden after having sustained critical spine injuries from a fall on an icy sidewalk. She came across a story in the Bible about a palsied, bedridden man who is forgiven by Christ and made to walk. She then formed her theory that the power to heal sin is the same power that heals the body. Indeed, she believed and got out of bed. Patterson left her that year, and, seven years later, Eddy divorced him.

After her transforming spiritual realization, she preached her discovery of Christian Science. She had found the answer to her quest for health, and she wrote her first book on the subject, *Science and Health with a Key to the Scriptures* (1875). And, in 1877, Eddy was married for a final time to Asa Gilbert Eddy.

Christian Science is based on her beliefs that anything associated with the physical world is an illusion (including pain), and that mind, life, and spirit are all that exist and are all part of God. Healing for her meant recognizing the error of believing in the flesh. Eddy's philosophy, however, cannot be considered a mind over matter philosophy because, in Christian Science, the concept of matter does not exist.

Eddy's writings and beliefs quickly helped her become the leader of thousands of people in the Christian Science movement. By the year 1900, only 34 years after her revelation and only 25 from the publication of her first book, over 900 churches participated in the Christian Science movement. Eddy obtained a nearly god-like status in her churches by her death in 1910.

The Christian Science Church, from its "Mother Church" headquarters in Boston, Massachusetts, has been a major media influence. *Science and Health,* reissued in 1994, immediately became an annual best seller among religious books. Eddy also wrote 20 other books and pamphlets, including other theology books and a book of her poetry and letters. In 1883, Eddy published the first issue of *The Christian Science Journal.* In 1899 she established both the *Christian Science Sentinel* and *Christian Science Quarterly.* She had a strong influence as editor of these periodicals. And, finally, in 1908 she requested that a daily newspaper be started called the *Christian Science Monitor.* Both the *Christian Science Journal* and the *Christian Science Monitor* are still in print and continue to be very well respected.

In 1989, the *Christian Science Monitor* launched The Monitor Channel, a cable network that failed and collapsed in 1992. At the same time, the church also started a radio network and a public affairs magazine that both fell through. Although Christian Science has remained politically powerful throughout the second half of the twentieth century, estimated membership totals have shown a drop, from 270,000 members before World War II to 170,000 in the 1990s. Branch churches have declined from 3,000 in 37 countries to fewer than 2,400 in the 1990s.

A major criticism of Christian Science is that its members are often unwilling to seek medical help for themselves or their critically ill children. In the last half of the twentieth century, Christian Scientists have even succeeded in most states to establish the right to deny their children medical treatment. Part of the decline of the church population is due to an increasing trust of traditional medicine.

The followers of Christian Science revere Mary Baker Eddy. Outside of the religion she is heralded as having made major feminist accomplishments. In *Science and Health,* she pushed for the equality of the sexes, female suffrage, and the right of women to hold and dispose of property. She also pushed for an understanding of both the motherhood and the fatherhood of God. Eddy's ideas, although spawned and proliferated in her time, have outlived her.

—Adam Wathen

FURTHER READING:

Beasley, Norman. *Mary Baker Eddy.* New York, Duell, Sloan, and Pearce, 1963.

Cather, Willa, and Georgine Milmine. *The Life of Mary Baker G. Eddy and the History of Christian Science.* Lincoln, University of Nebraska Press, 1993.

Dakin, Edwin Franden. *Mrs. Eddy: The Biography of a Virginal Mind.* New York, Charles Scribner's Sons, 1930.

d'Humy, Fernand Emile. *Mary Baker Eddy in a New Light.* New York, Library Publishers, 1952.

Orcutt, William Dana. *Mary Baker Eddy and Her Books.* Boston, Christian Science Publishing Society, 1991.

Peel, Robert. *Mary Baker Eddy.* New York, Holt, Rinehart and Winston, 1966.

Silberger, Julius, Jr. *Mary Baker Eddy: An Interpretive Biography of the Founder of Christian Science.* Boston, Little, Brown, 1980.

Thomas, Robert David. *"With Bleeding Footsteps": Mary Baker Eddy's Path to Religious Leadership.* New York, Knopf, 1994.

Wilbur, Sybil. *The Life of Mary Baker Eddy.* New York, Concord, 1908.

Zweig, Stefan. *Mental Healers: Franz Anton Mesmer, Mary Baker Eddy, Sigmund Freud.* New York, Viking Press, 1934.

Eddy, Nelson (1901-1967)

With his captivating good looks, military uniform, and baritone voice, Nelson Eddy was the epitome of the Hollywood musical hero in the 1930s and 1940s. He and Jeanette MacDonald became known as "America's Singing Sweethearts" because of their eight MGM film collaborations.

Born in Providence, Rhode Island, on June 29, 1901, Eddy grew up in a musical household. He sang major roles at New York's Metropolitan Opera before becoming known as a radio singer and eventually as a film star. Although he sang with such esteemed leading ladies as Eleanor Powell and Rise Stevens, it was with Jeanette MacDonald that he was most often associated. The films of the so-called "Beauty and the Baritone" included *Naughty Marietta* (1935), *Rose Marie* (1936), *Maytime* (1937), *The Girl of the Golden West* (1938), *The New Moon* (1940), *Bitter Sweet* (1940), and *I Married an Angel* (1942). Other Eddy films include *The Chocolate Soldier* (1941) and *Phantom of the Opera* (1943). In addition to his film appearances, Eddy made numerous recordings and sang frequently in concert and on the night club circuit. He died in Miami, Florida, on March 6, 1967.

—William A. Everett

FURTHER READING:

Castanza, Philip. *The Complete Films of Jeanette MacDonald and Nelson Eddy.* New York, Citadel Press, 1978.

Hamann, G.D. *Nelson Eddy in the 30s.* Hollywood, Filming Today Press, 1996.

Kiner, Larry F. *Nelson Eddy: A Bio-Discography.* Metuchen, New Jersey, Scarecrow Press, 1992.

Knowles, Eleanor. *Films of Jeannete MacDonald and Nelson Eddy.* South Brunswick, New Jersey, A. S. Barnes, 1975.

The Edge of Night

The Edge of Night, one of the top ten longest running soap operas in daytime television history, debuted on April 2, 1956 on CBS, along with *As the World Turns.* The two shows were the first soaps to air for a full half-hour on a major television network, and the enthusiastic audience response marked a new trend in the orientation of popular television. *The Edge of Night*'s original time slot, 4:30 p.m., inspired the show's title, but the title reflected the content, which was at times graphically violent. While some television critics, including the redoubtable *TV Guide,* have argued that *The Edge of Night* was technically a serialized melodrama rather than a soap opera, over its almost three-decade run the show turned to themes most commonly associated with soap opera drama: sex, romance, and family turmoil.

Set in Monticello, a turbulent midwestern town, *The Edge of Night* revolved around the criminal investigations of Mike Karr and his sometimes unorthodox detective work and courtroom tactics. After the first couple of seasons, Karr married his devoted assistant, Sara Lane, though the writers had her run over by a bus on the February 17, 1961 episode. Lane was the first major soap character to be killed off, and the high realism of the accident—the show was broadcast live until 1975—sent the audience into shock. Thousands of letters and phone calls deluged the network and prompted a televised announcement by Teal Ames and John Larkin, the actors who played Sara and Mike, explaining that Ames was fine in real life and had left the show to pursue other opportunities.

Over the years Mike Karr was played by three different actors—John Larkin from 1956 to 1961; Laurence Hugo from 1962-1971; and Forrest Compton from 1971-1984. Exemplifying a paradox that television audiences have simply come to accept, the three replacements were neither announced nor explained, but did nothing to disturb the sense of realism so central to *The Edge of Night*'s success. By the 1970s, however, the show's writers perhaps did push the limits of believability in the popular Adam-Nicole love story. Nicole (Maeve McGuire; later Jayne Bentzen and Lisa Sloan) had been killed off in a drowning during the explosion of a yacht, only to rejoin the show two years later when it was discovered that in fact she had survived the drowning, joined a gang in France, and suffered a long bout of amnesia before returning to Monticello.

After the show's sponsor, Procter and Gamble, requested a time change in the 1970s, *The Edge of Night* experienced a ratings slump from which it never recovered. The show moved to ABC on December 1, 1975, the first daytime serial to change networks, but was canceled on December 28, 1984. A few years later it enjoyed a short-lived cult revival in syndication on the USA cable network. Among the sophisticated luminaries who had early on enjoyed some of its 7,420 episodes were Cole Porter, P. G. Wodehouse, Tallulah Bankhead, and Eleanor Roosevelt.

—Michele S. Shauf

FURTHER READING:

Hyatt, Wesley. *The Encyclopedia of Daytime Television.* New York, Billboard Books, 1997.

McNeil, Alex. *Total Television.* New York, Penguin Books, 1996.

Edison, Thomas Alva (1847-1931)

Thomas Alva Edison, inventor of the phonograph in 1878 and the incandescent light bulb in 1879, is considered to be one of America's most creative minds. He is the only American to have patented an invention every year for 63 consecutive years, beginning in 1868 with his invention of an electrical vote recorder. Altogether, Edison held 1,093 patents including those for a stock ticker, a component of mimeograph systems, and a telephone transmitter that led to commercial telephone and radio broadcasting. Using a mobile studio and a photographic device he designed, Edison also created the first apparatus for projecting motion pictures. The invention, along with George Eastman's refinement of film, set the stage for the creation of the motion picture industry. It is appropriate that the creator of so many products, a man whose impact on America proved revolutionary, should have provided a symbol to represent originality and intelligence, the shining light bulb, used in logos to represent a "bright idea."

—Sharon Brown

FURTHER READING:

Baldwin, Neil. *Edison Inventing the Century.* New York, Hyperion, 1995.

Israel, Paul. *Edison: A Life of Invention.* New York, John Wiley & Sons, 1998.

Josephson, Matthew. *Edison: A Biography.* New York, John Wiley & Sons, 1992.

Edmonds, Kenneth

See Babyface

The Edsel

Announced with great fanfare in 1957 after almost a decade of planning, the Ford Motor Company's Edsel model car became one of the great flops in automotive history. The car was forecasted to sell over 200,000 units in its first year, but sold less than 85,000 during its three year run. Despite massive advertising—including pre-empting *The Ed Sullivan Show* with *The Edsel Show* featuring Bing Crosby and Frank Sinatra—the Edsel was the wrong car at the wrong time. The auto industry, after years of massive sales, hit a post-Sputnik slump and the new car, with its strange oval grille, was doomed. Named after Henry Ford's son Edsel, the name is now synonymous with failure. As such, Edsel is often used as a punchline and visual gag. The car can be seen in films such as *Pee Wee's Big Adventure,* and in *Airplane II,* where the engine from a 1959 Edsel is used to jumpstart a space shuttle.

—Patrick Jones

FURTHER READING:

Baughman, James L. "The Frustrated Persuader: Fairfax M. Cone and the Edsel Advertising Campaign." In *The Other Fifties: Interrogating Mid-century American Icons,* edited by Joel Foreman. Champaign-Urbana, University of Illinois Press, 1997.

Brooks, John. *The Fate of the Edsel and Other Business Adventures.* New York, Harper & Row, 1963.

Deutsch, Jan. *Selling the People's Cadillac: The Edsel and Corporate Responsibility.* New Haven, Yale University Press, 1976.

Warnock, C. Gayle. *The Edsel Affair.* Paradise Valley, Arizona, Pro West, 1980.

Edwards, James (1916?-1970)

With his thoughtful intelligent manner and splendid good looks, African American actor James Edwards came to epitomize the "new Negro" in post-World War II Hollywood film. His moderately successful motion picture acting career spanned four decades, from the late 1940s to his final appearance in 1970. His contribution to film history, however, is not attributed to a sterling performance in a wildly successful classic. Edward's legacy is that he was a groundbreaker, and his work helped to forge change during a significant period in American social history.

The 1958 Edsel Citation

Younger film devotees may find it difficult to appreciate the impact that black film stars such as Edwards and his contemporaries Sidney Poitier and Harry Belafonte had on the psyche of postwar Blacks and Whites, and on the state of race relations in the United States. Edward's portrayal as a victim of bigotry in *Home of the Brave* (1949) was widely hailed as the first feature film to deal honestly with race issues in America. It was an early example of the cycle of "message pictures" that appeared during the volatile period of bus boycotts, school desegregation, and protest against systematic discrimination.

Historically, African Americans had appeared in motion pictures as soon as the first murky images appeared in nickelodeons during the early days of the twentieth century. By the late 1910s, as filmmakers fine-tuned the possibilities of storytelling on film, Black people (along with recent immigrants, women, and Native Americans) found themselves viscously lampooned with the most egregious of film stereotypes. During the Golden Age of Hollywood (1929-1939) a number of Black film "types" appeared: Black film characters were relegated to a few roles as maid, butler or, most notably, comic-relief—the dim-witted, bug-eyed, darkie servant who was the butt of everyone's jokes. War and organized protest helped to forge change and by the postwar period, though the stereotypes had hardly disappeared and the number of roles for Black performers was small, Hollywood pictures could now feature Blacks as lawyers, teachers, soldiers, and otherwise contributing members of society.

Like Poitier, James Edwards began his acting career in theater. He was born in Muncie, Indiana, and attended Indiana and Northwestern University, earning a B.S. in 1938 for dramatics. As a lieutenant in the Army he was wounded in battle. Surgeons had to rebuild his face and he endured a long, painful convalescent period. It was suggested that he take lessons in elocution. Recovered, he pursued an acting career and appeared in the controversial 1945 stage production of *How Deep are the Roots* (in which he portrayed the love interest of a very white, Barbara Bel Geddes). His first film appearance appears to have been a bit part as a boxer in the 1949 film noir classic, *The Set-Up.*

The year was 1948 and President Harry Truman signed an order that would begin the long and painful process of desegregating the nation's armed forces. Far away from Washington, D.C., and working in total secrecy, young filmmaker Stanley Kramer worked on a film that intended to exploit the ramifications of Truman's order. Featuring James Edwards in the title role, the film *Home of the Brave* was released May 1949, less than a year after the president's missive. Based loosely on the stage play (which had anti-semitism as a theme), *Home of the Brave* told the story of a young Black soldier on duty in the Pacific who succumbs emotionally and physically to the torment of racial prejudice.

To contemporary viewers the film may appear contrived and corny, replete with staid dialogue and sometimes tacky sets. With its strong theme and frank language, however, it was praised by both the white press and black press—which noted with encouragement that Hollywood was finally putting the old film stereotypes of Blacks to rest. It also won recognition for Edwards in the form of an Oscar nomination for Best Supporting performance. He became a Black movie idol and his exploits were covered in the black fanzines of the time.

Issues of race were depicted in varying degrees in several of Edward's films. In 1951 he appeared in *Bright Victory,* portraying a blinded Black soldier whose white (and also blind) friend rejects him when he learns Edwards is black. In his role as Corporal Thompson in the Sam Fuller Korean War cult classic *The Steel Helmet* (1950), a Communist officer chides Edwards for risking his life for a country that requires him to sit in the back of bus. His other roles as a soldier include *Battle Hymn* (1957), *Men in War* (1957), *Blood and Steel* (1959), and the star-studded Lewis Milestone production of *Pork Chop Hill* (1959).

Bright, personable, and well-spoken, Edwards was a welcome alternative to the Black film stereotypes of the past. In effect, however, one stereotype replaced another. The bug-eyed comics of the 1930s were replaced in the 1960s by the "Good Negro"—intelligent, articulate, and most importantly, non-threatening.

But in some ways, Edwards was no Hollywood Negro poster-boy. He was an out-spoken critic of discrimination and he is said to have refused to testify during the infamous House Un-American Affairs Committee hearings of the 1950s. A 1953 article by Edwards appearing in the December issue of *Our World* magazine was titled "Hollywood: So What?" Unlike Poitier, who was seen at the time as, perhaps, a bit more accommodating, Edwards apparently spoke his mind.

Edward's other film roles include *Member of the Wedding* (1952), *The Joe Louis Story* (1953), *Seven Angry Men* (1955), *The Phenix City Story* (1955), *Battle Hymn* (1957), *The Killing* (1956), *Anna Lucasta* (1959), *Night of the Quarter Moon* (1959), *The Manchurian Candidate* (1962), *The Sandpiper* (1965), and his final appearance as a personal aid to General George Patton in the academy award winning 1970 production of *Patton.* Edwards was not to enjoy the success of *Patton.* He died in 1970 of a heart attack, leaving behind a wife and daughter. Curiously, obituaries list his age at the time of his death as anywhere from 42 to 58.

If not for the influence of cable movie channels and video collections, many of Edwards' films would have by now been relegated to the land of long-forgotten "B" movies. His legacy to film history, therefore, is not a classic film but his efforts and work as a Hollywood actor to help forge change in attitudes about race during a time in the social history of America when change was sorely needed.

—Pamala S. Deane

FURTHER READING:

Crowther, Bosley. "Home of the Brave." *New York Times.* May 19, 1949.

Edwards, James. "Hollywood: So What!" *Our World.* December 1953.

Franklin, John Hope, and Alfred A. Moss, Jr. *From Freedom to Slavery.* New York, Alfred A. Knopf, 1988.

Guernsey, Otis L., Jr. "Home of the Brave Proves Imagination, not Cash, Pays." *New York Herald Tribune.* May 15, 1949.

"Home of the Brave." *Variety.* May 4, 1949.

Kane, Kathryn. *Visions of War: Hollywood Combat Films of World War II.* Ann Arbor, UMI Research Press, 1982.

Nesteby, James R. *Black Images in American Films 1896-1954: The Interplay Between Civil Rights and Film Culture.* Lanham, Maryland, University Press of America, 1982.

Spoto, Donald. *Stanley Kramer, Filmmaker.* New York, G. P. Putnam's Sons, 1978.

Edwards, Jodie and Susie

See Butterbeans and Susie

Edwards, Ralph (1913—)

Television producer Ralph Edwards is best known for creating the game show *Truth or Consequences*. Edwards began his career in the entertainment industry as a radio announcer while attending the University of California, Berkeley. After graduating, Edwards moved to New York and became a nationally syndicated radio personality. In 1940 Edwards produced, wrote, and emceed the radio version of *Truth or Consequences,* which aired for 38 consecutive years on radio and television. Edwards introduced the ''live on film'' technique by having *Truth or Consequences* filmed before a live studio audience when it debuted on television in 1950; the show was hosted for 18 years by Bob Barker, who went on to become television's most durable game show host with *The Price Is Right*. Edwards produced dozens of television game shows, including *This Is Your Life, Knockout, Place the Face,* and *It Could Be You.* In 1981 Edwards teamed up with producer Stu Billett to create a show that introduced a new form of the reality genre to television; they called their show *The People's Court*.

—Lara Bickell

Ralph Edwards

FURTHER READING:

Fabe, Maxene. *TV Game Shows.* New York, Doubleday, 1979.

Graham, Jefferson. *Come On Down!!!: The TV Game Show Book.* New York, Abbeville Press, 1988.

Schwartz, David, et al. *The Encyclopedia of Television Game Shows.* New York, New York Zoetrope, 1987.

Eight, The

See Ashcan School, The

Eight-Track Tape

In the 1960s, the eight-track tape player was an ambitious attempt to employ magnetic prerecorded tape in a convenient format for use in home and automobile stereos. The eight-track was significant evidence that Americans now demanded music while they travelled and that the automobile had become a place to experience entertainment. By the early 1980s, however, the eight-track became a symbol of obsolescence in audio technology and an artifact of 1960s and 1970s nostalgia.

In the 1960s, several manufacturers developed tape cartridges as a format for recorded sound. The Lear Company, a manufacturer of executive jet airplanes, produced a continuous-loop cartridge with four sets of paired stereo tracks—thus the name eight-track. In 1964, representatives from Lear approached Ford Motor Company with a plan to introduce this format into automobiles. People wanted to select their own music to listen while travelling, and the eight-track tape was convenient for the driver because it could be inserted into the player with one hand.

Ford equipped millions of automobiles with eight-track players and millions more were manufactured for use in home radio/phonographs. Although the eight-track format became a major format for pre-recorded popular music in the 1960s and 1970s, it was not an entirely satisfactory product for the user who could not record on it and found it difficult to access selections. By the end of the 1970s, the eight-track tape had been overtaken by the compact cassette and dropped by audio manufacturers and record companies.

—Andre Millard

FURTHER READING:

Kusisto, Oscar P. ''Magnetic Tape Recording: Reels, Cassettes, or Cartridges?'' *Journal of the Audio Engineering Society.* Vol. 24, 1977, 827-831.

Millard, Andre. *America on Record: A History of Recorded Sound.* Boston, Cambridge University Press, 1995.

Einstein, Albert (1879-1955)

In the 1910s, Albert Einstein proposed a series of theories that led to new ways of thinking about space, time, and gravitation. For the continued his research and writing and in 1905 published a thesis entitled *A New Determination of Molecular Dimensions* that won him a Ph.D. from the University of Zürich. Four more important papers were published that year in the prestigious German journal *Annalen der Physik,* forever changing man's view of the universe.

Now accepted by his colleagues as one of Europe's leading physicists and much sought-after as a consultant, Einstein left the patent office and returned to teaching in universities in Switzerland and Germany. In 1914 he moved to Berlin, where he worked at the Prussian Academy of Sciences, doing his research on the general theory of relativity and lecturing occasionally at the University of Berlin. He published his findings in 1916 in an article entitled (in translation): "The Foundation of the General Theory of Relativity." He postulated that gravitation was not a force, as Newton had thought, but a curved field in a space-time continuum. This could be proved, he wrote, by measuring the deflection of starlight during a period of total eclipse. In 1919 British scientists photographed a solar eclipse from Principe Island in the Gulf of Guinea, and their calculations verified Einstein's predictions. Einstein was amazed at the world-wide acclamation he received, but he resented the constant interruptions his new fame brought. In 1921 he was awarded the Nobel Prize for Physics.

During the 1920s Einstein worked toward finding a mathematical relationship between electromagnetism and gravitation, thus relating the universal properties of matter and energy into a single equation or formula. This quest for a unified field theory, which occupied the rest of his life, proved futile. The rapidly developing quantum theory showed that the movement of a single particle could not be predicted because of the uncertainty in measuring both its speed and its position at the same time. The first version of the unified field theory was published in 1929, but the tentative, preliminary nature of the work was apparent to the scientific community.

In the 1930s, Einstein spent as much time championing the cause of peace as he did discussing science. He established the Einstein War Resisters International Fund to bring massive public pressure on the World Disarmament Conference, scheduled to meet in Geneva in 1932. After the failure of the conference, which he termed "farcical," Einstein visited Geneva to focus world attention on the failure and on the necessity of reducing the world's firepower.

When Adolf Hitler became chancellor of Germany in 1933, Einstein warned the world that Nazi Germany was preparing for war, then renounced his German citizenship and moved to America. He accepted a full time position at the newly formed Institute for Advanced Study at Princeton, New Jersey. Nazi storm troopers ransacked his summer home near Berlin in reprisal.

His life at Princeton remained the same for the next 20 years. He lived in a simple frame house, daily walking a mile or so to the Institute, where he worked on his unified field theory and talked with colleagues. In a 1994 movie entitled *I.Q.,* Walter Matthau played the role of Einstein enjoying his intellectual life at Princeton. Einstein rarely traveled, preferring to relax with his violin and sail on a local lake. He took no part in the work at Los Alamos, New Mexico, where the nuclear fission bombs were being made. When he died in his sleep on April 18, 1955, his wife found an incomplete statement, written to honor Israeli Independence Day, on his desk. It included this statement: "What I seek to accomplish is simply to serve with my feeble capacity truth and justice at the risk of pleasing no one."

—Benjamin Griffith

Albert Einstein

first time, the scientific world raced far beyond the theories of the seventeenth century English scientist Sir Isaac Newton, who began his study of gravity by observing an apple fall from a tree. Einstein's famous energy-mass equation, which asserts that a particle of matter can be transformed into an astounding quantity of energy, led to the construction of atomic and hydrogen bombs with unimaginable capacities for destruction. In his own time he was widely recognized as one of the most innovative geniuses in human history. Today, in the realm of popular culture, his name is synonymous with genius, and many a young prodigy has been called an "Einstein."

He was born in Ulm, Germany, on March 14, 1879, and grew up in Munich, where he was educated in public schools that he found to be boring, as well as highly regimented and intimidating. He showed such little ability as a student that his mother recommended that he study music, and he became an accomplished violinist, playing throughout his life for relaxation, not for public performance. Under the influence of two uncles, the boy Einstein began to develop a curiosity about science and mathematics, and at age 12 he announced that he would concentrate his mind on solving the riddle of the "huge world."

At age 15, with poor grades in languages, history, and geography, he left his German school without a diploma and moved with his family to Milan. He resumed his education at the famous Federal Polytechnic Academy in Zürich, where he completed four years of physics and mathematics. After graduating in the spring of 1900, Einstein began a two month tenure as a mathematics teacher before being employed as an examiner in the Swiss patent office in Bern. He

FURTHER READING:

Brian, Denis. *Einstein: A Life.* New York, Wiley, 1997.

Holton, Gerald James. *Einstein, History, and Other Passions: The Rebellion Against Science at the End of the Twentieth Century.* New York, Springer-Verlag, 1995.

Pais, Abraham. *"Subtle Is The Lord . . . ": The Science and Life of Albert Einstein.* New York, Oxford, 1982.

Eisner, Will (1917—)

With a career as a writer and artist that spans virtually the entire history of the medium, Will Eisner is one of the most innovative and influential creators of comic books and graphic novels. From his earliest work on the newspaper supplement, *The Spirit,* Eisner strove to understand and develop his chosen art form. His career has been driven by his canny business sense and by a belief that sequential art (as he prefers to call comic books and graphic novels) is a valid medium of artistic expression that deserves wider acceptance and respect.

As a teenager, Eisner's artistic talent simply represented a way out of the grim reality of Bronx tenement life during the Depression. After a brief stint studying at the Art Students League and working in a magazine advertising department, Eisner began writing and drawing comics for *Wow, What a Magazine!* in 1936. Samuel "Jerry" Iger was editing *Wow,* and when the magazine folded after four issues, Eisner and Iger formed their own studio to package comic book material for Fiction House, Fox Comics, and other publishers. At first, the prolific Eisner produced most of the work under different pen names. As the Eisner-Iger Shop flourished, however, the young Eisner began supervising a staff of artists that included Bob Kane and Jack Kirby.

In 1939 Eisner was approached by a features syndicate about producing a comic book supplement for newspapers. He jumped at the chance to reach a more mature audience through newspaper distribution. Because the syndicate had approached him—they were not likely to find anyone else capable of producing a complete comic book every week—Eisner was able to retain ownership and creative control of the feature. He sold his interest in the Eisner-Iger Shop to Iger and took four of the staff with him to form Will Eisner Productions.

The newspaper supplement that debuted in 1940 was simply called *The Comic Book Section,* but it became better known by the title of the lead feature, *The Spirit.* The syndicate saw the supplement as a way to benefit from the growing national market for comic books that was sparked by the appearance of *Superman* in 1938 and *The Batman* in 1939, and they envisioned the Spirit as a superhero very much in the mold of these two characters. Will Eisner was more interested in telling good stories, and his only concessions to the superhero concept were a simple domino mask and a pair of gloves.

When Eisner was drafted in 1942, his assistants, primarily Lou Fine, took over for the duration of the war. Fine was true to the style Eisner had set for the book, and it was a subtle change compared to what happened when Eisner returned from the Army. Many early stories from *The Spirit* were whimsical and fantasy-oriented, but when Eisner returned from the war his stories had greater realism and concern for the human condition—in his work that usually means the condition of humans crowded together by big city life. As Catherine Yronwode puts it in *The Art of Will Eisner,* "New York, or more

properly, Brooklyn and The Bronx, was, in Eisner's metaphoric world, transformed into a stage upon which the most wide-sweeping and the most intimate dramas of human life were enacted."

Eisner had used his art to escape from the tenements of New York, but eventually he used his art to explore the personal and universal meanings of those youthful experiences—it just took a while. Eisner stopped producing *The Spirit* in 1952 and devoted his time to his new venture, American Visuals Corporation, which was a successful producer of educational and corporate comics for the next 25 years. Then, in 1976, inspired by the decidedly non-adolescent material that he discovered in the underground comix of the late 1960s and early 1970s, he began creating a major comic book work that he hoped would find an adult audience. When his 192 page work, *A Contract With God,* appeared in 1978 it was not the first use of the graphic novel format (although Eisner did coin the phrase), but it was ground breaking in that it deviated from the usual adventure material to present more realistic and intimate human dramas. At 60, Eisner began blazing a new trail in the medium and followed his first graphic novel with innovative and deeply-felt works such as *A Life Force* (1983), *To The Heart of the Storm* (1991), and *Family Matter* (1998).

Eisner soon became the internationally acclaimed master of the comics medium. The major artistic awards of the American comic book industry, the Eisners, were named in his honor. He was asked to teach comics courses at the School of Visual Arts. Eisner reworked his lecture material and published two books, *Comics and Sequential Art* (1985) and *Graphic Storytelling* (1995), that have helped advance both artistic and critical understanding of the medium.

It was Eisner's experimentation with layout and composition in *The Spirit* stories that clearly established the comic book as a medium distinct from its comic strip origins. It was his championing of new forms and mature content in the graphic novel that helped establish comics as an art form. And, much of the visual language of the form was invented, or at least perfected, by Will Eisner. In the afterword to Eisner's *New York the Big City,* acclaimed comic book writer Alan Moore provides an eloquent statement of Will Eisner's importance to the medium: "He is the single person most responsible for giving comics its brains."

—Randy Duncan

FURTHER READING:

Harvey, Robert C. *The Art of the Comic Book.* Jackson, University Press of Mississippi, 1996.

Steranko, James. *The Steranko History of Comics.* 2 Vols. Reading, Pennsylvania, Supergraphics, 1970.

Yronwode, Catherine. *The Art of Will Eisner.* Princeton, Wisconsin, Kitchen Sink Press, 1982.

El Teatro Campesino

The United States' annexation of Mexico's northern territories in 1858 marked the beginning of the Mexican-American theater arts tradition. Mexican-American (California Chicano, Texas Tejano, and New Mexico Hispano inclusive) theater evolved as an amalgamation of Mexican street theater arts such as the carpa (traveling tent theater) and the zarzuela (Spanish comedic opera) with a European, Bertolt Brechtian brand of sociopolitical drama. Until the 1960s civil rights movements, however, Mexican-American theatrical arts had not received mainstream recognition. In 1965, two Chicano activists—the young, fiery new actor/director, Luis Valdez, and the powerful farmworkers' organizer César Chávez—teamed up during California's "Great Delano Strike" and founded El Teatro Campesino Cultural (The Workers' Cultural Center). Valdez drew on first-hand experience as an actor/director working in San Francisco's Mime Troupe and a broad knowledge of Mexican drama, history, and myth to train striking farmworkers to perform and write politically savvy, bilingual performances. Valdez writes in his book, *Actos: El Teatro Campesino,* of El Teatro Campesino's mission: "Chicano theater must be revolutionary in technique as well as in content. It must be popular, subject to no other critics except the pueblo itself; but it must also educate the pueblo toward an appreciation of social change, on and off the stage."

El Teatro Campesino's performances became well-known among those involved in the "Brown Power Movement" of the 1960s. For example, one of El Teatro's first productions, titled *Las dos caras del patroncito (The Two-Faced Boss)*, fully embodied El Teatro's ideal of developing a socially aware dramatic art form combining Aztec and European traditions. The loosely improvised, bilingually acted piece composed of ten to 15 minute actos, or skits—not only candidly addresses a farmworker's plight at the hands of a money-grubbing boss, but does so with a tinge of humor; the influence of satirically playful Italian comedia dell'arte allows the piece to both incite action and offer the audience the possibility of laughing at "The Boss," who dons a yellow pig-face mask and hides behind a rent-a-goon bodyguard.

In the late 1960s and early 1970s El Teatro performed a series of plays that utilized the mito, or culturally anchored act, to explore the plight of the Chicano/a dwelling increasingly in inner-city barrios ("neighborhoods"). For example, in *Las Vendidas (The Sell-Outs)*, the audience not only meets a Chicana Republican, Miss Jiménez, a gangbanger pachuco, and a revolucionario, but also gets a big taste of Aztec mythology and Mexican culture. *Las Vendidas* won the prestigious Obie Award in 1967. In 1971 Valdez and a professionalized El Teatro troupe moved to San Juan Bautista, where a range of performances continued to infuse the mythical dimension of Chicano/a identity—figures such as Huitzilpochtil (the Sun God), Quetzalcoatl, and the Virgin de Guadalupe would appear symbolically—to explore the everyday struggles of survival, from border crossing tragedies to romances and family breakups.

El Teatro's professionalization and broadened scope quickly led to recognition by mainstream critics. In the mid-1970s the famed British artistic director and drama critic Peter Brooks traveled to San Juan Bautista to work with El Teatro. The result: *The Conference of the Birds,* whose nation-wide success opened doors outside the Americas. El Teatro's follow-up production, *La Carpa de los Rasquachis (The Tent of the Underdogs),* toured eight European countries. And in 1979 El Teatro's *Zoot Suit*—a music-infused drama that retells the story of the 1942 Zoot Suit riots in Los Angeles of 1942 from a Chicano, Aztec-mythic point of view—was the first Chicano play to open on New York's Broadway. While *Zoot Suit* only had a short run, flopping at the box office, it received glowing critical reviews from drama critics.

Now in its thirtieth year as a professional theater-arts organization, El Teatro is recognized as a major contributor to dramatic arts. While El Teatro continues with performances in the Old Mission at San Juan Bautista—at Christmas they regularly perform their Chicano re-visioned miracle plays such as the *La Virgen Del Tepeyac* and

La Pastorela—the members continue to experiment with new forms and techniques. El Teatro has moved into television, and Valdez has directed several films. Finally, it is largely due to El Teatro's struggle to clear a space in the dramatic arts terrain that opportunity has opened up for many contemporary Chicano/a playwrights—Cheríe Moraga, Ricardo Bracho, and Octavio Solis, to name a few—to express a more complicated (queer sexuality and gender inclusive) vision of what it means to be Latino/a in the United States.

—Frederick Luis Aldama

FURTHER READING:

Tatum, Charles. *Chicano Literature.* Boston, Twayne Publishers, 1982.

Valdez, Luis. *Actos: El Teatro Campesino.* San Juan Bautista, Cucaracha Press, 1971.

El Vez (1960—)

Unlike most Elvis impersonators, Robert Lopez has created his own successful and unique character from the King's legacy. Looking back on his uneventful life growing up in Chula Vista, California, Lopez recalls that his uncles would wear "continental slacks and slight pompadours in that Elvis style." With this in mind, maybe it is not so surprising that the shy boy from Chula Vista would one day transform himself into the nationally acclaimed Virgin-de-Guadalupe, jumpsuit-wearing, sombrero-sporting, pencil-line-mustachioed Chicano musician/performance artist El Vez.

In 1988, while showcasing an Elvis-inspired kitsch/folk art exhibition at La Luz de Jesús Gallery on Melrose in Los Angeles, a 29 year-old Lopez received his true calling—to combine his talents as a musician (he used to play for the Southern California punk band The Zeroes) with his taste for Mexican kitsch and re-invent himself as El Vez. Just in time for Weep Week (the annual celebration of Elvis Presley's birthday), Lopez traveled to Memphis, Tennessee, where he secured himself a spot at Graceland's hot spot for Elvis impersonators, Bob's Bad Vapors. Lopez's over-the-top costume, super-gelled hair coif, "Mexican Elvis" identifying sign, and Mexican corrido (ballad) cut-n'-mixed into Elvis tunes were a huge success. With the help of newspaper wire services, Lopez became an overnight, nationally recognized celebrity. Certain of his destiny, El Vez—along with his Memphis Mariachis and the hip-gyrating Lovely Elvettes (Gladysita, Lisa María, Prescillita, and Qué Linda Thompson)—went on tour all over the United States and Europe and has received critical recognition and applause from the *New York Times* and *Rolling Stone*. He has appeared on such television shows as *The Late Night Show, Oprah,* and *CNN (Cable News Network)*. El Vez has a dozen CDs out, with titles such as *El Vez is Alive, Not Hispanic, G.I. Ay, Ay Blues,* and the album *A Merry Mex-Mus,* in which reindeer called Poncho and Pedro join Santa's team.

El Vez is certainly not only a novelty Elvis act. Along with Mexican mariachi tunes, Lopez uses a range of popular music sounds from the likes of Elvis, David Bowie, T. Rex, Queen, and The Beatles, to address issues such as California's anti-immigration act and California governor Pete Wilson's racism. The lyrics, for example, in his song "Chicanisma" (a version of Elvis' "Little Sister") are critical of the male-dominated Chicano community's oppression of women, while his revision of "Mystery Train" (called "Misery

Train'') tells the story of Pancho Villa and Los Zapatistas destroying ''los capitalistas.'' ''Viva Las Vegas'' is a crash course in pre-conquistador Mexican civilization, mixing musical styles and speeches to discuss the plight of the Mexican immigrant worker. In his album *Graciasland*—a rockabilly/country version of Paul Simon's *Graceland*—he identifies the Southwestern United States as the spiritual homeland, Aztlan, for Chicanos. As a reporter for the *New York Times* wrote in December 1995, ''He may look and dress like a young Elvis Presley (though Elvis never had El Vez's pencil-thin mustache), but El Vez is his own creation.''

—Frederick Luis Aldama

FURTHER READING:

Muñoz, José and Celeste Fraser Delgado. *Everynight Life: Dance, Music, and Culture.* Durham, Duke University Press, 1997.

Electric Appliances

By the turn of the twentieth century, it was common knowledge that the American home did not function efficiently. With increasing interest in efficiency, homemaking became more scientific. Instead of assigning more domestic servants to the task, home economists and other observers began analyzing the processes of the home and how they could be carried out more effectively. This sensibility provided the crucial entré for technological innovation to find its way into the American home.

Household technology, especially in the form of electric appliances, radically altered the American home in the twentieth century. These innovations, of course, relied on the inventions of Thomas Edison and others who would perfect the generation and transferral of

An electric iron.

electric energy for home use in the early 1900s. Many American homes would remain without electricity through World War II, but the American ideal of the electrified home had clearly been put in place.

To say that one single electric appliance altered American life more than another is difficult, but a good case could be made for the electric refrigerator, which, as it took form in the 1920s, revolutionized food storage capabilities in a fashion that dramatically altered American life. Improving upon the ''ice box,'' which was limited by the melting of a block of hand-delivered ice, electricity enabled the use of pumps relying on centrifugal pressure to push cooling fluids throughout an insulated box. Improved for safety reasons and efficiency, the refrigerator soon became the mainstay of any home. The refrigerator allowed homemakers to keep perishable items in the home, ending the necessary habit of frequent trips to the market. Moreover, this appliance allowed for the creation of the frozen food market. In 1941, 52 percent of American families owned refrigerators; ten years later, this proportion had risen to 80 percent and by 1980 refrigeration was almost universal.

Shifts in home technology after World War II were based most around labor-saving devices. Increased electrification, especially spurred by New Deal policies, offered the power source, and a new ideal of the American housewife offered suitable rationale. During these years, the growing middle class raised the national ideal of a standard of living to include the trappings of affluence that included electric kitchen appliances, washing machines, and televisions. In the late twentieth century, the cultural imperative for each American to own his or her own home was extended to shape expectations for the contents of the typical home. The re-formed cultural ideals identified the home as a self-sufficient support mechanism. The modern middle-class home became a facilitator that should ease the pressures of everyday life through the application of modern technology. Whereas domestic servants had aided many homemakers previously, the modern American housewife relied predominantly on the assistance of electric appliances.

The crystallizing moment of Americans' idealization of their new home is known as ''the kitchen debate.'' In this astonishing 1959 Cold War conversation, Vice-President Richard Nixon and Soviet Premier Nikita Kruschev discussed ideology and domestic technology in a ''model American home'' constructed in Moscow. Nixon drew attention to the washing machines and said, ''In America, these are designed to make things easier for our women.'' Kruschev countered Nixon's boast of comfortable American housewives with pride in the productivity of Soviet female laborers. In summing up the capitalist ideal, Nixon responded, ''What we want is to make easier the life of our housewives.''

No gadget sums up this desire to ease pressures better than the microwave. Perfected in 1946 but reaching widespread acceptance only in the 1980s, these ovens cook by heating water and chemical molecules in food with short-wave radio energy, similar to that used in radar and television. In addition to rapid heating without creating a heated environment, microwaves altered American patterns of life by making it much easier to defrost food items. In a recent survey by the appliance manufacturer Maytag, consumers chose the ubiquitous microwave as the most indispensable item in the kitchen.

Electric appliances changed the American home and gender roles after 1945. They continue to be a source of innovation and gadgetry as engineers try to solve the problems of the American home.

—Brian Black

FURTHER READING:

Cowan, Ruth Schwartz. *More Work for Mother: The Ironies of Household Technology from the Open Hearth to the Microwave.* New York, Basic Books, 1985.

Matranga, Victoria Kasuba, with Karen Kohn. *America at Home: A Celebration of Twentieth-Century Housewares.* Rosemont, Illinois, National Housewares Manufacturers Association, 1997.

Russell, Loris S. *Handy Things to Have around the House.* New York, McGraw-Hill Ryerson, 1979.

Electric Guitar

This instrument has dominated the production of popular music since its invention in the 1940s. Although primarily identified with both the sound and the image of rock 'n' roll, the electric guitar has made its mark on all genres of popular music, from country to world beat. Combined with an amplifier, and armed with a large inventory of special effects, the electric guitar is an extremely versatile instrument that can produce an infinite variety of sounds. Its ease of playing and low cost have made it an important consumer good of the twentieth century. It has given the baby boom generation the means to make their own music and emulate the great guitar heroes of their times.

Musicians began to consider electric amplification of the acoustic guitar during the 1930s when guitar players sat in the rhythm sections of the big bands and struggled to be heard. The Western Electric system of amplification was readily available and was soon employed to power the signal coming from the first primitive guitar pickups. The first electric guitars were hollow bodied acoustic models with pickups attached, but in the 1940s guitars were made with solid bodies to better suit electric amplification. Leo Fender was the first to mass produce solid bodied electric guitars and his Telecaster (1951)

Wes Montgomery playing an electric guitar.

and Stratocaster (1954) models remained in production in the 1990s. Fender established the basic layout of the electronics and the shape of his Stratocaster has been the most copied by other manufacturers of electric guitars.

The increased volume of the electric guitar was soon heard in popular music. Les Paul used a model of his own design to make successful records in both the country and popular fields in the 1940s and 1950s, but it took rock 'n' roll to showcase the power of the instrument and the great number of new sounds it could make. The electric guitar figured large in the two well springs of this new popular music: rhythm and blues from the black urban centers and rockabilly from the country. Blues musicians like Muddy Waters electrified a traditional music and brought it into the urban context, using the harder sounds of the electric guitar to make the blues more urgent and menacing. Country players had been the first to adopt the electric guitar perhaps because their audiences were used to the metallic sounds of the steel guitar which was extremely popular in the 1940s and 1950s. The high, ringing tones of the Fender guitar became the trademark of a new type of country music which was both more traditional than the popular records made in Nashville and more modern in its stark metallic tone. The Bakersfield sound of players like Merle Haggard and Buck Owens was created not far from the Fender factory in California and soon spread across the country.

The first rock guitarists—players like Scotty Moore, Chuck Berry and Buddy Holly—were inspired by both sides of the racial divide in popular music and the successful hybrid they produced came to be called rock 'n' roll. Buddy Holly was the most influential exponent of the rock guitar not only because of his playing, which used basic chords in an energetic and exciting way, but also because he popularized the all guitar lineup of the rock 'n' roll band: lead, bass (and later rhythm) guitars playing through the same amplification system in front of the drums. Holly's music was widely disseminated on records and the simplicity of his playing made it easy to copy; thousands of teenagers learned how to play rock guitar by listening to his recordings and many of them went on to form their own bands.

Leo Fender had designed his solid bodied guitars with ease of manufacture in mind and quickly moved into mass production. The unprecedented appeal of rock 'n' roll created an enormous demand for electric guitars and by the 1960s the production of instruments had become a highly profitable and crowded industry. Most of the manufacturers of acoustic guitars, such as Gibson and Gretsch, had moved into electric models and a host of new companies entered the field: including Mosrite and Peavey. There were also many new manufacturers of amplifiers and the effects boxes which added reverberation and echo to the sound of the guitar.

But rock 'n' roll music never relied on the sound of the electric guitar alone—the amplifier created the sound and the signal it received could be altered by the electronic circuits of the effect boxes. Thus the clear, high "Fender sound" heard on surf guitarist Dick Dales' records is not just the sound of his Fender Stratocaster but also of the Fender Showman or Bassman amplifier and the 6G-15 Reverb unit plugged in between guitar and amplifier. Musicians began to experiment with this technological system in their continual attempts to find new sounds. Pete Townshend of The Who was the great innovator in using all parts of the system to generate new sounds, his rapid turning on and off of the power switch on his guitar made a memorable ending to several of The Who's songs.

The man playing an electric guitar became a universally recognized image of rock 'n' roll and the instrument itself became a symbol of empowerment for a generation of teenagers who yearned for the abilities and successes of their guitar playing heroes. The myths of rock 'n' roll leaned heavily on the rags to riches tradition in the United States whereby ambitious immigrants could, with "luck and pluck," rise to the top of their profession and achieve the affluence and security of the American dream. The stories of the stars of rock 'n' roll followed this tradition and placed totemic importance on the tools of the trade: the electric guitar. Chuck Berry's "Johnny Be Goode," one of the great anthems of rock 'n' roll, tells the story of a young boy who leaves home, with only a guitar on his back, to seek out fame and fortune. This story resonated in thousands of other songs, most of which cast the hero as a guitar player.

The mass adulation of a few leading guitar players in the 1960s was a measure of the size of audience for the music and the market for the instruments. It also marked a return to an older tradition in the popular culture of the guitar, when the solitary bluesman was the center of attention. Several English musicians, including Jeff Beck and Eric Clapton, had spearheaded a blues revival in the early 1960s. This invigorated both blues and pop music and also created a new wave of guitar heroes who reflected some of the characteristics of the blues musicians who inspired them: outlaws and outcasts who travelled from place to place living on their wits and enjoying the rewards of their virtuosity on the guitar. The bluesman was a special person, either gifted or damned by the Gods, whose freedom and powers (especially over women) were highly valued in the popular culture of the 1960s. Jimi Hendrix was the greatest of all the guitar heroes; his unequalled virtuosity on the instrument was only matched by the excesses of his lifestyle which were also embodied in his songs.

The steady advance of the technology of electric guitars was centered on two main goals: increasing the volume and finding ever more electronic effects. In the 1960s amplifiers were made larger and more efficient and the separate amplifier unit and speaker boxes replaced the old amplifiers which had electronics and speakers in the same box. The banks of Marshall 4X12 speaker units became the backdrop for the typical rock 'n' roll performance. More complicated devices were used to manipulate electronic feedback and create new sounds. Guitar players could surround themselves with effects boxes, such as "fuzz" and "wah wah," that were operated by foot switches. The sound of psychedelic music of the 1960s was essentially the sound of controlled feedback from the electric guitar.

The increasing popularity of other methods of manipulating electronic sounds in the 1970s, such as the Moog synthesizer and electric organ, threatened to end the dominance of the electric guitar in popular music. But there were several sub genres of rock 'n' roll that were still completely dominated by its sound: heavy metal which made a cult of loudness and made futuristic guitars the center of theatrical stage shows; and punk which returned to the basic guitar sound of early rock 'n' roll. Punk musicians made a virtue out of amateurism in their rejection of the commercialization of pop music and the elevation of guitar virtuosos. They encouraged everybody to pick up a guitar and advised the aspiring musician that only a few chords needed to be mastered before forming a band. On the other hand, advocates of heavy metal wanted to be transported to an imaginary world of outlandish stage shows, outrageous costumes and unusual guitar shapes. Both groups of musicians used exactly the same equipment, but to different ends.

Although each decade after the 1960s produced an "alternative" music to rock 'n' roll, the electric guitar's ubiquitous presence in popular music was not challenged. Disco (1970s) and rap (1980s) still relied on the supple rhythm lines of the electric bass. The guitar based rock band continued to dominate both professional and amateur

music in the 1990s, ensuring that the instrument will prosper into the twenty-first century.

—Andre Millard

FURTHER READING:

Gill, Chris. *Guitar Legends.* London, Studio Editions, 1995.

Gruhn, George, and Walter Carter. *Electric Guitars and Basses: A Photographic History.* San Francisco, Miller Freeman, 1994.

Shaughnessey, Mary Alice. *Les Paul: An American Original.* New York, Morrow, 1993.

Smith, Richard R. *Fender: The Sound Heard Around the World.* Fullerton, California, Garfish, 1995.

Trynka, Paul, ed. *The Electric Guitar: An Illustrated History.* San Franciso, 1993.

Wheeler, Tom. *American Guitars: An Illustrated History.* New York, Harper, 1992.

Electric Trains

Even as transportation improvements accelerated through the twentieth century, the railroad still best symbolized the ability of mechanized invention to conquer distance; electric trains continue to epitomize this cultural belief in such technological progress. From children's playthings, they have evolved into accurately scaled and finely detailed models. Several gauges provide size options for modeling railroads, from the tiny N-scale and the highly popular HO at 1/87 scale, up to O-gauge and Standard gauge. In Europe, Märklin in 1901 manufactured the first model trains run by small electric motors. In 1910 the Ives Corporation of Bridgeport, Connecticut, introduced electric trains to this country; they remained their leading manufacturer up to the First World War. As the hobby caught on, other manufacturers began producing electric trains, including Marx, Varney, Mantua, American Flyer, and Lionel. Collecting and operating model trains is a pastime now enjoyed by people around the world.

—Robert Kuhlken

FURTHER READING:

Bagdade, Susan, and Al Bagdade. *Collector's Guide to American Toy Trains.* Radnor, Pennsylvania, Wallace-Homestead Book Co., 1990.

Carlson, Pierce. *Toy Trains.* Philadelphia, Harper and Row, 1986.

Williams, Guy. *The World of Model Trains.* New York, G.P. Putnam's Sons, 1970.

Elizondo, Hector (1936—)

A physically compact character actor with a brilliantly economical technique to match, Hector Elizondo delighted audiences and gained fame with his polished performance as the hotel manager in *Pretty Woman* (1990), one of several films he made for Garry Marshall. This New York-born actor of Hispanic parentage, who trained at the Actors Studio, proved exceptionally versatile, playing a wide range of supporting roles, utilizing different accents and dialects, and capturing the essence of a character, whether in drama or comedy, by an expert flick of expression. His multitude of television appearances include Sandy Stern in *Burden of Proof* (1992) and the put-upon hospital chief Dr. Philip Watters, authoritative, weary, and not always wise, in *Chicago Hope* from 1994. He came to television and film with an impeccable Broadway provenance, beginning his career in *Mister Roberts* (1961) for distinguished director Edwin Sherin.

—Robyn Karney

FURTHER READING:

Charity, Tom. "Hector Elizondo." *Who's Who in Hollywood.* Edited by Robyn Karney. New York, Continuum, 1994.

Elkins, Aaron (1935—)

Aaron Elkins is the creator of two mystery series. The Gideon Oliver novels feature a forensic anthropologist frequently compelled to work not with ancient bones, but with modern murders. *Fellowship of Fear* (1982) initiated the series, followed by *The Dark Place* (1983), an unusually poetic mood-piece, and *Murder in the Queen's Armes* (1985). *Old Bones* (1987) received the 1988 Edgar Award for Best Mystery Novel. Subsequent Gideon Oliver novels include *Curses!* (1989), *Icy Clutches* (1990), *Make No Bones* (1991), *Dead Men's Hearts* (1994), and *Twenty Blue Devils* (1997). The Chris Norgren novels, whose hero is a museum curator, include *A Deceptive Clarity* (1987), *A Glancing Light* (1991), and *Old Scores* (1993). He has also co-written golf mysteries with Charlotte Elkins: *A Wicked Slice* (1989), *Rotten Lies* (1995), and *Nasty Breaks* (1997). Elkins' forté lies in combining intriguing characters and plots with exotic settings, as far ranging as England, Germany, Mexico, Alaska, Egypt, Tahiti, and the Pacific Northwest.

—Michael R. Collings

Ellen
See DeGeneres, Ellen

Ellington, Duke (1899-1974)

Heralded by many as the greatest composer in jazz history, pianist and bandleader Duke Ellington composed and arranged most of the music played by his famous orchestra. His 1932 recording of "It Don't Mean a Thing (If It Ain't Got That Swing)" gave a name to the Swing Era, when jazz music and jitterbug dancing swept the nation in the late 1930s and early 1940s.

Born Edward Kennedy Ellington into a modestly prosperous family in Washington, D.C., he began studying piano at age seven. His graceful demeanor earned him the aristocratic nickname, Duke. Continuing to study piano formally, as well as learning from the city's ragtime pianists, Ellington formed his own band at age 19, and soon was earning enough playing for parties and dances to marry Edna Thompson. The band's drummer was his friend, Sonny Greer, who would anchor the Duke's rhythm section for the next 33 years.

Duke Ellington

After moving to New York City in 1923, Ellington began assembling jazz musicians whose unique sounds enhanced his own arrangements. With his new ensemble, he launched Duke Ellington and the Washingtonians. The band first worked for the legendary singer Ada Smith (better known later in European clubs as Bricktop). In 1924 Ellington wrote his first score for a revue, *Chocolate Kiddies,* which ran for two years in Germany, but was never produced on Broadway.

The band's big break came in 1927, when it began a five-year engagement at Harlem's Cotton Club, the site of frequent national broadcasts. Soon the Ellington name was widely known for Duke's signature style of improvisational and ensemble jazz. His earliest arrangements included what he at first called the "jungle style," which achieved unusual effects and rhythms through the use of plunger mutes on the trumpets and trombones. Major sidemen who joined the Duke Ellington Band in the Cotton Club era included Barney Bigard on clarinet, Johnny Hodges on alto and soprano sax, and Cootie Williams on the trumpet. The ensemble's first great recorded hit was "Mood Indigo" of 1930, which featured the band's inimitable tonal colors, made possible by the special sounds and styles of each individual musician. In 1933, a tour of England and the Continent brought the band worldwide fame.

With very little change in personnel over the beginning years, the orchestra was able to play with unheard-of ensemble precision. Such melodic recordings as "Solitude," "Sophisticated Lady," and "In a Sentimental Mood," won Ellington and his band a wide audience. But it was the uniquely orchestrated ensemble jazz in such pieces as "Daybreak Express," "Harlem Speaks," and "Rockin' in

Rhythm," that impressed fellow jazzmen such as Billy Strayhorn, who joined the band as assistant arranger in 1939. It was Strayhorn's composition "Take the A Train," which became the orchestra's theme song.

In 1943 the band began a series of annual concerts in Carnegie Hall that would continue until 1950. The first concert included Ellington's earliest attempt at a nearly hour-length jazz composition, *Black, Brown, and Beige*, which he envisioned as a "musical history of the Negro." It was his most ambitious work to date, one which musicologist and composer Gunther Schuller believes has "not been surpassed" in "scope and stature." In subsequent Carnegie Hall concerts Ellington played such lengthy compositions as *Deep South Suite, Blutopia,* and *New World A-Comin'. Harlem*, another suite, was the centerpiece of an Ellington concert at the Metropolitan Opera House in 1951.

Although the Ellington ensemble continued to be ranked as one of the top two or three jazz orchestras during the 1950s, their difficult repertoire, coupled with frequent personnel changes, led to spotty performances that were often disappointing to their fans. However, after giving a smash-hit performance at the Newport Jazz Festival in 1956, followed by a 1957 CBS-TV special on Ellington entitled *A Drum Is a Woman*, the band's fortunes were revived, and the Duke began a period of prolific composing. He and Strayhorn wrote a suite based on Shakespearean characters, *Such Sweet Thunder,* performed at New York's Town Hall in 1957. In 1958, his first European tour in eight years proved a stunning success—one that he repeated the following year. In 1959 Ellington wrote his first score for a film, Alfred Hitchcock's *Anatomy of a Murder*, which was recorded by Ellington's band.

Up until his death of lung cancer in May of 1974, Ellington continued to write important music, much of it devoted to other cultures and to religious themes. For more than a half century, Duke had led one of America's most popular and successful bands. As George T. Simon wrote, "No other bandleader ever did this nearly so long so well as Duke Ellington. No other bandleader created as much and contributed as much to American music." A chorus of jazz critics agrees that Duke may be the greatest single talent in the history of jazz.

—Benjamin Griffith

FURTHER READING:

Balliett, Whitney. *American Musicians.* New York, Oxford Press, 1986.

Schuller, Gunther. "The Ellington Style: It's Origins and Early Development." In *Jazz,* edited by Nat Hentoff and Albert J. McCarthy. New York, Da Capo Press, 1974.

Simon, George T. *The Big Bands.* New York, MacMillan, 1974.

Ellis, Bret Easton (1964—)

Born and raised in Los Angeles, writer Bret Easton Ellis belongs with novelists Jay McInerney and Tama Janowitz to New York's literary "brat pack," writers who achieved early success with their portraits of lonely types isolated in sparkling 1980s New York. Ellis has published four books: the novels *Less Than Zero* (1985), *The Rules of Attraction* (1987), and *American Psycho* (1991), and the

short story collection *The Informers* (1994). A rumored fourth novel on the world of fashion's top models remained unpublished in the late 1990s.

Published when Ellis was twenty-one years old, *Less Than Zero* narrates the sorry lives of a group of Los Angeles young people. No longer teenagers, these people epitomize what would later be known as "Generation X" in Douglas Coupland's popular phrase. The lives of the main character, Clay, and those of his well-to-do friends revolve around sex and drugs, in which they try to find the essence of a world that eludes them. Similar empty people populate the short stories of *The Informers*. Outstanding among them is the satirical "The End of the Summer," in which the Californians of *Less Than Zero* appear as happy vampires.

An ebb in Ellis's popularity came in 1987 when both the film adaptation of *Less Than Zero* and his novel about a triangular relationship, *The Rules of Attraction,* failed. But in 1991 he became a social phenomenon thanks to the publication of his outstanding *American Psycho,* the first-person narration of the exploits of serial killer Pat Bateman, a Manhattan yuppie. The extreme graphic violence and nihilism of the novel became controversial even before its publication. Following complaints by people working on the manuscript, Simon & Schuster withdrew the book from publication, losing a $300,000 advance. The excerpts published by *Time* and *Sky* contributed to the controversy. The book was finally published as a Vintage paperback, becoming a best-selling novel in the United States and abroad. Its publication was greeted with a barrage of criticism, especially from feminists, and lukewarm reviews that missed much of the book's originality to focus only on its nastier passages. Ellis himself confessed in an interview with Leslie White in 1994 that the controversy felt "like a joke, a huge postmodernist irony—the book was so badly misread."

David Skal complains in *The Monster Show* that "although the whole incident [involving Ellis's novel] was endlessly discussed in terms of taste, misogyny, and political correctness, a subtext of class snobbery predominated." Skal argues that what really irritated feminists and moral guardians alike is the fact that Bateman is upper-class and that Ellis's book is literature unlike the books by, for instance, Stephen King. This is possibly correct, yet *American Psycho*'s status as a literary text is still ambiguous. The book has sold remarkably well in many countries, creating a cult reflected in the many Internet websites devoted to its discussion, but critics and academics show an equivocal attitude toward it. Arguably, the book is commendable if only because it questions in depth the meaning of the word literature, together with the meaning of other relevant words such as homophobia, racism, misogyny, and classism.

American Psycho is essentially a radical indictment of the American culture of the Reagan era, a very bleak portrait of a time and place obsessed by money. Bateman's insanity is, nonetheless, close to the existentialism of characters such as the anonymous protagonist of Albert Camus's novel *The Outsider* (1946). In his lucidity Bateman is also a brother of the infamous Hannibal Lecter of the film *Silence of the Lambs* (also 1991) and of Mickey Knox in Oliver Stone's *Natural Born Killers* (1994). Bateman's diary narrates his frivolous life and that of the yuppie crowd that surrounds him. Bateman engages in a series of increasingly grisly murders of homosexuals, women, and male business colleagues which he describes with a stark, functional prose. This is hard to read because of its realism, but it may not be, after all, the true essence of the book. Perhaps a more remarkable peculiarity of Bateman's style is that his descriptions of characters and places abound with information about designer objects seemingly taken straight from catalogues. The violent passages that were published in isolation missed much of the irony of the book: characters mistake each other all the time because they all wear the same expensive clothes, Bateman's appraisals of pop idols such as Whitney Houston makes them appear trivial and boring, and restaurant surrealistic scenes are enriched by funny dialogue with plenty of non sequiturs showing the abysmal depth of the yuppies' ignorance.

It is undeniably true that many of the scenes in the book may offend the sensibilities of the average reader. But the fact that Bateman is addicted to Valium and Halcion suggests that, perhaps—hopefully, for some readers—the bloodbaths are just a product of his imagination, which is why nobody suspects him. Of course, this point is irrelevant to the question of what Ellis's intention was when writing such a remarkable book. Yet it is hard to see why so few reviewers have seen Ellis's fierce attack against yuppiedom. *American Psycho* shows no mercy at all with a society that allows people like Bateman a room at the top. The reading is, nonetheless, complicated by Ellis's risky choice of Bateman as both his mouthpiece and his target. The deep morality of the book is thus purposely blurred in a literary game of mirrors, but readers should not make the mistake of identifying character and author. Ellis does challenge the reader to face Bateman's cruelty for the sake of reaping the reward of the final message of the book: "Surface, surface, surface was all that anyone found meaning in . . . this was civilization as I saw it, colossal and jagged," Bateman says at the end of the novel. So does Ellis. After reading *American Psycho,* the reader can only sympathize with this view of life at the end of the twentieth century.

—Sara Martin

FURTHER READING:

Forrest, Emma. "On the Psycho Path." *The Sunday Times.* October, 23 1994, sec. 10, 18.

Punter, David. "Contemporary Gothic Transformations." *The Literature of Terror.* Vol. 2. London, Longman, 1980, 145-180.

Skal, David. *The Monster Show.* London, Plexus, 1994, 371-376.

Twitchell, James B. *Carnival Culture: The Trashing of Taste in America.* New York, Columbia University Press, 1992, 128-129.

White, Leslie. "Bleak as He Is Painted (An Interview with Bret Easton Ellis)." *The Sunday Times.* October, 23, 1994, 20-21.

Ellis, Perry (1940-1986)

Virginia-born Ellis took his talents from fashion merchandising to fashion design in 1975. In 1978, he founded Perry Ellis Sportswear, a name that immediately recognized his fashion niche. Strong color, luxury fabrics, and a rich-suburban nonchalance were chief characteristics: women prized his cashmere and silk hand-knitted sweaters and throws. He offered a young outlook on old-money styles. He also designed menswear and home fashions. A ruggedly handsome man and a famously affable figure in American fashion, he fell gravely ill in the mid-1980s, but denied that the cause was AIDS, then a scourge of New York design talent. Ironically, despite his denials, Ellis's struggle with disease and his early death was a point-of-conscience and conversion for the fashion industry which began aggressively to

raise funds for AIDS research. Since his death, Perry Ellis continues as a popular licensing name.

—Richard Martin

FURTHER READING:

Moor, Jonathan. *Perry Ellis.* New York, St. Martin's Press, 1988.

Ellison, Harlan (1934—)

Diminutive author Harlan Ellison has been called "one of the great living American short story writers." He has been called a lot worse by the many enemies with whom he has sparred in print, online, and in countless combative convention appearances. Ellison, whose major works include "I Have No Mouth and I Must Scream" and "Jeffty Is Five," began writing professionally at age 15, when his first story appeared in *The Cleveland News.* Since then he has been a prolific, at times logorrheic, presence on the American literary scene, penning essays, reviews, and teleplays in addition to his speculative fiction. A self-proclaimed humanist, Ellison writes dark fantasies that challenge the technological optimism prevalent in the science fiction genre. His idiosyncratic style has put off many mainstream science fiction readers, but few living scribes have been nominated for as many different honors (including, at last count, an Emmy, a Grammy, and a Humanitas Prize) as this complex, controversial figure.

—Robert E. Schnakenberg

FURTHER READING:

Ellison, Harlan. *The Essential Ellison.* Beverly Hills, Morpheus International, 1991.

Slusser, George Edgar. *Harlan Ellison: Unrepentant Harlequin.* San Bernardino, Borgo Press, 1977.

Ellison, Ralph
See Invisible Man

Elway, John (1960—)

With nicknames ranging from "The General" to "The Comeback Kid," National Football League quarterback John Elway of the Denver Broncos can add one more name to the list: "Super Bowl Champion." During his 16-year career in the NFL Elway earned a reputation as a fearless competitor, leading the Denver Broncos to five Super Bowls—three of which the Broncos lost. However, in his final two Super Bowl appearances (1998 and 1999), Elway led his team to victories over the Green Bay Packers and Atlanta Falcons, respectively, thus securing a place for the Broncos in the upper-echelon of NFL history and a place for himself in the NFL Hall of Fame. Although he often chose to run with the ball, sacrificing his body for an extra yard or two, Elway gained a reputation as a finesse quarterback. In addition to holding the record for most wins by an NFL quarterback, Elway also holds the record for most come-from-behind victories (45), and finished the 1999 season just behind Dan

John Elway

Marino of the Miami Dolphins in total career passing yardage. Elway earned the NFL's Most Valuable Player award for the 1987 season, and played in 8 NFL Pro Bowls. Elway retired from the NFL in 1999.

—Jason McEntee

FURTHER READING:

The Denver Broncos Official Home Page. www.denverbroncos.com. February 1999.

Latimer, Clay. *John Elway: Armed and Dangerous.* Lenexa, Kansas, Addax Publishing Group, 1998.

E-mail

The most important new medium of mass communication of the past 40 years was not in any way connected with television, moving pictures, or the recording industry; it initially emerged, instead, as a project of the U.S. Defense Department. In the 1960s, the department's Advanced Research Projects Agency, in coordination with several research institutions, came up with a system for connecting or "networking" distantly located computers using independent, dedicated telephone lines. Researchers using the system experimented with sending simple text messages to one another over the network. Soon, the trickle of research-oriented messages and data became a tidal wave of information exchange of all kinds. The new medium of

"electronic mail" eventually changed the way we interact with our friends, co-workers, and families. It also brought our everyday reality much closer to Marshall McLuhan's pipedream of a genuine world-wide community rooted in technology.

The practice of sending electronic messages from one person to another actually predated computer networking. A few years before the ARPANET, users of "time-sharing"-style computer consoles developed a simple system of sending memos to a central "mailbox" located on a mainframe computer used by a variety of users at different times. Each user had a file of their own to which the messages were directed and were able to pick up their messages during the time when they were using the computer. The practice was important to the future development of electronic messaging, but had little or no utilitarian value at the time; it was a mere toy. The ARPANET engineers later picked up on the idea and decided to see if they could send small messages and memos from one computer to another. It worked; they then began to send messages over the span of the nationwide ARPANET itself. To paraphrase one beneficiary of the ARPA's research, it was a small step for a few computer geeks, a giant leap for the global village.

The system was not only useful for the researchers but also proved to be a pleasant pastime—so pleasant, in fact, that ARPA director Stephen Lukasik worried that it could jeopardize the entire enterprise. In Katie Hafner and Matthew Lyon's history of the Internet, *Where Wizards Stay Up Late,* Lukasik said he told the researchers that if "you're going to do something that looks like it's forty thousand miles away from defense, please leave our name off of it." It was clear early on that e-mail was useful for much more than just the military and technological research for which the ARPA was founded in 1957.

By the mid-1970s, engineers discovered that messages could be sent through the ARPANET by those without official authorization to use it. The message-sending capability of this network was obviously universal, and through the demonstrated use of satellite technology, global. Anyone could tap into the network to send messages of any sort to virtually anyone else, anywhere else in the world. The message of this medium was limitless interactivity, not mere broadcasting. The ARPANET eventually gave way to a new, more enveloping network known as the Internet and the uses of e-mail quickly mushroomed.

The possibilities of the Internet were soon tested. In the early 1970s, individuals wrote anti-war messages and mass-mailed them; one electronically advocated Nixon's impeachment. Other mass-mailings became routinized around a variety of subject-headings that were of interest only to certain groups: this later became that part of the Internet known as Usenet. On Usenet, e-mail messages were sent to a central server and mass posted to a kind of electronic message board where all could read and even reply to the message. If one was interested in gardening and wanted to talk about it with other gardeners around the world, one could use software and server space to organize a group. Other forms of mass-e-mailings included discussion lists; in these, one needed to subscribe privately to the list and messages were routed directly to one's private mailbox rather than to a public message board.

E-mail also entertained in more traditional ways. Many used the Internet's e-mail capabilities early on to play fantasy role-playing games like Dungeons and Dragons. More serious uses of e-mail soon came to the attention of the U.S. Postal Service, and even President Jimmy Carter—who used a primitive e-mail system during his 1976 campaign—proposed ways of integrating the new technology into a postal system that originally delivered messages on the backs of ponies.

During the 1980s and 1990s, the culture that first blossomed in the 1970s began to flourish among a worldwide community of computer users. Hundreds of thousands of people now understood what it meant to be "flamed" (told off in a vicious manner). Multitudes decoded the meanings of the symbols called "emoticons" that attempted to convey facial expression through text. ;-) meant a wink and a smile: the messenger was "just fooling" and used the emoticon to make sure his plain text words were not misunderstood.

As the medium matured, private companies like Compuserve and America Online built private networks for individuals to dial in to send and receive electronic messages. New electronic communities formed in this way and were soon burdened with such "real world" issues as free speech, crime, and sexism. Many women complained of electronic abuse by the predominantly male on-line community. Predators sent electronic messages to children in attempts to commit crimes against them. Some of the private networks regulated speech in "public" forms of electronic communication and this met with scorn from the on-line community. Others used e-mail as an advertising medium, mass-mailing ads to hundreds of thousands of Internet users. This practice, known as "Spam," is held in almost universal disrepute, but is as unavoidable as smog in Los Angeles.

E-mail became ubiquitous by the late 1990s and the lines blurred between public, corporate, and private networks. By the late 1990s, many large corporations standardized their e-mail systems on Internet protocols so that interoffice mail shattered the physical boundaries of the "office" itself. Using e-mail, one could now effortlessly "telecommute" to work, rather than physically move from home to a separate workplace. With the boundarylessness of Internet-based e-mail, users could play at their work, and work at their play. The discovery of e-mail literally changed the ways that we live, work, and communicate with one another.

—Robin Markowitz

FURTHER READING:

Abbate, Janet. *Inventing the Internet.* Cambridge, Massachusetts, MIT Press, 1999.

Baty, S. Paige. *e-mail trouble: love and addiction @ the matrix.* Austin, University of Texas Press, 1999.

Brook, James, and Iain Boal, editors. *Resisting the Virtual Life: The Culture and Politics of Information.* San Francisco, City Lights Books, 1995.

Grey, Victor. *Web without a Weaver: How the Internet Is Shaping Our Future.* Concord, California, Open Heart Press, 1997.

Hafner, Katie, and Lyon, Matthew. *Where Wizards Stay Up Late: The Origins of the Internet.* New York, Simon and Schuster, 1996.

Wolinsky, Art. *The History of the Internet and the World Wide Web.* Springfield, New Jersey, Enslow Publishers, 1999.

Emmy Awards

The movies have their Oscars. Broadway has its Tonys. Off-Broadway has its Obies. And television has its Emmys. Ever since January 1949, when the Academy of Television Arts & Sciences first presented them at the Hollywood Athletic Club, the Emmy Awards have remained the most highly visible and coveted honor earned for

Best Actor and Best Actress in a Drama Series Emmy Award winners Andre Braugher and Christine Lahti with their statuettes, 1998.

achievement in television. The trophy's name was derived from "Immy," a word routinely employed to signify the image orthicon camera tube, which was in use during the early years of television. The statuette—a gold-plated winged lady hoisting a globe—was designed by television engineer Louis McManus, using his wife as a model. McManus himself was honored during that first ceremony with a special award "for his original design of the Emmy."

Over the years, the Emmy Awards have expanded and evolved. In 1949, six trophies were handed out; today, scores of Emmys are won each year for both national and local programs. The initial master of ceremonies for the awards was Walter O'Keefe, a long-forgotten radio quiz show emcee and celebrity interviewer. Across the decades since, the ceremony has been hosted by a gallery of star names, including Fred Astaire, Frank Sinatra, Bill Cosby and Johnny Carson; while among the many great acting legends who have won the award are Helen Hayes, John Gielgud, Julie Harris, Laurence Olivier, Dustin Hoffman, Bette Davis, Anthony Hopkins, Hume Cronyn, Jessica Tandy and Ingrid Bergman. The first Emmy recipient was Shirley Dinsdale and her puppet, Judy Splinters, categorized as "Most Outstanding Television Personality."

The Emmy categories, particularly during the early years, were frequently, and somewhat arbitrarily, re-named. Actor William Frawley, for example, was nominated for five successive years for his role as Fred Mertz in *I Love Lucy.* His first nomination, in 1953, was as "Best Series Supporting Actor"; the following four were re-designated annually as "Best Supporting Actor in a Regular Series," "Best Actor in a Supporting Role," "Best Supporting Performance By an Actor," and "Best Continuing Supporting Performance By an Actor in a Dramatic or Comedy Series." The procedure for securing nominations and naming winners also changed, while the number and variety of categories expanded. By the end of the 1990s, the most popular and high-profile awards—as with the Oscars—remained those for best performers and best programs, but established Emmy

Award categories had come to include directing, writing, casting, and hairstyling, and to acknowledge technological expertise with awards for technical direction, electronic camerawork, film editing, and videotape editing.

The Emmys have been fraught with controversy and internal conflict, characterized by in-fighting between the New York and Hollywood chapters of the Academy of Television Arts & Sciences, and disputes between other Academy factions, followed by lawsuits, rule changes and separations of power and responsibility. Some of the most publicized Emmy squabbles have involved boycotts. Upon learning that their awards would not be handed out during the televised broadcast, TV directors and writers banded together and threatened to boycott the 1974-75 show. In the previous decade, the news branches of CBS and ABC snubbed the 1963-64 Emmys. At the time, CBS News President Fred Friendly alleged that voting practices were ''unrealistic, unprofessional and unfair,'' and CBS News again refused to participate in 1964-65 and 1965-66. The 1979-80 affair was also boycotted—on that occasion by performers wishing to coerce the TV networks to resolve a seven-week-old strike by the Screen Actors Guild and the American Federation of Television and Radio Artists.

Another cause for concern is the situation whereby certain actors have amassed more trophies than can fit on their mantels for playing the same character year after year, while other equally fine performers have remained unrewarded. Susan Lucci, for example, nominated for umpteen Emmys for her performance as Erica Kane in the soap opera *All My Children*, and Angela Lansbury, similarly singled out for playing Jessica Fletcher in *Murder, She Wrote,* by the late 1990s had never won. Their failures to collect a single statuette became a national joke. Nonetheless, echoing the annual hype that surrounds the Oscars, critics and viewers continue to speculate as to the nominees and the winners, and gather before their television sets for the star-studded prime-time ceremony. And the winners, setting aside any behind-the-scenes tension, beam proudly for the cameras as, gratefully, they accept their gold-plated Emmys.

—Rob Edelman

FURTHER READING:

O'Neil, Thomas. *The Emmys: Star Wars, Showdowns and the Supreme Test of TV's Best.* New York, Penguin Books, 1992.

Empire State Building

Constructed in 1930-31, the Empire State Building was the tallest building in the world for forty years, until the construction of New York's World Trade Center in 1971 and, despite being overtaken in terms of its height, both in the United States and abroad, has remained America's most internationally famous architectural icon. It is both a shining example of the aesthetic and functional possibilities of the skyscraper form, and a potent symbol of the Manhattan metropolis it inhabits. The Empire State has played a prominent role in several Hollywood movies and has been the subject of countless

The Empire State Building, New York City.

essays and artworks, while an infinite number of products have been marketed, capitalizing on its familiar image.

The building demonstrated the extent to which corporate capitalism came to represent America to the rest of the world. It was the fruit of a speculative real estate venture by the Empire State Company, an organization whose major investors were John J. Raskob of General Motors and Coleman and Pierre du Pont. The former New York governor and presidential candidate Alfred E. Smith served as the company's president and front man. The project began with the purchase of land, formerly owned by the Astor family, on Fifth Avenue between 33rd and 34th Streets in midtown Manhattan. From the start, there was no ''anchor tenant'' or big company to occupy and associate with the building, unlike the nearby Chrysler Building or the famous downtown Woolworth Building. In 1929, just two months after the first public announcement of the Empire State venture, ''Black Friday'' struck on Wall Street, but the developers gambled on an economic turnaround and proceeded with their plans.

On May 1, 1931, at a ceremony attended by President Herbert Hoover and New York Governor Franklin Delano Roosevelt, the Empire State Building was officially opened. Construction had taken only 12 months—a remarkable rate of progress, during which the building's steel skeleton was erected in a mere 23 weeks. (During one period in 1930, workers put up 14 floors in ten days!) For promotional purposes, the developers had specifically set out to build the tallest building in the world. They achieved their goal. Reaching a height of 1,250 feet, the Empire State was almost 200 feet taller than its rival, the glitteringly flamboyant Chrysler Building, by comparison with which its design style, by the architectural firm of Shreve, Lamb and Harmon, was relatively sedate. The building's form was determined by its height and the setbacks required by the 1916 New York Zoning Laws. There was no elaborate decoration on the limestone exterior to attract the eye; instead, the building relied on its graceful form, enlivened by the conscientious use of setbacks, to provide an aesthetic effect. At the top, on the 102nd floor, was an open-air observation deck beneath a huge mooring mast intended by the developers to serve as an enticement for zeppelin landings. (No zeppelin ever docked, though).

The first years, however, were lean. The building was only half-full when it opened, and with only a twenty-five percent occupancy rate during the 1930s, was often dubbed the "Empty State Building." At times it seemed that only the income from the popular 86th and 102nd floor observation decks were keeping the premises alive. Nonetheless, almost immediately after opening, the Empire State Building became a cultural icon. In its first year of operation, over one million sightseers visited the observation decks, and Hollywood soon spotted its movie potential. The building's association with the movies famously began with *King Kong* in 1933, and surfaced as an integral plot strand many times since, including in *An Affair to Remember* (1957) and *Sleepless in Seattle* (1993). The building is a ubiquitous icon of the city's tourist trade, and millions of replicas of varying sizes have been sold to visitors and native New Yorkers alike.

There is no obvious explanation as to why the Empire State Building has continued to attract successive generations of visitors and admirers. People remain fascinated by the sheer (and ever increasing) size of skyscrapers, but impressive edifices such as Chicago's Sears Tower or New York's World Trade Center, have failed to capture the public affection in which the Empire State is held. The Empire State has not been the world's tallest building in decades; neither is it universally considered to be the most beautiful or the most interesting of the world's skyscrapers. Nevertheless, its special place in the hearts of Americans has not been superseded. During the Depression, the building was a stalwart symbol of optimism. As Alfred E. Smith said at the dedication ceremony, the Empire State Building is "the greatest monument to ingenuity, to skill, to brain power, to muscle power" And he might have added, to triumph in the face of adversity. After World War II, it was the emblem of America's triumphant emergence as the world's preeminent economic and cultural power; from the 1950s onwards, the building's elegant beauty put to shame (with certain honorable exception such as Mies van der Rohe's Seagram building) the forest of impersonal glass boxes that came to alter the face of Manhattan. With its many historic and romantic resonances, The Empire State Building represents much more than just a pioneering triumph of scale.

—Dale Allen Gyure

FURTHER READING:

Douglas, George H. *Skyscrapers: A Social History of the Very Tall Building in America*. Jefferson, North Carolina and London, McFarland & Company, Inc., 1996.

Goldman, Jonathan. *The Empire State Building Book*. New York, St. Martin's Press, 1980.

James, Theodore, Jr. *The Empire State Building*. New York, Harper & Row, 1975.

Reynolds, Donald Martin. *The Architecture of New York City*. New York, Macmillan Publishing Company, 1984.

Tauranc, John. *The Empire State Building: The Making of a Landmark*. New York, St. Martin's Griffin, 1997.

Willis, Carol, ed. *Building the Empire State*. New York, W.W. Norton, 1998.

Environmentalism

American environmental concern traces back to Jeffersonian ideas of a unique American connection to land and the romantic ethos of the nineteenth century. Open land, sometimes viewed as "wilderness," defined the New World for many European settlers. Thomas Jefferson argued that this open land could be transferred into an American strength if development were directed toward an agrarian republic. While much of the nation would pursue land-use similar to the landscape of Jefferson's ideal, some urban Americans remained intrigued by Jefferson's idea of a unique American connection to the natural environment. This can be seen in the adoption of European forms such as parks and gardens and in the intellectual tradition of romanticism and transcendentalism. By the end of the 1800s, wealthy urbanites pursued "wild" adventures in sites such as the Adirondacks, initiated organizations to conserve animal species or limit pollution, and, finally, set aside areas of nature from development. While the first national parks, Yellowstone and Yosemite, proved to be watershed events in environmental history, they were not initially set aside to protect wilderness areas.

Much nineteenth century environmentalism occurred without a strict organization or philosophy, and the first national parks are a primary example of this. Some scholars have chosen to view nineteenth century environmentalism as a product of Gilded-Age decadence and not an emerging new consciousness toward natural resource use. For instance, Yellowstone, established as the first national park in 1872, developed closely with railroad interests who hoped it would attract tourists to the American West. Its oddities—geysers, waterfalls—proved more important to observers than its unspoiled wilderness. They also made its utility for settlement questionable, which allowed its sponsors to dub the area "worthless for development." Such a designation made lawmakers more willing to sponsor setting it aside for altruistic reasons.

The progressive period energized many Americans to identify social ills and use the government to correct them. The impulse to discontinue waste of resources and the pollution, physical and spiritual, of American communities rapidly became an expression for Americans' unique connection to the land. The leadership of President Theodore Roosevelt and his Chief of Forestry Gifford Pinchot galvanized the upper-class interest with national policies. These policies deviated in two directions, preservation and conservation. Roosevelt greatly admired the national parks as places where "bits of the old wilderness scenery and the old wilderness life are to be kept unspoiled for the benefit of our children's children." With his spiritual support, preservationists linked securing natural areas apart from development to icons of Americanness, including Jeffersonian ideals and romanticism. Finally, though, preservationists argued that a society that could exhibit such restraint as to cordon off entire sections of itself had ascended to the level of great civilizations in world history. While Roosevelt is thought to have had preservationist convictions, his main advisor on land management, Pinchot, argued otherwise for the good of the nation.

Conservationists, such as Pinchot, sought to qualify the preservationist impulse with a dose of utilitarian reality. The mark of an ascendant society, they argued, was the awareness of limits and the use of the government to manage resources in danger. Forest resources would be primary to Pinchot's concern. The first practicing American forester, Pinchot urged Americans to manage forests differently than had Europe. Under Pinchot's advice, President Theodore Roosevelt moved the few National Forests created in 1891 out of the jurisdiction of the Department of Agriculture and into an independent Forest Service. During his administration, Roosevelt added 150 million acres of National Forests. The U.S. Forest Service became one of the most publicly-recognized government agencies of the Roosevelt era under Pinchot's direction. A mailing list of over 100,000, frequent public appearances, and penning articles for popular magazines combined with Pinchot's personal connections to help make forests a national cause celebre. This public standing, created through forest conservation, further inflamed the approaching altercation that would define the early environmental movement.

While the difference between preservation and conservation may not have been clear to Americans at the beginning of the twentieth century, popular culture and the writing of muckraking journalists clearly reflected a time of changing sensibilities. After the San Francisco fire, the nation confronted its feelings in order to define national policy. San Francisco, in search of a dependable supply of water, requested that the Hetch Hetchy Valley, located within the boundaries of Yosemite National Park, be flooded in order to create a reservoir to protect against future fires. Preservationists, rallied by popular magazine articles by naturalist John Muir, boisterously refused to compromise the authenticity of a National Park's natural environment. Reviving romantic notions and even transcendental philosophies, Muir used this pulpit to urge "Thousands of tired, nerve-shaken, over-civilized people are beginning to find out that going to the mountains is going home; that wildness is a necessity; and that mountain parks and reservations are useful not only as fountains of timber and irrigating rivers, but as fountains of life." He called those wishing to develop the site "temple destroyers." In reaction, Pinchot defined the conservationist mantra by claiming that such a reservoir represented the "greatest good for the greatest number" of people, and therefore should be the nation's priority. The dam and reservoir would be approved in 1913, but the battle had fueled the emergence of the modern environmental movement.

Environmentalism continued to emerge as a portion of twentieth-century culture throughout the period before World War II. Most importantly, the New Deal brought the connection of scientific understanding to the popular appeal of not abusing natural resources. Particularly as New Deal agencies strove to win public approval for their back-to-work programs, popular periodicals were deluged with scientifically-based articles discussing land-use practices being carried out by New Deal agencies. This development incorporated the emergence of ecology, also taking place in the 1930s, with federal policies to manage watersheds, maintain forests, teach agriculture,

and hold fast the flying soils of the Southern Plains. Press coverage of the "dust bowl" of the 1930s, for instance, presented a natural disaster caused by drought and bad luck. Through government-made documentary films such as *The Plow that Broke the Plains*, the New Deal infused a bit of ecological background to explain desertification and agricultural practices that can be used to combat it. In the process of a natural disaster, the American public learned a great deal about its role within the natural environment.

This lesson became more pronounced as Americans increased their lifestyle standards and their expectations for safety. Historians point to a clear correlation between the 1950s growth in the middle class and the popularity of environmentalism. Samuel P. Hays wrote that this era "displayed demands from the grass-roots, demands that are well charted by the innumerable citizen organizations. . . " that grew out of such public interest. Within growing suburbanization, middle-class Americans expected health and home safety. While there was as yet little regulative authority available, grass-roots environmentalists demanded their government to intercede and insure community safety. The groundswell of interest mobilized with the counter-culture movements of the 1960s, and activists seized a national stage to link scientific data with environmental concern.

The initial interest of the public in the 1940s and 1950s was garnered through an event similar to Hetch Hetchy. The Bureau of Reclamation, an agency developed by applying Pinchot's idea of conservation to waterways of the American West, set out to construct the Echo Park Dam along the Utah-Colorado border, and within a little used National Monument, named Dinosaur—even though most of its fossils and bones had been stolen. As Congress neared a vote on the issue in 1950, 78 national and 236 state conservation organizations expressed their belief that National Parks and Monuments were sacred areas. David Brower, executive director of the Sierra Club and Howard Zahniser of the Wilderness Society used the opportunity to create a model for environmental lobbyists to follow. Direct-mail pamphlets asked: "What is Your Stake in Dinosaur?" and "Will You DAM the Scenic Wildlands of Our National Park System?" Additionally, a color motion picture and a book of lush photos, each depicting the Echo Park Valley's natural splendor, were widely viewed by the public. Such images and sentiments forced Americans to react. With mail to Congress late in 1954 running at eighty to one against the dam, the bill's vote was suspended and the project eventually abandoned. The issues had been packaged by environmentalists to connect concerns with romantic images of the American past. The American public reacted as never before.

Zahniser identified this moment as the best to press for the environmental movement's greatest goal: a national system of wilderness lands. Based on the idealistic notion of pristine wilderness, such a system had been called for beginning with Aldo Leopold in the 1910s. With increased recreation in parks and public lands, argued Zahniser, it had become even more crucial that some of the land be set aside completely. His bill, introduced to Congress in the 1950s, precluded land development and offered recreational opportunities only for a few rather than for the great mass of travelers. Such an ideal goal required great salesmanship, and Zahniser was perfect for the job. As the political climate shifted in the early 1960s, lawmakers became more interested in wilderness. Finally, in 1964, President Lyndon Johnson signed the Wilderness Act into law. The United States had taken one of the most idealistic plunges in the history of environmentalism: nearly ten million acres were immediately set aside as ''an area where the earth and its community of life are untrammeled by man, where man himself is a visitor who does not remain.'' Additional lands were preserved in similar fashion by the end of the decade.

While the concept of wilderness forced the general American public to begin to understand ecosystems and the webs of reliance operating within natural systems, the application of scientific understanding to environmentalism occurred most often in other realms. Pollution composed the most frequent complaint, but its nuisance derived more from physical discomfort than a scientific correlation with human health. Rachel Carson, a government biologist turned nature writer, presented the American public with its lesson in science in 1962 with the publication of *Silent Spring*. The bestseller told the story of pollution (particularly that from the popular pesticide DDT) and its effect on ecological webs of life linked water runoff to fish health and then to depletion of the Bald Eagle population. Readers were left to infer the effects of such chemicals on humans. Flexing their increased environmental awareness, the American public scurried to support Carson's parade through television talk shows. The Kennedy administration appointed a commission to study Carson's findings and a year later banned DDT from use in the United States. Carson became identified with ''mother nature'' and a maternal impulse to manage the natural environment through federal regulation.

Over the next decade, a deluge of environmental legislation responded to the public's demand for action. The public outcry was so severe that even a conservative such as Richard Nixon could be deemed ''the environmental President'' as he signed the National Environmental Protection Act in 1969, creating the Environmental Protection Agency (EPA). The public entrusted the EPA as its environmental regulator to enforce ensuing legislation monitoring air and water purity, limiting noise and other kinds of pollution, and monitoring species in order to discern which required federal protection. The public soon realized just how great the stakes were. During the 1970s, oil spills, river fires, nuclear accidents, and petroleum shortages made it appear as if nature were in open rebellion. Rapidly, this decade instructed Americans, already possessing a growing environmental sensibility, that humans—just as Carson had instructed—needed to live within limits. A watershed shift in human consciousness could be witnessed in the popular culture as green philosophies infiltrated companies wishing to create products that appealed to the public's environmental priority. Recycling, day-light savings time, car-pooling, and environmental impact statements became part of everyday life after the 1970s.

The culture expressing this environmental priority has taken many forms since the 1970s. Earth Day 1970 introduced a tradition that has evolved into an annual reminder of humans' tenuous existence. As many as twenty million Americans participated in the first celebration. Some celebrants protested polluting companies, others planted trees, and still others cleaned up trash. Particularly for school-age children, a single day has evolved into continuous awareness. Ideas such as highway trash cleanup and recycling have become part of everyday American society. Many parents find children acting as environmental regulators within a household. Mixing science with action, environmentalism proved to be excellent fodder for American educators. More importantly, though, the philosophy of fairness and living within limits merged with cultural forms to become mainstays

in entertainment for young people, including feature films such as *Lion King* and *Fern Gully,* environmental music, and even clothing styles. The audience of children and youths quickly became an outlet for ideals for which many adults longed but from which society limited their access. In essence, after 1980 many American parents expressed their own convictions by supporting the environmental idealism of youth culture.

Earth Day 1990 continued such traditions, but also marked an important change in environmentalism's scope. Worldwide, 14 nations and more than 40 million humans marked some kind of celebration on Earth Day 1990. While a global perspective seemed inherent in the web of life put forward by Carson and others, it would take global issues such as the Chernobyl nuclear accident in 1986 and shared problems such as greenhouse gasses and global warming to bind the world into a common perspective, fueled to action by the Western environmental consciousness. Most importantly, the United Nations presented a tool for facilitating such efforts. With its first meeting on the environment in 1972, the global organization created its Environmental Program. This organization would sponsor the historic Rio Conference on the Environment in 1992 and that on global warming in 1997. In response to such activities, the U.S. federal government declared the environment a genuine diplomatic risk in global affairs by creating a State Department Undersecretary for the Environment in 1996. What began as an intellectual philosophy had so impacted the human worldview that it would now influence global relations.

By the late 1990s, polls revealed that nearly 70 percent of Americans referred to themselves as ''environmentalists.'' But of those who called themselves environmentalists most did not hold deep philosophical commitments. More often, they expressed themselves in reaction to mass mailings put out by any of the hundreds of environmental special interest groups developed by the 1990s. Starting from associations of conservation hunters, including the Audubon Society founded in the 1870s, organizations such as the Sierra Club, Wilderness Society, and the American Wildlife Federation have evolved with the environmental movement. Additionally, the global emphasis spawned Greenpeace, the world's largest environmental organization. Financial support from membership dues broadens the cultural impact of environmental philosophies while also allowing many Americans to define themselves as supporters while possessing little of the movement's primary convictions.

The twentieth century has witnessed the development of a consciousness that transcends the preservation of special places and the regulation of damaging pollutants. From romantic beginnings, Americans have been moved to ask serious questions about their very basic idea of progress. For many Americans, increased environmental awareness has moved them to alter their actions and priorities. American culture, though, has become more ''green'' for every observer.

—Brian Black

FURTHER READING:

Fox, Stephen. *The American Conservation Movement.* Madison, University of Wisconsin Press, 1981.

Nash, Roderick. *Wilderness and the American Mind.* New Haven, Yale University Press, 1982.

Sale, Kirkpatrick. *The Green Revolution.* New York, Hill and Wang, 1993.

Worster, Donald. *Nature's Economy.* New York, Cambridge University Press, 1977.

Equal Rights Amendment

While the history of slavery is well known in the United States, the fact that married women were legally subservient until the nineteenth century is less well known. The doctrine of *coverture,* practiced throughout the United States, meant that married women were covered by their husbands and had no separate legal existence. In practice, this resulted in the inheritance of women being assigned to their husbands, the guardianship of minor children being decided by the father, earnings of wives and minor children being claimed by the father, and lack of protection from abusive husbands. Many states allowed husbands to beat their wives to correct them as long as the means of punishment was no thicker than his thumb. This is where the rule of thumb derived. The Seneca Falls Convention in 1848 had paved the way for the rights of women, but it was not until 1920 that women had won the right to vote with the 19th Amendment. Once the vote was assured, women's groups launched a campaign to provide for equal rights amendments at both the state and national levels.

The push for equal rights was led by the National Women's Party (NWP) who succeeded in 1925 in convincing Congress to hold the first congressional hearings on the Equal Rights Amendment (ERA). The amendment stated that "men and women shall have equal rights throughout the United States and every place subject to its jurisdiction." The National Association for Women's Suffrage of America (NAWSA), headed by Carrie Chapman Catt, also worked for the passage of the Equal Rights Amendment. Alice Paul, a veteran of the English campaign for women's rights, joined Catt in her struggle and accepted the presidency of the NWP. She introduced the first version of the Equal Rights Amendment to Congress, arguing that the purpose of the amendment was to allow women to be all that they could be. Opponents to the ERA could be found both in and out of the women's movement. From within, Florence Kelly led the fight against it, believing that it would take away existing protections for which women had fought.

In 1940, the Republican party endorsed the Equal Rights Amendment, and the Democrats followed in 1944. In 1946, an attempt to steer the amendment through the Senate failed. By 1950 the intent of the amendment had been weakened by a rider that exempted all laws designed to protect women. Then in 1953, the amendment was sent to congressional committees where it remained for the next two decades.

When the "second wave" of the women's movement was launched in 1963 with the publication of Betty Friedan's *The Feminine Mystique,* new attention was focused on the Equal Rights Amendment. In 1923, support for the ERA had been considered radical, but in the 1970s support came from mainstream America as well as from more liberal elements. Advocates included The League of Women Voters, the Business and Professional Women, the Young Women's Christian Association (YWCA), the American Association of University Women (AAUW), Common Cause, and United Auto Workers (UAW).

Representative Martha Griffith reintroduced the Equal Rights Amendment in 1970, with a slight rephrasing: "Equality of rights under the law shall not be denied or abridged by the United States or by any state on account of sex." In 1972, the new version of the Equal Rights Amendment passed both houses of Congress with large majorities. The stiffest battle was still ahead, however, as supporters of the amendment set out to garner the necessary approval of three-fourths of the 50 states. It was not to be. Thirty-five states ratified, but the sophisticated organization of the opposition prevented passage in the three additional states needed for ratification.

Opponents to the Equal Rights Amendment pointed out that the 14th and Fifth Amendments to the United States Constitution contained guarantees of equality and that existing laws, such as the Civil Rights Act of 1964 and the Equal Pay Act provided practical protections of rights. They painted horrifying portraits of women in combat, co-ed restrooms, and working mothers who neglected their families. To no avail, supporters countered with arguments that laws were more transitory than amendments and that women had an equal responsibility to protect their countries. They pointed out that women already worked outside the home, and that traditional families were still the norm.

Most amendments are given seven years from the date of congressional approval to win ratification by the necessary 38 states. The Equal Rights Amendment was given an unprecedented three-year extension. But in 1983, the extension expired, and the Equal Rights Amendment was never made a part of the United States Constitution. Supporters of the amendment continue to offer it up for approval at both the national and state levels, but the urgency for its passage has dissipated. As a whole, women no longer feel as threatened by the lack of an ERA because they have enjoyed the successes of a society more open to women's rights and have reaped the benefits of Title VII of the Civil Rights Act of 1964, which banned discrimination based on sex. In a landmark case in 1972, the Supreme Court held in *Reed v. Reed* that legal classifications could not arbitrarily be based on sex. Subsequent cases have upheld women's right to serve on juries, to practice law and medicine, to work in bars, to be protected from pregnancy discrimination, and to take control of their reproductive lives. Ruth Bader Ginsburg, appointed to the Supreme Court by President Bill Clinton in 1993, successfully argued as a practicing lawyer that the Equal Protection Clause of the 14th Amendment should protect individuals from sexual discrimination. Even though the Equal Rights Amendment was never added to the United States Constitution, protection for those rights has now become part of the fabric of American law and society. While women continue to be discriminated against in practice, they are legally protected from intentional discrimination. It could be argued that the defeat of the ERA paved the way for the success of the goals of the amendment.

—Elizabeth Purdy

FURTHER READING:

Becker, Susan D. *The Origins of the Equal Rights Amendment: American Feminism between the Wars.* Westport, Connecticut, Greenwood Press, 1982.

Evans, Sarah M. *Born for Liberty: A History of Women in America.* New York, The Free Press, 1989.

Stetson, Dorothy McBride. *Women's Rights in the USA: Policy Debates and Gender Roles.* New York, Garland Publishing, 1997.

ER

The Emmy-Award-winning television drama *ER* premiered in the fall of 1994. It became the most richly compensated show in television history in 1998 when NBC agreed to pay the show's production company, Warner Brothers, 13 million dollars per episode for three seasons. Best-selling author and film producer Michael Crichton (*Jurassic Park, Disclosure*) created the hour-long drama, which centers on a staff of young medical professionals who work in the emergency room of an inner city hospital in Chicago. The show's collection of talented actors, writers, and producers garnered *ER* an average of 30 million viewers per episode. The show's blockbuster ratings and critical acclaim accelerated the 1990s trend toward cross-pollination between the television and film industries. Many members of the cast branched into film work while honoring contracts with the show. Crichton shared duties as executive producer with famous Hollywood producer and director Steven Spielberg and veteran television producers John Wells, Lydia Woodward, and Carol Flint.

The NBC-Warner Brothers financial agreement concerning *ER* signaled a shift in television economics. In the decade leading up to the deal, increased competition brought about by cable and satellite technology found traditional networks straining to maintain their dwindling audiences. Suddenly, exceptionally popular programs like *ER* enjoyed increased bargaining power. As a result, a two-tiered system took shape in which one or a handful of shows would carry a network—not necessarily by generating direct profits (although advertisers did pay $500,000 per 30 second spot during *ER* broadcasts),

ER cast members: (from left) NBC President Warren Littlefield, Laura Innes, series executive producer John Wells, Anthony Edwards, Julianna Margulies, George Clooney, Noah Wylie, Kellie Martin, and Gloria Reuben celebrate the show's 100th episode.

but by luring viewers to the network, thus generating interest on the part of advertisers to invest in less-popular shows.

Frenzied pacing and frankness in depicting emergency medical procedures characterized the show. Its immediate popularity also afforded *ER* directors considerable room for artistic experimentation. In attempting to reproduce an edgy documentary style, for instance, ''Ambush,'' the opening episode of the fourth season, was broadcast live and shot on video rather than on traditional film stock. The daring episode (which some called a publicity stunt) received mixed reviews. Ultimately, producers shifted the focus of the drama away from its hyperactive emergency scenes, toward the soap-opera-like personal lives of the characters.

Web sites centered on the show's doctors and nurses proliferated on the Internet. Viewers enjoyed the medical heroics performed by the characters, but also sympathized with the tragic humanity of their flaws and their weekly attempts to hold together their neglected personal lives. Series favorites include Dr. Mark Greene (Anthony Edwards), a senior attending physician whose career cost him his marriage; Dr. Doug Ross (George Clooney, whose 1999 departure from the show was one of the most-watched episodes), a handsome, philandering pediatrician; Dr. Peter Benton (Eriq La Salle), an intense and egotistical surgeon; Dr. John Carter (Noah Wyle), a well-intentioned but naive son of one of Chicago's wealthiest families; Carol Hathaway (Julianna Margulies), a compassionate, earthy nurse who struggles to determine her own self-worth; Jeanie Boulet (Gloria Reuben), an HIV-positive physician's assistant; Dr. Kerry Weaver (Laura Innes), an abrasive attending physician and administrator; and Dr. Elizabeth Corday (Alex Kingston), a winsome and intelligent visiting surgeon from England perplexed by the seriousness of her American colleagues. In addition to these favorites, series regulars have included various characters who lasted a season or two.

—Adrienne Russell

Erdrich, Louise (1954—)

Of mixed Chippewa and German-American ancestry, Louise Erdrich addresses the concerns of modern Native Americans in a way that appeals equally, if somewhat differently, to Native American and mainstream readers alike. ''Indianness'' matters in her work, but Erdrich is far more interested in affirming important aspects of Native American experience—attitudes toward sexuality and nature, women's power, and communal ethics and aesthetics in particular—than in accusing Euro-American culture (and readers) of past wrongs. Her Faulknerian preoccupation with place has led her to create a sprawling, loosely connected multi-novel saga that deals mainly, but not exclusively, with Native American life in the latter half of the twentieth century. Her fiction (she also writes poetry and essays) weaves together realism and fantasy, sensuality and lyricism, short story and novel, oral and written traditions, comic sensibility and tragic awareness. The popular and critical success of her National Book Award-winning first novel, *Love Medicine* (1984), and the physical attractiveness that led *People Magazine* to include her in its list of ''most beautiful'' people have helped make her one of the most recognizable and influential Native American writers of her generation.

—Robert A. Morace

FURTHER READING:

Chavkin, Allan, and Nancy Feyl Chavkin, editors. *Conversations with Louise Erdrich and Michael Dorris*. Jackson, University of Mississippi Press, 1994.

Chavkin, Allan, editor. *The Chippewa Landscape of Louise Erdrich*. Tuscaloosa, University of Alabama Press, 1999.

Erector Sets

Sets of metal girders, nuts, bolts, gears, and electric motors that could be used to build numerous structures and vehicles, Erector sets were a popular construction toy for decades and spawned other lines of construction sets, including Legos.

A. C. Gilbert, founder of the Mysto Magic Company in 1909, which sold magic trick equipment, introduced the Erector set in 1913. Inspired by the girders he saw being installed along the New Haven railroad, he was influenced by similar toy construction sets already on the market, including the English Meccano, which was made up of strips of metal, bolts, and nuts that could be put together to build various small models. Gilbert's Erector set, however, could use gears and electric motors, a feature which made Erector a leader among construction toys.

The success of the Erector set was due to its versatility and response to new technological developments. Gilbert originally created pieces and designs for his sets which could be put together to create square girders that allowed for the construction of impressive buildings and bridges in imitation of the engineering feats of the burgeoning skyscraper architecture. In the 1920s, Erector sets could build models of trucks, Ferris wheels, and zeppelins. In the 1940s, Gilbert introduced the Parachute Jump. Gilbert and his company produced his toys until his death in 1961. In 1965 Gabriel Industries purchased the A.C. Gilbert company, but by the end of the twentieth century, Meccano S. A., who had purchased the Erector trademark around 1990, produced Meccano sets labeled with the Erector name. But the nostalgia surrounding the original Erector sets made them collectors items.

—Wendy Woloson

FURTHER READING:

Hertz, Louis H. *The Handbook of Old American Toys*. Wethersfield, Conn., Mark Haber & Co., 1947.

———. *The Toy Collector*. New York, Funk & Wagnalls, 1969.

McClintock, Inez, and Marshall McClintock. *Toys in America*. Washington, D.C., Public Affairs Press, 1961.

Erhard Seminar Training

See est

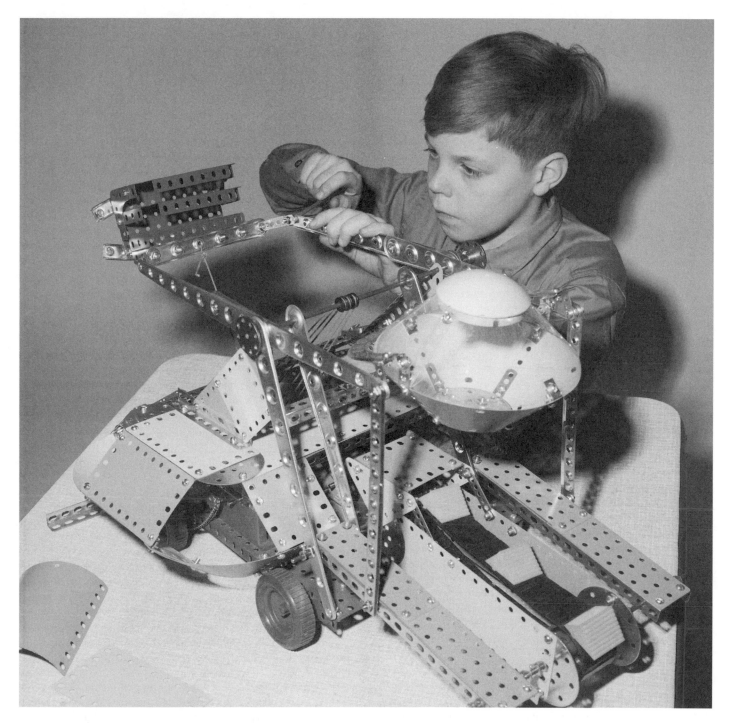

A young boy builds a "planetary probe" with his new Erector Set, 1963.

Ertegun, Ahmet (1923—)

Ahmet Ertegun is the foremost music entrepreneur of the rock 'n' roll age. He and partner Herb Abramson founded Atlantic Records in 1947 on a loan of $10,000. Under Ertegun's guidance, Atlantic Records was a key force in the introduction of rhythm and blues (R&B) and rock 'n' roll into the American mainstream. Atlantic has since become one of the top labels in the world. Ertegun's impact extends well beyond Atlantic Records. His astute guidance helped shape the career of dozens of other top music executives, among them mega-mogul David Geffen. Ertegun is also a founding member of the Rock 'n' Roll Hall of Fame and served as its chairman. He was inducted into the hall in 1987 and the museum's main exhibition hall bears his name. Interestingly, Ertegun was also instrumental in bringing soccer to the United States—he was president of the highly successful New York Cosmos team during the 1970s. Clearly an ingenious mind, Ertegun has also won many prestigious humanitarian awards for his tireless efforts on a number of civil rights and civil liberties fronts.

Ertegun's unique ear for talent and his penetrating insight into the music industry were developed early. A child of the Turkish Ambassador, Ertegun and his older brother Nesuhi spent many of their formative years in Washington D.C. where they became ravenous jazz and blues fans. Their teenage record collection is reported to have numbered in the thousands and long before they were of legal age, the brothers had seen many of the great jazzmen of the era, including Louis Armstrong and Duke Ellington.

While studying philosophy at St. John's College, Ertegun became increasingly frustrated in his search for the recordings of many of the jazz and blues performers he had seen live. In response, he decided to start Atlantic Records in order to record many of these unrecognized talents. Atlantic, however, was never intended to be an archival label. Ertegun envisioned Atlantic as a vehicle for mainstreaming blues and jazz. In order to realize this goal, Ertegun concentrated on finding and recording musicians that did not easily fit the dominant black music styles of the day.

Ertegun's reputation in the industry was built upon his great "ears" for talent. His intimacy with the black musical idiom and his willingness to scour clubs and juke joints in any neighborhood and any region of the country set him apart from other talent scouts of the day. His successes in the field of A&R stand still as the yardstick by which others are measured. Among the more influential artists Ertegun brought to Atlantic during the early years were Ray Charles, Big Joe Turner, Ruth Brown, The Drifters, The Clovers, and The Coasters. Jazz masters John Coltrane and Professor Longhair also recorded for Atlantic during this era. Once artists were contracted with Atlantic, Ertegun continued to work closely with them in the studio. On occasion he also wrote songs for his artists. Under the pseudonym "Nugetre" (Ertegun spelled backwards), he penned several hits, including "Don't Play that Song," "Chains of Love," "Sweet Sixteen," and "Mess Around."

More important, though, was Ertegun's ability to coax from a variety of musicians a sound that found widespread appeal among white audiences. The Atlantic sound evolved into a "danceable" compromise that borrowed from both country blues and big band jazz. It laid critical groundwork for the development of R&B (a genre label coined by Nesuhi Ertegun) and ultimately rock 'n' roll. By successfully bringing R&B to the mainstream market, Atlantic established itself as one of the first and most successful of the emergent "independent" record labels. Along with Chess and Sun Records, Atlantic eroded the corporate oligopoly of the recording industry (e.g., Columbia, RCA, and Decca).

In the early 1960s, when many independent labels faltered, Atlantic's successes mounted. Ertegun's musical instincts kept Atlantic from buying too heavily into the faddish teenybopper rock of that early period. Instead, the label concentrated on popularizing the emergent soul sound. Atlantic signed during this era soul legends Otis Redding, Wilson Pickett, Sam and Dave, and perhaps most importantly Aretha Franklin. In the later 1960s, Ertegun's insight into the nature of the British Invasion prompted him to lead scouting missions to England where Atlantic tapped into London's blues revivalism. Atlantic's discoveries during this era include megastars Cream and Led Zeppelin. Ertegun was also instrumental in bringing art-rock to American shores, signing or helping sign Genesis, Yes, and King Crimson. From the West Coast scene, Atlantic signed Buffalo Springfield, Crosby Stills and Nash, and Neil Young among others.

Although he sold the label in 1967 to Warner-Seven Arts, Ertegun stayed on as chairman of the Atlantic group and guided the label to greater glories in the 1970s. Atlantic's climb toward preeminence among rock labels was largely a product of Ertegun's personality and professional reputation. By the early 1970s, Ertegun had come to be regarded as one of the most knowledgeable, charismatic, and trustworthy industry executive. His abiding love of the music itself, his street savvy, and his legendary hedonism won him respect and admiration from musicians everywhere. In addition, his long-term friendship with Mick Jagger helped Atlantic steal the Rolling Stones from their long-time affiliation with Decca records, a deal which sealed Atlantic's standing as the preeminent rock label of the era. In 1997, Ertegun was still CEO at Atlantic, was still a vital personality on the New York nightclub circuit, and the label he founded 50 years earlier was the top market share holder.

—Steve Graves

FURTHER READING:

Ertegun, Ahmet, et al. *What'd I Say: The Atlantic History of Music.* New York, Welcome Rain, 1998.

Gillett, Charlie. *Making Tracks: Atlantic Records and the Growth of a Multi-Billion Dollar Industry.* New York, E.P. Dutton, 1974.

Wade, Dorothy, and Justine Picardie. *Music Man: Ahmet Ertegun, Atlantic Records, and the Triumph of Rock and Roll.* New York, W.W. Norton and Company, 1990.

Erving, Julius "Dr. J" (1950—)

Julius Erving led a revolution in the style and substance of the game of basketball beginning in 1971, when he joined the Virginia Squires of the American Basketball Association (ABA), following his junior year at the University of Massachusetts—it was playing college basketball that he earned his famous nickname, Dr. J. As a collegiate player with the Minutemen, Erving was one of only six players in NCAA history to average more than 20 points and 20 rebounds per game. During a professional career that spanned two leagues and 16 years, Erving redefined the role of a forward in not only the professional game, but in basketball as a whole. His athletic talents evoked an artistic flare that the professional game had never seen before. Erving also became an ambassador for the sport and a driving force in the revitalization of the game as a profitable spectator event.

During his five years in the ABA with the Squires (1971-1973) and the New York Nets (1973-1976), Erving was voted the league's Most Valuable Player (MVP) three times (1974, 1975, 1976), and led the Nets to the ABA Championship in 1974 and 1976. He was credited by many with single handedly keeping the financially strapped ABA afloat. Because the league had no national television exposure, many teams struggled at the box office. Arenas throughout the ABA, however, were consistently sold out for games in which the Nets and the flamboyant Erving participated. In his five ABA seasons, Erving averaged 28.7 points and 12.1 rebounds per game, led the league in scoring in 1973, 1974, and 1976, and was a four-time first team ABA All-Pro.

Following the 1975-76 season, four ABA teams merged with the larger and more financially stable National Basketball Association (NBA). This merger, which had been the initial hope and dream of the

Julius Erving, "Dr. J," in mid-air, gets ready to shoot.

original founders of the ABA, was due in large part to the popular and charismatic play of Julius Erving and a handful of other star ABA players.

After the NBA/ABA merger, Erving joined the Philadelphia 76ers, with whom he played for the next eleven years. During his NBA career, Erving was a five-time first team NBA All-Pro (1978, 1980, 1981, 1982, and 1983), and was voted the league's Most Valuable Player in 1981. In 1983, the 76ers, led by Erving and teammate Moses Malone, won the NBA Championship, the third championship of Dr. J's illustrious career. In addition to the 1983 title, the 76ers appeared in the Championship Series three other times during Erving's tenure with the club (1977, 1980, and 1982). As an NBA player, Dr. J averaged 22.0 points and 6.7 rebounds per game. Over the course of his career, Erving would leave his mark throughout the combined NBA/ABA record books, ranking in the top ten in career scoring (third), field goals made (third), field goals attempted (fifth), and most steals (first). At the time of his retirement in 1987, Dr. J was one of only three players to have scored over 30,000 points (30,026) as a professional player.

Julius Erving was chiefly recognized as a player who helped to establish the individual artistic creativity that has come to permeate professional basketball since the 1980s. Erving was the first player to win a league wide slam-dunk contest in 1976 while in the ABA, a feat he repeated several years later during his NBA career. He also possessed magnetic charm and an unquestionable dignity, which attracted the admiration of basketball fans and the general public in a manner few other players have enjoyed. The equally talented and charismatic Michael Jordan is known to have stated that he would

never have conceived of his basketball style without having seen Dr. J play during the prime of his professional career.

Since his retirement as a player, Erving continues to be a worldwide ambassador for the game, both through his personal business dealings and his regular appearances on NBA television broadcasts as a commentator. In 1993, Erving was inducted into the Basketball Hall of Fame in Springfield, Massachusetts.

—G. Allen Finchum

FURTHER READING:

Dickey, Glenn. *The History of Professional Basketball.* Briarcliff Manor, New York, Stein and Day, 1982.

Sachare, Alex. *100 Greatest Basketball Players of All Time.* New York, Pocket Books, 1997.

Escalona, Beatriz

See Noloesca, La Chata

Escher, M. C. (1898-1972)

With his fantastically precise, yet hallucinatory and illusional imagery, graphic artist M.C. Escher became a favorite of students and those who indulged in chemically altered states in the 1960s. Escher was best known for his tessellation, or repeating geometric patterns, and he also liked to draw scenes that incorporated several different spatial perspectives. In the course of time, his work became some of the most recognizable in the art world. Today, decks of playing cards and T-shirts decorated with his distinctive black and white patterns are usually found in museum gift stores next to the Van Gogh items— somewhat ironic in that, during his lifetime, Escher was dismissed by the traditional arts establishment as "too cerebral."

Escher died in 1972, not long after the heady counterculture of the 1960s had elevated his art to iconic status. "The hippies of San Francisco continue to print my work illegally. I received some of the grisly results through a friendly customer over there," he wrote in his journal on April 20, 1969. He was born Maurits Cornelis Escher in the Dutch city of Leeuwarden in 1898. As a youth he studied architecture, but then switched to graphic art. From 1923 to 1935 he lived in southern Italy, where he sketched traditional landscapes and architectural sites, from which he made woodcuts or lithographs. Some of this work, however, foreshadowed his later creativity; the pattern he painstakingly reproduced in *St. Peter's, Rome* (1928), for example, served as a precursor to his penchant for infinitely repeated abstractions, while his fascination with the hallucinatory is presaged in the 1935 woodcut *Dream,* in which an enormous insect visits the body of a recumbent bishop.

In the mid-1930s, the artist spent time in Spain, and his visits to Granada's Alhambra and the famed La Mezquita (mosque) of Cordoba gave him fresh inspiration. Both of these impressive architectural legacies from Spain's Moorish past housed a treasure of decorative art in abstract patterns, since Islamic art prohibited any representational imagery. At this point Escher began to think more about spatial relationships and the depiction of the infinite. His work soon took another direction when he began to fill space entirely with a repeating image.

In other works he would create a fantastical scene that had no counterpart in reality. The 1938 woodcut *Day and Night* depicts checkerboard farm fields, which morph into birds; the black birds are flying to the left into daylight, while the white flock heads toward darkness. Escher also somehow managed to mirror the opposite but concurrent hours into the landscape below them. Another famous work from this era, the 1942 lithograph *Verbum,* represents his fascination with the "closed cycle" in its images of reptiles that become fish who then become birds. Amphibians always remained a particular favorite for the artist: in the 1943 lithograph *Reptiles,* his subjects crawl off a piece of paper in a circular trajectory, during which they become three-dimensional; one exhales a little smoke before it returns to two dimensions.

These, and other creations, wrote Robert Hughes in *Time,* "are scientific demonstrations of how to visualize the impossible." Yet far from being a capricious fantasist, Escher was deeply interested in the hard sciences. The artist regularly corresponded with mathematicians, and had little contact or respect for other artists, especially those working in modernism. "I consider 60 percent of the artists nuts and fakes," he once said of those whose work hung in Amsterdam's famed Stedelijk Museum. He handled much of the business of art himself, selling his images directly to college professors who had requested them for use in mathematical textbooks. He also sold inexpensive prints of his works in college bookstores, which helped give him a certain cachet among the brainy. One of the most enthusiastic of American collectors during his lifetime was the engineer grandson of Teddy Roosevelt, Cornelius Van Schaak Roosevelt, but, for the most part, Escher was largely ignored by the art world. In the 1960s, among the very few periodicals that ran articles on him were *Life, Scientific American,* and *Rolling Stone*, whose issue No. 52 also ran an article speculating about the possible breakup of the Beatles.

A 1968 retrospective of Escher's work in The Hague, Holland's seat of government, gave his popularity something of an international boost, and an Escher Foundation was established in 1968 to market and promote his prints. Rock album covers began using his imagery, which further popularized it, and items with his signature double helixes or reptilian nightmares began appearing in the hippie mail-order bible, *The Whole Earth Catalog*. In 1971 the staid art-book publisher Abrams issued a well-received tome, *The World of M. C. Escher*. Shortly after his death in 1972, Washington D.C.'s National Gallery hosted an exhibition of Escher graphics. "Once the focus of a small, rather cultish, mostly non-art-world audience . . . Escher has in recent years become the focus of a *vast* rather cultish, mostly non-art-world audience," wrote Peter Schjeldahl in the *New York Times* that same year. The art critic, noting that Escher's fan base seemed confined to "scientists and stoned kids," observed dryly that the "psychedelic young" had seized upon Escher imagery in part because of his "terrific virtuosity" and "gamut of fanciful imagery," not to mention accessibility. "Renditions of easily grasped intellectual and sentimental conceits, laced with the bizarre, they yield their essences, it might be said, with alacrity," Schjeldahl declared. "They play intricate tricks in a direct, even blatant way, thus teasing the viewer and flattering him at once."

—Carol Brennan

FURTHER READING:

Albright, Thomas. "Visuals." *Rolling Stone.* 2 February 1970.

Bool, F. H., et al. *M. C. Escher: His Life and Complete Graphic Work.* New York, Abradale Press, 1992.

Davis, Douglas, "Teasing the Brain." *Newsweek.* 31 July 1972, 60-61.

Gardner, Martin. "Mathematical Games." *Scientific American.* April 1966, 110-1212.

Hughes, Robert. "N-dimensional Reality." *Time.* 17 April 1972, 64.

Schjeldahl, Peter. "The Games M. C. Escher Plays." *New York Times.* 23 July 1972, sec. II, 15.

The World of M. C. Escher (with texts by M. C. Escher and J. L. Locher). New York, Abrams, 1971.

ESPN

The Entertainment and Sports Programming Network (ESPN) has become the dominant sports network on cable television. ESPN started when cable television was available to less than 10 percent of the population. ESPN's irreverent style, brilliant advertising, and excellent programming and business decisions have catapulted it into over 70 million homes in the United States, as well as broadcasting in over 150 countries around the world.

When ESPN first began showing sports programming 24 hours a day in 1979, most industry experts concluded it had little chance of survival. With a limited budget and no connections to major sports programming, ESPN was forced to run such oddities as Australian Rules football, college lacrosse matches, and other rarely watched sporting events. Unable to raise the money to carry football, baseball, or any of the other major sports, ESPN concentrated its efforts on its news programming. Resources were poured into *Sportscenter,* the flagship news show for the network. In addition, network executives turned college basketball games and the National Football League draft into television events.

As ESPN gained in popularity, more and more sports fans began to subscribe to cable simply to get access to its excellent news coverage. By 1983, demand for ESPN became so great that the network was the first basic cable network to demand an operating fee from cable franchisers. As cable television continued to expand exponentially throughout the United States, ESPN became an integral part of any basic cable package.

In 1987, the network made two moves that would prove to be its most brilliant. The first move was the acquisition of the rights to televise National Football League games on Sunday nights, which immediately put ESPN in the same category as the major broadcast networks for sports coverage. The addition of football dramatically increased the network's visibility in the sports marketplace, and drew millions of new viewers to their other shows.

The second move was the hiring of John Walsh, who would transform *Sportscenter* into the must-see sports show on television. Walsh brought his background as managing editor of the weekly news magazine *U.S. News and World Report* to *Sportscenter,* transforming it into a news broadcast about sports, rather than a sports broadcast. Walsh created a network that no longer simply showed highlights but also covered the news like any other major nightly news show. ESPN

ABC-TV president Robert Iger (left) and NHL commissioner Gary Bettman at a press conference announcing the NHL's expanded distribution deal with ABC and ESPN through the 1999-2000 season.

added investigative news coverage with *Outside the Lines,* a show that was to examine such controversial issues as racism and gambling in sports. A regular interview show, *Up Close,* was also created and it featured the greatest names in sports on a daily basis. Walsh created a news organization that covered sports at a level of detail never before seen on television.

Walsh endeavored to give ESPN its own personality, one that was humorous, intelligent, and absolutely in love with all types of sports. He hired anchors for *Sportscenter* that epitomized this personality, including the dominant personalities of Dan Patrick and Keith Olbermann. Patrick and Olbermann became the must-see anchors on ESPN, throwing out catch phrases, humor, and information at a rapid-fire pace. Olbermann and Patrick's 11 p.m. edition of *Sportscenter* soon became known as the ''Big Show'' among sports fans, and the devotion the two received reached almost obsessive levels.

By the late 1980s, ESPN had become THE network for the serious sports fans and players alike. Professional athletes made it clear that making the highlight reel on *Sportscenter* was important to

them. Fans held up signs at games addressed to the *Sportscenter* anchors using the catch phrase of the week. The focus on *Sportscenter* became so strong that the anchors could literally create a trend overnight. During one news broadcast, anchors Olbermann and Craig Killborn shouted the word ''salsa!'' every time someone scored a basket in college basketball. The very next night, college basketball fans throughout the country were seen holding up ''Salsa!'' signs whenever the home team made a basket. ESPN had clearly become a dominant cultural phenomenon.

In the 1990s, ESPN's influence grew even further. ESPN radio debuted in 1992, and ESPN2, a second all-sports network, began broadcasting in 1993. The expansion continued, and by 1995 ESPN Sportzone became a presence on the internet, the all-news network ESPNews began in 1996, and *ESPN: The Magazine* emerged as a major competitor to the industry giant *Sports Illustrated* in 1998. In addition, the network began selling licensed ESPN sportswear and other products. ESPN programming now reaches over 70 million households in the United States, one of only three cable channels to have achieved that mark, and ESPN2 is close to reaching it as well. The demand for ESPN programming is so high that the network now commands the highest operating fees and advertising rates on cable. Through saturation and careful marketing, ESPN has become virtually synonymous with sports in the United States.

Before ESPN began broadcasting, most sports coverage was limited to eight minutes on local news channels. Although the major broadcast networks would occasionally run half-hour sports news shows on the weekends, the shows were generally little more than compilations of highlight films. ESPN provided the serious sports fan with a wide variety of news and sports coverage that was unmatched on the airwaves. Fans tuned in to *Sportscenter* to see a full hour of highlights and analysis focused exclusively on sports, a level of detail never before available outside of the sports sections of major newspapers.

Although the level of coverage clearly made ESPN popular, volume is no substitute for quality. If *Sportscenter* had simply been another bland collection of highlight reels, the network would not be the success it is today. Clearly, a large part of the network's success is its ability to tap into the mind of the sports fan. ESPN designed its programming to appeal to the serious fan. *Sportscenter* runs several times during the day, from 5 a.m. to midnight, each show covering the latest news from the sporting world. In addition, the personnel have a clear love for the sports they cover, and this is made apparent to the viewer. Anchors constantly rattle off detailed histories, statistics, and biographies, demonstrating their level of knowledge. ESPN also has succeeded in attracting a broad audience to its programming. Although viewers are predominantly male, their coverage of women's sports, including basketball, soccer, and gymnastics, has drawn more and more women into the ranks of ESPN viewers.

Finally, the anchors are not afraid to inject humor into their coverage. Rather than resorting to the slapstick "blooper" reels so commonly seen on local network television, ESPN anchors interject far more cerebral humor into their coverage. This humor, including a willingness to make fun of themselves, created a bond between the anchors and the viewer. The inside jokes and catch phrases created by the anchors became a language of its own, known only to the serious sports fans of the world.

While there are many things that ESPN did to become successful, one must also recognize that the network came along at just the right time. The 1980s was a decade in which sports franchises around the country experienced a resurgence in popularity. The decade saw the emergence of some of the greatest sports figures of all time, including Michael Jordan, Wayne Gretzky, Joe Montana, and Barry Bonds. Fans were flocking to sporting events in greater numbers than ever before, and ESPN was a clear beneficiary of it. In a symbiotic way, the resurgent popularity of sports drew more fans to ESPN and, in turn, the network created fans for other sports. ESPN's regular coverage of college and professional basketball, professional hockey, and professional soccer was at least partially responsible for the phenomenal growth in attendance for all four sports.

ESPN remains the dominant force in the sports news industry. Other cable networks have attempted to clone its success, but none of them have achieved anything close to their ratings. As the sports industry continues to grow, ESPN will continue to capitalize on that growth.

—Geoff Peterson

FURTHER READING:

Carvell, T. "Prime Time Player." *Fortune*. March 2, 1998, 135-44.

"ESPN International at 15." *Variety*. January 19, 1998, special section.

Mandalese, J. "Cable TV." *Advertising Age*. April 13, 1998, 6-18.

Esquire

From its Depression-era origins as a men's fashion magazine with high literary aspirations, through a brief period when it threatened to devolve into a semi-girlie pulp magazine, *Esquire* emerged by the 1960s as one of America's brashest and most sophisticated monthlies, with hard-hitting articles by the nation's leading writers and journalists on the hot-button cultural and political issues of the decade. At the same time, the periodical served as a Baedeker of sorts to a new generation of leisure-driven, style-conscious, sexually sophisticated men who were abandoning the austerity of the 1930s, the wartime privations of the 1940s, and the conformity of the 1950s for the more carefree, swinging lifestyle of the 1960s.

Esquire magazine was founded in 1933 by Arnold Gingrich and David Smart, who conceived of the publication as a magazine for the "new leisure," one that would be distributed largely through men's clothing stores, a plan that was quickly reversed when newsstands quickly and unexpectedly sold out their limited allotment of 5000 out of the 105,000 initial press run. From the beginning the magazine was known for its literary excellence—it published such authors as Erskine Caldwell, John Dos Passos, F. Scott Fitzgerald, Dashiell Hammett, and Ernest Hemingway—and for its lack of bigotry—it featured cartoons by E. Simms Campbell, the only black artist whose work appeared regularly in a mainstream national magazine, and fiction by Langston Hughes. Perhaps most notable, though, was the magazine's virtual reinvention of American masculinity. In place of the hard-working man of character who plodded through the pages of most American magazines, *Esquire* promoted men who were interested in leisure, were avid consumers, and had a keen interest in sex. Such representations of manhood were soon to become commonplace in American culture, but they first appeared regularly in *Esquire*.

Despite a cover price of fifty cents, double that of most magazines, circulation soared to 675,000 within a decade, emboldening its entrepreneurial founders to launch several other lifestyle magazines, including *Coronet*, *Verve*, and *Ken*. Another circulation-boosting factor was a series of controversial incidents in the early 1940s over the issue of censorship. *Esquire* first became the target of a boycott led by Roman Catholic leaders when *Ken* published some articles the church had found unpalatable. In another well-publicized case, *Esquire*'s practice during World War II of printing double-page pinups as a morale-booster for its military readership prompted the U.S. Post Office to deny the publication its second-class mailing privileges, a decision that was eventually reversed by the U.S. Supreme Court.

Arnold Gingrich withdrew from the publishing partnership soon after World War II, and Smart appointed Frederic A. Birmingham to assume the editorship. Under Birmingham's direction, the publication veered away from its original stylish and literary format in favor of more Western and detective stories, as in other popular pulp magazines of the time. "The design was garish, confused," wrote Carol Polsgrove in her 1995 book *It Wasn't Pretty Folks, But Didn't*

We Have Fun: Esquire in the Sixties. "Circulation stayed high—around 800,000 in the early fifties—but blue-chip advertisers, wary of Esquire's naughty wartime reputation, stayed away," she wrote.

In 1950, *Esquire* moved from Chicago to New York, with Gingrich returning as publisher just a few months before Dave Smart's death. Gingrich took on the task of trying to restore polish to the magazine, which over the next few years was forced to weather challenges from television and from other upscale periodicals like Hugh Hefner's *Playboy*. With his first priority the reestablishment of *Esquire*'s literary reputation, Gingrich asked authors like Paul Gallico, Aldous Huxley, and George Jean Nathan to come on board as regular contributors. By this time, L. Rust Hills had come on board as literary editor and took responsibility for organizing the magazine's annual literary symposia on college campuses. In 1956, Harold Hayes, who had worked for *Picture Week* and *Pageant* magazines, was hired by Gingrich, who wrote in his memoir, *Nothing but People,* "I took him in like the morning paper, knowing that in a Southern liberal who was also a Marine reserve officer I had an extremely rare bird." Gingrich began to withdraw in favor of a younger generation of editors. Ralph Ginzburg and Clay Felker became editors in 1957, and the young Robert Benton took over as art editor, solidifying a team that, despite an acrimonious working style and the sudden firing of Ginzburg soon afterwards, would remold the magazine to appeal to younger demographics and that would turn *Esquire* into the power magazine it would become in the 1960s.

By 1960, *Esquire* was already earning a reputation for publishing serious, even philosophical, articles that could appeal to a more educated audience, such as the correspondence between Elia Kazan and Archibald MacLeish during the production of MacLeish's drama, *J.B.* This editorial policy prompted Carol Polsgrove to declare that the *Esquire* editors were trying to "make thought entertaining. In an age where a whole generation of young men had gone to college on the GI Bill, why not put out a magazine for an audience that cared about rock and roll and the spiritual position of modern man, an audience that had heard of French playwrights and existentialists, an educated audience weary of television and eager to taste the delights of the mind, the cultivations of spirit and sense—and have fun doing it, too?"

Hayes was vowing to publish a magazine that would help America, particularly its men, resolve "a period of self-doubt and anxiety of great magnitude." His prescription was an *Esquire* with "humor, irreverence, fashion, fine writing, controversy, topicality and surprise." Diane Arbus was commissioned to do a photo spread of offbeat New York scenes and characters for a special July, 1960, issue on the city that included articles by James Baldwin, Gay Talese, and John Cheever. Among the many notable writers and journalists who would contribute to Hayes's mission over the next several years were Saul Bellow, Richard Rovere, Gloria Steinem, Malcolm Muggeridge, Dwight Macdonald, John Updike, Gore Vidal, and Norman Mailer. The latter had been assigned to cover the Democratic National Convention in 1960 that nominated the youthful John F. Kennedy for President, though Mailer vehemently quit the enterprise when he objected to *Esquire*'s editors changing a word in his title from "Supermarket" to "Supermart." Mailer was persuaded to return to the fold, however, and he was signed up to write a monthly column beginning in 1962, which quickly attracted critical attention for its audacity and imagination; Mailer later wrote a report on the Republican convention of 1964 that had nominated Barry Goldwater for president. It was also in 1962 that *Esquire* began bestowing its annual Dubious Achievements Awards, a semi-humorous feature concocted largely by a new member of the editorial staff, David

Newman. By this time, Hayes had assumed the role of editor-in-chief and brought in John Berendt as editor. It was also during the early 1960s that *Esquire* gained widespread reputation for publishing both serious and satirical articles on fashion, making the magazine the *de facto* arbiter of sartorial style for sophisticated and would-be sophisticated American men.

In the fall of 1963, when a fledgling writer named Tom Wolfe began to publish his onomatopoetic "new journalism" pieces in *Esquire,* the magazine's circulation had risen to 900,000 and it was being regarded as one of America's most influential publications. It devoted many pages over the next few years to some of the controversial social issues that were cleaving the American body politic, such as the militant black-power movement and the Vietnam war. Michael Herr went to Southeast Asia as a war correspondent for the magazine, and Tom Hedley contributed in-depth reports about unrest on American college campuses. Another young writer, Gary Wills, got his career underway under contract for *Esquire,* covering strife in the nation's black ghettos and the assassination of Rev. Dr. Martin Luther King, Jr. in 1968. Publication of contentious articles by the feuding William F. Buckley, Jr. and Gore Vidal in the summer of 1969 led to libel suits that were eventually settled in Buckley's favor. The following year, the magazine published John Sack's interviews with Lt. William L. Calley, Jr. about atrocities allegedly committed by American soldiers in Mylai, Vietnam. About that time, Gordon Lish, the new fiction editor, helped establish the career of writer Raymond Carver by publishing his short stories in *Esquire,* often over the objections of Hayes.

During most of the 1960s, the provocative and offbeat covers by George Lois were credited with helping stimulate newsstand impulse sales and by 1972, the magazine's circulation had peaked at 1.25 million. Newsstand sales soon began to decline, however, perhaps in part because the issues that had fueled *Esquire* during the turbulent 1960s were running out of steam. Many of the prominent writers who had brought the periodical to the pinnacle of literary and journalistic prominence, like Wolfe, Talese, and Vidal, could no longer be relied upon as regular contributors, and Mailer had again become estranged. In the fall of 1972, with the retirement of Gingrich, Hayes became editor and assistant publisher and Don Erickson was appointed executive editor. Hayes left *Esquire* in April of 1973 due to "irreconcilable differences" with management. Soon afterwards, George Lois ended his connection with the publication. Within the next three years, the magazine suffered sharp declines in readership and advertising lineage. In 1977, *Esquire* was sold to Associated Newspapers, a British concern that had a partnership agreement with Clay Felker. In 1979, the magazine was sold to Sweden's Bonnier Newspaper Group and a firm owned by Phillip Moffitt and Christopher Whittle, with Moffitt becoming editor. In 1987, *Esquire* was purchased by the Hearst Corporation, which continues as its publisher. Data posted on the magazine's website in early 1999 claimed a circulation of 672,073, of which 588,007 were subscription and 84,066 newsstand. The median age of its reader, says Hearst, is 42.6 years. David Granger, editor-in-chief, was quoted as saying "*Esquire* is special because it's a magazine for men. Not a fashion magazine for men, not a health magazine for men, not a money magazine for men. It is not any of these things; it is all of them. It is, and has been for sixty-five years, a magazine about the interests, the curiosity, the passions, of men."

—Edward Moran

FURTHER READING:

Breazeale, Kenon. "In Spite of Women: *Esquire* Magazine and the Construction of the Male Consumer." *Signs: Journal of Women in Culture and Society.* Vol. 20, No. 11, 1994, 1-22.

Gingrich, Arnold. *Nothing but People.* New York, Crown, 1971.

Kimball, Penn T. "The Non Editing of *Esquire.*" *Columbia Journalism Review.* Fall 1964, 32-34.

Lish, Gordon, editor. *The Secret Life of Our Times: New Fiction from Esquire.* New York, Doubleday, 1973.

Merrill, Hugh. *Esky: The Early Years at Esquire.* New Brunswick, New Jersey, Rutgers University Press, 1995.

Pendergast, Tom. "'Horatio Alger Doesn't Work Here Any More': Masculinity and American Magazines, 1919-1940." *American Studies.* Vol. 38, No. 1, Spring 1997, 55-80.

Polsgrove, Carol. *It Wasn't Pretty Folks, But Didn't We Have Fun? Esquire in the Sixties.* New York, W. W. Norton & Company, 1995.

Tebbel, John. *The American Magazine: A Compact History.* New York, Hawthorn Books, 1969.

est

Werner Erhard's est (Erhard Seminar Training and Latin for "it is"), established in 1971 in San Francisco, has come to epitomize the "me decade," a time when people began to focus on self-improvement and the articulation of identity. One of the more successful motivational therapy groups to spring from the "human-potential movement," est used strict training within a group format to build self-awareness and offer individual fulfillment, while training people to get "It." Est is an example of what psychologists call a Large Group Awareness Training program, in which dozens of people are given intense instruction aimed at helping them discover what is hindering them from achieving their full potential. Although est no longer exists in its original form, its offshoot, the Landmark Forum (launched in 1984), continues to attract people who have a growing need to see themselves in a new way, while capitalizing on the past success and popularity of est's teachings.

Like most people, Jack Rosenberg was interested in human development and potential. Confused about his own identity, Rosenberg, a used car salesman, walked away from his family and his life in 1960, in search of answers. Changing his name to Werner Erhard (taken from theoretical physicist Werner Heisenberg, and Ludwig Erhard, the West German Minister of Economics), he went to California to dabble in various human potential disciplines and Eastern religions. He became very interested in L. Ron Hubbard and the Church of Scientology's practices, concluding that "the course was brilliant," and progressing through five Scientology levels. That exposure catalyzed the birth of his own teachings, which caused some controversy with the Church as to their origins, though Erhard insisted the two were different: "Ron Hubbard seems to have no difficulty in codifying the truth and in urging people to believe in it . . . in presenting my own ideas . . . I hold them as pointers to the truth, not as the truth itself." Scientologists continue to accuse Erhard of having stolen his main ideas from Hubbard, while Erhard claimed the Church was behind attempts to discredit him, even hiring hitmen to kill him. An avid reader, Erhard used a mixture of ideas culled from existential philosophy, motivational psychology, Zen Buddhism, Alan Watts, and Sigmund Freud, among others, to build est. His own proverbial "enlightenment" occurred while driving across the Golden Gate bridge in San Francisco, where he says he was "transformed" into a state he described as "knowing everything and knowing nothing." The result was est.

The militant sessions (trainees were not allowed to speak to each other or take bathroom breaks) took place rigorously over two consecutive weekends. People were egged on by confrontational trainers who told them flatly "your life doesn't work" and to "wipe that stupid smile off your face, you a-hole." But the goal was "to get rid of old baggage" and to learn a "more profound sense of responsibility, a sense of potency," said Erhard in a 1988 interview. "My theory is that a person's vitality will generally equal their commitments, and if you'd like to have more vitality, make bigger commitments." Besides personal fulfillment, another benefit touted by the seminars was strengthening relationships. Although est helped many couples, Erhard couldn't do the same for his own two failed marriages.

Part of the controversy surrounding est (besides whether or not it should be classified as a cult) is its offering of quick-fix solutions in a psychologically manipulative setting, and its overly aggressive approach, which often continued after people finished their sessions, in the guise of persistent phone calls haranguing them to sign up for "follow-up" seminars, and forcing them to become recruiters. Erhard and est have had their share of lawsuits related to the seminars, but many who went through the program (an estimated 750,000 over the last 20 years, with centers in 139 cities throughout the world) maintain their loyalty. However, the organization, its lingo, and zealous followers were often satirized as self-obsessed cultists, who sported glazed, exuberant demeanors that made people uncomfortable. Characteristic of other similar movements, est attracted its share of celebrities who became public advocates of the program, such as actress Valerie Harper, singer John Denver, and artist Yoko Ono, which helped to bring the organization and its beliefs more into the public eye. Est and its buzz words started to become more a part of popular culture when advertisements capitalized on its popularity; for example, an ad campaign for MasterCharge used "master the possibilities," one of Erhard's famous aphorisms.

Erhard saw himself as a strict but passionate coach for people receptive to exploring life's possibilities through self-awareness and "transformation." Est "transformed" Erhard's life, making him a rich executive/guru who reigned over his self-help empire. But after it began to crumble in the 1990s, he vanished amidst reports of tax fraud (which proved false) and allegations of incest (which were later recanted), lurid details that continue to keep him alive in popular imagination.

—Sharon Yablon

FURTHER READING:

Ayella, Marybeth F. *Insane Therapy: Portrait of a Psychotherapy Cult.* Philadelphia, Temple University Press, 1998.

Carroll, Robert Todd. "Werner Erhard and est." *The Skeptic's Dictionary.* http://skepdic.com/est.html. January 1999.

Forum Graduate Association. *The Forum Graduate.* http://www.mnsinc.com/fgainc/tfg$_{25}$.html. January 1999.

Krasnow, Iris. *Transformation of est Founder Werner Erhard.* http://www.inlink.com/^dhchase/irikra.htm. January 1999.

MacNamara, Mark. *The Return of Werner Erhard: Guru II.* http://
www.inlink.com/^dhchase/marmac.htm. January, 1999.

Streissguth, Thomas. *Charismatic Cult Leaders.* Minneapolis, Oliver
Press, 1995.

Termayer, Charlotte Fal. *The Best of est?* Time Magazine, March 16,
1996, 52-53.

Yalom, Irvin D. *The Theory and Practice of Group Psychotherapy.*
New York, Basic Books, 1995.

E.T. The Extra-Terrestrial

Released in 1981, Steven Spielberg's *E.T. The Extra-Terrestrial*
touched the emotions and the collective imagination of moviegoers of
all ages, breaking all previous box-office records to become the most
profitable film of its time until it was ousted by Spielberg's own
Jurassic Park 12 years later. Exciting, moving, thought-provoking
and funny, as well as inventive and skillful, the film's importance,
however, transcends that of box-office success or entertainment value.

Made and released early in the Reagan years, *E.T.* exemplified a
shift in America's cultural values after the 1960s and 1970s, during
which the Vietnam War, the Watergate scandals, and the Iran hostage
crisis had convulsed the nation. The emergence, too, of the new youth
culture that had accompanied these turbulent decades, had manifested
itself in a new cinema that began with *Easy Rider* in 1969. With the
onset of the 1980s, Americans were seeking reconciliation and a
reassertion of family values. The perceived message of the times,
albeit clothed in political conservatism, was one of hope, love, and
nostalgia for a gentler past, which was faithfully reflected in the
majority of Hollywood movies.

Thus it was that Spielberg's film proved timely to its age,
reflecting the spirit and values that were being so eagerly sought by a
troubled nation, and thereby appealing to adults and children alike.
The expertise and imagination with which it was made, however,
gave it lasting properties well beyond the 1980s and has made it a
favorite film of audiences throughout the world. Indeed, it might be
seen as serving the same purpose and exerting the same degree of
magic as the perennially beloved *Wizard of Oz* (1939), although it is a
product of the technological age in both its vision and its realization.

Considered at the time to be Steven Spielberg's masterpiece, and
undoubtedly his most personal film, this story set in middle-class
suburbia grew out of the director's own lonely childhood in Scottsdale,
Arizona, the son of a father who left the family home. He has said, ''I
use my childhood in all my pictures, and all the time. I go back there to
find ideas and stories. My childhood was the most fruitful part of my
entire life. All those horrible, traumatic years I spent as a kid became
what I do for a living today, or what I draw from creatively today.''
E.T. was the culmination of several ideas that had germinated, been
explored, and even filmed, over a number of years. One of Spielberg's
major contributions to late-twentieth-century culture is the concept of
the benign alien. Virtually all previous science fiction films grew out
of fears of invasion, war, and the threat of nuclear annihilation that
loomed large during the Cold War years. It was posited that aliens
with the technology to reach Earth would also have the technology to
unleash incredible destruction; and these fears were reflected in
stories of invasion, aggression, colonization, and extermination. In
Spielberg's mind, however, ''Comics and TV always portrayed aliens
as malevolent [but] I *never* believed that. If they had the technology to
get here, they could only be benign.''

His first creative expression of this concept resulted in one of the
most profoundly searching and brilliantly executed films of the
century, *Close Encounters of the Third Kind* (1977), at the end of

Henry Thomas and E.T. in a scene from the film *E.T. The Extra-Terrestrial*.

which an alien creature steps off the ship—allowing Spielberg the opportunity to create and show an alien, even though the scene lasted only a half minute or so. Then, in 1979, after dreaming up an idea he called "Night Skies," a tale about 11 aliens terrorizing a farm family, he put the project into development at Columbia and turned it over to writer/director John Sayles to flesh out the script. Sayles made a number of changes that included the introduction of a friendly alien who befriends an autistic child, and ended his script with the kindly alien being stranded on Earth. This last scene became the first scene of *E.T.,* though Sayles never pursued screen credit, considering his script "more of a jumping-off point than something that was raided for material."

In 1980, while filming *Raiders of the Lost Ark* on location in Tunisia, Spielberg was turning over the idea of following *Raiders* with a simpler, more personal project. Looking for someone as a sounding board for his idea of an interplanetary love story, he turned to Harrison Ford's girlfriend, screenwriter Melissa Mathison, who had accompanied Ford to Tunisia. Mathison subsequently said the story was already half-created in Spielberg's mind, but she spent weeks pitching ideas back and forth with him for both the story and for the creature's visual image. Among other things, they decided that the creature's neck should elongate like a turtle's, so that the audience would instantly know that they were not watching an actor in costume, while Spielberg knew that he wanted the creature's communication to rest in emotion rather than intellect.

Back in the United States, while Spielberg edited *Raiders,* Mathison began writing the screenplay in earnest. An earlier version depicted E.T. as an interplanetary botanist stranded on Earth, at first more empathetic with plants than animals, and discussing with artichokes and tomatoes whether he should make contact with the humans. He finally does so by rolling an orange toward the boy Elliott's feet. In the hours spent by Spielberg and Mathison discussing changes, the orange became a baseball. Spielberg went to Columbia, which had already spent $1 million in development of "Night Skies" and offered them *E.T.* instead, but the studio, perceiving the idea as a children's picture with only limited commercial potential, said no. Universal was interested, but Columbia, because of their investment in "Night Skies," retained the rights to the property and refused to co-produce with Universal. They finally relinquished the rights in exchange for five percent of the net profits, and earned a fortune. (Spielberg, meanwhile, also convinced MGM to produce "Night Skies" which, after extensive rewrites to distance its subject matter from *E.T.,* became director Tobe Hooper's *Poltergeist,* 1982).

The storyline of *E.T. The Extra-Terrestrial* is simple enough: One night, in the woods behind a hillside development of split-level homes, a spacecraft lands, disgorging a group of strange little creatures who shuffle off into the night until the appearance of humans—menacing from their point of view—forces them to re-enter their craft and take off, with one of their number left behind. The terrified creature hides out in a back yard, and is found by Elliott, the youngest boy of the family and a child at once sensitive, bold, and canny. They form a close friendship, communicating largely through instinctive understanding (*E.T.* has telepathic powers), which ends when Elliott becomes sadly aware that the creature wants to go home. Within this plot, Spielberg unfolds an empathetic tale of love and sympathy, pitted against fear and suspicion. The characterizations, including those of Elliott's mother (Dee Wallace), his siblings (Drew Barrymore, Robert MacNaughton), and an initially menacing authority figure played by Peter Coyote, are richly three-dimensional. But the high ground is shared between Henry Thomas' enchanting,

fatherless Elliott, and the bizarre little alien, an Oscar-winning triumph of imagination, created and made by artist Carlo Rambaldi in accordance with Spielberg's humane vision.

More than one creature was built: there was a mechanically controlled version for scenes requiring large body movements, one with electronic controls for subtler articulation, and another to contain an actor (one of three used for the purpose) for the few scenes where E.T. has to lurch across the floor. Commentators have drawn parallels between E.T. and Christ, pointing to, among other aspects, the creature's arrival, his healing touch, his persecution by civil authorities, and his ascension into the heavens. Spielberg gave E.T. an appearance "only a mother could love," then wisely made him as afraid of Earthlings as they are of him, disarming Americans in particular, conditioned by years of Cold War sci-fi films to fear extraterrestrials. Interestingly, unlike the main character in *Close Encounters,* Elliott does not heed E.T.'s request, "Come," but chooses to stay behind with his family, perhaps reflecting Spielberg's own maturity and sense of responsibility. At the end, to lessen the pain of E.T.'s departure, Coyote's character, Keys, is subtly transformed from the antagonist to a possible new father, linked in two-shots with Elliott's mother as they watch the spaceship fly off.

The logistics, statistics, and tales both apocryphal and accurate surrounding the genesis and the making of *E.T.* have been frequently recounted in books and articles, but its importance lies in the finished product and the response it evoked, and continues to evoke, in all who see it. There is not a dry eye in the house at the film's climax, but the message is one of hope, within which is a serious subtext (shared by *Close Encounters*) that aims to defuse our nameless and parochial fears of "otherness." The film embodies its director's excursion into the wishes, dreams, and fantasies of his own past; but, significantly, that excursion brought audiences a return to innocence, love, and faith within a realistic contemporary social context.

With rare exceptions, the film, originally unveiled at the Cannes Film Festival, collected only superlatives from reviewers, and grossed millions for Spielberg personally, as well as for Universal studios. When the Academy Awards came around, *E.T.* lost out to *Gandhi,* but by the end of the twentieth century had become established as an acknowledged classic of the cinema.

—Bob Sullivan

FURTHER READING:

Baxter, John. *Steven Spielberg.* London, HarperCollins, 1996.

McBride, Joseph. *Steven Spielberg: A Biography.* New York, Simon & Schuster, 1997.

Taylor, Philip M. *Steven Spielberg.* London, Batsford, 1992.

Yule, Andrew. *Steven Spielberg: Father of the Man.* London, Little, Brown, 1996.

Etiquette Columns

Targeted primarily at women, etiquette columns have appeared in American newspapers and magazines since the mid-nineteenth century to guide readers through the tangled thickets of social convention and polite behavior. In part, these columns began as responses to the cultural anxieties of a newly emerging middle class, but they also derived from related American mythologies of moral perfection and self-improvement. And despite contemporary society's avowed indifference to propriety, these concerns clearly persist, as evidenced by the enthusiastic readership of Judith Martin's etiquette column "Miss Manners."

Godey's Lady's Book was among the first periodicals to dispense etiquette advice to American women. In the years before the Civil War, when literacy rates had reached 50 percent, *Godey's* enjoyed a circulation of 150,000. Editor Mrs. Sarah Josepha Hale was determined to avoid subjecting her subscribers to the day's political unpleasantness, so she frequently turned to contributor Mrs. James Parton, known to readers as Fanny Fern, for sharp and amusing columns on "Rules for Ladies."

Following the Civil War, publishers and editors were so concerned about the moral decay presumed to be an inevitable result of bad manners that etiquette columns began to appear further afield. *Appleton's Journal,* the *Atlantic,* the *Galaxy,* and the *Round Table* all tendered advice on appropriate behavior, though social education continued to be the special purview of women's magazines. Readers who had questions on both fine and general points of etiquette began directing their inquiries directly to the magazines. Among the first to address these questions in a regular column was the *Ladies Home Journal,* whose editor Edward Bok created "Side-Talks with Girls," written by "Ruth Ashmore" (actually Isabel A. Mallon), but it was not until 1896 that newspapers began to include subjects of special interest to female readers. That year "Dorothy Dix" (Mrs. Elizabeth M. Gilmer) started her etiquette column in the *New Orleans Picayune* and, soon after, etiquette columns appeared in newspapers throughout the country.

The nineteenth century's true expert on etiquette, however, was undoubtedly Mary Elizabeth Wilson Sherwood. Mrs. Sherwood first offered etiquette advice in a series of features for *Harper's Bazaar,* at the time noted for presenting European fashions to American women. Readers immediately took Mrs. Sherwood's advice as exact and authoritative. She greatly embellished her writing with florid details so that readers could visualize the fork or finger bowl she was describing, but it wasn't only this attention to detail that made her such a popular columnist. Unlike her predecessor Henry Tomes, whose etiquette columns from *Harper's* were eventually collected in an edition called the *Bazaar Book of Decorum,* Sherwood was convinced that American women were not crude by nature. They desperately wanted wise advice on manners and deportment, she argued, but existing articles and books were either inaccessible or wrought with error. Mrs. Sherwood thus set out to do more than codify the rules of good behavior; in *Manners and Social Usages* (1884), she sought to whet the nation's appetite for gracious living.

Although etiquette was to change dramatically in the new century, the first decade of the 1900s was seemingly obsessed with the subject. Over 70 books and at least twice as many magazine articles appeared between 1900 and 1910. Of these books, Marion Harland's *Everyday Etiquette* (1905) had the widest appeal. Miss Harland (the *nom de plume* of Mrs. Albert Payson Terhune, wife of a prominent clergyman) also wrote for many magazines. Another popular etiquette columnist at the time was Gabrielle Rozière, whose articles in the *Delineator* centered on the "E. T. Quette" family. Columns in *Current Literature, Munsey's, The Independent,* and *Century Magazine* all decried the decline of manners, especially the manners of women.

Of the early twentieth-century columnists, the best known were Florence Howe Hall, her sister Maude Howe, and their mother Julia Ward Howe, better remembered for her "Battle Hymn of the Republic." Like their fellow writers, the Howes avoided the term "society," which had, by the turn of the century, become equated with showy extravagance and vulgarity. In a similar fashion, the members of society likewise avoided "etiquette"—reasoning that those who required such advice did not really belong in society. But none of the hundreds of etiquette books and thousands of advice columns had the cultural impact of Emily Post's *Etiquette: The Blue Book of Social Usage* (1922). Almost immediately, Post became synonymous with etiquette. No one, it seemed, was embarrassed to have "Emily Post" on their shelves, and her book went immediately to the top of the nonfiction bestseller list.

As Post saw it, etiquette was nothing less than "the science of living," and her systematic approach to the subject promised firm guidance to everyone afloat in a sea of social uncertainty. Yet perhaps most important was the way Mrs. Post dramatized etiquette. She introduced characters such as the Oldnames, Mr. Richan Vulgar, and Mrs. Cravin Praise to personify elegance, rudeness, or gaucherie so that readers understood these were not abstractions but very real qualities (or shortcomings) embodied in real people. If earlier writers had used this technique, no one had deployed so extensive a cast. Post's *Etiquette* thus enjoyed popularity for two reasons. Certainly it was the manual of taste and decorum, but it also allowed average readers to glimpse through a keyhole into the world of footmen and debutante balls that they were unlikely to experience directly. Post's success might also be traced to the burgeoning advertising industry. Her book was heavily advertised and easily played into an advertising strategy as common then as now: exploiting the insecurities of the socially inexperienced.

Like Mrs. Sherwood before her, Mrs. Post was a socialite, and, until she came to write her own book, she had always considered etiquette advice to be an act of sabotage, an easy way for parvenus and social climbers to worm their way into society. She steadfastly maintained this view until she was approached by the editor of *Vanity Fair,* Frank Crowninshield, and Richard Duffy of Funk and Wagnalls to write an etiquette book. She refused until they sent her a copy of a new etiquette manual to review, which she found condescending and useless. Only then did Mrs. Post agree that a new book was badly needed.

With her impeccable background, Emily Post was an obvious choice for the job. Born in 1872 to a wealthy architect, Brice Price, and his wife, she debuted in 1892 and shortly thereafter married Edwin Post, an affluent financier. The couple eventually divorced amid some indiscretions committed by Post's husband. After her divorce Mrs. Post, who had been drawn to intellectual and artistic pursuits since childhood, turned to writing and enjoyed success as a novelist and feature writer before turning to etiquette. After the enormous popularity of *Etiquette,* she published many revisions of the book and in 1932 began a syndicated etiquette column that eventually appeared in 200 newspapers.

In its first 20 years, *Etiquette* sold 666,000 copies, and after its 50th anniversary "Emily Post" had been through 12 editions, 99 printings, and sold 12 million copies. For a time, it was used as a textbook in poise and good manners for high-school classes throughout the country, and by the late 1990s, Mrs. Post's great-granddaughter-in-law, Peggy Post, was writing the latest editions of the book. "Emily Post," which is now a registered trademark, remains the authoritative voice on all matters of good taste and polite behavior.

—Michele S. Shauf

FURTHER READING:

Aresty, Esther B. *The Best Behavior*. New York, Simon & Schuster, 1970.

Cable, Mary. *American Manners and Morals*. New York, American Heritage Publishing, 1969.

Carson, Gerald. *The Polite Americans*. Westport, Connecticut, Greenwood Press, 1966.

Lynes, Russell. *The Domesticated Americans*. New York, Harper & Row, 1963.

Post, Peggy. *Emily Post's Etiquette*. New York, Harper Collins, 1997.

Schlesinger, Arthur M. *Learning How to Behave*. New York, Macmillan, 1947.

Evangelism

From frontier camp meetings of the early 1800s, to the urban revivals of the late 1800s and early 1900s, to late twentieth century Christian television networks, evangelism has been a prominent feature of American Protestantism. The process of evangelism focuses primarily on encouraging others to accept Christianity, usually through a personal conversion experience; but in the United States, evangelism has also been closely related to revivalism, the process of encouraging existing believers to renew their commitment to particular forms of Christian practice and belief.

Evangelism emerged as an important feature of American religious culture for several reasons. The American policy of religious voluntarism, which rendered religious affiliation a matter of personal choice rather than civic obligation, precluded even large denominations from taking their membership for granted. Evangelical efforts to acquire new members and to retain existing ones became an important church function, particularly within the Protestant churches and among interdenominational movements such as fundamentalism and Pentecostalism. In addition, secular influences have had pronounced affects on American society as it has gone through the processes of modernization and urbanization. The weakening role of religion in many aspects of American life has in turn motivated religious leaders and institutions to increase their involvement in evangelistic endeavors. Finally, the evangelical Protestant denominations, which defined

An evangelist, the Rev. Jerry Falwell.

the nation's religious establishment during most of the nineteenth and early twentieth centuries, placed a strong doctrinal emphasis on evangelism and the conversion experience.

In promoting evangelism, different groups and individuals have developed diverse approaches to spreading their message. The most conspicuous form of evangelism early in the nineteenth century was the camp meeting, where believers would gather for several days of sermons, prayer, and religious testimony. Although the camp meetings were primarily a phenomenon of the frontier, many of their features persisted in the efforts of the itinerant evangelists who staged so-called tent meeting revivals in small towns and rural communities throughout the nineteenth century and well into the twentieth. As the United States became increasingly urbanized during this period, however, so did evangelistic activity; and by the early 1900s the most prominent evangelists worked primarily in urban settings. The urban revivals that they staged retained the focus on charismatic leadership and personal conversion, including the climactic ''altar call'' during which participants declared their faith; but the urban revivals reached audiences numbering in the millions, and produced converts by the thousands. The urban evangelists also incorporated a greater degree of showmanship, perhaps best exemplified by the garrulous, dramatic style of Billy Sunday during the 1910s.

Changing social conditions led to a decline in professional evangelism after World War I, particularly in urban settings. After World War II, however, a new generation of evangelists appeared on the American religious scene. These new crusaders became highly influential during the religious resurgence of the 1950s, although more so within the conservative wing of American Protestantism than among the mainstream churchgoers targeted by earlier revivalists. The leading figure in this new evangelical movement was Billy Graham, a conservative Baptist minister who spread his message through a wide variety of mass media, including radio, television, the cinema, and mass market publications. Graham's early use of television to promote evangelistic activities proved to be particularly important. By the 1970s, television had become a primary medium of mass evangelism in the United States—a position that was strengthened in the following decade as cable television enabled various Christian broadcasting networks to reach audiences dispersed throughout the country. As televangelism expanded, it also became increasingly associated with conservative perspectives in both religion and politics, and it generated considerable controversy during the 1970s and 1980s after a number of its major proponents lent their support to conservative political causes.

The shift in focus of mass evangelism during the twentieth century, from a broad connection to the Protestant mainstream to a narrower association primarily with religious conservatives, has had significant implications for its relationship to American cultural generally. The leading televangelists especially have become less exclusively concerned with the individual conversion experience, and increasingly concerned with general trends within American popular culture. In this sense, evangelism has evolved from a primarily religious phenomenon to one that has had significant impacts on politics and public policy in the United States.

—Roger W. Stump

FURTHER READING:

Ahlstrom, Sidney. *A Religious History of the American People.* New Haven, Yale University Press, 1972.

Bruns, Roger. *Preacher: Billy Sunday and Big-Time American Evangelism.* New York, W. W. Norton, 1992.

Hardman, Keith. *Seasons of Refreshing: Evangelism and Revivals in America.* Grand Rapids, Michigan, Baker Books, 1994.

Evangelists
See Religious Right, The

The Everly Brothers

One of the greatest singing brother duos of all time, the Everly Brothers' close harmonies became one of the most identifiable sounds of the early rock 'n' roll era of the late 1950s and early 1960s. Hits such as ''Bye Bye Love,'' ''Wake Up Little Susie,'' and ''Love Hurts'' are long ingrained in the memories of Americans who grew up listening to the Everly Brothers. While they were heavily influenced by other singing brother duos like the Delmore Brothers and the

The Everly Brothers: Phil (left) and Don

Louvin Brothers, the Everly Brothers went on to influence such groups as the Beatles and Simon & Garfunkel (who covered "Wake Up Little Susie" on their *Bridge Over Troubled Water* album). After their pop stardom declined, they followed the same path as Jerry Lee Lewis and other early rock 'n' rollers, becoming country music artists.

Phil (born January 19, 1939) and Don (born February 1, 1937) were raised in a musical family, singing with their guitarist father Ike and other family members on radio broadcasts in the early 1950s. Raised in Brownie, Kentucky, these brothers were heavily influenced by such country legends as the Louvin Brothers (and the Louvin's inspiration, the Delmore Brothers), as well as a number of other singing brother duo acts. After a very brief and unsuccessful stint at Columbia Records, the two did not hit their commercial stride until they joined Cadence records, which released the number two *Billboard* hit and rock 'n' roll classic, "Bye Bye Love." The two had a number of hits for Cadence including "Wake Up Little Susie," "Bird Dog," "('Til) I Kissed You," "All I Have to Do is Dream," and "When Will I Be Loved."

In 1960, the two joined Warner Brothers Records, hitting their commercial peak with songs such as "Cathy's Clown," helping to establish Warner Brothers as a major player in the music business in the process. In a similar way that their idols, the Louvin Brothers, succumbed to the pressures of success, Don Everly turned to drinking and drugs (in much the same way that Ira Louvin did), nearly dying of an overdose in 1962. Soon after their signing to Warner Brothers, the Everly Brothers hit a number of career setbacks, including the both of them being drafted into the Army and, a career killer for numerous early rock 'n' rollers, the British Invasion led by the Beatles.

After their last Top Ten hit, the aptly titled 1962 song "That's Old Fashioned," the group's career floundered as the two released a series of albums that were nothing less than careless contract fillers. In 1968, the Everly Brothers revived themselves, artistically at least, with *Roots,* a country-rock album that—along with the Byrd's *Sweetheart of the Rodeo*—became a major influence on the country-rock movement that inspired such groups as Poco and the Flying Burrito Brothers, as well as pioneering artists like Gram Parsons. Sibling rivalry and record industry-induced pressure led to the duo's dramatic demise at a 1973 concert in which Phil smashed his guitar and stormed off stage. After a decade of poorly received solo albums, the two resumed singing together in 1983, primarily performing on the oldies circuit.

—Kembrew McLeod

FURTHER READING:

Karpp, Phyllis. *Ike's Boys: The Story of the Everly Brothers.* Ann Arbor, Michigan, Popular Culture, 1988.

Spies, Jerry. *Phil & Don, Home Again.* Shenandoah, World Publishing, 1986.

Everson, Cory (1959—)

Best-known of all the Ms. Olympia winners, bodybuilder Cory Everson grew up in Deerfield, Illinois, where she was an outstanding athlete throughout high school and college. Everson, whose maiden name was Knauer, attended the University of Wisconsin and won the Big Ten Championship in the pentathlon for four consecutive years. While attending the university, Cory met Jeff Everson, a competitive

Cory Everson

weightlifter and bodybuilder who worked there as a strength coach. Following her marriage to Everson and her graduation from college, Cory began to train seriously as a bodybuilder. Blessed with outstanding genetics for bodybuilding, she made rapid progress, especially after she and Jeff moved to Los Angeles. She won the Ms. Olympia competition in 1984, the first time she entered, and won every year until 1989, when she retired. Everson soon became part of the fitness show phenomenon on cable television with her *Bodyshaping* program. She also had roles in such films as *Double Impact* (1991), *Natural Born Killers* (1994), and *Tarzan, the Epic Adventures* (1996). In the late 1990s she authored several fitness and health books, including *Cory Everson's Lifebalance* (1998).

—Jan Todd

Evert, Chris (1954—)

One of the greatest female tennis players of all time, Chris Evert ruled the sport for more than ten years (1974-1985) and established herself as a cultural icon in America and around the world. Born December 21, 1954 in Ft. Lauderdale, Florida, Christine Marie Evert started playing tennis at the ripe age of six. With her father (teaching pro Jimmy Evert) as coach, Evert showed promise early on, rising to number two in the United States in the 12-and-under age group. By the time she was 15, she had established herself as the country's top amateur player by defeating such stars as Billie Jean King, Virginia Wade, and the world's number one player at the time, Margaret Smith Court. At 16, she made it all the way to the semifinals of the U.S. Open. In 1972, Evert was a winner at both the Virginia Slims Championship and the United States Clay-Court Championship. In December of that same year, on her 18th birthday, Chris Evert turned professional.

In 1974, still only 19 years old, Evert won singles titles at Wimbledon, the French Open, and the Italian Open, lost in the finals at the Australian Open, and was a semifinalist at the U.S. Open. Already a popular player, the poise and intense concentration exhibited by Evert that year made her a favorite of sportswriters and spectators alike. Her engagement to budding American tennis hero Jimmy Connors (who was then 21) in late 1973 also contributed to Evert's rising fame. Dubbed the "King and Queen of tennis" by columnists, the couple called off the marriage in 1975. Four years later, Evert wed British Davis Cup player John Lloyd; the union lasted until 1987.

Evert won her first U.S. Open singles title in 1975, defeating Yvonne Goolagong in the finals at Forest Hills. She would keep her crown for the next three years, and finished her career a six-time U.S. Open champion. But her best surface was clay, and the French Open was where she had the most success. Evert made it to the finals at Roland Garros nine times, losing only twice; her seven French Open singles titles remain a record. Evert's career highlights also include

two Australian Open titles (1982 and 1984) and three Wimbledon titles (1974, 1976, and 1981). This last is all the more impressive considering Evert's reluctance to come up to net, a necessity on Wimbledon's grass surface according to conventional wisdom. Nor did her preference for staying at the baseline prevent Evert from winning three Grand Slam doubles titles. All told, Evert won at least one Grand Slam title per year for 13 straight years (1974-86), a statistic that testifies to her legendary consistency.

Evert's combination of charm and intensity helped attract large audiences and significant prize money to women's tennis. Nicknamed "The Ice Maiden" and "The Ball Machine" by her peers, Evert was extremely disciplined and almost never lost her composure on court. In this respect, she stood in stark contrast to other American tennis stars of the time, in particular Connors and John McEnroe. In 1976, Evert became the first female player to reach $5 million in career earnings. At risk of turning fans off by winning almost *too* easily, her rivalry with Martina Navratilova took on increasing importance. After 16 years, and dozens of hard-fought battles, Evert's career record against Navratilova ended at 37 wins and 43 losses. It should be noted, however, that the majority of these matches were not played on clay.

One year after a disappointing early exit in the 1988 Olympics, Evert retired from competitive tennis ranked number four in the world—her lowest ranking since turning pro 17 years earlier. Among Evert's immense list of on-court accomplishments, the following stand out: for 133 consecutive weeks (starting in 1975) she held the number one ranking in singles; she won 125 consecutive matches on clay—no one has won more matches consecutively on *any* surface; she took home a total of 157 singles titles, second only to Navratilova; and her career winning percentage of .900 (1309 victories against a mere 146 losses) ranks first in the history of the game. In 1995, Evert earned a rare unanimous selection to the International Tennis Hall of Fame.

It would be nearly impossible to overestimate Evert's popularity during her playing career. In 1985, the Women's Sports Foundation voted her Greatest Woman Athlete of the Last 25 Years. In November 1989, she became the first female athlete to host television's *Saturday Night Live*. In 1991, a poll conducted by American Sports Data, Inc. found her to be the most widely-known athlete in the nation. What accounted for her high degree of fame? One of the first players to rely on a two-handed backhand, Evert's unprecedented success with this stroke encouraged a generation of novices to copy her. Her grace and professionalism on and off the court led to her unofficial canonization as a role model for young people of both sexes. Her high-profile romances with male sports stars (in 1988 she married ex-Olympic skier Andy Mill, with whom she has three children) kept her in the gossip columns as well as the sports pages. But it was Evert's 17-year-long reign at or near the top of women's tennis that finally ensured her celebrity status. Although not blessed with prodigious athletic ability, Evert's honed-to-perfection strokes, along with a fierce will to win and an uncanny ability to exploit opponents' weaknesses, gave her an air of dominance that eventually became a source of national pride. Since her retirement, Evert has worked as a color commentator for network-television broadcasts of major tennis tournaments. She is also host of the annual Chris Evert Celebrity Tennis Classic in Boca Raton, a charity event that raises money to help drug-exposed, abused, and neglected children.

Chris Evert

—Steven Schneider

FURTHER READING:

Collins, Bud, and Zander Hollander, editors. *Bud Collins' Modern Encyclopedia of Tennis.* Detroit, Gale Research, 1994, 400-402.

Lloyd, Chris Evert. *Lloyd on Lloyd.* New York, Beaufort Books, 1986.

Lloyd, Chris Evert and Neil Amdur. *Chrissie: My Own Story.* New York, Simon and Schuster, 1982.

Existentialism

Existentialism is a term that incorporates both a specific philosophical history and its subsequent literary reception and popular use. Philosophically, "existentialism" loosely describes a reaction against abstract rationalist philosophical thought, and is mainly found in the work of Søren Kierkegaard, Friedrich Nietzsche, Martin Heidegger, Karl Jaspers, Jean-Paul Sartre, and Gabrielle Marcel (who in fact coined the term). Each of these thinkers argued in various ways for the irreducibility of the subjective, personal dimension of human life against the objective or formal considerations of "being" or "existence" found in other philosophical traditions. Existentialism generally holds that "Man" is a conscious subject, rather than a thing to be predicted or manipulated; he exists as a conscious being, and not in accordance with any pre-determined characteristics.

Given this, existentialist thought is largely concerned with the realms of ethics, politics, personal freedom, and will. Always central is the role of the individual in constituting these arenas. Difficulties arise for "existential man" in the clash between the preexisting material or social world and that same individual's will or real ability to constitute meaning or social relations on his or her own terms. One potential outcome of this conflict is pessimism, an attitude common among existential writers. Generally however it produces anxiety, a vague sense of unease regarding the structure of one's life, which in the absence of any external threat is considered to be a manifestation of one's own responsibility for this structure.

This emphasis on the individual and his or her problematic relation to the social whole becomes thematic in the existentialist literature of Albert Camus, Fyodor Dostoevsky, and Franz Kafka, and likewise in the drama of Samuel Beckett, Eugene Ionesco, the early Harold Pinter, and Sartre. Contemporary expressions of existentialism can be found in the novels of Milan Kundera (e.g., *The Unbearable Lightness of Being*), some films by Woody Allen (e.g., *Crimes and Misdemeanors*), and Peter Shaffer's play *Equus*. Although such an expansive list of figures emphasizes the wide influence of existentialism in cultural life, it also reveals its nebulous character. In common parlance, the term existentialism has been overused, becoming a mere catch-all for unconventional thought. The often spoken of "existential dilemmas" of the modern individual extend from the difficulties of adolescence to the mid-life crisis. Latent in these notions are the same concerns regarding freedom and choice that are central to philosophical existentialism. These issues have only become more dramatic in the wake of the post-WWII popularization of existential thought marked by the incorporation of existential tenets into the youth culture of the 1960s. From the "hippie" culture of that period to the Generation X of the 1990s, emphasis has been placed on questioning the predominantly middle-class social paradigm and its role in constituting the lives of an increasingly vocal and "self-actualized" youth. Existentialism can even be found underwriting popular "self-help" books and other works which attempt to give expression to the individual need to organize one's life according to a self-derived logic. In the face of decline of existential philosophy in academic circles, this dissemination into popular culture has assured its wide-ranging significance.

—Vance Bell

FURTHER READING:

Barrett, William. *Irrational Man: A Study in Existential Philosophy.* New York, Anchor Books, 1962.

Gordon, Lewis R., editor. *Existence in Black: An Anthology of Black Existential Philosophy.* London, Routledge, 1996.

Kaufmann, Walter. *Existentialism from Dostoevsky to Sartre.* New York, Meridian Penguin, 1989.

Olson, Robert G. *An Introduction to Existentialism.* New York, Dover Publications, 1962.

Sartre, Jean-Paul, *Essays in Existentialism,* edited by Wade Baskin. Citadel Press, 1993.

The Exorcist

The first major blockbuster in the history of horror cinema, William Friedkin's *The Exorcist* (1973) has exerted a powerful influence on the subsequent development of the genre and on public

Linda Blair (close-up) in the film adaptation of Peter Blatty's *The Exorcist.*

reception of it. Never before had a horror film been the subject of so much prerelease hype, so much gossip about postproduction strife, so much speculation as to why people of all ages would stand in line for hours to watch something reputed to induce fits of vomiting, fainting, even temporary psychosis. The cultural impact of *The Exorcist* can hardly be overestimated: it challenged existing regulations specifying what was acceptable to show on the big screen, stole U.S. newspaper headlines away from the ongoing Watergate scandal (at least for a little while), led to a detectable increase in the number of "real-life" possessions reported, and, in the words of gross-out film expert William Paul, "established disgust as mass entertainment for a large audience."

In 1949, reports came out in the press of a thirteen-year-old Maryland boy whose body was said to have been taken over by demonic forces. After seeing household objects fly around his room, the boy's distraught parents called in a Jesuit priest, who conducted a thirty-five-day-long exorcism with the help of numerous assistants. While the priests recited their holy incantations, the boy spit, cackled, urinated, writhed in his bed, and manifested bloody scratch marks on his body that spelled out words such as "Hell," "Christ," and the far more mysterious "Go to St. Louis." Fortunately for everyone involved, the alleged demon departed shortly after Easter. Novelist William Peter Blatty, inspired by this tale, made the possessee a girl (supposedly to protect the boy's anonymity, though his readiness to disclose information in later media interviews suggests this was unnecessary), sensationalized many of the details, added heavy doses of philosophical-theological speculation on the nature of evil, and came out with *The Exorcist* in 1971. An instant sensation, Blatty's novel would remain on the *Publishers Weekly* bestseller list for almost an entire year.

Even before its publication, Blatty signed a deal with Warner Brothers for the rights to make a film version of the novel. Warner agreed to Blatty's choice of director, William Friedkin, on the strength of his not-yet-released action movie, *The French Connection,* for which he won an Academy Award in 1971. After numerous and painstaking rewrites of the original script, Blatty finally came up with a screenplay of *The Exorcist* that managed to meet Friedkin's exacting demands for more mystery, more drama, and, above all, more direct confrontation between (good) priest and (evil) demon than were in the novel. For his own part—and with Warner's considerable financial backing—Friedkin employed a range of sophisticated cinematic techniques, along with state-of-the-art special-effects technology, to give the film's supernatural occurrences and gory physical details a degree of realism never before achieved.

The plot of *The Exorcist* is deceptively simple and has its roots in storytelling conventions well established in American cinema. After a lengthy prologue that is nearly incomprehensible to anyone who has not read the book, the first half of the film methodically develops the essential character relationships and establishes the crisis situation. Regan MacNeil (Linda Blair) is the adorable, almost-pubescent daughter of divorcee and well-known film star Chris MacNeil (Ellen Burstyn). After Regan prophesies the death of her mother's acquaintance and urinates (standing up, no less) in front of a roomful of shocked dinner guests, Chris starts to wonder what has "gotten into" her daughter. More odd behavior, and a wildly shaking bed, lands Regan in the hospital, where she is subjected to a battery of extremely invasive procedures best described as "medical pornography." A brain lesion is suspected, but the tests turn up nothing. When Regan, supposedly under hypnosis, responds to the smug questions of a hospital psychologist by grabbing his scrotum and rendering him immobile, it is recommended that Chris seek the Church's help. She does, pleading with doubt-ridden Jesuit priest Damien Karras (Jason Miller, Pulitzer Prize-winning playwright of *That Championship Season*) to perform an exorcism. The second half of the film culminates in an intense one-to-one fight to the finish between Karras and Regan's demonic possessor, after the more experienced exorcist on the scene, Father Merrin (Bergmanian actor Max von Sydow) dies in the struggle. Karras finally saves Regan by accepting the demon into his own body, only to throw himself (or at least allow himself to be thrown) out of a window to his death.

Although the Catholic Church originally supported Friedkin's efforts in the hopes that he would present Catholicism in a positive light, they ended up retracting that support after viewing the infamous scene in which Regan-demon violently masturbates with a crucifix in front of her powerless mother. For many audience members, the highly sexualized profanities spewing out of twelve-year-old Regan's mouth (the voice of the demon, Mercedes McCambridge, had to sue for credit) were as offensive as the green bile she vomited on Karras's face. In an era of student protest, experimental drug use, and general questioning of authority, *The Exorcist* allowed viewers to take pleasure in the terrible punishments inflicted on the rebellious ("possessed") Regan. But by making Regan-demon so fascinating to watch, so filled with nasty surprises, *The Exorcist* also allowed viewers to take pleasure in that rebelliousness.

The Exorcist did not merely give rise to a slew of imitations and variants on the possession theme, it made the child with special powers a dominant motif in modern horror cinema. Two mediocre sequels—*The Exorcist II: The Heretic* (1977) and *The Exorcist III* (1990)—followed, the second one written and directed by Blatty; neither involved Friedkin at all. Richard Donner's highly polished *The Omen* (1976) added an apocalyptic edge to the demonic infiltration theme. Linda Blair, who attained cult-figure status with her role as Regan, reprised it in a Leslie Nielsen spoof entitled *Repossessed* (1990).

—Steven Schneider

FURTHER READING:

Blatty, William Peter. *William Peter Blatty on "The Exorcist" from Novel to Film.* New York, Bantam, 1974.

Bowles, Stephen. "*The Exorcist* and *Jaws.*" *Literature/Film Quarterly.* Vol. 4, No. 3, 1976, 196-214.

Kermode, Mark. *The Exorcist.* London, BFI, 1997.

Newman, Howard. *The Exorcist: The Strange Story behind the Film.* New York, Pinnacle, 1974.

Paul, William. "Possession, Regression, Rebellion." In *Laughing, Screaming: Modern Hollywood Horror and Comedy.* New York, Columbia University Press, 1994, 287-318.

Travers, Peter, and Stephanie Reiff. *The Story behind "The Exorcist."* New York, Crown, 1974.

F

Fabares, Shelley (1944—)

In 1958, when Shelley Fabares was cast as Mary Stone in television's *The Donna Reed Show* at the age of 14, she was already an acting veteran. Born in Santa Monica, California, this niece of actress Nanette Fabray had been working in movies and on television since childhood, but it was as Mary Stone that she established her image as the ideal teenager: pretty, perky, smart, and sweet. After four years of the show's five-year run, its producer (and Donna Reed's husband) Tony Owen persuaded Fabares to record "Johnny Angel" and she lip-synched the tune on an episode in January 1962. By March, the single had climbed to number one on Billboard's Hot 100 chart, and eventually sold over three million copies. Shelley Fabares grew up on *The Donna Reed Show* and, as Mary, went away to college. In real life, she moved to the movies, donning a bikini to co-star with Fabian in *Ride the Wild Surf* (1964), and played leading lady to Elvis Presley in *Girl Happy* (1965), *Spinout* (1966), and *Clambake* (1967)—the only actress to do so three times—but her big-screen career never fulfilled the promise of her teenage years. Fabares continued to appear in a number of TV roles through the 1980s and 1990s, most notably as one of the central characters on the popular ABC comedy *Coach*.

—Jennifer Davis McDaid

FURTHER READING:

Bartel, Pauline. *Reel Elvis! The Ultimate Trivia Guide to the King's Movies*. Dallas, Taylor Publishing Company, 1994.

Fultz, Jay. *In Search of Donna Reed*. Iowa City, University of Iowa Press, 1998.

Geri, Brian. Liner notes for *The Best of Shelley Fabares*. Rhino Records R2 71651, 1994.

"Teens are Looking At . . . [Shelley Fabares]," *Seventeen*. November 1962, 52.

Fabian (1943—)

Perhaps the quintessential teen idol of the 1950s, Fabian was only fourteen when he was plucked from obscurity and thrust into the idol-making machinery by Philadelphia record producer-promoter Bob Marcucci. Though he had failed his high school chorus classes, the darkly handsome Fabian Forte hit the national charts with the off-key single, "I'm a Man." The hits "Turn Me Loose" and "Tiger" followed. Critics savaged him; *Time* labeled him a "tuneless tiger." But to teenage girls lamenting Elvis Presley's tenure in the U.S. Army, Fabian filled a void. Aware that he was being marketed like "a thing," Fabian left music in the early 1960s to pursue a Hollywood career. But after proving an affable co-star in popular movies such as *High Time* and *North to Alaska*, his career stalled. His career was

Fabian

revived in the 1980s by "golden oldies" tours, which continued into the 1990s.

—Pat H. Broeske

FURTHER READING:

Farley, Ellen. "The Story of Frank and Fabe and Bob." *Los Angeles Times,* November 23, 1980, 30-31.

Time. "Tuneless Tiger." July 27, 1959, 33.

Fabio (1961—)

The boom in romance novels in the mid-1980s propelled cover model Fabio to the heights of superstardom. With his broad, bare chest and long (dyed) blond hair, Fabio became an international sex symbol. Although his subsequent film and television career was limited to cameos playing himself, in the 1990s he parlayed his fame into a job as a spokesperson for I Can't Believe It's Not Butter and made it onto MTV with a spot in Jill Sobule's music video for "I Kissed a Girl." As his career as a model has faded, Fabio has returned to romance novels, this time as an author.

—Deborah Broderson

FURTHER READING:

Fabio. "The Trouble with American Women." *Penthouse.* September 1994, 128, 130-36.

Paul, Peter. *Fabio.* Livonia, Michigan, Stabur Corp., 1993.

Romantic Conventions. Bowling Green, Ohio, Bowling Green State University Popular Press, 1999.

Facelifts

"Facelift" is a term that encompasses a variety of surgical procedures intended to restore sagging facial skin to youthful smoothness. Conventionally, incisions are made around the frontal hairline and ears allowing the facial skin to be detached by inches and "buffed" underneath, then "lifted" in an upward pull, trimmed, and sutured. The aftermath includes bleeding, swelling, bruising, and sometimes regret and depression at electing to undergo this surgery. The facelift represents the consumer potential of post-World War II society to purchase beauty and success in addition to material goods. The decades since the 1950s have seen the term facelift generalized to include specific surgical facial enhancements, from eye-lid and jaw-line lifts, to nose reshapings and lip implants. Hi-tech tools of the 1980s and 1990s have produced specialty procedures, including laser hair removal and collagen and body-fat injections.

By the 1990s, the facelift was but a core element within a North American growth industry of medical procedures, out-patient clinics, and cosmetic products, all of which can be subsumed under the wider term "beauty culture." Beauty culture is nurtured by the print media, particularly glamour and lifestyle magazine genres (for example, *Vogue* and *Cosmopolitan),* sold in drugstores and convenience stores across the continent. Such mass-marketed magazines create and promote the illusionist images and ideology of beauty culture, often using teen models in advertisements and fashion spreads to emulate the sleek look of worldly women. Commonly, these magazines also feature culturally correct articles on the pros and cons of cosmetic surgery and related procedures. Drug and department stores, as well as specialty "anti-aging" shops, carry out the magazines' pervasive double-coded system of "dos" and "don'ts," selling treatment products, creams, and lotions whose packaging adopts the familiar language ("lift," "firming") of the surgical facelift and of advertising rhetoric.

Beauty culture underlies the American entertainment industry, with pop stars such as Michael Jackson and Cher reinventing themselves as plastic icons, as if they were born into their altered bodies. Over the course of their numerous surgeries, Jackson and Cher have become self-parodies; respectively, specimens of racial bleaching and frozen glamour. Cher was the central player in a television infomercial endorsing so-called revolutionary face-care products, the hypocrisy being that Cher's appearance is not the result of these potions.

The surgical lifts, implants, and failed body alterations of popular culture figures have been fodder for tabloid television and

newspapers, circulating a mixed message of celebrity surveillance and social warning. They reveal both the lure and baggage of the American star system in movies, pop music, and television. Pamela Anderson's Barbi-doll iconography has only shifted laterally between beach babe *(Baywatch),* centerfold *(Playboy),* movie vixen *(Barb Wire),* and sex object (x-rated "honeymoon" video with Tommy Lee). The processes of retaining a seemingly ageless public face have been taken up by figures in American political culture as well as by middle-class women, men, and even teens who can afford the procedures. When she was the First Lady of the United States, Nancy Reagan's perpetual startled expression in media images gave the impression of either too many facelifts or overdetermined surgery. The presumed power of looking white and Western is being adopted by women of China who, despite poor wages, pursue for themselves and their daughters the eyelid surgery that gives them the "fold" that Asiatics genetically lack. Skin bleaching among Chinese women is another signal that the West, especially American popular culture, sets global standards of beauty and achievement.

In 1982, filmmaker Michael Rubbo's documentary, *Daisy: The Story of a Facelift* addressed the processes and implications of the facelift in twentieth century culture. What he finds in his middle-aged title subject, Daisy, is a nostalgic desire to redress personal and emotional insecurity by making herself romantically fit, through a facelift, for a phantom suitor. The facelift scene in Rubbo's documentary is performed on a man who, like Daisy, also seeks an improved image for his personal security. Both Daisy and this man adopt the same path, cracking the gender assumption that only women are the subjects and consumers of the facelift. What we as privileged viewers observe through Rubbo's camera in the surgical theatre is a drama that resembles the gruesome imagery associated with the horror film. Rubbo's research prompted him to conclude that in North American the face is our most "mobile body part" ... "a moving image" in the desire for uniform, look-alike faces rather than unique physical character.

At the end of the twentieth century, when both visible and hidden piercings and tattoos are commonplace, it should not be surprising that even female genitalia must pass the test of the voyeur's gaze, as North American middle-class and "trophy" women apparently are flocking to cosmetic surgical clinics to undergo the labial "trim." This replication of the high production photographic look established by *Playboy* in the 1960s implies that the public and private body in contemporary culture is a series of discrete components that can be standardized in the industrial manner of auto-parts manufacturing.

—Joan Nicks

FURTHER READING:

Wolf, Naomi. *The Beauty Myth: How Images of Beauty Are Used against Women.* New York, William Morrow, 1991.

Factor, Max (1872-1938)

Best known for the cosmetic line that bears his name, Max Factor also pioneered screen makeup for motion pictures. When films were in their infancy, stage makeup was generally used on the actors but it did not photograph well. Factor created a makeup more suitable to film lighting. He also popularized the use of human hair in wigs. He later won a special Oscar in 1928 for his panchromatic makeup. He made what would become his most famous product, Pancake Make-up, when the advent of Technicolor film required a another new type of makeup. His line of skin-toned foundations disguised facial imperfections and was soon marketed for home use to mainstream America. Max Factor cosmetics remained one of the most popular brands of stage and street makeup into the 1990s.

—Jill A. Gregg

FURTHER READING:

Basten, Fred E. *Max Factor's Hollywood: Glamour, Movies, Make-up*. California, General Publishing Group, 1995.

Fadiman, Clifton (1904-1999)

Clifton Fadiman is a man of letters whose effectiveness as a broadcast personality helped him spread the gospel of the rewards of book reading to a wide public. A book reviewer for *The New Yorker* and other distinguished periodicals, Fadiman found fame in the late 1930s and most of the 1940s as the host of the radio quiz program, *Information, Please!* Taking advantage of his radio popularity, Fadiman appeared in magazines as an essayist and critic, and between hard covers as an anthology editor and introduction writer. Through his introductions and prefaces to the world's great books, he became one of the first and most distinguished of that unique breed of twentieth-century scribes: the "popularizer." The advent of television kept Fadiman in the public eye, and he continued to be an unpretentious but fervent advocate for the joys of reading and the pleasures of the civilized life.

Clifton (Paul) Fadiman ("Kip" to his friends) was born May 15, 1904 in Brooklyn, New York. Before he had graduated Phi Beta Kappa from Columbia University in 1925, he had already managed a bookstore, devised the standard translation of Nietzsche's *Ecce Homo*, and begun selling articles to national periodicals, including book reviews for the *Nation*. In 1927, Fadiman began a fruitful association with Simon and Schuster when he was hired as a reader and assistant editor. Within two years, he had been promoted to general editor, a position he held until the mid-1930s. While still with Simon and Schuster, Fadiman wrote book reviews for *Harper's Bazaar* and *Stage*; in 1933, he began a ten-year stint as the *New Yorker*'s book editor. Urbane yet unpretentious, Fadiman claimed that, "I look for clarity above all in what I read." These qualities—plus his penchant for the "atrocious" pun—made him the perfect person to peddle erudition to the masses when, in 1938, he was hired to moderate a distinguished but good-humored panel—Franklin P. Adams, John Kieran, and Oscar Levant—on the NBC radio program, *Information, Please!* Aided considerably by Levant's iconoclastic wit, the show, in which listeners competed for sets of the Encyclopedia Britannica by submitting questions with which they hoped to "stump the experts," became both a critical and popular success, running for the next ten years.

During this period, Fadiman expanded his activities to include writing introductions for such classics as *War and Peace* and *Moby Dick*. He left the *New Yorker* to join the editorial board of the Book-of-the-Month Club, but he continued to promote the classics through the writing and editing of various introductions and anthologies, and the creation of a *Lifetime Reading Plan. Information, Please!* faded in

the late 1940s, and the 1950s found Fadiman writing a series of essays in *Holiday* magazine under the title, "Party of One." He also had no trouble making the transition from radio to television, where he contributed his witty presence to such quiz shows as *What's in a Word?* and *The Name's the Same*, although probably closer to his heart was the radio show he co-hosted concurrently on NBC with Columbia Professor Jacques Barzun, *Conversation*.

In his writings, Fadiman came across as learned but genial, and far from snobbish (although he was not above quoting a remark of Dvorak without translating it into English). His inclusion of science fiction stories in his anthologies, *Fantastia Mathematica* and *Mathematical Magpie*, probably helped create the atmosphere in which that once-despised genre began acquiring literary respectability. To the general public, Fadiman so personified the world of great books that when one man was asked to name his favorite work of literature, he responded: "Clifton Fadiman's introduction to *War and Peace*."

—Preston Neal Jones

FURTHER READING:

Fadiman, Clifton. *Enter, Conversing*. Cleveland, World Publishing Co., 1962.

———. *Party of One: The Selected Writings of Clifton Fadiman*. Cleveland, World Publishing Co., 1955.

———. *Reading I've Liked*. New York, Simon and Schuster, 1941.

Fadiman, Clifton and John S. Major. *The New Lifetime Reading Plan*. New York, Harper Collins, 1997.

Fail-Safe

Released in 1964, Director Sidney Lumet's taut nuclear thriller is based on the 1962 Eugene Burdick and John Wheeler novel of the same title. Examining the changing face of war in the nuclear age, *Fail-Safe* depicts the possible consequences of the military's ever increasing reliance on computers. This is where *Fail-Safe* differs from its famous cousin of the genre, *Dr. Strangelove*, where a lone military madman plots an atomic attack upon the Soviet Union. In *Fail-Safe* nuclear apocalypse is at hand as an electronic error directs a squadron of U.S. long-range bombers to drop their nuclear payloads on Moscow. Through the exchange of sharp dialogue, the concepts of limited war in the nuclear age, the decreased time of humans to analyze potential nuclear strikes, and the survival of a nation's culture after the bomb are effectively challenged.

—Dr. Lori C. Walters

FURTHER READING:

Burdick, Eugene, and John Harvey Wheeler. *Fail-Safe*. New York, McGraw-Hill, 1962.

Fairbanks, Douglas, Jr. (1909—)

Although his famous father did not want him in the business, the son of swashbuckling actor Douglas Fairbanks, Sr. started acting at an

Douglas Fairbanks, Jr. (far left), in a scene from the film *Gunga Din*.

early age and eventually went on to become the first second-generation movie star. When he was barely a teenager, the studios sought to trade in on the Fairbanks name by casting Douglas Jr. in swashbuckling films, but ultimately he managed to carve his own niche as a debonair actor in supporting and leading roles. Although often overshadowed by other actors of the same type, he was always enjoyable to watch. When his career began to fade, Douglas Fairbanks, Jr. gracefully turned to producing and writing, although he occasionally returned to acting.

Born to one of the world's first movie stars, Douglas Fairbanks, Sr., and his first wife, Beth, initially the younger Fairbanks was not really interested in a career in acting. He eventually became drawn to it as a way, he hoped, of becoming closer to his distant father. Jesse Lasky of Paramount Pictures, eager to attract the loyal Fairbanks fans, cast Douglas Jr. in *Stephen Steps Out* (1923), when he was only thirteen. The film was a failure, but Fairbanks continued to try to make a name for himself. He was able to get a contract with Paramount, although his career did not go anywhere.

At seventeen, he co-starred in the silent version of *Stella Dallas* (1926), receiving critical acclaim but no notable follow-up work. Fairbanks continued to be cast in small parts, but was forced into work

as a title writer to make ends meet. Although he also did some stagework in Los Angeles, his career remained stagnant until he met and married a young starlet, Joan Crawford. The couple became the darlings of the Hollywood gossip columns and fan magazines.

The positive press he received because of his marriage led to some good parts, usually as villains. Metro-Goldwyn-Mayer (MGM) cashed in on fan interest in the couple by co-starring Fairbanks and Crawford in the motion picture, *Our Modern Maidens* (1929). However, it wasn't until Fairbanks appeared in two strong supporting roles in *Dawn Patrol* (1930) and the hit gangster film, *Little Caesar* (1931) starring Edward G. Robinson, that his talent was finally noticed. By this time his marriage was ending, but his career was progressing.

Warner Brothers Studios gave Fairbanks a contract which allowed the actor more control over his career; most of the roles that followed, however, were forgettable. He appeared with Katharine Hepburn in *Morning Glory* (1933), a film for which she won an Academy Award, but which did little for Fairbanks' career. In 1937 Fairbanks played the memorable villain in *The Prisoner of Zenda*. He then appeared in what is arguably his most famous role in the 1939 hit, *Gunga Din*, co-starring Cary Grant. In that same year he married his second wife, Mary Hartford. However, World War II was looming on the horizon and Fairbanks willingly put his career on hold to join the U.S. Navy. He became a Lt. Commander and was among the most decorated of all the Hollywood stars who served in the armed forces.

After the war, Fairbanks was knighted by the British Empire. Unfortunately, by the late 1940s, his career as an actor was in sharp decline. Although he appeared in the successful *Sinbad the Sailor* (1949), he had fallen out of the public eye during the time spent in the service, and his career had suffered. After appearing in *Mr. Drake's Duck* in 1951, he virtually retired from the screen, not appearing in another feature film for twenty years.

Fairbanks then began producing films, mostly for television. Occasionally, he also appeared in stage productions, including *The Pleasure of His Company* (1973) in London. The seventy-year-old actor had somewhat of a career resurgence when he appeared in the supernatural film, *Ghost Story* (1981) co-starring Fred Astaire. He also appeared with some regularity on popular television programs of the 1970s and early 1980s. Interest in his life and career was similarly revived by two very well received autobiographies, which appeared in 1988 and 1993. Mary died in 1988, and in 1991 he married Vera Shelton.

Although Douglas Fairbanks, Jr. may still be best remembered as the son of his famous father, he nonetheless managed to prove himself a worthy successor to the Fairbanks name. As a charming and debonair actor who created his own legacy as an actor, producer and writer, Fairbanks epitomized the elegance and manners of a bygone era of motion picture history.

—Jill A. Gregg

FURTHER READING:

Connell, Brian. *Knight Errant: A Biography of Douglas Fairbanks, Jr.* New York, Doubleday, 1955.

Fairbanks, Douglas. *A Hell of a War.* New York, St. Martin's, 1993.

———. *The Salad Days.* New York, Doubleday, 1988.

Fairbanks, Douglas, Sr. (1883-1939)

The silent-screen star who would become famous for his tireless energy and all-American attitude was born Douglas Ulman in Denver, Colorado, in 1883. Commentator Vachel Lindsay described Douglas Fairbanks, Sr.'s on-screen persona in terms of two key concepts: architecture-in-motion and sculpture-in-motion. In the 1910s and 1920s, the star's acrobatic stealth and extroverted performance style appeared to mirror the flickering electricity and seemingly endless possibilities of the newly emerging form of moving pictures. Always known for his insistence on maintaining a good deal of control over his films, Fairbanks was one of the founders of United Artists with Mary Pickford, Charlie Chaplin, and D. W. Griffith.

After leaving his mother and stepfather behind in Colorado when he was a teenager and surviving a brief stay at Harvard, Fairbanks tried his hand on the New York stage and soon made it to Broadway. In 1907, he married Anna Beth Sully and attempted to transform himself into her father's protege, first working as an executive in the family's soap company and then as a broker on Wall Street. The couple had a son, actor Douglas Fairbanks, Jr., in 1909. After a handful of years trying to conform to his wife's wishes for

Brandon Hurst (left) turned to Douglas Fairbanks, Sr., in a scene from the film *The Thief of Bagdad.*

him, Fairbanks returned to Broadway, achieving a successful comeback in *He Comes up Smiling* (1913).

Informed by his prejudice against the nascent industry of films, the star begrudgingly signed a contract with Triangle-Fine Arts in 1915 and made his debut in *The Lamb,* playing a wealthy, idle, relatively effeminate fellow who is disenchanted with life on Wall Street but decides to build himself up for the woman he loves. Fairbanks would develop this theme throughout his films of the teens, both with director Allan Dwan in films such as *The Half Breed* (1916) and *Manhattan Madness* (1916), and with director John Emerson and screenwriter Anita Loos in *His Picture in the Papers* (1916) and *The Americano* (1916).

His screen stories reinforced the philosophies he espoused in fan magazines and advice manuals (such as *Laugh and Live* in 1917 and *Making Life Worthwhile* in 1918), which followed Theodore Roosevelt's emphasis on clean living and hardy individualism. Fairbanks became a role model for young boys everywhere, evangelically touting, ''To be successful you must be happy . . . to be happy you must be enthusiastic; to be enthusiastic you must keep mind and body active.'' His intense love of activity was probably easier to read about in articles or watch on screen than to confront personally. Foreign dignitaries and royal guests were obligated to accompany the star to his private gymnasium on the studio lot and endure a "basic training" which left many of them crawling to the steam room.

In 1917, Fairbanks signed on as his own producer with Artcraft films, a subsidiary of Famous Players-Lasky. There, he continued his tradition of gymnastic stunts and masculine transformation in films such as *Wild and Woolly* (1917), *Reaching for the Moon* (1917), and *A Modern Musketeer* (1918). He then made a move which gave him full reign over his films when he cofounded United Artists in 1919. He starred in *The Mollycoddle* (1920) and *The Nut* (1921), among others, while beginning to make the transition to the swashbuckler, a genre for which he became famous. These costume dramas, such as *The Mark of Zorro* (1920), *The Three Musketeers* (1921), and *The Thief of Bagdad* (1924), offered him a formula by which he could continue his traditions of physically demanding stunts and chases but tailor them for his maturing persona.

Fairbanks has been congratulated for being a star auteur, one of Hollywood's first actors to exercise control over the development and production of his films. He participated in the scripting of many of his early films under the pseudonym Elton Thomas. By the middle 1920s, he demonstrated a keen understanding of the importance of publicity, going so far as to finance a New York City screening of *The Thief of Bagdad* in which he reportedly had the female ushers dress in harem costumes, serve Arabian coffee in the lobby, and waft perfumes from inside the auditorium.

Fairbanks married "America's Sweetheart" Mary Pickford in 1920, and, together, they reigned over Hollywood in their palatial Pickfair estate for more than a decade. His interest in overseas travel and international celebrity associations meant that the couple made a number of renowned world tours throughout the 1920s. Later, Pickford preferred to remain settled in California, and her husband would embark on these trips with comrades and often stay in Europe for months or years at a time.

Fairbanks was relatively successful in talkies (making his sound debut with Pickford in *The Taming of the Shrew* in 1929), and he was named the president of the Academy of Motion Pictures, Arts, and Sciences in 1927. But, because of his international interests, he came to be viewed as something of an expatriate by 1930. The star lost public favor to an even greater extent when he was named corespondent with British noblewoman Lady Sylvia Ashley in a divorce suit filed by Lord Ashley in 1933. An ex-chorus girl, Lady Ashley had been married three times by the time she was romantically linked with Fairbanks. The crumbling marriage of two of Hollywood's most famous stars played out turbulently in America's national press, with tabloid newspapers intercepting their private telegrams and publishing them as headlines. Pickford and Fairbanks divorced in 1936, after which he quickly married Lady Ashley and relocated to his house in Santa Monica, California. Though many of his friends said Fairbanks was content in his third marriage, it also was reported that the star spent many an afternoon sitting by the pool at Pickfair repeatedly mumbling his apologies to Pickford.

Once middle age required him to curtail his acrobatic characters, Fairbanks starred in a couple of travelogue-inspired films, *Around the World in 80 Minutes* (1931) and *Mr. Robinson Crusoe* (1932). His final film, *The Private Life of Don Juan* (1934), was directed by Alexander Korda and parodied the romantic image of hero Don Juan as he came to terms with his age and receding popularity, a commentary on the fleeting nature of fame notably coinciding with its star's own downward spiral.

Fairbanks died of a heart attack at the age of fifty-six. The prevailing consensus at the time was that Fairbanks had pushed his body so hard for so many years that his muscles literally turned in on him and caused his organs to degenerate.

—Christina Lane

FURTHER READING:

Carey, Gary. *Doug and Mary: A Biography of Douglas Fairbanks and Mary Pickford.* New York, E.P. Dutton, 1977.

Cooke, Alistair. *Douglas Fairbanks: The Making of a Screen Character.* New York, Museum of Modern Art, 1940.

Fairbanks, Jr., Douglas. *The Salad Days.* New York, Doubleday, 1988.

Hancock, Ralph, and Letitia Fairbanks. *Douglas Fairbanks: The Fourth Musketeer.* London, Peter Davies, 1953.

Herndon, Booten. *Mary Pickford and Douglas Fairbanks: The Most Popular Couple the World Has Ever Known.* New York, W.W. Norton & Company, 1977.

Lindsay, Vachel. "The Great Douglas Fairbanks." *Ladies Home Journal.* August 1926, 12, 114.

Schickel, Richard. *His Picture in the Papers: A Speculation on Celebrity in America Based on the Life of Douglas Fairbanks, Sr.* New York, Charterhouse, 1974.

Tibbets, John C., and James M. Welsh. *His Majesty the American: The Cinema of Douglas Fairbanks, Sr.* New York, A.S. Barnes and Company, 1977.

Fallout Shelters

Part of American culture since 1949, fallout shelters were inspired by fear of nuclear attack; and their subsequent waxing and waning popularity has been directly related to U.S.-Soviet relations. A fallout shelter, sometimes known as a bomb shelter, is a structure designed to allow those inside it to survive a nuclear blast and its likely aftermath of fire, radiation, and societal disruption. Although some large shelters were built by the U.S. government during the Cold War, most were smaller, designed to protect the family whose backyard they occupied. A prototypical fallout shelter was made of concrete and steel, and sunk in the earth for added protection, although those who could not afford such a construction project sometimes set aside a corner of their basement or dug a makeshift shelter under the crawlspace of a house. A shelter would usually be stocked with canned food, bottled water, medical supplies, a radio, a Geiger counter, and a chemical toilet, among other necessities.

The initial interest in fallout shelters within the United States can be traced to 1949, the year that President Harry Truman informed the nation that the Soviets had exploded an atomic bomb. This ended the American monopoly on nuclear weapons and introduced the world to the possibility of nuclear war between the two superpowers. Aside from the attack on Pearl Harbor, the United States had never, in all its wars, suffered such an attack from the air; but the nuclear age, with its long-range bombers and intercontinental ballistic missiles, made that threat very real.

Truman responded to the heightened public anxiety by creating the Federal Civil Defense Administration in 1951. Although scientists disagreed as to the effectiveness of shelters in the event of a nuclear war, Truman and his advisors knew that public belief that shelters worked would be a boon to morale in an otherwise nervous age. In fact, Truman was walking a tightrope in dealing with American public opinion about the Soviet menace. On the one hand, he was convinced that massive defense spending was essential if the United States were to stop Communist expansion throughout Europe. But postwar America was tired of high taxes and huge military budgets, and would only support these if the danger to the nation's security was both obvious and grave. On the other hand, Truman did not want fear of nuclear war to lead the public to outbreaks of panic, pacifism, or "Better red than dead" fatalism. Thus, fallout shelters were portrayed as realistic protection if worst should come to worst.

After President Truman left office in 1952, Americans' interest in shelters blew hot or cold in keeping with the temperature changes of the Cold War. There was relatively little interest in shelters during much of the Eisenhower administration until 1957—the year that saw both the launch of the first orbiting satellite (the Soviet *Sputnik*) and the release of the Gaither Report in the United States. The latter was the work of a blue-ribbon panel selected by Eisenhower to assess the relative nuclear capability and civil defense preparedness of the United States and the Soviet Union. The report concluded that the Soviets would soon surpass America in all categories of nuclear weaponry and that civil defense preparations in the USSR were already far ahead of American efforts. The supposedly secret document, which leaked to the press a week after being presented to President Eisenhower, led to an upsurge in public concern about fallout shelters, even though Eisenhower himself believed that true national security lay in U.S. superiority in offensive nuclear weapons.

The heyday of the fallout shelter occurred during the administration of John F. Kennedy, which saw both a rise in international tensions and Kennedy's advocacy of shelters as part of the American response. During the Berlin Crisis of 1961, precipitated by Soviet Premier Nikita Khrushchev's aggressive moves toward West Berlin, Kennedy gave a nationally televised speech explaining the gravity of the situation. He also endorsed the construction of fallout shelters, saying, "In the event of an attack, the lives of those families which are not hit in a nuclear blast and fire can still be saved if they can be warned to take shelter and if that shelter is available." If further inducement for building shelters was needed, it was provided fifteen months later by the Cuban Missile Crisis, in which the world came closer to nuclear war than it ever had before.

The popular culture of the late 1950s and early 1960s also contributed to public concern about nuclear war and hence increased interest in fallout shelters. The best-selling novel *Fail-Safe* (also made into a popular film) features a technical glitch that results in the nuclear destruction of both Moscow and New York. Other novels portrayed the aftermath of a nuclear exchange. Some, like Pat Frank's *Alas, Babylon,* were guardedly optimistic. Others, such as Nevil Shute's *On the Beach* and Walter Miller's *A Canticle for Liebowitz,* presented bleak and pessimistic visions.

Civil defense programs, sponsored by both federal and state governments, were designed to increase both Americans' optimism and their chances for survival in the event of nuclear attack. In addition to encouraging the building of shelters, the Federal Office of Civil and Defense Mobilization advised communities to conduct air-raid drills. The importance of such drills was emphasized by government-produced instructional films that were shown on television, as "short subjects" in movie theatres, and in schools. Some of these films manifest a degree of naive optimism about nuclear war that today seems absurd, such as a short animated film in which a

character named "Bert the Turtle" (a talking amphibian in a civil defense helmet) tells children that a nuclear blast can be survived by those who learn to "Duck and Cover" (crouch down and cover one's face and head).

Although concern about "The Bomb" was gradually replaced in American consciousness by the Vietnam War, interest in fallout shelters was revived in the 1980s. Consistent with its vigorously anti-Communist foreign policy, the Reagan administration devoted considerable rhetoric and resources to civil defense. This effort included the development of evacuation plans for people living near probable nuclear targets as well as a new shelter program designed to protect the rest of the population. However, the program languished during Reagan's second term as U.S. relations with the Soviet Union dramatically improved.

In the 1990s and beyond, the limited interest in fallout shelters (as evidenced by the dozen or so World Wide Web sites devoted to them) was apparently restricted to hard-core "survivalists," who wished to be prepared for anything, even the end of the world.

—Justin Gustainis

FURTHER READING:

Scheer, Robert. *With Enough Shovels: Reagan, Bush and Nuclear War.* New York, Random House, 1982.

Weart, Spencer R. *Nuclear Fear: A History of Images.* Cambridge, Harvard University Press, 1988.

Winkler, Alan M. *Life under a Cloud: American Anxiety about the Atom.* New York and Oxford, Oxford University Press, 1993.

Fame

See Celebrity

Family Circle

One of the most widely circulated magazines in the United States, *Family Circle,* like its sister magazines—*Ladies Home Journal, McCall's, Good Housekeeping, Better Homes and Garden,* and *Woman's Day*—, has not only disseminated and popularized expert knowledge about children, but has also been a major contributor to the nation's parent-education curriculum, a vehicle for the transfer of culture, and an exporter of American culture. It has been a medium through which information and ideas about children, adolescents, parenting, and the family have been transmitted to parents, especially, but not exclusively, to mothers, for over half a century. It has served, especially during the post-World War II era, as a guide and manual for families trying to make a comfortable home for themselves and their children with the limited resources at their disposal. Its readers were early proven to be good users of price-off coupons. Through most of its history it has been distributed in a way that has made it accessible to a very wide segment of the population, perhaps to a population that did not have easy access to other such media. When it first appeared, it was not available by subscription and was confined to chain grocery stores—whoever bought groceries in a supermarket all but inevitably saw it at the checkout counter.

In large measure *Family Circle,* like *Woman's Day,* has been overlooked by scholars and not received the attention they deserve, perhaps because they were started and continued for many years as magazines found only in grocery stores. Yet, their circulation has been greater than virtually all other similar magazines. While each has been described as belonging to the seven sisters—*Ladies Home Journal, McCall's, Good Housekeeping, Better Homes and Garden* (at times not included in this grouping), and *Cosmopolitan*—it may be more appropriate to view them as stepsisters. *Family Circle,* like *Woman's Day,* may justly be described as a store-distributed magazine, but neither is insignificant. There is no doubt that distributing magazines at the supermarket checkout stand was successful. In the 1930s and 1940s that spot was the exclusive domain of *Family Circle* and *Woman's Day.* They were joined there by *TV Guide* and *Reader's Digest* in the 1950s. By the early 1950s, according to *Business Week,* they were ''hard on the heels of the big women's service magazines.'' Subsequently, others wanted their place there too.

Family Circle began to assume its present form when the United States was in the midst of its new consumer culture, rearing the children who would express themselves as young adults in the late 1960s and early 1970s, and when the American household was, as historian William E. Leuchtenburg observed in *A Troubled Feast: American Society Since 1945,* adopting ''a style of consumption that was more sophisticated, more worldly [and] more diversified'' than ever before. As Landon Y. Jones recorded in *Great Expectations: America and the Baby Boom Generation,* it was the era during which the United States became a ''vast maternity ward.'' By the end of the 1950s, 40 million new babies had arrived, and the number of children between ages five and 13 was increasing by a million a year. *Family Circle* provided the parents of those new babies with information on how to feed, bathe, educate, entertain, and how not to spoil them. Indeed, from its very beginning, *Family Circle* offered parents advice about children's development and behavior. Its first issue (September 1932) included both Dr. Julius D. Smith's ''Judging the Health of Your Baby,'' information about baby's health, and what Dr. Arnold Gesell said they could expect from a child at six months.

The ways in which Americans lived changed significantly between the end of World War II and the beginning of the 1960s. The places and the social-economic context in which American children were reared were radically transformed. Those who gave birth to the baby boom were mostly born in the 1920s and experienced the Great Depression and World War II. Those to whom they gave birth had no such experiences, and many were brought up in what some believed would be an increasingly affluent society presided over by the organization man. A new culture was being made. Parents who were reared in either an urban neighborhood or a small town now lived and reared their children in a new kind of living place and dwelling, the developer's house in the suburb. *Family Circle* served as an inexpensive and handy directory and manual for families who were adjusting to and embracing the new way of life the affluent society seemed to be promising. According to *Business Week,* magazines such as *Family Circle* told ''the housewife how to cook economically, how to bring up her children, how to clothe them and herself, and how to take care of her house. To the budget-minded, this makes good sense.'' It was a ''good formula for many new and young housewives who want[ed] help at their new job.''

Family Circle's appearance in September 1932 was, as Roland E. Wolseley reported in *The Changing Magazine,* the beginning of ''the big boom in store-distributed magazines.'' Of the many store-distributed magazines founded since the 1930s—perhaps as many as a hundred—*Family Circle,* like *Woman's Day,* is one of the two that have survived and prospered. In *Magazines in the Twentieth Century,*

Theodore Peterson reported that ''when the old *Life* was undergoing one of its periodic readjustments, its managing editor, Harry Evans, joined with Charles E. Merrill, a financier with an interest in grocery chains, to start a magazine that would be distributed free but that would carry advertising.'' At the time, Merrill was a member of Merrill, Lynch, Pierce, Fenner, & Smith which controlled Safeway Stores. Evans reasoned that since radio programs were broadcast to listeners without charge, it should be possible to secure advertisers for a magazine for which the reader did not pay. His hope that *Family Circle* would reach a circulation of 3 million (almost ten times greater than the initial circulation) was soon realized. By the end of 1933, its circulation was nearly a million (964,690); it was slightly over a million (1,068,106) a few weeks later (February 9, 1934).

Family Circle's initial circulation of 350,000 was distributed through Piggly Wiggly, Sanitary, and Reeves grocery stores in Richmond, Baltimore, and Manhattan. The first issue of the 24 page gravure-printed tabloid weekly contained recipes and items on beauty, fashions, food, humor, movies, and radio, and was mostly written by Evans. It survived the years of the Great Depression, and was clearly prospering in the 1940s. It lost its giveaway status on September 3, 1946, became a monthly, and sold for five cents. It then assumed its present format and began its use of color. In the post-war era, it grew with the baby boom. In 1949, when the Kroger stores joined the other chains in selling it, its distribution was national. By 1952 it was available in 8,500 grocery stores and was able to guarantee its advertisers a circulation of 3.5 million. In 1958 when it took over *Everywoman's,* it announced a 5 million circulation rate base and was then able to claim that *Everywoman's Family Circle* would be available in nearly 12,000 chain stores (nearly all of which were self-service stores) in over 1,800 counties where 93 percent of all retail sales in the United States occurred. By the end of the 1950s, its circulation was 5.1 million. By the end of the 1970s, its circulation was over 8 million. At the end of the 1980s, its audience was over 21 million. It then claimed it was the ''World's largest women's magazine,'' a claim made on the Australian as well as the American edition.

Family Circle used celebrities as either authors or on its covers to increase its appeal and to satisfy the interests of readers. Covers of early issues featured Bing Crosby, Joan Crawford, and Douglas Fairbanks, Jr. Other early covers featured figures such as Mussolini, Stalin, Eleanor Roosevelt (December 29, 1933), and Amelia Earhart (December 8, 1933). During the Presidency of Franklin D. Roosevelt, Eleanor Roosevelt contributed articles to *Family Circle* as well as to its arch rival *Woman's Day.* In the April 1955 issue, Quentin Reynolds wrote about the problems of adolescence in an article called ''Help Over the Teen-Age Hurdle.'' The next month Art Linkletter explained ''Why People Are Funny,'' and in September, Herman Hickman explained that ''Football Is a Ladies' Game.'' When *Everywoman's* told its readers in 1958 that the next issue would be *Everywoman's Family Circle,* it also promised that in the first issue of the merged magazines Ivy Baker Priest, Treasurer of the United States, would switch to her role as a ''successful mother'' and ask: ''Are we neglecting our children enough?''

The use of celebrities has endured and has earned *Family Circle* free advertising. The *New York Times* reported in February 1976 that Susan Ford, daughter of President Ford, was in Palm Beach ''working as a model . . . for *Family Circle* magazine.'' It reported in 1981 that Nancy Reagan told *Family Circle* that she ''had just gotten out of the tub'' and Ronald Reagan was in the shower when ''President Jimmy Carter went on national television to concede the election.''

Charges that *Family Circle*'s content is primarily about economical cooking, styling hair, or that it is primarily a woman's magazine can be made only by those who have not bothered to turn the covers of the magazine. In *Magazines in the United States,* Wood reported that *Family Circle* was "a full magazine, carrying romantic fiction with housewife appeal, feature articles on such subjects of family interest as sports, law, divorce, teen-age problems, gardening, and travel." Its largest department was "All Around the House" which included material on food and its preparation, household equipment, decoration, home building, and home furnishings. In "Your Children and You," one found articles on child care, parent-child relationships, and how to organize successful parties for children. A typical issue contained sections by contributors headed "The Personal Touch," notices of new movies under "The Reel Dope," "Beauty and Health" departments, and a "Buyer's Guide" that told where and how the products mentioned in the magazine could be acquired. As was announced in its first issue, it was designed as a magazine with something for all members of the family. While a very large portion of its editorial content, probably a majority of it, was devoted to food, needlework, and other activities traditionally identified as women's activities, it did not ignore fathers and activities traditionally identified as men's activities.

Family Circle also included material directed to children and teenagers. For example, when the first monthly issue appeared in September 1946, it included "Teen Scene" by Betsy Bourne, a feature addressed not to parents but to teenagers themselves. It was similar to the feature *Woman's Day* introduced in 1939, Susan Bennett Holmes' "School Bus." Although most of it was addressed to females, some sections were addressed to males. Bourne, however, addressed only a portion of the nation's teenagers. There was no mention or acknowledgment of race. That may be explained by the period during which she was working, a period that ended with the *Brown* decision (1954). She further tacitly accepted that the families of the teenagers she addressed were all very much alike. There certainly was no significant acknowledgment of the great variety of familial forms and styles that prevailed throughout the nation. The topic that received most attention—Social Skills—told teenagers, especially girls, how they could manipulate and manage others—their parents and their peers—and how they could manage to get their own way. Girls were given instructions on how to catch boys and what to give and not to give boys.

Teenagers, especially the females, who followed Bourne's advice were being prepared to be good middle class wives. They would understand their husbands, be considerate, know how to dress, how to groom themselves, how to give parties, and how to participate in volunteer work. While they were being told how to manage, manipulate, and get their own way, they were not being told how to be independent or to pursue their own careers. Boys were given instructions on how to please girls. Presumably, that would transfer to pleasing their wives.

Family Circle has served as a successful exporter of American culture. In 1965 its Canadian circulation was 350,000. A British version appeared on September 23, 1964. By early 1966 it was the most successful monthly for housewives in Britain. Its initial circulation of 700,000, distributed through 9,000 markets, increased to 850,000 distributed by 13,000 stores by the beginning of 1966. On March 24, 1966, 5,000 self-service stores in Germany began distribution of a German edition, *Ich und meine Familie* with a circulation of 500,000 guaranteed through 1967. Most of its editorial content was to be provided by the Germans, but a significant portion of the material

on health and infant care was scheduled to come from *Family Circle.* An Australian edition appeared in Australian supermarkets in May 1973. *Family Circle* and Vanchen Associated of Hong Kong entered into a licensing agreement in 1984 to make it available in Hong Kong and Taiwan. The first issue was written in Chinese, but the recipe headings were in English.

—Erwin V. Johanningmeier

FURTHER READING:

"Food-Store Magazines Hit the Big Time." *Business Week.* No. 1171, February 9, 1952.

Jones, Landon Y. *Great Expectations: America and the Baby Boom Generation.* New York, Ballantine Books, 1981.

Leuchtenburg, William E. *A Troubled Feast: American Society Since 1945.* Boston, Little Brown and Co, 1979.

New York Times. February 20, 1976, 25.

New York Times. August 11, 1981, Section II, 10.

Peterson, Theodore. *Magazines in the Twentieth Century.* Urbana, Illinois, University of Illinois Press, 1964.

Taft, William H. *Americans Magazines for the 1980s.* New York, Hasting House Publishers, 1982.

Wolseley, Roland E. *The Changing Magazine.* New York, Hasting House Publishers, 1973.

Wood, James Playsted. *Magazines in the United States.* New York, Ronald Press, 1956.

The Family Circus

Bil Keane's daily single-frame comic strip began chronicling the mild misadventures of a white, middle-class suburban family on February 19, 1960 and is currently distributed to over 1,300 newspapers, making it the most popular panel in the world. Comics historian Ron Goulart has called *The Family Circus* "one of the gentlest and most heartwarming panels in comics history," and it is precisely this wryly humorous perspective which has made Keane's creation one of the clearest, most significant examples of the deep-seated American belief in the nuclear family as the moral center of domestic life. If a "circus" can be accurately described as a form of entertainment which displays human beings in control of both wild beasts and their own fears, then the ring which surrounds each panel of Bil Keane's strip is apt indeed, for *The Family Circus* takes everything that might be threatening or frightening about children or parenting and tames it with the whipcrack of a grin, the safety net of a smile.

Keane has reported that the idea for a comic strip poking fun at the foibles of family life occurred to him as early as 1952 while he was still involved in producing *Channel Chuckles,* a daily comic which encouraged readers to laugh at the new medium of television and at their own compulsive interest in it. Keane began keeping notes on 3x5 cards of the funny turns of phrase and humorous misunderstandings of his own children until, as he later said, he had "enough material for maybe 50 years.'' When *The Family Circus* debuted in 1960 (as *The Family Circle)*, the Keane family's ink-drawn counterparts consisted of a Daddy in horn-rimmed glasses, a pert and neatly dressed Mommy, and three children—seven-year-old Billy, five-year-old ponytailed Dolly, and three-year-old Jeffy. Another baby arrived two years later and PJ has since been permanently fixed at a toddling 18-months. Barfy the Dog and Kittycat are the pets of the family, and all are occasionally visited by a stereotypical crew of in-laws, neighbors, and schoolchums—with the principal focus remaining exclusively on the central family of parents and children. The perpetual preadolescence of the brood enables Keane to ignore the more disturbing issues of parenting which arise with puberty, and a typical *Family Circus* panel is a simple illustration of a child's malapropism, mild misunderstanding of the adult world, or parental eye-rolling. Any variation from this formula is usually confined to the more experimental (and larger) format offered by the Sunday panel, and here Keane makes regular, innovative use of an overhead perspective tracing one child's path through the neighborhood and of a version of the strip ''as drawn by'' little Bobby—usually as a Father's Day ''present'' to the hardworking Bil.

Keane has helped define the unique tenor of his strip by noting that ''There's a general tendency among people who want to be funny to exaggerate. I do just the opposite. I tone down every idea I get.'' While the resulting moderation can easily lull a reader into taking the strip for granted, the comic industry and the American public have been generous in their persistent recognition of Keane's consistently popular, understated art. The National Cartoonists Society has awarded Keane its highest honor, the Reuben, as Outstanding Cartoonist of the Year (1982), and *The Family Circus* characters themselves have appeared in three television specials, over 40 book collections, and uncounted calendars, figurines, advertisements, greeting cards, and Christmas ornaments.

While an occasional reference to contemporary matters helps keep the panel meaningful to its wide audience (e.g., a caption of Dolly advising Jeffy that ''Conscience is e-mail your head gets from Heaven''), the strip retains its focus upon the timeless center ''ring'' of the family—the mild pleasures, sighing frustrations, and deep love which makes the ''circus'' a place we want to visit whenever it comes to town or is delivered to our doorstep.

—Kevin Lause

FURTHER READING:

Goulart, Ron. *The Funnies: 100 Years of American Comic Strips.* Holbrook, Massachusetts, Adams Media Corporation, 1995.

Goulart, Ron, editor. *The Encyclopedia of American Comics from 1897 to the Present.* New York, Facts on File, 1990.

Horn, Maurice, editor. *100 Years of American Newspaper Comics.* New York, Random House, 1996.

Family Matters

The longest running black sitcom in history, *Family Matters* debuted in 1989 and aired on prime-time television for a total of nine

Jaleel White as Steve Urkel and Michelle Thomas as Myra Monkhouse in *Family Matters.*

years. Created by William Bickley and Michael Warren, the show featured a multi-generational, working-class black family living under the same roof. Originally a spin-off from *Perfect Strangers,* in which actress JoMarie Payton-France played an elevator operator, the series placed her character of Harriette Winslow in her own home with her husband, a Chicago police officer (Reginald Vel Johnson), and three children (Kellie Shanygne Williams, Darius McCrary, and Jaimee Foxworth). Other family members were Carl's mother, Estelle Winslow (played by Rosetta LeNoire) and an adult sister (Telma Hopkins).

Much as Henry Winkler's ''Fonzie'' unexpectedly stole the *Happy Days* thunder from his co-stars in the 1970s, *Family Matters* also witnessed the breakout performance of an actor named Jaleel White during its first season. Written into the script as the world's worst blind date—arranged for Laura by her father—12-year-old ''Urkel'' was a neighborhood goofball who fell instantly in love with the Winslows' daughter.

For his audition, White borrowed a pair of oversized work glasses from his dentist father, hiked his pants up to ''flood'' length, and proceeded to wheeze and snort his way into a character who would soon become television's most famous nerd. Urkel was an instant hit. In fact, White's performance was so stellar that producers quickly snatched him up as a regular cast member. Bickley claimed that he knew Urkel would be big after overhearing some teenagers imitating him in a shopping mall. As one reviewer put it, kids took to the character like quarters to arcade games. Before long there were Urkel t-shirts, jigsaw puzzles, and even a talking doll that recited favorite Urkel phrases such as, ''No sweat, my pet.''

In the midst of an otherwise unremarkable series, it was Urkel who drew both the bulk of criticism and praise for the program. Denounced as ''cartoonish'' by many he was, in many ways, a stereotypical buffoon. Even more insulting to many critics, was the show's cliched portrayal of the Winslow family's matriarch. Whereas her husband was often bumbling and unsure, Harriette Winslow was the sassy decision-maker; the domineering ''powerhouse of reality'' in the home. It could also be argued, however, that Urkel challenged racial stereotypes. Depicted as the son of a neurosurgeon, he was a studious bookworm with genius-like abilities in math and science; traits that made him a rare representation of black youth for prime-time television.

Nestled between *Full House* and *Perfect Strangers* on ABC's Friday night ''TGIF'' lineup, *Family Matters* was a black-cast series that found mainstream success among white, American audiences. Although it never won critical praise or Emmy awards, viewers were warmed by the show, which was a consistent favorite in its time slot. Unlike some of the more politicized black series of its era, such as *The Cosby Show* and *A Different World*, *Family Matters* did not emerge from a black sensibility. In fact, the white producing team of Bickley and Warren (who later created *On Our Own*, another black comedy for ABC) made a conscious effort to fashion a ''universal'' family, unmarked by racial difference. As actor Reginald Vel Johnson once noted, *Family Matters* was never nominated for any NAACP (National Association for the Advancement of Colored People) Image Awards. Despite its all-black cast, it was perhaps seen as being ''too white . . . to be considered a black show.''

Even after its retirement from prime-time, *Family Matters* continued to be a hit on cable. After a brief and unsuccessful run on the lily-white CBS, the series migrated to the Turner Broadcasting System (TBS) cable network, where it ranked number nine among cable programs for children in 1997.

—Kristal Brent Zook

FURTHER READING:

Curry, Jack, and Walter T. Middlebrook. ''*Family Matters.*'' *USA Today.* September 13, 1989, 4D.

McNeil, Alex. *Total Television.* New York, Viking/Penguin, 1996.

Family Reunions

The idea of gathering together all of one's family members at a central place and at a given time emerged as a popular American pastime in the 1960s, although family reunions had been held in the United States since the 1880s. Throughout the 1970s, 1980s, and 1990s, however, reunions grew in both popularity and scale as the baby boomer generation aged. To many people, reunions represent an opportunity to return to the "old days" when families resided in the same locale and knew each other very well. While many Americans attend family reunions for purely nostalgic reasons, others are motivated by the urge to get in touch with the family's "roots."

During the 1980s, the advent of computers and the Internet began an ongoing interest in amateur genealogy. The many Americans who trace their heritage are often the primary organizers of a family reunion. They wish to share their findings with family members as well as gather new information through personal contact. Furthermore, the Internet has made it easier to advertise reunions as well as to find and correspond with distant relatives.

Some reunions attract a gathering in the hundreds, often held at or near convenient popular resort areas, though smaller reunions remain common. Reunions are usually held in June, July, or August to correspond with family vacations and, since many are often held outdoors at state parks or campgrounds, to coincide with good weather. Making an occasion of mealtimes is an essential ingredient of the American family reunion, typically with each family contributing dishes to the large buffets that are held. The get-togethers might last anywhere between one and three days, with the participants enjoying pastimes that range from games and sports to sightseeing outings, but for many the most enjoyable pastime of all is sitting around talking. Recalling memories of youth, and passing those memories on to the next generation, are important goals of a family reunion. Many adults want their children to get to know their cousins or other extended family members, who influenced their own lives.

Because of their large scale, by the 1990s reunions had come to involve much careful planning and organization. Near the close of a reunion, families often hold a meeting to elect officers to organize the next get-together and perhaps set a date and place where it will be held. A family historian is usually entrusted with the task of recording the events of the reunion, as well as keeping the family history and genealogy up to date. Some families even appoint a fundraising committee to organize events that will pay the costs of getting everybody together and accommodating them. Despite the hard work and responsibilities that go into the arranging of a successful gathering, families enjoy being a part of the communal group that makes up a large reunion.

To commemorate the occasion, organizers often provide a variety of souvenirs for family members to purchase. T-shirts printed with the family name, and the date and place of the reunion are common, while other popular items might include caps, bumper stickers, tote bags, pencils, complete genealogies and family recipe books. Family members also take an abundant number of photographs and home videos to preserve the memory of the gathering.

By the 1990s it was estimated that over 200,000 American families attend a family reunion every year. In an age of smaller nuclear families and changing definitions of a family in general, reunions offer an opportunity for many people to feel a sense of belonging in a larger, extended family unit. Many families are forced to live far distant from their relatives because of work or other circumstances, and reunions give them an opportunity to keep in touch. Whatever a family's interests, or those of the individuals within it, reunions offer something for everyone to enjoy within the enhanced sense of close community that they create.

—Angela O'Neal

FURTHER READING:

Ayoub, Millicent R. "The Family Reunion." *Ethnology.* 1966, 415-433.

Mergenhagen, Paula. "The Reunion Market." *American Demographics.* April 1966, 30-34.

Swenson, Greta E. *Festivals of Sharing: Family Reunions in America.* New York, AMS Press, 1989.

Family Ties

President Reagan once named NBC's *Family Ties* his favorite show, despite the fact that the show was originally intended as a parody of Reagan-style values. The premise of the Emmy-winning series, which ran from 1982 to 1989, was the generation gap between the Keaton parents, who came of age in the 1960s and whose hippie leanings were evident from the opening sequence, and their children, who were products of the materialistic 1980s. The eldest child, Alex (Michael J. Fox, who became a star because of the series), wore suits, read the *Wall Street Journal,* and worshipped Richard Nixon and William F. Buckley. Middle child Mallory was rather dim and obsessed with shopping. The youngest, Jennifer, was a precocious sitcom kid. As viewers became more interested in the kids, the generation gap theme was dropped.

—Karen Lurie

FURTHER READING:

Brooks, Tim, and Earle Marsh. *The Complete Directory to Prime Time Network and Cable TV Shows 1946-present.* New York, Ballantine Books, 1995.

McNeil, Alex. *Total Television.* New York, Penguin, 1996.

Fan Magazines

Although many fields of endeavor such as sports, auto racing, radio, and music have all spawned "interest magazines" that provide inside information for devotees of a particular subject or pursuit, it is to the motion picture industry that America owes the long-established concept of the fan magazine. Conceived to promote, popularize, and trade off the fledgling art of film in early Hollywood, the publication of fan magazines dates back to 1911 when *Motion Picture Story* magazine and *Photoplay* first appeared. These magazines provided readers with an illusion of intimacy with the stars, and fed into their fantasies of the opulent lifestyles and sometimes scandal-ridden private lives of the famous. At the same time, they purported to reveal the mechanics of the star making process, allowing the average reader—an outsider looking in—to claim spurious knowledge and form a personal judgment as to a player's screen image, talent, off-screen personality and character, and to hold opinions about the best career moves for their favorites.

Initially, fan magazines relied on a formula that packaged a gallery of movie star portraits and illustrated stories of popular motion pictures, together with a few specialized features such as reader inquiries. Each issue was rounded off with short fictional pieces. However, as early as 1912, the magazines began to print interviews with stars, articles on various phases of film production, and even motion picture scenarios. The magazines were targeted to appeal primarily to female readers who, in the belief of most film industry executives, formed the large majority of the filmgoing public. By the same token, most of the magazine contributors were also women, and included such notables as Adela Rogers St. John, Hazel Simpson Naylor, Ruth Hall, and Adele Whitely Fletcher, who all wrote for several different publications under a variety of pen names. Other contributors came from the ranks of press representatives for both actors and film studios. Occasionally, a magazine would publish an article purportedly written by a star, or print an interview in which the actor or actress supposedly solicited readers' opinions on career moves, etc. Though these pieces were normally the result of collaboration between the editorial staff and the subject's press agent, there would be an accompanying photograph, or a set of handwritten responses to questions, supposedly supplied by the star, in order to lend authenticity to the enterprise. These editorial ploys gave the impression that the magazines were essentially uncritical mouthpieces, fawning on an industry that fed them tidbits so as to heighten the public's interest in films.

While this was not without some truth, fan magazines were, for the most part, published independently of the studios, although this did not always guarantee objectivity. The publications were dependent on the studios to organize interviews with actors and to keep them supplied with publicity releases and information about the stars and the films. Nonetheless, the magazines could be critical at times, particularly from 1915 when they began publishing film reviews. It was not uncommon to see both *Photoplay* and *Motion Picture Story* giving the "thumbs down" to pictures that they didn't think their readers would enjoy, although the sort of harsh criticism or expose that became a feature of the tabloids in the late decades of the twentieth century were generally avoided. Articles that dealt with the private lives of screen personalities tended to overlook any sordid doings and placed their emphasis on family values, domestic pursuits, and the aesthetics of the Hollywood home and hearth. From the 1930s onwards, it was commonplace to see major photographic features showing the famous names hard at work gardening, cooking, washing the car, or playing with the baby.

This was in extreme contrast to Hollywood coverage in the national press. The circulation of tabloid newspapers thrived through titillating their readers with detailed reportage of the numerous scandals that erupted in the early decades. A notorious example of this was the murder trial of Roscoe "Fatty" Arbuckle during the 1920s. The magazine *Screenland* (published from 1921 to 1927) took Hollywood's side against the sensationalism of the Arbuckle case by publishing a piece in defense of the comedian (later found innocent), but other fan publications, notably *Photoplay,* took a decidedly neutral stance on Hollywood scandal. Such incidents as the murder of director William Desmond Taylor, of which Mabel Normand was briefly suspected, Rudolph Valentino's divorce, and Wallace Reid's drug-related death, while prompting the implementation of the motion picture production code in the early 1930s, were pretty much neglected in the fan magazines, or treated in vague general terms within an article presenting a star and his family bravely overcoming adversity. That this approach worked as well as it did demonstrates the devotion of film fans to the romanticized image of their screen idols as peddled by the fan magazines. Most readers were well up on the current scandals, and when the fan magazines alluded to a star's "brave fight" or "lingering illness," they were knowledgeable enough to translate the terms into "drug addiction," or to know that "young foolishness," or "hot-headed wildness" meant sexual indiscretions of one kind or another.

Most film historians view the fan magazines of the silent era as having more scholarly validity than those after the advent of sound. Such publications as *Filmplay Journal, Motion Picture Classic, Motion Picture,* and *Movie Weekly,* gave readers well-written film reviews and factual, biographical information that could not be found anywhere else. They have come to provide modern scholars with fascinating sociological insights into the phenomenon of filmgoing in the first two decades of American motion picture history.

After the advent of sound, the fan magazines became less serious and more concerned with sensationalism and sex. The magazines played a major role in creating the lasting impression of Hollywood as the center of glamour during the 1930s. To a country mired in the economic consequences of the Great Depression, fan magazines presented an image of the American dream as attainable to the average person. They treated as gospel such myths as Lana Turner being discovered by a producer while eating a sundae at Schwab's Drug Store or Hollywood talent scouts combing the country for "unknowns" to be turned into stars. The myth-makers were preaching the messages of the Dream Factory to a nation only too willing to believe them. In the make-believe world that formed the setting of the majority of popular movies, crime was punished, courage was rewarded, and lovers lived happily ever after.

Fan magazines presented all movie actresses as icons of perfect beauty. At one end of the scale they were pictures of fresh prettiness (Fay Wray, Deanna Durbin); at the other, stylish and glamorous sophisticates (Garbo, Dietrich, or Myrna Loy). Their handsome male counterparts were either debonair (Cary Grant, Errol Flynn) or the epitome of masculine strength (Gary Cooper, Clark Gable). Everything about the stars was larger than life—their homes, their lifestyles, their passions, even their sins. In short, they had everything except the ability to visit with their fans. Hence, such magazines as *Modern Screen, Movie Action Magazine, Movie Classic, Movie Mirror, Silver Screen,* and *Motion Picture Classic* came into being to reveal the inside scoop on their lives to the fans. Articles such as "Jean Harlow—From Extra to Star"; "Shirley Temple's Letter to Santa"; "Motherhood: What it Means to Helen Twelvetrees"; and "The Bennetts Answer Hollywood Gossip" allowed the readers momentarily to forget their drab existence during the Depression and live vicariously through the pages of the magazines.

Conversely, the magazines also let the public know that these glamorous stars did not really have it all; indeed, they envied the simple pleasure enjoyed by their fans. Shirley Temple, they reported, wished she could visit a department store Santa; Deanna Durbin longed to eat fudge like an ordinary teenager, but couldn't lest she put on weight; Myrna Loy wanted the freedom to walk into a department store without being recognized. The conspiracy between editors and publicists that created this communication between the stars and their fans was a significant factor in keeping movie theaters filled with customers.

During the 1940s and 1950s, the pattern remained pretty much the same. The leading magazines during this period were *Photoplay, Modern Screen, Silver Screen, Movie Fan, Movie Stars Parade, Screen Album, Screen Stars,* and *Movie Story.* However, with the arrival of post-World War II affluence, the public grew less impressed with the wealth of the stars and more appreciative of pin-up poses of both sexes, and stories that revealed the less savory antics of stars such as Elizabeth Taylor, Errol Flynn, and Frank Sinatra. It was the beginning of the end of fan magazines as they had been known and loved for almost half a century. With the onset of the 1960s, they came increasingly to resemble the tabloids, trumpeting banner headlines such as "Liz will adopt a Negro Baby" (*Movie Mirror,* April, 1967), and containing little real news.

It was in the 1960s, too, that a number of specialty magazines began to appear. *Screen Legends* and *Film and TV Careers* devoted each issue to only one or two personalities, and included filmographies and interviews; *Famous Monsters of Filmland* dealt only with horror films and monsters; and *Serial Quarterly* concentrated on "cliffhangers" and Saturday matinee serials. As the traditional fan magazines fell away, eventually to disappear and leave the market to these specialist publications and to the scandal-mongering tabloids, a new style of movie magazine was created in the 1980s that has continued to fill the void. In the 1990s, film fans were buying magazines such as *Entertainment Weekly, Movieline* and, most notably, *Premier,* which blend interviews, filmographies, and production pieces with serious analysis of film trends and lifestyle fashion. They largely avoid sensationalism, but are not above criticism. They have become the new reading habit for the fans of an industry that is almost unrecognizable in terms of the old studio-based Hollywood, and the great gossip magazines, highly prized by collectors, have taken their place in Hollywood legend.

—Steve Hanson

FURTHER READING:

Levin, Martin, editor. *Hollywood and the Great Fan Magazines.* Revised edition. New York, Wings Books, 1991.

Older, Jon. "Children of the Night." *Magazines of the Movies.* No. 4, 1993, 14-16.

Slide, Anthony. "Fan Magazines." In *International Film, Radio and Television Journals.* Connecticut, Greenwood Press, 1985.

———, editor. *They Also Wrote for the Fan Magazines: Film Articles by Literary Giants from E. E. Cummings to Eleanor Roosevelt, 1920-1939.* Jefferson, North Carolina, McFarland & Company, 1992.

Studlar, Gaylyn. "The Perils of Pleasure? Fan Magazine Discourse as Women's Commodified Culture in the 1920s." *Wide Angle.* January, 1991, 6-33.

Tohill, Cathal. "Sleaze Town, USA." *Magazines of the Movies.* No. 4, 1993, 91-93.

Fantasia

A seminal film in the development of animated features, and a cultural cornerstone in leading children to classical music, Walt

The "Night on Bald Mountain" sequence from the film *Fantasia*.

Disney's *Fantasia* (1940) has entranced six generations of viewers in America and Europe. Named as one of the American Film Institute's Top 100 Movies of All Time in 1998, it has served as the inspiration for, among others, Bruno Bozetto's *Allegro Non Troppo* and Osamu Tezuka's *Legend of the Forest*. Although influential, it remains unique, one of the most masterful combinations of sound and images ever committed to celluloid.

Only the third full-length feature to be made by Walt Disney, at its inception it was one of the Hollywood film industry's most significant experiments since Warner Bros. introduced sound with *The Jazz Singer* 13 years earlier. The finished film, introduced by Deems Taylor, with the Philadelphia Orchestra under Leopold Stokowski providing the music, had grown out of a chance meeting between Stokowski and Disney. The famous conductor had expressed an interest in working with Disney; the master of animation was looking to restore Mickey Mouse to his former level of popularity. It was felt that a visual realization of composer Paul Dukas's "The Sorcerer's Apprentice" might do the trick.

Stokowski and Disney were both world-class showmen and in love with technological gimmickry. Stokowski was one of the earliest experimenters in stereophonic sound and suggested that the film's sound re-create that of a concert hall. This was done by recording the orchestra on three separate channels (right, left, and surround).

However, recording the sound to the conductor's satisfaction wound up costing more than it would have been possible to recoup on a short subject. Disney then committed to making what he initially called a "Concert Feature," a collection of shorts that would make up a concert. According to Stokowski, he wondered why Disney planned to stop at a short subject; why not a full-length film with several other musical works to suggest "the mood, the coloring, the design, the speed, the character of motion of what is seen on the screen," as he later expressed it. In short, a fantasia, which means a free development on a given theme.

It was decided to open the film with Stokowski's own orchestral transcription of Bach's "Toccata and Fugue in D Minor," complemented by visual detailing suggestive of falling asleep at the orchestra. Recalled Disney, "All I can see is violin tips and bow tips—like when you're half asleep at a concert," not, apparently, an uncommon occurrence for the easily bored studio executive. In preparing for *Fantasia*, Disney subscribed to a box at the Hollywood Bowl where, he told a colleague, he invariably fell asleep, lulled by the music and the warmth of the polo coat he liked to wear. There is also a story that he ridiculed an animator on the film, calling him homosexual for taking a music appreciation class in preparation for the project. However, when the film opened, Disney told the reporter from the *New York World Telegram,* "I never liked this stuff. Honest, I just couldn't listen to it. But I can listen to it now. It seems to mean a little more to me. Maybe it can give other people the same thing.''

The final film, a glorious marriage of sound and image, is not without flaws. Oskar Fischinger, an avant-garde painter who had worked with director Fritz Lang on the special effects for *Die Frau im Mond* (aka *The Woman in the Moon*) in Germany in 1929, helped design *Fantasia's* opening sequence. However, the literal-minded Disney, who denied him credit and had his designs altered, considered his vision too abstract. There were musical compromises, too.

Bach, best experienced with the original instrumentation, was given a bombastic transcription for full orchestra, and Igor Stravinsky's ''Rite of Spring'' was seriously distorted under Stokowsky's baton. (Disney offered the composer $5,000 for his work, pointing out that since Stravinsky's work was copyrighted in Russia, and as the United States had not signed the Berne copyright agreement, he could simply pirate the music). Beethoven's ''Pastoral Symphony'' was truncated, a problem exacerbated later when a piccaninny centaur was excised from the film on subsequent reissues as being in poor taste. The female centaurs in that sequence were originally bare-breasted, but the Hays office insisted that discreet garlands be hung around their necks.

Other aspects of the film have remained a continual source of delight. The design for the excerpts from Tchaikovsky's ''Nutcracker Suite,'' an enchanted forest peopled by mushroom Chinamen and Cossacks as dancing flowers, is a visual and aural feast; ''The Sorcerer's Apprentice'' starring, as intended, Mickey Mouse, is wonderfully inventive and amusing; ''The Dance of the Hours'' (from Ponchielli's opera *La Gioconda*) is a memorably comic sequence, with balletic ostriches and dancing hippopotami lampooning cultural pretensions.

Mussorgsky's ''Night on Bald Mountain,'' with its gargoyles, demons, and other frightening creatures of the night, remains the high spot of the film, accompanying a visual battle between the forces of good and evil. The spirits of the night rise from the local graveyard and travel to Bald Mountain for a celebration of Evil, a ritualistic bow to Tchernobog, the Black God. The flames transform into dancers, then animals, and then lizards, at the whim of the great Black God, who revels in the passionate exhibition. However, as morning approaches and church bells are rung, the Black God recoils in horror and is driven back until he is vanquished. The music segues into Schubert's ''Ave Maria,'' scored for solo voice by the composer, but here given a choral treatment (with new lyrics by Rachel Field) which blasts the preceding crescendo of magnificent malevolence out of existence.

Bela Lugosi was hired to perform the part of Tchernobog, a figure of ultimate evil. He was photographed miming the actions of the character—the legendary horror star's expressions on the character's face are unmistakable—and his image was then altered and incorporated by Vladimir Tytla, one of Disney's greatest master animators. (Tytla left Disney after the famous studio strike of 1941, brought on by Disney's refusal to allow a union, and went on to direct Little Lulu cartoons, among other things). Disney had been rotoscoping live action figures as guides to animation as far back as *Snow White* (1938) (despite Ralph Bakshi's claim of rotoscoping as an important innovation in the 1970s), and for *Fantasia* members of the Ballet Russe, notably Roman Jasinsky, Tatiana Riabouchinska, and Irina Baranova, modeled for the elephants, hippos, and ostriches (respectively) in the ''Dance of the Hours'' sequence.

The finale after ''Night on Bald Mountain'' is an anti-climactic version of Schubert's ''Ave Maria,'' which was innovatively filmed as one long continuous take that required five days to shoot. The first time it was attempted, someone had placed the wrong lens on the camera, thus exposing the background on each side of the artwork. A second attempt was made mere days before the film's opening and was briefly disrupted by an earthquake on the third day of filming, fortunately with no ill effect.

Disney had wanted to shoot the film in widescreen and offer it on a reserved-seat basis before giving it a general release; however, his bankers objected and the only innovation Disney was able to offer was ''Fantasound,'' an early stereo process that was available in only a few theaters.

By the time *Fantasia* opened, Disney had spent a fortune building his dream studio, but World War II shut down his foreign market and a significant portion of his revenues. The banks closed off his line of credit in 1940, and he was forced to offer stock to the public for the first time. *Fantasia* fared badly on its initial release, trimmed to 88 minutes, pleasing neither the audience (who wanted and expected more films like *Snow White*) nor the critics (who decried the misuse of classical music). However, Disney and *Fantasia* both survived, with the latter achieving classic status and more than recouping its costs (about $2,250,000). Until the film became available on video, it remained one of the classic Disney perennials, screened as a staple of children's vacation time.

One of Disney's ideas for the project was to periodically re-release it with the order and selection of musical programs altered. Such tunes as Debussy's ''Clair de Lune,'' Weber's ''Invitation to the Waltz,'' ''Humoresque,'' Sibelius' ''Swan of Tuonela,'' Wagner's ''Ride of the Valkries,'' and Prokofiev's ''Peter and the Wolf'' were considered for insertion into future releases. However, only ''Peter and the Wolf'' reached the animation stage in Disney's lifetime, narrated by Sterling Holloway in *Make Mine Music* (1938), though the ''Claire de Lune'' material formed the basis for Bobby Worth and Ray Gilbert's ''Blue Bayou'' in the same film.

Fantasia stands acknowledged as one of cinema's undisputed works of art, visually, musically and technically.

—Dennis Fischer

FURTHER READING:

Culhane, John. *Walt Disney's Fantasia.* New York, Abradale Press, 1983.

Heath, Robert. *Fantasia: The Making of a Masterpiece* (film).

Maltin, Leonard. *The Disney Films.* New York, Popular Library, 1978.

Peary, Danny. *Cult Movies.* New York, Dell Publishing, 1981.

Schickel, Richard. *The Disney Version.* New York, Avon Books, 1968.

Taylor, Deems. *Walt Disney's Fantasia.* New York, Simon & Schuster, 1940.

The Fantastic Four

The Fantastic Four is a comic book published by Marvel Comics since 1961. Created by Stan Lee and Jack Kirby, the Fantastic Four are a family of superheroes—Mr. Fantastic, the Invisible Girl (re-named the Invisible Woman in 1985), the Human Torch, and the Thing. The series departed significantly from previous superhero comic books by casting characters as distinct individuals plagued by human failings like self-doubt, jealousy, and even occasional antipa-thy toward the society that they have sworn to protect. With his monstrous orange rock-skinned appearance, the Thing especially was prone to alienation and periods of self-loathing. And he quickly emerged as the favorite among fans of the comic.

The Fantastic Four was the first of the Marvel comic books to predict the anti-conformist themes soon to become prevalent in the youth culture of the 1960s and subsequent decades. Along with *The Incredible Hulk* and *The Amazing Spider-Man*, *The Fantastic Four* formed the core of Marvel's 1960s comic-book publishing boom. It remained one of the company's most popular titles in the 1990s.

—Bradford Wright

FURTHER READING:

Daniels, Les. *Marvel: Five Fabulous Decades of the World's Great-est Comics.* New York, Harry N. Abrams, 1991.

Lee, Stan. *Origins of Marvel Comics.* New York, Simon & Schuster, 1974.

Fantasy Island

Producer Aaron Spelling once said that of all the characters he created, the one he most identified with was *Fantasy Island*'s Mr. Roarke, because he made dreams come true. Following *The Love Boat* on Saturday nights on ABC from 1978 to 1984, *Fantasy Island* offered viewers a chance to imagine romantic escapes and gave B-list celebrities such as Bill Bixby, Joseph Campanella, Adrienne Barbeau, Karen Valentine, and Victoria Principal another opportunity to ap-pear on the small screen. Unlike the comedic *Love Boat,* however, *Fantasy Island* was a romantic drama, complete with suspense and ironic twists. Each episode carried the implicit warning to be careful what you wish for.

The premise of *Fantasy Island* was simple: each of the three weekly visitors to the tropical Fantasy Island paid $10,000 to make a lifelong dream come true. Awaiting the visitors was their host, Mr. Roarke (Ricardo Montalban), a suave, mysterious man in a white suit, and his simiarly white-suited midget attaché, Tattoo (Herve Villechaize). Mr. Roarke managed the visitor's fantasies, directing his retinue to smile as the seaplane landed to Tattoo's now infamous call of "The Plane! The Plane!" From show to show the visitors' fantasies varied: one visitor was an ugly duckling who longed to be a sex symbol, another was a frustrated salesman looking for the business coup of a lifetime, yet another was a henpecked family man looking for a little respect. The visitors had one thing in common: they all imagined a life more glamorous or exciting than the one they left behind.

Roarke provided the magic that made fantasies come true, but he also proved a wise advisor to those guests who realized that their fantasies often led them where they did not want to go. When a

Ricardo Montalban and Hervé Villechaize in a scene from *Fantasy Island.*

pregnant woman certain to die during childbirth asks to see the life of her as yet unborn child, for example, she is horrified at the way the child's life turns out. As the guests' fantasies went awry, and they always went awry, Roarke was there to help his guests realize that some fantasies are best left fantasies. As the seasons went on, the show delved more into the supernatural. Roarke was suddenly able to bring about events from the future and the past, cast spells and mix up magic potions, and even do battle with the devil, played in a recurring role by a sinister Roddy McDowall. Was Roarke God? An angel? Or just a figure who let viewers indulge their taste for tropical fantasy while reassuring them that they were better off in the lives they had?

Fantasy Island was very much a product of its times, for it attempted to indulge the popular appetite for wealth and glamour that brought shows like *Dallas* and *Dynasty* such success. At the same time, the show addressed the age-old fears of those who worried that greed could only bring trouble. ABC brought back a revamped and "edgier" *Fantasy Island* in the fall of 1998, featuring Malcolm McDowell as Roarke, wearing a black suit this time, and accompa-nied by a few disgruntled assistants. Though the show had the basic same premise, it was far more interested in exploring the horror of a fantasy realized that was its predecessor. The revival was short-lived, leaving the air after just one season.

—Karen Lurie

FURTHER READING:

Brooks, Tim, and Earle Marsh. *The Complete Directory to Prime Time Network and Cable TV Shows 1946-present.* New York, Ballantine Books, 1995.

McNeil, Alex. *Total Television.* New York, Penguin, 1996.

Spelling, Aaron, and Jefferson Graham. *Aaron Spelling: A Prime-Time Life.* New York, St. Martin's Press, 1996.

The Far Side

Debuting in 1980, *The Far Side,* a single-panel comic strip written and drawn by Gary Larson, was different from anything previously seen on a comics page. Its offbeat and obscure humor drew epithets such as ''tasteless,'' ''sick,'' or ''demented,'' but the cartoon became immensely popular during its fifteen-year tenure, appearing in more than 1,900 daily and Sunday newspapers and being translated into seventeen languages. More than twenty *Far Side* collections and anthologies reached the bestseller lists and were available in bookstores long after Larson stopped producing the cartoon in 1995. *The Far Side* made its way to greeting cards, T-shirts, and calendars—including the especially popular desk calendars of 365 daily *Far Side* cartoons, which are produced and sold each holiday season.

Unlike other comics, *The Far Side* did not feature the same characters in each installment, although it did repeat types of characters. Farm animals, especially cows, chickens, and ducks, made frequent appearances. Among other animals featured were snakes and squids. Larson's love of biology showed itself in numerous insect jokes. (An entomologist even named a species of chewing lice after Larson for his contributions to biology. The insect was named strigiphilus garylarsoni. Larson considered it a great honor.) The people who appeared in *The Far Side* usually were similar in appearance: most of the children had big heads and glasses; the women had big hair and glasses; the men had long noses and often wore glasses. In fact, most of Larson's characters fit the stereotypical image of the nerd. Neanderthal men and aliens appeared as well.

The jokes found in *The Far Side* ranged from puns to the silly to the intellectual to the morbid. A cartoon about a sticky widget (a strange device covered in honey) could be followed by a joke referencing Mary and Louis Leakey and their discovery of Lucy. (That particular cartoon showed the Leakeys uncovering a cave painting of Lucy from the *Peanuts* cartoon strip.) On the morbid side, Larson often had animals or people meet their end in untimely and ironic ways. One panel showed a mother bear using the skulls of two young hunters to entertain her cubs. She had her hand inside each skull and mimicked the boys' last words about entering the cave. In fact, the panels that drew the most complaints usually depicted some cruelty done to an animal, usually by another animal. For example, one cartoon with the caption ''Tethercat'' showed a cat tied to a pole by its neck while two dogs batted it around. And as often as he got complaints, Larson got letters asking for him to explain the joke.

Larson also created an animated television special: *Gary Larson's Tales from the Far Side* (1994). Larson won the Reuben Award for

Best Cartoonist in 1991 and 1994. *The Far Side* was awarded the Max & Moritz Prize for best international comic strip/panel in 1993 and best syndicated panel in 1985 and 1987.

After Larson's retirement from the comics page, other single-panel comics that took up his style included *Off the Mark* and *Speed Bump.* Larson went on to other projects such as a book titled *There's a Hair in My Dirt: A Worm's Story* in 1998.

—P. Andrew Miller

FURTHER READING:

Larson, Gary. *The Far Side.* Kansas City, Andrews and McMeel, 1982.

———. *The PreHistory of The Far Side: A 10th Anniversary Exhibit.* Kansas City, Andrews and McMeel, 1989.

Fargo

In order to gain a piece of his father-in-law's fortune, a financially desperate husband (William H. Macy) hires two hitmen (Steve Buscemi and Peter Stormare) to fake a kidnapping of his wife in Joel and Ethan Coen's 1996 noir-comedy film, *Fargo.* Frances McDormand won a 1996 best actress Oscar for her portrayal of the pregnant police chief who cracks the botched-kidnapping, multiple-homicide case. More than murders, people-pulverizing woodchippers, and snowstorms, *Fargo* brought allegedly genuine midwestern mannerisms and dialect to urban America, and an Academy award for best original screenplay to the native-Minnesotan Coen brothers.

—Daryna M. McKeand

FURTHER READING:

Bennun, David. ''Coen for Gold.'' *Melody Maker.* June 1, 1996, 24.

Farm Aid

Farm Aid is an advocacy group that, since the mid-1980s, has called attention to the plight of the American family farm through a series of high-profile live concerts that feature many of the music industry's leading performers. Led by its president, country-music star Willie Nelson, and based in Cambridge, Massachusetts, Farm Aid was created in response to a comment by Bob Dylan at the 1985 Live Aid for Africa Concert: ''Wouldn't it be great if we did something like this for our own farmers right here in America?'' At the time, poor markets and high operating costs were driving an estimated 500 family farmers out of business every week. Nelson, Neil Young, and John Mellencamp responded immediately, and six weeks later the first Farm Aid concert, in Champaign, Illinois, attracted some 80,000 fans and raised over $7 million for the cause. Farm Aid II (1986) took place in Austin, Texas, and Farm Aid III (1987) in Lincoln, Nebraska. Participating artists have included performers as diverse as Bob Dylan, Lyle Lovett, Steppenwolf,

Willie Nelson performs at Farm Aid V in 1992.

Hootie and the Blowfish, Wilco, Loretta Lynn, the Beach Boys, Steve Earle, Elton John, Stevie Ray Vaughn, Johnny Cash, the Grateful Dead, Ringo Starr, Martina McBride, and Phish. Over the years, Farm Aid has raised $14 million and evolved into a two-part organization, one that produces the fund-raising concerts and another that administers support programs for family farmers and lobbies for political change. Farm Aid has also provided a forum for some exciting musical collaborations, such as Bob Dylan's work with Tom Petty and the Heartbreakers, which led to a substantial tour.

Farm Aid began to affect U.S. farm policy in 1987 when Nelson, Mellencamp, and a group of family farmers were called to testify before Congress, which later passed the Agricultural Credit Act. This act mandated that the Farmer's Home Administration could not foreclose on a family farmer unless the organization would make more money through foreclosure than it would by investing in the farm to make it profitable. Farm Aid saw this as a significant step forward.

In 1989, Nelson took Farm Aid on the road with 16 of his own shows, asserting that ''The fight to save family farms isn't just about farmers. It's about making sure that there is a safe and healthy food supply for all of us. It's about jobs, from Main Street to Wall Street. It's about a better America.'' In 1991, Farm Aid focused on dairy farmers who had experienced a sharp drop in prices and teamed with

ice-cream maker Ben & Jerry's. In 1993, Farm Aid raised money to aid farmers affected by the Mississippi River floods which destroyed 8 million acres of crops and damaged 20 million more. In 1994, Willie Nelson, on behalf of Farm Aid, successfully urged President Bill Clinton to pardon Nebraska farmer Ernest Krikava, who had been imprisoned for illegally selling hogs during a bankruptcy proceeding to feed his desperate and starving family. Farm Aid has also continued to emphasize the environmental responsibility of family farmers who, according to the organization, are more conscientious about land, water, and food purity.

Farm Aid's mega-concerts during the 1990s were produced in Indianapolis (1990), Dallas (1992), Ames, Iowa (1993), New Orleans (1994), Louisville (1995), and Columbia, South Carolina (1996). Even though the 1997 Farm Aid concert in Dallas was unsuccessful due to poor ticket sales, it rebounded with its 1998 concert in Chicago. According to its own literature, since 1985, Farm Aid has ''granted over $14 million to 100 farm organizations, churches, and service agencies in 44 states. Nearly half of those grants are used for direct services such as food, emergency aid, legal assistance, and hotlines.'' Other funds are ''distributed as 'Program Grants' to promote outreach, education, and the development of long-term solutions.''

—S. Renee Dechert

FURTHER READING:

"Country." http://www.country.com/tnn/farm-aid/farm-aid-content.html. March 1999.

"Farm Aid." http://www.farmaid.org. March 1999.

Farr, Jamie (1936—)

Jamie Farr is best known as Maxwell Q. Klinger, the soldier who wore women's clothing in an attempt to get an insanity discharge in the Korean War sitcom *M*A*S*H* (1972-1983). Late in the show's run, Klinger stopped wearing dresses and took over as his unit's company clerk after "Radar" O'Reilly (Gary Burghoff) left the show in 1979. Klinger married a Korean woman, Soon-Lee (Rosalind Chao), in the show's final episode, and their life in America was chronicled in the spinoff *After M*A*S*H* (1983-1984). Farr's film work includes *Blackboard Jungle* (1955—credited as Jameel Farah), *With Six You Get Eggroll* (1968), and *The Cannonball Run* (1981).

—Christian L. Pyle

FURTHER READING:

Farr, Jamie. *Just Farr Fun.* Clearwater, Florida, Eubanks/Donizetti, 1994.

Fast Food

Even more than hotdogs and apple pie, the hamburgers and french fries found at ubiquitous fast food restaurants represent America's quintessential food and, in many ways, America's quintessential culture.

The rise of the fast food restaurant would not have been possible without concomitant changes in American culture. Beginning in the 1920s, thanks in large part to developments in technology and industry, the American lifestyle began to change. Formerly distinctive regional and ethnic cultures were now meeting up with each other, blurring differences in identity. More people were moving off the farm and into the city in search of lucrative and exciting careers. In addition, the widespread use of inventions like the telephone and the increasing acceptance of mass media meant that there was a larger degree of cultural interaction.

The development of an affordable automobile and the simultaneous governmental support of new road systems physically reinforced this cultural melding, enabling car owners, especially, to go to places they had never been before. This sparked a boom in the tourist industry: travelers who once went by rail, boat, or horse, were now moving faster by car, and began to value things such as speed and convenience as part of their trips. Not only did they need affordable and reliable places to stay, but they also needed similarly reliable places to eat.

While local diners and eateries offered good, wholesome home-cooked meals, they were often located far away from main thoroughfares, making them inconvenient for the interstate traveler. Travelers, however, were not the only ones eating on the run; private dining, once a formal ritual among family members and close friends, was

A Taco Bell fast food restaurant.

becoming a thing of the past, and eating in public was becoming much more acceptable for everyone. The increased pace of life, especially in urban areas, meant that people no longer ate as a group around the table, but favored sandwiches and other foods that could be eaten quickly and on the go. Food carts had been familiar urban sites since the late 1800s, eventually evolving into more permanent "short order" joints and diners. Cafeterias like Horn and Hardart in Philadelphia featured Automat systems in the early 1900s that allowed people to extract foods such as pies, sandwiches, and entrees from vending machines for a penny or nickel. Food was becoming merely a fuel, like gasoline, for the human working machines.

The need for fast, reliable, affordable, and convenient food, along with an increasing acceptance among Americans of a more homogenous culture, led to the rise of the fast food industry, and in particular, of the hamburger's and french fries it served. Purveyors of fast food sprang up in both urban areas and along the nation's highways. During the 1920s, the hamburger experienced a complete change of identity that attested to Americans' collective willingness to accept the new culture of food service. At the beginning of the decade the humble meat patty, served between layers of bun and often garnished with onions, ketchup, and mustard, was considered a lowly, working-class food held largely in disrepute. At this time, most hamburger stands were located close to factories and in working-class neighborhoods. By the end of the decade, however, the hamburger had come into its own, gaining widespread popularity and being considered a staple food, as evidenced by the overwhelming success of the "hamburger stand." The cartoon Popeye even featured a character, Wimpy, who gorged himself on nothing but hamburgers.

The most successful of these stands quickly multiplied, taking advantage of the growing popularity of this new "fast" food and applied industrial principles of standardization to its development. White Castle, founded in Wichita, Kansas, in 1921 by Billy Ingram and Walt Anderson, is considered the first fast food restaurant. Anderson had originally been a fry cook who perfected one version of the hamburger—square with small holes for better cooking, topped with fried onions and placed on a bun of soft white bread. Ingram recognized the potential of this relatively simple food, devised a limited menu around it, and standardized its production so that the White Castle hamburger could be found in many different cities, but would be uniform. While White Castle was never the largest of the fast food chains, it was the first and most influential, beginning the franchise system that inspired many imitations, including White Tower, White Clock, Royal Castle, and White Palace.

The methods and success of White Castle outlets had many implications for business and culture. They sold their five-cent burgers "by the sack," and encouraged carry-out for those customers on the go. They also developed standard floor plans and architectural designs that could be easily duplicated wherever a new White Castle was to be erected. They standardized the operations of the cooks so that even human workers behaved like machine mechanisms. All of these things were implemented in order to produce a uniform product and to divest the hamburger of its formerly negative reputation as a working-class foodstuff made of dubious ingredients. In order to implement these ideas, White Castle even adopted a system of vertical integration: the company produced the white porcelain and steel panels used for its buildings, owned the bakeries that made its buns, and even started a company to make the disposable paper hats and aprons worn by its employees.

White Castle hamburgers were so tasty, affordable, and increasingly ubiquitous that there was a marked increase in beef production in addition to the mass consumption of hamburgers. As historian David Hogan has remarked, "White Castle advanced food production and distribution to the volume demanded by the expanding population, and it gave an American democracy an accessible, egalitarian, and standardized style of eating. It also supplied America with a distinctive ethnic symbol: people the world over now readily identify fast-food hamburgers as the food of Americans." By the end of the decade, White Castle had brought their burgers and cultural ethos to Omaha, Kansas City, St. Louis, Minneapolis, Indianapolis, Louisville, Cincinnati, Chicago, and finally to the east coast in 1929, inspiring successful imitators wherever they went, and making "White Castle" almost a generic name for hamburgers by the end of the 1920s.

The hamburger fulfilled economic as well as cultural needs. During the Depression, affordable food like that found at the local hamburger stand was a godsend, especially to those who were unemployed; White Castle's hamburgers, for example, cost just five cents each until 1946, when the price doubled due to beef shortages caused by World War II. At the end of 1930, the company had sold over 21 million hamburgers; at the end of 1937, this number had increased to over 40 million.

Even though the first drive-in restaurant, Royce Hailey's Pig Stand in Dallas, Texas, was opened in 1921, it was not until nearly three decades later that the drive-in restaurant enjoyed a degree of success. Drive-ins, another fast food institution, celebrated the cultural importance of the automobile, allowing the car itself to be a dining room of sorts, from which people could order their food and eat it in the open air without having to unbuckle their seatbelts. "Car hops,"

as they were also called, became familiar congregation centers for teenagers as well.

At the same time, various businessmen, impressed by the enduring success of hamburger stands, especially White Castle, capitalized on these cultural shifts by developing sophisticated franchise operations to run new fast food companies. The franchise was a distinct business strategy that standardized not only the specific product sold, but the very institution that sold it. This form of organization exploited economies of scale and therefore was highly successful; as one entrepreneur remarked, there was "more money to be made selling hamburger stands than hamburgers."

Franchises were not unique to the 1950s; they had been around since the early decades of the twentieth century, patronized by a public increasingly used to and insistent upon the supposed reliability and trustworthiness of branded goods. White Castle was one of the first successful franchises, but was quickly followed by A & W Rootbeer in 1925, and Howard Johnson's, which began operations in 1935. But it took the ideals of postwar culture to wholly support the fast-food franchises and make many of them into companies worth billions of dollars. The idea of the franchise operation itself was attractive, melding otherwise conflicting postwar desires: after the War, the big business economy was a reiteration of American power; that this economy was made up of small businesses simultaneously expressed traditional American values.

McDonald's, the most successful fast food franchise, was started in 1955 by Ray A. Kroc (1902-1984), a Chicago milk shake machine salesman. While Kroc did not invent the hamburger, nor the concept of the hamburger stand, nor even the franchise system, he combined these elements in such an astute way as to make both his name and his company synonymous with fast food. When Kroc sold some of his milk shake equipment to Richard and Maurice McDonald of San Bernardino, California, for their popular hamburger stand, he was so impressed with their operation that he joined them in partnership in 1955. The first McDonald's outlet opened in Des Plaines, Illinois, that same year. By 1960, Kroc had opened 228 of these "golden arches" drive-ins, selling fifteen-cent hamburgers, ten-cent french fries, and twenty-cent milkshakes; in 1961 Kroc bought out the McDonald brothers, name and all. Original McDonald's architecture was red and white tile with a golden arch abutting each end of the building. Criticized as too gaudy, McDonald's moved to a more modest brown brick design with a shingled mansard roof in the mid 1960s, but kept the golden arches, now attached to form an "M," as their widely recognized logo.

Kroc's success lay in his approach not specifically to cooking individual food items, but in conceiving of his franchise operation in its entirety. His outlets were food factories—everything was systematized to ensure sameness, even the smiles on the clerks' faces. Kroc did not promise the best burger in the world, but the same burger throughout the world; indeed, the public came to accept this dictum, preferring predictability over quality. Every McDonald's had the same menu and the same general layout (with minor variations to acknowledge regional differences). The workers, all dressed alike, used the same techniques and equipment to prepare the food in the same way. In addition, Kroc established these as "family" restaurants that were clean, well-lit, and free from pay phones and pin ball machines that would encourage loitering.

McDonald's periodically introduced new products in response to perceived consumer demand and competition from other chains. The Filet-O-Fish entered the menu in 1962 in at attempt to attract

Catholic customers on Fridays. The "Chevy of Hamburgers," the Big Mac, appeared in 1967 to directly compete with Burger King's The Whopper. In 1971 McDonald's introduced the Egg McMuffin, and developed an entire breakfast line from it. Chicken McNuggets were added in 1981.

The 1960s through the 1990s was considered the "golden age" of fast food, and saw the explosion of various fast food chains and the subsequent creation of "the strip" in almost every town—the piece of road or highway flanked by franchise after franchise—which became a trademark feature of the suburban landscape. Fast food restaurants along the strip sold not only hamburgers, but also hotdogs, fish, pizza, ice cream, chicken, and roast beef sandwiches. Their brightly colored, neon signs advertised such various businesses as A & W, Arby's, Big Boy, Blimpie, Burger Chef, Burger King, Carrol's, Church's Chicken, Dairy Queen, Domino's Pizza, Hardee's, House of Pizza, Howard Johnson's, Jack in the Box, Kentucky Fried Chicken, Long John Silver's, Pizza Hut, Ralley's, Red Barn, Roy Roger's, Royal Castle, Sandy's, Shakey's Pizza, Taco Bell, Taco Time, Taco Tito's, Tastee Freez, Wendy's, White Castle, White Tower, and many others.

McDonald's experienced its stiffest competition in the 1960s from Burger Chef, which was eventually sold to General Foods and absorbed by Hardee's in the early 1970s. Burger King was a more enduring rival. It began in 1954 as a "walk-up" called InstaBurger King, and offered no interior seating. Dave Edgerton and Jim McLamore, its Miami founders, shortened the name to Burger King in 1957. While the business featured hamburgers, similar to McDonald's and White Castle, it set itself apart by offering the "flame-broiled" Whopper—a much larger hamburger (one quarter of a pound compared to the 1.6 ounce McDonald's hamburger)—and instituted an advertising campaign that promised people could "Have It Your Way," by letting customers choose their own toppings.

Kentucky Fried Chicken, also a viable competitor to McDonald's, took a different approach by offering stereotypical southern food—buckets of fried chicken, coleslaw, mashed potatoes, and biscuits and gravy. Founded by "Colonel" Harlan Sanders (1890-1980) in 1954, the franchise that made chicken "Finger Lickin' Good" consisted of over 300 outlets by 1963 and was enjoying revenues of over $500,000; by 1966 KFC had a gross income of $15 million.

There were other fast food franchises that bear mentioning. Arby's first appeared in 1964 in Boardman, Ohio, and was the brainchild of Forrest and Leroy Raffel, who tried to attract a more discriminating clientele by offering roast beef sandwiches, using an old west decor, and featuring more expensive menu items. Dairy Queen, started in 1944 by partners Harry Axene and John McCullough of Davenport, Iowa, sold hotdogs and ice cream, and had 2,500 outlets by 1948. Domino's, with delivery-only pizza service, was founded by Tom Monaghan, who opened his first shop in 1960 and turned to franchising in 1967. At the end of 1986, Domino's sold over 189 million pizzas, accruing sales of $2 billion. Hardee's, largely an imitation of Burger King, began in Greenville, North Carolina in 1961, and its outlets numbered over 900 by 1975. Howard Johnson's, named for its founder and known for its bright orange rooftops and homemade ice cream, started out as a set of franchised roadside restaurants in 1935. By 1967 "HoJo's" boasted over 800 restaurants, but was a victim of the "burger wars" in the 1980s, eventually going out of business.

Expanding into "ethnic food," Taco Bell originated in 1962 in San Bernardino, California. Even though it came from the idea of Glen Bell, a telephone repairman, John Martin better merchandised the company beginning in 1983, and was responsible for much of its success. Among other things, Martin omitted all ethnic symbols to counteract the negative associations people made with Mexican restaurants; he even changed the logo from a sleeping Mexican with a sombrero to a pastel-colored bell. Wendy's, specializing in bigger, better, and more expensive hamburgers, introduced the first drive-thru windows at their restaurants, which were so popular that Burger King and McDonald's had to follow suit. Founded in 1972 by R. Dave Thomas in Columbus, Ohio, it had 9 outlets and sales of $1.8 million at the end of that same year.

McDonald's, Burger King, Taco Bell, Wendy's, and Kentucky Fried Chicken remained the most successful fast food chains at the end of the twentieth century, edging out most of their competitors during the "burger wars" of the late 1970s and 1980s, a time when large companies bought up fast food franchises and either made them more successful or put them out of business. There were other factors that also led to many franchise downfalls. Beginning in the 1970s, these operations were faced with increasing criticism about everything from employees' working conditions and the nutritional value of the food they served, to the impact the "fast food" mentality was having on the public at large.

Franchise success was almost wholly based on the principles of standardization and a machine ethic. This included the laborers working within, who were treated as parts of the machine meant to run as efficiently as possible. Training was based on the idea that basic skills substituted for high turn-over rates—the guarantee that the food could still be made the same even from unskilled hands. The short order cook of the early diners, who was considered an artisan of sorts, was replaced by teenager working for minimum wage and no benefits.

Nutritionists targeted the composition of the meals themselves, identifying them as laden with too much fat, cholesterol, and sugar, and not enough vegetables. They worried that people eating a steady diet of fast food would go without basic nutriments, and also become too accustomed to unhealthy meals. Historian David Hogan underscored this point by remarking that "Americans consumed 50 percent more chicken and beef in 1976 than they had in 1960, mainly because the fast-food chains usually served only those two meats."

Critics coined the pejorative phrase "fast food culture" as a metaphor for the quick-service industries and excessive standardization seen in late-twentieth-century culture and consumption. This homogenization, they believed, not only affected American culture, erasing once vibrant ethnic and regional traditions, but also was beginning to influence the entire world—a cultural imperialism enacted on an international level.

The major franchises tried to combat these critiques to greater and lesser success. They hired older workers in an attempt to seem beneficent, giving job opportunities to those past retirement age while never addressing the real issue of wages. To counter the protests of nutritionists, they introduced salad bars and "lean" burgers, which were largely ignored by fast food customers. They tried to soften their image in a number of ways, chiefly by marketing themselves as family restaurants.

They also targeted children, creating loyal future consumers as well. Most chains had mascots. McDonald's had Ronald McDonald, a clown who debuted in 1963. (Ronald was so successful that a study conducted in 1973 found that 96 percent of American children recognized him, second only to Santa Claus). Ronald's friends who lived in "McDonaldland" with him included Grimace, the Hamburglar,

Mayor McCheese, Captain Crook, and the Professor. McDonald's also built brightly-colored playgrounds at their restaurants beginning in the 1980s. Burger King's mascot was the Magic Burger King. Kentucky Fried Chicken used the colorful Colonel himself as a spokesman long after he had sold the rights to his company. Most fast food franchises also introduced specially packaged children's meals that contained prizes; many were even sites for children's birthday parties. In addition, these franchises openly founded or contributed to charitable organizations. McDonald's established Ronald McDonald houses which provided lodging to parents whose children were getting treatment in nearby hospitals. Both Burger King and Wendy's supported programs for needy children, and Colonel Sanders was an outspoken supporter of the March of Dimes.

By the final decades of the twentieth century, Americans had fully embraced their "fast food culture." In 1994 alone, fast food restaurants in the United States sold over 5 billion hamburgers, making it a favorite meal and an important commodity. In 1996, seven percent of the population ate at the 11,400 McDonald's each day; males from their mid-teens to their early 30s comprised 75 percent of this business. By this time, fast food had become a cultural phenomenon that reached beyond America's borders. In 1996 McDonald's owned over 7,000 restaurants in other countries, including: 1,482 in Japan; 430 in France; 63 in China; two each in Bulgaria and Andorra; and one in Croatia. These outlets acknowledged some cultural differences—in Germany they sold beer, in France they sold wine, and in Saudi Arabia they had separate sections for men and women and closed four times a day for prayers. But for the most part the fast food fare was the same, homogenizing culture on an international level. The overwhelming success of the fast food culture invasion, and of McDonald's in particular, was realized when that chain opened its first store in India in 1996, and sold no hamburgers at all.

—Wendy Woloson

FURTHER READING:

Boas, Max, and Steven Chain. *Big Mac: The Unauthorized Story of McDonald's.* New York, E.P. Dutton, 1976.

Dicke, Thomas S. *Franchising in America: The Development of a Business Method, 1840-1980.* Chapel Hill, University of North Carolina Press, 1992.

Fishwick, Marshall, editor. *Ronald Revisited: The World of Ronald McDonald.* Bowling Green, Ohio, Bowling Green University Popular Press, 1983.

Hogan, David. *Selling 'em by the Sack: White Castle and the Creation of American Food.* New York, New York University Press, 1997.

Jackson, Kenneth T. *Crabgrass Frontier: The Suburbanization of the United States.* New York, Oxford University Press, 1985.

Kroc, Ray. *Grinding It Out: The Making of McDonald's.* Chicago, Contemporary Books, 1977.

Love, John. *McDonald's: Behind the Arches.* New York, Bantam Books, 1995.

Luxenberg, Stan. *Roadside Empires.* New York, Viking, 1895.

McLamore, James W. *The Burger King: Jim McLamore and the Building of an Empire.* New York, McGraw-Hill, 1998.

Monaghan, Tom. *Pizza Tiger.* New York, Random House, 1986.

Pearce, John. *The Colonel: The Captivating Biography of the Dynamic Founder of a Fast Food Empire.* Garden City, New York, Doubleday, 1982.

Fatal Attraction

Released in 1987 by Paramount Pictures, *Fatal Attraction* was one of the biggest box-office attractions of the year. More than just a popular success, the film, directed by Adrian Lyne, was a cultural phenomenon, inspiring discussion across the nation. The film is the story of an extramarital affair between Dan Gallager, played by Michael Douglas, a married attorney and father of one, and Alex Forrest, a single, successful professional played by Glenn Close. After a brief, and seemingly uninvolved two night fling, Gallagher is stalked and terrorized by the obsessed Alex. The film sparked a new genre—that of the female psychopath—that included such films as *The Hand That Rocks the Cradle* (1992), *Single White Female* (1992), and *Basic Instinct* (1992). Though dangerous women have existed long before *Fatal Attraction,* the murderous female characters in these films were more violent, sexualized, and devious. Many critics view *Fatal Attraction* as characteristic of the 1980s and 1990s backlash against the feminist movement. The character of Alex, with her gender-neutral name, financial independence, and ability to express and act on her desire, though a far cry from the traditional Hollywood depiction of women as passive sexual objects, presented female power as destructive and deadly.

—Frances Gateward

FURTHER READING:

Holmlund, Chris. "Reading Character with a Vengeance: The Fatal Attraction Phenomenon." *The Velvet-Light-Trap.* Spring 1991, 25-36.

Father Divine (18??-1965)

Despite certain ambiguities of character, the self-appointed Father Divine was undoubtedly both charismatic and clever and prospered in one of the few leadership roles open to black males in early twentieth-century America. Divine's theology blended various Christian traditions with a belief in positive thinking in ways that foreshadowed a number of contemporary New Age spiritual trends; and his career demonstrated how a promise of religious salvation, political progress and the philanthropic provision of basic social services can attract a large following in times of racial and economic turmoil. From obscure and humble origins Father Divine fashioned himself into a cult leader of god-like pretensions and created a controversial church whose beliefs fascinated America throughout the 1930s and 1940s.

There are a number of competing versions of the history of his early life—sources conflict as to his birthdate, variously noted as between 1874 and 1882—but the most plausible account is that

Father Divine

Divine was born George Baker to ex-slave parents in a Maryland African-American ghetto in about 1880. By the early years of the twentieth century he was traveling with a wandering evangelist who styled himself Father Jehovia, while the young Baker called himself the Messenger. After some years of preaching together they parted, and Baker began to refer himself as Major Jealous Devine and to proclaim himself as God. With a small band of followers in tow, he moved to New York where he changed his name yet again to Father Divine.

By 1919 he had obtained a base for his new Universal Peace Mission Movement in Sayville, Long Island, where his preaching initially attracted a mainly black audience. The years following World War I had seen a massive migration of southern African Americans to northern industrial cities, and Divine's message of self-respect and racial equality drew an increasingly large following. The Universal Peace Mission mandated celibacy and modesty and shunned improvidence and debt, but it was its provision of employment, cheap lodgings, and inexpensive food to its adherents during the Great Depression that brought thousands of worshippers, white as well as black, flocking to Sayville. The influx aroused the ire of local residents whose complaints resulted in Father Divine's arrest. He was charged with disturbing the peace, convicted in 1932, and sentenced to a year in jail. The court proceedings brought Divine widespread

notoriety when, two days after sentencing him, the judge suffered a fatal heart attack. From his prison cell, the self-styled "God" proclaimed "I hated to do it"—a remark that, trumpeted by the media, confirmed their leader's claims to divine being among his followers.

Moving the mission's headquarters to Harlem, Divine continued to attract national attention on two fronts: by his lavish lifestyle and rumors of his sexual adventures, and by the progressive social ideas his believers practiced. The Mission's services were scrupulously integrated racially, and the movement led the way in pressing for anti-lynching laws and for public facilities to be open to all races. In a time of economic disaster it rejected relief and welfare and bought hotels, which it termed "heavens," where its members could live modest, mutually supportive lives free of alcohol, tobacco and reliance on credit.

In 1946 Divine was again in the headlines when he married one of his young followers, a white Canadian woman named Edna Rose Hitchings, also known as Sweet Angel. By the 1950s, however, he was in deteriorating health. His public profile dwindled alongside the importance of his movement as other, less outrageous, African-American leaders rose to prominence. Father Divine died in 1965 at his Philadelphia estate, where his wife, known as Mother Divine, was still presiding over the remains of the Universal Peace Mission Movement in the late 1990s.

—Gerry Bowler

FURTHER READING:

Burnham, Kenneth E. *God Comes to America: Father Divine and the Peace Mission Movement.* Boston, Lambeth Press, 1979.

Watts, Jill. *God, Harlem, U.S.A.: The Father Divine Story.* Los Angeles, University of California Press, 1992.

Weisbrot, Father. *Father Divine and the Struggle for Racial Equality.* Urbana, University of Illinois Press, 1983.

Father Knows Best

Father Knows Best, which began life as a radio series in 1949, evolved into a CBS television sitcom in 1954. An archetypal representation of 1950s ideals of family life, it came to be regarded as an important influence on American family values. Actor Robert Young (the only member of the original radio cast who continued his role on television) starred as Jim Anderson, an agent for the General Insurance Company, who lived with his wife, Margaret, and their three children at 607 South Maple Lane in Springfield, a wholesome Midwestern suburban community. Jane Wyatt co-starred as Margaret Anderson, and their offspring—17-year-old Betty (called "Princess" by her father), 14-year-old Jim Jr. (or Bud), and Kathy, the baby of the family at age nine and fondly known as "Kitten" to her dad, were played by Elinor Donahue, Billy Gray, and Lauren Chapin respectively. The stories revolved around the various exploits of the Anderson family, whose problems were neatly solved in each 30-minute episode by listening to Father (and, by extension, Mother) and doing the right thing.

Although critically acclaimed, the show's initial season on television in the Sunday 10:00 p.m. slot was considered a ratings failure, and CBS canceled it in the spring of 1955. Despite the ratings, the cancellation brought protests from viewers, who demanded not

The cast of *Father Knows Best*.

only the return of the show but an earlier time slot to allow the youngsters to watch it. This audience reaction brought a response from NBC, who picked up the show, aired it earlier, and were rewarded with a hit. Robert Young decided to leave in 1960, but such was the show's popularity that CBS, in a highly unusual move for network television, aired re-runs in prime time for two more years.

The most remarkable episode of *Father Knows Best*, however, was never seen on television. In a move that pointed toward the national importance it had assumed in its healthy depiction of family life, the U.S. Treasury Department commissioned a special episode in 1959 to be distributed to schools and civic organizations throughout the country. Titled "24 Hours in Tyrantland," the story disseminated a masterful piece of Cold War propaganda through the plot device of Jim Anderson being asked to head Springfield's U.S. Savings Bond drive. Delighted at being charged with this worthwhile task, Jim decides to enlist the help of his family in the campaign. Predictably, Margaret is entirely supportive, but the kids, caught up in other concerns, are less than enthusiastic. Upset by their unwillingness to help, Jim strikes a bargain: he gives them each the cost of a U.S. Savings Bond, but decrees their home a Communist state for 24 hours. If, he tells them, they can stand to live in "Tyrantland" for 24 hours, they can keep the money to use however they choose. If they don't make it, they have to use the money to buy a bond and help him in the drive. Throughout the day, "tyrant" Jim works them to the bone and taxes them into poverty, while they repeatedly assert the unfairness of the situation. Jim reacts to their complaints as would a man who has no concept of fairness. The children make it through the 24 hours, but, just when time is up and Betty is about to go out on her Saturday evening date, Jim turns back the clock an hour. The tyrant is all-powerful; he can even reverse time. This is too much for Betty, who breaks down and sees the error of her ways. She is now proud to help sell bonds, and her siblings follow suit.

Over a 20-year period from the 1970s, reruns of *Father Knows Best* have frequently been seen on television, offering a nostalgic reminder to the baby boomers who came of age watching this almost perfect suburban family. Like many a sitcom of its period, it came to acquire the camp appeal of the quaintly outmoded, particularly in its treatment of gender issues. Women knew their place in the Anderson family (and in 1950s America), and in the rare instances when they momentarily lose sight of that place, some revelatory incident gently nudges them into submission, because "Father knows best."

—Joyce Linehan

Father's Day

The origin of Father's Day represents a grassroots phenomenon that characterizes American reverence for the family. Although deeply rooted in North American social culture, the popularity—and, some might say, the commercial exploitativeness—of Father's Day has crossed national boundaries to become popular in other countries such as Canada and Britain. Americans and Canadians set aside the third Sunday in June as the day when children show their appreciation and gratitude for their fathers, but the earliest Father's Day celebration on record appears to have been held on July 5, 1908, in a church in Fairmont, West Virginia.

Father's Day was first celebrated in local towns and cities scattered across America. The citizens of Vancouver, Washington claim to have been the first town to officially hold a Father's Day ceremony, beginning in 1912. In 1915, the president of the Uptown Lions Club in Chicago was hailed as the "Originator of Father's Day" when he suggested that the Lions hold a Father's Day celebration on the third Sunday in June of that year. The day was chosen as being closest to President Wilson's birthday.

Perhaps the most famous promoter of this holiday, though, was Sonora Smart Dodd of Spokane, Washington. Her inspiration for a Father's Day celebration came while she was listening to a Mother's Day sermon in 1909. Dodd wished to show appreciation to her own father because he had raised six children after her mother died in 1898. Her own father's birthday was June 5, so she petitioned the Spokane Ministerial Association to set aside that day in June of 1910 as a special day to honor fathers. The Association honored her request, but changed the date of the celebration to June 19. On that day, the city of Spokane became the first city to honor fathers in this way, beating Vancouver's official claim by two years.

The governor of Washington took note of the celebration and declared that the entire state should observe the day as Father's Day. Newspapers around the country carried stories about Spokane's celebration of Father's Day, and the celebration soon received national recognition. In 1916, President Woodrow Wilson joined in a celebration of Father's Day by pressing a button in Washington D.C. which caused a flag to unroll in Spokane. In 1924, President Calvin Coolidge recommended that the third Sunday in June be set aside as "Father's Day" in all states.

In the following years, there were several attempts to pass a resolution in Congress declaring Father's Day an official holiday. In 1957, Senator Margaret Chase Smith attempted to pass such a resolution, arguing that it was the "most grievous insult imaginable" that Father's Day had not been recognized as an official holiday, despite the fact that Mother's Day had been celebrated as a national holiday since 1914. Finally, in 1972, President Nixon signed a law making Father's Day an official national holiday.

This holiday is marked by many interesting traditions. Roses are worn to honor Fathers: red for living fathers and white for those who have died. Many families celebrate the day by preparing the father's favorite meal, while children often buy special gifts for their fathers. The necktie is a perennial favorite, though power tools have become a popular choice in smaller towns, especially in the northern states. In larger cities, where a growing number of employers allow casual dress at work, sports shirts have become a popular gift. Thus, the customs of Father's Day can be seen to have evolved to reflect social change. Over two thousand different Father's Day cards are available each year—less than the variety on offer for Mother's Day and Valentine's Day—but Father's Day cards hold the distinction of having the highest percentage of humor. Approximately 100 million of these cards are sold annually, compared to sales of around 150 million Mother's Day cards, but both are far outstripped by the almost 900 million Valentine's Day cards given each year.

Numerous churches continue the century-long tradition of recognizing fathers. Sermons often honor fathers and deliver encouragement to stronger family relationships. Indeed, for all the commercial and private family aspects of Father's Day, churches in America have remained the backbone of organized Father's Day celebrations, continuing to pay tribute to the work and dedication of fathers in a society that has seen many changes and convulsions in family life during the late twentieth century.

—James H. Lloyd

FURTHER READING:

Hatch, Jane M. *American Book of Days*, 3rd ed. New York, Wilson, 1978.

Klebanow, Barbara. *American Holidays: Exploring Traditions, Customs, and Backgrounds*. Brattleboro, Vermont, Pro Lingua Associates, 1986.

Myers, Robert. *Celebrations: Complete Book of American Holidays*. New York, Doubleday, 1972.

Santino, Jack. *All Around the Year: Holidays and Celebrations in American Life*. Urbana, University of Illinois Press, 1995.

Faulkner, William (1897-1962)

William Faulkner is widely regarded not only as the greatest American novelist but also as one of the great novelists of world literature. Born September 25, 1897, in New Albany, Mississippi, Faulkner spent most of his life in Oxford, Mississippi, the small town that provided inspiration for his novels. He began his writing career as a poet, but soon turned to prose, although he retained a poetic, flowery style. His first novel, *Soldier's Pa* (1926), was a typical postwar novel of disillusion. *Mosquitoes* (1927), a Huxley-style novel of ideas, concerned a group of artists and intellectuals. Not until *Flags in the Dust* did Faulkner find inspiration in his Southern heritage. He invented the town of Jefferson, Mississippi, modeled after his own Oxford, and peopled it with dozens of characters based on his family

William Faulkner

and townsmen, most of whom reappear in later novels. In the Southern setting Faulkner found the great themes that would occupy him for the remainder of his career: family curses, the burden of guilt that slavery had left upon whites, the romance of the Southern aristocracy and its ghostly influence upon modern social codes, the transmission of a defeated culture through the telling of stories and gossip, the advent of the automobile and its intrusion upon the settled ways of the rural South. In these themes one finds the clash of old and new, past and present, fiction and reality, absolutism and relativity, which Faulkner would develop further in later novels. *Flags* was a long, complex, and fragmented novel, and the editors drastically cut the manuscript and published it as *Sartoris* in 1929. (A partially restored edition was published as *Flags in the Dust* in 1973).

Upset by the changes and convinced that he would never make money from novels, Faulkner began writing for himself rather than for the public. He wrote *The Sound and the Fury* (1929), a book that he thought no one would ever understand. It is indeed one of the most difficult novels ever published, but it is also one of the greatest. Abandoning the rambling, omniscient style of *Sartoris,* Faulkner utilized several modernist techniques: multiple narrators and jumbled chronology that had been used so successfully by Joseph Conrad, and the James Joyce-ian stream-of-consciousness technique that meticulously reports the thoughts of characters without the filter of dialogue or paraphrase. Thus, the simple story of Caddy, a rebellious girl who loses her virginity, becomes very complex: each of the first three sections is told by one of her three brothers, who reveal through their thoughts what Caddy's loss of virginity means to them. The final section is told by an omniscient narrator, but focuses on the family's servant, an aged black woman who knows that Caddy's loss of virginity does not *mean* anything at all.

It is ironic, but highly significant, that Caddy does not tell her own story. This decentralization of the main character has significant modernist implications: Faulkner implies that there is no objective reality, that all exists in the eyes of the perceiver, that meaning does not inhere in facts and deeds but is assigned to them by the perceiver—hence the objective, meaningless *sound* and the subjective, interpretive *fury*. Thus, concepts like virginity, honor, and sin are not God-given constants; they are social constructs created within a patriarchal society. These modernist ideas reverberated throughout the century. However, *The Sound and the Fury* is no mere novel of ideas. It is a gripping, passionate tale of human love and suffering. Faulkner's genius lies in the artistic union of the universal and the particular: the treatment of cosmic themes through vivid, sympathetic portraits of believable characters.

After *The Sound and the Fury,* Faulkner continued to experiment with narrative techniques and to explore universal themes through the microcosm of the South. *As I Lay Dying* (1930), *Light in August* (1932), *Absalom, Absalom!* (1936), and *Go Down, Moses* (1942) are all considered masterpieces of modernist fiction. Less experimental but also great are *Sanctuary* (1931), *The Unvanquished* (1938), and *The Hamlet* (1940).

Unfortunately, only *Sanctuary,* a stark potboiler about gangsters and prostitutes, sold well, and Faulkner was forced to write for Hollywood in order to make money. His screen credits included *To Have and Have Not* (1944) and *The Big Sleep* (1946). The drunken screenwriter in the film *Barton Fink* (1991) seems to be based on Faulkner during his Hollywood years.

In 1946, when all his novels were out of print, *The Portable Faulkner* was published. This anthology gradually exposed him to a wider audience, and in 1950 Faulkner was awarded the 1949 Nobel Prize, followed by the Pulitzer Prize in 1954. Faulkner's career in the 1950s was devoted to filling in the history of the mythic town of Jefferson and Yoknapatawpha County. This work is marked by continuing experimentation, but also a decline in emotion, giving way to a hyperbolic rhetoric that makes the some of these novels almost unbearable. These problems may have been related to his life-long battle with alcoholism. Faulkner died on July 6, 1962, leaving scholarships for black students and grants for the advancement of American literature.

Because of his radical experiments, his recondite diction, and his long, convoluted sentences that sometimes last several pages, Faulkner is notoriously difficult, and has never attained widespread readership. Nevertheless, his books sell by the thousands each semester in college bookstores, and students find their efforts rewarded by a powerful intellectual experience. He had a great influence on the French "New Novelists" of the 1950s and Latin American authors of the "Boom" period of the 1960s. As one of the great modernists, Faulkner has influenced almost every writer today, whether they have read him or not. Often noted for his cinematic qualities, many of Faulkner's techniques are now used routinely in movies and television (notably *The Godfather Part Two*). Whether we realize it or not, we are more sophisticated viewers and readers because of Faulkner.

Another more amusing legacy is the annual Faux Faulkner contest. A prize is awarded to the writer of the funniest parody of Faulkner's distinctive style. The contest is sponsored by Jack Daniels Distillery.

—Douglas Cooke

FURTHER READING:

Blotner, Joseph. *Faulkner: A Biography* (One-Volume Edition). New York, Vintage Books, 1991.

Cowley, Malcolm. *The Faulkner-Cowley File: Letters and Memories, 1944-1962*. New York, Viking Press, 1966.

Faulkner, John. *My Brother Bill: An Affectionate Reminiscence*. New York, Trident Press, 1963.

Kawin, Bruce F. *Faulkner and Film*. New York, Frederick Ungar Publishing Co., 1977.

Volpe, Edmond L. *A Reader's Guide to William Faulkner*. New York, Noonday Press, 1964.

Fauset, Jessie Redmon (1882-1961)

Writer Jessie Redmon Fauset represented the emergence of an authentic African-American voice in American literature. Fauset corresponded with W.E.B. Du Bois while she attended language courses at Cornell University. Impressed by her writing, Du Bois invited Fauset to join the staff of the National Association for the Advancement of Colored People's (NAACP) magazine, *The Crisis*. As literary editor from 1919 to 1926, Fauset encouraged black writers, serving as a mentor to such artists as Langston Hughes, who said she was one of the "midwives" of the Harlem Renaissance. Fauset wrote four novels, *There Is Confusion* (1924), *Plum Bun* (1929), *The Chinaberry Tree* (1931), and *Comedy, American Style* (1933). Racial identity was a major theme of Fauset's work. Her writing stressed her belief that middle class African Americans could overcome prejudice but not self-loathing. Through her characters,

Fauset revealed the complex literary and artistic lives of Harlem Renaissance figures, including herself. Hoping to mitigate racism, she wanted to enlighten white Americans about the realities of African-Americans' experiences. Fauset also developed *The Brownies' Book*, a monthly publication for black children in 1920 and 1921. Fauset's novels were reprinted during the 1960s Civil Rights Movement.

—Elizabeth D. Schafer

Further Reading:

Allen, Carol. *Black Women Intellectuals: Strategies of Nation, Family, and Neighborhood in the Works of Pauline Hopkins, Jessie Fauset, and Marita Bonner.* New York, Garland Publishing, 1998.

McLendon, Jacquelyn Y. *The Politics of Color in the Fiction of Jessie Fauset and Nella Larsen.* Charlottesville, University Press of Virginia, 1995.

Sylvander, Carolyn Wedin. *Jessie Redmon Fauset, Black American Writer.* Troy, New York, Whitston Publishing Company, 1981.

Fawcett, Farrah (1947—)

Best known for her role in the television series *Charlie's Angels*, which ran on ABC from 1976-1981, Farrah Fawcett became one of the biggest influences on American style during the late 1970s. With a

Farrah Fawcett

plot that revolved around a trio of female private investigators—Fawcett and costars Kate Jackson and Jaclyn Smith—the campy TV show relied heavily on the physical attributes of its leading actresses. As the standout on the series during its first season, the blonde, attractive Fawcett set the trend for millions of women, who copied her trademark feathered hair and bought hair care products marketed under her name. But it wasn't only women who liked Farrah. The most popular poster of the decade, featuring Fawcett's toothy smile, flipped-back, bushy mane, and slim, athletic physique shown off in a wet swimsuit, became a staple on untold numbers of boys' bedroom walls during the era. After becoming a superstar on the top-rated show during the 1976-77 season, Fawcett left to pursue more serious acting roles, but met with little success. She never reclaimed the status that she once held, although she continued to appear regularly on television and in films into the 1990s and retained a cult following by those enamored with 1970s nostalgia.

Mary Farrah Leni Fawcett was born on February 2, 1947, in Corpus Christi, Texas. She attended Catholic school until the sixth grade, after which she went to public school at W. B. Ray High School. She then enrolled at the University of Texas in Austin, where she planned to study microbiology, but later changed her major to art. In college, she began modeling for newspaper advertisements and art classes. When she was voted one of the ten most beautiful women on campus, a publicist contacted her and suggested that she pursue a career in entertainment. At the end of her junior year, Fawcett went to Hollywood, landed an agent, and met actor Lee Majors, who helped jumpstart her acting career. They married in 1973 but divorced in 1982.

During the 1960s, Fawcett guest starred on a number of popular television shows, while maintaining a lucrative career on the side as a model. She appeared in top magazines and on commercials for Noxzema shaving cream, Ultra-Brite toothpaste, and Wella Balsam shampoo. In 1969 she saw her screen debut in the French film *Love Is a Funny Thing,* and in the early 1970s she began to find work in television movies. Her big break came in 1976, when she was cast as one of three attractive female private eyes, who work for a mysterious, wealthy man, in *Charlie's Angels.* Playing the athletic Jill Munroe, Fawcett's character was known for her sense of humor and card skills. Kate Jackson was cast as the intelligent Sabrina Duncan, while Jaclyn Smith provided street smarts as Kelly Garrett.

Charlie's Angels became the top-rated show of the 1976-77 season, thanks to its appeal to both men and women. Men enjoyed watching the women clad in scanty costumes as they went undercover as prostitutes or go-go dancers, and they relished the melodramatic situations that found the trio tied up by ne'er-do-wells. However, women also enjoyed the program, finding a feminist slant amid the eroticism because the program broke ground as a prime-time action-adventure program that featured the women in a variety of daring situations. Women viewers appreciated the Angels' courage, quick thinking, and resourcefulness—they were quick draws and could hold their own in a fight—in addition to their stylish sensuality.

Fawcett quickly emerged as the most popular of the three stars. Her wholesome likeness spawned a cottage industry of merchandise, including one of the defining pieces of 1970s popular culture: the famous Farrah Fawcett poster. An estimated six million of these pictures were eventually sold, and Farrah's image also landed on T-shirts, lunch boxes, and more. Salons nationwide turned out scores of women with the curled-back, mussed-up coiffure, and teenage boys everywhere tacked the picture to their bedroom walls. With her career at its peak, Fawcett left *Charlie's Angels* after the first season to pursue more serious drama.

Farrah initially found it hard to break away from her *Charlie's Angels* image and at first her foray into serious acting met with little luck. Finally, in 1981, Fawcett landed a role in the comedy *Cannonball Run,* starring Burt Reynolds, and also that year starred in the made-for-television movie, *Murder in Texas.* Fawcett subsequently found her niche in made-for-TV movies, particularly those based on true stories, and was highly acclaimed for her role in the 1984 television movie, *The Burning Bed*, an emotional tale of domestic abuse. Her acting in *Extremities,* a dramatic film about a woman who is attacked by a rapist in her own house, was also highly praised. Fawcett made news again in 1995 after posing for nude pictures in *Playboy* magazine and a video. Two years later, the media focused positive attention on her acting again for her role in *The Apostle* (1977).

Fawcett began a long-term relationship with actor Ryan O'Neal in the early 1980s and has a son, Redmond O'Neal, with him, but the couple broke up in 1997. Fawcett later began dating producer James Orr, who was convicted of assaulting her in 1998 in a highly publicized scandal, that was played up in the tabloids. Though Fawcett has never been one of Hollywood's top leading actresses, and has enjoyed only a sporadic television career, she made a lasting imprint on the style of the 1970s during her heyday and is still regaled on a number of fan web sites by nostalgia buffs and longstanding fans.

—Geri Speace

FURTHER READING:

Mortiz, Charles, editor. *Current Biography Yearbook.* New York, H.W. Wilson, 1978.

Fawlty Towers

Fawlty Towers was a British television comedy starring John Cleese as hotel proprietor Basil Fawlty. Cleese, one of the original members of *Monty Python's Flying Circus,* returned to television as the writer and star of *Fawlty Towers.* Although only twelve episodes were produced (six in 1975, six in 1979), it remains one of the most widely syndicated comedy series in television history, and continues in regular syndication on public television stations throughout the United States to this day. Much as *All in the Family* broke ground by portraying a flawed family, *Fawlty Towers* took the premise to its comedic extreme. Fawlty and his wife constantly argued, insulted each others' intelligence, and generally made each other miserable. Their pointed barbs and insults marked a new high (or low) in television dialogue. *Fawlty Towers* proved critically, if not commercially, successful. The series garnered two British Association of Film and Theatre Actors awards for Best Comedy Series and Cleese received an award from The Royal Television Society for his writing and acting.

—Geoff Peterson

FURTHER READING:

Cleese, John, and Connie Booth. *The Complete Fawlty Towers.* London, Methuen, 1988; New York, Pantheon, 1989.

Margolis, Jonathan. *Cleese Encounters.* New York, St. Martin's, 1992.

FBI (Federal Bureau of Investigation)

The Federal Bureau of Investigation is housed under the Department of Justice with field offices throughout the country. Its agents are responsible for federal cases as diverse as white collar crime, serial killing, and espionage. Attorney General Charles Bonaparte and President Theodore Roosevelt established the forerunner of the FBI in 1908 with the designation of Special Agents assigned to the Department of Justice. Their desire to create a bureau of agents to strengthen the Federal Government's crime fighting capabilities grew out of the early nineteenth-century Progressive era's desire for reform. The Department of Justice's agents later formed the Bureau of Investigation, the United States Bureau of Investigation, and finally, in 1935, the Federal Bureau of Investigation. The American public calls the agency simply by its initials or as the Bureau.

Known individually as the dashing secret agent saving America from communism or as the mysterious man in black, FBI agents have enjoyed a leading role in American popular culture almost since the Bureau's inception. Radio shows, movies, novels, magazines, and television shows have all featured the FBI agent and his adventures. The American public called both real life and fictional FBI agents ''G-men.'' The FBI's public popularity demonstrates the American public's fascination with crime and punishment as moral drama between good and evil. As scholar Richard Gid Powers notes, ''a formula adapts the universal myth to the national experience so that national history might be understood as an instance of the eternal struggle between good and evil.'' The FBI and its agents became potent forces in this eternal struggle as it played out in American popular culture.

The FBI gained power and popular notoriety during the gangster era of the 1920s and 1930s. This era was characterized by a general sense of lawlessness accompanying the Constitutional Amendment prohibiting the use of alcohol as well as the despair and fear brought about by the 1929 stock market crash and the Great Depression. Organized crime became increasingly visible because of its involvement in the production and distribution of illegal alcohol. Americans felt that they were witnessing illegal activity with increasing frequency and that criminals were lurking on every corner. The famous kidnapping and murder of Charles Lindbergh's infant son and the crimes of the legendary gangster Al Capone captured Americans' imaginations and they demanded revenge. Powers explained that the American public feared that this seeming crime explosion was undermining the country's moral base. These developments led to a desire for a strong national crime fighting presence both in reality and in popular culture. People also sought escape from the troubling times through popular entertainment. Popular culture anointed the FBI as the nation's solution to the problem of the mythical public enemy. Gangsters and their FBI pursuers quickly found their way into movies, detective fiction, magazines, and radio shows. Popular culture helped the FBI agent become a beacon of hope that American values would survive the crime wave and the economic despair of the nation.

No figure has been more closely associated with the popular image of the FBI as national defense against crime than J. Edgar Hoover, the Bureau's most infamous leader. President Calvin Coolidge selected Hoover as the young Bureau's next head in 1924. Hoover quickly gave the Bureau a more professional image and greater strength by firing unqualified agents and establishing formal

A kidnapping victim's body is carried away by FBI agents after being discovered in a shallow grave in St. Joseph, Missouri, 1953.

training for all agents at the newly created National Academy in Quantico, Virginia. He also oversaw the creation of the FBI's Technical Laboratory and the establishment of a nationally centralized fingerprint database to aid in tracking criminals. Hoover was not only a great leader, he was also a great publicity agent who carefully presided over the growing public popularity of both himself and his organization. In his day, Hoover was a dominant presence that the government, his agents, and the public both feared and admired. Though Hoover and his G-Men set the early standard for the quintessential FBI agent, Hoover's image did not survive his death in 1972 and a subsequent public reevaluation of his methods. He became widely associated with the negative image of government as "Big Brother," spying on the average citizen and maintaining secret files. He also gained much notoriety with his widely rumored penchant for cross-dressing. Hoover's legacy also became entwined with the increasingly negative American popular images of government that began in the late 1950s and 1960s.

The middle decades of the twentieth century witnessed a growing public distrust of government and its official representatives for a number of reasons. The FBI was not immune to this image problem. Some of the government's most notorious actions involved the witchhunts for suspected communists that dominated the World War I, World War II, and Cold War periods. The FBI assisted Attorney General A. Mitchell Palmer during World War I in the quest to expose American communists and communist sympathizers. The FBI then gained its own power to investigate subversives during World War II. When Senator Joseph McCarthy and the House Un-American Activities Committee went too far in the minds of most Americans, all government officials involved in the hunt for communists were caught in the scandal. The FBI's role in detecting subversion, sabotage, and espionage had at first enhanced its image as protector of the American way of life but ultimately led to a more negative image of the FBI as "Big Brother." During the 1960s, the FBI's image suffered again. Many Americans found the FBI's overall treatment of minorities and those people the Bureau labeled as subversives to be questionable at best. Many citizens felt that the FBI unjustly persecuted anti-establishment groups such as anti-Vietnam War demonstrators, radical students, and minority activists. The FBI was also involved in such controversial 1960s civil rights investigations as the Mississippi murders of three civil rights workers later immortalized in the movie *Mississippi Burning*. The culmination of the growing popular cynicism toward government and authority, however, is widely regarded as the 1970s Watergate scandal that brought down the Presidency of Richard Nixon.

The FBI also garnered a negative image by figuring prominently in a number of conspiracy theories that captured the American imagination. Perhaps the most famous of these theories have revolved around the 1963 assassination of President John F. Kennedy. Much controversy surrounded the official Warren Commission's report of the events responsible for Kennedy's death and the naming of Lee Harvey Oswald as the sole killer. Oliver Stone offered one of the most famous treatments of these conspiracy theories in his movie *JFK*. Conspiracy theories have also circulated widely on the question of whether UFOs existed and whether the government was responsible for covering up any such knowledge. Many rumors centered on the alleged crash of one such UFO at Roswell, New Mexico. The popularity of the 1990s television show *The X-Files* proved that the popularity of these theories of alien contact continued to thrive into the late twentieth century. The show portrayed two FBI agents assigned to investigate unexplained X-File cases of possible paranormal and extraterrestrial activity as well as government conspiracies to conceal the truth. Lingering questions over FBI involvement in hampering the search for truth in matters such as what really happened to John F. Kennedy and are we alone in the universe continued to hurt the Bureau's credibility.

The latter decades of the twentieth century witnessed a revival of the get-tough-on-crime stance that first made the FBI popular in the 1920s and 1930s. The largely positive response from the American public to this stance was due to an alarming growth of terrorist incidents, the illegal drug trade, and white collar crime. Infamous serial killers such as Ted Bundy and Jeffrey Dahmer also instilled fear into the American public. But crime fighting techniques were developed to combat these threats. The FBI behavioral sciences unit pioneered the technique of profiling violent and serial offenders as DNA technology greatly aided the fight against crime. The television show *America's Most Wanted* as well as the Bureau's Ten Most Wanted lists involved the public in the FBI's manhunts.

Despite the events that recaptured the "tough guy" image of the FBI, other incidents challenged the public's views of the Bureau's policies. The 1992 death of a U. S. Marshall led to a standoff at Ruby Ridge, Idaho, between the FBI and fugitive Randall Weaver during which Weaver's wife was accidentally killed by a sniper's bullet. The Branch Davidians led by David Koresh isolated themselves in their compound near Waco, Texas, leading to another FBI siege in 1993. This siege later ended amid much controversy when some cult members deliberately set fire to their compound rather than surrender. The negative publicity garnered by these events and led to governmental inquiries into the FBI's conduct. They also quickly became made for television movies. While the FBI's role has always centered on the mythical struggle between the forces of good and evil, the FBI's changing image shows that it is often difficult to distinguish between these seemingly diametrically opposite forces.

—Marcella Bush Treviño

FURTHER READING:

Breuer, William B. *J. Edgar Hoover and His G-Men.* Westport, Praeger, 1995.

Cook, Fred J. *The FBI Nobody Knows.* New York, Macmillan, 1964.

North, Mark. *Act of Treason: The Role of J. Edgar Hoover in the Assassination of President Kennedy.* New York, Carroll and Graf, 1991.

Potter, Claire Bond. *War on Crime: Bandits, G-Men, and the Politics of Mass Culture.* New Brunswick, Rutgers University Press, 1998.

Powers, Richard Gid. *G-Men: Hoover's FBI in American Popular Culture.* Carbondale, Southern Illinois University Press, 1983.

Sullivan, William C., with Bill Brown. *The Bureau: My Thirty Years in Hoover's FBI.* New York, Norton, 1979.

Turner, William W. *Hoover's FBI: The Men and the Myth.* New York, Dell, 1971.

Feliciano, José (1945—)

José Feliciano is one of the most passionate balladeers and guitar virtuosos on the popular music scene. Because of his bilingual abilities, Feliciano has achieved popularity throughout the Americas where his English and Spanish language albums have often topped the charts. His 1968 *Feliciano!* is today considered a classic as is his number one hit single "Light My Fire."

Born the second of twelve children on September 10, 1945, in Puerto Rico, Feliciano was raised on the Lower East Side of New York City. Feliciano was born blind from congenital glaucoma, but nevertheless was a musical prodigy who by age six was playing instruments. Today, he is known to perform credibly not only on his

José Feliciano

favorite, the guitar, but also on the bass, banjo, organ, mandolin, harmonica, piano, harpsichord, and several Afro-Caribbean percussion instruments. Because of his exposure to both Latin and American pop musical traditions, Feliciano developed an eclectic taste and style, and has been able to master folk, flamenco, salsa, rock guitar, and vocals. His folk-rock performances got him onto stages at the beginning of his career during his teens, in Greenwich Village cafes. At age 17, Feliciano dropped out of high school to become a professional musician, with his first road show booked at the Retort Coffee House in Detroit in 1963. He soon signed a recording contract with RCA Victor and became a frequent performer at coffees houses and night clubs around the country and in San Juan, Puerto Rico resort hotels.

Feliciano's first album, *The Voice and Guitar of José Feliciano*, appeared and went unnoticed in 1964, and both he and RCA experimented for the next few years in finding an appropriate niche for the eclectic singer and musician. In those years, the greatest success came with Feliciano's Spanish language recordings and his Latin American tours; in 1966, for instance, his concert in Buenos Aires drew an audience of 100,000. Finally in 1968, his album *Feliciano!*, which included the Doors' "Light My Fire," achieved mainstream success. "Light My Fire" became the third most popular single that year and *Feliciano!* reached number two on the album charts. To top this, Feliciano won Grammy awards for Best New Artist of 1968 and Best Contemporary Male Pop Vocal Performance for "Light My Fire."

After 1968, Feliciano has continued as a standard and recognized artist in both American and Latin pop music, but has never again achieved the popularity or success in the United States that he had that stellar year. One tune, however, has made Feliciano a seasonal staple—his bilingual classic "Feliz Navidad (I Wanna Wish You a Merry Christmas)." Feliciano has, however, remained enormously popular internationally, especially in Latin America and Europe. He has earned 40 international gold and platinum records and won Grammy awards for best Latin pop performance in 1983, 1986, 1989, and 1990.

In the mid-1970s, Feliciano left RCA and went on to record with a number of other houses. At times, his relationships with the studios have been rocky because the performer insists on his unique style and on "doing it my way." Feliciano's way has pioneered a place for intercultural musicians and opened up a new space for Hispanics in American pop culture.

—Nicolás Kanellos

FURTHER READING:

Rees, Dafydd, and Luke Crampton. *Rock Movers and Shakers*. Santa Barbara, ABC-CLIO, 1991.

Rubiner, Julia M., editor. *Contemporary Musicians*. Detroit, Gale Research Inc., 1994.

Tardiff, Joseph T., and L. Mpho Mabunda, editors. *Dictionary of Hispanic Biography*. Detroit, Gale, 1996.

Felix the Cat

The creation of Otto Messmer (1892-1983) and Pat Sullivan (1885-1933), Felix the Cat first appeared as an animated cartoon character (under another name) in 1919 in *Feline Follies*. Felix had a lively personality, an expressive manner, and solved problems in a creative fashion. For this later facet of Felix's personality his creators took full advantage of the animation medium and metamorphosed body parts into useful tools. The first major funny animal character to star in a series of animated cartoons, Felix appeared in some 150 shorts in the 1920s before the introduction of new sound technology saw his popularity wane. Meantime, however, King Features had commenced a Felix the Cat comic strip in 1923 and his trademark likeness had been licensed to many products.

Not only was Felix the first star of animation, he was also the product of a particular business arrangement that would become commonplace in animation studios. Messmer and Sullivan were the creative force behind the character. Messmer, a talented artist, took creative control of the movies and Sullivan, a lesser artist but a driven entrepreneur, arranged distribution and licensing. Sullivan retained all rights for the character and for many years his was the only name publicly associated with Felix. Messmer remained an employee.

Messmer, the son of German immigrants, was born just across the river from New York in Union City. Before joining Sullivan he worked variously as a scene painter, cartoonist, and as an animator for Henry "Hy" Mayer. Sullivan, of Irish heritage, was born in a tough working class neighborhood of Sydney, Australia. After some limited success as a cartoonist, during which time he shortened his name from O'Sullivan, he departed Australia for London in 1907. By 1909 he was in New York where in 1911 he found work as an assistant to William F. Marriner on his comic strip *Sambo and His Funny Noises*. Felix would later demonstrate some of Sambo's trickster qualities.

When Messmer and Sullivan joined forces in 1916, the worldly Sullivan had established his own animation studio releasing Sammy Johnsin animated shorts based on the Sambo strip, but renamed to avoid litigation. Sullivan's studio, however, was put on hold in 1917 when he was convicted of rape and sentenced to two years in Sing Sing. Messmer went back to work for Mayer before being drafted. The two met up again in 1919 on Messmer's return from the First World War and Sullivan's release from jail. They collaborated on the aforementioned *Feline Follies,* which helped re-establish the Sullivan studio.

The 1920s were Felix's decade. Sullivan shopped his character around film distributors. Historian John Canemaker has estimated that some 30 Felix shorts were released through Famous Players - Lasky from 1919-1921. In 1922, finding himself without a distributor, but with the ownership of an established character, Sullivan struck a deal with distributor Margaret J. Winkler and from 1922 to early 1925 her company distributed 50 Felix animations. In these years Bill Nolan influenced Messmer to soften Felix's features and a rounder Felix became the cartoon norm.

In 1925 Sullivan broke his ties with Winkler and signed a new distribution contract with Educational Films. Winkler turned to a young Walt Disney who had already turned out a Felix clone named Julius in a series distributed by Winkler. Disney's new character, Oswald the Lucky Rabbit, had many similarities to Felix. In 1928 Disney lost control of Oswald to Winkler and had to create a new character: Mickey Mouse.

Meanwhile, Felix had been licensed extensively to doll, toy, and pencil manufacturers, as well as cigarette companies. He was also the subject of popular songs and generated income for Sullivan from sheet music sales. The comic strip, which according to Canemaker was not widely popular, nonetheless appeared from coast to coast in the papers of William Randolph Hearst. Felix was also extremely popular in the United Kingdom and Sullivan's native Australia. In 1928 Felix was at the height of his fame. So ubiquitous was his fame and appearance that NBC used a Felix doll to test television cameras and transmission. In the strong visual presence of Felix lay the seeds of his downfall.

Disney's debut of Mickey Mouse in the sound film *Steamboat Willie* introduced a new dimension to animated shorts. Felix embodied the perfect characteristics for silent animation. To meet the challenges of sound he had to change, and the change undermined his character. Moreover, whereas Disney carefully pre-planned his animation to fit music and sound effects, the Sullivan studio, when it eventually introduced sound, did so as a post animation process. Inevitably the Disney product was superior.

By 1930 Felix had faded from the screen. Sullivan died in early 1933 from the effects of alcoholism. His heirs and lawyer briefly revived Felix in film in 1936, but the lackluster efforts were short lived. Felix lived on in a weekly and daily comic strips which ran to 1943 and 1967 respectively. He also appeared monthly in a Dell comic book. In 1959 Joe Oriolo revived Felix in a series of cartoons for television. Oriolo resurrected Felix again in another television series in 1982. Retrospectives of early Felix shorts were held at the Whitney Museum of American Art and at the Museum of Modern Art in 1977. In the late 1980s, Felix cropped up in a number of licensed merchandise ventures.

Felix is an icon of twentieth-century American popular culture. That he was created by an Irish-Australian and a German-American and was popular world-wide reminds us of the transnational character of popular culture in the twentieth century.

—Ian Gordon

FURTHER READING:

Canemaker, John. *Felix: The Twisted Tale of the World's Most Famous Cat.* New York, Pantheon, 1991.

Fellini, Federico (1920-1993)

Italian film director Federico Fellini helped bring the cinema to a mature state of expressive quality, introducing an eye-opening kaleidoscope of psychological symbolism and sometimes bawdy imagery to popular audiences and art-house denizens alike. Beginning in film as a screenwriter for famed filmmaker Roberto Rossellini, Fellini came into his own directing a number of masterpieces in the 1950s which expanded upon the natural, visually stark style of Italian Neorealism pioneered by Rossellini. Most notable of these were *La Strada* and *Nights of Cabiria,* both of which boasted emotionally rich performances by Fellini's wife, the gamin-faced Giulietta Massina. However, it was during the 1960s that Fellini reached the height of his international stature with films such as *La Dolce Vita, 8 ½,* and *Juliet of the Spirits,* wherein Fellini evinced a circus-like, sometimes surreal, and always highly personal vision of the world that could only be achieved through the cinema. Fellini continued directing films until his death in the early 1990s, consistently creating worlds so unique that the word "Felliniesque" found its way into the popular vocabulary.

—Shaun Frentner

FURTHER READING:

Baxter, John. *Fellini.* London, Fourth Estate, 1993.

Bondanella, Peter. *The Cinema of Federico Fellini.* Princeton, Princeton University Press, 1992.

Fellini, Federico. *Fellini on Fellini.* London, Faber and Faber, 1995.

Feminism

Feminism, the ideology that supports uplifting the status and improving the rights of women, has been one of the most influential political ideas of the nineteenth and twentieth centuries. Since its inception, it has been both hailed as a profound liberation of society, and condemned as a philosophy of victimhood, responsible for the breakdown of the nuclear family and the degradation of society in general. There is no doubt, however, that the work of feminist activists and reformers has been responsible for enormous improvements in the position of women in the United States over the past 200 years. Equally indisputably, a glance at the power structure of most of the world's governments and businesses shows that male dominance is still very much a reality. In spite of this, feminism has changed the American social order, from the superficial, such as media portrayals of women, to the deepest underlying assumptions of science and religion.

Throughout Europe and the United States, the eighteenth and nineteenth centuries were a time of sweeping ideological changes. A new humanism was developing, with a focus on the "rights of man." The principles of both the American and French revolutions of the late 1700s and the publication of the Communist Manifesto in 1848 were examples of this new atmosphere of brotherhood and justice. As white males were discovering and outlining their inalienable rights, women were still largely trapped within a patriarchal family system, kept there by economic necessity and rigid social convention. Basically considered the property of husband or father, women were not permitted to vote, own property, operate businesses, attend colleges, or make legal decisions concerning their children or themselves. Politically aware women had already began the work to change these conditions, such as Abigail Adams and Mercy Otis, who unsuccessfully lobbied the authors of the United States Constitution to include women's rights in their plan for the new country, and Britain's Mary Wollstonecraft, who published the landmark *Vindication of the Rights of Women* in 1792.

By the early 1800s, many progressive men and women began to join the abolitionist movement to work for the end of slavery. One liberation ideology led naturally to another, and a number of abolitionist women drew parallels between the slavery they fought and the plight of women. "The investigation of the rights of the slave has led me to a better understanding of my own," wrote anti-slavery activist Angelina Grimke in 1836. This growing understanding of the condition of women led to the first Women's Rights Convention in Seneca Falls, New York, in 1848. Organized by abolitionists Elizabeth Cady Stanton and Lucretia Mott, the convention drew dozens of women and a number of supportive men as well. Together, convention participants drew up the Declaration of Sentiments, outlining both the rights of women and a set of demands, such as equality in law, education, and wages and the right to vote.

By the 1860s, the fight for women's rights led to a split in the abolition movement. Some anti-slavery activists felt that women

A feminist protest of the Miss America Pageant 1968.

should step back and focus on the fight against slavery, even if that meant prioritizing the rights of black men, while others felt that changes in the status of slaves and changes in the status of women must go hand in hand. Foreshadowing a recurrent issue in the struggle for women's rights, men's role in the women's movement also became controversial. In 1867, as the 15th Amendment to the Constitution was giving the vote to black men, the abolitionist movement divided. The National Women's Suffrage Association, led by Stanton and Susan Brownell Anthony, was an all-women's organization which opposed the 15th Amendment. The American Women's Suffrage Association, led by Lucy Stone and Julia Ward Howe, supported legalization of black male suffrage and included men in its membership.

By the 1890s however, both factions reunited to push for the still-elusive women's suffrage. Women's clubs began to form to foster discussions about politics, culture, and education. In 1896, The National Association of Colored Women formed, uniting the separate black women's clubs. Other important women's organizations were the temperance societies. Often mocked as prim and puritanical, the temperance societies were in reality an attempt to protect women and children from the abuse and poverty that were often a result of male drunkenness. Toward the end of the suffrage battle, the word "feminism" first came into use. The feminists differed from the suffragists

by claiming to work for a broader liberation of the social order than would be achieved simply by attaining the vote.

Gradually, some states began to grant the vote to women in local elections. In 1917, Jeannette Rankin of Montana became the first woman elected to the U.S. Congress, and in 1920, women finally won the vote. Within two years of the ratification of the 19th Amendment to the Constitution, the National Women's Party proposed an Equal Rights Amendment, which was defeated.

Both before and after suffrage was attained, feminist activists continued to work on gaining a measure of control over their lives, bodies, and property. Gradually they chipped away at the laws that put women in the power of men, and women won the right to own property, attend college, and many of the other rights they had demanded at the Seneca Falls convention. Because childbirth and the work of raising children has affected women's lives so deeply, birth control and abortion have always been central issues in any feminist movement. The American Birth Control League, organized by Margaret Sanger in 1921, was one of the earliest attempts to make family planning available to U.S. women.

The "Roaring Twenties" was a decade of new independence for women. Once women were able to vote and obtain birth control, even fashion followed suit, as Coco Chanel and other modern designers discarded the painful, restrictive corsets women had once laced around themselves. The new fashions emphasized freedom and even androgyny, as women cut off long, time-consuming tresses and sported the free and easy bobs that symbolized the era. With the approach of the depression of the 1930s, the feminist movement subsided into quiescence for several years. Though women were given unprecedented opportunities to work in male dominated industries during World War II, when the war ended, they were unceremoniously sent back home. The 1950s was a paradoxical decade, conventional and conformist on the exterior, and seething underneath with repressed rebellion. In the upper and middle classes, more women than ever before were attending college, where they developed intellectual comradeships and learned to take themselves seriously before being isolated and often ignored raising families in suburban homes. In the working class, women were frequently stuck in repetitive dead-end jobs, which generally paid them around 50 cents for every dollar earned by the men working next to them. Within all these women the knowledge began to slowly awaken that something was not working in their lives.

The dilemma of the middle class woman was articulated powerfully in a pivotal book published in 1963. *The Feminine Mystique* by Betty Friedan marked the official beginning of the "second wave" of U.S. feminism. Describing the stultifying life of women in American suburbs, Friedan captured the deep longing within girls and women for "something more" than their prescribed roles as cheerleaders and helpmates for men and caretakers for children. It was a message women had been waiting to hear, and around the country they began to discuss an innovative concept: women's liberation.

Just as nineteenth century feminism had been a part of a larger social liberation movement, the second wave of feminism was fired by the same energy that fueled the civil rights movement, the anti-war movement, and the gay and lesbian liberation movement. In the same way that the female abolitionists had been inspired by the fight against slavery to fight for their own rights, women in the civil rights and other movements began to feel empowered to challenge their own second-class citizenship, not only in the larger world but even among their male colleagues within the movement.

Following the passage of Title VII of the Civil Rights Act of 1964, prohibiting discrimination based on sex, race, religion, or national origin, government agencies began to document cases of sex discrimination. Even women themselves were appalled to see the evidence of so much blatant discrimination. They began to gather in "consciousness raising" groups to discuss their own experiences. Women's isolation was beginning to break down, and the competition and mistrust that had been fostered among women by patriarchal society, began to be replaced by communication and alliance. Though the National Organization for Women (NOW) was formed by Friedan and others in 1966, it was the solidarity created by the consciousness raising groups that was the heart of the new movement. Though threatened males of every political stripe ridiculed the personal and revelatory nature of the groups, the feminists responded by saying "the personal is political." The phrase became the very basis of women's liberation, meaning that each individual life has political meaning and each personal action requires responsibility.

By the early 1970s, NOW had over 400 chapters around the country, working to change the laws that oppressed women and to raise women's consciousness about their own potential. In 1972, Title IX of the Education Amendments prohibited sex discrimination in all education programs receiving federal funds, an act that promised to revolutionize women's education. In 1973, the landmark *Roe v. Wade* decision in the Supreme Court made legal abortions available to

women throughout the United States, ending decades of dangerous and traumatic illegal abortions and unwanted childbirths.

The ideas and energy of women's liberation spread around the country, touching women from the university towns to the suburbs and from the PTA to the factory floor. Feminists began to create a "woman's culture" where women could gather to discuss and disseminate the new ideas. Women's bookstores, coffeehouses, journals, publishing houses, and community centers were energized by the new spirit of sisterhood. Women's Studies courses were introduced at colleges and universities to focus on women's history and perspectives. Feminist health care workers created women's clinics to prioritize issues of women's health. Women, who had been encouraged to view their bodies as inferior and even slightly disgusting, attended classes where they learned to appreciate and understand their bodies. Feminist psychotherapists developed feminist therapy that included an analysis of women's oppression. Rape crisis centers opened to publicize and fight violence against women. From family to language to religion, no nook or cranny of modern society or history escaped the feminist critique as feminists sought to reinterpret a male-defined world from a women's perspective.

The media also responded to the new movement, at first with ridicule, then with more serious analysis. In 1972, the premier issue of *Ms.*, the first national feminist magazine, appeared on newsstands. Even on television, that most conservative organ of the status quo, independent women began to spring up on sitcoms and dramas of the 1970s. Mary Richards, solid, sensible heroine of *The Mary Tyler Moore Show* (1970-1977) was a single career woman, who had real friendships with her more flighty woman friends, not just double dates or competitions over boyfriends. Maude Findlay, outspoken, bitchy, and unashamedly middle-aged, appeared first on *All in the Family* (then was given her own spinoff *Maude* (1972-1978) as audiences responded enthusiastically to the non-stereotypical portrait of a wife and mother. Though it did not debut until 1982, *Cagney and Lacey* was also part of the wave of feminist television. The show, an innovative police drama, paired tough-talking, hard-drinking single girl Chris Cagney with down-to-earth happily married mama Marybeth Lacey. Neither silly nor superhuman, Cagney and Lacey brought a sympathy and compassion to the police show that drew audiences for six years.

Though the feminist ideal of sisterhood was exhilarating, it was also flawed. Lesbians, who were naturally drawn to a movement that empowered women, had been among the first activists of women's liberation, but straight women immediately sought to disassociate them from the movement. Calling the issue the "lavender menace," many heterosexual feminists were uncomfortable with the idea of lesbianism and feared that inclusion of gay women would discredit the movement. Lesbians fought for recognition of their place within the women's movement, but many were hurt by the movement's denial of them, and remained mistrustful. Some even withdrew from feminism, calling themselves lesbian separatists, and began focusing on lesbian issues only.

Women of color and working-class women also had to fight for their place in the women's liberation movement of the 1970s. Though the intellectual ideology of the movement had been developed in universities among largely white, middle-class academia and suburban housewives, working-class women and women of color often had the largest stake in the feminist cause. Issues of pay and advancement at work, abortion and birth control within the body, and abuse at home were often survival issues for working-class women. Though many working-class women and women of color were active in the movement, white feminists often had to be compelled to confront their own racism and classism, and many did little to fight the media stereotype of feminism as a white, middle-class movement.

The 1980s saw a sharp backlash to the advances made by women in the 1970s. While most people, even feminism's enemies, professed to believe in "equal pay for equal work," many were threatened by the deeper societal changes suggested by feminist analysis. Using the age-old weapons of ridicule and threat, anti-feminist writers and pundits announced that women had achieved equality and no longer needed to be liberated. (This cheery mythology has continued through the 1990s, even in the face of the fact that in 1998, women still earned only 76 cents for every dollar earned by men.) In the 1980s feminism's critics threatened women by describing a world where women had unprecedented equality in the work place, but were frustrated, unhappy, and unfulfilled in their personal lives. Conservative religious leaders assured women that their place in the home was divinely ordained. Popular feminist novels of the 1970s like Erica Jong's *Fear of Flying* (1973) and Marilyn French's *The Women's Room* (1977) were replaced in the 1980s by grim tales of the price of independence, like Gail Parent's *A Sign of the Eighties* (1987) and Freda Bright's *Singular Women*. In film too, *Kramer vs. Kramer* (1979) won an Oscar for punishing a confused mother who leaves her child with his father so that she can explore her own identity.

The 1990s have left the most virulent phase of the backlash behind, merely using the phrase "post-feminist" to describe the lack of need for a women's liberation movement. Though in a *Time*/CNN poll in 1998, over 50 percent of women, aged 18 to 34, said they had "feminist values," there is little public support for calling oneself a feminist. Young women of the 1990s have developed a feisty culture of "grrl power" that promises to support strength in a new generation of women, but the anti-feminist media has succeeded in turning the word "feminist" into a pejorative for many people.

Feminist activists still proudly claim the title however, and many still work for change in the status of women independently or in local or national groups. Many of the old issues remain: women are still paid less than men for identical or comparable work, and advance less quickly and less far on the job; sexual harassment, domestic violence, and rape continue unabated; childcare remains prohibitively expensive and stigmatized as the choice of selfish mothers. Even causes that were once won, such as abortion rights and welfare rights for single mothers, have returned to be fought for again as conservative forces gain power.

However, though feminism has not totally succeeded in achieving economic and political equality for women, the various feminist movements have dramatically improved women's position in American society. The feminist critique has challenged patriarchal interpretations of history and science and brought the light of public discussion to issues of women's lives once considered matters of personal decision for husbands and fathers. Feminism has embraced the question of children's rights, the politics of the family, and internationalism. Like the abolitionist/suffragists of the nineteenth century, feminists approaching the twenty-first century seek to unite the struggles of the helpless and disenfranchised.

—Tina Gianoulis

FURTHER READING:

Berg, Barbara J. *The Women's Movement Today: A Hot Issue.* Springfield, New Jersey, Enslow Publishers, 1999.

Berkeley, Kathleen C. *The Women's Liberation Movement in America.* Westport, Connecticut, Greenwood Press, 1999.

Collins, Patricia Hill. *Black Feminist Thought: Knowledge, Consciousness, and the Politics of Empowerment.* New York, Routledge, 1999.

Faludi, Susan. *Backlash: The Undeclared War Against American Women.* New York, Doubleday, 1991.

Marilley, Suzanne M. *Woman Suffrage and the Origins of Liberal Feminism in the United States, 1820-1920.* Cambridge, Massachusetts, Harvard University Press, 1996.

Yeo, Eileen Janes, editor. *Mary Wollstonecraft, and 200 Years of Feminism.* London, New York, Rivers Oram Press, 1997.

Fenway Park

Together with Chicago's Wrigley Field and New York's Yankee Stadium, Boston's Fenway Park is one of the archetypal American baseball facilities. Called "a lyric little bandbox" by no less an eminence than John Updike, the park's idiosyncratic design is as legendary among baseball aficionados as is the futility endured by its home team, the Boston Red Sox. Together, team and park have suffered all manner of near-miss and could-have-been finishes since the stadium's triumphal opening in 1912.

The ballpark derived its name from the Fenway Realty Company, the business that owned the plot of marshland on which the ballpark was constructed. The Osborne Engineering Company of Cleveland designed the concrete and steel structure, which was modeled in part on Philadelphia's Shibe Park. The famous wall in left field, known popularly as the "Green Monster," was not part of the original ballpark. Fenway's asymmetrical configuration was largely a function of location, nestled as it was just across the Massachusetts Turnpike from bustling Kenmore Square.

Fenway Park opened on April 20, 1912. The sinking of the Titanic was still front-page news in the *Boston Globe* that morning as the Red Sox prepared to play the New York Highlanders before a crowd of twenty-four thousand. Boston Mayor John F. "Honey Fitz" Fitzgerald threw out the ceremonial first pitch, and the hometown club went on to win 7-6 on an extra-inning single by Tris Speaker. The Highlanders, later rechristened the Yankees, were to remain integrally intertwined with the ballpark's history over the ensuing decades.

At first, the new park seemed to be a good-luck charm for the Red Sox. The team won the American League pennant in 1912, as Fenway played host to its first World Series in October. Fred Snodgrass's error in the tenth inning of the deciding game gave the series to the Sox, four games to three, over the New York Giants. But what seemed like an auspicious beginning to the Fenway Era was actually the start of one of the longest championship droughts in baseball history.

Fenway Park took a major step forward in its evolution in 1934, when the original wall in left field was leveled and a thirty-seven-foot-high metal fence was installed. Initially covered with advertising signs, in 1947 the wall was painted green. The Green Monster would go on to become one of the most distinctive features of any American ballpark. Officially listed as 315 feet from home plate (though some aerial photographs have indicated that 300 feet is more likely), the Green Monster continues to bedevil American League left fielders while providing an all-too-tempting target for right-handed power hitters looking to pull a ball out of the park.

One such power hitter was New York Yankee Bucky Dent, a diminutive shortstop who clouted one of the signature home runs in Fenway Park's history on October 2, 1978. The towering pop fly off Red Sox pitcher Mike Torrez landed on the screen above the Green Monster and helped the Yankees capture the American League East Division championship in a one-game playoff. Dent's blast was just one in a long line of tragic moments for the Red Sox's long-suffering fans, who have watched their beloved team fail time and time again in their quest to capture the franchise's first World Series title since 1918.

The Red Sox returned to the World Series in 1946 and again in 1967 but were turned away in seven games on both occasions. They took the Cincinnati Reds to seven thrilling games in 1975 in one of the greatest championship sets ever played. That series saw Fenway play host to one of the most dramatic games in baseball history, the sixth game in which Boston catcher Carlton Fisk clouted a twelfth-inning, game-winning home run just inside the left field foul pole. True to form, the Red Sox proceeded to lose the decisive game in heartbreaking fashion.

As the twentieth century draws to a close, Fenway Park remains one of Major League Baseball's oldest, smallest, and most revered ballparks. Besides the Green Monster, its distinctive features include one of the last remaining hand-operated scoreboards (the initials of the club's late owner, Thomas A. Yawkey, and his wife, Jean R. Yawkey, are inscribed vertically in Morse code on the face of the scoreboard) in the majors. In typically eccentric Fenway fashion, only the American League scores are recorded.

Despite its aesthetic and historic value, the park faces an uncertain future. Its seating capacity (about thirty-five thousand) is woefully small by modern ballpark standards, and there are few provisions for such revenue-generating gewgaws as luxury boxes and interactive entertainment centers. The club was said to be actively seeking a new home for the next millennium. Red Sox fans could only hope that a new facility retained the charming architectural features and rich sense of place that marked the original.

—Robert E. Schnakenberg

FURTHER READING:

Gershman, Michael. *Diamonds: The Evolution of the Ballpark.* New York, Houghton Mifflin, 1995.

Huntington, Tom. "There Is No Finer Place in the World to Watch Baseball." *Smithsonian.* October 1994.

Lowry, Philip J. *Green Cathedrals: The Ultimate Celebrations of All 273 Major League and Negro League Ballparks Past and Present.* Reading, Massachusetts, Addison-Wesley, 1992.

Ferrante and Teicher

Piano stylings of pop music themes were in vogue during the post-war "lounge music" or "mood music" style, and Arthur Ferrante (1921—) and Louis Teicher (1924—) were the duo-piano team that capitalized most prolifically on this genre during the 1960s. Imitating the sound of the Romantic-era piano concerto, and at times including novelty effects such as "prepared" pianos, Ferrante and Teicher recorded lush arrangements of film themes, Broadway tunes, and other melodies backed by full orchestra and chorus. Both pianists pursued their early training at the Juilliard School in New York, but gradually dropped their classical repertoire in favor of pop and light comedy performance elements. After signing with United Artists in 1960, they had their first American chart hits with the million-plus seller theme from *The Apartment* and Ernest Gold's main theme from *Exodus;* in 1969, their arrangement of "Midnight Cowboy" was a Billboard Top 10 single. Their discography numbers over 60 albums and compilations.

—Ivan Raykoff

FURTHER READING:

Ferrante, Arthur, and Louis Teicher. "Two Pianos? It'll Never Sell!" *Music Journal.* September, 1965, 42-43.

Fetchit, Stepin (1902-1984)

The first black actor to receive featured billing in Hollywood movies, Stepin Fetchit has passed into the culture as an emblem of the shameful racial stereotyping that reflected early twentieth century America's perception of blacks as servile, lazy, feckless, and stupid. However, throughout the gravy years of his career during the 1930s,

Stepin Fetchit

this talented actor entertained movie audiences with his skillfully comic portrayals of slow-talking, dim-witted, shuffling slaves and servants, and earned a large, albeit temporary, fortune.

Born Lincoln Perry in Key West, Florida, on May 30, 1902, he went on the road as an entertainer in medicine shows and vaudeville before arriving in Hollywood in the late 1920s. His stage act with comic Ed Lee was spotted by a talent scout, engaged by Fox studios, and he took his screen name, which turned out ironically appropriate to many of his screen roles, from a racehorse on whom he had placed a winning bet. He was in the 1929 part-talkie version of *Show Boat*, the same year that he played a major role in the first all-black musical, *Hearts of Dixie*. As Gummy, a workshy layabout on a cotton plantation, Fetchit stole the show, but none of the several subsequent musicals in which he was cast gave him a similar opportunity to shine with such prominence.

Fetchit worked steadily throughout the 1930s, rapidly becoming one of the best known, best-loved, and most instantly recognizable of black actors. However, by virtue of his color, he was more often than not confined to cameos and small featured roles. Among the 26 films he made between 1929 and 1935 were three with Shirley Temple, most noticeably in *Stand Up and Cheer* (1934), and five for director John Ford. The Ford films included *Steamboat 'Round the Bend* (1935), one of four popular Will Rogers films in which Fetchit played the star's servant and comic sidekick.

Invariably typecast as the arch-coon, a tall, bald servant wearing a grin and hand-me-down clothes too large and loose for his lanky frame, his servile image eventually alienated him from black audiences and offended civil rights advocates. Walter White of the NAACP declared that Fetchit's flunky roles reinforced the white man's racist image of blacks, while the black press repeatedly criticized his perpetuation of unwelcome stereotypes. By the mid-1940s, these protests against his racist caricatures curtailed his career. Moreover, he had dissipated his wealth on the extravagant lifestyle he had adopted—at one time he owned six houses and 12 cars, and employed 16 Chinese servants—and was forced to declare bankruptcy in 1947, the year he starred in *Miracle in Harlem*.

In the early 1950s, after making only a handful of movies, some of them all-black productions, Fetchit disappeared from the screen for 20 years and, in the late 1960s, having suffered his share of personal tragedy with the death of his son by suicide, he converted to the Black Muslim faith. In 1970, he unsuccessfully brought a defamation suit against CBS for using "out of context" clips from his work to demonstrate black caricature in American movies. The 1970s, brought something of a renaissance to the then almost forgotten actor. He returned to the Hollywood screen with roles in *Amazing Grace* (1974) and *Won Ton Ton the Dog Who Saved Hollywood* (1975); in 1976, his earlier perceived slights on his own people forgiven, he received a special Image Award from the Hollywood branch of the NAACP, and in 1978 he entered the Black Filmmakers Hall of Fame.

Stepin Fetchit died in Woodland Hills, California, on November 19, 1984. Over the years, film scholars had come to recognize the wealth of comic talent and the flawless timing that underpinned the characters who defined his screen image. Robert Townsend paid him lasting tribute with his brilliant impersonation of Fetchit in his own independent film, *Hollywood Shuffle* (1987), and, thanks to television reruns of movies, he lives on for later generations as more than just a quaint name.

—Peter C. Holloran

FURTHER READING:

Bogle, Donald. *Toms, Coons, Mulattos, Mammies, and Bucks: An Interpretive History of Blacks in American Films.* New York, Continuum, 1989.

Cripps, Thomas. *Slow Fade to Black: The Negro in American Film, 1900-1942.* New York, Oxford University Press, 1977.

Leab, Daniel J. *From Sambo to Superspade: The Black Experience in Motion Pictures.* Boston, Houghton Mifflin, 1975.

Patterson, Lindsay, ed. Black Films and Film-Makers: A Comprehensive Anthology from Stereotype to Superhero. New York, Dodd, Mead, 1975.

Fibber McGee and Molly

Out of Fibber McGee's famous closet came a 24-year radio run whose success and innovation were matched by few broadcasters in the 1930s and 1940s. The series helped forge the genre later called "situation comedy"; it also invented the concept of the "spin-off," with not one but two popular supporting characters winning their own series in the 1940s. Through it all, Jim and Marian Jordan continued as Fibber and Molly, their program setting both ratings records and a patriotic example during the war years, its stars perhaps more deserving of the title "beloved" than any other performers of network radio's glory days.

The Jordan's early broadcasting careers were inauspicious at best. The couple were already battle-worn vaudevillians when, on a bet, they performed on a Chicago radio station in 1924. But their obvious talent soon won them their own music and patter series. By the early 1930s, Jim and Marian Jordan had hosted or appeared on numerous local music and banter programs; their work gradually evolved into a series that would finally win them a spot on a national NBC hookup.

For *Smackout*, the Jordans teamed up with Don Quinn, the gifted writer with whom they would collaborate for more than 15 years. In the new series, the couple played multiple roles, among them the proprietors of a depression-era grocery always "smack out" of everything. An existing 1931 recording reveals that Marian perfected her "Teeny" character, the precocious adolescent she would continue to portray when *Smackout* gave way to *Fibber McGee and Molly* in 1935.

After years of work, it was undeniably the "big break" for the Jordans and writer Quinn. From Chicago, *Fibber McGee and Molly* was broadcast nationwide over the NBC network on April 16, 1935 to middling reviews; the premiere show was an uneasy mix of swing music and comedy segments in which Molly was an unadulterated battle-ax who spoke in a thick Irish brogue, and Fibber was a tale-spinning loudmouth who more closely resembled his *Smackout* character Uncle Luke than the character the nation would come to know as Fibber McGee. Yet the series became a moderate success, at least winning time to develop its style and characters. Within a year, Quinn and the Jordans had shaped the characters into the warmer, funnier personas they would inhabit for the rest of their careers.

The scripts were pure corn, with each episode revolving around the thinnest of plots. Fibber remained a big-talking but inept spinner of yarns; Molly was his long-suffering but big-hearted companion. The couple had no obvious source of income; most of their Tuesday night adventures took place in the McGee home at 79 Wistful Vista, with a company of popular supporting characters parading through the house for brief appearances. Even announcer Harlow Wilcox was made a character, his job being to work in a clever plug for sponsor Johnson's Wax. Many of the supporting characters were played by Bill Thompson, a genuine vocal acrobat who brought life, among others, to "Wally Wimple," a perpetually henpecked husband whose every syllable bespoke his suffering; and the "Old Timer," a talkative curmudgeon whose catchphrase "That ain't the way I hear'd it!" became national slang by 1940.

In the late 1930s, the series weathered a crisis that threatened its very existence. Marian Jordan was forced off the show for health reasons in November, 1937; her hiatus ultimately lasted 18 months. Fans and historians have spent the intervening decades debating the true nature of her absence: press accounts at the time said only Marian had been sent to a "sanitarium" for a "rest," while fans have long whispered she had actually suffered a nervous breakdown. In 1998, radio historian John Dunning, citing an impeccable but anonymous source, revealed that Marian was actually battling alcoholism during her absence. The show limped along without her under the title *Fibber McGee and Company.* Marian—and Molly—returned on April 18, 1939, her reappearance drawing both press attention and a huge ovation from the studio audience.

Then, seemingly out of the blue, the series' popularity simply exploded. Paired with Bob Hope's new NBC series on Tuesday night, *Fibber McGee and Molly* suddenly found itself shooting to the very top of the ratings chart—part of a late-1930s spate of new radio hits that included stars such as Hope, Red Skelton, and Edgar Bergen. One of the Jordans' supporting cast proved so popular during this period that he was given his own show: broadcasting's first "spin-off" was *The Great Gildersleeve* (1941), in which Hal Peary reprised his role of bombastic-but-lovable Throckmorton P. Gildersleeve, who had delighted audiences for several years as Fibber's ever-feuding next-door neighbor.

Fibber's famous closet was opened for the first time on March 5, 1940, in a sound effects extravaganza in which years' worth of piled-up junk came pouring out to the delight of the audience; the oft-repeated gag became one of the best known in broadcast history.

The series was one of the first to go for all-out flag waving upon the outbreak of war on December 7, 1941; two days later, Marian Jordan may have uttered the first broadcast joke of World War Two (Gale Gordon's Mayor LaTrivia tells Molly he's shopping for a globe. "You want a globe with Japan on it?" Molly asks. "Then you better get one quick!"). The series almost weekly featured patriotic themes during the war years; an April, 1943 program in which Fibber buys and then gets sick from black market meat is a perfect example—forceful without being preachy, and very funny. The McGees even took in a boarder at mid-war, opening their home to war-plant worker Alice. By February, 1943, *Fibber McGee* was drawing record ratings—quite a feat considering a significant percentage of the population was off fighting the war!

The series suffered a major hit during this period, when actor Bill Thompson joined the service. The slack, however, was taken up in large part by the appearance of the McGee's feisty maid Beulah: a giggly, vivacious—and African-American—bundle of energy whose catchphrases "Somebody bawl fo' Beulah?" and "Love that man!" became two of the most popular slang phrases of the war. The character's popularity only increased when the audience learned the black female Beulah was actually portrayed by a white man—actor Marlin Hurt, who became so famous in the role that he, too, was given his own series. *Beulah* premiered in 1945; upon Hurt's sudden death

the next year, it became the first radio comedy to feature a black actress in a starring role—perhaps making up somewhat for the unapologetic caricature which had first given the series life.

The McGees' ratings suffered only slightly after the war, but the late 1940s proved more troublesome. Bob Hope never recaptured the overwhelming success of his war-years tours of service camps; the entire NBC Tuesday schedule suffered somewhat as Hope's ratings fell. By 1950, the previously obscure CBS sitcom *Life with Luigi* was besting Hope's ratings. But the biggest threat was television: the new medium's first real sensation—Milton Berle's *Texaco Star Theatre*—was slotted on Tuesday night, directly opposite Hope and the McGees. *Fibber McGee and Molly* performed impressively against long odds, but NBC radio's Tuesday night glory days were clearly over.

By then it barely mattered; the series had long ago crossed the line from popular entertainment to American institution. The Jordans stayed with NBC when many of the chain's top comedians bolted to CBS in the 1948-'49 talent raids; writer Quinn departed in 1950. Longtime sponsor Johnson's Wax dropped the series the same year; later sponsors included Reynolds Aluminum (which used its commercial time to introduce a revolutionary new product—Reynolds Wrap!) and Pet Milk. In 1953, with network radio dying, the Jordans gave up their weekly series and embarked on a nightly 15-minute version of *Fibber McGee and Molly*; this ran four years. The McGees were still on the air performing short segments on NBC's innovative *Monitor* series into 1958 and 1959.

By then the "golden age" of radio was long over; the Jordans' refusal to appear in a television version of their creation virtually guaranteed failure upon its premiere in 1958. Marian Jordan died in 1962; Jim lived another quarter century. They had set a decent, honest example for their audience during the era of depression and war; they had also invented and honed many of the formats and techniques broadcast writers and comedians utilize to this day. The phrase "Fibber's Closet" may be a distant memory, but the McGee's legacy is alive and well.

—Chris Chandler

FURTHER READING:

Dunning, John. *On the Air: The Encyclopedia of Old-Time Radio.* New York, Oxford University Press, 1998.

Price, Tom. *Fibber McGee's Closet: The Ultimate Log of Performances by Fibber McGee and Molly, 1917-1987.* Monterey, California, T. A. Price, 1987.

Stumpf, Charles, and Tom Price. *Heavenly Days!: The Story of Fibber McGee and Molly.* Waynesville, North Carolina, World of Yesterday, 1987.

Fiddler on the Roof

One of the most important musicals of the 1960s, in many ways *Fiddler on the Roof* represents the end of the classic mid-twentieth century American musical theater. The tale of Tevye, a Jewish peasant in turn-of-the-century Russia, and his difficulties with maintaining tradition in the midst of change, has had universal appeal ever

Zero Mostel in *Fiddler on the Roof*.

since its premiere in 1964. The score includes the hit songs "Tradition," "To Life," "If I Were a Rich Man," and "Sunrise, Sunset."

In the early 1960s, composer Jerry Bock, lyricist Sheldon Harnick, and librettist Joseph Stein decided that they wanted to write a musical together. After looking at numerous potential plot sources, they chose Sholom Aleichem's short story "Tevye and His Daughters." The trio persuaded Harold Prince to produce the show, who in turn advised them to engage Jerome Robbins as director-choreographer. With Prince and Robbins—two of Broadway's most significant creative personalities—involved with the production, its success was virtually secure.

Fiddler on the Roof takes place in the Jewish village of Anatevka, Russia, in 1905. Its plot revolves around Tevye, a dairyman, his wife Golde, and their five daughters. Tevye reveals his creed in his opening monologue:

> A fiddler on the roof. Sounds crazy, no? But in our little village of Anatevka, you might say every one of us is a fiddler on the roof, trying to scratch out a pleasant, simple tune without breaking his neck. It isn't easy. You may ask, why do we stay here if it's so dangerous? We stay because Anatevka is our home. And how do we keep our balance? That I can tell you in a word—tradition!

Tevye's world is challenged by impending change. Tzeitel, his eldest daughter, marries a poor tailor after Tevye has promised her to a

wealthy widowed butcher. Hodel, his second daughter, marries a revolutionary and follows him to Siberia, while Chava, his third daughter, marries a Christian. At the end of the musical, the Czar's Cossacks destroy Anatevka as Tevye and his family leave for an unknown future in America. The show's title—a fiddler on the roof who tries to maintain his balance while playing—suggests the desire for constancy in the face of mutability. The image itself was inspired by Marc Chagall's painting *The Green Violinist.*

Fiddler on the Roof opened on Broadway on September 22, 1964, at the Imperial Theater, where it played for 3,242 performances—the longest run in the history of the American musical theater to that time. Zero Mostel created the role of Tevye. Other original cast members included Maria Karnilova, Beatrice Arthur, Joanna Merlin, Julia Migenes, Bert Convy, and Tanya Everett. The musical garnered numerous Tony Awards, including best musical, score, book, actor (Mostel), featured actress (Karnilova), choreographer (Robbins), and costumes (Patricia Zipprodt). Topol starred in the London production, which ran for over 2,000 performances, as well as in the 1971 film version.

The success of the show was due largely to its superb musical score. The opening number, "Tradition," is a joyous celebration of life, as is the wedding number "To Life." The waltzes "Matchmaker" and "Sunrise, Sunset" capture the nostalgia of bygone traditions and the passing of time, while Tevye's splendidly dramatic monologue, "If I Were a Rich Man," is one of the great soliloquies of the musical theater. Tevye and Golde's comic duet "Do You Love Me?" is a frank expression of the love that can develop between two people over a lifetime. This expression of matrimony based on traditional matchmaking is contrasted with the "modern" concept of marriage based on love and choice in "Now I Have Everything" and "Miracle of Miracles." The music of *Fiddler on the Roof* does not generally fit into the standard mold of Broadway show tunes; traditional folk idioms fill the score and infuse it with a particular yet accessible ethnic character that distinguishes it from other shows of its era. As such, it opened the door for more variations on the traditional American musical theater genre through the end of the century.

Fiddler on the Roof is imbedded within its Jewishness without being parochial. The show's emphasis on family and religious interactions against a backdrop of a disintegrating social order gives it a universality that transcends time, place, and ethnicity. Its popularity through professional, amateur, and school productions remains as strong as ever more than thirty years after its premiere.

—William A. Everett

FURTHER READING:

Robbins, Harold. *Harold Prince Presents Zero Mostel in Fiddler on the Roof: Director's Book.* New York, J. Robbins, 1970.

Slobin, Mark. "Some Intersections of Jews, Music, and Theater." In *From Hester Street to Hollywood: The Jewish-American Stage and Screen,* edited by Sarah Blacher. Bloomington, Indiana University Press, 1983.

Suskin, Steven. *Opening Night on Broadway: A Critical Quotebook of the Golden Era of the Musical Theatre, Oklahoma! (1943) to Fiddler on the Roof (1964).* New York, Schirmer Books, 1990.

Swain, Joseph P. *The Broadway Musical, A Critical and Musical Survey.* New York and Oxford, Oxford University Press, 1990.

Fidrych, Mark "Bird" (1954—)

The American League's Rookie of the Year for 1976, pitcher Mark Fidrych briefly captured the imagination of baseball fans with his bizarre on-the-field antics. Dubbed the "Bird" for his lanky, ostrich-like frame, the 6'3" right-hander with the mop of curly blonde hair won 19 games for the Detroit Tigers that season, compiling 24 complete games and a 2.34 earned run average. But it was the *way* he pitched more than the results that filled ballparks that summer. Fidrych was far more animated than any pitcher before him: he talked to the baseball and shook hands with his infielders after good plays. After one stellar season, however Fidrych blew out his arm and never regained his rookie form. He attempted several abortive comebacks and retired in 1983.

—Robert E. Schnakenberg

FURTHER READING:

Amos, Ken. "Still the Bird." *Los Angeles Times.* November 3, 1996.

Pepe, Phil. *Talkin' Baseball: An Oral History of Baseball in the 1970s.* Beverly Hills, Morpheus International, 1991.

Ziegel, Vic. "Former Tigers Goofball Fidrych Remains A Different Sort of Bird." *St. Louis Post-Dispatch.* July 23, 1993.

Field and Stream

Field and Stream magazine, America's fishing and hunting bible, was born in a Minnesota duck blind in 1895. With contemporaries such as *Sports Afield* and *Outdoor Life,* it challenged the nineteenth-century stereotype that hunting and fishing were the domain of fur trappers and frontiersmen such as Daniel Boone, Davy Crockett, and Christopher "Kit" Carson, or amusements for the idle rich. Coupled with technological innovations that made shooting and fishing more accurate and easier, the new magazines demonstrated that hunting and fishing were recreational activities that could be enjoyed by all, especially the growing middle class. Through the twentieth century, *Field and Stream* has crusaded for conservation measures, developed a library of wildlife film and video, and commissioned wildlife images by well-known artists and photographers without ever forgetting its basic purpose, to provide the stuff of dreams for generations of hunters and fishermen.

The Civil War marked a new interest among Americans in sporting activities, most notably horse racing, boxing, track and field, and the relatively new sport of baseball, but also in hunting, fishing, and other outdoor activities. *The Sporting News* debuted in St. Louis in 1885, and its quick success encouraged newspaper publishers such as Joseph Pulitzer to add sporting news sections to their daily newspapers. Sports were considered entertainment and a form of escapism from what the late nineteenth century considered a frantic lifestyle, but they also taught an important lesson, especially to the young. Like life, sports had rules, and one needed to learn and obey them to succeed and win. The alternative, disobedience, meant failure, disgrace, and perhaps even death in a society obsessed with social Darwinism.

Magazine publishers were not far behind their newspaper counterparts in filling the new void for sports information. *Sports Afield* was founded in 1887, followed by *Outdoor Life,* which began as a Denver-based bicycling magazine in the early 1890s. John P. Burkhard and Henry W. Wack were talking in their duck blind in September 1895 about the wholesale slaughter of wildlife by so-called sportsmen. The conservation movement was in full swing, inaugurated by the establishment of Yellowstone National Park in 1872 and fanned by advocates such as John Muir and Gifford Pinchot. Burkhard and Wack disapproved of thrill shooting and set out to preach the new gospel of conservation to middle-class hunters and fishermen in their publication, *Western Field and Stream,* which was published in their hometown of St. Paul, Minnesota.

Theodore Roosevelt was the first of many notable conservationists to appear in the publication. Writing in January 1899, the president-to-be noted of the grizzly bear, "He has been hunted for sport, and hunted for his pelt, and hunted for the bounty, and hunted as a dangerous enemy to stock, until, save the very wildest districts, he has learned to be more wary than a deer." Another article on childhood hunting observed a few years later, "All little boys crave the out-of-doors—when they don't get enough of it." The magazine was moved to New York in the first years of the twentieth century and its title modified, but it continued to struggle financially. Reportedly Henry Ford offered Burkhard and Wack $1,200 worth of stock in his new motor car company in 1905 in exchange for twenty full-page advertisements, but the pair turned him down because they were desperate for cash. Eltinge Warner, a printing salesman and circulation manager, took over the business side of the magazine in 1906 and purchased the publication upon Burkhard's death in 1908.

Circulation climbed, and *Field and Stream* prospered as conservation measures advocated by the magazine increased animal and fish populations. Warner became involved in the motion picture industry and published other magazines using profits from *Field and Stream,* but his first magazine kept to its original course. "When trout are rising, hope is strong in the angler's heart, even though he may not have determined in what position or upon what insects the fish are feeding," a *Field and Stream* article on fly-fishing maintained in 1912. An article on a shark attack in 1933 portended, "terrible things . . . there in the murky water and the misty moonshine." The magazine also featured the self-depreciating humor of Gene Hill and the off-the-wall antics of Ed Zern.

A boon in men's magazines during and after World War II expanded the circulation of *Field and Stream.* By 1963, *Sports Afield, Outdoor Life,* and *Field and Stream* had a combined circulation of 3.7 million. Warner sold *Field and Stream* to the book-publishing house of Holt, Rinehart, and Winston in 1951, which was subsequently absorbed by CBS magnate William S. Paley and reorganized into the CBS Magazine division in 1971. The magazine peaked in size at about 200 hundred pages per issue during the 1970s, because of the payment method for writers. "We don't pay by the word any more," said managing editor Margaret Nichols in 1995. "Long ago, when we paid a nickel a word, some people let their stories drag on and on. Fish would jump, then jump again and again and again." The circulation plateaued at two million during the 1980s and 1990s, but the venerable *Field and Stream* faced two new challenges. It was sold twice, ending up with Times Mirror Magazines, the publisher of *Outdoor Life,* in 1987. And a host of more health and fitness-conscious men's outdoor magazines, with titles such as *Outside, Backpacker,* and *Bike,*

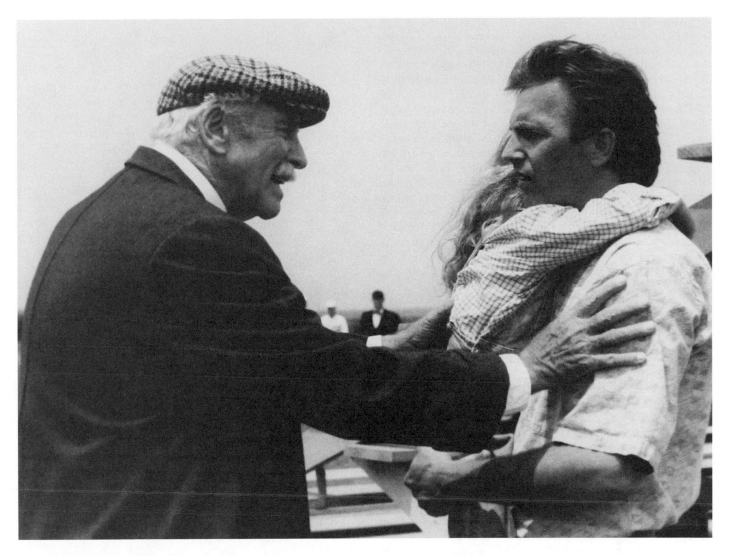

Burt Lancaster (left) and Kevin Costner in a scene from the film *Field of Dreams*.

stagnated advertising and circulation rates and left more traditional outdoorsmen's publications like *Field and Stream* hunting for a new image.

—Richard Digby-Junger

FURTHER READING:

Egan, D'Arcy. "Hunting, Fishing Bible Turns 100: Field & Stream Takes Readers Back to the Adventures They Grew Up On." *Cleveland Plain Dealer,* July 14, 1995, 9D.

Merritt, J. I., and Margaret G. Nichols. *The Best of Field & Stream: 100 Years of Great Writing from America's Premier Sporting Magazine.* New York, Lyons and Burford, 1995.

Mott, Frank L. "The Argosy." *A History of American Magazines.* Vol. 4. Cambridge, Harvard University Press, 1957, 417-423.

Peterson, Theodore. *Magazines in the Twentieth Century.* Urban, University of Illinois Press, 1964, 367-368.

Tanner, Stephen L. "The Art of Self-Depreciation in American Literary Humor." *Studies in American Humor.* Fall 1996, 54-65.

Field of Dreams

Ostensibly about baseball, the emotional, magical *Field of Dreams* became more than just a movie for many people following its release in 1989 to both critical and popular acclaim. Directed by Phil Alden Robinson and starring Kevin Costner, James Earl Jones, and Ray Liotta, the film made almost sixty-five million dollars at the box office and another forty million in video rentals and purchases.

Based on W. P. Kinsella's book *Shoeless Joe, Field of Dreams* is a story of faith, forgiveness, and redemption. Iowa corn farmer Ray Kinsella (Costner) and his family lead a normal, if boring, existence until, during one of his regular inspection walks through the cornfields, Kinsella hears a ghostly voice whispering the phrase " . . . if you build it, he will come." At first Kinsella assumes he is hallucinating, but the voice returns. After seeing a vision of a baseball diamond in the middle of his corn, Kinsella plows up the corn and builds a ballpark, although doing so puts his family and farm in a precarious financial position. Just at the point when Kinsella is convinced he has gone mad, Shoeless Joe Jackson (Liotta), Kinsella's late father's favorite player, walks out of the corn to play baseball on the field.

Although Kinsella believes he has fulfilled his mission to bring Shoeless Joe back to redeem himself, he continues to hear messages from the voice in the corn. The voices eventually lead him to Terence Mann (Jones), an author and activist Kinsella followed in the 1960s. Mann has given up his activism and become a software designer. Kinsella convinces Mann to return to Iowa with him, and on their way, they are told by the voice to find an old country doctor, Moonlight Graham (Burt Lancaster), who played one game in the major leagues but never got to bat. Although the doctor is long dead, he appears as a young man to Kinsella on his way back to Iowa. When Kinsella, Mann, and the teenage Graham return to Iowa, Kinsella meets the ghost of his father as a young minor league baseball player. For the first time, Kinsella is able to understand his father and the deeper meaning behind his father's obsession with baseball and Shoeless Joe Jackson. Not long after this, bankers come to foreclose on the farm. As Kinsella begins to realize the extent of his plight, an enormous line of cars begins to form outside of his home—people wanting to pay to watch Shoeless Joe and his fellow ghosts play baseball on Kinsella's field.

Field of Dreams touched a particular chord with baby boomers. Kinsella himself represents the average boomer male, forgetting how important baseball was to him as a child. Mann is clearly symbolic of all of the activists in the 1960s who sold out their principles to make money. The bankers foreclosing on the Kinsella farm represent the faceless corporations that now own baseball teams, focusing entirely on profits rather than a love of the game. The connection between boomer children and baseball is perhaps best explained by Mann, who looks out onto the field of ghost players and proclaims, "The one constant through all the years, Ray, has been baseball. America has rolled by like an army of steamrollers. It's been erased like a blackboard, rebuilt, and erased again. But baseball has marked the time. This field, this game, is a part of our past, Ray. It reminds us of all that was once good, and what could be good again."

Field of Dreams started a resurgence of baseball nostalgia, with dozens of books and movies recounting the "good old days" when children collected baseball cards for trading, rather than saving them as an investment. The actual "Field of Dreams" movie site on the Lansing Farm in Dyersville, Iowa, continues to be one of the top ten tourist attractions in the state. People flock from all over the United States to visit the field, trying to make the same connection with the lost innocence of youth that the film so effectively portrayed.

—Geoff Peterson

FURTHER READING:

Kinsella, W. P. *Shoeless Joe.* Boston, Houghton Mifflin, 1982.

Will, G. *Men at Work: The Craft of Baseball.* New York, Macmillan, 1990.

Field, Sally (1946—)

From perky, surf-loving Gidget in 1965 to gray-haired, frumpy Mrs. Gump in 1994, Academy award-winning actress Sally Field has exhibited a wide range of talent and an enduring likability in a profession that too often ignores women over the age of 40. If her roles have a common theme, it is that women are intelligent, strong, and capable of heroic deeds. Born in Pasadena, California, on November 6, 1946, Field was brought up by her actress mother and

Sally Field

her step-father Jock Mahoney. At 17, while most young women were deciding whether to go to college or to get married, Field won the starring role in the television show *Gidget* (1965-66), a role originally played by Sandra Dee in the hit movie of the same name. Gidget epitomized the typical teenager of the early 1960s, and Field was ideal for the role, establishing herself as a television star that gave young women a positive role model: enthusiastic and slightly goofy, but always inherently obedient and moralistic. The role of Gidget was followed by the even more endearing role of Sister Bertrille in *The Flying Nun* (1967-70). Ironically, Field was pregnant with her son Peter while flying through the air around the convent. She had married her high school sweetheart Steve Craig in 1968. Field gave birth to a second son, Eli, but the couple divorced in 1975. Field's last series, *The Girl Was Something Extra* (1973-74), told the story of a young newlywed who had extra-sensory perception (ESP).

The breakout performance of Field's early career came with the role of Sybil in 1976. Playing a young woman with multiple-personality disorder, Sally Field sealed her place in American television history and won an Emmy for her efforts. Sybil was as different from Gidget as it was possible to be. Bound up in her mental illness, Sybil took no pains with her appearance and had very few people skills—traits that were the essence of Gidget. While she met the challenges of this difficult role with apparent ease, Field paid a price for playing against type. She was no longer perceived as an attractive leading lady. In 1977 she took on a different type of challenge with the role of young, attractive, fun-loving Carrie who accepts a ride from trucker Burt Reynolds while fleeing her wedding in *Smokey and the Bandit* (1977, 1980, 1983). With their seven-year alliance, the two became constant fodder for tabloids. However, while Field was entering her prime as an actress, Reynolds entered a period of decline, and the romance ended.

In 1979, Sally Field won her first of two Academy awards as Best Actress for her role in *Norma Rae,* the story of an Alabama textile worker who fought for unionization. When Field, as Norma Rae, stood up, holding her placard for union rights, and faced down irate mill owners, no one thought of Gidget. It was a moment that cemented the maturity of Sally Field as an actress and illustrated the gains made by women in American film. Unlike earlier female stars who had become known mostly for romantic and maternal roles, women of the 1970s, 1980s, and 1990s were allowed to become heroes by standing up for what they thought was right. Field's second Academy Award for Best Actress came with 1984's *Places in the Heart.* Playing Edna Spaulding, a Depression-era widow and the mother of two who fought to save her farm with only the help of a black man and a blind man, Field demonstrated that heroes could be more traditional than Norma Rae and still be memorable. Field said in a 1984 interview that Edna was her favorite role because she identified with her fierce love for her children and her strong will to survive. It was when accepting this Academy award that Field won a unique place in the award's history. Accepting the honor as proof that she had surpassed the roles of Gidget and Sister Bertrille, Field effused: "You like me—You really like me!" Rather than being accepted as the words of a woman who had matured from being a little girl struggling to please her absent father to a mature actress accepted by her peers, critics, and comedians had a "field" day with her acceptance speech.

Throughout her career, Sally Field has demonstrated versatility as an actress. In 1984's *Absence of Malice* with Paul Newman, Field played a reporter determined to get her story even at the cost of destroying innocent people. In 1985, Field played the much-younger love interest of veteran actor James Garner. Even though the movie was a romantic comedy, Field managed to strike a blow for women's rights with the role of a single-mother trying to raise her son by boarding horses. In 1989, Field led an all-star cast in *Steel Magnolias,* a fact-based story of six southern women who hang out at a beauty shop, loving and supporting one another and remaining strong even when death claims one of their group.

Continuing to take chances, Sally Field played the stable wife of a forever-youthful Robin Williams in *Mrs. Doubtfire* (1993), the voice of Sassy the cat in the two *Homeward Bound* (1993, 1996) movies, and justice-seeking mothers of an abducted daughter in *Not without My Daughter* (1991) and of a slain daughter in *Eye for an Eye* (1996). She again became involved in an Academy award-winning movie in 1994 when she accepted the role of Mrs. Gump in *Forrest Gump.* Ironically, Field played the mother of Tom Hanks, who had played opposite her six years before in *Punchline.* In 1998, Field continued to hold her own in the world of entertainment. She directed and starred in a segment of Tom Hank's phenomenal *From the Earth to the Moon* (1998) and remains active in improving the image of women in the entertainment industry and in a number of charitable works.

—Elizabeth Purdy

FURTHER READING:

Bandler, Michael J. "Sally Field: Sweetness and Might." *Ladies Home Journal.* 1 July 1991, 73-76.

Craig, Peter. *The Martini Shot.* New York, William Morrow, 1998.

Hallett, Lisa. "Field Day." *Emmy.* 1 January 1995, 18.

Sachs, Aviva. "Spunky Sally Field." *McCall's.* November 1989, 10.

Fields, W. C. (1879-1946)

One of film comedy's best-loved performers, W. C. Fields has inspired countless impersonators but few imitators. In more than forty films over three decades, the bulbous-nosed actor perfected a unique comic persona marked by a love of whiskey, a hatred of small children and animals, and a love of underhanded chicanery. Among the memorable quotes attributed to Fields are "Anyone who hates dogs and kids can't be all bad" and "A thing worth having is a thing worth cheating for." His famous epitaph, "All things considered, I'd rather be in Philadelphia," paid mocking tribute to his birth city.

Born William Claude Dukenfield, Fields left home at age eleven to escape his abusive father. By age thirteen he was a skilled pool player and juggler, and was soon entertaining customers at amusement parks. By the age of twenty-one, he was one of the leading lights of Vaudeville. He played the Palace in London and starred at the Folies-Bergere in Paris. He appeared in each of the Ziegfeld Follies from 1915 through 1921. Fields's stage act, which featured both

W. C. Fields with Charlie McCarthy.

comedy and juggling, was immortalized in 1915 in his first silent film, *Pool Shark.* He devoted himself to films throughout the 1920s, though his comic persona did not find full flower until the advent of sound in the next decade.

Fields's best silent feature, *It's the Old Army Game* (1927), was later remade as his breakthrough talkie, *It's a Gift* (1934). That film, which cast Fields as a grocery clerk who moves his family west to manage a chain of orange groves, established for all time the incomparable W. C. Fields persona. His nose reddened by excessive drink, speaking sarcastic asides in a comic snarl, forever bedeviled by animals and children, Fields was the cantankerous bastard inside of every moviegoer, the personification of the male id unleashed. This emerging comic identity was also on view in a series of classic shorts he made for Mack Sennett. Most notable among these are *The Dentist* (1932), *The Barber Shop,* and *The Pharmacist* (both 1933).

Fields proved himself more than a mere clown, however. He also found a niche playing character roles in adaptations of the classics. He portrayed Humpty Dumpty in the all-star 1933 film version of *Alice in Wonderland,* then replaced Charles Laughton as Micawber in the 1935 adaptation of *David Copperfield.* Fields was also given serious consideration for the title role in 1939's *The Wizard of Oz,* though that part eventually went to Frank Morgan.

As the 1930s drew to a close, Fields began work on one last stretch of classic films. He teamed up with ventriloquist Edgar Bergen and his dummy Charlie McCarthy for the 1939 circus farce *You Can't Cheat an Honest Man. My Little Chickadee* (1940) paired Fields with Mae West, an inspired bit of casting that produced some of their best work. *The Bank Dick,* which Fields wrote using an alias, was perhaps his finest starring vehicle. Fields's last full-length starring feature was 1941's *Never Give a Sucker an Even Break,* an anarchic comedy whose plot outline Fields reportedly sketched out on a cocktail napkin.

Battling poor health, Fields continued acting in bit parts well into the 1940s. His infirmities eventually caught up with him, and he died of pneumonia on Christmas Day, 1946. In the decades after his death, Fields's filmic oeuvre generated a vibrant cult following. His works became a staple of late-night art house film festivals, and he was particularly beloved on college campuses. In 1976, Rod Steiger gamely impersonated the comic legend for a well-received biopic *W. C. Fields and Me.*

—Robert E. Schnakenberg

FURTHER READING:

Deschner, Donald. *The Complete Films of W. C. Fields.* Secaucus, New Jersey, Citadel Press, 1989.

Louvish, Samuel. *Man on the Flying Trapeze: The Life and Times of W. C. Fields.* New York, W. W. Norton, 1997.

Fierstein, Harvey (1954—)

The gravel-voiced Harvey Fierstein was one of the first openly homosexual American actor/playwrights who lent his name and support to gay rights and AIDS (Acquired Immune Deficiency Syndrome) activism during the 1980s and 1990s. His breakthrough work was the autobiographical 1982 play *Torch Song Trilogy*, dealing with a young man's coming out and his relationship with his mother. Fierstein became familiar to moviegoers for his work as a supporting

actor in such blockbuster hits as *Mrs. Doubtfire* (1993) and *Independence Day* (1996) and he narrated the 1984 Oscar-winning documentary *The Times of Harvey Milk,* about an assassinated gay politician.

—Andrew Milner

FURTHER READING:

Fierstein, Harvey. *Torch Song Trilogy.* New York, Random House, 1984.

''Harvey Fierstein.'' *Current Biography.* Vol. 45, 1984.

The Fifties

The 1950s were a time of rapid change and lock step conformity, of new forms emerging out of old, and technical innovations proceeding at a breakneck pace. For all the talk of traditional American values, the country was shedding its past as a snake sheds its skin. By the decade's end, so much had changed—internationalism replacing isolationism; rampant consumerism replacing thrift; the extended family network, once the social glue binding the country, superseded by the suburban nuclear family—that the country was scarcely recognizable. Yet, the 1950s continues to be perceived as the ultra-American decade. Nostalgic for a time when America was without question the most powerful nation on earth, and, like the biblical land of milk and honey, overflowing with bounty, America has projected its anxieties back to this supposedly Golden Age. This perception does not bear scrutiny. At the time, it seemed as if overnight a familiar way of life had been replaced by shopping malls and prefabricated suburbs, the atom bomb and television sets—especially television sets.

It is almost impossible to calculate the effect television had in the first decade of its usage. Television intruded into every aspect of American life, leaving almost nothing untouched. Book sales declined; radio listenership slumped precipitously; the film industry, already in shambles, was dealt a staggering blow. By 1951, movie theaters had begun to close throughout the country—134 in Southern California alone—and even cities with only one television station were reporting drops in film attendance of between 20 and 40 percent. So fascinated was the public with this new medium, according to a 1951 study, that when a popular program was on, toilets would flush throughout the city as if on cue, in concert with commercial breaks or the conclusion of a program. Television altered the country's mores and conventions, its collective vision of the nation and the world, and the very nature of electoral politics. Television brought America the wars abroad and the war at home—the Arkansas National Guard blocking court-ordered school desegregation in Little Rock, the French Catastrophe at Dien Bien Phu—and the confluence of these forces, racial tension and American internationalism, would foster the more radical changes of the 1960s.

Nowhere was the effect of television so pervasive as in advertising, and so great was the effect of television advertising on consumer habits, it was almost Pavlovian. ''Television was turning out to be a magic machine for selling products,'' writes David Halberstam, author of an exhaustive survey of the decade, ''and the awareness of that was still dawning on Madison Avenue in the late 1950s.'' Six months after Revlon began sponsoring the popular game show, *The $64,000 Question,* for instance, the company's revenues had risen 54 percent. The next year sales had risen to $85.7 million, a $33 million increase, a figure close to Revlon's total profits prior to television. Obviously, there were winners and losers in this equation. The companies that could afford national advertising gained market share, and smaller companies lost it. In short, television furthered the subsumption of market capitalism under the hegemony of multinational corporations, a profound blow to the free-market that television so zealously trumpeted.

Television advertising was also used to great effect in politics. The campaign commercial became an integral part of the American electioneering, as did television coverage, replacing the whistle-stop tour as a tool of effective voter-outreach. Television could make or break a candidate: it was Richard Nixon's famous televised "Checkers" speech that saved his 1952 vice-presidential candidacy, and television again that proved his undoing against John F. Kennedy in 1960. In their debate, Nixon, exhausted by his arduous campaign schedule, and with the sweat washing away his makeup, appeared so haggard and pale that acquaintances called afterwards to inquire after his health. Kennedy, on the other hand, having spent the previous week relaxing poolside in Southern California, literally radiated vitality; the choice was apparently between a derelict used car salesman and a bronzed demi-god.

There was a schizoid quality to life in the 1950s, a manic oscillation between paranoia and omnipotence. The disjunct was fueled by the long shadow of the Depression and among certain parties, a blind, unreasoned hatred of Communism. "You and I were trained for a conflict that never came," writes D. J. Waldie in his memoir of life in Lakewood, California, the second, mass-produced suburb built in America (Levittown, New York, was first). "At my grade school, the Sisters of St. Joseph made me hate Communists, then intolerance, and finally everything that could break the charmed pattern of our lives. I am not sure the Sisters of St. Joseph expected this from their daily lessons on the Red threat." One might attribute this hyper-vigilance to a form of collective post-traumatic stress disorder, a reaction to defeating the Nazis, as if prosperity—linked as it was to war production—was contingent on possessing a worthy enemy to defeat.

In fact, this was precisely the case. The American economy had become beholden to Keynesian theory, perpetual war production. As it was, America had already experienced a series of recessions since the end of the war. The more leftist historians of the age would argue that the bellicose nature of our foreign policy—Korea, our material support of France's struggle in Indochina, our numerous covert actions in places like Guatemala and Iran—and our strident anti-Communism was in fact a method of keeping the war machine chugging away full blast. It was the Monroe Doctrine expanded to include the entire world. In addition, our numerous foreign interventions coincided with vested interests, and it was often at the behest of large corporations that foreign policy was molded. One seldom mentioned proof of this thesis is the new zeal with which Americans were taxed—they were spending more, but they were also, many for the first time, paying an income tax, much of which went to supporting our foreign excursions. By the end of the decade, even Eisenhower could not ignore the changes the cold war had wrought, and his farewell address carried a dire warning.

Above all else, red-baiting made for effective campaign politics. Richard Nixon, perhaps America's most opportunistic politician, first saw the value of red-baiting, using the Alger Hiss hearings before the House Un-American Activities Committee (HUAC) as a bully pulpit, pushing anti-Communist legislation through sub-committee when the matter seemed all but dead. Nixon then seized the moral high ground

in his 1950 senatorial race, mercilessly baiting his liberal opponent, Helen Gallagher Douglas, at every opportunity. Senator Joseph McCarthy became the most notorious red-baiter of all, stepping into the role of what David Halberstam called an "accidental demagogue" when he casually mentioned a fictitious list of State Department Communists at a Lincoln Day Celebration in Wheeling, West Virginia. McCarthy's campaign to ferret out Communism lasted four long years, fueled as much by a lust for headlines as by ideological conviction. It ended with his ill-conceived attack on the U.S. Army, leading to his censure by the Senate and political disgrace. The red scare was, as Maryland Senator Millard Tydings said of Joseph McCarthy, "a hoax and a fraud ... an attempt to inflame the American people with a wave of hysteria and fear on an unbelievable scale." As such, it was a smashing success. Nixon was victorious in his senatorial campaign against Douglas in 1950. Tydings, whose comments exposed him to the full brunt of far right wrath, was not: he lost his seat in 1956.

If America was exporting spear rattling abroad, at home the good life was being rationalized as never before. Technology and the mania for speedy service had crept into almost every facet of commerce from restaurants (McDonald's) to motels (Holiday Inn) to shopping (E.J. Korvetts, and the many discount department stores Korvetts inspired) to farming itself. Family farms disappeared at a staggering rate, replaced by large agribusiness conglomerates, whose indiscriminate use of pesticides and feed additives, along with promotion of the beef industry, changed forever the American diet. Whatever product or service could be performed, could be performed better and more efficiently as part of a chain, or so it was thought. Ray Kroc, the original franchiser of McDonald's, demonstrated this with stunning success. It was part of a democratization of goods and services. What had formally been the province of the upper-middle class—leisure, cars, houses—was now available to the working man, albeit in a watered-down form. Nowhere was this dual relationship—technology and egalitarianism—in commerce more apparent than in the housing industry.

Housing had suffered from the paucity of building supplies during World War II. In 1944 there had been a mere 114,00 new house starts, and with the return of America's soldiers, the housing shortage became a housing crisis. Bill Levitt, himself a veteran of the Seabees, began thinking about applying assembly line techniques to housing before the war, and had bought a plot of farmland on Long Island with his brother for that very purpose. Levitt wanted to bring housing to the working class and emancipate them from the inner city. Following the war, Levitt, with the aid of Federally-insured mortgages, began building a community of 17,000 minimalist Cape Cod houses, a scale of production heretofore unknown. Everything was pre-fabricated and transported to the building site, where specialized crews moved from one lot to the next in assembly-line fashion performing their single task. Construction was finished within a matter of months.

"This is Levittown! All yours for $58. You're a lucky fellow, Mr. Veteran," proclaimed an ad in the *New York Times*. "Uncle Sam and the world's largest builder have made it possible for you to live in a charming house in a delightful community without having to pay for them with your eye teeth." Veterans stormed Levitt's sales office; in one day alone 1,400 contracts were drawn up. The new owners were pioneers in what became a mass exodus from city to suburb as all across the nation similar projects were initiated. Levitt himself built several other Levittowns along the East Coast. It was a revolutionary change in living for the nuclear family. In 1955, Levitt-type suburbs accounted for 75 percent of the new housing starts. Within thirty years some 60 million people had moved to the prefabricated suburbs Levitt had helped to create, while fifteen of the twenty-five largest cities had declined in population, a massive migration that would have dramatic consequences in the ensuing years.

The ranks of the suburbanized middle class were swelling, but what was the price of this newfound affluence? The suburbs were clean and safe, but living in them could be enervating, especially to college-educated women who had forsaken careers for domesticity and child-rearing. Nor were men spared the malaise. It was ironic, an irony not lost on many returning veterans, that having risked their lives in war, they had returned to another kind of death, that of the colorless organization man. In 1950 sociologist David Reisman published *The Lonely Crowd*, his psychological exploration of middle class anomie. Shortly thereafter, Sloan Wilson quit his advertising job to write *The Man in the Gray Flannel Suit*, his 1955 novel portraying the emptiness of the suburbs. "Have we become a nation of yes-men?" these books asked. Was solace to be found in blind materialism? Many sensed the danger, but could not resist the allure. "*The Lonely Crowd* was anatomized in 1950," wrote Richard Schickel, "and the fear of drifting into its clutches was lively in us. *White Collar* [C. Wright Mills' truculent attack on conformist culture] was on our brick and board bookshelves, and we saw how the eponymous object seemed to be choking the life out of earlier generations . . . though of course, even as we read about these cautionary figures, many of us were talking to corporate recruiters about entry-level emulation of them."

While the nation fell further under the sway of homogeneity, it was no surprise that a kind of exaggerated rebel would become a popular cultural icon, an omnipresent figure in literature (the Beats), in rock and roll, and the movies. Stars such as James Dean, Marlon Brando, and Montgomery Clift assayed a new type of masculinity; sensitive, brooding, and rebellious, while Elvis Presley, and to a greater degree, Jerry Lee Lewis, comported themselves with a haughty menace. These sneering film and music stars were America's surrogate rebels, acting out in ways most people could ill afford to chance. America's contempt for what it had become was caught in the sneer, an expression that, when employed by Marlon Brando or James Dean or Elvis Presley, contemptuously leveled the organization man and the carrot-on-a-stick world of nine-to-five.

Rock and roll was this rebellious spirit's most potent manifestation. The culmination of years of cross-cultural evolution, teenagers began enthusiastically seeking out "race" music, one of a variety of blues and rhythm and blues (R&B), in the early 1950s, an enthusiasm all the more attractive for the disapprobation with which parents reacted to it. Rock and roll was unabashedly sexual, exuberant, and raucous. To parents everywhere it represented a threat, an insidious menace crawling up from the cellars of the lower classes. In 1951, a Cleveland record store owner reported this new craze to DJ Alan Freed, then playing classical music on a late-night show, and prevailed upon him to change his show to the nascent rock and roll, making Freed one of the first disc jockeys in the country to program bi-racially. Previously, a Memphis DJ, Dewey Phillips, had devised a show, Red, Hot and Blue, that had become the rage among Memphis's hip youth. Memphis was thoroughly segregated, but on Phillips show one could hear Ike Turner, Fats Domino, and B. B. King alongside Bill Haley, Hank Williams, Johnny Cash; in short, the two styles from which rock and roll derived played side-by-side.

Elvis Presley, who listened religiously to Phillips show, exemplified this hybrid, blending country-western, blues, and evangelical mania, presented with a sneer ripped straight off the face of James

Dean, whom the young Elvis worshipped. Linking the surliness of Dean with the frenzy of the gospel revivalist was an inspired combination. "This cat came out in a coat and pink shirt and socks and he had this sneer on his face and he stood behind the mike for five minutes, I'll bet, before he made a move," said country singer Bob Luman in recalling an early Elvis show. "Then he hit his guitar a lick and he broke two strings. . . . So there he was, these two strings dangling, and he hadn't done anything yet, and these high school girls were screaming and fainting and running up to the stage and then he started to move his hips real slow like he had a thing for his guitar." This was the threat that parents worried over, why religious groups burned rock and roll records, and why the music was ineluctably attractive to the kids, and the nature of music, and musical celebrity would never be the same.

The change in rock and roll over the course of the decade, from unbridled passion to commercial product, was an early lesson in co-optation. But for the Beat writers, defiance to American values, such as they were, was a central tenet of their thinking, and they were regularly castigated for it. Writing in the November 1959 issue of Life, Paul O'Neill called the Beat writers "undisciplined and slovenly amateurs who have deluded themselves into believing their lugubrious absurdities are art simply because they have rejected the form, styles, and attitudes of previous generations." The Beats rejected American consumerism and the plastic world of mortgages and car payments, living, instead, on the periphery. "In their discontent with American values," writes Ted Morgan, William S. Burroughs' biographer, "with cold-war suspicion, with loving the bomb, with a society shaped by corporate power and moral smugness, they had come up with something more vital. . . . In their rejection of the boring, the conventional, and the academic, in their adoption of a venturesome lifestyle, they gave everyone the green light to plumb their own experience." And while they were derided in the 1950s, endlessly examined for moral failings, labeled as naysayers and saddled with the diminutive, Beatnik (after Sputnik), America could not be rid of them. Within a few short years, their progeny, the baby-boomers who read them in high school, were omnipresent.

The most common representation of the 1950s is a sort of glossy coffee table *histoire*, heavy on photographic images and short on historical fact. It is these images of tail fins and spotless kitchens and poodle skirts that endure, as if the other America, the America of violent racist attacks, of Little Rock and Montgomery—the incipient racism and paranoia of the most powerful country on earth—never existed. "One reason that Americans as a people became nostalgic about the 1950s more than twenty-five years later," writes Halberstam, "was not so much that life was better in the 1950s (though in some ways it was), but because at the time it had been portrayed so idyllically on television. It was the television images of the era that remained so remarkably sharp in people's memories, often fresher than memories of real life. Television reflected a world of warm-hearted, sensitive, tolerant Americans, a world devoid of anger and meanness of spirit and, of course, failure." Those aficionados of the decade who dress in vintage clothing, drive 1950s-era cars, and listen to the music, have made of the 1950s a virtual cult of style. Their strivings to elude the present constitutes a nostalgic retreat, a harkening back to a Golden Age through the mute power of artifacts. This beneficent image, the make-believe world represented by such movies and television shows as *Grease, Happy Days, Sha Na Na,* and *Laverne and Shirley,* constitutes an evasion, a return to a time of clear cut values, which is all the more insidious for being a fiction. As a decade, the 1950s represents a sort of idealized America, but this image has more to do with the 1970s television show, *Happy Days,* than with any objective reality.

It is perhaps to be expected, then, that, compared to the abundance of memoirs, histories, analyses, and so on published about the 1960s, there is such a paucity of historical material on the 1950s. Ironic, and unsettling, because the America we have inherited, and with which some take umbrage, was shaped in great part by the 1950s. Much of the landscape we take for granted—fast food franchises and foreign policy, corporate hegemony and interstate freeways—was brought into being during that era, as was the generation that went to college, protested the war, took acid, and wrote a memoir. They prefer to remember the 1950s as a bad dream.

—Michael Baers

FURTHER READING:

Arnold, Eve. *The Fifties.* New York, Pantheon, 1985.

Carter, Paul A. *Another Part of the Fifties.* New York, Columbia University Press, 1993.

Chancellor, John. *The Fifties: Photographs of America.* New York, Pantheon, 1985.

Escott, Colin. *Sun Records: The Brief History of the Legendary Recording Label.* New York, Quick Fox, 1980.

Ginsberg, Allen. *Ginsberg Journals: Mid-Fifties, 1954-1958.* New York, Harper Collins, 1995.

Gruen, John. *The Party's Over Now: Reminiscences of the Fifties by New York's Artists, Writers, and Musicians.* New York, Viking Press, 1972.

Friedan, Betty. *The Feminine Mystique.* New York, Norton, 1963.

Halberstam, David. *The Fifties.* New York, Villard Books, 1993.

Harvey, Brett. *The Fifties: A Women's Oral History.* New York, Harper Collins, 1993.

Jezer, Marty. *The Dark Ages: Life in the United States 1945-1960.* Boston, South End Press, 1982.

Mills, C. Wright. *White Collar.* New York, Oxford University Press, 1951.

Morgan, Ted. *Literary Outlaw: The Life and Times of William S. Burroughs.* New York, Henry Holt and Company, 1988.

Riesman, David. *The Lonely Crowd.* New Haven, Yale University Press, 1950.

Waldie, D. J. *Holy Land: A Suburban Memoir.* New York, W.W. Norton & Company, 1996.

Wilson, Edmund. *The Fifties.* New York, Farrar, Straus & Giroux, 1986.

———. *The Fifties: From Notebooks and Diaries of the Period.* New York, Farrar, Strauss & Giroux, 1986.

Wilson, Sloan. *The Man in the Gray Flannel Suit.* New York, Simon and Schuster, 1955.

Film Noir

The genre known as film noir emerged from economic, political, and moral crises in European and American cultures in the years leading up to World War II. Its American origins are in the "tough-guy" and "hard-boiled" novels that became popular in the 1920s and 1930s, and which, as Hollywood became more liberal in the 1940s and 1950s, could more easily be adapted for the movies than before. Such novels were also popular in Europe, particularly in France, where they were known as "romans noirs," and were published under imprints with titles such as "La Série Noire." When the embargo on American films that existed in France under German occupation was lifted in 1944, many of the films that first arrived were based on hard-boiled novels, and it seems natural for French critics to have begun categorizing these films as "film noir." The European influence on film noir is not restricted to its name, however. Many of the cinematic techniques, and the overall pessimistic outlook of these movies, can be found in French "poetic realist" films made in the 1930s, and more especially, the work of German Expressionist film makers, many of whom emigrated to the United States to escape the Nazis and went on to work in Hollywood.

German directors such as Fritz Lang and Robert Siodmak, and cinematographers, such as Hungarian-born John Alton, used contrasting light and shade, odd camera angles, and scenes dominated by shadow, to reproduce on screen the bleak vision of hard-boiled writers such as Dashiell Hammett, Cornell Woolrich, and others. Movies in the film noir style can be recognized by their visual dependence on the effect of *chiaroscuro,* the contrast between light and shade. Characters and objects in film noir are often backlit, so that they cast long shadows and their features are obscured, or else the principals are brightly lit from the front so that the background is dark. Faces are pictured half-obscured by darkness, or crosshatched by the shadows of prison bars, window frames, or banister rods; the corners of rooms are dark and the interiors of cars provide a gloomy, claustrophobic setting.

Although many of its visual codes are familiar, the overall concept of film noir is notoriously difficult to pin down; although their plots usually center on crime, films included in the corpus cannot easily be identified as belonging to one particular genre. For example, Howard Hawks's *The Big Sleep* (1946), an adaptation of Raymond Chandler's novel of the same name, is a detective thriller, while Charles Laughton's *The Night of the Hunter* (1955) concerns an ex-con's search for the proceeds of a robbery committed by his former cellmate. Billy Wilder's *Sunset Boulevard* (1950) depicts a vain and ageing star of silent movies obsessed with loyalty, her lost beauty and star status; it ends with her murder of the young man who rejects her and is narrated, famously, by the victim, face down in the swimming pool. What these films do have in common, however, is a fascination with psychological instability, sexual obsession, and alienation. Unlike the "Hollywood Gothic" of films such as *Dracula* (1931) or *The Bride of Frankenstein* (1935), what appears as monstrous in film noir derives not from the half-human horrors of the vampire or Frankenstein's monster, but from the all too human characteristics of jealousy, greed, lust, and ruthless self-interest.

Such themes are by no means exclusive to film noir, of course, and film categories must be defined as much by their technical and visual features as by thematic and formal tendencies. If film noir is difficult to define in terms of the plots of the films it includes, the problem is hardly eased by critics' reliance on terms such as "style," "mood," and "sensibility" when discussing films of "noir" pedigree. Rather than seeing film noir as a genre, many critics instead view it as a movement, a set of films and filmmakers expressing a common approach to life using similar literary sources, narrative structures, and visual codes.

The difficulties of describing film noir as a genre combine the problem of the sheer variety of different types of stories such films encompass, and the question of what it is exactly that distinguishes them from other films. Many films, for example, use *chiaroscuro* but can be described only as *noir*-ish, while others, such as *Gilda* (1946) are accepted as film noir, but betray their otherwise pessimistic tone with a happy ending of sorts. A further complication is that while genres seem not to be trapped in a particular time or place, film noir is very closely linked with the Hollywood of the 1940s. A significant proportion of films in the film noir mode that have been made since then refer back, in some way, to the immediate post-war period, and many of the reasons for film noir's appearance at that time and place have to do with the particular culture of Hollywood. Financial restrictions on filmmakers during the war have already been mentioned, but other factors, such as the perception of German Expressionist style as "quality," and the need among the smaller studios for new and distinctive film products, are also important. The opportunities film noir gave for directors and cinematographers to "show off" their talents, combined with the gradual relaxation of the Hays Code, which controlled the "moral content" of movies, made Hollywood cinema receptive to the content, mood, and style of film noir in the 1940s.

Because most noir films were "B" movies, or at least made much of their money in the so-called "grind houses"—small theatres playing a rolling program and catering for people on the move from one town to another—budgets for sets, costume, and film stock were limited. This was particularly the case with films made during and just after the war, when money for new sets was restricted to $5000 per film. The shadowy look of what has become known as film noir could be used to conceal props and sets lacking in detail, or perhaps missing altogether. While much of this could be achieved by lighting effects alone, cinematographers such as John Alton, or Gregg Toland, who worked on Orson Welles's famous early noir film, *Citizen Kane* (1940), enhanced and spread out the darkness in their pictures by underexposing slow film. Faster film stock, which had only recently become available, was, in any case, much more expensive.

Besides economic considerations, the visual style of film noir owes much to the ideas and techniques of émigré directors such as Lang, Siodmak, and Wilder. Lang's German film, *M* (1931), for example, uses shadowy streets, empty, darkened office buildings, and unlit attics to depict the inner turmoil of the child murderer, played by Peter Lorre. If the chaos of the murderer's mind is represented by the cluttered attics in which he hides, so the dank, half-lit cellar in which he is lynched by a mob of "decent" people suggests that humanity at large is troubled by a dark inner life. This view of the human psyche as dark and troubled, brought by directors such as Lang and Siodmak from Nazi Germany, appears too in the "tough" stories written in America during the 1920s and 1930s. Combining such a view of humanity with the American themes of urban alienation, organized crime, and fear of failure, such stories became ideal vehicles for the émigrés and their followers, and it is from this combination that the mood and sensibility of film noir developed.

Robert Siodmak's 1946 film of Ernest Hemingway's short story "The Killers" (1927) is a good example of the interplay between the look of film noir and its exploration of the ambiguities of the human psyche. *The Killers* concerns a man known as "The Swede" (Burt Lancaster) who waits in his small, dark room for his killers to arrive, accepting his fate because "I did something wrong. Once." Hemingway's story takes us only to the moments before the killers arrive,

while the film uncovers what it was he did wrong through a narrative constructed mainly from flashbacks. The images of The Swede's last moments include shots of him, in a darkened room, lying half-dressed on the bed, deep in thought. The impenetrable shadows around him suggest the impenetrability of his thoughts. His enigmatic and ambiguous answer to the man who warns him of his approaching death suggests the possibility of regret for a criminal past, but turns out to refer to his obsession with a woman. Through flashbacks, and the insurance investigator's haphazard reconstruction of events, it emerges that what The Swede has "done wrong" has nothing to do with the fact of his criminal past but with the psychological reasons for it.

This emphasis on The Swede's psychological state is representative of film noir's fascination with psychoanalysis. Frank Krutnik suggests in *In a Lonely Street* (1991) that Freudian psychoanalysis became popular in America during the late 1930s and 1940s and coincided with the adaptation of hard-boiled crime stories such as "The Killers" by Hollywood. Krutnik argues that the shift in crime thrillers towards highlighting the psychological reasons for and consequences of crime can be attributed to this popularization of psychoanalysis. This is evident, he thinks, in the complex narrative structures of many films noirs, including *The Killers*. In these films, "the process of storytelling becomes submerged"; it becomes unclear who is telling the story, whose version is true, and what their motives are for telling it in a particular way. *Citizen Kane*, for example, addresses directly the process of telling and retelling stories, being the story of the rise and fall of a newspaper magnate. In *Citizen Kane*, as in film noir in general, the margins between fantasy, psychosis, and reality become blurred; the film emerges as the story of Kane's psychological flaws, centering on an incident from his childhood. All of these signs of unstable psychological states are enhanced by film noir's adoption of techniques from Expressionist cinema; exaggerated darkness and light/shade contrast, strange camera angles, and plain, unrealistic sets.

While the political conditions of Europe in the 1930s affected the American film industry through the arrival of talented filmmakers, film noir is also a product of the political instability of the period during and after World War II. Critics point to a crisis in American national identity, the problems of war veterans readjusting to civilian life, and the new threats of the atom bomb and the Cold War, as possible cultural reasons for the flourishing of film noir in the period 1941 to 1958. Certainly the aftermath of war meant that large numbers of young men, to some extent institutionalized by life in the forces, and often physically or psychologically damaged, now had to look after themselves and find work in a competitive labor market that included many more women than before. They returned from war anxious that their contribution be acknowledged, yet questioning what they had fought for, given the new threat that was emerging in Eastern Europe and the Far East. On a more personal level, many returned to wives and families who were no longer dependent on them for financial or emotional support, whose lives had continued without them for several years, and who were unable to understand the ordeal they had suffered. All of this contributed to a sense of instability and hostility in the culture at large that is a central feature of film noir.

Like many films of the time, *The Blue Dahlia* (1946) makes direct reference to the concerns and problems associated with returning war veterans. The story revolves around the return of Johnny Morrison (Alan Ladd) from service in the Navy and his discovery of his wife's infidelity. Helen Morrison (Doris Dowling) represents the new moral possibilities for women in the years following the war, abandoning the traditional roles of wife and mother and declaring her freedom to go where and do what she wants. She goads Johnny into using violence against her, and so unwittingly makes him a suspect for her murder. The exchanges between her and Johnny represent a challenge to old-fashioned versions of masculinity, based on physical strength and power over women and the family. While Johnny's violence is presented in the film as unacceptable and excessive, the idea that he is in some way struggling to come to terms with a changed world presents itself as a way of understanding his actions. The male characters in this film, like The Swede in *The Killers,* and men in film noir in general, command our sympathy because they have all in some way been deprived of their defining masculine roles by forces beyond their control. As is also common in film noir, Johnny finds emotional support in his relationships with other men. Frank Krutnik suggests that the problems Johnny experiences in his conventional family are offset by the stability of the ''all-male Navy family'' that consists of his friends George and Buzz.

Women in film noir tend to fall into two main categories: those who support the hero as good, wives, or pliant molls, and those who use their sexuality in an explicit way to manipulate men and get what they want. Women in this second group, a key feature of film noir, are known as ''femmes fatales,'' dangerous women who encourage the hero's obsessive sexual interest to the point where he will risk his job, his freedom, or even his life for her. The insecurity of the hero's identity, outlined above in the case of The Swede in *The Killers,* leads him to ''over-invest'' in a version of her sexuality which he himself has invented; the femme fatale is awarded power over the hero by the (weakened) hero himself. Her inevitable death can be seen as punishment for her ''unfair'' exploitation of her advantage.

The many examples of cheating wives like Helen Morrison, and more obvious femmes fatales whose overt sexuality plays a part in the hero's misery, is often given as evidence of film noir's inherent misogyny, of a conservative core in what otherwise appears to be a subversive alternative to classical Hollywood cinema. But the femme fatale is usually drawn in at least as much psychological detail as her male counterpart, and the emergence of that unexpected complexity often takes the place of the quest or mystery plot at the center of the hero's attentions. She rejects classical Hollywood cinema's version of passive womanhood and, by whatever means she has at her disposal, actively seeks independence and freedom from men. She is remembered by audiences not for her death, but for her strength in life, her sexual power, and the deadly challenge she represents to the male's attempt to solve the mystery or reach the end of his quest. If film noir is concerned with exploring ambiguities of perspective (through voice-overs and flashbacks), the limits of subjective vision (through the use of shadow, and unnatural camera angles), and the instability of the human psyche, then the femme fatale represents a further interference with clarity of vision. Like the heroes of film noir, the femme fatale is an ambiguous figure, at once the victim of society's restrictions and the defiant answer to them. Her strength, sexual independence, and freedom pose a direct challenge to the masculine gaze of the hero and the male majority of film noir's original audience.

The origins of film noir in the political turmoil of pre-war Europe, and post-war America and Hollywood would seem to limit its scope to the historical period from which it springs. Although film noir was at its most popular during the late 1940s and 1950s, ''noir'' and ''neo-noir'' films have appeared right up to the 1990s. Some of these, like *Farewell, My Lovely* (1975), have been remakes of films made in the 1940s; others, such as *Chinatown* (1974), recreate the

look of 1930s Los Angeles. *Taxi Driver* (1976) and *Seven* (1995) bring ''noir'' sensibilities to their contemporary settings, while *Blade Runner* (1982) adds a futuristic, science-fiction setting that compounds the ambiguities, instabilities, and uncertainties of more conventional film noir. If film noir viewed 1940s America through the bleak sentiments of pre-war Europe, it remains a ''dark mirror'' in which we look to find out who we are, and what we might become.

—Chris Routledge

FURTHER READING:

Christopher, Nicholas. *Somewhere in the Night: Film Noir and the American City.* New York, Free Press, 1997.

Copjec, Joan, editor. *Shades of Noir: A Reader.* London and New York, Verso, 1993.

Crowther, Bruce. *Film Noir: Reflections in a Dark Mirror.* London, Columbus Books, 1988.

Hannsberry, Karen Burroughs. *Femme Noir: Bad Girls of Film.* Jefferson, North Carolina, McFarland, 1998.

Kaplan, E.A., editor. *Women in Film Noir.* London, British Film Institute, 1980.

Krutnik, Frank. *In a Lonely Street: Film Noir, Genre, Masculinity.* London and New York, Routledge, 1991.

Naremore, James. *More Than Night: Film Noir in Its Contexts.* Berkeley, University of California Press, 1998.

Stephens, Michael L. *Film Noir: A Comprehensive, Illustrated Reference to Movies, Terms, and Persons.* Jefferson, North Carolina, McFarland, 1995.

Tuska, Jon. *Dark Cinema.* Westport, Connecticut, Greenwood Press, 1984.

Firearms

The right to carry a gun, whether for purposes of self-protection or hunting animals, is an emotional issue embedded deep in the cultural consciousness of the United States. By the 1990s, after some eight decades of destruction wrought by the use of guns by organized crime, political assassins, and dangerous psychopaths, many Americans were growing disturbed by their gun heritage, but they remained in a hopeless minority when it came to effecting anti-gun legislation.

The American love of firearms probably originated in a combination of frontier actuality and propaganda coup. When English colonists and Native American cultures collided, the usual result was gunfire from the colonists, who won the Pequot and King Philip's wars and secured their toeholds in North America. When Revolutionaries created an icon of independence, it was the Minute Man, usually portrayed with plow in the background and long rifle in hand. According to Samuel Adams and the Concord Battle Monument, it was the Minute Man who defeated the British and won the Revolution. That heroic figure of the liberty-loving, citizen-soldier hovers over all twentieth-century discussions of gun control and the Second Amendment to the U.S. Constitution, whose complete text reads, ''A well-regulated Militia, being necessary to the security of a free State,

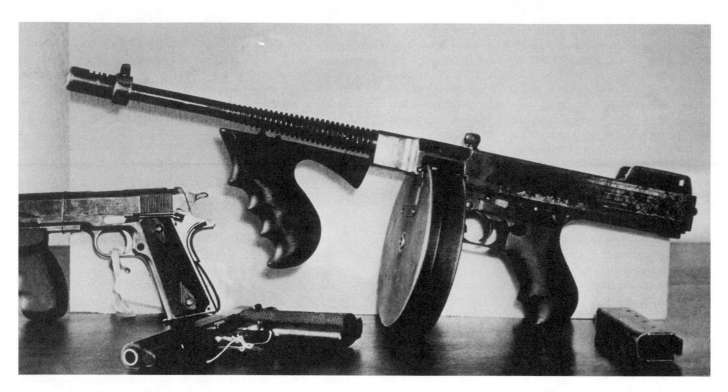

A Thompson Machine gun and a Colt .45.

the right of the people to keep and bear arms, shall not be infringed." Those individuals and organizations like the NRA (National Rifle Association) who favor individual gun ownership stress the last two phrases of the Second Amendment. Those who support gun control or elimination argue that the complete Amendment provides for police organization, not for an individual right.

In the twentieth century, certain specific weapons have achieved iconic status for Americans. In popular military imagination, there are only two American rifles. The first is the M1, or Garand Semi-Automatic Rifle, which General George S. Patton memorialized in his famous assertion, "In my opinion, the M1 rifle is the greatest battle implement ever devised." The M1 is the final development of infantry doctrine which stresses target selection, accuracy, and measured fire. (The original design specifications excluded full automatic firing.) For perhaps 25 years (1944-1969), the M1 was a symbol of American might, rooted in GI grit and bravery, and reluctantly deployed in order to save the world. Some of the best movie images of M1s in skilled acting hands can be seen in William Wellman's *Battleground* (1949) and Samuel Fuller's *Fixed Bayonets* (1951).

The second legendary American military weapon is the M16 rifle. Imaginatively speaking, the M16, which can be toggled for either semi-automatic or full automatic firing, figures in the moral ambiguities of the late Cold War and post-Cold War periods. Late twentieth-century infantry doctrine takes as fundamental the statistical fact that, under fire, the majority of riflemen in World War II did not fire their weapons, and those who did tended to fire high. The M16, with its automatic-fire option and light recoil, lets a soldier "cover" a target area without particular target selection. Probability, more than aim, determines the results.

One of the most enduring and disturbing images of the M16 resides in a television interview during the 1968 Tet Offensive in Vietnam. The reporter questions a rifleman (Delta Company, 5th Brigade, 1st Marine Division) who repeatedly jumps into firing position, shoots a burst of automatic fire, and drops down to relative safety. He first tells the reporter, "The hardest thing is not knowing where they are." After another burst, he says, "The whole thing stinks, really."

When such confusion, which must be common to the experience of all soldiers in the field, is replayed uncensored on television, the iconography shifts from democratic Dogface to enduring but victimized Grunt, doing the will of (at best) deluded leaders. The M16 shares in this imaginative legacy of the Vietnam War, whereas M16s in the hands of young, drug-busting Colombian soldiers, or crowd-controlling Israeli soldiers are more likely to provoke sympathy for peasants and protesters than concerns for enlisted men.

The counterpart to the M16 is the Soviet AK47, which expresses the same combat doctrine. With its characteristic banana-clip and crude wooden stock and fore-piece, the AK47 has a somewhat sharper emblematic presence than the high-industrial M16, perhaps because it is associated with the uprising of the oppressed. It was the weapon of the victorious North Vietnamese Army, and figures in the artful, controlled imagery from that side of the war. In contemporary Mexico, the contrast between M16 and AK47 is stark. The army is equipped with M16s. When one of their most militant opponents, Sub-commander Marcos of the Zapatista National Liberation Army, appears for photo opportunities, he does so "in full military garb with an AK47 automatic rifle strapped across his chest" according to the *New York Times*.

The M16 carries its ambiguous military significance into equivocal imaginations of civilian life. While there are relatively few images of the M1 deployed on American streets, the M16 figures prominently in urban American drug movies. Police SWAT teams carry the weapons in various configurations, ever more technically advanced. In such modern, nihilistic gangster movies as Michael Mann's *Heat* (1995),

Val Kilmer's split devotion to family and to casually murderous excitement has him emptying uncounted magazines of .223 ammunition at expendable policemen, his weapon always toggled to full automatic. The camera delights in shattered windshields, while the exquisite audio-track records the counterpoint of firing with the clinking sound of spent cartridges hitting the streets and sidewalks.

Moving from long guns to hand guns, the American pistol that probably holds pride of place in twentieth-century civilian imagination is the ".45 Automatic," Colt's Model 1911, semi-automatic military side-arm whose high-caliber, relatively low-velocity cartridge was meant to knock a man down, wherever it struck him. It had a name-recognition advantage, since the other Colt .45, a six-shooter, is the favorite gun of such Western movies as *High Noon* (1952). A presentation-grade version of the 1911 Semi-Automatic Colt .45 appears in the movie *Titanic* (1997). The counter-image to the .45 automatic is the German Luger, officer issue in the German army. The pistol's narrow barrel and curved trigger-guard give it a sinuous, European quality, in contrast to the bluff (and heavy) American .45. In cinematic imagination, seductively evil men use Lugers in such movies as Clint Eastwood's *Midnight in Garden of Good and Evil* (1997).

The more visually and audibly stimulating weapon associated with mid-twentieth-century urban mayhem is the "Tommy gun," whose movie and comic-strip rat-a-tat-tat! lights up the seemingly countless gangster-vs.-cops movies. A Tommy gun is the .45 caliber, fully automatic Thompson sub-machine gun. The "sub" simply means that it is smaller in size and magazine capacity than a military machine-gun. There is a famous photograph of smiling John Dillinger, with a drum-magazine Tommy gun in one hand, a small Colt automatic pistol in the other. The most eroticized, cinematic realization of the Tommy gun's power is in the slow-motion shooting of Warren Beatty and Faye Dunaway at the end of Arthur Penn's *Bonnie and Clyde* (1969).

Other handguns permeate late-twentieth-century popular culture. The *James Bond* novels and movies briefly popularized the Walther PPK, and Clint Eastwood's *Dirty Harry* series gave us "Go ahead, make my day," but few know the make of gun down which he speaks (it's a Smith & Wesson .44 Magnum). There are Uzis (Israeli micro sub-machine guns) and the MAC-10, but none of these weapons has the imaginative staying power of the M1, M16, AK47, Colt .45, Luger, and Tommy gun.

—Jonathan Middlebrook

FURTHER READING:

D'Este, Carlo. *Patton: A Genius for War*. New York, Harper-Collins, 1995.

Gerson, Noel B. *The Grand Incendiary; A Biography of Samuel Adams, by Paul Luis*. New York, Dial Press, 1973.

Krakow, Stanley. *Vietnam: A History*. 2nd Rev. Ed. New York, Penguin Books, 1997.

Lepore, Jill. *The Name of War*. New York, Alfred A. Knopf, 1998.

Newton, Michael. *Armed and Dangerous: A Writer's Guide to Weapons*. Cincinnati, Ohio, Writer's Digest Books, 1990.

Toland, John. *The Dillinger Days*. New York, Random House, 1963.

———. *Reporting World War II*. 2 Vols. New York, Literary Classics of the United States, 1995.

Firesign Theatre

With their education, artfulness, attention to detail, and full use of the newly emerging multitrack technologies, the four members of The Firesign Theatre—Peter Bergman (1939—), David Ossman (1936), Phil Proctor (1940—), and Phil Austin (1947)—were the Beatles of recorded comedy. Writing and performing their own material, they created multi-layered surrealist satires out of the very stuff of popular culture: television shows, the Golden Age of Radio, old movies, commercials, literature, music, etc. At a time when the Who was pioneering the rock concept album, Firesign was pioneering the comedy concept album. Their humor reflected the times; complaints about their occasional drug references may be misplaced, since it would be difficult to represent southern California in the 1960s and 1970s without mentioning drugs. But their comedy was much more than an amalgam of cultural references. One 40-minute album might be as tightly structured as a one-act play, achieve real poignancy, and convey new ways of looking at things, new connections; the first cut on their first album, for example, presents a brief aural history of the United States from the Indians' point of view. The group's comedy albums are among the few that can be listened to repeatedly and still be enjoyed, each new listening revealing subtle asides, missed connections, and hidden messages.

Bergman and Proctor first met while studying playwriting at Yale, and Bergman went on to work on a British radio show with Goon Show alumnus Spike Milligan. While in England, Bergman saw the Beatles for the first time, and vowed someday to become part of a four-man comedy team. The foursome came together in 1966 as part of "Radio Free Oz," a free-form late-night FM radio show on KPFK in Los Angeles, hosted by Bergman. Guests included Andy Warhol and Buffalo Springfield, but the show developed a cult following because of the group's improvisations. No one was aware of the size of their following until the group began promoting a Love-In (a word coined by Bergman) in Elysian Park in Los Angeles, and 40,000 hippies showed up. Seeing the commercial potential, CBS record producer Gary Usher signed the group to a record contract. Their first four albums for CBS remain the core of their work, include their best albums, and show the group's evolution: the transition from shorter pieces to album-length fantasies, and the emergence of the Fifth Crazee Guy. The Firesign Theatre's publishing company is called 4 or 5 Crazee Guys Publishing because the group found that, when all were contributing and when each had ultimate veto power (if anyone of them didn't like a line, it was out), a tangible entity emerged that was much more than the sum of its parts: the Fifth Crazee Guy. According to Austin, "It's like, suddenly there is this fifth guy that actually does the writing." And who is the Fifth Crazee Guy? He's Clem riding the bus, he's George Leroy Tirebiter, he's Mr. and Mrs. John Smith from Anytown, USA, he's the audience's laughter, he's an everyman (and everywoman) reflecting our culture and our collective unconscious. To begin to grasp how the Fifth Crazee Guy manifests itself on Firesign albums, imagine someone who had The Goon Show and the Beatles as parents but grew up in America, and then, at some point, was sucked into an alternate universe.

Their first album, *Waiting for the Electrician or Someone Like Him* (1968), contains several short pieces on Side One (including the Indians'-eye view of American history and some drug humor), with all of Side Two taken up by a comic nightmare journey through Turkish security, complete with the now-classic game-show sendup Beat the Reaper. That album sold poorly, but their sophomore effort,

How Can You Be in Two Places At Once When You're Not Anywhere At All (1969), benefitted from the emergence of FM radio as a significant force and the willingness of FM deejays to play long cuts. The title piece is a sonic delight that puts you behind the wheel of a motor home with climate control that changes the climate as no car ever has before. And Side Two contains the piece that is most likely to convert the uninitiated: Nick Danger, Third Eye, a pun-filled satire of noir radio dramas involving a Peter Lorre soundalike and bizarre time-travel convolutions. Their third and fourth albums, considered to be their best, each contain one long cut (interrupted only by the pre-CD need to turn the album over). *Don't Crush That Dwarf, Hand Me the Pliers* (1970), the first of their albums recorded on 16 tracks, mingles the recollections of film producer George Leroy Tirebiter with footage from one of his teen comedies, "High School Madness," to produce a moving nostalgia piece loaded with laughs. But nothing could prepare fans for the total sonic immersion of *I Think We're All Bozos On This Bus* (1971), a sensurround trip to and through the Future Fair—a cross between Disneyland and a World's Fair—complete with clones, computers, and holograms, where our hero, Clem, eventually breaks the president and has a showdown with the computer controlling everything. Repeated listenings reveal hidden subtleties. The fourth time through the listener may realize that, while passengers are warned to pump their shoes before walking across the water, Clem gave up shoes years ago. And the sixth listening might reveal that, when Clem talks about how he's going to just "sink in" to his bus seat and the P.A. says to get "in sync," the words "sink" and "sync" are, in fact, in sync. At the end of the millennium, Firesign was still going strong, producing the album *Give Me Immortality or Give Me Death* (1998), set at Radio Now (a station so cutting-edge that it changes formats every commercial break) on the last hour of the last day of 1999. And individual troupe members continued to lend their vocal talents to everything from *The Tick* TV series (1995) to *A Bug's Life* (1998).

—Bob Sullivan

FURTHER READING:

"Firesign." www.firesigntheatre.com. February 1999.

Smith, Ronald L. *Comedy on Record: The Complete Critical Discography.* New York, Garland Publishing, Inc., 1988.

Fischer, Bobby (1943—)

In 1972, American Robert "Bobby" James Fischer became the world's chess champion after defeating Soviet Boris Spassky. This match, set against the backdrop of Cold War rivalries, marked the pinnacle of Fischer's often turbulent career. In 1975, Fischer was stripped of his title after refusing to defend it. Despite his eccentricities, Fischer's demands initiated improvements in playing conditions and the financial rewards of professional chess. In the western world, Fischer's dramatic rise to international prominence revitalized popular interest in chess.

In 1992, Fischer, still claiming to be the legitimate world champion, ended his self-imposed exile to play a return match against Spassky. Played in war-torn Yugoslavia in violation of United States and United Nations sanctions, this match again made Fischer the center of popular controversy. Fischer defeated Spassky with 10 wins, 5 losses, and 15 draws, and received $3.65 million as the winner's share of the prize fund. Following the match Fischer returned to seclusion.

—Christopher D. O'Shea

FURTHER READING:

Brady, Frank. *Profile of a Prodigy: The Life and Games of Bobby Fischer.* New York, David McKay Co., 1965.

Evans, Larry. "Bobby's Back!" *Chess Life.* Vol. 47, No. 11, 1992, 56-59.

Forbes, Cathy. "Bobby Fischer, the Holy Grail - A Balkan Odyssey." *Chess Life.* Vol. 48, No. 3, 1993, 26-28.

Huntington, Robert. "Observations from THE MATCH." *Chess Life.* Vol. 48, No. 2, 1993, 37-40.

Roberts, Richard. *Fischer/Spassky: The New York Times Report on the Chess Match of the Century.* New York, Bantam Books, 1972.

Steiner, George. *Fields of Force: Fischer and Spassky at Reykjavik.* New York, Viking Press, 1972.

Fisher, Eddie (1928—)

For a brief time, Eddie Fisher was the most popular male vocalist in America, but for a longer period, the affable crooner was the center

Eddie Fisher

of a highly-publicized series of romantic entanglements, involving some of the most famous celebrities of his generation.

One of seven children of a Jewish grocer in South Philadelphia, Edward Fisher had a Depression-era childhood of poverty and frequent moves. He sought a singing career from an early age, and became a regular performer on Philadelphia radio by the age of fifteen. Two years later, the seventeen-year-old Fisher obtained a tryout with the Buddy Morrow band in New York, but he was only employed for a few weeks. Calling himself Sonny Edwards, Fisher haunted the city's nightclubs for months, searching for work. In an audition at the Copacabana, Fisher impressed the owner with his voice, but his immature looks and manner detracted from his talent. Fortunately, the nightclub owner put Fisher in touch with publicist and celebrity manager, Milton Blackstone, who in turn found the youthful entertainer a summer job at Grossinger's resort hotel in the Catskills. There Fisher set about learning as much as possible, not only by honing his own skills, but also by studying the behavior of the famous acts that performed at Grossinger's.

In the fall of 1946 Fisher returned to the Copacabana, where he was given a small job, and the ambitious young singer spent the next three years in a vain effort at becoming a star. Frustrated with his progress, in 1949 Fisher put himself fully under the control of Blackstone, and made one last effort at establishing himself as a singing sensation. Now 21, he was more mature and his stage presence had greatly improved, so Blackstone decided to manufacture a groundswell of popularity for Fisher, and persuaded the famous comedian Eddie Cantor to "discover" Fisher during a performance at Grossinger's.

Blackstone paid for "fans" to sit throughout the hall, and to cheer wildly during Fisher's act. Cantor set up the audience to love Eddie Fisher, and Fisher performed very well. Several reporters, who had been alerted by Milton Blackstone of a breaking show-business story, covered the "discovery" for major newspapers. A star was born in one hour of conniving, where four years of talented and honest effort had achieved nothing.

Cantor then took Eddie Fisher under his wing, giving him a place on his current national tour and television show, and even wrangling invitations for the young singer on other major television programs. Finally, Cantor and Blackstone arranged for Fisher to sign with RCA Victor, one of the biggest recording companies. Throughout the rest of 1949 and all of 1950, Fisher's career grew at a rapid pace. He had several hit records, performed frequently on television and on tour, and was given *Billboard* magazine's award as Most Promising Male Vocalist of 1950.

Early in 1951, Eddie Fisher was drafted into the Army during the Korean War. But Blackstone used his influence to ensure that Fisher would spend his two years in the military crooning with the U.S. Army Band. In fact, given that his recording dates, television appearances, and tours continued without a hitch, Fisher's career probably benefited from his military service. Not until Fisher made a personal request to President Truman did the Army allow him to visit Korea and entertain fighting troops.

Returning to civilian life in early 1953, Fisher found that his handlers had set up a television program for him to host, a twice-weekly show on NBC. Sponsored by the Coca Cola corporation, the show was called *Coke Time*, as Fisher's popularity with teenagers made soft drinks a logical sponsor. The show lasted over three years on radio as well as on television; when it ended, NBC found another show (albeit a less successful one) for him until 1959.

Television was just part of Fisher's hectic performance schedule, which included tours as well as frequent live shows in New York. After excessive singing began to harm his voice, Fisher was taken to celebrity physician Dr. Max Jacobson and given an injection of special vitamins, or so he was told. He felt better immediately, and turned to Dr. Jacobson more and more often in the years to come. The shots were a mixture of substances, but mostly amphetamines or "speed;" Jacobson would eventually lose his license to practice medicine, but not before Eddie Fisher had become a confirmed drug addict.

Fisher's youth, fame, and wealth carried him through the next several years, and his records continued to sell well. Drug use made Fisher easier for his handlers, who booked him into almost continuous performances, to manage. His income and popularity soared. In 1954 Fisher won the *Cash Box* magazine Top Male Vocalist award.

In the same year, Fisher began seeing a young but already established movie star named Debbie Reynolds. His base of operations in New York and hers in Los Angeles limited their interaction, but they became close. The media quickly promoted Fisher and Reynolds as America's sweethearts, but when marriage began to appear imminent Fisher's fans (mostly young and female) turned on him. Record sales declined, and Fisher's managers attempted to block the marriage. Finally in late 1955 Fisher and Reynolds were married at Grossinger's.

Throughout 1956 Fisher experienced a career decline. Coca Cola cancelled his program, his records were not selling well, and rock and roll was erupting into the popular music scene. Almost from the outset, Fisher's marriage was in trouble too. The media once again made much of this celebrity couple, chronicling the supposed ups and downs of the marriage, casting Fisher as the thoughtless villain and Reynolds, whose film career as a sweet young thing was at its height, as the put-upon wife. There was a lot of truth in what the reporters wrote. Fisher was a dope addict, an irresponsible husband and father, and a compulsive gambler. He still made a huge income, but he was virtually spending it all.

After the death of one of Fisher's closest friends, the producer Mike Todd, Fisher's marriage disintegrated completely, and he began dating Todd's widow, actress Elizabeth Taylor. The media responded predictably to this famous romantic triangle, casting Taylor as the evil "other woman." Eddie and Debbie were divorced in February 1959. (Their daughter, Carrie, would go on to become famous as *Star Wars'* Princess Leia and as a bestselling author.) Three months later, Eddie married Liz. Fisher's career had slipped so badly by that point that he has never been able to make an effective comeback.

Fisher had hoped to parlay his singing success into a movie career, and in 1956 he had starred with then-wife Reynolds in *Bundle of Joy*. It was no more successful than his performance opposite Taylor in *Butterfield 8* in 1960; she won the Academy Award for Best Actress, but Fisher was never again invited to act in a major film. A year later on another film set, the epic *Cleopatra*, Taylor switched allegiances once more, this time to co-star Richard Burton. Fisher was the media's innocent, sympathetic character this time, in an orgy of gossip reporting that outdid all earlier efforts.

The next several decades followed a sad pattern for Eddie Fisher—high profile romantic involvements, attempts to get off drugs, failed comebacks, and tax troubles. Even a former celebrity can earn a lot of money in America, but Fisher could never get ahead. His drug habit and erratic behavior kept him from building a strong second career from the wreckage of the first. He was the last of the old-style crooners, and the least capable of recovering from changes in American popular music.

—David Lonergan

FURTHER READING:

Fisher, Eddie. *Eddie: My Life, My Loves*. New York, Harper and Row, 1981.

Greene, Myrna. *The Eddie Fisher Story*. Middlebury, Vermont, Paul S. Eriksson, 1978.

Fisher-Price Toys

One of the most famous American toymakers, Fisher-Price has been part of children's play for almost seven decades. While Fisher-Price is still creating low-cost and durable playthings for infants and preschoolers, older Fisher-Price toys are now prized collectibles, coveted by the same owners—now adult toy aficianados—who once clutched them in crib and playpen. From Granny Doodle and Snoopy Snuffer in the 1930s, through the decades with Tick Tock Clock, Pull-a-Tune Xylophone, and Little People, to computer software for toddlers in the 1990s, the Fisher-Price name has long been in the forefront of imaginative and educational play for children.

The company was founded in 1931 in East Aurora, New York, by Herman G. Fisher, Irving Price, and Helen M. Schelle, who began with $5,000 and the idea of creating an innovative line of toys for very young children. Though they managed to build their factory and began producing toys during the difficult Depression years, few had money to spend on luxuries, and during World War II the factory was refitted to produce goods needed for the war effort. By the 1950s, however, toy production was up and running again, which coincided with the arrival of the Baby Boomer generation during a more prosperous period when more disposable income was available for spending on leisure-time products like toys. With the demand for toys skyrocketing, Fisher-Price was forced to build another plant. For the first time, the company began to make its own metal parts for toys and to make them with an exciting and popular new material—plastic.

By the 1960s, Fisher-Price produced twice as many toys as in the three previous decades combined. Discretionary income of American families would continue to vary, but by the 1960s the idea had been firmly established that "store-bought" toys were necessities for children. Television commercials for toys began to be aimed at children themselves, who became the best lobbyists for toy companies. In 1969 Quaker Foods bought the toy company, and the 1970s saw the opening of new Fisher-Price plants in New York, Texas, Mexico, Belgium, and England.

Much of Fisher-Price's success was due to its focus on and understanding of toys for infants and preschool children. The darkest days for the company came in the 1980s when it attempted to branch out into toys for older children. This new line included make-up kits and battery-powered sports cars, and even a toy video camera that used audiotapes that could be played back through a television. The new products failed miserably. This failure, coupled with large order cancellations caused by Fisher-Price's inability to meet delivery deadlines, gave competing toy manufacturers Mattel and Hasbro a significant advantage. In 1991, Fisher-Price went back to its specialty: producing simple toys beloved by infants and toddlers. The company streamlined its operation and regained its status among toymakers. In 1993, competing toy giant Mattel acquired Fisher-Price and continues to expand the Fisher-Price niche in the United States and abroad.

As toys have grown more and more sophisticated, Fisher-Price has kept up, producing educational computer games for two and three-year-olds. But the Fisher-Price standbys remain its most popular items. The Bubble Mower, which emits a stream of soap bubbles as it "mows" the floor, the Corn Popper, a clear plastic dome in which colored balls jump energetically as it is pushed, and SnapLock Beads, which teach dexterity, are among the favorites. Perhaps the most popular of all are the Little People, small wooden figures that are little more than colorful heads on wooden pegs that fit into various vehicles and toy houses. Created decades ago, the older Little People are valued by adult toy collectors, while the newer ones, little changed except for racial diversity and wider plastic bodies, are equally in demand in the playroom. These toys are durable in every sense of the word, their appeal is diminished neither by time, nor by the vigorous chewing of a two-year-old.

—Tina Gianoulis

FURTHER READING:

Fox, Bruce R., and Murray, John J. *A Historical, Rarity, and Value Guide: Fisher- Price 1931-1963*. New York, Books America, 1993.

"The Magical World Of Fisher-Price: Collectible and Memorabilia Web Site." Unofficial Fisher-Price website. http://www.mwfp.com. May 1999.

Fisk, Carlton (1947—)

Despite the fact that he holds the all-time major league career records for games played and home runs by a catcher, Carlton Fisk will always be remembered for his dramatic, extra-innings, game-winning home run in game six of the 1975 World Series. With the score tied in the bottom of the twelfth inning and his Boston Red Sox trailing the Cincinnati Reds three games to two, he hit a long line drive down the left field line. As the ball started curving foul, Fisk hopped down the first base line and waved his arms towards fair territory willing the ball to stay in play. After the ball bounced off of the foul pole for the series-tying home run, he jumped in the air, arms outstretched in celebration. Although the Sox would lose the series the next day, Fisk's spontaneous and joyous reaction captured the public's imagination, as it seemed to exemplify the purity and innocence of baseball during a time of contentiousness and increasing labor strife in the game. Fisk was traded to the Chicago White Sox in 1980 after eight years with the Red Sox and retired in 1993.

—Gregory Bond

FURTHER READING:

Gammons, Peter. *Beyond the Sixth Game*. Boston, Houghton-Mifflin, 1985.

McKelvey, G. Richard. *Fisk's Homer, Willie's Catch and the Shot Heard Round the World: Classic Moments from Postseason Baseball, 1940-1996*. Jefferson, North Carolina, McFarland and Company, 1998.

Thorn, John, et al. *Total Baseball*. New York, Viking Penguin, 1997.

A Fistful of Dollars

The film *A Fistful of Dollars,* released in 1964, was the first of the ''spaghetti Westerns'' to gain a large audience in the United States. Directed by Sergio Leone, it starred Clint Eastwood, who was then best known to American audiences as a supporting actor on the television Western *Rawhide*. Eastwood's television character, the fresh-faced, slightly naive Rowdy Yates, was far removed from his first starring film role as the unshaven, cigarillo-smoking, deadly bounty hunter known only as ''The Man with No Name.''

The plot was blatantly lifted from Akira Kurasawa's Japanese classic *Yojimbo*. In both films, a mercenary shows up in a town that is being terrorized by two rival gangs. The stranger cleverly plays each gang off against the other, then ruthlessly wipes out those who are left. This storyline was revived yet again for the 1996 Bruce Willis vehicle *Last Man Standing.* The worldwide success of the film led to Eastwood's reprising his role in two Leone-directed sequels: *For a Few Dollars More* (1965) and *The Good, the Bad, and the Ugly* (1966).

—Justin Gustainis

FURTHER READING:

Weisser, Thomas. *Spaghetti Westerns: The Good, the Bad, and the Violent.* Jefferson, North Carolina, McFarland & Co., 1992.

Fitzgerald, Ella (1918-1996)

The flawless voice and delivery of singer Ella Fitzgerald is woven tightly into the tapestry of American popular music. Her place in the canon of jazz artists was ensured early on in her career, while she reached a wider audience throughout the world with her renditions of those enduring songs that have come to be known as standards. Her name is almost synonymous with the compositions of Irving Berlin, George Gershwin, Rodgers and Hart, and Cole Porter, as well as the music of Duke Ellington. Her interpretation of their music is forever enshrined in her famous ''Song Book'' series of albums, in which she uniquely included the verses to the songs. Billed as ''The First Lady of Song,'' she commanded sell-out attendance at her concerts at home and abroad, touring extensively from the

Clint Eastwood in a scene from the film *A Fistful of Dollars*.

Ella Fitzgerald

mid-1940s onwards, but her unique integrity to the music and the high standards she set herself never wavered in the face of her immense popularity.

Born in Newport News, Virginia, and raised in Yonkers, New York, Ella Fitzgerald was discovered at the age of 16 while singing in a talent contest at the Apollo Theater in Harlem. She joined the Chick Webb band in 1935 and became the idol of Harlem's Savoy Ballroom. She was featured on most of Webb's recordings, and Decca was committed to pushing her recording career, which began with "Love and Kisses" in 1935. She had her first hit with the humorous and perkily tuneful ditty, "A-Tisket, A-Tasket," in 1938, which propelled her to the top of the charts. In the course of her subsequent recording career, she made over 250 albums and won 13 Grammy Awards.

Ella inherited Webb's band after his death in 1939, and just muddled along until Norman Granz, later her manager (and instigator of her "Song Book" albums), began to feature her in his Jazz at the Philharmonic Concerts. Mingling with great jazz musicians at a time when jazz drew enormous audiences and dominated the popular music scene, gave her the exposure and education that allowed her to move to the front rank of vocalists. Her live recordings demonstrate the musical affection she and her audience shared. *Ella in Berlin,* for example, has her forgetting the words to her version of "Mack the Knife," but she keeps going, making it up as she playfully teases herself. The audience loved it. This moment would probably have been cut out of a studio recording. Ella enjoyed touring and continued to do so for most of her life until ill health prohibited her from doing so. She generally appeared with a trio, but was also frequently found at festivals where she would join groups of varying sizes. Fortunately,

many of these live performances, in which she was in great form, were recorded.

Ella Fitzgerald was blessed with a crystal clear voice and perfect pitch. Indeed, the Memorex Corporation capitalized on her ability to break glass in their famous commercials that asked whether it was Ella or Memorex tape. Her tone was generally bright and cheerful, and some critics caviled that her sense of fun got in the way of her overall art, depriving her of emotional depth. In fact, her technique enabled her to do anything she desired with a song, and she loved what has come to be termed the Great American Songbook (Berlin, Porter et al.). Her clarity of diction was the admiration of her peers, including her male counterpart of perfection, Frank Sinatra, and her live performances were suffused with warmth and a quality of youthful vulnerability that she never lost.

Ella Fitzgerald is often bracketed with Billie Holiday, her contemporary, as among the greatest of jazz vocalists, but although she could, and did, swing and scat with the best of them, her repertoire was not jazz dominated. Holiday is generally defined as the more emotional and sensual of the two, implying her greater depth and sophistication, while Fitzgerald is considered to have greater simplicity and directness. Her dexterity was considered equal to that of the best horn players, and Bing Crosby was not alone in saying she had "the best ear of any singer ever" and called her "the greatest."

Duke Ellington said that Ella's skill (she is commonly referred to simply as Ella) "brings to mind the words of the maestro, Mr. Toscanini, who said concerning singers, 'Either you're a good musician or you're not.' In terms of musicianship, Ella Fitzgerald was beyond category." Mel Torme marveled that "Anyone who attempts to sing extemporaneously—that is, scat—will tell you that the hardest aspect is to stay in tune. You are wandering all over the scales, the notes coming out of your mouth a millisecond after you think of them. . . . Her notes float out in perfect pitch, effortlessly and, most important of all, swinging." Ella loved Louis Armstrong, and the three albums and many radio checks she made with him can be placed with her best work. The respect and affection these artists had for each other shines through their recordings, and their *Porgy and Bess* album remains essential to any jazz collection.

A favorite guest artist on television programs—Dinah Shore and Bing Crosby featured her often—Ella was in particularly good form on the *Swing into Spring* programs of 1958 and 1959, and in a program produced by Norman Granz on PBS in November 1979, which featured Count Basie and his Orchestra, Roy Eldridge, Zoot Sims, Joe Pass, and many other leading jazz artists. She also made a number of cameo appearances in movies, and was featured more substantially in *Pete Kelly's Blues* (1955) and *St. Louis Blues* (1958).

Ella Fitzgerald came of age in a period that respected elegance and artistry. She continued to hone her craft throughout her long career, and her fans instinctively appreciated her note-perfect musicianship and precise technique that was so admired by the cognoscenti. Her long career saw her singing in numerous and varied settings and winning fans across several generations. She rose from simple origins to become a good will ambassador for America.

In 1947 Ella married bass player Ray Brown and the couple adopted a son, Ray Brown, Jr., before divorcing in 1953. She suffered some eye trouble in the 1970s, but continued to perform happily at concerts and festivals until the late 1980s when she grew debilitated as a consequence of the diabetes from which she had suffered for a number of years. In 1992, she had to have a toe removed as a result of the disease, and gave the final concert of her career in Palm Beach,

Florida, in December of that year. The following year both her legs were amputated, and she died three years later at the age of 78.

—Frank A. Salamone

FURTHER READING:

Colin, Sid. *Ella: The Life and Times of Ella Fitzgerald.* London, Elm Tree Books, 1986.

Fidelman, Geoffrey Mark. *First Lady of Song: Ella Fitzgerald for the Record.* Secaucus, New Jersey, Carol Publishing Group, 1994.

Gourse, Leslie, editor. *The Ella Fitzgerald Companion: Seven Decades of Commentary.* New York, Schirmer Books, 1998.

Kliment, Bud. *Ella Fitzgerald.* New York, Chelsea House, 1988.

McDonough, John. "Ella: A Voice We'll Never Forget." *Down Beat.* Vol. 63, No. 9, September 1996.

Nicholson, Stuart. *Ella Fitzgerald: A Biography of the First Lady of Jazz.* New York, Da Capo Press, 1995.

Fitzgerald, F. Scott (1896-1940)

Perhaps because so much of his writing is autobiographical, F. Scott Fitzgerald is as famous for his personal life as he is for his writing. In his career as a writer, Fitzgerald proved to be gifted in a

F. Scott Fitzgerald

number of forms—he excelled as a novelist, a short story writer, and an essayist. But because his personal and professional histories paralleled the times in which he lived and wrote, Fitzgerald will be forever identified with The Jazz Age of the 1920s and the ensuing Great Depression of the 1930s.

F. Scott Fitzgerald was born on September 24, 1896, the namesake and distant cousin of the author of the National Anthem. His father, Edward, who viewed himself as an old Southerner, was from Maryland, while his mother, Mary (Mollie) McQuillan, was the daughter of an Irish immigrant who was a successful St. Paul grocery wholesaler. After Fitzgerald's father failed as a businessman in St. Paul, Minnesota, he relocated the family to upstate New York, where he worked as a salesman for Procter and Gamble. In 1908 Fitzgerald's father was let go and he moved the family back to St. Paul. After two years at the Newman School, a Catholic Prep school in New Jersey, Fitzgerald enrolled at Princeton in the Fall of 1913.

It was during his years at Princeton that Fitzgerald first applied himself to the pursuit of a literary life. He wrote for the Princeton Triangle Club's musicals and also contributed pieces to the *Princeton Tiger* and the *Nassau Literary Magazine.* In addition, he cultivated life-long relationships with fellow students who also went on to achieve literary success, including Edmund Wilson and John Peale Bishop. Unfortunately, Fitzgerald's dedication to the literary life resulted in his neglecting his studies. In 1917, after being placed on academic probation and realizing that he was unlikely to graduate, Fitzgerald dropped out of Princeton and joined the army, in which he was commissioned a second lieutenant in the infantry.

Like so many others who were slated to see action in Europe, Fitzgerald was certain his days were numbered. Accordingly, he quickly turned out a novel entitled *The Romantic Egoist,* which was an autobiographical work chronicling the Princeton years of "Armory Blaine." Although the novel was rejected by Charles Scribner's Sons, it was praised for its originality and invited to be resubmitted after revision. In the summer of 1918 Fitzgerald was assigned to Camp Sheridan, outside of Montgomery, Alabama. While there he met Zelda Sayre, the debutante youngest daughter of an Alabama Supreme Court Judge. Thus began one the most famous tragic romances in American history. Fitzgerald pursued Zelda with vigor, but was not particularly well liked by her family; who thought he was an ill-suited match for Zelda. He placed high hopes in Scribner's accepting his revised novel, which would, he hoped, make him worthy of Zelda's hand. They rejected it, which ultimately resulted in Zelda breaking off their engagement. Shortly before Fitzgerald was to go overseas, the war ended and he was discharged. In 1919 he left for New York intending to make his fortune in order to persuade Zelda to marry him.

Amazingly, Fitzgerald succeeded. After a brief stint in New York, he returned to St. Paul to dedicate himself to rewriting his novel yet again. The finished product, *This Side of Paradise,* was published on March 26, 1920. The novel was an immediate smash hit, making Fitzgerald suddenly famous as the voice of his generation. A week later he married Zelda in New York and the couple began their life together as young celebrities. In order to support their lavish lifestyle, Fitzgerald wrote short stories for mass-circulation magazines, which he did for the remainder of his life. Most of his stories were published in *The Saturday Evening Post,* which resulted in his becoming known as a "*Post* Writer." Since he wrote many of them for money, Fitzgerald often felt that his short stories were not artistic achievements on par with his novels. However, literary history has proven

Fitzgerald's estimation of his short stories wrong. Fitzgerald published some 160 magazine stories in his lifetime, an extraordinarily high number by any count. Although many of these are second rate, his finest pieces nevertheless rank at the forefront of American short stories. Among his best are "Bernice Bobs Her Hair," "May Day," "The Diamond as Big as the Ritz," "Winter Dreams," "The Rich Boy," "Babylon Revisited," and "Crazy Sunday."

After spending a summer in Connecticut the Fitzgeralds moved to New York City, where Fitzgerald wrote his second novel, *The Beautiful and the Damned* (1922), which tells the story of the dissipation of Anthony and Gloria Patch. Much of the book's events were inspired by the Fitzgeralds' drunken lifestyle, particularly during their time in Connecticut. The novel was not particularly well received, nor did it make much money. The Fitzgeralds, especially Scott, where quickly gaining a well-deserved reputation as hard drinkers. Although he claimed never to have worked while under the effects of "stimulant"—and judging by the quality of his work it's likely the truth—Fitzgerald's reputation as a carouser hurt his literary standing.

After their first trip to Europe, the Fitzgeralds returned to St. Paul, where in October of 1921 Zelda gave birth to, their only child, a daughter, Frances Scott (Scottie) Fitzgerald. In the mean time, Fitzgerald wrote *The Vegetable,* a play he was sure would result in financial riches. The Fitzgeralds moved to Great Neck, Long Island in order to be closer to Broadway. Unfortunately, the play bombed at its tryout in November of 1923. Fitzgerald was bitterly disappointed. The distractions of New York proved too much for Fitzgerald. He was not making progress on his third novel, and he and Zelda were increasingly fighting, often after heavy drinking. The Fitzgeralds retreated to Europe in an attempt to find peace.

In April of 1925 Fitzgerald published *The Great Gatsby,* the book that was to become his literary legacy. Through the recollections of Nick Carraway, *The Great Gatsby* recounts the history of Jay Gatz and his love for Daisy Buchanan. As Matthew Bruccoli writes in his introduction to *A Life in Letters,* "Fitzgerald's clear, lyrical, colorful, witty style evoked associations with time and place. . . . The chief theme of Fitzgerald's work is aspiration—the idealism he regarded as defining American character. Another major theme was mutability or loss. As a social historian Fitzgerald became identified with 'The Jazz Age': 'It was an age of miracles, it was an age of art, it was an age of excess, and it was an age of satire.'" *Gatsby* is the essential Jazz Age document—the work most commonly considered an accurate reflection of the ultimately irresponsible optimism of the Roaring Twenties boom years. Jay Gatz started off with a traditional American work ethic, but in his pursuit of the American Dream his ethic eventually gave way to the pursuit of money. The inevitable failure of his dreams, which were all along founded on a fallacy, anticipated the demise of the postwar prosperity that characterized the 1920s, which officially came to a close with the stock market crash on October 29, 1929.

Fitzgerald knew *Gatsby* was good, but the reviews were lukewarm and sales were extremely disappointing. In fact, at the time of his death the book had sold less than 23,000 copies. But in the end, Fitzgerald was proved correct; in the years following his death, *The Great Gatsby,* along with the rest of Fitzgerald's work, underwent a remarkable renaissance. Beginning in the 1950s, Fitzgerald's literary reputation skyrocketed. Book after book was reissued and numerable new collections of his stories were released to keep up with demand. In the 1990s, *The Great Gatsby* remained by far the most frequently assigned book in American high schools and colleges.

After being labeled the voice of his generation and experiencing fame and notoriety as someone whose life was representative of the Jazz Age, Fitzgerald, like the nation around him, fell on extremely hard times. In 1930 Zelda experienced her first mental breakdown. Her mental problems lasted the remainder of her life, which she spent in and out of sanitariums. Zelda's medical condition was of great concern to Fitzgerald, who by all accounts never stopped loving her. Unfortunately, his drinking increased concurrently with his need for more money. Scottie was in private schools and Zelda's medical expenses were immense. From the publication of *The Great Gatsby* in 1925, Fitzgerald had been writing almost exclusively short stories in order to counteract cash flow problems. But in the early 1930s his price, which had peaked at $4,000 per story for his *Post* stories, began to plummet. Fitzgerald's *Post* stories no longer had an audience; the country, deep in economic depression, no longer wanted to read about the Jazz Age. In truth, Fitzgerald's stories are often neither optimistic nor do they always end happily. But Fitzgerald's reputation as Jazz Age figure could not be separated from his fiction. His star fell rapidly.

Fitzgerald's final completed novel was *Tender is the Night,* a tale about the fall of Dick Diver loosely based on Fitzgerald's experiences with Zelda's various breakdowns. The 1934 publication was a critical and financial failure. Although not as well crafted as *Gatsby, Tender* has since earned its proper place as an American masterpiece. For the remainder of his life, Fitzgerald scrambled to make a living, writing essays and stories for magazines and spending time in Hollywood as a contract writer. Towards the end of his life he appeared to have finally put things in order. He was sober, in a stable relationship with Hollywood movie columnist Sheilah Graham, and in the midst of writing *The Last Tycoon,* which even in incomplete form has the characteristics of his finest work. Just as America appeared to be coming out of the Depression, so too did Fitzgerald seem to be on the brink of making a return to his former glory. But such was not to be. On December 21, 1940, Fitzgerald died of a heart attack in Graham's apartment. He was 44 years old.

Despite his meteoric posthumous rise to the forefront of American letters, the myth of Fitzgerald as an irresponsible writer has persevered. In fact, Fitzgerald was a meticulous craftsman—a dedicated reviser who went through countless drafts of everything he ever wrote. But when we think of Fitzgerald, we think of a raucous prodigy whose Jazz Age excesses became larger the life. Or perhaps we think of the tragic figure of the 1930s whose fall from grace somehow seemed to be the inevitable price he had to pay for his earlier actions. Either way, Fitzgerald's art ultimately supersedes his life. The events of his life will continue to fascinate us as legend, but the grace and beauty of his uniquely American works will forever serve as a testament to the truth of Fitzgerald's opinion of himself: "I am not a great man, but sometimes I think the impersonal and objective quality of my talent, and the sacrifices of it, in pieces, to preserve its essential value has some sort of epic grandeur."

—Robert C. Sickels

FURTHER READING:

Berman, Ronald. *The Great Gatsby and Modern Times.* Urbana, University of Illinois Press, 1994.

Bloom, Harold, editor. *F. Scott Fitzgerald.* New York, Chelsea House, 1985.

Bruccoli, Matthew J. *A Life in Letters: F. Scott Fitzgerald.* New York, Simon and Schuster, 1994.

———. *Some Sort of Epic Grandeur: The Life of F. Scott Fitzgerald.* New York, Harcourt Brace Jovanovich, 1981.

Donaldson, Scott. *Fool For Love: F. Scott Fitzgerald.* New York, St. Martin's Press, 1983.

———, editor. *Critical Essays on F. Scott Fitzgerald's The Great Gatsby.* Boston, G.K. Hall, 1984.

Kuehl, John. *F. Scott Fitzgerald: A Study of the Short Fiction.* Boston, Twayne Publishers, 1991.

Mellow, James R. *Invented Lives: F. Scott and Zelda Fitzgerald.* Boston, Houghton Mifflin, 1984.

Seiters, Dan. *Image Patterns in the Novels of F. Scott Fitzgerald.* Ann Arbor, UMI Research Press, 1986.

Tate, Mary Jo. *F. Scott Fitzgerald A to Z: The Essential Reference to His Life and Work.* New York, Facts on File, 1998.

Flack, Roberta (1939—)

One of the most popular female singers of the early 1970s, Roberta Flack was critically praised for her impressively beautiful and classically controlled voice, as well as her performance style: powerful, yet intimate in its delivery. Flack was a musical prodigy, and achieved her mastery of song interpretation early on. After years of study and working as a music teacher, she began recording professionally in 1969. Her biggest success came in 1971 with the song "The First Time Ever I Saw Your Face." By the following year, it was the number one song in America, popularized in part through its inclusion in the soundtrack of Clint Eastwood's *Play Misty for Me.* Over the next two decades Flack's successes were sporadic, but interest in her music surged again in the late 1990s, inspired by the Fugees' popular hip-hop remake of her 1973 song "Killing Me Softly."

—Brian Granger

FURTHER READING:

Whitburn, Joel. *The Billboard Book of Top 40 Hits.* New York, Billboard Publication, Inc., 1996.

Flag Burning

Though the burning of the American flag does not occur very often, when it does it leads to strong emotions from both supporters and those who oppose the activity. The issue of flag burning reached the Supreme Court in 1989 in the *Texas v. Johnson* case. In this case, Texas resident Gregory Johnson was convicted of flag desecration. Justice William Brennan, writing for the Court, said "to say that the Government has an interest in encouraging proper treatment of the flag, however, is not to say that it may criminally punish a person for burning a flag as a means of political protest," allowing that a person has the right to burn the flag as political protest.

Many groups have led the charge to add a flag desecration amendment to the Constitution. The proposed amendment has passed the House of Representatives, but by the end of 1998, had not achieved the necessary 67 votes in the Senate before it could be sent to the states for ratification. Those who did not endorse the amendment believed that one should not limit the right to protest, protected under the First Amendment. As Robert Justin Goldstein noted in his 1996 book concerning the issue of burning the flag, "forbidding flag burning as a means of peaceful political protest will surely diminish the flag's symbolic activity to represent political freedom." The issue is sure to spark heated debate for some time to come.

—D. Byron Painter

FURTHER READING:

Goldstein, Robert Justin. *Burning the Flag: The Great 1989-90 American Flag Desecration Controversy.* Kent, Ohio, Kent State University Press, 1996.

Lockhart, William B., et al. *Constitutional Rights and Liberties: Cases, Comments, Questions.* St. Paul, West Publishing Company, 1991.

Flag Clothing

In the United States, flag clothing is highly subjective; it can be either seditious or patriotic, depending upon context. Radical Abbie Hoffman was arrested in the disestablishment year 1968 for wearing a flag shirt; beginning in 1990, designer Ralph Lauren had knitted or applied the flag into sweaters and sportswear almost as a brand logo, and by 1995, so had designer Tommy Hilfiger. Actress Sherilynn Fenn appeared on the July 7, 1990 cover of *New York* Magazine wearing only the Lauren hand-knitted "Betsy" throw. In 1998, Lauren gave the Smithsonian $13 million to restore the Star Spangled Banner, a less than equal return on the money Lauren had made on the flag. Critics continue to ponder whether flag clothing amounts to desecration or exaltation, whether it's equivalent to flag burning or flag waving.

—Richard Martin

Flagpole Sitting

One of the more outlandish fads associated with the Roaring Twenties, flagpole sitting, like marathon dancing and bunion derbies, was an endurance feat performed for fame and money during a decade of change and restlessness. Less well known than Bobby Jones, Babe Ruth, Henry Houdini, or Charles Lindbergh, Alvin "Shipwreck" Kelly traveled across America, setting up and sitting on flagpoles through extremes of weather for increasingly longer periods of time. Seated atop a flagpole, he took only liquids for nourishment (hoisted to him by rope and pail), voiding his waste through a tube attached to the pole. In 1927, he perched on a flagpole in Baltimore for 23 days and 7 hours, while thousands stood and gaped, a feat which has become a metaphor for an American obsession with endurance feats and records, crazy thrills, and outlandish exploits.

—John R. Deitrick

FURTHER READING:

Allen, Frederick Lewis. *Only Yesterday*. New York, Harper-Collins, 1957.

Flappers

In the 1920s a new and popular model of modern womanhood dominated the American cultural scene. Although not all American women of the early twentieth century would emulate the flapper model, that model quickly came to represent the youthful exuberance of the post-World War I period. According to F. Scott Fitzgerald, the author whose novels set a tone for the 1920s, the ideal flapper, representing the ideal modern woman, was "lovely, expensive, and about nineteen." Originally merely a symbol of young and daring female chic, the flapper came to embody the radically modern spirit of the 1920s. Not merely a fashion trend, "flapperhood" came to represent an entire new set of American values.

The term "flapper" originated in England, where it was used simply to describe girls of an awkward age. American authors like Fitzgerald transformed the term into an iconic phrase that glorified the fun-loving youthful spirit of the post-war decade. The flapper ideal,

A flapper girl, c. 1922.

along with the look, became popular, first with chic young moderns, then with a larger body of American women. The flapper was remarkably identifiable. With her bobbed hair, short skirts, and penchant for lipstick, the starlet who had "it," Clara Bow, embodied the look. Other celebrity women, from the film star Louise Brook to the author Dorothy Parker, cultivated and popularized the devil-may-care attitude and fashion of the flapper. America's young women rushed to emulate the flapper aesthetic. They flattened their chests with tight bands of cloth in order to look as young and boyish as possible. They shortened the skirts on their increasingly plain frocks, and they bought more cosmetics than American women ever had before.

But flapperhood was more than mere fashion. To an older generation of Americans the flapper symbolized a "revolution in manners and morals." Flappers did not just look daring, they were daring. In the 1920s growing numbers of young American women began to smoke, drink, and talk slang. And they danced. Not in the old style, but in the new mode inspired by jazz music. The popularity of jazz and dancing hinted at new attitudes toward sexuality. The image of the "giddy flapper, rouged and clipped, careening in a drunken stupor to the lewd strains of a jazz quartet," gave license to new ideas about female sexuality. As F. Scott Fitzgerald claimed, "none of the Victorian mothers . . . had any idea how casually their daughters were accustomed to being kissed." Flappers presented themselves as sexual creatures, radically different to the stable maternal women who epitomized the ideal of the previous generation.

And yet the popularity of the flapper did not, as one might suppose, signal the triumph of feminism in the early twentieth century. For the flapper, for all her sexual sophistication and her rejection of her mother's Victorian values, did not pose any real threat to the gender status quo. Although the flapper presented a positive image for modern women, with her athleticism and her adventurous spirit, the flapper remained a soft creature who demurred to men. Indeed, it was precisely the flapper's "combination of daring spirit and youthful innocence that made her attractive to men." The flapper was a highly sexualized creature, but that sexuality retained an innocent, youthful, romantic quality. Ultimately, flappers married and became the mothers of the 1930s.

Although flappers presented a new model of single womanhood that would have positive ramifications because it gave license to women to work and play alongside men, that model had its limits. The transformative cultural promise of the flapper moment would recede just like the fashion for short skirts and short hair. In the long years of the Depression the desire to emulate reckless rich girls faded along with the working girl's ability to afford even the cheapest imitation of flapper chic. Remnants of the flapper lifestyle, however, remained popular—a youthful taste for music and dancing, smoking and swearing, sex and sexiness. And the market for goods that had emerged to meet the consuming passions of flapper women gained in strength and power. Even after the flapper disappeared from the American scene the feminine ideal that she had popularized lingered—along with a culture of consumption designed to help women pursue that impossibly impermanent idea. For the ideal modern woman of America's imagination, although no longer officially a "flapper," was to remain infuriatingly "lovely . . . and about nineteen."

—Jackie Hatton

FURTHER READING:

Allen, Frederick Lewis. *Only Yesterday: An Informal History of the 1920s*. New York and London, Harper Brothers, 1931.

Coben, Stanley. *Revolt Against Victorianism: The Impetus for Cultural Change in 1920s America.* New York, Oxford University Press, 1991.

Fass, Paula. *The Damned and the Beautiful: American Youth in the 1920s.* New York, 1977.

Marchand, Roland. *Advertising the American Dream: Making Way for Modernity 1920-1940.* Berkeley, University of California Press, 1985.

Flash Gordon

The most successful of the *Buck Rogers* imitators, *Flash Gordon* began as a Sunday page early in 1934. It was drawn by Alex Raymond, written by erstwhile pulp magazine editor Don Moore, and syndicated by King Features. The strip commenced with handsome, blond Flash and lovely Dale Arden, destined to be his love interest for the life of the strip, taking off in a rocket ship with brilliant, bearded Dr. Zarkov. Due to a miscalculation, they ended up on the planet Mongo, a considerable stretch of which was ruled over by a ruthless dictator known as Ming the Merciless. A combination of all the terrible qualities of Fu Manchu, Hitler, and the villain of a Victorian melodrama, Ming became Flash's prime antagonist. Flash and his friends underwent a series of picaresque adventures that took them, often while aiding local guerilla activities, to dense jungles thick with monsters, to strange arboreal kingdoms, to realms beneath the sea, and to whatever other stock science fiction locales Moore could borrow from the pulps. While the writing, which appeared in captions below the drawings, was stodgy and noticeably purple, Raymond quickly developed into a first-rate illustrator. Within a year the feature was one of the best-looking and most impressive in the Sunday funnies. In those pages, as one comics historian has noted, readers were able to see their "adolescent dreams of romance and adventure . . . given life."

Flash Gordon soon began being reprinted in comic books and Big Little Books and within two years was also in the movies. Universal produced three extremely popular serials based on the strip. Loosely adapted from some of Moore's newspaper continuities, they starred Buster Crabbe, his hair dyed blond, as Flash. Jean Rogers was Dale in the initial two, Frank Shannon portrayed Zarkov in all three and Charles Middleton, a veteran cinema villain, brought just the right degree of camp to the part of Ming. The first of the chapter plays, titled simply *Flash Gordon,* was released in 1936. *Flash Gordon's Trip to Mars* came along in 1938, followed by the more flamboyantly titled *Flash Gordon Conquers the Universe* in 1940. Filled with rocket ships, ray guns, mad-doctor apparatus, and young women in skimpy costumes, the Flash Gordon serials aren't noted for their state-of-the-art special effects. Yet they do possess a sort of tacky charm and the performances make up in exuberance for what they lack in dramatic depth.

Such was the popularity of the strip that King decided to add a daily in the spring of 1940. Raymond chose to devote all of his time to the Sunday, while his longtime assistant Austin Briggs, an established magazine illustrator in his own right, drew the weekday version. Never a particular success, it was dropped in 1944. About that time Raymond entered the Marines and Briggs took over the Sunday *Flash Gordon.* Determined to abandon comics eventually and devote himself full-time to illustration, Briggs never signed the page. He quit in 1948 and went on to become one of the highest paid magazine and

advertising artists in the country, as well as a founder of the Famous Artists School.

Mac Raboy, a comic book artist who had drawn such superheroes as Captain Marvel, Jr. and the Green Lama, followed Briggs on the Sunday page, doing a flamboyant and formidable job. In the early 1950s the daily version was revived with Dan Barry, another very good alumnus of comic books, as the artist. Various science fiction writers, including Harry Harrison, wrote the scripts. Barry added the Sunday page to his chores after Raboy's death in 1967; eventually he turned over the drawing to Bob Fujitani. In the late 1990s, *Flash Gordon,* was once again only a Sunday, appearing in a handful of newspapers and written and drawn by Jim Keefe.

—Ron Goulart

FURTHER READING:

Barry, Dan, and Harvey Kurtzman. *Flash Gordon.* Princeton, Kitchen Sink Press, 1988.

Marschall, Richard. *America's Great Comic Strip Artists.* New York, Abbeville Press, 1989.

Raymond, Alex. *Flash Gordon.* Franklin Square, Nostalgia Press, 1967.

Flashdance Style

The 1983 film *Flashdance* was an instant phenomenon in the United States. It not only created a new fashion style instantaneously embraced by females of all ages, but also introduced the world to actress Jennifer Beals and the wholesome but sexy character she played who welded by day and danced by night. The "look" consisted of worn-in sweatshirts ripped at the neckline that slipped off the shoulder casually, revealing some but hinting at more. Combining comfort with sexuality, the style also embraced an athleticism for women by making workout wear sexy. In the early 1980s, punk music and its fashions were starting to fade, and break dancing was the new fad—and with it, a new style was born: sportswear worn as everyday wear. Moving away from lace and other classic feminine clothing, the Flashdance look celebrated a new kind of woman, independent and down-to-earth, athletic and sexy.

—Sharon Yablon

FURTHER READING:

Bailey, Bill, and Frank Hoffman. *Arts and Entertainment Fads.* New York, Haworth, 1990.

Fresh, Mr. *Breakdancing.* New York, Avon, 1984.

Sewall, Gilbert T., editor. *The Eighties: A Reader.* Reading, Massachusetts, Addison-Wesley, 1997.

Traube, Elizabeth G. *Dreaming Identities: Class, Gender, and Generation in 1980s Hollywood Movies.* Boulder, Westview Press, 1992.

Flatt, Lester (1914-1979)

Born in Sparta, Tennessee, Lester Flatt's friendly, down-home vocal style, solid rhythm guitar, and songwriting were instrumental in both creating and popularizing bluegrass music. Joining Bill Monroe's Blue Grass Boys in 1945, Flatt's warm lead vocals were an integral part of the original bluegrass sound created in 1946-48, as was "the Lester Flatt G-run," a guitar figure used to punctuate song verses. Together with Earl Scruggs, he departed in 1948 to form the Foggy Mountain Boys, and throughout the 1950s and early 1960s the ensemble was one of the most visible and successful bluegrass acts. Creative differences led to a breakup in 1969, and Flatt formed a new band, the Nashville Grass, to pursue the earlier act's more traditional sound. With both former Foggy Mountain Boys and new musicians backing him up, Flatt remained a popular elder statesman of bluegrass until his death.

—Jon Weisberger

Flatt, Lester

See also Foggy Mountain Boys, The

Flea Markets

Markets where hundreds and sometimes thousands of people gather to buy and sell goods, flea markets are literally a material accumulation of American culture in a concentrated area. At a single flea market one can see—and buy—lamps, cookbooks, shoes, tools, clocks, toys, uniforms, salt-and-pepper shakers, cookie jars, ratchet sets, tarpaulins, radios, paintings, porcelain sinks, drinking glasses, bookends, duct tape, and candy dishes. The variety of goods constitutes the very nature of the flea market. New but discounted merchandise is common and runs the gamut from pet supplies, housewares, and tube socks to boxes of laundry detergent, canned goods, and toothpaste. Used items are generally household cast-offs, including baby clothes, furniture, stereo equipment, carpeting, and automobile tires. Flea markets contain objects both of the past and present, revealing obsolete technologies like eight-track players and Atari video games, and out-of-date clothing like bell-bottom pants, wide ties, and polyester shirts. Some people even sell antiques, not higher-end goods like Tiffany lamps and fine china, but more affordable collectibles like vintage pottery and prints. Flea markets may offer fresh produce from local farms, plants, and sometimes pets. Flea market operators often put restrictions on the types of things that are sold and usually prohibit the sale of firearms and other deadly weapons, stolen property, illicit drugs, pornography, and liquor. While most also officially prohibit "gray market" (counterfeit) items, these goods are usually in evidence at every flea market, with vendors selling imitation designer sunglasses, T-shirts, watches, and jewelry. Many medium-sized towns enjoy their own weekly or monthly flea markets.

Also known as swap meets, trade days, and peddlers' fairs, the flea market derives from the Greek *agoras* and other open-air markets of ancient times. It is believed that the term "flea market" comes from the French *Marché aux Puces,* the name of an outdoor bazaar known for the fleas that infested the upholstery of used furniture sold there. A popular pastime for people who frequent them regularly, flea markets allow people of all classes to enjoy a degree of economic power and autonomy—being able to buy or sell what they want at a price they more or less determine—outside of the highly regulated, inflexible, and taxable sphere of retail commerce.

Ubiquitous across the country for more than a century, one of the first American flea markets was the Monday Trade Days in Canton, Texas, which began in 1873 as a place where people would go to buy horses; later, they brought their own goods to sell or trade. Other towns quickly adopted this pattern of trade, but the modern flea market was supposedly the brainchild of Russell Carrell, an east-coast antique show organizer. Working as an auctioneer in Connecticut, Carrell thought to run an antique show like an outdoor auction, only forgoing the tent, which because of fire hazards was too expensive to insure. Carrell's 1956 Hartford open-air antiques market, he claimed, was the first modern incarnation of the flea market, although the true flea market does not consist of professional antique dealers, but rather of people looking to make some extra money on the side.

The different characteristics of flea markets reflect the diversity of the goods they offer and the people who attend them. Some are completely outside, others take place indoors, while still others have both inside and outside areas to sell goods. They usually take place at drive-ins, parking lots, race tracks, and fairgrounds. Paying a flat fee to the flea market's organizer (about ten to twenty dollars per day in the 1990s), vendors come equipped with tables, racks, and shelves on which to display their merchandise, or merely a sheet or blanket to cover the ground. Flea markets usually take place on the weekends, although not always: some convene on Fridays or on particular weekdays. Northern markets sometimes shut down during the winter while southern ones do the same in the hot summer months.

For all of their differences, flea markets and the people who frequent them have some things in common. Flea markets are characterized by the unpredictability in goods offered and the prices asked. Most certainly, every buyer is looking for a bargain—some hope to find valuable antiques and collectibles hidden among the cast-offs, while others look for utilitarian goods that are cheaper than in the retail marketplace. To this end, "haggling" is commonplace at flea markets, with buyer and seller both working to agree on a fair price, but using their own strategies. The seller "talks up" his or her merchandise to make it as appealing as possible, while the buyer points out defects or claims to have only a certain amount of money left in his or her pocket. Other tactics include, conversely, coming early to get first pick of the goods, and staying late, hoping that sellers will be more willing to unload items cheaply rather than taking them home.

—Wendy Woloson

FURTHER READING:

Freund, Thatcher. *Objects of Desire: The Lives of Antiques and Those Who Pursue Them.* New York, Penguin, 1993.

LaFarge, Albert. *U.S. Flea Market Directory.* New York, Avon Books, 1996.

Fleetwood Mac

Founded as a British blues band in 1967, Fleetwood Mac exploded as an American rock 'n' roll phenomenon in 1975, when a pair of young Californian songwriters joined the group. The bewitching Stevie Nicks and guitar genius Lindsey Buckingham rounded out the band of songwriter/keyboardist Christine McVie, bassist John McVie, and drummer Mick Fleetwood. Their first album together, the eponymous *Fleetwood Mac* (1975), hit number one with three hit

The 26th Street Flea Market in the Chelsea neighborhood of New York.

singles; but these merits were far overshadowed by the follow-up album, *Rumours* (1977). Songs of love, anger, heartbreak, and hope launched the band into stardom, but the drama between the grooves mirrored that raging between the members of the band: Christine and John McVie divorced after seven years of marriage, Stevie Nicks and Lindsey Buckingham ended their long-time romance, and Mick Fleetwood split with his wife, Jenny Boyd.

Audiences sang along and sympathized, sending *Rumours* to the top of the charts and winning it the title of best selling album of all time to date. Fleetwood Mac continued to tour and make music together for the next ten years, while four of the five members also began solo careers. Of these Stevie Nicks garnered the greatest success, with her husky voice, mystical lyrics, boots and shawls, touring in support of *BellaDonna, The Wild Heart,* and other records, magnifying her identity as a popular culture icon. (New York City holds a Night of 1000 Stevies each year, when thousands of men and women pay tribute to the woman and her style by emulating her dress and gestures.) Lindsey Buckingham self-produced two albums, *Law and Order* and *Go Insane,* during this period as well, and Christine McVie made a self-titled LP.

Continuing tensions and creative dissention caused Buckingham to leave after 1987's *Tango in the Night* album, and Stevie Nicks and Christine McVie followed not long after. As he had in the past, Mick

Fleetwood again scouted out new talent to keep the band going: Bekka Bramlett, Billy Burnette, and Rick Vito toured and recorded with the band's founders, but the *Rumours* line-up re-joined to perform at President Bill Clinton's inauguration in 1993, and continued to flirt with group projects, culminating in a CD, tour, and video, called *The Dance,* in 1998. After several road dates, the band disbanded once again, citing old difficulties, both personal and creative. Nonetheless, Fleetwood Mac not only remains synonymous with the 1970s, but their musical and pop cultural influence endures.

—Celia White

FURTHER READING:

Carr, Roy, and Steve Clarke. *Fleetwood Mac: Rumours n' Fax.* New York, Harmony Books, 1978.

Fleetwood, Mick, and Stephen Davis. *Fleetwood: My Life and Adventures in Fleetwood Mac.* New York, Morrow, 1990.

Furman, Leah. *Rumours Exposed: The Unauthorized Biography of Fleetwood Mac.* Secaucus, New Jersey, Carol Publishing, 1999.

Graham, Samuel. *Fleetwood Mac: The Authorized History.* New York, Warner Books, 1978.

Fleming, Ian (1908-1964)

Writer Ian Fleming created one of the major male icons of the second half of the twentieth century, the spy James Bond—as Alan Barnes suggests, "the only fictional character of the twentieth century to have acquired the aura of myth." The series of novels containing Bond not only concocted a new heroic figure, its immense success and popularity (Fleming had sold thirty million books by the time of his death) kick-started indigenous spy writing in America. Bond on film was also hugely successful, adding to the lustre of the spy and increasing the popularity of British music and cinema in 1960s America.

Son of a major and member of the British parliament, and younger brother of author Peter Fleming, Ian Fleming's English background was privileged and reflected the expected route of one of his class (Eton, Sandhurst, a job in the "City") rather than the adventurous spirit of his most famous creation. It was Fleming's periods as a journalist in Moscow at the beginning and end of the 1930s, along with his work in World War II as a high-ranking officer in naval intelligence, that provided much of the background for the novels. Fleming was in his forties when he began his writing career with *Casino Royale* in 1953 followed by ten more Bond novels (the best of which were written in the 1950s) and two collections of short stories. Fleming also wrote a column under the pseudonym Atticus for the London *Sunday Times* in the 1950s and contributed to other magazines. He had one son, named Caspar.

The plots of the Bond stories reflect the heritage of the previous half century of British popular spy and thriller writing. Fleming laid out "the right ingredients" for these works in *Dr. No* (1958): "physical exertion, mystery and a ruthless enemy . . . a good companion," and a certainty that the "cause was just." The James Bond character was based on a number of soldiers and agents Fleming knew during the war, but the author, as quoted in Andrew Lycett's biography, wanted the character to be "unobtrusive": "Exotic things would happen to and around him, but he would be a neutral figure—an anonymous blunt instrument wielded by a government department." Bond's enemies and their conspiracies took their power from an almost mythical badness, and the battles were more parables of good and evil than political thrillers. Yet Fleming covered these parables with a veneer of reality, which, in its intensity, was perhaps his biggest influence on the genre. His prose describes closely many of the most attractive and expensive places in the world, from beautiful islands to expensive restaurants. He also described in detail the possessions of the rich and successful, whether it be the most reliable guns or smoothest cigarettes, the finest car or best mixed cocktail. Comparable to this closely described visible consumption was the depiction of women, built to Playboy specifications, whom Bond seduced, bedded, and discarded with astonishing ease. There was something of the Playboy philosophy to Fleming's novels, of men as adventurous and potent while still at ease with consumer society.

Fleming's work did much to change attitudes toward the figure of the spy in American culture. Fleming's Bond was praised by John F. Kennedy and recommended by Allan Dulles, head of the CIA. Bond made the spy acceptable, shifted the perception from 1950s associations with the Rosenbergs and muddied the moral problems the spy had always held in the American psyche. Bond was a very English figure, of class and with imperial concerns, but he was also an international, professional figure fighting evil. As America moved to the forefront of world politics, its own intelligence service could be drawn in such a light, an international, professional movement against evil.

The Bond novels reflect a moment in time after World War II, beyond rationing in Britain and beyond the darkest days of the cold war in America when tourism, visible consumption, and sexual freedom came to the fore. It was at this point in the early 1960s that they made it onto the screen. Cubby Broccoli, producer of the majority of the Bond movies, pinpoints the strengths Fleming's work offered: "a virile and resourceful hero, exotic locations, the ingenious apparatus of espionage and sex on a fairly sophisticated level." It was these elements that would sell the films as the racism and misogyny (in their most extreme forms) and much of Fleming's British imperial nostalgia were sloughed off. Bond, as a character, was fleshed out by Sean Connery into a less one-dimensional character with a more attractive and humorous rebelliousness. *Dr. No*, the initial film, came out in 1962, quickly followed by *From Russia with Love* (1963) and *Goldfinger* (1964). These films showed the British industry turning away from the "kitchen sink" dramas of the previous few years to more slick and upbeat movies that were enormous commercial successes in America, increasingly interested in British pop music and culture. *Dr. No* had been made cheaply, but a great deal of American money was pumped into its sequels—money well spent, as the series became successful on an increasingly global scale.

—Kyle Smith

FURTHER READING:

Barnes, Alan, and Marcus Hearn. *Kiss Kiss Bang! Bang!: The Unofficial James Bond Film Companion.* London, Batsford, 1997.

Broccoli, Albert R. ("Cubby"), and Donald Zec. *When the Snow Melts: The Autobiography of Cubby Broccoli.* London, Boxtree/ Macmillan, 1998.

Lycett, Andrew. *Ian Fleming.* London, Weidenfield & Nicholson, 1995.

Fleming, Peggy (1948—)

Peggy Fleming remains the best-known and universally respected American figure skater in history. After an outstanding amateur career capped by her winning the 1968 Olympic Ladies' Figure Skating gold medal in Grenoble, France, Fleming embarked on a career as a professional skater, signing first with the Ice Follies and then pioneering as a solo act on television specials when the professional skating field was largely limited to ice shows. Corporate endorsements were minute compared to the enormous financial rewards available to most competitors today, but Fleming broke new ground here, too, becoming the spokesperson for over 30 sponsors in her career. In 1981, she became an anchor of ABC Television's figure skating coverage, usually paired with Dick Button, two-time men's Olympic champion and skating entrepreneur. With grace and ability, Fleming has maintained a presence in the world of figure skating for over 30 years. Known for her poise, elegance, and professionalism, Peggy Fleming has been the inspiration for three generations of skaters, all hoping to achieve her prominence in the sport.

Peggy Gale Fleming was born July 27, 1948 in San Jose, California, the second of four daughters. The Fleming family was often short on cash, and one summer, the entire family camped out in Oregon while her father worked; the girls never suspected they were

Peggy Fleming

homeless because they were enjoying their adventure. A tomboy, Peggy began skating at the age of nine and won her first competition at ten. Her mother Doris is credited by Dick Button as being "... forceful, domineering, and the perfect mother for Peggy''; Mrs. Fleming's role as the quintessential skating mother is well-known. Doris Fleming pushed her daughter to excel, providing an A to Z support system for the young skater: making all her costumes, driving her to practices, grilling her coaches on Peggy's progress, and generally stage-managing her career. Her father Al, a newspaper pressman, believed his working-class daughter could succeed in the sport of the well-to-do; Peggy's family moved constantly to support her career. Another skater would not have done well with such an unsettled life style, but Peggy seemed only to improve with such unorthodox training routines.

In 1961 an unprecedented tragedy in the sports world pushed Peggy Fleming to the forefront of skating; a plane carrying the entire United States Figure Skating Team crashed near Brussels, killing all aboard, including Fleming's coach. She was noticed as an up and coming competitor and in 1964, she had a stunning victory at the National Championships. Still only 15, she was suddenly propelled into the international spotlight when she headed the American team going to the Olympics at Innsbruck, Austria. She placed sixth, performing with a high fever but gaining invaluable experience on the world stage.

After the Olympics, Doris Fleming sought the best coach for her daughter and selected Carlo Fassi, whom she believed would help Peggy with "school figures"—the grueling and precise art of tracing figures in the ice which at that time was the major part of a skater's

marks. Fassi and Fleming proved to be a perfect match in every respect—a coach of rare ability and artistic refinement, he brought out the best in the young woman who continued to improve and win every title in her progress towards the Olympic gold medal. She became World champion in 1966 in a major upset and retained her National and World titles in 1967. Grenoble was the pinnacle of her amateur career—in a chartreuse costume sewed by her mother, Peggy Fleming won the gold medal (the only one for the United States in those Winter Games). Known for her balletic style that incorporated superior jumps with graceful moves such as her trademark layback spin (the pose made famous by a well-known Olympic photo), Fleming set the sport a new level of achievement that has been approached by only a few skaters since: Dorothy Hamill, Kristi Yamaguchi, and Michele Kwan are the three most often cited.

Her popularity was tremendous, and almost immediately Peggy was approached to make television skating specials which drew high ratings and critical approval—her Sun Valley special won two Emmy awards and *Peggy Fleming in the Soviet Union* (1974) made history as a television first, a cooperative venture between America and Russia. The professional success of Peggy Fleming was important beyond skating; she was arguably the first female sports superstar. In 1994, *Sports Illustrated* named Peggy one of "40 for the Ages": "40 individuals who have most significantly altered or elevated the world of sports in the last 40 years."

Her private life has been quietly successful as well; Fleming met Dr. Greg Jenkins, her future husband, when both were pupils of Carlo Fassi. They married in 1970, and Peggy remained active as a skater without significant interruptions to her family life. She is the mother of two sons, Andrew (born 1977) and Todd (born 1988). Although her relationship with her mother was often strained by Doris' need to control Peggy's life, she speaks with great affection of both her parents, now deceased. Al Fleming died at 41 of a heart attack shortly after driving across country to see his daughter perform after capturing a World title.

Peggy Fleming made news on the eve of the Michelle Kwan-Tara Lipinski battle for the Olympic gold medal in 1998. Diagnosed with breast cancer, she withdrew from her commentator duties for ABC and had successful surgery followed by chemotherapy. Characteristically, she began to speak out on breast cancer awareness immediately; her self-detection and her candor about her experience have motivated a noticeable increase in women seeking medical attention. Throughout her career, she has worked for numerous charities (March of Dimes, Osteoporosis Foundation, Kidney Foundation) but now her advocacy is more significant due to her successful return to skating and her characteristically modest account of her remarkably rapid recovery. A decidedly low-key ice princess, Fleming has retained her striking good looks and has never suffered any bad publicity, the lot of nearly every skater since Sonja Henie.

—Mary Hess

FURTHER READING:

Brennan, Christie. *Inside Edge: A Revealing Journey into the Secret World of Figure Skating.* New York, Anchor Books, 1996.

Fleming, Peggy. *The Official Book of Figure Skating: The U.S. Figure Skating Association.* New York, Simon & Schuster, 1998.

Guthrie, Patricia. "Fleming Speaks Out on Breast Cancer." *Atlanta Journal and Constitution.* October 8, 1998.

Hiestand, Michael. "Cancer Surgery Can't Ruin Fleming's Upbeat Outlook." *USA Today*. February 18, 1998.

Lessa, Christina, editor. *Women Who Win: Stories of Triumph in Sport and Life*. New York, Universe Publishing, 1998.

Vecsey, George. "New Role in Sports for Peggy Fleming." *New York Times*. September 6, 1981.

The Flintstones

Every prime-time animated television series traces its lineage back to *The Flintstones,* the first show to disprove the notion that cartoons are suited only for children. From 1960 to 1966, the comical adventures of the stone-age Flintstone family unfolded weekly on ABC. Essentially a pre-historic version of *The Honeymooners*, the program revolved around Fred Flintstone, an irascible blowhard (voice of Alan Reed), his pliant pal Barney Rubble (voice of Mel Blanc), and their long-suffering spouses. Cartoon veterans William Hanna and Joseph Barbera produced the cheaply-animated half hour. A live action movie version, starring John Goodman as Fred, was produced in 1994, but was not as popular with audiences as the original cartoon.

—Robert E. Schnakenberg

FURTHER READING:

Adams, T. R. *The Flintstones: A Modern Stone Age Phenomenon.* New York, Turner Publishing, 1994.

Flipper

The bottlenose dolphin star of two 1960s feature films, a television series from 1964 to 1968, and a 1996 film revival, Flipper educated Americans about the intelligence, loyalty, and compassion toward humans that characterizes the several dolphin species. Flipper rescued people from perilous situations, fought sharks, and warned individuals about impending dangers. Through Flipper, viewers were entertained by an unusual animal friend with a built-in smile, and were made aware of a dolphin's ability to communicate with and respond to people.

Flipper was born of the vision of movie and television underwater stuntman Ricou Browning. While watching *Lassie* on television with his children, Browning was inspired to invent an underwater counterpart to the courageous collie and wrote a story about a boy and a dolphin named Flipper. He offered the property to Ivan Tors, the producer of the successful television series *Sea Hunt* (1957-1961). Tors was fascinated by the idea and agreed to produce a feature film.

Browning acquired a dolphin named Mitzi and began training her for the stunts in the film, which included having a boy ride on her back. The training for this stunt required Browning to get into the water with the dolphin, a technique that was highly unusual for the time—trainers who worked with dolphins generally remained outside the water, but Browning discovered that being in the water with Mitzi seemed to accelerate her learning process.

Flipper saves a puppy in an episode of his television series.

The stunt that required Mitzi to carry a boy on her back was one of those that gave her the most difficulty. Browning finally overcame the problem by employing a variation of the retrieving behavior with the assistance of his son, Ricky. Browning picked up Ricky, commanded Mitzi to fetch, and then threw the boy into the water near the dock where the training session was being conducted. After several attempts, Mitzi grabbed Ricky, he took hold of her fins, and she pulled him back to Browning. The trainer was thrilled that his dolphin had been able to master this routine, considered to be an impossible feat.

Mitzi starred, with Luke Halpin as the boy, in the feature film *Flipper* (1963) and in the sequel, *Flipper's New Adventures* (1964), both filmed in the Bahamas. The commercial success of the movies led to the television series, *Flipper* (1964-1968), which aired on NBC, starring Brian Kelly as Porter Ricks, a ranger in Coral Key Park, Florida; Luke Halpin as his elder son, Sandy; and Tommy Norden as his younger son, Bud. The episodes related the adventures of the boys and their aquatic pet, who rescued them from many dangerous situations.

A dolphin named Suzy was selected as the lead dolphin for the television series, and quickly learned the 35 to 40 behaviors necessary for any script circumstance. However, some behaviors she seemed to exercise on her own. For example, before diving with Suzy, Luke Halpin gulped air from the surface then plunged beneath the water, holding onto the dolphin as she swam toward the bottom. The actor noticed that whenever he needed more air, Suzy returned to the surface. Since she repeated this behavior regularly, Halpin concluded that Suzy's keen hearing and sonar ability probably allowed her to monitor his heart and respiration rates and thus know when the boy needed air. Offscreen, Suzy demonstrated a newly learned trick to producer Ivan Tors. While visiting the set, Tors walked down to the dock and greeted Suzy, who returned the courtesy by squirting water on his shoes.

For three consecutive years from 1965-1967, "Flipper," who enthralled, entertained and enlightened millions, was honored with three PATSY Awards (Performing Animal Top Stars of the Year), the animal equivalent of the Academy Award, given by the American Humane Association. The Flipper idea was revived in the 1990s—as part of a general revival of television shows from the 1960s—with the movie *Flipper* (1996) and the television series of the same name (1995). The Flipper legacy lives on in increased interest, awareness, and concern for dolphins.

—Pauline Bartel

FURTHER READING:

Brooks, Tim, and Earle Marsh. *The Complete Directory to Prime Time Network TV Shows 1946-Present*. New York, Ballantine Books, 1979.

Edelson, Edward. *Great Animals of the Movies*. Garden City, New Jersey, Doubleday, 1980.

Paietta, Ann C., and Jean L. Kauppila. *Animals on Screen and Radio: An Annotated Sourcebook*. Metuchen, Scarecrow Press, 1994.

Rothel, David. *Great Show Business Animals*. San Diego, A.S. Barnes & Company, 1980.

Terrace, Vincent. *Encyclopedia of Television Series, Pilots, and Specials 1937-1973*. New York, Zoetrope, 1986.

Florida Vacations

For much of the twentieth century, Florida's warm sunshine and long sandy beaches have been associated with an exotic escape from the northern states' frigid winter weather. Though Florida vacations were once luxurious adventures for the wealthy, mass transporation soon opened the state to all. But it was not Florida's warm climate or accessibility that made the state one of the most popular vacation spots in the world. Walt Disney would combine the grand and luxurious image of the Florida vacation and create a comparable entertainment palace, the Magic Kingdom. As construction continued, the Walt Disney resort complex, Disneyworld, attracted visitors from all over the world, making the Florida vacation one of the most treasured winter escapes in the world.

While the heyday of vacations to the "Sunshine State" lies in the post World War II era, its foundation is set firmly in the nineteenth century. At a time when few individuals ventured more than one hundred miles south of the Florida-Georgia border, entrepreneur Henry Flager envisioned Florida as a winter vacation playground for wealthy northern tycoons. To access the southern portion of the state and its warm year round climate, Flager forged a railway through its dense natural vegetation to open the palatial Ponce de Leon hotel and introduce the wealthy winter weary to St. Augustine's pristine beaches in 1888. Visitors flocked to the hotel, inspiring Flager to continue expansion southward with his railway line and accompanying hotels. By 1894, the Royal Poinciana Hotel opened in Lake Worth near Palm Beach, accommodating 1,200 guests. As his railway stretched down the coast, with its terminus in Key West, Henry Flager succeeded in

making the warmth of Florida a mere thirty-six hour train ride from the frozen north.

Spurred by cleverly designed advertisements in national magazines and northern newspapers featuring bathing beauties basking in sunshine during the dead of winter, vacationing to Florida continued to grow. Immediately following World War I the newly affordable mass-produced automobile opened the state to many average Americans who could not manage the considerable railway fare and rates of the posh established hotels. Funneled into Florida via the "Dixie Highway" network of roads, this new breed of tourist came complete with their own tents and food provisions. In an era before motels, "tin can tourist camps" sprang up around the state to assist in accommodating the budget-conscious travelers. However, the onset of Great Depression stifled the burgeoning middle-class tourist trade.

During World War II, Florida became a center for training military personnel, exposing an incredible number of servicemen to its attractive winter climate. With fond recollections of sunshine many returned to the state with young families in tow following the war's conclusion. Other concurrent factors assisted in Florida's ascendance as a tourist mecca in the 1950s and 1960s. First was an incredible period of national economic prosperity providing expendable cash for vacations. Also, the development of the interstate highway system reduced automobile travel time, permitting more relaxation time at the vacation destination. Finally, perhaps most important of all, the rise of affordable air conditioning opening the state to year-round tourism by making the humid summers comfortable.

The Gold Coast, stretching from Vero Beach south to Miami Beach along the Atlantic, became the destination of choice for vacationers. Its semi-tropical climate permitted Americans to visit the tropics without necessity of a passport or knowledge of another language. While southeast Florida may have been their ultimate destination, a multitude of tourist attractions popped up along the major traffic arteries. A few captured the natural beauty of Florida, most notably Silver Springs with its glass bottom boats. Others capitalized on "Florida living" activities such as the water skiing extravaganzas at Cypress Gardens or the underwater mermaids at Weeki Wachee. Gatorland and the famous "gator jumparoo show" became an instant hit with children. The tacky tourist emporiums did not stop once families reached the Gold Coast. In Miami there was Parrot Jungle, Monkey Jungle, the Miami Seaquarium, and perhaps most memorable of all, the Miami Serpentarium. Audiences thrilled to death defying Bill Haast milking venom from cobras and other poisonous snakes. With a drive south to the Keys children could even see the real "Flipper."

Though tacky tourist attractions proliferated, Florida, and especially Miami Beach, remained the ultimate prestige vacation to an entire generation. The Fontainbleau and Eden Roc were veritable land-locked luxury cruise ships rivaling the Queen Mary. James Bond stayed at the Fontainbleau in *Goldfinger*. Jackie Gleason touted Miami Beach as the fun and sun capitol of the world on the *Honeymooners*. And America watched as Lucy, Ricky, and the Mertzes took off to Miami Beach for a holiday in the sun on the television show *I Love Lucy*.

Florida vacationing reached a transition phase in the 1970s. The rise of the popularity of jet aircraft and decreased airfares led many vacationers to seek out new winter destinations. Bermuda, the Bahamas, or even Hawaii were now within the grasp of many. A series of racially-motivated riots at the decade's end tarnished the image of South Florida. Miami Beach no longer held the same mystique as it had during the 1950s and 1960s. But with the decline of fun in the sun vacation in the southern portion of the state, central Florida witnessed the birth of the greatest tourist attraction in Florida's history. The Magic Kingdom, the first phase in the Walt Disney World resort complex, opened its gates in 1971. The entertainment theme park building bonanza that ensued transformed Orlando into one of the most popular vacation destinations in the world and preserved Florida's long vacation heritage.

—Dr. Lori C. Walters

FURTHER READING:

Flynn, Stephen J. *Florida: Land of Fortune.* Washington, Luce, 1962.

Tebeau, Charlton W. *A History of Florida.* Coral Gables, University of Miami Press, 1980.

The Flying Nun

Julie Andrews, Whoopi Goldberg, and Mary Tyler Moore have all played nuns, but the most notorious TV nun was played by Academy Award-winner Sally Field, much to her chagrin. *The Flying Nun* television series soared on ABC from 1967 to 1970, bringing viewers a concept that still seems ridiculous years later. Sister Bertrille (Field) was a bubbly young ninety-pound novice at the

Sally Field as the flying nun.

ancient Convent San Tanco, which sat on a hilltop in Puerto Rico. Whenever a stiff wind caught the starched cornette worn by her order, Bertrille was lifted into the air, becoming the "flying nun." The convent's conservative Mother Superior, Reverend Mother Plaseato (Madeleine Sherwood), wasn't too impressed, but Sister Bertrille did get along well with wise and humorous Sister Jacqueline (Marge Redmond) and Sister Sixto (Shelley Morrison), a Puerto Rican nun who had trouble with English. And, because even a show about nuns needed to have a little sex appeal, Bertrille was admired from a distance by Carlos Ramirez (Alejandro Rey), a wealthy, handsome playboy, owner of a discotheque in town, and patron of the convent.

Bertrille's avian ability got her into some hot water, sometimes literally: she was occasionally dunked into the ocean. Once she was almost shot down because she was mistaken for an enemy aircraft; another time a pelican fell in love with her. The novice took it all in sunny stride, but Sally Field was anything but sunny about this role, as she explained in *Playboy* in 1986: "In *Gidget,* I had things to play, scenes with fathers and people; here I had nothing. Just complete silliness—someone got into the convent who shouldn't have and we'd have to hide him. . . There were no life problems going on, nothing I could relate to. It made no sense to me. I started refusing press interviews and getting a bad reputation. But I couldn't go and hype the show, saying, 'I'm having such a good time' when I wanted to say, 'Let me out of here!' Flying Nun was a one-joke show, and I don't know why it was successful."

Field took the role because she was a teenager and believed she'd never work again after *Gidget* made her, or at least her character, the butt of jokes. Comics like Bob Hope had a "field day" making cracks about the series and turning all of the standard nun jokes into flying nun jokes. Besides feeling hurt by the jibes and feeling the ennui of an actor with no challenge, Field had another problem during her holy tenure—she was pregnant with her first child. During filming she had to carry books in front of herself to hide her growing belly.

For Field, there was one good thing that came of the role. Castmate Madeleine Sherwood took her to the Actors Studio, where Field could hone her craft with the likes of Ellen Burstyn, Jack Nicholson, Sally Kellerman, Bruce Dern, and Lee Strasberg. "It changed my life," she said in *Playboy.* "I found a place where I could go and create." But before Field left the world of light, gimmicky sitcom fare to begin her career as one of America's finest actresses, she would complete her wacky TV trilogy with *The Girl with Something Extra,* in which her character has ESP.

Not everyone hated *The Flying Nun* as much as Field; after all, it lasted three years. In a 1996 article in *Psychology Today,* Will Miller wrote, "This show is actually a provocative lesson about personal power . . . this show says, if you'll stop resisting the environment, if you'll only attune yourself to nature, to the direction and flow of the world's winds, you too can fly!" *The Flying Nun* was also commended by religious orders for "humanizing" nuns and their work. The series was based on the book *The Fifteenth Pelican* by Tere Rios.

—Karen Lurie

FURTHER READING:

Brooks, Tim, and Earle Marsh. *The Complete Directory to Prime Time Network and Cable TV Shows, 1946-present.* New York, Ballantine, 1995.

McNeil, Alex. *Total Television.* New York, Penguin, 1996.

Miller, Will. "Mental TV." *Psychology Today*. November-December 1996, 56.

Nelson, Craig. *Bad TV*. New York, Dell, 1995.

"Playboy Interview: Sally Field." *Playboy*. March 1986.

Flynn, Errol (1909-1959)

The facts of Errol Flynn's life and work reveal a pathetic tragedy of self-destruction and wasted gifts. His place in popular culture was assured equally by fame and notoriety. A heroic swashbuckler on screen, seducing audiences with his fresh charm, devil-may-care personality, athleticism, and dazzling good looks, he scandalized the public and his peers with his private exploits. A boon to gossip columnists he undoubtedly was, but while they charted his barroom brawls and questionable boudoir escapades (which gave the English language the expression "In like Flynn"), he steadily disintegrated, dying of drink, drugs, and despair at the age of 50.

From an early age, Flynn's nature—adventurous, reckless, unstable—was evident. Born into a comfortable and well educated

Errol Flynn in a scene from the film *The Sea Hawk*.

family in Hobart, Tasmania, he was expelled more than once from the good schools to which he was sent and became a shipping clerk at the age of 15. He had an affinity with boats and sailing and, still in his mid-teens, went wandering in search of gold. At 21 he bought a boat in which he made a seven month journey to New Guinea where he worked on a tobacco plantation and was a correspondent for an Australian newspaper. Back in Sydney, his looks brought an offer to play Fletcher Christian in a semi-documentary film *(In the Wake of the Bounty,* 1932), and he caught the acting bug. He went to England, joined a provincial repertory company, and played the lead in a B-picture which led to a contract with Warner Brothers.

Flynn arrived in Hollywood in 1935, married actress Lily Damita, and made brief appearances in a couple of low budget movies. Before the year was out, he played *Captain Blood,* surgeon-turned-pirate during the reign of James II, and became a star. This first foray into swashbuckling adventure demonstrated his grace and agility in wielding a sword, notably in a brilliant duel with Basil Rathbone's villain, and the public responded favorably to the combination of Flynn and then relative newcomer Olivia de Havilland. Backed by a stirring score from composer Erich Korngold, Warners' experienced craftsman Michael Curtiz directed with panache.

The studio was quick to grasp that they had found a winning formula and the natural heir to Douglas Fairbanks. De Havilland co-starred with Flynn in another seven films and, more significantly, Curtiz directed him in a further ten, beginning with *The Charge of the Light Brigade* (1936) and ending with *Dive Bomber* (1941). These ten included the actor's first Western, *Dodge City* and the same year—1939—*The Private Lives of Elizabeth and Essex* in which Flynn, bravado substituting for skill and experience, played second fiddle to Bette Davis' awesome Virgin Queen. He was never a great actor and his range was limited, but when the beguiling personality matched well with the vehicle, it did not seem to matter. Such was the case with the most memorable of the Curtiz collaborations, *The Adventures of Robin Hood* (1938). Indeed, the film endures as a classic in its own right, distinguished by outstanding Technicolor and Academy Award-winning design, a host of marvelous supporting performances, and what David Thomson aptly calls Flynn's "galvanizing energy" and "cheerful gaiety." It is as Robin Hood, handsome, dashing, brave, and humorous that Flynn is, and should be, best remembered.

Many commentators consider that the actor owed much of his success to the good fortune of being assigned first to Curtiz, then to the more serious-minded Raoul Walsh. They made seven films together, beginning with *They Died With Their Boots On* (1941), in which the star was a sympathetic General Custer, and including what is arguably his best performance, as prizefighter *Gentleman Jim* (1942). *Objective Burma* (1945), however, gave much offense to the British for creating the impression that the Americans single-handedly conquered the Japanese in Burma; and Flynn, although winningly portraying the heroic leader of a crucial and life-endangering mission, already looked weary and older than his years.

In truth, his notoriety had been rising in direct proportion to his stardom. He was tried, and eventually acquitted, for the rape of two teenage girls aboard his yacht in 1942, the year he was divorced from Lily Damita (by whom he had a son); in 1943 he married Nora Eddington (they divorced in 1949 and he married the last of his wives, Patrice Wymore, in 1950); his heavy drinking and smoking was on the increase and he began experimenting with drugs.

From the late 1940s on, Flynn's life and career reflected a downward slide. Weary of swashbuckling and looking for new directions in his work, he left Hollywood for Europe in 1952, played in several films probably best forgotten, and bankrupted himself in a failed attempt to finance a production of *William Tell*. He sailed around aimlessly in his yacht, and returned to Hollywood in 1956, a ravaged shadow of his former self, to face the final irony of his self-destruction: praise for his performance as a drunken wastrel in *The Sun Also Rises* (1957). He played two more drunks the following year in *Too Much Too Soon* (as John Barrymore) and in Huston's *The Roots of Heaven,* and ended his career, shortly before his death, with the nadir of his achievements, a semi-documentary about Fidel Castro called *Cuban Rebel Girls* which he wrote, co-produced, and narrated.

Movie stars biographer Charles Higham, in *Errol Flynn: The Untold Story,* suggested that the actor had been a Nazi agent for the Gestapo and a bisexual who had affairs with several famous men. Needless to say, the object of these scurrilous accusations was no longer alive to defend himself, and it is kinder and rather more rewarding to remember him for the considerable pleasure he gave at the height of his popular success.

—Robyn Karney

FURTHER READING:

Flynn, Errol. *My Wicked, Wicked Ways*. London, Heinemann, 1960.

Godfrey, Lionel. *The Life and Crimes of Errol Flynn*. New York, St. Martin's Press, 1977.

Thomas, Tony, et al. *The Films of Errol Flynn*. New Jersey, Citadel, 1965.

Thomson, David. *A Biographical Dictionary of Film*. New York, Alfred A. Knopf Inc., 1994.

Flynt, Larry
See Hustler

The Foggy Mountain Boys

Created in 1948 by Lester Flatt and Earl Scruggs, the Foggy Mountain Boys were one of bluegrass music's most popular acts, introducing millions of listeners to the style through their association with well-known movies and televisions shows in the 1950s. Though the act's full name was Flatt and Scruggs and the Foggy Mountain Boys, they were widely referred to as Flatt & Scruggs, as the two co-leaders were the sole permanent members of the band during its almost 20-year existence.

The Foggy Mountain Boys' first recordings were made shortly after Flatt and Scruggs left Bill Monroe's Blue Grass Boys in 1948, and in the space of little more than a year they created 28 of the most influential and enduring songs in the style, virtually all of which have become standards. With John Ray "Curly" Seckler singing tenor harmony to Flatt's genial lead vocals, and Scruggs providing the lower, baritone harmony part, the band sought to distinguish itself from Monroe's by downplaying the role of his instrument, the mandolin, featuring instead Scruggs' dazzling banjo picking and the work of a succession of fiddlers, including Benny Sims, "Chubby" Wise, "Howdy" Forrester, and Benny Martin. Where Monroe's sacred ("gospel") songs were performed with spare backing featuring the mandolin, Flatt and Scruggs opted to retain the full band's

sound, with the substitution of Scruggs' bluesy, finger-picked lead guitar for his banjo. Working for a succession of radio stations in places like Danville, Virginia; Bristol, Tennessee; Atlanta, Georgia; and Versailles, Kentucky, they quickly built a devoted following that made them an attractive acquisition for the Columbia label, whose roster they joined in 1950, remaining for the duration of the band's career.

While the Foggy Mountain Boys scored their first charting record in 1952, "'Tis Sweet To Be Remembered," their real breakthrough came when the Martha White Mills signed on as their sponsor, a relationship that was to continue for as long as the band existed. The deal gave Flatt and Scruggs an early-morning show on Nashville's WSM, the radio home of the Grand Ole Opry, starting in the spring of 1953, which led to regular weekly appearances on a Martha White-sponsored portion of the Opry, as well as a series of television shows that aired in cities around the South. Together with a busy touring schedule and regular recording sessions and releases, these appearances kept the Foggy Mountain Boys before an increasingly devoted audience, while the security of their Martha White sponsorship allowed them to retain a relatively stable lineup—Paul Warren on fiddle, Burkett "Uncle Josh" Graves on dobro (resonator guitar), Seckler and English "Jake" Tullock on string bass—at a time when other bluegrass acts were suffering the economic effects of the rock'n'roll boom of the late 1950s.

Indeed, Flatt and Scruggs' defied conventional wisdom by achieving their greatest success during a period when many country and bluegrass acts were suffering hard times. On the one hand, their increasingly sophisticated recorded sound—often augmented by drums, additional guitars, and other instruments—found favor on the country charts (they placed six singles in the Top 40 between 1959 and 1962), while on the other, Earl Scruggs' brilliance on the banjo brought the act attention from the growing numbers of urban folk revival enthusiasts, which was carefully tended to by his wife, Louise. The greatest boost to their popularity, however, was their recording of the theme song for television's *Beverly Hillbillies*, which spent three weeks at the top of the country chart and exposed millions of viewers to their music—and to the co-leaders directly, as they made several guest appearances on the show. When they appeared at Carnegie Hall in New York the same December, 1962, week that "The Ballad Of Jed Clampett" reached #1, it was apparent that the Foggy Mountain Boys had reached hitherto unattained heights of popularity for a bluegrass act.

From then on, the band led what amounted to a double life, aiming single records at country radio, LP albums at the folk audience, and making appearances at both folk and country venues, including at the prestigious and increasingly well-attended Newport Folk Festivals in the mid 1960s. Though the strategy worked well from a commercial point of view, many of their fans were dismayed by the resultant changes to their music, which drew increasingly from the folk realm, both older, traditional numbers as well as songs written by newer, urban folk artists such as Bob Dylan. The Foggy Mountain Boys' sound moved increasingly in the direction of folk-rock, with an ever-growing number of studio musicians playing a prominent role in their recordings; the change was further sharpened as Earl Scruggs, encouraged by his teenaged sons, began to develop a greater interest in contemporary popular styles, while Flatt yearned for a return to the more countrified, strictly bluegrass sound of the 1950s and early 1960s editions of the band.

By 1969, despite even greater popularity resulting from the prominent use of their "Foggy Mountain Breakdown" as background music in the movie *Bonnie and Clyde*, both Flatt and Scruggs were unwilling to maintain their association, and the Foggy Mountain Boys disbanded shortly after Scruggs' appearance with his sons at an anti-Vietnam War demonstration in Washington, D.C. Both of the leaders established their own groups, Flatt forming The Nashville Grass, with a more traditional sound, Scruggs creating the Earl Scruggs Revue with his sons and other young musicians interested in a bluegrass-rock hybrid. The Foggy Mountain Boys passed into history. The band's reputation, tarnished by the end, rebounded as their earlier recordings were reissued, and their influence has proven to be both immense and enduring; most of their recordings from the band's first 15 years of existence have become staples of the bluegrass repertoire, and virtually no bluegrass festival takes place without the performance of a healthy number of the Foggy Mountain Boys' classic songs.

—Jon Weisberger

FURTHER READING:

Cantwell, Robert. *Bluegrass Breakdown: The Making of the Old Southern Sound.* Urbana, University of Illinois Press, 1984.

Kochman, Marilyn, editor. *The Big Book of Bluegrass.* New York, William Morrow, 1984.

Rosenberg, Neil V. *Bluegrass: A History.* Urbana, University of Illinois Press, 1985.

Willis, Barry R. *America's Music, Bluegrass.* Franktown, Colorado, Pine Valley Music, 1992.

Folk Music

Before the twentieth century, a dichotomy prevailed between cultivated music, by educated, formally trained musicians and composers, and folk music, performed by everyone else. Cultivated music was created by and for the upper classes, and was taught and transmitted within a written tradition, while folk music was created by and for the lower classes, and was transmitted orally. Since folk songs were remembered rather than written down, they changed over time—sometimes gradually over centuries, sometimes all at once at the hands of a particularly innovative interpreter. The changes might be accidental, resulting from a lapse of memory, or a deliberate improvement. This communal re-creation is one of the defining characteristics of folk music. The songs and variation belonged to the whole community and were not associated with specific individuals. The names of great classical composers were transmitted in the written tradition along with their compositions, but traditional folk songs are anonymous. Cultivated music had to please the wealthy patron who paid the composer, but a folk song had to appeal to the entire community in order to survive over generations. Thus cultivated music was aristocratic and folk music was communal. Each reflected its audience's values. Cultivated music was often quite complex and required specialized musicians who were hired to perform it, whereas folk songs remained simple, so that anyone could memorize, sing, or play them.

One innovation which compromised the oral nature of folk music was the broadside. Broadsides were lyrics printed on large sheets of paper and sold at the marketplace. There was often an instruction to sing the lyrics to the tune of a well-established song.

Folksinger Buffy Sainte-Marie, 1971.

This introduced a degree of literacy to folk music, and many "broadside ballads" exhibit literary qualities. But the major change that permanently affected folk music was the advent of mass media. Records, movies, radio, and television all gave rise to popular music accessible to everyone from coast to coast. Individuals were able to become rich, or at least make a living, by performing music which appealed to millions of people. This has caused difficulty for musicologists in defining folk music. Popularity itself does not disqualify a song as folk music, but some musicologists claim that it ceases to be folk when it conforms to mainstream styles and tastes. In the latter half of the twentieth century there are very few communities unaffected by mainstream culture (with the exception of isolationist communities like the Amish). One may be immersed in one's own regional or ethnic tradition, but hardly anyone is completely sheltered from mass media. Consequently, individual traditions have shed their particularities and conformed to mainstream tastes. Folk has given way to folk rock and folk pop. The same can be said of blues, bluegrass, and country. These were originally types of folk music which have been popularized into mainstream genres.

American folk music is among the richest and most variegated in the world, owing to the many ethnic groups that make up the American people. The major strains of American folk music are Irish, Scottish, English, and African. Other European traditions, notably

Spanish, have also exerted some influence. The American Indians have a rich musical heritage, but it was never integrated with the European or African traditions. Some instruments of American folk music are the guitar, string bass, mandolin, autoharp, dulcimer, fiddle, and banjo.

The most intriguing genre of the American folk song is the ballad, a song which tells a story. The earliest American ballads came from the British Isles and thrived for centuries in Appalachian areas. Ballads can often be traced to mythic or epic traditions. "Polly Vaughan" (Peter, Paul and Mary) can be traced back to Celtic mythology. (Note: in this discussion, examples of ballads will be followed by popular performers who have recorded the song. More traditional versions of many of these ballads may be explored in Child's *English and Scottish Popular Ballads.*) "Polly Vaughan" tells the story of a hunter who accidentally kills his wife, having mistaken her for a swan. The story has a supernatural element: in some versions Polly is resurrected as a swan; in others her ghost visits the courtroom where her husband is tried. "John Riley" (Joan Baez, the Byrds) tells of a man who, returning from a seven-year expedition, disguises himself from his wife to find out if she has been faithful. John Riley has obvious parallels with the Greek Odysseus. Many ballads derive from the Biblical tradition, as in "Samson and Delilah," also called "If I Had My Way" (Grateful Dead, Peter, Paul and Mary).

Although there are some comic ballads, most ballads are tragic and have a tone of inevitability which exerts a strange power over the listener. Many tell of the hero's ruin and seek to deter the listeners from a similar fate by delivering a moral at the end. "The House of the Rising Sun" (Bob Dylan, Joan Baez, Odetta, the Animals), tells the tragic tale of a woman lured into prostitution and warns the listener "not to do what I have done." The fidelity of women is a common theme, as in "John Riley" mentioned above, and "Gallows Tree," also called "Hangman" (Peter, Paul and Mary, Odetta), which tells of a man at the gallows abandoned by father, mother, and brother, until his true love finally comes to pay his fee (a very different version of this song is recorded by Led Zeppelin as "Gallows Pole"). The infidelity of men is an equally common motif, as in "Come All Ye Fair and Tender Ladies," also known as "Tiny Sparrow" (Peter, Paul and Mary).

Ballads may be inspired by local events, such as battles, uprisings, disasters, trainwrecks, and shipwrecks (including the *Titanic*). A shipwreck is the subject of "Sir Patrick Spens," one of the oldest and most famous of all British ballads, often included in literature anthologies for its deft, concise poetry and symbolism. Train songs are very common. The advent of the train captured the folk imagination for its great economic and cultural impact upon rural America. "John Henry" (Odetta) tells of a railroad laborer who tried to outperform the steam drill using his bare hands to drill the railroad tracks. "Casey Jones" tells of an engineer who died in a trainwreck (the Grateful Dead's "Casey Jones," from the album *Workingman's Dead*, is their own composition, only marginally related to the original). The Badman Ballad was also popular. Often petty criminals and bandits attained legendary status and became tragic or ironic antiheroes in ballads such as "Jesse James" or "Pretty Boy Floyd."

One of the major genres of American folk music is the protest song. Wars have always been a topic of protest songs. "Cruel War" (Peter, Paul and Mary) goes back to the American Revolution. But in this century it was the "union singers," declaiming the atrocious labor conditions of the Industrial Age, that made protest songs notorious. One of the first union singers was a Swedish immigrant named Joe Hill. He was a member of the Industrial Workers of the

World and contributed to their book, *Songs to Fan the Flames of Discontent.* He was executed in 1915, accused of murdering a businessman. (Joan Baez commemorated him in the song "I Dreamed I Saw Joe Hill.")

But the great flowering of protest songs arose from the hardships of the Great Depression. Notable among these are the Dust Bowl ballads of Woody Guthrie. Guthrie added his own lyrics to folk and country songs to tell what he saw and suffered in his travels across America during the Depression. He modified the Badman Ballad to write songs about good men down on their luck. Thus one of his major contributions was the emphasis on new lyrics. Guthrie traveled with folksingers like Ramblin' Jack Elliott, Cisco Houston, and Huddie (Leadbelly) Ledbetter. In 1941 he joined the Almanac Singers, who played topical songs that would inform people of current events which might not be covered honestly in the media. They formed a commune in Greenwich Village and charged 35 cents for daylong performances which demanded audience participation. (Such group participation in folk music is called a hootenanny.) The purpose of these folksingers was to promote group solidarity and rally listeners into supporting workers' rights by joining unions. Though Guthrie and his companions would be hailed as "authentic" folksingers by a later generation, many folk musicologists of the time objected to this popularization of folk music for the sake of political causes. Guthrie himself denied that he was a folksinger. He hated the beautifully sad songs of the "silk-stocking balladeers" of an ancient British tradition which held no hope of social mobility for the lower classes.

Another important folksinger of the period was Pete Seeger, a musicologist and Harvard dropout who, like Guthrie, was bent upon traveling and recording his experiences in song. He traveled to other countries, learned their traditions, and included them in his repertoire. Seeger also joined the Almanac Singers, though he was more famous for his next band, the Weavers. Seeger, Guthrie, and others were affiliated with Communism, like many left-wing activists of the time. In 1953, the Weavers disbanded, effectively silenced by the House Committee on Un-American Activities. In 1954 Guthrie entered the hospital, debilitated by Huntington's Chorea. He ceased to write songs, though he did not die until 1967. Without these major players, folk music subsided in the mid-1950s, forgotten by the mainstream amid the excitement of a thrilling new sound called rock 'n' roll.

But folk music became chic among certain middle-class college students who disdained rock 'n' roll as an inane, fleeting fad. Eventually folk scenes arose in Berkeley and Cambridge, and Albert Grossman opened the Gate of Horn folk club in Chicago. Grossman was also responsible for producing the Newport Folk Festival, which became an annual event. The first festival, in 1959, introduced Joan Baez. But the most exciting folk scene was in Greenwich Village, in coffee houses like the Bitter End and the Gaslight Cafe. (This scene was later satirized in Dylan's "Talking New York," and commemorated more abstrusely in Simon and Garfunkel's "Bleecker Street.") Grossman visited Greenwich Village, and, moved by the devotion of college students buying expensive coffee while watching grubby folksingers, he decided the time was right to cash in on folk. He converted three clean-cut California boys into the Kingston Trio in 1957. They recorded "Tom Dooley" (1958), a traditional ballad about a man sentenced to death, which sold two million copies. Soon a proliferation of polished, cleancut folkies imitated the Kingston Trio: the Folkswingers, the Limeliters, the Ramblers Three, the Brothers Four, the Chad Mitchell Trio, the New Christy Minstrels, and Peter, Paul and Mary. But a remarkable new talent distinguishing himself from the crowd was Bob Dylan, who wrote his own material in addition to covering traditional songs. Dylan was audacious, perhaps even pretentious: his "Song for Woody" compared his own travels to the hardships Guthrie endured during the Depression. However, Dylan soon proved to be a poet worth listening to. When his songs were covered by Peter, Paul and Mary they became hits, and Dylan finally got his deserved recognition. Soon the folk popularizers, and then mainstream acts, were covering his material. But a more significant outgrowth of Dylan's success was the emergence of folksingers who, rather than simply covering his songs, were inspired by Dylan's example to write and perform their own songs. Tom Paxton, Tim Hardin, Phil Ochs, Judy Collins, and Gordon Lightfoot were all indebted to the standard of originality, creativity, and intelligence established by Dylan. Peter, Paul and Mary's reputation hovered between the popularizers and the earnest folkies, until Dylan's nostalgic poem commemorating their performances at the Gaslight was published on their album *In the Wind* and boosted their credibility. In February 1964, Peter, Paul and Mary were at the height of their popularity, with all three of their albums in the top ten, when the Beatles invaded America and awoke the sleeping giant of rock 'n' roll.

It was inevitable that folk and rock would merge. Rock was always an eclectic genre, born of blues and country music, and was always ready to absorb influences. After the Beatles began to dominate the charts, other bands sought some something new to hook fickle teen tastes. In September 1964, the Animals attacked "House of the Rising Sun" with electric guitars and organ. The song was a hit, and suggested to the folkies that they too could cash in on the hybrid.

1965 saw the explosion of folk rock. This year was important for several reasons. In January, Bob Dylan shocked the folkies by "going electric" on the single "Subterranean Homesick Blues." They hoped the new style was a put-on, a satire of the rock craze, but these hopes were shattered in March by the equally electric album *Bringing It All Back Home*. At the Newport Folk Festival in July Dylan and his electric guitar were booed offstage after three songs, despite the fact that Muddy Waters had played an electric guitar at the 1964 festival. Meanwhile, the Byrds had released *Mr. Tambourine Man* (June 1965), featuring Dylan songs and other folk songs revitalized by their electric twelve-string guitars and harmonies. They followed this up with another fine album in December, *Turn! Turn! Turn!* The Byrds were essentially folk musicians, who shrewdly recognized rock as the new direction in popular music. Simon and Garfunkel were also urban folkies transformed into folk rockers. Their first album, *Wednesday Morning, 3 A.M.*, was, like Dylan's first album, a mixture of traditional folk songs and authentic-sounding original compositions. In spite of its great musical and lyrical qualities, the album did not sell well. But when their producer added electric guitars and drums to one of these songs, "Sounds of Silence," and re-released it as a single, it reached the top of the charts. Fortunately, Paul Simon was able to live up to the expectations stirred by the folk rock version. He had been uncomfortable with the "authenticity" demands of the folkniks and proved to be an original and intelligent songwriter, free of Dylan's evasiveness and posturing. Simon created much of folk rock's finest music throughout the rest of the decade.

Meanwhile, the Beatles also had come under the influence of Dylan. Inspired by his mellow introspection and elusive symbolism, Lennon responded with "You've Got To Hide Your Love Away," and McCartney offered the folksy, wordy "I've Just Seen a Face" (*Help!*, August 1965). By December the Beatles were rising to the challenge of the upstart Byrds, and exhibited a more pronounced folk

influence on *Rubber Soul.* It never occurred to the Beatles to explore their own British tradition of folk music. This task was taken up by the Scottish troubadour Donovan Leitch. Donovan combined the ballad tradition of the British Isles with Dylanesque lyrics and was quickly hailed the "Scottish Dylan."

By 1966 folk rock was seemingly everywhere. Worthy folk rockers included the Lovin' Spoonful, the Mamas and Papas, Buffalo Springfield, and the Turtles. But the "folk" label was often abused as a marketing device applied to anyone slightly eclectic, from Janis Joplin to the Youngbloods. Even Sonny and Cher were considered folk rock. On the other hand, the Grateful Dead are rarely considered folk, but produced great folk rock on *Workingman's Dead, American Beauty,* and later *Reckoning* by mingling blues, country, jugband, bluegrass, and Appalachian styles. The Dead's lyricist, Robert Hunter, was a poet whose literary qualities rivaled Paul Simon or Dylan. His terse, ironic tales of the struggles and adventures of simple folks were closer to genuine folk song than many others ever came.

Much of what passed for folk rock was the appropriation of several features with varying relevance to traditional folk song. First of all, anyone holding an acoustic guitar was called a genuine folkie, and the electric twelve-string guitar was also labeled folk, based on the Byrds' precedent. And then there were the vocal harmonies associated with Peter, Paul and Mary (though these were just as often borrowed from the Beatles or the Everly Brothers). Finally, "sensitive" lyrics, whether political or personal, were a sure sign of folkdom. Dylan's songwriting was the widest and most enduring influence, though not always for the best: his style of protest—detached, ironic, and accusing—was eventually imitated in every area of popular music, reaching a crescendo of sanctimony in the "Art Rock" of the 1970s. The "other side of Bob Dylan," his cryptic autobiographies, also exerted an unfortunate influence, as less skilled writers began to bare their soul with diminishing subtlety and sophistication. The 1960s spirit of togetherness, embraced by everyone from Peter, Paul and Mary to Crosby, Stills and Nash, was abandoned in the 1970s as these and so many other groups splintered into solo artists. Retreating from the political chaos of the late 1960s, the singer/songwriters resorted to whiny introspection and self-infatuation. Some of them, such as John Prine and Jim Croce, maintained a sense of humor and irony which made them worthy folksingers. Others, such as Joni Mitchell and Leonard Cohen, relied on their literary prowess to grace their gloom with a little dignity.

Folk rockers of the British Isles tended to avoid the singer/songwriter malady. In the late 1960s and 1970s, Fairport Convention, the Incredible String Band, Jethro Tull, Led Zeppelin, and Irish guitar maestro Rory Gallagher successfully blended folk influences into their eclecticism. These were usually musical influences, without the ideological baggage associated with folk music. The folk spirit of protest, homespun integrity, and anti-corporate independence was eventually seized by a new and very different breed of "simple folks"—the punk rockers.

—Douglas Cooke

FURTHER READING:

Anthology of American Folk Music. Folkway Records (FP 251-253), 1952.

Cantwell, Robert. *When We Were Good: The Folk Revival.* Cambridge, Harvard University Press, 1996.

Child, Francis James. *English and Scottish Popular Ballads.* New York, Dover Publications, 1965.

Folk Song and Minstrelsy. Vanguard (RL 7624), 1962.

Lang, Dave, et al. *Electric Muse: The Story of Folk to Rock.* London, Methuen Paperbacks, 1975.

Nettl, Bruno. *Folk Music in the United States.* 3rd edition. Detroit, Wayne State University Press, 1976.

Pollock, Bruce. *When the Music Mattered: Rock in the Sixties.* New York, Holt, Rinehart and Winston, 1984.

Vassal, Jacques. *Electric Children: Roots and Branches of Modern Folkrock.* Translated and adapted by Paul Barnett. New York, Taplinger, 1976.

Folkways Records

Founded by Moses "Moe" Asch in 1948, Folkways Records evolved into perhaps the most important independent record label in the history of American popular culture. Determined to document the authentic musical traditions of the world, Asch assembled an eclectic catalogue of more than 2,200 titles that featured such artists as Huddie "Leadbelly" Ledbetter, Woody Guthrie, Pete Seeger, Coleman Hawkins, Mary Lou Williams, and John Cage. In addition to assembling an impressive collection of children's and world artists, Folkways played a prominent role in shaping the canon of American folk music, exerted tremendous influence on left-wing culture, and, in part, inspired the folk revival of the 1960s.

Born in 1905 in Warsaw, Poland, in 1914 the nine-year-old Moses Asch emigrated with his family to New York City, where his father, the renowned Yiddish novelist Sholem Asch, sought to forge relationships with other Jewish intellectuals. In 1923, Sholem sent his son to Germany to study electronics, and when Moe returned to New York in 1926, he opened a radio repair shop and pursued a career as a sound engineer. Eager to gain his father's approval, he then sought a more literary occupation. During his sojourn in Germany, he had read John Lomax's *Cowboy Songs* (1910), which sparked his interest in American folklore and convinced him that folk music constituted the literature of the "common" people. In 1939, he established Asch Records to document their voices, recording traditional Yiddish folk songs and cantorials. Asch's repertoire expanded in 1941 when he released a collection of children's songs performed by Leadbelly, the former Lomax protégé who would become central to the label's success.

The release of Leadbelly's material as well as *The Cavalcade of the American Negro* (1941) underscored Asch's commitment to preserving the cultural heritage of African Americans. These racial politics were indicative of his general leftist sympathies. Reared in a family of socialists, he enthusiastically embraced the Popular Front, a loose affiliation of left-wing and liberal artists and intellectuals who, at the suggestion of the Communist Party International, committed themselves to the defeat of European fascism and the promotion of racial and economic equality. Although Asch was wary of communism, in 1944 he opened his studio, now under the banner of Disc Records, to the leftist American Folksong Movement. Seeger and his Almanac Singers, Cisco Houston, Brownie McGhee, Sonny Terry, and Woody Guthrie gathered to record traditional tunes and politically-inflected songs. Folkways was particularly supportive of Guthrie's

career and, between 1944 and 1945, Asch recorded nearly 140 Guthrie selections and meticulously archived the musician's voluminous notebooks, letters, and drawings.

Disc Records ended in bankruptcy, but when Asch and his assistant, Marian Distler, launched Folkways in 1948, he refused to make efforts to sign commercially successful artists. Marquee performers, he worried, would compromise the label's integrity among academics as well as his attempts to chronicle the lives of "real" folk. As a result, he continued to record music that appealed to small but well-defined audiences: white leftists, jazz aficionados, librarians, and teachers. In its fledgling years, Folkways rereleased Guthrie's *Dust Bowl Ballads* (which RCA originally recorded in 1940), expanded its jazz catalogue, and, under the direction of ethnomusicologist Harold Courlander, promoted the Ethnic Series.

In 1952, Asch hired Harry Smith to assemble the *Anthology of American Folk Music,* a compendium that introduced a new generation, notably Bob Dylan and Bruce Springsteen, to the genre. This seminal album became a cultural touchstone for the many white students who, inspired by the success of the Weavers and the Kingston Trio, sought to celebrate folk musicians and their traditions. Under Asch's auspices, Mike Seeger, Pete's half-brother, reclaimed and recorded Southern traditions, while Ralph Rinzler documented such virtuosos as Clarence Ashley and Arthel "Doc" Watson. A burgeoning interest in folk music opened a new market to Asch, impelling him to rerelease older materials and to issue new recordings by such legends as Sam "Lightnin'" Hopkins and Big Joe Williams.

This renaissance gained momentum when, in the early 1960s, Dylan and Joan Baez began to write and perform topical songs that both reflected and shaped the politics of the Ban the Bomb and Civil Rights Movements. Interested in the New Left's use of the folk idiom, Folkways created the Broadside label to document songs written for the radical underground publication of the same name. Replete with Dylan compositions, the *Broadside Ballads* featured a host of folksingers, including Seeger, Phil Ochs, and Dylan himself, performing under the pseudonym Blind Boy Grunt. Folkways captured other sounds of the decade by employing Guy and Candie Carawan to record the music and speeches of the Civil Rights Movement.

A sizable catalogue, a vault of vintage recordings, and a handful of new projects sustained Folkways through the 1970s, but as the 1980s approached, Asch focused on finding a way to preserve his life's work. Moe Asch died in 1986 and, in 1987 the Smithsonian Institution acquired his collection and reorganized the company under the rubric Smithsonian-Folkways. To fund the venture, the Smithsonian enlisted a coterie of popular musicians to cover material for an album entitled, *A Vision Shared: A Tribute to Leadbelly and Woody Guthrie* (1988). The artists who participated in this effort attest to the enduring legacy that Folkways and its most recognizable legends passed to American popular music. Dylan, Springsteen, Willie Nelson, Little Richard, John Cougar Mellencamp, and Emmylou Harris were among those who identified Leadbelly and Guthrie as their cultural forebears. The Smithsonian agreed to keep each of Asch's original titles in print and has continued to issue previously unreleased materials from his archives.

—Bryan Garman

FURTHER READING:

Goldsmith, Peter. *Making People's Music: Moe Asch and Folkways Records.* Washington, D.C., Smithsonian Press, 1998.

Follett, Ken (1949—)

Writer Ken Follett burst upon the American fiction scene in 1978 with his mystery spy story *Eye of the Needle*. A taut thriller, it portrayed a central female character rising to heroism and a humanized villain together with a convincing image of World War II lifestyles, sensibilities, and attitudes. Characterized by fast-paced action and an economic, readable style, the book was greeted with enthusiasm by public and reviewers alike. It became an American Literary Guild selection garnering sales of more than ten million copies. This was to be the start of Follett's continued success in America from the 1970s through the 1990s. With *Eye of the Needle,* he gained the coveted "Edgar" award from the Mystery Writers of America, a prize honoring the father of the American detective story, Edgar Allan Poe. The novel was later adapted for the screen by Stanley Mann, starring Donald Sutherland and Kate Nelligan. With its release in 1981, the film secured Follett's reputation as a top-notch writer in the spy genre.

He followed his first success with four more best-selling thrillers: *Triple* (1979), *The Key to Rebecca* (1980), *The Man from St Petersburg* (1982), and *Lie Down with Lions* (1986). American television miniseries of both *The Key to Rebecca,* starring Cliff Robertson and David Soul, and *Lie Down with Lions* in 1994, starring Timothy Dalton, enhanced his popular reputation. A further miniseries of *On Wings of Eagles* (1983), a true story of an Iranian rescue mission, cemented his standing and following.

Pillars of the Earth, which has since achieved a worldwide cult status, was published in 1989. It was a radical departure from Follett's spy stories. The novel about building a cathedral in the Middle Ages was on the New York Times best-seller list for 18 weeks. This book was followed by *Night Over Water, A Dangerous Fortune,* and *A Place Called Freedom,* which again were not in the spy genre, but had elements of suspense and intrigue. In 1997, Follett's thriller *The Third Twin,* a suspense novel about a young woman scientist who stumbles over a genetic engineering experiment, was ranked number two in the world, beaten only by John Grisham's *The Partner.* Miniseries rights for the book were sold to CBS for $1,400,000, and its broadcast in 1997 was a further indication of Follett's rank in American popular culture. *The Hammer of Eden* (1998) is a contemporary suspense story with all of the elements of fast pace and intriguing characters established in his earlier efforts.

Follett began his career as a fiction writer while working for the *London Evening News.* He produced a series of mysteries and thrillers under various pseudonyms until he felt he had learned enough and written well enough to author under his own name. His early works were, in Follett's words, "intentionally very racy, with lots of sex."

Each of his best works grew out of news stories and historical events. Cinematic in conception, they follow a hunter-hunted pattern that leads to exciting chase scenes and games of wit and brinkmanship. His most successful works have dealt with World War II, perhaps because he requires a wide backdrop and world-shaking events to justify the tumultuous passions he instills in his characters. At its best, Follett's prose is lean and driven. His forte lies in setting up a chain of events in chronological sequences. Follett's ideal is a compromise between the serious and the popular, the "plot, story, excitement, sensation and the world outside the mind" that he believes serious writers often ignore merged with the graceful, powerful prose and more complex "character development" that mass-market writers fail to take time for.

Born in Cardiff, Wales, on June 5, 1949, Follett was encouraged to read from a very early age, openly acknowledging his debt to the access to free books he had from the local library, and often saying in lectures that it is axiomatic that a writer is also a reader. He attended University College, London, where he received a BA in philosophy in 1970. While at University, he married his first wife, Mary Elson, and had a son and daughter. His second wife, Barbara Follett, became the Member of Parliament for Stevenage in Hertfordshire. Follett has major interests in music, playing bass guitar in a band called Damn Right I Got the Blues; the theater, especially Shakespeare; and his work as president of the Dyslexia Institute.

—Jim Sinclair and Joan Gajadhar

FURTHER READING:

Atkins, John. *The British Spy Novel: Studies in Treachery.* London, Calder, 1984.

"Ken Follett." http://members.aol.com/hnmibarich/follett.htm.

"Ken Follett." http://www.ken-follett.com/f,ndex.html. April 1999.

McCormack, Donald. *Who's Who in Spy Fiction.* London, Elm Tree/ Hamilton, 1977.

Fonda, Henry (1905-1982)

Although cast in a similar mold to his contemporaries Gary Cooper and James Stewart, Henry Fonda was one of the most distinctive American screen actors. Tall, dark, good-looking, and quietly spoken, he exuded decency, sincerity, and understated authority, and spent much of his 46-year career being offered up as a repository of honesty, a quiet American hero and man of the people. He will forever be remembered as the incarnation of the president in *Young Mr. Lincoln* (1939), Steinbeck's Tom Joad in *The Grapes of Wrath* (1940)—both for John Ford, with whom he did much of his finest work—and the subtly persuasive jury member in *Twelve Angry Men* (1957), but his roles ranged wide and his successes were numerous. He was an engagingly absent-minded dupe, turning the tables on Barbara Stanwyck in Preston Sturges's sparkling comedy *The Lady Eve* (1941), the voice of conscience in William Wellman's *The Ox-Bow Incident* (1943), and a memorable Wyatt Earp for Ford in *My Darling Clementine* (1946). He created the role of *Mister Roberts* on Broadway and on-screen, and played presidential candidates in two of the best political films of the 1960s, *Advise and Consent* (1962) and *The Best Man* (1964).

Fonda was born on May 16, 1905 in Grand Island, Nebraska. After high school, he enrolled for a degree in journalism at the University of Minnesota, but dropped out and became an office boy. Asked to play a role in an amateur production with the Omaha Community Players, he found his calling, went on to work in summer stock, and joined the University Players, a new group of students who aspired to the theater. The guiding light was future director Joshua Logan, and the young company included James Stewart and Margaret Sullavan. From there, with his friend Stewart, he made his way to

Henry Fonda

New York and the Broadway stage in the early 1930s, and married Margaret Sullavan—the first of his five wives—in 1932. The marriage was over in 1934, the year when, having enjoyed a Broadway success in *The Farmer Takes a Wife,* he signed a contract with film producer Walter Wanger.

Victor Fleming's film version of *The Farmer Takes a Wife* (1935) marked Henry Fonda's screen debut. He repeated his lead role, cast opposite Janet Gaynor, and progressed steadily to popularity and stardom through the rest of the decade. He played a backwoods pioneer in the first outdoor Technicolor adventure movie, *The Trail of the Lonesome Pine* (1936), the film that established his idealistic resolute persona (cartoonist Al Capp later claimed that he had based L'il Abner on Henry Fonda), and in 1937 was invited to star in the first British Technicolor picture, *The Wings of the Morning.* In 1938 he played Frank James in the first Technicolor Western, *Jesse James,* making him Hollywood's first Technicolor star. However, his best work of this early period was in Fritz Lang's social conscience drama, *You Only Live Once* (1938). Set against the background of the Depression, Fonda played a fundamentally decent young man driven to crime by force of circumstance and on the run with his wife (Sylvia Sidney). Other career highlights of the 1930s were William Wyler's Civil War melodrama *Jezebel* (1938), in which he costarred as the exasperated but intractable beau of a willful Bette Davis, and the start of his collaboration with John Ford. *Young Mr. Lincoln,* in which he limned a dreamy, political calm while maintaining a commitment to justice and decency, found him perfectly cast. His frontier pioneer in *Drums Along the Mohawk* (also 1939) followed, and confirmed (after his Frank James) that Fonda, who detested guns and didn't care

much for horses, was nonetheless a sympathetic candidate for the Westerns genre.

He played Frank James again in *The Return of Frank James* (1940), a memorable but sadly underrated Western from Fritz Lang, but it was indubitably Ford who engraved Fonda's image on the Western. In Ford's hands, Fonda was a kind of Sir Galahad of the Prairie: polite, laconic, slow to anger, but a man of his word who means what he says. They made only one more Western together (*Fort Apache,* 1948), but Fonda's mature postwar demeanor served Anthony Mann's *The Tin Star* (1957) and Edward Dmytryk's uneven *Warlock* (1959). Meanwhile, there was Tom Joad.

Although a major star by 1940, Fonda, dissatisfied with his material, wanted out of his contract with 20th Century-Fox and Walter Wanger. However, he desperately wanted to play Joad, and reluctantly signed a seven-year deal with Fox in order to get it. Ford directed *The Grapes of Wrath* from his own screenplay adaptation of the novel. It was a powerful depiction of the plight of the Dust Bowl migrants, in which Fonda's Joad, a decent man just out of jail after killing in self-defense, is dismayed to find his family farm a ruin. Undaunted by adversity, he helps his family make it to California against the odds, only to find the poor are oppressed there, too. Following the death of Casey (John Carradine), an inspirational figure, Joad, in a classic speech lifted directly from Steinbeck's novel, vows to fight injustice wherever it may be. Fonda was Oscar-nominated for his performance but lost, ironically, to his close friend James Stewart's comedy performance in *The Philadelphia Story.*

In 1936, Fonda had married socialite Frances Brokaw. The marriage lasted until 1950 when, following a mental breakdown, she committed suicide. Brokaw, the second Mrs. Fonda, was the mother of future actors Jane and Peter. In the early 1940s, Fonda was able to escape from a couple of years of his contractual obligations to Fox thanks to active service during World War II. His postwar return was *My Darling Clementine,* and after a handful of films, ending with *Fort Apache,* he deserted Hollywood for the Broadway stage, and was off the screen for eight years. During this time, his notable successes included *The Caine Mutiny Court Martial* and *Mister Roberts,* the play that brought him back to the screen when John Ford insisted he recreate his stage role for Warner Bros.' 1955 film version. (Warner Bros. had wanted William Holden or Marlon Brando to star). Sadly, the filming was marked by dissension between star and director, and Ford's increasing illness, and the picture was completed by Mervyn Le Roy.

In 1956, the actor starred as Pierre, opposite Audrey Hepburn's Natasha in King Vidor's lumbering, multi-million-dollar version of *War and Peace.* Fonda insisted on wearing spectacles to give the character a suitably distracted, intellectual air but, unfortunately for the film, as *Time* magazine noted, Fonda gave "the impression of being the only man in the huge cast who had read the book." Also in 1956, Fonda's third wife divorced him, citing his affair with Adera Franchetti, who became his fourth wife in 1957. That year, he starred in one of his biggest successes of the decade, Alfred Hitchcock's *The Wrong Man,* playing the victim of a case of mistaken identity, fighting to save himself from a wrongful charge of murder. The 1960s began with a fourth divorce, and brought marriage (in 1965) to his fifth and last wife, Shirlee Mae Adams. During this decade, too, his public profile became somewhat eclipsed by those of his children, notably his daughter Jane, who was a prominent political activist as well as an increasingly successful actress. Both children were publicly outspoken in their criticism of their famous father, and his image as the nicest guy in town was somewhat tarnished.

On the professional front, he continued active. He made a number of television specials, including *Clarence Darrow,* and produced and starred in *The Deputy* from 1959 to 1961; and alternated between the live theater and films, but the Hollywood glory days were over and the good roles were few and far between. There were exceptions, notably in three overtly political films to which the gravitas of his demeanor was perfectly suited, and in which he was uniformly excellent. He was the candidate running for the office of Secretary of State, but dogged by a dark secret, in Otto Preminger's *Advise and Consent* (1962); an Adlai Stevenson-like presidential nominee with high ideals in Franklin Schaffner's adaptation of Gore Vidal's Broadway play, *The Best Man* (1964); and a heroic president staving off a nuclear holocaust by extreme means in Sidney Lumet's *Fail Safe* (1964). He made cameo appearances in such major, all-star productions as *The Longest Day, How The West Was Won* (both 1962), *Battle of the Bulge* and *In Harm's Way* (both 1965), and, in a late reprise of his Westerns career, but in a reversal of his "good guy" image, starred as a ruthless gunman in Sergio Leone's epic *Once Upon a Time in the West* (1969).

During the 1970s, with ill health gradually creeping upon him, Henry Fonda's illustrious career gradually wound down, though never quite out. In 1974, he was a presenter at the Tony Awards, was honored by the American Civil Liberties Union, and narrated a history film series for colleges and universities. He also opened on Broadway in the one-man show *Clarence Darrow,* but the show closed after 29 performances when Fonda collapsed in his dressing room from total exhaustion. He was rushed to the hospital and a pacemaker was implanted, but he later revived the play at the Huntington Hartford Theater in Los Angeles, where it was taped and presented on NBC later the same year. In 1977 he made a splash as a crusty old Supreme Court Judge in Robert E. Lee and Jerome Lawrence's *First Monday in October,* which played in Los Angeles, on Broadway, and in Chicago.

In between work, Fonda found time to paint (his watercolors hang in several galleries), do needlework, and experiment with haute cuisine. He was honored by the American Film Institute with a Lifetime Achievement Award in 1978, and by the Kennedy Center for the Performing Arts, and was given an honorary Oscar at the 1981 Academy Awards ceremony "in recognition of his brilliant accomplishments."

Henry Fonda stepped into the Hollywood spotlight once more to costar with Katharine Hepburn in *On Golden Pond* (1981). The film went some way to healing the rift with his daughter Jane, who played his daughter in the film, and, at age 76, he became the oldest recipient of the Best Actor Oscar—the first of his long and distinguished career—for his performance as a retired professor grown curmudgeonly with age and the fear of approaching death. He was, alas, too ill to attend the Oscar ceremony in March 1982, and Jane Fonda, herself a nominee that year, collected the statuette on her father's behalf. Henry Fonda, one of the best loved actors of Hollywood's Golden Age, and of the Broadway theater, died in August of that year.

—Dennis Fischer

FURTHER READING:

Fonda, Henry, with Howard Teichman. *Fonda: My Life.* Orion, 1981.

Goldstein, Norm, and the Associated Press. *Henry Fonda: A Celebration of the Life and Work of One of America's Most Beloved Actors.* Holt, Rinehart and Winston, 1982.

Parish, James Robert, and Don E. Stanke. *The All-Americans.* Rainbow Books, 1977.

Thomas, Tony. *The Complete Films of Henry Fonda.* Citadel Press, 1983.

Fonda, Jane (1937—)

A popular culture icon alternately revered and reviled by American audiences, Jane Fonda is an actress whose career often has been overshadowed by her very public personal life. The quintessentially mod sixties cinematic sex symbol in *Barbarella,* Fonda soon became one of America's most controversial figures following her highly publicized trip to Vietnam in which she spoke out against the war. Despite public disapproval, Fonda nonetheless became one of Hollywood's most popular actresses, nominated for six Academy Awards and winning two. Off-screen, Fonda has been known as a dedicated political activist, a hugely successful workout guru, and wife to three prominent men—French film director Roger Vadim, politician Tom Hayden, and media mogul Ted Turner.

A member of Hollywood's aristocracy since birth, Jane was born in New York City to the legendary Henry Fonda and his socialite wife, Frances Seymour Brokaw. Jane spent her early years at the Fonda home in the mountains above Santa Monica, California, where Tomboy Jane and her younger brother, Peter, spent an idyllic childhood climbing trees and riding horses. After World War II, Henry returned to Broadway to star in *Mister Roberts,* and the family moved

Jane Fonda

to Connecticut, where the Fondas hoped to raise their children away from the Hollywood limelight. But the marriage quickly disintegrated after Henry fell in love with Susan Blanchard, the twenty-one-year-old stepdaughter of composer Oscar Hammerstein. Shortly thereafter, Frances, who had long suffered from depression, had a series of nervous breakdowns and was committed to a sanatorium, where she committed suicide by slashing her throat. Feeling that his twelve-year-old daughter and ten-year-old son were too young to know the truth, Henry told his children that their mother had died of a heart attack. Both Jane and Peter later learned the truth through the press.

As a teenager, Fonda showed little interest in following in her father's footsteps. Educated at the elite girls' school Emma Willard and later at Vassar, she earned a reputation as a free spirit and rebel whose chief interests were boys and art. But when the opportunity came to costar with her father and Dorothy McGuire at the theatre where the two stars had made their debuts, Fonda accepted and, in 1954, made her own acting debut in the Omaha Playhouse production of *The Country Girl.* Yet, she continued to envision a career as a painter, studying at the Ecole des Beaux Arts in Paris and the Art Students League in New York.

After meeting famed acting teacher Lee Strasberg in 1958, Fonda became interested in acting but was afraid of being compared to her famous father. It wasn't until Strasberg told the twenty-one-year-old Fonda she had talent that she decided to become an actress. Fonda joined the Actors Studio in 1958 and two years later made her film debut opposite Anthony Perkins in *Tall Story.* Fonda soon found regular work on Broadway and in Hollywood, where her beauty and talent won her a growing public following. During the sixties, she starred in such popular films as *Walk on the Wild Side, Cat Ballou,* and Neil Simon's *Barefoot in the Park* with Robert Redford.

In 1965, Fonda married French director Roger Vadim, and it was her controversial nudity in Vadim's futuristic film *Barbarella* which catapulted her to international stardom. Her next two films, *They Shoot Horses, Don't They?* and *Klute,* revealed her growing reputation as one of Hollywood's top actresses, earning her two Academy Award nominations. In 1971, Fonda took home the Oscar for best actress for *Klute.*

In 1972, Fonda traveled to North Vietnam. Shocked by the devastation, she agreed to make ten propaganda broadcasts to U.S. servicemen. This earned her the pejorative nickname "Hanoi Jane," and her speeches, calling U.S. soldiers war criminals and urging them to disobey orders, were carried around the world, along with pictures of her on the North Vietnamese guns used to shoot down American planes. Fonda's fame skyrocketed as she became both the darling of the antiwar movement and the sworn enemy of the Establishment, the U.S. military, and countless Vietnam veterans. For the rest of her life, Fonda would be associated with her trip to Vietnam, greeted with praise or literally shunned and spit upon.

Following her divorce from Vadim, Fonda became increasingly politically active after marrying radical politician Tom Hayden in 1972. The Haydens supported countless liberal causes, becoming one of Hollywood's most outspoken political couples. Fonda's reputation as an actress continued to grow. During the late seventies, she appeared in such film classics as *Julia, Comes a Horseman,* and *Coming Home,* for which she won her second Oscar.

In 1981, Fonda finally was given the opportunity to act opposite her father on film. *On Golden Pond,* starring Henry, Jane, and the inimitable Katharine Hepburn, would be Henry's last film and would earn the ailing actor an Academy Award. Jane continued to make movies throughout the eighties, appearing in *Agnes of God, The Morning After,* and *Old Gringo,* but much of her time was taken up with a new role, as she once again became an iconic figure in a new movement—the fitness revolution. She produced "The Jane Fonda Workout" series of fitness videos, which became national bestsellers even as the money they earned benefited the liberal political causes she and Hayden espoused.

In 1988, during an interview with Barbara Walters on television's *20/20,* sixteen years after her trip to Vietnam, Fonda publicly apologized for her bad judgment in going to Vietnam and particularly rued the effects her trip had had on Vietnam veterans. She would later meet with Vietnam veterans in a semi-successful effort to heal old wounds.

In 1989, Fonda and Hayden were divorced. After a difficult period of adjustment, Fonda began dating Ted Turner. They married in 1991, and their union is thought to be a happy one. So happy, in fact, that Fonda has retired from acting, preferring to devote her time to her marriage and to the social causes she continues to support. As Jennet Conant wrote in an April 1997 *Vanity Fair* article, Fonda is now "the star turned supporting player, the activist turned philanthropist." After a lifetime in the public eye, the more private Jane Fonda nonetheless remains one of America's most intriguing popular culture icons.

—Victoria Price

FURTHER READING:

Andersen, Christopher. *Citizen Jane: The Turbulent Life of Jane Fonda.* New York, Henry Holt and Company, 1990.

Conant, Jennet. "Married ... With Buffalo." *Vanity Fair.* April 1997, 210-30.

Freedland, Michael. *Jane Fonda: A Biography.* London, Weidenfeld & Nicolson Limited, 1988.

Haddad-Garcia, George. *The Films of Jane Fonda.* Secaucus, New Jersey, Citadel Press, 1981.

Fonteyn, Margot (1919-1991)

Prima ballerina of the British Royal Ballet for over forty years, Margot Fonteyn was one of greatest dramatic dancers of the twentieth century. Fonteyn was the first ballerina trained in a British school and company to achieve international stature. Artistic partnerships were integral to her career; her forty-year collaboration with Frederick Ashton was the longest between a ballerina and choreographer in dance history. As she prepared to retire at age 43 in 1962, her career was revitalized by her partnership with Rudolf Nureyev, who, at age 24, had just defected from the Soviet Union. "It was an artistic love affair conducted in public" said dance critic Clement Crisp. Fonteyn's career was unusually long for a ballet dancer and she continued to perform until her mid-sixties.

—Jeffrey Escoffier

FURTHER READING:

An Evening with the Royal Ballet, with Rudolf Nureyev and Margot Fonteyn (film). Kultur International Films.

Macauley, Alastair. *Margot Fonteyn,* London, Sutton Publishing, 1998.

Ford, Glenn (1916—)

One of the most pleasing, consistent, thoughtful, and prolific of screen actors, Glenn Ford (born Gwyllym Newton in Quebec) was a regular feature of the Hollywood landscape, particularly the sagebrush, given the large number of Westerns in which he starred. Initially a leading man of the second rank, he enjoyed full stardom from 1946 until the late 1950s. He owed his elevation to *Gilda,* Charles Vidor's classic *film noir* in which he tangled angrily and enigmatically with Rita Hayworth in a seedy South American nightclub, and subsequently demonstrated his worth and versatility in a wide range of material. He subsumed his natural likability to play hard men (e.g. *3.10 to Yuma,* 1957) and revealed comedy talent in *Teahouse of the August Moon* (1956), but his most memorable performances were as the revenge-obsessed detective in Fritz Lang's *The Big Heat* (1953) and the teacher dealing with delinquents in *The Blackboard Jungle* (1955). His star waned in the 1960s, owing to poor material, but he proved his durability on TV and made a noteworthy appearance in *Superman* (1978).

—Robyn Karney

FURTHER READING:

Ford, Glenn, and Margaret Redfield. *Glenn Ford, RFD.* Beverly Hills, Hewitt House, 1970.

Shipman, David. *The Great Movie Stars: The International Years.* London, Angus & Robertson, 1980.

Ford, Harrison (1942—)

Starring in two of the most successful film trilogies of all time, the *Star Wars* and Indiana Jones adventures, actor Harrison Ford became the action hero for a new generation of blockbusters in the 1970s and 1980s. Throughout the 1990s he further consolidated his film star appeal and was voted ''The Greatest Movie Star of All Time'' by *Empire* magazine in October 1997.

Ford's most notable roles prior to *Star Wars* were appearances in George Lucas's *American Graffiti* (1973) and Francis Ford Coppola's *The Conversation* (1974), establishing him as a competent character actor and, more importantly, making him known to the ''Movie Brat'' directors who came to dominate commercial cinema in the 1970s and 1980s. The most famous biographical fact about Ford was that he was working as a carpenter to the stars when Lucas called him in to take part in auditions for a new science-fiction project. Breaking all box office records and establishing the trend for special-effects blockbusters, *Star Wars* (1977) was a much bigger film than any of its actors;

Harrison Ford in a scene from the film *Raiders of the Lost Ark.*

but Ford's Han Solo clearly had the edge as an attractive rogue—a cowboy in the first film, a romantic hero in *The Empire Strikes Back* (1980), and a freedom fighter in *Return of the Jedi* (1983).

Apart from a lighthearted cowboy role in *The Frisco Kid* (1979), for a while it seemed that Ford was going to be typecast in war movies, as the Vietnam veteran in *Heroes* (1977), the action man in *Force 10 from Navarone* (1978), the romantic hero in *Hanover Street* (1979), and the sum of his associations as Captain Lucas in Coppola's *Apocalypse Now* (1979). But it was with the release of Steven Spielberg's *Raiders of the Lost Ark* in 1981 that Ford was able to take center screen in an altogether different, but still highly familiar set of adventures. As an archaeologist in the 1930s, the Indiana Jones character was able to combine all of the essential action fantasies of the Lucas-Spielberg team; as typified by the first film, for example, this adventurer could take part in a mythic quest against the Nazis— fantasy and war movie heroics lovingly packaged in Saturday morning serial form. The two sequels, *Indiana Jones and the Temple of Doom* (1984) and *Indiana Jones and the Last Crusade* (1989), clearly established Ford as the family action hero of the decade, an actor who combined elements of Humphrey Bogart, Gary Cooper, and Cary Grant, partly in his looks and his acting style, partly in the types of pastiche films which he chose, and all in contrast to the solely musclebound poundings of Sylvester Stallone and Arnold Schwarzenegger.

Ford's performances in Ridley Scott's *Blade Runner* (1982) and Peter Weir's *Witness* (1985) may, in fact, remain his most interesting in this respect. Not overtly commercial films, they nevertheless established Ford as an actor with understated authority, comparisons with 1940s film noir in the former and *High Noon* in the latter, serving to enhance, rather than detract from his contemporary generic appeal. Although possibly Ford's least favorite film, *Blade Runner* nevertheless gained cult and now classic status, and for *Witness* he gained his only Academy Award nomination. Ford probably demonstrated his greatest acting range as a stubborn inventor in Weir's *The Mosquito Coast* (1986), but it is still a performance in a film without simple generic identity, balanced by his next two films, Mike Nichols's romantic comedy *Working Girl* (1987) and Roman Polanski's Hitchcockian thriller *Frantic* (1988).

Ford's attractiveness lies in the fact that he's something of a reluctant star who can nevertheless bring authority and appeal to the most generic of films. Part of his ongoing success has been due to the deliberation and discrimination with which he has chosen his films, taking care to alternate action with light comedy and drama, and working with the most professional directors available. After two of his most mediocre films, Alan J. Pakula's solid courtroom drama *Presumed Innocent* (1990) and Mike Nichols's sentimental *Regarding Henry* (1991), Ford had the sense to move on to action thrillers, starring as Jack Ryan in the high-tech Tom Clancy adaptations *Patriot Games* (1992) and *Clear and Present Danger* (1994), and as the innocent doctor on the run in *The Fugitive* (1993).

Two of Ford's most ill-received films appeared in 1995 and 1996; in the old-fashioned remake of *Sabrina* he played the Bogart role, and in *The Devil's Own* he courted controversy. Though Ford often noted that he choose films with "strong" stories, some of his films have had controversial political agendas. Both *Patriot Games* and *The Devil's Own* offered a simplistic vision of the IRA situation in Ireland. *Clear and Present Danger,* however, is actually quite radical in its attack on sub-Republican government, while *Air Force One* (1997) offers a more populist political agenda. Directed by Wolfgang Peterson, *Air Force One* is an undeniably professional action film, but with Ford playing a U.S. president who gets to fight back at terrorists, too contemporary, perhaps, to avoid "political" readings. From these films with deliberate political currents, Ford moved on to Ivan Reitman's lightweight "castaway" comedy *Six Days, Seven Nights* (1998), playing the sort of cantankerous figure Cary Grant played in his later years. Another classic comparison for an actor who also happens to be one of the most important stars of the contemporary era.

—Stephen Keane

FURTHER READING:

Clinch, Minty. *Harrison Ford: A Biography.* London, New English Library, 1987.

Jenkins, Garry. *Harrison Ford: Imperfect Hero.* London, Simon & Schuster, 1997.

Ford, Henry (1863-1947)

As founder of the Ford Motor Company, Henry Ford epitomized the can-do optimism of the industrial age. His homespun, folksy persona charmed Americans and redefined an alternate image of the wealthy industrialist. His Model T automobile, rolled out of his Michigan headquarters in 1908, was the first car to capture the national imagination and the first to sell in mass quantities. Upon doubling his workers' wages in 1914, Ford became an overnight celebrity.

Though he earned his fame as a wealthy industrialist, Ford grew up on a modest family farm. Born July 30, 1863, in Dearborn, Michigan, he spent his early years doing chores and tinkering with watches and steam engines. At age seventeen, he left home to take a job in Detroit for a manufacturer of railroad boxcars. For the next twenty years, he worked at a succession of technical jobs, eventually landing the position of chief engineer at a power company. All the

while, he tinkered in his off-hours with homemade steam and, ultimately, gasoline powered engines and vehicles.

In 1899, at age thirty-eight, Ford quit the power company and, with some partners, founded his first automobile manufacturing enterprise. While this attempt failed, as did a second, his third try, the Ford Motor Company, founded in 1903, grew into one of the largest, wealthiest companies of the century. The introduction of the Model T in 1908 revolutionized the young industry. Ford quite intentionally set out to, in his words, "build a motor car for the great multitude." Ford continually reduced the retail price, bragging "Every time I reduce the charge for our car by one dollar, I get a thousand new buyers." Each price decrease was heralded by national press coverage. The first car aimed at the middle class, the Model T was an immediate best-seller—so much so that building enough cars to meet public demand became a significant challenge.

Ford worked with his team to develop a number of refinements to the production process, culminating, in 1913, with an assembly line, where each worker had one small task to repeatedly perform and remained in place while an automated belt rolled the cars past. These improvements cut production time by 90 percent. Ford's competitors were forced to adopt the same methods, and the assembly line became a standard fixture of manufacturing operations.

Previously, craftsmen had worked on a job from beginning to end, but the division of labor necessary to boost efficiency on an assembly line required the breaking of the production process into a series of repetitive, boring, less-skilled tasks. The implementation of the assembly line increased worker turnover and absenteeism. Soon the Ford Motor Company was spending $3 million a year training new workers to replace those who had quit. In response, Ford raised the daily wage of his laborers from $2.35 to $5.

While the success of the Model T gained Ford some renown as a successful inventor and industrialist, the "five-dollar day," as it became known, heralded his arrival as a national celebrity. All the newspapers of the day reported it, many editorializing for or against.

Becoming a household name, Ford was asked to opine on all manner of popular issues and eagerly did so with a commonsensical folk wisdom that endeared him to many. Ford's populist pronouncements, such as "the right price is the lowest price an article can be steadily sold for and the right wage is the highest wage the purchaser can steadily pay," set him in stark contrast to the monopolistic robber barons of the previous era such as Andrew Carnegie, John D. Rockefeller, and Cornelius Vanderbilt. The left-wing magazine *The Nation* marveled that this "simple mechanic" didn't need "combination or manipulation or oppression or extortion" to dominate his market but instead "distanced his competitors by no other art than that of turning out his product by more perfect or more economical methods than they have been able to devise or execute."

Ford basked in the favorable attention lavished on him, but he was unprepared for the increased scrutiny he received in the public eye. In 1915 the national press ridiculed him when, in an effort to avoid war with Germany, he chartered an ocean liner to take himself and his "delegates" to Europe to mediate and negotiate for peace. In 1918 he was chastened by the personal attacks he and his family endured as a result of his narrowly unsuccessful run for the Senate. In 1919 Ford sued the *Chicago Tribune* when it labeled him "ignorant." In the ensuing trial and surrounding media circus, the *Tribune*'s lawyer proceeded to humiliate Ford by exposing his utter lack of historical knowledge.

Ford nonetheless became a folk hero to the public in the 1910s and 1920s. He was a man of little formal education who, through his

Henry Ford

own wits, became one of the richest men in the country, yet continued to espouse populist values, paying his workers well and lowering the price of his cars nearly every year. A 1923 *Collier's* poll showed him far ahead of Warren G. Harding, Herbert Hoover, and everyone else in a theoretical presidential race. It has since become routine to accept populist political and social wisdom from wealthy titans of industry such as Lee Iacocca and Ross Perot.

Ford, the farmer, tinkerer, inventor, industrialist, and populist social critic, died in 1947. The automobile had long since become an American icon, as had the man himself.

—Steven Kotok

FURTHER READING:

Collier, Peter, and Chris Horowitz. *The Fords: An American Epic.* New York, Summit Books, 1987.

Lewis, David L. *The Public Image of Henry Ford.* Detroit, Wayne State University Press, 1976.

Nevins, Allan. *Ford: The Times, the Man, the Company.* New York, Scribners, 1954.

Sward, Keith. *The Legend of Henry Ford.* New York, Russell & Russell, 1968.

Ford, John (1894-1973)

Film director John Ford is a profoundly influential figure in American culture far beyond his own prolific, wide-ranging, and often impressive output in a 50-year plus cinema career that began in the silent era with *The Tornado* (Universal, 1917). Despite the variety of subject matter he tackled for the screen, he remains historically, critically, and in the public consciousness, as the architect of the Western, the genre on which he cut his teeth during the silent era. It was, however, not only the numerous popular and acclaimed Westerns he made for which he is important: his romantic, émigré's vision of the Old West and the pioneering spirit has crept into the perception of American history, blending idealized fiction into the harsher truth of fact for generations of Americans and, certainly, for non-Americans in the many countries where his work is regarded as a classic staple of Hollywood cinema at its best.

John Ford is the most decorated director in Hollywood history, and his four Academy Awards as best director in part illustrate his range while, curiously, ignoring his westerns (from which he took a decade-long break from 1927). He won his first Oscar for a return to the political roots of Ireland with *The Informer* (RKO, 1935), a tale of a simple-minded Irishman (Victor McLaglen) who betrays an IRA leader. It was garlanded with Oscars and extravagant critical praise for its stylization and grim atmosphere. Ford returned to Ireland again for *The Quiet Man* (1952), a Technicolor comedy, vigorous and funny. In between, he was honored by the Academy for *The Grapes of Wrath* (1940), from Steinbeck's novel about a family trekking to California to escape the disaster of the 1930s dust-bowl, and *How Green Was My Valley* (1941), a nostalgic tearjerker set in a Welsh mining community. To these films, add *The Whole Town's Talking* (1935), a comedy melodrama with Edward G. Robinson; the Shirley Temple vehicle *Wee Willie Winkie* (1938), set in colonial India; *Young Mr. Lincoln* (1939), *What Price Glory* (1952), *Mogambo* (1953) and his last feature, *Seven Women* (1966), set in an isolated Chinese mission in the 1930s, and one gets an inkling of the depth and range of Ford's interests and his professional skill.

Ford was born Sean O'Feeney in Portland, Maine, on February 1, 1894, one of the many children of his first-generation Irish immigrant parents. Of his siblings, he was closest to his brother Francis, some 12 years his senior. Always restless, Francis ran away from home to seek his fortune at an early age, changed his name to Ford, and forged a modest acting career in the theater, before moving into the film business with Edison and Biograph. By 1913, he was in Hollywood, writing, directing, and acting in silent action serials at Universal Studios, where, in 1914, his younger brother joined him. Known initially as Jack Ford—the name under which he was credited when he began directing, changed to John in 1923—Ford learned the rudiments of filming as gopher, jack-of-all-trades, and apprentice to Francis, eventually being allowed a hand in acting, writing, and camera work. In 1917, just as Francis Ford's star was fading, Universal's founder and chief Carl Laemmle made John Ford a director, entrusting him with *The Tornado*, a two-reel short. The film was a success, and thus launched the most prolific directing career in film history. In Ford's four and a half years at Universal he made his reputation as a director of westerns, and forged a significant creative relationship with actor Harry Carey, whom he later frequently cited as having been the most important influence on his work outside of his brother Francis. When the fledgling director met Carey, 16 years his senior, the actor had already worked in almost 200 films, and would appear in 25 of Ford's 39 films for Universal. By 1921 Universal had relegated Carey to "B" westerns, but Ford's stock had risen considerably. He had proved himself capable of making films that came in on time, often under budget, and generally turned a profit.

Ford used his increasing reputation to jump ship to Fox, where he made 50 films. The move was well-timed: within a few years after his arrival, Fox rose from a second tier studio to an industry leader, and although Ford, always stubborn, had run-ins with management from time to time, for the most part he enjoyed a freedom few of his counterparts could claim. By 1939 Ford's stock could not have been higher, but he had been absent from his first love, the western, for some ten years. Aware that the genre was not taken seriously by critics but that he certainly was, he determined to use his reputation and influence to bring prestige to westerns. The first fruit of his ambition was *Stagecoach* (1939), a watershed film that marked the first of the director's nine films to be set in his signature landscape of Monument Valley, and the first of his famous collaborations with John Wayne. Contemporary audiences think of the Valley as a cowboy movie cliché, but *Stagecoach* was its first appearance and it owes its resonance and associations to Ford's work. As Jane Tompkins argues, for a western film "not just any space will do. Big sky country is a psychological and spiritual place known by definite physical markers. It is the American West, and not just any part of that but the West of the desert, of mountains and prairies, the West of Arizona,

Utah, Nevada, New Mexico, Texas, Colorado, Montana, Wyoming, the Dakotas, and some parts of California." Ford's repeated use of Monument Valley caused it to become an archetypal mythic landscape, a virtual stand-in for any and all of the above named places. Never identified by name in any of the Ford films in which it is featured, Monument Valley serves to represent locations as diverse from one another as the city of Tombstone, Arizona (*My Darling Clementine*, 1946) and the Texas plains (*Rio Grande*, 1950, *The Searchers*, 1956).

Stagecoach is in many ways essentially a "B" western, rife with stereotypes, that follows the structure of what would later be known as a "road movie." However, Ford was fully aware of the stereotypes, the use of which, as Richard Slotkin observes, "allowed him to take advantage of genre-based understandings—clichés of plot, setting, characterization, and motivation—to compose an exceptional work marked by moral complexity, formal elegance, narrative and verbal economy, and evocative imagery." Stereotypes or no, the characters were given rich life by a superb cast led by Wayne, Claire Trevor, and Thomas Mitchell, who won an Oscar. The film also won for its music score, and garnered five additional nominations, including those for picture and director. Exquisitely photographed, critic Frank Nugent has called it "A motion picture that sings the song of camera," while John Baxter, writing in 1968, identifies it as "The basic western, a template for everything that followed."

With the huge critical, popular and financial success of *Stagecoach*, Ford earned the freedom to make just about any western he wanted. By 1941, however, his Hollywood career was on hold while he served as Lieutenant Commander Ford attached to the Navy during World War II. Appointed Chief of the Field Photographic Branch of the Office of Strategic Services, he made two Academy Award-winning documentary propaganda films, *The Battle of Midway* (1942) and *December 7* (1943). After the war Ford returned home and, although he made many other films in between, focused steadily on the estern, beginning with *My Darling Clementine* (1946), starring Henry Fonda, which marked the beginning of a near ten-year period of filmmaking by Ford that frequently reflected mainstream America's post-war optimism. As Mark Siegel notes, "*Clementine* seems to reflect an America looking back on the recent world war. One image Americans held of their participation in World War II was that . . . America needed not just to revenge itself but to make the world a safe and decent place in which to live. . . . [T]he hopefulness of this movie, which shows Tombstone as an increasingly civilized social center, seems typical of American optimism immediately after World War II." Ford's optimism continued throughout the late 1940s and early 1950s, evidenced by such films as his marvellous Cavalry Trilogy, starring Wayne—*Fort Apache* (1948), *She Wore a Yellow Ribbon* (1949), and *Rio Grande* (1950)—and *Wagon Master* (1950). But that optimism would not last.

According to Peter Stowell, most of Ford's westerns presented America as a "strong, vibrant, frontier culture that must retain its strength through a wilderness frontier hero, while it demonstrates its progress through a series of civilizing factors." Thanks to Ford's influence, most classic Hollywood westerns share these traits, but towards the end of his career Ford's optimism turned to cynicism, and he began lamenting the progress he had once celebrated. In his later films, most notably *The Searchers* (1956)—a bitter revenge western starring John Wayne and considered by many to be the director's masterpiece—*The Man Who Shot Liberty Valance* (1962) and *Cheyenne Autumn* (1964), he began to question the myths that he, more than any other filmmaker, had played such a central role in creating.

As Jon Tuska observes, "memories, instead of being cherished, became bitter; progress became a hollow drum that beat mechanically." While Ford's earlier westerns established the tone and morality that typify the classic Hollywood western, these late works, notably *The Man Who Shot Liberty Valance,* paved the way for the moody revisionism that has characterized much of western cinema since.

John Ford died of cancer on August 31, 1973. Shortly before his death he was made the recipient of the first American Film Institute Lifetime Achievement Award. Since that time Ford's reputation as a filmmaker has continued to grow, and by the end of the twentieth century he was widely considered the most influential director in Hollywood history. His gifts and his influence have been acknowledged over the decades by the finest of his peers throughout world cinema, and Orson Welles spoke for many when, asked which American directors most appealed to him, he replied, "The old masters . . . by which I mean John Ford, John Ford, and John Ford."

—Robert C. Sickels

FURTHER READING:

Bogdanovich, Peter. *John Ford.* Berkeley, University of California Press, 1967, 1978.

Darby, William. *John Ford's Westerns: A Thematic Analysis with Filmography.* Jefferson, McFarland & Co. Inc., 1996.

Davis, Ronald L. *John Ford: Hollywood's Old Master.* Norman, University of Oklahoma Press, 1995.

Gallagher, Tag. *John Ford: The Man and His Films.* Berkeley, University of California Press, 1986.

McBride, Joseph, and Michael Wilmington. *John Ford.* New York, Da Capo Press, 1975.

Siegel, Mark. *American Culture and the Classic Western Movie.* Tokyo, Eihosha Ltd., 1984.

Slotkin, Richard. "The Apotheosis of the 'B' Western: John Ford's *Stagecoach*." In *Gunfighter Nation.* New York, Atheneum, 1992, 303-11.

Tompkins, Jane. *West of Everything: The Inner Life of Westerns.* New York, Oxford University Press, 1992.

Tuska, Jon. *The Filming of the West.* New York, Doubleday & Co. Inc., 1976.

Yawn, Mike, and Bob Beatty. "John Ford's Vision of the Closing West: From Optimism to Cynicism." *Film & History.* Vol. 26, No. 1-4, 1996, 6-19.

Ford Motor Company

By 1920, the immense scale Henry Ford's international fame could be matched only by the size of his financial assets and the magnitude of his ego. Though Henry would not wrest sole control of Ford Motor Company—the automobile manufacturer he founded with twelve investors in 1903—until the 1920s, the wild success of the car maker was attributed entirely to his individual genius. During Ford's early years, the company was virtually indistinguishable from its founder. "Fordism," as it came to be known—a system of mass

production which combined the principles of "scientific management" with new manufacturing techniques, such as the assembly line—created more than fantastic profits for his company: it literally revolutionized industry on a global scale within twenty years of its implementation at Ford's factory in Highland Park, Michigan. Away from the factory, the Model T, produced between 1908 and 1927, defined the mass consumer market of the 1920s, and in the process helped make the automobile an essential component of American culture. After Henry's resignation in 1945 and series of problems throughout the 1950s, the remarkable success of the Mustang in the 1960s re-established the prominence of Ford Motor Company in the postwar era.

The rapid growth of Ford Motor Company during the first twenty years of this century was due to the astounding sales record of the Model T, or "Tin Lizzie" as it came to be known. Because the cost of early automobiles was prohibitive for most Americans, cars were essentially luxury items and few manufacturers saw the potential for mass appeal of the motorized vehicle. With a debut price of only $850, significantly less expensive than its competitors, the Model T was within the budget of many potential consumers. Because Ford's ingenious labor-saving techniques were not yet available—the assembly line, for instance, would later quadruple productive capacities and reduce labor expenses—Ford kept costs for the Model T low by producing only one type of car (other companies tried to build several different models simultaneously) but assembling it with interchangeable body styles. Due to its functional simplicity, the car was often ridiculed for its aesthetic shortcomings, and Ford himself boasted that consumers could purchase the Model T "in any color they want so long as it's black."

Despite its competitive price, the Model T did not sell particularly well during its initial release. It was aggressive marketing that turned the Model T into the best selling car in history. Henry Ford had originally won financial backing for Ford Motor Company by racing cars and he turned to racing once again in an effort to sell his new product. This competition, however, was a much-publicized transcontinental race. Though the winning Ford car was later disqualified for irregularities, the Model T gained enormous notoriety for its victory and Ford turned that success into massive sales. Later, Ford would market the Model T by appealing to his own person: purchasers could buy a piece of Henry Ford's genius as well as a part of America itself.

To a large extent, we can trace the evolution of America's "car culture" to Ford and the Model T. It was the first car marketed to a large consumer audience, and this alone redefined the role of the automobile industry in the United States. In their famous sociological study *Middletown,* Robert and Helen Lynd conclude that the automobile, by 1925, was already an accepted and indispensable part of American life. It is no exaggeration to suggest that the Model T permanently changed the geography of this country: the popularity of the car made the huge suburban building booms of the 1920s possible, while millions of miles of paved roads were built in response to the demands of new motorists. In addition to the changes brought by the automobile, Ford's production of tractors and other internal combustion farming equipment had a lasting effect on the rural landscape and the agricultural business. Though Henry himself came from a farming community and had nostalgic sympathies for the family farm, his products made life difficult for many small farmers who could not afford (or make profitable) the new harvesting machines. As much as Henry may have loved the farmer, he hated the inefficiency of small operations and imagined an agriculture of mass scale.

The unveiling of the Ford Motor Company's Mustang, 1964.

By 1911, the popularity of the Model T began to present fresh challenges to Ford and its management team. The young company had already moved its base of operations to Highland Park after reaching productive capacity at its Detroit shop and was rapidly approaching its limit once again. The appetite of consumers was far from sated, but labor shortages and productivity ceilings were arresting further plans for expansion. Over the next five years or so, Henry Ford began to develop the concept of "Fordism," an industrial regime which would shortly revolutionize factory production on a global scale. In its early years, the philosophy of Fordism rested on two simple strategies: the invention of the assembly line and the increase of wages. Before the introduction of linework at Ford, the bodies of cars remained stationary while teams of workers moved from station to station. By simply putting the unfinished body on rails and attaching it to a drive train, Ford could move the car from point to point while groups of laborers remained at their assigned posts. This new method allowed for greater specialization of tasks among the workers and permitted management to monitor the efficiency of laborers. And though Henry Ford did not "invent" the assembly line, he has been credited with the development and refinement of this manufacturing technique.

One of the earliest and most persistent critiques of the assembly line came from craftsmen who complained that the division of labor reduced the level of skill required for employment. The assembly line created a distinct division of labor, and the standardization of tasks it required led to a more general deskilling of workers. In order to induce workers to accept this new industrial regime, Ford decided to raise wages. Although this contradicted the logic of supply and demand (with the assembly line, fewer workers could produce more), Ford reasoned that workers would only accept more mundane work in return for better compensation. With the introduction of the eight-hour, five-dollar day (more than doubling the average daily pay) in 1914, Ford single-handedly revolutionized wage structures. Thousands of job-seekers flooded employment offices across the Detroit area looking for positions at Ford, and Henry himself later said that the five-dollar day was the best idea he ever had.

Ironically, the concept of higher wages also permitted the company to discriminate in the workplace. Employees of eastern European and middle-eastern descent were given the most dangerous and physically taxing jobs, while African-Americans were not hired until World War I and women were a rarity before World War II. Meant to bring stability to the organization, the five-dollar day was introduced as part of a larger profit-sharing scheme: workers were only eligible after six months at the company and had to pass a battery of "tests" in order to qualify.

To this end, Ford recruited an army of "social workers," whose ranks included physicians, nurses, and sociologists, to inspect the habits and living arrangements of its employees. To his credit, Henry seemed genuinely concerned with the safety of his employees and built a hospital where they could receive treatment at any time of day. Ford's paternalistic attitude towards his employees, however, had more questionable results in other areas. The company produced a series of "instructional manuals" through the 1910s and 1920s, encouraging its employees to practice thrifty lifestyles and conform to "American" ways of living. Employees who were unmarried or did not live in "sanitary" homes were consistently denied a share of profits. To assist its many immigrant employees, Ford established an official program of "Americanization" that included English language training, courses on household thrift, and moral instruction.

Not surprisingly, employees of "British" descent often qualified for profit-sharing with little scrutiny; most other immigrants had to pass the course of "Americanization" before they could hope to realize the five-dollar wage.

The glory years of Ford ended during the 1930s, and the next thirty years were a very tumultuous time for the company. In keeping with his philosophy, Ford actually raised wages after the stock market crash of 1929 in an effort to stimulate demand. Unwilling to find other supporters in industry, Ford was compelled to reverse his policy shortly thereafter. Labor unrest and unionization during the 1930s forced Ford to reassess his authoritarian discipline and recognize the power of organized labor. Henry stepped down as President in 1945, and though profits had been maintained during the war, Ford's arcane organizational structure was limiting profitability, and the ensuing power struggle eventually led to Ford's public stock offering. The Edsel, Ford's economy model of the late 1950s, named after Henry's son, was the most spectacular failure in the history of American automobile production and symbolized the mood in the company and its public reputation. Although Ford kept its position as an industrial giant (it has consistently been the third largest American manufacturer during the postwar era), General Motors established itself as a much larger and more profitable rival.

On the road, Ford maintained its visibility during the 1950s with the Thunderbird. Its eight cylinder engine was one of the most powerful in its time, but its size necessitated a fairly large body. Because it was priced in the range of other luxury cars (the Chevrolet Corvette was the only true sportscar made in the United States), the Thunderbird faced stiff competition from sleek foreign models though it always achieved high sales figures. New technology of the early 1960s allowed for more streamlined vehicles, and Ford responded by releasing the Mustang in 1963 (under the direction of a young Lee Iaccoca). Smaller and more affordable than the Thunderbird, the Mustang became all things to all people: at once a sports coupe and a touring sedan, it offered a unique combination of practicality and flair. Its remarkable success helped invent the genre of the sports-sedan and reinvigorated Ford's lagging profits. Although the 1970s and early 1980s were a difficult time for Ford and the other American auto manufacturers—the oil crisis of 1973 and competition from Japanese firms sapped profits, while the well-publicized safety problems of the Pinto did little to enhance the company's image—Ford re-emerged during the 1980s with the Escort, a functional, economy car designed for the growing legions of suburban Americans. The Escort was the best-selling car in the world for a number of years during that decade and it helped catapult Ford into a period of renewed profitability. With the Escort, Ford returned to its roots, using the principles of functionality and reliability to once again capture a mass consumer audience.

—Peter Kalliney

FURTHER READING:

Flink, James J. *The Automobile Age*. Cambridge, Massachusetts, and London, MIT Press, 1988.

Miller, Ray. *Mustang Does It: An Illustrated History*. Oceanside, California, Evergreen Press, 1978.

Nevins, Allan. *Ford: Expansion and Challenge, 1915-1933*. Vol. 2. New York, Charles Scribner's Sons, 1957.

————. *Ford: The Times, the Man, the Company*. Vol. 1. New York, Charles Scribner's Sons, 1954.

———. *Ford: Decline and Rebirth, 1933-1962.* Vol. 3. New York, Charles Scribner's Sons, 1963.

Raushenbush, Carl. *Fordism, Ford, and the Community.* New York, League for Industrial Democracy, 1937.

Stern, Philip Van Doren. *Tin Lizzie: The Story of the Fabulous Model T Ford.* New York, Simon & Schuster, 1955.

Ford, Tennessee Ernie (1919-1991)

With his smooth bass voice and warm country charm, Ernest Jennings "Tennessee Ernie" Ford became one of the first country music stars to cross both musical and cultural boundaries to reach a truly national audience during the 1950s. Working as a disk jockey and radio performer in California after World War II, Ford came to the attention of Capitol Records, which signed him in 1949. A string of hits followed, most of them in the "country boogie" style he helped pioneer that married boogie-woogie rhythms with country music themes and instrumentation, including "The Shot Gun Boogie," "Anticipation Blues," and "I'm Hog-Tied Over You." He became a national figure when his recording of "Sixteen Tons" became both a country and pop hit in 1955. He starred in his own television programs between 1955 and 1961 and later recorded a number of highly successful gospel albums.

—Timothy Berg

Tennessee Ernie Ford (right) with Gary Crosby on the Tennessee Ernie Ford Show.

FURTHER READING:

Malone, Bill C. *Country Music U.S.A.: A Fifty Year History.* Austin, American Folklore Society, University of Texas Press, 1968.

Stambler, Irwin, and Grelun Landon. *Country Music: The Encyclopedia.* New York, St. Martin's Press, 1997.

Sixteen Tons of Boogie: The Best of Tennessee Ernie Ford. Rhino Records, 1990.

Ford, Whitey (1928—)

Edward Charles "Whitey" Ford was the dominating left-handed pitcher for the New York Yankees from 1950-67, a 17-year period that coincided with the team's greatest success. Manager Casey Stengel nicknamed Ford "Slick," with good reason: Ford, born and raised in New York, was a city slicker who often relied on guile—and perhaps a scuffed ball on the mound—and liked to take a drink now and then. "The Chairman of the Board," as he was known, chalked up a career record of 236-106, the highest winning percentage for any twentieth-century pitcher, and came to hold a nearly unsurpassable World Series record for wins, strikeouts, and consecutive scoreless innings. Whitey Ford, Mickey Mantle, and Billy Martin constituted a New York trio in the 1950s that shared a public passion for baseball, drinking, and women. They did much to establish the image of the baseball player as an overgrown boy: silly, crude, and outrageous, but basically harmless.

—Jon Sterngass

FURTHER READING:

Ford, Whitey, and Phil Pepe. *Slick: My Life in and Around Baseball.* New York, William Morrow, 1987.

Foreman, George (1949—)

Boxer George Foreman is best known not as the fierce young heavyweight fighter of his youth, but as the oldest man ever to claim the heavyweight championship. Foreman has had a boxing career in two distinct eras, the first spanning the glory years of heavyweight boxing in the late 1960s and 1970s, and the second defined by his astonishing comeback in the 1990s. The forty-plus-year-old Foreman's comeback earned him the status of an American icon, and as he boxed and boasted about his ability to eat, he became a symbol of determination for a generation many considered over the hill.

In 1968 Foreman won an Olympic Gold medal in Mexico City. After turning professional he beat Joe Frazier to capture the world heavyweight championship. In one of the most publicized fights in history he lost his championship to Muhammad Ali in Zaire. By 1977 Foreman had retired from boxing and become a preacher. But he returned to the ring a decade later, an object of ridicule because of his weight and age. In 1994—at the age of forty-five—he recaptured the heavyweight crown.

Foreman was born January 10, 1949, and was reared in an impoverished area known as the Fifth Ward of Houston, Texas, by his mother. Foreman dropped out of school in junior high, and earned a

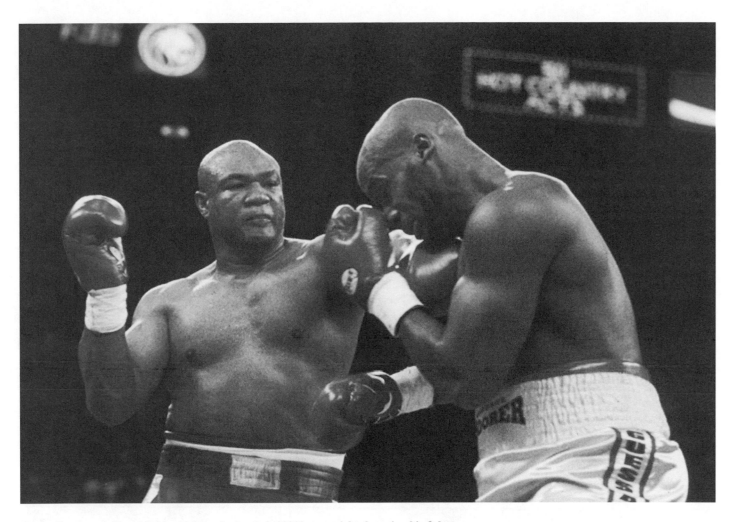

George Foreman (left) and Michael Moore during their 1994 heavyweight championship fight.

reputation as a fighter. After quitting school, Foreman joined the Job Corps. He was shipped first to the Fort Vanney Training Center outside Grant Pass, Oregon, then to the Parks Job Corps Center outside Pleasanton, California. After years of being a bully, this is where Foreman began to box. After graduating from the Job Corps, Foreman worked at the Pleasanton Center and continued to train as a fighter. As an amateur Foreman went on the win the gold medal in the tumultuous 1968 Olympics. John Carlos and Tommie Smith, two American sprinters, had been expelled from the Olympic Village for flashing the Black Power salute during their medal ceremony. Foreman waved a small American flag after winning his gold medal match.

After the Olympics, Foreman turned pro and in his first professional fight knocked out Don Waldheim on June 23, 1969, in Madison Square Garden. Foreman advanced through the heavyweight ranks and on January 22, 1973, in Kingston, Jamaica, Foreman knocked out Joe Frazier in the second round to win the heavyweight championship.

After compiling a record of 40-0, Foreman lost his first professional fight and the heavyweight crown to Muhammad Ali on October 30, 1974, in Zaire. His second loss came to Jimmy Young in March of 1977 in San Juan, Puerto Rico. After his loss to Young, Foreman experienced a religious conversion, retired from boxing, and became a street preacher and ordained minister. He eventually became a radio evangelist in Los Angeles and Houston and, finally, established his own church in Houston. He also established the George Foreman Youth and Community Center.

In an effort to raise money for his youth center—at the age of 37 and 10 years removed from professional boxing—Foreman decided to return to the ring. Foreman's comeback began in March of 1987 in Sacramento against Steve Zouski. The first loss of Foreman's comeback came on April 19, 1991, in Atlantic City, when he lost a 12-round decision in a heavyweight championship bout with Evander Holyfield. However, on November 5, 1994, at the age of 45, Foreman recaptured the heavyweight championship with a 10th round knock-out of Michael Moore.

Foreman's return to boxing prominence was accompanied by a rush of media attention, and Foreman proved himself as adept a media celebrity as he was a boxer. With his bald pate, broad smile, and massive physique, Foreman made good copy as he boasted about the numbers of hamburgers he loved to eat. Quipped Foreman to a reporter, ''Today the biggest decisions I make aren't related to the heavyweight title. They are whether I visit McDonalds, Burger King, Wendy's, or Jack-in-the-Box.'' It might have all seemed a joke had he not backed up his words with a powerful punch. In 1999, with a career record of 76-5, Foreman's fans wondered if he could win his next championship in his fifties.

—Kerry Owens

FURTHER READING:

Foreman, George, and Joel Engel. *By George.* New York, Villard Books, 1995.

Mailer, Norman. *The Fight.* Boston, Little, Brown, 1975.

''Welcome to George Foreman's Place.'' http://www.georgeforeman.com. June 1999.

Forrest Gump

The film *Forrest Gump* represents the ultimate American dream in a land of opportunity. It is a history lesson that takes the viewer from Alabama, where Forrest Gump, an improbable modern hero and *idiot savant,* was born, across America, and back again to the fishing village of Bayou La Batre on the Gulf coast. Governor George Wallace is once again seen standing in the schoolhouse door as he vows ''segregation now, segregation forever''; Coach Paul ''Bear''

Bryant, the legendary University of Alabama football coach, recognizing how Forrest can run, makes him a Crimson Tide gridiron star. Eventually Forrest comes home again to his sweet home Alabama (represented also in song) and makes a fortune in a shrimping business. He had promised his ''best good friend,'' Bubba, that he would go into business with him when the two boys returned from the war. But Bubba was killed and didn't return, so Gump gives half of the million dollars he makes to his friend's family in the small fishing village of Bayou La Batre.

Based upon the novel by Winston Groom, Eric Roth transformed the book into a screenplay that grossed over $636 million dollars and also won the Oscar for Best Picture of 1994. The film affirms possibility and hope: no matter how grim things may seem, it is possible, as Gump says, ''to put the past behind you and move on.'' He shows that a gimpy kid in leg braces can become a football hero, win a Congressional Medal of Honor for bravery in Vietnam, become a Ping Pong champion, crisscross America from sea to shining sea, and marry his childhood sweetheart, who bears him a son to carry on the father's good name.

Tom Hanks in *Forrest Gump.*

In spite of the film's positive message, life, as portrayed in *Forrest Gump,* is not "just a box of chocolates." It is more than candy-coated sentimentality. The viewer witnesses the assassination attempt on George Wallace, and the assassinations of John F. Kennedy and Robert Kennedy; the struggles over civil rights; and the war in Vietnam. Lieutenant Dan (Gary Sinise) portrays the bitter horror of what it is like to lose both legs and live as a cripple. Jenny (Robin Wright), born in poverty and molested by her father, becomes a stripper and a slut, a drug addict caught up in the counterculture of love-ins and psychedelics, flower power and antiwar demonstrations. Though Jenny becomes pregnant with Forrest's child and eventually marries him, she lives a short, unhappy life that is only a questionable testimony to the overriding power of love. Forrest tells her "I'm not a smart man, but I know what love is"—but it isn't enough to save her life or that of his friend, Bubba, or to prevent Lieutenant Dan from losing his legs. At the beginning of the film, a feather floating in the wind lands at Forrest's feet; he picks it up and places it in his worn copy of *Curious George,* the book his mother used to read to him. At the end of the film, he passes the book on to his son with the feather intact. "What's my destiny?" Forrest once asked his mama. *Forrest Gump* shows that every man and woman, idiot or President of the United States may be blown about by the whims of chance or fate, but that it is still possible to prevail.

In addition to the Oscar for Best Film, *Forrest Gump* earned five more Academy Awards. Tom Hanks was voted Best Actor for his masterful portrayal of Gump, and Robert Zemeckis was awarded the Oscar for Best Director. The film also won awards for Film Editing, Best Adapted Screenplay, and for Visual Effects. It is the masterful visual effects that enabled Forrest to shake the hand of President John F. Kennedy, have Lyndon B. Johnson place a Congressional Medal around his neck, meet Richard Nixon and Ronald Reagan, not to mention John Lennon, Dick Cavett, Bob Hope, Captain Kangaroo, and Chairman Mao. Elvis Presley, the King, even learns to swivel his hips by watching little crippled Forrest dance.

Although some critics are not enchanted with the fantastic Gump, the movie affirms the values that Americans hold dear. Forrest's mother exemplifies the ideals associated with motherhood. Over and over, Forrest repeats: "As my Mama always said," and his words reverberate almost as a refrain throughout the movie. "Don't ever let anybody tell you're they're better than you," she tells her boy, even though he has an IQ of 75. Life, after all, is a box of chocolates. Even if "you never know what you're going to get," *Forrest Gump* gives people hope.

—Sue Walker

FURTHER READING:

Groom, Winston. *Forrest Gump.* Garden City, Doubleday, 1986.

Forsyth, Frederick (1938—)

Frederick Forsyth shot to fame in America in 1971 as a top thriller writer with the publication of *The Day of the Jackal,* which dealt with the attempt by a hired killer, "the Jackal," to murder French president Charles de Gaulle. In it, Forsyth meticulously and precisely described how things worked, ranging from the construction of a special rifle to the last detail of the "procedure" the Jackal used to acquire his new passport, a style which was to be the hallmark of his books, a meticulous attention to realistic detail. In researching the book, Forsyth consulted a professional assassin, a passport forger, and an underground armourer. In later best-sellers he improvised car bombs (*The Odessa File,* 1972), gunrunning (*The Dogs of War,* 1974), the innards of oil tankers (*The Devil's Alternative,* 1979), and the assembly of miniature nuclear bombs (*The Fourth Protocol,* 1984). *Icon* (1996), a spine-chilling action thriller which deals with an ex-CIA agent returning to Moscow on the brink of anarchy, has been another in his long list of best-sellers. His popular appeal has been fueled by the blockbuster films made of his books. He has won the Edgar Allan Poe Award from the Mystery Writers of America twice.

Forsyth's books have been criticized for containing recipes for forged passports and explosive bullets. And some actual crimes have seemed to be copycats of crimes described in Forsyth's books. Some examples include: After Yigal Amir was arrested for the assassination of Yitzhak Rabin in 1995, Israeli police searching his apartment found a copy of *The Day of the Jackal* among his Orthodox Jewish literature; John Stonehouse, former British labour minister, faked his death in Florida and began a new life in Australia with a new partner; when geophysicist Karen Reid was shot dead in May 1994, mercury bullets were found near the scene.

Forsyth's interests lay in the relationship of an individual to the organization. In his suspense thrillers, a man of action, a consummate professional, is pitted against an establishment, bureaucracy, or organization. The hero, a maverick who succeeds by cutting through standard procedure, often has difficulty in fitting into society. Forsyth suggests that it is the lone professionals, whether opposed to the organization or part of it, who truly create history, but a history which is only barely represented on the front pages of newspapers. His technique suggests a hidden pattern governing a great event, a pattern not always obvious even to the participants, much less to newspaper readers or devotees of CNN. It is a style very similar to a docudrama which was very popular in the American sixties with such books as Truman Capote's *In Cold Blood* and Norman Mailer's experiments with fact and the novel form.

Forsyth was born in Ashford, Kent, in 1938 and educated at Tonbridge School where he studied French and German. He ended his formal education at the age of seventeen. His background as pilot, journalist, world traveller, and speaker of several languages has served him well in his writing career, where he employs a terse journalistic style using real people, places, and events. From 1958 to 1961 he was a reporter for the *Eastern Daily Press,* first in Norwich and later in King's Lynn, Norfolk. In 1961, he was a Reuters correspondent travelling between Paris, London, and East Berlin, serving as bureau chief in the East German capital because of his knowledge of languages. Next he acted as a BBC radio reporter in London between 1965 and 1967, and as an assistant diplomatic correspondent for BBC television in 1967 and 1968, when he was recalled after his pro-Biafran coverage offended Sir David Hunt, British High Commissioner in Lagos.

Forsyth enjoys fishing in the streams on his leafy country estate in Hertfordshire where he lives with his second wife, Sandy, and two sons, Frederick and Shane. A serious angler who also enjoys the calm of fishing in the Caribbean, Mauritius, and the Andaman Sea, he says the plots of some of his best-sellers gel in his mind during hours of staring into space. He also says that the weirdest and loneliest job in the world is being a writer. An actor has a cast, a pilot has a crew, a doctor a patient, but a writer has only himself. His own life is reflected in the characters depicted in his nine thrillers and anthology of short stories, *No Comebacks* (1982). The effect he achieves is less that of fiction than a projection into real lives.

—Joan Gajadhar and Jim Sinclair

FURTHER READING:

Atkins, John. *The British Spy Novel: Studies in Treachery.* London, Calder, 1984.

McCormick, Donald. *Who's Who in Spy Fiction.* New York, Taplinger, 1977.

Merry, Bruce. *Anatomy of the Spy Thriller.* Dublin, Gill & MacMillan, 1977.

Panek, LeRoy L. *The Special Branch: The British Spy Novel, 1890-1980.* Bowling Green, Ohio, Bowling Green University Popular Press, 1981.

Pate. *The Book of Spies and Secret Agents.* London, Gallery Press, 1978.

Fortune

Despite an inauspicious launch in February 1930, just four months after the Wall Street Crash, *Fortune* magazine became established as the premier business publication in the United States. Symbolic of the success and status of *Fortune,* its annual listing of the top performing companies—the Fortune 500 (est. 1955)—rapidly became, and remains, the highest accolade of American business. Determined to avoid the banality of the trade journal, *Fortune* aimed instead to become "the literature of enterprise." To this end, the magazine published high quality copy, written by established intellectual figures like Dwight MacDonald, in a high quality, glossy format. *Fortune* humanized the world of commerce by combining its stories and values with those of the broader social and political world, and it presented the face of business through the inventive use of photojournalism. Both approaches were to profoundly influence Time Inc.'s next publication, the more populist *Life* magazine, which in turn was to influence a whole generation of journalists and publishers.

—Emma Lambert

FURTHER READING:

Tebbel, John, and Mary Ellen Zuckerman. *The Magazine in America, 1741-1990.* Oxford, Oxford University Press, 1991.

Fortune Tellers
See Psychics

42nd Street

The first of a series of Depression-era musicals released by the Warner Brothers Pictures, *42nd Street* is notable for its role in reviving and redefining a cinematic genre which had begun to fade by 1933. Following the industrywide adaptation of sound films in 1929, Hollywood promptly released a plethora of musicals to excited audiences. Unfortunately, the majority of these products were hastily

conceived and often hindered by the still unresolved technical mysteries of "talking" pictures. Such artistic shortcomings conspired with a saturation of the marketplace, and the public's enthusiasm for such fare rapidly faded.

The successful release of *42nd Street* in March of 1933 reversed this trend, and convinced the major studios to reexamine the commercial possibilities for screen musicals. By the end of the year, Warner had released two follow-up films, *Goldiggers of 1933* and *Footlight Parade.* Other studios embraced this trend, most notably RKO-Radio that began production of a series of pictures starring Fred Astaire and Ginger Rogers. In general, musicals would remain a significant component of Hollywood's product well into the World War II era.

The plot of *42nd Street* revolves around the efforts of a Broadway director (Warner Baxter) struggling to revive his failing reputation with the creation of a lavish extravaganza. The majority of the film details the rigors and hardships of backstage life with a clear eye for the steamier side of show business. On the eve of the show's debut, the leading lady breaks her leg, leaving the director no recourse but to take a chance on a neophyte but determined chorus girl (Ruby Keeler). Following Baxter's now legendary warning—"You're going out a youngster, but you've got to come back a star!" Keeler takes the stage and delights the audience. Although this should provide Baxter's triumph, the film ends on a somber note. As the director stands outside of the theater to assess the comments of the exiting crowd, the loudest sentiments are complaints about the position of Baxter's name on the marquee. To the audience, it was the dancer, not the director who deserved the credit for the show's success.

While the backstage setting of *42nd Street* would be used in dozens of subsequent musical films, the basic story was not an innovation at the time. Earlier productions, most notably MGM's *Broadway Melody* (1929), had focused on a similar theme without such lasting impact. What set *42nd Street* apart from its predecessors was a unique collaboration of actors, songwriters, and directors. The film benefitted from a strong cast; Baxter and Keeler shared the screen with Bebe Daniels, Ginger Rodgers, Dick Powell, Allen Jenkins, Una Merkle, and Guy Kibbee. The team of Al Dubin and Harry Warren composed the music. Although the picture was directed by the dependable craftsman Lloyd Bacon, the musical numbers, which were the main focus of the film, were staged and created by Busby Berkeley.

This assemblage of talent formed a reliable unit that continued to produce highly successful musicals throughout most of the 1930s. Although actors came and went over time, Powell and Keeler were often the focus of these films. Joan Blondell soon joined the stock company as a frequent co-star, while Jenkins and Kibbee routinely provided support. Dubin and Warren were prolific songwriters and seldom failed to include at least one tune per film that would become a popular standard. For *42nd Street,* the duo provided "Shuffle off to Buffalo." In subsequent movies, they debuted soon to be familiar titles such as "We're in the Money," "I Only Have Eyes For You," "Don't Give Up the Ship," and "The Lullaby of Broadway." Although Bacon continued to direct musicals such as *Footlight Parade, Wonder Bar* (1934), and *In Caliente* (1935), he was a versatile filmmaker, and the studio often utilized his talents on other projects. At various times, Mervyn LeRoy, Ray Enright, and Frank Borzage directed musicals for Warner.

The dominant figure in the creation of the Warner musicals was Busby Berkeley. Rising to prominence as dance director for Broadway showman Florenz Ziegfield, Berkeley came to Hollywood in

The chorus line from *42nd Street*.

1931 to work for Samuel Goldwyn. In 1933 Warner signed Berkeley to a lucrative seven-year exclusive contract with *42nd Street* as his initial assignment. Berkeley's work is best described as kaleidoscopic. Employing a system of overhead and moving cameras, Berkeley organized his dancers into a dizzying array of geometric patterns. Such activity could occur on stages as diverse as an indoor waterfall or a gigantic typewriter. The dancers might possess props as innocuous as parasols or as surreal as neon-trimmed violins. Berkeley's imagination seemed endless, and with each film, the musical numbers became increasingly outlandish.

The fantasy world of Berkeley's dance numbers provided the perfect counterpart to the back stage grittiness of *42nd Street*. As a tremendously popular film released in the depths of the Great Depression, the movie remains a valuable key to the needs and tastes of the American public at a specific time in history. The story focuses on the hopes of the downtrodden, and through luck and determination, a hero emerges. At the same time, the swirling elegance of the elaborate musical numbers provided a healthy dose of escapism from the worries of the day. However, the topical nature of the film should

not be over exaggerated. Some fifty years later, the story would be revived as a major Broadway play.

—J. Allen Barksdale

FURTHER READING:

Barrios, Richard. *A Song in the Dark: The Birth of the Musical Film.* New York, Oxford University Press, 1995.

Rubin, Martin. *Showstoppers: Busby Berkeley and the Tradition of the Spectacle.* New York, Columbia University Press, 1993.

Sennett, Ted. *Hollywood Musicals.* New York, H.N. Abrams, 1981.

Fosse, Bob (1927-1987)

Director-choreographer Bob Fosse forever changed the way audiences around the world viewed dance on the stage and in the film

Bob Fosse

industry in the late twentieth century. Visionary, intense, and unbelievably driven, Fosse was an artist whose work was always provocative, entertaining, and quite unlike anything ever before seen. His dances were sexual, physically demanding of even the most highly trained dancers, full of joyous humor as well as bleak cynicism—works that addressed the full range of human emotions. Through his films he revolutionized the presentation of dance on screen and paved the way for a whole generation of film and video directors, showing dance through the camera lens as no one had done before, foreshadowing the rise of the MTV-era of music video dance.

Robert Louis Fosse was born in Chicago, Illinois, on June 23, 1927. Bob was the youngest of six children and quickly learned to win attention from his family through his dancing. It was not long before he was recognized as a child prodigy. His parents sent him to formal lessons, where he immersed himself in tap dancing. A small boy who suffered from nagging health problems, he nevertheless was so dedicated that by the time he reached high school, he was already dancing professionally in area nightclubs as part of their sleazy vaudeville and burlesque shows. The sexually free atmosphere of these clubs and the strippers with whom Fosse was in constant contact made a strong impression on him. Fascinated with vaudeville's dark humor and teasing sexual tones, he would later develop these themes in his adult work. After high school, Fosse enlisted in the navy in 1945. Shortly after he arrived at boot camp, V-J day was declared, and World War II officially came to an end. Fosse completed his two-year duty and moved to New York City.

For the next seven years, Fosse went through two rocky marriages with dancers Mary Ann Niles and Joan McCracken, all the

while performing in variety shows on stage and on television. He had a few minor Broadway chorus parts, but his big break came with his brief appearance in the 1953 MGM movie musical *Kiss Me Kate.* Fosse caught the immediate attention of two of Broadway's acknowledged masters: George Abbott and Jerome Robbins.

Fosse's first fully choreographed show was 1954's *The Pajama Game.* Directed by Abbott, the show made Fosse an overnight success and showcased his trademark choreographic style: sexually suggestive forward hip-thrusts; the vaudeville humor of hunched shoulders and turned-in feet; the amazing, mime-like articulation of hands. He often dressed his dancers in black and put them in white gloves and derbies, recalling the image of Charlie Chaplin. He incorporated all the tricks of vaudeville that he had learned—pratfalls, slights-of-hand, double takes. Fosse received the first of his many Tony Awards for Best Choreography for *The Pajama Game.*

His next musical, *Damn Yankees,* brought more awards and established his life-long creative collaboration with Gwen Verdon, who had the starring role. With her inspiration, Fosse created a stream of classic dances. By 1960, Fosse was a nationally known and respected choreographer, married to Verdon (by then a beloved Broadway star) and father to their child Nicole. Yet Fosse struggled with many of his producers and directors, who wished him to tone down or remove the ''controversial'' parts of his dances. Tired of subverting his artistic vision for the sake of ''being proper,'' Fosse realized that he needed to be the director as well as the choreographer in order to have control over his dances.

From the late 1960s to the late 1970s, Fosse created a number of ground-breaking stage musicals and films. These works reflected the desire for sexual freedom that was being expressed across America and were huge successes as a result. Before Fosse, dance was always filmed either in a front-facing or overhead view. In his 1969 film version of *Sweet Charity* (Fosse's 1966 stage version was based on an earlier movie by Italian director Federico Fellini, about a prostitute's search for love; the film was commissioned by Universal Studios after the success of the stage version) and in later works, Fosse introduced unique perspective shots and jump cuts. These film and editing techniques would become standard practice for music video directors decades later.

His 1972 film *Cabaret* was based on Christopher Isherwood's stories of pre-Weimar Germany. Articles on the film appeared in all the major magazines. Photos appeared on the covers of *Time* and *Newsweek.* The film was Fosse's biggest public success and won eight Academy Awards. Fosse's *Pippin* (1972) became the highest earning Broadway show in history, as well as the first Broadway show to advertise on national television. *Pippin* was awarded five Tony Awards for the 1972-73 season, one of them given to Fosse for best direction and choreography. Fosse staged and choreographed a variety show special for NBC starring Liza Minnelli, *Liza with a Z,* which brought Fosse an Emmy Award and made him the first person to ever win top honors in three entertainment mediums—stage, film, and television.

Two stage musicals followed: *Chicago* (1975) and *Dancin'* (1978). During rehearsals for *Chicago,* Fosse suffered a heart attack. He survived and used much of that traumatic experience in 1979 in his semiautobiographical dance film *All That Jazz.* Two other films, *Lenny* (1974) and *Star 80* (1983), were not the popular successes that his other shows had been. *Big Deal,* Fosse's last musical, was also poorly received. During a rehearsal for *Big Deal,* Fosse suffered a massive heart attack and died on the way to the hospital. Fosse's contribution to American entertainment continued after his death via show revivals and dance classes. His most prominent contribution was through the body of his work recorded on film and video.

—Brian Granger

FURTHER READING:

Beddow, Margaret. *Bob Fosse's Broadway.* Portsmouth, New Hampshire, Heinemann, 1996.

Grubb, Kevin Boyd. *Razzle Dazzle: The Life and Work of Bob Fosse.* New York, St. Martin's Press, 1989.

Foster, Jodie (1962—)

Actress Jodie Foster earned a reputation as a precocious, complicated preteen in Martin Scorsese's *Taxi Driver* (1976) and went on to prove herself as a no-nonsense actress/producer/director in the 1990s. When, in 1981, the tabloid spotlight unexpectedly hit her following John Hinckley, Jr.'s attempt to assassinate President Ronald Reagan, she displayed a grace and reserve to the media that reinforced her status as an intelligent woman. Having won two Academy Awards for Best Actress, Foster has established herself as one of Hollywood's most powerful women and one of the few female stars able to guarantee astronomical box-office receipts in the increasingly important global market.

Jodie Foster

In 1962, Alicia Christian Foster was born the youngest of four siblings in Los Angeles, California. She was tightly bonded to her mother, Evelyn "Brandy" Foster, in part because her father had abandoned the family before she was born and in part because her mother actively promoted Foster's acting talents from an early age. Foster made a popular Coppertone commercial when she was three years old and garnered a minor television role on *Mayberry RFD,* a program in which her brother Buddy was also a star.

Her film debut came with Disney's *Napoleon and Samantha* (1972), and she went on to play a number of children's roles on-screen. It was her infamous performance as Iris, a child prostitute who soberly and unaffectedly carried her pain and powerlessness through a New York City world of moral corruption, opposite Robert De Niro in *Taxi Driver,* which won her a National Film Critics Award. This part also affirmed the fact that the capricious, nimble-witted characters she took on at Disney made her incredibly well-suited for more adult material. After *Taxi Driver,* she starred in *Freaky Friday* (1977), a family film in which her character finds herself in the skin of her mother (Barbara Harris) for a day, as she humorously confronts the realities of being an adult housewife.

While actively pursuing her career as a performer, Foster graduated and was valedictorian at the Lycée Français in Los Angeles and went on to earn a cum laude degree in literature at Yale University. It was while she was at Yale that she was stalked by John Hinckley, Jr., whose obsession with *Taxi Driver* motivated him to shoot President Reagan in 1981. Though Foster was trying to carry on the life of a "normal college student," she immediately held a press conference on campus in hopes of containing the publicity and went on to write an article titled "Why Me?" for *Esquire* magazine which explained her experiences as one of Hinckley's targets.

Once out of college, in an attempt to recharge her acting career, Foster lobbied for the role of a working-class rape victim in *The Accused* (1988). She won a difficult competition among a number of up-and-coming female stars, even dropping weight for the part upon request from studio executives, and went on to score her first Academy Award. She battled yet again for the role of FBI agent Clarice Starling in the thriller *The Silence of the Lambs* (1991), convincing director Jonathan Demme that she had a better psychological understanding of the "rising heroine" character than the other top-notch stars he preferred. This performance garnered her a second Best Actress Oscar.

Foster moved into the role of director with two Hollywood feature films, *Little Man Tate* (1991) and *Home for the Holidays* (1995). The former film tells the story of a young child prodigy and his complicated relationship with his struggling, little-educated, waitress mother, played by Foster. At the release of the film, Foster admitted that her interest in it partially stemmed from her own experiences as a child living in a world beyond her years. With *Home for the Holidays,* which was produced through Foster's company, Egg Pictures, the director follows an insecure single mother (Holly Hunter) as she journeys home to her eccentric family for Thanksgiving.

While increasing her power as a producer/director, Jodie Foster continued to turn in remarkable performances in films such as *Nell* (1994), in which she plays a rugged wild child brought painfully into contemporary society, and *Contact* (1997), an adaptation of Carl Sagan's science fiction story about a woman who explores the possibility of life in outer space.

Foster developed a reputation as an anti-establishment pragmatist who remained within the Hollywood system in order to transform its representations of women and bring unconventional character pieces to the screen. She is also known as a down-to-earth, democratic star who, throughout her twenties, lived in the less-than-glamorous "valley" of Los Angeles and reportedly refused to rely on a personal assistant for mundane tasks such as picking up dry cleaning or going to the post office. Foster fiercely protects her private life, having earned the respect and protection of Hollywood trade reporters and mainstream journalists. She became mother to a boy, Charles Foster, in the summer of 1998, provoking a relatively minor outcry when she refused to name the baby's father.

In films such as *Silence of the Lambs* and *Contact,* Foster drew on the androgyny and maturity of her childhood characters and solidified a reputation as an actress who rebelled against traditional feminine stereotypes and sought out complex acting opportunities that had been relatively unexplored by female stars. She became notorious for taking disenfranchised, scrappy characters and moving them closer to heroic self-empowerment. In a 1993 discussion of Hollywood, Foster explained, ". . . 95 percent of the people will always try to maintain the status quo. It's the other five percent that move the art form further. . . . What's different about [women] is that we identify with the underdog, so we spend a lot of time thinking about who's left out. When you sit around a table like this with a bunch of guys, they spend a lot of time thinking about who's on top." The first three decades of Foster's career leave little doubt that she stands within "the other 5 percent" and that, despite her immense Hollywood power, she has spent considerable efforts "thinking about who's left out."

—Christina Lane

FURTHER READING:

Chunovic, Louis. *Jodie: A Biography.* Chicago, Contemporary Books, 1995.

Foster, Buddy. *Foster Child.* New York, Penguin/Putnam Books, 1997.

Kennedy, Philippa. *Jodie Foster: A Life on Screen.* New York, 1996.

Lane, Christina. "The Liminal Iconography of Jodie Foster." *Journal of Popular Film and Television.* Winter 1995, 149-153.

Rich, B. Ruby. "Never a Victim: Jodie Foster, A New Kind of Female Hero." *Sight & Sound.* December 1991, 50-61.

Smolen, Diane. *The Films of Jodie Foster.* Seacaucus, Citadel Press, 1996.

Fourth of July Celebrations

As the day designated to commemorate the signing of the Declaration of Independence and the anniversary of America's birth, the Fourth of July has been celebrated since the Revolutionary War Era. However, after the war was over it was only sporadically celebrated and did not become a regular observance in many parts of the country until after the turn of the nineteenth century.

Although the Continental Congress formally passed the resolution for independence on July 2, 1776, it was not until July 4, 1776 that Congress finally voted to approve the Declaration of Independence, which stated the reasons for the break with England. In fact, on July 3, 1776, John Adams wrote his wife that July 2, 1776 would be "the most memorable epocha in the history of America," according to historian Daniel Boorstin. Adams then outlined the contours of the

"great anniversary festival" which he thought should include: ". . . solemn acts of devotion to God Al-mighty . . . with pomp and parade, with shows, games, sports, guns, bells, bonfires, and illuminations from one end of this continent to the other. . . ."

While it is a mystery to historians why July 4th was designated to commemorate independence and the signing of the Declaration, this date marked the annual official celebration during the Revolutionary War period. Afterwards, official festivities became sporadic and eventually evolved into incredibly partisan events, which persisted for more than three decades. These often included separate observances held by the different political parties. As a day of political dissension, the celebrations at times erupted into violence. In particular, it was used by both the Federalist and Republican parties to hold what amounted to political rallies, with separate orations, dinners, and processions.

It was not until 1826, after a second successful war against Britain and the commemoration of the 50th anniversary of the new nation, that newspapers across the country called for an end to partisanship. They encouraged plans for orations, military processions, private gatherings, public dinners, and picnics to celebrate American independence. As this day became popular as a community event, its rituals affirmed community ties as well as national identity and became linked to other community events such as ground breakings, building dedications, and rededications of historic sites.

Communitywide celebrations continued in popularity from the early nineteenth century until the Civil War, and included parades, ceremonies, sporting events, and fireworks. During the Civil War, Independence Day celebrations were no longer held in many parts of the country, especially in the South.

In the postwar era, the urban celebrations on the East Coast were often sites for clashes between the upper and middle classes and the working class (especially immigrants) over the style of celebration and the use of public space. A genteel or "respectable" celebration was favored by the middle and upper classes, with an emphasis on picnics, private gatherings, games like croquet and lawn tennis, and retreats into the countryside. The working class, however, typically favored rowdy and carnivalesque festivities such as unruly parades, drunkenness, rough games, and noisy discharges of firecrackers and fireworks.

Significantly, celebratory styles were debated back in the Revolutionary Era in hopes of standardizing festivities throughout the Colonies. Members of the Continental Congress weighed the advantages of the rowdy or carnival style of celebration—with its ability to stimulate crowds and allow the venting of tensions—in contrast to the solemn style—with its ability to unify a diverse populace. Eventually, in the interests of national unity, the solemn or respectable style was favored and became associated with the notion of civil religion. In newspaper accounts of Independence Day thereafter, celebrations in this style were typically emphasized while coverage of regional Fourth of July celebrations and their local variations in the carnival style were often neglected.

Although incompatible with urban order, the rowdy style of celebration regained popularity with immigrants in many urban areas in the early nineteenth century. Rooted in the European carnival customs of the working class, these celebrations included masking, charivaris (noisy demonstrations to humiliate someone publicly), and calithumpian parades (parades of urban maskers whose "rough music" mocked "real music"). Over time, tamed versions of these working-class practices were adopted and modified to accommodate

Fourth of July fireworks in downtown Detroit, Michigan.

urban order and to avert class conflicts that had previously erupted over the clash of styles.

In the late nineteenth century, the Safe and Sane Fourth of July Program promoted standardized Fourth of July celebrations across the country, emphasizing the solemn or respectable style of celebration. Aimed at the socialization and ''Americanization'' of immigrants, the program was developed by progressive reformers to promote safety and to establish social order. A primary goal of this program was to legitimate the respectable style as ''American'' behavior. This program banned all firecrackers and encouraged noise abatement. Reformers produced and disseminated a standardized format in which a formal program was devoted to promoting the values of social order, solemn patriotism, and moderation. In addition, the program emphasized speeches and orations related to the Declaration of Independence. Progressive reformers also encouraged parades featuring patriotic pageantry with selected folk traditions to model the respectable version of America's history.

In many small towns and remote areas, the Fourth of July has typically been a communitywide celebration in which distinctive rituals and traditions have reflected the interests of the residents. In Lititz, Pennsylvania, for example, community members prepare for

the Fourth by producing thousands of tallow candles in old-fashioned molds during the winter in a tradition dating back to 1843. The town's Fourth of July festivities begin with a baby parade in which children dressed in patriotic costumes ride on floats decorated in red, white, and blue. A queen of candles is chosen from the senior high school class to preside over the evening ceremony in which boys of the town light many of the candles in the park and float them on the water. In the town of Bridgeport, California, the Declaration of Independence has traditionally been read at the county courthouse, children ride in a parade on decorated bicycles, and a pie-eating contest is a featured event. The participants include community members as well as Native Americans and cattlemen from neighboring ranches who ride in a parade on decorated horses. Other events include picnics, sporting events, and a barbecue.

For more than 100 years, Biwabik, Minnesota, a town of 1,500, has seen its population grow to more than ten times its size during the Fourth of July. Its traditional celebration includes patriotic and calithumpian parades, fireworks, and games like egg-tossing contests and three-legged races. In some of the western states like Colorado and Texas, Fourth of July celebrations have often revolved around rodeos featuring events like roping and riding contests. In 1959 when

Alaska became the 49th state and in 1960 when Hawaii was added as the 50th state, commemorations of these occasions were held across the country on the Fourth of July.

Although Independence Day has been celebrated since the Revolutionary War Era, it was not made a federal legal holiday until 1941. Most recently its status as a holiday from work has taken precedence over the emphasis on commemorating America's birthday, and in some parts of the country celebrations are no longer held. In addition, a pattern of waxing and waning of interest in holding Independence Day programs is evident in many urban areas. The years in which its popularity has peaked were during periods of patriotic fervor such as the centennial in 1876, the years after both World War I and World War II, the 175th anniversary in 1951, and the Bicentennial in 1976. The turn of the century in the year 2000 is also expected to stimulate a resurgence of interest in Fourth of July celebrations across the country.

—Mary Lou Nemanic

FURTHER READING:

Bodnar, John. *Remaking America: Public Memory, Commemoration and Patriotism in the Twentieth Century.* Princeton, Princeton University Press, 1992.

Boorstin, Daniel J. *The Americans: The National Experience.* New York, Random House, 1965.

Cohen, Hennig, and Tristam Potter Coffin, editors. *The Folklore of American Holidays.* Detroit, Gale Research Company, 1987.

Davis, Susan G. *Parades and Power: Street Theatre in Nineteenth-Century Philadelphia.* Philadelphia, Temple University Press, 1986.

Glassberg, Philip. *American Historical Pageantry: The Uses of Tradition in the Early Twentieth Century.* Chapel Hill, North Carolina, University of North Carolina Press, 1990.

Foxx, Redd (1922-1991)

Born John Elroy Sanford in St. Louis, Missouri in 1922, Redd Foxx became one of America's most beloved comedic figures in the 1970s. Called Redd because of his complexion, he took the last name of baseball star Stan Fox—though by adding his distinctive double "x," nobody would have known this—, and left home at the age of 16 to join a New York street band. Through the 1940s and 1950s, Foxx worked as a stand-up comedian and became known for his "party records," recordings of his bawdy stand-up act. The most famous of these was 1955's "Laff of the Party," but he recorded many more. Over 15 million copies of his records were reportedly sold, although Foxx claimed to have received no royalties.

Redd Foxx is best remembered for his role as junk dealer Fred G. Sanford, the cantankerous but lovable elderly widower of NBC's hit comedy *Sanford & Son* (1972-1977). The show was the second smash hit (after *All in the Family*) for Norman Lear and Bud Yorkin, whose topical comedies of the 1970s addressed issues of bigotry regarding race, gender, and sexuality to a degree that had never been seen on American television before. Fred Sanford was a black counterpart to *All in the Family*'s Archie Bunker. *Sanford & Son* was based on the hit British comedy *Steptoe & Son*, which revolved around a cockney junk dealer. The American version was set in the Watts section of Los Angeles, where Fred and his son Lamont (played by Demond Wilson)

are partners in the business. Fred is content to eke out a living as a junkman, though he is constantly hatching all kinds of get-rich-quick schemes, which make Lamont crazy. Lamont, by contrast, is seeking a better life, and many of the sitcom's conflicts arise out of Lamont's desire to get out of the junk business and Fred's attempts to make him stay. Their arguments frequently end with Fred feigning a heart attack, clutching his chest, and calling to his dead wife, "I'm coming to join you Elizabeth!" With this conflict between family and ambition at the center, the Sanfords interact with other engaging characters, many of them played by older black actors who Redd Foxx had worked with in his early stand-up days. The results were hilarious.

Foxx left *Sanford and Son* at the end of the 1976-77 season amidst reported contract disputes with the producers and an argument with NBC over an appropriate dressing room. He signed with ABC for the *Redd Foxx Comedy Hour,* in which he spotlighted some of his old show business friends, and communicated his version of events in American history in a regular spot called "The History of the Black in America." The show, however, proved a ratings bomb and lasted only a few months.

After a few years working in Las Vegas clubs and making guest appearances on other people's variety shows, Foxx returned to television in 1980 when NBC tried to revive the earlier hit series as *Sanford.* The cast of characters was new, the writing poor, and that show, too, suffered the fate of his *Comedy Hour,* lasting only a few months. In 1986, *The Redd Foxx Show* attempted to present its star in an entirely new guise as a kindly newsstand operator with a white foster daughter. It was retooled after a couple of episodes when network research showed that Americans liked Foxx better as a grumpy character. The daughter was written out and a nagging ex-wife was written in. The series failed to survive.

In the late 1980s, Foxx was forced to file for bankruptcy. Three divorces and an extravagant lifestyle had forced him into a position where the IRS seized most of his assets, but 1989 brought a change of fortune. He appeared in Eddie Murphy's film *Harlem Nights,* received good notices and went on to a role in a new Murphy-produced series called *The Royal Family.* On October 11, 1991, after filming only seven episodes, Redd Foxx collapsed on the set during rehearsals, provoking laughter from cast and crew who thought he was doing his "Elizabeth, I'm coming to join you!" routine from *Sanford and Son.* He had, however, suffered a fatal heart attack, dying in harness as he no doubt would have wished.

—Joyce Linehan

Foyt, A. J. (1935—)

A. J. Foyt is one of the premier names in motor sports, having enjoyed an auto racing career that spanned four decades, beginning in the 1950s. No other driver achieved such a unique combination of longevity, dominance, and versatility in motor sports, on which he left a permanent mark wherever he raced. Known as "Supertex" to his many fans, Hoyt gained a reputation for a uniquely tough and aggressive style that brought a new excitement to the sport, and he is probably the most popular driver ever to have run at "The Greatest Spectacle in Racing," the Indianapolis 500.

Anthony Joseph Foyt, Jr. was born on January 16, 1935 in Houston, Texas, where he became familiar with racing cars from an

Redd Foxx

early age. His father owned the Burt and Foyt Garage that specialized in the vehicles, and Foyt had already decided to make a career of racing when he was no more than five years old. By his late teens he was driving midget racers on the Midwestern circuit.

In the years that followed, A. J. Foyt firmly established himself in various aspects of the sport: midgets, sprints, stock cars, sports cars, and Indy cars. He emerged from quarter-mile dirt ovals to become arguably the most dominant driver in the history of the Indianapolis 500. At Indianapolis, Foyt qualified for a record 35 consecutive races, and was the first driver to win Indianapolis four times, a feat later matched only by Al Unser and Rick Mears. By the late 1990s, he still held the record for the most Indy Car wins with 67 victories and has thus far remained the only driver in the history of the sport to win seven national Indy car titles.

Foyt was also highly successful in other areas of car racing. He won the 24 Hours at Le Mans in 1967, captured the 24 Hours at Daytona in 1983 and 1985, and was victorious at the 12 Hours of Sebring in 1985. Perhaps one of the most amazing aspects of Foyt's career is that so successful an Indy car driver was also able to achieve

victories in major stock car events. After recording 41 wins in United States Auto Club (USAC) stock car racing, he joined the famous Wood Brothers team and became a significant force on the NASCAR circuit, winning seven NASCAR Winston Cup races, including the 1972 Daytona 500. His astonishing record was enhanced even further when he captured the world closed course speed record for an Oldsmobile in 1987, recording a 257-m.p.h. lap in a Quad-4 powered Aerotech.

In 1993, at the age of 58, A. J. Foyt announced his retirement from race-car driving. However, he retained his connection with the sport as a car owner, including his proprietorship of A. J. Foyt Honda in Houston. He also bought several cattle and horse ranches in Texas, and was appointed to the boards of both Riverway Bank and Service Corporation International. He continued living in Houston with his wife Lucy. Of Hoyt's four children, three have followed in their father's footsteps: Jerry pursues a career in stock car racing, Larry races go-carts, and A. J. Foyt IV races junior dragsters.

—James H. Lloyd

A. J. Foyt crosses the finish line at the 1967 Indianapolis 500.

FURTHER READING:

A. J. Foyt: Champion for Life. Videocassette. Greenwich, Connecticut, Cabin Fever Entertainment, 1992.

Engle, Lyle Kenyon. *The Incredible A. J. Foyt.* New York, Arco, 1977.

Foyt, A. J., and Bill Neeley. *A. J.* New York, Times Books, 1983.

Libby, Bill. *Foyt.* New York, Hawthorn Books, 1974.

Motor Sports Hall of Fame "'A. J.' Foyt." http://www.mshf.com/hof/foyt.htm. March 1999.

Wilker, Josh. *A. J. Foyt: Race Car Legends.* New York, Chelsea House Publishers, 1996.

Francis, Arlene (1908—)

During her long career as one of television's most versatile hostesses, Arlene Francis was the quintessence of wit and charm.

Beginning her career as an actress on the stage and screen, Francis hosted a precursor to *The Dating Game,* called *Blind Date,* for three years in the early 1950s, while also emceeing the talent shows *By Popular Demand* and later, *Talent Patrol.* At the same time she radiated sophistication and good cheer as a regular panelist on *What's My Line,* the popular game show with which she was associated for 25 years. In 1954 NBC president Sylvester "Pat" Weaver chose Francis as host and editor-in-chief for a new concept in daytime television, *Home,* a serious talk show for women. The three year run of *Home* established Francis' credentials as a pioneer in the talk format. She returned to public affairs television in the early 1980s when she hosted a New York program, *The Prime of Your Life,* a noteworthy series for senior citizens.

—Ron Simon

FURTHER READING:

Francis, Arlene, with Florence Rome. *Arlene Francis: A Memoir.* New York, Simon and Schuster, 1978.

Francis, Connie (1938—)

In the late 1950s and early 1960s, singer Connie Francis reigned as America's top-selling female vocalist and the female counterpart to teen idols such as Frankie Avalon and Fabian. Cute, as opposed to glamorous, the diminutive brunette with the perky demeanor typified the girl next door. Teenage girls wanted to be her best friend; teenage boys dreamed of dating her. The media called her ''America's sweetheart.''

Born Concetta Rosa Maria Franconero in Newark, New Jersey, Francis was just three years old when her roofing-contractor father presented her with an accordion. A year later she was performing at family events, churches, and hospitals. She was eleven when her father took her to Manhattan to meet the producer of the TV show *Startime,* which featured child performers; she appeared on the program for the next four years. She was later showcased on TV variety shows, including Arthur Godfrey's *Talent Scouts.* It was Godfrey who suggested that she change her name. He also suggested that she put away her accordion to concentrate on singing.

Francis began her recording career cutting demo records for various music publishing companies. Then came a 1957 recording contract with MGM and ten failed singles. It was at her father's suggestion that she did an up-tempo version of the 1923 standard

Connie Francis

''Who's Sorry Now?'' for what she anticipated would be her final recording session for the label. To her surprise, the record found favor with Dick Clark, congenial host of the popular *American Bandstand.* Touting the new ''girl singer,'' Clark played her record on a 1958 New Year's Day telecast. Over the next five weeks, the record sold a million copies to become Francis's first gold record. Francis, who became a frequent guest on *Bandstand,* later admitted that were it not for Clark and his support, she would have given up on her musical career.

She instead became a perennial on the charts. Along with outselling all other female artists from 1958 to 1964, she became the first female singer to have consecutive number-one hits with the 1960 songs ''Everybody's Somebody's Fool'' and ''My Heart Has a Mind of Its Own.'' A household name, her likeness appeared on paper dolls, diaries, and other merchandise aimed at teenage girls. Then came a quartet of MGM films. First and most memorable was *Where the Boys Are* (1960), about college girls looking for love during spring break in Ft. Lauderdale, Florida. Though the film is today best known for its heartfelt title song, performed by Francis, its plot and setting were mimicked myriad times in succeeding decades, especially during the 1980s when youth-oriented movies were the rage.

As her fame grew, Francis began recording songs with adult appeal; the Italian-American also recorded albums in numerous foreign languages. As a result, the mature Francis was able to establish herself as a strong nightclub draw. In the late 1960s, during the cultural revolution which saw American audiences clamoring for performers with British accents, Francis took her act overseas.

But there were personal trials, including failed marriages and disagreements with her domineering father-manager. Then came an emotionally shattering rape and beating, which she suffered hours after performing at Long Island's Westbury Music Fair in late 1974. The headline-making experience left Francis psychologically unable to perform. Three years later she suffered another setback, when cosmetic surgery on her nose affected her voice. It was a 1978 television concert show, hosted by longtime friend Dick Clark, that marked Francis's return, but unbeknownst to audiences, the still-fragile Francis had to lip-sync to a prerecorded medley of her hits. Three years later, she suffered yet another crisis, the 1981 gangland-style murder of her younger brother, but she went on to face a live audience later that year. In fact, she bravely played the same venue where she had performed the night of her rape and beating. Explained Francis, ''I had to put my fears to sleep.''

Sadly, Francis's various fears continued to resurface. The recipient of sixteen gold records suffered nervous breakdowns, involuntary confinements in mental facilities, and was diagnosed as a manic-depressive. In interviews and in her 1984 autobiography, she attributed some of her woes to her relationship with her overprotective father: ''Thanks to my father, I [grew up] the typical horribly repressed Italian girl. I was this nice little girl that no man was supposed to touch.... Probably the biggest regret of my life is that I allowed him to exercise all that control. It was a form of emotional abuse....''

Still, through the 1990s, Francis has made intermittent comebacks. In performance, the woman who led the way for today's female superstars, including Madonna, Janet Jackson, and Celine Dion, continues to project the engaging demeanor of the girl next door, albeit one who is sadder but wiser.

—Pat H. Broeske

FURTHER READING:

Bronson, Fred. *The Billboard Book of Number One Hits*. New York, Billboard Publications, 1988.

Francis, Connie. *Who's Sorry Now?* New York, St. Martin's Press, 1984.

Hunt, Dennis. "Connie Francis Gets It All out of Her System." *Los Angeles Times*. November 23, 1984, 22.

Levinson, Bill. "Where the Boys Aren't." *American Weekly*. January 1, 1961, 7.

Francis the Talking Mule

Francis was the smart, sassy talking mule who led a bumbling but sincere human sidekick into and out of trouble in seven films for Universal Pictures from 1949 to 1956. For all but the last film, the sidekick was played by singer/dancer Donald O'Connor, and the voice of Francis was supplied by character actor Chill Wills. The special effect of talking was achieved by feeding a strong thread from the bridle to the mule's mouth. A gentle off-camera tug on the thread caused the animal to try to dislodge the annoyance by moving its lips. The film series was considered silly by the critics, but moviegoers enjoyed the antics of a mule who not only talked but who was more intelligent than his owner. As the first non-cartoon talking movie animal, Francis paved the way for television's talking horse, *Mister Ed*.

—Pauline Bartel

FURTHER READING:

Edelson, Edward. *Great Animals of the Movies*. Garden City, New York, Doubleday, 1980.

Rothel, David. *Great Show Business Animals*. San Diego, A.S. Barnes, 1980.

Frankenstein

On the shores of Lake Geneva in the summer of 1816, nineteen-year-old Mary Wollstonecraft Shelley (1797-1851), her future husband, Percy Shelley, and their charismatic friend Lord Byron engaged in a ghost-story contest. After seeing a vision of what she called "the hideous phantasm of a man," Mary Shelley began writing *Frankenstein, or The Modern Prometheus,* the gothic novel that would bring her lasting fame. Even before Shelley's name was widely known, theatrical versions of her novel—the tale of Victor Frankenstein and his monster—frightened and appalled audiences all over Europe. The popularity of stage adaptations in the nineteenth century foreshadowed the emergence of the Frankenstein monster as an icon of film, television, and other forms of popular culture in the twentieth century, including everything from comic books to Halloween costumes. Indeed, the creature's deformity and pathos have earned it such an indelible position in the popular imagination that the name "Frankenstein" has come to denote not the scientist who bears the name or even the novel which gave it life, but rather the image of a scarred and lumbering monster in angry revolt against its creator and society. On one level, the creature exists simply as a horror-movie staple, like Dracula or the Wolf Man. But it is the monster's value as a powerful symbol of our fears regarding the dangers of science, technology, and industrialization, as well as the perils of man's hubristic attempts to control nature, that has given Shelley's "hideous progeny" such an enduring and ubiquitous afterlife.

No other medium exploited, influenced, and perpetuated the Frankenstein myth like film. One of the first movies ever made, Thomas A. Edison's sixteen-minute silent film *Frankenstein* (1910), began the transformation of Shelley's literary creation into its numerous cinematic offspring. But it was the 1931 Universal Studio release of director James Whale's *Frankenstein* that exerted the greatest impact on Frankenstein mythmaking. In his career-making performance as the monster, Boris Karloff reduced Shelley's articulate, intelligent, and agile creature to a silent brute that was nevertheless endearing in its child-like innocence. Ironically, Karloff's monster—furnished with a protruding and stitched forehead, eyes devoid of intelligence, and electrodes in his neck—all but replaced Shelley's original creation in the popular imagination. As well as cementing Karloff's creature as a cinematic icon, the film also gave rise to enduring "Frankenstein movie" conventions such as the elaborate creation scene, the mad doctor's laboratory, his demented hunchback assistant, Fritz, his infamous ecstatic cry at the moment of creation ("It's alive!"), and the angry torch-carrying rabble who pushed the monster to its fiery death. For two decades, Universal profited immensely from the Frankenstein series with the much-praised *Bride of Frankenstein* (1935) and several lesser but popular sequels, such as *Frankenstein Meets the Wolf Man* (1943). The film series also yielded several spin-off characters, including Elsa Lanchester's Bride of Frankenstein, whose teased-up hair with white "lightning streaks" made her a comparable, though lesser known, pop icon.

Embodying the postwar optimism and prosperity of the late 1940s, the Frankenstein monster shifted into the comic genre when Universal released *Abbott and Costello Meet Frankenstein* in 1948. This "horror-comedy" approach to the Frankenstein myth, complete with slapstick gags, marked a departure from Whale's more serious pictures of the 1930s. But the title's explicit focus on the Frankenstein monster—and the film's positive reception with audiences and critics—evinced the creature's ongoing mass-market appeal and presaged the onslaught of low budget films such as *I Was a Teenage Frankenstein* (1957) in the following decades.

After Abbot and Costello's satire of "classic" monster movies proved that the more serious Frankenstein formula had grown tired, Frankenstein films suffered a hiatus until the British studio Hammer Films released *The Curse of Frankenstein* in 1957. The movie marked the beginning of a more serious and gory approach to big-screen versions of the Frankenstein story. Peter Cushing, who played Baron Frankenstein in numerous films for the Hammer series, captured the psychological struggle of the "mad" scientist so memorably that his character soon overshadowed the monster in much the same way that Karloff's creature had usurped the fame of his creator in the Whale films.

This focus on the psychology of the mad scientist, however, was short-lived. Capitalizing on the prevailing counter-cultural climate and the renewed popularity of classic horror characters in the 1960s and 1970s, the Frankenstein monster made a comeback as a popular symbol of nonconformity. Exemplary of this new trend, interpretations of Frankenstein in the 1970s subverted and even perverted more traditional representations. In 1974, cult artist Andy Warhol produced *Flesh for Frankenstein* (or *Andy Warhol's Frankenstein*), an ultra-gory retelling in which Baron Frankenstein and his "zombies" display overtly homoerotic, sensual, and necrophilic behavior. In the same year, Mel Brooks's *Young Frankenstein* cleverly parodied the

A scene from the film *Frankenstein*, with Boris Karloff (standing) and Mae Clarke, 1931.

Frankenstein myth and answered the long-unspoken question about the monster's sexual girth. The cult film *The Rocky Horror Picture Show* (1975) even featured a transvestite named Frank-n-Furter and his creation Rocky Horror.

The Frankenstein monster also infiltrated America's rising TV culture in two very similar shows about eccentric nuclear families. Both *The Munsters* (CBS, 1964-66) and *The Addams Family* (ABC, 1964-66) featured a Frankenstein-like character that was essentially a nostalgic reproduction of Karloff's famous creature. In telling the weekly stories of these suburban families who were, besides their monster-movie appearance, normal in every respect, these shows satirized the quaint, white, middle-class family sitcoms of an earlier decade and capitalized on the comic implications of a "domesticated" Frankenstein's monster. (In *The Addams Family,* for instance, the creature named Lurch served as the terse family butler.) The popularity of such series in TV reruns and feature films suggested that the Frankenstein monster, and its attending creature culture, had become a cuddly household commodity now endlessly recycled for comic effect and commercial gain. It was not until the 1990s, in fact,

that any significant attempt was made to reestablish a more serious approach to this material. Kenneth Branagh's 1994 film *Mary Shelley's Frankenstein* returned to Shelley's original novel and captured much of its gothic terror but also added popular movie formulas such as the creation of the monster's bride.

Despite the endless dilutions, distortions, and recyclings, the force of the Frankenstein myth remains undiminished as contemporary society continues to incorporate technological advances—in fields such as genetic engineering—into everyday life while growing increasingly apprehensive about their potential dangers. Each version of Frankenstein's monster acts not only as a potent reminder of the dark side of man's creative idealism—the dangers of trying to play God—but also as a powerful representation of the collective fears and desires of the particular era in which it was conceived. The Frankenstein legend continues to endure as a deformed mirror held up to human nature, *re*-formed from parts of the dead past—with our imagination providing the electrical spark.

—Kristine Ha

FURTHER READING:

Glut, Donald. *The Frankenstein Catalog.* Jefferson, North Carolina, McFarland & Company, 1984.

————. *The Frankenstein Legend: A Tribute to Mary Shelley and Boris Karloff.* Metuchen, New Jersey, Scarecrow Press, 1973.

Haining, Peter, ed. *The Frankenstein File.* London, New English Library, 1977.

Levine, George, ed. *The Endurance of Frankenstein: Essays on Mary Shelley's Novel.* Berkeley, University of California Press, 1979.

Mellor, Anne Kostelanetz. *Mary Shelley, Her Life, Her Fiction, Her Monsters.* New York, Methuen, 1988.

Shelley, Mary W. *Frankenstein or the Modern Prometheus.* New York, Penguin Books, 1992.

Franklin, Aretha (1942—)

As the career of singer, songwriter, and pianist Aretha Franklin makes evident, the black church—its ministers, its members, and its music—have had a profound influence on popular music. A fruit of the black Baptist church, Franklin is one of the most important female artists to translate gospel music—with all its intensity—into soul music. Her talent was nurtured by a who's who of gospel song—Clara Ward, James Cleveland, and Mahalia Jackson—and her father, Reverend C. L. Franklin, was a gospel singer in his own right. For the past thirty years, Franklin has reigned as the "Queen of Soul," winning more Grammy Awards than any other female vocalist—at least one a year from 1967 through 1974 and then in 1981, 1985, and 1987. From 1960 to 1992, 89 of her songs were in the pop or R&B Top Forty, with twenty of them reaching number one on the R&B chart. Franklin was the first African-American woman to appear on the cover of *Time* magazine (in June, 1968), and in 1987 she became the first woman to be inducted into the Rock and Roll Hall of Fame. By the mid-1980s, Franklin had racked up a total of twenty-four gold records. The state of Michigan has designated her voice as a natural resource.

The eldest of three sisters, Aretha Franklin was born in Memphis, Tennessee, on March 25, 1942. During her childhood, her family moved to Buffalo and then to Detroit, where she grew up. Her father, the celebrated Reverend C. L. Franklin, ministered the 4,500 member New Bethel Baptist Church. Rev. Franklin was one of the first ministers to have a nationally broadcast radio program, and at one time he earned up to $4000 per sermon. His eldest daughter taught herself to play the piano at the age of eight. Her father's national stature and influence drew such well-known gospel singers as James

Aretha Franklin

Cleveland, Mahalia Jackson, and Clara Ward to their home for improvisational praise sessions. Two of the Clara Ward Singers helped rear Aretha after her mother's separation from the family. Franklin absorbed the rich black musical experience in her father's church and by the age of twelve began touring with him, singing solos.

Her recording career began in 1951 when she and her sisters Carolyn and Erma made a 78, singing behind their father on the Gotham label. In 1956, Franklin recorded the hymn ''Where We'll Never Grow Old,'' profoundly influenced by her mentor, Clara Ward. Following the path of one of her idols, Sam Cooke, who had made a successful transition from gospel to pop, at the age of eighteen Franklin left Detroit for New York, where Major Holley, a bass player for jazz pianist Teddy Wilson, helped look after her while she made the rounds in an attempt to be discovered. John Hammond, the legendary impresario who had encouraged Columbia Records to sign Mahalia Jackson, among other talents, heard Franklin and encouraged the company to sign her. While with Columbia, Franklin released a number of recordings: ''Today I Sing the Blues'' and ''Won't Be Long'' were moderately successful R&B hits.

After her contract expired with Columbia, Franklin signed with Atlantic Records in 1967. With the savvy producing skills of Jerry Wexler, Franklin recorded ''I Never Loved a Man (The Way I Love You)'' with the Muscle Shoals, Alabama, rhythm section, her own piano accompaniment, and the backup vocals of her sisters. The single and the album of the same title achieved gold status, and Aretha had arrived. A string of gold records followed, including ''Respect,'' her first single to top both the R&B and Pop Charts. The album also included such popular hits as ''Dr. Feelgood,'' ''Baby, I Love You,'' ''Chain of Fools,'' and ''Since You've Been Gone.'' Her next hit songs, ''Think'' and ''I Say a Little Prayer,'' went gold, along with her *Lady Soul* album in 1968. In 1969, ''See Saw'' and the album *Aretha Now* similarly attained gold status. ''Don't Play that Song'' in 1970 and her 1971 version of Simon and Garfunkel's ''Bridge Over Troubled Water'' also were hits. In 1972, she won two Grammys for the albums *Young, Gifted, and Black* and *Amazing Grace.* In 1973, Franklin scored again with ''Master of Eyes'' and in 1974 with ''Ain't Nothin' Like the Real Thing.''

The mid- to late 1970s saw a dry spell in Franklin's creative hitmaking. Disco had begun to gain favor, adversely impacting the sale and popularity of soul and R&B. In 1980, Franklin signed with Arista Records, and by 1982 she had made a successful comeback with the album *Jump on It.* In 1985, the *Who's Zooming Who* album, with the hit ''Freeway of Love,'' went gold. But in 1987, Franklin returned to her roots with the album *One Lord, One Faith, One Baptism,* her first gospel collection in fifteen years. A duet with George Michael entitled ''I Knew You Were Waiting'' became her second number one Pop hit.

Franklin's relentless productivity, diverse repertoire, and sheer volume of recordings make a simplified overview of her style difficult. To be sure, if one were to distill her style, it would boil down to her rhythmic gospel piano style and arrangements that accompany her voice with all its ecstatic tension. Beginning with her recording for Atlantic, Aretha Franklin essentially defined soul music as vital, genuine, sexual, and visceral, reflecting the struggles and triumphs of the human spirit. ''It is her fierce, gritty conviction. . . . She flexes her rich, cutting voice like a whip; she lashes her listeners—in her words—'to the bone,' for deepness,'' *Time* magazine observed. All in

all, it has been Franklin's faith and ''hard knocks'' that enabled her to embrace a song, dramatizing it and making it her own.

The early Columbia sessions were a fallow period in terms of her mature individual stylistic development, persistently marred by the company's attempt to pigeonhole her style into jazz and pop arrangements, not allowing for her freedom of expression. But at Atlantic, the arrangements of Franklin's music were based on her piano accompaniment to her voice. Upon her arrival at the studio to record, arrangers such as Arif Mardin would base everything around her piano and voice renditions, adding the backup vocals of sisters Carolyn and Erma. Atlantic allowed Franklin to exercise a great deal of artistic control, encouraging her creativity and a selection of songs that meant something to her. The first album, *I Never Loved a Man (The Way I Love You),* paid homage to her musical idols: Sam Cooke in ''A Change Is Gonna Come'' and ''Good Times,'' and Ray Charles, who had previously merged gospel with pop beginning with the recording of ''I've Got a Woman,'' is represented in a moving and undeniably convincing ''Drown in My Own Tears.''

Franklin's personal life has been a turbulent one. During her childhood she faced one traumatic experience after another. At the age of six, her mother abandoned the family, leaving Aretha's father to provide the nurturing and support of the children. From a young age, Aretha toured on the gospel highway, where the attendant pitfalls that she encountered on the road were not always in her best interest. She was the mother of two boys by the time she reached seventeen. Her marriage to her manager, Ted White, who had been known to rough her up from time to time, ended in divorce. Her second marriage to actor Glynn Turman also ended in divorce. In 1979, her father was shot by a robber in his home and remained in a coma for several years, never recovering. Through it all, Franklin has ardently guarded her private life and remained the ''Queen of Soul.''

Franklin has been active for several social causes and an activist for black pride and Civil Rights. Her father was a friend of the late Dr. Martin Luther King, Jr.; Franklin sang at King's funeral. She recorded ''Young, Gifted and Black'' as an affirmation of positive black consciousness and pride. Her unabashed celebration of sexual liberation with ''sock it to me'' in ''Respect'' and ''taking care of business is really this man's game'' in ''Dr. Feelgood'' was liberating to many women. Franklin sang for the Democratic National Convention in 1968, for the inauguration of President Jimmy Carter in 1977, and again for the inauguration of President Bill Clinton in 1993. Three television specials—*Aretha* in 1986; *Aretha Franklin: The Queen of Soul* in 1988; and *Duets* in 1993—have featured Franklin's life and music.

Franklin has shared her songs of love, hurt, respect, and black pride, but not much of her personal life. The Queen of Soul may soon talk in the form of an autobiography in collaboration with David Ritz, biographer of B. B. King, Marvin Gaye, Etta James, and Ray Charles. Whether singing gospel or pop, music is a balm and an alter ego for Franklin. ''It does get me out of myself. . .'' she has said. ''I guess you could say I do a lot of traveling with my voice.''

—Willie Collins

FURTHER READING:

Bego, Mark. *Aretha Franklin, The Queen of Soul.* New York, St. Martin's Press, 1989.

Franklin, Bonnie (1944—)

An actress and dancer best known for her portrayal of Ann Romano—TV's first "Ms."—on Norman Lear's sitcom *One Day at a Time,* Bonnie Franklin was born January 6, 1944, in Santa Monica, California. She started tap dancing when she was nine years old, appearing with Donald O'Connor on the *Colgate Comedy Hour,* and began teaching at the age of twelve. Franklin appeared in the original *Munsters* and *Man from U.N.C.L.E.* but became a household name from 1975 to 1984 on Lear's sitcom. Franklin dabbled in directing (*New Munsters*), TV movies (*Portrait of a Rebel: The Remarkable Mrs. Sanger*), and exercise videos (*I Hate to Exercise—I Love to Tap*). In the 1990s she could be found doing regional theater.

—Karen Lurie

FURTHER READING:

Franklin, Bonnie. "Bonnie Franklin." *Ladies Home Journal.* February, 1983, 90.

Frasier

Frasier, a popular situation comedy starring Kelsey Grammer as the pompous, insecure psychiatrist Dr. Frasier Crane, first premiered

The cast of *Frasier*: (from left) David Hyde Pierce, Peri Gilpin, Kelsey Grammer, Jane Leeves, John Mahoney, and Moose.

on NBC in September 1993. The character had appeared originally in the long-running and much-loved comedy show *Cheers,* with which *Frasier* shared the same creative team. *Frasier* relocated the doctor from his original *Cheers* setting in a Boston tavern to Seattle, where he became the host of a call-in radio show on fictional local station KACL. *Frasier* immediately won accolades for its sophisticated humor and literate dialogue, and secured a consistent position in the top 15 network shows. In 1998, the show became the first to win five consecutive Emmy awards for Outstanding Comedy Series, ensuring its place in television history.

Grammer's character was moved to Seattle in order to give the show enough distance with which to create a sense of identity separate from *Cheers,* yet the choice of Seattle also meant that the show reflected (and contributed to) the heightened profile of the Northwest City in the 1990s and a range of popular accounts that hailed Seattle as a desirable and sophisticated place to live. For example, in place of the Cheers tavern, one of the main settings of *Frasier* is the upscale Café Nervosa, where Frasier and his snobbish brother, fellow psychiatrist Niles (David Hyde Pierce) sip their cappuccinos and lattes. Much of the show's best comedy lies in the ensuing conversations between the two brothers, sharp retorts flying as each tries to undermine and outdo the other in everything, from successful careers to suit fabrics.

The brothers are of one mind, however, when dealing with their father, retired ex-cop Martin Crane (John Mahoney). Gruff and blue-collar, Martin was forced to move into Frasier's expensive, lofty apartment after being injured in the line of duty. With his dog, Eddie, (recipient of much fan mail) and his liking for beer, hot dogs, and *Monday Night Football,* Martin constantly frustrates Frasier's attempts to create a tasteful, chic ambience for the apartment. Martin's English live-in homecare provider, Daphne Moon (Jane Leeves), also provides the object of Niles's frustrated affection and adds another hilarious dimension to the complex domestic dynamics.

Critics have noted the way that the best episodes feel like little 22-minute plays because of the combination of high quality writing and ensemble acting. The episodes often take place within one confined, high-pressure setting, such as Frasier's apartment or the radio station, where the doctor battles against a constant stream of irritating callers with his slightly jaded producer, Roz (Peri Gilpin).

Off-screen, Kelsey Grammer had some well-publicized battles with substance abuse; he checked himself into the Betty Ford Clinic in the fall of 1996. On-screen, the show continued to move smoothly from strength to strength, and in November 1997 celebrated its one hundredth episode by uprooting from its studio in Hollywood to shoot on location in Seattle. Eschewing its usual stage-bound format, the episode took in the sights of the city and starred the real mayor of Seattle, Norm Rice, who declared it "Frasier Day" in Seattle.

The show's reward for continued critical and ratings success was in taking over for *Seinfeld* in the coveted NBC prime-time slot in the fall 1998 schedule. This slot had been filled previously by some of the most successful and critically acclaimed series in American television history, including *The Cosby Show, Hill Street Blues,* and *L.A Law.* What made *Frasier*'s rise to the number one comedy slot all the more unusual was that it bucked the trend in situation comedy in the 1990s. Instead of building itself around a celebrity personality (often a stand-up comedian), as in the case of *Seinfeld, Roseanne,* or *Ellen, Frasier* relied upon the continuing appeal of a well-drawn fictional character.

—James Lyons

FURTHER READING:

Bailey, David, and Warren Martyn. *Goodnight Seattle: The Unauthorized Guide to the World of Frasier.* London, Virgin, 1998.

Graham, Jefferson. *The Frasier Companion.* London, Simon & Schuster, 1996.

Frawley, William (1887-1966)

William "Bill" Frawley left his mark on American cinema during the 1930s as one of the medium's first character actors. Appearing in more than 150 films from *Miracle on 34th Street* to *Huckleberry Finn,* the strong-faced Iowan depicted surly, middle-aged men who hid their compassion behind masks of crustiness. He later adapted his trademark role to the small screen where he created two of television's most memorable supporting roles: Fred Mertz on the *I Love Lucy* show (1951-1957) and "Bub" O'Casey on *My Three Sons* (1960-1964).

Lucille Ball and Desi Arnaz selected Frawley for the role of Fred Mertz after their first choice, Gale Gordon, turned out to be unavailable. CBS executives warned Ball and Arnaz against the choice: Frawley had a reputation for heavy drinking. Yet the veteran actor rose to the occasion and created in Fred Mertz the prototype of the stick-in-the-mud husband and penny-pinching landlord. He even managed to tolerate Vivian Vance, who played his on-screen wife Ethel Mertz, although the two strongly disliked each other. "She's one of the finest girls to come out of Kansas," he once observed, "But I often wish she'd go back there." After the *I Love Lucy* show, Frawley created the role of Michael Francis "Bub" O'Casey, Fred MacMurray's gruff father-in-law and housekeeper on the sitcom *My Three Sons.* William Demarest replaced him on his retirement in 1964. Fittingly, Frawley's last television appearance was a cameo on a 1965 episode of Lucille Ball's *The Lucy Show* entitled "Lucy and the Countess Have a Horse Guest." On that episode, Lucy Carmichael (Ball) jokes about how familiar Frawley seems to her. As Fred Mertz, whose name is almost synonymous with the old neighborhood landlord, Frawley is equally familiar to us all.

—Jacob M. Appel

FURTHER READING:

Andrews, Bart. *Lucy & Ricky & Fred & Ethel: The Story of "I Love Lucy."* New York, Dutton, 1976.

Wyman, Ric B. *For The Love of Lucy: The Complete Guide For Collectors and Fans.* New York, Abbeville Press, 1995.

McClay, Michael. *I Love Lucy: The Complete Picture History of the Most Popular TV Show Ever.* New York, Warner Books, 1995.

Frazier, Joe (1944—)

Joe Frazier was a quintessential pressure fighter. He came forward at all costs, throwing his vaunted left hook at opponents until he broke their spirits or bodies or, as was often the case, both. A great heavyweight champion by any standard of measurement, Frazier left his mark in his three-fight series against Muhammad Ali. In 1967, Ali had been stripped of his heavyweight crown and his license to box for refusing induction into the United States Army during the Vietnam War. In Ali's absence, an elimination tournament was held to determine his successor to the heavyweight throne. Frazier won the tournament, tearing through the division's contenders and establishing himself as the best active heavyweight in the world. When Ali's license to box was reinstated, a superfight was made between Joe Frazier, the undefeated reigning champion, and Muhammad Ali, the undefeated former champ. The fight, which promised to be a thrilling encounter pitting Ali's speed and athleticism against Frazier's strength and determination, was billed as the "Fight of the Century." On March 8, 1971, at New York City's Madison Square Garden, Ali and Frazier split what was then a record-setting purse of five million dollars, and staged a fight that may have even exceeded its hype.

The fight was of such import that singer, actor, and pop culture icon Frank Sinatra was enlisted as a photographer for *Life* magazine. The bout's significance owed not merely to the high quality of the match itself, but also to the social and political symbolism attached to its participants. While Ali's refusal of induction into the armed forces and his outspoken stances on various political and religious issues made him a representative, in the eyes of many, of oppressed people all over the world, Frazier unwittingly came to represent the establishment and the status quo of the white American power structure. Smokin' Joe, as he was nicknamed for his relentless style, resented the perception of himself as the "white hope." Frazier was proud of his racial identity and noted on several occasions that, ironically, he was darker complected than Ali. Nevertheless, Ali vilified Frazier as representing white America, and in turn an enraged Frazier handed Ali his first professional loss, a 15 round unanimous decision defeat. Frazier even knocked Ali down in the last round for good measure.

The two boxers fought a rematch three years later, this time with no title on the line (as Frazier had lost his title in a humiliating knockout at the hands of the murderous hitting George Foreman). This time Ali took revenge with a 12 round unanimous decision victory. The third and final meeting rivaled their fist encounter as the most famous heavyweight title fight in history. Dubbed by Ali "The Thrilla in Manilla," this 1975 classic was a contest of wills unlike anything witnessed in the division's illustrious history. Ali was champion by this time, having knocked out the same George Foreman who so easily beat Frazier. Figuring that Frazier would be old and ineffective this time around (though Ali himself was the elder of the two by two years), Ali took him lightly and did not expect a tough fight. To add insult to injury, Ali took to calling him "The Gorilla." Frazier's pride was hurt once again by his antagonist, and he presented Ali with the toughest test of his career—14 grueling rounds, ending only when Frazier's chief cornerman, the venerable Eddie Futch, refused to let Joe whose eyes were swollen nearly shut, come out for the last round. Cast unwillingly in a role he despised, Joe Frazier nevertheless etched his name into the American consciousness. If Muhammad Ali was the greatest heavyweight champion who ever lived (and even if he was not), then Joe Frazier was his greatest rival. Their names go down in history together, as Frazier himself said, "whether he [Ali] likes it or not."

—Max Kellerman

FURTHER READING:

Frazier, Joe. *Smokin' Joe: The Autobiography of a Heavyweight Champion of the World.* New York, Macmillan, 1996.

Pepe, Phil. *Come Out Smokin': Joe Frazier—The Champ Nobody Knew,* New York, Coward, McCann & Geoghegan, 1972.

Frazier, Walt "Clyde" (1945—)

Walt Frazier was the epitome of "cool" in a basketball era that worshiped the style that the flamboyant "Clyde" came to symbolize. Frazier was an All-American at Southern Illinois University, and led his team to the 1967 National Invitational Tournament (NIT) Championship, coincidentally in New York's Madison Square Garden, where he would continue his career as a professional. Frazier was an All-Star guard for the New York Knicks from 1967-1977, and was the undisputed floor leader of two Knick teams that won National Basketball Association (NBA) titles in 1970 and 1973. Combined with his smooth and explosive offensive talents, he was also one of the league's premier defensive players, always assigned to control the opponents' primary outside offensive threat. Frazier is most remembered, however, for his resplendent wardrobe, as well as his calm and dignified demeanor that earned him the nickname "Clyde." Frazier was inducted into the Basketball Hall of Fame in 1987.

—G. Allen Finchum

FURTHER READING:

Dickey, Glenn. *The History of Professional Basketball.* Briarcliff Manor, New York, Stein and Day, 1982.

Sachare, Alex. *100 Greatest Basketball Players of All Time.* New York, Pocket Books, 1997.

Freak Shows

By the mid-twentieth century the display for profit and entertainment of people known in the United States as "freaks" had for the most part become an anachronism. Parading disabled people before a staring public for amusement has, along with public executions, become socially unacceptable. But as our lingering collective memory of P. T. Barnum suggests, from about 1830 to 1940 in the United States, as well as in Europe, people with congenital disabilities or other physical traits that could be turned into curiosities were displayed on stages, in dime museums, in circuses, and at fairs as a part of a growing culture of popular performance that was driven by the increased commercialism, leisure, and urbanization of modernity. Whereas the term "freak" now connotes a negative departure from the norm, in the nineteenth century "freak" meant a whimsical fancy. This shift in meaning suggests the long history of exhibiting people whose bodies are presented as extraordinary and the enduring interest that they inspire in the popular imagination.

Extraordinary bodies have obsessed humankind since antiquity. The nineteenth century "freak" was known as a "monster" in ancient times and considered to be a prodigy. The birth of such an individual, as with natural events such as comets and earthquakes, was thought to portend grave or disastrous events. Stone-age cave drawings record monstrous births, while prehistoric grave sites evince elaborate ritual sacrifices of such bodies.

As the narrative of the natural world shifted from one of divine determination to secular explanations, early science viewed exceptional bodies as indices to the order of things or proof of God's abundance, but also as sources upon which to hone medical expertise. Early scientists and philosophers kept cabinets of curiosities full of items like shark's teeth, shrunken heads, and bottled fetuses that they regarded with a mixture of awe and curiosity. At the same time, these extraordinary bodies were commercialized at public fairs, like London's famous Bartholomew Fair, and on streets by monster mongers who charged for viewings and sold pamphlets called monster ballads, which offered morals drawn from the wondrous bodies. Congenitally disabled newborns, called monstrous births, continued to be interpreted as exegeses of the divine and natural orders by figures as respected as Cotton Mather and John Winthrop well into the seventeenth century. Disabled people were often celebrities or kept at court as "Fools" or in the role of pets, as were many dwarfs. For example, a powdered and wigged Matthew Buchinger, who was virtually armless and legless, dazzled eighteenth century Europe with his conjuring, musical performances, calligraphic skills, and marksmanship with the pistol. These monsters filled their viewers with awe and curiosity; they were seen as "marvels" and "wonders," not as what the twentieth century observer would interpret as abnormal or inappropriate to stare at.

By the 1840s, P. T. Barnum—nineteenth-century America's Walt Disney—institutionalized the once itinerant practice of showing monsters in halls and on streets when he opened in New York his American Museum, which aspired to middle-class status with temperance tracts, appeals to education, entrepreneurship, and other gestures toward bourgeois respectability. An entertainment industry in freaks and other curiosities flourished in dime museums and later as circus sideshows throughout Victorian America. The secularizing, mobile, rapidly changing social order dominated increasingly by market economics, individualism, and a developing mass culture generated this boom in staring at "curiosities," which was part of a larger culture of display manifest in museums, circuses, grand expositions, photographs, parades, theater, department store displays, and what Thorstein Veblen called "conspicuous consumption."

These shows gathered an astonishing array of wonders, from Wild Men of Borneo to Fat Ladies, Living Skeletons, Fiji Princes, Albinos, Bearded Women, Siamese Twins, Tattooed Circassians, Armless and Legless Wonders, Chinese Giants, Cannibals, Midget Triplets, Hermaphrodites, Spotted Boys, and much more. Augmenting these marvels were ancillary performers like ventriloquists, performing geese, mesmerists, beauty contestants, contortionists, sharpshooters, trained goats, frog eaters, sword-swallowers, and tumbling monkeys. From Queen Victoria and Henry James to families and the humblest immigrants, Americans gathered together in this most democratizing institution to gaze raptly at freaks of display. Freaks were the highest paid performers in the industry; many such as Tom Thumb were celebrities, who made their handlers rich. But freaks were more than simply disabled people; they were figures created by the shows' sensationalized and exaggerated conventions of display. Elaborate costuming, exotic sets, bizarre "true-life" pamphlets, the hyperbolic rant of the pitchmen, photographs for audiences to collect, and scientific testimonials all surrounded these bodies to produce freaks and marvels from people who had unusual bodies that could be appropriated for the shows.

Into the nineteenth century, scientists and doctors participated in the show culture by examining the performers for scientific study and by verifying the freaks' authenticity, lending prestige to the exhibitions. Alongside its involvement with the entertainment industry, however, science institutionalized its preoccupation with monsters by 1832 with the development of teratology, the scientific study of monsters. Teratology endeavored to harness the ancient power of prodigies by creating pigs with cleft palates and elaborate taxonomies of physical deviation. As science and medicine began to separate from the shows and become more elite, such developments as statistics, the idea of the average man, the pathologizing of disabilities, and the eventual belief that extraordinary bodies should be standardized for the good of both the individual and society helped turn the wondrous freak into the medical problem.

A complex, interrelated combination of historical and social factors ended the immense popularity and proliferation of the freak show by the mid-twentieth century. The medicalization of disability, the rise of the bourgeoisie, the sentimentalizing of disabled people as pathetic rather than wondrous, and the sinking of freak shows to lowbrow culture, among other developments, snuffed out the form of the freak show that Barnum so masterfully exploited. Its allure lingers nevertheless in such transmuted forms as talk shows, bodybuilding, and wrestling matches, science fiction narratives like *Star Trek,* or even performers such as Michael Jackson.

—Rosemarie Garland Thomson

FURTHER READING:

Altick, Richard D. *The Shows of London.* Cambridge, Belknap Press, 1978.

Bogdan, Robert. *Freak Show: Presenting Human Oddities for Amusement and Profit.* Chicago, University of Chicago Press, 1988.

Daston, Lorraine, and Kathryn Park. *Wonders and the Order of Nature: 1150-1750.* New York, Zone Books, 1998.

Dennett, Andrea Stulman. *Weird and Wonderful: The Dime Museum in America.* New York, New York University Press, 1997.

Fiedler, Leslie. *Freaks: Myths and Images of the Secret Self.* New York, Simon and Schuster, 1978.

Jay, Ricky. *Learned Pigs and Fireproof Women.* New York, Villard Books, 1986.

Mannix, Daniel P. *Freaks: We Who Are Not as Others.* San Francisco, Re/Search Publications, 1990.

Mitchell, Michael. *Monsters of the Gilded Age: The Photographs of Charles Eisenmann.* Toronto, Gage Publishing Limited, 1979.

Pare, Ambroise. *On Monsters and Marvels.* Trans. Janis L. Pallister. Chicago, University of Chicago Press, 1982.

Thomson, Rosemarie Garland. *Extraordinary Bodies: Figuring Physical Disability in American Literature and Culture.* New York, Columbia University Press, 1997.

Thomson, Rosemarie Garland, editor. *Freakery: Cultural Spectacles of the Extraordinary Body.* New York, New York University Press, 1996.

Freaks

Perhaps the most unsettling horror film to follow in the wake of *Frankenstein*'s enormous financial success in 1931, *Freaks* (1932) tells the story of seemingly childlike carnival "freaks" who wreak unspeakable revenge on two able-bodied swindlers. Adapted from the Tod Robbins short story "Spurs" and directed by Tod Browning, this untidy little film shocked audiences with its use of actual disabled performers: midgets, an armless woman, a "living torso" (a man whose body ended slightly below his ribcage), and many others.

Receiving mostly negative reviews and faring poorly at the box-office, *Freaks* ran afoul of censorship boards across the United States and was banned in Great Britain for three decades. After playing the exploitation-film circuit for years, it received acclaim at the 1962 Venice Film Festival and enjoyed some popularity among counterculture "freaks" during the late 1960s and early 1970s. The Library of Congress honored *Freaks* by adding it to the National Film Registry in 1994.

—Martin F. Norden

FURTHER READING:

Norden, Martin F. *The Cinema of Isolation: A History of Physical Disability in the Movies.* New Brunswick, Rutgers University Press, 1994.

Skal, David J., and Elias Savada. *Dark Carnival: The Secret World of Tod Browning.* New York, Anchor Books, 1995.

Frederick's of Hollywood

Frederick's of Hollywood is an innovative lingerie company established by Frederick N. Mellinger on New York's Fifth Avenue in 1946. A year later he moved his business to the West Coast. Originally a mail-order house, by 1998 it had expanded to include 205 retail outlets and an on-line presence at its web site at www.fredericks.com. For many years, corporate headquarters were located at 6608 Hollywood Boulevard and housed in an art deco building, which was informally known as the Purple Palace for its garish lavender facade.

During World War II, Mellinger was stationed in Europe, where he noticed the French preference for black undergarments at a time when Americans preferred white. Mellinger formulated a theory of female pulchritude centered on proportional perfection. When he returned to the United States, he studied anatomy so as to be better prepared to contend with such phenomena as sagging breasts, midriff bulges, lackluster posteriors, and something that he referred to as "piano legs," to name a few. Stern and Stern, in *The Encyclopedia of Bad Taste,* proffer the following quote, which addresses the issue of Mellinger's motivation: "I knew there had to be ways to reproportion women and give every lovable one of them EQUAL OPPORTUNITY in the eyes of men." A popular Mellinger slogan—"Came in looking like a Chevy and left looking like a Cadillac"—epitomizes the Frederick's philosophy throughout much of the company's history.

Frederick's-style perfection can be achieved with the assistance of a number of innovative products. For the poorly contoured buttocks, there is the Living End padded girdle. For the woman who requires flexibility in regard to bust size, there is the Light 'N' Lovely Air-Lite Inflatable Bra, whose cups can be expanded to the desired degree with the aid of straws. Or, for those who prefer a brassiere that more nearly approximates tactile perfection, there is the H_2O Water Bra, which features pads containing a water-and-oil mixture. A salient nipple effect can be achieved with the aid of prosthetic-nipple-pad bra inserts.

The Mellinger concept of femininity, the one that Frederick's has projected throughout much of its history, extolled the symmetrical, the curvaceous, the buxom, and the docile: the image of the sex kitten and the harem girl, adumbrations of which were even evident in

Tod Browning (wearing sweater) and the cast of the film *Freaks*.

some of the company's product names—Sheik's Choice pajamas, for instance. Males made many of the purchases or told their women what to buy. The image of Mellinger as "Mr. Frederick" appeared throughout the catalogue proffering tips on such subjects as male preferences and drooping breasts. The male orientation of the firm was unmistakable.

In an era when many American women are financially independent of their male partners, and rapid progress has been made toward sexual equality, it is not surprising that Frederick's, with the death of Mr. Mellinger in 1991, has considered altering its image. *New York Times* contributor Jennifer Steinhauer related Frederick's CEO Terry Patterson's plans for the company: "Over all . . . Frederick's of Hollywood stores would attempt to whisper seductively to the modern female consumer, instead of simply leering salaciously at her boyfriend. 'I'm dressed, I'm corporate, I'm successful, I can play with the big boys . . . And you don't know I'm a Frederick's woman.' That is where I see the company now."

—William F. O'Connor

FURTHER READING:

Saari, Laura. "Naughty but Nice." *Pittsburgh Post-Gazette.* July 1, 1996, D-1.

Steinhauer, Jennifer. "What Becomes a Legend?" *New York Times.* February 13, 1998, D-1.

Stern, Jane, and Michael Stern. *The Encyclopedia of Bad Taste.* New York, HarperCollins Publishers, 1990.

Free Agency

Free agency has created a controversial revolution in professional athletics since the 1980s. Free agency is the ability of professional team athletes to change teams when their contracts expire. Players can entertain offers from the teams interested in signing them and choose from the available choices. In theory, players use the principles of a free-market economy to receive salaries commensurate with their abilities. Some pundits believe that free agency has been extremely beneficial to professional sports, allowing the best players to be paid what they are worth. Others argue that the dramatic increases in salaries and the tendency of players to change teams every few years has been detrimental.

For most of the history of professional athletics, players were forced to stay with the team that drafted them through a "reserve clause" in their contracts. The only way an athlete could change teams was to be traded by the team's management. Athletes' salaries were completely at the discretion of the owners. Professional baseball, football, basketball, and hockey players found themselves completely at the mercy of the team owners and managers. Stories abound of players who were named the Most Valuable Player or won a league scoring title only to find their salaries stagnate or even decrease. The athletes found themselves bound to their teams regardless of their wishes, and they could be traded to other teams without being consulted.

Anger over the reserve system grew in professional sports. In 1969, Curt Flood, a center fielder for the St. Louis Cardinals, was traded to the Philadelphia Phillies, one of the worst teams in the league. Flood had played for the Cardinals for twelve years, earning a reputation as an outstanding center fielder (226 consecutive games without an error) and an excellent hitter (lifetime average of .293). In addition, Flood was deeply involved in the community and well-liked by the people of St. Louis. Flood asked the commissioner of baseball to declare him a free agent so that he could decide for himself where he would end his career. The commissioner refused, and Flood took major league baseball to court. The case eventually wound up in front of the Supreme Court. In 1972, the Supreme Court ruled by a five to three margin against Flood, but the door had been opened. Although Flood would never return to the sport he loved, he had paved the way for the current system of free agency.

In 1976, pitcher Bill Campbell successfully negotiated a free agent contract with the Boston Red Sox. By the start of the 1980s, free agency was a fact of life in baseball. Players' salaries began to increase rapidly, with Nolan Ryan becoming the first player in history to sign a contract worth $1 million per year. The concept of free agency spread to other team sports throughout the decade. By the early 1990s, all professional team sports had some form of free agency, although some were more restrictive than others.

As more players began changing teams and increasing their salaries, team owners began to argue against the free agent system. They argued that teams based in smaller cities, such as St. Louis or Portland, could not offer comparable salaries to teams based in New York and Los Angeles. This growing gap between small-market and large-market teams was addressed in most sports (with the exception of baseball) through revenue sharing and the implementation of a salary cap on the total amount a team could spend on its players.

Free agency has been a boon to professional athletes, but it also has many detractors. Traditionalists argue that fan support has faded as players move from team to team for financial gain. Many critics believe that the constantly changing rosters alienate fans who can no longer find players to support. To counter that argument, supporters of free agency point out that attendance at sporting events has increased dramatically in the past twenty years. If fans were truly feeling alienated by the roster changes, then attendance should be decreasing.

—Geoff Peterson

FURTHER READING:

Klatell, D. *Sports for Sale: Television, Money, and the Fans.* New York, Oxford University Press, 1988.

Klatell, D., and N. Marcus. *Big Time Sports: Television, Money, and the Fans.* New York, MasterMedia, 1996.

Weiss, A. *Money Games: The Business of Sports.* Boston, Houghton Mifflin, 1993.

Free Speech Movement

The Free Speech Movement started as a dispute over 26 feet of sidewalk and escalated into a pitched battle for control of the University of California at Berkeley. In the process, an entire school, students and faculty alike, was polarized into two camps fundamentally at odds with each other, both ideologically and in terms of rhetoric. The Free Speech Movement represented the adoption of civil rights protest techniques—pickets, sit-ins, and other non-violent methods—in a hitherto untested arena, the university. As it turned out, it was the opening salvo in a long, drawn-out battle, a tumult that would ultimately affect one out of every ten college and university campuses nationwide (a conservative figure), rending the country in two along ideological and generational lines.

Over the summer of 1964, the administration of the UC Berkeley changed its rules on political activism on campus, eliminating a narrow strip of sidewalk at the intersection of Telegraph Avenue and Bancroft Way that had been a main point of egress to the campus, and a traditional location for political activity. To the student activists, the administration's ruling was an attack not only on their individual rights but also on the civil rights movement itself. Concerned student activists met with administrators, and were able to win back their right to set up tables, but the administration refused to budge on matters of fund-raising or political advocacy.

This set the stage for a series of escalating protests, as students tested the power of their as-yet-untried political muscle. Fundraising and advocacy activities resumed at the Bancroft/Telegraph intersection under the auspices of the United Front, an ad-hoc organizing committee, and after a week had passed without incident, new tables were set up at Sather Gate, a hundred yards inside the campus. On September 30, five students were cited for manning them. Five hundred students signed a letter of complicity, crowded Sproul Hall, which they occupied until early morning, and demanded that the administration discipline all of them. Eight students were suspended indefinitely, and the following day Jack Weinberg, a recent graduate and a leader of the campus Congress of Racial Equality (CORE), was arrested as he manned a table. Hundreds of students surrounded the police car containing Weinberg and, for the next 32 hours, the crowd maintained a vigil, with speakers holding forth from atop the car's bonnet.

The more intransigent the administration appeared, the more radicalized the movement became. "Beginning with concern about rights to a small strip of territory," wrote Max Heirich, a sociologist who studied the movement as it was happening, "the students had shifted their focus to freedom of expression and advocacy on the campus as a whole. After the arrest of October 1, they began to talk about the proper purpose of the university." The weeks wore on without resolution and more students were swept up in the conflict, forced to choose a side amidst the growing rancor. Chancellor Edward Strong remained firmly opposed to any concessions, convinced that student opinion was volatile and would peter out of its own accord. There were indeed indications that the protest was losing steam: after the UC Board of Regents ruled against the FSM in a November 20 meeting, a rally and sit-in the following Monday ended in disarray, with the student leadership disheartened and student support flagging. Over the Thanksgiving break, however, disciplinary letters were sent to four FSM leaders, rekindling the fickle flames of student unrest and inflaming the FSM leadership by this show of bad faith. The FSM reacted by submitting an ultimatum to the administration—if the charges were not dropped, a sit-in would begin on Wednesday, December 2, followed by a general strike.

The administration did not deign to respond, and students set about occupying Sproul Hall. Far from housing an angry mob, the occupied premises had a festive air as the students passed the time square dancing, and conducting teach-ins and religious services. Joan Baez led a folk singalong; Laurel and Hardy films were shown. On Governor Pat Brown's orders, police officers began clearing Sproul Hall early Thursday morning. By daybreak, the exhausted police officers were growing rough with the students—who went limp in classic civil rights fashion—and those en route to their morning classes were treated to the sight of fellow students being manhandled by the California Highway Patrol, and cries of police brutality echoing through Sproul Hall. The next day pickets appeared.

In the end, the administration capitulated. Perhaps it was the threat of a prolonged strike, perhaps the pressure of faculty members, who voted at an Academic Senate to support the students' demands. However, the tenor of the conflict can be summed up in a single event: at an assembly on the Monday following the successful strike, the entire student body watched as Mario Savio, one of the most charismatic of the movement's leaders, strode to the lectern, only to be tackled by Berkeley policeman and quickly hustled offstage. Savio had been forbidden to address the students, and his decision to take the platform appeared to be calculated for maximum impact. The incident had the desired effect, cementing student support for the FSM. In the weeks following the strike, Chancellor Strong was relieved of his duties by the regents, and a chancellor who was sympathetic to FSM goals was appointed. In the elections held the week following the strike, FSM candidates swept into ASUC office. In the space of a semester, the climate of UC Berkeley changed irrevocably from comfortable complacency to overt radicalism. The campus would remain at war for the next five years.

The triumph of the Free Speech Movement against Berkeley's administration encouraged a wave of protests over alleged administrative abuses nationwide. The following year, 14 schools experienced outbreaks of student unrest, and student revolt developed into a worldwide phenomenon, culminating in the massive protests, strikes, and general unrest of 1968. Berkeley itself became the site of bitter, protracted battles that eventually led to fatalities. Max Heirich wrote, of the protests that followed, "With increasing momentum each side seemed to create its own 'self-fulfilling prophecies' of what opponents would do," adding to the rampant paranoia.

Nowhere, then, was the revolt as typical as at Berkeley, where the privileged sons and daughters of the middle class had risen up with such force and determination. Theirs was a political conversion unique in world history—a revolution fomented by abundance. "... We were the first generation in the history of the world that had never gone hungry," wrote David Lance Goines, one of the eight students suspended on October 2, 1964. "Our parents trembled at the memory of the Great Depression, but it meant nothing to us. We didn't have much notion of not getting what we wanted, when we wanted it." True to Goines' appraisal, Berkeley students got what they wanted—indeed, perhaps rather more.

—Michael Baers

FURTHER READING:

Anon. *Berkeley: The New Student Revolt.* New York, Grove Press, 1965.

Goines, David Lance. *The Free Speech Movement: Coming of Age in the 1960s.* Berkeley, Ten Speed Press, 1993.

Heirich, Max. *The Beginning: Berkeley, 1964.* New York, Columbia University Press, 1970.

Kitchell, Mark. *Berkeley in the Sixties* (documentary). Los Angeles, Pacific Art, 1992.

Rorabaugh, W.J. *Berkeley at War: The 1960s.* New York, Oxford University Press, 1989.

Warshaw, Steven. *The Trouble in Berkeley.* Berkeley, Diablo Press, 1965.

Freed, Alan "Moondog" (1921-1965)

One of the most popular and influential pioneering radio disc jockeys, Alan "Moondog" Freed helped make Cleveland, Ohio, an early hotbed of rock 'n' roll music through the programs that he hosted on radio station WJW there in the 1950s. Moving to WINS Radio in New York, he soon became a nationally-known celebrity as one of the first important supporters of the new youth-oriented music that was sweeping the country during that decade. His theory that white teenagers would listen to and purchase rhythm and blues records by black artists proved insightful. For more than a decade, Freed constantly promoted the emergent music format via stage shows, national radio, television, and in a series of movies. Although he did not coin the phrase "rock 'n' roll," he is credited with popularizing the term which had originally been a euphemism for sexual intercourse on "race" records beginning in the 1920s. Freed's

Alan Freed

talent for promotion soon became his downfall as he and other disc jockeys across the nation were implicated in the payola scandals in 1959. Author John Jackson underscores Freed's contribution to contemporary American music by stating he "proved how essential the disc jockey was to the growth of rock & roll."

Aldon James Freed, who was born on December 21, 1921, and raised in rural Salem, Ohio, had a strong interest in music from childhood. While attending Ohio State University he became fascinated with the activity at WOSU Radio, the university station. He did not become involved with the station during his stay at the university, but, instead, enrolled in a broadcasting school in Youngstown, Ohio. Throughout the 1940s he toiled at a variety of small, local radio stations in Pennsylvania and Ohio where he held numerous positions such as sweeping floors, news and sports announcing, and playing music. The young announcer's fortunes changed dramatically when he took a position with Cleveland's WJW (850 AM) as host of a rhythm and blues program in 1951. He adopted the name "Moondog" from a raucous recording featuring a howling dog titled "Moondog Symphony." Freed's on-air antics soon made him a popular personality with Cleveland's young black community. Six months after the debut of his late night radio broadcast, he and the owner of the area's largest record store entered a partnership to promote a dance called the "Moondog Coronation Ball." On March 21, 1952, more than 10,000 mostly black teens packed the Cleveland Arena to see rhythm and blues performers Paul Williams, Varetta Dillard, and the Dominoes. The arena became so overcrowded with the unexpectedly large mass of people that city officials were forced to stop the show for safety reasons. The Moondog Coronation Ball is considered a significant moment in the development of rock 'n' roll. Bill Randle, one of the nation's most respected deejays in the 1950s, characterizes Freed's 1952 event as the "beginning of the acceptance of black popular music as a force in radio. It was the first big show of its kind where the industry saw it as big business."

By 1954, Freed's relentless promotion of himself as well as the rhythm and blues style cemented his position as the music's chief spokesperson. Increasingly, young white record buyers began to cross the racial barrier that had separated mainstream pop songs from rhythm and blues. Freed was further able to enlarge his growing white audience when he moved his program to the powerful WINS radio station in New York. The disc jockey became a national figure through his syndicated radio program, many television appearances, and his role in the film *Rock Around the Clock* (1956). Playing himself, Freed portrayed a disc jockey encouraging adults to accept the new rock 'n' roll music as sung by Bill Haley and the Comets. The film's great success in the United States and across Europe significantly boosted the exposure of rock music to new audiences.

As the influence of rock 'n' roll spread worldwide, Freed became embroiled in a scandal that would tarnish the remainder of his career. The House Subcommittee on Legislative Oversight, which in 1959 had concluded its investigation of corruption on television quiz shows, began to probe charges that songs heard and heavily promoted on the radio were selected for airplay due to commercial bribery. These secret payments in return for record promotion were known as "payola," a portmanteau word combining "payoff" and "victrola." After years of legal wrangling and a steadily diminishing career, Freed eventually pleaded guilty on December 10, 1962, in the New York Criminal Court to accepting payments and gifts from Superior Record Sales and the Cosant Distributing Corporation "without the knowledge and consent" of his employers. He was sentenced to a six-month suspended jail term and fined $500. He later noted that payola

practices had not been ended despite all the government's efforts. Freed never regained his earlier prominence and died on January 20, 1965, after a long illness.

Alan Freed has secured a place in American music history as the first important rock 'n' roll disc jockey. His ability to tap into and promote the emerging black musical styles of the 1950s to a white mainstream audience is seen as a vital step in rock's increasing dominance over American culture. Freed's contribution to the music he sold so successfully was honored in 1986 by the Rock 'n' roll Hall of Fame, which selected him as one of the first inductees in the special "non-performer and early influences" category. In 1995, the city of Cleveland hosted the Rock 'n' roll Hall of Fame and Museum's dedication not far from the site of Freed's Moondog Coronation Ball and the radio station where he popularized the phrase "rock 'n' roll."

—Charles Coletta

FURTHER READING:

Jackson, John. *Big Beat Heat: Alan Freed and the Early Years of Rock & Roll.* New York, Schirmer Books, 1991.

Sklar, Robert. *Rocking America.* New York, St. Martin's, 1984.

Freedom Rides

Throughout the long struggle for civil and political rights, African Americans utilized a number of protest methods. One of the most favored of these were the "Freedom Rides" that captured the country's attention and imagination in the early 1960s, and successfully influenced the cultural consciousness of the nation with regard to matters of racial prejudice. The goal of the freedom rides was simply to end segregation in interstate travel. Although the United States ruled the segregation of interstate facilities unconstitutional, the edict went largely ignored in the Jim Crow South.

In 1949 the Congress of Racial Equality (CORE) and the Fellowship of Reconciliation (FOR) launched a freedom ride throughout the upper South to highlight the discrimination African Americans faced when traveling below the Mason-Dixon Line. However, the efforts of these interracial, nonviolent, and pacifist organizations were unsuccessful, largely because they were unable to attract press attention. Nonetheless, the foundation was laid for a tactic that came to achieve amazing results in the early 1960s.

As the federal government began to illustrate a sincere concern for the rights of African Americans in the aftermath of the 1954 *Brown v. Board of Education* decision, CORE once again launched the idea of "Freedom Rides" to the same purpose as before. For CORE leader James Farmer the concept was simple: (1) have an interracial group take a bus across the South (2) demand service at all terminals, and (3) if arrested, refuse bail and fill up the jails. The entire program was designed to attract media attention to the brutal conditions that black people faced in the Southern states.

CORE's initial "freedom riders" left Washington, D.C. in May 1961, and headed for the South. All was well until they approached Anniston, Alabama, on Mother's Day, when they were greeted by mobs of whites who beat them severely. They encountered further trouble in Birmingham where the local Ku Klux Klan (which had been granted 15 minutes of immunity by the local police force) unleashed their frustrations upon the riders. The protest was postponed when the riders could not find a driver to continue the trip.

A group of freedom riders.

Ironically, however, the brutality was instrumental in awakening the consciousness of Americans to the appalling plight of the freedom riders because the national media gave extensive coverage to the incident and disseminated the images of the badly beaten protesters.

After a cooling-off period the freedom ride continued from Birmingham to Montgomery. Upon arriving in Montgomery the courageous protesters were hit with pipes, baseball bats, billy clubs, and other such objects, and once again the national media was there to give the incident widespread coverage. In the aftermath of the Alabama beatings, young SNCC (Student Non-Violent Coordinating Committee) activists wanted to continue the rides, in spite of the reluctance of CORE and the SCLC (Southern Christian Leadership Conference). They did. In late May SCLC initiated a ride from Montgomery to Jackson, Mississippi, hoping to encounter brutality which would then be broadcast to the world. Contrary to their expectations, however, on their arrival they were peacefully arrested. This response by the Jackson Police Department established a pattern for future "Freedom Rides."

In the summer of 1961 the traditional civil rights organizations created the Freedom Rides Coordinating Committee (FRCC) which sponsored Freedom Rides throughout the country. As a result of the continued protest, the Interstate Commerce Commission (ICC) banned racial segregation and discrimination in interstate travel. Although many civil rights leaders took credit for the legislation, the victory belonged to CORE, who had initiated the protest, and to the young activists in SNCC who were persistent in their quest for civil rights. The ruling by the ICC dealt a massive blow to Jim Crow.

—Leonard N. Moore

FURTHER READING:

Carson, Clayborne. *In Struggle: SNCC and the Black Awakening of the 1960s.* Cambridge, Harvard University Press, 1981.

Fairclough, Adam. *To Redeem the Soul of America: The Southern Christian Leadership Conference and Martin Luther King, Jr.* Athens, University of Georgia Press, 1987.

Farmer, James. *Lay Bare the Heart: An Autobiography of the Civil Rights Movement.* New York, Plume, 1985.

The French Connection

The French Connection, the 1971 Best Picture Oscar winner, remains the best existential cop film ever made, contains arguably the best chase sequence ever committed to film, and turned Gene Hackman into a major star. The film is based on the real-life French connection heroin bust by NYPD narcotics division detectives Eddie ''Popeye'' Egan and Sonny ''Cloudy'' Grosso. That investigation lasted from the night of October 7, 1961 when off-duty detectives Egan and Grosso noticed Pasquale Fuca talking with some known drug dealers in the Copacabana nightclub to the day four months later when Fuca and five others were arrested for drug trafficking.

Producer Philip D'Antoni owned the rights to Robin Moore's book about the case, and when William Friedkin agreed to direct the film, a succession of writers was hired. Ernest Tidyman finally wrote a screenplay good enough to get the project green lighted by Twentieth Century-Fox. Friedkin, who began his career making documentaries on topics ranging from law enforcement to pro football for a Chicago television station and then ABC, brought a documentarian's sensibilities to the project. When he decided to direct the film, he strapped on a .38 pistol and spent nearly a year riding around with Egan and Grosso, visiting drug houses and shaking down bars. Once production began, Friedkin had immediate problems directing his actors. We first see Jimmy ''Popeye'' Doyle (Hackman) dressed as Santa Claus, and he and his partner, Buddy ''Cloudy'' Russo (Roy Scheider), sprinting after and catching a fleeing suspect. Friedkin decided to stage the interrogation scene as it usually happens in real life, with the suspect sitting in the squad car and being grilled by the two detectives. Dissatisfied with the dialogue as written, Friedkin wrote some dialogue based on actual interrogations he had seen Egan and Grosso conduct, dialogue which he later referred to as Pinteresque. But thirty-two takes later, Friedkin still didn't have anything on film that satisfied him. According to Friedkin, he realized later that night what was wrong with the scene: ''This is not Harold Pinter. This is a street show. I've got to let them improvise that scene.'' The scene was reshot in an open courtyard—one take, two cameras—and Friedkin used the best moments captured on film. Many other scenes were likewise improvised, with Hackman and Scheider taking their cues from Egan and Russo: Egan really did dress up as Santa and really did ask suspects if they ''picked their feet in Poughkeepsie.''

The film itself is brilliantly photographed and edited, making superb use of visual storytelling. Friedkin has pointed out that, of the film's twelve reels, six contain no dialogue at all, yet the silence isn't conspicuous because the acting is so good that viewers can almost hear what the characters are thinking. An excellent example of this is the cat-and-mouse game Popeye plays with Frog One (Fernando Rey) on the New York City subways, an incident that actually happened the way it was shown on film. Another example involves something D'Antoni and Friedkin had agreed to include in the film, even though it never happened in real life and wasn't in the book or screenplay: a car chase. The sequence starts when Frog Two (Marcel Bozzuffi) tries to shoot Popeye from a rooftop; Popeye runs after him, Frog Two hops on an elevated train, and Popeye commandeers a car to chase him. The ten-minute virtually wordless sequence has pedestrians and other cars in almost every shot, so Friedkin knew he couldn't undercrank the camera to simulate speed. The feeling of speed was ultimately obtained by having someone actually driving through New York streets at speeds approaching ninety miles per hour. What was to have been a near miss accidentally became the chase sequence's first collision. Most of this sequence, like 70 percent of the rest of the film, was shot with hand-held cameras, adding to the documentary feel.

Although Hackman wanted to humanize his character, Friedkin kept insisting, ''No, this man is a pig. He's as rotten as the criminals he's chasing.'' This characterization also adds to the realism and is perhaps the most divisive aspect of the film. Popeye is portrayed as

brutal, racist, foulmouthed, lecherous, and continuously violating suspects' rights—unlike the way cops are usually portrayed on film. Many saw the film as being right-wing because it humanized cops trampling on civil liberties, and many saw it as being left-wing because it showed cops as they really are, so Friedkin thought he'd achieved the correct balance. What he was striving for was a kind of hyperkinetic activity for its own sake, to little or no avail. Friedkin has said that the police really work hard, killing themselves and sometimes other people, ''yet basically they're involved in a line of work that is frustrated, ineffectual.'' He believes narcotics is an impossible job, with too many ways to get drugs into the country and too many people wanting them. Friedkin and his actors capture this frustration while telling a gripping tale that proves a police procedure can be fast-paced and riveting if the storytelling and performances are so good that viewers really care what happens to the characters.

—Bob Sullivan

FURTHER READING:

Clagett, Thomas D. *William Friedkin: Films of Aberration, Obsession and Reality.* Jefferson, North Carolina, McFarland, 1990.

Moore, Robin. *The French Connection.* Boston, Little Brown, 1969.

Segaloff, Nat. *Hurricane Billy: The Stormy Life and Films of William Friedkin.* New York, William Morrow, 1990.

French Fries

America's love affair with french fries started in 1789 when Thomas Jefferson, fancier of French cuisine and especially of *pommes frites,* introduced the delicacies to his fellow citizens when he returned home after serving as American ambassador to France. Two

French fries, cheeseburger, and a soft drink.

centuries later, french fries, those thin strips of potato cut lengthwise that have been deep-fried until crisp, are internationally associated with hamburgers and fast-food meals. Their popular success benefitted from advances in food processing and the growth of the fast-food trade. They became a fetish of the McDonald's corporation: "The french fry would become almost sacrosanct for me, its preparation a ritual to be followed religiously" wrote Ray Kroc in his book *Grinding It Out: The Making of McDonald's.* Famous for their high quality, McDonald's french fries are essential to the chain's success, with more than 6.8 million pounds prepared every day in 1998. On the eve of the twenty-first century, french fries changed national identity as fast-food ventures in Japan and Southeast Asia promote them as "American fries."

—Catherine C. Galley & Briavel Holcomb

FURTHER READING:

Kroc, Ray. *Grinding It Out: The Making of McDonald's.* Chicago, Contemporary Books, 1977.

Meltzer, Milton. *The Amazing Potato: A Story in Which the Incas, Conquistadors, Marie Antoinette, Thomas Jefferson, Wars, Famines, Immigrants and French Fries All Play a Part.* New York, HarperCollins, 1992.

Salaman, Redcliffe N. *The History and Social Influence of the Potato.* Cambridge, Cambridge University Press, 1985.

Freud, Sigmund (1856-1939)

Sigmund Freud

Sigmund Freud is widely known as the founding father of psychoanalysis, and is probably the most famous and influential theorist and practitioner in the field of psychology to date. His works are studied not only by mental health professionals, but by students of philosophy, humanities, art, literature, and culture as well. Probably Freud's most widely known contributions are his theories about the motivating force of the libido, his descriptions of the effect of childhood experiences on the adult psyche, and his theories of dreams, the mind, and the unconscious. His writings have been translated into most modern languages, and are collected in twenty-four volumes in *The Standard Edition of the Complete Works of Sigmund Freud,* but people who have never read a word Freud wrote or even an essay about him are familiar with the Freudian implications of dreams. Many of Freud's concepts have been popularized by their usage in novels, movies, and self-help movements, and Freud himself is a widely recognized icon in Western societies, so much so that the standard film and television stereotype of a psychiatrist or psychologist will have a beard, a cigar, and an Austrian accent.

Freud's theories have always aroused controversy. Many of his contemporaries greeted Freud's ideas with overt hostility and ridicule. Some of this was due to widely prevalent anti-Semitism and some was due to the Victorian sexual standards of his day, which found his graphic discussion of sexuality distasteful. Since the women's liberation movement of the 1970s, feminists have questioned Freud's understanding of women, and blamed his male-identified theories for much of the damage done to women by mental health institutions. Other psychiatrists and psychologists began to challenge what they call the "hero worship" of Freud. Writers like

Richard Webster and Frederick Crews accuse the father of psychotherapy of fraud, saying he stole many of his ideas and often forced patients to conform to his theories.

Freud was born May 6, 1856, in the small town of Freiberg in the Austro-Hungarian Empire. The son of a moderately successful Jewish wool merchant, Freud was raised in Vienna. Though an innovative thinker, Freud was most definitely a product of his time. The mid-nineteenth century was at a crossroads between the Romantic movement and a new orientation toward the scientific. Freud was deeply interested in Romantic subjects like philosophy and the humanities, and felt it necessary to balance this passion with the study of science. His work came from that blending of the intensely humanistic notion of the value of the individual experience and the new growth of medical science, along with influences from the Germanic *Naturphilosophie* and the Jewish philosophers of his own heritage. Though his contributions were in part scientific, the way his theories have shaped the public imagination for decades may have more to do with their mythical power.

Freud studied medicine at Vienna University and later worked at the Salpetriere hospital in Paris, where Jean-Martin Charcot was director. Charcot's influence on Freud was significant: the famous French professor of neurology was the leading expert on hysteria, the study and treatment of which eventually led Freud to develop the theory and method of psychoanalysis. Hysteria was an ailment presumed to afflict a large number of women at the time. While its symptoms—such as paralysis, seizures, anorexia, and aphasia—had previously been viewed as resulting from a literal irritation of the uterus (the word hysteria derives from the Latin for uterus), Charcot viewed hysteria as a neurological disorder that was caused by trauma, and could be treated through hypnosis. Charcot's idea that a person's experiences, thoughts, or emotions might cause physiological symptoms had a profound influence on Freud's subsequent work.

In *Studies on Hysteria* (1895), Freud and his colleague, Josef Breuer, proposed the radical thesis that hysteria was in fact caused by sexual traumas—specifically, childhood sexual abuse, and quite often incest—that the patient was re-enacting through her bodily symptoms. Freud's radical insight about the origins of hysteria led to his revolutionary theory of the unconscious mind, which he conceived as a literal place in the brain to which intolerable memories, thoughts, feelings, desires, and conflicts were relegated. Freud's and Breuer's treatment of women diagnosed with hysteria also led to the development of the "talking cure," the cornerstone of the psychoanalytic method. The "talking cure" began with Breuer's treatment of "Anna O." (Bertha Pappenheim), an hysteric patient who was resistant to hypnotic suggestion, but found that "talking out" her memories and experiences had the cathartic effect of "talking away her symptoms."

In 1896, Freud renounced his original theory that hysteria was caused by the patient's real traumatic experiences of childhood sexual abuse, and instead began explaining patient's symptoms in terms of their own incestuous desires and fantasies. This evolved into Freud's well-known theories of infantile sexuality—which include the oral, anal, and phallic drives—and the postulation of a universal "Oedipus complex," named for the Greek tragic hero who killed his father and married his mother. According to this theory, childhood development involves a progression from oral desires (for the mother's breast); through anal drives (the desire for mastery and control of one's bodily products); and culminates in overtly genital sexuality, which for Freud is always phallic.

For boys, the Oedipus stage of development as Freud describes it involves incestuous desires toward the mother, and feelings of rivalry toward—and fear of retaliation from—the father. This retaliation is also understood in terms of male genital sexuality as the threat of castration. According to Freud's theory, the psychological conflicts of desire, guilt, and castration anxiety must be resolved in favor of the boy's gender identification with his father, and sublimation of his incestuous desires toward his mother. Freud postulates that the lack of such resolution is the root of much adult male psychopathology.

In the female version of the Oedipus complex, Freud believed the young girl must first shift away from her primary (originally oral) desire for her mother, toward a more mature oedipal desire for her father. The girl's normal development involves a recognition that because she lacks a penis, she cannot fulfill her sexual desire for her mother, nor identify with her father, but must accept her role as the passive recipient of men's desire. Further, in discovering that she lacks a penis, the girl must contend with the realization that she is "already castrated," mutilated, and inferior. Freud described the inability of some female patients to accept their lack of a penis, to renounce their "phallic" (clitoral) desire, and to accept and embrace the passive feminine role, as "penis envy," which he considered a common female psychopathology.

Freud's theories of female sexual development have engendered decades of debate both within psychoanalysis and beyond. For example, feminists have pointed out that Freud's conceptualization of both normal and pathological female development require the girl's renunciation of some part of herself—either her agency as an active, desiring subject, or her feminine gender identity. Freud has been sharply criticized for his equation of sexual activity with masculinity,

for his arguments that women are biologically, intellectually, and morally inferior to men, and for his insistence that, in female development, "Anatomy is destiny." From Freud's contemporaries Karen Horney and Joan Riviere, to modern feminists such as Nancy Chodorow and Jean Baker Miller, Freud's theories of female psychology have undergone intense scrutiny and revision.

The shift in Freud's focus from real sexual traumas to infantile sexuality and incestuous desires has itself been the subject of controversy. Freud's followers believe that his shift from real incest to oedipal fantasies reflected a more mature and sophisticated understanding of the mind and of personality formation and allowed for the recognition of infantile sexuality and the psychological importance of fantasies, guilt, and repression. On the other hand, many contemporary scholars have argued that Freud's original belief in the reality and psychological significance of child sexual abuse was scientifically valid, while his later reversal was personally, professionally and culturally motivated. According to his critics, Freud's reversal denied the role that actual incestuous abuse had played in the emotional problems of his patients, and contributed to a cultural refusal to acknowledge the realities of widely prevalent sexual abuse and other traumas experienced predominately by women and children in a patriarchal society.

Despite Freud's theoretical shift from exploring real traumas to emphasizing unconscious desires and conflicts, Freud continued to develop and employ the "talking cure" that he and Breuer had used in treating hysterics. This cathartic method evolved into the technique of free association and interpretation that characterizes psychoanalytic practice, and has had a profound influence on nearly all other forms of psychotherapy. While subsequent practitioners have differed from Freud in their use of techniques—such as free association, hypnosis, the analytic couch, and interpretation—the essential practice of encouraging patients to talk about their experiences and express their deepest thoughts, feelings, wishes, and fears has remained a central part of psychotherapy since Freud.

While Freud's psychoanalytic method had a profound influence on psychotherapeutic practice, it is his theories of the mind—and particularly his conceptualization of the unconscious—that have arguably been his most important and influential contributions to contemporary thought. Freud conceived of the mind in spatial terms, viewing the unconscious as the area to which our socially unacceptable desires and fantasies are relegated, and well as the area from which jokes, slips of the tongue, dream imagery, and much of our creative ideas flow. Freud elaborated a schematic of the mind that corresponded with his view of personality development. The *id* consisted of the primary drives and impulses, such as oral and sexual desire and the aggressive instincts. The *superego* was the internalization of familial and social rules, particularly the prohibitions against primitive desires and instincts. And the *ego* was essentially the socialized self, capable of defenses, sublimation, rational thought, and creativity. While these theories have been elaborated and debated within psychoanalytic circles, the rudimentary concepts are familiar to most people in western cultures, and have been largely, if crudely, incorporated into contemporary thinking about the mind and the personality.

In addition to Freud's profound influence on ideas of the mind, the significance of early life events, and the dynamics of personality development, contemporary culture owes many of its assumptions about the symbolism of dreams, jokes, and cultural products to Freud's writings. Freud considered his seminal and perhaps most famous text, *The Interpretation of Dreams* (1899), to be the key to his work, and pronounced dreams "the royal road to the knowledge of the unconscious." His understanding of dreams, jokes, and slips of the tongue as laden with unconscious meanings has permeated western thinking. Terms such as "repression," "projection," "ego," and "superego" have become part of everyday parlance; and it is common for inadvertent—yet potentially significant—errors in speech to be referred to as "Freudian slips" (such as the postcard from the erring husband to his unsuspecting wife which reads, "Wish you were her.") Freud himself applied many of his theories to the study of art and literary texts—including the works of Da Vinci, Goethe, Michelangelo and, of course, Shakespeare—and many culture scholars since Freud have used psychoanalytic ideas about desire, fantasy, language and the unconscious in their interpretations of artist's works.

The notion of repression of memory has particularly grasped the modern imagination. From Henry James' *Turn of the Screw* (1898), which was written in Freud's time, to such modern classics as *The Manchurian Candidate* (published 1959; filmed 1962) and *Psycho* (filmed 1960), audiences have been fascinated with the potential depths of the mind, and the horrors that can be stored there, just out of reach. Even Homer Simpson, *pater familias* of the wacky television cartoon family portrayed on the television series *The Simpsons* (1989—), understands the uses of repression, when he tells his daughter: "The important thing is for your mother to repress what happened, push it deep down inside her, so she'll never annoy us again."

One of Freud's most significant impacts on modern culture has been the popularization of psychotherapy. While once reserved for the rich and introspective, psychotherapy is now widely available to a broad spectrum of people. As the stigma of seeing a "headshrinker" has lessened, therapy has become an increasingly popular way of dealing with life's troubles. In the United States alone, over 10 million people talk out their problems with psychiatrists, psychologists, and psychiatric social workers. Untold numbers of others see marriage counselors and other, often self-styled, therapists. All of these counselors are direct descendants of Freud's "talking therapy."

The idea that people's adult actions are influenced by their childhood experiences has become a widely held social belief. While this has led, on the one hand, to a certain "democratization" of mental and emotional problems and has inspired social reform movements, some social critics believe it has also led to a failure to take personal responsibility for one's actions, since everything can be traced back to parental abuse or rejection. From the notorious Menendez brothers, who insisted that constant childhood abuse led them to murder their parents, to Kitty Dukakis, wife of 1988 presidential candidate Michael Dukakis, who wrote an autobiography attributing her adult alcohol and drug abuse to her mother's rejection, the idea that parental failings cause our adult pain has taken root in society. Freud's belief that our lives are determined by how we come to terms with our sexuality shows up at the center of serious social analysis as well as cocktail party chat, and in cultural representations from Broadway theater (*Equus, Who's Afraid of Virginia Woolf?*) to soap operas.

Much is known about Freud's life because of his prolific correspondences with friends, colleagues, students and patients—many of whom were famous figures in their own right—and because of his self-analysis. At the same time, much about Freud has been obscured—both by his own silences and contradictions, and by the deliberate obfuscations of those who have wished to discredit or to protect him. Freud himself was sharply aware of his place in history and zealously guarded his image, hoping to control the picture of him that would be written down in history. Modern critics accuse Freud of failing to acknowledge the contributions of his mentors. Some even charge him with outright theft of his ideas of the unconscious and his "talking therapy" from such influential teachers as Josef Brauer and Wilhelm Fleiss. Many of Freud's detractors also point to his practice of bullying patients into agreeing with his pre-conceived theories. They quote Freud himself, who advised his students:

> The work [of therapy] keeps coming to a stop and they keep maintaining that this time nothing has occurred to them. We must not believe what they say, we must always assume, and tell them too, that they have kept something back.... We must insist on this, we must repeat the pressure and represent ourselves as infallible, till at last we are really told something....

Critics contend that this image of the infallible psychiatrist has been the most damaging influence of psychotherapy. Still others call psychotherapy itself a fraud, especially Freud's model of psychoanalysis, saying that there is no real evidence that it works.

Freud's persona itself shows up regularly in the popular media, whether it is the actual character of Freud assisting fellow cocaine addict Sherlock Holmes with cases (as in *The Seven Percent Solution*, 1976) or merely his voice speaking through controversial television heroine Murphy Brown when she intones the famous Freud quote, "Sometimes a cigar is just a cigar." Freud has been the prototype for many popular culture representations of psychologists, psychiatrists, and psychoanalysts. His face and habits—such as his cocaine use and his cigar smoking—are widely recognized icons even seven decades after his death in 1939. Many have argued that Sigmund Freud was the most influential thinker of the twentieth century. Others have insisted that his theories reflect a decidedly nineteenth-century emphasis on biological determinism, sexuality, and bourgeois patriarchal values. For better or worse, Freud has had a profound impact not only on psychological theory and practice, but on culture and the way we understand it.

—Tina Gianoulis and Ava Rose

FURTHER READING:

Brennan, Teresa. *The Interpretation of the Flesh: Freud and Femininity*. New York, Routledge, 1992.

Chodorow, Nancy. *Femininities, Masculinities, Sexualities: Freud and Beyond*. Lexington, Kentucky, University of Kentucky Press, 1994.

Freud, Sigmund. *Standard Edition of the Complete Psychological Works of Sigmund Freud*. General editor, James Strachey. London, Hogarth Press, 1953-74.

Gay, Peter. *Freud: A Life for Our Time*. New York, W.W. Norton, 1988.

Masson, Jeffrey Moussaieff. *The Assault on Truth: Freud's Suppression of the Seduction Theory*. New York, Harper Perennial, 1984.

Roazen, Paul, editor. *Sigmund Freud*. New York, Da Capo Press, 1985.

Slipp, Samuel. *The Freudian Mystique: Freud, Women, and Feminism*. New York, New York University Press, 1993.

Webster, Richard. *Why Freud Was Wrong: Sin, Science, and Psychoanalysis.* London, Harper Collins, 1995.

Friday, Nancy (1938—)

There is a cliché in American culture that men are principally interested in sex, while women are mostly concerned with love. In helping to debunk this myth, Nancy Friday has performed an invaluable national service. She is one of the relatively small number of modern writers who has gathered and published evidence that women's fantasies are often as sexually explicit as men's. Her books devoted to relating women's sexual fantasies work effectively on several levels: as psychology, as sociology, and as pornography. In addition, Friday has produced several other important books on subjects of interest to modern women: jealousy, beauty, and the mother-daughter relationship.

Nancy Friday grew up in Charleston, South Carolina, the child of a single mother. She moved to New York City in the early 1960s, where she was simultaneously introduced to the sexual revolution and the women's movement, both of which would influence her life, and writing, profoundly. She worked at *Cosmopolitan* magazine and *The Examiner* before deciding to devote her energies to writing books.

Friday's first book, *My Secret Garden: Women's Sexual Fantasies,* appeared in 1973. It attracted considerable attention, partly because of its sexually explicit language and subject matter, but

Nancy Friday

mostly because these "nasty" words and scenarios were coming from the minds of women. In 1973, the idea that respectable, normal women had such steamy, even "kinky" thoughts was considered something of a revelation. The book was a bestseller, as was its 1975 sequel, *Forbidden Flowers.*

Her third book was something of a departure. *My Mother/My Self,* which appeared in 1977, was an exploration of the mother/adult daughter relationship, including the ways that mothers' implicit messages can influence their daughters long past childhood. The book was a huge success, and interest in the subject was suddenly on the public agenda, spawning workshops, TV programs, and books by a host of authors.

In her next work, Friday returned to familiar territory, but with a twist. *Men in Love* (1980) was a collection of male sexual fantasies. Friday's choice of title was a reflection of her conclusion after reading the anonymously submitted fantasy material. Contrary to widely held belief, Friday said, men's fantasies about women were mostly not violent, hateful, or exploitative; instead, they were passionate, inventive, and, yes, loving.

Friday waded into another subject of intense interest to many women with her 1985 book, *Jealousy.* An immense volume (running over 500 pages), the book combines a discussion of the psychological literature on the subject with interview material and Friday's brutally honest account of how jealousy had played such a major role in her own life. Friday admits that her principal reasons for approaching the project were personal, and much of the book is a description of her own personal struggles with the "green-eyed monster."

With *Women on Top,* Friday returns to the milieu of women's sexual fantasies, but the book's subtitle is her justification for visiting the territory again: *How Real Life Has Changed Women's Sexual Fantasies* (1991). Friday wanted to find out whether the passage of fifteen or so years since her last visit had changed the landscape of women's private sexual longings. Her conclusion: women have ceased to dream of passivity and submission. They now are excited by thoughts of sexual power, aggression, and dominance. The fantasies submitted for consideration this time, she found, were much more likely to portray the woman as taking change of her partner, her relationship, and her own sexual satisfaction.

The year 1996 saw the publication of *The Power of Beauty,* possibly Friday's most ambitious work yet. As with her earlier books on mother/daughter relationships and jealousy, Friday combines survey research, psychological insights, and her own candid history into a meditation on the ways that physical attractiveness (or the lack thereof) influences, for good or ill, many aspects of modern life—from who you will marry to where you will work, to the degree of success you will enjoy in your job.

Nancy Friday established her own web site in 1997. It allows users to read Friday's thoughts on a variety of subjects, leave their own messages for her, share their sexual fantasies, and read excerpts from several of Friday's books.

—Justin Gustainis

FURTHER READING:

Friday, Nancy. *Jealousy.* New York, William Morrow and Co., 1985.

———. *Men in Love: Men's Sexual Fantasies, the Triumph of Love over Rage.* New York, Delacorte Press, 1980.

———. "Nancy Friday." http://www.nancyfriday.com. March 1999.

—. *Women on Top: How Real Life Has Changed Women's Sexual Fantasies.* New York, Simon & Schuster, 1991.

Friday the 13th

Made on a budget of less than $600,000, with mostly unknown actors, corny dialogue, and a hastily prepared script (completed in under two weeks), the original installment of *Friday the 13th* in 1980 nevertheless went on to gross over $70 million at box offices around the world and launch a cottage industry of sequels, spoofs, spin-offs, and outright rip-offs. No modern horror film monster, save perhaps for Freddy Krueger, has managed to capture our culture's collective imagination as much as has Jason Voorhees, the speechless, seemingly immortal psychopath with a hatred for promiscuous adolescents. Along with John Carpenter's *Halloween* (1978), *Friday the 13th* is credited with initiating the notorious "stalker cycle" of horror films—an immensely popular, and heavily criticized, subgenre that would continue to draw huge audiences through the mid-1980s.

Jason from *Friday the 13th, Part IV*.

Whereas *Halloween* is best known for the cinematic conventions it helped to establish, *Friday the 13th* has managed to transcend the world of film. The series has come to serve as a point of departure in public debates over the consequences of exposing youths to representations of graphic violence in the name of entertainment.

Sean Cunningham, producer, director, and co-writer of the original *Friday the 13th,* had gained a measure of infamy in film circles for producing Wes Craven's ultra-violent underground hit, *Last House on the Left,* in 1972. (Craven, who would go on to direct *A Nightmare on Elm Street* (1984) and *Scream* (1996), returned the favor by doing some uncredited editing on the first *Friday.*) But this infamy turned out to be a benefit, as Paramount, United Artists, and Warner Brothers—all eager to repeat the commercial success of the independently produced *Halloween*—entered into a bidding war for Cunningham's low-budget vehicle about a psychopath determined to kill off all the counselors at Camp Crystal Lake (otherwise known as "Camp Blood"). Paramount won the war and launched *Friday the 13th* with a $4 million advertising campaign. The studio's confidence was quickly rewarded, as the film grossed $31 million in its first six weeks alone, surpassing such major productions as Stanley Kubrick's *The Shining* and James Bridges' *Urban Cowboy.* On the strength of Tom Savini's make-up and special effects wizardry, the progressively gory murders taking place in *Friday the 13th* ensured that whatever the movie lacked in narrative sophistication, it would more than make up for in violent spectacle.

Although it was not the very first stalker film, *Friday the 13th* is widely regarded as the prototype of the subgenre. In sharp contrast to *Halloween,* fans, critics, and theorists alike have emphasized the movie's essential reliance on formula and convention, denying it any claim to cinematic originality. Andrew Tudor, in his influential history of the horror film, writes that "in practice, *Friday the 13th* is no more than a crude template for the creation of formula *Halloween* clones." It is true that the subjective ("point-of-view") camera work, the cat-and-mouse-style killing of vapid, horny teenagers, the prolonged final battle pitting psychopath against virginal, sensible, ultimately victorious "good girl," all come straight out of *Halloween.*

But it is also important to note the ways in which *Friday the 13th* breaks with stalker convention and establishes precedents of its own. Contrary to popular belief, the killer in Part One is not Jason, but Mrs. Voorhees, who blames her son's drowning death in 1958 on the camp counselors who neglected their responsibilities. Twenty years later, she seems not to care that the counselors have changed; nor does she seem to care about the gender of her victims. All this creates difficulties for those who would argue that modern horror film monsters represent nothing more than the sadistic wish-fulfillments of misogynistic male viewers. Furthermore, the surface normality of Mrs. Voorhees—she looks and talks just like a conservative, middle-class mom when she's not slitting people's throats—anticipates the all-too-realistic serial killers populating such films as *The Stepfather* (1987), *White of the Eye* (1988), and *Henry: Portrait of a Serial Killer* (1990).

With the disfigured Jason taking over his mother's murderous attacks in *Friday the 13th, Part 2* (1981), and especially after his decision to don a goalie mask in *Friday the 13th, Part 3: 3D* (1982), the series' transformation was complete. Under the direction of Steve Miner, these films saw the replacement of a human psychopath whose actions are at least somewhat explicable in quasi-Freudian terms with a supernatural agent of evil whose sole intent seems to be the violent eradication of America's adolescents. Jonathan Crane asserts that "Jason, as well-known as any prominent American personality, ranks among the foremost of all popular signs embodying meaning's demise.'' It is not only the apparent randomness with which Jason chooses his victims that leads Crane to this conclusion. It is the fact that Jason's single-minded devotion to murder, his virtual indestructibility, and, above all, his inevitable return from the dead all serve as prime sources of pleasure for the mostly teenage audiences who, well into the 1990s, came out in droves to see the further adventures of their ''hero.''

Besides its record number of sequels (eight and counting), *Friday the 13th* has been the inspiration for parodies such as *Saturday the 14th* (1981), generic rip-offs such as *Campsite Massacre* (1983), a Canadian television show (1987-90), a series of young adult novels, a heavy metal song by Terrorvision, and a successful run of porno movies that began with *Friday the 13th: A Nude Beginning* (1987). In the late 1990s, blockbuster ''neo-stalkers'' such as *Scream* and *I Know What You Did Last Summer* (1997) scored points with audiences by explicitly foregrounding a number of *Friday*'s plot devices. All of which supports the view that *Friday the 13th,* despite being nominated worst picture at the 1981 Razzie Awards, inaugurated the most successful franchise in modern horror cinema.

—Steven Schneider

FURTHER READING:

Crane, Jonathan Lake. ''Jason.'' *Terror and Everyday Life: Singular Moments in the History of the Horror Film.* Thousand Oaks, Sage Publications, 1994, 132-58.

Dika, Vera. *Games of Terror: ''Halloween,'' ''Friday the 13th,'' and the Films of the Stalker Cycle.* East Rutherford, Fairleigh Dickinson University Press, 1990.

Tudor, Andrew. *Monsters and Mad Scientists: A Cultural History of the Horror Movie.* Oxford, Basil Blackwell, 1989.

Friedman, Kinky (1944—)

Founder and leader of the Texas Jewboys, an iconoclastic country and western band of the 1970s, Richard ''Kinky'' Friedman has since become better known as a comic novelist.

Born in Chicago (not—as often claimed—in Palestine, Texas) on Halloween, Friedman was the son of a psychology professor and a speech therapist. The family moved to Texas during his childhood, buying a ranch near Medina to create the Echo Hill Ranch summer camp for boys. Interested in both music and chess from an early age, Friedman was chosen when he was seven years old to be one of fifty local chess players to challenge Polish-born U.S. grand master Samuel Reshevsky to simultaneous matches in Houston. While Reshevsky won all fifty matches, Friedman was by far the youngest competitor.

Friedman was a junior counselor at Echo Hill Ranch and then an honors psychology student at the University of Texas (B.A., 1966). He spent the next two years as a Peace Corps volunteer in the Southwest Pacific, ostensibly as an agricultural extension agent. According to Friedman, his greatest achievement in the Peace Corps

was to introduce the Frisbee to Borneo. Upon his return to America he pursued a career in country music; he had already been in a moderately successful rock 'n' roll band in Austin, while an undergraduate. This band, King Arthur and the Carrots, had a local hit with ''Schwinn 24,'' a parody of Beach Boys-type drag racing songs, this one about a boy and his bicycle.

In the early 1970s Friedman formed his own band, the Texas Jewboys. The name is a multilayered pun on Bob Wills and His Texas Playboys, a famed Depression-era country band. Many musicians performed with Friedman, so there is no one correct lineup for the band. A central factor in the band's material, almost all of which was at least co-written by Friedman, is the tension in his background as a Jewish intellectual raised in rural Texas. His songs explore many topics, including feminism, racial relations, the stresses of a musician's life, and nostalgia for the past, but anti-Semitism and clashes with rednecks are frequent concerns. Among his most famous songs are ''They Ain't Makin' Jews Like Jesus Anymore'' and ''Ride 'Em Jewboy.'' The latter song, in which the Holocaust is compared with a cattle drive, is a beautiful ballad with eerie lyrics, considered to be Friedman's most affecting song.

Some of Friedman's songs are strictly played for laughs, and a few are more traditional country tunes without an overt sermon, but most have some kind of social message embedded in them. His audiences have frequently mistaken Friedman's song persona for his authentic feelings and social agenda, as when the National Organization for Women gave him its Male Chauvinist Pig of the Year award in 1974 for ''Get Your Biscuits in the Oven and Your Buns in the Bed,'' a satirical song about a redneck and his women's-libber girlfriend.

The band was heckled for that and other songs, and some of their bookings were canceled, but this notoriety also led to greater success. In 1973 Friedman obtained a recording contract with Vanguard, releasing *Sold American* later that year. Another album followed in 1974, and in 1976 Friedman achieved his musical high-water mark with an album on the Epic label, *Lasso From El Paso.* (The song was originally titled ''Asshole from El Paso,'' a parody of Merle Haggard's ''Okie from Muskogee,'' but Epic required a title change before issuing the record.) On Lasso, Friedman had guest artists like Eric Clapton and Bob Dylan, having met Dylan and gone on his Rolling Thunder Revue tour the year before. Other important songs on his early albums include ''Sold American,'' ''Wild Man from Borneo,'' and ''Homo Erectus.'' More recently, he has released *From One Good American to Another,* and a ''greatest hits'' compilation entitled *Old Testaments And New Revelations.*

Friedman spent several years living in a Greenwich Village loft in New York City. While there, he was a frequent performer at the Lone Star Cafe, a Texas-themed hangout in Manhattan. His act and a bit of his lifestyle are described in *No Laughing Matter,* by Joseph Heller and Speed Vogel, and *Thin Ice: A Season In Hell With The New York Rangers,* by his close friend Larry Sloman. In the early 1980s Friedman returned to the Echo Hill Ranch, eager to make a radical change in his life after seeing several friends die from drug-related causes. Back in Texas, Friedman began writing comic mystery novels, set in New York, with a fictionalized version of himself as the sleuth. He has published nearly one every year since 1986, with such memorable titles as *A Case of Lone Star* (1987), *Elvis, Jesus, and Coca-Cola* (1993), and *God Bless John Wayne* (1995). The fame resulting from his second career has helped create a renewed demand

Kinky Friedman

for his recorded music, though he expresses little interest in performing again.

—David Lonergan

FURTHER READING:

"Friedman, Kinky." *Contemporary Authors,* Vol. 147. Detroit, Gale Research, 1995.

"Kinky Friedman." *The Illustrated Encyclopedia of Country Music.* London, Salamander Books, 1977.

Sloman, Larry. *On the Road with Bob Dylan: Rolling with the Thunder.* New York, Bantam Books, 1978.

Stambler, Irwin, and Grelun Landon. *The Encyclopedia of Folk, Country and Western Music.* 2nd Ed. New York, St. Martin's Press, 1983.

Friends

Six attractive, barely employed but financially comfortable Manhattanites in their twenties constituted the eponymous core of *Friends,* the TV sitcom that burst onto NBC for the first time during the 1994-1995 season, and rocketed to instant, "must-see" popularity. Single young viewers, bored with sitcoms about family life, latched enthusiastically onto this group of pals in cute clothes and trendy haircuts, who spend much of their time sitting around in a coffee bar conversing and exchanging banter, and who treat each other like family. *Friends* is an ensemble show that appeared to have been directly modeled after the Fox sitcom *Living Single,* which began its run a year earlier and featured an almost identical premise except that the cast was African American.

Created by Marta Kauffman and David Crane, the group of friends is divided equally between the sexes. The girls are Monica Geller (Courteney Cox), a chef and a neatness freak, her old high school friend and roommate Rachel Green (Jennifer Aniston), and the flighty Phoebe Buffay (Lisa Kudrow). Phoebe is Monica's college friend and a massage therapist and guitarist who plays at the coffee bar/hangout Central Perk. (her signature song is "Smelly Cat"). Rachel began the series by leaving her daddy's financial support and her dentist fiancé at the altar to make it on her own. Monica's slightly older brother Ross (David Schwimmer) is a well-meaning paleontologist whose wife divorced him upon realizing that she's a lesbian; Ross' college pal Chandler Bing (Matthew Perry) lives across the hall from Monica and is the smart-ass of the group, while his roommate Joey

Tribbiani (Matt LeBlanc) is a none-too-bright aspiring actor who completes the sextet.

The show's theme song, The Rembrandts' Beatle-esque "I'll Be There For You," is insidiously infectious, a suitable metaphor for the show itself. Each week, this clique of attractive idlers discusses life in general and relationships in particular, with the on-again, off-again romance between Ross and Rachel a recurrent theme, and an almost constant cliffhanger. Ross is wild about Rachel; so much so that, even at the altar about to marry Emily (Helen Baxendale) in 1998, Ross said, "I, Ross, take thee Rachel."

The best known cast member when the show started was Courteney Cox, who had made a few movies and was on *Family Ties* for a season as Michael J. Fox's girlfriend. She no doubt felt immediately at home with Matthew Perry's Chandler, whose comic timing and delivery is heavily reminiscent of Fox. And Lisa Kudrow's Phoebe appears to have borrowed most of her mannerisms from Teri Garr, who was brought on to play Phoebe's long lost mother briefly in 1997.

Cox, Aniston, Perry, LeBlanc, Kudrow, and Schwimmer all became household names as a result of *Friends*. Not only are they a beguiling and talented assembly, but the show has the weight of an incomparable publicity machine behind it, and these six people, together and separately, have appeared on the cover of almost every entertainment magazine in the United States. All have tried to cultivate movie careers, with Aniston, by the late 1990s, having had the most success with big-screen ventures.

All the episode titles of *Friends* start with "The One with. . ." as in, "The One with the Embryos" and "The One with George Stephanopolous." Many critics might well name the whole series "The One with the Hairdos." No television show has influenced hairstyles as much as *Friends* has done, with variations on "the Rachel" still in evidence four years after the show premiered. The enormous popularity of the series spawned dozens of imitator shows in the 1990s, all of which featured attractive, witty young men and women hanging out together, but *Friends* had outlasted them all by the end of the decade. This can mostly be credited to the high standard of witty, imaginative and well-constructed scripts, which have helped garner critical acclaim and ratings success for a series that, by 1999, had received 14 Emmy nominations.

Notwithstanding its popularity and success, the series does have its share of vehement detractors. Certainly, not much happens on the show and the charm of its stars, along with the witty one-liners, is what carries it. For those who fail to find the *Friends* charming, there isn't much reason to tune in (but the same could be said of *Seinfeld*). Critics have maintained that the show bears no resemblance to reality, from the trouble these gorgeous people have finding love interests (so

(From left) Matt LeBlanc, Courteny Cox, Matthew Perry, Jennifer Aniston, and David Schwimmer.

much so that they seem to be turning to each other), to the one-dimensional nature of the characters, to the fact that no one ever seems to be working, and those who do, don't do it much. The fans answer that there are plenty of workplace comedies out there, but this show is about hanging out with your friends. And that's what the characters do—hang out with their friends.

—Karen Lurie

FURTHER READING:

Brooks, Tim, and Marsh, Earle. *The Complete Directory to Prime Time Network and Cable TV Shows 1946-present*. New York, Ballantine Books, 1995.

McNeil, Alex. *Total Television*. New York, Penguin, 1996.

Frisbee

The Frisbee, a plastic flying disc, has been a required component of any American child's toy collection for most of the latter half of the twentieth century. It is widely believed that Ivy League students began flinging and catching pie and cookie tins in the 1920s and 1930s, naming the practice "Frisbee-ing," after a local pie company. Wham-O Toy Company, producers of the Hula Hoop, began mass production of Frisbees in 1957.

An affordable and portable toy with no set rules, the Frisbee enjoyed a boom in sales and public familiarity in the anti-establishment atmosphere of the late 1960s. This new generation of Frisbee fans invented Frisbee Golf, Guts, and Ultimate Frisbee, but it was freestyle frisbee, with its behind-the-back and between-the-legs catches, trick throws, and leaping, Frisbee-catching dogs, that did the most for visibility of the growing sport. By the end of the twentieth century, over 50 colleges featured interscholastic Ultimate Frisbee teams, and Frisbee Golf courses peppered suburbs across the continent. And it was still a mark of pride among American youth to be able to fling a Frisbee straight and far.

—Colby Vargas

FURTHER READING:

Johnson, Dr. Stancil E. D. *Frisbee: A Practitioner's Manual and Definitive Treatise*. New York, Workman Publishing Company, 1975.

A group of frisbee enthusiasts.

Frizzell, Lefty (1928-1975)

One of country music's greatest vocal stylists, Lefty Frizzell's syllable-stretching, note bending style has influenced singers like Merle Haggard, George Jones, Willie Nelson, George Strait, and Randy Travis. Frizzell's meteoric rise to fame in country music may be unparalleled. Both sides of his first single (''If You've Got the Money I've Got the Time'' b/w ''I Love You a Thousand Ways'') for Columbia Records in 1950 hit number one on the country charts, and at one point in 1951, he had four singles in the top ten. Largely because of his alcoholism and brushes with the law, Frizzell's career suffered ups and downs. From 1953 to 1958, though he continued to tour and record, he had no hits. In 1959 he staged a comeback with ''Long Black Veil,'' followed a couple of years later by the number one hit ''Saginaw Michigan.'' Lefty continued to work until his death from a stroke in 1975.

—Joyce Linehan

FURTHER READING:

Cooper, Daniel. *Lefty Frizzell: The Honky-Tonk Life of Country Music's Greatest Singer*. Boston, Little Brown, 1995.

From Here to Eternity

First as a novel and then as a film, *From Here to Eternity* enjoyed enormous critical and popular success in the early 1950s. The novel, the first published work of James Jones, is a long and powerful fictional treatment of the United States Army climaxing with the December 7, 1941, Japanese attack on U. S. military installations at Pearl Harbor. The bulk of Jones's novel relentlessly exposes the exploitation of enlisted men by a cynical officer class. Its naturalistic descriptions of an inhumanly brutal stockade constitute some of the most harrowing passages in American fiction. Still, the novel is, to a large degree, a kind of elegy for the sustaining camaraderie among enlisted men as well as for the sanctuary that the army offered the economically destitute during the Great Depression. It is then a unique variation on proletarian fiction with officers equated to corrupt capitalists and enlisted men to oppressed workers. Jones's book was awarded the National Book Award for 1952, received overwhelmingly favorable reviews, and became a sensational best-seller (in no small part because of an elaborate publicity campaign by its publisher, Scribner's). The novel's two central characters, Robert E. Lee Prewitt, a boxer and bugler of unusual talent and unyielding principles, and Sergeant Milton Anthony Warden, also a man of integrity but a master manipulator and covert enemy of the officer class as well, are exceptionally well realized.

Largely because of its unrelenting expose of the corrupt officer class in the old peacetime army and the frankness of its treatment of sexuality, *From Here to Eternity* benefitted, in its popular success, from the public's appetite for sensationalism. These two motifs are carefully intertwined in Jones's text. For instance, Warden sets out to seduce Karen Holmes, the allegedly promiscuous wife of his corrupt commanding officer, merely as a political statement but quickly finds himself falling in love with her. Prewitt, after being forced to desert the army following a horrendous experience in the stockade during which he experiences physical torture and sees another soldier die at

the hands of Sergeant ''Fatso'' Judson, seeks refuge with his prostitute girlfriend, Alma Schmidt, who has taken the professional name of Lorene. The novel contains a comically graphic scene in the brothel where Alma works and in which Prewitt finds relief from the endless harassment which he is receiving at the direct orders of Lieutenant ''Dynamite'' Holmes. In the scene, Prewitt is accompanied by the only friend that he has in C Company, Private Angelo Maggio, an enormously likeable but recklessly defiant young man from Brooklyn.

Despite (or because of) the novel's sensational elements, producer Harry Cohn of Columbia Pictures eagerly purchased the rights to film it and hired Jones, who had by then become something of a celebrity (partly because of extensive coverage in *Life* magazine) to write the screenplay. Cohn also acquired the services of Fred Zinnemann, the acclaimed director of *High Noon* and other successful films. Jones's screenplay was rejected in favor of a subsequent effort by film writer Daniel Taradash. Because of the novel's emphasis upon memorable characters, Cohn and Zinnemann realized that casting would be a crucial element in the success of their final work. In this, they were to be extremely fortunate. For the crucial role of Prewitt, Cohn initially pushed for actor Aldo Ray, but ultimately yielded to Zinnemann's insistence upon the casting of Montgomery Clift, whose ability to project a threatened sensitivity had been established in such films as George Stevens's *A Place in the Sun* (1951). Burt Lancaster and relative film newcomer Ernest Borgnine were easy choices to portray Sergeant Milt Warden and ''Fatso'' Judson, but the casting of the two female roles surprised many Hollywood observers. Initially, Joan Crawford was chosen to play Holmes, but she withdrew from the project before filming began and was replaced by Deborah Kerr, unquestionably a fine actress, but one best-known for portraying genteel and sometimes aloof characters. The choice of Donna Reed for the role of Alma was unexpected for comparable reasons. Even though the script overtly made her a dance-hall hostess instead of a prostitute, the character's original identity as conceived by Jones in his novel was more than implied; and Reed was known for such ''wholesome'' performances as the wife of James Stewart in Frank Capra's *It's a Wonderful Life* (1946). The process of choosing the actor to play Angelo Maggio became the stuff of Hollywood and pop legend. Then at the nadir of his career as a singer, Frank Sinatra, who had read Jones's novel and identified with Maggio, campaigned tirelessly for the part and was somewhat reluctantly given it. This episode would be fictionalized by Mario Puzo in his novel *The Godfather*.

Taradash's screenplay downplayed Jones's depiction of military corruption. For instance, the corrupt Captain ''Dynamite'' Holmes is exposed and disgraced in the film, when Jones's novel last shows him rising higher in the military command; and the stockade sadism is largely kept offscreen. Still, the finished film, released in 1953, captured much of the novel's emotional power primarily because of Zinnemann's directing and the exceptional performances of his cast. Critics Pauline Kael and Michael Gebert have correctly observed that Clift's inspired interpretation of Prewitt is the real heart of the film and is so intense as to be almost unbearable at times. Lancaster and Kerr are exceptional in playing off each other, and a scene in which, dressed in bathing suits, they kiss while lying on a beach with the waves splashing over them is probably the movie's best-known single image (ironically the scene does not exist in the novel). Sinatra, Read, and Borgnine are perfect in their secondary roles.

Not surprisingly, the film gathered a number of major awards. Out of thirteen Academy Award nominations, it won eight, including

Deborah Kerr and Burt Lancaster in a scene from the film *From Here to Eternity*.

best picture, Zinnemann as best director, Taradash for writing, and Sinatra and Reed as supporting actor and actress (Clift, Lancaster, and Kerr were also nominated). It also received the best picture award from the New York Film Critics Circle, and Zinnemann was named the year's best director by that organization and by the Directors Guild of America. In 1953, much of the film's power originated in its being filmed in black and white in a technicolor-dominated age. This deliberately anachronistic approach achieved the realistic effect that Zinnemann wanted.

Both as novel and as film, *From Here to Eternity* occupies an important place in American culture. In the conformist and sexually repressive 1950s, its advocacy of oppressed enlisted men and its frank depiction of their sexual hunger seemed daring and even revolutionary. Some of the images from the film (Lancaster and Kerr on the beach, Montgomery Clift playing "Taps" for the dead Frank Sinatra) are indelibly engraved on the consciousness of a generation of moviegoers; and Jones's novel remains perhaps the best fictional treatment of the U.S. Army. Despite its considerable length, it was, in fact, conceived by Jones as the first volume in an "Army trilogy," the last two volumes of which appeared as *The Thin Red Line* (1962) and *Whistle* (published posthumously in 1978).

—James R. Giles

FURTHER READING:

Garrett, George P. *James Jones.* New York, Harcourt Brace Jovanovich, 1984.

Gebert, Michael. *The Encyclopedia of Movie Awards.* New York, St. Martin's, 1996.

Giles, James. *James Jones.* Boston, Twayne, 1981.

Giles, James, and J. Michael Lennon. *The James Jones Reader.* New York, Birch Lane, 1991.

Harkness, John. *The Academy Awards Handbook.* New York, Windsor, 1994.

Hendrick, George, ed. *To Reach Eternity: The Letters of James Jones.* New York, Random House, 1989.

Kael, Pauline. *I Lost It at the Movies.* Boston, Atlantic Monthly Press, 1965.

LaGuardia, Robert. *Monty: A Biography of Montgomery Clift.* New York, Arbor House, 1977.

McShane, Frank. *Into Eternity: The Life of James Jones.* Boston, Houghton Mifflin, 1985.

Whipple, A. B. C. "James Jones and His Angel." *Life.* May 7, 1952, 143ff.

Frost, Robert (1874-1963)

The image of Robert Frost nurtured by most Americans is of a white-haired, rustic saint writing poems about the mellow glories of nature and the pastoral idylls of New England rural life. When not shining in this bucolic light, he glows with a patriotic aura as America's Poet Laureate reading his work at the inauguration of John F. Kennedy, presaging through his presence the imminent wonders promised by the young president's election. But this idealistic image of Frost was more the product of marketing by the poet himself than a true reflection of any innate homespun charm. Frost was, indeed, a great poet, but he was also a bitter, egotistical writer who resented the late recognition of his genius. To understand how he came to be both the great poet and bitter man requires foraging in the woods of his life.

Robert Frost was born in San Francisco, California, on March 26, 1874, the son of William Prescott Frost and Isabelle Moodie. Frost's father was a journalist whose drinking habits led to an early death by tuberculosis at age 34 in 1885. After his death, Frost's mother moved the family to Massachusetts, where Frost graduated as one of two valedictorians in 1892 from Lawrence High School. His co-valedictorian was his future wife, Elinor Miriam White. After high school, Frost enrolled at Dartmouth College, while Elinor attended St. Lawrence. Frost left Dartmouth early, unable to contain his bouts of jealousy over Elinor's refusal to leave her studies and marry him. After Elinor graduated in 1895, she took a teaching position at the school Frost's mother had started and shortly afterwards married Frost. Frost at the time worked as a teacher and reporter, publishing

Robert Frost

what little poetry could get past the stodgily Victorian editors who ruled the world of American letters. The Frosts started bearing children shortly after their marriage, increasing the pressure on Frost to make good on his own evolving opinion of himself as a poet worth serious consideration. Financial strains were eased when Frost's grandfather let the entire family reside at Derry Farm in New Hampshire. (The farm was shortly afterwards bequeathed, with a small annuity, to the still growing family.)

By 1907, Frost had six children and still no steady form of income beyond the annuity. On October 23, 1912, Frost left America for England, fed up with the obtuseness of the American poetry establishment. In England, he discovered an entirely new and altogether exciting world of letters. There were the modernist giants—Ezra Pound, T. S. Eliot, Ford Maddox Ford, William Butler Yeats—fashioning with great broad strokes a new poetic reality. Frost published his first book of poetry, *A Boy's Will,* in April 1913, which was favorably reviewed in Ezra Pound's *Poetry* within a month. Many of the poems featured in *A Boy's Will* had been written during Frost's years at Derry Farm, as were the poems in his next two works, *North of Boston* (1914) and *Mountain Interval* (1916). *North of Boston* offered some of Frost's best work, including ''After Apple-Picking'' and ''The Wood-Pile,'' while *Mountain Interval* featured ''The Road Not Taken'' and ''An Old Man's Winter Night.''

Frost returned to the United States after the publication of *North of Boston* to resounding critical praise. He was named Phi Beta Kappa Poet by Tufts University and a few years later at Harvard as well. His election to the National Institute of Arts and Letters and appointment as a professor at Amherst College assured the recognition he had always craved and the income he and his family had to do without for so long. In 1922, he received his first of four Pulitzer Prizes for poetry with his collection *New Hampshire,* which included ''Fire and Ice,'' ''Two Witches,'' and his most famous work, ''Stopping by Woods on a Snowy Evening.'' Five years later *West-Running Brook* appeared, again to high praise, but featuring, as did *New Hampshire,* individual poems with a decidedly political cast. In 1930, he received his second Pulitzer Prize for *Collected Poems of Robert Frost,* while in 1936 a third was awarded for the much more openly political *A Further Range.* Yet despite the obvious compliment implied in winning a third Pulitzer, *A Further Range* drew fire from major literary critics such as Newton Arvin and R.P. Blackmur for Frost's conservative overtones, which ran contrary to the general political feeling during the Great Depression.

In 1942, Frost received his fourth and last Pulitzer Prize for poetry. The collection responsible was *A Witness Tree,* which included ''Beech,'' ''The Most of It,'' ''November,'' and the poem he would read at Kennedy's inauguration 20 years later, ''The Gift Outright.'' Afterwards, Frost was never quite the same as a poet, despite the occasional powerful lyric. *Steeple Bush* (1947), *A Masque of Mercy* (1947), *A Masque of Reason* (1948), and *In the Clearing* (1962) were themselves vitiated by a writer whose creative genius had run its course and whose destiny appeared for the final 20 years of his life to be one of putting out collections of his earlier poetry and racking up all of the remaining accolades except the one he desired most, the Nobel Prize for literature.

Frost's genius emanated in large part from his conscious decision during the modernist era not to follow the lead of his fellow poets and experiment with *vers libre.* Frost's poems were thematically and metrically unified by his belief in the idea—shared by other American modernists like Wallace Stevens—that the chaos of reality is given order by the extension of the perceiver's will. A cross between the stoic naturalism of Jack London and Frank Norris and the American-ized Nietzcheanism of William James and John Dewey, Frost's poetry illustrates the ways in which the decaying effects of nature are held at bay by the forms into which we mold our understanding of our environment. As a result, Frost integrates the formal rigidities of blank verse and sonnet with a distinctly regional coloration that depends heavily on the use of common speech, standard word order, and metaphors grounded in natural events. Although, like other contemporaries, Frost saw in free verse an opportunity to retreat from the high diction of earlier poetical traditions, the chaotic freedom of its metrical format could not accommodate a personal philosophy that saw the economy and rhythm of poetry as an instrument for taming the uncertainties of lived reality. Thus in a poem like "Nothing Gold Can Stay," it is the simple rhyme scheme that staves off the decay of nature. Or consider his "Once by the Pacific," which attempts to contain the dark irony of the inherent destructiveness of nature in a highly structured metrical format. Even "Stopping by Woods on a Snowy Evening" manages to restrain the suicidal intensity of the narrator's tone, rhythmically counterbalancing his response to the woods "lovely, dark and deep" with the "promises" left "to keep." Frost's dark vision may belie the idyllic sweetness that has grown up around the image of him, but in many ways they represent far more closely the anxieties he sought to capture of the American spirit seeking to understand the limits of freedom and the wisest use of it.

—Bennett Lovett-Graff

FURTHER READING:

Frost, Robert. *Selected Letters of Robert Frost.* Edited by Lawrance Thompson. New York, Holt, Rinehart, & Winston, 1964.

Greiner, Donald J. *Robert Frost: The Poet and His Critics.* Chicago, American Library Association, 1974.

Lentricchia, Frank. *Robert Frost: Modern Poetics and the Land-scapes of Self.* Durham, Duke University Press, 1975.

Pritchard, William H. *Frost: A Literary Life Reconsidered.* New York, Oxford University Press, 1984.

Thomson, Lawrance. *Robert Frost: The Early Years, 1874-1915.* New York, Holt, Rinehart & Winston, 1966.

———. *Robert Frost: The Later Years, 1938-1963.* New York, Holt, Rinehart & Winston, 1976.

———. *Robert Frost: The Years of Triumph, 1915-1938.* New York, Holt, Rinehart & Winston, 1970.

Frosty the Snowman

Frosty the Snowman has entertained American children during the winter holidays since his creation in 1950. Frosty originated in the song, "Frosty the Snowman," by Steve Nelson and Jack Rollins which then inspired the Golden Book of 1951 adapted by Annie North Bedford and illustrated by Corine Malverne. The song and book tell of a snowman that comes alive and takes the children who created it on sledding and ice-skating adventures. But Frosty melts when he and the children go to the village to see the shop windows. Golden Books kept Frosty popular for later generations with an animated video narrated by Jimmy Durante (1969). For half a century, the song has

been included on Christmas albums by popular performers. The concept was also used in *Jack Frost* (1998), a motion picture starring Michael Keaton as a deceased father who comes back to life in the snowman built by his children.

—Sharon Brown

FURTHER READING:

Bedford, Annie North, and Corinne Malverne. *Frosty the Snowman.* New York, Simon and Schuster, 1951.

Frozen Entrées

Frozen entrées, appetizing or otherwise, came to revolutionize the social culture of America and, in due course, the entire First World. Although the science of quick freezing had its beginnings early in the century, by the 1950s, the development of the process and the successful marketing of frozen food products came both to reflect and advance wider changes in working, family, and social habits. Despite the criticism that has always attached to frozen cuisine by those of more discerning palates, convenience has triumphed over considerations of taste in sufficient quantity to support a massive frozen food industry. By the end of the twentieth century, these "instant meals" had become an accepted constituent of American domestic life.

People who lived in harsh winter conditions with access to ice and snow, had always slow-frozen foods as a means of preserving them. Slow freezing, however, causes irreparable harm to the cellular structure of organic material, making it barely edible when thawed out. Clarence Birdseye was the first to accomplish quick-freezing, inspired by his work as a naturalist and then a fur trader in Montana from 1910 to 1917. When Birdseye noticed that fish caught at temperatures of 50 degrees below zero froze almost immediately, and upon being thawed, were still fresh and tasty, he was inspired to develop his own quick-freezing techniques. He first employed these in 1924, freezing fish, fruits, and vegetables. He had two methods: to chill foods by means of a very cold (-40 to -45 degrees) calcium chlorate solution, or, through the vaporization of ammonia, to chill foods to -25 degrees. The other important component of successful quick-freezing, Birdseye discovered, was to encase the food in protective packaging before freezing it, and thus to protect it from the deleterious effects of direct contact with the cold.

In 1929, the Postum Company (founded by C. W. Post) bought Birdseye's frozen haddock factory and became General Foods. The first line of Birdseye frozen foods, which included peas, spinach, raspberries, cherries, meats, and fish appeared in 1930, but struggled to catch on in the marketplace for several reasons. The public was inclined to view the frozen foods with suspicion, considering that they were inferior in quality and fit only for institutional use, or even that they had been accidentally exposed to cold and then resold as "frozen." In addition, during the 1930s fewer than half of Americans had iceboxes or electric refrigerators, and fewer still had mechanical freezers in which to store frozen food. The first dual-compartment, dual-temperature refrigerator came on the market in 1939, promising greater success for frozen foods, but World War II forced appli-ance manufacturers to turn their production efforts toward war materials instead.

The end of the war brought a boom in retail manufacturing and sales, and also a new American ethos that began to value convenience over quality. General Foods had offered a few frozen dinners, such as Irish stew, in the 1930s, but the post-war culture saw a great expansion in frozen dinner lines. In 1945 Maxson Food Systems, Inc. introduced "Strato-Plates," individual frozen meals on trays for both military and civilian airplane passengers. In 1951 Swanson came up with Pot Pies, and followed these with their mass-marketed "TV Dinners" in 1955. A turkey dinner with cornbread dressing, gravy, peas, and sweet potatoes comprised their first offering and sold for about one dollar. Roast beef, fried chicken, Salisbury steak, and ham with raisin sauce quickly followed as additional entrée choices. Other companies eventually joined in the trend, among them Stouffer, Banquet, and On-Core. According to *Consumer Reports,* "By 1959 frozen dinners had become the best-selling of all frozen food items, outstripping the ever-popular meat pot pie." Americans bought 70 million dinners in 1955, 214 million in 1960, and an incredible two billion in 1994.

The first frozen dinners came in compartmentalized aluminum trays which held meat, vegetables, a starch (usually mashed potatoes), and dessert. The entire meal was baked in an oven anywhere from 45 minutes to two hours. These dinners represented a revolution in food preservation technology and, more significantly, a change in American eating patterns. The frozen dinner meant that American family members no longer had to eat the same thing at the same time; and the American housewife did not have to cook it. Children and husbands could prepare frozen dinners, and they could be eaten in front of the television on "TV trays," rather than at the dining room table. Further, people were no longer tied to the seasons or regions for their choice of food—quick-freezing meant that they could have any meat, fruit, or vegetable at any time.

Swanson launched the "Hungry Man's Dinner" in 1972, appealing to those who wanted larger quantities of meat and potatoes. During the 1970s the company also changed its product name from the "TV Dinner"—which had become a generic term in the American vocabulary—to the "Frozen Dinner." The 1980s saw an influx of new products. Individual dinners were broken up into individual components, with "frozen entrées" overtaking dinners in popularity. In 1986, the four-section aluminum tray had been superseded by plastic serving dishes, which could be placed in the microwave oven for quicker heating. These contained more specialized meals to suit various palates and dietary needs, and by 1990, 651 new entrées came on the market, compared with 55 dinners that same year. Companies introduced ethnic cuisine, pizzas, gourmet meals, side dishes, cakes, and pies. Lean Cuisine, Budget Gourmet, Le Menu, Weight Watchers, and Healthy Choice were among the main market competitors producing these ranges.

For all the apparent variety that frozen entrées offer, people generally agree that the food is mediocre at best. Meats contain fillers and constitute only a small percentage of the total food in the dinner, while vegetables taste bland and too often need the addition of salt. Nonetheless, with the development of domestic technologies, leading to the widespread popularity of freezers and microwave ovens in the home, attitudes to eating have changed. Where once the evening dinner was a requisite social activity that reinforced familial bonds, by the 1990s people were content to eat their own individual meals alone, sacrificing taste and conviviality for standardization and convenience.

—Wendy Woloson

FURTHER READING:

"Better than TV Dinners?" *Consumer Reports.* March 1984, 126-127, 170.

I'll Buy That! 50 Small Wonders and Big Deals that Revolutionized the Lives of Consumers. Mount Vernon, New York, Consumers Union, 1986.

Stern, Jane, and Michael Stern. *The Encyclopedia of Bad Taste.* New York, HarperCollins, 1990.

Volti, Rudi. "How We Got Frozen Food." *Invention and Technology,* Spring 1994, 47-56.

Fu Manchu

First introduced to western reading audiences in 1913 by Sax Rohmer (pseudonym of Arthur Sarsfield Wade, 1883-1959), Fu Manchu quickly became considered the quintessential sinister Chinese villain. Featured in over a dozen books, Fu Manchu used blackmail, kidnapping, and murder in his efforts to achieve world domination. The popularity of Fu Manchu increased when the character with the long face, goatee, and wispy mustache hit the silver screen (1920s), radio airwaves (1920s-30s), comic books (1930s), and television (1950s). Since his creation, Fu Manchu has become a damaging stereotype for Asians, suggesting that they are inscrutable and evil. Fu Manchu has also become the name for a style of beard (goatee and thin mustache), and a popular California rock band that released its first album in 1990.

—Midori Takagi

FURTHER READING:

Van Ash, Cay. *Master of Villainy; A Biography of Sax Rohmer.* Ohio, Bowling Green University Popular Press, 1972.

The Fugitive

A man wrongly convicted of the murder of his wife escapes the train taking him to death row. He wanders America in search of the real killer, a one-armed man, pursued by the lieutenant who investigated the murder and lost the prisoner. This was the story of the ABC television drama *The Fugitive.* The saga of Dr. Richard Kimble and Lt. Gerard, a mix of *Les Miserables* and a real life case, produced not only the highest rated television series broadcast of the 1960s, but also a hit movie and a sequel in the 1990s.

The series first aired September 17, 1963. Roy Huggins, who had created *Maverick* and would co-create *The Rockford Files,* devised *The Fugitive* based heavily on the Victor Hugo novel *Les Miserables,* with Lt. Gerard based on Inspector Javert, the indefatigable pursuer. But *The Fugitive* was also inspired by the real-life case of Dr. Sam Shepard, who was sentenced to prison for killing his wife after a sensational trial. He always maintained someone else had killed his wife and in fact he was later acquitted after winning a new trial. (The appeal, based on the circuslike atmosphere of the original trial, went to the United States Supreme Court and launched the career of F. Lee Bailey. Shepard died a few years after his release, tarnished

David Janssen, star of the television show *The Fugitive.*

by the case. His son is still trying to have the state of Ohio pardon his father, due to the fact that later DNA testing of blood evidence indicates that Shepard may not have been the murderer.)

Huggins devised the basic plot, explained in the opening narration of each episode. Dr. Richard Kimble, convicted of killing his wife, was riding to prison on a train, shackled to Lt. Gerard. Kimble was still insisting a one-armed man killed his wife. The train crashed, Kimble was thrown clear, and escaped. Dyeing his hair, changing his name, he traveled America, working a series of odd jobs and intruding on guest stars' crises, always eluding Lt. Gerard. David Janssen, with his world-weary manner and voice, played Kimble; Barry Morse showed up several times a season as Gerard. Bill Raisch played the one-armed man. The series trademark was actor William Conrad's dramatic voiceover in the title sequence, explaining the backstory, and announcing "The Fugitive—A QM Production." (QM stood for producer Quinn Martin). The series won an Emmy for best Drama in 1965-66 (its only nomination), and Janssen was nominated several times for best actor (1963-64, 1964-65, and 1966-67).

In 1967, ABC cancelled the series and producers decided to go out with a flourish, wrapping up the story in a two-part episode airing at the very end of *The Fugitive*'s last season. The final episode, airing August 29, 1967, had Kimble corner the one-armed man and Gerard arrive in time to hear the man confess. Conrad read the closing narration, "August 29. The day the running stopped." The episode was the most viewed episode of a regular series until that time and its 72 percent share of the viewing audience stood as a landmark until the "Who Shot JR?" resolution episode of *Dallas*. Ironically, the show's famous ending was said to have worked against it. While ABC ran

daytime repeats of the series the following year (April 1967 to March 1968), the series was never a big hit in syndication.

In the 1990s, with the burgeoning market for revivals of old TV series, *The Fugitive* seemed to be a natural, despite the death of Janssen. It took a while to get off the ground, but the movie finally made it to the screen in August 1993. Dr. Richard Kimble became a top-notch surgeon in Chicago, whose wife is murdered by a one-armed man as part of a plot to cover up a medical company's corruption. Again, Kimble escapes in a spectacular train crash. However, he's hunted by a federal officer this time, U.S. Marshal Sam Gerard, who has no connection with the case (and, famously, when Kimble insists "I didn't kill my wife" responds, "I don't care").

The movie focused on Kimble's efforts to track the one-armed man while Gerard and his oddball team try to track Kimble. Gerard investigates the crime in an effort to find Kimble, but he uncovers more and more evidence that Kimble didn't commit the crime until, like the original Gerard, he is on Kimble's side when he confronts the villain. The presence of Harrison Ford as Kimble, plus the taut script, made the movie a hit, but it was Tommy Lee Jones as Gerard who stole the show, and the Oscar and Golden Globe for Best Supporting Actor. The film's other Oscar nominations were for Best Picture, Sound Effects Editing, Film Editing, Original Score, and Sound.

After much wrangling over whether Ford would be back for the inevitable sequel, it was Jones and his ragtag team who made it to the 1998 sequel, *U.S. Marshals,* in which they sought another fugitive.

—Michele Lellouche

FURTHER READING:

Robertson, Ed. *The Fugitive Recaptured: The 30th Anniversary Companion to a Television Classic.* Beverly Hills, California, Pomegranate Press, 1996.

Fuller, Buckminster (1895-1983)

Best known as the inventor of the Geodesic Dome, engineer, architect, inventor, and philosopher Buckminster Fuller epitomized old-fashioned American know-how, and was an apostle of the democratizing possibilities of technology. Convinced his inventions and designs might prove the salvation of the human race, for more than 50 years the diminutive autodidact talked a blue streak, tirelessly lecturing to audiences around the world, all the while churning out a seemingly endless procession of designs and elaborations on earlier designs. Circumnavigating the globe twice in the year of his death, he went to his grave convinced of the efficacy of these beliefs—that one day, his inventions would revolutionize human life.

Born to an illustrious New England family, Richard Buckminster Fuller (nicknamed Bucky as a child, an appellation he would never outgrow) was an awkward child with poor eyesight and mismatched legs requiring the insertion of a lift in one shoe. His physical defects were countered with a precocious intelligence and startling perspicacity, abetted, in fact, by his poor eyesight, which taught him not to trust overly the verity of physical appearances. A late bloomer, Bucky twice was sent down from Harvard, and at nineteen his family apprenticed him to a Canadian cotton mill.

In 1922, Fuller was again out of work when his four-year-old daughter, Alexandra, died, victim to the postwar influenza epidemic. Fuller would later credit this event with sparking his interest in housing, becoming obsessed with the part drafty houses played in spreading the contagion. As a salesman for his father-in-law's company, selling a new building technique, he rose to vice president before his father-in-law sold his shares and Fuller was let go. Contemplating suicide on the shores of Lake Michigan, a "private vision" spoke to Fuller, saying, "You do not have the right to eliminate yourself. You do not belong to you. You belong to the universe." Like Saul's vision on the road to Damascus, this experience galvanized Fuller into action.

He removed his small family (a second daughter having been born in 1927) to a Chicago tenement, beginning a year of intense introspection. Fuller devoured books at a fantastic rate and emerged from his year of unceasing cerebration the author of an impenetrable thirty-thousand-word essay alternately titled "4-D" or "Timelock," and designer of a mass-produced house, also called 4-D. The former was privately published and sent out to two hundred notables, many of whom professed incomprehension. The latter, whose patent application had been turned down, was presented as a gift to the American Institute of Architects, who imperiously rejected it, saying they could not endorse "pea in a pod" designs.

Fuller was nothing if not resolute. He spent the 1930s refining his Dymaxion house design—interrupted by three years devoted to a revolutionary but flawed vehicle called, fittingly enough, the "Dymaxion car." Frequently, he wrote about technology for *Fortune* magazine and published his own journal, *Shelter*. During World War II, Fuller served under Henry J. Kaiser on the Board of Economic Warfare and used his position to promote the Dymaxion house. In 1944, he submitted a proposal to Kaiser in which he craftily combined the exigencies of economic conversion with the anticipated housing shortage brought on by the legions of returning vets. His solution was to refit aircraft manufacturing to mass-produce his house, using the same light-weight duralumin used to manufacture planes. Kaiser thought enough of the idea to finance its development. The 1946 Wichita house, produced at Beech Aircraft's Wichita facility, was the first successful application of Fuller's precepts, anticipating the mass-produced suburbs of the 1950s. Some 60,000 houses were ordered, but Fuller insisted on further refinements, and in his intransigence, he lost his backers; Fuller Houses, Inc., dissolved into nothingness.

This failure drove him into the world of academia. Always loquacious, the job of lecturer was perfectly suited to Fuller and gave him the opportunity to refine his ideas without the fickle backing of industry. He moved from university to university, and while in residence at the now-famous experimental Black Mountain College, Fuller built his first Geodesic Dome. It was made from vinyl louvers and collapsed within seconds of erection. But in 1949, Fuller received a patent for the Geodesic Dome and founded Geodesics, Inc. He received royalties for each dome built, so for the first time in his life, Fuller was free from economic woes. He could devote more time to what he called "thinking out loud." Traveling incessantly, circling the globe so often he was given to wearing five watches at a time, Fuller would talk to audiences for four or five hours at a stretch.

By the 1960s, he had become a counterculture legend, the messiah of modern technology, and film exists of the diminutive Bucky, with his thick glasses, close-shorn white hair, and conservative, three-piece suits, lecturing to auditoriums full of ecstatic hippies. His commission for the 1967 Montreal Expo, and perhaps his crowning achievement, was a magnificent seventy-six-meter-wide dome encased in transparent plastic tiles; it was photographed endlessly, gracing magazine covers worldwide. One visitor wrote: "Inside the dome the walls start going away from you . . . suddenly you realize the walls are not really there . . . And it was not done according

to the aesthetics of architecture as it had been practiced up to then. It was done simply in terms of doing the most with the least."

For the rest of his life, Fuller refined and expanded upon the implications of this idea. Martin Pawley writes, "Fuller had converted the Bauhaus epigram 'Less is more' into its Dymaxion derivative 'More for less.'" The domes themselves were the first link in this thought-chain; tensegrity, a building application utilizing continuous tension/discontinuous compression, was a further refinement. Tensegrity made building structures of enormous size and tensile strength—for instance, a three-kilometer dome that could enclose a part of Manhattan—a possibility. Fuller published elaborate schemata for these and other ideas verging upon science fiction. He envisioned enormous housing developments, self-sufficient islands set offshore, or kilometer-high pyramids, one of which he imagined as replacing a blighted Harlem. Fuller had logged out a logarithm of human need, and he would follow its varied implications to their logical conclusions. In 1983, he collapsed and died at his wife's bedside; she died thirty-six hours later.

From his "silent year" in Chicago onward, Fuller had worked ceaselessly for the betterment of mankind, seeing in his creations the means to realize a more equitable society. But outside of certain limited applications, (the Geodesic Dome house enjoyed a brief vogue with hippies, although industrial applications have proved more enduring), Fuller's inventions failed to revolutionize modern culture. The philosophical underpinnings of his inventions (altruism, ephemeralization, mass housing) remained unpopular ideas—if intermittently expedient. But Fuller saw his creations as part of the evolutionary process, envisioning that his revolutionary designs would inevitably supplant conventional architecture. One day history may prove him correct.

—Michael Baers

FURTHER READING:

Fuller, R. Buckminster, and Robert Marks. *The Dymaxion World of Buckminster Fuller.* Garden City, Anchor Press, 1973.

Kenner, Hugh. *Bucky: A Guided Tour of Buckminster Fuller.* New York, Morrow, 1973.

Meller, James, ed. *The Buckminster Fuller Reader.* London, Jonathan Cape, 1970.

Pawley, Martin. *Buckminster Fuller.* New York, Taplinger Publishing Company, 1990.

Ward, James, ed. *The Artifacts of R. Buckminster Fuller.* Vols. I-IV. New York, Garland Publishing, 1985.

Fundamentalism

The emergence, growth, and entrenchment of fundamentalism as an active ideological stance in the course of the twentieth century became a major source of social and cultural controversy within the United States. As the twentieth century began, the effects of modernism and secularism on American culture produced a growing sense of alarm among conservative Protestants, who believed that these innovations threatened to undermine the traditional values and moral authority of evangelical Christianity. They responded by reasserting their unyielding commitment to certain fundamental beliefs, such as the divine authorship and literal truth of the Bible, and by working to ensure the survival of those beliefs in American institutions and public life. By the 1920s, this movement came to be known as fundamentalism, and, since that time, its views have permeated swathes of the social and cultural fabric of America. The fundamentalists' stand against innovations in theology and their strict adherence to Biblical doctrine have repeatedly placed them in conflict with mainstream trends in American popular culture—not only in religion, but in the realms of education, politics, entertainment, and the arts. In resisting such trends, fundamentalists have also engaged in various forms of activism, from public demonstration to political organization, and in the process have made their influence felt throughout American society.

The fundamentalist movement originated within the evangelical Protestant churches, particularly among Baptists and Presbyterians. An emphasis on revivalism and the conversion experience had contributed to the rapid growth of the evangelical churches during the 1800s, and by the end of the century they defined the mainstream of religious life in the United States. As they grew, however, these groups found it increasingly difficult to maintain a denominational consensus on certain theological issues. One major source of controversy was the doctrine of biblical inerrancy, which asserted that the Bible is literally true in every detail. Liberal adherents of the evangelical churches gradually abandoned this doctrine, arguing that the Bible must be reinterpreted within the context of contemporary thought. In their view, for example, the biblical account of creation could not be taken literally because it conflicted with the findings of modern science. Conservatives, on the other hand, rejected modernist revisions of the meaning of scripture, holding to the idea that the Bible contains factual truth, and believing that to say otherwise undermined the certainties of their faith.

Another important controversy developed around the doctrine of dispensational millennialism, which became widely accepted among conservative Protestants late in the 1800s. According to this doctrine, human history comprises a series of distinct eras, or dispensations. During each dispensation, humanity is subjected to a divine test which it ultimately fails, resulting in a catastrophic event such as the banishment from Eden, the Flood of Genesis, or the crucifixion of Christ. Dispensational millennialism asserts that the end of the next-to-last dispensation is approaching, and will be followed by the final dispensation, the ''Millennial Age,'' during which Christ will rule on earth for a thousand years. Although this doctrine was not universally accepted by conservatives, it became a major theme in the thinking of key fundamentalist leaders during the late nineteenth and early twentieth centuries, clearly setting them apart from moderate and liberal Protestants who, by this time, had begun to de-emphasize the supernatural aspects of Christian belief.

As these theological controversies developed, liberals and conservatives within the evangelical Protestant denominations found themselves increasingly at odds with one another. Both sides tried to ensure that their point of view would define their denomination's policies and statements of faith; as a result, bitter disputes developed within several of the larger Protestant groups. Some of the evangelical denominations actually experienced little conflict, because one side or the other dominated their membership so thoroughly. The widespread acceptance of modernist theology by Congregationalists, for example, precluded extensive debate within that group, as did, conversely, the widespread rejection of modernism by the Southern Baptists. But within other groups, such as the Northern Baptists, Northern Presbyterians, and Disciples of Christ, the diversity of beliefs led to serious conflict. In each of these denominations,

however, fundamentalists in the end lacked the numbers needed to ensure that their views would prevail. Realizing that the spread of modernism had made it impossible for them to take control of these groups, the fundamentalist faction within each split off from its parent body to start a new denomination.

The fundamentalists' failure to control most of the large evangelical denominations did not deter them from promoting their views. They established a variety of programs and organizations that focused on advancing the fundamentalist cause outside of the existing structure of Protestant denominations. An early example of these non-denominational efforts was the publication of a series of booklets, entitled *The Fundamentals*, which described and justified various conservative theological positions. Distributed to religious leaders, students, and pastors throughout the English-speaking world, these booklets helped spread the fundamentalist message, and provided the source of the fundamentalist movement's name. Fundamentalists also established dozens of non-denominational Bible institutes and colleges during the early twentieth century, in part to provide clergy for the many independent fundamentalist churches organized during this period. And as the century progressed, fundamentalists became very active in religious broadcasting, which enabled them to disseminate their beliefs to much larger audiences than they could reach within the confines of their own congregations.

While developing its own institutional structure, the fundamentalist movement adopted an increasingly oppositional stance with respect to contemporary culture, and began to develop strategies to reform American society. The first major issue raised by the fundamentalists in this context was the teaching of scientific concepts that contradicted traditional interpretations of the Bible. They focused in particular on the teaching of evolution in public schools and universities, which they sought to ban either by legislation or through the regulations of local school districts. Anti-evolution laws were subsequently enacted in a number of states, primarily in the South where the influence of fundamentalism was greatest. The controversy surrounding these laws became widely publicized during a celebrated case in Tennessee, the so-called Scopes Monkey Trial, in which biology teacher John Scopes was tried in 1925 for violating the state ban on teaching Darwin's theory of evolution. Although this event provided a forum for one of the most eloquent supporters of the fundamentalist position, William Jennings Bryan, it also subjected fundamentalists to widespread criticism and ridicule in the national and international press, perhaps most notably by columnist H. L. Mencken. As a result, the movement lost much of its credibility, and became increasingly alienated from the mainstream of American popular culture.

Following their defeats within the mainstream denominations and in the public debate over the teaching of evolution, fundamentalists entered a period of withdrawal and consolidation. Rather than attempting to reform society at large, they concentrated on building a separate structure of religious institutions consisting of Bible colleges and institutes, non-denominational fundamentalist churches, independent missionary organizations, revival meetings, and the like. They also became increasingly involved in religious broadcasting, first in radio and then television. Televangelism provided an especially effective outlet for the fundamentalists' efforts to expand their base of support. By enabling them to operate outside traditional institutional structures, it gave them a means of addressing new, untapped audiences as well as their existing followers. The broadcast media also suited the preaching style of many of the leading fundamentalist evangelists, who relied heavily on their personal charisma. Through such efforts, fundamentalism remained an active if unobtrusive force within American culture during the 1950s and 1960s.

A conservative turn in American politics during the 1970s gave fundamentalists a new opportunity to bring their agenda before the public. Through movements such as the Moral Majority and the Christian Coalition, fundamentalists became extensively involved in political action during the 1970s and 1980s, and formed the core of the "new religious right." Although the religious right supported a range of conservative positions on policy issues, the fundamentalists' primary goal was again to reform American society by addressing issues of faith and morality. They were especially concerned with trends that appeared either to undermine traditional religious belief or to limit the traditional role of religion in American life. They again confronted the issue of the teaching of evolution in public schools, now cast as a conflict between Darwinian theory and creationism, a defense of the Biblical account of creation presented in scientific terms; and in a number of locales, primarily in the South and West, they succeeded in influencing curricular policies, although not to the point of banning evolution from science classes. Their concern with the public role of religion not only involved them most directly in the effort to restore prayer to the public schools, but also engaged them in the debates over a variety of social issues and public policy that they believed should be guided by religious principles. These issues included gay rights, pornography, immorality in the entertainment industry, and equal rights for women. They continued to face strong opposition from moderates and liberals on these issues, but, nonetheless, their efforts to organize politically substantially enhanced their influence on American culture, particularly during the Reagan administration of the 1980s, when candidates such as Pat Robertson entered the active political arena.

During the 1990s, fundamentalists maintained their commitment to political action, although developments at the national level, such as Pat Robertson's failed bid for the Republican presidential nomination in 1988, led many to focus on local or grassroots efforts. Control of local school boards became one of the most common objectives of fundamentalists in their attempts to influence public policy. They also adopted a more direct approach to expressing their opposition to trends within the entertainment industry through boycotts of entertainment production companies and their advertisers. Thus, although its prominence in national politics had declined, fundamentalism continued to offer a substantive critique of mainstream American culture. Finally, it has also provided a model for understanding the resurgence of militant religious traditionalism in other regions of the world, within religious cultures as different as Islam, Judaism, and Hinduism. In this sense, the term "fundamentalism" now applies not only to a conservative wing of evangelical Protestantism in the United States, but to a variety of analogous social trends, sometimes accompanied by the violence of "Holy war," that have developed around the globe.

—Roger W. Stump

FURTHER READING:

Ammerman, Nancy T. *Bible Believers: Fundamentalists in the Modern World*. New Brunswick, New Jersey, Rutgers University Press, 1987.

Brasher, Brenda E. *Godly Women: Fundamentalism and Female Power*. New Brunswick, New Jersey, Rutgers University Press, 1998.

Carpenter, Joel A. *Revive Us Again: The Reawakening of American Fundamentalism*. New York, Oxford University Press, 1997.

Lawrence, Bruce B. *Defenders of God: The Fundamentalist Revolt Against the Modern Age*. San Francisco, Harper and Row, 1989.

Marsden, George M. *Fundamentalism and American Culture: The Shaping of Twentieth Century Evangelism, 1870-1925*. New York, Oxford University Press, 1980.

Marty, Martin E., and R. Scott Appleby, editors. *Fundamentalisms Comprehended*. Chicago, University of Chicago Press, 1995.

Sandeen, Ernest R. *The Roots of Fundamentalism: British and American Millenarianism, 1800-1930*. Chicago, University of Chicago Press, 1970.

Funicello, Annette (1942—)

During the height of her fame at Walt Disney Pictures, *Mickey Mouse Club* star Annette Funicello received more mail than the studio's two most popular leading "men": Mickey Mouse and Zorro. To young people she was, quite simply, the quintessential dream girl. Males liked her because, over the course of the series' run, from 1955 to 1959, she blossomed into a buxom beauty before their eyes. Females liked her for her sweetness and sincerity, and for her winning smile. She was so beloved that she became known, and was often billed, by her first name alone.

Annette Funicello

Born in Utica, New York, Annette was twelve years old when Walt Disney saw her dancing the lead in *Swan Lake* at a school recital. Annette had dreamed of becoming a ballerina. She instead donned mouse ears to become an original member of Disney's pioneering children's show. Emerging as the series' most popular performer, Annette was increasingly showcased, even starring in her own *Mickey Mouse Club* serial, "Annette." Disney also licensed Annette merchandise, including paper dolls, lunch pails, and jewelry. And in the tradition of "girl detectives" Nancy Drew and Trixie Belden, a fictional Annette starred in a series of books in which she helped solve mysteries.

Meanwhile, fan magazines recounted the seemingly fairy-tale existence of the real-life teen idol. Readers learned of her romance with another teen idol, Paul Anka, which was inspiration for his hit tune "Puppy Love." Fans likewise were treated to details about her customized T-Bird, with its forty coats of purple paint, purple tuck-and-roll upholstery, and purple carpeting. Along with cruising the streets of Burbank, home to the Disney studio, Annette cruised the airwaves. It was her popularity, more than vocal talents, that led to strong record sales for songs including "Tall Paul," "First Name Initial," "How Will I Know My Love?" and "Pineapple Princess." Among the 15 albums she turned out on the Disneyland/Vista label were those bearing the titles *Hawaiiannette, Italiannette,* and *Danceannette.*

When the *Mickey Mouse Club* ended its run, Annette was the only Mouseketeer to remain under contract to Disney. She appeared in a string of movies for the studio including *The Shaggy Dog* (1959) and *Babes in Toyland* (1961), and then segued to American International Pictures for *Beach Party.* The 1963 sand-and-surf youth picture found her cast opposite Frankie Avalon, whom she had dated in the 1950s. In *Beach Party,* the raven-haired Annette managed to be both voluptuous and wholesome. Honoring the request of her mentor, Walt Disney, she would not wear a navel-baring bikini. Nor would her screen character succumb to her boyfriend's romantic urges. As an unapologetic Annette once related, "My big line was always, 'Not without a ring you don't'. . . [and] I believed what I was saying wholeheartedly." In large part because of the Avalon-Funicello chemistry, *Beach Party* spawned a series of sequels, including *How to Stuff a Wild Bikini* (1965) and *Pajama Party* (1964). Annette also ventured into the fast track with a pair of innocuous car-racing movies opposite Avalon and Fabian, respectively. And she put in a cameo in the 1968 cult picture *Head,* starring the Monkees.

During the 1970s and for much of the 1980s, the twice-married mother of three made only intermittent appearances on TV, including as a pitch woman for products such as Skippy peanut butter. She did not return to the screen until 1987's *Back to the Beach,* in which she and Avalon poked fun at their anachronistic images. Their reunion prompted a wave of nostalgic publicity. In fact, such was Annette's status that her watershed moments have become media milestones. When she was married for the first time, the famed *Peanuts* comic strip depicted Snoopy the dog lamenting, "I can't stand it! This is terrible! How depressing—Annette Funicello has grown up!" A more sobering milestone was Annette's 1992 disclosure that she suffered from multiple sclerosis. An entire generation suddenly felt much older, as well as sadder.

Despite her illness, Annette went on to launch several new business ventures, including a line of collectible teddy bears. She also authored an optimistic, scandal-free autobiography, which became a highly rated TV movie. With hopes of finding an eventual cure for MS and other neurological disorders, she has also set up the Annette Funicello Research Fund for Neurological Diseases.

—Pat H. Broeske

FURTHER READING:

Anderson, Nancy. "What Is an Annette? Who Is She? How Did She Get That Way?" *Photoplay.* September 1959, 57-58, 71-72.

Broeske, Pat H. "Annette, Frankie on Nostalgia Wave in Beach Film Update." *Los Angeles Times.* August 3, 1987, VI, 1, 8.

Funicello, Annette, with Patricia Romanowski. *A Dream Is a Wish Your Heart Makes: My Story.* New York, Hyperion, 1994.

Santoli, Lorraine. *The Official Mickey Mouse Club Book.* New York, Hyperion, 1995.

Funk

A rhythmically-driven, bass-heavy form of Black music, funk provided the bridge between 1960s soul music and late-1970s Disco. Emerging in America at the same time as the civil rights movement, funk became implicitly associated with Black pride because of its unapologetic celebration of traits that were often negatively associated with Black people. The key attributes that separated funk from other forms of popular music were expressiveness, unbridled sexual energy and a raw, gritty attitude. After its 1970s commercial heyday, funk continued to influence a variety of genres, most notably hip-hop—with the massive back-catalog of funk records providing a large reservoir of different sounds.

As a musical form, credit for funk's origins is overwhelmingly given to James Brown. As a bandleader, he developed the use of the guitar, horns, and keyboards as purely rhythmic instruments used to support the bass and drum rhythm section. One of the first funk recordings is considered to be James Brown's 1965 single "Papa's Got a Brand New Bag," which provided the syncopated blueprint for many of his later recordings such as "Cold Sweat," "Funky Drummer," and—the quintessential Black pride song—"Say it Loud, I'm Black and I'm Proud." The rhythmic experimentalism of these songs would widely be imitated, and expanded upon, by the likes of Sly & the Family Stone, Parliament-Funkadelic and Curtis Mayfield.

As a genre, funk's lineage can be traced relatively easily. But as a term, "funk's" origins are more unclear, though the following explanations are most likely. Just like jazz and rock 'n' roll, funk was used as a euphemism for sexual activity in many African-American communities throughout much of the twentieth century. Funk was used to connote something that is dirty and sexual, and by the late 1960s it soon became associated with the most earthy, gritty, and raw dancable forms of Black music.

Though it is possible to overemphasize Brown's importance in the development of funk, it is hard to do because many of the players pulled into Brown's orbit and schooled by him went on to become key players in the genre. Most notably, Fred Wesley, Pee Wee Ellis, Maceo Parker, and Bootsy Collins went on to play in Parliament-Funkadelic, Fred Wesley's Horny Horns, Bootsy Collins' Rubber Band, and a slew of lesser-known but no less significant outfits.

Funk was rife with fusion. Jazz musicians immediately gravitated toward funk, with Miles Davis, Herbie Hancock, Lonnie Smith, and Donald Byrd (who formed the popular Blackbyrds in the 1970s) pioneering Jazz-fusion. Jimmy Castor and Rufus Thomas used funk to score a number of weird, dancable novelty hits, while other acts like War, Graham Central Station, and Mandrill fused rock with funk by adding a heavier beat and more distorted guitars.

Artists like Bootsy Collins, particularly during his tenure in the George Clinton-masterminded operation Parliament-Funkadelic, pushed the envelope of what was acceptable in Black and popular music. And others like Sly & the Family Stone blurred the lines between rock, soul, and funk music on dense, high concept albums like *There's a Riot Goin' On.* Silky-smooth soul stars soon incorporated funk into their music, with musicians like Curtis Mayfield, Stevie Wonder, Al Green, and Marvin Gaye making some of the best music of their careers using strains of funk.

Though the genre was dominated by men, which was typical of any genre of the time, Millie Jackson, Betty Davis, and Jean Knight proved that women could add a female-centered perspective to the music, and still be just as tough and assertive as their male counterparts.

By the late 1970s, the experimental left-of-center nature of funk had been largely smoothed over by the standardized pulsating beat of disco. During the 1980s, when slickness ruled the R & B and pop airwaves, the raw crudeness that characterized funk made it a dirty word again—commercially speaking, at least. At this time, many of the most essential funk recordings had gone out of print, and interest in the genre had waned. But the emergence of hip-hop, with its widespread use of 1960s and 1970s funk samples, rejuvenated interest in classic funk recordings by the late 1980s. Referring to a hip-hop song by Eric B. & Rakim that sampled James Brown, hip-hop group Stetsasonic rapped in their song 1988 song, "Talkin' All That Jazz": "Tell the Truth/James Brown was old/Til Eric B. came out with 'I Got Soul'/Rap brings back old R & B/If we would not/People could have forgot."

As the result of hip-hop artists sampling old funk records and the extensive reissues of funk albums on compact disc, Bootsy Collins, George Clinton, Maceo Parker, James Brown, and others maintained modestly successful careers throughout the 1990s, touring and releasing records.

—Kembrew McLeod

FURTHER READING:

George, Nelson. *The Death of Rhythm and Blues.* New York, Plume, 1988.

Vincent, Rickey. *Funk: The Music, the People and the Rhythm of The One.* New York, St. Martin's Griffin, 1986.

Fusco, Coco (1960—)

Born Juliana Emilia Fusco Miyares in New York City, Coco Fusco is a Cuban-American performance artist, writer, teacher, and cultural critic. After earning a B.A. in Semiotics and Literature and Society from Brown University in 1982 and an M.A. from Stanford University's Modern Thought and Literature program in 1985, Fusco first worked as a curator and writer and then turned primarily to developing sociopolitically infused performance art that would, as she writes in her book *English Is Broken Here,* "make sense out of the clashes between cultures" that shape U.S. Latino/a identities. One of her more controversial *tableaux vivants,* titled "Two Undiscovered Aborigines Visit. . ." was first performed in 1992 to critique the quincentennial celebration of Columbus' discovery of America. Fusco and collaborator Guillermo Gómez-Pena posed as "exotic" Caribbean islanders in a museum cage for three days, performing what anthropologists call "traditional tasks." As a symbolic act expressing five hundred years of resistance to colonial oppression, the piece, as Fusco states in *English Is Broken Here,* performs a "reverse ethnography," blurring the distinctions between art object and body, reality and fantasy, history and dramatic enactment. In 1993 "Two Undiscovered Aborigines Visit. . ." was invited to several international exhibitions including the 1993 Whitney Biennial, the 1992 Sydney Biennial, and the 1992 Edge Festival in London and Madrid.

Fusco has brought her performance art on tour to Europe, Australia, the United States, New Zealand, South Africa, Canada, and Latin America. She is also actively committed to identifying—through her journalism, teaching, and curatorial work—films and other art media that have been censored within the U.S. and abroad. Coco Fusco's performance art and other critical inquiries into Latino/a culture have complicated the erstwhile notion of an "authentic" Latino identity; her interrogation of identity as formed by senses of nation, race, sexuality, gender, and class has helped to dramatically alter the way ethnic identity is understood today.

—Frederick Luis Aldama

FURTHER READING:

Fusco, Coco. *English Is Broken Here: Notes on Cultural Fusion in the Americas.* New York, New Press, 1995.

G

Gable, Clark (1901-1960)

An icon of Hollywood's Golden Age, Clark Gable was dubbed "The King," and so he remained, a symbol of commanding virility through dozens of indifferent films, three generations of leading ladies, and the eventual decline—but never the entire death—of his popularity. His own golden age was the 1930s, and his image—tough, confident, and handsome—reached its apogee and has spoken to all generations since in the guise of Rhett Butler, famously and frankly not giving a damn about loving and leaving the ravishing Scarlett O'Hara (Vivien Leigh) in *Gone with the Wind* (1939).

The word macho, not yet in use in the 1930s, might have been coined for Clark Gable. The rough-hewn independence of his screen persona cannot have been unconnected to his own background. Born William Clark Gable in Ohio, the son of an itinerant oil-driller, he left school at fourteen to labor in an Akron factory. It was there that he first saw a play, determined on a life in the theater, and got himself some bit parts with a stock company before his father took him away to drill oil until he was twenty-one. Penniless, he worked at lumberjacking and other odd jobs until he joined a touring theater company run by Josephine Dillon, a veteran actress fourteen years his senior.

Clark Gable

The young Gable was then a gangling youth with jug ears and bad teeth, which Dillon paid to have fixed. She also coached him in acting and, in 1924, became his first wife. (They divorced in 1930.) The couple settled in Hollywood where Gable picked up a few engagements as a movie extra before going on the road again, eventually making it to Broadway and thence to the lead in the Los Angeles production of *The Last Mile*. MGM and Warners both rejected him after screen tests, but he played a villain for Pathe in a William Boyd Western, *The Painted Desert* (1931), and MGM came back with a contract.

In 1931, Gable began his twenty-three-year tenure at MGM with a bit part as a milkman in *The Easiest Way;* by the end of the year he was a star. Not yet sporting his trademark mustache, the actor had a threatening mien well-suited to playing brutes and roughnecks, which he did in several supporting roles before starring as Norma Shearer's gangster lover, slapping her around in *A Free Soul;* costarring in two of seven films—*Laughing Sinners* and *Possessed*—with Joan Crawford, a pairing that made for a potent sexual charge on screen (and off); and essaying a nobler character as Garbo's ill-used swain in *Susan Lenox: Her Fall and Rise.* Also that year, he married wealthy socialite Rhea Langham, seventeen years his senior.

Swiftly established as the archetypal "man's man," tough, rugged, and confident, whose good looks and earthy sex appeal also fed the fantasies of legions of women. Gable's rating rose even higher in 1932 with the studio's incendiary combination of the actor with their newest female star, Jean Harlow, in *Red Dust.* They made three more films together before Harlow's untimely death during the filming of their last, *Saratoga* (1937). However, despite his popularity, MGM's choice of vehicles for their premier male star often appeared decidedly odd. Throughout his career, much of the material foisted upon him was run-of-the-mill, and it seemed as though, rather than capitalizing on his charisma to create films of real quality, the bosses exploited his drawing power to sell the mediocre. Efforts in 1932 to lift him out of the rut of his typecasting were even odder: reunited with Norma Shearer in the film version of Eugene O'Neill's *Strange Interlude* and quaintly, even bizarrely miscast as a clergyman restoring a fallen woman (Marion Davies) to grace in *Polly of the Circus.* But nothing seemed bad enough to tarnish his image or diminish his popularity.

Gable himself, though, was increasingly unhappy and made his dissatisfaction felt. In what he viewed as disciplinary action to contain his money-making asset's recalcitrance, Louis B. Mayer loaned a reluctant Gable to the then Poverty Row studio, Columbia, for a comedy to be directed by Frank Capra. The film was *It Happened One Night* (1934), with Claudette Colbert as a runaway heiress who found herself embroiled with a broke journalist looking for a scoop. The film was a masterpiece of screwball comedy, and Capra took full advantage of Gable's range. With the famous mustache now well in place, he delivered a thoroughly delightful characterization embodying his down-to-earth practicality, good-natured cockiness, recklessness, charm, humor, and tenderness. It was neither the first nor last newspaperman he played, but this one brought Gable his only Academy Award and the first of his two most enduring successes.

Back at MGM, it was much the same mixture as before: Gable met the challenge of Fletcher Christian with an Oscar-nominated performance in *Mutiny on the Bounty* (1935), was perfectly cast in *San Francisco* (1936), survived a disaster as the Irish politician *Parnell* (1937), and was everybody's ideal *Test Pilot* (1938). But 1939 was the year in which Gable ensured his immortality as Rhett Butler. *Gone with the Wind* swept the board at the Oscars, except for the leading man, who, though nominated, lost out to Britain's Robert Donat. Gable, separated from his second wife since 1935, had become involved Carole Lombard, his costar in *No Man of Her Own*. She proved the great love of his life, and, in the midst of filming *Gone with the Wind,* Gable married her in a partnership that was swiftly recognized as a fairy-tale romance. Three years later the beautiful and gifted Lombard was killed in a plane crash.

A devastated Gable dealt with the shock by joining the United States Air Force, rising to the rank of major, and was off the screen until 1945. His return to MGM in *Adventure,* publicized with the phrase "Gable's Back and [Greer] Garson's Got Him," was not successful and began the slow decline of the star's postwar career. Prematurely aged and drinking heavily, he attempted unsuccessfully to find happiness in a brief fourth marriage to Lady Sylvia Ashley, something of a Lombard look-alike, while his film output steadily decreased, despite teamings with stars such as Lana Turner and Hedy Lamarr. His public still held him in affection, however, and there were a few last successes, notably *The Hucksters* (1947), with Deborah Kerr, and *Mogambo* (1953), a remake of *Red Dust* with Ava Gardner subbing for Jean Harlow, in which Gable was as charismatic as ever.

Gable's MGM contract expired in 1954, and his last years were spent as a freelance in films of little distinction except for a few interesting Westerns (e.g., *The Tall Men,* 1955) in the "veteran cowboy" tradition to which he had proved himself well suited. In 1955 he married his fifth wife, Kay Spreckels, another Lombard type, who was pregnant in 1960 when her husband joined Marilyn Monroe and Montgomery Clift on location in the Nevada desert for John Huston's *The Misfits*. Written by Arthur Miller, this bleak and powerful portrait of lost men roping wild stallions to sell was deeply ironic in that the protagonists were as doomed off-screen as their characters were in the film. The production was fraught with difficulties, and Gable, who insisted on doing his own stunts, was exhausted by the physical demands this made on him. His weighty performance, considered by some his best ever, was his last. He lived neither to receive the critical acclaim that greeted it, nor to see his first and only child, a son, who was born after his death. Gable suffered a fatal heart attack at age fifty-nine, shortly after *The Misfits* finished shooting, and Hollywood mourned the passing of its only king.

—Robyn Karney

FURTHER READING:

Samuels, Charles. *Clark Gable*. New York, Coward-McCann, 1962.

Shipman, David. *The Great Movie Stars: The Golden Years*. London, Angus & Robertson, 1982.

Thomson, David. *A Biographical Dictionary of Film*. New York, Alfred A. Knopf, 1994.

Tornabene, Lyn. *Long Live the King*. London, W. H. Allen, 1977.

Gambling

From TV programs such as *Wheel of Fortune* to daily point spreads in newspaper sports pages, the gambling spirit is everywhere in American life. Casinos have spread beyond tawdry, out-of-the-way locations such as Las Vegas to Indian reservations and cities across the country. Riverboats, with their poker machines and blackjack tables, ply the nation's great rivers again, as their predecessors did over a century ago. The gambling and casino boom has breached even the citadel of middle-class respectability in the form of hotels such as Las Vegas' Circus Circus and Treasure Island, featuring "family" entertainment within yards of slot machines. Variously blamed on de-industrialization, a decline in the American work ethic, and a lapse in moral values, gambling's something-for-nothing mentality has become an important part of the American consciousness. Long a refined diversion for the wealthy and a desperate last chance for the poor, it is perhaps only technology and style that separates twentieth century gambling from its primeval counterparts.

Gambling, the betting or staking of something of value, is as old as humankind itself. Betting on horses began as soon as the animals were domesticated, and gambling's ties to sports date back as far as 1450 B.C.E., when Egyptians competed against each other in jumping, wrestling, and ball game competitions, centuries before the first Greek Olympics. As many as 250,000 spectators watched, and gambled on, chariot races in Rome's Circus Maximus. Gospel writers Matthew and Mark report that Roman guards gambled for Jesus' garments following his crucifixion, "casting lots upon them, what every man should take." Towns challenged towns in medieval archery matches, and gambling was an ever present accompaniment as sports competitions became organized in Europe during the Renaissance and early Modern periods.

In the New World, special days were set aside by the Northwest Coast Indians for "mook-te-lo," or wagering on games. The Iroquois played a betting game called "hubbub" with dice made from peach stones. Participants hit themselves on the chest and thighs, crying "hub hub hub" so loudly that they could be heard a quarter-of-a-mile away according to a contemporary report. The first deck of cards to be manufactured in the Western hemisphere was made by Columbus' crew in 1492. According to the story, the sailors threw their European cards overboard because they believed gambling was bringing them ill fortune during their long voyage. Once ashore in the New World, they regretted their impulsive behavior and made substitute decks from the large leaves of the copas tree. Lotteries, begun in England in 1566, were approved for the new Jamestown settlement in Virginia by King James I in 1612. Proceeds were used to sustain the struggling colony until the king withdrew his permission in 1621.

The Puritans first objected to popular recreations like gambling during the seventeenth century because they violated Sabbatarian principles. In the Puritan's distinctive mixture of capitalism and Calvinism, gambling was a double sin, a violation of the Lord's day of rest and an ungodly diversion from work the other six days of the week. Puritans had little success convincing Europeans to stop betting but they established strict statutes against gambling and other worldly distractions in their early American settlements beginning in 1638. Lotteries were unnecessary appeals to providence, according to Puritan minister Increase Mather, who believed that "God determines the cast of the dice or the shuffle of the cards, and we are not to implicate His providence in frivolity." The Puritans' holy opposition to gambling faded in the New England colonies during the eighteenth

The Argosy Gaming Boat, Lawrenceburg, Indiana.

century, and they had never had much influence on mid-Atlantic and southern colonists, but the Puritan association of gaming and wagering with alcoholism, idleness, and ungodliness became a recurrent theme in numerous anti-gambling crusades during the nineteenth and twentieth centuries.

Lotteries were a common recourse for eighteenth-century American colonists in search of funds for wars, schools, charities, or other purposes. George Washington himself bought and sold lottery tickets, and Benjamin Franklin spoke in favor of a lottery to finance the purchase of a cannon battery for Philadelphia in 1748. In 1758, once-Puritan Massachusetts authorized a lottery to fund an expedition against Canada during the French and Indian Wars. Gambling was still considered a vice, however, and during the first days of the American Revolution, various colonial "committees of safety" opposed gambling as a means of galvanizing public morality. General Washington, a frequent gambler at cards, forbade gambling among his soldiers when it distracted them from their military duties, even during the grueling winter at Valley Forge. However, the Continental Congress sponsored a national lottery in 1777, promoting it as a contribution "to the great and glorious American cause," only to be disappointed by the proceeds because the loosely-knit colonists failed to gamble as freely as their more sophisticated English counterparts.

On the rough-and-tumble borders of the new country, however, gambling was a primary diversion. Thoroughbred horse racing, cockfights, card games, billiards, and fighting over the outcome of such contests were favorite past times of eighteenth-century frontier inhabitants, and gambling, alcoholism, prostitution, and related social vices continued to be associated with the American frontier as it spread westward throughout the nineteenth century. The 1803 Louisiana Purchase opened the western Ohio and Mississippi, and as commerce developed on the waterways, so did gambling. New Orleans evolved as America's first gambling city as flatboat men,

farmers, and plantation owners played a French card game named "poque." With a few modifications, draw "poker" became the quintessential American card game. Gambling was outlawed in the rest of the huge Louisiana territory in 1811 in the wake of a popular anti-gambling tract written by Mason Locke Weems (better known for authorship of the myth about George Washington chopping down the cherry tree), but gambling remained a critical component of New Orleans' economy and politics for another century.

The first American gambling casino was opened in New Orleans around 1822. Owner John Davis provided gourmet food, liquor, roulette wheels, faro tables, poker, and other games, made certain that prostitutes were never far away, and kept his club house open twenty-four hours a day. Dozens of imitators soon made gaming, drink, and women of easy virtue the primary attractions of New Orleans. The city's status as an international port and its thriving gambling industry created a new profession, the card "sharper." Professional gamblers and cheats gathered in a waterfront area known as "the swamp," an area even the police were afraid to frequent, and any gambler lucky enough to win stood a good chance of losing his earnings to thieves outside of the gambling rooms and saloons. The slot machine, invented by Charles Fey in San Francisco in 1895, first became popular with New Orleans gamblers. Reform movements struggled to limit gambling and prostitution to a red light district until military restrictions put the halls and brothels out of business during World War I.

The nineteenth-century relationship between gambling and western expansion was epitomized by the early West's favorite son, President Andrew Jackson. Jackson was not the first president to gamble openly, but he bet with such an intensity that he created an image that came to stereotype all Westerners. He bet on cards, lotteries, and cockfights, but he preferred horse racing, a sport suited to his western Tennessee roots. Jackson hated losing, and his advice to a nephew summarized not only his personality but the mood of entire nation during his presidential term: "You must risk to win." New frontier settlements risked everything for success, and those that prospered almost always embraced gambling. Chicago became a city in 1837, the same year it ostensibly outlawed gambling, but gaming "hells" continued to flourish along with drunkenness and prostitution. By 1849, there were as many gambling establishments in Chicago per capita as New York City and more than 1,000 women were said to be employed as prostitutes in 1856. The New England-bred Mayor "Long" John Wentworth ordered the destruction of gambling houses along Chicago's notorious Sands riverfront district in 1857, but the denizens simply moved to more law-abiding sections of the city where open gambling continued until 1904 when Mayor Carter Harrison closed all of the city's horse-racing tracks.

Gambling thrived in the South as well. Horse racing was the most popular sport for betting, and formal racing sessions were organized by the upper class in Williamsburg, Fredericksburg, Annapolis, and Alexandria well before the Revolutionary War. Slaves rode Southern race horses until replaced by white riders after the Civil War, inspiring the black jockey lawn ornaments that persisted into the twentieth century. The development of the telegraph, especially a modification permitting the transmission of more than one message at a time, allowed betting from a distance and made betting on the races a major business in the South. The first sports pages in American newspapers were reports on horse racing until the rise of professional baseball after the Civil War. Baseball, too, attracted gamblers. The Chicago "Black Sox" scandal of 1919, which saw the best team in baseball lose a World Series on purpose, was predated by the Louisville Greys, who threw enough games to go from a comfortable first place in the National League standings to late season also-rans in 1877.

Steamboats and riverfront gambling houses along the lower Mississippi attracted swarms of professional gamblers. A host of companies specialized in manufacturing and selling card cheating devices. One riverboat gambler named George Devol was so proud of his ability to slip a stacked deck into a game that he once used four of them in one poker hand, dealing four aces to each of his four opponents. Devol bragged of his exploits in his 1887 memoir, *Forty Years a Gambler on the Mississippi*. Children looked upon such professional gamblers as heroic figures. "To me as a boy, the gambler was an object of awed admiration," sportswriter Hugh Fullerton recalled of his Southern boyhood in the 1870s. But anxious townsfolk viewed the presence of such confidence men as a vestige of an unruly frontier past. Five "sharps" were lynched by vigilantes in Vicksburg, Mississippi, in 1835, less for religious reasons than to preserve civic respectability, and other river cities applied similar, if less stringent preventatives. Still, the riverboat gambler came to symbolize freedom in dime novels and other popular literature, even though most died poor.

California established a reputation for professional gambling as well. In the wake of the state's 1848 gold rush, European traveler Friedrich Wilhelm Christian Gerstacker observed that "gambling houses are now to California what slave-holding is to the United States." Professional gamblers became so wealthy and influential that they managed to become controlling political forces in the state for short periods of time. In San Francisco, gamblers played all day and all night at games that were refined into a high-volume industry. Rather than cheating and deceit, the city's gambling saloons relied on percentages and odds for their profits, foreshadowing the Las Vegas casinos a century later. Miners did not seem to mind. San Francisco gambling mirrored the entire gold rush mentality that "the fun would

be worth a fortune almost," as one contemporary wrote. Professional gamblers were an implicit, if not sanctioned, part of the casino scene until journalist and businessman James King launched such a vigorous crusade against them that he was murdered in 1856. In revenge, his alleged killer and a professional dealer named Charles Cora were lynched by vigilantes. Nonetheless, gaming continued in San Francisco, on a less ostentatious scale, into the 1910s.

Gambling flourished in other Western mining camps and towns that supplied the prospectors. Virginia City, Comstock, and Deadwood became as well known for faro and gunfights over card games as they did for mineral wealth. Even cattle towns such as Dodge City, Kansas, had forty saloons and gambling houses to cater to the cowboys, buffalo hunters, and railroad workers that visited it in 1875. But prohibition was in the wind. Scandals involving lottery ticket sales, including a massive fraud in the Louisiana lottery in 1894, the rise of baseball and other spectator sports, and a revival of moral concerns against idleness, drunkenness, and debauchery led to laws against lotteries and gambling in most states by 1910. "Puritanism [was] the inflexible doctrine of Los Angeles," one historian noted. By 1908, 289 of the nation's 314 thoroughbred horse race tracks had been closed.

Horse racing was the first gambling industry to be reborn. Colonel Matt J. Winn, president of Churchill Downs, dusted off old pari-mutuel machines stored in the back of the track's storehouse, banished illegal bookmakers, and made sure the state of Kentucky got a share of every bet made at his track. Pari-mutual horse wagering was legalized in other states, especially during the cash-strapped Depression years. State racing boards or commissions supervised the tracks, reducing cutthroat competition and providing an aura of respectability for a public concerned about the connection between gambling and crime. Professionals gamblers remained, epitomized by George E. Smith, better known as "Pittsburgh Phil," who made horse betting into a science. Bookmakers prospered as well, off track, aided by advances in communication such as radio. Although state lotteries were not revived until 1964, numbers games were introduced to Harlem by West Indian immigrants in the 1920s and spread to other cities. Manufactured games such as pull tabs and punch boards appeared in rural areas, as did illegal slot machines and other electronic devices. Almost 25 percent of Americans admitted gambling on church-sponsored bingo games and lotteries in a 1938 Gallop poll. New York Mayor Fiorello LaGuardia stated the obvious, "if bingo is unlawful in one place, it cannot be lawful in another." Politicians have tried to resolve this dilemma over the remainder of the twentieth century.

Most casinos and "gambling hells" were shut down during the early 1900s, even in obscure locations such as French Lick, Indiana, and Canton, Ohio. True to the worst fears of the Puritans, gangsters combined liquor and gambling in New York, Cleveland, Chicago, and other cities during the 1920s. Florida temporarily legalized slot machines during the depths of the Depression at about the same time that El Monte and Gardena, California, licensed poker. But it was a dusty little Nevada town located on the old Spanish Trail that reintroduced casinos and gambling to twentieth-century America.

Las Vegas was established as a Mormon mission before the Civil War. Its future was assured when the San Pedro, Los Angeles & Salt Lake railroad laid track in 1904 and three other railroads, including the Union Pacific, soon followed suit. The railroads were the town's primary employer but the providing of ice, refreshments, shelter, and other amenities became almost as important. Although gambling was banned in Nevada in 1909, Las Vegas continued to grow, reaching a population of 5,165. It remained a railroad town until divorce and gambling laws were relaxed and the federal government began the construction of Hoover Dam in 1930. The first major hotel, the 100-room Apache, opened in 1932 to augment an active red light district patronized by dam workers. So many workers and their families poured into Las Vegas that the *New York Times* claimed the city had "a touch of Mexico's Tijuana" in 1936. Still, Las Vegas continued to be outpaced by its primary competitor, Reno, and boasted only six casinos and sixteen saloons by 1939.

The post-World War II improvement of automobiles and high-ways, especially to and from Los Angeles, forever changed Las Vegas. Downtown's Fremont Street became "Glitter Gulch" and the vacant Las Vegas Boulevard was renamed the "Strip." Three casinos opened in 1946 including mobster Benjamin "Bugsy" Siegel's Flamingo Hotel. The Horseshoe Club began hosting the World Series of Poker in 1951. Motion pictures such as the 1952 *Las Vegas Story*, staring Jane Russell and Victor Mature, and the 1959 *Oceans Eleven*, which featured the "rat pack," Peter Lawford, Sammy Davis, Jr., Frank Sinatra, Dean Martin, and Joey Bishop, promoted the growing sophistication of Las Vegas. The movies also helped establish gambling as an adult entertainment in a decade noted for juvenile attractions from Elvis Presley (who later became a Las Vegas star) to McDonald's. They also helped erase gambling's disreputable, low-class image. Las Vegas' gambling industry survived and even thrived under scrutiny from investigators led by Senator Estes Kefauver. His Senate Special Committee to Investigate Organized Crime leaned heavily on gambling during the early 1950s, but only a few of the committee's proposals were legislated.

The Golden Nugget was the first Las Vegas property created specifically as a hotel-casino, but every hotel provided gambling. Eventually all would feature big-name entertainment, led by pianist Liberace, who headlined the new Riviera in 1955. The city's reputation as the "last" frontier served not only as a recurring casino and hotel theme, but intensified the gambling experience. Just as thrill seekers had swarmed San Francisco's casinos a century earlier, gamblers escaped their ordinary lives in the fantasy world of Las Vegas, surrounded by flashing lights and jingling coins, visual and auditory "noise" that heightened their sensations of gambling. Sports betting became popular, influenced in part by the banning of Pete Rose from baseball in 1989. The first theme property, the Circus Circus Hotel Casino, opened in 1968, was joined by the Mirage in 1989, the Excalibur in 1990, and Treasure Island in 1993, attracting a new type of visitor, the middle-class family. The introduction of gambling in Atlantic City and other locations induced Las Vegas to reinvent itself once again, providing educational attractions such as dolphin habitats and family entertainment acts like magicians Siegfried and Roy.

Beginning in New Hampshire in 1964, lotteries spread to more than thirty states, usually claiming to devote a large percentage of the profits to state education. Multi-state lotteries offered payouts of over one hundred million dollars. The first legal casino in the United States outside of Las Vegas opened on Atlantic City, New Jersey's Broadwalk in 1978, providing an influx of jobs and money even as the outer city remained impoverished. Deadwood, South Dakota, opened its streets to gambling in 1989. Gaming on Indian Reservations, the so-called "return of the buffalo," was re-legalized by Congress in 1988. Dozens of tribes across the country competed to provide casinos and hotel-casinos almost as glitzy as Las Vegas and used the profits to bolster their dying cultures and communities. River and lake boats, off-track and bingo parlors, dog and horse racing tracks, all vied for what economists called discretionary funds. In every case, what had been once a sin, like divorce or deficit spending, was re-merchandised into an economic and social virtue. Even the Indian casinos and the state lotteries, however, must continually fight against gambling's shadowed twin, corruption. The same qualities of desperation and greed that guarantee success to gambling enterprises, also impel those who try to "beat the system." "Gambling is the child of avarice, the brother of iniquity, and the father of mischief," wrote George Washington, and, whether the gambling is for fun or for charity, that lineage seems to remain the same.

—Richard Digby-Junger

FURTHER READING:

Brenner, Reuven. *Gambling and Speculation: A Theory, A History, and a Future of Some Human Decisions.* Cambridge, Cambridge University Press, 1990.

Burnham, John C. *Bad Habits: Drinking, Smoking, Taking Drugs, Gambling, Sexual Misbehavior, and Swearing in American History.* New York, New York University Press, 1993.

Christiansen, Eugene Martin. "Gambling and the American Economy." *The Annals of the American Academy of Political and Social Science.* Vol. 556, 1998, 36-52.

Fabian, Ann. *Cardsharps, Dreambooks, and Bucket Shops: Gambling in Nineteenth-Century America.* Ithaca, New York, Cornell University Press, 1990.

Findlay, John M. *People of Chance: Gambling in American Society from Jamestown to Las Vegas.* New York, Oxford University Press, 1986.

Lane, Ambrose I., Sr. *Return of the Buffalo: The Story Behind America's Indian Gaming Explosion.* Westport, Connecticut, Bergin and Garvey, 1995.

Sasuly, Richard. *Two Hundred Years of Gambling.* Fort Worth, Texas, Holt, Rinehart, and Winston, 1982.

Weyler, Karen A. "'A Speculating Spirit': Trade, Speculation, and Gambling in Early American Fiction." *Early American Literature.* Vol. 31, No. 3, 1996, 207-42.

Game Shows

It is not surprising that the game show has been one of the most enduring mass media formats. Combining entertainment and competition, celebrities and ordinary people, populism and the promise of instant success, game shows have tapped into elemental parts of the collective American psyche. America's most acute "quiz mania" occurred during the decades from the 1930s until the mid-1950s as a new incarnation of the American dream in which ordinary people, through luck and pluck, could rise from rags to riches overnight.

One of the first quiz programs appeared fairly early in radio's history. To increase its readership, *Time* magazine aired current events quizzes over the radio with *The Pop Question Game*, which lasted from 1923 to 1926. Other early radio contests of the 1920s included *The Brunswick Hour Musical Memory Contest, The Radio*

A fun-filled moment during the game show, *Let's Make a Deal*.

Digest, Do You Know, and *Ask Me Another.* The Depression years also encouraged Americans' interest in game shows and quiz contests. Because listening to the radio was still free in an era of tight budgets and unemployment, people flocked to their sets for diversion. Local movie theaters picked up on the game craze by offering bingo games and bank nights to lure people in with the promise of affordable entertainment and the possibility of winning prize money. People were attracted to quizzes for these practical purposes, but the shows also tapped into more elemental needs and desires like the pursuit of fame. During the Depression people experienced both economic and social hardships, often feeling like they were "lost in the crowd," their individual needs abandoned by governmental and financial institutions. In 1932, workers at the Houston radio station KTRH tried to counteract this malaise by taking a microphone outside and asking passersby their opinions on the Roosevelt/Hoover election and other more random questions. First called *Sidewalk Interviews* and later renamed *Vox Pop,* the show, which offered prize money to its participants, lasted until 1948, and spawned similar interview shows all across the country.

Professor Quiz, originating in 1937 in Washington, D.C., was the first genuine money quiz. The show not only awarded money to individual contestants, but also sent money to people who submitted questions used on the air, immediately increasing participation from

the on-air contestants to, potentially, the entire listening audience. In this way, even the early radio quiz shows spurred national interest and involvement, making them games of mass culture and mass appeal. *Professor Quiz,* for example, was so successful that within two years it had inspired over 200 variations, including a very popular version called *Dr. I.Q.* Other shows emphasized mental acuity by asking difficult questions. Of these, *The Answer Man* was one of the most popular, running for 13 years. It combined information and entertainment, becoming a frequent bet settler and voice of authority. The format of another show, *Information Please,* was designed to stump a panel of experts rather than the common man. Indeed, appearing as the weekly guest on the panel was a source of prestige, and often attracted entertainers and politicians to sit with the regular panelists. Created by Dan Golenpaul and launched in 1938, *Information Please* was so popular that in 1939 it had boosted sponsor Canada Dry's sales by 20 percent. In addition, in one of the first quiz show promotional tie-ins, there were items of spin-off merchandise, including *Information Please* home games and the still-active *Information Please Almanac and Yearbook.* This game and others like it (including a version for younger participants called *Quiz Kids*) gave the public new role models beyond sports and film stars, adding credibility and worth to intellectuals and academicians. Quiz language even entered the vernacular: the phrase "the $64 question," meaning a particularly tough question, came from *Take It or Leave It*, a popular gambling-based game show.

Like other media programming, quiz shows reflected the interests of the times. The Big Band influence of the late 1930s led to the creation of Kay Kyser's *Kollege of Musical Knowledge,* which ran for 13 seasons, *Melody Puzzle, Beat the Band,* and *So You Think You Know Music,* among others. During World War II, "quiz programs and audience-participation shows stressed themes of patriotism and sacrifice, while boosting morale and offering a measure of 'escapist' cheer," in the words of historian Thomas DeLong. These shows often featured members of the armed forces, asked questions about the War itself, encouraged enlisting, raised money for war bonds, and frequently awarded war stamps and bonds as prizes.

After the war, quiz shows once again returned to emphasizing individual pursuits and pleasures, clearly expressing America's post-war preoccupations. Consumption and the possession of goods were seen as a solution to many personal problems and served as psychological and material relief after war-time rationing. Beginning in 1946, manufacturers shifted their production away from military products and back to domestic goods, but these items were still in short supply. Many game shows whetted the consumer appetite by taking place on location in department and grocery stores—traditional sites of merchandise display and mass consumption. Their titles included *Bride and Groom, Second Honeymoon, Missus Goes a-Shopping,* and *Give and Take.* In 1948 the four major radio networks alone gave away about $90,000 a week in merchandise spread over 54 programs, totaling $4.5 million by year's end. *Go For the House* offered the grand prize of a fully furnished $7,000 house; *Break the Bank* presented the chance at a $5,000 jackpot; and *Stop the Music,* hosted by Bert Parks, featured, in addition to a wealth of prizes, a jackpot that accrued weekly. This show and others like it, in which the studio called a random person who was listening to the show at home, even sparked an increased purchase of telephones so that people could feel as if they had an equal chance of participating.

Encouraging women's return to the domestic sphere after their war-time factory work, many shows blatantly pandered specifically to perceived female desires. *Ladies Be Seated,* hosted by Johnny Olson, involved women performing pranks for merchandise. Perhaps the most unfortunate example of this genre was *Queen for a Day* (1945-64), which was more an audience-participation show than a quiz show. On this program women told various tales of woe, from dead or out of work husbands to sick relatives and impending house foreclosures. The "winner"—the woman whom the judges deemed to be in the worst straits—received prizes meant to fulfill her special wishes. In 1946 alone over 40 companies supplied $250,000 worth of products to the show. *Queen for a Day* did not showcase the intellect of the common man, but instead spotlighted and exploited the financial and emotional burdens of the common woman, an early form of mass media therapy and confessional that presaged the daytime television talk shows of the 1980s and 1990s. Another show, *Strike It Rich,* similarly exploited people's misfortunes, but also required them to answer questions to receive cash and prizes. Various sponsors telephoned the "Heart Line," offering donations to these needy people while at the same time receiving on-air promotions. *New York Times* critic Jack Gould said at the time that the show "callously exploits human anxiety to sell the product of a soap manufacturer and does it with a saccharine solicitude that hits the jackpot in bad taste."

Successful radio emcees of the 1940s included John Reed King, Bert Parks, Bud Collyer, Jack Barry, Johnny Olson, Bill Slater, and Bill Cullen, and many of them were equally successful when the quiz shows went to televised broadcasts. The first televised quiz shows appeared in 1941 with *Uncle Jim's Question Bee* (hosted by Bill Slater) and *Truth or Consequences* (hosted by Ralph Edwards). Indeed, many of these former radio shows easily translated to television, and were often broadcast simultaneously in both mediums. New shows were also developed to take advantage of the visual aspects of television and its burgeoning stable of talent. *Telequizzicals* and *Pantomime Quiz* were both based on charades, and the latter featured guest appearances by actors such as Roddy McDowell, Jimmy Durante, Lucille Ball, Steve Allen, and Danny Thomas. In 1949, *Pantomime Quiz* won television's first Emmy as its most popular show.

However, tremendous popularity often brings a backlash, and, in the late 1940s game shows experienced a wave of negative publicity. People began to feel that the shows emphasized money at the expense of talent and intellect. The 1950 film *The Jackpot*, starring Jimmy Stewart, depicts the problems a man faces after winning prize money, which, far from bringing instant happiness, almost ruins his life. In effect a morality tale, the film points out many of the reservations people had about instantly winning, rather than earning, money and merchandise. In addition, in 1948, the FCC, in an attempt to improve the quality of programming in general, tried to outlaw most quiz shows as a form of a broadcast lottery, which was then illegal. After many legal maneuverings, the courts ruled in 1953 that banning quiz shows from the airwaves would constitute censorship, and thus allowed them to continue. The standard game shows of the late 1940s and early 1950s nevertheless sank in popularity and were replaced with comedy shows. The game shows that did appear on the air were, not surprisingly, influenced by this new trend and included such offerings as *Tag the Gag, Stop Me If You've Heard This One, Draw Me a Laugh, Draw to Win, Doodles,* Groucho Marx's *You Bet Your Life,* and *Beat the Clock.* The last, the most popular of the comedy-quiz shows, was born of the prolific game show production team of Mark Goodson and Bill Todman. *Beat the Clock*, combining circus influences and sight gags, required people to successfully perform very difficult stunts in a limited amount of time. Future playwright Neil Simon helped write the show's stunts, while future actor and screen idol James Dean auditioned them in front of test audiences.

The early 1950s also saw the winning combination of Hollywood talent and intellectual prowess in popular panel games which featured celebrities and were hosted by academicians. The number of veterans who had recently completed their studies with the help of the GI Bill meant that there were more educated people who found entertainment both as contestants and audience members for quiz shows. The stars who appeared on these panels also benefited from this arrangement—the work paid well, afforded good publicity for an entertainer, showcased comedic talent, and often helped revitalize the careers of older comedians and actors. *What's My Line*, which began in 1950, was one of the longest running shows on television, becoming a Sunday night fixture on CBS for over 17 years. In this program panels, by asking yes or no questions, were enlisted to guess the unusual occupation of the night's guest. Over the years, panelists included such well-known entertainers as Steve Allen, Fred Allen, Arlene Francis, Errol Flynn, Ronald Reagan, Ernie Kovacs, and Jane Powell. Special guests included actor Frederic March, Mike Todd and his new wife Elizabeth Taylor, Frank Lloyd Wright, Gerald Ford, Jimmy Carter, Milton Berle, and Art Carney. *What's My Line* inspired a slew of more and less successful imitations including *The Name's the Same, I've Got a Secret* (with Bess Myerson, Henry Morgan,

Betsy Palmer, and Bill Cullen), and *To Tell the Truth* (with Kitty Carlisle, Peggy Cass, Tom Poston, and Orson Bean). The panel shows amassed devoted followers who tuned in every week to witness the banter of their old friends; these followers were so loyal that they guaranteed the success of the shows even in the face of the quiz show scandals of the mid-and late 1950s.

The $64,000 Question (1955-58) was the first big-money television quiz show and was inspired by *Take It or Leave It*'s "$64 question." Incorporating a televisual aesthetic that would reappear in shows like *The Price is Right* and *The Wheel of Fortune, The $64,000 Question* was described by *Newsweek* at the time of its first airing as "vaguely sleazy . . . compounded of beaverboard and sequins, liberally decorated with the name of the sponsor." The show was also referred to as the "Mount Everest" of quizzes because, to reach the peak prize, contestants had to return in subsequent weeks to risk their winnings to date for double the amount, beginning at $8,000. *The $64,000 Question* along with *The $64,000 Challenge* and *Twenty-One* created ongoing televisual dramas that pitted contestants against each other and provided suspense for the viewing audience. In addition, these shows created overnight folk heroes in their winners, who were equal parts intellectual and common man. Many were offered university lectureships, commercial endorsements, and guest appearances on television shows.

Although audiences believed that the player-against-player drama was naturally inspired by the tension of the games themselves, in actuality many of the contestants were coached by show producers. *Twenty-One* was the first show to blatantly use coaching as a method to create more on-air drama and to force larger stakes in order to draw a larger viewership. Out of greed and actual financial need, Herbert Stempel, a homely Jewish ex-soldier working his way through the City College of New York, knowingly participated in the fraud perpetuated by producer Daniel Enright. While Stempel had a photographic memory, Enright continued to coach him about the correct answers to questions to be posed on air. When Enright realized that Stempel was not a popular contestant, he recruited Charles Van Doren, tall, aristocratically handsome, and an Ivy League graduate who wanted the prize money to be financially independent of his family. Although Van Doren was at first reluctant to cheat, the producers convinced him that his repeated appearances on *Twenty-One* would be a good influence on national attitudes about teachers, education, and intellectual life. He relented, lasting 15 telecasts, accumulating $143,000 (the most single amount ever won on a quiz show), marriage proposals, a regular spot on *The Today Show,* and a teaching position at Columbia.

Stempel, angered at having to "take a dive," began to expose the quiz show rigging to journalists, who in 1957 discovered more jilted contestants and began formal investigations into the fraud at this and many other shows, including *Tic Tac Dough* and *Dotto.* Van Doren, after numerous protestations to the contrary, finally testified before a grand jury in 1959, admitting his collusion in the rigging of *Twenty-One.* The next day, he resigned his position at Columbia and the day after that was fired from *The Today Show.* Eventually he took a position as a columnist for *Leisure* magazine, and found regular employment at the *Encyclopedia Britannica.* Ironically, Van Doren was seen by many as a sympathetic figure, and the media compared him to "Shoeless" Joe Jackson, who fixed the 1919 baseball World Series.

The scandals not only ended the impressive reign of the quiz shows, but also forced larger cultural discussions about the nature of American morality and the role of television "entertainment." To the media's chagrin, the general public lacked outrage, believing the issue to be irrelevant. Some in the television industry, in fact, claimed that the print media exaggerated the scandal in order to penalize a rival medium; yet these same people took steps to minimize the scandal's fallout, canceling all dubious shows and temporarily banning canned laughter and applause. CBS even went so far as to cancel Edward R. Murrow's six-year-old and respected *Person To Person* interview show because it was "rehearsed."

The Price Is Right, which first aired in 1956, weathered the scandal days to become one of the most popular game shows in America. Originally hosted by Bill Cullen, it encouraged the American consumer ethos by not only awarding prizes, but also rewarding people who were good shoppers—people who could come closer than their rivals to guessing the retail prices of goods (anything from a box of detergent to a yacht) without going over, would then win those goods. After a three-year hiatus, *The Price Is Right* returned to the air in 1972 hosted by the avuncular Bob Barker. It featured a glitzy studio and beautiful models who caressed the items "offered up for bid" and were as objectified as the goods themselves. Chosen middle-American audience members were exhorted by the announcer to "Come on down!" to be the next contestant, echoing the populist strains of the early quiz shows.

The quiz shows of the 1960s, in order to distance themselves from the scandals, renamed themselves "game" shows, and stayed away from big money prizes. *Jeopardy*, created by former game show host Merv Griffin in 1964, reversed the normal question and answer format by providing an answer and requiring contestants to supply the question. It was wildly popular especially among college students who regularly skipped class to watch it. Its original host, Art Fleming, was replaced by Alex Trebek in 1984. The 1970s saw a decrease in the number of and enthusiasm for game shows. As Thomas DeLong has written, "It seemed clear that prize money had become less of a riveting attraction to viewers and contestants alike. For the thousands who lined up at a game show studio with the hope of being selected as a contestant, it was less the promise of dollars and merchandise. The lure was television itself." Producer and game show host Chuck Barris, who referred to his shows as "popcorn for the mind," capitalized on this new attitude with the double entendre-filled *The Dating Game, The Newlywed Game,* and *The Gong Show. Let's Make a Deal* with Monty Hall also lured Americans looking for televised attention—the most outlandishly costumed people were chosen out of the audience by Hall to be the day's contestants. These shows reflected the increasing desire among the populace for fame rather than fortune. The longing to appear on television in front of millions of viewers seemed to take precedence over anything else—even prize money.

Notable shows of the 1970s included *The $100,000 Pyramid* with Dick Clark, and new versions of old shows like *Super Password, The $1,000,000 Chance of a Lifetime, The $128,000 Question,* and *Tic Tac Dough* (with game show veteran Wink Martindale). *Family Feud* with Richard Dawson, added a twist that seemed particularly suited to the conformist backlash of the late 1970s. Rather than coming up with the *right* answer to a question, *Feud*'s teams of families had to guess which answer most people would give. Among the most outstanding shows beginning in the 1970s was the wholesome *Wheel of Fortune*, combining the children's game of Hangman with a Las Vegas-like spinning wheel to determine prize money. Originally hosted by Chuck Woolery (who later went on to host *Love Connection* and *Scrabble*), *Wheel* gained its greatest popularity in prime time when it was hosted by Pat Sajak and featured the fashionably bedecked former Miss America Vanna White as the letter turner. Still a favorite in the late 1990s, this show is often televised in conjunction with *Jeopardy* during early prime time hours, and the two together are a study in contrasts: *Wheel* relies partly on luck, celebrates the simple accomplishments of the common man, and encourages a camaraderie where contestants clap in support for one another. *Jeopardy,* in contrast, maintains a more reserved atmosphere. It is strictly an answer-and-question game that hearkens back to the intellectual challenges of *Twenty-One* and *Information Please,* requiring smart players to answer difficult questions before their opponents do.

Game shows have had a difficult time competing with the drama found in the daytime talk shows of the 1980s and 1990s. No longer do producers have to pay or reward people to come on television and tell their stories—people do it for free just for the temporary chance at fame and the spotlight. *The Price Is Right* has remained daytime television's game show mainstay, accompanied mostly by soap operas and talk shows. Prime time hours during these decades have witnessed the entrenchment of *The Wheel of Fortune* and *Jeopardy,* and the resurgence of *Hollywood Squares,* a celebrity-based show, modeled on tic tac toe. In addition, in the late 1990s, shows like *Jeopardy* and *Wheel of Fortune* have developed interactive computer games that allow people to play at home, and The Gameshow Network, which televised both classic game shows and new ones, debuted in 1998, at once reviving the game show format and relegating it to a single marginalized cable network.

—Wendy Woloson

FURTHER READING:

Anderson, Kent. *Television Fraud: The History and Implications of the Quiz Show Scandals.* Westport, Connecticut, Greenwood Press, 1978.

DeLong, Thomas A. *Quiz Craze: America's Infatuation with Game Shows.* New York, Praeger, 1991.

Holbrook, Morris. *Daytime Television Game Shows and the Celebration of Merchandise: The Price is Right.* Bowling Green, Ohio, Bowling Green State University Popular Press, 1993.

Stone, Joseph, and Tim Yohn. *Prime Time and Misdemeanors: Investigating the 1950s TV Quiz Scandal—A D.A.'s Account.* New Brunswick, New Jersey, Rutgers University Press, 1992.

Gammons, Peter (1945—)

During the 1980s and 1990s, respected baseball analyst Peter Gammons has become virtually ubiquitous as a commentator on America's "national pastime," both in print and on television. Gammons writes a regular Sunday newspaper column for the *Boston Globe,* which refers to Gammons as the "Unofficial Commissioner of Baseball," covering issues dealing with both the local Boston Red Sox as well as the sport of baseball as whole. Since 1988, Gammon has served as a studio analyst and regular reporter for the cable television Entertainment and Sports Programming Network during the baseball season, offering a popular report called "Diamond Notes" during the network's *Sportscenter* program.

Gammons grew up in Groton, Massachusetts, as a lifelong Red Sox fan. He attended the University of North Carolina in the late

1960s, and after his graduation in 1969 began a seven-year stint as a sportswriter for the *Boston Globe.* In 1976, Gammons left the *Globe* to work for the prestigious national weekly *Sports Illustrated* until 1978, during which time he covered college basketball, the National Hockey League, and Major League baseball. As a senior writer from 1986 to 1990, he concentrated on Major League baseball. He has worked for the *Globe* again since 1990.

Gammons offers penetrating insights on the state of the game of baseball, including its past and future, instead of simply discussing day-to-day events. He has been highly critical of skyrocketing player salaries and the emphasis of baseball owners on television revenues, as evidenced by his book with Jack Sands, *Coming Apart at the Seams: How Baseball Owners, Players, and Television Executives Have Led Our National Pastime to the Brink of Disaster* (1993). He also has written *Beyond the Sixth Game* (1985), which deals with the issue of free agency in baseball, and he helped former Boston Red Sox pitcher Roger Clemens write his autobiography, *Rocket Man: The Roger Clemens Story* (1987).

Gammons was voted the National Sportswriter of the Year in 1989, 1990, and 1993 by the National Sportscasters and Sportswriters Association. He also received an honorary Pointer Fellowship from Yale University. In a July 1998 chat session on the ESPN SportsZone web site, Gammons offered the following advice for aspiring sportswriters: "Take as many English, Political Science and History classes as you can. Then try to write for as many publications that will take your copy. Doesn't matter if it's a small-town, weekly newspaper or collector's news or *Sports Illustrated.* The more you write, the better you get."

—Jason George

FURTHER READING:

Coleman, Ken, and Dan Valenti. *The Impossible Dream Remembered: The 1967 Red Sox.* Lexington, Massachusetts, Stephen Greene Press, 1987.

"Peter Gammons." *ESPN SportsZone.* http://espn.go.com/espninc/ personalities/petergammons.html. April 1999.

Sand, Jack, and Peter Gammons. *Coming Apart at the Seams: How Baseball Owners, Players, and Television Executives Have Led Our National Pastime to the Brink of Disaster.* New York, MacMillan, 1993.

Shaugnessy, Dan. *At Fenway: Dispatches from Red Sox Nation.* New York, Crown Publishers, 1996.

Gangs

Youthful street gangs have become a seemingly ineradicable fixture of American urban life. Stories abound of well-armed black or Latino teenagers locked in heated battle, often to the death, with their rivals, growing rich off the profits of drug dealing, and swelling the ranks of already overcrowded state prisons. By the end of the twentieth century, as hysteria over the existence of these gangs increased, a sort of historical amnesia appeared to take hold of the press and the general public. It is easy to forget—or so it would seem—that the existence of gangs has been a consistent social phenomenon since the nineteenth century, causing sociologists to

Crips gang members in Los Angeles.

lock horns in debating the origins and motivation of the street gang. Common sense, however, dictates that any group, such as deprived inner-city youth, excluded from the general prosperity, will compensate for deprivation by staking a claim to their neighborhood, to the square blocks of ghetto they can control with relative impunity, and will profit from their position by any means at hand.

Prior to the Civil War, gangs of young Irish toughs were common in New York City. (In the field of gang studies, New York virtually monopolized the attention of sociologists, criminologists, psychologists, and others until the mid-twentieth century.) These youths had, by all accounts, provoked and fanned the draft riots that consumed New York in 1863, leaving an estimated 5,000 dead. With colorful names—such as the Pug Uglies (who took their name from their battered pug hats), the Dead Rabbits, and the Swamp Angels— and distinctive costumes, the different gang contingents were easily recognizable to each other and had an unsettling effect on the more genteel folk in the neighborhood. They engaged in street crime and extortion, murder and mayhem for hire, their services itemized in a price list that gang-members often carried with them. Such a list carried by one Piker Ryan priced ear removal at 15 dollars; murder itself commanded a mere 100. As an additional source of revenue, certain gangs leased their services to Tammany Hall politicians, intimidating voters and controlling elections. With the support of the

corrupt Tammany Hall politicians, and payoffs to local police, the street gangs could indulge in all manner of petty larceny, and were much feared in the neighborhoods they controlled. In reading accounts of their activities, the parallel with gang activities in the South Central area of Los Angeles in the late twentieth century is striking, but with two major differences: the early gangs were white (''no dogs and Irish'' signs appeared in New York business premises at the time), and they did not carry automatic firearms.

By the turn of the century, politicians were forced to buckle under public pressure and withdraw their patronage from the gangs, and with it, police protection for their illicit activities. By then, the hegemony of Irish gangs throughout the Eastern seaboard was being challenged by successive waves of immigrants from Europe, and Italian and Jewish street gangs mushroomed, impinging on Irish territory and profits. In a perverse example of market demand, the price for strong-arm services fell to a new low. Many gangs began diversifying their activities, adding union-busting (or striker protection) to their racketeering in extortion and protection. It was a volatile situation. ''By the latter part of 1913,'' wrote the historian Herbert Asbury, ''it is likely that there were more gangs in New York than in any other period in the history of the metropolis; the number and the ramification of their alliances were so bewildering that of hundreds there now [1927] exists no more than a trace. . . .''

Less than ten years later, gangs were spoken of in the past tense; an overly optimistic assessment as many gang members, cognizant of street crime's limitations, had simply gone professional, attaching themselves to one or another of the Irish, Jewish, or Italian mobs. In the 1920s, Prohibition provided ample and lucrative opportunities in the bootlegging trade, and with newfound wealth came a patina of respectability. The now fully fledged criminals forsook raffish outfits for smart, if ostentatious, business wear, bought fancy cars, and acquired a certain prestige in their communities; money brought them the temporary illusion that they had transcended their marginal social position.

Inner city neighborhoods are like fragile ecological systems, their balance of power disrupted by new arrivals. In New York waves of Puerto Rican and black immigrants arrived throughout the 1930s, 1940s, and 1950s. They came to seek an escape from rural impoverishment, but found, instead, its urban corollary. Following a by then familiar pattern, neighborhood youths organized under distinctive names, using the local candy store or soda shop as a base from which to enforce their territorial prerogative. They established alliances and bitter rivalries, often but not exclusively along color lines, and made war in the time-honored fashion. Now street fighting was called "rumbling," and it was fought with knives, chains, and homemade zip guns, but seldom with actual firearms. Of course, in this more civilized age, mayhem no longer had the same fiduciary incentive, and street gang crime was petty rather than serious. In short, the newer generations seemed more driven by the emotional need to form bonds and establish a distinctive identity.

The public, however, reacted to the mid-century gangs as if they were some fascinating new phenomenon. Their very existence may have been seen as an affront by the police, but sociologists studied them intently and a regular cottage industry was comprised of professors writing about "alienation and the juvenile delinquent." Hollywood capitalized on the *sturm und drang* of disturbed youth, romanticizing their fashions, their primitive chivalry, and their violence. To all appearances, it was as if the term juvenile delinquent, having been thus coined, made the problem more comprehensible, but it was never clearly understood. Perhaps Hollywood came closest to doing the topic justice. Broadway's hit musical *West Side Story* (subsequently filmed) gave a romantic gloss to the subject of gang warfare by very virtue of the music, dance, and love story at its center, but *The Blackboard Jungle* (1955) caught the tenor of urban alienation, and *Rebel without a Cause*, released the same year, captured the flavor of suburban teendom and the ways in which it aped the anomie of the ghettoes. A consequence of these films was to inspire teenagers everywhere to adopt the "delinquent" style of dress—black leather jacket, greased hair, tight jeans—and to unleash a wave of mindless and destructive middle class hooliganism.

By the 1960s, many gangs had assumed a radical agenda, as much a sign of the changing times as the radicalization of the poor. In an inversion of this trend, the Black Panther Party adopted a stylized version of gang-wear, sporting uniform black leather suit-jackets and berets. The Panthers, who could not technically be considered a gang, as well as bona fide gangs, initiated community self-protection (and self-help) programs, while joining the throngs in search of War on Poverty grants and lobbying the Federal government for funding. In his long essay, *Mau-Mauing the Flak-Catchers*, Tom Wolfe caught the methods of intimidation—not so different from the tactics adopted when extorting money from neighborhood businesses—used by gang members to cash in on the Federal largesse. With the collapse of the War on Poverty, economic and territorial imperatives reasserted

themselves and gangs returned to the petty crimes and drug dealing that had long supported them.

Out of the wreckage of the 1960s, new gangs emerged, and with them, a new hysteria. Left to their own devices, gangs in public housing projects, like the infamous Cabrini Green in Chicago, turned to drug dealing, especially after the introduction in the early 1980s of crack cocaine, a cheap, smokable, and virulent form of the drug. Projects and ghetto neighborhoods like South Central Los Angeles became no-go areas, patrolled by the new breed of gangster, or gang-bangers as they called themselves, well-armed, tightly-organized cadres inured to violence and ready to give their lives for their colors. Especially in Los Angeles, the new breed of gangs—the Crips, the Bloods, the Mexican Mafia—introduced a paramilitary discipline to their activities, enforcing the age-old territorial imperative with an impressive array of weaponry. These gangs became one of Los Angeles' most talked-about exports, with Crips and Bloods appearing as far afield as small towns in the Midwest.

The "rumble" was a thing of the past. Now gangs engaged in a sort of automotive warfare, the drive-by shooting, that bore as much resemblance to the rumble as a duel to an air raid. And once again, Hollywood turned the social unrest to its advantage, churning out a string of dystopic (*The Warriors,* 1979) or topical (*Colors,* 1988, *New Jack City,* 1991) gang films, while gangsta rap, a sub-genre of rap that celebrated the gang-banging lifestyle in graphic terms, made billions for record companies. Young white suburbanites did not fail to appreciate the nuances of "the life," and gangster slang and fashion overran white America, much to the distress of suburban parents. As in the 1950s, a cognitive dissonance developed between the fictitious depiction of gangs in music and film, enormously popular amongst white suburban teenagers, and the gangs themselves, who were vilified in the press and subjected to increasingly restrictive police measures. But no one would argue that cost in human life merited the celebration, especially after several high-profile rappers died (most prominently, Tupac Shakur, the son of a Black Panther, who had already survived one murder attempt) as the result of bi-coastal gang feuding; was it art imitating life or life imitating art?

It would appear that few social problems have remained as intractable as the street gang. But are street gangs a genuine danger or simply a bugbear, conveniently trotted out to justify the growth of police departments? This is of some import since, historically, gangs are depicted in the language of crisis. It becomes difficult to separate the phenomenon itself from the overlay of media coverage that concurrently obscures and defines the street gang. But for the atomized middle class public towards whom most media is slanted, gangs remain a disturbing phenomenon. That the media hysteria itself might not have an agenda is seldom discussed. It may be true that over the years the excesses of street gangs have become more alarming (there is no way to put a positive spin on the spate of random assaults and murders that have plagued New York, the result of "wilding," that is, young gangs hunting in packs for their human prey), but those who would vilify poor colored youth, fail to see their relationship to the problem, a relationship as intractable as the problem itself. John Q. Public would do well to read accounts of gang activity in the nineteenth century. He would soon realize that gangs are inextricably related to socio-economic conditions, and not a sign of impending societal collapse—the barbarians clamoring at the gate. The barbarians have always been among us.

—Michael Baers

FURTHER READING:

Haskins, James. *Street Gangs: Yesterday and Today.* New York, Hastings House, 1974.

Salisbury, Harrison. *The Shook-Up Generation.* New York, Crest, 1958.

Shakur, Sanyika, aka Kody Scott. *Monster: The Autobiography of an L.A. Gang Member.* New York, Penguin Press, 1994.

Whyte, William Foote. *Street Corner Society.* Chicago, The University of Chicago Press, 1943.

Wolfe, Tom. *Radical Chic and Mau-Mauing the Flak-Catchers.* New York, Farrar, Strauss and Giroux, 1970.

Gangsta Rap

Gangsta rap is the most controversial style of the rap music genre. It has achieved global prominence through its vivid sexist, misogynistic, and homophobic lyrics, as well as its violent depiction of urban ghetto life in America. Gangsta rap has also helped bring attention to other styles of rap music.

Although gangsta rap originated in New York in the late 1970s, it has widely become associated with the West Coast, particularly Los Angeles, due to the multi-million sales of rappers such as Ice Cube, Ice T, Dr. Dre, and Snoop Doggy Dogg. Los Angeles might proclaim itself as the home of gangsta rap, but gangsta lyrics and style were part of the hip-hop scene from its origins in the South Bronx in the mid-1970s. The inspiration behind the specific style known as gangsta rap in the late 1990s was Schooly D's *Smoke Some Kill* (1987) and Boogie Down Production's *Criminal Minded* (1987). In particular, the latter's track "9mm Goes Bang" has been seen as a pioneering force in gangsta rap's development. However, it was West Coast based Ice T's *Rhyme Pays* (1987), which ranged from humorous boasts and tales of crime and violence to outright misogyny, together with N.W.A.'s (Niggaz With Attitude) underground album *Straight Outta Compton* (1988) that established gangsta rap firmly within the American music scene. Its keynote track "F*** Tha Police" was considered so shocking that radio stations and MTV refused to play it. Nonetheless, the album went platinum. N.W.A. and gangsta rap's popularity was compounded with the release of their second album *EFIL4ZAGGIN* in 1991, which debuted at number two in the *Billboard* chart with neither a single nor a video and became the first rap album to reach number one. Snoop Doggy Dogg then became the first rapper to go straight to number one with his album *Doggystyle* (1993).

Gangsta rap is distinctive for its rich descriptive storytelling laid over heavy funk samples from Parliament-Funkadelic, Sly Stone, James Brown, Rick James, Average White Band, Ohio Players, and George Clinton. Although it originated in New York, gangsta rap has evolved a unique West Coast flavor. Its roots can be traced to early depictions of the hustler lifestyle and low-budget blaxploitation movies of the 1970s, which glorified blacks as criminals, pimps, pushers, prostitutes, and gangsters. And since many of rap's early pioneers were gang members, gangsta rap came from the life experiences of the rappers. Gangsta rappers have become high-profile figures, many of them featured in Hollywood films such as *Boyz 'n' the Hood* (1991), *New Jack City* (1991), and *Menace II Society* (1993), which have brought views of ghetto life to the masses.

The reliance on crime in the lyrics of gangsta rap fuels much of the controversy surrounding the musical style. Too Short, Above the Law, Mr. Scarface, and Big Daddy Kane, for example, all celebrate pimping. While it has been criticized for glorifying the negativity of the streets, gangsta rap's defenders claim that the rappers are simply reporting what really goes on in their neighborhoods; that drugs, prostitution, violence, and sexual promiscuity are all features of their daily existence. As N.W.A. proclaim, "It's not about a salary, it's all about reality." Nonetheless, this has led to suggestions that rap reinforces negative stereotypes of the black community and lionizes anti-social behavior. What is more, many of gangsta rap's high-profile rappers have acquired public notoriety. Some like Snoop Doggy Dogg have been implicated in gangland murders, while others such as Tupac Shakur and the Notorious B.I.G. have been killed.

Gangsta rap has become popular with those who have no direct experience with the lifestyle it depicts. The sexually explicit lyrics combined with graphic portrayals of gang killings have appealed to many middle-class white male youths. Indeed, some critics have suggested that a directly proportional relationship has developed between gangsta rap's explicitness and the sale of its records. Critics note that the violence and gangsterism has been over-exaggerated as a highly effective marketing ploy by the white-owned record companies. This has been helped by the addition of "parental advisory" stickers to many of their albums. For white middle-class male youths, gangsta rap possibly fulfills the same role as the blaxploitation films, attracting listeners for whom the "ghetto" is the location of adventure, violence, erotic fantasy, an alternative to the conformity and banality of suburbia. This voyeurism helps to explain gangsta rap's large following outside its communities of origin.

—Nathan Abrams

FURTHER READING:

Fernando, S. H., Jr. *The New Beats: Exploring the Music Culture and Attitudes of Hip-Hop.* Edinburgh, Payback Press, 1995.

Kelley, Robin D. G. "Kickin' Reality, Kickin' Ballistics: 'Gangsta Rap' and Postindustrial Los Angeles." In *Race Rebels: Culture, Politics and the Black Working Class.* New York, Free Press, 1994, 183-227.

Toop, David. *Rap Attack 2: African Rap to Global Hip Hop.* London, Serpent's Tail, 1991.

The Gap

The Gap casual apparel stores have become a ubiquitous fixture in malls and urban shopping districts around the world. Their high-quality, classic designs have remained wardrobe staples for youthful customers, older shoppers, and their children, bridging that "generation gap" that originally gave rise to its name. Founded in San Francisco in 1969 by Donald and Doris Fisher as a place for youngsters to buy jeans in a variety of sizes, The Gap by the 1990s warranted mentions and appearances in films and television shows, winning a prominent place in the 1994 hit movie *Reality Bites* and spawning a satire on the skit program *Saturday Night Live*. Detractors criticize the store's style as generic, but steadily increasing sales have made it a multibillion dollar company.

—Geri Speace

FURTHER READING:

Caminiti, Susan. "Competition: Will Old Navy Fill the Gap?" *Fortune*. March 18, 1996, 59.

Rudnitsky, Howard. "Widening the Gap." *Forbes*. September 13, 1982, 205.

Garbo, Greta (1905-1990)

Swedish actress Greta Garbo accomplished in less than two decades what advocates for women's rights had sought for centuries: she showed the American public that feminine sexuality was compatible with intelligence. During the 1920s, when liberated flappers still attracted scorn from mainstream society, Garbo's depiction of independent yet feminine beauties helped convince millions of American women that sexual initiative was not a man's prerogative. Garbo "was allowed the right to have amorous needs and desires," according to biographer Karen Swenson, and her popularity with both sexes enabled her to challenge "traditional roles with few negative consequences." At the same time, Hollywood's highest paid female star eschewed media attention and created a mystical image around her indifference to public opinion. At the age of thirty-six, Garbo retired to a life of almost hermetic seclusion. Film critic David Thomson saliently observed that "in making the journey away from fame into privacy she established herself forever as a magical figure, a true goddess, remote and austere, but intimate and touching."

Greta Garbo

Hollywood's Viking beauty began life as Greta Lovisa Gustafsson on September 18, 1905. She grew up in an impoverished Stockholm household and went to work as a lather girl in a barber shop at age fourteen. By sixteen, the aspiring actress had garnered admission to Sweden's exclusive Royal Dramatic Theater Academy. She soon impressed Scandinavia's foremost director, Mauritz Stiller, with her perfect instincts and dignified beauty. He gave her the stage name Garbo and cast her as Countess Elizabeth Dohna in the silent screen masterpiece *The Story of Gosta Berling*. A leading role in G. W. Pabst's *Joyless Street* (1925) soon followed. The part, that of a struggling Viennese women on the verge of prostitution, permitted Garbo to explore sexuality on screen for the first time. The film itself shattered box office records and became an enduring masterpiece of realistic cinema. Garbo's great break occurred when Louis Mayer of Metro-Goldwyn-Mayer recruited Stiller for his Hollywood studios. The established director insisted that his relatively obscure nineteen-year-old starlet accompany him to the United States. Stiller was soon exported back to Stockholm while Garbo became a box office sensation.

The eleven silent movies that Garbo filmed between 1925 and 1929 earned her critical claim as Hollywood's most talented female actress. Starring across from leading man John Gilbert in *Flesh and the Devil* (1927) and *Love* (1927) she awed audiences and shocked censors with her forthright sexuality. Garbo displayed her wide range playing a Spanish opera singer in *The Torrent* (1926), a Russian spy in *The Mysterious Lady* (1928), an English aristocrat in *A Women of Affairs* (1928) and a southern belle in *Wild Orchids* (1929). The star's appearance influenced an entire generation as millions of female fans copied her tastes in clothing and hair styles. Crazes for artificial eye lashes and cloche hats swept the nation. Meanwhile Garbo, whom Claire Booth Luce described as "a deer in the body of a woman living resentfully in the Hollywood zoo," distanced herself from both the public and the Los Angeles social scene.

Garbo may have been one of the leading box office draws of the silent era but few critics expected her to make the transition to talkies. The advent of sound ended the careers of most silent stars and the Swede's deep voice and heavy accent were expected to turn off audiences. Instead, the twenty-five-year-old actress gave her most compelling performance in an adaptation of Eugene O'Neill's play *Anna Christie* (1930). She played a waterfront streetwalker searching for her barge-captain father. Her opening words, at that time the longest sound sequence ever heard in a film, are cinematic legend: "Gimme a whiskey, ginger ale on the side . . . and don't be stingy, baby!" Other hits followed. *Mata Hari* (1932), *Queen Christina* (1935), *Anna Karenina* (1935) and *Camille* (1936) confirmed her reputation as the leading lady of the early sound era. Garbo's greatest role, that of the suicidal Russian dancer Grusinskaya in *Grand Hotel* (1932), ranks among the best female leads ever seen on the large screen. It is here that she declares her haunting wish: "But I want to be alone." After surprising success as the comic lead in *Ninotchka* (1939), Garbo filmed the lackluster *Two-Face Woman* (1941) and then retired from the public eye. She was thirty-six years old.

During the last five decades of Garbo's life, "The Scandinavian Sphinx" established herself as cinema's leading enigma. She travelled extensively but turned down all requests for public appearances. Instead, she entertained such close friends as Winston Churchill and Martha Graham in her posh New York City apartment. As one of the *grande dames* of American cinema, her intimates included William Paley, Anthony Eden, Jean Cocteau, Irwin Shaw, Dag Hammarsjokld, Cole Porter, and Jacqueline Kennedy. She also devoted herself to amassing an internationally renowned art collection which boasted masterpieces by Renoir and Bonnard. Garbo received an Honorary Academy Award in 1954 for "unforgettable screen performances." She died in New York City on April 15, 1990.

Greta Garbo entered the American consciousness during the mid-1920s at an historical moment when gender roles were in flux. The young actress came to represent a palatable form of female liberation and brought the icon of the independent woman home to Middle America. As biographer Karen Swenson described the star, "Her intimate posture and kisses suggested a woman—not a vamp— who was secure in her sexuality." Garbo's influence endured long after she became film's most celebrated recluse. Throughout her life, she remained private, elusive, and conspicuously unmarried. "There is no one who would have me. I can't cook," she once joked— displaying the combination of independence and feminine intelligence which made her famous.

—Jacob M. Appel

FURTHER READING:

Affron, Charles. *Divine Garbo*. Paris, Ramsay, 1985.

Bainbridge, John. *Garbo*. New York, Holt, Rinehart and Winston, 1971.

Brion, Patrick. *Garbo*. Paris, Chene, 1985.

Broman, Sven. *Garbo on Garbo*. London, Bloomsbury, 1991.

Carr, Larry. *Four Fabulous Faces: The Evolution and Metamorphosis of Garbo, Swanson, Crawford and Dietrich*. New Rochelle, Arlington House, 1970.

Durgnat, Raymond and John Kobal. *Greta Garbo*. New York, Dutton, 1965.

Gronowicz, Antoni. *Garbo*. New York, Simon and Schuster, 1990.

Paris, Barry. *Garbo: A Biography*. New York, Knopf, 1994.

Sands, Frederick. *The Divine Garbo*. New York, Grosset and Dunlap, 1979.

Sjolander, Ture. *Garbo*. New York, Harper and Row, 1971.

Swenson, Karen. *Greta Garbo: A Life Apart*. New York, Scribner, 1997.

Vickers, Hugo. *Loving Garbo: The Story of Greta Garbo, Cecil Beaton and Mercedes de Acosta*. London, Jonathan Cape, 1994.

Gardner, Ava (1922-1990)

Film actress Ava Gardner was the last, and least typical, of the screen's Love Goddesses, superseding Rita Hayworth and outliving Marilyn Monroe. As the hard-bitten press agent (Edmond O'Brien) in *The Barefoot Contessa* (1954) says of the Madrid slum gypsy (Gardner) elevated to screen stardom, "Whatever it is, whether you're born with it, or catch it from a public drinking cup, she's got it; and the people with the money in their hands put her there." Joseph L. Manckiewicz's film was dubbed "a trash masterpiece" by critic Pauline Kael, but trash or not, it perhaps gave the fullest expression to the magic sensuality of its titular star. Tall and lissome, Gardner was frequently likened to a panther and her sinuous grace inspired publicists for *The Barefoot Contessa* to trumpet her as "The World's Most Exciting Animal." Dark-haired, smokily glamorous, and husky-voiced, her sex appeal was subtly come-hither, and with her "natural" quality she was a beauty both dazzling and refreshingly uncontrived.

Frank Sinatra and Ava Gardner

To quote from *The Barefoot Contessa* again, "Life, every now and then, behaves as though it has seen too many bad movies." Spoken by Humphrey Bogart, the words might well have reflected the less happy aspects of Ava Gardner's life although, by all accounts, she was a warm, generous, witty, and life-loving free spirit. However, she was as famed for her torrid love affairs and her heavily publicized marriages as for her legendary looks. Indeed, fame first came her way not for her work, but for her first marriage to an unlikely husband, the pint-sized Mickey Rooney, in 1942. It lasted 17 months, and her second, to bandleader Artie Shaw in 1945, was even shorter. Most famously, her third and last husband was Frank Sinatra. They married in 1951, separated in 1954, and divorced in 1957, but it was a grand passion and a tempestuous liaison that resonated for years to come in their lives and in the pages of an eager tabloid press.

Popular myth has it that Ava Gardner (her real name) suffered an unhappy childhood as a daughter of dirt-poor tenant farmers in North Carolina. In reality, life was a struggle for her Depression-hit family, but nobody went hungry. In 1940, aged 18, Ava visited her married sister in New York where she intended to become a secretary. Her photographer brother-in-law took pictures of her and sent them to somebody at MGM, resulting in a screen test and a seven-year contract with the studio that boasted "more stars than there are in heaven." It took six years before Gardner was one of them. She was put through the usual rigors of studio training in how to walk, how to talk, how to pose for publicity pictures (of which, in her case, there would be thousands), but MGM initially failed to realize her potential. She was given small roles in a variety of films and lent to other studios. It was only after she played the sultry temptress opposite Burt

Lancaster in *The Killers* (1946)—on loan to Universal—that stardom beckoned. The path to the top was uneven—leads alternating with supporting roles. She played her first starring role, appropriately as a goddess, in the none-too-successful *One Touch of Venus* (1948), but the public was entranced by her. Whether playing secondary parts or leads in less than distinguished films, she retained top star status until her career ended in 1982, her beauty matured but intact.

Gardner's high public profile, arising from her private life— after parting from Sinatra she lived for a time amidst the Jet Set in Madrid, romancing with playboys and matadors—tended to obscure her professional accomplishments. Cinema historian David Shipman wrote "Ava Gardner has seldom been accused of acting," and many considered that she held the world in thrall with her ravishing looks but had little talent. Time proved this a common misperception. Although her range was limited, her intelligence was unmistakable, and she revealed a touching vulnerability that enhanced characters as diverse as her critically well-received mulatto Julie in *Show Boat* (1951), her gutsy Hemingway woman in *The Snows of Kilimanjaro* (1952), the half-caste Anglo-Indian of Cukor's *Bhowani Junction* (1956), and the small but significant role of the patriotic discarded mistress of a deranged general (Burt Lancaster) in *Seven Days in May* (1964).

Gardner was never more beautiful than as Pandora in the mythical, mystical hokum that was *Pandora and the Flying Dutchman* (1951), ensnaring and redeeming eternally wandering sea captain James Mason; and she was nominated for an Academy Award for her performance as a tough-talking, witty good-time girl, costarring with Clark Gable in *Mogambo* (1953), a remake of his outing with Jean Harlow in *Red Dust* (1932). To her detractors, the biggest surprise was her performance in John Huston's screen version of *The Night of the Iguana* (1964). No longer youthful, but still oozing sexual charisma, she did creditable justice to Tennessee Williams's play, at the center of things as the heavy-drinking hotel keeper lusting after Richard Burton's defrocked priest.

Ava Gardner retired from the screen in 1982 and made a late television debut in 1985 in *Knot's Landing*. She played three more roles on television, notably as the scheming Agrippina in the miniseries *AD,* before settling to a reclusive life in London, England, where she died of pneumonia at the age of 67. Her autobiography, compiled by Alan Burgess and Kenneth Turan from interview tapes, was published posthumously.

—Robyn Karney

FURTHER READING:

Daniell, John. *Ava Gardner.* New York, St. Martin's Press, 1982.

Gardner, Ava. *Ava: My Story.* New York, Bantam Books, 1990.

Shipman, David. *The Great Movie Stars, The International Years.* London, Angus & Robertson, 1980.

Garfield, John (1913-1952)

The original movie rebel, ruggedly handsome John Garfield rose to fame with his post-Depression portrayals of cynical men who reflected the era's social unrest. As depicted by Garfield, characters no longer were readily identifiable as either good or evil—the rebel

John Garfield

characterization which became the calling card of iconoclastic actors including Marlon Brando, Montgomery Clift, James Dean, Steve McQueen, and Al Pacino. Garfield also endures as a strong sexual presence, particularly in his teaming with Lana Turner in the 1946 adaptation of James M. Cain's steamy *The Postman Always Rings Twice,* and, a year later, opposite Joan Crawford in *Humoresque.*

Born Julius Garfinkle on New York's Lower East Side, Garfield was the son of a coat presser and cantor, and a mother who died when he was seven. He spent much of his childhood on the streets, where he ran with Bronx gangs. As a teenager, his life took a turn when he came under the tutelage of noted educator Angelo Patri, who encouraged him to study drama. "Julie," as Garfield was called throughout his life by friends and family, went on to earn a drama scholarship at the Heckscher Foundation Drama Workshop. Through the workshop he met playwright Clifford Odets, who helped to pave his way into the innovative Group Theater.

It was in a Group Theater February 1935 performance of Odet's play *Awake and Sing* that Garfield first caught the attention of reviewers. Yet, he might have remained a stage performer if not for his disappointment over the casting of Odets's *Golden Boy.* Though the central role had been written with Garfield in mind, it instead went to the director's brother-in-law. Garfield, who took a lesser role, was primed for a career change when he was approached by Warner

Brothers. Then known for its movies for and about the working class, the studio signed him to a contract.

Garfield's talents and rebellious persona were apparent with his first film, *Four Daughters,* for which he was nominated best supporting actor of 1938. As Mickey Borden, an orchestrator who comes into the life of a sunny blonde and her musical family, he sardonically surmised, "The fates are against me. They tossed a coin—heads, I'm poor, tails I'm rich. So what did they do? They tossed a coin with two heads." That sense of fatalism would become a Garfield motif. Indeed, he enjoyed his only traditionally heroic role in the 1945 title *Pride of the Marines,* which followed the return home and rehabilitation of real-life marine Al Schmid. Blinded during a bloody night attack on Guadalcanal, Schmid nonetheless machine-gunned some two hundred Japanese soldiers.

An actor who identified with characters who lived on the edge, Garfield also tackled roles because of his admiration for particular artists and themes. He starred in *The Sea Wolf* (1941) because he revered the writings of Jack London. He took a supporting role in the seminal movie *Gentleman's Agreement* (1947) because it examined anti-Semitism. Said Garfield, "That was a part I didn't act. I felt it with all my heart."

Frequently, the men he played were on the run—from themselves as well as from the law. In *They Made Me a Criminal* (1939) he was a prizefighter who headed west following his involvement with a murder; in *Dust Be My Destiny* (1939) he was an escapee from a prison work farm; in *The Breaking Point* (1950) he was a boat captain who smuggled illegal aliens; in his final film, the 1951 *He Ran All the Way,* his character goes into hiding following his involvement in a payroll robbery in which a policeman is killed.

Within the Garfield oeuvre, redemption came at a significant price. *Body and Soul* (1947), about an unscrupulous prizefighter, climaxes when Garfield's character refuses to throw a fight. "What are you gonna do, kill me? Everybody dies," he says, in a defiant but downbeat climax. Renowned for its realistic boxing sequences, the movie earned Garfield a best actor Oscar nomination. In the similarly dark *Force of Evil* (1948), Garfield was a crooked lawyer involved in a numbers syndicate. Both movies, which were produced by Garfield's own company, continue to enjoy cult status, in part because of the involvement of filmmaker Abraham Polonsky, who was later blacklisted.

Because of his own outspoken liberal views, Garfield also came under the scrutiny of the House Un-American Activities Committee during its investigation of the Communist infiltration of Hollywood. During his 1951 testimony, Garfield surprised friends and associates by contradicting his well-known viewpoints. In the aftermath of his testimony, major film offers ended. The actor was estranged from his family when he succumbed to a heart attack at age thirty-eight. Those closest to him claimed that the stress of the investigation contributed to his death.

Because Garfield had an off-screen reputation as a lothario, and because he died in the bed of a female friend, there have long been rumors regarding details of his death. In the 1993 movie *Indecent Proposal,* in which multi-millionaire Robert Redford has a contract drawn up regarding a pending sexual liaison with Demi Moore, the lawyer adds a "John Garfield clause," explaining, "That's if you die in the act." But the sexual lore about Garfield pales alongside his fiercely memorable screen images. With his tousled hair, ubiquitous cigarette, and embittered world-weariness, he is a reminder that life is a survival course.

It could also be said that the original movie rebel helped to make possible a far more legendary career: Garfield originally was sought for the role of Stanley Kowalski in the Broadway play *A Streetcar Named Desire.* He turned it down, believing that the character of Blanche du Bois overshadowed Kowalski. The role went to a twenty-four-year-old unknown named Marlon Brando. In essence, one rebel passed the torch to another.

—Pat H. Broeske

FURTHER READING:

Beaver, James N., Jr. *John Garfield: His Life and Films.* New York, A. S. Barnes and Co., 1978.

McGrath, Patrick J. *John Garfield: The Illustrated Career in Films and On Stage.* North Carolina, McFarland & Co., 1993.

Morella, Joe, and Edward Z. Epstein. *Rebels: The Rebel Hero in Films.* New York, Citadel Press, 1971.

Swindell, Larry. *Body and Soul: The Story of John Garfield.* New York, William Morrow and Co., 1975.

Garland, Judy (1922-1969)

At the end of the twentieth century, 30 years after her tragically premature death, Judy Garland is still a legend to legions of fans the

Judy Garland

world over, who recognize in her one of the twentieth century's all-time great American talents. As Dorothy in *The Wizard of Oz* (1938), she symbolized the innocence and hope that would both desert her in her own life, which came to represent an unhappy paradigm of the fate that befell so many child stars who were victims of the old Hollywood studio system. As an MGM "triple threat" from 1938 to 1950, she acted, danced, and sang her way through more than two dozen feature films, many of which are now considered classics of the Hollywood musical genre. She possessed a powerful and expressive voice, unique in tone, and full of pain and vulnerability—she once said, "I have a voice that hurts people when they think they want to be hurt." She recorded nearly 100 singles and more than two dozen albums with that voice. Diminutive, but vibrating with nervous energy and charisma, she became a gay icon among show business devotees, much as Maria Callas did among opera buffs. Her life was turbulent and terrible, her legacy a joyous inspiration. She was an underused and brilliant actress as well as one of the greatest-ever popular singers. Above all, she had that indefinable quality that makes a star.

Garland was born Frances Gumm on June 10, 1922 in Grand Rapids, Minnesota, to vaudevillian parents Frank and Ethel Gumm. From the time she was a toddler, "Baby Gumm" performed with her two older sisters in a stage act called "The Gumm Sisters Kiddie Act." Her rendition as a two-year-old of "Jingle Bells," performed on stage at the New Grand Theater (her father's cinema), brought the house down. The act later became the "Garland Sisters," with Judy billed as "the little girl with the great big voice." Her own name was changed when she was 12—comedian George Jessel gave Judy and her sisters the moniker Garland when he introduced them at the 1934 World's Fair in Chicago, and she herself chose Judy, after the title of a Hoagy Carmichael song.

In 1935, at the age of 13, Garland signed a contract with MGM. In November of that year, she did several radio broadcasts, singing "Broadway Melody" and what would later become one of her several signature songs, "Zing! Went the Strings of My Heart." A few days later, her father died of spinal meningitis; Judy's reaction was a day-long crying binge, indicative of the raw emotionalism that would dog her always. Initially, studio chief Louis B. Mayer was unsure how to use Garland. Her vocal quality was so adult, it was feared that audiences would not believe it came from the child, but they put her into a two-reel short called *Every Sunday* (1936) with another youthful newcomer named Deanna Durbin. Durbin was dropped and Garland kept on, but her first feature, *Pigskin Parade* (1936) was made on loan-out to Fox. Then, in 1938, she virtually stole the show from a starry cast in MGM's *Broadway Melody of 1938*, tremulously singing "Dear Mr. Gable/ You Made Me Love You" to a photograph of the macho star.

In 1937 Judy appeared in *Thoroughbreds Don't Cry*. The film was neither here nor there, but marked a significant first pairing with the other multi-talented performing child genius of the age, Mickey Rooney, with whom she would co-star nine times in all. With the young Lana Turner, she appeared with Rooney again in *Love Finds Andy Hardy* (1938), an entry in America's most famous ever "family entertainment" screen series. But the film that elevated her to superstardom was *The Wizard of Oz* (1939), in which the studio cast her with some reluctance when Mayer failed to get his chosen Dorothy, Shirley Temple.

The role of Dorothy, who yearns for a place where "the dreams that you dare to dream really do come true," only to discover after a series of fantastic adventures, that "home is best," unleashed and

defined Garland's extraordinary talent, and revealed the heartbreaking vulnerability that uniquely characterized her persona. Garland's portrayal of Dorothy was the defining role of her life, while "Somewhere Over the Rainbow" pursued her for the rest of her life. It became an anthem of hope in England during World War II, and later, she would sing the last eight bars over the phone to President John F. Kennedy whenever he needed cheering up. No concert audience would have permitted her to leave the stage without performing the number, which she generally used as her finale; it had profound personal significance for her and for the concert fans, who often shed a tear when listening.

The Academy Award-nominated film lost out to *Gone with the Wind,* but 16-year-old Judy Garland, an instant legend, received a special miniature Oscar in recognition of her performance. Meanwhile, off-screen, her personal life was already subject to the patterns that would destroy her. Controlled by an archetypal stage mother on the one hand and the ruthless rules of the studio on the other, she was put on a strict diet to contain a tendency to over-weight. A doctor recommended appetite suppressants. Simultaneously, the pressures of work were taking their toll and soon she was living on pills—diet pills, pills to sleep, pills to keep awake. At 19 she married orchestra leader David Rose, the first of her five husbands. Two years later they were separated and officially divorced in 1945, by which time she had made several in the cycle of juvenile, "lets-put-on-a-show" musicals with Mickey Rooney that remain classics of their kind—exuberant, and bursting with the combined powerhouse of dancing, singing, and acting talent provided by their young stars. The cycle began with *Strike Up the Band* in 1940, and included *Babes on Broadway* (1942) and *Thousands Cheer* (1943) along the way.

In 1944 Judy starred in one of the American cinema's landmark musicals, *Meet Me in St. Louis*, directed by the great colorist of the musical screen, Vincente Minnelli. The film yielded another of Garland's signature tunes with "The Trolley Song" and led to her second marriage. Minnelli became her husband in 1946, and the father of her daughter Liza. The marriage was over by 1949 but, under her husband's direction, Garland made *The Clock* (1945). Co-starring Robert Walker, the small-scale, black-and-white film concerned the meeting of a girl and a soldier under the clock at Grand Central, and their brief idyll and marriage during his 24-hour leave. Charming and poignant, it marked a departure for Garland, who revealed her considerable talents as a straight actress.

While the systematic disintegration of her health and psyche continued, rendering her subject to professional unreliability, the star continued to make millions for MGM. She starred in *The Harvey Girls* and *Ziegfeld Follies* in 1946 and *In the Good Old Summertime* (1949); her guest appearance in *Till the Clouds Roll By* (1946), in which, as Broadway star Marilyn Miller, she memorably rode bareback in a circus, sang "Who (stole my heart away)," and, smudge-nosed and aproned, rendered "Look for the Silver Lining" while up to her ears in a pile of dirty dishes, were among the highlights of a film packed with them. The most enduring musical of the period saw her paired with Fred Astaire in *Easter Parade* (1948), the film in which, dressed in tattered top hats and tails, the pair famously sang "A Couple of Swells."

By 1950, however, Garland's increasing failure to appear on set and her emotional setbacks, which caused monumental difficulties for *Summer Stock* with Gene Kelly, had become intolerable, and MGM fired her. She published a somewhat disingenuous open letter (doubtless concocted by her publicist or some such person) to her fans in *Modern Screen,* saying she had suffered from depression and a "mild inferiority complex," and needed a vacation. Garland thanked her fans for their stalwart support and said, "A lot of fanciful stories have depicted me as the victim of stark tragedy, high drama, and all sorts of mysterious Hollywood meanderings. All that is bunk. Basically, I am still Judy Garland, a plain American girl from Grand Rapids, Minnesota, who's had a lot of good breaks, a few tough breaks, and who loves you with all her heart for your kindness in understanding that I am nothing more, nothing less."

In 1951, Garland and her third husband, Sid Luft, staged her first big "comeback"—a concert appearance at the Palace Theater on Broadway. The record-breaking show ran for 21 weeks. She continued to appear on the international concert circuit through the 1950s and 1960s—when, that is, her shaky emotional stability allowed her the strength to keep her engagements, but her film career shuddered to an almost total halt, but for perhaps her greatest screen achievement, as Esther Blodgett/Vicki Lester in Warner's 1954 remake of *A Star is Born* (1954). Co-starring James Mason and directed by George Cukor, the film showcased an amalgam of all the Garland gifts, both musical and dramatic, highlighting her vulnerability, her intensity, her energy and her sense of humor. It is a spectacular performance in a spectacularly good film (musical highlights include "The Man That Got Away" and "Born in a Trunk") and she was nominated for the Best Actress Oscar. In a decision that remains an eternal blot on the Academy's integrity, the coveted statuette went to Grace Kelly for *The Country Girl,* rendering Garland a body blow.

She remained an Academy Award nominee only again in 1961, deservedly acknowledged for her heart-rending straight dramatic performance in Stanley Kramer's *Judgment at Nuremberg.* Another dramatic performance, opposite Burt Lancaster in Kramer's *A Child is Waiting* (1963), was even more heart-rending, as was the film itself, set in a home for autistic children. On CBS television, *The Judy Garland Show* during the early 1960s was short-lived, but her Carnegie Hall appearance, in 1962, the recording of which received an unprecedented five Grammy Awards, including Album of the Year, was a now legendary success. At this concert, and those at the Palace and the London Palladium (where she appeared in an emotional shared concert with Liza), the hysterical screaming and crying was comparable only to that found at rock concerts. There was a real chance that "The World's Greatest Entertainer" would collapse or fail on stage, but audiences were rooting for her; they loved not only Garland's voice and talent, they loved *her.* Legend has it that once, when she called for requests, one audience member yelled, "Just stand there!"

In 1963, Judy Garland made the last, and least, of her films. Indeed, *I Could Go on Singing,* opposite Dirk Bogarde, was a travesty and a humiliation as the once great star played herself—a dumpy, frowsty, unhappy washed-up singing star attempting to make a comeback amid the ruins of her private life. That, fortunately, is not how she is remembered.

Her marriage to Sid Luft (the father of her children Lorna and Joey) was over in the early 1960s, and their divorce in 1965 followed an exhausting battle over custody of the children. In the wake of Luft, she married an unsuccessful actor named Mark Herron, seven years her junior, but they were separated after only six months. Worn out from long years of concert tours, lawsuits, depression, substance abuse, nervous breakdowns, failed marriages and suicide attempts, Garland went to London in early 1968, married her fifth husband—35-year-old disco manager Mickey Deans—and appeared for a three-week season at The Talk of the Town.

She was clearly in a bad way, and drew unsympathetic audiences who were vocal in their hostility. The run was a humiliating fiasco, but she planned yet another comeback at the same venue the following year. Garland once said she'd had so many comebacks that every time she came back from the bathroom it was regarded as a comeback. It was an ironic comment: On June 22, 1969, she never came back from the bathroom of her London hotel suite where Deans found her, dead of a drug overdose. Alas, although millions grieved, few were surprised. Vincent Canby wrote in the *New York Times,* "The greatest shock about her death was that there was no shock." She was 47 years old and died four million dollars in debt.

While Garland attracted a wide cross-section of the population, both at home and abroad, she held a particular appeal for gay men, and her status as a gay icon remains probably unmatched. She collected a gay following quite early on in her career and by the 1970s the phrase "a friend of Dorothy" was understood as describing someone as gay. She was adored by drag queens, an idolatry that led to a line in the play, (and film) *The Boys in the Band* where one character rhetorically asks, "What's more boring than a queen doing a Judy Garland imitation?" Even the gay pride rainbow symbol connects to her most famous iconic image. Garland's frequent suicide attempts became a bizarre element of her legend, and with each new attempt reported in the tabloids, gay fans wore Band-Aids on their wrists in solidarity. Some say Garland's New York City funeral contributed to the power of the pivotal Stonewall rebellion. With emotions running high in the aftermath of the funeral, gay and lesbian patrons at the Stonewall Inn in Greenwich Village fought gay-bashing police and sparked a series of riots in New York that heralded the beginning of the gay liberation movement.

A powerful, and sad, echo of Judy Garland has lived on in the voice, persona, and tortured personal life of her gifted daughter, Liza Minnelli, while Lorna Luft, too, pursued a show business career and wrote a tell-all book about her mother, *Me and My Shadows: A Family Memoir* (1998). Her great legacy, though, rests in the films and recordings by which she lives on and, as Frank Sinatra so aptly put it after her death, "the rest of us will be forgotten—never Judy."

—Jessy Randall

FURTHER READING:

Fricke, John. *Judy Garland: World's Greatest Entertainer.* New York, Holt, 1992.

Goldman, William. *The Season: A Candid Look at Broadway.* New York, Harcourt Brace, and World, 1969.

Kaiser, Charles. *The Gay Metropolis: 1940-1996.* San Diego, Harcourt Brace, 1997.

Rainbow: A Star-Studded Tribute to Judy Garland. Edited by Ethlie Ann Vare. New York, Boulevard Books, 1998.

Shipman, David. *Judy Garland: The Secret Life of an American Legend.* New York, Hyperion, 1993.

Garner, James (1928—)

Playing wandering gambler Bret Maverick in the television western *Maverick* (1957-60), James Garner established the persona of the cynical, witty anti-hero, a persona which he would carry with him in the majority of his later roles. Garner enjoyed television success again in *The Rockford Files* (1974-80) as crusty private eye Jim Rockford, a role which earned him an Emmy (1976). In films such as *The Americanization of Emily* (1964), *Support Your Local Sheriff!* (1969), *H.E.A.L.T.H.* (1979), *Victor/Victoria* (1982), and *Barbarians at the Gate* (1993), Garner has proven that his trademark persona has an enduring popularity.

—Christian L. Pyle

FURTHER READING:

Strait, Raymond. *James Garner: A Biography.* New York, St. Martin's Press, 1985.

Garvey, Marcus (1887-1940)

As an activist who promoted Black pride, Marcus Garvey founded one of the largest mass movements of Black Americans. Garvey's United Negro Improvement Association (UNIA) offered

Marcus Garvey

new hope for working-class Blacks in the 1920s. At the same time, Harlem Renaissance artists also encouraged racial pride like Garvey, but within that movement opportunities came to only a limited number of creative African American individuals. Garvey's clarion call for Black nationalism resonated primarily among lower- and working-class blacks and inspired numerous Black mass-appeal leaders and movements. The appeal of Garvey himself faded by the late 1920s, but he remained a complex and controversial figure for his views on Black nationalism and cultural militancy, which energized many Black Americans in the post-World War I era.

Although he would become a pioneering Black nationalist in the United States, Garvey grew up in rather inauspicious surroundings in Jamaica. He was born on Saint Ann's Bay, Jamaica, on August 17, 1887. As a young man, Garvey moved to Kingston, where he worked as a printer and editor. After traveling extensively in the West Indies and Central America and living briefly in England, Garvey became convinced that Black people suffered a sort of universal cultural and economic exploitation wherever they lived outside Africa. Garvey worked to resolve this by preaching cultural unification of Blacks worldwide, stressing the idea of going back to Africa. In 1914, Garvey organized the Universal Negro Improvement Association in Jamaica as the organizational arm of his Black nationalist "Back to Africa" Movement. Soon his oratorical skills drew many supporters. By the time Garvey moved to the United States in 1916, the UNIA had become a budding international movement for downtrodden Blacks seeking help in improving their lives as a collective voice. It was the desperate post-World War I Black population of inner-city New York that provided Garvey with the most recruits and support.

By the early 1920s, Garvey had made Harlem the home base for the UNIA. During numerous rallies, parades, and similar demonstrations, Garvey preached a message of racial pride and cultural unity to millions of Blacks throughout the United States and the world. Garvey's then-radical message appealed especially to Black Americans who, as a result of the "Great Migration" of the early twentieth century (which had moved millions of blacks from the rural South to the urban North), could easily spread Garvey's message through their new urban-based culture. Garvey's fervent nationalism became epitomized in his cry, "Up, Up You Mighty Race! You Can Accomplish What You Will!" By the mid-1920s, the UNIA claimed almost two and a half million members and sympathizers, although in retrospect that number seems inflated.

Yet, by the late 1920s, the mass cultural appeal of Marcus Garvey and the UNIA quickly decreased. In 1925, Garvey received a five-year prison sentence for mail fraud, even though the evidence indicated that his subordinates may have committed the crimes without Garvey's knowledge. In 1927, President Coolidge commuted Garvey's sentence and ordered him deported to Jamaica. Without the dynamic Marcus Garvey as its leader, the UNIA quickly disintegrated into a moribund movement. As the Great Depression swept America in the 1930s, Garvey's once forceful movement slipped into anonymity. Garvey sought to resurrect the movement in London in 1935, but gained little success and died a largely forgotten man in London in 1940.

Though Garvey faded from popularity after his incarceration in 1925, his teachings and ideas became a lasting legacy. His emphasis on racial pride, understanding the African heritage, and Black unity shaped the thinking of Malcolm X (whose father was a Garveyite) and the program of the Black Muslims in the 1930s. Garvey's memory also inspired the Black Power movement of the 1960s. Moreover,

Garvey's stress on self-reliance is still an important theme among many African-American community leaders. Marcus Garvey remains an undisputed icon of Black pride.

—Irvin D. Solomon

FURTHER READING:

Cronon, E. David. *Black Moses: The Story of Marcus Garvey and the Universal Negro Improvement Association.* Madison, University of Wisconsin Press, 1969.

Garvey, Amy Jacques, editor. *Philosophy and Opinions of Marcus Garvey, or, Africa for the Africans.* London, Cass, 1967.

Hill, Robert A., editor. *The Marcus Garvey and Universal Negro Improvement Association Papers,* 7 Vols. Berkeley, University of California Press, 1983-90.

Jamaica Library Service. *Garvey Centenary, 1887-1987: A Select Bibliography.* Kingston, Jamaica Library Service, 1987.

Martin, Tony. *Race First: The Ideological and Organizational Struggles of Marcus Garvey and the Universal Negro Improvement Association.* Westport, Connecticut, Greenwood Press, 1976.

Stein, Judith. *The World of Marcus Garvey: Race and Class in Modern Society.* Baton Rouge, Louisiana State University Press, 1986.

Garvey, Steve (1948—)

Baseball great Steve Garvey was one of the most popular and successful players in Major League Baseball during the 1970s. Garvey was named the National League's Most Valuable Player in 1974 and went on to play in four World Series as first baseman with the Dodgers. He was voted to the All-Star team eight times as a Dodger, and was named the All-Star Game's Most Valuable Player twice, in 1974 and 1978. He and wife Cynthia Garvey, who had a very successful television career, became known as the ''Barbie and Ken'' of baseball because of their good looks and apparent perfect lifestyle. Marital infidelity plagued both of the Garveys, and the couple eventually divorced. Garvey completed his playing career with the San Diego Padres where he retired in 1987.

—Jay Parrent

FURTHER READING:

Garvey, Cynthia, and Andy Meiser. *The Secret Life of Cyndy Garvey.* New York, St. Martin's Paperbacks, 1989.

Garvey, Steve, and Skip Rozin. *Garvey.* New York, Times Books, 1986.

Gas Stations

Gas stations are embedded in our urban and rural landscape, pervasive symbols of the automobile's domination of twentieth-century society. Like the fast-food restaurant, the motel, and the shopping mall, gas stations are buildings whose very existence was generated by the automobile. The gas station also demonstrates the extent of corporate control over our lives. On a more philosophical note, they represent what one writer has referred to as ''a potential point of pause'' in our unceasingly mobile culture.

Gas stations have changed over the course of the century from strictly functional to multipurpose. Their evolution allows us to glimpse the development of a consumer society in the twentieth century, fueled by the power of advertising and increasing corporatization. Early motorists purchased their gasoline by the bucket from a dry goods or hardware store. The first gas stations were simple sheds or shacks with a gas pump. By the 1910s, however, they began to take on a unique identity in the landscape. Oil companies created standardized buildings for the distribution of their product. The Texas Company (Texaco), for example, constructed its first station in 1916. Each distinct station provided a means of corporate identity. Since the motorist was in no position to judge the quality of gasoline and therefore distinguish any one brand from another, the oil companies had to instill brand loyalty in their customers. The distribution of gasoline was therefore linked from the beginning to a marketing/advertising system. Corporate logos and slogans were created to help the public identify with the company. Visible gasoline pumps, which allowed the motorist to see the product as it was pumped into the car, led to the practice of dyeing gasoline with colors like red, blue, or purple in an effort to distinguish one brand from another. Companies also began to diversify the range of products and services available to the public. Maintenance and repair services turned the filling station into the all-around car-care station.

The standardization of the 1910s gave way to the eclecticism of the 1920s. Oil companies' drive to make their product identifiable led to the creation of exotic eye-catching buildings designed to look like Greek temples, Chinese pagodas, and Swiss chalets. By the end of the 1920s, a nationwide gasoline distribution system was in place in America that has not changed since. At the same time, a highway-building boom allowed motorists to expand their range of travel. Gas stations arose along the new highways to provide necessary and convenient services. These non-urban stations were dedicated as much to the customer as the car—they offered amenities for the new long-distance traveler unnecessary in urban locales. Stations offered clean rest rooms, free maps, soft drinks, and snacks. As traffic increased and the automobile culture expanded, gas stations attracted other businesses, such as motels and diners, to their location. The desire to make the customer feel comfortable also led these early stations to clothe their employees in military-style uniforms, which added an air of legitimacy to a still relatively novel enterprise. Slogans like Texaco's ''You can trust your car to the man who wears the star'' also encouraged consumer comfort.

In the 1930s and 1940s, the eclectically styled gas stations of the previous decade diminished as a new, ''modern'' design aesthetic—reflecting public fascination with images of the future—swept through the industry. Stations emphasized clean surfaces and streamlined curves. ''Art Deco'' or ''Moderne'' style gas stations became popular symbols of the new machine age. Oil companies hired famous designers to update and promote their image. In 1934, Norman Bel Geddes provided a new design for the Socony-Vacuum Oil Company (now Mobil), which proved too avant-garde and was never built. In the same year, Walter Dorwin Teague was hired by Texaco for the same purpose. His streamlined box design was an instant success and was used in more than 10,000 stations across the country. Teague

An early Gulf gas station.

created a universally adaptable form and an immediately recognizable symbol for Texaco products. Other companies attempted to duplicate this achievement but were not as successful.

By the 1950s, a "functional" aesthetic began to prevail in the design of gas stations across the country. Historic and modern elements were rejected in favor of a design that emphasized function. Logos became more important as symbols of corporate identity. The impact of television as an advertising medium lessened the need for the gas station to serve as a three-dimensional billboard. For example, the Pure Oil Company sponsored a television quiz show in 1950, in which the company's slogan "Be Sure with Pure" was constantly repeated. The Texaco Star Theatre, with Milton Berle, was the most successful of these ventures—the show was the most popular television program in America in the 1950s.

The nature of the gas station began to change in the 1960s with the emergence of self-service stations and convenience stores. Self-service actually dated back to the 1930s, but in the interim most states had passed legislation requiring that only station personnel attend the pumps. The link between gas station and grocery store was even older; in the 1910s, many general stores in rural areas also had a gas pump. Also developing during this time period were truck

stops and "highway hubs"—small nodes of consumerism at highway interchanges.

In the late twentieth century, as repair and maintenance services have come increasingly within the purview of specialty shops and automobile dealerships, and gasoline pumps have been added to convenience stores as a secondary service, the traditional filling station is almost extinct, but as long as our society remains dependent on the automobile, the gas station, in whatever form it may take, will be a permanent part of our landscape.

—Dale Allen Gyure

FURTHER READING:

Jakle, John A., and Keith A. Sculle. *The Gas Station in America.* Baltimore and London, The Johns Hopkins University Press, 1994.

Jennings, Jan, ed. *The Automobile in Design and Culture.* Ames, Iowa State University Press, 1990.

Vieyra, Daniel I. *"Fill 'er Up": An Architectural History of America's Gas Stations.* New York, Collier Macmillan Publishers, 1979.

207

Witzel, Michael Karl. *The American Gas Station: History and Folklore of the Gas Station in American Car Culture.* Osceola, Wisconsin, Motorbooks International Publishers & Wholesalers, 1992.

Gated Communities

Gated communities are residential areas, ranging in size from individual streets and neighborhoods to entire cities, enclosed by walls and gates that are intended to prevent unauthorized entry by nonresidents. In many gated communities further protection against the outside world is provided by private security guards and electronic security systems. Most such communities operate as Common Interest Developments in which residents collectively own the common spaces or shared amenities, and a private homeowners association oversees community affairs. The population of these fortified enclaves tends to be overwhelmingly middle- or upper-class, white, and middle-aged or older. The primary reason they settle in such places, according to surveys, is to escape the crime, traffic, and noise of the cities and ungated suburbs. To many observers, the rising number of gated communities constitutes, in the words of Clinton Administration Labor Secretary Robert Reich, "the succession of the successful" from the civic life of the broader society.

Although gated communities in one form or another have existed in America since the colonial era, up until the late 1960s they were popular only with the ultra-rich and privacy-conscious celebrities. In the 1970s, developers built a few master-planned walled subdivisions aimed primarily at senior citizens and retirees. By the 1980s and 1990s, gated communities designed for ordinary middle-class families were proliferating at a rapid rate, particularly throughout the Sun Belt states. Researchers agree that middle-class fears about rising crime and concerns about the deterioration of municipal services are the most important factors behind the boom in gated developments. In their book *Fortress America,* Edward Blakely and Mary Gail Snyder estimate that by 1997 the United States had approximately 20,000 gated communities with some three million units of housing and 8.4 million residents. Some of the gated developments being built in the 1990s attempt to incorporate all the traditional features of city living behind their walls. An excellent example of this trend is Green Lake, Nevada, a sprawling walled suburb outside Las Vegas that is expected to have 60,000 residents by the year 2005. It is divided by house size and cost into prefabricated "villages," each with its own meeting hall, recreational center, school, park, and in the more exclusive tracts, an entrance with a manned guardhouse. At the same time, more and more preexisting neighborhoods and suburbs are walling themselves off from surrounding cities by barricading public streets and installing gates and security systems.

In the majority of gated developments that are organized as CIDs, homeowners associations function as a kind of private government. People who buy property in such developments are forced to join the association, pay dues, and agree to abide by its rules. Homeowners associations deliver such traditionally public services as trash collection, policing, snow removal, road maintenance, and street lighting. They also make regulations governing all aspects of life in the community, including rules limiting the hours and frequency of visitors, setting the minimum age of residents, banning the display of flags, prohibiting certain kinds of pets, and specifying what color paint owners can use on their houses. Fairbanks Ranch, an affluent gated community in Southern California, is patrolled by private security officers who enforce a speed limit set by the homeowners association which fines repeat speeders $500 and bans them from the community's streets for a month. A few gated communities have succeeded in incorporating themselves as full-fledged municipalities (in which the elected city government usually defers to the rule-making authority of the homeowners association).

As the proportion of the population living in them has risen, gated communities have gradually become a political force to be reckoned with. In California, private homeowners associations have lobbied state legislatures for the right to deduct homeowner dues from state income taxes. In New Jersey, private homeowner associations in 1990 pushed legislation through the state legislature which entitles their members to rebates on the property taxes they pay to support city services.

Yet even as gated communities were beginning to enjoy the fruits of their new-found power, there were signs in the late 1990s of a growing backlash against what planner Norman Krumholtz has called the "balkanization" of America's cities. Four communities in suburban Dallas—Addison, Plano, Richardson, and Southlake—decided to prohibit barriers on public roads and even placed moratoriums on the construction of private gated developments. In 1995, both San Diego and Portland began studying policies that would limit the spread of gates within their boundaries. Proposals to erect walls around existing communities and close public streets have been successfully fought in courts and city councils in Los Angeles, Chicago, Atlanta, Sacramento, and elsewhere.

Ultimately, however, whether the number and population of America's fortified enclaves continues to expand will be determined less by political battles than by the desires and decisions of millions of home buyers in the years to come. As long as fear of crime and the desire for peace and quiet outweigh the lure of public life in the minds of those who can afford to choose where they live, gated communities will continue their inexorable spread across the nation's landscape.

—Steve Macek

FURTHER READING:

Blakely, Edward, and Mary Gail Snyder. *Fortress America: Gated Communities in the United States.* Washington, D.C., Brookings Institution Press, 1997.

Judd, Dennis. "The Rise of New Walled Cities." *Spatial Practices: Critical Explorations in Social/Spatial Theory.* Edited by Helen Liggett and David Perry. Thousand Oaks, California, Sage, 1995, 144-166.

McKenzie, Evan. *Privatopia: Homeowner Associations and the Rise of Residential Private Government.* New Haven, Connecticut, Yale University Press, 1994.

Stark, Andrew. "America, the Gated?" *Wilson Quarterly.* Winter 1998, 58-79.

Gay and Lesbian Marriage

The advent of marriage between same-sex couples marked one of the major cultural and social changes of the twentieth century in the United States. In 1970 gay and lesbian couples requested so many marriage licenses from the Los Angeles County Clerk, that the Clerk's office requested the California legislature tighten California marriage laws. However, despite this auspicious start, and the continued efforts of gay and lesbian activists and their supporters, it was not until the late 1980s that homosexual marriage was again hotly contested in the courts, the state and national legislatures, by the public at large, the mass media, and within the gay and lesbian community itself.

In 1971, Richard John Baker and James Michael McConnell brought the first case of same-sex marriage to court in Minnesota. Along with arguing their constitutional rights, they cited recent anti-miscegenation laws in support of their plea, all of which the court rejected. The first lesbian case, *Jones v. Hallahan*, was brought in Kentucky in 1973. Again, as would continually happen, the case was lost on the grounds of falling outside the "dictionary" definition of marriage. During the 1970s, a number of other court cases were lost, though there were a few small victories, such as a marriage license granted to a gay couple in Boulder, Colorado, which encouraged numerous gay and lesbian couples to apply successfully for marriage licenses. However, the decision was later overturned by the Attorney General and all licenses were revoked. In 1975 the Arizona legislature passed an emergency bill defining marriage as only being possible between a man and a woman. This bill set up a precedent for other state legislatures.

From the 1970s through the mid-1980s the rise of radical lesbian-feminism, coupled with AIDS concerns, dominated political energy and time within the lesbian and gay communities. Early radical lesbian-feminist theory argued against the institution of marriage in general, and many lesbians questioned the focus on lesbian and gay marriage rights. The graver issue of the AIDS epidemic so dominated people's lives that comparatively lesser issues such as marriage rights became secondary. Yet, ironically, it might be argued that both the lesbian-feminist movement and AIDS activism may have provoked the issue of same-sex marriages to re-surface by encouraging more people to come out. By politicizing increasing numbers of homosexuals, raising public consciousness about lesbian and gay issues, and attempting to eradicate the image of gays—most particularly men—as promiscuous people incapable of long-term relationships, the marriage issue once more came up for discussion. Additionally, the feminist movement's push towards passing the Equal Rights Amendments later had a great effect on an extremely prominent same-sex marriage case in Hawaii in the 1990s, where the state ERA was used as an argument for legalizing such marriages.

In 1986, the American Civil Liberties Union declared that they would seek to eliminate those legal barriers preventing lesbians and gays from marrying. In 1989, the San Francisco Bar Association called for gay and lesbian marriages, and two gay Chicago journalists filed complaints with the Illinois Department of Human Rights, accusing the state of sex discrimination for refusing gay marriages. By the 1990s, many activists were trying to force the passing of pro-marriage bills, while license applications and court cases continued, along with the filing of discrimination complaints with Human Rights Commissions. The issue started gaining momentum in the general public and, in 1989, a *Time* magazine poll reported 69 percent disapproval, 23 percent approval, and eight percent unsure on the issue of legalizing same-sex marriages. Three years later, in a 1992 *Newsweek* survey, the figures had altered to 58 percent against, 35 percent for, and seven percent unsure.

The most well-known court case to act as a catalyst in advancing the cause of same-sex marriage was that of *Baehr v. Lewin*, heard in Hawaii in 1991. Three same-sex couples sued the state of Hawaii for refusing to issue them marriage licenses, claiming that the refusal violated Hawaii's state Equal Rights Amendment (ERA) barring discrimination on the basis of sex. In May 1993, for the first time in U.S. legal history, the Hawaii Supreme Court ruled in favor of lesbian and gay marriage. In a December 1996 trial, Circuit Judge Kevin Chang ruled against the state of Hawaii on almost all counts, declaring that the state could not deny marriage licenses to same-sex couples and ordering the state to pay the plaintiffs' litigation costs. The next day, the judge stayed his decision pending appeal to the Hawaii Supreme Court.

Anti-gay groups and political leaders feared that lesbians and gays would flock to Hawaii to marry. They furiously worked to change the constitutional mandate providing interstate recognition of marriage whereby each state must recognize and honor a marriage license granted in any other state. The biggest blow to the gay and lesbian community came with the passage of the Federal government's Defense of Marriage Act (DOMA) in 1996, which defined marriage for federal purposes as a legal union between one man and one woman, and permitted states to ignore out-of-state gay and lesbian marriages, despite constitutional law that ruled otherwise. Activists planned to challenge DOMA.

By the late 1990s, over 30 states enacted some type of anti-same-sex-marriage legislation, explicitly limiting marriage to one man and one woman. These 1990s laws differed from those passed in the 1970s because they discussed marriages within their own state as well as the interstate recognition of marriages. In the November 1998 elections Hawaii voters passed a ballot saying there should be a constitutional amendment defining marriage as one man and one woman. Although a blow to advocates of gay and lesbian marriage, a committee had yet to draft an amendment on which a vote would be taken. If passed, the amendment would make it more difficult, but not impossible, for a judge to declare same-sex marriage legal.

While conservative and right-wing elements battled against the gay marriage activists, the lesbian and gay communities also debated the issue. Many fought for same-sex marriage rights, believing they deserved the same civil rights as heterosexual couples. Others felt fighting for marriage rights was a middle-class white issue that detracted from broader issues, and that fighting for marriage rights was bowing to a conservatism to be "just like everyone else." Some lesbians and gays felt it was more important to fight for domestic partnership rights for all and abolish the age-old unjust institution of marriage for everyone.

Both within the lesbian and gay communities and the heterosexual constituencies, the heated debate as to what defines marriage continues to rage, and plays into the hands of the Moral Majority. Irrespective, however, to which side of the argument any one individual, state, or religious body adheres, the issue is one of major significance for legal and civil rights in both the national and local political arenas of the United States.

—tova gd stabin

FURTHER READING:

Dunlap, David. "Panel in Hawaii Recommends Legalizing Same-Sex Marriage." *The New York Times*. December 11, 1995, A18.

Feldblum, Chai R. "A Progressive Moral Case for Same-Sex Marriage." *Temple Political & Civil Rights Law Review.* Vol. 7, No. 2, 485.

"Fever." *The Advocate,* No. 712, July 23, 1996, 22.

Goldstein, Richard. "The Great Gay Marriage Debate." *The Village Voice.* January 9, 1996, 24.

Kopels, "Sandra. Wedded to the Status Quo: Same-Sex Marriage After *Baehr v. Lewin." Journal of Gay & Lesbian Social Services,* Vol. 8, No. 3, 1998, 69.

Marcus, Eric. *Together Forever: Gay and Lesbian Marriage.* New York, Doubleday, 1998.

Martinac, Paula. *The Lesbian and Gay book of Love and Marriage: Creating the Stories of Our Lives.* New York, Broadway Books, 1998.

Patten, James M. "The Defense of Marriage Act: How Congress Said 'No' to Full Faith and Credit, and the Constitution." *Santa Clara Law Review,* Vol. 38, No. 3, 939.

Stiers, Gretchen A. *From This Day Forward: Commitment, Marriage, and Family in Lesbian and Gay Relationships.* New York, St. Martin's Press, 1999.

Gay and Lesbian Press

For fifty years gay and lesbian presses in America have published papers and magazines that give a distinctive voice to their concerns. Their editorial approach and journalistic style— unabashed, irreverent, and confrontational—reflect a commitment to bolstering the strength of the gay community that they serve, and to documenting the homophobic attitudes of society. The dissemination of ideas through the written word of the gay and lesbian presses has been a building block in the development of the gay subculture. The publications act as a powerful resource in the promotion of homosexual rights on a national and international scale, and as a coalescing agent in bringing together gay activists and closeted individuals, those from rural areas and urban gay ghettos. Mirroring the diversity of the gay and lesbian community, its presses are as varied as the interests of its constituency. Some publishers focus upon either gay or lesbian issues, while others maintain a more inclusive gender stance.

The core of the press group is comprised of a small collection of specialist presses, along with a widespread array of local and national newspapers and magazines. Historically, the distribution of gay and lesbian books was generally through privately owned gay and lesbian bookstores, located in urban gay neighborhoods. Initially there was strong opposition by regular booksellers to stocking gay and lesbian titles, but this changed by the 1990s when booksellers, along with other commercial enterprises, had come to recognize the gay and lesbian market as a vast untapped resource. It was predicted that by the year 2000, more than 20,000 gay and lesbian titles would be published.

During the first half of the twentieth century most of the materials published that provided a positive viewpoint on homosexuality were issued through private presses. Often the publications produced were of poor quality, frequently printed by hand, typed, or copied on mimeograph machines. In this discrete endeavor, the print runs were necessarily small, though there were notable exceptions in the literary field, where homosexual concerns were explored under the guise of metaphorical language and symbolism. The precursor to the modern-day gay and lesbian presses can be observed in two early twentieth-century German periodicals, *Der Eigene* and *Jahrbuch fur Sexuelle Zwischenstufen.*

The sexologist Magnus Hirschfeld was the editor of the *Jahrbuch fur Sexuelle Zwischenstufen* from 1899 to 1923. Published in Berlin, the journal contained an academic perspective on homosexuality featuring full-length articles, bibliographies of new books, and articles by Eugen Wilhelm. *Der Eigene,* headed by Adolf Brand, was devoted to the field of arts, and later developed into a publication of Gemeinschaft der Eigenen, a German homosexual movement. The publication was high in quality, with many black and white, sepia, and color illustrations. *Der Eigene* was published from 1898 to 1930, until the rise of the National Socialist movement in Germany, which culminated in the upswing of Nazi persecution of homosexuals in the mid-1930s, bringing the flourishing gay presses to an abrupt halt.

During the 1920s small and secretive gay presses started to emerge in the United States. The first gay publication to emerge was Henry Gerber's short-lived *Friendship and Freedom* (1924). The magazine was published by the Society for Human Rights, founded by Gerber in Chicago. Two issues were published, produced on a mimeograph machine and running to approximately 100 hundred copies. When police learned of the activities of the Society for Human Rights they seized the remaining copies of *Friendship and Freedom* and arrested the membership of the group, including Gerber, who was dismissed from his postal job as a result of his activities. He also worked on another publication, *Chanticleer,* during the 1930s, of which 50 percent of the contents were devoted to homosexual issues and the remaining proportion to atheistic advocacy. Gerber also published a single-sheet mimeographed newsletter for Contacts pen pal club from 1930 to 1939. The newsletter contained a few short news articles and was distributed among 30 to 70 members of the club. None of these publications were able either to appeal to or demand a large readership due to limited publishing numbers, geographic constraints, and the restrictive attitudes of society. Most existed on the margins of journalism, fearing the intervention of the police or government officials under one pretext or another.

Following World War II there was a revival of the Homophile Movement in the United States, and new gay and lesbian journals began to emerge. The earliest surviving publication, *The Ladder,* dates back to 1947, and was edited by Lisa Ben in Los Angeles. Lisa Ben was the author's pseudonym, an anagram for lesbian, used to conceal her actual identity. Small press runs of *Vice Versa* were printed from 1947 to 1948. Typical of publishing during the era, the periodical was typed on a dozen carbon copies and distributed by hand at several Los Angeles lesbian bars. *Vice Versa* helped to lay the groundwork for the creation of a gay and lesbian press in the United States. Early in 1953 Martin Block, Dale Jennings, and Bill Lambert planned what would become the first openly sold gay and lesbian magazine in the nation. The title, *ONE Magazine,* was derived from the Carlyle quote "A common bond of brotherhood makes all men one." Martin Block edited the first issues of *ONE* in 1953, and Dale Jennings took over for the final part of the year. The format was small, a six by seven-inch pamphlet, with only 500 copies printed, and sold for 20 cents. Distribution and sales occurred primarily at gay and lesbian bars and organized homophile meetings. Most of the issues focused on news, homosexual persecution, and police harassment, but the journal went further than some of its predecessors and included fiction, poetry, and theoretical and political articles. The mission of the editors and staff of *ONE* was to remove homophobic attitudes from within the homosexual community as well as from society at large, while simultaneously creating and nurturing the community and its culture. From *ONE Magazine* also sprang the membership newsletter, *ONE Confidential,* and the first scholarly treatment of homosexual issues, *ONE Institute Quarterly of Homophile Studies.*

Jim Kepner joined the staff of *ONE Magazine* in 1954. A victim of police harassment in a bar raid, Kepner's writings advocated the need for gay self-respect, education, community-building, and gay identity. While the writings of Kepner and others at *ONE* took a militant stance, *The Mattachine Review*, established by Harold Call in 1955, subscribed to an assimilationist and conformist viewpoint. A squeaky clean image was advocated and promoted by the *Mattachine Review* and by *The Ladder,* a Daughters of Bilitis publication, as the tool for gays and lesbians to gain entree into a society known to repress homosexuals. In spite of the fact that these early gay presses worked collegially well together, *ONE* was frequently chastised by *Mattachine* for its aggressive and confrontational attitudes, while the Daughters of Bilitis were offended by it. The women of the Daughters of Bilitis, *Mattachine,* and *ONE* denied that there were separate women's issues as such during this period. Many insisted they were just like everyone else, with a strong sense of commitment to the gay community. Many women were included as authors in *One Magazine,* with an all-women's issue printed in February of 1954. Topical concerns and coverage of women was also a key facet of *ONE Magazine.*

By the end of the 1950s, monthly homosexual magazines were being discreetly mailed, first class, in plain brown wrappers to avoid interception by postal authorities. The contents mainly contained news articles, editorials, literature, and non-erotic illustrations that were subtly suggestive rather than graphic. Personal ads did not appear due to legal and societal constraints.

The turbulence of the 1960s saw both a changing attitude towards homosexuality and the development of an underground press, which acted as fertile ground for new gay publishers. These unprecedented materials held a hard edge and bite. Obscene language appeared frequently in the articles, and personal ads became a regular feature, in which the authors would express their most intimate desires and fetishes. The Gay Liberation Movement had found its voice by the end of the decade in publications such as *The Advocate, The Body Politic* (Toronto), *Come Out, Gay Community News* (Boston), *Gay Sunshine,* and *Gay* (New York).

During the 1970s gay and lesbian presses grew and flourished. More magazines, newspapers, and newsletters began to appear, many with a specialized identity featuring religious, political, or professional interests. Local and regional publications also burgeoned, and as the proliferation of gay and lesbian periodicals increased so did the ''in your face'' frankness of the content. New homosexual organizations were created on both sides of the gender divide, many of them distributing their own publication. Some of the new periodicals had a short life, while others have continued printing to the present day.

Glossy illustrated magazines focusing on male nudity, erotic illustrations, short stories, and personal and classified advertisement rich in graphic detail became a common feature of the gay press during this period. Magazines such as *Blueboy, In Touch,* and *Mandate,* became more readily available on the newsstands or by subscription. Their articles and editorials quickly reached a nationwide audience, creating a norm of taste and attitude within the gay community. Beyond the major urban centers, many smaller cities began producing local gay newspapers. Often distributed at the gay bars, some became known as ''bar rags.'' Many of these newspapers joined forces to found the Gay and Lesbian Press Association. More importantly, new scholarly journals such as the *Gai Saber* (1997-1978), *Gay Books Bulletin/Cabirion* (1979-1985), and *Journal of Homosexuality* (1974—) provided an academic basis for the pursuit of in-depth gay and lesbian research and university studies.

The gay and lesbian press market has predominantly been segregated by gender. Book sales are ranked on separate male and female bestseller lists, with few bestsellers appearing simultaneously on both. During the 1960s and early 1970s many of the lesbian publications were usurped under the feminist banner. Signs of a developing lesbian press could be observed from Marie Kuda's Lesbian Writers Conferences, which were held annually from 1974 until 1979. The establishment of lesbian-friendly presses made it possible for fiction and non-fiction to be published in book form rather than in small circulation magazines. Support for lesbian writing was due in large part to women's bookstores across the country, which made lesbian books more accessible than ever before. These bookstores have continued to play a significant role in the sale of lesbian materials.

Through the power of the written word gay and lesbian presses have created a common language and a shared frame of reference for a diverse population of gays and lesbians. Bonding together through periodicals and books, the specter of isolation has been removed, and replaced by a sense of ''gay identity.'' The presses have also created a window through which the outside world can look at the many aspects of gay life, and have provided a written record for deeper understanding and further research.

—Michael A. Lutes

FURTHER READING:

Kepner, Jim. *Rough News, Daring Views: 1950s Pioneer Gay Press Journalism.* New York, Haworth Press, 1998.

Long Road to Freedom: The Advocate History of the Gay and Lesbian Movement. New York, St. Martin's Press, 1994.

Malinowsky, H. Robert. *International Directory of Gay and Lesbian Periodicals.* Phoenix, Oryx Press, 1987.

Miller, Alan. *Our Own Voices: A Directory of Gay and Lesbian Periodicals, 1890-1990: Including the Holdings of the Canadian Gay Archives.* Toronto, The Archives, 1991.

Streitmatter, Rodger. *Unspeakable: The Rise of the Gay and Lesbian Press in America.* Boston, Faber and Faber, 1995.

Gay Liberation Movement

The tidal wave of social change that began with the black civil rights movement of the early 1960s carried many other social movements on its crest. These included the anti-Vietnam War protests, women's liberation, and the gay and lesbian liberation movement, and all of these movements owed tremendous debts to each other. Many gay men and lesbians worked in the civil rights, anti-war, and feminist movements and their labor to fight oppression in these movements sparked dissatisfaction with the hidden oppression in their own lives. Many people, even those working politically in other

A group of gay rights demonstrators.

movements, saw sexual orientation as a personal issue, removed from politics. Even progressive activists, who were sympathetic and respectful of many differences among people, often ridiculed gays as savagely as their conservative counterparts. Feminism, in particular, began to change this perception, with its emphasis on the political meaning in each person's experience. Gays began to view their sexuality as a political issue rather than a shameful personal secret.

Though there had been work historically to improve the status of homosexuals, the beginning of the gay liberation movement is often officially marked on the night of June 28, 1969 at the Stonewall Inn, a gay bar in New York's Greenwich Village. In the pre-gay liberation 1950s and 1960s, even in known gay neighborhoods like the Village, gay bars were shadowed places. Gay people kept their sexuality hidden, and much about homosexuality was illegal, from cross-dressing to same-sex dancing. Gay bars were one of the few places gays could meet in public, and these bars were often run by members of organized crime, who were happy to profit from the illegitimate status of homosexuality. Police frequently raided gay bars, where proprietors sometimes had warning systems so that gay men and lesbians could switch partners quickly when the police entered a bar. Gay bar raids were also often an opportunity for police to brutalize gays, with little fear that their victims would report them and chance being publicly labeled "queer." Those who looked most obviously

gay—the drag queens in dresses and high heels and the lesbians in men's suits—were singled out for harshest treatment. That June night at the Stonewall Inn, the patrons of the bar did not respond in the passive way gays had usually responded to attacks by the police. Tired of being helpless victims, the gays fought back, rioting in the streets of "their" neighborhood, shouting the new rallying cry, "Gay Power!" The riots lasted for three days and received unprecedented media coverage.

Popular mythology says that the riots occurred on the day that singer Judy Garland died from a drug overdose, thought by many to have been intentional. Many gays, especially gay men, identified strongly with Garland's ravaged vulnerability and passionate singing style, and the story goes that when the police arrived to harass a gay community grieving over the loss of an idol, something snapped and anger and pride welled up to take the place of shame. In fact, Garland's death took place almost a week before the riots, on June 22. But there is a truth that underlies all mythology, and the truth is that the Stonewall riots were a watershed that marked a change in gays' and lesbians' perceptions of themselves. The status of homosexuals did not change overnight, but neither could things ever go back to the way they had been before the riots. Almost as if they had been waiting for a catalyzing event, gay liberation organizations began to spring up across the United States and around the world.

There had always been gay men and lesbians, and they had been more or less visible and more or less oppressed, depending on their time in history and their cultural context. In previous centuries, for example, upper-class women had lived together in lesbian relationships called "Boston marriages" which were socially tolerated. It was not uncommon for women in pioneer country to pass as men to attain some of the freedom of movement and financial independence denied to them as women, and frequently these women married and lived with their "wives." Many Native American cultures made a place for both women and men who did not identify with their traditional gender role, or who had same-sex lovers. In the early part of the twentieth century, African-American drag "debutante" balls, were major social events that drew elite society, straight and gay alike. These balls were satirical reproductions of the traditional balls where young women were presented to society, and it is from them that we derive the term "coming out," for gays and lesbians publicly announcing their gayness. The more repressive connotation, that of gays "coming out" of a dark closet, did not arrive until the 1950s, and the less socially lighthearted atmosphere of that decade.

In Europe, World War II meant Nazi aggression and the attempted genocide of European gays. However, the upheaval of war brought openness and opportunity to gays in the United States, whether in the military or on the home front. Military service had always provided a same-sex environment and gays often connected there, and the necessities of war did not permit an anti-gay campaign which would reduce U.S. forces. The defense industry attracted thousands of people to urban centers where gays who had formerly been isolated in small towns around the country could find each other. Once the war was over, society took on the job of repressing those women and gays who had found unusual freedom during wartime. Heterosexual women were sent home to be housewives, and gays and lesbians were the subject of a concerted "witch hunt" by the Truman administration. Hundreds of gays working for the government lost their jobs.

Gay and lesbian organizing itself did not originate with the 1970s gay liberation movement. As early as 1924 Henry Gerber was jailed and fired from his job for founding the gay and lesbian Society for Human Rights in Chicago. In Los Angeles, in 1950, foreshadowing the connection of gay liberation and leftist politics, a group five men, three of them Communist Party members founded the Mattachine Society. The group's goal was "to promote a sense of solidarity and group identity among homosexuals." Mattachine was one of a number of early "homophile" associations which included the lesbian group Daughters of Bilitis, founded in San Francisco in 1955. These groups promoted acceptance of homosexuals; their members wrote, spoke, and even picketed in defense of that cause. Their other function was to provide a safe place for lesbians and gays to meet, apart from the bars. Certainly the idea of social safety for gays was radical enough, but by the 1970s, influenced by the civil rights movement and feminists, gays demanded more.

Following the Stonewall Riots, new gay liberation organizations began forming. Some, like New York's Gay Liberation Front and Radical Fairies had chapters across the country. Others were smaller, local organizations, created by activists in many urban areas and progressive small towns nationwide. The Furies in Washington, DC, the Lesbian Alliance in St. Louis and the Atlanta Lesbian Feminist Alliance (ALFA) were only a few of hundreds of groups that formed and re-formed. Political gays and lesbians began by reclaiming the names that had been used against them. "Gay" itself, once a general term for immorality, had been used by gay men in the 1920s and 1930s as a code word to identify each other. Once the term "gay" had

been reclaimed by homosexuals to describe themselves, radicals began to look for ways to disempower the anti-gay epithets that had been hurled at them. They began to reclaim words such as "dyke" and "faggot" for use among themselves, thus denying the words their negative power, much as African Americans had reclaimed racist slurs for an exclusive usage that reinforced black solidarity.

With few exceptions, homosexuality had previously been treated in American society as either a crime or a disease. Homosexuals who did not regularly end up in jail, often ended up in mental hospitals subjected to various brutal "cures," such as aversion therapy and electroshock therapy. Since any deviation from their prescribed societal role often landed women in mental hospitals, many lesbians suffered this form of oppression. After the Stonewall Rebellion, as it came to be called, gay activists began to work not only for social acceptance, but for legal rights. They demanded the right to live and work, free from discrimination, and they demanded that homosexuality be removed from the American Psychiatric Association's list of mental diseases. In 1973, thanks to the work of lesbian and gay activists, the APA did remove homosexuality from the list.

Gays also began to work on decriminalizing homosexuality, which was illegal in many states. In 1962, Illinois became the first state to repeal its anti-gay laws, and activists kept up the pressure until by 1998, only 19 states still had anti-gay laws on the books. Not content with mere legality, gay rights activists worked for gay rights protections with varying degrees of success. One example: in 1973, the city council in the liberal university town of Boulder, Colorado voted in a gay rights law. Outraged, the conservative citizenry not only repealed the law, but voted to recall every member of city council that voted for it.

With the new movement and the increasing number of new organizations inevitably came differences and conflict. Older gays who had come out without the support of a very public movement resented the often dismissive attitudes of the young "liberated" gays. Younger gays challenged the political conservatism and butch and femme gender roles that had often been practiced by their predecessors. Some gays, many of them white men, were fairly comfortable with their place in society, and felt that changing society's attitudes about homosexuality was all that was needed. Others saw many things about American society that needed to be changed and viewed gay liberation as inevitably connected to other progressive liberation movements. This argument over whether gay rights was a "single issue" fight or part of a larger leftist liberation struggle was to become perhaps the second biggest split in the movement.

Possibly the biggest split was between men and women. Some lesbians, coming to the movement through feminism, questioned their commonalities with gay men, preferring to ally themselves with heterosexual women instead. Insisting that "gay" was a word that defined gay men, many chose to distinguish themselves by using the word "lesbian" or "dyke." The feminist movement began by resisting accusations of lesbians in its ranks, fearful that identification of lesbians with feminism would undermine the legitimacy of women's liberation. However, many of the feminist leaders were lesbians, and, in the increasing atmosphere of gay openness, they demanded recognition. More divisions followed: lesbian feminists threatened not only the heterosexual male establishment, but also heterosexual feminists and non-feminist lesbians. Lesbian feminists themselves split, dividing those who still identified with heterosexual women's issues from the separatists, who tried to have as little as possible to do with men or non-lesbian women. While these splits created discord and discomfort, they also created an energy that propelled dozens of groups, conferences, newspapers, bookstores, and small presses throughout the country. The new atmosphere of gay liberation was creating a frenzy of dialog on subjects that had once been shrouded in silence.

Though, as with feminism, the gay liberation movement was usually presented by the press as a white and middle-class movement, gay activists came from all classes, races, and ethnic backgrounds. Many of these activists attempted in their agendas to focus on the racism, classism, and sexism within the movement, though their attempts were not always successful. Some gays of color and Jewish gays formed their own groups, seeking solidarity and support. Events such as the 1976 West Coast Conference on Faggots and Class Struggle in Eugene, Oregon, and the Dynamics of Color lesbian conference in San Francisco in 1989 are examples of the many efforts made to address difficult intra-movement conflicts.

Perhaps the most controversial aspect of the gay and lesbian liberation movement was its connection to the counterculture. Movement gays were no longer content to ask for acceptance by society; they demanded that society change to reflect the evolving definitions of gender and gender roles. Radical gays challenged the ideas of nuclear family, of monogamy, of capitalism, and, though not all gays agreed, the movement brought up topics of discussion, and those discussions would forever change the way American culture saw itself.

Lesbians were intent on creating and developing ''women's culture'' that included new forms of spirituality, literature, and music, all stemming from and connected to lesbian feminist politics. Lesbian music became a growing art form and women's recording artists gained popularity on both coasts and in the midwest. In 1975, hundreds of women attended Michigan Women's Music Festival. The Michigan festival, organized by lesbians, combined concerts and political workshops and was the largest of many regional women's cultural events.

The notion of free sex, espoused by the counterculture hippies had opened up acceptance of differing sexual lifestyles among the young, as well as legitimizing styles of dress and appearance formerly considered outlandish. Gay men in particular reveled in the new sexual openness. Their celebratory exuberance resulted in the rocketing popularity of the disco phenomenon. As gay identity became more proud and less shameful, the image of the gay bar as a dark hideaway also changed. Gay disco bars, which had flashing lights and loud music with a driving sexual beat became the social centers for gay men, and, to a lesser extent, lesbians. The trendy, exciting bars also attracted straight people, and this moved gay culture into the mainstream in a way that demonstrations could not accomplish. The disco scene was also heavily associated with casual sex and recreational drug use, which in part was responsible for its end.

By 1981, medical authorities were beginning to identify a new virus the called GRID or Gay Related Immune Deficiency. Soon, they had changed the name of the disease to Acquired Immuno-Deficiency Syndrome (AIDS) and re-evaluated its connection to the gay community. Though AIDS is not a gay disease, it is sexually transmitted and the promiscuous lifestyle and drug use common within many gay male communities made them an ideal place for the virus to spread. It did spread, and, as thousands of gay men died, AIDS became a focus for the work of gay rights activists.

By the late 1970s, the revolutionary fervor that had characterized early gay liberation politics, had succumbed to the same backlash that had quieted much of the 1960s activism. Fundamentalist Christians were particularly threatened by any legitimization of gay lifestyles, and the anti-gay agenda became a platform issue for conservative Republicans. Right-wing Christian activist Anita Bryant launched her anti-gay Save Our Children campaign in 1977, and many gay rights advances were threatened. Though leftist gay activists continued to fight the challenges of the right wing, the excitement of the nation-wide movement had been dampened. In 1987, the AIDS Coalition to Unleash Power (ACT-UP) formed to fight for de-stigmatization of the AIDS virus, money for AIDS research, and other AIDS related issues. The arrival of ACT-UP with its 1960s-like aggressive street tactics, politicized the gay male community and many supportive lesbians around the issue of AIDS, and led the way to other ''second generation'' activist organizations such as the Lesbian Avengers, which originated in New York and expanded to chapters across the country. The first gay and lesbian rights march in Washington, D.C., in 1979, attracted one hundred thousand marchers. By 1993, when the third march on the capitol was held, almost a million people attended.

Of all the contributions that gay activism has made to society, one of the most unexpected is that it has given young gays a very public older generation. As in every other grouping, an older generation supplies mentors and role models—and something to rebel against. Like other children of the baby-boom generation, the 1970s gay activists have been nonplussed to find their own ''children'' espousing quite different politics and beliefs than the ones that drove them. Where post-Stonewall gays rejected gender roles, 1990s gay youth has rediscovered and embraced butch and femme. While feminism provided the foundation for many 1970s lesbians to discover and acknowledge their own identities, some lesbians in the 1990s call themselves ''post feminist'' and reject what they see as the unnecessary polarity that feminism espouses. Their gay liberation movement has expanded to include bisexuals and transgendered people.

The Stonewall riots are commemorated each year around the end of June on Gay Pride Day. In cities all over the world, gays gather for parades, marches, celebration, and political action. The 1990s have brought renewed energy to right-wing attacks on gay rights as well as ''gay bashing'' and other violent attacks on gays. Media coverage of gays and lesbians is limited to gays that fit the conservative ''middle America'' stereotype, and coverage of radical gays is almost non-existent. Disagreements among gays over sex, race, class, and politics continue. Gay and lesbian identity is still stigmatized, and ''coming out of the closet'' is still an act of personal courage and risk that many feel unable to perform. However, gays are no longer invisible figures of the shadows. Gay characters appear on many prime-time network television shows and on the covers of national magazines, not only as political figures or as curiosities, but as celebrities and role models. Gay and lesbian youth, while still at risk in many ways, no longer have to rely on whispered epithets to learn what the words ''gay'' and ''lesbian'' mean. The decades of secrecy, shame, and oppression that culminated in three days of rioting in Greenwich Village ended that summer, and a new era began. That era is still unfolding.

—Tina Gianoulis

FURTHER READING:

Cruikshank, Margaret. *The Gay and Lesbian Liberation Movement.* New York, Routledge, 1992.

D'Emilio, John. *Sexual Politics, Sexual Communities: The Making of a Homosexual Minority in the United States.* Chicago, University of Chicago Press, 1983.

Grahn, Judy. *Another Mother Tongue: Gay Words, Gay Worlds.* Boston, Beacon Press, 1990.

Johnston, Jill. *Lesbian Nation: The Feminist Solution.* New York, Simon and Schuster, 1973.

Vaid, Urvashi. *Virtual Equality: The Mainstreaming of Gay and Lesbian Liberation.* New York, Anchor Books, 1995.

Gay Men

While homosexuality has been documented in most cultures throughout history, the modern American gay male community began to form itself in the early 1900s. The word "gay," once widely used in the nineteenth century to describe any sort of debauched behavior, gained a new meaning when gay men in the 1920s and 1930s used it as a code word to identify each other. Though their communities were kept underground for decades, hidden from a larger society, which for the most part condemned homosexuality as immoral and perverted, gay men have exerted a tremendous influence on that society. Through arts, fashion, literature, entertainment, and politics, gay men, both visible and invisible, have been one of the major forces in shaping the twentieth century.

Around the 1920s, urban gays had begun to find ways to meet and socialize. Most gay meeting places were clandestine, but some were tolerated or even considered fashionable by straight society, such as the African-American drag "debutante" balls of the early twentieth century, which were major social events that drew elite society, straight and gay alike. "Drag," where men dress in women's clothes, complete with wigs and makeup, has long been a staple of some men's gay identity, and the gay drag queen is both stereotype and icon.

The 1940s were a galvanizing time for gay communities. World War II caused major population shifts, as young people left rural areas to join the army or get jobs in cities in the defense industry. Gays began to find each other in unprecedented numbers, and, having made these connections, they were reluctant to return to the isolation of small town life. Many remained in urban centers and developed their communities, opening clubs and bars where they could meet and socialize.

The return to "normalcy" after the war led to increased repression and even "witch hunts" for gays in the late 1940s and 1950s, but, like a pressure cooker, repression eventually led to release. The black civil rights movement of the 1960s and later the anti-war movement and women's liberation inspired gays to seek their own rights. In 1969, decades of repression exploded in the "Stonewall Rebellion," three days of rioting in the gay section of New York's Greenwich Village. In the forefront of the riots were the drag queens, the most visible of gay men. By the 1970s, gays enjoyed a visibility and freedom previously unknown in American history.

Though male homosexuality has been stigmatized by mainstream culture both historically and in the present, it is widely known that many men who would never identify themselves as gay have had sexual experiences with other males. In situations where a same-sex environment is enforced, such as prisons and male boarding schools, it is recognized, if not totally accepted, that men and boys will "make do" with other males until females are available to them. That this behavior is considered inevitable has to do in part with the view of male sexuality, which is often seen as a driving force which must be satisfied, quite apart from affection and romance. Gay men, freed from the constraints of female expectations around sexuality, have often reveled in sex itself, creating clubs and baths for easy access to anonymous sex and claiming areas of public parks as "cruising" areas. While there are certainly many gays who are celebate or monogamous, many gay men freely admit to dozens or even hundreds of sexual partners.

The gay liberation movement of the 1970s, while challenging the oppression of gays, also offered gay men a new pride in their sexuality. As gay identity became more proud and less shameful, the image of the gay bar as a dark hideaway also changed. Gay disco bars, which had flashing lights and loud music with a pounding, sexual beat became the social centers for gay men. The trendy, exciting bars also attracted straight people, moving gay culture dramatically into the mainstream. The disco scene was also heavily associated with casual sex and recreational drug use, which in part was responsible for its end.

By 1981, medical authorities were beginning to identify a new virus the called GRID or Gay Related Immune Deficiency. Soon, they had changed the name of the disease to Acquired Immuno-Deficiency Syndrome (AIDS) and re-evaluated its connection to the gay community. Though AIDS is not a gay disease, it is sexually transmitted and the promiscuous lifestyle and drug use common within many gay male communities made them ideal conduits for the virus to spread. The virus did spread, and, as thousands of gay men died, AIDS became a focus for the work of gay rights activists. Galvanized by the deaths of their friends and lovers, gay men began to organize to fight for de-stigmatization of the AIDS virus, money for AIDS research, and other AIDS related issues.

Because AIDS affects them so deeply, it has continued to be a central issue for the gay men's community into the 1990s. Controversy continues over community response to the virus. Some insist that modification of gay male sexual behavior, such as safe sex and monogamy, is the only responsible way to confront the disease, while others argue that such modification erodes the fabric of promiscuity that is the very basis of gay male identity. Some support Human Immuno-deficiency Virus (HIV) testing, while others question the connection between HIV and AIDS, and most are suspicious of the willingness of government or society to guard the health and rights of gay citizens.

Gay men have been severely punished for their sexual preference by ridicule, threats, and physical abuse. Perhaps because of the misogyny that is rampant in U.S. society, tomboyish behavior in girls is often tolerated and even rewarded, while feminine behavior in a male is almost universally condemned. Boys who are small, gentle, or artistic will in all likelihood, be taunted, sneered at, or beaten at school and even within their own families. "Gay bashings," vicious physical attacks on those suspected of being gay, are still common occurrences. Many states continue to allow a so-called "unwanted homosexual advance" defense for such assaults, the argument being that a flirtation or proposition from a gay is so repugnant that one may be excused for responding with violence.

While gayness has been highly stigmatized, there has been a traditional acceptance, even expectation of gay men in certain occupations. Hairdressers and interior decorators are generally supposed to be gay, and many are, if only because these are occupations that have traditionally been open to identifiably gay men. Fields such as music, art, and theater, have also attracted gay men who wish to be open about their lifestyle, since the arts community tends to be tolerant. Writers like Walt Whitman and James Baldwin, musicians like Cole Porter, and playwrights like Noel Coward are only a small sampling of the many gay men who have made unparalleled cultural contributions.

Gay men have not only been influential in the arts, but also in many other areas where it has been more necessary to keep their sexual preference a secret. On two ends of this spectrum we find Bayard Rustin and J. Edgar Hoover. Rustin, a civil rights leader on a par with Martin Luther King, Jr., was forced to downplay his public identification with the movement by those who thought his gay identity would harm the black struggle. Hoover, head of the Federal Bureau of Investigation for almost 50 years, hid his longtime relationship with Clyde Tolson, his second in command at the FBI, while using his knowledge of the power of such information to manipulate public policy by keeping files on the guilty secrets of public figures.

One well-known facet of gay male culture is the glorification of the diva. Perhaps because they can identify so strongly with public vulnerability, gay men have traditionally selected certain female stars to revere and emulate. Some of these, like singers Barbra Streisand and Bette Midler, owe their propulsion into stardom to their gay male audiences. Others, like Judy Garland and Joan Crawford, simply became icons, one the vulnerable waif, the other the tough bitch, that many gay men identified with.

The identification with the diva is part of another cultural phenomenon, the friendship between gay men and straight women. Sometimes derisively called "fag hags," straight women who choose gay men for friends are usually seeking a non-threatening relationship with a man. Gay men may also offer more emotional depth in a friendship with a woman than a heterosexual man. Similarly, a gay man may find it comforting to receive emotional support from a source that is not sexual. Such relationships between straight women and gay men (even though the men may not always be overtly gay) have been depicted in films such as *Breakfast at Tiffany's* (1961), *Cabaret* (1972), and *My Best Friend's Wedding* (1997). Even on television, where homosexuality has been scarce, shows like *Love, Sidney* (1981-1983) and *Will and Grace* (1998—) have found success by the safe pairing of gay men with straight women.

While gay-identified men are often oppressed, some social analysts argue that American society itself has a male homosexual perspective that stems from its sexism and patriarchy. Like ancient Greece, where love between men was viewed as the highest form of spiritual and physical connection, American society endows male friendship with a loyalty and honor it does not deem possible in heterosexual relationships. Much is made of male bonding rituals, and, while a slap on the back or a punch in the jaw might take the place of a kiss, nonetheless, male bonding is deeply physical and emotional. A man might never expect to share the intimacy with his wife that he does with his football, hunting, or poker buddies, and, indeed, heterosexual men often voice a low opinion of women. Perhaps it is because gay men demonstrate the tenderness of this male bonding that they are so threatening to a society where men must be rough, tough, and in charge of women. Perhaps in the long run, gay liberation, will result in nothing less than a wider liberation of the social order.

—Tina Gianoulis

FURTHER READING:

Hardy, Robin. *The Crisis of Desire: AIDS and the Fate of Gay Brotherhood.* Boston, Houghton Mifflin, 1999.

Harris, Daniel. *The Rise and Fall of Gay Culture.* New York, Hyperion, 1997.

Nardi, Peter M. *Gay Men's Friendships: Invincible Communities.* Chicago, University of Chicago Press, 1999.

Gaye, Marvin (1959-1984)

During his tenure at Motown records, vocalist and songwriter Marvin Gaye expanded the boundaries of what soul music could address *and* how it could sound. His early Motown hits "How Sweet It Is (To Be Loved by You)," "Ain't That Peculiar," and "Ain't Nothing Like the Real Thing" (with Tammi Terrell) helped define the 1960s Motown sound. His 1968 "I Heard It through the Grapevine" became Motown's biggest-selling record to date. On genre-defying albums such as 1971's *What's Going On*, Gaye opened soul music to allow for overt political protest, while on 1978's *Here, My Dear* he reduced his subject matter to a level of pain and honesty that had rarely been touched in any form of popular music. During his lifetime, Gaye battled many demons—the most significant of which was his father, a man with whom Gaye had an ongoing, troubled relationship. That relationship ended tragically April 1, 1984, when Gaye's father gunned him down in his parents' home after a heated argument.

Born Marvin Pentz Gaye, Jr. to a devoutly religious family that belonged to the House of God (a conservative Christian sect that drew from Pentecostalism and Orthodox Judaism), Marvin had a troubled childhood growing up in Washington, D.C. Gaye was beaten almost daily by his father, an ordained minister at the local House of God church, and felt stigmatized and out of place among his peers because of his shy nature and the gossip-attracting, flamboyant personality of his father. Gaye grew up amid perpetual confrontations with his father and, by most accounts, was an unhappy child, except when he was singing.

Marvin Gaye

Starting at a very early age, Gaye buried himself deep in music, learning to play drums and piano in church, and later becoming a soloist in his father's church choir. Upon graduating from high school, Gaye enlisted in the Air Force to escape his family life, but after his discharge he returned to Washington, D.C., and sang around town in a number of Doo-Wop groups. During a tour stop as a backing vocalist with the Moonglows in Detroit, Gaye caught the attention of Motown founder Berry Gordy Jr., who hired him as a session musician and eventually signed him as a Motown artist in 1961. Gaye got to know, and fell in love with, Gordy's sister, Anna (who was 17 years Gaye's senior). They were married in late 1961.

After a few minor hit singles and a poor-selling album in the style of his hero, Nat King Cole, Gaye scored his first Top Ten hit with the up-tempo "Pride and Joy." But Motown's pigeonholing of Gaye as an upbeat party song singer ran in opposition to his desire to sing sweet, romantic ballads and resulted in Gaye's long-running conflicts over artistic direction and control of his career. In addition to churning out up-tempo numbers, Gaye also became known as a duet singer, his most beautiful and gut-wrenching songs sung with Terrell. This pairing generated such classics as "Ain't No Mountain High Enough," "Your Precious Love," and "You're All I Need to Get By." Their musical affair sadly ended when she collapsed in his arms onstage, eventually dying of a brain tumor in 1970. By all accounts, Gaye never emotionally recovered from the loss of Terrell, a woman with whom he had a deep emotional connection, though not a romantic relationship.

By the end of the 1960s, America was in the middle of a social upheaval generated by, among other things, the Civil Rights Movement and the Vietnam War. Gaye wanted to find a way to musically address his social concerns but found Motown's assembly-line hit-making method increasingly constraining. Gaye fought against Motown for the release of *What's Going On* (1971), his personal testament against the horrors of the Vietnam War, environmental destruction, and the indignities of ghetto life. Opening with the strains of his tenor voice singing "Mother mother / there's too many of us dying," *What's Going On* was a landmark album. Released to universal critical praise in magazines from *Rolling Stone* to *Time* (which devoted a long, two-column review to the album), the album freed soul music from the limiting subject matter of simple love songs. It also featured more complex and jazzy arrangements that used strings, as well as songs that seamlessly segued into each other. The album became the best-selling album of Gaye's career, a demonstration that an artist's muse and commerce could successfully coexist.

In 1972 Gaye followed up *What's Going On* with the soundtrack to the blaxploitation flick *Trouble Man*, and in 1973 he released the deeply erotic *Let's Get It On*. It, too, was a massive hit. Now at the high point of his career, he sank to one of the lowest points in his life. Severely depressed, he increasingly took large amounts of cocaine while his marriage to Anna dissolved. During the course of his marriage, Gaye's weakness for women made him unfaithful, but the last straw for Anna occurred when he had a second child with Janis Hunter (whom he later married). In a bizarre divorce settlement, Gaye agreed to pay the entirety of royalties for his next album to Anna. Briefly contemplating making a toss-off album, he instead delved deep into their relationship and created what is among the most unusual albums in popular music history, *Here, My Dear*, a double concept album that documented the rise and fall of their marriage, his unfaithfulness, his cocaine habit, his obsession with prostitutes, and other very personal subjects with songs such as "When Did You Stop Loving Me, When Did I Stop Loving You?" and "You Can Leave,

but It's Going to Cost You." Even the album's cover art visually represented their crumbling marriage. Confronting an audience that was clearly unprepared for such a display of raw emotion and dirty laundry, the album flopped.

Gaye sank deeper into a drug-induced depression and financial collapse. He moved to Europe, where he pulled himself out of his hole and recorded 1982's *Midnight Love,* an album that contained his last big hit and winner of two Grammy Awards, "Sexual Healing." Marvin Gaye was shot and killed by his father in 1984; he was posthumously inducted into the Rock and Roll Hall of Fame in 1987.

—Kembrew McLeod

FURTHER READING:

Davis, Sharon. *Marvin Gaye.* New York, Proteus, 1984.

Ritz, David. *Divided Soul: The Life of Marvin Gaye.* New York, Da Capo, 1985.

Ward, Brian. *Just My Soul Responding: Rhythm and Blues, Black Consciousness and Race Relations.* Berkeley, University of California Press, 1998.

Gehrig, Lou (1903-1941)

Baseball great Lou Gehrig (the "Iron Horse") was, alongside teammate Babe Ruth, a powerhouse player on the New York Yankees

Lou Gehrig

during the 1920s and 1930s until his career was cut short by the degenerative disease that bears his name. Born Henry Louis Gehrig in 1903, he was the son of German immigrants who were living in Manhattan. Gehrig's high-school accomplishments earned him an opportunity to play sports at Columbia University, but he was coaxed into signing a professional contract with Hartford of the Eastern League under the surname Lewis. Gehrig hid his identity but not his talent, and the ruse was soon discovered. Columbia University promptly declared him ineligible for the 1921-1922 school year, but in his second year of college, he played exceptionally in both football and baseball. Paul Krichell of the New York Yankees discovered Gehrig in 1923 and offered him a $1,500 signing bonus, which Gehrig accepted despite his parents' objections. He played most of the year in the minors before making his Yankee debut in September. Likewise, Gehrig spent most of the 1924 season playing in the minors, but in June of 1925, he began a consecutive game streak that would not end until 1939.

Lou Gehrig made an immediate impact on the Yankees, and his ability to hit propelled him to national stardom by the late 1920s. He hit behind Babe Ruth on baseball's most powerful lineup, which the press nicknamed ''Murderer's Row,'' and succeeded in outhitting Ruth by the early 1930s. Gehrig compiled a streak of thirteen consecutive years with more than 100 runs and runs batted in, and a 12-year streak of hitting over .300. He led the American League in home runs three times and in runs four times, and ranks third all-time in RBIs and slugging percentage. The durable first baseman was selected as the American League's Most Valuable Player twice, won the Triple Crown in 1934, and won six world championships as a Yankee.

Statistics alone did not endear Lou Gehrig to the nation. Representing the tireless worker during the Great Depression, the ''Iron Horse'' established a record for the number of consecutive games played: 2,130 games in succession from 1925 to 1939. Gehrig's consecutive game streak continued despite back spasms, a broken toe, a broken thumb, and 17 different hand fractures. This record stood for more than half a century until it was surpassed in 1995 by Cal Ripken, Jr. of the Baltimore Orioles.

Gehrig's statistics began to slip in 1938, and he lacked his usual strength and mobility. When Gehrig's teammates congratulated him on a routine ground ball in 1939, he knew it was time to take himself out of the game, and he never again played for the Yankees. His ailing health led him to the Mayo clinic where doctors diagnosed him with a rare and fatal degenerative disease called amyotrophic lateral sclerosis (ALS). Since his diagnosis, ALS has been commonly called Lou Gehrig's disease.

On July 4, 1939, the Yankees honored the newly retired Lou Gehrig in front of 62,000 fans. He received awards, retired his number, and then gave one of the most famous speeches in baseball history. Gehrig thanked the many people who touched his life, telling the crowd ''Yet today I consider myself the luckiest man on the face of the earth.'' The powerful speech electrified the nation and epitomized his humble nature.

Gehrig spent the remaining two years of his life working for the New York City Parole Commission and spending time with family and friends. The Baseball Hall of Fame exempted him from the five-year waiting period, and he was honored by induction in Cooperstown in 1939. The story of unconditional love between Lou and his wife, Eleanor, received national attention, and shortly after Gehrig's death, Hollywood made *Pride of the Yankees,* a movie about his life and marriage that starred Gary Cooper as Lou Gehrig. The movie was a box-office success and was nominated for Best Picture.

—Nathan R. Meyer

FURTHER READING:

Gallico, Paul. *Lou Gehrig, Pride of the Yankees.* New York, Grosset and Dunlap, 1942.

Gehrig, Eleanor. *My Luke and I.* New York, Crowell, 1976.

Robinson, Ray. *Iron Horse: Lou Gehrig in His Time.* New York, W. W. Norton, 1990.

Geisel, Theodor

See Dr. Seuss

The General

Johnnie Gray (Buster Keaton) has two loves: his locomotive The General and Annabelle Lee (Marion Mack). As the Civil War begins, both The General and Annabelle are captured by Union spies and taken north across enemy lines. Johnnie follows and rescues both his loves. Although it was a flop when it was first released in 1927, *The General* is probably the best known and most popular of Keaton's films; it has a more cohesive plot than many of his other works and a larger background with an elaborate battle sequence. Johnnie is consistent with other Keaton characters: he meets every adversity with a solemn lack of facial expression and an unbeatable determination.

—Christian L. Pyle

FURTHER READING:

Buster Keaton's The General. New York, Flare-Avon, 1975.

Rubinstein, E. *Filmguide to ''The General.''* Bloomington, Indiana University Press, 1973.

General Hospital

Created by writers Frank and Doris Hursley, *General Hospital* was one of two hospital-based daytime dramas to premiere on April 1, 1963 (The other was *The Doctors*). Though pre-dating the height of the feminist movement by several years, it nonetheless appealed to a female audience that enjoyed broadening its attention beyond the home by shifting the conventions of the soap opera from the kitchen to the workplace, and from a focus on the family dynamics to one on relationships between coworkers. The show's developers created the hospital staff as a large surrogate family, and wrote storylines that were in a constant state of flux between the personal and professional challenges presented to the main characters.

During its first few years the drama centered on the friendship of Dr. Steve Hardy and nurse Jessie Brewer, and on their complicated love lives. The self-sacrificing Brewer had suffered for years in a marriage to an unfaithful husband who was much younger than she; although she went on to have a number of relationships and several

Emily McLaughlin and John Beradino in a scene from the television show *General Hospital,* **1972.**

marriages, she always seemed to return to her original spouse and to further abuse until his death finally freed her. For his part, Dr. Hardy faced his own problems due to an on-again, off-again relationship with an ex-stewardess named Audrey March. In one storyline Audrey becomes pregnant by artificial insemination during a separation from Steve, goes to Vietnam, returns, marries someone else, becomes pregnant again as a result of marital rape, leaves that husband, and reconciles with the always understanding Steve, who adopts her child.

General Hospital seemed to lose its focus during the late 1970s despite the efforts of the Hursleys and later writers, including their daughter Bridget, to stick to themes that had brought the show success in the past. When ratings hit rock bottom in 1977 and ABC was considering canceling the program, a last ditch effort at resuscitation brought in writer Douglas Marland, who had created a number of highly successful, youthful storylines on *The Doctors,* and Gloria Monty, who had directed *Secret Storm,* as the new producer. Monty infused the show with prime-time production values by introducing new scenery, crosscutting, and new lighting, and demanding that the actors speed up the pace of the show. Marland created a new storyline centered on 15-year-old Laura Vining (Genie Francis), a previously peripheral character, and her relationship with Scotty Baldwin (Kin Shriner). The story was further complicated by the introduction of a new rival for Laura, the scheming Bobbie Spencer. When Laura killed a taunting older lover in a rage and allowed her self-sacrificing mother to take the blame, the show's ratings really took off, bringing in a younger audience who became particularly hooked on the unfolding tragedy of the mother and daughter.

While Marland continued to develop the stories into the 1980s, Monty continued to shorten scenes, emphasize action over dialogue, and synthesize emerging trends into the show's plots. The efforts of the two practitioners returned *General Hospital* to a top-ten spot in the ratings.

The show reached its peak in popularity in the early 1980s following the departure of Marland and the hiring of his replacement Pat Falken Smith. Smith created what many considered the most controversial story in soap opera history, that of having Laura marry Scotty, but then become fascinated with an older, more sophisticated man, antihero Luke Spencer (Anthony Geary), who raped her in his deserted disco. The show couldn't afford to slow its pace by having a trial or ordering the incarceration of Luke, so the incident was passed off as a seduction, although Laura subsequently spent a year in therapy trying to recover from the emotional damage done by the attack. Nonetheless, whether it was rape or seduction, the chemistry between the two characters incited fan interest to a fever pitch and, despite critical outcries denouncing the producers for condoning rape, the show began to increase its focus on Luke and Laura. As this happened, mainstay characters Steve and Jessie were demoted to supporting status with but a few lines of dialogue each week.

Luke and Laura's wedding on November 16 and 17, 1981, became the most-watched event in the history of daytime TV, even attracting a guest appearance by Elizabeth Taylor, a fan of the show. Monty then steered the show in a more fanciful direction by having Luke and Laura confront the efforts of a mad scientist who, in an attempt at global domination, decides to freeze the world. Although the storyline disappointed *GH* purists, the theme attracted a new teenage audience, and ratings soared. Within a couple of years, however, both actress Genie Francis and writer Pat Falkin Smith departed the show to develop their careers further. Monty assumed the role of head writer. Although plots were both hit and miss among fans, the ratings continued to increase.

By early 1985, after a succession of writers had tried to move the show in different directions with limited success, Smith returned many of the original characters to prominent roles while his focus continued to be on action-adventure themes. When Smith was succeeded by Claire Labine in the 1990s, the emphasis shifted to social issues such as AIDS, organ transplants, and other emerging medical/ethical issues, and *General Hospital* came full cycle, returning, at least in part, to its original premise of drama in the lives of hospital personnel.

—Sandra Garcia-Myers

FURTHER READING:

Allen, Robert C. *Speaking of Soap Operas.* Chapel Hill, University of North Carolina Press, 1985.

Groves, Seli. *The Ultimate Soap Opera Guide.* Detroit, Visible Ink Press, 1985.

LaGuardia, Robert. *Soap World.* New York, Arbor House, 1983.

Mumford, Laura Stempel. *Love and Ideology in the Afternoon: Soap Opera, Women, and Television Genre.* Bloomington, Indiana University Press, 1995.

Schemering, Christopher. *The Soap Opera Encyclopedia.* New York, Ballantine Books, 1985.

Warner, Gary. *General Hospital: The Complete Scrapbook.* Los Angeles, General Publishing Group, 1995.

General Motors

The impact of auto manufacturer General Motors on American culture, the economy, and politics is staggering, as is the sheer size of the corporation. For years, GM was the largest corporation on earth, its value greater than most nations. It was the first company to gross more than one billion dollars a year. When GM had a bad year in 1957, commentators said, "GM sneezed and the economy caught a cold," so interdependent were the U.S. GNP and the fortunes of GM. Controlling more than half of the market and creating more cars than its domestic rivals combined, GM made and sold cars everywhere in the world. Although regulation, foreign competition, and oil shocks have rocked GM the past few decades, for most of its history it has towered over not just the auto industry, but all industry. And from the farmer-friendly, half-ton pick-ups of the 1930s, to the luxurious Cadillac Coup De Villes or the space-age looking Buick LeSabre of the 1950s, to the Pontiac GTO for the youth longing for "muscle cars" in the late 1950s, to the "uniquely American" 1957 Chevy, to sports cars like the Pontiac Trans-Am of the 1970s, to the one and only Chevy El Camino half car/half pick-up of the same decade, GM has produced not just cars, but symbols of American culture.

While Henry Ford staked his claim on manufacturing genius, the "father" of General Motors, Billy Durant, brought to the industry "the art of the deal." Durant was not just an entrepreneur, he was an expert dealmaker who merged companies and formed GM as a large holding company. GM started with Olds and Buick in 1908, then added Cadillac a year later. Durant, however, expanded too quickly and was forced out by bankers. Undeterred, Durant hired a racecar driver named Louis Chevrolet to design a new car, and in 1915, Durant merged the two companies and regained control. Durant continued to buy not only auto companies, but also suppliers (Fisher Body) and related companies (Frigidaire, which was sold in 1979). Yet, again, Durant overextended and was forced out in 1920, his place soon taken by Alfred Sloan.

If Ford created modern manufacturing techniques (Fordism) to conquer the massive scale of making automobiles, then Sloan created management techniques (Sloanism) to master the managing of a large-scale firm. Sloan's management ideas on hierarchical line authority became the model for all large corporations for years. Sloan also became the first GM president to engage in collective bargaining when the United Auto Workers staged a series of successful sit-down strikes in GM plants in Flint, Michigan, in 1937. But Sloan's greatest triumph was his creation of a styling and color department under the direction of designer Harley Earl in 1927. From this concentration on styling, thus on marketing, GM cemented in the American psyche the fact that, according to David Halberstam, "the car was not merely transportation, but a reflection of status, a concept to which most Americans responded enthusiastically as they strove to move up into the middle class, and then the upper middle class." With the annual model changes—which were often only cosmetically different from the previous year—new car buyers were hooked. It was Sloan and Durant's vision of a car for every market niche: new car buyers could start cheap with a Chevy and then, as they earned more, work their way up to an Olds, and everyone would dream of owning a Cadillac.

The war years made GM rich, but its wealth became unprecedented in the 1950s with a combination of pent-up demand, the need for a car for suburban living, and the coming of the interstate highway system. In addition to lobbying for the automobile as *the* mode of transportation for Americans, GM also did its best to destroy the competition. In 1949, GM, Standard Oil, Firestone, and other companies were convicted of criminal conspiracy to replace electric transit lines with gasoline or diesel buses. GM had replaced more than one hundred electric transit systems in forty-five cities with GM buses. Despite a fine and the court ruling, GM would, with the aid of urban planners like Robert Moses, block efforts at mass transit.

With Earl's love of the "jet engine look" GM cars came to resemble planes, loaded with chrome and fins. Advances in engineering could have made cars more fuel efficient; instead, GM opted to make cars more powerful and loaded with expensive options like air-conditioning. GM showed off its cars with road shows called Motoramas, which annually drew more than one million spectators. The Motoramas ended in 1961 as GM concentrated its advertising dollars on television. During the 1960s, GM divisions sponsored hundreds of TV shows. With famous ads like "See the USA in the Chevrolet," GM created a national car culture, made even more attractive with the coming of color television.

Yet, the events of the 1960s also brought about the first chinks in GM's armor. A poorly designed knock-off called the Corvair inspired a young lawyer named Ralph Nader to write a book about auto safety (or the lack thereof) called *Unsafe at Any Speed*. While the book was troubling to GM, more embarrassing was GM's clumsy attempt to investigate and intimidate Nader. This led to the spectacle of GM issuing Nader a public apology. The safety issues led to more government regulation of the auto industry, which escalated with emissions and other standards enacted in the 1960s and 1970s. Like all large institutions, GM found itself under attack in the 1960s, but nothing compared to the shocks it would face in the next decades.

Beginning with a lengthy UAW strike in 1970, through oil embargoes, inflation, and recessions, GM lost profit, market share, respect, and dominance into the 1990s. The company underwent a series of huge reorganizations coupled with a titanic downsizing of its work force. The devastating effect of GM's layoffs is best chronicled in Michael Moore's bitterly funny 1989 film *Roger & Me*. After a series of management shake-ups, some at the behest of new board member Ross Perot (whose Electronic Data Systems Corporation had been purchased by GM in the 1980s), GM tried to reinvent itself with the Saturn project in 1984. Saturn was an attempt to develop not just a new car, but a new method of manufacturing and selling automobiles based on the Japanese model. While new, Saturn also represented something old in GM's past: producing the right car for the right market.

—Patrick Jones

FURTHER READING:

Automobile Quarterly Magazine editors. *General Motors, the First 75 Years of Transportation Products.* Princeton, Automobile Quarterly Incorporated, 1990.

Cray, Ed. *General Motors and Its Times.* New York, McCraw-Hill, 1975.

Flink, James J. *The Automobile Age.* Cambridge, MIT Press, 1988.

———. *The Car Culture.* Cambridge, MIT Press, 1975.

Halberstam, David. *The Fifties.* New York, Villard Books, 1993.

Keller, Maryann A. *Rude Awakening: The Rise, Fall, and Struggle for Recovery of General Motors.* New York, Morrow, 1989.

Maynard, Micheline. *Collision Course: Inside the Battle for General Motors.* New York, Birch Lane Press, 1995.

Nader, Ralph. *Unsafe at Any Speed.* New York, Grossman, 1965.

Sloan, Alfred P. *My Years with General Motors.* New York, Doubleday & Company, 1996.

Generation X

Throughout the twentieth century, American historians and social commentators have placed labels on various generations in an effort to capture their characteristic spirit. Generation X—roughly defined as the more than 79 million people born between 1961 and 1981—has been characterized by the media as lazy, laconic, and unfocused, but in the eyes of many, the pejorative label represents propaganda rather than reality. For those outside this generation, the X stands for some unknown variable, implying young adults searching aimlessly for an identity. Many members of Generation X think otherwise, however, and they fill in the blank with such descriptors as diverse, individualistic, determined, independent, and ambitious.

The term "Generation X" worked its way into popular vernacular after the release of Douglas Coupland's 1991 novel, *Generation X: Tales for an Accelerated Culture,* about three twentysomethings who are underemployed, overeducated, and unpredictable. Other nicknames have emerged, such as the more neutral "13ers" (which indicates the 13th generation since the pilgrims landed at Plymouth Rock). However, most of the other markers have negative overtones, such as "slackers," "latch-key generation," "MTV generation," and "baby busters." Many members of this generation reject these labels for they not only stigmatize and stereotype, but also reinforce the negative behavior they describe. On the other hand, Karen Ritchie, author of *Marketing to Generation X,* actually prefers the label "Generation X," for she sees "something anticommercial, antislick, anti-Boomer, and generally defiant about the 'X' label." She also predicts that soon enough, and rightly so, this generation "will name themselves."

The members of Generation X can be seen as natural products of the intellectual atmosphere in which they have grown up, for they are the first generation to be raised in the age of postmodernism—a widespread cultural development of the last quarter of the twentieth century. Understanding the often rocky transition from modern to postmodern culture is necessary to understanding how many members of Generation X think and operate. While modernism values a single world view rooted in objective science, postmodernism values multiple world views based on subjective experiences and contingencies. Information and knowledge is gathered in a linear fashion by the modernists, but for postmodernists, particularly those of Generation X, information comes from fragmented and non-linear sources, often in the form of hypertext or visual images. While the modernists revere the classics of art and literature, postmodernists have a broader frame of reference: they not only revere the classics, but they also grant status and value to the productions of popular culture. Ethics for the modernists can be rigid, even self-righteous, but postmodernists have a more situational ethic that resists the concept of "Universal Truth." Monolithic institutions such as government, education, corporations, and the press which are seen as authoritative by the modernists are viewed with caution and distrust by members of Generation X.

Xers have grown up during the cultural transformation from modernism to postmodernism. The sensibilities of postmodernism are naturally appealing to many members of Generation X, because their young adulthood has been constructed by the postmodern society. Paradoxically, they have simultaneously been victimized by

a society trying to come to terms with a paradigm shift that many find threatening. Members of Generation X often represent that threat to their elders. As a result, these youth are both the product and the scapegoat of a culture in a state of flux.

True to this variable spirit of postmodernism, Generation X defies homogeneity. Extremely diverse in race, class, religion, ethnicity, and sexual orientation, Xers often feel a collective uniqueness that has emerged from shared experiences and cultural circumstances. The unrest of the late 1960s and early 1970s, followed by the uneasy discomfort of the late 1970s and the self-involved consumption of the 1980s, have been the foreground to the 1990s—a decade laden with problems. Social ills like the rise in teen suicide, widespread homelessness, proliferating toxic waste, violent crime, the AIDS epidemic, and a "down-sizing" workforce, coupled with fundamental changes in social structures like the family, caused by rising divorce rates and working parents, have been the realities of the world as Generation X has come of age. Like most younger generations, many Xers resent their parental generation—the baby boomers—for leaving them to repair or endure a society on the brink of collapse. Considering the problems Xers face, it is perhaps no wonder that one of their favorite T-shirt slogans is "NO FEAR," and it is also representative of the contradictions of their culture that NO FEAR is the corporate brand name of a line of sports clothes.

Lack of fear, however, is not enough to manage America's social problems, and many baby boomers voice concern that most members of Generation X evince distaste for politics and public affairs. The trust of all Americans in their government has reached increasingly low levels in the 1990s, as members of Generation X have come of age politically. Because they view politics as a hostile and corrupt environment, Xers have tended to be disgusted by political machinations, and thus often disengaged. Political apathy among young people is not a new phenomenon; personal challenges such as education, careers, and relationships often consume their time and energy, leaving little left over for political affairs. Furthermore, political scientists report that, historically, levels of public participation increase with age. However, Xers have never experienced political innocence and have lived within a negative climate of politics their entire lives. This climate has caused many to turn their backs on political involvement, in turn causing a potentially devastating problem in terms of Xers' future civic and political responsibility.

Neil Howe and Bill Strauss provide a more pragmatic perspective in their oft-cited *13th Gen: Abort, Retry, Ignore, Fail?,* in which they lay out a five-point political credo of Xers: 1. "Wear your politics lightly"; 2. "Survival comes first"; 3. "Try to fix only what's fixable"; 4. "Clean up after your own mess"; and 5. "Personal style matters." Howe and Strauss posit that for the 13th Generation, "national politics will drift toward the personal, no-nonsense, survivalist approach." Xers are already employing this do-it-yourself attitude by saving early for their retirement. According to Richard Thau, in a 1994 poll of 18-34 year olds, 82 percent believe that Social Security, the U.S. government's largest benefit program, will deconstruct before their retirement. Thau is the Executive Director of the Third Millennium, a political advocacy group centered in New York with hundreds of members who are dedicated to speaking out on behalf of the interests of the Generation X age group. Likewise, Hans Riemer and Chris Cuomo cofounded 2030, what they describe as a "political action-tank" for Generation X. In Riemer's words, "so much of what is going wrong today requires innovation and new thinking, and we can respond to these requirements at a more rapid pace than other generations could." These informed Xers are responding to the concerns of "massive ignorance" through practical action.

Xers' cautious and fiscally conservative sensibility has been a challenge to America's mostly middle-aged advertisers and marketers who have recognized Generation X as a viable and large market. However, they are also the best educated generation in America's history and were raised on commercial hyperbole. While Xers might respect and enjoy advertisements that are crisp, sophisticated, humorous, and informative, they are savvy enough to realize when hype or insincerity is at work. Karen Ritchie recognizes that "no icon and certainly no commercial is safe from their irony, their sarcasm or their remote control. These are the tools with which Generation X keeps the world in perspective."

Xer Richard Thau confirms such use of satire and irony in explaining the wild popularity of the "fictional buffoons" who have largely defined Generation X for the nation: Beavis and Butthead, Bill and Ted, Wayne and Garth, Bart Simpson, and the children who live in South Park. Members of Generation X, claims Thau, are clearly educated enough to enjoy "watching these morons because they satirize the image older generations have of us." Shows like *Friends, ER, Seinfeld, Melrose Place, The X-Files,* and *Party of Five* are popular among Xers because they employ friends as family, serialized story lines, and the use of music, three ingredients favored by Generation X viewers. The effect of Generation X on current TV programming can clearly be measured by the launching of three broadcast networks—Fox, UPN, and WB—specifically targeted at Generation X.

Perhaps one of the more joyful memories from the early days of Xers is those three-minute jingles that provided Saturday morning lessons in grammar, math, civics, and science: ABC's *Schoolhouse Rock.* Rob Owen, author of *Gen X TV,* claims that "these little ditties entered the Gen X consciousness and stayed there." He also posits that these musical education segments were the forerunner to what we later came to know as music videos. Unlike any preceding generation, the visual element is essential to Xers. Since they have grown up with television, video games, and computers, it is natural that theirs is the generation that added pictures to rock songs. Owen contends that the introduction of the Music Television channel (MTV) "raised the ante" in the entertainment industry when television producers blended music, visuals, and quick cuts for the sophisticated viewing demands of Generation X. When MTV went on the air in August, 1981, targeting the 12-34 age group, members of Generation X responded immediately, so much so that Xers are criticized for having an MTV-attention span, alluding to the quick-cut and fast-paced conventions of music videos. Despite this criticism, the attraction of MTV remains constant, explains Meredith Bagby, because MTV has quite literally made it their business to keep up with the changes in Generation X.

The musical interests of Xers are as diverse as the members themselves. In the early 1990s, many members of Generation X revered grunge rock groups like Nirvana with their furious, angst-ridden lyrics and wailing guitar licks. Nirvana railed against the establishment and a decaying society—issues with which Xers could readily identify. Kurt Cobain was their poet, but his suicide in April, 1994 brought his anguished alienation to a crashing halt. The bullet that ended Cobain's life created a collective heartache for many members of Generation X. While Cobain screamed in despair, rappers continue to provide their version of the nightly news concerning the happenings on America's urban streets. Hip-hop and rap music appeal to members of Generation X across all race and ethnic

lines, for like Cobain, rappers speak of the issues of the day while simultaneously affirming black identity. Howe and Strauss describe inner-city Xers as "unmarried teen moms and unconcerned teen fathers; lethal gangsters . . . and innocent hiphoppers who have no illusions about why older white guys cross the streets to avoid them." Rappers like Tupac Shakur, Queen Latifah, Snoop Doggy Dogg, Master P, Puff Daddy, and Dr. Dre are significant voices for many members of Generation X. The success of Black Entertainment Television (BET), a music network which focuses on urban contemporary sounds, attests to the far-reaching appeal of black music among Generation X. In addition to alternative rock and rap, other genres of GenX music include ska, techno, industrial, country, reggae, and goth.

Though many Xers have a deep connection to music, they are not merely tuning in to the various music networks and dancing at all-night raves. Some have a strong entrepreneurial spirit that belies their media reputation for laziness and lack of focus. For example, Jerry Yang and David Filo, both graduate students at Stanford, cofounded Yahoo!, the first online navigational guide to the Web. Xer Adam Werbach is the youngest president of the Sierra Club, the largest grass-roots environmental organization. Xer Eric Liu edited a collection of essays about Generation X called *Next* and is a foreign-policy speech writer for Bill Clinton. At age 25, Steve Frank became a journalist for the *Wall Street Journal.* Jonathan Karl was hired as a reporter for CNN to represent his generation. Xer David Mays is the founder and editor-in-chief of *The Source,* the immensely popular magazine of hip-hop music, culture, and politics. Twentysomething Kevin Smith financed his first movie, *Clerks,* on his credit card and then went on to make *Chasing Amy,* which earned him the respect of mainstream moviemakers. Beth Kobliner, writer for *Money* magazine, also wrote the bestseller on personal finance for Generation X, *Get a Financial Life!* At only 26, Jeff Shesol is considered an acclaimed historian for his book *Mutual Contempt* about Robert Kennedy and Lyndon Johnson; Shesol also serves as a presidential speech writer for Bill Clinton. Although the title of the 1991 movie, *Slackers,* has been used to label members of Generation X, the above accomplishments clearly negate such a reputation.

In the face of dismissive and stereotypical media portrayals as they learn to navigate the increasingly fast-paced world around them, members of Generation X have learned to cope with guarded optimism, and practical confidence. Although they may be cynical about the conditions of the world in which they came of age, they do embrace an American Dream, albeit a different one from that of their predecessors.

—Judy L. Isaksen

FURTHER READING:

Bagby, Meredith. *Rational Exuberance: The Influence of Generation X on the New American Economy.* New York, Dutton, 1998.

Bennett, Stephen Earl, and Eric W. Rademacher. "The 'Age of Indifference' Revisited: Patterns of Political Interest, Media Exposure, and Knowledge among Generation X." *After the Boom: The Politics of Generation X.* Lanham, Maryland, Rowman & Littlefield, 1997, 21-42.

Coupland, Douglas. *Generation X: Tales for an Accelerated Culture.* New York, St. Martin's Press, 1991.

Howe, Neil, and Bill Strauss. *13th Gen: Abort, Retry, Ignore, Fail?* New York, Vintage Books, 1993.

Owen, Rob. *Gen X TV: The Brady Bunch to Melrose Place.* Syracuse, Syracuse University Press, 1997.

Ritchie, Karen. *Marketing to Generation X.* New York, Lexington Books, 1995.

Thau, Richard. "So-Called Generation X: How Do You Target a Market that Wants to Be Left Alone?" *Vital Speeches of the Day.* Vol. LXII, No. 21, 1996, 664-67.

Gentlemen Prefer Blondes

Novel, stage play, and, most notably, popular 1953 film *Gentlemen Prefer Blondes* began as a series of satiric sketches written by Anita Loos and published by *Harper's Bazaar* in 1925. The series featured two pretty and bright but unschooled flappers, Lorelei Lee and Dorothy Shaw, who joyfully infiltrated the bastions of the ruling class. "The strength behind Loos's heroines lies not in their sexuality per se," as Regina Barreca notes, "but on the fact that they remain on the periphery of social and cultural structures." Their profound hunger to be fully accepted into society is at odds with their outsider's recognition of society's entrenched moral hypocrisy. The series struck a chord with readers, and by the third installment, *Harper's Bazaar* had tripled its newsstand sales.

Loos developed the premise into a novel, which was translated into thirteen languages and adapted into a stage play the following

Marilyn Monroe (left) and Jane Russell in a scene from the film *Gentlemen Prefer Blondes.*

year. The narrative took the form of a diary written by Lorelei, whose attempts to sound cultured resulted in malapropisms ("A girl like I") and whose childlike observations satirized the surrounding society ("He really does not mind what a girl has been through as long as she does not enjoy herself at the finish"). The first film version premiered in 1928 to rave reviews. "Those two energetic and resourceful diamond diggers, Lorelei Lee and Dorothy, have come to the Rivoli Theatre in a splendid pictorial translation of Anita Loos's book," wrote Mordaunt Hall for the *New York Times;* "This film is an infectious treat." The story was transformed into a Broadway musical that made Carol Channing a star in 1949. It was produced as an elaborate technicolor film by Twentieth Century-Fox in 1953, revived as a musical entitled *Lorelei* in 1974, and enacted as a stage play by the National Actors Theatre in 1995. But the most influential vehicle for the story is undoubtedly the 1953 film.

Directed by Howard Hawks, *Gentlemen Prefer Blondes* starred Marilyn Monroe as Lorelei and Jane Russell as Dorothy. The film rose to number one in the nation in August 1953 and generated more than $5 million for Fox by the end of the year. Monroe got second billing, earning less than one-tenth of Russell's $200,000 for her work on the film. She was even refused her own dressing room, since she wasn't considered a star. By the end of the year, however, Monroe had starred in three hit films, appeared on the cover of *Look* magazine, and was voted top female box-office star by American film distributors. *Playboy* magazine took advantage of Monroe's sudden celebrity by putting her on the cover of its first issue in December and printing five-year-old nude photographs of her as its first centerfold. The embodiment of the *Playboy* philosophy—combining desirability with vulnerability and exuding sexuality as something natural and innocent—Monroe was perfect for the role of Lorelei, who, as one critic remarked, sometimes "employs an imploring expression, one which seems to imply that she is totally ignorant of her physical attraction." Monroe's star persona coalesced with the film, and thereafter roles such as Pola in *How to Marry a Millionaire* (1953), "The Girl" in *The Seven Year Itch* (1955), and Sugar in *Some Like It Hot* (1959) were written with her specifically in mind.

In the early 1970s, film critics such as Molly Haskell criticized Monroe for "catering so shamelessly to a false, regressive, childish, and detached idea of sexuality." It might seem surprising, then, that *Gentlemen Prefer Blondes* was revived as "a feminist text" by film scholars in the early 1980s. Lucie Arbuthnot and Gail Seneca, for example, pointed out that "Given the mammary madness of the fifties, it is striking that Hawks chose to dress Monroe and Russell in high-necked sweaters and dresses." Actually, the costumes—including skin-tight, red-sequined dresses with thigh-high slits—are far from modest. And the high necklines were not Hawks's choice, but the result of the Motion Picture Association of America going "on breast alert," insisting on seeing costume stills for each of the outfits the two stars would wear in advance. The MPAA red-lined suggestive phrases such as "bosom companions" but allowed lines like the famous "Those girls couldn't drown" to remain in the finished film.

Feminist scholars made a stronger case for the film's progressive depiction of female friendship: "the absence of competitiveness, envy or pettiness" between Dorothy and Lorelei. By many accounts, this reflects a genuine affinity between Russell and Monroe, belying rumors that Monroe couldn't get along with other women. The popular press predicted a giant feud between the two stars during filming, a "Battle of the Bulges" as one male columnist inevitably called it. In fact, according to Todd McCarthy, Russell "welcomed

Monroe at once and gained her confidence professionally and personally.'' In Monroe's last interview with *Life* magazine, conducted just two days before her death in August 1962, she recalled that Russell ''was quite wonderful to me.''

Perhaps most strikingly for contemporary feminists, *Gentlemen Prefer Blondes* can be said to draw a moral parallel between the motivations of women who pursue men for their money and men who pursue women for their beauty. Hollywood, of course, has traditionally vilified the former as gold digging and celebrated the latter as love at first sight. But songs like ''Diamonds Are a Girls' Best Friend'' suggest that men are fickle and women have but one commodity to exchange under patriarchal capitalism: their youthful beauty. ''Men grow cold as girls grow old / And we all lose our charms in the end / But square-cut or pear-shaped / These rocks won't lose their shape / Diamonds are a girl's best friend.'' Proving herself not to be as dumb as her future father-in-law thinks, Lorelei proclaims that ''A man being rich is like a girl being pretty. You might not marry a girl just because she's pretty, but my goodness, doesn't it help?''

''The line which separates celebration from satire in American culture is perniciously thin,'' as Maureen Turim writes, and ''no place is that lack of differentiation more evident than in Howard Hawks's *Gentlemen Prefer Blondes.*'' It is not surprising, then, that Madonna, whose work is characterized by a similar ambiguity, chose to restage Monroe's ''Diamonds Are a Girl's Best Friend'' performance in her 1985 hit music video ''Material Girl.''

—Jeanne Hall

FURTHER READING:

Arbuthnot, Lucie, and Gail Seneca. ''Pretext and Text in *Gentlemen Prefer Blondes.*'' *Issues in Feminist Film Criticism.* Edited by Patricia Erens. Bloomington, Indiana University Press, 1990.

Dyer, Richard. *Heavenly Bodies.* New York, St. Martin's Press, 1987.

Haskell, Molly. *From Reverence to Rape: The Treatment of Women in the Movies.* New York, Penguin Books, 1974.

Loos, Anita. *Gentlemen Prefer Blondes.* New York, Penguin Books, 1998.

McCarthy, Todd. *Howard Hawks: The Grey Fox of Hollywood.* New York, Grove Press, 1997.

Rollyson, Carl E. *Marilyn Monroe: A Life of the Actress.* Ann Arbor, UMI Research Press, 1986.

Turim, Maureen. ''Gentlemen Consume Blondes.'' *Wide Angle.* Vol. 1, No.1, 1979, 52-59.

Gere, Richard (1949—)

Actor Richard Gere has evolved from a typically brash young leading man, whose career was based primarily on his sexy good looks, into a devoted Buddhist and champion of oppressed people.

A deft musician, composer, and gymnast in high school, Gere attended college on a gymnastics scholarship, then dropped out to pursue a career in music. Acting and composing in summer stock led to a position as an understudy for the lead in the Broadway production of the rock musical *Grease* in 1972, then the opportunity to play the lead in the London production the following year. This was followed by the rare opportunity (for an American actor) to play a season with

Richard Gere

the Young Vic Company in such offerings as *The Taming of the Shrew* in 1974.

His film debut in 1974 was in a bit part as a pimp in *Report to the Commissioner,* which was followed by a more high-profile but similar role as a sexually charged street hustler involved with Diane Keaton in 1977's *Looking for Mr. Goodbar,* and his status as a sex symbol was confirmed by his starring role in the breakthrough hit *American Gigolo* in 1979. His career then suffered a marked decline due to inferior choices of roles; critics claimed that it was because his film work came second after his burgeoning interest in Buddhism. Having studied the religion, Gere made a visit to the Tibetan refugee camps in Nepal in 1978, and after meeting with the Dalai Lama, declared himself a disciple.

Following his embrace of Buddhism, Gere attempted to break free of his sex-symbol status and try more character-driven work. Returning to the stage in a highly praised performance as a gay concentration camp prisoner in the Broadway play *Bent,* he then accepted an equally challenging role as a desperate young man struggling to get through brutal military officer's training in *An Officer and a Gentleman* (1982), which proved a box office hit and suggested Gere possessed untapped skills as an actor. However subsequent misfires such as the remake of *Breathless* (1983), *Beyond the Limit* (1983), *King David* (1985), and even Francis Ford Coppola's ill-fated *The Cotton Club* (1984) lowered his credibility until his unexpected breakthrough performance opposite Julia Roberts in 1990's megahit *Pretty Woman,* caused producers to take notice. Since that time Gere has re-established his leading-man status in respectable films such as 1993's *Sommersby* (the remake of the French film *The Return of Martin Guerre*), and thrillers such as *Primal Fear* (1996) and *The Jackal* (1997). But Gere's "heart project" was *Red Corner* (1997), which allowed him to bring his career and private concerns together in the story of an American businessman visiting China who is framed for a murder, wrongly imprisoned, and forced to struggle against China's rigidly oppressive legal system.

Devout in his religion, Gere maintained that he meditated daily and spent his time between projects in India with the exiled Tibetans. In fact his very public twenty-year devotion to the faith led the Dalai Llama to personally request Gere's high-profile assistance in the crusade to end China's tyrannous rule of Tibet—a cause which Gere championed to the extent of making a very public plea at the Academy Awards, which in turn led to his banishment from the event. He was also actively involved in campaigning to raise public awareness of the religious and cultural heritage of Tibet in an effort to push for an American boycott of China. Gere has also published a book of photographs he has taken of Tibetans, *Pilgrim,* the proceeds of which were donated to the cause of Tibetan autonomy.

Gere's sense of universal responsibility has also extended to his taking up the cause of oppressed Central American refugees by lobbying Congress on their behalf in 1986, and launching an AIDS awareness program in India, for which he received a Harvard Award in 1997.

—Rick Moody

FURTHER READING:

Gere, Richard, with foreword by the Dalai Lama. *Pilgrim.* Boston, Little, Brown, 1997.

Parker, John. *Richard Gere: The Flesh and the Spirit.* New York, Headline Book Publishing, 1997.

Gernsback, Hugo (1884-1967)

An American publisher, editor, and author, Gernsback is perhaps best known as the founder of the modern science fiction literary genre. It was his publication of *Amazing Stories* (1926) that gave him this distinction and drew Americans into reading stories about an unknown future. Indeed, Gernsback's imagination was not only limited to the abstract—not in the sense that what he wrote about was impossible—but his speculation about future technological advancements had a solid basis in science . . . as any good science fiction does. In this sense, he was one of the twentieth century's greatest visionaries.

Gernsback immigrated to the United States from Luxembourg in 1904 and established The Electro Importing Company, the first electrical importing business in America. In 1905 he designed and produced the world's first home radio set and began publishing a mail-order catalog, which he filled with articles discussing new technologies. By 1908, Gernsback's mail-order catalog had grown and evolved into *Modern Electrics,* the first electronics magazine of its kind in the world.

Gernsback began experimenting with science fiction as a way to speculate on the new technologies that exploded on the scene at the start of the twentieth century. He serialized his first such story, "Ralph 124C 41+: A Romance of the Year 2660," in *Modern Electrics* from April 1911 to March 1912. Though clumsy and simplistic by today's standards, "Ralph 124C 41+" was based on solid scientific principles and made a number of remarkable technological predictions: fluorescent lighting, plastics, synthetic fabrics, stainless steel, juke-boxes, hydroponics, tape recorders, loudspeakers, microfilm, television, radio networks, vending machines, nuclear weapons, and solar energy. Gernsback's story proved so popular among his mostly young and technologically curious readers, that he began including at least one such story in each issue.

Gernsback sold *Modern Electrics* in 1912 and started a larger periodical, *The Electrical Experimenter,* in 1913, which he retitled *Science and Invention* in 1920 (later absorbed into *Popular Electronics).* By this time Gernsback was publishing two or more stories in each issue of *Science and Invention* as well as in its companion publication *Radio News,* and he began to suspect there might be a market for an all-fiction science magazine. In August 1923 he found out when he published a special "Scientific Fiction Number" of *Science and Invention,* which contained six new "scientifiction" stories (Gernsback's term for the new genre) and cover art depicting a man in a space suit. It was so successful that on April 5, 1926, the enterprising Gernsback launched the first magazine in the world devoted exclusively to science fiction, *Amazing Stories.*

Aware of the "historical interest" posterity would have in this new genre, Gernsback stressed both literary quality and scientific accuracy in his new magazine. At first he filled its pages with reprints of stories by Jules Verne, Edgar Allan Poe, and H.G. Wells. But Gernsback quickly attracted such visionary writers as E.E. "Doc" Smith, Jack Williamson, Ray Cummings, and John W. Campbell, whose groundbreaking stories would map out science fiction's major themes. Gernsback also hired Austrian-born artist Frank R. Paul to provide illustrations for many of the magazine's covers and interior stories. Paul's bold style, vivid use of color, and imaginative depiction of scientific gadgetry, future cities, and alien worlds gave *Amazing Stories* a distinctive look and was an important factor in the magazine's success. Bolstered by that success, Gernsback followed *Amazing Stories* with an expanded edition of the magazine titled *Amazing Stories Annual,* which was so popular Gernsback immediately changed it to the more frequent *Amazing Stories Quarterly.*

Gernsback lost control of *Amazing Stories* in 1929 in a bizarre legal maneuver rumored to have been orchestrated by one of his competitors. Within a month, however, the crusading editor launched four new science fiction magazines: *Science Wonder Stories, Air Wonder Stories* (both merged in 1930 as *Wonder Stories),* *Science Wonder Quarterly,* and *Scientific Detective Monthly.* Gernsback's new magazines were an overnight success, in part because of Gernsback's solid reputation, but also because he took with him Frank R. Paul and many of *Amazing Stories'* best science fiction writers. But it is Gernsback's editorial in the first issue of *Science Wonder Stories* that is of particular interest to the history of popular culture. It is there he gave the world the term "science fiction."

Scholars have noted that if Gernsback had not launched the first science fiction magazine in 1926, someone else would have seen the market opportunities and published something very similar. As important as timing was in the success of Gernsback's magazines, however, his contribution to the genre goes far beyond having an uncanny business sense. Gernsback had a genuinely altruistic, though perhaps simplistic, belief that technology could bring about a human utopia, and he saw it as his role to instill a love of science and technology in his mainly adolescent readers. His argument that science could not only be extrapolated but also taught through fiction was one he returned to over and over, and one that was not lost on his readers.

Throughout his life Gernsback continued to invent electronic devices, patenting nearly 80 before his death in 1967. And though he published more than 50 magazines devoted to such diverse topics as radio, humor, sex, economics, crime detection, and aviation, it was with the publication of *Amazing Stories* that he achieved his lasting fame and exerted his most profound influence on popular culture. Shortly after its publication, magazines and newspapers began to carry science fiction stories geared for a wider audience and science fiction quickly began appearing in nearly every artistic medium including books, radio, film, comic books, and television. Moreover, Gernsback's actions inspired two generations of readers and writers and played a major role in establishing science fiction as an independent literary genre. As a tribute to Gernsback's overall contribution to the field, in 1953 the prestigious Science Fiction Achievement Awards were named the "Hugo" Awards.

—Anthony Ubelhor

FURTHER READING:

Aldiss, Brian W. *Trillion Year Spree*. New York, Avon Books, 1988.

Moskowitz, Sam. *Explorers of the Infinite: Shapers of Science Fiction*. Westport, Connecticut, Hyperion Press, 1974.

Gertie the Dinosaur

Billed as "The Greatest Animal Act in the World," the animated cartoon *Gertie the Dinosaur* premiered in Chicago in February 1914. "She eats, drinks, and breathes! She laughs and cries! Dances the tango, answers questions and obeys every command! Yet, she lived millions of years before man inhabited this earth and has never been seen since!!" claimed the posters. Though Gertie was not the first cartoon character to come alive on screen, she might as well have been. As American film critic Leonard Maltin has written, "One might say that Gertie launched an entire industry." Created by the American comic strip artist Winsor McCay, Gertie's silent debut preceded Walt Disney's Mickey Mouse sound film, *Steamboat Willie*, by 14 years. Though animated cartoons date to experiments in Thomas A. Edison's film studio as early as 1906, it was McCay's sophisticated drawings, charming story, and ingenuity that first really gave "life" to animated characters. It was Gertie's charming personality that captured the imagination of filmgoers.

Popular comic strips were made to move early in the history of cinema, but the development of the art and craft of animation was initially inhibited by economic constraints. While audiences and exhibitors expected animated cartoons to be produced with the same frequency as newspaper comic strips, one minute of an animated cartoon required about 1000 drawings (each film frame was one drawing, and passed at the speed of 16 frames per second). The speed of production precluded much analysis of the art, and early animators had to depend on visual gags and dialogue balloons to get a laugh.

McCay, a well-known newspaper cartoonist, inspired by his son's flip-up books and the pioneering films of J. Stuart Blackton, began experimenting with cartoons and motion pictures in 1907. Four years later, in April, 1911, he premiered his first animated cartoon, *Little Nemo*, based on one of his popular comic strip characters. This short film had no story. Instead, the character asked the audience, in a dialogue balloon, to watch him move as he jumped, flipped, ran, and bounced. To create this short film, McCay hand-colored four thousand frames of 35mm film. He incorporated *Little Nemo* into his vaudeville act and the audience loved it.

Next, McCay created *The Story of a Mosquito,* which took him about a year to make. This new cartoon advanced the techniques used for *Little Nemo,* this time telling a story—of a mosquito's experience with a drunken man. Although McCay's second film, which also premiered as part of his vaudeville act, was well-received, audiences and critics had a hard time accepting that drawings could be brought to life on film, and suspected that the movement was some sort of trick produced with wires and figures.

Gertie the Dinosaur was McCay's answer to the sceptics. He chose a dinosaur as his character because the animal was long extinct and no one could claim that the artist was employing trickery to make her move. The idea of a dinosaur as the subject of an animated drawing was far-fetched. McCay's ingenuity, however, lay in the manner in which he presented the one-reel film in his vaudeville act. As Leonard Maltin describes it, McCay performed on-stage with the cartoon, playing Gertie's trainer and interacting with the motion picture. Gertie "obeyed" his commands, cried when he reprimanded her, ate the snacks he tossed her, and playfully teased her trainer. At the end of the film, McCay walked onto the screen, becoming part of the animation, and together he and Gertie walked away.

Gertie the Dinosaur was a one-reel film, lasting about 12 minutes. To create his memorable character, McCay inked 10,000 drawings on rice paper and then mounted them on cardboard. He invented a flip machine to check the animation. Most astonishing, perhaps, for current aficionados accustomed to animation cells and computer-generated animation, McCay had to redraw the dinosaur and her background for every frame. He drew over 10,000 Gerties himself, and enlisted John A. Fitzsimmons to reproduce the backgrounds, often by tracing.

The film and its "leading lady" were wildly popular and the dinosaur became an instant star. McCay, however, had little desire to remain involved in the industry that his work had spawned. He preferred, instead, to continue with his newspaper comic strips and vaudeville acts, and to work on his films for his own satisfaction. In further developing the art of animation, McCay created, among others, *The Centaurs* and *The Sinking of the Lusitania.* In these, as in *Gertie,* his graphic precision was far more sophisticated than that of his contemporary animators. Eventually, McCay stopped making films altogether, although early animators, including John Randolph Bray, the inventor of the cell, considered McCay to be the father of their art and their craft. Indeed, McCay himself is reported to have proudly christened himself "the creator of animated cartoons."

—Ilene S. Goldman

FURTHER READING:

Maltin, Leonard. *Of Mice and Magic: A History of American Animated Cartoons.* Revised ed. New York, Penguin Books, 1980.

Piring, Jayne, editor. *A Reader in Animation Studies.* Australia, John Libbey and Company, 1997.

Van Eaton Galleries. "A Brief History of Gertie the Dinosaur." http://vegalleries.com/gerthistory.html. May 1999.

Get Smart

The James Bond craze of the 1960s produced a host of spy heroes eager to cash in on the popularity of 007. Some were slavish imitations, but others reflected a willingness to poke fun at the genre. One of the most successful satires, created by Mel Brooks and Buck Henry, was the television series *Get Smart,* which ran on NBC from 1965 to 1970.

Don Adams played Maxwell Smart, Agent 86 of CONTROL. Barbara Felton was Smart's partner, Agent 99. The inept spy and his far more capable partner fought against the evil organization KAOS. They usually won, mostly due to Smart's tendency to do the right thing for the wrong reason. The show made two contributions to popular culture in the late 1960s—the phrase ''Sorry about that, Chief,'' and a running gag built around the question ''Would you believe,'' as in, ''Would you believe you're surrounded by 100 armed agents?'' ''No, I wouldn't.'' ''Would you believe four Boy Scouts and an angry nun?''

—Justin Gustainis

FURTHER READING:

Green, Joey. *The Get Smart Handbook.* New York, Collier Books, 1993.

Meyers, Richard. *TV Detectives.* San Diego, A.S. Barnes and Co., 1981.

Ghettos

If it is true that the poor will always be with us, then, by extension, one can argue that ghettos, ''the huts where poor men lie,'' to quote the poet Wordsworth, are equally eternal, a seemingly insoluble social problem with a long past. The word ghetto carries dark and distressing historical resonance for the Jews of Russia and Europe who, for centuries, culminating in the Nazi atrocities of World War II, were segregated into particular areas by governmental decree. The appalling living conditions that characterized these ghettos carried over to the modern United States, whose cities contain areas that exemplify the dictionary definition of a ghetto as ''a densely populated area of a city inhabited by a socially and economically deprived minority.'' The existence of American ghettos, determined by specific social and economic contingencies, are also too often dictated by ethnicity, providing a disturbing echo of disadvantage based on race or color for those whose fate has confined them to ghetto conditions.

The ghettos of America began as virtual warehouses for cheap immigrant labor in the late nineteenth century, and evolved into holding pens for disadvantaged humanity, a lost and forgotten segment of the populace. Between 1970 and 1990, the number of persons living in ghettos grew by 92 percent, a figure that continued to rise throughout the 1990s. In this era of global economy, industrial flight threatens to turn not only cities, but also suburbs into new ghettos, which stand as a bleak testament to the vicissitudes of economic exigency that is fed by the manic flight of capital into and out of cities, and, finally, abroad.

Through the late nineteenth century, as coal and electricity supplanted water power, industry moved from riverside factory towns to cities. Proximity to markets, rail transport, and the availability of

Children play on a street in Harlem, 1941.

cheap labor provided economic incentives for the industrial migration, which gave rise to sub-standard housing for the work force built adjacent to the factories with little regard to hygiene or creature comforts. Hence, conditions were crowded and unsanitary. Nonetheless, the dreadful conditions that prevailed in these early ghettos were ameliorated somewhat by the strong social and cultural ties that held the immigrant communities together. For example, Yiddish newspapers and theaters thrived within the close confines of New York's lower East side in the early 1900s, while the 1920s and 1930s saw the process repeated in the black community of Harlem (where, incidentally, middle class Jews had moved to escape the confines of the East side), ushering in the artistic and intellectual burgeoning of the Harlem Renaissance. While the ghettos grew out of economic exploitation and crime flourished in their streets, they housed viable communities to whom the street became a meeting place for the people and an extension of the tenement apartments they occupied. Thus, the ghettos functioned as tight social entities that belied their external appearance of chaos and disorder.

As industry increasingly clogged the inner cities, wealthier residents sought escape from the noise and pollution, and thus began an exodus to bedroom communities outside the city proper. The poor filled the vacuum, occupying once upscale neighborhoods vacated by the affluent where mansions were turned into rooming houses and residential hotels. Bunker Hill, for example, with its stately Victorian mansions situated west of downtown Los Angeles, had been the premier neighborhood in the 1890s. But as the city encroached upon the area and its wealthy residents fled, the stately mansions were parceled into boarding houses for the poor and elderly, a process that repeated itself in every neighborhood adjacent to the downtown. Over time, these areas became not only physically dilapidated but also morally impoverished. Through newspapers, books—Raymond Chandler in particular, linked Bunker Hill with vice and depravity—and films, the association of ghettos with every manner of social ill spread through the public mind. During the 1940s and 1950s, *film noir* movies frequently used Bunker Hill locations as representative of an imaginary ghetto, a place blighted and beyond redemption. The process of ghettoization was not particular to Los Angeles, but typical of virtually every major American city.

Ironically, as congestion and union activism began to undermine the economic gains that had initially prompted industry moves to central cities, manufacturing, too, abandoned the city, relocating in the suburbs, and away from the threat of union activism. Then, too, the migration of African Americans and other people of color to the cities added to the disfavor in which ghettos were held. For European immigrants, ghettos had often been the first step in a trajectory that led to full assimilation. This could not be said of people of color, large numbers of whom have tended to remain economically, politically, and socially disenfranchised, creating a permanent underclass, trapped in a culture of poverty with few avenues of escape.

Stripped both of employment in industry, and the wealth-creating proximity of middle-class urbanites, poverty-stricken neighborhoods sank deeper into decline as a result of neglect and increasing crime. By the 1940s inner city decline had become a matter of paramount importance to the Federal government. Following World War II, urban theorists began mapping strategies to save the decaying inner cities or, alternatively, to contain the spreading contagion of poverty. Whole city blocks in inner cities were red-lined as slums, thus effectively depriving residents of bank loans, and were subsequently purchased under eminent domain laws, razed to the ground, and replaced by high-rise apartment buildings.

There were several reasons for this particular approach to the problem. It has often been asserted that these planners were utopians, wishing to overlay their international modernist vision on the inner city. In many cases they knew little about how neighborhoods operated, but these massive public works netted huge profits for large-scale contractors, while providing a short-term solution to a desperate housing shortage, and infused massive amounts of Federal funds into the local economy. Unfortunately, Project Housing, as it became known, failed to provide a convivial living environment, neither did they foster stable neighborhoods. The consequence of high-rise projects was further to contain and isolate disadvantaged groups from society at large, causing a concomitant rise in chronic unemployment, youth gangs, and crime—all of the ills, in short, that these projects had sought to eradicate. Neighborhood streets once lined with small businesses and apartment buildings were replaced by sterile plazas, arid and inhospitable; amenities that had once been close at hand now required a trip outside the immediate neighborhood, thus further disabling local economies and rendering them increasingly reliant on Federal assistance.

Racism was implicit in the planning of these massive construction projects, designed to contain and quarantine poor minority groups. Lewis Mumford once wrote that the function of a city street is "to permit . . . the greatest potential number of meetings, encounters, challenges, between all persons, classes, and groups." This was a view antithetical to the utopian planners. "In the view of the planners," writes Marty Jezer, "slums and overcrowding were the root cause of crime. The new high-rise red brick housing projects were seen as antidotes to crime, and this became their most spectacular

failure." In San Francisco's Western Addition area, a bustling black neighborhood west of the civic center, more than 300 apartment buildings and small businesses were razed, replaced by barracks-like public housing. A functioning neighborhood was thus obliterated in the service of an idea, grim proof of the adage that sometimes the cure is worse than the disease. Perhaps the most significant refutation of postwar urban policy was seen in the 1960s, and again in the 1990s, when overcrowding, misery, frustration, poverty, and despair erupted into riot and conflagration. By the 1990s, projects had become the breeding ground for a major escalation of the trade in and addiction to crack cocaine, with appalling social consequences. Projects have undoubtedly served to intensify African-American and Hispanic feelings of disenfranchisement, and can be pointed to as the match that lit the powder kegs of violence.

The monumental failure of public housing lay in its attempt to impose a bird's-eye view on social organizations without consideration for the lived experience at ground level. Caught in a spiral of increased public expenditure without the tax base to sustain them, many cities slipped into a long period of decline. In once thriving rust belt cities such as Detroit and Milwaukee, the entire inner city was in effect a ghetto, ringed by suburban bedroom communities. In addition, many inner city projects are being torn down, replaced by middle-income housing (the land is now too valuable to be occupied by the poor), and their former residents dispersed throughout metropolitan areas in a deliberate policy of "spatial deconcentration" intended to offset the possibility of further large-scale riots.

In the postwar era, the creation of ghettos could at times be attributed to the political disenfranchisement of poor people. Massive public works projects such as highways, freeways, and parkways could change a neighborhood from stability to impoverishment by destroying the built environment. Often political expediency rather than sensible and equitable planning determined the route of such public works. Robert Moses, the longtime planning commissioner of New York, leveled 54 six- and seven-story apartment buildings in East Tremont, a Bronx neighborhood inhabited by elderly Jews and Eastern Europeans, in order to build the Cross-Bronx-Expressway. Another route, which would have destroyed fewer residences, but not spared several commercial structures, was available, but the factory owners had the influence that the residents of East Tremont sorely lacked. Soon East Tremont became a no-man's-land of condemned apartments and vacant streets. Large swathes of the Bronx suffered a similar fate, making it one of the most desolate and inhospitable urban neighborhoods within the United States, and a reproach to the urban policies of modern America.

In the last three decades of the twentieth century, as the existence of ghettos proved an intractable problem, sociologists postulated various hypotheses to explain the ghetto. De-industrialization, industrial relocation, and neighborhood sorting (the tendency for minorities to leave a neighborhood once a certain economic status is reached) have all been offered as reasons for the proliferation of ghettos in the postwar period. "Neighborhood poverty is not primarily the product of the people who live there or a ghetto culture," writes sociologist Paul Jaworsky, "but the predictable result of the economic status of the minority communities and the degree to which minorities are segregated from whites and from each other by income." The problem has been further exacerbated by gentrification (the reclamation of inner city housing by middle-class whites) on the one hand, and further spatial isolation on the other. Indeed, the more desirable inner-city locales become, the more impacted the plight of the poor. The result has been intermittent rioting and a culture of desperation. Nevertheless, the by-products of ghetto culture—gangster rap, drugs, clothing styles, and drugs—find ready buyers in white, middle-class America. This is perhaps the greatest paradox of the ghetto, that while experiencing almost total disenfranchisement, the music, fashions, and ethos of its inhabitants had come to dominate the trendy styles of the late-twentieth century.

With the present-day policy of destroying the high-rise projects, combined with the cessation of welfare, the ghetto stands to become a much more mobile phenomenon, a ghetto made of shopping carts, cars, vans, and prison cells. The criminalizing of larger sectors of the population is one of the more obvious consequences of the "War on Drugs," which is in effect a war on the urban poor. Forty years of government policy has done little to ameliorate the problem of the ghetto. If anything, the problem has been exacerbated by Federal intrusion. One is finally drawn to the inescapable conclusion that, unless society finds the will and the means to educate and employ all its members, it will continue to be plagued by a permanent and destabilizing underclass.

—Michael Baers

FURTHER READING:

Caro, Robert A. "The City-Shaper." *New Yorker*. January 5, 1998.

Jargowsky, Paul A. *Poverty and Place: Ghettos, Barrios, and the American City.* New York, The Russell Sage Foundation, 1997.

Jencks, Christopher, and Paul E. Peterson, editors. *The Urban Underclass.* Washington, The Brookings Institution, 1991.

Jezer, Marty. *The Dark Ages: Life in the United States 1945-1960.* Boston, South End Press, 1982.

Kotlowitz, Alex. *There Are No Children Here: The Story of Two Boys Growing Up in the Other America.* New York, Doubleday, 1991.

Mumford, Lewis. *The City in History.* New York, Harcourt, Brace & World, 1961.

Thomas, Piri. *Down These Mean Streets.* New York, Alfred A. Knopf, 1967.

Whyte, William Foote. *Street Corner Society.* Chicago, University of Chicago Press, 1955.

Wilson, William Julius. *The Truly Disadvantaged: The Inner-City, the Underclass and Public Policy.* Chicago, University of Chicago Press, 1987.

GI Joe

The GI Joe action figure, a plastic doll twelve inches tall and dressed as a military man, was the first action figure and the first exclusively boy's doll, disguised as a war toy. Extremely popular, it was at the same time controversial because of the fighting in Southeast Asia: its introduction by Hassenfeld Brothers in 1964 coincided with the U.S. Congress' passing of the Gulf of Tonkin Resolution which escalated American involvement in Vietnam. Invented by Stanley Weston, GI Joe was inspired by Mattel's Barbie, which made its debut in 1959, but GI Joe was different from Barbie in that it had twenty-one movable joints, enabling it to be configured in various combat poses. In the "razor and razor blade" principle of marketing, GI Joe, like Barbie, was "accessorized"; that is, designed to need

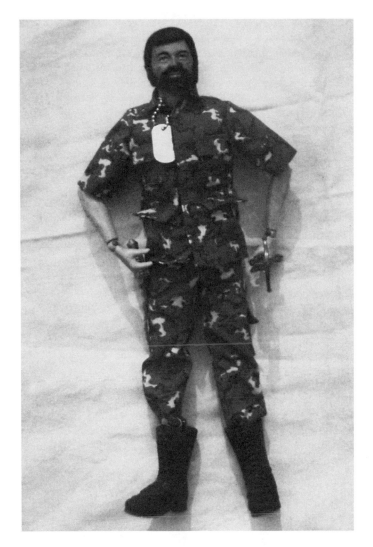

A GI Joe action figure.

additional paraphernalia. "Items sold separately" was the saying which accompanied every advertisement for the dolls.

Although the GI Joe action figure originated during the Cold War, it was nonetheless made in the image of the World War II fighting man. According to Hassenfeld's promotional campaign, the face of GI Joe comprised a composite of the faces of twenty Medal of Honor recipients from the war. American television and cinema were, at the time, frequently glorifying the soldier of the "Good War" in adventure series (*Combat, The Lieutenant,* and *Rat Patrol*), docu-cameo-epics (*The Longest Day, The Battle of the Bulge,* and *In Harm's Way*), and big-war films (*The Great Escape* and *Von Ryan's Express*). Comic books made the World War II fighter a hero as well, represented by DC Comics' "Sgt. Rock" and Marvel Comics' "Sgt. Fury." America's fascination with the World War II past may have been linked to the uncertainties felt during the Cold War era, as was their fascination with the GI Joe action figure.

A year after its introduction, the GI Joe line was augmented by an action nurse, featuring blonde rooted hair and painted green eyes; and a black soldier heralded as "Action Negro." Neither sold well, and the nurse was discontinued soon thereafter. On the other hand, GI Joe accessories like the plastic jeep and space capsule were very popular. In 1968 the Talking Joe offered combat discourse, eight phrases per action figure, produced by the pull of a color-coded string. Not everything that GI Joe said was celebratory (for example, "Medic, get that stretcher up here" and "Prepare wounded for helicopter pick-up"), although it was certainly less negative than what a real soldier would have said slogging in the mire of Vietnam. When war protests grew more bitter, fighting Joe dolls were converted into the Adventure Team to look for buried treasure or to capture wild animals. The logo worn by the Adventure Team uncannily resembled a peace sign. By 1976, the GI Joe action figure became Super Joe and was reduced in size to eight inches, for cheaper production and to enable the selling of more affordable accessories. Two years later, with Kenner dominating the market with its Star Wars action figures, racking up nearly $100 million in sales, GI Joe was discontinued.

The GI Joe story does not end there, however. Many children wrote Hasbro (Hassenfeld's later name), asking for the toy soldier's return. In the year of Ronald Reagan's first inauguration, GI Joe was reintroduced as "A Real American Hero." Standing at less than four inches tall, a size based on the Star Wars figures, the new GI Joe was the best-selling toy of the 1982 holiday season. This was quite a feat considering that Mattel at the same time introduced its He-Man and Masters of the Universe action figures. The following year, Mattel hired a film company to create a TV cartoon series based on the Masters of the Universe, inspiring Hasbro to do the same for Joe. In 1983 Mattel sold twenty-three million Masters of the Universe figures, and in the following year sales increased to $250 million. In 1984 Tonka entered the competition with its GoBots, and Hasbro responded with its Transformer line featuring "good" Autobots and "evil" Decipticons.

In the meantime, the second wave of GI Joe dolls continued to fill a niche, dealing with new foes such as "Destro" and "Drednoks." In 1986, GI Joe had $185 million in sales. Two years later, Hasbro claimed that two-thirds of American boys between the ages of five and eleven owned GI Joe dolls. What was new was the official narrative offered by the GI Joe animation series (1983-1987, 1989) and the comic book *G.I. Joe: A Real American Hero* (1982-1994), creating a need for clear enemies. In 1986, the line encompassed all four branches of the American military and was augmented by Japanese, German, Russian, British, French, and Australian fighters. This was in keeping with its World War II theme. Even so, little was suggested by the manufacturer on how boys should play with these figures.

If by the Reagan years it was necessary for a story line to be more explicit, World War II seemed too remote for development. On the other hand, a plot directly focusing on the Cold War was risky during the era of Mikhail Gorbachev. The comic book and animation series created fictional events and a line of enemy soldiers known as Cobra, a group of warriors who sought "to conquer the world for their own evil purposes!" The Gulf War did inspire Hasbro to create a "Duke" figure, a friendly soldier dressed in camouflage fatigues, back at the original twelve inches of height. By alluding to the film actor John Wayne, Duke linked not only World War II (a la *Sands of Iwo Jima*) with the Cold War (as in *The Green Berets*), but also the New World Order (represented by the international coalition which opposed Iraq). Among Hasbro's new GI Joe offerings for 1998 was the General Colin Powell doll.

—Roger Chapman

FURTHER READING:

Cross Gary. *Kids' Stuff: Toys and the Changing World of American Childhood*. Cambridge, Harvard University Press, 1997.

Engelhardt, Tom. *The End of Victory Culture: Cold War America and the Disillusioning of a Generation*. New York, BasicBooks, 1995.

Fraser, Antonia. *A History of Toys*. Frankfurt-am-Main, Delacorte Press, 1966.

Miller, G. Wayne. *Toy Wars: The Epic Struggle between G.I. Joe, Barbie and the Companies That Make Them*. New York, Times Books, 1998.

Young, Robert. *Action Figures*. New York, Dillon Press, 1992.

Giant

George Steven's 1956 film *Giant* reveals the ethics and personalities of the Texas oil industry as it shifted from individually driven concerns to large-scale corporate dominance. Rock Hudson plays Bick Benedict, who presides over the 595,000-acre Benedict Reata Ranch. James Dean plays the film's most memorable character, Jett Rink, the rebellious upstart who labors on the ranch before striking oil on his small plot of land. Dean, drenched in crude, arrives at Reata in a great moment in American film. Rink becomes the symbol of "new money," a corrupt, flamboyant oil tycoon and he and Benedict battle for the affections of Leslie Lynton, played by Elizabeth Taylor. *Giant* was Dean's last film; he died in a car accident on the Texas highway just as the filming was completed.

—Brian Black

Gibson, Althea (1927—)

Althea Gibson is one of the foremost names in American tennis and in African American history. In a prejudiced, segregated society, and in the even more segregated world of tennis, she carved out a place for herself with her aggressive serve and volley game. She won four grand-slam tournaments and several international titles, in both singles and doubles. But in the United States of the 1950s and 1960s there were few financial rewards for a black woman athlete, and Gibson grew discouraged and reclusive. While her name is known and celebrated by many, few know of the poverty and obscurity in which she currently lives.

Gibson was born in August 1927 on a Silver, South Carolina, cotton farm, the oldest of five children. In 1930, her family moved to Harlem, where her aunt made a living selling bootleg whiskey. The difficulties of growing up on the streets were tempered by the supportive black community atmosphere of Harlem. Tall and strong, Gibson played basketball with the boys and shot pool in the corner pool halls, but it was the game of paddle ball, played in streets blocked to traffic, where she excelled. When blues musician Buddy Walker observed how she easily defeated all comers, he bought her a tennis racquet and arranged for lessons for her at the Cosmopolitan Tennis Club in Harlem.

Gibson once said, "No matter what accomplishments you make, somebody helps you." In her own case, she received encouragement not only from Walker, but from boxer Sugar Ray Robinson and from

Althea Gibson

doctors Hubert Eaton and Robert Johnson, all of whom took particular interest in encouraging young black athletes. With their support, she began to play in tournaments through the American Tennis Association, the oldest black sports organization in the United States. Gibson won the girl's singles championship in 1944 and 1945, and, starting in 1947, she continued to win the title for ten years in a row.

Though Gibson dropped out of high school, her mentors helped her to return, and in 1949, she received a tennis scholarship to Florida Agricultural and Mechanical University in Tallahassee. In 1950, she broke into the world of white tennis. Former tennis champion Alice Marble pleaded her cause with the U.S. Lawn Tennis Association, and Gibson was allowed to play in their famous tournaments at Forest Hills, New York. Though she won her first tourney, she lost the second and became discouraged. The pressure of serving as a role model for her race coupled with persistent money troubles almost forced her to quit the game, but in 1955 the USLTA and the U.S. State Department chose Gibson to represent the United States on a goodwill tennis tour of Asia. This sign of acceptance by the white tennis establishment restored much of her confidence and renewed her commitment to tennis.

Gibson was almost thirty years old when she began the most dramatic phase of her career. She became the first African American to win an international championship when she won the French Women's Singles in 1956. She then went on to win the Italian championship in 1957, and Wimbledon and the U.S. Nationals two years in a row in 1957 and 1958. She was part of the winning doubles team for three years at Wimbledon, as well as in the French Open and the Australian Open. Her powerful game became legendary. "People

thought I was ruthless," she wrote later, "which I was. I didn't give a darn who was on the other side of the net. I'd knock you down if you got in my way."

In 1958, Gibson was the top-ranked women's tennis player when she decided to go professional. Financially, she simply could not afford to continue on a strictly amateur basis. However, her professional career never took off the way she had hoped. She did have a successful run touring with the famous Harlem Globetrotters, playing exhibition tennis games as an opening act before their novelty basketball games. Otherwise, she did not get many offers to play for money and had little success in her bids to initiate a film or recording career. In the 1960s she played professional golf, becoming the first African American member of the Ladies Professional Golfers Association, but her golfing career was undistinguished. After that, she earned a living by working as a tennis coach and for state government sport agencies in New Jersey, where she lived.

Gibson was elected to the Tennis Hall of Fame in 1971. In 1997, she was honored as a barrier-breaking African American athlete at the dedication of the Arthur Ashe Stadium in New York City. Gibson herself did not attend the ceremonies, but few knew it was because she had suffered several strokes and was living in poverty in East Orange, New Jersey, depressed, reclusive, and gravely ill. Some women athletes and coaches were horrified to learn of Gibson's circumstances. Pooling their energies and resources, these women staged a benefit and tribute for Gibson, raising more than thirty-five thousand dollars to help with medical bills and other expenses and to found an Althea Gibson Trust Fund to grant scholarships for women athletes. When she learned of the work that had been done on her behalf, and was given a video in which old friends and young newcomers alike testified how Gibson's life had inspired their own careers, her spirits were lifted immeasurably.

Though she contributed greatly to the sport of tennis, Gibson had to fight against prejudice throughout her career, whether it was a hotel that refused to book a luncheon in her honor or the unwritten prohibition against women earning money from sports. Her career is both an inspiration and a cautionary tale for aspiring young athletes: some games cannot be won with skill and aggressive determination. Perhaps a whole life will only be one point won in the game of changing a culture.

—Tina Gianoulis

FURTHER READING:

Biracree, Tom. *Althea Gibson.* New York, Chelsea House, 1983.

Davidson, Sue. *Changing the Game: The Stories of Tennis Champions Alice Marble and Althea Gibson.* Seattle, Seal Press, 1997.

Gibson, Althea. *I Always Wanted to Be Somebody.* New York, Harper, 1958.

———. *So Much to Live For.* New York, Putnam, 1968.

Gibson, Bob (1935—)

Bob Gibson's pitching for the St. Louis Cardinals earned him a dominant place in baseball history. The 6'1" right-hander used an overwhelming fastball and a peerless array of breaking pitches to strike fear in the hearts of National League batters throughout the

Bob Gibson

1960s and early 1970s. Gibson reserved his finest performances for the biggest games, outshining all competitors in the three World Series in which he pitched.

A frail child who suffered from a heart murmur, Gibson was encouraged to pursue sports by his older brother, a YMCA athletic director. He signed with the St. Louis Cardinals in 1957 for $4000, but did not crack the team's starting rotation until 1961. His breakthrough season came in 1963, when he went 18-9, and the Cardinals emerged as a contender for the National League pennant.

Gibson earned a reputation as the ultimate big game pitcher by winning the clinching games of the 1964 and 1967 World Series. In 1964, he held a powerful New York Yankees lineup in check on only two days of rest. In 1967, he beat the Boston Red Sox almost single-handedly, recording three of the Cardinals' four victories. All these wins were just a prelude for what was to come, however.

In 1968, Gibson enjoyed one of the finest seasons ever registered by a major league pitcher. He won 22 games against only nine losses, including a streak of 15 consecutive victories. He recorded 13 shutouts, highlighted by a stretch of 92 innings in which only two runs

were scored against him. His earned run average of 1.12 set a National League record, and was the lowest recorded for a pitcher since 1914. For his efforts, Gibson was voted the National League Cy Young Award by the Baseball Writers Association of America.

As impressive as he was in the regular season, Gibson was even more dominant in the World Series. He struck out a record 17 Detroit Tigers in the opening game of the Fall Classic, prevailing 4-0 over 30-game winner Denny McLain. He won Game Four as well, 10-1, to run his World Series record to 7-1. But when he tried to pitch the deciding seventh game on just two days of rest, even the unhittable Gibson met his match. He carried a shutout into the seventh inning but was beaten by the Tigers' Mickey Lolich, 4-1. It was Gibson's last World Series game.

Thanks in large measure to Gibson's efforts, 1968 went down in baseball history as the ''Year of the Pitcher.'' To compensate for a perceived imbalance, the next season Major League Baseball lowered the pitcher's mound, giving batters a fighting chance against the new breed of power pitchers led by Gibson and the New York Mets' Tom Seaver. Despite these adjustments, Gibson continued to dominate

National League batters well into the 1970s. He won 20 games in each of the next two seasons and was named to the All-Star team both years.

Gibson was feared around the league as one of the most intense, aggressive competitors in baseball. He believed it was a pitcher's right to knock down a batter with a high, inside fastball if the occasion demanded it. Gibson's intimidating demeanor even extended to his own teammates. On one occasion, when catcher Tim McCarver approached the mound for a conference, Gibson glowered at him angrily. ''The only thing you know about pitching is you can't hit it,'' he informed the terrified receiver. McCarver slunk back behind the plate with his words of advice still stuck in his gullet.

Although the Cardinals did not return again to the World Series, Gibson continued to reach personal milestones. He registered 56 total shutouts and became the second pitcher in major league history to amass 3000 strikeouts. When a series of injuries to his arms and legs began to take a toll on him, Gibson realized the end of his career was at hand. After Pete LaCock, a light-hitting first baseman known primarily for being the son of *Hollywood Squares* host Peter Marshall, crushed a grand slam off him in September of 1975, Gibson decided to call it quits. He retired as the winningest pitcher in St. Louis Cardinals history.

In recognition of his achievements, Gibson was elected to the Baseball Hall of Fame in 1981. He worked as a baseball broadcaster, a Major League pitching coach for several teams, and in 1998 he accepted a position as an advisor to the commissioner of baseball. He continued to speak out on the art of pitching and the state of the game at the close of the century.

—Robert E. Schnakenberg

FURTHER READING:

Deane, Bill. *Bob Gibson.* New York, Chelsea House, 1993.

Shatzkin, Mike. *The Ballplayers: Baseball's Ultimate Biographical Reference.* New York, William Morrow, 1990.

Gibson Girl

A creation from the pen of illustrator Charles Dana Gibson (1867-1944), the Gibson Girl came to be viewed as an ideal image of youthful femininity in the early 1890s. Statuesque and athletic, she was a contemporary incarnation of the beautiful, desirable, and modern woman. In one drawing from around 1900 she is pictured on the golf course in her signature long skirt and blouse. She stands tall and straight, one hand planted firmly on her hip, and lifts her head

Charles Dana Gibson's illustration of ''The Weaker Sex.''

majestically. Her male partner stands well to the side and stares in rapt admiration. The captivating Gibson Girl appealed to the imagination of a nation that craved an image of femininity that was fresh and uniquely American.

Gibson, the most popular illustrator in the United States at the turn of the century, began his career in New York during the early years of what has come to be known as the golden age of American illustration—the mid-1880s. By 1890 he was drawing for *Life, Scribner's Magazine, Century, Harper's Magazine,* and *Harper's Weekly.* He began drawing the Gibson girl in the early 1890s. She was featured in the first folio edition of his work, which appeared in 1894, and soon became a national sensation. Gibson's wife, the aristocratic Irene Langhorne Gibson, whom he met in 1893 and married in 1895, was widely believed to have been the inspiration behind her husband's creation, but she could not have been his original model. There was, in fact, no single model for the Gibson Girl, and the artist himself claimed that he had used several; moreover, he said that he had never intended to represent any one particular type of woman. Many young society women did actually seek out the illustrator, hoping to enhance their social standing further by posing for the famous Gibson Girl.

As Lois Banner observes, the Gibson Girl has often been identified with high society, the American "aristocracy" to which Gibson himself belonged. Nonetheless, she had qualities that also endeared her to the working class. Two working-class women, in particular, were thought to have been her inspiration: Minnie Clark, a professional model with an Irish working-class background, and the unnamed personal maid to the dancer Loie Fuller. The Gibson Girl, however, was rarely pictured as a working girl, and the settings in which she appeared were almost invariably fashionable. We see her at fancy dress balls, musical and theatrical events, and engaged in then-elite sporting activities. She was essentially a privileged socialite and her image, despite its modern trappings, incorporated traditional aspects of femininity. Contemporary feminists, such as writer Charlotte Perkins Gilman, saw in her the strength, ability, and freedom of the "new woman," although her fundamental appeal was her feminine beauty. Charles Dana Gibson emphasized her decorative qualities when he designed wallpaper for bachelors' rooms featuring a dense pattern of Gibson Girl faces.

The popularity of the Gibson Girl was reflected in many related phenomena in American popular culture. She was a paragon of beauty and style for millions of American women, who sought to emulate her in dress and hairstyle. Songs and plays were written about her, and her image was reproduced everywhere: on dishes and clothing, tablecloths and pillow covers, ashtrays and umbrella stands. For almost two decades she wielded a powerful influence in American popular culture. By the early 1910s, however, her vogue began to wane as a new image of femininity began to emerge—that of the liberated style and daring spirit that would culminate in the Jazz Age flapper at the end of World War I.

—Laural Weintraub

FURTHER READING:

Banner, Lois W. *American Beauty.* Chicago, The University of Chicago Press, 1983.

Banta, Martha. *Imaging American Women: Idea and Ideals in Cultural History.* New York, Columbia University Press, 1987.

The Gibson Girl and Her America: The Best Drawings of Charles Dana Gibson. New York, Dover Publications, Inc., 1969.

Van Hook, Bailey. *Angels of Art: Women and Art in American Society, 1876-1914.* University Park, Pennsylvania State University Press, 1996.

Gibson, Mel (1956—)

American-born, Australian-reared actor Mel Gibson has remained one of the world's most popular film stars for nearly 20 years, and his reputation as a producer and director is on the ascendancy in the late 1990s. With his natural good looks, highlighted by piercing blue eyes, his rich speaking voice, and humorous "bad boy" manner, he long ago went beyond the label *People* magazine placed on him in 1985 as their first ever "Sexiest Man Alive."

Gibson first came to international attention in his second picture, the low-budget 1979 Australian film *Mad Max.* As Max Rockatansky, a highway patrolman living in postapocalyptic Australia, the then 23-year-old Gibson was a bit wooden, but his screen charisma, good looks, and emotional intensity were a hit with audiences throughout the world. Despite the fact that Gibson's then-strong Australian accent was dubbed by an American for U.S. release, the film has remained a cult favorite. Gibson has maintained the "Mad Max"

Mel Gibson

mantle, portraying characters on the edge, from *Lethal Weapon*'s Martin Riggs, his most financially successful characterization, to Scottish patriot William Wallace in *Braveheart* to the lovable paranoid cabby Jerry Fletcher in *Conspiracy Theory*.

Following *Mad Max*, Gibson appeared in several more Australian films. He won an Australian Academy Award for Best Actor for *Tim*, a sentimental love story about a slow-witted man who falls in love with a middle-aged business woman. This was followed in 1981 by an outstanding performance in Peter Weir's antiwar masterpiece *Gallipoli* and an enormously popular cult film *The Road Warrior* (released internationally as *Mad Max 2*).

Although Gibson's early post-Australian films were critically and financially mixed, his reputation grew internationally. Some of his early U.S. films faltered at the box office: *The River, Mrs. Soffel, The Bounty,* and the Australian-made Warner Brothers release *Mad Max Beyond Thunderdome* were made within an 18-month period in the mid-1980s, and only *Thunderdome* proved financially successful.

The stress of work, success, and long separations from his wife and growing young family proved troublesome for Gibson personally. An arrest for drunk driving in Toronto while filming *Mrs. Soffel* and subsequent bouts of erratic behavior and drinking almost brought his career to an end and earned Gibson the moniker "Mad Mel." To address his problems, Gibson returned to his ranch in Australia and did not make any pictures for almost two years. His next film, the 1987 Richard Donner-directed *Lethal Weapon,* costarring Danny Glover, proved to be his greatest career success to that time and placed him on the level of solid international stardom.

In the early 1990s, Gibson moved permanently from Australia to the United States and began to take charge of his career, moving into the area of producing and directing. With partner Bruce Davey, Gibson had formed Icon Productions in 1989. In addition to producing or coproducing many of Gibson's own star vehicles, Icon turned out more than a dozen films in the late 1990s, including some small films ranging from *Immortal Beloved* to *87*. Its most financially and critically successful film was Gibson's second directorial effort, *Braveheart* (1995), which grossed more than $200 million worldwide and earned five Oscars, two of which went personally to Gibson, as director and as producer, along with Davey and Hollywood veteran Alan Ladd.

Following on the heels of *Braveheart*'s success, Gibson immediately made the intense action drama *Ransom,* directed by Ron Howard. The film was an immediate hit, earning more than $300,000 worldwide and bringing Gibson his first Golden Globe Award nomination as best actor. The period 1994-1997 was a high point in Gibson's career, with three of his films earning more than $1 million domestically, including a fourth installment of the *Lethal Weapon* series. In addition, Gibson cemented his position as a Hollywood mainstay by winning his second People's Choice award for favorite actor and a firm position either at the top or near the top of the annual Harris Poll of America's favorite actors and the world's list of top box-office stars.

On the personal side, unlike most Hollywood stars, Gibson has maintained a solid life away from show business, having married his wife, Robyn Moore, in 1980 and produced seven children. Gibson's religious and political views remain conservative, and his Catholicism has led him to espouse views often unpopular in Hollywood against abortion rights and abortion. His highly publicized distaste for political correctness, love of practical jokes, and bad puns have sometimes gotten him into trouble, as have comments that have occasionally labeled him as anti-feminist and anti-gay.

In early 1999, Gibson and Davey made the decision to move Icon from Warner Brothers (which had been the headquarters since the company was founded and had been Gibson's primary studio for more than a decade) to the Paramount lot in Hollywood, where Gibson had recently completed work on the film noir *Payback,* whose tagline was "prepare to root for the bad guy." In addition to his contacts with Paramount, and the possibility of releasing at least one additional film as part of his 1996 deal with Warner, Gibson and Davey were partnered with Rupert Murdoch in a new Australian studio, planned as the site of Gibson's next directorial effort, an adaptation of Ray Bradbury's *Fahrenheit 451*.

—Steve Hanson

FURTHER READING:

Clarks, Wesley. *Mel: The Inside Story.* London, Blake Publishing Ltd., 1993.

Grobel, Lawrence. "Mel Gibson." *Playboy.* July 1995, 51-63.

McCarthy, John. *The Films of Mel Gibson.* Secaucus, New Jersey, Citadel Press, 1997.

Pendereigh, Brian. *Mel Gibson and His Movies.* London, Bloomsbury Publishing, 1997.

Ragan, David. *Mel Gibson.* New York, Dell Publishing, 1985.

Gibson, William (1948—)

An American science-fiction writer most renowned for coining the term "cyberspace" in *Neuromancer* (1984), the book hailed by many critics and technology buffs as the seminal work in the cyberpunk genre, William Gibson is most poignant in simultaneously relishing and demonizing the technologies which increasingly shape human relationships at the end of the millennium. The now-legendary idea of cyberspace, defined in *Neuromancer* and employed throughout his fiction, anticipated the Internet as a virtual playground where information is exchanged and where corporations rise and fall: "A consensual hallucination experienced daily by billions of legitimate operators, in every nation, by children being taught mathematical concepts . . . A graphic representation of data abstracted from the banks of every computer in the human system. Unthinkable complexity. Lines of light ranged in the nonspace of the mind, clusters and constellations of data. Like city lights, receding." In a November 1994 interview for the Swedish news program *Rapport* (which is appropriately available on the Internet), Gibson calls the Internet "as significant as the birth of cities" and "a new kind of civilization" in its being primarily user-driven and transnational. Nevertheless, he also admits to not using "too glamorous" e-mail or even "browsing the 'Net," despite their correlation to his fiction, because of their great time investment and tendency to mark elitist distinctions of social class. As quoted by many of the Internet sites dedicated to his work, Gibson has said, "I'm not a techie. I don't know how these things work. But I like what they do, and the new human processes that they generate."

Gibson grew up in a small town on the edge of the Appalachian Mountains, dropped out of high school in 1967, and ended up in Toronto, Ontario, Canada. There he married Deborah Thompson in 1972. The couple has two children. He later earned a B.A. in 1977 from the University of British Columbia. By the early 1980s, Gibson was making a name for himself with stories such as ''Johnny Mnemonic'' and ''Burning Chrome,'' many published in *Omni* magazine.

In his debut novel *Neuromancer,* Gibson evokes a near-future world organized by technological-corporate enclaves that circulate power through an elite of specialized information-manipulators. The players are typically ''console cowboys'' (cyberspace operators) who navigate the hallucinatory data-field which is cyberspace, ''razor girls'' (free-lance cybernetic assassins) who roam the ''Sprawl'' (the extended and dirty metropolis of discarded and constantly renovated technology), and a myriad of Japanese and Chinese syndicates who pull the strings. Hailed by the science-fiction community at its inception and increasingly studied at the university setting, *Neuromancer* won the prestigious Hugo Award, the Philip K. Dick Memorial Award, and the Nebula Award for best novel. It is the first of the Sprawl trilogy, a series which charts how disconnected members of a technological elite inadvertently make possible an AI (artificial intelligence) which covertly seeks to revolutionize human-machine relations. The equally compelling *Count Zero* (1986) and *Mona Lisa Overdrive* (1988) complete the trilogy.

Gibson's real-life fear of technology-born inequality also shows itself in his fiction. Written during a robust 1980s economy which saw unprecedented economic mergers, the Sprawl trilogy resonates with a new sense of the corporation (''zaibatsu'') as an indomitable Hydra: ''the multinationals that shaped the course of human history, had transcended old barriers. Viewed as organisms, they had attained a kind of immortality. You couldn't kill a zaibatsu by assassinating a dozen key executives; there were others waiting to step up the ladder, assume the vacated position, access the vast banks of corporate memory.'' In the *Rapport* interview though, Gibson reveals more real-world optimism in having ''great hopes for the Internet'' of individual initiative and ''very little hope for commercial versions.'' Making a prophetic gesture before the National Academy of Sciences in May 1993 with colleague Bruce Sterling, Gibson advocated enhanced online teaching, free software to *all* teachers, and corporate-provided computers to *only* the most economically disadvantaged school districts as an equalizing move for the United States.

Hollywood brought Gibson to the silver screen with *Johnny Mnemonic* (1995), an adaptation of his short story published in the Nebula award-winning *Burning Chrome* (1987), a collection of Gibson's short fiction. The film stars Keanu Reeves as an ''information-courier'' whose cerebral data capacity is dangerously overloaded with information critical to an anti-technology resistance movement. Despite its often lethargic plot and juvenile characterization, the film is most successful in casting rapper Ice-T and singer Henry Rollins as prominent ''Lo Teks,'' a band of renegade fighters which quietly undermines corporate power. The film therefore continues the idea of an ''underground'' use of discarded technology, established in his fiction, as the ground for resisting larger institutions.

Gibson also has written *Dream Jumbo* (1989), a text to accompany performance art; *Agrippa, A Book of the Dead* (1992), a poem about his father which was encoded on computer disk and eroded rapidly after being read; and, with novelist Bruce Sterling, *The Difference Engine* (1991), a retroactive science fiction novel set in Victorian England. Gibson's latest prose works, *Virtual Light* (1993) and *Idoru* (1996), continue the provocative vision established in the Sprawl trilogy. Although he spends no time there, the Internet is fertile with talk of Gibson and itself resonant with the implications of his work.

—Anthony Cast

FURTHER READING:

Trosky, Susan M., ed. *Contemporary Authors*. Vol. 133. Detroit, Gale Research, 1991.

Gifford, Frank (1929—)

On the football field, Frank Gifford starred for the New York Giants in the 1950s and early 1960s during the final days of the two-way player. Away from the game, his movie-idol visage made him a larger-than-life sports hero, a figure synonymous with another famous New Yorker of the 1950s, ball player Mickey Mantle. But it was a book about failure that cemented Gifford's cultural standing. The football star was cast as a central figure in Frederick Exley's autobiographical novel, *A Fan's Notes*. After retiring from the Giants in 1964, Gifford married television personality Kathie Lee Johnson, and joined the Monday Night Football broadcasting team helmed by Howard Cosell. He made headlines again in the late 1990s when a tabloid newspaper paid a former flight attendant to seduce him in a bugged hotel room. When the scandal hit, Gifford's fairytale marriage seemed to be over, but Kathie Lee stood by her man and Frank Gifford's late-life sin did little to change his standing as an All-American icon.

—Geoff Edgers

FURTHER READING:

Exley, Frederick. *A Fan's Notes*. New York, Harper & Row, 1968.

Gifford, Frank, with Harry Waters. *The Whole Ten Yards*. New York, Random House, 1993.

Gifford, Kathie Lee, with Jim Jerome. *I Can't Believe I Said That!* New York, Simon & Schuster, 1992.

Gillespie, Dizzy (1917-1993)

On stage, wearing his black beret, goatee, and wire-rimmed glasses, Dizzy Gillespie was the much-imitated archetype of the jazz hipster. When he raised his trademark bent horn and began to play, cheeks puffed out like a giant chipmunk, he created a sound that defined American jazz, and many of his compositions become lasting jazz standards. Gillespie came of age during a golden time in jazz. In the 1930s and 1940s, brilliant musicians like Gillespie, Charlie Parker, Thelonious Monk, Miles Davis, and Max Roach were playing together in wildly creative jam sessions that would change the face of American music. Though Gillespie's technical expertise and soaring harmonies on the trumpet made him an integral part of this new movement, perhaps his greatest contribution was his ability to thrive as an African-American musician and public figure in the inhospitable climate of the pre-civil-rights United States. During a career that

Dizzy Gillespie

lasted six decades, Gillespie's upbeat attitude, personal stability, and charismatic showmanship were major factors in the popularization of jazz.

Gillespie was born John Birks Gillespie, the youngest of nine children, in the small town of Cheraw, South Carolina. His working-class parents had little energy to devote to their youngest son's education, but Gillespie's father was a part-time bandleader on his weekends off from his bricklaying job. Young John practiced on the band instruments around the house, learning piano and percussion before finally settling on the trumpet as his favorite. When a Works Progress Administration job convinced him he did not want to do manual labor, Gillespie got a scholarship to attend the all-black Laurinburg Technical Institute in North Carolina. There he began to study music theory and the principles of harmony with which he would experiment throughout his career.

In 1935, Gillespie quit school to move to Philadelphia, where he honed his skills on the horn in jam sessions and joined his first band. By 1937, he had arrived at the new jazz mecca, Harlem. Gillespie began to prove himself to the great New York bandleaders and soon had a job in Cab Calloway's band, wowing audiences and musicians alike with his creative virtuosity and stage antics. Fellow trumpeter Palmer Davis gave him the name Dizzy because of his childlike exuberance and zaniness on stage. "Man, this is a dizzy cat," Davis said, and the name stuck. Adding to Gillespie's eccentric image was his unique trumpet, the horn of which was bent almost straight up. Created by accident when a drunken reveler stepped on it, Gillespie insisted on keeping his "bent horn," claiming he could hear his own sound better.

Though it endeared him to fans, Gillespie's unbridled humor got him in trouble more than once, and he lost his job with Calloway in the mid-1940s when the bandleader tired of being the butt of jokes. It was then that Gillespie joined the famous Harlem jam sessions that produced the wildly radical, urgent beat that came to be known as bebop. Polished and developed by Gillespie and saxophonist Charlie "Bird" Parker, bebop got its name from Gillespie's chanted intro to the songs: "Dee-ba-pa-'n-bebop. . . ." Soon fans were yelling, "Play some of that bebop music." Bebop gave jazz a deeper and more complex dimension, and Parker and Gillespie's innovations continue to influence the development of jazz. Though jazz is perhaps the most intrinsically American of all music forms, like everything in America, it is a combination of many influences. Early in his career, Gillespie was introduced to Cuban music, with its roots in the rhythms of Africa. Together with Cuban musicians like Charo Pozo, Gillespie was instrumental in developing the genre of Afro-Cuban jazz, which he worked to popularize up until his death. In 1946, Gillespie started his first big band, where he introduced Pozo on the conga drum. This was an historic event because African-style drums had been banned since the days of slavery, and Gillespie's band marked the first time a jazz drummer had used his hands rather than sticks to play his instrument. It was by such subtle, yet joyously radical maneuvers that Gillespie managed to challenge the racist system while keeping his good nature and popularity. The 1989 film *A Night in Havana* documents Gillespie's connection to Cuban music and culture.

Unlike many other jazz musicians, Gillespie did not fall victim to substance abuse or a self-destructive lifestyle. He married dancer Lorraine Willis in 1940 and remained happily married to her until his death in 1993. In the 1960s, he converted to Baha'i, a religion of Persian origin that focuses on tolerance and love. Gillespie himself was widely loved and respected, even in unexpected places. In 1956, the State Department chose Gillespie as a good will ambassador and sent him to the Middle East and Latin America. Principled as ever, the jazz man refused to speak for the government. Instead, he got to know individuals, played free concerts for children and the poor, and brought back rhythms like the samba and bossa nova to enrich American musical culture.

In 1964, Gillespie surprised the public by running for president. Running on a platform that included abolishing racism and uniting the world's people, Gillespie as always had his tongue in cheek, proposing that the White House be renamed the "Blues House" and suggesting Miles Davis as CIA chief and Malcolm X as attorney general. One of his campaign songs advised, "Your politics oughta be a groovier thing / So get a good President who's willing to swing."

Until his death from cancer in 1993, Gillespie maintained a vigorous schedule, releasing more than five hundred recordings and performing in close to three hundred live concerts a year. His contribution to jazz and to American music in general resides not only in his considerable legacy of classic hits such as "A Night in Tunisia," "Groovin' High," and "Salt Peanuts," but also in his down-to-earth ability to make his music accessible and transcendent at the same time. Drummer Max Roach said of him, "Dizzy was the catalyst, the man who inspired us all."

—Tina Gianoulis

FURTHER READING:

Gillespie, Dizzy, with Al Fraser. *To Be or Not . . . to Bop: Memoirs.* Garden City, New York, Doubleday, 1979.

Gourse, Leslie. *Dizzy Gillespie and the Birth of Bebop*. New York, Simon & Schuster, 1994.

McRae, Barry. *Dizzy Gillespie: His Life and Times*. New York, Universe Books, 1988.

Shipton, Alyn. *Groovin' High*. New York, Oxford University Press, 1999.

Gilligan's Island

Airing only three seasons, 1964-1967, *Gilligan's Island* remains one of the best-known shows in television history. The premise of the show is basic: seven castaways are shipwrecked on an uncharted island following a storm and have to survive until they are rescued. The show is remarkable in its popularity and longevity almost in spite of itself. In its first season it received almost universally terrible reviews from television critics. It is still seen by many as one of the dumbest and most absurd shows on television, but its 98 episodes have been in constant syndication since it went off the air more than 30 years ago. Three reunion/sequel television movies in the late 1970s and early 1980s all received good ratings, and the show was the inspiration for two children's animated series.

Gilligan's Island was created and nurtured by Sherwood Schwartz (who would go on to create that other astounding hit of the 1960s and 1970s, *The Brady Bunch*). In fact, the show would not have been made at all except for Schwartz's persistence; his book *Inside Gilligan's Island* describes the long struggle to get the show made against the desires of the CBS network chief. Winning its time slot in each of its three seasons, it was abruptly cut from the lineup to make room for the network president's favorite show, *Gunsmoke*.

In describing *Gilligan's Island*, Schwartz said that his plan was to create a microcosm of society. The characters in this society were extremes in social, financial, and intellectual terms: the leader—Skipper (Alan Hale, Jr.), the bumbling sidekick—Gilligan (Bob Denver), the wealthy—Mr. and Mrs. Howell (Jim Backus and Natalie Schafer), the country girl—Mary Ann (Dawn Wells), the movie star—Ginger (Tina Louise), and the academic—Professor (Russell Johnson). Indeed, the Skipper tries to lead, the Professor is looked to for solutions to problems, the rich people and the movie star sit in an island version of luxury, and Gilligan and Mary Ann are left to do much of the manual labor.

The actual stories relied on slapstick humor. Ostensibly, the castaways wanted to be rescued from their isolation on the island, and in almost every episode they were presented with a possibility of escape. Invariably something happened to foil the plan, usually involving an innocent accident on the part of Gilligan. Quite often the viewer is required to suspend disbelief and accept the fact that the same group that can create elaborate equipment and solve problems with items available on this ever-abundant island is somehow incapable of making good on the many possibilities of rescue. What's more, though upset at the failings, they seem content with their home. They accept each other for their characteristics and their weaknesses, and persist.

Even though this was an uncharted island, many stories included the arrival and departure of a new person to the island only to leave the main characters stranded once again. These guests included everyone from Russian cosmonauts to natives to Hollywood producers to foreign spies and South American dictators, and allowed for comment on contemporary issues and events of the day such as space flight, South American politics, radioactivity, surfing, spies, and Mars pictures.

One of the highest rated film specials in television history, *Rescue from Gilligan's Island* finally brought the castaways home in 1978 where each one found unhappiness with his former way of life. At the end of the movie, they are contentedly shipwrecked again on the same island. The *"Castaways" on Gilligan's Island* (1979) was

The cast of *Gilligan's Island* as they appeared in the 1978 television movie *The Return from Gilligan's Island*.

an attempt to make a new series in the mode of a Fantasy Island/Love Boat resort on their island. *The Harlem Globetrotters on Gilligan's Island* followed in 1981.

—Frank E. Clark

FURTHER READING:

Denver, Bob. *Gilligan, Maynard & Me.* New York, Citadel Press, 1993.

Green, Joey. *The Unofficial Gilligan's Island Handbook.* New York, Warner Books, 1988.

Marc, David, and Robert J. Thompson. *Prime Time, Prime Movers: From I Love Lucy to L.A. Law—America's Greatest TV Shows and the People Who Created Them.* Boston, Little, Brown & Co., 1992.

McNeil, Alex. *Total Television: A Comprehensive Guide to Programming from 1948 to the Present.* 3rd ed. New York, Penguin Books, 1991.

Schwartz, Sherwood. *Inside Gilligan's Island: From Creation to Syndication.* Jefferson, North Carolina, McFarland, 1988.

Stoddard, Sylvia. *TV Treasures: A Companion Guide to Gilligan's Island.* New York, St. Martin's Press, 1996.

Allen Ginsberg

Ginny Dolls

Ginny is an American made 8-1/2 inch doll immensely popular from 1951 through 1959. Produced by Jennie Graves, owner of Vogue Doll Company, Ginny was made of hard, durable plastic developed first for war uses. The doll's size and durability made it convenient for her to accompany a child everywhere. Storybooks relating Ginny's activities such as a trip around the country piqued children's imaginations while quantities of meticulously designed outfits and accessories encouraged play related to the doll's activities. Ginny was a forerunner of action figure dolls that contribute to children's development by encouraging factual-based play. The reasonably priced Ginny dolls were sold many places including drugstores and department stores.

—Taylor Shaw

FURTHER READING:

Izen, Judith, and Carol Stover. *Collector's Encyclopedia of Vogue Dolls: Identification and Values.* Paducah, Kentucky, Collector Books, 1998.

Mandeville, A. Glenn. *Ginny, America's Sweetheart.* Grantsville, Maryland, Hobby House Press, 1998.

Ginsberg, Allen (1926-1997)

The poet Allen Ginsberg, an iconoclast in both his politically charged writing and unconventional lifestyle, epitomized the antiestablishment "Beat" movement of the 1950s and 1960s. In the midst of a generation shaped by the aftermath of the Holocaust and the atomic bomb, mass conformity, the hysteria of McCarthyism, and government censorship of personal liberties and civil rights, Ginsberg became a popular voice of artistic defiance. In American popular and academic culture, Ginsberg's influence as a poet, musician, artist, professor, and agitator has continued to grow even after his death. Bearing unofficial titles such as the "father of the Beat Generation," the "prophet of the 1960s," and the "guru of the counterculture movement," Ginsberg remains a cultural icon of one of America's most socially and politically turbulent eras.

Along with other Beats like Jack Kerouac and William S. Burroughs, Ginsberg embraced Eastern philosophies and African American culture, experimented with various drugs, used the raw materials of life as the basis for his art, and subverted numerous societal and middle-class conventions in order to achieve spiritual, political, and sexual liberation. The opening lines of Ginsberg's *Howl*, the poetic manifesto of Beat attitudes and Ginsberg's most widely known work, exemplifies the gritty nature of his poetry: "I saw the best minds of my generation destroyed by madness, starving / hysterical naked, dragging themselves through the negro streets at dawn looking for an / angry fix." Because of its graphic sexual references, *Howl*, became the subject of a 1957 obscenity case that resulted in a landmark acquittal of the poem's publisher, Lawrence Ferlinghetti of City Lights Books. The trial's notoriety pushed Ginsberg into the public spotlight and ensured his status as a popular poet, an indelible symbol of Beat defiance, and a lasting representative of the rebellious spirit of the 1960s.

Despite his reputation as a boisterous nonconformist, Ginsberg grew up shy. He was born in New Jersey on June 3, 1926, to Louis Ginsberg, a moderate socialist and an accomplished lyric poet, and to Naomi Ginsberg, a radical communist during the Depression, who suffered from psychotic delusions until her death. Ginsberg discovered the poetry of Walt Whitman in high school, which sparked his interest in becoming a poet. However, upon his father's advice, he entered Columbia University in the mid-1940s with the intent of becoming a labor lawyer. At Columbia, he joined a circle of friends that included Kerouac, Burroughs, and Neal Cassady. They exposed him to Manhattan's varied subcultures and fostered his artistic, philosophical and sexual development; each of them would contribute greatly to the Beat movement a decade later.

Ginsberg eventually changed his major to literature and after receiving his bachelor's degree in 1948 was hired as a market researcher in New York City. During this time, Ginsberg experienced a vision of William Blake and awoke, in his own words, "into a totally deeper real universe." He introduced himself to fellow New Jersey poet William Carlos Williams, whose poem about Paterson, New Jersey, moved Ginsberg greatly; Ginsberg would eventually incorporate Williams's broad narrative style into his own poetry. Ginsberg quit his job and left New York in 1953, traveling to Cuba and Mexico. Bearing a letter of introduction from Williams, he arrived at San Francisco in 1954 to meet Kenneth Rexroth and the group of poets, writers, artists, filmmakers, and avant-gardists who would later be at the core of the Beat movement. It was here that Ginsberg composed and first read *Howl* as part of the Six Gallery reading in October 1955.

Not since Brook Farm (a transcendentalist utopian community established in Massachusetts in 1841) had an American cultural-literary group enjoyed such cohesion as the Beat and counterculture movements. At the center of the community was Ginsberg—who coined the term "flower power" in 1965—promoting free love, LSD, and group living in San Francisco's Haight-Ashbury district, the national epicenter of counterculture. He also stood out as a major figure in Vietnam War protests. He was arrested in 1967 in an antiwar demonstration in New York City along with Dr. Benjamin Spock, the famed child psychologist.

In the post-Vietnam War years, Ginsberg's reputation as an agitator grew even more widespread when countries such as Cuba, the former Soviet Union, and Poland deported him for speaking against communism and the persecution of homosexuals while he attempted to establish residency. Within the United States, he participated in the antinuclear, environmental, and gay liberation movements in the 1970s and 1980s. During the first term of the Reagan administration, the FBI placed him on a list of people deemed "unsuitable" as government paid speakers abroad, a list on which black leader Coretta Scott King, feminist Betty Friedan, and consumer advocate Ralph Nader also appeared.

Ginsberg wrote more than forty books of poetry in his lifetime, working up to his death in 1997. His uncensored free-verse style produced as much controversy among academics as his profanity did among the government authorities. However, despite the stones of disdain and censorship thrown in Ginsberg's path, *Howl* has become required reading on college campuses throughout the United States, and his *Fall of America* won the National Book Award in 1972. He was also a member of the American Institute of Arts and Letters.

Ginsberg's love for poetry inspired him to take an active and highly public role in its promotion. In 1974, he helped found the Jack Kerouac School of Disembodied Poetics at the Naropa Institute, the first accredited Buddhist college in the Western world, located in Boulder, Colorado. He also taught English at Brooklyn College in New York. During the 1970s and 1980s, Ginsberg recorded spoken words and songs, and sometimes toured with popular musicians such as the Clash, and Bob Dylan, who cited Ginsberg as one of the few literary figures he could stand. In the 1990s, Ginsberg made more

recordings, collaborating with artists such as Paul McCartney and Phillip Glass. Ginsberg also had a talent in photography; he depicted his subjects—many of whom were people—with great depth of character, expressing visually what he achieved poetically. In 1996, his photographs were displayed in "Beat Culture and the New America: 1960-1965," an exhibition organized by the Whitney Museum of Art, suggesting that Ginsberg's anti-establishment life and work had, near the end of his life, become fully embraced by the country's most entrenched cultural institutions.

—Nancy Lan-Jy Wang

FURTHER READING:

Ginsberg, Allen. *Howl and Other Poems*. San Francisco, City Lights, 1956.

Holmes, John Clellon. *Nothing More to Declare*. New York, Dutton, 1967.

Kramer, Jane. *Allen Ginsberg on America*. New York, Paragon House, 1969.

Girl Groups

"Girl group" is a popular descriptive term referring to a genre of all-female singing groups and to the distinctive style of music such a

The Chiffons

group performs. Sexual desire is essential to the girl group image and sound. The genre was nonexistent in the sexually restrictive, first half of the twentieth century, although some all-female groups (like the Boswell and Andrews Sisters) existed. The rise of the genre helped challenge sexual mores in society and helped nurture the growth of a youth-driven culture in America. By 1960, the image of the girl group was everywhere in popular culture—spread across the nation through radio and television. The genre had its ultimate expression in the Supremes in the 1960s. By the 1990s, the image of the girl group, such as the Spice Girls, had become an established musical and cultural symbol.

The girl group image alludes to both youthful innocence and sexual desire (desire usually for the heterosexual men for whom the groups were originally marketed). Traditionally a trio or quartet in number, members are young, attractive women who are groomed in a noticeable way—they appear in matching clothes, for example, or wear designer dresses. Their hair is styled fashionably and members often wear makeup. The image is one of a young woman representing the heterosexual man's ideal woman or Dream Date. She is pretty, she is all made-up, and she is dressed for a lovely dinner, a night of dancing, or a romantic movie. Sex is always a part of the image, although this theme has been used in different degrees throughout the genre's history. The Dream Date is multiplied in the image of her sister singers, and so, together, the group appears as a harem of sorts, ready to entertain and please the man lucky enough to choose (or be chosen by) the women.

Musically, the girl group sound is meant to complement this narrow but highly identifiable physical image of youthful, desirable women. To emphasize the notion of youth, all members generally have young-sounding voices: thin, high alto to soprano range, sometimes nasal in tone. The thinness of each woman's voice allows for easy blending and a uniformity of tone. A voice that is low—say, tenor range—or too full or distinctive is uncommon in the genre, as such voices are considered too mature to convey qualities of youth or too individual to blend invisibly into the sound of the other members' voices. To emphasize the notion of sex, sometimes the voices are decidedly breathy—borrowed from the popular images of the Hollywood sex symbols (such as Marilyn Monroe) of the first half of the twentieth century. As with much popular music, the songs themselves are short and repetitive, therefore memorable, and usually address or convey a situation or emotion right away, allowing the remainder of the song to be used as a showcase for the group's romantic or sexual appeal. The lyrics of girl group songs deal with predicaments of love and sexual relationships, often revolved around precoital stress. Before the "Sexual Revolution," many lyrics were controversial, for it was not considered proper for a woman—whose cultural image in America had long been synonymous with virginity—to consider or voice her own thoughts about sexual intercourse, especially in a public forum.

The barriers to what was lyrically acceptable had come down in the 1950s with male musicians such as Chuck Berry, Elvis Presley, and Jerry Lee Lewis, solo artists who were writing and performing songs that entertained and were relevant to teenage experience—particularly the desires for freedom and sexual expression that teenagers were developing from beneath the oppressive morality of the 1940s and early 1950s. By the mid-1950s, these themes of love and sexual relationships were being explored by groups of male singers, and the genre of all-male singing groups became popular. Finally, five classmates at a school in Harlem decided to form an all-female group similar to the male groups that were so popular. Known

as the Bobbettes, they recorded their smash, top ten hit song "Mr. Lee" in 1957. The song had both the flavor of doo-wop (a style many male singing groups were having success with at that time) and many of the characteristics of what would become the "girl group" style: the lyrics were simple and repetitive, and the song emphasized youthful innocence and budding sexual desire. In this case, the song concerned a girl's affection for her favorite teacher. The Bobbettes' later recordings never achieved the level of success that their first single had reached, but another girl group called the Chantels released their first song only a few months after the appearance of "Mr. Lee," and so a trend had begun.

A year later, four other high school girls formed a group of their own. Fans of the Bobbettes and the Chantels, they called themselves the Shirelles and soon became one of the most popular girl groups in the rock 'n' roll era. Their biggest hit was "Will You Still Love Me Tomorrow?" The lyrics described a young girl musing on the loss of her virginity and were well ahead of the times. The song raced to the number one spot on the record charts, making the Shirelles the first black all-female group to have a number one record. Within a few years, dozens of girl groups formed and recorded records, all with varying degrees of success. All followed the girl group format, using slight variations to distinguish themselves from one another. Some of the most popular groups were the Crystals, the Marvelettes, the Chiffons, and the Shangri-Las. Two groups—Martha and the Vandellas, and the Ronettes—brought their own self-confident, "tough girl" innovation to the girl group sound.

Prior to the 1960s, audiences knew a singer's physical image from the live performance. Records were popular, but artists were, in the beginning, rarely shown on the covers of rock 'n' roll records. As girl groups began to appear more regularly on teen-oriented television shows such as Dick Clark's American Bandstand, and as their pictures began to show up on record covers, the idea of developing a visual image that supported either a group's tough or softly sweet (but in any case, sexually appealing) sound also became common.

The Motown Records company knew exactly how to use public visual image to their advantage. With shrewd business savvy, the company turned the Supremes—one of the many groups they managed—into the most successful girl group in popular music history. The Supremes capitalized on the use of a group name that implied divinity, on a public image that strove for larger-than-life beauty and sexual appeal, and through the sheer number of record-breaking achievements (including 12 number one hit records). A charm school run by the company taught the three young girls how to behave, dress, dance, and present themselves as young ladies. The Supremes' music was true to the girl group mold—simple, highly repetitive songs about love, yet audiences all over the world took notice of lead singer Diana Ross's breathy, seductive voice—light and thin but unquestionably distinctive. Their performances showcased their graceful, thoroughly choreographed routines and their often dazzling designer dresses. Motown owner Berry Gordy assembled a gifted team of writers to supply the Supremes with an almost endless stream of popular songs. The Supremes also appeared almost weekly on television variety shows and commercials, so by the end of the 1960s their name was household, and their image had become almost the sole representation of the term "girl group": three beautiful women, shining in sequined dresses, singing seductively to the listener. So completely did the Supremes seem to embody the concepts of the girl group that all other girl groups were subjected to a doomed comparison. Through the 1970s and 1980s a number of innovative all-female or female-led groups appeared (the Pointer Sisters, Heart, the Go-Gos, the Bangles), but these were of a very different sort. Any female group performing in the "girl group" style—now embodied by the Supremes—was guaranteed to fail in the public's eye as mere imitators.

Girl groups were often hired by other musicians to perform as background singers, so even when the genre began to move out of the public's eye, its influence was present in much of the subsequent popular musical work that was done in America. By the 1990s, the term "girl group" had developed a negative connotation for some, drawing on the worst stereotypes of the style: music thought of as shallow, low on talent, or vocal beauty but high on studio polish and gimmickry; highly sexual lyrical content; simplistic lyrical texture; and heavy emphasis on public image and physical sexual appeal rather than on the quality of the musical product or performance. In the 1990s a resurgence in the girl group style occurred in rhythm and blues music. Of these groups, a talented few (such as En Vogue) arose that functioned traditionally in many ways, yet embodied the best of what the genre had to offer and received, in return, their share of recognition. However, most of the girl groups in the 1990s had to struggle, in the general public's eye, to prove themselves against the later, negative image of the girl group.

—Brian Granger

FURTHER READING:

Gaar, Gillian G. *She's a Rebel: The History of Women in Rock & Roll.* Seattle, Seal Press, 1992.

Grieg, Charlotte. *Will You Still Love Me Tomorrow?: Girl Groups from the 50s On. . . .* London, Virago, 1989.

O'Brien, Lucy. *She Bop: The Definitive History of Women in Rock, Pop and Soul.* New York, Penguin Books, 1995.

Ryan, Thomas. *American Hit Radio: A History of Popular Singles from 1955 to the Present.* Rocklin, California, Prima Publishing, 1996.

Warner, Jay. *The Billboard Book of American Singing Groups: A History 1940-1990.* New York, Billboard Books, 1992.

Girl Scouts

The Girl Scouts would probably never have come into being if the Boy Scouts had not been exclusively for boys. During the first decade of the twentieth century several thousand girls had wanted to join the new youth group created by General Sir Robert Baden-Powell in England shortly after the Boer War in South Africa, and a parallel organization called the Girl Guides had been quickly organized, with Baden-Powell's sister Agnes at its head.

Juliette Gordon Low, a native of Savannah, Georgia, had married an Englishman; at the time that she met the Baden-Powells in 1910, she was a wealthy widow who had survived her increasingly abusive marriage, and now had both energy and funds to spare. After a turn at leading a Guides group in Scotland, Low threw herself with gusto into creating an American analogue to the organization, and on returning to Savannah in 1912 formed the first troops in the United States with the eager support of a distant cousin, Nina Anderson Pape, and a naturalist, W. J. Hoxie. Hoxie also collaborated with Low on

revising Agnes Baden-Powell's Girl Guides handbook for American consumption, including writing some new chapters on camping and nature lore. The first edition of *How Girls Can Help Their Country* was published in 1913. In 1915 the name of the American organization was changed from Girl Guides to Girl Scouts and its headquarters moved from Savannah to Washington; in 1916 the national office moved to New York, where it remained for the rest of the century.

Robert Baden-Powell saw Scouting for boys as a means to a specific end: "to help them become handy, capable men and to hold their own with anyone," he wrote, adding that a woman with similar training as Girl Guides "can be a good and helpful comrade to her brother or husband or son along the path of life" and that the Girl Guides during the First World War had "quickly showed the value of their training by undertaking a variety of duties which made them valuable to their country in her time of need." So Girl Scouts, like Boy Scouts, were taught how to survive in the wilderness and the basics of water safety and first aid, and encouraged to learn how to handle firearms. With the motto "Be prepared," members of both organizations still promise "to do my duty to God and my country, to help other people at all times, and to obey the Scout Laws." Both groups award merit badges for the acquisition of particular skills. And both sexes wear uniforms—the Girl Scouts' originally were blue like the Girl Guides' but were soon switched to khaki, green uniforms being substituted in the late 1920s.

Nevertheless, the separation of the two branches meant that there was less emphasis on a military agenda for the Girl Scouts, and more on developing proficiency in skills rooted in a gendered division of labor. In addition to scoutcraft (woods lore, trailblazing, and mapping, Morse and semaphore flag signaling, and other outdoor skills) the first Girl Scout handbooks contained highly practical instructions in hygiene, cooking, housekeeping, gardening, and child care.

As in England, girls flocked to join the movement in America. Like female suffrage, Scouting implicitly challenged the Victorian ethos of women's assignment to a male-protected domestic sphere. By getting girls outdoors and into each other's company, the Girl Scouts offered mastery of real-world skills and gender solidarity. The separate governance of the two organizations also allowed the Girl Scouts to continue to follow a policy of inclusiveness when, in the early 1990s, the Boy Scouts took a stand against membership for religious nonbelievers and homosexuals (losing, as a result, some financial support from corporations and foundations with nondiscrimination policies).

Funding for the Girl Scouts was seeded by Juliette Low's personal fortune, but the organization remained throughout the century the only entity of its size supported primarily by a bake sale: the annual Girl Scout Cookie drive. The shortbread trefoils and chocolate mints became as much a part of American popular culinary culture as apple pie. Individual member dues are *not* a major source of revenue: at the end of the century, membership was just six dollars a year.

Original Girl Scout Laws mandating kindness to animals and thrift were later broadened into the ecological and social directives to "use resources wisely" and to "make the world a better place." A significant difference is the extension of the old "clean in thought, word, and deed" rule from personal and public health to include instruction on how to deal with sexual harassment and psychological challenges of adolescence such as stress, moodiness, and self-esteem. One clause which has not changed is the commitment to "be a sister to every Girl Scout," a fellowship which transcends national barriers. Girl Scouts of the U.S.A. is a member of the World Association of

A Girl Scout troop, c. 1920s.

Girl Guides and Girl Scouts (WAGGGS), which has eight million members in 100 countries, and international meeting centers in England, Switzerland, India, and Mexico.

Girl Scouts range in age from Kindergarten-aged Daisies (named after Juliette Low, whose childhood nickname was Daisy), Brownies (ages 6 through 8), Junior Girl Scouts (aged 8-11), Cadettes (aged 11-14), and Senior Girl Scouts (aged 14-17). A girl may become an Adult Scout at age 18. Not all Scouts follow the progression from Daisy all the way up through Senior, as the many other activities of adolescence, including boys, make competing claims on their time. (''We are feminist rather than feminine,'' explained a former Scout leader in the 1990s.) And some girls abandon Scouting because of what they saw as excessively religious undercurrents, despite the organization's efforts to be nonsectarian and inclusive. Nevertheless, many American women regard Scouting as a happy aspect of their childhood, and one they would readily see their own daughters experience as well.

—Nick Humez

FURTHER READING:

Bacon, Josephine Daskam, editor. *Scouting for Girls.* New York, Girl Scouts, Inc., 1920.

Baden-Powell, Agnes. *The Handbook for Girl Guides, or, How Girls Can Help Build the Empire.* London, Thomas Nelson and Sons, 1912.

Bergerson, Chris, et al. *Junior Girl Scout Handbook.* New York, Girl Scouts of the U. S. A., 1994.

Ciraco, Candace White, et al. *Brownie Girl Scout Handbook.* New York, Girl Scouts of the U. S. A., 1986.

———. *Outdoor Education in Girl Scouting.* New York, Girl Scouts of the U. S. A., 1984.

Degenhardt, Mary, and Judith Kirsch, compilers. *Girl Scout Collector's Guide.* Lombard, Illinois, Wallace-Homestead Book Company, 1987.

Eubanks, Toni, et al. *Cadette Girl Scout Handbook.* New York, Girl Scouts of the U.S.A., 1995.

Girl Scouts of the U.S.A. *The Wide World of Girls Guiding and Girl Scouting.* New York, Girl Scouts of the U.S.A., 1980.

Low, Juliette Gordon. *How Girls Can Help Their Country.* Savannah, Press of M. S. & D. A. Byck Company, 1916.

Philmus, H. C. *Brave Girls: The Story of the Girls Scouts and Girl Guides in the Underground.* New York, Girl Scouts National Organization, 1947.

Shultz, Gladys Denny, and Daisy Gordon Lawrence. *Lady from Savannah: The Life of Juliette Low.* New York, Lippincott, 1958.

Gish, Dorothy (1898-1968)

One of the pioneering actresses of silent film, Dorothy Gish starred in over 20 films directed by legendary filmmaker D. W. Griffith. Like her older sister and co-star, Lillian, Gish played roles that embodied Griffith's vision of ideal womanhood—charming, chaste, and strong-willed. In particular, Gish earned acclaim for her comic portrayal of ''The Little Disturber'' in Griffith's *Hearts of the World* (1918) and as the blind Louise in *Orphans of the Storm* (1921). Even though Gish left film for a successful stage career in the 1930s, in the eyes of the public she remained forever Griffith's *gamine.*

—Samantha Barbas

FURTHER READING:

Borden, DeWitt. *More from Hollywood: The Careers of 15 Great American Stars*. South Brunswick, A.S. Barnes, 1977.

Gish, Lillian. *Dorothy and Lillian Gish*. New York, Scribner's, 1973.

Gish, Lillian (1893-1993)

Both frail and tough, innocent and powerful, charming and serious, actress Lillian Gish has defied both categorization and convention. Best known for her work with director D. W. Griffith, in her younger years Gish portrayed pale, waiflike heroines who used emotional strength, hard work, and persistence to protect their chastity—and spirit—from destruction at the hands of lustful men. To many filmgoers, Gish served as a bridge between nineteenth- and twentieth-century values, uniting Griffith's Victorian views on sexual purity with the strong-willed independence of the "modern" girl. Even after Gish left Griffith's studio in 1923, she continued to shy away from overtly sexual roles, and for the rest of her career, Gish remained an

Lillian (left) and Dorothy Gish in a scene from the film *Orphans of the Storm*.

icon of propriety—and a firm believer in the dignity of acting. Gish, who pioneered many of the acting techniques of silent film, worked tirelessly to elevate the cinema from the status of mere entertainment to serious art.

For an actress who championed the respectability of film, Gish's introduction to the world of drama was less than highbrow. At the age of five, Gish debuted in a vaudeville melodrama called "In Convict's Stripes," and a few years later, Gish, her mother, and her sister Dorothy had joined vaudeville touring companies and were traveling around the country with a child actress named Gladys Smith. In New York in 1912, Lillian and Dorothy went to visit Smith, who had been renamed Mary Pickford and was working at D. W. Griffith's Biograph studio. Pickford urged Griffith to hire the Gish sisters, and in the next three years Lillian and Dorothy appeared in over 35 short films. In 1914, Gish starred in her first feature-length film, *Judith of Bethulia,* and in 1915 played heroine Elsie Stoneman in *The Birth of a Nation.* During the next seven years, Gish developed and refined her on-screen persona: in *Hearts of the World (1918), Broken Blossoms* (1919), and *Orphans of the Storm* (1922), Gish played downtrodden characters who survived poverty, abandonment, and abuse through tenacity, sacrifice, and luck. In the most famous of these roles, in *Way Down East* (1921), Gish's character Anna Moore floated down a river on an ice floe, hand and hair dragging in the frigid water, until saved by her lover. Prevented by the silent film medium from using spoken words, Gish perfected the art of facial expression, and Griffith, the pioneer of the close-up shot, used Gish's wide eyes and cautious smile to create a depth and intensity unparalleled in early film.

In 1923, a dispute with Griffith over her salary drove Gish to Inspiration Pictures, where she appeared in *Romola* (1924) with William Powell; in 1926, she moved to MGM and starred in *La Bohème* (1926), *The Scarlet Letter* (1926), and *The Wind* (1928). Gish's films at MGM, though, were largely box-office failures, and production head Irving Thalberg suggested that the studio invent a scandal for Gish to boost her popularity. Gish refused, leaving MGM and signing with rival United Artists in 1930. Soon afterwards, when *One Romantic Night* (1930) proved a commercial disappointment, Gish asked to be released from her contract, thus concluding her most productive and creative years in film. As actress Louise Brooks lamented, "Stigmatized as a grasping, silly, sexless antique... the great Lillian Gish left Hollywood forever, without a head turned to mark her departure." Brooks, however, turned out to be wrong. Although Gish devoted most of the next five decades to the stage, she returned to Hollywood for a few notable films. In 1947, Gish received an Academy Award nomination for her role in *Duel in the Sun* and, in 1955 she gave a powerful performance as an old woman protecting a group of children from a maniacal killer in *The Night of the Hunter.* No longer the gamine, Gish increasingly portrayed mature, if not spinsterish characters. In 1960, Gish played Burt Lancaster's mother in *The Unforgiven,* and in 1969 she appeared in a television version of "Arsenic and Old Lace," playing one of the spinster sisters with Helen Hayes. In real life, Gish did not marry, although she was admired by many suitors. When asked in the 1920s why he was so fascinated with Gish, co-star John Gilbert, one of her more ardent followers, replied, "Because she is unattainable."

By the 1970s, Gish was widely celebrated as "the first lady of film," and in 1971 she received an honorary Academy Award for her contribution to motion pictures. "This beautiful woman so frail and pink and so overwhelmingly feminine has endured as a working artist from the birth of the movies to its transfiguration," Melvyn Douglas read at the ceremony, "for underneath this wisp of a creature there is hard steel.'' Gish's iron constitution served her well: in her eighties, Gish continued to act in television, theater, and film, giving her final performance in *The Whales of August* in 1987. She died in 1993, leaving a legacy of hard work, creativity, and versatility. While Hollywood vamps, goddesses, and bombshells came and went, Gish remained a testament to the timelessness of the fine art of acting.

—Samantha Barbas

FURTHER READING:

Affron, Charles. *Star Acting: Gish, Garbo, Davis.* New York, Dutton, 1977.

Gish, Lillian. *Dorothy and Lillian Gish.* New York, Scribner's, 1973.

———. *The Movies, Mr. Griffith, and Me.* Englewood Cliffs, New Jersey, Prentice Hall, 1969.

Shipman, David. *The Great Movie Stars: The Golden Years.* New York, Crown, 1970.

The Glass Menagerie

Tennessee Williams's 1944 drama *The Glass Menagerie,* his self-described ''memory play,'' has been considered a classic of the American Theatre since its debut. The play is Tom Wingfield's reminiscence of his youth living in a St. Louis tenement in the 1930s with his domineering mother Amanda and his handicapped sister Laura. The 1945 Broadway production was awarded The New York Drama Critic's Circle ''Best American Play.'' Since that time, the play has gone on to be performed internationally and adapted several times to film. Its success is attributed to its autobiographical story, its poetic language, and its vivid characterizations.

—Michael Najjar

FURTHER READING:

Leverich, Lyle. *Tom: The Unknown Tennessee Williams.* New York, Crown Publishers, Inc., 1995.

Parker, R. B., editor. *The Glass Menagerie: A Collection of Critical Essays.* New Jersey, Prentice-Hall, Inc., 1983.

Presley, Delma E. *The Glass Menagerie: An American Memory.* Boston, Twayne Publishers, 1990.

Williams, Tennessee. *Memoirs.* Garden City, New York, Doubleday & Company, Inc., 1975.

Gleason, Jackie (1916-1987)

As his sobriquet, The Great One, implies, Jackie Gleason was a comedian of superlative talents, but one whose persona housed enormous contradictions. A literally larger-than-life performer who became a star on the small screen when he failed to achieve headline status on stage and in the movies during the 1940s, Gleason became ''Mr. Saturday Night'' during the next two decades, and helped to define the comic possibilities of television. Although he hosted a variety series for over 20 years, the corpulent comedian is best remembered for a situation comedy that lasted only one season: *The*

Honeymooners. A high-living *bon viveur,* Gleason achieved success by never forgetting the lowly ''Ralph Kramdens'' who populated his boyhood.

In a medium where understatement is the cool virtue, broad physicality and verbal bombast were the red-hot core of Jackie Gleason's game. Even as the medium became more refined, extravagance was Gleason's badge of distinction. His programs were always lavish spectacles, highlighted by gaudy dance numbers and glamorous starlets. On stage and off, Gleason presided like a monarch.

But poverty and abandonment defined Gleason's childhood and his later conception of himself. Even in his glitziest productions, there was always a reminder somewhere of the tough mean-streets of his youth. He was born in an impoverished section of Brooklyn on February 26, 1916. His brother died when Jackie was three and his father, an insurance clerk, deserted the family when he was eight. Gleason's mother supported her son by working in a subway token booth and living with rented furniture.

Jackie quit school at an early age and worked as a pool hustler, comic high diver, and carnival barker to pay the rent. He found his calling as a master of ceremonies at Brooklyn's Folly Theater, and across the Hudson River at Newark's Miami Club. His quick wit with hecklers and his energetic charm landed him steady employment at Club 18, a cabaret in Manhattan. Movie executive Jack Warner caught his act and signed him to a Hollywood contract. Beginning in 1941, he played minor parts in a series of movies, including the musical *Navy Blues* (1941) with his idol, Jack Oakie, and *All Through the Night* (1942), a gangster yarn with Humphrey Bogart. Unrecognized by the movie crowd, he returned to New York in 1944 and began to attract notice on Broadway. His appearance in *Artists and Models* led to a larger role in the musical comedy *Follow the Girls*, for which *Time* lauded him as a ''likably Loony comic.'' Gleason stole the show by impersonating a female naval officer, proving to himself that he could ''get away with more as a fat man.'' Offers began to pour in: he replaced Bob Crosby on a Sunday night radio show and emceed at Billy Rose's Diamond Horseshoe. In 1949 he was featured in the Broadway revue *Along Fifth Avenue* with comedienne Nancy Walker. Brooks Atkinson of *The New York Times* recognized Gleason's ability to move on stage as ''a priceless accomplishment in a man who wants to be funny.''

Later in 1949, Gleason returned to Los Angeles to star in a blue-collar situation comedy, *Life of Riley*, a television adaptation of a popular radio series about a bumbling aircraft worker. Producer Irving Brecher was unable to sign the lead of the original radio program, William Bendix, because of movie commitments. Gleason was recruited to play the goodhearted but incompetent Chester A. Riley in one of television's first comedies recorded on 35mm film. Chester's catchphrase, ''What a revoltin' development this is!'' caught on, but Gleason's edginess and *joie de vivre* were missing without an audience. Although the series received an Emmy Award for ''Best Film Made For and Viewed on Television'' (there wasn't much competition), *Life of Riley* was canceled after 26 weeks. Bendix revived the role for television in 1953, and that incarnation ran for five years.

Several months after the cancellation, Gleason landed a television role that was totally suited to his strengths. He was hired as host of the live variety series, *Cavalcade of Stars*, on the DuMont television network. DuMont was a struggling fourth network with little money for programming, but proved an excellent training ground for future stars on the established networks. Both previous

Jackie Gleason

hosts of *Cavalcade,* Jack Carter and Jerry Lester, were stolen by NBC for big-time variety shows. In the two years that Gleason hosted the low-budget DuMont show, he laid the groundwork for his impending future success.

On *Cavalcade* the comedian developed the variety format, and his repertory of characters that would serve him well for the next 20 years. Unlike other variety hosts, such as Milton Berle or Sid Caesar, who relied mostly on new sketches each week, Gleason based his comedy on recurring characterizations, many of which were comic extensions of people he grew up with in Brooklyn. There was the ever complaining Charles Bratton, known as The Loudmouth; the sweetly meek Fenwick Babbitt, who would sometimes explode; the hapless Bachelor, a silent figure struggling to cope alone; and garrulous Joe the Bartender, caught in an endless monologue about the idiosyncratic patrons of his establishment. Two creations revealed the polar sides of Gleason's sensibility: the innocent savant, The Poor Soul, a silent homage to the vulnerable, saintly Little Tramp of Charlie Chaplin, and the ostentatious playboy, Reginald Van Gleason III, a baroque vision of wealth and grandeur.

Jackie's most famous character, Ralph Kramden, debuted later than the others, but was probably Gleason's best understood creation. There were, as he explained, "hundreds of them in my neighborhood." Gleason was so close to the yearning and unquiet desperation of his bus driver that he gave him the same address as his boyhood residence, 358 Chauncey Street. *The Honeymooners* began modestly enough as a six-minute sketch portraying a long-married working-class couple who stayed together despite life's blows and disappointments. Unlike the foolishness of *Life of Riley,* Gleason wanted this pair based on realism; he instructed his writers "to make it the way people really live." Pert Kelton first played Alice, the wife, and gave her a battle-scarred feistiness. To everyone's surprise, the audience identified with the Kramden's struggles and *The Honeymooners* sketches became longer and richer in comic incident.

For an early Reggie van Gleason sketch, the show hired an agile player from *The Morey Amsterdam Show,* Art Carney. Gleason and Carney hit it off immediately and remained partners in one way or another until the end. Carney had a cameo in the first *Honeymooners* sketch as a policeman, but he was so adept at playing sidekicks that the role of Ralph's buddy, the sewer worker Ed Norton, was quickly created for him. This pairing eventually developed an archetypal resonance with Carney who would be a Sancho Panza to Gleason's Don Quixote.

The other networks quickly recognized Gleason's popularity on DuMont. He appeared as a special guest star on CBS' *The Frank Sinatra Show* and there was talk about making him a regular. He also hosted *The Colgate Comedy Hour* on NBC, and in 1952 William Paley, Chairman of CBS, lured Gleason and his staff to CBS by quintupling his salary. The bigger budget for *The Jackie Gleason Show*, which premiered on September 20, 1952, allowed for splashier production numbers, including an opening extravaganza with the June Taylor dancers which Busby Berkeley would have been proud to own. Gleason also employed beautiful chorines, known as the Glea Girls, to introduce segments of the show, while he himself became one of the show's grand inventions, sipping his "tea" as if it were laced with alcohol and uttering his trademark phrases "How sweet it is," "You are a dan-dan-dandy crowd," and "And Away we go!" Soon the Gleason show owned Saturday nights and was second in the overall ratings, behind *I Love Lucy*.

On top for the first time, Gleason pushed himself into other creative arenas. Although he could not read music, he composed the signature melody for his variety show, *Melancholy Serenade*. Deciding that the common man needed background music for his pleasures, he composed over 40 mood albums, beginning with *Music for Lovers Only*, whose collective sales reached 120 million. He scored an "original symphony in ballet," entitled *Tawny*, which *The New York Times* called "a poem for eye and ear, a simply superb example of inspired television artistry." In 1954 Gleason also produced a summer music show for the Dorsey brothers,Tommy and Jimmy, which became the regular series, *Stage Show*. The comedian took personal credit for giving Elvis Presley his first network exposure on the Dorsey program.

In 1953 Gleason made his dramatic acting debut, portraying a manipulative comic in a *Studio One* production. He starred in several live television dramas, which led to the resurrection of his movie career. He received an Academy Award nomination for his role as Minnesota Fats in *The Hustler* (1961) and critical acclaim for his sleazy boxing manager in *Requiem for a Heavyweight* (1962), but was less successful as a deaf mute in *Gigot* (1962), a sentimental tale that he also wrote. In 1959 he made a triumphant return to the stage as an irresponsible drunk in *Take Me Along*, a musical adaptation of Eugene O'Neill's *Ah, Wilderness!*

Gleason strayed several times from his successful variety formula. In 1955 Buick offered him one of the largest contracts in television history to produce *The Honeymooners* on film, but Ralph and Alice (played by Audrey Meadows since the move to CBS) did not click with the audience. Eventually, however, these 39 episodes of *The Honeymooners* became a financial bonanza in syndication. In 1961 Gleason inexplicably tackled the quiz show format, and his *You're in the Picture* became one of television's most notorious debacles, lasting only one week. During the early 1960s he launched *The American Scene Magazine*, using his characters to comment on societal change. In 1964, when he relocated his television series to Miami Beach, "the Sun and Fun Capitol of the World," he reverted to his characteristic brand of splashy entertainment. Although the variety format was losing its luster, Gleason remained in the Nielsen Top Ten throughout the decade.

After his move to CBS, Gleason insisted on total control of his variety series. He participated in every aspect of production, from casting to set design to merchandising. With Orson Wellesian bravado, his end credit proclaimed, "Entire Production Supervised by Jackie Gleason." As he once explained, "I have no use for humility . . . In my work, I stand or fall by my own judgment."

Gleason emerged in an era of live television when comedians dominated the airwaves. Despite changes in American culture and television, he was able to produce and star in his type of variety program until 1970. After that, he revived *The Honeymooners* as holiday specials and starred as a Southern sheriff in several *Smokey and the Bandit* movies. When he died on June 24, 1987, the country was rediscovering the "lost" episodes of *The Honeymooners* from the 1950s. Gleason demonstrated that commercial television could be a medium for original comic expression, and his work has spoken to the American Everyman. As critic Tom Shales has noted, "Gleason was perhaps as much the auteur as Chaplin was or as Woody Allen is."

—Ron Simon

FURTHER READING:

Bacon, James. *The Jackie Gleason Story.* New York, St. Martin's Press, 1985.

Bishop, Jim. *The Golden Ham: A Candid Biography of Jackie Gleason.* New York, Simon and Schuster, 1956.

Cresenti, Peter, and Bob Columbe. *The Official Honeymooners Treasury.* New York, Perigee Books, 1985.

Henry, William. *The Great One: The Life and Legend of Jackie Gleason.* New York, Doubleday, 1992.

Meadows, Audrey. *Love, Alice: My Life as a Honeymooner.* New York, Crown Publishers, 1994.

McCrohan, Donna. *The Honeymooners' Companion.* New York, Workman Publishing, 1978.

The Museum of Broadcasting. *Jackie Gleason: "The Great One."* New York, 1988.

Weatherby, W. J. *Jackie Gleason an Intimate Portrait of The Great One.* New York, Pharos Books, 1992.

Glitter Rock

From 1972 to 1974, a wave of primarily British rock acts—dubbed Glitter Rock—emerged to enjoy massive success with a sound that marked a radical departure from the peace/love/sandals vibe of the recent past. The new movement celebrated the superficial, made androgyny look cool, and marked a complete departure from the more earnest "save the world" sentiments of the hippie era. *Rolling Stone* writer David Fricke described glitter rock as "the tidal splash of pop guitars, raging puberty, and elegant anarchy." Male singers often sported shag haircuts, eyeliner, lipstick, outrageous clothing, and towering platform shoes with abandon. Yet the music that came out of this era—David Bowie and Roxy Music would create some of glitter's greatest sonic legacies—would land an assured place in the annals of rock history, and the genre has been posited as the most innovative event to sweep through the pop music landscape before punk rock.

"Glitter was urban panic music," wrote Jon Savage in *Gadfly*, in describing the marked distinction between glitter rock and hippie

Glitter rock artist Gary Glitter.

rock. "Instead of natural fibers, you had crimplene, glitter, fur; instead of LSD, alcohol and downers; instead of albums, singles were the focus; instead of authenticity, synthetic plasticity ruled; in place of a dour, bearded machismo, you had a blissful, trashy androgyny." The summer of 1972 is usually tagged as the moment of glitter's genesis, and London the place, but the chart-success version of glitter—called glam in the United Kingdom—did owe a small debt to an obscure young American band, the New York Dolls. Living in Greenwich Village and originally playing Otis Redding covers in what was called the "Oscar Wilde Room" at the Mercer Art Center, the Dolls had long hair, dressed in platform shoes, and wore a great deal of makeup. Part of their inspiration came from the late 1960s Greenwich Village theater scene—particularly the gross doings of the Ridiculous Theater Company—and they became the next hot band to catch when Andy Warhol and his entourage began frequenting the Mercer shows.

A management team thought it better to launch the Dolls first in London, and they flew over and found instant success. Contracted to open for Rod Stewart, they became the first group in music history to tour with a major rock act without ever having produced an album or even a single. Then one of the Dolls, Billy Murcia, died of a Quaalude

overdose, and the band was eulogized in the music press for a time. They emerged again with a new drummer in December of 1972, signed to the Mercury label, but their career fizzed after just two albums. To add to the band's troubles, American audiences assumed that they were gay at a time when homosexuality was a new and very controversial topic for many.

Back in London, however, the vibe was quite different. Glitter/ glam rock was huge by the summer of 1972. Its precursor came in the spring of 1971 with a young and attractive singer, Mark Bolan, and his band T. Rex. "Get It On (Bang the Gong)" and subsequent tracks like "20th Century Boy" and "Diamond Meadows" came to be deemed classics of glitter. Like most pop culture movements, glitter originated as a reaction against something else. In this case it was the ubiquity of the hippie. By 1972 the long-hair-and-granola look was even being coopted in advertising images. The Beatles were gone, and bands like Yes, the Moody Blues, Fleetwood Mac, and Led Zeppelin were huge, as was country rock; long dirge-like tunes were in vogue. Glitter celebrated artifice and the soignée, and through it ran strong elements of camp. Furthermore, the spectacle of men wearing makeup was still enough to make people halt on the street and cause periodic uproars in the mainstream press. Homosexuality had only been decriminalized in Britain in the late 1960s, and the gay-rights movement in the United States only dated back to the summer of 1969. The average man or woman of a certain age still found it dreadfully uncomfortable even admitting that gay men and women existed at all, so taboo was the topic prior to these years. Thus glitter rock and its accoutrements— the weird album covers, the high-resolution rock poster, the aping of the look of one's favorite singer—found great resonance with the teen generation.

Several crucial albums were released in 1972 that portended a new era in rock. Roxy Music, led by Bryan Ferry and including Brian Eno at the time, has been termed the ideological vanguard of the movement. Their self-titled debut LP and the single "Virginia Plan" both arrived in the summer of 1972 to massive success. Very rock-guitar chords and booming drums melded with Ferry's arch, almost poetic lyrics, and made Roxy perhaps the most enduring of all glitter bands, and one that virtually never fell out of critical favor. This Eno period is usually termed their zenith; they disbanded after the release of *Country Life* in 1974 and subsequent reformations never really achieved the initial edge.

David Bowie and his Ziggy Stardust persona is also inextricably linked with glitter rock. His massive success with androgynous outfits and spacey lamé bodysuits was the mainstream rock manifestation of the whole glam movement. His 1972 album *The Rise and Fall of Ziggy Stardust and the Spiders from Mars* is deemed one of the quintessential releases of the genre. Moreover, Bowie would produce a number of significant albums in a short span of time, also vital to the glam-rock discography: Mott the Hoople's *All the Young Dudes,* Lou Reed's *Transformer,* and Iggy Pop and the Stooges' *Raw Power,* all released in 1972. That same year, Bowie told an interviewer in the British music paper *Melody Maker* that he was gay (later amending it to "bisexual"), which caused a huge stir. He became the first pop star to ever to make such an admission.

Further musical events that summer of 1972 made glam/glitter a commercially viable movement. Gary Glitter, a forgotten English singer from the 1950s and 1960s, had a huge hit with the kazoo-like guitars and one-word lyrics ("Hey!") in "Rock and Roll (Part II)." A massive success in England that reached the Top Ten in the United States, the single would go down in history as the essential sports-stadium rouser by the 1990s. "Instantly nostalgic, but like nothing else on earth, 'Rock and Roll' cut through everything that was around that English summer, through the T. Rex sparkle and David Bowie sashay, through Slade's patent stomp and Sweet's candied pop,'' wrote Dave Thompson in *Goldmine*, ''and though it didn't quite make #1, it hung around the chart so long there's not another song on earth that recaptures the moment like [this] one.''

Several other tracks signify the glitter rock moment, such as the cult favorite ''Baby's on Fire,'' from a Brian Eno solo project. Other British bands quickly climbed onto glam once its moneymaking potential had been established, but produced music with far less panache and artistic endurance than Bowie, Roxy, or T. Rex. Slade and Sweet were two such acts, and would become the begetters of the 1980s glam metal movement; Queen also grew out of this era, and surprised many by successfully riding the glitter rock well past its announced demise. Glitter rock also marked a turning point in pop music: prior to 1972, American and British tastes had more or less corresponded. Yet glam failed to catch on in the United States as it did in Britain, and the shock-rock proto-Goth Alice Cooper was its only true homegrown commercial success.

By 1974, the New York Dolls had disintegrated after more problems with drugs, the Stooges broke up, Bowie released an album of vintage cover tunes, and Elton John—perhaps the most commercial and internationally successful manifestation of glitter rock—was a huge success. The cross-dressing camp of glitter rock was successfully translated into a stage play, *The Rocky Horror Picture Show*, which became a cult film almost from its debut in 1975. The last gasp of real glam in the United States came with Sweet's Top Ten hit, ''Ballroom Blitz,'' in the summer of 1975.

Already by that summer, punk was in its nascent stages in England and would hit full-force the following year. Hallmarked by vulgarity, tattered clothing, and almost unlistenable, anything-but-melodic music, punk was, not surprisingly, a reactionary movement—against the satiny, coiffed look of glitter with its electric pianos and Wildean sentiments. A little over a decade later the outlandishness and alternative sexuality of glitter rock were standard pop music clichés, embodied most successfully by Boy George, Prince, and even Madonna. *Velvet Goldmine*, a 1998 film by Todd Haynes, borrowed its title from a Bowie song of the era and was heralded as a sign of glitter rock's revival. Set in London in the early 1970s, it follows the rock 'n' roll love story of a bisexual rock star in space-age apparel and his far punker American friend, a clear stand-in for Iggy Pop. Numerous luminaries from alternative music stepped in to create and/or record for the *Velvet Goldmine* soundtrack, and filmmaker Todd Haynes recalled in interviews how profoundly some of the music and imagery from the glitter rock era had affected his adolescent years. ''It was a moment when it was cool even for straight people to appear bisexual,'' the film's editor, Jim Lyons, told Amy Taubin in the *Village Voice*. ''There's a clear nostalgia for that period when we believed that we were going to have a better and better society, and that feminism would win, and homosexuality would be completely accepted.''

—Carol Brennan

FURTHER READING:

Fricke, David. ''Weird Scenes from the Velvet Goldmine.'' *Rolling Stone,* November 26, 1998, 64-67.

Goldman, Albert. ''Rock Goes Holl-Ly-Wooood!'' *Sound Bites.* New York, Random House, 1992.

Klawans, Stuart. ''All that Glitters.'' *Nation.* November 30, 1998, 32-34.

Lim, Dennis. ''The Music Choice Artifacts and Inspired Counterfeits.'' *Village Voice.* November 3, 1998, 50.

McCormick, Moira. ''International 'Velvet' Mines Glam's Riches.'' *Billboard.* October 3, 1998, 22.

McNeil, Legs, and Gillian McCain, *Please Kill Me: The Uncensored Oral History of Punk.* New York, Penguin, 1997.

Savage, Jon. ''Divine Decadence: Memories of Glam.'' *Gadfly.* October 1998.

Stambler, Irwin. ''David Johansen.'' *The Encyclopedia of Pop, Rock & Soul.* New York, St. Martin's, 1989, 339-41.

Taubin, Amy. ''All that Glitters.'' *Village Voice.* November 18, 1997, 64-66.

Thompson, Dave. ''Gary Glitter.'' *Goldmine,* July 4, 1997, 20-30.

Gnagy, Jon (1906?-1981)

Jon Gnagy was a man who taught himself how to draw and then taught millions of youngsters how to follow in his footsteps, thanks to the then-new medium of television. With his checkered shirt and vandyke beard, Gnagy was one of the fixtures of 1950s television, demonstrating simplified techniques of line and shade to children, many of whom were drawing along in front of their television sets at home with the aid of one of Gnagy's *Learn to Draw* workbooks. Although criticized in some esoteric art circles, Gnagy defended his methods, which enabled him to remain popular on the tube from the beginning of the 1950s until the middle of the decade. In the years since, other telegenic art instructors have found similar success by patterning their shows after the man who introduced a generation of baby-boomers to the world of do-it-yourself art.

The Kansas-born Gnagy taught himself how to create art while recovering from a childhood illness. The skill later helped him earn a living as everything from a sign-painter to an advertising art director. He started teaching his techniques—based on Cezanne's fundamentals, he claimed, using the basic tools of cube, ball, and cone—on experimental video outlets in 1946. CBS started featuring Gnagy nationally in 1950 on 15 minute shows known variously as *Draw with Me, You Are an Artist,* and *Jon Gnagy Learn to Draw.* Though criticized for oversimplification and for promoting imitation rather than creativity, Gnagy felt that his methods were appropriate for his medium and his audience. There was no quarrel from the many youngsters who faithfully watched his shows and had their parents buy his instruction kits throughout the early 1950s. After leaving television, Gnagy continued to lecture on his favorite subject. He died in 1981 at age 74.

—Preston Neal Jones

FURTHER READING:

Grossman, Gary H. *Saturday Morning TV.* New York, Dell Publishing Co., 1981.

The Godfather

One of American popular culture's most resilient narratives is that of the Mafia and its antiheroic gangsters, and one of this genre's most popular and poignant products is Francis Ford Coppola's *The Godfather* trilogy, based on Mario Puzo's novel of the same name. Released in 1972 to universal acclaim and rewarded with several Academy Awards, including Best Picture, *The Godfather* instantly fixed its place in the American cultural psyche, establishing itself as the de facto gangster film to which all other subsequent exercises in the genre would be compared.

Powered by Marlon Brando's timeless delivery of the film's namesake, Godfather Vito Corleone, the film also established the futures of Hollywood royalty Al Pacino (Michael Corleone), Robert Duvall (Tom Hagen), and James Caan (Sonny Corleone), all of whom are most recognized for the roles they played in this sprawling and sensitive study of two generations of Mafia membership and power—especially Pacino, who would go on to the starring role in *The Godfather Part II* (1974) and *The Godfather Part III* (1990). More importantly, the blinding success of the first two *Godfather* films immediately marked Coppola as a major player in Hollywood, allowing him green lights on almost any project he set his hands on, leading to the legendary conflicts with his producers as well as

Brando during the shooting of *Apocalypse Now* (1979) and his ambitious attempt to form his own studio/distributor conglomerate, Zoetrope Studios, in 1980.

In 1972, Coppola adapted Mario Puzo's popular novel for the screen, and although the two worked together on the script, Coppola dramatically shaped the project during the shooting. The second installment was entirely his creation. Cutting out much of the novel's romanticized violence, the director decided to instead focus on the Corleone family dynamics, personalizing the film in accordance with his own experience growing up as the second-generation son of an Italian immigrant. The Mafia, as always, was the perfect vehicle for the consideration of American culture and values, Coppola asserted in an interview: ''I feel that the Mafia is an incredible metaphor for this country. Both America and the Mafia have roots in Europe . . . both the Mafia and America feel they are benevolent organizations. Both the Mafia and America have their hands stained with blood from what it is necessary to do to protect their power and interests. Both are totally capitalistic phenomena and basically have a profit motive.''

Indeed, the strength of *The Godfather* trilogy's appeal lay in the collusion of the two phenomena, one which ran throughout the genre in its most moving expressions, from Paul Muni's bravura performance in *Scarface* (1932) to Martin Scorsese's immediately canonical *GoodFellas* (1990). All installments in the gangster genre engaged

The cast of *The Godfather*: (from left) Al Pacino, Marlon Brando, James Caan, and John Cazale.

the audience's sympathies for the lead character as an independent businessman living out his version of the American Dream. In fact, there is a built-in bias toward the Mafia, especially within *The Godfather,* as a conglomerate of well-intentioned businessmen looking out for the best interests of their families; as critic Roger Ebert has explained, ''During the movie we see not a single actual civilian victim of organized crime . . . The only police officer with a significant speaking role [Sterling Hayden] is corrupt.'' The ideas of law and order are specific to the machinations of the various families of the Mafia, replacing the exterior world with the cloistered, fiercely loyal world of organized crime; in fact, one of the first scenes in *The Godfather* involved Brando castigating an undertaker, who describes himself as a ''good American,'' for going to the police for help. Interestingly enough, the film's violent finale, which juxtaposes the exhaustive murders of each of Michael Corleone's opponents (a figurative baptism of Corleone power through death) with the literal baptism of his child, was cheered by audiences as a shining example of American triumph. This moral ambiguity and veiled criticism of the American legal and political system's inefficacy is one which has coursed through popular culture's fascination with organized crime, one which was an interesting accident to Coppola, who had actually structured his movie to be a criticism of the ethnic and religious hypocrisy within the Mafia. Instead, the audiences were attracted by the poignant scenes of family cohesion in the face of social and economic pressure; in this sense, Coppola's film had the endearing, if violent, nature of some of the best work of Frank Capra, including his classic *It's a Wonderful Life.*

The Godfather Part II applied Coppola's intended criticisms of organized crime and religious hypocrisy even further, culminating in Michael Corleone's assassination of his own brother Fredo and his disruption of his marriage for the sake of the family business. There is no noble Brando figure in the second installment: everyone from Michael, his family, the Nevada governor, and local citizenry is completely corrupt. The ethnic cohesion and protection which coursed through the first installment is totally disrupted, a monumental disappointment augmented by Coppola's insertion of an earlier scene of a cheerful birthday party for Vito Corleone at the end of the film. An ultimately tragic figure, Michael Corleone, by the end of *The Godfather Part II,* has compromised not only his Italian heritage, his ethnic identity, and his family, but has positioned himself as the type of win-at-all-costs American immigrant criticized in the first installment, one who, even in the possession of unquestionable power and influence, can no longer trust anyone because he can be trusted by no one. By *The Godfather Part III,* Michael has extended his power as far as the Vatican, which he implores for redemption for the murder of his brother, but he still ends up powerless as his daughter is murdered at his side by the end of the film.

Resistant to the idea of establishing his *Godfather* series as a trilogy for years (Coppola asserted that if he ever did make a third installment, it would have to be a farce), the failure of his Zoetrope Studios (in which a good deal of his personal funds were invested) and the relative failure of his artistic product following *The Godfather* and *The Godfather Part II* (only one of his post-*Godfather* films, *The Outsiders* in 1983, met with any measurable mainstream success), Coppola capitulated to the American infatuation with the Corleone family business and released *The Godfather Part III,* inciting further controversy by casting his own daughter, Sofia, as Andy Garcia's love interest. Sofia Coppola's mediocre delivery shattered the prodigious but deteriorating reputation of her father, whose legendary status seemed to exist parallel to the lasting impact of the trilogy. But

it did not diminish the technical skill, daunting vision, and deeply personal attention which Coppola nevertheless employed in his following films. Regardless of his future projects, Coppola has assured himself immortal status in film history on the strength of *The Godfather* trilogy alone. *The Godfather Part III,* predictably, was a moderate success at the box office, garnering $70 million, but it was another star vehicle for Pacino and newcomer Andy Garcia. It also fulfilled American popular culture's desire for closure while fulfilling Coppola's desire for a sharp critique of the inherent destruction and corruption within the relentless pursuit of power and wealth which lies at the heart of the American Dream.

—Scott Thill

FURTHER READING:

Bergan, Paul. *Francis Ford Coppola—Close Up: The Making of His Movies.* New York, Thunder's Mouth Press, 1998.

Cowie, Peter. *Coppola: A Biography.* New York, Da Capo Press, 1994.

Lebo, Harlan. *The Godfather Legacy.* New York, Simon and Schuster, 1997.

Lewis, Jon. *Whom God Wishes to Destroy: Francis Coppola and the New Hollywood.* Durham, Duke University Press, 1995.

Godfrey, Arthur (1903-1983)

The arrival of genial, folksy Arthur Godfrey on television was the most publicized event of the 1948-49 season. The reviewers pulled out all the stops in praising ''the old redhead,'' and he became the only personality in TV history to have two top-rated programs run simultaneously in prime time for an extended period. *Arthur Godfrey's Talent Scouts* aired on Mondays and *Arthur Godfrey and His Friends* on Wednesdays for eight-and-a-half seasons. In 1952-53, the programs ranked two and three, just behind *I Love Lucy.* Even more remarkably, Godfrey's morning radio show, every Monday through Friday, continued during this time with high ratings, his fan base growing with multiple exposures. TV critic Ben Gross of the *New York Daily News* summed up Godfrey's appeal: ''It is his friendliness, his good cheer, his small-boy mischievousness, and his kindly philosophy.''

Godfrey's Talent Scouts brought little known or newly discovered professional talent to perform before a live nation-wide audience, with an applause meter deciding the winner. The host's witty banter and interviews with contestants plus a high quality of talent delighted the listeners. Some of the winners—including Pat Boone, Carmel Quinn, the Chordettes, and the McGuire Sisters—later became regulars on *Arthur Godfrey and His Friends.* Also appearing on the show were many other soon-to-be-famous performers, including Rosemary Clooney, Tony Bennett, Connie Francis, Steve Lawrence, Leslie Uggams, and Patsy Cline. Two big stars missed by the show's screening staff, Elvis Presley and Buddy Holly, both flunked the show's auditions.

For his weekly variety hour, Godfrey assembled a personable group of talented regulars, chosen with an eye to audience demographics. Frank Parker and Marion Marlowe sang romantic duets for the mature audience, and Julius LaRosa was the bright young singer with appeal to bobby-soxers. There was also the bashful Hawaiian singer, Haleloke, as well as the Chordettes, a squeaky clean

Arthur Godfrey

barbershop quartet from Wisconsin. Other popular regulars were Janette Davis, Bill Lawrence, and the Toppers. Tony Marvin was the mellow-voiced announcer, while Godfrey enhanced the proceedings, sometimes playing his ukulele and singing in a gravelly croon. As he had on radio, Godfrey kidded his sponsor's products, but he refused to endorse any product he did not like personally.

When Godfrey underwent surgery for a hip replacement in May 1953, it almost seemed as though the whole country sent him get-well cards. The press continued to revere him until October of that year, when a dramatic turnaround occurred and Godfrey became controversial—suddenly maligned by columnists who had praised him. The controversy was ignited by his firing members of his popular TV family of stars for what seemed to be petty reasons. He dismissed Julius LaRosa on the air in October 1953, charging that he ''had become too big a star.'' He told the press that LaRosa had lost his ''humility,'' a remark that was to come back and plague Godfrey for the rest of his career. LaRosa made immediate well-publicized appearances on *The Ed Sullivan Show,* cut several hit records, and was given a series of his own, before his career faded after a few years. In April 1955, Godfrey fired Marion Marlowe, Haleloke, and the Mariners in one fell swoop.

Part of the public forgave him. His *Talent Scouts* continued until July 1958, and the *Friends* show until April 28, 1959, but his popularity never matched that of the sensational early 1950s. Godfrey survived an operation for lung cancer in 1959 but, except for a brief interval on television's *Candid Camera* in 1960-61, his television career was over. He worked on radio until 1972, when he broadcast a tearful farewell over CBS. Coincidentally, it had been tears that

brought him to national attention as he gave a touching description of President Franklin D. Roosevelt's funeral in 1945.

—Benjamin Griffith

FURTHER READING:

Brooks, Tim, and Earle Marsh. *The Complete Directory to Prime Time Network TV Shows: 1946 to Present.* New York, Ballantine, 1980.

Lackmann, Ron. *Same Time . . . Same Station: An A-Z Guide to Radio from Jack Benny to Howard Stern.* New York, Facts on File, 1996.

Sackett, Susan. *Prime-Time Hits: Television's Most Popular Network Programs.* New York, Billboard Books, 1993.

Godzilla

The lead monster character in a series of successful Japanese science fiction films, Godzilla has rampaged across movie screens worldwide for over 40 years. His popularity and recognition rivals that of Superman and Mickey Mouse. In Japan, where he is known as Gojira, he has dominated popular fantasy for every generation to come of age since the 1950s. The films have inspired toys, games, clothes, model kits, comic books, novels, fan magazines, candy, television commercials, and countless imitations. Godzilla movies are often lumped in with B-grade and camp cinema in America, where audiences almost exclusively see edited, badly dubbed versions of the Japanese originals. Fans who investigate the series carefully discover that many entries, particularly the early ones, are thoughtful, well-crafted efforts by respected members of the Japanese film community. Though an American remake in 1998 did not fare as well as expected, the character maintains a loyal following in the United States and abroad. The ''King of the Monsters,'' as he has been called often, is likely to reign for years to come.

Godzilla's screen debut was in Toho Co. Ltd.'s *Gojira* (1954). The name, meaning ''whale-ape,'' was allegedly inspired by a burly studio employee. *Gojira* was, at the time, the most expensive movie ever produced in Japan, costing around $900,000. The film was a huge success—grosses topped $7 million—and the film spawned a new style of Japanese cinema: the *kaiju eiga,* or giant monster genre.

Toho producer Tomoyuki Tanaka was first inspired to make a monster movie by the successful reissue of RKO's *King Kong* (1933) in 1952. By the next year, a new breed of American science fiction creature, the giant monster, was drawing audiences to U.S. theaters and the newly popular drive-ins. Films like *The Beast from 20,000 Fathoms* (1953) and *Them!* (1954) played off Cold War anxieties; the monsters' creation and/or release on the world was the result of nuclear energy. The terror of nuclear war took physical form as the atomic mutant. As the only nation ever attacked by atomic weapons Japan had its own reasons to fear such mutations, and memories of the Hiroshima and Nagasaki bombings were still fresh in the early 1950s. *Gojira* turned these fears and memories into cinematic terror.

As an enduring character Godzilla is largely the product of four men. Producer Tanaka oversaw the original *Gojira* and remained with the series through the 1990s. Director Ishiro Honda was a friend and colleague of Akira Kurosawa, arguably Japan's greatest cinematic genius. A visit to Hiroshima in 1946 inspired in Honda a desire to tell the story of atomic devastation on film. He regarded monsters as

Godzilla

tragic figures, the result of mankind's abuse of technology. Special effects director Eiji Tsuburaya was an admirer of Willis O'Brien's stop-motion effects in *King Kong*. His work in the Godzilla films pioneered what would come to be called "suitmation" (suit + animation); his monsters were played by actors in molded latex suits. The process eventually became synonymous with Japanese monster movies, though not everyone could do it as well as Tsuburaya. Composer Akira Ifukube was a respected classical musician and scholar. His score, parts of which reappear subsequently in the series, became nearly as recognizable as Godzilla himself. The booming contrabass perfectly symbolizes the monster's rumbling gait.

Gojira came to America two year later as *Godzilla, King of the Monsters* (1956). B-movie producers Richard Kay and Harold Ross purchased the American distribution rights from Toho and, along with Joseph E. Levine, adapted the film for U.S. audiences. The dialogue was dubbed in English (as would be all successive U.S. theatrical and TV releases of Godzilla movies.) The producers reconstructed the original sets to shoot new footage with Raymond Burr as American newspaper reporter Steve Martin. All mentions of the atomic bombs dropped on Hiroshima and Nagasaki were edited out. *Godzilla, King of the Monsters* opened in New York City in April, 1956. Levine promoted the film heavily, and it proved a huge hit in the United States, becoming the first Japanese picture to play outside art cinemas, in mainstream first-run theaters.

In film, success breeds sequels. Toho released its second Gojira film, *Gojira No Gyakushu* (1955) ("Gojira's Counterattack") only months after the first, and a year before the creature's American debut. With this feature, Toho began its longstanding practice of

selling the rights to each of its monster movies individually. Warner Brothers acquired *Gojira No Gyakushu* for the American market. They did not, however, acquire the name Godzilla, even though Toho owned it and could have sold it to them. Consequently, the film was released as *Gigantis the Fire Monster* (1959).

The sequel received a somewhat shabbier treatment than its predecessor. Warner originally intended to construct an entirely new film using only the special effects sequences from *Gojira No Gyakushu,* but it was never made. Instead the Japanese original was dubbed in English. Voice performers include George Takei, who gained fame as *Star Trek*'s Mr. Sulu, and *Kung Fu*'s Keye Luke, best known then as Charlie Chan's number one son. (In 1978 he would again lend his voice to a Japanese-to-American adaption when Sandy Frank brought the animated *Science Ninja Team Gatchaman* to America as *Battle of the Planets*.) Narration was provided by Daws Butler, who gave voice to a number of Hanna-Barbera's animated characters. Stock footage of rockets and creature effects was added. The original score by Masaru Sato was replaced with music from Universal's film music library, including the theme from *The Creature from the Black Lagoon* (1954). Upon release *Gigantis the Fire Monster* was placed on a double feature with the American *Teenagers from Outer Space* (1959), a film so bad its director was never allowed to make another.

Godzilla disappeared from theaters until 1962 while Toho and Ishiro Honda branched out to other creature features like *Radon* (1956) (called *Rodan* in America) and *Daikaiju Baran* (1958) (U.S. title *Varan the Unbelievable*). The monster's return came about due to the efforts of Willis O'Brien. His concept for a *King Kong* sequel, wherein the giant ape fought a rebuilt Frankenstein monster, was purchased by Toho. They took out Frankenstein and added Gojira. Tanaka, Honda, Tsuburaya, and Ifukube all returned to the positions they held on *Gojira*. The film they made, *Gojira tai Kingukongu* (1962), departed from the atomic age terror themes of the first two films, taking a more comedic, family-friendly tone with elements of slapstick and satire. It became the most widely seen Gojira film in Japan.

The U.S. release, Universal's *King Kong vs. Godzilla* (1962), loses much in the translation. Sequences are cut, and scenes of English-speaking television reporters are added in a attempt to clarify the truncated action. Ifukube's score is gone, replaced by music from the distributor's previous films. Without the subtleties of the original, the film is little more than an extended build-up to a fight between two men in monster costumes. For the first time, American audiences received a taste of what the genre would devolve into in a few short years.

For years after the film's release a rumor circulated among fans that there were two different endings to *King Kong vs. Godzilla*. Allegedly, Godzilla is triumphant in the Japanese version, but the outcome was changed to please U.S. audiences by having "their" monster win. The story, though, is apocryphal. Kong is, and always was, the winner.

Gojira/Godzilla returned in 1964 in *Mosura tai Gojira,* known in the U.S. as *Godzilla vs. The Thing*. This time Godzilla's enemy is a Toho-created monster, the title creature of *Mosura* (1961), called *Mothra* in America (she is a benevolent giant moth). In this film the creative team of Tanaka, Honda, Tsuburaya, and Ifukube delivered a somewhat different, but extremely enjoyable, spin on the *kaiju eiga* motif. For the last time until 1984 Godzilla is portrayed as a threat to the world. Mothra is called upon to fight the lizard, though she has just laid an egg and is about to die. A battle royal ensues. In what is likely the most touching sequence in the entire series, Mothra sacrifices herself fighting Godzilla. Soon after she dies, her egg hatches—and two larval Mothras emerge. They spin a cocoon around Godzilla, who falls into the ocean in defeat. The film reprises the more purely fantasy atmosphere of *Mothra,* bringing back the two pretty, six-inch-tall female fairies who act as heralds to the creature. The women are as memorable a part of the film as the monsters: they speak in unison, and sing a song to Mothra whenever they wish to call her. The emotional core of *Godzilla vs. The Thing* has long made it a favorite of fans, many of whom regard it as the high point in the series.

Godzilla, Mothra and the twin fairies, and Rodan returned only nine months later in *Ghidrah, The Three-Headed Monster* (1964). While not on the level of its immediate predecessor, it is an exciting film with much action and excellent suitmation effects. It is most notable as the beginning of Godzilla's "good monster" phase. Godzilla, Rodan, and Mothra team up to rid the earth of the menace of Ghidrah, a golden, fire-breathing dragon from outer space. In Japan, the monster was understood to be a metaphorical representation of China, symbolizing Japanese fears of Maoist expansionism. This was largely lost on American matinee audiences. Mothra, always a good monster, jumps into the fray immediately, but Godzilla and Rodan would at first rather fight each other. They eventually experience a change of heart (after a "discussion" in monster growls and roars) and the three earth creatures drive Ghidrah back into space.

For the rest of the 1960s and into the 1970s, the Godzilla films closely followed a formula established by the next entry, *Kaiju Daisenso* (1965). The title translates as "The Giant Monster War" though the U.S. title is *Monster Zero,* or *Godzilla vs. Monster Zero* for home video versions. In this film, an alien race tries to take over earth using a monster. Godzilla stops them. It was the first Godzilla film to use an American actor, Nick Adams, in the original cast. Director Ishiro Honda left the series for a time after this film, citing his reluctance to humanize Godzilla. His vision and style would be sorely missed.

Godzilla releases had become an annual event for Toho, but with increased quantity came decreased quality. *Ebirah, Horror from the Deep* (1966)—better known as *Godzilla vs. the Sea Monster*—saw Jun Fukuda step in as director. Akira Ifukube was replaced. Godzilla is missing from the first half of the picture, which is padded out by a story of a group of young men who discover an island where the natives are being enslaved by a vaguely defined paramilitary organization based on another island. Godzilla fights their monster and puts things right. *Son of Godzilla* (1967) is an outright children's film. Godzilla and his little mutant lizard son, Minira (Minya in the U.S.), battle a giant spider. The baby Godzilla is laughable; he resembles Barney the Dinosaur far more than he does Godzilla. His freakish appearance and strange, crying noises make him Toho's most annoying creation.

Kaiju Soshingeki (1968), released in the U.S. as *Destroy All Monsters,* was the last vestige of the exciting and creative original Godzilla series. In an attempt to regain its older fans, Toho pulled out all the stops. Honda returned, and so did most of Toho's stable of monsters. As the film begins all of the monsters are exiled to a peaceful life on a remote island. But aliens again attack earth, taking control of the monsters and unleashing them on major cities. After much destruction, the earth people regain control of the creatures and turn them on the aliens—only to have Ghidrah appear out of space, leading to a final decisive showdown. Naturally, the good monsters win. The film offers more action than the previous two combined. For a brief moment, the excitement which spawned the films' earlier success was back.

From *Godzilla's Revenge* (1969) and through the 1970s the Godzilla films went steadily downhill. Eiji Tsuburaya died and Ishiro Honda left Toho. Fukuda returned as director. *Godzilla vs. the Smog Monster* (1971) tries, unsuccessfully, to integrate anti-pollution messages with its juvenile monster story. While the monster Hedora (meaning "pollution") is an interesting amalgamation of aquatic creature and industrial waste, he is not nearly enough to redeem the picture. *Godzilla on Monster Island* (1972), known on home video and cable as *Godzilla vs. Gigan,* sees the lizard destroying an amusement park (complete with Godzilla attraction) which serves as a base for aliens and their monster. In a creative move perhaps more misguided than the creation of Minira, Godzilla speaks. In *Godzilla vs. Megalon* (1973), he is teamed with Jet Jaguar, a robotic rip-off of the popular television character Ultraman (who was, ironically, the creation of Eiji Tsuburaya). The series was now firmly lodged in juvenile territory. *Megalon,* along with *Sea Monster,* would eventually become fodder for cable's *Mystery Science Theater 3000,* wherein a man and his robot puppets mercilessly mock the worst movies ever made. *Godzilla vs. the Cosmic Monster* (1974) featured a robotic "Mechagodzilla." Honda and Ifukube returned for *Terror of Mechagodzilla* (1975), but it was too late. There would be no more Godzilla movies for nine years.

Godzilla was temporarily gone, but definitely not forgotten. By this time his name and image had entered the popular consciousness. In the United States the movies played as reruns on local television. With *Star Wars* (1977) creating a boom in science fiction, the door was open for new Godzilla product. In the fall of 1978, NBC offered *The Godzilla Power Hour* as part of its Saturday morning children's lineup. The series was an animated adventure from Hanna-Barbera. Ted Cassidy (Lurch of *The Addams Family*) provided Godzilla's roars. Godzilla's adventures were packaged with other animated shows in various combinations and aired until May, 1981.

Godzilla's true return came with the remake/sequel *Gojira* (1984), released in the United States a year later as *Godzilla 1985.* Based on an original story by Tomoyuki Tanaka, the film takes Godzilla back to his origins as a city-stomping bad monster. Raymond Burr returns (in the American version) as the reporter Martin (but not Steve this time), the only living American who had seen Godzilla during his initial attack. The story ignores the sequels. Heavy promotion on both sides of the Pacific helped the film achieve some financial success, despite a nearly universal critical drubbing. Godzilla's new profile even earned him appearances in TV advertisements for Nike shoes and Dr. Pepper soft drink.

The King of the Monsters was back. Toho's new sequels, starting with *Gojira tai Biorante* (1989), never reached American theaters, though it did receive an official U.S. home video release as *Godzilla vs. Biollante.* As they became available on VHS and laserdisc in Japan (and sometimes before), the new Godzilla films began to be traded among tape-collecting fans in America. These unauthorized copies, known as "bootlegs," kept Godzilla alive in front of the eyes of a small but very dedicated and resourceful group of monster-movie lovers. Toho continued through the early 1990s, as Godzilla once again met Ghidrah, Mothra, and Mechagodzilla, as well as Space Godzilla. The new series climaxed with *Gojira tai Desutoroia* (1995). Godzilla is apparently wiped out by a weapon called the "oxygen destroyer," the same device which had dispatched him in the 1954/1955 film. His end came mainly to make way for yet another incarnation: a big-budget, Hollywood treatment of the story.

An American Godzilla film seemed only logical given the success of Steven Spielberg's dinosaur epic *Jurassic Park* (1993). Digital technology made realistic dinosaurs possible on the screen. A script was written which had the lizard being discovered in the Pacific and shipped to New York City for study, where he breaks loose and wreaks havoc. Jan DeBont, fresh from his success on the film *Speed* (1994), was set to direct. DeBont believed only a huge epic could sell Godzilla to a 1990s audience. "You can do a Godzilla movie two ways," he declared, "like the Japanese do it with men in costumes and miniatures . . . the other way is to do it right." Though he stressed the need for a compelling story, he still seemed to view the digital special effects as the key. Fortunately for him, it was two other filmmakers who would learn firsthand how wrong he was.

DeBont left the project over TriStar's refusal to let the budget exceed $100 million. The studio was subsequently acquired by Sony, who could afford to put that and more into a film. The project fell into the hands of Dean Devlin and Roland Emmerich, creators of the hugely successful alien invasion movie *Independence Day* (1995). Hopes were high among fans and studio executives when the pair announced that their next project would be a Godzilla adaptation. It soon became the most anticipated film of 1998. Posters, merchandise, and theatrical trailers (which did not show the monster) whetted the public's appetite. Other studios shuffled their summer release schedules; none wanted to open their event movie (expected blockbuster) against the King of the Monsters. Box office gross in the United States alone was expected to reach $250 to $300 million.

Trouble appeared even before the film's release. Devlin and Emmerich scrambled to make the announced release date of May 18, 1998. Time to finish the digital effects grew short. Many full-body shots of the monster were replaced with quicker, cheaper ones of the feet or tail. Fans and the press wondered why no still photos of the monster were being released. The budget reached $125 million, with tens of millions more spent on promotion.

Godzilla (1998) opened big, but disparaging reviews and bad word-of-mouth soon took their toll. Many fans were left unimpressed by the redesigned Godzilla, who looked and moved like a Tyrannosaurus Rex. The scaled-down effects were further diminished by much of the action taking place at night, in the rain. The slim plot lifted elements from previous science fiction hits, including *Alien* (1979) and *Jurassic Park*. Large quantities of tie-in merchandise went unsold. Hardcore fans took to referring to the new monster by the acronym GINO: Godzilla in Name Only. The dank, charmless film earned $138 million dollars in America, and another $221 million overseas. *Godzilla* became the latest example of a relatively new species in Hollywood: the $100 million-plus grossing flop. While not a financial disaster of *Waterworld* (1995) proportion, it was nonetheless a major disappointment in relation to cost and expectation. Most in Hollywood agreed that, at least in the immediate future, a sequel was unlikely.

All was by no means lost for Toho's best known creation. The 1998 movie was released on VHS, laserdisc, and DVD, earning more than respectable figures on sales and rentals. Fan publications such as *G-Fan* and countless internet sites feed the public's appetite for news and discussion on the character. In 1999 Toho announced tentative plans for a new Japanese film which would take Godzilla into the new millennium. More importantly, the character is alive in the imagination of moviegoers worldwide. Godzilla is like Dracula or the Frankenstein monster: he will never die, no matter how many times movie heroes might kill him. He is inescapable, a part of our culture and language. His shadow looms large not only over Tokyo Bay, but anywhere lovers of fantastic films sit facing a lighted screen or cathode ray tube, awaiting the next jolts of excitement and adventure. The King of the Monsters has well and truly earned his throne.

—David L. Hixson

FURTHER READING:

Aberly, Rachel. *The Making of Godzilla*. New York, HarperPrism, 1998.

Bock, Audie. *Japanese Film Directors*. Tokyo, New York, and San Francisco, Kodansha International, 1978.

Bueher, Beverly Bare. *Japanese Films: A Filmography and Commentary, 1921-1989*. Jefferson, North Carolina, McFarland, 1990.

Galbraith, Stuart, IV. *Japanese Science Fiction, Fantasy, and Horror Films: A Critical Analysis of 103 Features Released in the United States, 1950-1992*. Jefferson, North Carolina, McFarland, 1994.

Glut, Donald. *Classic Movie Monsters*. Metuchen, New Jersey, Scarecrow, 1978.

Harmon, Jim. *The Godzilla Book*. San Bernardino, California, Borgo Press, 1986.

Lees, J. D., and Marc Cerasini; compiled and edited by Alice Alfonsi. *The Official Godzilla Compendium*. New York, Random House, 1998.

Lent, John A. *The Asian Film Industry*. London, Christopher Helm, 1990.

Lovece, Frank. *Godzilla: The Complete Guide to Moviedom's Mightiest Monster*. New York, Morrow, 1998.

Kalat, David. *A Critical History and Filmography of Toho's Godzilla Series*. Jefferson, North Carolina, McFarland, 1997.

Mellen, Joan. *Voices from the Japanese Cinema*. New York, Liveright, 1975.

Tucker, Guy Mariner. *Age of the Gods: A History of the Japanese Fantasy Film*. Brooklyn, New York, Daikaiju Publishing, 1996.

Waldecki, Michael E. *Godzilla Goes to Hollywood*. M. E. Waldecki, 1985.

Gold, Mike (1893-1967)

Born to Jewish immigrants on New York's Lower East Side, Itzok Issac Granich changed his name to Mike Gold to avoid persecution in the Red Scare of 1919. A Harvard dropout, Gold entered Greenwich Village circles in 1914 and became perhaps the most influential leftist literary critic of the 1920s. After authoring "Towards Proletarian Literature" (1921), a radical manifesto that encouraged writers to promote revolution, Gold assumed editorship of *New Masses* in 1926. In 1930, he published *Jews Without Money*, a work of autobiographical fiction inspired by his tenement-house childhood. He spent the Depression decade writing for the Communist *Daily Worker*. Brash, irreverent, and dogmatic, he praised the class-conscious radicalism of Woody Guthrie and Langston Hughes and assailed Ernest Hemingway and Thorton Wilder for failing to promote social change. His politics confined him to France in the late 1940s and 1950s, and to relative obscurity in American literary history. His influence on radical writers, however, has been recovered in the late 1990s.

—Bryan Garman

FURTHER READING:

Bloom, James D. *Left Letters: The Culture Wars of Mike Gold and Joseph Freeman.* New York, Columbia University Press, 1992.

Folsom, Michael, editor. *Mike Gold: A Literary Anthology.* New York, International Publications, 1972.

Goldberg, Rube (1883-1970)

Rube Goldberg was a professional cartoonist for over 60 years, the creator of more than a dozen nationally syndicated comic strips, and the winner of a Pulitzer Prize for political cartooning, yet he is remembered at the end of the twentieth century chiefly for one thing—the Rube Goldberg Invention. In various strips over the years he concocted elaborate, multi-part machines to perform the simplest of tasks. These struck readers as extremely apt comments on the overly complicated and often circuitous lives led by just about everybody in modern society. Eventually, Goldberg's inventions earned him a listing in most dictionaries and made his name part of the language. Rube Goldberg Machine competitions continue to be held in high schools and colleges around America, and Purdue University has an annual National Competition for the best Goldberg variations.

Born Reuben Lucius Goldberg into an affluent San Francisco family, Goldberg attended the University of California at Berkeley and majored, at his father's urging, in engineering. But he was also in on the founding of the college humor magazine, *The Pelican,* to which he became a contributing cartoonist. By 1904, in spite of his engineering degree, young Goldberg was working on the *San Francisco Chronicle,* and a year later he was drawing sports cartoons for the *San Francisco Bulletin.* Soon he moved to New York City to draw for an assortment of newspapers, starting with the *Evening Mail,* at impressive increases in salary each time he moved to the next publication. He drew such daily strips and panels as *Mike and Ike, They Look Alike, Lunatics I Have Met, I'm The Guy, Cartoon Follies, The Candy Kid,* and *Foolish Questions.* This last-named panel, much imitated

Rube Goldberg

over the years, offered rude answers to obvious inquiries—"Q. Did your hat fall in the water? A. No, I threw it in there for some frogs to use as a ferry boat. Q. Is this number 99? A. No, mister, it's number 66—we turned the house upside down just for a change."

Goldberg began including inventions in his strips, often attributing them to Professor Lucifer Gorgonzola Butts, a sort of screwball anagram of his own full name. The inventions, which were presented in cartoon diagram form, involved not only sundry mechanical devices, especially pulleys, but ingredients that were not always readily available to more conventional inventors. These included a hungry goat, a dancing Eskimo, a miniature elephant, waltzing mice, a college boy, a penguin, an electric eel, Miss Las Vegas, and a palooka hound, plus numerous bowling balls, pistols, midgets, fish, and umbrellas. The components of each mechanism were labeled with letters of the alphabet so that a reader could construct his own intricate machine to perform such simple tasks as opening a can, uncorking a bottle, or slicing bread. The typical description accompanying a Goldberg invention is exemplified by that for a device designed to wash dishes while one is out. It begins, "When spoiled tomcat (A) discovers he is alone he lets out a yell which scares mouse (B) into jumping into basket (C), causing lever end (D) to rise and pull string (E)," etc. Goldberg sometimes admitted that an invention might not function perfectly and so he offered alternatives. The dishwashing instructions concluded with, "If the cat and turtle get on to your scheme and refuse to cooperate, simply put the dishes on the front porch and pray for rain."

Goldberg's major Sunday page, *Boob McNutt*, began in 1915 and survived until 1934. The strip was syndicated in the Hearst papers by the McNaught Syndicate. It starred a plump, redheaded, and accident-prone young man, dressed somewhat like a silent movie comedian, and, as his name implied, was naïve and none too bright. The feature has been described as "an eclectic jumble of satire, burlesque, fantasy and cockeyed technology." From 1922 onward Boob was preoccupied with the courtship of a pretty girl named Pearl, who was the target of many a fiendish scheme constructed by the strip's villains. Mike and Ike, their panel defunct, joined the cast, along with Bertha the Siberian Cheesehound. Goldberg had done a mock adventure strip, *Bobo Baxter,* in the middle 1920s, and in the early 1930s he drew a serious daily. *Doc Wright* was ahead of its time, trying soap-opera continuities years before *Mary Worth* made them fashionable, but it lasted less than two years.

Lala Palooza came along in 1936, daily and on Sundays, and concerned itself with the humorous adventures of the plump, rich Lala and her layabout brother Vincent. Even though Vincent now and then came up with an invention in the Professor Butts vein, *Lala* was not successful and ended in 1939. Next came Goldberg's last go-round in the funny papers with *Side Show*, a Sunday page that offered a hodgepodge of different features under one roof: *Crackpot College, Little Butch, Brad and Dad* and, of course, a *Weekly Invention.* By then, Goldberg was getting considerable help with the drawing from his longtime assistant Johnny Devlin. He and Devlin also had a hand in putting together *Feature Funnies* in 1937. When the comic book ceased reprinting *Lala Palooza* pages in its lineup, Devlin drew new ones, glamorizing and streamlining Lala considerably.

Goldberg began drawing political cartoons in the early 1940s for the *New York Sun,* and after the paper suspended publication he signed with the *New York Journal American* and King Features Syndicate. He had quite a bit of help from Warren King, who later became the political cartoonist for the *New York Daily News.* One of these collaborations won Goldberg a Pulitzer in 1948. He also put

together many cartoon books, wrote a novel, and helped found the National Cartoonist Society. The highest annual NCS award is called a Reuben in his honor.

—Ron Goulart

FURTHER READING:

Goulart, Ron, editor. *The Encyclopedia of American Comics.* New York, Facts on File, 1990.

Kinnaird, Clark, editor. *Rube Goldberg vs. The Machine Age.* New York, Hastings House, 1968.

Goldberg, Whoopi (1949—)

Whoopi Goldberg rose from humble circumstances and a troubled youth to become a highly respected and successful actress. As one of the first African American actresses to maintain mainstream success, she personifies America's growing acceptance of performers from across the racial spectrum. Her outspoken nature and willingness to present her offscreen persona to the public has made her one of the most high-profile African Americans of the 1990s.

Rising to prominence in the mid-1980s, Goldberg became one of the most recognizable faces in the entertainment industry as she moved easily between comedy and drama on both stage and screen.

Whoopi Goldberg

Her outspoken humor reflected her experiences as a former drug addict and welfare mother who had moved from the depths of poverty to the heights of celebrity. Goldberg first appeared onstage at the age of eight but did not gain attention until 1982 with the premiere of *Spook Show,* a one-woman review in which she played several characters. She made her film debut in *The Color Purple* (1985). Offscreen, she occasionally found herself at the center of controversy as she sparred with other prominent African Americans.

Born Caryn Johnson on November 13, 1949 (some sources list the year as 1955), the girl who would later assume the name of Whoopi Goldberg was raised in the multicultural section of New York City called Chelsea. She was an imaginative child who was encouraged to become a performer by her mother. Her life took a downward spiral, however, when she dropped out of school in the ninth grade. She began to use drugs, had several abortions, and found herself living on the streets. By age seventeen she had weaned herself off heroin, and she eventually married her drug counselor. The couple had one daughter, but the marriage was short-lived. As a single mother, Goldberg survived on welfare and through a series of temporary jobs such as bricklayer and mortician's make-up artist. Throughout this period she was determined to have a career in theatre. In the mid-1970s, Caryn Johnson decided to change her professional name to "Whoopi Cushion" so agents and audiences would remember her. Her mother suggested she use the last name "Goldberg" because it sounded more serious. Author James R. Parrish notes Goldberg's gimmicky name soon gained her great attention: "Audiences were forever surprised that the owner of this odd Jewish-sounding name turned out to be an African American who had a strange hairdo and a very special look."

Goldberg moved to the West Coast in 1974 to perform with several drama and improvisation groups in the San Diego and San Francisco areas. Her reputation grew with the premiere of *Spook Show,* which showcased her range of characterizations. Among her most popular personas were "Little Blonde Girl" and "Fontaine," an educated junkie. Goldberg populated each performance with more than a dozen alter egos engaging audiences with their provocative views on contemporary society. In early 1984, director Mike Nichols saw her show and immediately offered to produce it on Broadway. Nichols's interest in the young actress gained her much media attention and shifted her career into high gear. Steven Spielberg cast Goldberg as the abused Celie in the film version of Alice Walker's *The Color Purple.* Her movie debut won raves, and she was nominated for an Academy Award. After her promising start in film, Goldberg's career began to skid as she appeared in a series of forgettable and overly- broad comedies like *Jumpin' Jack Flash* (1986), *Burglar* (1987), and *Fatal Beauty* (1988). She rebounded in 1990 as Oda Mae Brown, a storefront medium, in the popular film *Ghost.* This performance earned Goldberg an Academy Award for best supporting actress and made her the first black woman to win an Oscar since Hattie McDaniel in 1939. Goldberg's subsequent film work offered audiences a strong mix of comedy and drama. In *The Long Walk Home* (1990) she played a Southern maid in the 1950s, while Robert Altman's 1992 *The Player* showcased her as a no-nonsense detective. She endeared herself to children as the voice of a hyena in *The Lion King* (1994) and enjoyed much acclaim for her *Sister Act* nun comedies in 1992 and 1993.

Goldberg's TV career failed to match the success of her movie work. In 1990 she starred in *Bagdad Café,* a mediocre sitcom, and 1992 saw her as host of a syndicated talk show. She did, however, find some small-screen success through a recurring role as an alien on *Star Trek: The Next Generation* and as the center square on 1998 revival of the game show *Hollywood Squares.* Goldberg twice hosted the Academy Awards.

Goldberg's on-screen persona has tended to be that of a sassy, self-reliant, and always likable woman. Away from the set, however, she became known for being unafraid to court controversy. She angered Jews with several ethnic jokes in her selection "Jewish American Princess Fried Chicken" in the book *Cooking in Litchfield Hills.* Other high-profile blacks, including Jesse Jackson and Spike Lee, criticized her for her infamous 1993 appearance at the Friars Club with then-companion Ted Danson. Public outrage ensued as Danson appeared in blackface mouthing offensive jokes written by Goldberg. The pair later apologized for the incident. On the other hand, Goldberg has garnered respect for her appearances as a co-host, with Billy Crystal and Robin Williams, at the annual Comic Relief telethons for the homeless.

—Charles Coletta

FURTHER READING:

Adams, Mary Agnes. *Whoopi Goldberg: From Street to Stardom.* New York, Dillon Press, 1993.

Bogle, Donald. *Blacks in American Films and Television.* New York, Garland Publishing, 1988.

Parrish, James. *Whoopi Goldberg.* Secaucus, Carol Publishing Group, 1997.

Golden Books

From its humble beginnings in the Midwest, Golden Books publishers developed into the most successful publisher and entertainment company for children in North America with such classics as *Pat the Bunny* and *The Poky Little Puppy.* By the end of the century, in addition to storybooks, Golden Books Entertainment products included children's television productions, audio and video recordings, interactive software, educational workbooks, craft products, puzzles, party accessories, gift-wrap products, invitations, and stationery. As of Golden Books' fiftieth anniversary in 1992, there were more than one thousand Golden Books titles.

In 1907, Edward Henry Wadewitz purchased a small printing company for less than three thousand dollars. He and his partner, Roy A. Spencer, operated it in the basement of a building in Racine, Wisconsin. Incorporating small publishers, puzzle makers, playing card manufacturers, and stationery engravers and adding high-volume printing equipment, the company grew under the name of Western Printing and Lithographing. The leap toward children's publishing began in 1933, when Wadewitz signed a contract with Walt Disney for exclusive book rights to all Disney licensed characters. In 1939, with Simon and Schuster, Western printed Walt Disney's *Bambi,* the precursor to the Golden Books that would dominate the juvenile book market for the rest of the twentieth century. The series developed, by 1942, into Simon and Schuster's

"Little Golden Books" line of hardcover, forty-two page, illustrated story books for children.

Little Golden Books became standard fare in home libraries from that decade on through the 1960s. In part, their appeal went beyond entertainment to include a smattering of educational value: the books' title pages included a note that the stories were "prepared under the supervision of Mary Reed, Ph.D., [who was associated with] Teachers College of Columbia University." But the main attraction came in owning these brightly illustrated, neatly bound, and affordable stories at a time before local public libraries included much in the way of children's literature. For the children who read them and the adults who purchased them, they suggested a value beyond their twenty-five-cent price. The books appeared to be expensive with a distinct, gold-colored, foil trim along their spines. They contained a decorative space on the inside cover that read "This Little Golden Book belongs to" with a line for the child to personalize. And children loved the famous characters in the stories. With these features, the company created a sense that Golden Books provided a special treasure for each child who owned one.

In association with Whitman Publishing Company, Dell Publishing Company, Simon and Schuster Incorporated, and Walt Disney, Western Printing maintained the lead in children's favorites. Western moved its corporate headquarters to Fifth Avenue offices in New York and changed its name to Golden Books Family Entertainment Incorporated. Golden Books printed many popular titles that continue to be sold from generation to generation. *Pat the Bunny*, first published in 1940, is noteworthy as one of the first touch-and-feel books for children and has been a continual best-seller among children's books. *The Poky Little Puppy* (1942), one of the original twelve Golden Books, tells the story of an adventurous puppy; its sales exceeded fourteen million copies by the end of the century. Other celebrated publications from the company's early years include books about Lassie, the Lone Ranger, Mickey Mouse, Donald Duck, and other animated Disney characters, and a holiday collection including *Frosty the Snow Man, Rudolph the Red-Nosed Reindeer,* and *Baby's Christmas*. Religious titles include *David and Goliath, Noah's Ark,* and *My Little Golden Book about God*.

The company's early domination of the children's book market enabled it to continually secure contracts with well-known children's authors, illustrators, and entertainers. Golden Books produced popular works by Margaret Wise Brown, Richard Scarry, and Mercer Mayer. Jim Henson's Muppets and Sesame Street characters have been featured in Golden Books since the 1970s. Other popular stories to which Golden Books secured printing rights are Winnie-the-Pooh, Tarzan, and Star Wars. In the 1990s, Golden Books bought rights to Shari Lewis productions, including videos and television shows featuring the famous Lamb Chop and Charley Horse puppets. Even a European favorite, Ludwig Bemelmans' *Madeline,* became property of Golden Books with the production of Golden Books Entertainment videos based on Bemelmans' books.

—Sharon Brown

FURTHER READING:

Jones, Dolores Blythe. *Bibliography of the Little Golden Books. Bibliographies and Indexes in American Literature, No 7.* Westport, Connecticut, Greenwood Publishing Group, 1987.

Santi, Steve. *Collecting Little Golden Books: A Collectors's Identification and Value Guide.* Florence, Alabama, Books Americana, 1994.

Golden Gate Bridge

The Golden Gate bridge, with its soaring art deco design, its ability to sway 27.5 feet in high winds, and its arches posed against the backdrop of the sea, more than any other monument symbolizes San Francisco. It spans a submerged cleft in the coastal mountain range, dubbed the "Golden Gate" by prospectors on their way to California's gold fields in the mid-1800s. When completed in 1937, it was the world's longest suspension bridge (1.86 miles) and the highest structure west of New York (745 feet). Its chief engineered was Joseph Strauss.

Its daily load of approximately 100,000 cars is supported by cables that are three feet in diameter. When the thick fog pours in rendering it invisible from land, the bridge's distinct color, "international orange," keeps seagulls from crashing into it.

—Adrienne Russell

The Golden Gate bridge, in San Francisco.

The Golden Girls

The situation comedy *The Golden Girls,* which aired on NBC from 1985 to 1992, was one of television's first successful representations of the lives of older women and an unlikely hit in a television landscape populated by young, sexy performers in shows designed to appeal to a youthful audience. The series focused on four single women living together in Miami as they faced the issues of aging in America. Created by veteran television writer and producer Susan Harris, the show balanced controversial social themes with raucous, often ribald, humor. Starring a cast of seasoned actresses, who were all in their late fifties or early sixties, *The Golden Girls* emphasized that life does not end with menopause and that older women are still vital, energetic, and worthy of the attention of the mass viewing audience. Audience acceptance of the series was immediate. It placed in the top ten its premiere season by winning a following among all age groups. Strong public approval was matched by much critical praise. The series was twice named best comedy, and each of the leads earned Emmy awards for their performances.

One of TV's dominant female voices, Harris (who wrote for *All in the Family* and *Maude,* and created *Soap*) earned her greatest critical and commercial success with *The Golden Girls,* representing a breakthrough for women on television both in front of and behind the camera. In 1984, actress Selma Diamond appeared in a brief sketch titled ''Miami Nice'' at an NBC affiliates meeting. The performance was designed to test the audience's reaction to a comedy revolving around an older woman. The positive response to the piece encouraged NBC to purchase a pilot of the premise written by Harris. She assembled a strong cast of actresses to play the group of women facing their ''golden years'' together. Bea Arthur, the star of *Maude,* played Dorothy, a loud divorcee and substitute teacher. She lived with housemates Blanche (Rue McClanahan), a lusty Southern widow, and Rose (Betty White), a naive widow from a tiny town in Minnesota. The trio was joined by Sophia (Estelle Getty), Dorothy's Sicilian mother who moved in after a nursing-home fire. The pilot episode also featured actor Charles Levin as the women's gay housekeeper, but the character was dropped by the second show. The friendship of the ''girls'' as they supported each other through various problems became the core of the series.

The series' humor grew from Harris's distinctive writing and her actresses' strong characterizations. Arthur's Dorothy was an extension of her Maude character. Divorced from a husband who betrayed her with a younger woman, no-nonsense Dorothy embodied the sense of reason for the series as she demonstrated that a woman did not need a man to be happy. Throughout the series her more flighty roommates tested her patience. Blanche appeared to have stepped from a Tennessee Williams play, the Southern belle struggling to hold onto her former glory. Much of the show's raunchy humor came from her recounting a lifetime of wild sexual exploits. Rose provided a contrast to Blanche in that she was more innocent and conservative. A highlight of many episodes consisted of her telling stories about the loony inhabitants of her hometown of St. Olaf. The series' most popular character was the octogenarian Sophia, played by the much younger Getty. Her sarcasm was said to come from the effects of a stroke that destroyed the ''tact'' portion of her brain. This allowed the character to speak her mind and make jokes at the others' expense.

Harris gave her characters many opportunities to discuss issues beyond aging. Dorothy faced clinical depression, Rose befriended a lesbian, Blanche was distant with her children, and Sophia briefly

remarried. Most of all, they displayed the strength of female bonding. In 1992, the series ended as Dorothy married and moved away. The remaining cast returned to TV the following year with the short-lived sitcom *The Golden Palace,* in which Rose, Blanche, and Sophia ran a small hotel on Miami Beach.

The Golden Girls proved both that audiences would accept older female characters on series television and that a woman could helm a series and provide it with a distinctive voice and personality. Television historians David Marc and Robert Thompson view the series as an indicator of future programming as baby boomers age and begin to demand more senior characters on the small screen.

—Charles Coletta

FURTHER READING:

Cotter, Bill. *The Wonderful World of Disney Television.* New York, Hyperion, 1997.

Marc, David, and Robert Thompson. *Prime Time, Prime Movers.* Boston, Little Brown & Co., 1992.

White, Betty. *Here We Go Again: My Life in Television.* New York, Scribner, 1995.

Goldwyn, Samuel (1879-1974)

One of the most successful of the early independent film producers, Samuel Goldwyn will be remembered for many of his classic films, for his uncultured style, and for his misuse of the English language—so-called Goldwynisms such as ''a verbal agreement isn't worth the paper it's written on.'' Goldwyn was one of a pioneering group of immigrant men who came to America and helped shape the Hollywood studio system.

He was born Samuel Gelbfisz in Minsk, Poland. At 16, he emigrated to London and then New York state to make his fortune. Once in America, Goldfish, as he was now called, obtained work at Louis Meyers and Son as a glovemaker and by age 18 was one of the top glove salesmen in the world and a partner in the Elite Glove Company. When the woman he was trying to court married Jesse Lasky instead, Goldfish was introduced to Lasky's sister, Blanche. They married in 1910 and had a daughter, Ruth.

In 1913 Goldfish became interested in a career in the motion picture industry. From his initial idea of owning movie theaters he progressed to a desire to be a motion picture producer. Eventually he persuaded his brother-in-law to join him, and together they formed the Jesse Lasky Feature Play Company with Goldfish managing sales for the company. In 1914 the company had its first release with Cecil B. DeMille's successful *The Squaw Man,* one of the first feature-length films made in Hollywood. In 1916 the Goldfishes divorced, and it was only a matter of time before Goldfish had a falling out with his Lasky. The company's partners overthrew him, but when the company merged with Adolph Zukor's Famous Players to form Famous Players-Lasky Corporation, Zukor named Goldfish chairman of the board. By the end of 1916, however, Goldfish had managed to sabotage his position there and was forced to resign.

In November 1916 Goldfish formed a partnership with the Selwyn brothers and formed Goldwyn Pictures. The company selected the original Leo the Lion as its company logo, and eventually Goldfish changed his last name to Goldwyn. He broke away from

Samuel Goldwyn

Goldwyn Pictures in 1922 after a contract dispute and was therefore only a stockholder when it merged to form Metro-Goldwyn-Mayer. He immediately formed a new Goldwyn Pictures Company and produced projects independently through United Artists. His first success as an independent producer, *The Dark Angel* starring Ronald Colman, was released in 1925, the same year he married Frances Howard. The couple later had a son, Samuel, Jr.

While his output could not match the major studios, Goldwyn produced several successful movies. Colman, the only star he had under contract, starred in several of these: *Bulldog Drummond* (1929), *Stella Dallas* (1929), and *Dodsworth* (1936). In the early 1930s Goldwyn had what was probably his greatest failure. He discovered a Swedish actress named Anna Sten and was convinced he had found a star who would be greater than Greta Garbo. Unfortunately, Sten had a problem with the English language and did not show much talent. It took Goldwyn several years and several bad films before he admitted his mistake and released her from her contract.

The year 1939 is considered special for the number of classic films it produced. One of these was the Goldwyn film *Wuthering Heights,* starring Laurence Olivier and Merle Oberon. That same year James Roosevelt, son of the U.S. president, was selected as president of United Artists. By 1940, Goldwyn and United Artists were calling it quits, and Goldwyn thereafter distributed his work through RKO

Studios. Goldwyn continued producing films that would become classics, such as *The Little Foxes* (1941) and *The Best Years of Our Lives* (1946), generally considered his finest. Its unflinching look at veterans returning home after World War II won nine Academy Awards.

In 1954 Goldwyn paid $1 million plus 10 percent of profits for the film rights to the Broadway musical *Guys and Dolls*—the largest sum paid to that time. While that film in 1955 and Goldwyn's final film, *Porgy and Bess,* in 1959 were minor successes, Goldwyn's time had passed, and he knew it. The golden era of Hollywood was over, and many of his contemporaries were dead. Goldwyn would survive until 1974, but his career was finished.

—Jill A. Gregg

FURTHER READING:

Berg, A. Scott. *Goldwyn: A Biography.* New York, Knopf, 1989.

Easton, Carol. *The Search for Sam Goldwyn; A Biography.* New York, Morrow, 1976.

Marx, Arthur. *Goldwyn: A Biography of the Man behind the Myth.* New York, Norton, 1976.

Golf

Golf is the strangest of games. Invented by the Scots perhaps as early as the 12th or 13th century, it is played in an area that can vary in size anywhere from 30 to 200 acres; it can be an individual or a team sport; it is essentially a mental game rather than a physical one; and it pays homage to a concept largely ignored in other sports: aesthetics. Golf also has an established code of honor that is a rarity in most sports. When a player breaks a rule, accidental or not, they are expected to penalize themselves. To the eye, golf appears a sedate game devoid of action. To the player, it is a mind-numbing, physically demanding, and more often than not, demeaning, sport—a test of character more than athletic ability. It is game played in the mind, on a field awash with lush grass, stately trees, meandering creeks, and manicured greens, each of which are physically endearing but taken together represent an obstacle course to be negotiated for 18 arduous holes. The ultimate and all-too-simple goal: to hit the ball as few times as possible.

The story of golf is as much a tale about change as it is tales about great players, miraculous shots, and dramatic victories. Great players have been the constant in a game that has changed dramatically over the last 700 years. From wooden balls (prior to 1440), to feather-stuffed, leather-covered balls known as "featheries" (1440 to 1848), to gutta percha balls made from the sap of trees indigenous to Malaysia (1848 to 1901), to rubber balls made from winding rubber thread around a solid rubber core (1901 to the present), to the solid core balls commonly used today, the game has relentlessly evolved. And, of course, as balls changed, so did clubs. The first clubs had shafts made of wood, probably ash. Wood clubs had long, broad heads while the irons tended to have large faces, square toes, and nicked sockets. Sometime during the feather ball period, perhaps in the late 1770s, club-making became profitable enough that artisans began taking up the craft. By the 1800s most shafts were made from ash or hickory, while all sorts of woods—beech, pear, apple—were used to fashion the heads of wooden clubs. Depending on the course, the number of holes also varied, usually ranging from five to 18. The shape and size of club heads also regularly were changed in the early years of the game, either to improve accuracy or increase distance, or both. As time passed, the number of clubs also increased: from two or three in the 1600s, to four or five in the 1700s, to five or six in the 1800s, to eight or nine or even ten by the late 1900s. Today, a normal set of clubs numbers 14, and can be made of materials with space age sounding names like graphic, tungsten, and titanium. Every year hundreds of companies produce thousands of variations of golf clubs in what appears to be a never-ending technological war, all with the purpose of helping a golfer hit a little white ball toward a very small hole an awful long distance away.

Not surprisingly, the first golf club and course was established at St. Andrews, Scotland, in 1754, the place many golf historians believe the game was first played (Some historians argue that the game may have been invented much earlier by the Romans, but there exists little substantial evidence to support this theory.). One hundred and three years later, in 1857, St. Andrews hosted the first National Club Championship with 11 clubs participating. Three years later Willie Park became the first British Open champion when he won at Prestwick. The popularity of golf in the British Isles spread throughout the second half of the nineteenth century, and by 1888, the first club in the United States, also called St. Andrews, was open for play. In 1895, the United States Golf Association (USGA) sponsored its first championship: the Men's Amateur. Before the end of the year, however, two other championships were contested: the Men's Open and the Women's Amateur. Championship golf was embraced by both the British and Americans, and would lay the groundwork for golf's vast growth in the twentieth century on both the amateur and professional levels.

Although the history of the game is difficult to compartmentalize because of its longevity, once golf clubs began to open and championships were initiated, three distinct periods can be discerned—the early period (1896-1916), the golden age (the 1920s, 1930s, and 1940s), and the television era. The beginning of the early period is marked by Harry Vardon's victory in the British Open in 1896 and ends with the formation of the Professional Golfers' Association (PGA) in 1916. The golden age was marked by some of the greatest legends the game has seen. In the 1920s, two players dominated the game, Bobby Jones and Walter Hagen. By the 1930s, men like Gene Sarazen, Lawson Little, Sam Snead, Ben Hogan, Ralph Guldahl, Craig Wood, Henry Picard, and Jimmy Demaret pushed the game to even greater popularity. In the early 1950s, Ben Hogan and Sam Snead held sway, but the popularity of the game reached an all-time high with the coming of Arnold Palmer and the television era. With his trademark attacking style and charismatic personality, Palmer revolutionized the game from a marketing standpoint, and television rushed in to capitalize. Although the game was still considered one played by the well-to-do, Palmer's dynamic style of play and his incredible popularity brought the game to millions of Americans who previously displayed little interest in the game.

Palmer's emergence in the 1950s as the dominant player also laid the groundwork for a recurring theme in golf—head-to-head competition for the top spot. In the 1920s, Jones and Hagen battled; in the 1940s it was Hogan and Snead. By the 1960s Palmer and Jack Nicklaus had become the marquee players. In each instance the result was the same—the game grew in popularity. Although Nicklaus has since been named golfer of the century, he, too, was challenged by players like Tom Watson, Johnny Miller, and, later, Greg Norman. By the 1990s, the newest "personalities" in golf—Tiger Woods and the

Ryder Cup (a team competition between the best golfers in Europe and the United States)—have been responsible for popularizing the sport to heights never previously attained.

At the professional level, golf appears to be in an upward growth pattern. Besides the PGA pro tour in the United States, professionals play on tours in Asia, Europe, Africa, and Latin America. There is a women's tour, the LPGA, a senior tour, and the Nike tour, for players attempting to earn their way unto the more lucrative PGA tour.

Golf, however, still exists primarily for the amateur player. Perhaps the most dramatic change in recent years (besides the ongoing technological changes in club design and composition), has been demographic. More Americans than ever play—26.5 million in 1997—and more blue-collar workers—about 34 percent of all golfers—have taken up what once was once termed the "Royal and Ancient Sport." In the United States, woman now comprise almost 22 percent of the golfing population, and because of the influence of players like Tiger Woods, more minorities and children are playing the game. Since 1970, the number of players has increased by more than 15 million while the number of golf courses has risen by almost 6,000, from 10,848 to 16,010 in 1997. While the game has traditionally been considered one played by rich people on private courses, more than 70 percent of the courses in the United States are open to the public, and four out of every five courses being built are public facilities.

However, the exclusion of minorities from many private clubs, at least until recently, had for years been golf's "dirty little secret." The original constitution of the PGA of America required that members be Caucasian, and not until black golfer Bill Spiller filed suit against the PGA did that change in the early 1950s. Unfortunately, conservative traditionalism blended with elitism to keep most private country clubs "white only" facilities well into the 1980s. When it was revealed that Shoal Creek Country Club near Birmingham, Alabama, the site of the 1990 PGA championship, had no black members, adverse publicity seemed to accomplish what years of criticism failed to yield—a realization among many private clubs that exclusionary policies were both racist and non-productive. Within a year of the 1990 PGA, both Shoal Creek and Augusta National, the home of The Masters golf tournament and generally considered the last bastion of segregated golf, had black members. Other clubs around the country followed suit. With the emergence in the 1990s of Tiger Woods, who was part African American, as one of the best players in the world and the biggest drawing card since Arnold Palmer, the golfing public was more integrated than ever before.

—Lloyd Chiasson, Jr.

FURTHER READING:

Atha, Anthony. *World of Golf: The History, the Classic Players, the Major Tournaments.* New York, Smithmark, 1997.

Barkow, Al. *Gettin' to the Dance Floor: An Oral History of American Golf.* New York, Atheneum, 1986.

Browning, Robert. *History of Golf.* Norwalk, Connecticut, Classics of Golf, 1985.

Concannon, Dale. *Golf: The Early Days.* New York, Smithmark, 1995.

Grimsley, Will. *Golf: Its History, People, and Events.* Englewood Cliffs, New Jersey, Prentice-Hall, 1966.

Rice, Grantland, from the writing of O. B. Keeler. *The Bobby Jones Story.* Atlanta, Tupper & Love, 1953.

Gone with the Wind

Gone with the Wind, the epic Civil War-era novel and film, described as "the romance of a baggage and a bounder," has no peer in literary history when its longevity and profitability are considered. Beloved by readers and filmgoers throughout the world for over sixty years, *Gone with the Wind* continues to captivate audiences and generate profits, and for many Margaret Mitchell's novel supersedes history in depicting "the War Between the States." Called racist and inaccurate by historians who find its sugarcoating of the Old South and the Ku Klux Klan appalling, nonetheless it has created an industry of literary and commercial output that shows no sign of slowing down as *Gone with the Wind* approaches its 70th anniversary. Its appeal is worldwide, and the epic is particularly popular in Japan, Germany, and Russia, perhaps indicating that *Gone with the Wind* has a special resonance for nations who have experienced defeat and occupation. The ur-text of "The Lost Cause," *Gone with the Wind*'s most powerful moment comes when a famished and exhausted Scarlett, defiant, vows: "As God is my witness, I won't let them lick me! If I have to lie, steal, cheat, or kill—I'll never be hungry again!"

The author, Margaret Mitchell, reluctantly allowed her manuscript to be published in 1936, and then was stunned and overwhelmed by its success. The book has sold more copies than any book besides the Bible, and won the Pulitzer Prize in 1936, a sensation in Depression-era America. The film adaptation premiered in 1939 to immediate acclaim, culminating in 10 Academy Awards. *Gone with the Wind* reigned supreme as the box office champion until the 1970s and remains the most popular film of all time (when dollars are adjusted for inflation). As with the novel, the love story of Scarlett O'Hara and Rhett Butler has fared less well at the hands of some critics, notably author Lillian Smith, who described the novel as "slick, successful but essentially mediocre fiction. . . "; [*Gone with*

Vivien Leigh and Clark Gable in a scene from the film *Gone with the Wind*.

the Wind] "wobbles badly like an enormous house on shaky underpinnings." Despite its flaws, what is obvious is its staying power, proof of *Gone with the Wind*'s timeless appeal for its fans.

Gone with the Wind is a rich, sentimental, and starkly partisan story of a Southern belle, charming and selfish, who recklessly pursues the wrong man (the genteel Ashley Wilkes) throughout the narrative which spans the Civil War and Reconstruction, marrying three times, enduring war, famine, and personal tragedy. At the story's end, after the death of the saintly Melanie Wilkes, who resolutely loved Scarlett despite her pursuit of her husband, she finally recognizes that her now-departing husband Rhett Butler is indeed her true love. Rhett, weary of her contrivances, answers her heartfelt "Oh, where shall I go, what shall I do?" with one of the best-known exit lines in literary history: "Frankly, my dear, I don't give a damn." Not be outdone, Scarlett sniffs a bit, then declares brightly: "I'll get him back . . . I'll think about that tomorrow. After all, tomorrow is another day!"

Much has been made of the connections between Scarlett, the flirtatious and determined heroine, and her creator. Margaret Mitchell (who had first named her character Pansy) was a young reporter who stubbornly went her own way throughout life: routinely flying in the face of Atlanta society, marrying (and divorcing) the unsuitable and abusive Red Upshaw, then marrying his best friend, John Marsh. Marsh is best known for his literary midwifery: he brought a typewriter to his restless wife, then mending from an accident, and suggested she write her novel. From these modest beginnings came the phenomenon of *Gone with the Wind*: "I would go to the apartment and frequently she was at that little table where she worked," recalled Harvey Smith, a friend of Mitchell's. "We all joked about it: 'Well, you know she's writing the world's greatest novel.' . . . And, by God, she was."

Peggy Mitchell furtively wrote her epic novel in a tiny, cramped apartment in a down-at-the-heels house in midtown Atlanta; she affectionately called the place "The Dump." While Mitchell drew on her own life to create her characters, her primary inspiration was her family lore: her mother Maybelle and particularly her grandmother Fitzgerald were her models for Scarlett. Mitchell's Irish Catholic background allowed her to further enhance her tale; a successful immigrant plantation owner, Gerald O'Hara rebukes his frivolous daughter and evokes her spiritual connection to Tara, the family plantation. "Why, land's the only thing in the world worth working for, worth fighting for, worth dying for, because it's the only thing that lasts" is the unifying theme of *Gone with the Wind.*

Ignoring the standard wisdom that Civil War films were "box office poison," producer David O. Selznick fought to bring the novel to the screen, and in wheeling and dealing in pursuit of his goal lost the majority of the financial rights to the film to MGM in return for the coveted services of the "King of Hollywood," Clark Gable. The film's pre-production has generated legends of its own, from the discovery of the manuscript by Selznick assistant Kay Brown (sold for a record $50,000) to the "Search for Scarlett"—a publicity stunt dreamed up by publicist Russell Birdwell, a nationwide search for the right woman to portray Mitchell's heroine. The episode was portrayed amusingly by Garson Kanin in his novel and television film *Moviola: The Scarlett O'Hara War* (1979 and 1980, respectively). The screen tests of actresses famous and on the rise are an indication of how fiercely this battle raged in Hollywood: Paulette Goddard, Bette Davis, and Alabama-born Tallulah Bankhead claimed they alone could portray Scarlett, and even arch-Yankee Katherine Hepburn was discussed. Although there is considerable dispute about the way

Selznick found Vivien Leigh, the exquisite British actress who would win an Oscar for her portrayal, the legend is that Selznick's brother Myron, a leading agent, brought Leigh to the set of the "Burning of Atlanta" scene, arguably the most famous sequence of the film. "I want you to meet Scarlett O'Hara," said Myron, as the flames consumed old sets and illuminated Leigh's lovely face. In fact, she had been brought to his attention earlier, but the contrived "introduction" may indeed have persuaded Selznick, as he confided to his wife Irene in a letter, calling her "the Scarlett dark horse—she looks damn good."

Casting the other leads proved to be problematic as well, especially in the case of Leslie Howard, who, like Gable, resisted being cast. Gable, the overwhelming choice of the public, feared he wasn't able to handle the part of the blockade-running romantic lead. Said Gable: "It wasn't that I didn't appreciate the compliment the public was paying me," he said. "It was simply that Rhett was too big an order. I didn't want any part of him. . . . Rhett was too much for any actor to tackle in his right mind." Howard believed himself too old and miscast as the hopelessly idealistic and weak-willed Ashley. Olivia de Havilland, under contract by Warner Brothers, effectively wore down the resistance of the studio heads with her persistence; she knew Melanie was the role to establish her as a serious performer. One of the film's finest performances is Hattie McDaniel's Mammy; her sensitive and slyly subversive portrayal won the best supporting actress Academy Award, the first Oscar for a black actor. Butterfly McQueen, so memorable and very controversial as Scarlett's skittish and indolent servant Prissy, similarly transformed what might well have been a one-note characterization by a lesser talent.

Further complicating matters were the three directors of *Gone with the Wind*: George Cukor was fired early in the production, although de Havilland and Leigh secretly sought his advice during filming, then Victor Fleming, Gable's close friend and a "man's director," (also director of *The Wizard of Oz*) walked off the picture, and Sam Wood was brought in; he and Fleming split up the work, which was staggering by any measure. Vivien Leigh, featured in nearly every scene, worked constantly, and permanently damaged her fragile health. Sidney Howard's script trimmed some characters and plot, yet remained remarkably faithful to the book. Finally, after 11 months of shooting and over four million dollars spent, *Gone with the Wind* at last premiered in a much-ballyhooed spectacle staged by the city of Atlanta in 1939, attended by the stars, Selznick, and Mitchell herself.

The cultural impact of the film is hard to overestimate—in southern theaters as late as the 1960s, the technically astonishing and highly effective crane shot of the ragged Confederate flag fluttering over the vast assembly of Atlanta's dead and wounded provoked sobs, applause, and spontaneous emotion, including the occasional "rebel yell." The film's length of 222 minutes (punctuated by an intermission) deterred few, swept up as they were by the storyline. Max Steiner's stirring "Tara's Theme" is ubiquitous among movie scores, a perennial favorite. Film historian Leonard Maltin called *Gone with the Wind* "if not the greatest film ever made, certainly one of the greatest examples of storytelling on film. . . ." Even in numerous re-releases, and after being shown on television many times, *Gone with the Wind* continues to do well; in 1998, a restoration of the film's original negative led to lucrative video and DVD releases, as well as a theatrical re-release. A spectacularly visual film, *Gone with the Wind* used Technicolor to its greatest effect; William Cameron Menzies' brilliant cinematography remains a landmark achievement.

Gone with the Wind has unlimited kitsch potential: from Madame Alexander dolls to Scarlett Christmas ornaments, souvenir books (including the *Gone with the Wind Cookbook,* which has plenty of recipes from Mammy and Melanie, but none from Scarlett), fan clubs, online websites crammed with *Gone with the Wind* trivia and news, and in—an echo of the "Search for Scarlett"—"lookalike" contests and professional Scarlett, Melanie, and Rhett lookalikes, the story continues to fascinate. Bed and Breakfasts (notably the "Inn Scarlett" in Georgia) offer the fan a *Gone with the Wind* immersion experience, and exact replicas of the famed "Green Curtain" dress or "the Barbecue dress" are widely available. *Gone with the Wind* has been the subject of many parodies—memorably by comedian Carol Burnett, who lampooned Scarlett while wearing the "curtain dress" with the rod intact. "The Dump," now handsomely restored by German company Daimler-Benz and a favorite tourist destination, survived two arson attempts and opened in 1997.

The literary reputation of Mitchell's book has been favorably reassessed by numerous critics, and with the rise of Southern history and literature as a subject of scholarship, *Gone with the Wind* has become a touchstone, spawning numerous symposiums and studies, with Scarlett herself lionized as "modern" and a feminist heroine. In 1988, the Mitchell estate finally allowed an authorized sequel; *Scarlett* (by romance writer Alexandra Ripley) appeared in 1991. Panned by critics but financially successful, the CBS 1996 miniseries similarly proved popular.

—Mary Hess

FURTHER READING:

Behlmer, Rudy, editor. *Memo from David Selznick.* New York, Viking Press, 1972.

Dooley, Roger. *From Scarface to Scarlett: American Films in the 1930s.* New York, Harcourt, Brace, Jovanovich, 1979.

Dowling, Claudia Glenn. "The Further Adventures of Scarlett O'Hara." *Life.* November, 1988.

Flamini, Roland. *Scarlett, Rhett, and a Cast of Thousands: The Filming of "Gone with the Wind."* New York, Macmillan, 1975.

Hanson, Elizabeth I. *Margaret Mitchell.* Boston, Twayne Publishers, 1991.

Haver, Ronald. *David O. Selznick's "Gone with the Wind."* New York, Bonanza Books, 1986.

King, Richard H. *A Southern Renaissance: The Cultural Awakening of the American South, 1930-1955.* New York, Oxford University Press, 1980.

Mitchell, Margaret. *Gone with the Wind.* New York, Macmillan, 1936.

Myrick, Susan, and Richard Harwell, editors. *White Columns in Hollywood: Reports from the "Gone with the Wind" Sets.* Macon, Georgia, Mercer University Press, 1982.

O'Dowd, Niall. "Frankly, Scarlett . . . We Do Give a Damn." *Irish America.* November, 1981.

Pratt, William. *Scarlett Fever: The Ultimate Pictorial Treasury of "Gone with the Wind," Featuring the Collection of Herb Bridges.* New York, Macmillan, 1977.

Pyron, Darden Asbury, editor. *Recasting "Gone with the Wind" in American Culture.* Miami, University Presses of Florida, 1983.

Taylor, Helen. *Scarlett's Women: "Gone with the Wind" and Its Female Fans.* New Brunswick, New Jersey, Rutgers University Press, 1989.

Good Housekeeping

By dint of its very title, *Good Housekeeping* magazine stands as a symbol of a past era in American life. Along with *Redbook, Woman's Day, Ladies' Home Journal,* and others, *Good Housekeeping* belongs to what is known in industry parlance as the "Seven Sisters" of women's service magazines, and achieved its most pervasive success in an era when the bulk of middle-class women stayed at home and focused their energies on cooking, cleaning, and their children. *Good Housekeeping* and its cohorts "gradually built up the power of the matriarchy," wrote John Tebbel and Mary Ellen Zuckerman in *The Magazine in America, 1741-1990.* "Mom was . . . a figure of responsibility, dignity, and authority in the magazines." *Good Housekeeping,* however, differed from the other women's service magazines in its slightly elitist air; clearly aimed at women running economically stable households, in its heyday the periodical featured articles on how to choose a children's camp while, in a 1998 issue, readers received a run-down on the capital-gains tax.

Good Housekeeping began in 1885 as a ten-cent bi-weekly founded in Holyoke, Massachusetts, by Clark W. Bryan, a local journalist. Following on the heels of the success of *Ladies' Home Journal,* from the start *Good Housekeeping* catered to the young, affluent homemaker, a distinction that would later set it apart from its competitors in the field. It did not shy away, for instance, from feature stories on how to deal with hired help around the house. The first edition solicited reader contributions for a write-in contest on the topic "How To Eat, Drink and Sleep as a Christian Should." In 1891 it became a monthly, and in 1911 it was acquired by the Hearst publishing empire and its offices relocated to New York City.

From the start *Good Housekeeping* offered domestic guidance in the form of recipes, etiquette advice, and child care issues; it also contained more fiction and poetry in its pages than other women's magazines. In 1900, the magazine founded its famous Good Housekeeping Institute, which moved to state-of-the-art facilities in New York in 1912 and came under the guidance of a renowned former chemist from the United States Department of Agriculture. The GHI conducted research into food purity, tested products for safety, and in general brought a scientific approach to housekeeping. Its findings often became editorial features in the magazine itself, and from 1902 the magazine offered its "Ironclad Contract," the promise that any product advertised in *Good Housekeeping* would perform as promised. The "Seal of Approval" evolved over the next few decades in legal language and scope of guarantee, in order to deal with enforced compromises that result from this problematic mix of editorial focus and advertising revenue.

Circulation achieved the one-million mark in the 1920s, and the magazine—like much of the old-money, upper middle class in America—was virtually unaffected by the Great Depression of the 1930s, though its competitors suffered. Much of *Good Housekeeping*'s tone was set in the years between 1913 to 1942 under the editorship of William Frederick Bigelow. (The magazine would not

have its first female editor until 1994.) Bigelow introduced renowned writers such as W. Somerset Maugham and Booth Tarkington to the roster of fiction contributors, and the illustrations came from the pen of celebrated American artists such as Charles Dana Gibson. Keeping true to the magazine's focus on the sanctity of motherhood, its cover featured illustrations of children, at least through the 1950s; adult celebrities began appearing in the 1960s, but the December issue almost always still features an elaborate gingerbread house, with instructions inside on how to bake and construct this time-consuming *piece de resistance* of holiday festivities.

In the golden era of the Seven Sisters—the 1950s and 1960s when circulation and advertising pages reached an all-time high—*Good Housekeeping* continued to set itself apart, and above, its competitors in the field. It maintained its policy against liquor or tobacco advertising, and shied away from the tragic first-person tales found in other women's magazines, but did have an advice column written by Dr. Joyce Brothers. An etiquette column from Elizabeth Post, a descendant of the legendary authority Emily Post, gave readers advice about table manners and dealing with nosy neighbors; Elizabeth Post's daughter-in-law Peggy continued the column in the late 1990s.

After a circulation high of 5.5 million in 1966, *Good Housekeeping* lost readership and with that, advertising revenues, over the subsequent decades, as more American women entered the workforce on a full-time, permanent basis throughout the 1970s and 1980s. *Redbook* and other service publications responded to the trend, focusing their features and advice on how to manage both a household and a job outside the home, but *Good Housekeeping* did not. By the early 1990s, this orthodoxy had served the magazine well, and it began positioning itself toward a new demographic: career women who were giving up work in their thirties to become full-time suburban moms. The magazine launched its "New Traditionalist" ad campaign to attract readers and revenue with this focus. It remains one of the top performers in the Hearst media empire.

—Carol Brennan

FURTHER READING:

Endress, Kathleen T., and Therese L. Lueck, editors. "Good Housekeeping." *Women's Periodicals in the United States: Consumer Magazines.* Westport, Greenwood Press, 1995, 123-30.

McCracken, Ellen. "*Good Housekeeping* and *McCall's*: Safe Consumerism and Ideological Formation." *Decoding Women's Magazines: From "Mademoiselle" to "Ms."* New York, St. Martin's Press, 1993.

Mott, Frank Luther. "Good Housekeeping." *A History of American Magazines.* Vol. 5. Cambridge, Harvard University Press, 1968, 125-43.

Peterson, Theodore. *Magazines in the Twentieth Century.* 2nd ed. Urbana, University of Illinois Press, 1964.

Tebbel, John, and Mary Ellen Zuckerman. *The Magazine in America, 1741-1990.* New York, Oxford University Press, 1991.

"The Way We Were! The Way We Are!" (special supplement). *Good Housekeeping.* February, 1990.

Wood, James Playsted. *Magazines in the United States.* 3rd ed. New York, Ronald Press, 1971.

The Good, the Bad, and the Ugly

The last and most expensive of director Sergio Leone's "Dollar" trilogy grossed a respectable $6.1 million in 1966 and solidified Clint Eastwood's status as a major Western star. Following the success of Leone's *A Fistful of Dollars* (*Per un pugno di dollari,* 1964) and *For a Few Dollars More* (*Per qualche dollaro in piu,* 1965), *The Good, the Bad, and the Ugly* (*Il buono, il brutto, et il cattivo,* 1966) signifies the aesthetic high point of the Italian-produced spaghetti westerns, which revitalized the western hero through Eastwood's portrayal of the calculating "Man with No Name." Energized by Leone's vibrant film style and Ennio Morricone's didactic score, *The Good, the Bad, and the Ugly*'s international influence permanently altered popular conceptions of the western and its themes.

The Good, the Bad, and the Ugly's plot follows the progress of three ruthless gunfighters racing to obtain $200,000 in stolen Confederate gold. Beginning the film with a series of three lovingly constructed murder scenes, Leone employs extreme long shots and close-ups, piercing sound spikes, and dramatic freeze frames that introduce Tucco the Ugly (Eli Wallach), Angel Eyes the Bad (Lee Van Cleef), and "Blondie" the Good (Clint Eastwood) with his signature style of bravado exposition. As the story unfolds, all three principals form and break alliances in search of Bill Carson's hidden treasure.

The epic design of Leone's scenarios redefined the film image of the American West. After early collaborations with innovators like Michelangelo Antonioni and Robert Aldrich, Leone invested his

Clint Eastwood in a scene from the film *The Good, the Bad, and the Ugly.*

western scenes with an obviously distorted, often frenetic perspective. Unlike the stagy studio sets of B-grade Hollywood Westerns, Leone's plastic camera expanded adobe farm houses and barren deserts into exaggerated oceans of space peopled by minuscule though deadly specks of humanity. No Westerns since John Ford's dramatic Monument Valley films had offered such profoundly dynamic compositions. Leone's wild spectacles of dueling gunfighters, public hangings, Civil War battles, and prison camps create an darkly comic, self-consciously chaotic view of western society. At one point, Tucco and Blondie engage a pack of Angel Eyes' assassins in the middle of a bombed-out ghost town. While artillery continues to demolish the buildings around them, Tucco and Blondie nonchalantly utilize the rising dust as cover and peep out of new bomb craters to survey their enemies. Leone's freewheeling camerawork reaches its expressive heights during the montage of whip pans and zooms that describe the finale of an absurdly bloody Civil War battle on a bridge, and during the tension-building long shots that commence the climactic three-way gunfight in a sprawling deserted cemetery.

Much of *The Good, the Bad, and the Ugly*'s success depends on Ennio Morricone's infamously parodic score. As a discordant aural accompaniment to the crazed animations and incongruous antique fonts that constitute the title sequence, Morricone's campy revision of distinctive western sounds gives all three "Dollar" films a Monty Python-flavored musical edge. For *The Good, the Bad, and the Ugly,* Morricone deconstructs clichés of the western soundtrack to create a distinctively catchy theme of shriek-propelled, psychedelic yodeling that became as popular as Eastwood's nameless hero. In the spring of 1966, *The Good, the Bad, and the Ugly*'s main theme went to No. 1 on the American billboard charts alongside the Rolling Stones' "Jumpin' Jack Flash." With all its crazed energy, Morricone's score thematically accentuates key moments of Leone's narrative through its invocation of familiar western harmonies. In *Once upon a Time: The Films of Sergio Leone,* Robert Cumbow explains:

> The score to *The Good, the Bad, and the Ugly* taps Civil War movie conventions in its use of a lilting sentimental ballad played off a recurring march tune. The ballad, "Story of a Soldier," is derivative of the Confederate standard "Lorena" (a leading motif in Max Steiner's score to *The Searchers* . . . and in David Buttolph's music for *The Horse Soldiers,* for which it is the main theme). Sung phonetically by an Italian chorus, the lyrics of the song are only sporadically intelligible, but they reflect an antiwar tone consistent with both the film's treatment of war and the prevailing mood of ballads appearing during the period.

Cumbow also notes the innovative use of human voices and unconventional instruments in the soundtracks to all three "Dollar" films as an especially affecting element of "Morricone's offbeat orchestration." In *The Good, the Bad, and the Ugly,* Morricone's campy vocal orchestrations amplify not only the opening credits but also the introductory vignettes and Tucco's frantic, nearly orgasmic search for the buried gold in the cemetery.

In many ways, the spectacle of Eli Wallach's drunken, disheveled Tucco embodies the heart of Leone's film. Eastwood is undoubtedly the box-office star, but the plot and the camera continually privilege Tucco's furious escapades. Grinning, chuckling, and thieving his way through crowds of bitterly serious supporting characters, Tucco's vulgarity, tenacity, and humor make him the most endearing of the three mercenaries. Leone gives Tucco the most entertaining scenes as he crashes half-shaven through a barbershop window after plugging three bounty hunters, makes faces at an appalled elderly bystander during his own execution, and surprises a would-be assassin by hiding his pistol under the froth of his bubble bath. Tucco even rules the final moments of Leone's 160-minute film as his cursing of Blondie rises in a shocking echo that initiates the last flourish of Morricone's score. Tucco clearly personifies the aesthetic agenda of Leone's entire ''Dollar'' trilogy. In *The Good, the Bad, and the Ugly,* themes of war, murder, and greed fuse into a pseudo-serious, gore-punctuated epic that intercuts Tucco's torture scene with the lilting strains of a band in a Civil War prison camp. Combining the deadly serious with the sickly comic, Leone's entertaining, anarchic western formula parallels James Whale's Universal horror films, Stanley Kubrick's satirical science fiction, and Tim Burton's gothic *Batman* series.

—Daniel Yezbick

FURTHER READING:

Cumbow, Robert. *Once upon a Time: The Films of Sergio Leone.* Metuchen, New Jersey, Scarecrow Press, 1987.

Frayling, Christopher. *Spaghetti Westerns.* London, Routledge, 1981.

Newman, Kim. *Wild West Movies.* London, Bloomsbury, 1990.

Good Times

Throughout its initial success and later criticism, sitcom *Good Times* revolutionized prime-time television. While the story lines of 1950s and early 1960s television sitcoms provided little more than cautious counsel on the minor vicissitudes of family life, the decade of the 1970s ushered in what came to be known as the era of relevancy in television programming. In *Good Times,* which aired on CBS from February 1974 to August 1979, suburban street crime, muggings, unemployment, evictions, Black Power, and criticism of the government were frequent and resounding themes. The show is regarded as perhaps the first in prime-time television to tackle such issues with any measure of realism. It stretched the boundaries of television comedy and provided a different view, not only of black family life, but of the social fabric of 1970s American society in general.

Good Times, along with *Maude, Sanford and Son, The Jeffersons,* and television's most controversial sitcom *All in the Family,* was the creation of independent producer Norman Lear, whose programs, built on confrontational and ethnic-style humor, helped revolutionize prime-time television during the 1970s. *Good Times* was developed as a spin-off of the earlier hit show *Maude,* which starred Bea Arthur and Bill Macy, and featured the sometimes controversial machinations of a well-appointed, middle-aged, married couple. Their black housekeeper, Florida, was portrayed by veteran actress Esther Rolle, who was chosen to star as Florida Evans in *Good Times.*

The appearance of *Good Times* is noteworthy in that, along with *The Jeffersons* and *Sanford and Son,* it was one of the first prime-time television sitcoms featuring a mostly African-American cast since the controversial *Amos 'n' Andy* show had been canceled amid a firestorm of protest in 1953. *Good Times* was also unique in its funny but sometimes poignant portrayal of an African-American family eking

out an existence in a high-rise tenement apartment in an urban Chicago slum. The program exploited, with comic relief, such volatile issues as inflation, unemployment, discrimination, and the apparent reluctance of the government to do anything about them. In addition to the Florida character and James (John Amos), her frequently unemployed, but looking-for-work husband, the cast of *Good Times* included their teenage son, J.J., portrayed by comedian Jimmie Walker; their grown daughter, Thelma (Bernadette Stanis); and an adolescent son, Michael, portrayed with gusto by a talented young Ralph Carter. A fortyish woman named Wilona (Ja'net Dubois) made frequent appearances as the Evans's supportive neighbor. Later in the series, a very young Janet Jackson of the musical Jackson Family fame joined the cast as Wilona's adopted daughter.

Good Times's popularity and good ratings were rooted in the fact that it offered solace for a TV audience fed up with the Vietnam War, Watergate, high interest rates, and unemployment. Both blacks and whites could identify with the difficulties the Evans family faced, and the show became a champion for the plight of the underclass. Black viewers especially appreciated how the program highlighted the good parenting skills of James and Florida. In spite of their difficult situation, they never shirked on their responsibility to teach their children values and accountability. The Evans's ability to remain stalwart in the face of difficult odds was the underlying theme of many episodes.

Good Times is also significant for the controversy that haunted the show's production. Disputes developed about the program's changed direction; in particular, the ever-popular J.J. character. J.J.'s comical, but at times undignified, antics raised the resentment of many in the black community. With his toothy grin, ridiculous strut, and bug-eyed semblance, to some he had metamorphosed into a coon-type stereotype of former times. More and more episodes were centered around his farcical exploits, featuring his trademark exclamation, ''DY-NO-MITE!'' All but forgotten was the daughter Thelma, James's search for a job, Michael's scholastic interests, and family values. ''We felt we had to do something drastic,'' Rolle stated in the *Los Angeles Times* in 1978, ''we had lost the essence of the show.'' After both Rolle and Amos left the program in protest, attempts were made to soften the J.J. character and continue the program without the James and Florida characters. But with an employed and more mature-acting J.J., and the return of Rolle, ratings for *Good Times* declined. The program failed, and the series was canceled but continued to enjoy success in syndication.

—Pamala S. Deane

FURTHER READING:

Barnow, Eric. *Tube of Plenty.* Oxford University Press, 1982.

Brooks, Tim, and Earle Marsh. *The Complete Directory of Prime Time Network TV Shows, 1946-Present.* New York, Ballantine Books, 1985.

MacDonald, J. Fred. *Blacks and White TV: Afro-Americans in Television Since 1948.* Chicago, Nelson-Hall Publishers, 1983.

Marc, David, and Robert J. Thompson. *Prime Time, Prime Movers: From I Love Lucy to L. A. Law, America's Greatest TV Shows and the People Who Created Them.* Boston, Little, Brown and Co, 1992.

Margulies, Lee. ''Ester Rolle: Coming Home.'' *Los Angeles Times.* May 12, 1978.

(From left) Ralph Carter, Ja'Net DuBois, Jimmie Walker, Esther Rolle, and John Amos in a scene from the television show *Good Times*.

Taylor, Ella. *Prime Time Families: Television Culture in Postwar America.* University of California Press, 1989.

Goodbye, Columbus

A collection of five stories and one novella, *Goodbye, Columbus,* Philip Roth's first book, published in 1959, introduces the basic themes that Roth explores more fully in the novels that have followed and that have in turn been shaped by the critical response to *Goodbye, Columbus.* Published at a time when anti-Semitism was still prevalent in the United States and memories of the Holocaust still fresh, *Goodbye, Columbus* led a number of influential Jewish readers to question Roth's depiction of American Jews from the perspective of a writer for whom Jewishness was more cultural than religious, and assimilation and individual identity more pressing matters than survival and collective memory. While some charged Roth with disloyalty and self-hatred, others welcomed *Goodbye, Columbus'*

author into the front rank of the diverse group of Jewish-American writers then beginning to dominate American fiction. The less specifically Jewish implications of Roth's comic genius and irreverence were underscored by the release of the successful film version of the title novella in 1969, two years after *The Graduate.*

—Robert A. Morace

FURTHER READING:

Cooper, Alan. *Philip Roth and the Jews.* Albany, State University of New York Press, 1996.

Halio, Jay L. *Philip Roth Revisited.* New York, Twayne, 1992.

Gooden, Dwight (1964—)

Pitcher Dwight Gooden enjoyed one of the fastest rises to stardom in baseball history, but he ended up the sport's major casualty in the 1980s war against cocaine. Gooden won the National League Rookie of the Year Award in 1984 for the New York Mets; the following year, at the age of 20, he became the youngest pitcher ever to win the Cy Young Award. Heralded as "Doctor K," Gooden quickly became the toast of New York, but by 1987 the young pitcher was forced to enter a drug rehabilitation center for his cocaine addiction. Repeated violations of league drug policy limited Gooden's effectiveness and ultimately resulted in his suspension from baseball for the 1995 season. He subsequently kicked his drug habit and enjoyed some success with the New York Yankees and the Cleveland Indians in the late 1990s, notably in pitching a no-hitter against the Seattle Mariners on May 14, 1996.

—Scott Tribble

FURTHER READING:

Shatzkin, Mike, editor. *The Ballplayers: Baseball's Ultimate Biographical Reference.* New York, Arbor House, 1990.

GoodFellas

Chosen by the American Film Institute as one of the 100 greatest American films of the last 100 years, Martin Scorsese's *GoodFellas* (1990) has done more to demythologize organized crime than any other major contemporary film, while cementing its maker's reputation as, arguably, America's greatest director still living and working at the end of the twentieth century. *GoodFellas* was based on Nicholas Pileggi's 1985 bestseller, *Wiseguy: Life in a Mafia Family*, which recounted the true story of Henry Hill. A low-level mobster who rose up through the ranks, Hill was involved in the biggest cash robbery in America's history, was caught dealing cocaine, turned

The cast of *GoodFellas* (l-r) Ray Liotta, Robert De Niro, Paul Sorvino, and Joe Pesci.

State's evidence, and entered the Federal Witness Protection Program. Behind its glossy and absorbing gangster-thriller surface, the film offered an unvarnished account of Mafia brutality that came to set a standard—seldom achieved since—for the moral focus of serious crime films, and illuminated public understanding of the culture in which organized crime flourishes.

Set in Scorsese's home ground of New York City, whose underbelly he had so successfully exploited in many of his films, including the early *Mean Streets* (1973) and the masterly *Taxi Driver* (1976), *GoodFellas* marked the climactic contribution to the director's cycle of underworld subjects, and the one to which he successfully brought an epic approach. His by now practiced craft and brilliantly individual brand of expressionistic realism imbued *GoodFellas* with black comedy, often memorably ironic, sharp social observation, and scenes of deeply shocking but never gratuitous violence. The film is very long, but absolutely enthralls in its unfolding of a tale in which audiences watch the young lad Hill grow to manhood in the Mafia, and was lent further power by a large cast that, as British critic Max Loppert wrote, was "a galaxy of New York character acting at its athletic, up-front best." At the center was Ray Liotta as Hill, surrounded and supported by, among others too numerous to mention, a menacingly detached Robert De Niro, Oscar-winning Joe Pesci as the viciously manic Tommy DeVito, Paul Sorvino as Mafia boss Paul Cicero and, as Hill's middle-class Jewish wife, a superb Lorraine Bracco. Together, this ensemble vividly and realistically impersonated the real-life sociopaths they were portraying, articulating a world of men whose daily business embraces every known felony from arson and extortion through dealing in drugs and firearms to cold-blooded killing in the pursuit of money and power.

Hill was an insider who remained outside; although he was involved in the mob's scams, thefts, and murders, he was half-Irish and half-Sicilian, and only thoroughbred Sicilians could become "made men" within the Mafia. While the book dealt with the facts of the case, Scorsese puts flesh on the bones by making choices as to what he includes and how he treats it. The book, for example, detailed the 1978 theft of six million dollars from a Lufthansa cargo at Kennedy Airport, but where a lesser director would show the theft in all its detail, Scorsese shrewdly omits it entirely; his concern is with the lives of the perpetrators and how they are affected in the aftermath of the operation. The haul is so huge that a number of them, though warned to lie low, start living extravagantly, thus worrying De Niro's Jimmy Conway that their behavior will tip off the cops. He deals with their indiscretion by having each of them—some ten in all—killed, fully aware that their elimination will bring the added advantage of increasing his own percentage of the take.

This expert and imaginative ability to transpose and select creates dramatic juxtapositions from the start. Pileggi's book began with Hill describing his childhood, lived across the street from a cab stand controlled by the mob. He reveals how he was attracted by the apparent glamour of the mobsters' lives, admiring them for their power and wealth so that, from the age of 12, his dream was to be one of them. By contrast, *GoodFellas* opens midway through the story, with the adult Henry driving along a deserted road at night, accompanied by Jimmy and Tommy. He hears a strange thumping sound, speculates on its cause (a flat? Did he hit something?), and they pull over to investigate. The three men climb out, circle to the back of the car, and Henry opens the trunk to reveal a beaten and bloody cohort who, to their collective astonishment, is still breathing. Tommy lunges forward with a huge knife and brutally stabs him, after which Jimmy pumps four bullets into him. As the stunned Henry moves to close the trunk, he says in voice over, "As far back as I can remember, I always wanted to be a gangster."

The story then flashes back to Henry's formative years across from that cab stand, his first youthful errands for the mob, and his meeting of Jimmy and Tommy. In a now classic scene, Tommy is first spotted telling an anecdote that has his fellow mobsters in stitches and Henry saying, "You're funny." Tommy suddenly becomes threateningly confrontational. "Funny how? . . . I mean funny like I'm a clown? I amuse you? I make you laugh?" The tension builds until Henry finally realizes that Tommy is putting him on, and everyone laughs. From then on, whenever Tommy starts down the same confrontational road with someone else, audiences are lulled into thinking he's kidding again, so that his eventual explosion into uncompromisingly bloody violence is all the more shocking.

The film moves at a dazzlingly fast but perfectly controlled pace, its imagery enhanced by freeze-frames, jump-cuts, continuous takes, voice-overs, and on-screen date-and-place information that emphasizes its biographical origins. Unlike the book, which ends with Henry purporting to be happily ensconced in the Witness Protection Program, the movie ends with a distraught Henry trapped in suburbia. As he picks up the morning paper from the front porch of a row of identical houses, he says in voice over, "I'm an average nobody. I get to live the rest of my life as a schnook."

Comparisons with Coppola's *The Godfather* and its sequel proved inevitable—they are great films, epic in scope, and making much of the Family's code of honor. But as Nicholas Pileggi told the *New York Times,* "The honor code is a myth. These guys betray each other constantly. Once Henry's life is threatened, he has no qualms about testifying. He does no soul-searching, because he has no soul." *GoodFellas* is mired in the minutiae of everyday life, set among the lawns and shrubs of suburbia and stripped of other than fleeting, vulgar, and spurious glamour. The beatings and killings are always sick and brutal, never macho or alluring. The effect is to expose the sickening reality of the criminal lifestyle, revealing it in all of its violence, dishonor, and empty aspirations.

—Bob Sullivan

FURTHER READING:

Brunette, Peter, ed. *Martin Scorsese: Interviews (Interviews With Filmmakers Series).* Jackson, University Press of Mississippi, 1998.

Friedman, Lawrence S. *The Cinema of Martin Scorsese.* New York, Continuum Publishing Group, 1997.

Linfield, Susan. "'Goodfellas' Looks at the Banality of Mob Life." *New York Times,* September 16, 1990, sec. II, 19.

Pileggi, Nicholas. *Wiseguy: Life in a Mafia Family.* New York, Pocket Books, 1985.

Thompson, David, and Ian Christie, editors. *Scorsese on Scorsese.* London, Faber and Faber, 1989.

Goodman, Benny (1909-1986)

Known as the "King of Swing," bandleader Benny Goodman left his mark on the swing era of the late 1930s and early 1940s in several important areas. He adapted both jazz and popular songs into a unique style of big band jazz. His superb technique and distinctive

Benny Goodman

solo style made him the outstanding clarinetist of that era. During a time of racial segregation, he became the first leader to include African Americans in his orchestra. He innovatively returned jazz to its roots by using band members in small combos—from trios to sextets. His career was long-lasting, and when almost seventy, he impressed jazz critic John McDonough as "the only bankable jazz star left who can fill a concert hall all by himself," adding that "the Goodman mystique has not only survived, it's thrived."

When Chicago-born Benny was ten he joined a synagogue boys band, immediately showing a natural aptitude for the clarinet. Within a year he enrolled in the boys' band at famous Hull House, which offered free instruction in the arts to children of immigrant families. There his teacher was Franz Schoep, an instructor of woodwinds in the Chicago Symphony. Benny was twelve when he appeared on stage in Chicago doing an impersonation of clarinetist Ted Lewis, even then attracting the attention of bandleader Ben Pollack, who later hired him. At thirteen Goodman was playing phenomenal jazz solos with the famous Austin High Gang, which included such stars-to-be as saxophonist Bud Freeman, drummer Dave Tough, cornetist Jimmy McPartland, and clarinetist Frank Teschemacher. When he first jammed with the band, McPartland said, "This little monkey played about sixteen choruses of 'Rose' and I just sat there with my mouth open."

At thirteen, he was a full member of the musicians' union and working several nights a week in clubs and dance halls. In August 1925, the sixteen-year-old prodigy left Chicago wearing adolescent knickers to join Ben Pollack's band in Los Angeles. Pollack led one of the best jazz bands in the United States during the late 1920s and early

1930s. By 1927 Goodman was gaining the respect of other musicians, and that same year Melrose music publishers issued a folio called *One Hundred Jazz Breaks by Benny Goodman*. In 1928 he left Pollack briefly for the Isham Jones band, but when Pollack got a job that year in New York City, young Goodman rejoined him for the chance to play regularly with such standout jazzmen as Bud Freeman, Jimmy McPartland, Glenn Miller, and Jack Teagarden. He was undaunted by his fellow stars, and Pollack commented that "Benny Goodman was getting in everybody's hair about this time, because he was getting good and took all the choruses."

In 1929 he began a successful career as a freelancer in New York City, playing in Broadway pit bands and on recordings and radio. Of the 130 recording dates Goodman made during this period, only about fifteen were genuine jazz sessions. In these, however, he played with such jazzmen as Bix Beiderbecke, Red Nichols, Joe Venuti, Fats Waller, blues queen Bessie Smith, and even his early idol, Ted Lewis.

By 1933, having determined the kind of music he wanted to play, Goodman began making plans to organize his own band, and in 1934 the Benny Goodman Orchestra was featured on an ongoing NBC radio series called "Let's Dance." After a few recordings on Columbia, he signed a long-term contract with Victor in 1935 and took his band on the road. Success was gradual at first, but with the extraordinary arrangements of Fletcher Henderson, enhanced by the solos of Goodman, trumpeters Bunny Berrigan, Ziggy Elman, and Harry James; pianists Jess Stacey and Teddy Wilson, and drummer Gene Krupa, the band attained phenomenal nation-wide success in 1936. On January 16, 1938, Goodman, wearing white tie and tails, led his band into Carnegie Hall for the first pure jazz concert held there. The vocals of Peggy Lee—including "Why Don't You Do Right?" and "My Old Flame"—helped the orchestra remain a prime attraction until it was disbanded in mid 1944 to allow Goodman to focus on concerts with his combo groups.

He reorganized his big band in 1945 and appeared as its leader off and on until 1950, when he toured Europe with a sextet. After that, he fronted the big band on only one brief tour in the spring of 1953, involving himself in a number of other projects. He assembled a special band in 1955 to record the soundtrack for the film *The Benny Goodman Story,* starring Steve Allen as Goodman.

A wide variety of projects drew his attention: in the winter of 1956-57 he toured the Far East and in 1962 the Soviet Union, both for the State Department; sandwiched between were appearances with the Budapest String Quartet as well as concerts of works he had commissioned from Bartok, Hindemith, and Copland.

In the early 1970s he presented a television show from Carnegie Hall in which he reunited his original quartet and played a memorable version of "I'm a Ding Dong Daddy from Dumas." The same group, with an ailing Gene Krupa, played the 1973 Newport Jazz Festival.

By the 1980s Goodman's health problems began to increase as he suffered from arthritis in his fingers and a heart ailment that required a pacemaker. As late as 1986 he continued to play with a big band on occasional radio broadcasts. His biographer, Russell Connor, found these performances "brilliant, effortless, faultless, inspiring," adding that the sidemen were "visibly impressed."

The respect of his peers was far more important to Goodman than the long string of victories in jazz polls taken by *Downbeat, Metronome, Playboy,* and *Esquire*. His special niche was to change the course of jazz during the swing era. He was the "King of Swing," who, as James L. Collier wrote, "opened the door for the bands which rushed through the gap—among them Basie, Herman, Barnet,

Lunceford, Berigan, Crosby, Webb, Shaw, and eventually Kenton, Raeburn and the modernists."

—Benjamin Griffith

FURTHER READING:

Collier, James Lincoln. *Benny Goodman and the Swing Era.* New York, Oxford University Press, 1989.

Connor, D. Russell. *Benny Goodman: Listen to His Legacy,* Lanham, Maryland, Scarecrow Press, 1988.

Schuller, Gunther. *The Swing Era.* New York, Oxford University Press, 1989.

Goodrich, William

See Arbuckle, Fatty

Goodson, Mark (1915-1992)

Fondly known as the godfather of television game shows, Mark Goodson produced and created some of television's top-rated and most enduring programs, including *The Price Is Right, The Match Game,* and *Family Feud*.

Born in Sacramento, California, to Russian immigrant parents, Goodson was a shy and introverted child. Despite his reserved character, he pursued a career in the radio industry. In 1937 he landed his first job as a disc jockey at radio station KCBS in San Francisco. Two years later he was hired by Mutual Broadcasting System as an announcer, newscaster, and station director. In 1941 Goodson moved to New York to work as a radio announcer. It was here that he first became involved with game shows by emceeing the radio quiz show *The Jack Dempsey Sports Quiz*. In addition, Goodson tried his hand at acting while performing on the radio program *We the People* that aired during the Second World War; Goodson depicted the characters who had German and Japanese accents. In 1943 Goodson created his first network show for ABC, *Appointment with Life,* a dramatic series based on the files of a marriage counselor. During this time Goodson was also writing and directing installments of *The Kate Smith Variety Hour*.

In 1946, Goodson teamed up with Bill Todman to form Goodson-Todman Productions. Their first creation was a radio game show entitled *Winner Take All,* which aired on CBS. During the next couple of years, the two created several more successful radio shows, thereby creating a strong presence in network television. Goodson created the duo's first television program, *What's My Line*, which premiered on CBS on February 1, 1950. The program was an overnight success, airing weekly for seventeen years. Over the next thirty years, Goodson-Todman Productions continued to produce hit game shows and develop the widely used formats.

Complementary opposites, Todman managed the business side, while Goodson was the creative and productive force. Goodson created many of the essential attributes that define game shows. For example, Goodson-Todman Productions was one of the pioneers in set design, using bright colors and flashing lights. Goodson also pioneered the celebrity panel on the game show. In an attempt to boost ratings, Goodson introduced the celebrity panel in the 1950s on

What's My Line? The program featured a panel of four celebrity guests who guessed the occupations of the contestants. Over the years Goodson perfected the practice of the celebrity panels on programs such as *Password* and *The Match Game.* Goodson's celebrity panels were and still are imitated by other game show producers.

In 1979 Bill Todman died, leaving all of Goodson-Todman Productions in control of his partner. The name of the company was changed to Goodson Productions, and Goodson continued to focus on producing game shows and expanding his media group. In 1986, Goodson created the Goodson Newspaper Group, which consolidated several daily and weekly newspapers. By 1992 the group published eight daily, six Sunday, and twenty-five weekly newspapers.

Two weeks before his death in December 1992, Goodson was inducted into the Academy of Television Arts and Sciences Hall of Fame. This award topped a long list of other achievements that included three Emmy awards, the National TV award of Great Britain, and a star on the Hollywood Walk of Fame.

Yet nothing represents Goodson's contribution to television better than the longevity of the shows themselves. There has not been a weekday since 1946, when *Winner Takes All* premiered on radio, that a Goodson program has not been on the air. Goodson-Todman's thirty-plus game shows include *Winner Takes All* (1948-52); *Beat the Clock* (1950-62, 1968-71, 1979-80); *What's My Line?* (1950-74); *The Price Is Right* (1956-65, 1972—); *To Tell the Truth* (1956-77); *Password* (1961-67, 1971-75, 1979-81, 1985—); *The Match Game* (1962-69, 1973-82); *He Said, She Said* (1969); *Concentration* (1973-79); *Tattletales* (1974-80, 1982-84); *Mindreaders* (1979); *Blockbusters* (1980-82, 1987); *Match Game/Hollywood Squares Hour* (1982-83); and *Trivia Trap* (1984).

Goodson-Todman also produced a few episodic shows: *The Rebel, Jefferson Drum, The Richard Boone Show, Philip Marlowe,* and *The Don Rickles Show.*

—Lara Bickell

FURTHER READING:

Broughton, Irv, editor. *Producers on Producing.* Jefferson, North Carolina, McFarland & Company, 1986.

Fabe, Maxene. *TV Game Shows.* New York, Doubleday and Co., 1979.

Graham, Jefferson. *Come on Down!!!: The TV Game Show Book.* New York, Abbeville Press, 1988.

The Mark Goodson Collection, UCLA Film and Television Archive, Los Angeles, California.

Scheuer, Steven H., ed. *Who's Who in Television and Cable.* New York, Facts on File, 1983.

Schwartz, David, et al. *The Encyclopedia of Television Game Shows.* New York, New York Zoetrope, 1987.

Gordy, Berry (1929—)

Founder of the Motown music empire, Berry Gordy was for many years America's most successful black businessman.

Gordy was one of eight children from a middle-class family in Detroit; his father, Berry Gordy, Sr., was a contractor and entrepreneur. The elder Gordy's gospel of achievement and competition found a respectful audience in his son, but Berry Gordy, Jr., always sought wealth rather than merely middle-class success. Gordy dropped out of high school to pursue a career in boxing and fought in 19 mostly successful professional bouts, but he quit the ring after concluding that he would never be great. Shortly afterwards he was drafted, serving in Korean War combat.

Returning to Detroit in 1953, Gordy started a jazz record store with borrowed money. It failed after a short time, and he next took an assembly line job at a Ford plant. Gordy's sisters had by then obtained the cigarette concession at one of Detroit's better black nightclubs, and he began spending much of his free time there. He was composing songs in his head during his long, boring shifts at Ford, and attempted to persuade the nightclub's talent to use his material. In 1957, with the first of his marriages falling apart, Gordy quit his Ford job to devote himself to composing full-time.

It was Jackie Wilson, an old acquaintance from his boxing days, who first recorded songs by Berry Gordy. Wilson was just on the brink of success when Gordy gave him "Lonely Teardrops" and several other songs to use, but he quickly discovered that a composer's royalties were very small, especially in the frequently corrupt music business of the day. He started doing freelance record producing as well, learning valuable lessons but still not making much profit.

In 1959, on a shoestring budget, Berry Gordy founded his own music production company. He named it Motown after Detroit, the Motor City, and brought several of his siblings and their spouses into the business. One brother-in-law was writer/producer/singer Harvey Fuqua of Harvey and the Moonglows; another was Marvin Gaye, who would become one of Motown's biggest, and most troubled, stars. Gordy also employed a number of would-be singers and writers in secretarial and production capacities, thus assuring a constant supply of willing talent at very little cost to himself.

Berry Gordy's earlier careers had prepared him well for Motown. From the outset he was a stickler for high production values, and quickly created a recognizable "Motown sound." He also sought to broaden his appeal beyond his core customer base of young black people to a larger and more affluent older white audience. In order to mask how many records Motown was releasing, Gordy created and managed a variety of labels, such as Tamla, Soul, Gordy, Rare Earth, and many others.

Early acts produced by Motown included Smokey Robinson and the Miracles, Mary Wells, Marvin Gaye, the Temptations, Martha and the Vandellas, the Spinners, the Marvelettes, and Stevie Wonder. In the years to come, Gordy would sign up such performers as the Four Tops, Gladys Knight and the Pips, Junior Walker and the All-Stars, the Isley Brothers, the Commodores, and the Jackson Five. In many cases, after a few years in Motown's mixture of production wizardry and tight-fisted, arbitrary control, the now-established stars left for greener pastures. Some critics argue that few ever sounded as good after Motown as they had as part of it.

Gordy retained almost complete ownership of his company, making him a very wealthy man. When his struggling female group, the Supremes, finally began to make a name for themselves, he determined to make Diane Ross—as she was then known—into a major star. Diane Ross was a skinny schoolgirl when the Supremes started with Gordy's record label, and was plunged, like many other new acts, into Motown's whirlwind of training bent on making stars. Following the practice of the big Hollywood studios, Motown's Artist Development Department coached the youngsters on speech, choreography, stage behavior, costume, and of course on singing. Diane, soon Diana, Ross of the Supremes was Motown's greatest success story, rising from poverty in Detroit to international stardom, just as Berry Gordy willed it. His strategy was methodical. First, he put

Berry Gordy (right) receiving the NAACP Award of the Year from commentator Barry Gray, 1968.

Ross's name ahead of the group, then he fired Florence Ballard, her former equal and arguably the best singer ever to call herself a Supreme. Next, he separated Ross from the group and built her up as a solo act. Finally, he began to invest some of his millions in motion picture production, but only when Diana Ross was given the lead in each film. *Lady Sings the Blues* (1972), a biographical film about Billie Holiday, was a smash hit.

During production of the next film, *Mahogany* (1975), the producer's suggestions came so often that the director resigned, and Berry Gordy eventually took directorial credit for the film. It was

quite successful; other films in which Gordy was involved were less so. *The Wiz* (1978) was an abject flop, losing millions despite the presence of Ross and Michael Jackson. Gordy left the movie business shortly thereafter. In 1972, much to the chagrin of Detroit residents and his employees, Berry Gordy relocated Motown to Los Angeles.

Gordy lived through many changes in the American recording industry, and left an indelible mark on popular music. A list of the artists who recorded for Motown's many labels over a 35-year period would include a disproportionate number of major stars whose songs created a musical dynasty. It was the end of an era when Berry Gordy sold Motown to the media conglomerate MCA in 1994.

—David Lonergan

FURTHER READING:

Benjaminson, Peter. *The Story of Motown.* New York, Grove Press, 1979.

George, Nelson. *Where Did Our Love Go? The Rise and Fall of the Motown Sound.* New York, St. Martin's Press, 1985.

Gordy, Berry. *To Be Loved.* New York, Warner Books, 1994.

Gospel Music

Gospel music is arguably the most important African-American musical tradition. Throughout the twentieth century it has managed to instill a vision in African-Americans with its message of hope, love, and compassion through the power of Jesus Christ. Gospel music has also had a profound influence on religious and secular music, enabling it to become a part of the broader American culture.

During the Antebellum period, African-Americans used religious and sacred songs as a tool of liberation in order to help them survive the terrible institution of slavery. Once emancipation had been achieved, they then relied upon spirituals such as "Nobody Knows the Trouble I See," "Steal Away," "Didn't My Lord Deliver Daniel," "Ezekiel Saw the Wheel," and "In that Great Gettin' up Morning," to help them make the transition from slavery to freedom. Beginning in the early twentieth century, however, African-American religious music would enter a new age with the birth of black Pentecostal churches and denominations. With a strong worship emphasis on emotionalism and speaking in tongues, many traditional hymns were instantly "gospelized" by increasing the tempo and, at times, by adding percussion accompaniment. Instrumental in this phenomena was Charles Price Jones of Jackson, Mississippi, founder of the Church of Christ (Holiness) USA, who as the father of African-American Pentecostalism composed over 1,000 songs for his congregation. Jones' songs—such as "I'm Happy With Jesus Only" and "Jesus Only"—were unique in that they expressed the feelings and expressions of African-Americans after slavery.

Beginning in the 1920s, black religious music was introduced to the Quartet movement. Whereas most sacred music was sung by congregations, The Fisk Jubilee Singers of Nashville were responsible for popularizing the groups as they sprang up east of the Mississippi River. Because of their amazing popularity, record companies such as RCA Victor, Paramount, and Columbia, cashed in on the demand for this type of music in the Urban North by recording and promoting the quartet sound. Radio stations also sought to capitalize on the growing popularity of black religious music. Stations such as WLAC of Nashville, with its 50,000 watts, played the music at night to listeners as far away as Chicago, Philadelphia, and New York.

Seeking to take advantage of the growing popularity of black religious music, Thomas A. Dorsey of Chicago took African-American religious music to a new level by combining blues and jazz rhythms to traditional hymns; he labeled his sound "gospel." Dorsey, a former jazz and blues pianist, decided to give his talents to "the Lord" in 1932 and in that same year he organized a gospel choir at Chicago's Pilgrim Baptist Church. One year later he organized the

National Convention of Gospel Choirs and Choruses (NCGCC). Thus, he had begun a career that would eventually lead him to compose over 500 songs. His most famous was "Take My Hand Precious Lord." In addition to directing and composing, Dorsey also opened a gospel music publishing house and soon thereafter he was labeled the "Father of Gospel Music." Although Dorsey was indeed a prolific songwriter, he did not operate in isolation. He worked with other artists such as Sallie Martin and the popular Mahalia Jackson. Between 1938 and 1947 Jackson made several recordings, but her most popular—"Move On Up A Little Higher"—catapulted her into gospel music fame. On the heels of the popular recording she secured a weekly CBS radio program and she also made a number of appearances at the famed Apollo Theater and the on *Ed Sullivan Show.* Since she was one of the first gospel artists to take her work to a secular audience, Jackson quickly became an international star and many today consider her the "World's Greatest Gospel Singer."

Beginning in the 1950s, other artists—the Dixie Hummingbirds, the Blind Boys of Alabama, and the Sensational Nightingales—filled churches, auditoriums, and jazz festivals with their unique style as they followed Jackson's lead in taking their message to a broader audience. Again, the media sought to take advantage of the popularity of gospel music by establishing such nationally syndicated television programs as *TV Gospel Time.* Although the show had a short existence it was nonetheless instrumental in bringing gospel music to a non-religious crowd.

While some artists were bringing gospel to new listeners, others such as James Cleveland were gaining notoriety within traditional gospel circles. Born in 1930 in Chicago, Cleveland served as composer, arranger, and pianist for several gospel groups before starting his own, the James Cleveland Singers, which performed many of his 500 songs. What made Cleveland unique was that he introduced the nation to the "Gospel Choir." At times, his choirs would number several hundred as they entertained audiences with their hand clapping, dancing, and singing, while arrayed in their fashionable robes. In 1968 Cleveland organized the Gospel Music Workshop of America (GMWA) and because of his success he received three Grammy Awards; in 1981 he was awarded a star on the Hollywood Walk of Fame.

In spite of Cleveland's broad appeal, there was a faction inside the gospel music industry that wanted to take gospel into the mainstream; quite simply, they wanted to imitate the more popular rhythm and blues songs. Leading this movement was Edwin Hawkins, who in 1969 recorded "Oh Happy Day," which rose to number one on the Top Fifty Chart with its catchy beat and rhythmic sound, but without any references to God or Jesus. A new generation of gospel was born.

Other artists such as Andrae Crouch followed Hawkins' crossover success by writing gospel lyrics for more popular secular songs. Although Hawkins and Crouch were forerunners of this "new gospel music," their popularity was still largely confined to the ears of black churchgoers. Beginning in the late 1980s, however, contemporary gospel groups such as Take 6 and the Winans began to take the gospel message to an ever wider audience. During their heyday both groups could easily fill a concert hall as they played their new style to the sacred and the secular. By the 1990s gospel music had grown to a billion-dollar industry, thanks in part to such artists as Kirk Franklin, whose debut album *Why We Sing* reached number one on the Billboard Gospel Chart and Number 13 on Billboard's Rhythm and Blues listing. Today, gospel music continues to be an important thread in the fabric of American popular music.

—Leonard N. Moore

FURTHER READING:

Allen, Ray. *Singing in the Spirit: African-American Sacred Quartets in New York City.* Philadelphia, University of Pennsylvania Press, 1991.

Boyer, Horace, and Lloyd Yearwood. *How Sweet the Sound: The Golden Age of Gospel.* Washington, Elliott and Clark Publishing, 1995.

Harris, Michael. *The Rise of Gospel Blues: The Music of Thomas Andrew Dorsey in the Urban Church.* New York, Oxford University Press, 1992.

Reagon, Bernice Johnson, editor. *We'll Understand It Better By and By: Pioneering African-American Gospel Composers.* Washington, Smithsonian Institution Press, 1992.

Gossip Columns

As America shed its provincial nineteenth-century sensibilities and slowly entered the modern era, the media emerged as one of the twentieth century's most powerful forces. But until the early 1920s, journalism was still influenced by an older ethos of taste and good

Gossip columnist Hedda Hopper in 1959.

breeding—until Walter Winchell. An ambitious young New York newspaperman, Winchell brought gossip into the mainstream media, breaking longstanding taboos in favor of a press for whom nothing was sacred and no one was guaranteed privacy. During his heyday, two-thirds of the adult population of America listened to Winchell's radio broadcast or read his column, as America clamored to learn "the dirt" about the rich, the famous, and the powerful. The ultimate tool of a democracy, gossip became the great leveler, breaking down distinctions of class, race, and gender, in favor of a society where no one is above reproach and everyone is the subject of gossip. His influence was pervasive, spawning such hugely successful gossip mongers as Hollywood's Hedda Hopper and Louella Parsons, whose fame soon came to exceed even Winchell's. What once was shocking soon became expected and, over the course of the twentieth century, gossip has become an integral component of mainstream journalism from which no one has become exempt—not even, as the world found out in 1998, the President of the United States.

The emergence of gossip columns and columnists as powerful new journalistic forces and voices during the early twentieth century would not have been possible without the creation of a new class of Americans: celebrities. The invention of motion pictures and their consequent development into an immensely popular form of entertainment gave birth to a new kind of fame—celebrity. Where once fame had been the result of heroism, genius, talent, wealth, or aristocratic birth, the movie industry promoted their new personalities to bring in audiences. A truly democratic art form, movie actors may have been more beautiful, more ambitious, and sometimes even more talented than the average American, but they were generally no better born. Celebrities were thus tantalizing to the American public, who saw in them the breakdown of an old social order and new possibilities for themselves. The public clamored to know as much as possible about celebrities and the media tried to meet their demand. This reciprocal relationship spawned the mass media frenzy that has defined the twentieth century.

Gossip has always existed, but it did not become a big business until the 1920s in the United States. Although Walter Winchell made gossip a staple of the modern press, as his biographer, Neal Gabler, has written, the tough-talking Winchell "no more invented gossip than he invented slang." During the 1880s, Louis Keller, a New York patent attorney, published a rag called *Town Topics,* devoted exclusively to the goings on of high society and the nouveau riche—as Gabler notes, "the bawdier the better." Soon most of the major papers had society columns, but most stayed clear of hard line gossip. In the 1920s, however, Stephen Clow started *Broadway Brevities and Social Gossip,* on the premise that he could make money by getting people to pay him not to print gossip about them. Clow was later brought to trial, but the idea stuck and would continue to crop up throughout the twentieth century. Still, the traditional press tried to avoid engaging in libelous gossip, particularly after Supreme Court Justice Louis Brandeis wrote an important article in the *Harvard Law Review* condemning gossip and arguing for the legal right to privacy. But the tide was turning.

Neal Gabler writes that the media "were exerting an almost inexorable pressure toward gossip by engendering a fascination with personalities. In the movies, magazines and the tabloids, personalities were sales devices; once the public became aware of these personalities, its curiosity was insatiable. With the interest in place, all that was needed to cross the line to gossip was someone with the audacity and nerve to begin writing frankly about the various private doings of the celebrated—someone who would defy the taboo. That was where Winchell came in.''

Although the ''respectable'' papers refused to have anything to do with reporting gossip, for the tabloids the line was a little blurrier. In 1924, a new tabloid called the *Graphic* hit the streets—a publication dedicated to the masses that would not be afraid to splash sex across its front pages. On the staff of the *Graphic* was a 27-year-old former vaudevillian named Walter Winchell, who had spent the past four years establishing his reputation as a Broadway reporter; Winchell loved gossip, and he longed to print it in his column.

Inspired by the *Graphic*'s dictum to print ''Nothing but the Truth,'' Winchell's Monday column, ''Mainly About Mainstreeters,'' stunned the theater and journalism worlds. He printed straight gossip. Sex, extra-marital affairs, and illegitimate children all found their way into Winchell's Monday pieces. Nothing was out of bounds. And Winchell made it additionally juicy by printing the gossip in bold type, virtually creating a new gossip lingo composed of innuendo, double entendre, and slang. Gabler writes:

> Not surprisingly, the journalistic Old Guard was en-raged by the affront to privacy, but the avidity with which the Monday column was devoured by readers left no doubt that Walter had tapped into the American psyche, into something beyond voyeurism, even if it would always be difficult to define precisely what he had struck. Part of it was the general interest in anything that had to do with the new class of celebrities. Part of it may have been attributable to urbanization ... As the twenties transformed America from a community into a society, gossip seemed to provide one of the lost ingre-dients of the former for the latter: a common frame of reference. In gossip everyone was treated as a known quantity ... Like slang, gossip also made one feel knowing, ahead of the curve ... The rich, the powerful, the famous and the privileged had always governed their own images. Now Winchell, with one act of defiance, had taken control and empowered his readers.

Walter Winchell once said, ''Democracy is where everybody can kick everybody else's ass. But you can't kick Winchell.'' During the height of his power, Winchell was untouchable. He struck fear into the hearts of the rich, famous, and vulnerable, even as he delighted a national audience of millions. He became one of the most powerful men in America, a friend to J. Edgar Hoover, an advisor to Franklin Delano Roosevelt, and, later, a staunch supporter of McCarthyism. The puissance of his pen became the scourge of his enemies, for although he could make someone's reputation, he could also break it. Yet, as Alistair Cooke once wrote, his devastating power ''was the promise of American freedom and uninhibited bounce, he was Americanism symbolized in a nose-thumbing at the portentousness of the great.''

There were, of course, many others who jumped on the gossip bandwagon. Ed Sullivan began his career writing a theater column for the *Graphic*. Other major gossip columnists would include Dorothy Kilgallen, Sidney Skolsky, and, of course, Louella Parsons and Hedda Hopper. Hopper and Parsons would, in fact, come to rule Hollywood much as Winchell did New York.

More than 15 years younger than Winchell, Louella Parsons was a large, strong-willed woman who carved out a career for herself when she was in her thirties, working as a Chicago reporter on the fledgling movie business. When she moved to New York in 1918, she began campaigning to earn the attention of media mogul William Randolph Hearst, by inserting glowing praises and weekly mentions of his paramour, actress Marion Davies, in her weekly column. By the early 1920s, Hearst had given Parsons a job and by the mid-1920s, she had moved to Hollywood and had become globally syndicated. She quickly became the most powerful woman in Hollywood, demanding and receiving every scoop in the movie business. Like Winchell, she was unafraid to print the truth, to sniff out scandal, and to tell secrets.

In the mid-1930s, a former actress named Hedda Hopper was hired to write a competing column. Though she and Parsons had once been friends, they soon became arch-enemies, competing for every scoop. Their rivalry upped the ante immediately, and gossip flew from their dueling pens. For almost 30 years, Hollywood was held in their grasp—as Hopper and Parsons made and ruined careers. When Louella Parsons broke the story of Ingrid Bergman's illegitimate child with director Roberto Rossellini, the actress did not work in Hollywood for almost a decade. Neither Parsons nor Hopper were above being vindictive and destructive, and both could inspire genu-ine rage among members of the motion picture community helpless to fight them. When Joseph Cotten once kicked the chair on which Hopper was sitting to bits, after having an extra-marital affair announced in her column, his house was filled with flowers and telegrams from others who had been similarly maligned. But like Winchell, when Hopper and Parsons liked someone, nothing was too much to do to help—and their power could become a boon for someone struggling to make it in movies.

As the Golden Age of Hollywood ended and the studio system crumbled, Hopper and Parsons no longer wielded the clout they had once had when all the moguls were forced to kowtow to them. Winchell, too, began to lose his former hegemony, as his New York connections no longer gave him the edge on gossip in film and television. But the die was cast. Gossip had become an integral part of the media, carried on not only by actual gossip columnists such as Liz Smith, but also by mainstream journalists, eager to spice up the news to make a good read.

With the evolution of the Internet, gossip found another happy home. And when Internet gossipmonger Matt Drudge began to spread rumors of President Clinton's extra-marital affairs, it was not long before it became mainstream news. But the political and media crisis of 1998 has spawned a new debate. Has the media gone too far in reporting the private affairs of public people? Is the press telling the public more than it wants to know? Seventy-five years after Walter Winchell introduced gossip into the mainstream media, we are still reeling from the results. The public debate will undoubtedly continue. The fact, however, remains—American popular culture is saturated with gossip, and its effect will always be felt.

—Victoria Price

FURTHER READING:

Collins, Amy Fine. ''Idol Gossips.'' *Vanity Fair*. April 1997, 357-75.

Eels, George. *Hedda and Louella: A Dual Biography of Hedda Hopper and Louella Parsons*. New York, Putnam, 1972.

Gabler, Neal. *Winchell: Gossip, Power, and the Culture of Celebrity*. New York, Alfred Knopf, 1994.

Spacks, Patricia Meyer. *Gossip*. New York, Alfred A. Knopf, 1985.

Goth

Although members of this youth subculture may differ in their own definitions, goth can be characterized by a fascination with all things otherworldly, from vampires to magic and beyond. Like punk, goth comprises a musical genre as well as an attitude, represented by somber acts like Bauhaus, Dead Can Dance, Christian Death, and Faith and the Muse. Often perceived by the general public as little more than "kids who wear black clothes," the goth scene is in fact a fusion of attitudes stemming from the sublime emotion of Romantic poetry, the macabre images of decadent Victorian poetry, and the contempt for normative bourgeois complacency found in the punk movement. While it is true that goth has been centered around themes of death and morbidity, what often goes unnoticed is goth's sense of humor—albeit a decidedly black one.

—Shaun Frentner

FURTHER READING:

Edmundson, Mark. *Nightmare on Main Street: Angels, Sadomasochism, and the Culture of the Gothic.* Cambridge, Harvard University Press, 1997.

Mercer, Mick. *The Hex Files: The Goth Bible.* New York, Overlook Press, 1996.

Gotti, John (1940—)

Known as the "Teflon Don" for his ability to win acquittal during several criminal trials and as the "Dapper Don" for his penchant for expensive, custom-tailored suits, John Gotti was the most visible organized crime figure of the late twentieth century. A media celebrity in the late 1980s and early 1990s, the boastful Gotti offered a public image of macho ultra-confidence that many admirers associated with the iconic American figure of the rebel, and crowds of his supporters often gathered outside the court during his trials. Within the mob, Gotti was reportedly a ruthless enforcer who controlled New York's Gambino crime family after the 1985 assassination of Paul Castellano outside a Manhattan restaurant. Gotti was ultimately betrayed by his closest associate, Salvatore "Sammy the Bull" Gravano, and convicted on federal racketeering and murder charges in 1992. In addition to Gravano's devastating testimony, thousands of hours of taped conversations in which Gotti discussed criminal activities with his top associates secured the government's case against him. He is serving a life sentence in the maximum security federal penitentiary in Marion, Illinois.

—Laurie DiMauro

FURTHER READING:

Davis, John H. *Mafia Dynasty. The Rise and Fall of the Gambino Crime Family.* New York, HarperCollins, 1993.

Dorigo, Joe. *Mafia.* Seacaucus, New Jersey, Chartwell Books, 1992.

Nash, Jay Robert. *World Encyclopedia of Organized Crime.* New York, Da Capo Press, 1993.

John Gotti

Grable, Betty (1916-1973)

The most popular pinup of American servicemen during World War II, actress, dancer, and singer Betty Grable was the symbol of an era. Dressed in a bathing suit and looking over her shoulder at the camera in her famous pinup, she radiated the optimism of an all-American girl and gave the American servicemen a vision of what they were fighting for. Not only did her image adorn barracks all over the world, but her likeness was used by the military to teach their men how to read grid maps. The star of Technicolor musicals at Twentieth Century-Fox, she reigned supreme, registering as the number one box office star in 1943 and appearing on the list of top stars from 1942-1951. Her legs were considered so close to perfection that they were insured by Lloyd's of London for one million dollars as a publicity stunt.

Born Ruth Elizabeth Grable in St. Louis, Missouri, her starstruck mother, Lillian, determined to make one of her daughters a star. She failed with elder daughter Marjorie, but Betty, as she was called, not only had talent but was enthusiastic about a show business career herself. She studied dance, singing, and the saxophone. She appeared in her first movie at the Fox Studios in the chorus of *Happy Days* (1929) in a black-face number. She was signed to a one-year contract by lying about her age, but when the executives discovered she was only thirteen, they dropped her option. Her mother was not deterred and arranged for her to appear in Eddie Cantor's *Whoopee* (1930). Betty was signed as a Goldwyn Girl with a five-year contract, but her career still did not take off. She appeared in a few other films, then

Betty Grable

signed to the Frank Fay musical *Tattle Tales,* which closed after only a few performances.

With her film career going nowhere, Grable spent time as a vocalist for several orchestras. During the mid- to late 1930s Grable appeared in more than a dozen films, but it was an appearance in a Fred Astaire/Ginger Rogers film that first brought her some notice. In 1934's *The Gay Divorcee* Grable did a dance number with character actor Edward Everett Horton called "Let's K-knock K-knees." In 1937 Grable married former child actor Jackie Coogan, who at the time was embroiled in a lawsuit against his parents regarding his earnings, and this put much strain on the marriage. Coogan and Grable appeared together in *Million Dollar Legs* (1939), but they later divorced.

Grable was finally being noticed, and Daryl F. Zanuck of Twentieth Century-Fox signed her to a contract. He did not have any immediate plans for Grable, so he allowed her to appear in a musical called *DuBarry Was a Lady* on Broadway. The show starred Ethel Merman and Bert Lahr, but it was Grable who caused a sensation performing the number "Well Did You Evah" with Charles Waters. In 1940 Grable left the show to replace an ailing Alice Faye in *Down Argentine Way.* The film was a huge success, and Grable immediately became a superstar. To follow her "instant" success Grable appeared in musicals such as *Moon over Miami* and *Springtime in the Rockies.* It was during the latter film that she met bandleader Harry James, whom she married in 1943 and with whom she had two daughters.

Although her famous pinup may have been her greatest contribution to the war effort, Grable joined other stars in war bond rallies, entertaining the troops, and appearing at the Hollywood Canteen.

Grable continued to make successful films, although after the late 1940s her popularity began to wane. She also fought with Zanuck, who wanted to put her in serious films, but which Grable knew was not her forte. To make Grable toe the line, Zanuck brought several blond starlets to the studio. Grable appeared with Marilyn Monroe in *How to Marry a Millionaire* (1953), and rather than being threatened she took the younger woman under her wing. Grable had had it with Twentieth Century-Fox, however, and left shortly after. When *Millionaire* was released, it was Grable who received the most critical praise, and she was persuaded to return for the film *How to be Very, Very Popular* (1955), a flop which was Grable's last film.

Grable continued to make successful appearances on television and in live theater productions such as *Guys and Dolls* and in a touring company of *Hello Dolly.* While things were still going well for Grable careerwise, her personal life was not. In October of 1965 she divorced James after more than twenty years of marriage.

In 1969 Grable went to London for the production of a new musical, *Belle Starr,* which was written especially for her. It flopped and closed after sixteen performances. In 1972, shortly after appearing on the Academy Awards telecast, Grable was diagnosed with cancer. After extensive treatments she decided to return to work appearing in *Born Yesterday* in Florida. Unfortunately, the cancer had spread, and within a few months Grable died.

—Jill A. Gregg

FURTHER READING:

McGee, Tom. *Betty Grable: The Girl with the Million Dollar Legs.* New York, Vestal Press, 1995.

Pastos, Spero. *Pinup, the Tragedy of Betty Grable.* New York, Putnam, 1986.

Warren, Doug. *Betty Grable, the Reluctant Movie Queen.* New York, St. Martin's Press, 1981.

Graceland

Graceland mansion, home to rock-and-roll phenomenon Elvis Presley for the twenty years preceding his 1977 death, became world-famous after it was opened to the public in 1981. Before the end of its first decade as a tourist attraction (or pilgrimage destination for some fans), Graceland had hosted more than one million tourists, and by the late 1990s it served as a symbol of both the indefatigable hope and immense costs of the American Dream.

Named after the first owner's aunt Grace, Graceland was built in the 1930s to resemble an antebellum, plantation-style manor home. Elvis paid $100,000-plus for the mansion in 1957. Located on "Elvis Presley Boulevard," a portion of Highway 51 South in Memphis, Tennessee, the majestic-looking Georgian mansion sits amidst an extraordinarily overflowing mass of plasticized suburban sprawl. There are an astounding number of fast-food establishments within a one-mile radius of the estate.

Inside, the front rooms of the house have been designed for the eyes of "company"; in this case, company that would be curious to

The Graceland mansion in Memphis, Tennessee.

know how a poor farmhand's son would live in an atmosphere of newly acquired wealth. There is the obligatory glitzy chandelier in the foyer, an elegant dining room, marble and glass-topped tables, fine porcelain statuary, a gilded piano, overdone white carpeting, yards of gilt-edged draperies hanging about the rooms—in fact, just about everything is trimmed in gold—and much else to indicate wealth and status. A television set sits smack in the middle of one of the front rooms.

Visitors are guided down a dark staircase with carpeted walls and a mirrored ceiling to Elvis's pleasure palace in the basement. One room sports a blinding yellow, white, and black color scheme; one wall of the room houses three built-in TV sets, side by side. Elvis got the idea from President Lyndon Johnson, who needed to monitor all of the evening newscasts at the same time, but Elvis wanted to watch all of the Sunday football games at once. The billiards room is entombed in yards of printed, pleated fabric that covers the walls and ceilings and that enforces a sensation of profound claustrophobia even in those not ordinarily afflicted. Although the pool table was torn years before Presley's death, and he never had it fixed, the keepers of Graceland decided to maintain most such flaws to create a sense that the home is frozen in time. This is a well-intended, though inaccurate depiction of Graceland as it was when Elvis lived there; many of Elvis's latter-day decorating decisions have been swept away. The blood-red carpeting and drapes were changed to a more pleasing blue hue, and a rotating glass statue in the foyer that spurted water was simply discarded as an embarrassment.

There was no way, though, that the keepers could enforce any more than the smallest degree of upper-class nobility upon Graceland. The coup de grace is what everyone at Graceland calls "the jungle room." According to Graceland-approved legend, Elvis and his father happened upon a most intriguing collection of "Polynesian" wooden and fake fur furniture at a Memphis establishment called

Donald's Furniture in the early 1960s. Vernon Presley remarked that it was the ugliest furniture he'd ever seen in his life. Elvis arranged to buy the entire collection. The "throne," as it might be called, features a wooden owl's head at the top and claws dangling from each arm. Fake greenery languishes about the room, and a small waterfall flows behind the throne. The jungle room is at once horrifying and hilarious.

—Robin Markowitz

FURTHER READING:

Eggleston, W., and M. Filler. "Elvis Presley's Graceland—An American Shrine." *House and Garden.* March 1984.

Marcus, G. *Mystery Train—Images of America in Rock 'n' Roll Music.* New York, E. P. Dutton, 1975.

Marling, K. A. *Graceland—Going Home with Elvis.* Cambridge, Harvard University Press, 1996.

Mills, C. W. "The Celebrities." *The Power Elite.* New York, Oxford University Press, 1956.

Sims, J. "At Last—The First Elvis Presley Movie." *Rolling Stone.* November 9, 1972.

The Graduate

For some the 1967 film *The Graduate* was a sex farce, for others, a generation gap comedy, and for still others, a ballad of alienation and rebellion. In the film, Benjamin Braddock (Dustin Hoffman), a recent graduate of an Eastern college, comes back to his parent's California home with no ambition, no plans, and no self-esteem. He wanders through a maze of suburban clichés and expectations looking

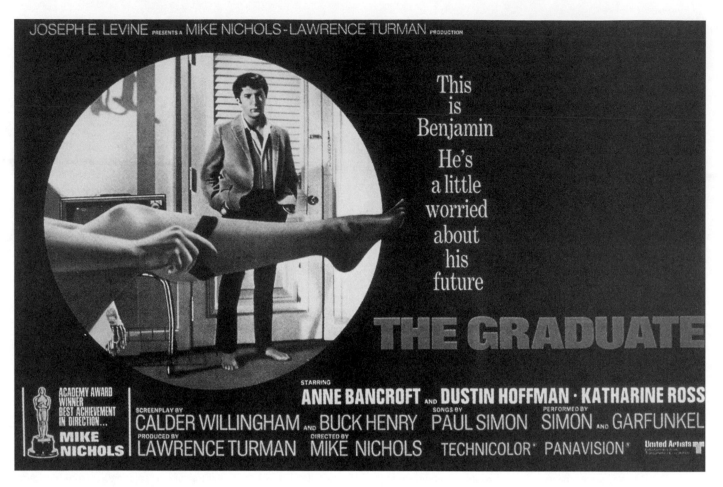

An advertising poster for the film *The Graduate*.

for something to care about, feeling like a pawn in society's chess game. Along comes Ben's father's partner's wife, Mrs. Robinson (Anne Bancroft), offering something to wake him out of his stupor—herself. Content for a while, Ben soon finds his tryst depressing; he is, after all, still aimless. His parents, trying to focus him on something, have picked the perfect girl for him, Elaine Robinson (Katherine Ross), Mrs. Robinson's daughter. Mrs. Robinson forbids the date, and Ben tries to prove Mrs. Robinson right by humiliating Elaine at a strip club, but they end up connecting, and Ben finally feels something. Mrs. Robinson tries to end the relationship by telling her daughter about the affair, but Ben has decided that only Elaine can save him. He pursues her to Berkeley, learns she's about to be married, and barges in on the wedding. Elaine leaves the altar and runs off with Ben; they hop on a passing bus and ride off together.

Happy ending? Those who wanted this to be a romantic comedy thought so. But these virtual strangers barely look at each other on the bus, the triumphant smiles fade from their faces, and they don't utter a word as the haunting beginning of the song "Sounds of Silence" rises on the soundtrack: "Hello darkness, my old friend. . . ." This late 1960s movie took a different look at the generation gap than, say, *Easy Rider.* There were no hippies or protests in this film, no talk of the Vietnam War, and no rock music; easy-listening bards Simon and Garfunkel provided the soundtrack. All of that might have kept the film from being dated, but the film still managed to tell a tale of distinctly generational woe.

The Graduate, which was directed by Mike Nichols, is filled with delightful moments: the fleeing lovers use a giant cross to lock their families in the church; an alienated Ben is decked out in scuba gear like an astronaut landing on the Planet of the Parents; a corporate wonk at his parents' party tells Ben that he should think about one word, "plastics"; a classic shot views Ben as a small, frightened man seen under the arch of Mrs. Robinson's bent leg; Ben calls his now-regular lover by the appellation "Mrs."; and perpetual landlord Norman Fell asks Ben if he's "one of those outside agitators." He's not; in fact, Ben may not even be a rebel. He seems to enjoy the products of the corporate culture he despises, like his graduation present, a new Alfa Romeo, and his parent's swimming pool. The real rebel against the status quo, at least at first, is Mrs. Robinson. Aside from depictions of prostitutes, when had a woman with such sexual authority, confidence, and cool intelligence ever been portrayed on screen? But Mrs. Robinson is transformed into a demon. She forbids Ben to see Elaine, not because she wants him to herself, but because the guy she commits adultery with is no longer good enough to date her daughter.

As an odd representative of purity, Elaine falls into a marriage with someone she's "sort of" engaged to, mostly because it's what her parents want. Doesn't she represent what Ben hates? Not to Ben. She's safe, clean, and forgiving, nothing like her mother, and in the same boat as he is. Young Ben, hating everything his parents stand for but never articulating why, gets to screw them in the person of his father's partner's wife. But ultimately, he ends up with the girl his parents picked for him, and he's still aimless. The film seems to deliberately sow confusion. When he gets off the bus, will Ben look into a future in plastics? Will the lovers live without their parents' financial help? Will they even stay together? These unanswered questions are part of the meaning of the film.

Though Hoffman had been in a few movies, Ben is the role that brought him (and director Nichols, who won an Oscar) fame. Hoffman was 30 when he played the 20-year-old Ben, and Bancroft was only 36. Robert Redford turned down the role of Ben out of fear that he wouldn't be able to convey Ben's naivete. Charles Grodin was cast in the role, but there was a salary dispute. Anne Bancroft wasn't the first choice for Mrs. Robinson, either. The role was offered to Patricia Neal, who was ill, and Doris Day, who was reportedly offended by the character.

The Graduate made the third highest box-office profit of any American film up to that time. Written by Calder Willingham with help from Buck Henry (who has a cameo as the hotel clerk), it was based on the novel by Charles Webb. Ironically, the Simon and Garfunkel song ''Mrs. Robinson'' as we know it was not on the movie's soundtrack—only an instrumental part was. After the film's successful release, Nichols persuaded Paul Simon to write an actual song with lyrics, for use as a marketing tool. It became a huge hit.

—Karen Lurie

FURTHER READING:

Macklin, F. Anthony. '''Benjamin Will Survive. . .': Interview with CharlesWebb.'' *Film Heritage.* Vol. 4, 1968, 1-6.

Webb, Charles. *The Graduate.* New York, New American Library, 1963.

Graffiti

People have been scribbling on walls as long as they have been building them. ''Graffiti''—the word comes from the Italian verb *graffiare,* ''to scratch''—covers a wide range of public inscriptions, from the early paintings on the walls of caves at Lescaux to quips hastily inked up on contemporary bathroom stalls. The late-twentieth century has seen the development of a market for graffiti as an art form, although the majority of graffiti remains unsolicited and anonymous.

Historically, graffiti has been used primarily as a form of personal communication. One of the earliest uses developed in the United States among hobos who rode the rails across the country in the first decades of the twentieth century. The complicated symbolic language of these transients was scratched in chalk on fence posts and other unobtrusive spots to communicate the receptivity of the townspeople to future travelers.

One of the most famous examples of graffiti in the twentieth century came in the image of Kilroy. James J. Kilroy, a shipyard inspector during World War II, wrote the words ''Kilroy was here'' in chalk on bulkheads to indicate that he had inspected the riveting. U.S. troops added the scribbled drawing of Kilroy leering over a wall to accompany the inscription ''Kilroy was here'' and Kilroy became an internationally known phenomenon during the 1940s and 1950s. Kilroy turned up in some very odd places; his first appearance is reputed to have been on the side of the battleship *New Yorker,* discovered by U.S. inspectors after the atomic bomb test at the Bikini atoll, but he has also appeared on top of the torch of the Statue of Liberty and under the Arc de Triomphe.

While American soldiers were spreading Kilroy across the globe, another ultimately more influential form of graffiti was developing in the United States during the 1940s. The exterior walls of

A graffiti-covered wall in Venice Beach, California.

buildings in Hispanic communities in postwar Los Angeles were increasingly decorated with a kind of marking subsequently designated as "old school." Before the advent of spray paint, these black-and-white drawings were realized entirely in marker to communicate the boundaries of neighborhoods controlled by rival gangs.

Although graffiti continued during the 1960s, it was not until the 1970s that it started attracting public attention as a serious social problem. The visibility of graffiti had steadily been increasing, as graffiti artists started using spray paint to cover larger areas more colorfully than was previously possible. One of the first graffiti artists to achieve notoriety was a tagger, or name-writer, whose signature "Taki 183" began appearing on walls in four boroughs of New York in 1971. Taki was followed by a hoard of fellow taggers, and by the mid-1970s the primary target of graffiti artists hungry for name-recognition had become the trains of the New York City subway system. Throughout the decade, the city of New York fought a battle with enterprising taggers, whose projects grew rapidly from quick signatures to elaborately stylized versions of their street names, dubbed "Wild Style," that could cover an entire subway car. Even as the transit authorities struggled to remove the colorful paintings, or "throw-ups," New York graffiti was achieving international recognition as part of a nascent hip-hop culture that included rap music and break dancing. Several films immortalize this period, including *Wild Style* (1982) and *Beat Street* (1984).

Eventually, a coating was developed that inhibited the application of spray paint onto the surfaces of trains, and in the 1980s a booming art market developed an interest in graffiti marketed as an art form. Several galleries in Manhattan began specializing in graffiti art, and former graffiti artists such as Keith Haring, who got his start doing quick marker drawings in his characteristic outline style, and Jean-Michel Basquiat became instant celebrities, with works selling for hundreds of thousands of dollars. The public fascination with graffiti faded by the end of the decade, as graffiti became increasingly associated with the activity of urban gangs.

—Deborah Broderson

FURTHER READING:

Phillips, Susan. *Wallbangin': Graffiti and Gangs in LA*. Chicago, University of Chicago Press, 1999.

Reisner, Robert. *Graffiti: Two Thousand Years of Wall Writing*. New York, Cowles Book Company, 1971.

Wiese, Markus. *New York: Graffiti 1975-1995*. Moers, Edition Aragon, 1996.

Wimsatt, William. *Bomb the Suburbs: Graffiti, Freight-Hopping, Race and the Search for Hip-Hop's Moral Center*. Chicago, Subway and Elevated Press, 1994.

Grafton, Sue (1940—)

Along with fellow writers Sara Paretsky and Marcia Muller, Sue Grafton has been credited with popularizing the mystery sub-genre of the female private eye. Although there have been female detectives almost from the beginnings of mystery fiction, in the past they were almost exclusively amateur sleuths rather than detectives for hire. The tough female private eye, written in the tradition of a Mike Hammer or a Philip Marlowe, was unheard of until the late 1970s. Women

writers of this type of mystery were also rare. Due to the growing popularity of Grafton, Paretsky, and Muller, however, other authors have begun to introduce many new female detectives. However, Grafton's Kinsey Milhone remains among the most popular.

It now seems almost inevitable that Grafton would become a mystery writer. She was born in Louisville, Kentucky, the daughter of teacher Vivian Harnsberger and attorney, C. W. Grafton, himself a mystery writer of some note who had several books published in the 1940s and 1950s. She earned her Bachelor of Arts degree from the University of Louisville in 1961 with a major in English Literature. After graduation, Grafton worked in the medical field in various capacities while pursuing her writing. She also married twice and began a family that would eventually include three children.

Grafton's initial forays into novel writing were not in the mystery realm. Her first novel, *Keziah Dane,* was published in 1967. Her second novel, *The Lolly Madonna War,* published in 1969, was made into the motion picture *Lolly-Madonna XXX* in 1973, with Grafton co-writing the screenplay. This led to her early career as a writer for television. During that time she wrote episodes for several television programs such as *Rhoda* and *Seven Brides for Seven Brothers.* Grafton was also a prolific writer of made-for-television movies, such as *Walking through Fire,* for which she won a Christopher Award; the critically acclaimed *Nurse,* which starred Michael Learned; and *Sex and the Single Parent.* With third husband and writing partner, Steven Humphrey, she adapted two Agatha Christie novels for TV—*A Caribbean Mystery* and *Sparkling Cyanide.* It was the experience of working as a writer of television and movies that later made Grafton vow that no Kinsey Milhone novel would ever be used for a motion picture.

Although she was a successful screenwriter, Grafton was determined to leave Hollywood. She planned to try her hand at a mystery novel, as her father had forty years before, and she decided her main character would be a female private detective. Grafton based Kinsey Milhone largely on herself. In 1982 she began the alphabet mystery series with *'A' is for Alibi,* for which she won an Anthony Award. She plans to continue the series through the letter Z and, at her current rate of one Milhone book a year, she should reach that goal about the same time she turns seventy years old. Grafton has won many awards since the first Milhone book, including three more Anthony Awards, a Shamus Award, and an American Mystery Award.

Sue Grafton has had an impact on television and its culture with her screenplays and television shows. However, it is with the popular Kinsey Milhone that she has continued to stretch not only the boundaries of mystery fiction, but also those of acceptable behavior for women, whether fictional or flesh and bone.

—Jill A. Gregg

FURTHER READING:

Kaufman, Natalie Hevener, and Carol McGinnis Kay. *"G" is for Grafton: The World of Kinsey Milhone.* New York, Henry Holt, 1997.

Graham, Bill (1931-1991)

Bill Graham revolutionized the music industry by providing a forum for the explosion of artistic expression in rock and roll during

Bill Graham

the 1960s. A teetotaling prime mover of the psychedelic movement, Graham used his shrewd business acumen to present music to the world, making it profitable and self-sustaining. In the process, Graham drew attention to this brilliant period of cultural revolution and focused its creative energy into a performance ethic that has become the standard for live stage presentation.

Born Wolfgang Grajonca January 8, 1931, in Berlin, Graham was the only son in a large Russian-Jewish family. He was sent away to school to escape the Hitler Youth movement, and later, when Hitler invaded Poland in 1939, Bill and his younger sister were transported to France as deportation to labor camps became inevitable. Graham developed few memories of his family, having spent his formative years surrounded by air raids and bomb shelters, and as the Nazis pushed into France in 1941, Bill was separated from his ailing sister as he fled (mostly on foot) with the other refugees. Meanwhile, all but two of his sisters were deported to the concentration camp at Auschwitz.

Like many Jewish refugees during World War II, Bill was sent to New York City. He languished in a foster home until he was adopted by Alfred and Pearl Ehrenreich in 1941, and he quickly learned English from his step-brother Roy. Though he was not a United States citizen, and was ridiculed for his heavy German accent, he became an active, integral part of his ethnic community. When World War II ended he corresponded, and later was reunited, with his surviving sisters.

In high school and in community college, Bill was a hard worker if not a stellar pupil. He worked several jobs and enjoyed the positive reinforcement of a good tip for a job well done, especially as a waiter at various resorts in the Catskills Mountains in the late 1940s. Here he also developed his passion for show business and immersed himself

in theater, film, and Latin music while rubbing elbows with pretentious, high-society vacationers and the stars they came to see. In 1950, though, Graham was drafted at the onset of the Korean War. In the army, he changed his name to Bill (the American equivalent of Wolfgang) Graham (closest to G-R-A-J in the phonebook) and served until 1953, receiving a Bronze Star for valor and—at last—United States citizenship.

Discharged and aimless, he hitchhiked across America and worked with theater troupes in New York City and San Francisco, eventually meeting his future wife Bonnie as well as finding a steady job with the San Francisco Mime Troupe, a politically aware artists' collective. It was when the group was arrested for performing in a public park without a permit that Graham discovered his true organizational calling.

In 1965 Graham arranged a benefit to raise bail money for the Mime Troupe and, seeing a business opportunity, set to work organizing larger and more elaborate community events. A strange synthesis was brewing in San Francisco. The rise of a counter-culture involved attempts at changing society. Performers did more than entertain; they also educated and informed, but too often without a legitimate venue in which to express themselves. Bill Graham filled this void by opening the Fillmore Auditorium, which quickly became the performance space for important cultural and musical events.

Charging nominal fees, Graham exposed the general public to local groups (Grateful Dead, Jefferson Airplane) as well as eclectic opening bands (Ravi Shankar, Miles Davis), claiming "vegetables before dessert" were important. He also supported performance artists, acid tests, be-ins, love-ins, and any other human social experiment in need of a decent sound system. Light shows backed up the music, and shows were advertised by local artists in psychedelic poster art. The Fillmore thus became the entertainment nexus of San Francisco counterculture.

As the 1960s wore on, and more and more initiates were "turned on" to the hippie aesthetic, Graham branched out and opened auditoriums on both coasts. He made a sizable profit from the flower power phenomenon which caused some tension between him and his more obstinate cohorts from the early days. As ticket prices increased so did the pretensions of many performers, and Bill was also often regarded as one of Them—a member of the Establishment. Yet he managed to straddle the line between exploiter and exploited, earning the trust of many musicians and artists whom he helped to foster.

Inevitably, his grassroots business went national. Bill was an integral organizer of the legendary Monterey Pop Festival, and though he only advised its organizers, he made Woodstock possible as well. Due to the widening gulf between audiences and performers in the 1970s, however, Graham closed his Fillmores and began promoting tours to properly present rock and roll to the world. In the 1980s, as behemoth sports arenas seating thousands of people became the standard venue, Bill's production company, "Bill Graham Presents," pioneered the rock concert as a social statement while his t-shirt and poster business boomed. He promoted some of the first rock concerts in Eastern Europe and organized historic benefits such as Amnesty International's Conspiracy of Hope tour and the Live Aid concert which brought famine relief to Ethiopia.

On October 25, 1991, while leaving a concert he had promoted, Bill Graham was killed in a helicopter crash. A week later, Bill Graham Presents put on a massive free concert in his honor at the Polo Field in Golden Gate Park in San Francisco, the site of many past benefit concerts Bill had organized. Though there was no announcement made regarding who would play, the crowd was estimated at nearly half a million. Many important groups to whom Bill had given their first break paid tribute to this capitalist who played no instrument, yet whose influence over music and public presentation forever changed popular culture and its interpretation by mass media. He was inducted into the Rock and Roll Hall of Fame in 1992.

—Tony Brewer

FURTHER READING:

Graham, Bill, and Robert Greenfield. *Bill Graham Presents: My Life Inside Rock and Out.* New York, Doubleday, 1992.

Graham, Billy (1918-)

Billy Graham, one of the most prominent of America's Protestant evangelists, has preached to more than 200 million people in his many crusades throughout the world, and to countless other millions through the media of radio and television. Considered one of the most successful evangelists in the history of Christianity, he is admired even by many who do not share his religious beliefs. For five decades Americans have named him to the Gallup Poll's lists of the "Ten Most Admired Men in the World." Graham has spoken intimately with many of the most powerful figures of the twentieth century, including ten American presidents, Winston Churchill, Mikhail Gorbachev, Kim Il Sung, and Pope John Paul II. Former President

Billy Graham

George Bush has called him "America's pastor," but Graham's influence is global.

When he was born on November 7, 1918, in Charlotte, North Carolina, there was nothing to suggest that William Franklin Graham, Jr., would become a world-renowned personality. His parents were God-fearing country people who reared Billy Frank and his siblings to read the Bible, pray often, and work hard on the family's dairy farm. Graham was 16 years old when Mordecai Ham, a fire-and-brimstone evangelist, came to Charlotte. Like most adolescent males, Billy Frank was more interested in cars, baseball, and girls than in anything an evangelist had to offer. Even after his confession of faith at a Ham service, visible changes in him were slight. Graham admits in his 1997 autobiography, "Although I had been converted, I did not have much of a concept of my life coming under some kind of divine plan. . . . I had no inkling of what my life work would be." He was certain, however, that undertaking and preaching could be ruled out.

Nevertheless, by 1938, Graham, who by this time had dropped the "Frank," felt that God had called him to preach. From that moment his commitment was unswerving. During his years at the Florida Bible Institute, young Graham preached in small churches, in mission services, and on street corners. Later studies at Wheaton College in Illinois gave Graham a liberal arts background and reinforced his conservative biblical interpretation. Time would mellow Graham in many respects; his staccato delivery would become more conversational, his Protestantism would become more ecumenical, his social views would become less judgmental, but he would never swerve from his allegiance to what "the Bible says."

Another significant event of his Wheaton years was his encounter with Ruth Bell, daughter of medical missionaries, who had spent her first 17 years in Asia and was planning to return as a missionary to Tibet. Instead, in 1943, she became the wife of Billy Graham. The young Grahams served briefly as pastor and wife, but Graham soon resigned his church to become a charter vice-president and the first full-time evangelist of Youth for Christ International. He covered the country, conducting YFC meetings in Atlanta, Norfolk, Indianapolis, Princeton, and dozens of other cities.

It was a fortuitous moment. Post-World War II America was a nation of seekers; church membership, sales of religious books, and enrollment at religious institutions were all on the rise. Predictably, so were evangelists. Among their number were some that were no more than confidence men and others who soon fell prey to the temptations of the flesh and the world. Graham, concerned with what he referred to as the Elmer Gantry problem, called together his associates during a Modesto, California campaign. In what came to be known as the Modesto Manifesto, team members agreed that the sponsoring committee would be asked to handle funds with no contributions passing through the hands of the Graham team. They further agreed that each would avoid situations that would place him alone with a woman not his wife. These simple but effective measures protected the Graham team from the scandals that toppled many other evangelists.

A year later California was again the setting for a Graham milestone. The young evangelist had been invited to be the featured speaker at the annual Christ for Greater Los Angeles revival. The Graham team began an operation that would in its general shape become their operating policy for the next five decades: preparatory revivals, small group-prayer meetings, area-wide choir recruitment, counselor training—nine months of preparation in all coupled with thousands of dollars worth of publicity. Despite these efforts, attendance at the services was not extraordinary. Celebrity conversions resulted in a flurry of interest, but then William Randolph Hearst gave the order that became part of Graham legend: ''Puff Graham,'' he instructed his papers. The result was media saturation that no amount of money could have purchased. Headlines in Hearst papers were followed by wire-service coverage that was followed by coverage in national newsmagazines. By the time Graham left Los Angeles, the revival had run for eight weeks, the aggregate congregation had reached into the hundreds of thousands, and Billy Graham had become a national celebrity.

A 12-week crusade in London, followed by a European tour where he preached to record crowds in Stockholm, Amsterdam, and Berlin, proved Graham's appeal was not limited to Americans. Nevertheless, his greatest triumph may have been the 1957 New York crusade where he preached to two and a half million people in services that lasted from mid-May through Labor Day. The New York Crusade was important for more than its numbers. Graham, whose critics have long faulted him for failing to use his status more aggressively for social causes, integrated his own team with the addition of Howard O. Jones, an action that led to a wave of protests from segregationists. Graham also met privately with Rev. Dr. Martin Luther King, Jr., and invited King to be a platform guest. There can be little question that Graham was uncomfortable with confrontation, and that the concept of civil disobedience troubled the evangelist whose patriotic fervor and anti-Communist rhetoric had been part of his early appeal. But Graham was convinced of the immorality of racism, and as early as 1952 had refused to hold segregated services in Jackson, Mississippi and other Southern cities. Graham's actions may have made a stronger statement to other moderates than his critics recognize.

The New York crusade was also important because for the first time a Graham crusade was broadcast on network television. Graham had already shown himself astute in utilizing media to promulgate his message. *The Hour of Power* radio broadcasts reached millions, as did his syndicated newspaper column ''My Answer.'' The Billy Graham Evangelistic Association would go on to use film, video, and the Internet to reach target audiences, but perhaps no other avenue did so much to make Graham known and admired by most Americans as did the intimate medium of television which brought his crusades into the living rooms of Americans of all creeds, classes, and colors. By the late 1990s the audience for Graham's televised crusades reached 60 million annually.

The 50 years after the New York crusade saw Graham preach in hundreds of countries across the face of the globe. He organized crusades in the former Eastern bloc nations, the People's Republic of China, and, in 1973, one in South Korea where he addressed 1.2 million people, the largest public religious gathering in history. He also served as an unofficial spiritual adviser to President Richard M. Nixon during the Watergate crisis. Thus, Graham had literally taken his message ''unto all the world.''

His audiences may be worldwide, but Billy Graham remains a peculiarly American figure. His rise from North Carolina farm boy to become the companion of presidents; his curious mix of religion, politics, and celebrity; his eagerness to be liked; his simple faith; his paradoxical blend of ego and humility are all elements of the American psyche. Graham has been presented with the Presidential Medal of Freedom, the Congressional Gold Medal, and a star on Hollywood Boulevard. But Graham answers reporters' queries about how he wishes to be remembered with the single word ''integrity,'' a word that means not only honesty but also completeness, a lack of division. At the end of his autobiography, Graham regrets lost time with his family, lost opportunities for study, and foolish slips into partisan politics. The one thing for which he has no vestige of regret is his ''commitment many years ago to accept God's calling to serve Him as an evangelist of the Gospel of Christ.''

—Wylene Rholetter

FURTHER READING:

Aikman, David. *Great Souls.* New York, Word, 1998.

Frady, Marshall. *Billy Graham: A Parable of American Righteousness.* Boston, Little, Brown, 1979.

Graham, Billy. *Just As I Am: The Autobiography of Billy Graham.* New York, HarperCollins, 1997.

Martin, William. *A Prophet with Honor: The Billy Graham Story.* New York, William Morrow, 1991.

Graham, Martha (1894-1991)

The greatest and most influential choreographer of modern dance, Graham built on the foundations created by American pioneers like Isadora Duncan, Ruth St. Denis, Ted Shawn, and Doris Humphrey. She created and codified a dance language that stressed the downward pull of gravity and balance—and, along with it she identified a series of gestures and movements to express particular emotions in dance. Early in her career she explored American experience in such works as *Steps in the Streets* (1936) about homelessness, *El Pentitente* (1940) about a religious cult in the Southwest, and a Shaker wedding in *Appalachian Spring* (1944). Later, Graham explored the spiritual and psychological meaning of classical myths like, for example, the myth of Oedipus in *Night Journey* (1944) and *Clytemnestra* (1958). She began dancing in 1916

Martha Graham

and retired as a dancer in 1970, although she continued to choreograph for her company until her death at 96.

—Jeffrey Escoffier

FURTHER READING:

de Mille, Agnes. *The Life and Work of Martha Graham.* New York, Random House Vintage Books, 1991.

Grandmaster Flash (1958—)

Grandmaster Flash (Joseph Saddler) was a hip-hop pioneer. Using his skills as an electronic engineer he perfected the art of punch phasing and mixing by constructing the first twin-deck turntable using a mixer, headphones, and a monitor switch. Flash polished his technique on the "wheels of steel" and took the art of "scratching" to a new level. He has been imitated by rap deejays ever since. His quick mixing and scratching skills can be heard on his *The Adventures of Grandmaster Flash and the Wheels of Steel,* which was the first rap record to use samples. Flash began to add snippets of rhyme and boasting to his deejaying and soon formed The Furious Five, who did the rapping for him. Together they released the seminal track "The Message" (1982), a vivid portrayal of the underside of the American Dream in New York's urban ghettos. Flash's early experimenting with the new hip-hop genre helped to bring it out of abandoned buildings in the South Bronx and into the homes of millions worldwide.

—Nathan Abrams

FURTHER READING:

Fernando, S. H., Jr. *The New Beats: Exploring the Music Culture and Attitudes of Hip-Hop.* Edinburgh, Payback Press, 1995.

Larkin, Colin, editor. *The Guinness Who's Who of Rap, Dance and Techno.* London, Guinness Publishing, 1994.

Toop, David. *Rap Attack 2: African Rap to Global Hip-Hop.* London, Serpent's Tail, 1991.

Grand Ole Opry

The longest-running radio show in broadcasting history, the *Grand Ole Opry* has long been the symbolic center of country music. It represents the pinnacle of success for performing artists, for whom the *Grand Ole Opry* is the country music equivalent of playing Carnegie Hall. The *Opry* is, however, much more than simply a prestige performance venue. Since its inception in 1925, it has brought country music to listeners all across the United States, helping to transform the genre from a regional musical form to a national one. For its rural listeners, spread out across the vast stretches of open space, the *Opry* became part of the common bond that united rural folk across the country, not only providing musical entertainment, but also creating a cultural home for its many thousands of rural listeners.

In the early 1920s, radio was still a new means of communication. As its commercial potential grew, certain radio stations began to broadcast programs with special appeal to rural listeners. In 1925, George D. Hay, formerly an announcer at WLS in Chicago, which featured a country music program called *The National Barn Dance,* took a job as station director at the new WSM radio station in Nashville, Tennessee. Hay's first program was the WSM *Barn Dance,* a copy of the WLS show in Chicago which featured just two performers, 77-year old fiddle player Uncle Jimmy Thompson and his niece, pianist Eva Thompson Jones. The hour-long show consisted of nothing more than fiddle tunes with piano accompaniment, but the show drew such a favorable response that the format was continued for several weeks. Soon, however, the roster and the repertoire broadened, as other local musicians, including banjo and guitar players, came to perform on the show. Most were amateurs and none were paid. The image of *Barn Dance* as a rural program was important, and Hay made sure his performers kept things "down to earth."

The show's success continued, and in 1927 George D. Hay changed the name of the show to the *Grand Ole Opry.* The name "Opry" was an intentional jibe at the world of classical music, often perceived as pretentious, and the *Grand Ole Opry* followed NBC's national *Musical Appreciation Hour,* a show devoted to classical music and opera. Hay announced one evening that although listeners had spent the last hour hearing grand opera, he would now present what he called the "Grand Ole Opry." The name proved popular, and it became the official name of the show that year. Hay, who called himself the "Solemn Old Judge," opened the show every Saturday night with the words "Let her go, boys." And off they went. Among the early popular favorites were banjo player and singer Uncle Dave Macon, African-American harmonica player Deford Bailey (the only African-American performer until Charley Pride in the mid-1960s), and Dr. Humphrey Bate, who hosted one of the many string bands featured on the early *Opry.* As the show grew in popularity, the station's power grew as well. By the early 1930s, the station's signal could reach 30 states and parts of Canada.

In the 1930s, the emphasis of the *Grand Ole Opry* shifted away from its rough rural edge and moved more in the direction of modern country music. The *Opry* had proved that country music had a wide appeal, and the potential of that appeal to turn profits for country musicians and for the corporate sponsors of radio programs like the *Opry,* moved the show in a new direction—toward the creation and marketing of country music "stars." In 1928, Harry Stone joined WSM as an announcer and quickly assumed supervisory duties, replacing George Hay who was relegated to announcing duties on the *Grand Ole Opry.* With his brother David Stone, and stage manager Vito Pellettieri, Harry Stone furthered the commercial potential of the *Opry.* In 1934 Pellettieri began dividing the show into sponsored segments as a way of increasing revenue. Commercial sponsorship of the *Grand Ole Opry* was still very inexpensive in the mid-1930s; a 15-minute segment cost a sponsor only $100. Promoting new star talent, however, was where the real money could be made. Stone moved the *Opry* away from the amateur string band sound favored during the 1920s, and began promoting new individual stars such as singer Roy Acuff. Stone also managed WSM's Artist Service, which booked *Opry* stars for personal appearances within the territory reached by WSM's radio signal. Stone used the *Opry* as an avenue to promote individual stars, whose personal appearances could make good money, of which the *Opry* got a cut as manager. Performers were paid very little for their appearances on the show, but the exposure was invaluable in providing opportunities for stardom, while ensuring that the artists made a living from concert appearances.

This star system, very much akin to the system used to promote Hollywood movie stars at the time, brought new talent to the *Opry* in the 1930s and 1940s. Notable among them were the Delmore Brothers, Eddy Arnold, Hank Snow, Pee Wee King, Ernest Tubb, Minnie Pearl, Bill Monroe, and others, all of whom were among the biggest names in country music. The biggest newcomer to the *Opry* in the 1930s was Roy Acuff, who joined it in 1938. Acuff had worked earlier in his life as a musician with a traveling medicine show. He recorded his first songs in 1936, and had an early hit with "The Great Speckled Bird." With his band the Tennessee Crackerjacks (later renamed the Crazy Tennesseans and, later still, the Smoky Mountain Boys), Acuff soon became the leading performer on the *Grand Ole Opry*. At a time when cowboy music was sweeping country music, Acuff managed to prosper under the *Opry*'s new star system, while still keeping close ties to his own southern rural roots, which he had in common with his listeners. Those rural roots were also kept alive by the emerging bluegrass sound of Bill Monroe and his Bluegrass Boys, who were developing a new, hard-driving, string-band sound that combined virtuoso musicianship with close harmony vocals. Among the *Opry*'s biggest female stars in the 1940s and beyond was Minnie Pearl, one of country music's greatest comediennes, known for her flower hats with the price tag attached, her high-pitched "Howdeee!" greeting, and her routines that lovingly chronicled rural life. In the late 1940s, one of country music's biggest stars, Hank Williams, became an *Opry* regular, thrilling audiences with his honky-tonk sound until his unreliable appearance schedule led to his dismissal in 1952, followed shortly thereafter by his death in 1953.

The *Opry* continued to grow during these years, playing to a continually expanding audience. In October 1939, the *Opry* went national when a half-hour of the show was featured on NBC's national Saturday night line-up. This was known as the *Prince Albert Show,* sponsored by Prince Albert Tobacco. The *Opry* was also the subject of a motion picture in 1940, called simply *Grand Ole Opry,* and featuring Uncle Dave Macon, Roy Acuff, George Hay, and others. In 1943, the show moved its location to Nashville's historic Ryman Auditorium in order to accommodate the increased demand among fans to attend the live performances. In 1948, the *Opry* expanded to include a spin-off show on Friday nights on WSM called *Friday Night Frolics.*

During the 1950s, the *Opry*'s sound moved further and further away from its rural origins. New *Opry* managers Jim Denny and Jack Stapp attempted to modernize the show, and although old-timers like Roy Acuff, Bill Monroe, and Hank Snow still made appearances, often hosting their own segments, the *Opry* continued to use its star system approach, promoting younger stars to add to the roster of older, established stars. The *Opry* in the 1950s remained a crucial stepping stone for country talent, hosting such emerging stars as George Jones, Johnny Cash, Webb Pierce, Stonewall Jackson, Little Jimmy Dickens, Porter Wagoner, and others. These trends continued in the 1960s, a decade that saw the emergence of Loretta Lynn, Jim Reeves, Patsy Cline, and Dolly Parton.

By the late 1960s, however, even though the *Grand Ole Opry* remained a prestige performance venue for country musicians, it no longer had the same star-making power. This was a reflection of the declining influence of Nashville, brought about by the realization that it was not the nation's sole preserve of country music. In the 1960s, California country artists such as Buck Owens and Merle Haggard had demonstrated that country music talent could come from anywhere, and often with a more authentic sound than the more commercial country-pop Nashville had been offering since the late 1950s.

Other factors also reduced the *Opry*'s influence. It refused to acknowledge the growing popularity of rockabilly and rock 'n' roll music in the 1950s, both of which had country influences, and as a result the show lost a portion of its younger audience. Also, early in the 1960s, the *Opry* lost two major stars with the deaths of Patsy Cline and Jim Reeves. Matters were not made any easier by the fact that the *Opry* paid its performers poorly. Contracts with musicians stipulated a certain number of appearances each year, but the high number of appearances at union scale wages made touring for some of the stars difficult. Consequently, staying close to Nashville in order to fulfill their contractual obligations cut into their income potential from concert performances.

In the 1970s, 1980s, and 1990s, the *Opry* largely redefined itself as a repository for country music's historic traditions. The show moved out of the Ryman Auditorium in 1974 and into more modern and spacious accommodations in the new Opryland amusement park outside Nashville. There, it continued to draw huge crowds each week, an indication that many were hungry for a taste of this country past. By the end of the 1990s, the *Opry* was still a prestige venue for both established and up-and-coming stars. The relaxation of contractual obligations, put in place by *Opry* manager Hal Durham during the 1970s and 1980s, allowed such younger stars as Clint Black, Reba McEntire, Vince Gill, Alan Jackson, Alison Krauss, and Garth Brooks, among others, to make occasional appearances on the show without cutting too heavily into their concert schedules. Despite the rarity of appearances by country stars of this stature, and the fact that the Opry has become home more regularly to older or lesser stars who are no longer making hit records, the *Grand Ole Opry* remains one of the greatest of country music traditions. Most importantly, it has preserved the old-time radio show format that began entertaining country music audiences back in the 1920s.

—Timothy Berg

FURTHER READING:

Hagan, Chet. *Grand Ole Opry.* New York, Owl Books, 1989.

Malone, Bill C. *Country Music U.S.A.: A Fifty Year History.* Austin American Folklore Society, University of Texas Press, 1968.

Stambler, Irwin, and Grelun Landon. *Country Music: The Encyclopedia.* New York, St. Martin's Press, 1997.

Grant, Amy (1960—)

Bringing a flamboyant and youthful sound to what had generally been considered a stiff and formal musical field, Amy Grant changed the face of Christian music. When Grant emerged on the Christian music scene in the 1980s, four categories existed: classical, traditional, gospel, and Jesus rock. Seeing the need for the expression of personal feelings, Grant developed her unique style, which made the old form of Jesus rock acceptable to a greater audience. The Christian message reached a mainstream following of teenagers, college students, and twenty-somethings, through Grant's use of a rock beat. Contemporary Christian music finally had a young, visible face with a vibrant sound.

Born in Augusta, Georgia, on November 25, 1960, Amy Lee Grant moved to Nashville, Tennessee, as an infant. Religion played an important role in her family life, with her strong belief being

Amy Grant

reflected in the songs that she wrote as a teenager. Reflecting what were sometimes intensely personal feelings, her songs served as an outlet through which Grant expressed her thoughts.

Amy Grant's career was launched when Chris Christian played a tape, which Grant had made for her parents, for the Christian music company, Word. Word and the Myrrh label offered the teenage Grant a recording contract, allowing her to present her first album to the Christian market at age 16. The eponymous work, *Amy Grant,* was recorded in Christian's home basement studio. Beginning with this album's release, a gradual change in religious music took place, bringing Jesus rock into a new era. Grant gave contemporary Christian music a revitalized image.

Through her high school and college years, Grant continued to record and perform. Her life revolved around family, church, school, and friends. With each new album, her audience grew, as did her appeal. People began to accept her style, unique sound, and the fresh messages found in the lyrics of her songs. Grant also branched out to record works written by others, most notably her future husband, Gary Chapman (''Father's Eyes''), and a young man, Michael W. Smith (''Thy Word''), who served as her co-writer and eventually followed her into the contemporary Christian field. Grant's popularity continued to increase, as did her honors, awards, and media recognition. Winning numerous Grammys and GMA Dove Awards, her albums have received gold and platinum awards from the music industry.

While Grant's earlier recordings include deeply religious works such as ''El Shaddai'' (1982) and ''Thy Word'' (1984), her music began to change with the release of the album, *Unguarded* (1986).

This album created controversy especially the song, ''Find a Way.'' The video for this particular number caused Christian traditionalists concern because of the lack of references to God both in lyrics and imagery. That same year, Grant recorded ''Next Time I Fall'' with Peter Cetera, which raised more questions about the type of music she was choosing to record.

In spite of these concerns in the Christian community, Grant's popularity continued to grow. She countered the worries on the Christian music front with the album *Lead Me On* in 1988. In 1991, A & M Music, in conjunction with Word, released Grant's first pop collection *Heart in Motion,* in both the Christian and secular markets. With songs like ''Baby, Baby,'' which Grant wrote for her infant daughter, her music reached the Top 40 echelon and her songs became standards. Her critics, however, found the song too sexual in content for a Christian singer. While the album was not overtly religious, the music still carried messages of hope, love, and family. In 1994, Grant released *House of Love,* which combined secular and Christian music with powerful messages regarding all varieties of love—including God's love. Her 1997 album, *Behind the Eyes,* returned Grant to her musical roots as a solo performer using acoustical guitar accompaniment with thought provoking but not necessarily Christian lyrics.

Grant's tours have played to diverse audiences. In the beginning of her career, she performed as a solo act on a bare stage. By 1981, Grant had added a live band and a new performing image. She exhibited dance movements on stage that were more common to rock performers than to Christian singers. Not afraid to let her emotions show, Grant expressed her feelings through both facial expressions and heartfelt pleadings. This exuberance led to a steady increase in young adults attending her concerts, which in turn increased the exposure of a growing contemporary Christian music field. Grant's performance at the Grammy Awards in 1985 gave contemporary Christian music an unprecedented exposure during a primetime live network broadcast, at a time when the musical form needed exposure to the masses. She served as a pioneer in the field, thus opening the door for a wider range of contemporary Christian artists, including the pop stylings of Michael W. Smith, the hard rock sound of Petra, and rap by DC Talk.

—Linda Ann Martindale

FURTHER READING:

Long, Jim and Michael Long. ''Amy Grant: Another New Beginning.'' *Campus Life.* July/August, 1994, 17-22.

Millard, Bob. *Amy Grant.* Garden City, New York, Dolphin/ Doubleday, 1986.

Grant, Cary (1904-1986)

A top box-office draw from the 1930s through the 1960s, movie star Cary Grant personified the ideal attributes of the ''leading man'' during the golden age of Hollywood. Darkly handsome, with that trademark cleft chin, elegantly attired whether in dinner clothes or soldier's uniform, meeting every challenge with self-deprecating savoir-faire, ready with witty banter or eloquent gesture and possessing a flair for comic timing second to none, Grant was adored by women and admired by men for three decades. Though he occasionally veered from his popular image by attempting more serious roles,

Cary Grant

Cary Grant's forte was light, romantic comedy. He brought to his films a buoyant charm and an effortless improvisational quality that belied the hard work spent making it look so easy. He was Fred Astaire minus the music and plus the chiseled good looks.

The persona the world came to know as "Cary Grant" was the carefully crafted creation of Alexander Archibald Leach, born in Bristol, England, in 1904. As a teenager, Leach forsook an unpromising existence in Bristol for the uncertainties of a theatrical career, joining Bob Pender's theatrical troupe in vaudeville performances throughout England. Pender's Troupe eventually played America, and young Archie went with it. After deciding to settle in the United States, Leach occasionally found vaudeville work, but just as often found hard times. Once in 1922, he earned his keep as a Coney Island stiltwalker. By the late 1920s, Archie's perseverance was finally paying off in leading roles on Broadway. His first film appearance, as a sailor in *Singapore Sue,* a musical short shot at New York's Astoria Studio, led to a contract with Paramount in Hollywood, where he began acting under his new moniker, Cary Grant.

Grant's earliest film roles reveal that he had already developed his "Cary Grant voice," with its unique inflection of Americanized Cockney, impossible to place geographically and therefore concealing his humble origins. But the process of becoming Cary Grant was a slow one, evolving from film to film. "I guess to a certain extent I did eventually become the characters I was playing," Grant once confessed. "I played at being someone I wanted to be until I became that person. Or he became me." At first, nothing more was required of Grant than that he be the stalwart leading man, though he soon displayed hints of the charm to come in his badinage with Mae West in *She Done Him Wrong* and *I'm No Angel,* (both 1933). Under George Cukor's direction, Grant began to loosen up and find himself, portraying a Cockney con-man opposite Katharine Hepburn in *Sylvia Scarlett* (1936). Playing a devil-may-care ghost in 1937's *Topper* seems to have freed Grant still further. That same year's *The Awful Truth* featured Grant's first full-out comedy star-turn. Leo McCarey's direction encouraged improvisation, and the interplay between Grant and Irene Dunne delighted audiences. This hit was immediately followed by Howard Hawks's *Bringing Up Baby,* again co-starring Katharine Hepburn. It was a box-office disappointment but is now recognized as one of the archetypal classics of screwball comedy.

Once he had hit his stride, Grant moved from strength to strength as one of the first big stars to become an independent agent and shop his wares at different studios, thus enabling him to have his pick of the best scripts, directors, and co-stars. Grant proved he could shift suavely from the knockabout Kipling adventure of *Gunga Din* (1939) to the sophisticated romance of *The Philadelphia Story* (1940). Alfred Hitchcock was the first director to take advantage of a certain dark undercurrent in Grant by casting him as a murder suspect in *Suspicion* (1941), though the studio insisted the story be re-written to exonerate Grant's character at the fade-out. Hitchcock and Grant would team memorably thrice more, with *Notorious* (1946), *To Catch a Thief* (1955), and *North by Northwest* (1959). Highlights of Grant's romantic-comedy filmography include *His Girl Friday* (1940, with Rosalind Russell), *The Bachelor and the Bobby-Soxer* (1947, Shirley Temple and Myrna Loy), and *That Touch of Mink* (1962, Doris Day). Grant's career as a top box-office draw was a long one, sustained partly by his shrewd emphasis on the light romantic fare his public seemed most to favor—although there were occasions when Grant attempted a "stretch," as with "Ernie Mott," the impoverished Cockney he played in Clifford Odets' *None but the Lonely Heart* (1944).

In many ways, Ernie Mott was the man Archie Leach might have become had he never left Bristol. An important element of *Lonely Heart* was Ernie's relationship with his mother, played by Ethel Barrymore. Archie's own mother had strangely disappeared for a time when he was a boy, and the adult Cary Grant's relations with women were not as effortless in life as they were on the screen; he was married five times and divorced four. Grant's search for meaning in his life at one point led him to participate in early clinical experiments with LSD, which he claimed were beneficial. Still handsome in his sixties, but growing uncomfortable at playing love scenes with younger actresses, Grant retired from the screen after playing his first character lead in *Walk, Don't Run* in 1966. Film offers kept coming his way, but Grant was content to pursue other business interests and, more importantly, spend time with his daughter Jennifer, the product of his marriage to wife number four, actress Dyan Cannon. In 1986, while on a speaking engagement in Davenport, Iowa, with his wife Barbara Harris, Grant suffered a fatal stroke.

Much though he doted on his real-life role as father, Grant's image in the public mind would always be the dashing chap in the tuxedo who was never at a loss for the right words to charm Grace Kelly or Audrey Hepburn. Thanks to such 1990s films as *Sleepless in Seattle,* Grant's 1957 *An Affair to Remember* remains evergreen in the popular consciousness as the epitome of movie romance. Cary Grant never fully abandoned Archie Leach, and Grant has also come to symbolize the power of creating one's own persona, thus giving a world of Archie Leaches hope for the fulfillment of their own dreams. Once, when told that every man would like to be Cary Grant, the actor replied, "So would I."

—Preston Neal Jones

FURTHER READING:

Deschner, Donald. *The Films of Cary Grant.* Secaucus, Citadel Press, 1973.

Donaldson, Maureen and William Royce. *My Life with Cary Grant.* New York, G. P. Putnam's Sons, 1989.

Harris, Warren G. *Cary Grant: A Touch of Elegance.* New York, Doubleday, 1987.

McCann, Graham. *Cary Grant: A Class Apart.* New York, Columbia University Press, 1996.

Nelson, Nancy. *Evenings with Cary Grant.* New York, William Morrow and Co., 1991.

Peary, Danny, editor. *Close-Ups: The Movie Star Book.* New York, Simon and Schuster, 1978.

Wansell, Geoffrey. *Haunted Idol: The Story of the Real Cary Grant.* New York, William Morrow and Co., 1983.

The Grapes of Wrath

Written by John Steinbeck and published in 1939, *The Grapes of Wrath* describes the Depression era journey of the fictional Joad family from the Dust Bowl of Oklahoma to the agricultural fields of California. A film version of the novel, directed by John Ford and starring Henry Fonda, followed in 1940. Together with evocative photographs by Dorothea Lange, the novel and film focused national attention on the plight of migrant farm workers in California and earned Steinbeck the Pulitzer Prize in fiction in 1940.

The novel recounts the westward journey of the Joads, a three-generation Oklahoma family pushed off their land through a combination of dust storms and foreclosures. Eldest son Tom returns home from the state penitentiary to find the family preparing to head to California in the hopes of obtaining work and eventually a farm of their own. Tom, along with parents, grandparents, an uncle, siblings, and a brother-in-law, are joined in their trek by Jim Casy, an ex-preacher looking to fill the void left by his loss of "the Holy sperit." After leaving Oklahoma, they discover that California is not the land of milk and honey where they can become independent farmers, but rather it is a cold, harsh, uninviting environment, in both the towns and the countryside. Through their journey, Tom and Casy learn about the exploitative practices of landowners and the avenues open to farm laborers to challenge the power of the farm owners. Ma Joad learns, over the course of the novel, that her responsibilities extend beyond the limits of the "fambly" to "the people." She learns the importance of solidarity in regaining and maintaining human dignity, just as Tom learns the value of solidarity in gaining respect in labor. This message is reinforced in the novel's final scene, in which Tom's sister, Rosasharn (Rose-of-Sharon), having just given birth to a stillborn child, gives her maternal breast to a dying man. By the end of the novel, the Joad family has grown to include the family of man.

The Grapes of Wrath is a prime example of the proletarian novel that was popular during the Great Depression in which ordinary working class families (especially agricultural workers) became the focus. Steinbeck strongly believed in the power of literature to bring about change in society through education and example. By exposing the corrupt ways of agribusiness and the benefits of government intervention into the agricultural economy, Steinbeck sought to bring about the creation of a farm labor proletariat. The novel ignited an explosion of controversy over the problems of migrant labor. Accusations about the novel's accuracy led to debates such as the 1940 radio broadcast of "America's Town Meeting of the Air," which addressed the issue "What should America do for the Joads?" Criticisms about the representations of California growers and Oklahoma natives resulted in bans on the book in communities across the nation and most publicly in Kern County, California, a heavily agricultural region of the state.

Stylistically, the novel also recalls the documentary movement of the 1930s in its use of interchapters which depart from the narrative of the Joad family and describe phenomena representative of the migrant population as a whole. The interchapters authenticate the narrative by placing the plight of the Joads within the larger context of Dust Bowl migrants, the agricultural economy, and the American proletariat. Steinbeck portrayed the "Okie" migrants as uneducated, unsophisticated, earthy, and decent folk whose humanity provided a counterpoint to the inhumanity of industrial/agribusiness exploitation. Much like the photography of Margaret Bourke-White, Dorothea Lange, and Walker Evans; and documentary books like Bourke-White and Erskine Caldwell's *You Have Seen Their Faces* (1937), Lange and Paul Taylor's *An American Exodus: A Record of Human Erosion* (1939), and Evans and James Agee's *Let Us Now Praise Famous Men* (1941), *The Grapes of Wrath* sought to improve society through the presentation of information in a highly emotionally charged narrative.

Upon publication, Daryl Zanuck of Twentieth Century-Fox studios acquired the rights to the novel and set screenwriter Nunnally

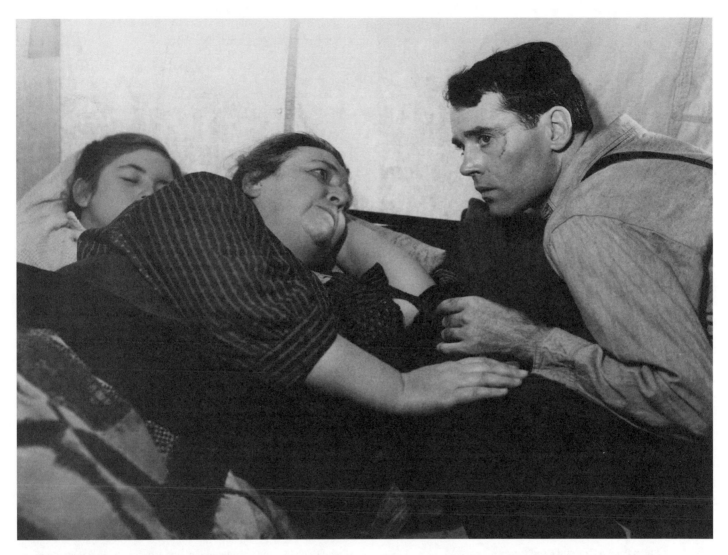

Henry Fonda (right) at the bedside of Shirley Mill (left) and Jane Darwell in a scene from the film *The Grapes of Wrath*.

Johnson to the task of adapting Steinbeck's prose into a screenplay. Production proceeded under tight security conditions as controversy over the novel mounted. Renowned western director John Ford gathered together a cast of actors including Henry Fonda (Tom Joad), Jane Darnwell (Ma Joad), and John Carradine (Preacher Casy). The film's look, through the stark cinematography of Greg Toland, recalls the documentary vision of government photographers like Russell Lee, Arthur Rothstein, and Dorothea Lange. While more optimistic in tone than the novel, the film presents a bleak look at the conditions of migrant farm workers during the Great Depression. John Ford received the Academy Award for Best Director for *The Grapes of Wrath*.

—Charles J. Shindo

FURTHER READING:

Benson, Jackson J. "'To Tom Who Lived It': John Steinbeck and the Man from Weedpatch." *Journal of Modern Literature*. Vol. 5, April 1976, 151-224.

French, Warren. *Filmguide to "The Grapes of Wrath."* Bloomington, Indiana University Press, 1973.

French, Warren, ed. *A Companion to "The Grapes of Wrath."* New York, Penguin, 1963.

Millichap, Joseph. *Steinbeck and Film*. New York, Frederick Unger, 1983.

Steinbeck, John. *Working Days: The Journals of "The Grapes of Wrath."* Edited by Robert DeMott. New York, Viking, 1989.

Wyatt, David, ed. *New Essays on "The Grapes of Wrath."* New York, Cambridge University Press, 1990.

The Grateful Dead

The Grateful Dead, with its notorious founding member Jerry Garcia, was a band that epitomized the psychedelic era of American rock 'n' roll music from the 1960s to the 1990s. Even after Garcia's death in 1995, members of the band continued to tour, in part to satisfy the yearnings of the most dedicated group of fans ever to bind themselves to a musical group, the so-called Dead Heads.

A backstage pass from a Grateful Dead concert.

the early 1960s by artists such as Bob Dylan and Joan Baez. The Dead continued to play folk classics like ''Peggy-O,'' ''Jack-a-Roe,'' and ''Staggerlee'' until the end. The grounding of the Grateful Dead in the American folk tradition contradicts its image as a corrupt purveyor of hallucinatory drugs, but their roots can also be traced to free-spirited Ken Kesey's Merry Pranksters and Beat figures like Neal Cassady. Jerry Garcia acknowledged this very explicitly in a 1991 interview with *Rolling Stone*: ''I owe a lot of who I am and what I've been and what I've done to the beatniks of the Fifties and to the poetry and art and music that I've come into contact with. I feel like I'm part of a continuous line of a certain thing in American culture. . . .'' Like the Beats, the hippies and their house band the Grateful Dead continued the rebellion against the conformist 1950s and the middle class culture that had by and large given birth to them.

Some of the Grateful Dead's first concerts were known as the Acid Tests of the San Francisco Bay area where psychedelic music, visuals, and hippies all came together as harbingers of the raves of the 1990s and the Dead's concerts between the 1970s and the 1990s. They spawned bands like Phish, which recreated the Dead's spontaneity in improvisation, and in its nomadic fans and epic tours that extended across America and sometimes Europe.

The Grateful Dead cult started after a call to fans, ''Dead Freaks Unite—Who Are You? Where Are You?'' was published in the 1971 album *Grateful Dead* (also known as *Skull and Roses*). The Dead fans who answered received concert updates and news that would eventually result in the band's formation of Grateful Dead Ticket Sales, which successfully bypassed music company and corporate control by selling up to half the tickets to concert venues by mail. From 1973 to 1976 the band also had its own recording company, Round Records/Grateful Dead Records. However, this collective thumbing of noses at the recording industry came at a price, costing them the respect of critics who saw the band as an aberration and a throwback.

There was another downside to the burgeoning Grateful Dead industry. In his last few years Garcia occasionally wearily commented on the fact that a whole group of people—not just the traveling circus of Dead Heads and unauthorized vendors, but the Grateful Dead ticketing and merchandising industry controlled by the band— were dependent on the Dead. Ironically, as the Dead found more popular success after issuing *In the Dark* (1987), problems abounded with unruly fans who crashed the concert gates and participated in uncontrolled vending, sometimes even of controlled substances.

The Grateful Dead's cult following was almost religious in its intensity. Dead Heads, as they were known, showed their loyalty (or perhaps obsession) by watching *Dead-TV,* a television cable program that first aired in 1988; hitting Grateful Dead-related computer online groups like Dead-Flames, DeadBase, and Dead.net; reading Dead theme magazines like *Relix* and *Golden Road* and the compendium of Dead statistics known as *DeadBase*; tuning into the nationally broadcast Grateful Dead radio hour, aired weekly from the San Francisco Bay Area's KFOG radio station by long-time fan and Dead historian David Gans; buying the recordings that continued to be issued even after Garcia's death from the band's own master sound board tapes of concerts in the ''Dick's Picks'' series; and trading the ''bootleg'' tapes of Dead concerts recorded by fans almost from the beginning, a practice the band in the end condoned. Garcia didn't make the mistake John Lennon made of comparing his band's popularity to that of Jesus Christ, but he did remark on the ritualistic nature of its concerts in *Rock and Roll: An Unruly History:* ''For some people, taking LSD and going to a Dead show functions like a rite of passage. . . . Each person deals with the experience individually; it's an adventure that

Garcia and friends Bob Weir, Ron ''Pigpen'' McKernan, Bill Kreutzmann, and Phil Lesh formed the band in the San Francisco Bay Area in 1965 after various incarnations as a blues and bluegrass influenced jug band (Mother McCree's Uptown Jug Champions) and a blues/rock ensemble (The Warlocks). The various members, especially keyboard players, who were to come and go, included Tom Constanten, Donna and Keith Godchaux, Brent Mydland, Bruce Hornsby, and Vince Welnick. Mickey Hart joined the band shortly after its inception, complementing Kreutzmann as a second drummer, left for a while after his father ripped off the band, and later rejoined them. Pigpen died and the band kept on playing, but with the death of Jerry Garcia the remaining members finally disbanded. They kept playing in their various individual bands, however, and in a combined band called The Other Ones, which approximated the Grateful Dead and continued the Dead's summer tour tradition.

According to Garcia, he found the name ''Grateful Dead'' by randomly opening a book and coming upon a dictionary entry describing the legend of those who, returned from the dead, reward a living person who had unwittingly aided them. The folk derivation of the name was fitting, since it summed up the roots of the founding members in the bluegrass, blues, and folk music that was performed in you can have that is personalized. But when people come together, this singular experience is ritualized. I think the Grateful Dead serves a desire for meaningful ritual, but it's *ritual without dogma.*''

Also unlike the Beatles, fans were allowed this great road adventure because the band preferred making its money by touring (or perhaps was forced to tour because of the lack of conventional success) rather than by recording studio albums. Garcia explained in an interview published in *Rock Lives,* ''Mostly we're always on the road, because we earn our living by playing. So we haven't had much of the luxury where you just go into the studio for no particular reason to screw around.'' At the time of Garcia's death, the band was in its 30th year.

In a 1989 *Rolling Stone* interview, Jerry Garcia talked about the last adventure in America that touring with the band allowed. Asked why the fans kept coming back, he answered:

> They get something. It's their version of the Acid Test, so to speak. It's kind of like the war-stories metaphor. Drug stories *are* war stories, and the Grateful Dead stories are their drug stories, or war stories. It's an adventure you can still have in America, just like Neal [Cassady] on the road. You can't hop the freights any more, but you can chase the Grateful Dead around. . . . You can have something that lasts throughout your life as adventures, the times you took chances. I think that's essential in anybody's life, and it's harder and harder to do in America. If I were providing some margin of that possibility, then that's great. That's a nice thing to do.

Though Garcia was certainly the charismatic spokesman for the band in its later years, early on Pigpen was the draw for the band. The son of a San Francisco Bay area disc jockey, Ron McKernan was steeped in the blues, playing organ and harmonica, and singing in a harsh, anguished voice perfect for the medium. It was Pigpen who largely set the tone of albums like *Workingman's Dead* and *American Beauty,* classic Dead recordings. It wasn't until 1970 with *Live/Dead* and *Workingsman's Dead* that the band's records really began attracting a sizable number of fans outside of the San Francisco Bay area, and the band toured extensively. Pigpen sang many of the tunes that characterized the Dead at that time, and some which they kept playing until the end—covers such as ''Good Morning Little School Girl,'' ''Viola Lee Blues,'' ''In the Midnight Hour,'' ''Beat It On Down the Line,'' and ''Cold Rain and Snow.'' His death at 27 in 1973 from liver damage was a serious blow, although before his death his absence from gigs due to deteriorating health had begun to lessen his influence on the band. After Pigpen's death, Donna and Keith Godchaux joined the band as keyboard player and vocalist, respectively. As William Ruhlmann points out in *The History of the Grateful Dead,* both events caused the band to diversify its repertoire and approach. Hank Harrison puts it differently in *The Dead,* claiming that the old band also died with Pigpen.

Other neglected de facto ''members'' of the band included their frequent lyricists, Robert Hunter and John Barlow. Hunter collaborated with Jerry Garcia, while Barlow worked with Bob Weir, and, while he was in the band, Brent Mydland. Robert Hunter, himself a musician, was a member of the San Francisco scene from the beginnings of the Grateful Dead. He never played with them, but penned several of their trademark songs, including ''Terrapin Station,'' ''Touch of Grey,'' ''Jack Straw,'' ''Tennessee Jed,'' ''It Must

Have Been the Roses,'' ''Playing in the Band,'' and ''Truckin'.'' Most of the time Hunter collaborated with Garcia in composing songs. In a 1988 interview with David Gans, published in *Conversations with the Dead,* Hunter was asked why he didn't collaborate with other members of the band more often. He replied that ''Garcia makes it easy. You know, he makes himself available to do it, and when I give him a piece of material he'll either reject it or set it, and he gives me changes, which I *will* set, generally—he doesn't give me anything I don't like . . . he's a genius, he's got an amazing musical sense, and no one else makes themselves available or particularly easy to work with.''

Hunter was probably referring to the Dead's other primary singer, Bob Weir, who could be difficult to work with. John Barlow, a childhood friend of Weir, referred to himself in interviews with David Gans as ''the Grateful Dead's word nigger,'' but explains that although sometimes Weir may abuse him, he is ''only that way when he's feeling a bit uptight and overworked. Then he gets very head-strong about certain creative decisions, and I'm not in a position to gainsay him because he's got to get out in front of a whole bunch of people and sing that stuff.'' Barlow, an active member of cyberspace by the late 1990s, started out as a poetry and fiction writer, but Weir persuaded him to try his hand at song lyrics after Weir joined the Dead. Barlow's patience was in evidence when the very first song he wrote, ''Mexicali Blues,'' was transformed into a polka number by Weir, something that Barlow hadn't envisioned. As with those lyrics, Barlow often infuses a Western flavor into his songs; they include ''Estimated Prophet,'' ''Looks Like Rain,'' ''Cassidy,'' ''Hell in a Bucket,'' ''Heaven Help the Fool,'' and ''Black Throated Wind.'' Collaborations with Brent Mydland include ''Easy to Love You,'' and ''Just a Little Light,'' while ''Throwing Stones'' was a Barlow, Weir, and Mydland effort. Mydland's death in 1990 of a drug overdose ended what had promised to be a fruitful collaboration.

Studio albums present polished versions of the Dead's songs, but the concert experience was the essence of the Dead. Improvisation was their chosen method; they claimed never to perform with a set list (although drummers Hart and Kreutzmann admitted practising the famous extended drum solo features known as ''Space'' that were a capstone of a Dead show's second set). This is one reason why, perhaps, the Dead could keep filling large stadiums on their tours, even in the early 1990s when the live concert industry hit a slump. In 1991 they were the top grossing concert band in the United States. The Dead never had a number one hit— in 1987 the Hunter/Garcia song ''Touch of Grey'' went only to number nine—but their music was being listened to, and no one knows how many bootleg tapes were trading, and continue to trade, hands.

Every former member of the Grateful Dead, except Bill Kreutzmann, formed a separate band with which they performed, toured, and recorded. Lesh, the only classically trained musician in the group, played on occasion with the San Francisco symphony until he underwent a liver transplant in 1998; upon his remarkable recovery from this operation, Lesh immediately began performing occasional gigs with a roving cast known as ''Phil and Friends.'' Mickey Hart, the most eclectic member of the band, went on to compose and perform experimental pieces, even contributing a composition used in the opening ceremony of the 1996 Olympic Games in Atlanta. He also composed music for Francis Ford Coppola's film *Apocalypse Now* (1979).

At the end of the twentieth century, members of the Grateful Dead were continuing as an industry unto themselves. The band is the most complete and longest lasting representation of the San Francisco counterculture, begun in the 1950s with the Beats and flowering in the 1960s with the hippies. The band helped to propagate and preserve the spirit of 1960s America at home and abroad with its recordings and tours. That it was never in need of reviving, and continues to thrive in various guises, attests to a thread of continuity in fast-paced American pop culture.

—Josephine A. McQuail

FURTHER READING:

Brandelius, Jerilyn Lee. *The Grateful Dead Family Album.* New York, Warner, 1989.

Gans, David. *Conversations with the Dead: The Grateful Dead Interview Book.* New York, Citadel, 1991.

Gans, David, and Peter Simon. *Playing in the Band: An Oral and Visual Portrait of the Grateful Dead.* New York, St. Martin's Press, 1985.

Goodman, Fred. "The *Rolling Stone* Interview: Jerry Garcia." In *Garcia,* edited by the editors of the *Rolling Stone.* New York, Little, Brown, 1995, 170-79.

Harrison, Hank. *The Dead.* Millbrae, California, Celestial Arts, 1980.

Henke, James. "The *Rolling Stone* Interview: Jerry Garcia." In *Garcia,* edited by the editors of the *Rolling Stone.* New York, Little Brown, 1995, 180-89.

Jackson, Blair. *Goin' Down the Road: A Grateful Dead Traveling Companion.* New York, Harmony, 1992.

Palmer, Robert. *Rock & Roll: An Unruly History.* New York, Harmony, 1995.

Ruhlmann, William. *The History of the Grateful Dead.* New York, Gallery, 1990.

White, Timothy. "Grateful Dead." In *Rock Lives. Profiles and Interviews.* New York, Henry Holt, 1990. 259-79.

Womack, David. *Aesthetics of the Grateful Dead.* Palo Alto, Flying Public Press, 1991.

Gray Panthers

The Gray Panthers seek to redefine old age in America. Founder Maggie Kuhn emphasized that "ageism" diminishes all people by stigmatizing young and old people as less than full members of society. Their mission statement affirms the importance of their relationship: "The Gray Panthers is an intergenerational advocacy organization. We are Age and Youth in Action—activists working together for social and economic justice. Our issues include universal health care, jobs with a living wage and the right to organize, the preservation of Social Security, affordable housing, access to quality education, economic justice, environment, peace and challenging ageism, sexism and racism." The Gray Panthers work with other organizations (notably AARP—the American Association of Retired Persons) for issues of common interest (e.g. preserving Social Security), but they are distinctive in placing a primary emphasis on activism, particularly for those not normally active in the political process.

Philosophically, the Gray Panthers are to the left of AARP, which is more conservative and allied with a variety of businesses and services. For over 25 years, the Gray Panthers have advocated social change, inspired by the dynamic example of founder Maggie Kuhn, who urged, "Speak your mind. When you least expect it, someone may actually listen to what you have to say. Even if your voice shakes, well-aimed slingshots can topple giants."

Maggie Kuhn (1905-1995) had been an activist for many causes during her life, but the organization that made her famous came about when she was forced to retire from the job she loved as an executive of the United Presbyterian Church at age 65. Infuriated by the wasteful nature of bureaucracies that mandated retirement for workers at 65, Kuhn began the process of organizing an advocacy group for older Americans. She recalled the awakening of her consciousness in her autobiography, *No Stone Unturned:* "Something clicked in my mind and I saw that my problem was not mine alone. I came to feel a great kinship with my peers and to believe that something was fundamentally wrong with a system that had no use for us." She believed that the talents, energy, and wisom of older Americans were being wasted.

With five friends, Kuhn began to hold meetings to try to address the problem, and it quickly grew from six to a hundred members in a year. The original name of the group was the Consultation of Older Persons, which was changed to the Gray Panthers when a member of the media suggested it to Maggie Kuhn as a better fit for her activist organization. This caused some confusion for people who were intimidated by the name, which recalled the Black Panthers, a militant activist organization of the Civil Rights movement. One woman wrote to Kuhn that she wanted to join but didn't want to be part of any "bombings." The new organization was helped significantly by consumer advocate Ralph Nader, who incorporated his own seniors group (Retired Professional Action Group) into the Gray Panthers. His organization had investigated the hearing aid industry, and he published an exposé, "Paying through the Ear." Nader also contributed $25,000 to the Gray Panthers, which helped significantly as they began their next campaign for nursing home reform. Their efforts (in conjunction with the National Citizen Coalition for Nursing Home Reform) produced a handbook, "Nursing Homes: A Citizen Action Guide," which documented nursing home abuses. By 1974, the Gray Panthers were making their influence felt across the country.

Annoyed by television talk-show host Johnny Carson's character "Aunt Blabby," Kuhn turned her guest spot on the show in 1974 into a tour de force, charming Carson and not incidentally promoting the Gray Panthers. In 1975 the Gray Panthers established a National Media Task Force, which documented ageist stereotyping in broadcasting, which led the National Association of Broadcasters to amend the Television Code of Ethics to include "age along with race and sex." In 1978, the Gray Panthers won perhaps their most satisfying reward for their efforts: the Age Discrimination in Employment Act was passed, raising the mandatory retirement age from 65 to 70. The 1980s were a very successful decade for the organization; the Reagan era provided a spur to activist groups and the Panthers reached an all-time high of 80,000 members. While the Gray Panthers have a much lower profile than the AARP, Maggie Kuhn had a keen sense of what the press would pick up on and always provided them with good copy. She once said, "Old age is an excellent time for outrage. My goal is to say or do at least one outrageous thing every week." In that same spirit, membership materials affirm that "the Gray Panthers movement is in the trenches fighting for the values in which we believe—taking the far out positions which lead to real change."

The Gray Panthers have a strong bond with organized labor and walked the picket line in the successful 1997 United Parcel Services strike. The organization has requested all members who are also union retirees to identify themselves as such so that the Gray Panthers can continue to solidify the close relationship with the AFL-CIO and other unions in their quest for social and economic justice. Many members of the Panthers are lifetime activists, participating in union and progressive politics at a level of commitment that makes them extremely skillful as organizers. Networking is crucial to the success of the Gray Panthers: rather than employ the high-power lobbying techniques of AARP to influence members of Congress, the organization uses its modest resources to work directly with other progressive organizations such as Food First (The Institute for Food and Development Policy).

In 1995, the 10th Biennial Convention honored Founder and National Convener Maggie Kuhn. Kuhn passed away shortly after the convention, and on what would have been her ninetieth birthday, August 3, 1995, the Gray Panthers celebrated her memory in ceremonies across the country. The Panthers' most important achievement after Kuhn's passing was a joint event with the United States Student Association, the first "Age and Youth in Action Summit" in Washington, D.C. in 1996. The next year the organization regrouped and focused attention on producing a successful convention. With the election of a new national chair, 55-year-old Catherine DeLorey, president of the Women's Health Institute, the organization seeks to reaffirm its intergenerational character as it moves into the twenty-first century.

—Mary Hess

FURTHER READING:

Brazil, Eric. "Gray Panthers Hope to Attract New Blood." *San Francisco Examiner*. September 27, 1997.

Gottlieb, Martin and Kurt Eichenwald. "A Hospital Chain's Brass Knuckles, and the Backlash." *New York Times*. May 11, 1997.

Gray Panthers. "Age and Youth in Action." Final Report. Washington, D.C., Gray Panthers, 1996.

———. "Bridging Generations for a New Social Contract." Report. Washington, D.C., Gray Panthers, 1997.

Hessel, Dieter T., editor. *Maggie Kuhn on Aging: A Dialogue*. Philadelphia, Westminster Press, 1977.

Kay, Jane Holtz. "Asphalt Nation: How the Automobile Took Over America and How We Can Take It Back." *New York Times*. July 20, 1997.

Kuhn, Maggie. *No Stone Unturned: The Life and Times of Maggie Kuhn*. New York, Ballantine Books, 1991.

Great Depression

Starting in 1929 and ending with America's entry into World War II in 1941, the Great Depression marked a turning point in American history by establishing the enlarged federal bureaucracy associated with the post-WWII state. While first and foremost an economic event, the Great Depression affected every aspect of

Workers on relief line during the Great Depression.

American political, social, and cultural life. It was during the depression that the radio and film industries, along with developments in documentary photography, reportage, and literature, helped to develop a national culture based in uniquely American practices, environments, experiences, and ideals.

While the stock market crash of October 1929 is often viewed as the start of the Great Depression, it was by no means the cause of the depression. The crash, and its aftermath of unemployment, bank closures, bankruptcies, and homelessness, were caused by fundamental flaws in the prosperity of the 1920s. The availability and widespread use of credit, the increasingly unequal distribution of wealth, the problems of falling farm prices, and the corporate consolidation of American industry all contributed to the overproduction of farm and industrial goods and the overexertion of credit and speculation. In the wake of the crash, American industrial output decreased rapidly, reaching in 1932 the same level of production as in 1913. Employment reached an all-time low, with 13 million people out of work, roughly 25 percent of the population. For farmers, crop prices had fallen drastically; a bushel of wheat that sold for three dollars in 1920 brought only thirty cents in 1932.

The effect of the depression on American culture was felt in both the public and private sectors. The federal government, through its New Deal programs, subsidized writers, composers, musicians, performers, painters, sculptors, and other artists, and it developed and encouraged cultural programs which focused attention on the United States, its history, traditions, and native arts and crafts. The Federal Writers Project employed writers, editors, and researchers to not only produce works of fiction, usually with American themes, but also to create several series of books such as the *State Guide Series,* consisting of all-purpose guide books for each state of the union. The Federal Arts Project hired painters and sculptors to create public art for post offices and other public buildings, and developed a network of community art centers in cities and towns across the country. The Federal Theater Project sought to bring the dramatic arts to the general public through local programs such as the Living Newspaper, in which local news stories were acted out in community theaters. Additional programs employed musicians, composers, architects, and other artists. Preservation programs such as the Index of American Design and the Library of Congress' Archive of Folk Song sought to preserve the inherently American character of folk arts. In all, the cultural programs of the New Deal focused attention on the unique aspects of American culture, not only in past arts and crafts, but also in the creation of new works of art.

The mass-media industries of broadcasting and motion pictures responded to the economic realities of the depression and the government sponsored trend towards reinforcing traditional American values. In the 1930s, radio dominated Americans' leisure time. Nearly one third of all Americans owned at least one radio, and even those who did not own a radio usually had access to one through family, friends, or neighbors. The potential radio audience for any program was estimated at sixty million people. As a result of these vast audiences and the huge profits to be made, the radio industry became big business with production companies selling "pre-packaged" shows to sponsors and stations, along with syndicates and networks developing and growing. During the 1930s, comedians were the most popular radio personalities. Jack Benny, Fanny Brice, George Burns and Gracie Allen, Bob Hope, Milton Berle, and Jimmy Durante all had popular radio shows. Musical shows were also a favorite of audiences as almost every station presented remote broadcasts from hotel ballrooms featuring dance orchestras and jazz bands such as Paul Whiteman ("The King of Jazz"), Ralph Ginsberg and the Palmer House Ensemble, and Phil Spitalny and his All-Girl Orchestra, featuring Evelyn and her Magic Violin. Daytime programing was dominated by the soap opera, so named because most were sponsored by soap manufacturers. Writer James Thurber described soap operas as "a kind of sandwich, whose recipe is simple enough. . . Between thick slices of advertising, spread twelve minutes of dialogue, add predicament, villainy, and female suffering in equal measure, throw in a dash of nobility, sprinkle with tears, season with organ music, cover with a rich announcer sauce, and serve five times a week." As opposed to daytime serial dramas, evening dramas contained much better production values and more sophisticated material featuring famous actors. *The Texaco Theater, The Philip Morris Playhouse, Grand Central Station,* and other hour-long programs presented serious dramatic fare, but the most popular shows were the half-hour long crime-suspense-adventure shows, including *Sam Spade, Jack Armstrong: the All-American Boy, The Thin Man, Sargent Preston of the Yukon, The Green Hornet, The Shadow,* and *The Lone Ranger.* Even news reporting took on a more entertaining flavor as radio newsmen became celebrities, such as Lowell Thomas, Edward R. Murrow, and Floyd Gibbons, who introduced himself as "the fastest talking man in radio." Forty percent of all Americans preferred to get their news and information from radio, more than any other single source.

Radio took on a whole new importance in the wake of the Depression, primarily through the use of the medium by President Franklin D. Roosevelt. In his "fireside chats," Roosevelt addressed the country directly from the White House. This mediated communication, due to the intimacy associated with radio broadcasting, developed a more personal relationship between the president and the public than ever before, reinforcing the expansion of federal, especially executive, authority. Radio became much more than a source of local information and entertainment; it became a vital tool of the government to promote and support its programs. Roosevelt's first "fireside chat," explaining the purpose of the bank holiday and subsequent banking legislation, produced enough confidence in Roosevelt and the government that the following day bank deposits outnumbered withdrawals for the first time since the stock market crash almost four years earlier. Radio not only informed people, but also brought them under the influence of a centralized medium which homogenized the information it was disseminating. As Warren Susman argues in his essay "The Culture of the Thirties," radio "helped mold uniform national responses; it helped create or reinforce uniform national values and beliefs in a way that no previous medium had ever been able to do." Illustrating one such uniform national response was the euphoria witnessed in communities, both black and white, over Joe Louis' heavyweight title fights in 1937 and 1938. Informing the public became such a vital part of the radio industry, and so accepted by the public, that a fake "emergency bulletin" as part of Orson Welles' 1937 radio production of H. G. Wells' *War of the Worlds* created pandemonium in towns and cities across America.

As a result of the depression, Hollywood experienced a decline in movie attendance, and it compensated by using the latest technology to its fullest impact to produce movies which would appeal to adult males, the segment of the movie audience that had declined the most. War films such as *All Quite on the Western Front* (1930) and *The Dawn Patrol* (1930); horror films such as *Dracula* (1931), *Frankenstein* (1931), and *King Kong* (1933); gangster movies such as *Little Caesar* (1930), *The Public Enemy* (1931) and *Scarface* (1932) all took advantage of sound technology to enhance the filmgoing experience. Movies such as Marlene Dietrich's *Blonde Venus* (1932), Jean Harlow's *Red Dust* (1932), and Irene Dunn's *Back Street* (1932) all challenged the prevailing notions of respectable women's roles. Even the glamorous Greta Garbo, in her sound film debut, did not play a socialite, but rather a prostitute. The long awaited moment when Garbo first spoke on film was in *Anne Christie* (1930) as she addressed a waiter in a waterfront dive: "Gimme a viskey. Ginger ale on the side. And don't be stingy, ba-bee." Even a film as superficial as *Gold Diggers of 1933* implied that for women there were limited career paths. In the film's most memorable song, "We're in the Money," chorus girls joke that if they had to give up performing they would have to enter into the world's oldest profession: "We're in the money. We're in the money. We've got a lot of what it takes to get along." Even comedies emphasized this tendency towards anarchy and sex. The most popular film comedians, the Marx Brothers and Mae West, relied heavily on sound to convey their primarily verbal humor, yet both also depended on visuals for the strong physical presence necessary in both slapstick comedy and body enhancing sexual innuendo.

This "golden age of turbulence," according to film historian Robert Sklar in *Movie-Made America: A Cultural History of American Movies,* lasted from 1930 to 1934 when Hollywood, under pressure from civic organizations like the Catholic Church's League of Decency, discovered there was as much, if not more, profit to be made on supporting traditional American values as there was in challenging them. With the 1934 introduction of the Breen Office (officially the Production Code Administration, but popularly named after Joseph Breen, the film industry's self-imposed censor who had absolute power), the movie industry stopped challenging traditional values by becoming one of their most staunch supporters.

The Breen Office brought about the "golden age of order" in which the social order was restored in films that reinforced traditional notions about social roles and American ideals. Screwball comedies set among the upper classes, such as *Bringing Up Baby* (1938) and *The Philadelphia Story* (1940) replaced the anarchic vision of the Marx Brothers and the brazen sexuality of Mae West. Gangster movies focused not on the lawless, but on the government agent, the G-man. And Hollywood began producing socially conscious films such as *The Grapes of Wrath* (1940) and the films of Frank Capra.

Frank Capra best exemplifies the "age of order" with his morality plays set among the common people of America. Capra produced films which encouraged Americans to reaffirm their beliefs in democracy, community, and humanity. In his "American trilogy," of *Mr. Deeds Goes to Town* (1936), *Mr. Smith Goes to Washington* (1939), and *Meet John Doe* (1941), Capra presented American democracy at its best with each protagonist (Deeds, Smith, and Doe) overcoming the challenges to honesty and decency through perseverance. In *Mr. Deeds,* Gary Cooper stars as Longfellow Deeds, who plans to use his inherited millions on establishing farmers on their own small plots of land in an attempt to recreate the Jeffersonian vision of the democratic yeoman farmer. In *Mr. Smith,* James Stewart stars as Jefferson Smith, a junior senator who envisions a boys' camp in the western wilderness to teach boys the virtues of independence, self-sufficiency, and frontier democracy. And in *John Doe,* Gary Cooper once again stars, this time as Long John Willoughby, a down-and-out baseball player recruited by a big city newspaper to play the role of John Doe, a "common" man who has threatened to end his life as a protest against modern society. John Doe not only becomes a circulation booster, but his simple ideas about neighborly consideration and the "little guys" watching out for each other is readily picked up by an eager public searching for solutions to the depression. The John Doe Movement, with the establishment of John Doe clubs, is manipulated by the tyrannical newspaper owner D. B. Norton, who aspires to political office. Norton and Willoughby come into conflict when Norton's machinations are revealed and Willoughby seeks to stop him. Norton exposes the "fake" John Doe and the movement crumbles. In the end, Willoughby seeks to follow through on "John Doe's" original promise to jump off the city hall tower on Christmas Eve. Like all Capra movies, the honest and decent hero survives the attacks against him through the faith of a loving woman and the eventual realization of "the people." Capra reaffirms traditional ideas about self-help and the private function of charity in the face of adversity, as opposed to more modern ideas in which the federal government assumes responsibility for the health and welfare of individual citizens. Despite the revolutionary medium of motion pictures, late 1930s movies overwhelmingly reinforced traditional values.

In general, the reaction to the Great Depression, by the federal government and the mass media industries, served to maintain traditional American values in the face of economic, political, and social change.

—Charles J. Shindo

FURTHER READING:

Hilmes, Michelle. *Radio Voices: American Broadcasting, 1922-1952.* Minneapolis, University of Minnesota Press, 1997.

McElvaine, Robert S. *The Great Depression: America, 1929-1941.* New York, Times Books, 1984.

Sklar, Robert. *Movie-Made America: A Cultural History of American Movies.* New York, Vintage Books, 1975.

Shindo, Charles J. *Dust Bowl Migrants in the American Imagination.* Lawrence, University Press of Kansas, 1997.

Susman, Warren I. *Culture As History: The Transformation of American Society in the Twentieth Century.* New York, Pantheon Books, 1985.

The Great Train Robbery

Made in 1903, Edwin S. Porter's eleven minute *The Great Train Robbery* is a landmark in the evolution of film editing. Porter's film, in its cutting back and forth between multiple simultaneous story lines, showed that movies need not be restricted to linear story-telling. *The Great Train Robbery* is also interesting as a transitional film; in some scenes the backgrounds are clearly painted, while in others, such as the famous train-top fistfight scene, the action is thrillingly "real."

—Robert C. Sickels

FURTHER READING:

Kauffmann, Stanley. "The Great Train Robbery." *New Republic.* Vol. 213, No. 10, 27-28.

Kirby, Lynne. *Parallel Tracks: The Railroad and Silent Cinema.* Durham, North Carolina, Duke University Press, 1997.

Great War, The
See World War I

Greb, Harry (1894-1926)

Edward Henry "Harry" Greb epitomized the Roaring Twenties. Middleweight champion by 1923, "The Pittsburgh Windmill" lived hard, played harder, and fought hardest. Greb made the sports pages for his myriad, perhaps even historically unparalleled, accomplishments inside of the ring, and he made the front pages for his antics outside of it. Affairs with married women, car crashes, drunken brawls, law suits: Greb was the original media bad boy. He once fought fellow Hall of Famer Mickey Walker outside a pub, several hours *after* their bruising title fight (Greb won the title fight, Walker the street brawl). His non-stop attack and indomitable fighting spirit seemed to carry over from the ring to his personal life, and in spite of his negative press (and maybe in part, because of it), Harry Greb was a beloved sports icon. According to boxing historian Bert Randolph Sugar, Ernest Hemmingway once accused another writer who did not know who Greb was of "not knowing one of our greatest Americans."

—Max Kellerman

Harry Greb

FURTHER READING:

Fair, James R. *Give Him to the Angels: The Story of Harry Greb.* New York, Smith and Durrell, 1946.

Greed

The bowdlerization of Erich von Stroheim's *Greed* (1924) is almost more famous than the film itself. An adaptation of *McTeague,* Frank Norris' epic novel of avarice, desire, and disintegration, it stars Gibson Gowland as the dentist McTeague, ZaSu Pitts as the wife he murders for money, and Jean Hersholt as the brute Marcus with whom he fights to their mutual destruction in Death Valley. In realizing a cherished dream to do literal justice to the book, Stroheim broke new ground in cinematic realism, both in characterization and the use of actual locations in San Francisco and Death Valley, but emerged with a 42-reel, ten-hour film. Producer Irving Thalberg, the director's nemesis with whom he had previously tangled, ordered cuts and Stroheim tried to oblige. The film, however, was taken away from him and the cuts became a massacre. The final release version was a little short of two hours, with much careful detail lost and the dramatic balance seriously upset by the removal of sub-plots and subsidiary

characters. Nonetheless, *Greed* remains a powerful masterpiece of the silent cinema from one of the medium's few geniuses.

—Robyn Karney

FURTHER READING:

Curtiss, Thomas Quinn. *Erich von Stroheim.* New York, Farrar, Strauss, & Giroux, 1971.

Koszarski, R. *The Man You Love to Hate.* United Kingdom, Oxford University Press, 1983.

Roud, Richard. *Cinema: A Critical Dictionary.* London, Secker & Warburg, 1980.

Greeley, Andrew (1928—)

A self-described "faintly comic Celtic Lancelot" and "perennial dissident priest," Catholic priest, sociologist, and writer Andrew Greeley has stirred frequent controversy within and outside the Church and produced enormous amounts of written work in widely different fields. Beginning late in the 1950s and continuing at a relentless pace thereafter, the water-skiing, celibate priest published countless articles in newspapers, magazines, and scholarly journals, as well as more than 100 books. These range from obscure sociological tracts on religion and ethnicity in the United States to racy bestselling novels filled with sex and corruption, as well as works on relationships, photography, and mysteries. If a central theme ties his work together, it may be his possibly quixotic crusade to "free the riches of the Catholic tradition from the stranglehold of a decrepit and corrupt bureaucracy" and to bring a sense of "God's merciful love" to readers.

A lifelong resident of Chicago, Greeley has been a professor at both the University of Chicago and at the University of Arizona and a longtime researcher at Chicago's National Opinion Research Center. He has become embroiled in numerous controversies, offending persons of all political stripes. His advocacy of liberalization of Church policies on birth control, divorce, and women in the priesthood has angered a conservative Catholic hierarchy, while his opposition to abortion and support of priestly celibacy has offended many liberals. Despite his success as a writer of bestselling novels, he claims his primary occupation as a parish priest and cites his popular books as his most successful outreach.

As a youth Greeley attended Catholic schools and admired the works of G. K. Chesterton, Graham Greene, and other Catholic writers. He decided he wanted to be a priest in second grade and was ordained in 1954. While serving as an assistant pastor in Chicago, he began writing articles for religious publications under a pseudonym and later under his own name. His first book, *The Church and the Suburbs* (1959), grew out of two of his articles that examined the effects of increased affluence on religious belief. In 1962 he earned a doctorate in sociology from the University of Chicago. His sociological work, often based on surveys generated at NORC, has included studies of Catholic education, the priesthood, the paranormal, ethnicity and alcoholism, and Irish Americans, among other things. Religious works like *The Mary Myth* (1977) suggest the "womanliness of God," a recurrent theme in Greeley's nonfiction and fiction. Books like *The Unsecular Man* (1972) make a case for the persistence of religious belief in a supposedly secular age.

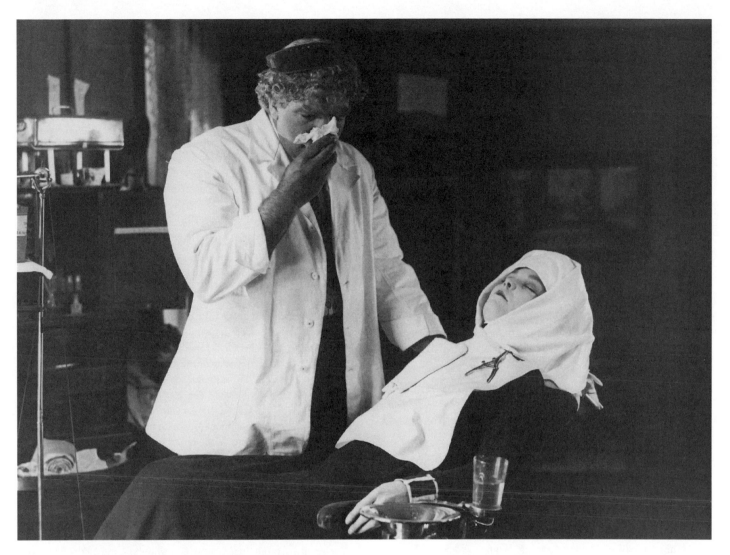

Gibson Gowland (left) and ZaSu Pitts in a scene from the film *Greed*.

One of Greeley's main offenses against conventional Catholic doctrine has been to suggest that sex is a sacrament and an expression of God's love rather than a sin when it is not a means of procreation. His outspokenness on this and other issues brought him into conflict with leading church authorities, including John Cardinal Cody of Chicago. Greeley's most critically-acclaimed work of popular nonfiction, *The Making of the Popes, 1978: The Politics of Intrigue in the Vatican* (1979), examines papal politics in Rome in the style of Theodore White, deglamourizing, demystifying, and exposing the papal selection process as an unfair practice in which popes are chosen secretly, undemocratically, and often ineptly. Although the book sold only moderately well, it earned plaudits for its close observation, detailed reporting (much of it thanks to a source Greeley termed "Deep Purple"), and analysis of a rite that has remained shrouded in secrecy for centuries.

In the mid-1970s, convinced that the power of storytelling and emotion rather than dry exposition and philosophy were key to religious belief, Greeley began writing poetry and fiction. His first two novels sold poorly, but his third, *The Cardinal Sins* (1981), made him an overnight celebrity. The story of two boyhood friends, one who goes on to become a simple parish priest and the other who becomes a cardinal, is laced with sex and corruption. It remained on bestseller lists for more than a year, selling more than three million copies. Greeley followed with dozens of other novels, many of them bestsellers that often included sex, corruption, and violence, set in Chicago, and featuring religious or mystical characters. Like *The Cardinal Sins*, many were better received by the public than by reviewers, who often have complained that Greeley's writing is stiff and his characters two-dimensional. Catholic officials (many of whom, Greeley claimed, never read the books) often criticized the novels for their sex scenes, although Greeley has defended his depiction of sex as tasteful and claimed his own surveys show that his books brought a majority of Catholic readers closer to the Church. He described his novels as "comedies of grace"—parables of God's grace through love—and "the most effective priestly activity in which I have ever engaged," and blamed the anger of his priestly critics on their envy of the wealth and fame his books brought him. Though he has owned expensive houses and cars, he claims he has given away most of his earnings to charity.

Reaching his 70th birthday in 1998, Greeley, who has attributed his productivity to celibacy and long hours at the computer terminal, allowed that he would slow down his pace. But the previous decade had brought little evidence of declining energy. He produced more than a score of books of nonfiction and fiction. Although the latter earned many unfavorable reviews, they continued to receive an enthusiastic reception from loyal fans. According to Greeley, readers who write him often tell him that his stories have had "an enormous effect on their personal and religious lives, giving them new hope and a new (or renewed) sense of God's forgiving love." Among his later works were mysteries somewhat reminiscent of Chesterton's Father Brown series that feature the adventures of Father Blackwood Ryan, monsignor, who represents the best attributes of Catholic priests: "intelligence, pragmatism, zeal, wisdom, and wit," rather than the selfishness and insensitivity of other priests portrayed in the books. Greeley also continued to write popular books on relationships, including *Sexual Intimacy: Love and Play* (1988) and *Faithful Attraction: Discovering Intimacy, Love, and Fidelity in American Marriage* (1991).

—Daniel Lindley

FURTHER READING:

Greeley, Andrew. *Confessions of a Parish Priest: An Autobiography.* New York, Simon and Schuster, 1986.

Shafer, Ingrid H. *Eros and the Womanliness of God: Andrew Greeley's Romances of Renewal.* Loyola University Press, Chicago, 1986.

———, editor. *The Incarnate Imagination: Essays in Theology, the Arts and Social Sciences in Honor of Andrew Greeley: A Festschrift.* Bowling Green, Ohio, Bowling Green State University Popular Press, 1988.

Green, Al (1946—)

Admirers call eight-time Grammy winner and Rock 'n' Roll Hall of Fame inductee Al Green "the quintessential soul man." Born in Arkansas, Green grew up in Michigan, and as a youngster toured with his father in a family gospel quartet. He formed his own group "The Creations," in the mid-1960s, later becoming lead singer for "The Soul Mates." A solo career with Memphis-based Hi Records rocketed him to fame in the 1970s, becoming "that decade's most popular purveyor of soul music," according to the Rock and Roll Hall of Fame. In eight years, Green co-wrote thirteen charting singles including "Tired of Being Alone," and "Let's Stay Together." Fourteen of Green's albums have appeared on the Top 200 charts; five went gold. Ordained in 1976, he serves as pastor and proprietor of Memphis' Full Gospel Tabernacle, and recorded nine bestselling gospel albums in the 1980s.

—Courtney Bennett

FURTHER READING:

MCA Records. "Al Green," http://www.mca.com/mca_records/library/bios/bio.algreen.html. December 1998.

Rock and Roll Hall of Fame and Museum. "Al Green: 1995, Performer," http://www.rockhall.com/induct/greeal.html. December 1998.

The Green Bay Packers

As the National Football League's most successful franchise, with 12 titles since 1929, the Green Bay Packers overcame early financial hardship and a location in a city smaller than any other professional sports team to become one of the most popular teams in all of American sport. In addition to their 12 league titles, the Packers have placed 19 members into the Professional Football Hall of Fame, and they are the only NFL franchise to win three straight league titles, having done so twice (1929 to 1931 and 1965 to 1967). With this long history of amazing success, the Packers have even given a nickname to their hometown of Green Bay, Wisconsin—Titletown, USA. However, the city has undoubtedly earned its strong connection to the club, as city leaders and citizens have aided the team many times since it was founded.

Founded by Earl L. "Curly" Lambeau and George Calhoun in 1919, the Packers owe their team name to the Indian Packing Company, a meat-packing firm in Green Bay. The company, which employed Lambeau at the time as a meat cutter, provided the initial funds for necessary equipment, and allowed the club to use their private athletic fields for practice sessions. Due to the strong debt initially owed to the packing house, the team chose to use "Packers" as their name, Calhoun was named club president, and Lambeau was elected as vice-president and coach, a position he would hold for 30 years. In their first season the Packers won 10 of 11 games against other club teams in the Wisconsin area, but after this auspicious start even bigger things were on the horizon.

In 1921, officials of the company encouraged Calhoun and Lambeau to secure a franchise in the new national professional football league that had formed a year earlier, and would later become the modern National Football League (NFL). Following this grand leap, a long string of financial troubles beset the team, the first of which allowed Lambeau to take full ownership of the club in 1922. The financial difficulties continued throughout the 1920s, however, and it was during this decade that Lambeau sought citywide assistance for the club and formed the Green Bay Football Corporation with financial help from business leaders throughout Green Bay and the surrounding region.

Once the corporation was established, and with it a more stable financial base, Lambeau was able to secure the services of better players and acquire first-rate equipment, allowing the team to become more competitive in the growing professional football world of the late 1920s. By 1929 the Packers had won the first of three consecutive NFL titles during what is commonly known as the Iron-Man Era of professional football, when players commonly played both offense and defense for the entire game. Following these early championships, legal problems in the mid-1930s led the club into financial problems once more, but the local business community again came to the rescue with an infusion of capital, and the team was saved.

In 1935 a new weapon was added to the Packers' arsenal of great football players, a young end from the University of Alabama named Don Hutson. He became an immediate star in the fledgling NFL, so great that he would be named to the 75th Anniversary Team in 1994, 50 years after his retirement. Hutson led the league in receiving seven times, scoring five times, and also set an all-time record in 1945, personally scoring 29 points in one period. In the Hutson era, the

The Green Bay Packers with head coach Vince Lombardi, 1967.

Packers won three more NFL titles (1936, 1939, and 1944). During this period the Packers gained national recognition with their success on the gridiron, and fans throughout the country began to follow the team and the legendary Hutson.

Following Hutson's retirement in 1945, the Packers' fortunes on the field began to decline, along with their gate receipts. By 1949 the club was yet again struggling financially, this time nearing complete bankruptcy. The situation led Lambeau to search for greener pastures, and he left the club to become coach of the Chicago Cardinals. However, the community would not forsake their beloved Packers, and in 1950 a giant public stock sale was organized that raised $125,000 to save the club from dissolution. This sale, the third such effort by the club since 1923 and the first to be open to the general public, formed a stable financial base for the franchise that has continued ever since. While the club was only moderately successful throughout the remainder of the 1950s, the ground had been laid to set the course for the greater success yet to come.

In 1959 the Packers hired Vince Lombardi, an assistant coach from the New York Giants, to become only the fifth head coach of the team in 40 years. Over the next nine years, Lombardi became a legend in Green Bay and throughout the country, both because of the success to which he led his teams, and for the unswerving loyalty he demonstrated to his players, friends, and colleagues in Wisconsin and

the pro football community. By Lombardi's third season as coach (1961) he had transformed the Packers from a mediocre club to NFL Champions, a feat the team would repeat four more times under his (1962, 1965, 1966, 1967). Within this span the Packers won the first two Super Bowls in 1966 and 1967, setting in motion the development of the Super Bowl as America's premier one-day sporting spectacle. The team's dominance was so commanding during this era that the NFL named the Super Bowl Championship trophy after the Packers legendary leader, the Vince Lombardi Trophy. This honor could be attributed in part to Lombardi's phenomenal success as a coach in Division and League Championship games alone, winning nine out of ten such games in which his teams participated.

During the Lombardi era, Green Bay was not only blessed with exceptional coaching, but also with a collection of Hall of Fame caliber players seldom matched in the history of the NFL. Lombardi himself was inducted into the Hall of Fame in 1971, and ten players who played for him in Green Bay are now also enshrined in the Pro Football Hall of Fame in Canton, Ohio. These players are Jim Taylor, Forrest Gregg, Bart Starr, Ray Nitschke, Herb Adderley, Willie Davis, Jim Ringo, Paul Hornung, Willie Wood, and Henry Jordan. Starr led the Lombardi-era teams as quarterback, and later followed his legendary mentor as Packers Head Coach from 1975 to 1983. His successor in that position was his Green Bay teammate and fellow

Hall of Fame member Forrest Gregg, who led the team from 1984 to 1987, having previously taken the Cincinnati Bengals to Super Bowl XVI in 1982. All of Lombardi's players praised their demanding coach for pushing them to give their very best, but also for his undying loyalty to those men who showed their dedication to him. The influence of Lombardi's charismatic leadership ability has remained evident in the way that many coaches and business executives have continued to follow his axioms, while some even continue to play taped speeches he made regarding leadership, effort and teamwork.

Following the Lombardi era, the Packers slipped into another period of on-field mediocrity, although the fans in Green Bay and throughout Wisconsin continued to support the team unfailingly with their attendance at games in Lambeau Field. During this period, some critics, skeptical of the Packers' location in a small, mid-western city, blamed the team's poor performance on their hometown. However, the residents of Green Bay, as well as Packer fans throughout Wisconsin and across the country, never lost hope that the team would return to greatness. Following the Starr and Gregg coaching periods, Green Bay hired noted offensive innovator Lindy Infante to coach the team, but nobody was able to emulate the success of coaching legends Lambeau and Lombardi. Throughout the 1970s and 1980s, therefore, the Packers remained a second division team in the NFC Central Division, making the league playoffs only twice between 1968 and 1993.

In 1992 the Packers hired Mike Holmgren, the offensive coordinator of the San Francisco 49ers as Head Coach, and a new era of success dawned. By Holmgren's third season new players had been brought in through the college draft, shrewd trades, and free agency, who would help lead the Packers back into the NFL elite. These players included a young quarterback acquired from the Atlanta Falcons named Brett Favre and a talented veteran defensive leader named Reggie White who was signed as a free agent from the Philadelphia Eagles. These players would lead the Packers on the field as Holmgren and his coaching staff devised schemes that would confound opponents into numerous strategic errors, in a manner similar to the Lombardi era. In 1994 the Packers returned to the playoffs for the first time since 1983, and by 1996 the team had risen to the top of the league, winning Super Bowl XXXI. In 1997 the Packers again reached the Super Bowl, but were forced to bow to the Denver Broncos in one of the closest and most hard fought battles the game had seen in many years. During this dramatic run of success, Favre proved the greatest beneficiary of Holmgren's coaching, moving from a reserve player with the Falcons to winning the League MVP award for three consecutive seasons from 1995 to 1997.

Through all of the team's successes and hardships, the citizens of Green Bay and fans throughout the United States have always supported the Packers. While playing in the smallest city to hold an NFL franchise, the Packers have enjoyed unparalleled fan support, ranging from consistent sell-outs at Lambeau Field to the financial aid of the stock sales that have made the team the only publicly held franchise in professional sports. The Packers have become an institution in American sport, and a "pilgrimage" to Lambeau Field is among the most cherished events for many professional football fans throughout the country. Legions of Packer fans have come to be known as "Cheeseheads" for their devotion to the club, and the comical cheese-wedge shaped hats they wear in honor of the state's most famous dairy product. The cheese-adorned paraphernalia, which

Packer fans wear in concert with the club's green and yellow colors, are among the most popular souvenirs for NFL teams, as well as in all of sport. No other professional franchise enjoys the complete support of its community in quite the same manner as the Green Bay Packers.

—G. Allen Finchum

FURTHER READING:

Packer Legends in Facts: The Green Bay Packers 75ᵗʰ Year in the NFL Anniversary. Germantown, Wisconsin, Tech Data Publications, 1995.

Schapp, Dick. *Green Bay Replay, The Packers Return to Glory.* New York, Avon Books, 1997.

Green Lantern

Green Lantern is one of the oldest and most popular comic-book superheroes. The character first appeared in DC comic books in 1940. Wielding a magic power-ring capable of performing a variety of feats, Green Lantern spent his early years championing the interests of common citizens against crooked stock brokers, greedy businessmen, and corrupt politicians before taking on America's enemies in World War II.

Although his initial comic-book series was canceled in 1949, DC revived and revised the character ten years later and has kept him in publication ever since. The "modern" Green Lantern uses his power-ring in the service of an intergalactic police force. In 1970, Green Lantern's comic book became a vehicle for "relevant" stories that critiqued America's social ills.

—Bradford Wright

FURTHER READING:

Daniels, Les. *DC Comics: Sixty Years of the World's Favorite Comic Book Heroes.* Boston, Little, Brown, 1995.

O'Neil, Dennis. *Secret Origins of the Super DC Heroes.* New York, Warner, 1976.

Greenberg, Hank (1911-1986)

Noted as the first Jewish baseball star, Hank Greenberg became a hero to a generation of Jewish fans and led the way for greater Jewish opportunities in baseball. Greenberg debuted at first base for the Detroit Tigers in 1933 and faced anti-Semitism from fans and opposing teams. Yet "Hammerin' Hank" withstood this and managed to win two Most Valuable Player awards, earn four batting titles, hit 58 home runs in 1938, and get inducted into the Baseball Hall of Fame in 1956. Greenberg fought over four years in World War II, and set a precedent after the war by becoming the first Jewish owner and general manager in baseball. Greenberg's popularity changed America's perspective on Jews, and he has come to symbolize a hero who overcame prejudice to lead his baseball team, his country, and his faith.

—Nathan R. Meyer

FURTHER READING:

Greenberg, Hank, with Ira Berkow. *Hank Greenberg: The Story of My Life.* New York, Times Books, 1989.

Greene, Graham (1952—)

His Academy Award nomination for the supporting role of Kicking Bird in *Dances with Wolves* (1990) has made Graham Greene one of the most recognized Native American actors. Greene, a full-blooded Oneida Sioux, was born on the Six Nations Reserve near Brantford, Ontario, and at age 16 left the Reserve to pursue a variety of careers, including welder, drafter, and roadie. He began acting in Toronto in 1974 and landed his first film roles in the early 1980s with roles in *Running Brave* (1983) and *Revolution* (1985). In 1989 he received the Dora Mavor Moore Award of Toronto for best actor for

Graham Greene in a scene from the film *Dances with Wolfs.*

the play *Dry Lips Oughta Move to Kapuskasing.* After *Dances with Wolves,* he went on to appear in numerous films, including *Clearcut* (1992), *Thunderheart* (1992), and *Die Hard with a Vengeance* (1995). In addition to television appearances on *Lonesome Dove: The Series* (1992) and *Northern Exposure* (1990), he starred in the 1992 HBO film *The Last of His Tribe.*

—Eugenia Griffith DuPell

FURTHER READING:

Johnson, Brian D. "Dances with Oscar: Canadian Actor Graham Greene Tastes Stardom." *Maclean's.* March 25, 1991, 60-61.

Malinowski, Sharon, editor. *Notable Native Americans.* Detroit, Gale Research, 1995.

Pollock, Sean R., editor. *Newsmakers: The People Behind Today's Headlines.* Detroit, Gale Research, 1998.

Greenpeace

Formed in 1971 by a group of Canadian and expatriate American Sierra Club members who wanted a more active form of environmentalism, Greenpeace is a global environmental organization with offices in 23 countries and international headquarters in Amsterdam. Its major campaigns include Atmosphere and Energy, Nuclear Weapons and Nuclear Power, Tropical Rainforests, Toxics, and Ocean Ecology. Its mission combines both environmental and peace issues. Since its inception, Greenpeace has been involved in hundreds of highly publicized direct-action campaigns against major polluters and government nuclear testing. Its flamboyant protests in the cause of ocean ecology in the 1970s heightened public awareness to environmental abuses around the world and drew millions of people to its membership list. Political pressure exercised by Greenpeace led to global treatise protecting whales and dolphins. It shocked public sentiment into action with graphic footage of baby seals being bludgeoned to death. In 1998, Greenpeace, one of the world's largest, wealthiest, and most successful environmental groups, had a membership totaling over 5 million people worldwide.

Greenpeace relies heavily on canvassing, telemarketing, and direct mail campaigns for mobilization, retention, and fund raising. Not allied with any political party, it accepts no corporate donations, and ninety percent of its revenues come from membership dues and other contributions. To promote their confrontational tactics, Greenpeace operates an international information service that consists of four units: Hard News and Features, Film and Video, Photo Desk, and Publications Division. It also runs mass-media crusades, drafts and lobbies for international conventions, participates in educational campaigns, and sells Greenpeace merchandise such as T-shirts and posters. Greenpeace concerts, albums, and compact discs, featuring groups such as U2, REM, and other major acts, market the organization's message to the world's youth.

The elemental principle behind the operation of Greenpeace is the American Quaker tradition of "bearing witness"—drawing attention to objectionable activity by unwavering presence at the site of abuse. The organization has a "navy" of eight ships, an "air force" of one hot air balloon and two helicopters, as well as an "action bus." Its bold protests have included sailing into nuclear testing zones, intercepting whaling vessels, and hanging banners from bridges,

A Greenpeace activist hangs on the anchor of a Japanese whaling ship, 1998.

in 1993 pointed out, "The moral imperative of demonstrators and direct action to save whales on the high seas was set against rationalizations and sales images of conventional commerce, and the whales won." The mythology of Moby Dick and Captain Ahab that had dominated human consciousness about whaling for over a century had been destroyed. The story became one of courageous whales fighting men in giant boats. Greenpeace's media exploits and public relations drives were the centerpiece of its strategies and the prototypes for other social movements striving to assert a presence in the electronic age. With its reputation as an effective, persistent, and uncompromising environmental organization, grown from its prowess as an efficient publicity machine, Greenpeace has been instrumental in alerting people around the world to environmental evils. Together with other organizations, it succeeded in moving the protection of the environment from a marginal to a central public and moral concern.

—Ken Kempcke

FURTHER READING:

Brown, Michael and John May. *The Greenpeace Story.* New York, Dorling Kindersley, 1991.

Rose, Chris. "Beyond the Struggle for Proof: Factors Changing the Environmental Movement." *Environmental Values.* Vol. 2, 1993, 185-98.

Wapner, Paul. "Politics Beyond the State: Environmental Activism and World Civic Politics." *World Politics.* Vol. 47, No. 3, 1995, 311-30.

Greenwich Village

Greenwich Village's known history dates back to the sixteenth century, when it was a marshland called Sapokanikan by Native Americans who fished in the trout stream known as Minetta Brook. When the Dutch first settled on Manhattan in 1621, naming the area New Netherlands, all but a small area on the Southeastern tip of the island was left untouched by the Europeans. When the colony passed to British hands in 1664 and became New York, a few farms and estates emerged some miles to the north of the city; the settlement evolved into a country hamlet, first designated Grin'wich in 1713 Common Council records.

The village was transformed overnight in 1828, when yellow fever caused thousands of city dwellers to flee to the Greenwich countryside. Many of these displaced city-folk enjoyed the country, and throughout the following decade the village grew as businesses and residents moved their permanent homes there.

As the population of Manhattan grew, the city felt the need for northern expansion in an orderly fashion. The city council adopted a grid plan in March 1817 which would have placed gridded streets running from river to river, cutting through the heart of the fledgling village. The village people were outraged. During the year that the grid war waged, an anonymous 62-page pamphlet was submitted to the city laying out an argument against the plan. Soon after, the council backed down and limited the grid to the east of what is now Sixth Avenue and north of what is presently Fourteenth Street.

During the early nineteenth century, as New York University grew on the east side of Washington Square, religious denominations

skyscrapers, and smokestacks. In the 1970s and 1980s, these demonstrations drew enormous media attention and Greenpeace became a model for other organizations by utilizing the mass media to influence public opinion. As a result of its campaign against the killing of harp seals, people around the globe changed their buying habits and stopped purchasing products made out of the seal pelts. In 1985, After protests against nuclear testing in the South Pacific, the French government sabotaged the organization's flagship, the *Rainbow Warrior*, in New Zealand. The sinking killed Fernando Pereira, a Greenpeace photographer, and sparked worldwide condemnation against France. This incident resulted in a doubling of the group's membership and a tripling of its revenues. It became the organization of choice for many high-profile celebrities and the pet issue for many Western politicians. The French government eventually paid Greenpeace $8 million in compensation for the destruction of the *Rainbow Warrior*.

During the 1990s, Greenpeace increasingly moved into the corporate board rooms, law offices, and scientific laboratories of the mainstream, but direct action—nonviolently confronting polluters and marine mammal killers—is what Greenpeace is best known for in the public mind. As Chris Rose, program director of Greenpeace UK

A Greenwich Village street at night, 1955.

commissioned buildings with elaborate decorative schemes and the neighborhood soon became the site of art clubs, private picture galleries, learned societies, literary salons, and libraries. Fine hotels, shopping emporia, and theaters also proliferated. The character of the neighborhood changed markedly at the close of the century when German, Irish, and Italian immigrants found work in the breweries, warehouses, and coal and lumber yards near the Hudson River and in the Southeast corner of the neighborhood. Older residences were subdivided into cheap lodging hotels and multiple-family dwellings, or demolished for higher-density tenements.

The Village at the turn of the twentieth century was a quite picturesque and ethnically diverse area. By the start of World War I it was widely known as a bohemian enclave with secluded side streets, low rents, and a tolerance for radicalism and nonconformity. Attention became increasingly focused on artists and writers noted for their boldly innovative work. The bohemian atmosphere helped to make Greenwich Village an attraction for tourists. Entrepreneurs provided amusements ranging from evenings in artists' studios to bacchanalian costume balls. During Prohibition local speakeasies attracted uptown

patrons. Decrepit rowhouses were remodeled into "artistic flats" for the well-to-do, and in 1926 luxury apartment towers appeared at the northern edge of Washington Square. The stock market crash of 1929 halted the momentum of new construction.

During the 1930s, galleries and collectors promoted the cause of contemporary art. Sculptor Gertrude Whitney Vanderbilt opened a museum dedicated to modern American art on West 8th Street, now the New York Studio School. The New School for Social Research, on West 12th Street since the late 1920s, inaugurated the "University in Exile" in 1934.

The Village had become the center for the "beat movement" by the 1950s, with galleries along 8th Street, coffee houses on MacDougal Street, and storefront theaters on Bleecker Street. "Happenings" and other unorthodox artistic, theatrical, and musical events were staged at the Judson Memorial Church. During the 1960s a homosexual community formed around Christopher Street; in 1969 a confrontation by the police culminated in a riot known as the Stonewall Rebellion, regarded as the beginning of the nationwide movement for gay and lesbian rights. Greenwich Village became a rallying place for antiwar protesters in the 1970s and for activity mobilized by the AIDS epidemic in the 1980s.

—Anna Notaro

FURTHER READING:

Banes, Sally. *Greenwich Village 1963: Avant-Garde Performance and the Effervescent.* Durham, North Carolina, Duke University Press, 1993.

Beard, Rick, and Leslie Cohen, editors. *Greenwich Village: Culture and Counterculture.* New Brunswick, New Jersey, Rutgers University Press, 1993.

Gold, Joyce. *From Trout Stream to Bohemia: A Walking Guide to Greenwich Village History.* New York, Old Warren Road Press, 1996.

Gross, Steve, et al. *Old Greenwich Village: An Architectural Portrait.* Washington, D.C., Preservation Press, 1993.

Kellerman, Regina M., editor. *The Architecture of the Greenwich Village Waterfront: An Archival Research Study Undertaken by the Greenwich Village Society for Historic Preservation.* New York, New York University Press, 1989.

Kugelmass, Jack, et al. *Masked Culture: The Greenwich Village Halloween.* New York, Columbia University Press, 1994.

McDarrah, Fred W., and Gloria S. McDarrah. *Beat Generation: Glory Days in Greenwich.* New York, Simon and Schuster, 1996.

Selzer, Jack. *Kenneth Burke in Greenwich Village: Conversing with the Moderns, 1915-1931* (Wisconsin Project on American Writers). Madison, University of Wisconsin Press, 1996.

Ware, Caroline F. *Greenwich Village 1920-1930: A Comment on American Civilization in the Post-War Years.* Berkeley, University of California Press, 1994.

Greeting Cards

Forms of correspondence with preprinted written sentiments and illustrative pictures, greeting cards have in many ways replaced more traditional and personalized forms of communication like letter writing by appealing to the needs of busy Americans and their willingness to mark an increasing number of holidays and events in largely commercialized ways. Rather than writing lengthy missives by hand, Americans since the turn of the century have found it easier to purchase prewritten sentiments in the form of greeting cards that they need only sign, address, and mail.

The earliest objects resembling greeting cards were handmade Valentines, popular in Europe and America in the eighteenth and nineteenth centuries. By the 1840s, both English and German chromolithographers had developed techniques allowing them to publish full-color postcards commemorating, primarily, Christmas and Valentine's Day. These enjoyed large commercial success in America as well as Europe, beginning what would become an American habit of sending manufactured rather than personal correspondence. The popularity of these early holiday cards also marked the increasing mobility of Americans and their need to communicate with friends and relatives now miles rather than blocks away, and appealed to the needs of busy people.

After the Civil War, the United States experienced what historian Leigh Eric Schmidt has termed the "commercialization of the calendar," an increasing prevalence of business-inspired holidays that were marked in increasingly homogenous ways. In about 1866, Louis Prang, a Boston printmaker, perfected his "chromo" process and was therefore able to produce finely detailed printed images in full, bright colors. Prang applied his talents to media of all sorts, including advertising trade cards, fine art prints, and calendars. His work producing Christmas cards, beginning in 1874, was the start of American greeting card production and the gradual unseating of European imports. Soon after Prang's first cards, he added birthday, New Year's, and Easter cards. These early cards, still in postcard form, were often embellished with detailed surface embossing, applied glitter, and silky fringe.

In the first decade of the twentieth century American producers completely overtook European manufacturers, creating a new sensibility for greeting cards and establishing the most enduring form of the greeting card, the folded piece of paper with a picture on the front, a written sentiment of verse inside, and a size-matched envelope. These early companies included the A. M. Davis Company, Rust Craft Publishers, the Keating Company, the Gibson Art Company, Hall Brothers, and American Greetings, which all enjoyed industry solidarity after the formation of the National Association of Greeting Card Manufacturers (later, The Greeting Card Association) in 1913. The success of these companies relied on Americans' increasing propensity to acknowledge a greater number of holidays: Mother's Day, Father's Day, and St. Patrick's Day were quickly added to the modern celebratory schedule. The greeting card industry worked together with the floral, jewelry, and confectionery industries not only to ingrain the importance of holiday celebrations in the collective American psyche, but also to make Americans feel more comfortable about relying on premade commodities to do so.

The most enduring of the early greeting card manufacturers were Hallmark, American Greetings, and Gibson Greetings, all founded between 1907 and 1914. Hallmark, established in 1914 in Kansas City, Missouri, by Mr. Joyce C. Hall and his brother Rollie, was the most successful of the three—in 1995, Hallmark possessed 42 percent of the market, followed by American Greetings with 35 percent and Gibson with 8 percent. With revenues estimated at $3.8 billion in 1994, it is no wonder that Hallmark has been called the "General Motors of emotion." As such, the company also cultivated its image of being a producer of down-home, conservative sentiments. J. C. Hall was a close friend of Walt Disney, and often incorporated wholesome Disney images into his cards, along with the works of other traditional illustrators like Norman Rockwell. In addition, Hallmark sponsored television's well-known drama series, the Hallmark Hall of Fame, beginning in the 1950s, and coined the slogan, "When You Care Enough to Send the Very Best." To critics, Hallmark had achieved the dubious reputation of being a purveyor of bland, mass-produced feelings that reflected the most banal of middle-American thoughts.

Greeting cards have not only tapped into, but also reflected changing American sentiments, aesthetic preferences, and preoccupations throughout the twentieth century. During the Depression, some Mother's Day cards came embellished with a precious piece of lace; and special Mother's Day cards during World War II were made and sent to women who had lost their sons in the war. Continuing to tap into the contemporary zeitgeist for their success, card companies in the late 1970s responded to a growing American cynicism, producing "alternative" humor lines alongside their more conservative and sentimental staples. By the mid-1980s larger companies began to capitalize on baby boomers' growing desire for self-expression and feelings of individuality by developing more specific lines of greeting cards. By the 1990s Hallmark itself had its own alternative humor card line called Shoebox Greetings. Its Mahogany line, targeted toward African-American audiences, strove to open up the world of greeting cards to nonwhite faces and sensibilities. Hallmark's Recovery line offered cards for former addicts, and the Thinking of You line included cards for such late-century concerns as downsizing, the needs of caregivers, new divorcees, PMS, and the struggles of weight loss.

With the help of women, who purchased more than 85 percent of all greeting cards in 1998, Hallmark enjoyed $3.7 billion in revenue, while American Greetings took in $2.2 billion. Card companies have also realistically acknowledged the potential encroachment of computers into their businesses by setting up in-store kiosks where one can create one's own computer-generated card. Hallmark has even developed a computer program that allows one to produce individualized cards at home.

—Wendy Woloson

FURTHER READING:

Chase, Ernest Dudley. *The Romance of Greeting Cards*. Cambridge, University Press of Cambridge, 1956.

Hall, Joyce. *When You Care Enough*. Kansas City, Missouri, Hallmark, 1979.

Hirshey, Gerri. "Happy [   ] Day to You." *New York Times Magazine*. July 2, 1995, 20-7+.

Schmidt, Leigh Eric. *Consumer Rites: The Buying and Selling of American Holidays*. Princeton, New Jersey, Princeton University Press, 1995.

Stern, Ellen Stock. *The Very Best from Hallmark*. New York, Abrams, 1988.

Gregory, Dick (1932—)

Dick Gregory brought a unique approach to political activism: he was one of the first African Americans to use his celebrity to promote a variety of political causes. He has intertwined his political beliefs with his work as an athlete, comedian, author, actor, and nutritionist since the 1950s. As the first Black comedian to work in "top-of-the-line" white nightclubs and on television, Gregory was one of the first African Americans to define Black issues for a mainstream white audience. He reached millions with his popular satirical comedy, bringing to light such issues as racism, civil rights, segregation, and nonviolence. He also used his humor to promote his

Dick Gregory

ideals in his movie appearances and books. In the 1960s, Gregory used his visibility as an entertainer to bring political causes like the civil rights movement, the antiwar movement, and the fight against violence, hunger, drug and alcohol abuse, and poor health care to popular attention. He combined his celebrity with such "attention-getting" tactics as fasts for political causes.

Born Richard Claxton Gregory on October 12, 1932, he was raised in poverty in St. Louis, Missouri. Gregory realized the power of politics at an early age; while in high school he was president of his graduating class and organizer of a march against conditions in segregated schools. With his interest in activism, Gregory soon learned the benefits of combining fame with politics. An athletic scholarship to Southern Illinois University (SIU) helped him achieve athletic fame on the track team as the fastest half-miler ever at SIU, and, in 1953, he was the first Black student awarded the school's Outstanding Athlete of the Year award. Gregory used his prominence to desegregate Carbondale's only movie theater.

While in the Army, Gregory performed comedy shows, and by the late 1950s he had begun working in Chicago nightclubs. He parlayed a one-night gig at the prestigious Playboy Club into a six-week run that brought him national recognition, winning him coverage in *Time* magazine and an appearance on the popular *Jack Paar Show*. He subsequently had gigs at numerous nightclubs, concerts, and on other television shows. Gregory's unique ability to use humor and wit to publicize political discourse to a large cross-section of the general population also brought the attention of Medgar Evars and Martin Luther King, Jr., who asked him to become more involved with the civil rights movement. He performed at benefits for groups like the National Association for the Advancement of Colored People (NAACP) and Congress of Racial Equality (CORE). He became involved with Martin Luther King, Jr.'s Southern Christian Leadership Conference programs, and in 1963 he helped collect and deliver 14,000 pounds of food to people in Leflore County, Mississippi. A strong advocate of King's non-violent movement, he was often jailed with King for civil disobedience.

In the 1960s Gregory wrote a number of books which continued his campaign for the civil rights movement. He titled his 1964 autobiographical work *Nigger* as a shock tactic. The tactic seemed effective as the book sold over a million copies. Gregory ran for mayor of Chicago in 1966 and for president of the United States in 1968. Those experiences were recounted in his book *Write Me In.* Gregory continued his fight to promote civil rights and his theories on how the government has tried to kill the civil rights movement and its leaders in books like *No More Lies: The Myth and the Reality of American History* and *Code Name Zorro: The Murder of Martin Luther King,* which he co-authored with Mark Lane. In addition to his books, Gregory made social commentary comedy records to spread his message even further. One of his records was the first "talk" record to sell over a million copies.

By the late 1960s and early 1970s, Gregory had expanded his activism to address issues including the Vietnam war, healthcare, capital punishment, Native American land and fishing rights, violence, and world hunger. Gregory began using fasts to bring attention to issues. In the tradition of Ghandi, Gregory began one of his many fasts in 1967 to protest the Vietnam War. His forty-day fast was sprawled over the media. Since that first fast, Gregory has fasted over 100 times for political causes, including one fast of 71 days.

In addition to his political causes, Gregory became one of the first celebrities to strongly advocate vegetarianism, becoming an expert on nutrition and a marathon runner in the 1970s. He jogged across the country to gain recognition for his political analysis of health and nutrition issues and his belief that nutritional solutions can help alleviate world hunger. In 1973, he published *Dick Gregory's Natural Diet for Folks Who Eat: Cooking with Mother Nature* and formed Dick Gregory Health Enterprises, Inc. around his nutritional product, the chemical-free, dairy-free Bahamian Diet in 1984. Gregory focused his health work on the African American community, blaming their lower life expectancy on poor nutrition and alcohol and drug addiction. To do his part to alleviate world hunger, he donated 2,600 pounds of his nutritional formula to starving Ethiopians. Gregory's approach to nutrition brought together issues of healthy eating, world hunger, and racism.

Throughout the 1990s, Gregory continued fighting for and gaining recognition for a wide spectrum of political causes. Despite being credited with "opening the door" for many Black comedians, Gregory stayed out of the entertainment business. Instead, his ability to combine wit, intelligence, humor, and political conviction continued to help support many political causes.

—tova stabin

FURTHER READING:

Buyukmihci, Hope Sawyer. "A Thinking Man's Journey." *The av magazine.* Vol. 102, No. 6, June 1, 1994, 17.

Gregory, Dick. *Dick Gregory's Political Primer.* Edited by James R. McGraw. New York, Harper & Row, 1972.

———. *Nigger: An Autobiography.* New York, Dutton, 1964.

———. *No More Lies.* Cutchogue, Buccaneer Books, 1993.

———. *No More Lies: The Myth and the Reality of American History.* Edited by James R. McGraw. New York, Harper & Row, 1971.

———. *Up from Nigger.* Edited by James R. McGraw. New York, Stein and Day, 1976.

Gretzky, Wayne (1961—)

The greatest hockey player of his generation and one of the greatest of all time, Wayne Gretzky's greatest contribution to the sport is his part in helping to popularize it throughout the United States. The National Hockey League has successfully expanded in California and across the Sun Belt (often, it must be said, at the expense of the game's Canadian roots); NHL-licensed apparel is worn by millions of American young people; and an increasing percentage of players joining professional teams are from the United States.

Gretzky was born in Brampton, Ontario, Canada, began skating at age two-and-a-half, and was taught hockey by his father, Walter. Even as a small child Gretzky's hockey skills were remarkable—at age ten he scored 378 goals in 69 games for a local peewee team,

Wayne Gretzky.

attracting the attention of professional scouts and the national media. When the up-start World Hockey Association began signing players at a younger age than the established NHL, Gretzky became a pro at the age of seventeen, agreeing in 1978 to a contract with the Indianapolis Racers. Like many other WHA teams, the Racers were under-financed, and owner Nelson Skalbania was forced to sell the skinny center to the Edmonton Oilers in one of the most ill-conceived transactions in the annals of professional sports.

In Edmonton, Gretzky joined a team possessed of a number of promising young players. After one year the Oilers organization joined the National Hockey League and Gretzky was able to demonstrate his talents to a larger audience. Despite doubters who pointed to his slight build and lack of speed, in 1979-1980, his first season in the NHL, Gretzky won the Rookie of the Year award. In his second campaign he broke Phil Esposito's single-season points record, and in his third he smashed his own record with an astonishing 92 goals and 212 points. In a sport where fifty goals in a season of eighty games denoted a superstar, Gretzky raised the level of superlatives by reaching the mark of fifty goals in thirty-nine games. In the mid-1980s, the Edmonton Oilers were one of the most exciting and successful teams in league history, winning the Stanley Cup in 1984, 1985, 1987, and 1988.

By 1988, however, Gretzky's talents could command more in salary than a small-market team like the Oilers claimed they could afford, and he was dispatched to Los Angeles for a package of players, draft choices, and $15 million. The trade that was a disaster for Edmonton fans turned out to be a gift to professional hockey in general and the Los Angeles Kings in particular. With Gretzky's marquee presence in a major mediacentre, the profile of the sport was raised enormously in California and throughout the United States. Gretzky's amiable features appeared in national endorsements, he hosted *Saturday Night Live,* gave interviews to Johnny Carson, and was even cast in a television soap opera. The Forum arena was sold out for the entire season, celebrities flocked to games, and more American children started to play hockey.

The same level of success on the ice was harder to come by. Despite leading the Kings to the Cup finals in 1993, where they lost to the Montreal Canadiens, Gretzky found team management unable to assemble a supporting cast of players as talented as he had enjoyed in Edmonton. At his request, he was traded to the St. Louis Blues in 1996, but this proved to be an unhappy experience, and after that season he signed with the New York Rangers. Once more, his arrival in a large American market sparked media interest, but again his skills, declining with age though still considerable, were insufficient to lift his team to cup-winning form. Gretzky retired from the game on April 18, 1999.

Gretzky holds sixty-one NHL individual records. He won the scoring championship ten times and was voted Most Valuable Player nine times; eighteen times he was voted to the All-Star team (and three times he was the game's MVP). Along with his four Stanley Cups, he played a leading part in three of his country's Canada Cup victories.

—Gerry Bowler

FURTHER READING:

Messier, Mark, Walter Gretzky, and Brett Hull. *Wayne Gretzky: The Making of the Great One.* New York, Beckett Publications, 1988.

Grey, Zane (1875-1939)

Author Zane Grey had a significant and lasting influence on American culture. Considered the creator of the modern Western novel, his work shaped the imagery of the West in the popular imagination. Many evaluations of the genre concentrate on the literary attributes of its writers. These literary considerations tend to outweigh the cultural resonance of the Western's popular appeal and often lead to the underrating of Grey's work in particular. As well as his ability to establish place and evoke the landscape of the mythical West, Grey endowed his work with a sense of popular history. He also negotiated cultural tensions that revolve around such issues as the coming of modernity, marriage, religion, and the returning veterans of World War I, which appealed to an exceptionally broad range of readers. He was serialized in the *Ladies Home Journal* as well as *Colliers Country Gentleman* and *McCalls,* and numerous books of his were translated into films, some made by his own company. He insisted that these were shot on location, thus introducing, through the cinema, a very particular visual depiction of the West that still endures. Arizona is now known to tourists as Zane Grey country.

Grey was born in Zanesville, Ohio, in 1875. He studied dentistry at Pennsylvania University, and then practiced in New York, where he published his first novel *Betty Zane* under his real name, Pearl Grey. His first books, set in Ohio, were based on family history of the pioneer period, and followed in the tradition of James Fennimore Cooper. However, although filled with adventure, they did not really convey the sense of the Wild West in a cohesive or effective form. Then, in 1907, at the Campfire Club in New York, Grey met Charles Jesse "Buffalo" Jones, a conservationist who labored to save the buffalo from extinction. He joined Jones as a writer and photographer on a trip to Arizona and across the Painted Desert and the Grand Canyon, and during these travels met and lived with Native Americans, cowboys, and Texas rangers; thereafter his writing evolved into authentic and convincing descriptions of the West. He wrote his first account of his travels in *Last of the Plainsmen* (1908), but did not become successful until the publication of *The Heritage of the Desert* (1910), which established his individual style. In the prefatory note to *Last of the Plainsmen,* Grey writes, "As a boy I read of Boone with a throbbing heart, and the silent moccasined, vengeful Wetzel I loved. I pored over the deeds of vengeful men—Custer and Carson, those heroes of the plains. And as a man I came to see the wonder, the tragedy of their lives, and to write about them."

Grey's novels use the frontier west of the 98th Meridian to create a new landscape for the West. This rugged and exacting territory, inhabited by extremes of good and evil, legitimates violence, yet offers redemption. It also provided Grey with a fictional space through which to address the anxieties of the period in which he was writing, and to offer the prospect of escape from them. *The Heritage of the Desert* opens with intense religious imagery projected on to the desert landscape and leads into a dramatic romantic adventure. The eastern hero is nursed back to health by a Mormon, and falls in love with his half Navajo, half Spanish adopted daughter. The girl needs to be rescued from an impending marriage to the villain, a circumstance that culminates in a climactic shoot out. It was, however, with *Riders of the Purple Sage* (1912) that Zane Grey made his name. Originally rejected by the publishers because of its harsh treatment of Mormon

Zane Grey

culture, the novel went on to sell two million copies. Grey continued to travel throughout his career and incorporated his experience of landscape and knowledge of oral history directly into his fiction. He published 54 novels in his lifetime, and more were released posthumously. For the most part, they have very simple adventure plots, but are structured into thrilling and romantic episodes sustained by their evocative settings.

At the height of his popularity between 1917 and 1924, Grey's novels made Bookman's top ten bestseller list every year. *The U.P. Trail* (1918) and *The Man of the Forest* (1920), the two major bestsellers, illustrate the appeal of Grey's work. *The U.P. Trail* is based very specifically on the history of the Union Pacific Railroad between 1864 and 1869, and incorporates the endurance of the pony express rider and the introduction of the telegraph to the West. The background to the narrative accords with popular memory. *The Man of the Forest* is set in 1885, within living memory, and the story follows the integration of a woodsman into the community of the West through his romance with a spirited eastern girl. She finds her full potential in the West and is ready to build a homestead in ''Paradise Park.'' Novels such as *The Desert of Wheat* (1919), *The Call of the Canyon* (1924), *The Vanishing American* (1925), *Under Tonto Rim* (1926), and *The Shepherd of Guadaloupe* (1930) are set contemporaneously and deal with modern issues and recent changes. They therefore establish the ethos of the West as a living idea rather than a lost ideal.

The formula that Grey established for the modern Western is one of moral regeneration or redemption, with heroic individuals proving themselves by living up to basic code of American values. His characters live by a ''Code of the West'' that differentiates between hero and villain, and leads to inevitable confrontation. He presented the Western hero in a manner that would become a central convention. He pays much attention to details of dress, appearance, and stance of his heroic characters. In *Riders of the Purple Sage,* for example, Lassiter is the mysterious gunfighter delineated by his fast draw, his costume, his honor, and his shady past. Here Grey introduced the professional gunman as a hero, but in the majority of his Westerns the older heroes are ready to be re-incorporated into society or commit themselves to very independent heroines. In most cases these women also come to recognize higher moral values through their experience in the West.

Although women are largely absent in the action of the Western, Grey's novels often feature a female protagonist, or pioneer characters. Heroines true to romantic formula are introduced at a stage where they have lost their social identity, which is restored in the course of the narrative through their own test of character in the Western landscape and not merely by the hero. In *Riders of the Purple Sage* Jane Withersteen attempts to stand up to the patriarchal Mormon power structure in which she has been orphaned. Part of the oppression she faces is the terrorism of a gang of outlaws, especially ''The Masked Rider'' who is revealed to be a girl brought up in the immoral culture of men. Grey is often accused of priggishness in his depiction of his heroes, and this tendency is also found in his heroines. He perfected two extremes of heroine: the cold, flirtatious, eastern sophisticate who reveals her deep and passionate love for the hero, and the practical, unladylike western girl, whose seeming promiscuity proves to be a blind.

These simplistic characters, and his constant appeal to religious symbolism and heightened moral codes, lead Grey's stories very easily into the realm of melodrama and sentimentality in which the stories address particular fantasies of freedom away from the corruption and constraints of city life. His characters frequently confront the dilemmas of modern life, as does the flapper heroine of *Code of the West* (1934) who chooses marriage to the hero because she recognizes his worth. More pointedly, a similarly drawn heroine in *The Call of the Canyon* (1924) marries a shell-shocked World War I veteran and chooses the harsher, but more essentially American West in which to raise a family. The Western landscape, with its promise of abundant riches, offers the protagonists a chance to re-make their lives according to higher moral values, in contrast to their old life and that of those around them.

Grey is often accused of being either ambivalent or complacent about the Native Americans who feature in his stories. For *The Vanishing American* (1925) he adopted the melancholy stance of Fennimore Cooper regarding the inevitably doomed fate of Native American culture; while the nobility of the Indian is part of the Western myth, he cannot win against the dishonesty of the white man. Regret at the passing of the buffalo herds and other species of wildlife and their habitats can also be detected in Grey's writings, and *The Vanishing American* gives evidence of Grey's grounding in other contemporary concerns, such as corruption in the U.S. Bureau of Indian Affairs, which is exposed by the narrative.

After 1925, Grey no longer appeared on the bestseller list, but his influence continued during the 1940s and 1950s through films based on his books, as well as through *Zane Grey's Western Magazine* and television's *Zane Grey Theatre* (1956-61). However, the Western film as a high budget production went into decline after 1930 until the formula was successfully reworked in John Ford's *Stagecoach* (1939). Although based on an Ernest Haycox story, the film—shot in Arizona and famously featuring Monument Valley—was a perfect expression of Zane Grey's articulation of the West. The revitalized formula, of which Ford was the master, explored the psychological depth of its characters at a time when the morality and romance of the 1920s Westerns seemed old-fashioned and melodramatic to Depression audiences with more complex concerns. Grey continued to publish fiction until his death in 1939, and sold his version of the winning of the West to an international audience, sustaining a myth that remains embedded in popular culture.

—Nickianne Moody

FURTHER READING:

Blake, K. S. ''Zane Grey and Images of the American West.'' *Geographical Review.* Vol. 85, No. 2, April 1995.

Cawelti, J. G. *Adventure, Mystery and Romance.* Chicago, University of Chicago Press, 1976.

Gruber, F. *Zane Grey.* Cleveland, World, 1970.

Jackson, Carlton. *Zane Grey.* Boston, Twayne, 1989.

Kimball, Arthur G. *Ace of Hearts: The Westerns of Zane Grey.* Forth Worth, Texas Christian University Press, 1993.

May, Stephen. *Zane Grey: Romancing the West.* Athens, Ohio University Press, 1997.

Ronald, Ann. *Zane Grey.* Boise, Idaho, Boise State University Press, 1975.

The Greyhound "Highway Traveler," 1948.

Scott, Kenneth William. *Zane Grey, Born to the West: A Reference Guide*. Boston, G. K. Hall, 1979.

Greyhound Buses

There is barely a town or a city in the United States that is not served by Greyhound bus lines, which began operating in 1914 and became a romantic emblem of America, its wide open spaces and its freedom to travel cheaply and explore the horizons of the country. Swedish immigrant Carl Eric Wickman began the enterprise in Hibbing, Minnesota, shuttling miners to and from work in a seven-passenger Hupmobile. He quickly expanded his operation and began buying out competitors; by 1935 the Greyhound Corporation owned 1,726 buses running over 46,000 route miles. Although their surrounding neighborhoods may have come to seem dilapidated, bus stations often served as the focal point of many a downtown district. Even in this age of the frequent flyer, Greyhound transports more than 45 million passengers annually. The well-known slogan "Go Greyhound . . . and leave the driving to us" rests within our collective consciousness, and the familiar red, white, and blue bus with its

painted profile of an outstretched racing dog has become as much a part of popular culture as any single icon of the road.

—Robert Kuhlken

FURTHER READING:

Jackson, Carlton. *Hounds of the Road: A History of the Greyhound Bus Company*. Dubuque, Iowa, Kendal/Hunt Publishing Co., 1984.

Schisgall, Oscar. *The Greyhound Story: From Hibbing to Everywhere*. Chicago, J. G. Ferguson, 1985.

Grier, Pam (1949—)

In the early to mid-1970s, American actress Pam Grier emerged as a tough heroine in the genre of "blaxploitation" films. With Hollywood's history of relegating African Americans to demeaning roles and women to love interests or other support positions, Grier quickly stood out as a groundbreaker. Though she got her start in "B" movies such as *The Big Bird Cage* and *Beyond the Valley of the Dolls* in 1969, Grier soon rose to stardom playing grass roots vigilantes in

Coffy (1972) and *Foxy Brown* (1974). Many critics faulted her films for their violence, sensationalism, and reliance on her attractive physique, but also recognized them as vanguard vehicles for portraying blacks as smart and self-sufficient, as well as giving women an important place as strong, confident, and active players. The rise in women's rights and civil rights at the time probably played a factor in the success of Grier's films.

—Geri Speace

FURTHER READING:

Smith, Jessie Carney, editor. *Notable Black American Women, Book II*. Detroit, Gale Research, 1996.

Speace, Geri. "Pam Grier." *Newsmakers 1998, Issue 3*. Detroit, Gale Research, 1998.

Griffin, Merv (1925—)

Talk show host Mervyn Griffin began his entertainment career as a singer and emcee with the Freddy Martin big band in the late 1940s. Griffin parlayed his quick wit and affable personality into movie acting opportunities as well as hosting television game and travel shows in the 1950s. He earned his place in the public consciousness, though, as the host of *The Merv Griffin Show,* which ran for 24

Merv Griffin

years from 1962 to 1986. This highly popular television show was, at various times, syndicated by Westinghouse Broadcasting Company and Metromedia as well as playing on the NBC and CBS networks. Known for his jovial, friendly style, Griffin was disparaged as a "softball" questioner by some, and accused of being more concerned with ingratiating himself with his guests than with being a "tough" interviewer. He also founded Merv Griffin Productions, making a fortune producing his talk shows, and packaging dozens of game shows that have continued to grip the nation such as *Jeopardy* and *Wheel of Fortune*. Griffin later made an even larger fortune as an owner of hotels and casinos across the country.

—Steven Kotok

FURTHER READING:

Druxman, Michael B. *Merv.* Leisure Books, New York, 1980.

Griffin, Merv with Peter Barsocchini. *Merv: An Autobiography.* Simon and Schuster, 1980.

Griffith, D. W. (1875-1948)

Considered the father of the motion picture and the first great artist of the cinema, director D. W. Griffith revolutionized filmmaking with technical innovations and a narrative structure still in use at the end of the twentieth century. His most significant and controversial movie, *The Birth of a Nation* (1915) established the feature-length film and the Hollywood star system. After a private viewing at the White House, President Woodrow Wilson reportedly remarked that the film "was like writing history with lightning." Released on March 3, *The Birth of a Nation* was not only the longest and most expensive movie to date, but it was the most popular movie of its time and the most politically explosive film in American history.

David Wark Griffith was born on January 23, 1875, in the town of Crestwood in Oldham County, Kentucky. He was an aspiring actor from 1897-1907, traveling from Portland, Oregon, to Boston, Massachusetts, working in stock companies under the name Lawrence Griffith. In 1906, while in Boston, he married his first wife, Linda Arvidson Johnson. His days as a stage actor were unfruitful.

In 1908, the famed director Edwin S. Porter introduced Griffith to his associates at the Biograph Company on 14th Street in Manhattan. Here the young actor gave up his first love to sell stories and ultimately to begin making movies himself. Along with his trusted and accomplished cameraman, G. W. "Billy" Bitzer, Griffith worked at a tremendous pace. From August 1908 through August 1911, he completed an astonishing 326 one-reel films. Through these early years, Griffith experimented with different camera angles, editing, and narrative styles. He used close-ups to produce greater emotional drama and sharp cuts between scenes to quicken a story's pace, believing that action rather than written titles should propel the movie's plot. In 1912 Griffith made a short, *The New York Hat,* with Lionel Barrymore and a young Mary Pickford based on a story submitted by sixteen-year-old Anita Loos, soon to be the most sought-after scenarist in Hollywood. Griffith stayed with Biograph just one more year, but he made his longest and most elaborate film to

D. W. Griffith (third from left) on location.

date in 1913, *Judith of Bethulia.* At four reels, it was four times longer than the standard movie.

Griffith reportedly convinced Bitzer to leave Biograph by telling him that he planned on making the greatest film in history. As an independent producer, Griffith acted as director, producer, distributor, and press agent for his epic *Birth of a Nation.* Based on Thomas Dixon's novel *The Clansman* (1905), Griffith's movie faithfully depicted the Reconstruction Era that immediately followed the U.S. Civil War as a period in which African-American men threatened the purity of the white race politically, socially, and sexually. From 1915 to 1946, a reported two hundred million people saw the film. During the first weeks of the movie's release, Americans lined up along sidewalks and in New York City paid the extraordinary price of $2.00 a seat for a chance to see the most talked-about movie of the year. With more than twelve reels of film, it ran a record two hours. The movie cost more than $100,000 to film but grossed an astonishing $18 million.

The technical innovations that Griffith employed to make his film have continued to impress viewers and film historians alike since 1915. For example, Griffith had Bitzer set up his camera at ground level to capture the power and frantic torrent of horse hoofs at full gallop on a dusty road. Such a scene illustrated the capabilities of the movie camera if freed from its stationary position in front of a stage. Using an array of camera angles—close-ups, long shots, cutbacks—Griffith proved that directors could make long movies and still hold the audience's attention. Parallel editing—cross-cutting footage of different events—achieved suspense and created the illusion of simultaneous action.

Repugnant to modern audiences yet reflecting widespread American sentiments at the time, the overt racist and nativist imagery, specifically the sympathetic portrayal of the Ku Klux Klan, throughout *Birth of a Nation* provoked the NAACP, a young organization in 1915, to rally black and white people around the country to picket theaters showing the movie. Surprised by the strong reaction to the film and believing it threatened his freedom of speech and, perhaps more importantly, his artistic integrity, Griffith released the antibigotry epic *Intolerance* in 1916. As popular as *Birth of a Nation* was, *Intolerance* proved to have a stronger effect on other directors. Among those under Griffith's influence was the famous Soviet director Sergei Eisenstein, who believed the American's style of rapid-fire editing had advanced filmmaking by a decade.

Griffith directed another twenty-six features between 1916 and 1931 but never again enjoyed adulation as the world's most brilliant director. He ended his career working from his Mamaroneck studio, a suburb of New York City, to be closer to the financial center of the movie industry.

—Ray Haberski, Jr.

FURTHER READING:

Barry, Iris. *D. W. Griffith: American Film Master.* New York, Museum of Modern Art, 1965.

Carter, Everett. "Cultural History Written with Lightning: The Significance of *The Birth of a Nation.*" *Hollywood as Historian.* Edited by Peter Rollins. Lexington, University of Kentucky Press, 1998.

Cripps, Thomas. "The Reaction of the Negro to the Motion Picture *The Birth of a Nation.*" *Historian.* Vol. 25, 1963.

Franklin, John Hope. "Birth of a Nation—Propaganda as History." In *Hollywood's America: United States History through Its Films,* edited by Steven Mintz and Randy Roberts. New York, Brandywine Press, 1993.

Graham, Cooper C., Steven Higgins, Elaine Mancini, and Joao Luiz Vieira. *D. W. Griffith and the Biograph Company.* Metuchen, New Jersey, Scarecrow Press, 1985.

Gunning, Thomas. *D. W. Griffith and the Rise of the Narrative Film.* Urbana, University of Illinois Press, 1991.

Litwack, Leon F. "The Birth of a Nation." In *Past Imperfect: History According to the Movies,* edited by Mark C. Carnes. New York, Henry Holt and Company, 1995.

Schickle, Richard. *D. W. Griffith: An American Life.* New York, Simon and Schuster, 1984.

Stern, Seymour. "The Birth of a Nation." *Film Culture.* Vol. 36, Spring-Summer, 1965.

Williams, Martin. *Griffith: First Artist of the Movies.* New York, Oxford University Press, 1980.

Griffith, Nanci (1954—)

Almost alone among commercially successful singer-songwriters within folk and country music, Nanci Griffith represents a refreshing contrast to the bland offerings of the music industry's hit-making machinery. Defying easy categorization into the standard pigeonholes, Griffith once described her own style of music as "folkabilly." After 15 albums Nanci Griffith still seems to be steaming ahead at full throttle. No longer scaling the heights but rather traversing the summit ridge of her creative powers, several of her most recent releases have been met with widespread critical acclaim. She has also captivated a legion of loyal fans.

Nanci Caroline Griffith was born July 6, 1953 near Austin, Texas—a town full of good music, where she penetrated the competitive ranks of a near legendary songwriting tradition. She has portrayed her parents as "beatniks" who enthusiastically supported her attempts to become a folksinger. Nanci's first paid gig was at the age

Nanci Griffith

of 14, when she played at the local Red Lion and made $11. She graduated from Austin's Holy Cross High School, where she strummed guitar for folk mass, then stayed in the neighborhood by enrolling at the University of Texas. Nanci began playing every Sunday night—and would continue to play for five years—at the Hole in the Wall, a dingy little bar across the street from campus. The bar became her proving ground, for—as she once described it—if you can get loud beer-drinkers to hush up a moment and listen to your songs then you must be doing something right. She tried teaching kindergarten for a while, but by this time her heart was firmly attached to her true calling.

Nanci writes and plays folk music. Not one to shy away from this particular "f-word," she capitalizes the term because the people are important to her and so is the music. Invoking the muses of this particular genre has turned into a one-woman crusade to resurrect what's good and true among the earthier forms of the American song canon. In 1994 Griffith won a Grammy Award for her 1993 album *Other Voices, Other Rooms,* which paid tribute to songwriters she has come to admire. Her 1998 release, *Other Voices, Too (A Trip Back to Bountiful),* serves as a continuation of this project. She cites Carolyn Hester as an influential figure in her early career, but also draws motivation from the Carter Family, Buddy Holly, and the Everly Brothers. By all accounts, Nanci is even more popular in the British Isles than in the United States. Perhaps this stems from her own Anglo ancestry, or perhaps because British sensibilities allow for greater sophistication in popular music. It may also reflect her residential choices: she has maintained a loft in Dublin for more than a decade, and now divides her time between Ireland and a small farm south of Nashville.

Nanci's first album was recorded in 1978 and subsequently reissued by folk-oriented Philo/Rounder Records (as were her next three). A good representation from this initial foray into record making would be the 1984 title, *Once In a Very Blue Moon*. In 1987 she switched to the predominantly country label MCA, and over the next five years released a series of rich offerings with more production input than the spare earlier records. It was also during this time period that Griffith assembled a first-rate touring band—the Blue Moon Orchestra—that has stayed together and backed her efforts for over a decade. Since 1992 Nanci has recorded on the Elektra label, which has given her wide latitude to experiment with new ambitions and soundscapes. Unanimously well received by critics was a 1994 album, the very personal and heartfelt *Flyer*. She has also recorded with artists as diverse as Bruce Cockburn, John Gorka, The Chieftains, and Hootie and the Blowfish. Her songs have been covered—often as hit records—by many other performers, including Willie Nelson, Suzy Boguss, and Kathy Mattea.

Stylistically, Griffith is capable of assuming many postures. Her voice, at once so full and supple, can be delicate and hesitant one moment, and growling with anger or unassailable determination the next. That soft Texas twang is never too far away. A true storyteller, she likes to experiment with dialect and playful pronunciation. She has great range of expression, and uses her vocal chords like a richly textured instrument. Whether accompanied only by acoustic guitar or backed with a full string orchestra, it makes no difference; Nanci Griffith is able to reach out and tell us about ourselves through song. Thematically, Griffith takes on the broad sweep of land and life, especially trials of the common person trying to negotiate the lonely distances of modern times. There are accounts of working in orchards and on street corners, of dusty towns, drive-in movies and dashboard lights. She writes of rivers and lakes and fields of bluebonnets, geographical metaphors for sensing our place; there are also railroads and highways, and always the alternative of moving on. She accusingly points to racism, violence, and the inexcusable folly of warfare as pernicious tragedies we can ill afford. An avid reader, Nanci credits writers such as Larry McMurtry, Carson McCullers, and Eudora Welty as major inspirations. Her own stories put to song are situated squarely within the great literary tradition of the South, where the people, the lives they lead, and the land they live on are all worthy of notice. But there is something sad and melancholy about this artist's persona, reflecting bittersweet memories of lost loves and roads not taken. There have been some hard times, perhaps even a few regrets. In this, there is more than a hint of autobiography, thereby lending authenticity to its emotional impact. Her characters often live alone, their broken or half-baked dreams seeing them through one day at a time. Yet there is always hope, the yearning for fulfillment and intimacy never quite extinguished. Such an undeniably romantic vision is usually sustained at great cost. Deep down inside Nanci knows that love is a choice we make—though she can never bring herself to venture a decision.

Fortunately her fans do not face the same dilemma. In one of those paradoxes of popular culture, it seems the more things become homogenized and mass-produced, the more we yearn for interaction with a genuine and distinct expression of artistry. Well loved by a devoted group of admirers, Nanci Griffith has one of the more active news groups on the Internet. Members of "NanciNet" discuss everything from favorite albums and musical influences to the social and political commentary inherent in Griffith's songs. Numerous web pages exist that pay tribute to her artistic achievements. For this

reclusive, self-avowed folk singer, such grass roots activism by the people must be gratifying indeed.

—Robert Kuhlken

FURTHER READING:

Griffith, Nanci, and Joe Jackson. *Nanci Griffith's Other Voices: A Personal History of Folk Music.* New York, Three Rivers Press, 1998.

Vaughan, Andrew. *Who's Who in New Country Music,* New York, St. Martin's Press, 1989.

Grimek, John (1910-1998)

During John Grimek's career as a weightlifter, bodybuilder, and magazine editor—which began in the late 1920s and ended in the mid-1980s—he saw weight training change from being an activity shunned by athletes and exercise scientists into an activity universally embraced by these groups. What's more, because of his remarkable combination of muscle mass, athleticism, and flexibility, he was one of the main instigators of the change in attitude. In the mid-1920s, when young John first began to lift, following the example of his older brother George in Perth Amboy, New Jersey, there were very few men and virtually no women in the United States who trained with heavy weights. It was not that heavy lifting was unknown; it was that lifting was anathema throughout the culture. How such nonsense came to be believed by so many people is important to an understanding of the role John Grimek played in demystifying the notion of heavy lifting.

Beginning in the latter half of the nineteenth century, several influential writers began to argue that the lifting of heavy weights would make a person slow and inflexible, and a new word came into the English language: musclebound. These writers, who included Dr. Dio Lewis, William Blaikie, and Dr. Dudley Allen Sargent, warned prospective weight trainers that, in the words of Blaikie, "If you do work suited to a draft horse, you will surely develop the ponderous qualities of that worthy animal." The arguments of these men, who misunderstood genetics as thoroughly as they misunderstood physiology, were soon bolstered by a group of unscrupulous lifters who had built muscular bodies with weight training and wanted to use those bodies to make money. These lifters realized that it would be difficult to prosper by selling barbells and dumbells through the mail because such weights were expensive to manufacture and costly to ship. However, they also realized that if they denounced heavy weight training in their mail order advertisements, they could then either sell equipment that was very light (e.g., rubber expanders) or simply sell a course of instruction explaining how to do various callisthenic exercises that required no apparatus.

Together, the misguided writers and the dishonest entrepreneurs gave birth to the myth of the musclebound weightlifter, and almost all coaches, athletes, and trainers came to believe that the worst thing an athlete could do was to lift heavy weights. Thus it was that, throughout the first half of the twentieth century, young men such as John Grimek were looked on with suspicion and even hostility as they pursued their dreams of size and strength. Perhaps because of the belief that weights would make a person slow and "tie you up," many lifters during that period worked on their flexibility and athleticism so they could disprove the belief. As for Grimek, it became especially important, as he gained muscular size very quickly and easily. In a few short years, his robust constitution and genetic predisposition combined to produce a body of previously unsurpassed perfection.

During most of the 1930s, there were no bodybuilding contests, and the only place where a young lifter/builder could compete in the "iron game" was on the weightlifting platform. Grimek's first competition was the New Jersey State Championships in Newark, which he won easily, lifting in the heavyweight class (over 82.5 kg or 181.75 pounds). Later that same year he entered the U.S. National Championships, and exceeded the national record in the press, with 242.5 pounds. He moved to York, Pennsylvania, in 1936 to train with the York Barbell Club and to work for the York Barbell Company, and by winning the National Championships that year he qualified for the 1936 Olympic Games in Berlin.

For the next several years, Grimek continued in competition, reaching his best total in 1940 at the National Championships with a press of 285 pounds, a snatch of 250, and a clean and jerk of 325. That same night, he won his first Mr. America title, and by that time he was far more famous in the small subculture of heavy lifting as a bodybuilder than as a weightlifter. In order for him to compete with the true heavyweights in America and around the world, some of whom weighed up to 300 pounds, it would have been necessary for him to gain 40 or 50 pounds, which would have spoiled the symmetry of his already legendary physique. Robert (Bob) Hoffman, the coach of the York Barbell Club team and owner of the York Barbell Company, analyzed the situation correctly: "I frequently say that a man can't have everything. John Grimek has more than his share and has done more than his share for weightlifting.... He became a weightlifter to prove that there is power in a shapely physique ... Grimek would be stronger if he was heavier, but he would not have his present physique. I think his physique does weightlifting and the entire cause of weight training more good than would his winning of the world's championship."

One of the ways Grimek helped the "cause of weight training" was to serve as the prime example of flexible muscle in Bob Hoffman's magazine, *Strength & Health*, for which Grimek worked as a writer/editor. From 1932 on, in every issue of his magazine, Hoffman hammered away at the myth of the musclebound lifter and Grimek was his biggest weapon. Photographs of Grimek's flexibility and stories of his athleticism filled the pages of *Strength & Health* and helped to convince skeptical readers that heavy weights would help them, as Hoffman always said, "in their chosen sport." Another important way in which Grimek helped the "cause" was by taking part in the many exhibitions arranged by Hoffman. Whenever Hoffman was asked to bring some lifters and put on an exhibition, he would accept if at all possible. He knew that only by exposing the public to the truth that heavy lifting would help a man or a woman at his or her chosen sport, could he hope to dispel the myth of the musclebound lifter. All of these exhibitions chipped away at the myth, as audiences saw for themselves how quick and flexible the lifters were, but in the spring of 1940 Hoffman took a group of lifters, including John Grimek, to Springfield College in Massachusetts. What happened there became a pivotal event in the destruction of the myth.

Fraysher Ferguson, a student at Springfield College (where most of the country's Y.M.C.A. directors were trained), invited Hoffman to bring the lifters to Springfield for an exhibition because none of his professors believed him when he said that his lifting helped him as an athlete. One of those professors was Dr. Peter Karpovich, the most widely respected physical educator in America at that time and an avowed enemy of heavy lifting. The hall was packed with students and staff that day, and after Hoffman introduced the two top lifters, John Grimek and world heavyweight champion John Davis, Davis did some heavy lifting and Grimek gave a posing exhibition. Although physiques such as Grimek's had become common by the last decades of the twentieth century, none of the people in attendance in 1940 had ever seen a man with such huge, defined muscles. Following the exhibition, Hoffman invited questions, and the students turned to Dr. Karpovich. True to form, he rose and asked if "Mr. Grimek would mind scratching the back of his neck." After drawing a laugh by saying his neck didn't itch, Grimek obliged, then went on to a series of stunts that included standing on a low stool and touching the floor, straightlegged, with his fingertips and then doing a full side to side leg split. John Davis then did a back flip while holding a 50-pound dumbell in each hand. The audience burst into shocked applause at each new shattering stunt, and afterward Karpovich came down and privately apologized, vowing to undertake research studies that would help him understand how he could have been so mistaken. Indeed, though World War II intervened, when Karpovich returned to his lab in the late 1940s he directed a series of studies that proved to his satisfaction that far from slowing a person down, weight training increased a person's speed. In time, these studies were published in the most important journals in the field, and the musclebound theory was gradually laid to rest.

It is doubtful whether a person with significantly less muscle mass could have caused such a change in the thinking of those who saw Grimek perform his feats of flexibility. If anyone appeared visually to symbolize the word "musclebound" it was John Grimek during the 1930s and 1940s. Yet if such a man was both limber and graceful, it flew in the face of the myth. Part of Grimek's power as a performer came from his dramatic ability to pose his body. Many who saw him in his prime have said that his posing was a "ballet of power," in which he moved from pose to pose in a fluid, natural manner. Most historians of physical culture place Grimek above all bodybuilders before or since in his mastery of physical display. According to Joe Weider, who began his publishing empire in 1940, Grimek "invented modern posing, and no one has ever matched his ability on the posing platform." Films that remain of Grimek on the platform reveal a performance that combined grace, power, drama, masculinity, and beauty. He was never defeated in bodybuilding competition, and he was the man to whom all other lifter/builders would point when they were told that "lifting will make you musclebound." As Grimek himself told a group of skeptical Y.M.C.A. directors after an exhibition in which he posed and performed his seemingly miraculous stunts, "Can you do what I do? If you can't, then you're the ones who are musclebound."

—Jan and Terry Todd

FURTHER READING:

Fair, John. *Muscletown USA: Bob Hoffman and the Manly Culture of York Barbell*. State College, Pennsylvania State University Press, 1999.

Todd, Jan and Terry, editors. "John Grimek: The Man." In Special Commemorative Issue of *Iron Game History*. Vol. 6. April 1999.

Grisham, John (1955—)

John Grisham's contributions to the world of popular culture in the late twentieth century are enormous. Not only is he largely responsible for the elevation of legal thrillers to a level of popularity never before seen in literary circles, but he has also transcended that genre as his books are eagerly anticipated by those in the movie industry. Ironically, the best-selling author did not find instant success. While working as a lawyer and a Mississippi state legislator, Grisham took four years to write his first novel, *A Time to Kill.* When he finished in 1987, he sent the manuscript to 16 agents, finally connecting with agent Jay Garon. Over two dozen publishers rejected the book before Wynwood Press accepted it. Wynwood decided on a small print run, only 5000 copies, and paid Grisham a mere $15,000 for what many believe to be his finest book. This, however, would be the last time Grisham was to meet with such difficulty in getting his work published.

Grisham wrote *The Firm* based on guidelines in a *Writer's Digest* article on writing a suspense novel. Paramount bought the film rights for $600,000 in 1990 before the novel even had a publisher. After the film rights sold, publishers lined up to offer Grisham a

John Grisham

contract. Doubleday, one of the many publishers that rejected *A Time To Kill,* won out and signed Grisham to a three book contract. Grisham closed his law practice and began devoting his time entirely to writing. He wrote his third book, *The Pelican Brief,* in only 100 days. He took six months to write his next book, *The Client.* Grisham found himself in 1993 with *The Client* at number one on the *New York Times* hardcover bestseller list, and *The Pelican Brief, The Firm,* and *A Time to Kill* within the first five slots on the *New York Times* paperback bestseller list.

Grisham has not only had a huge impact on the publishing industry. Almost all of his novels have been made into relatively successful films. They have been directed by such big-name directors as Joel Schumacher, Sydney Pollack, and Francis Ford Coppola. They have attracted such critically acclaimed and popular actors as Susan Sarandon, Tommy Lee Jones, Tom Cruise, Gene Hackman, Denzel Washington, Julia Roberts, Matt Damon, Danny DeVito, and Claire Danes. *The Gingerbread Man,* a film released in 1998, was based on Grisham's first original screenplay.

As bestsellers, Grisham's novels have received a great deal of critical attention, and the reviews have been mixed. He is most often criticized for writing formulaic novels and sacrificing character development for plot. Still, even his critics usually admit that he writes a thrilling page-turner. He is often compared to his contemporary Scott Turow, best-selling author of legal thrillers *Presumed Innocent* and *Burden of Proof.* Grisham and Turow, whose first book appeared in the year Grisham finished *A Time to Kill,* are credited with making legal thrillers a hot commodity in the 1990s, adding fuel to the careers of such authors as Richard North Patterson, Steven Martini, and Brad Meltzer.

Grisham's books appeal to a sense of paranoia that prevailed in the 1990s. His books and the films they inspire often deal with people who are fighting corruption and others' self-serving interests at every turn. In *The Firm,* Mitchell McDeere is stuck between the corrupt firm that lured him straight out of law school with an $80,000 salary and a new BMW, and the FBI agents who are trying to bully him into helping them bring the firm down. In *The Pelican Brief,* law student Darby Shaw stumbles on the truth behind the assassination of two Supreme Court justices and finds herself pursued not only by the man behind the assassinations, but also by various government representatives. The American public seems very ready and willing to believe that the wealthy and the government are corrupt and in cahoots with one another, and that an earnest and intelligent person can get out of even the worst of situations.

Indeed, the 1990s saw an explosion of legal thrillers in print, film, and television. From 1991 to 1998, Doubleday released a new Grisham novel every spring. In a *Publishers Weekly* article, Jeff Zaleski describes the frenzy this begets: "To accommodate it, booksellers around the country clear miles of shelf space; book and audio clubs quicken to fill orders; motion picture studios cajole and connive to get a first peek at galleys." Grisham's impact on publishing is obvious, he is the kind of author, in company with such mega-selling authors as Stephen King and Danielle Steel, who creates big sales for publishers and bookstores alike. His influence reaches into the entire entertainment industry, where film and television studios look to capitalize on Grisham's popularity.

—Adrienne Furness

FURTHER READING:

Ferranti, Jennifer. "Grisham's Law." *Saturday Evening Post.* March/April 1997, 42-45.

"Grisham, John." *Current Biography.* September 1993, 21-24.

Olsen, Mark. "Grishamovies." *Film Comment.* March/April 1998, 76-80.

Zaleski, Jeff. "The Grisham Business." *Publishers Weekly.* January 19, 1998, 248-51.

Grits

Made from finely ground dried and hulled corn kernels, or hominy, grits are a central feature of Southern foodways. Grits are commonly eaten for breakfast and complimented by a wide variety of condiments; including red-eye gravy, butter, cheese, ham, bacon, salmon, shrimp, and sausage. While generally boiled to a porridge-like consistency, grits can also be served with milk and sugar or even cold-sliced and fried. Generations of Southerners have enjoyed grits since Native Americans first introduced Virginia colonists to unrefined hominy, but this Southern staple apparently has little culinary currency outside the region. Indeed, grits are an important element of Southern distinctiveness and celebrated in the region through festival, humor, literature, and song. Packaged instant or quick, grits are a key ingredient in Southern cooking and an enduring feature of Southern identity.

—Stephen C. Kenny

FURTHER READING:

Egerton, John. *Southern Food: At Home, on the Road, in History.* Chapel Hill, University of North Carolina Press, 1993.

Wilson, Charles Reagan, and William Ferris, editors. *Encyclopedia of Southern Culture.* Chapel Hill, University of North Carolina Press, 1989.

Grizzard, Lewis (1946-1994)

Lewis McDonald Grizzard, Jr., was a popular and sometimes controversial newspaper columnist who gained fame in the 1980s and 1990s with his popular syndicated newspaper column. Throughout his career, Grizzard's wit entertained readers with a commentary that was unabashedly pro-Southern. His love for his alma mater, the University of Georgia, his attitude toward Yankees, and his well-known marital failures all provided material for his columns, numerous books, audiocassettes, and personal and television appearances. But it was in his life-and-death struggle with heart disease that he touched the hearts of his loyal readers.

Grizzard grew up in the small town of Moreland, Georgia, where he had been born on October 20, 1947. He attended the University of Georgia in Athens, but because he accepted a job with the *Atlanta Journal-Constitution* in his senior year, he did not graduate until years later. Despite his delayed graduation, Grizzard was awarded the distinguished alumni award from his alma mater's College of Journalism and Mass Communication.

Before settling down as a syndicated newspaper columnist, Grizzard worked as sports editor at newspapers in Atlanta and Chicago. By the time of his death in 1994, his columns had appeared in more than 200 newspapers across the United States, and he had authored 14 books of his collected humor. Many of Grizzard's books found their way to the *New York Times* best-selling list, and most remain in print years after his death. True to his persona as a southern "good old boy," he never used a word processor or computer, preferring instead an old manual typewriter.

While his humor won him fame, Grizzard often endured conflicting attitudes toward his work. Some condemned his brand of humor as sexist, homophobic, jaded, and cynical, while others praised him as a great storyteller and a modern-day Mark Twain. A publisher once compared the writer to Faulkner, but implied that Grizzard was more attuned to the average person. Grizzard met criticism of his work with an honesty that marked his writing and humor as distinctly his own. His popularity quickly spread from syndicated columns to books to audiotapes and personal appearances. Probably his best-known appearance was on the sitcom *Designing Women,* in which he played Julia and Suzanne Sugarbaker's (Dixie Carter and Delta Burke) half-brother.

Despite his commercial success, Grizzard's personal life seemed far from successful. He had three failed marriages, which he often wrote about in his columns and books. He married his fourth wife, Dedra, just days before his death. Grizzard had one stepdaughter and no children of his own.

After years of illnesses and surgeries, Grizzard died from complications following heart surgery in Atlanta. After his death, the Lewis Grizzard Museum, operated by the Lewis Grizzard Memorial Trust, was established in his hometown of Moreland. Though admission is free, visitors may donate one dollar to support the Lewis Grizzard Scholarship. Visitors can view such items as the writer's baseball glove, his letter jacket, and his childhood rocking chair among other mementos. Grizzard's book *I Took a Lickin and Kept on Tickin* is a posthumous compilation of previously published essays employing humor to detail his battle with the heart disease that eventually led to his early death.

—Kimberley H. Kidd

FURTHER READING:

Grizzard, Lewis. *I Took a Lickin and Kept on Tickin.* New York, Ballantine, 1995.

———, and Chuck Perry. *Don't Fence Me In: An Anecdotal Biography of Lewis Grizzard.* Atlanta, Longstreet Press, 1995.

Groening, Matt (1954—)

Matt Groening graduated from Evergreen State University in 1977 expecting to become a writer, but cartooning became his claim to fame. By 1991, the creator of the animated television series *The Simpsons* and the nationally syndicated comic strip *Life in Hell* had received his first two Emmys and was listed as one of the Forbes Top 40 earners in the entertainment industry.

Groening's struggles as a writer in Los Angeles after college led to the creation of *Life in Hell,* a comic strip about Binky, a hostile,

Matt Groening

frustrated rabbit (the only recognizable animal Groening could draw). Instead of sending correspondence to his relatives and friends, Groening sent his first comics because they communicated his feelings. He also tried to sell booklets of his comic strips in the "punk" section of the record store where he worked. In 1978, *Wet,* a magazine which showcased unconventional graphics, ran a few installments of the strip. In 1980, the Los Angeles *Reader,* a weekly alternative paper, hired Groening as circulation manager and began to run *Life in Hell* regularly. Groening transformed Binky from a grouchy pessimist to a hapless victim. He added several characters, Binky's son, Bongo; his girlfriend, Sheba; and Akbar and Jeff, the identical fez-wearing entrepreneurs. By 1983, the strip was being published in twenty papers and its success led to Groening's first book, *Love Is Hell,* published in 1984. By 1997, Groening had published twelve *Life in Hell* books, and that year the comic appeared in more than two hundred newspapers.

In 1985, Groening resigned from the *Reader* along with Deborah Caplan (who worked in the paper's advertising department). Together they established Life in Hell, Inc., with Caplan as the company's business manager. They married on October 29, 1986, and later had two children—Homer and Abraham. In 1987, James L. Brooks (creator of the television shows *Taxi* and *The Mary Tyler Moore Show,* and director of *Terms of Endearment* and *As Good as It Gets*) approached Groening to create short animated segments of *Life in Hell* for the Fox network's *The Tracey Ullman Show.* Groening agreed to do segments for the show but, unwilling to relinquish the rights to *Life in Hell,* created an entirely new set of characters—the Simpsons, a blue-collar family including parents Homer and Marge, son Bart, and daughters Lisa and baby Maggie.

By 1989, the Simpsons had become so popular on *The Tracey Ullman Show* that Fox commissioned thirteen episodes for the 1989 fall season. After a delay, the first episode of *The Simpsons* aired in

January 1990, and, within two months, the show was ranked in the Nielson's top fifteen most watched shows on American television. The creator, developer, animator, director, and executive producer of *The Simpsons,* Groening was nominated for an Emmy for outstanding animated program every year the Simpsons appeared on *The Tracey Ullman Show* and won Emmy awards in that category for each of *The Simpsons'* first two seasons. He won again in 1994, 1996, and 1998. In 1997, Groening was awarded the George Foster Peabody Award for excellence in broadcasting for *The Simpsons.*

Groening further broadened the appeal of *The Simpsons* in 1993 when he started the Bongo Comics Group (for which he received the Diamond Distribution Gem Award for new publication of the year), which included four monthly comic books—*Simpsons Comics, BartMan, Itchy & Scratchy,* and *Radioactive Man* (Bart Simpson's favorite comic book hero). In 1995, Groening founded and published Zongo Comics, established to publish the work of alternative independent artists, which includes the titles *Jimbo, Fleener,* and *Hopster's Tracks.* He added *Krusty Comics* and *Lisa Comics* to the Bongo Comics Group, and *Roswell* in 1996.

Groening's philosophies are deeply integrated into *The Simpsons.* As he indicated in a 1993 interview with the *Washington Post,* the Simpsons are a blue-collar family similar to cartoon greats like the Flintstones and the Jetsons, but *The Simpsons* tries to go for "real emotions." Although the characters encounter exaggerated events, the writers have tried to make them react as people would. Episodes of *The Simpsons* are replete with cultural references, from "Dr. Zaius," the song referring to the 1968 film *Planet of the Apes* sung to the tune of Falco's 1985 hit "Rock Me Amadeus," to Mayor Quimby's Kennedy-esque Boston accent.

The Simpsons have become one of the most recognizable television families in the world. Bart Simpson even made *Time* magazine's list of the one hundred most important people of the twentieth century as one of the top twenty Artists and Entertainers. Groening's show has not only captured the television market, but has overwhelmed the commercial market with the Simpsons appearing as toys, in their own video game, on T-shirts, as product endorsers, on compact disks, and on their own Internet web page.

Groening has a second project in production with Fox: an animated series called *Futurama*. Beginning mid-season 1999, *Futurama* is an animated story about a twentieth-century man dealing with life in the year 3000.

—Adam Wathen

FURTHER READING:

Authors and Artists for Young Adults. Vol. 8. Detroit, Gale Research, 1992.

''The Groening of America: Once a Doodler on the Fringe, Bart's Bad Boy Is Now a Millionaire Slob.'' *Washington Post.* May 13, 1993, C1.

Hile, Kevin S., ed. *Something about the Author.* Vol. 81. Detroit, Gale Research, 1995.

''Matt Groening.'' *Contemporary Theatre, Film and Television,* Vol. 17. Detroit, Gale Research, 1997.

Newsmakers: The People Behind Today's Headlines. Detroit, Gale Research, 1990.

Olendorf, Donna, ed. *Contemporary Authors.* Vol. 138. Detroit, Gale Research, 1993.

Riley, Sam G., ed. *Biographical Dictionary of American Newspaper Columnists.* Westport, Connecticut, Greenwood Press, 1995.

Grunge

Grunge is the name given to the hard rock music produced by bands such as Nirvana, Soundgarden, and others, in Seattle, Washington, from the mid-1980s through the mid-1990s. While the term provides a convenient blanket description, it also hides fairly substantial stylistic differences between the bands. Few, if any, of those groups ever described themselves as ''grunge,'' and the stereotyping of grunge as humorless and angst-ridden is a serious distortion. Nonetheless, the same media scrutiny that bred those misrepresentations turned grunge into a worldwide phenomenon that shaped not only music, but also other aspects of popular culture such as fashion.

Through the late 1970s and early 1980s, punk and hard-core rock had embraced a do-it-yourself attitude in defiant opposition to the bombast and big money of heavy metal and arena rock. However, as the hard-core and punk movements began to wane in the mid-1980s, many of those independent bands retained their amplifiers and distortion pedals but began slowing the tempos of their songs considerably. As a result, many bands (intentionally or not) began to reproduce the sound of the arena rock bands on which they had originally turned their backs. Although this trend occurred throughout America, it became particularly noticeable in two groups of musicians in Seattle, The Melvins and Green River. Hailing from Aberdeen, Washington, The Melvins played a particularly sludgy form of hard rock, touring with their friend Kurt Cobain at the wheel of their

Members of the grunge band Nirvana, from left: Chris Novoselic, Dave Grohl, and Kurt Cobain.

tour bus before he formed Nirvana. Green River also received some attention in independent music circles, before splitting up to re-form as Mudhoney and Mother Love Bone.

Those two groups nicely illustrate the two poles of the grunge movement. Fronted by flamboyant lead singer Andrew Wood, Mother Love Bone's music clearly indicated the band's commercial ambitions, and after just a handful of shows they secured a contract with PolyGram Records—a situation amounting to heresy in the independent music scene. After Wood's death in 1990 from drug-related causes, members of the band secured the talents of San Diego-based singer Eddie Vedder and formed Pearl Jam.

In contrast to Mother Love Bone, Mudhoney openly satirized the entire notion of rock stardom. Their sound was considerably rougher, with front man Mark Arm's vocals closer to a hoarse shout than to singing. Taking their name from the title of a soft-core film directed by Russ Meyer, they embraced a *faux*-sexism that simultaneously spoofed and celebrated the excesses of big-name rock bands.

Soundgarden fell somewhere between the blatant commercialism of Pearl Jam and the unpolished garage sound of Mudhoney. Lead singer Chris Cornell possessed a powerful falsetto that went well beyond that of Black Sabbath's Ozzy Osbourne, his most obvious influence. Soundgarden built its reputation as an independent band, satirizing the misogyny of heavy metal in songs such as ''Big Dumb Sex,'' but a lot of listeners seemed to miss the joke. The group's 1989 album, *Louder than Love,* was nominated for a Grammy, and *Superunknown,* released in 1994, debuted at number one on the *Billboard* charts. By that time the band's sound was closer to

Metallica or Guns 'N' Roses (with whom they had once toured) than to Mudhoney or Nirvana. Soundgarden broke up in 1997.

It is likely that many of these bands would have vanished quietly, or perhaps not even formed at all, if it were not for Sub Pop Records. Founders Bruce Pavitt and Jonathan Poneman recognized the strength of the Seattle music scene and, like Berry Gordon, whose Motown label had popularized the pop and rhythm-and-blues of Detroit in the 1960s, they set out to promote their city's bands. From the label's inception, they showed an ambition previously absent from independent labels. Sub Pop's first release, a compilation of bands who, for the most part, weren't from Seattle at all, described the label as "The new thing, the big thing, the God thing: A multi-national conglomerate based in the Pacific Northwest." Most people thought it was a joke, but Pavitt and Poneman weren't kidding.

Many independent record labels in America had been releasing excellent music that never achieved any degree of commercial success, but Pavitt and Poneman were shrewd marketers with an unrivaled gift for generating hype. They hired a British press agent to promote their bands, and paid a correspondent from the British music newspaper *Melody Maker* to come to Seattle. They believed—correctly—that the best way to promote their bands in the United States was through a reputation that was build abroad. Soon the city was renowned as one of the foremost centers of independent music in the world.

Nonetheless, by early 1991, Sub Pop was nearing bankruptcy. Its salvation came from the wholly unexpected success of Nirvana's first full-length album, *Nevermind*. When David Geffen's DGC label signed Nirvana, the contract stipulated that Sub Pop would receive a two percent royalty if the album sold more than 200,000 copies. Most observers expected it would sell a fraction of that number. However, "Smells Like Teen Spirit," the album's first single, became an overnight anthem, combining an infectious riff with a heavy guitar sound and lyrics which expressed a wry world-weariness. A few months earlier, Nirvana had been known to only a small number of independent music cognoscenti; now they were receiving airtime on top 40 rock and alternative stations throughout the world. Within a year, *Nevermind* had sold four million albums. Pearl Jam's *Ten* was released the same month as Nirvana's album, and although sales were initially slower, it sold an equal number of copies during its first year.

With the success of Nirvana and Pearl Jam, journalists, film crews, and fashion designers began flocking to Seattle to cash in on the music, which the world outside Seattle was calling "grunge." The flannel shirt became the ultimate symbol of grunge couture, although flannels had been popular for years in the national hard-core scene because they were cheap, comfortable and durable. Soon, upscale stores were selling "designer grunge," a bizarre inversion of a look essentially the opposite of fashion. Seattle bands on tour often found crowds dressed in flannels, ripped jeans, and Doc Marten boots: "more Seattle than Seattle" as one musician observed.

Many bands who had prided themselves on a punk ethos now found themselves signing very lucrative contracts. A popular tee-shirt in Seattle depicted the irony. It featured a large picture of a heroin syringe with the caption "I came to Seattle to score, and all I got was this stupid recording contract." The standard defense was an equally ironic pose. Kurt Cobain appeared on the cover of *Rolling Stone* with a hand-lettered tee-shirt which read "Corporate mags still suck"—an allusion to the bumper-sticker "Corporate music still sucks." Even Mudhoney signed with a major label and, in concert, began changing the lyrics of their song "Touch Me, I'm Sick" to "Fuck Me, I'm

Rich." While those might have been effective comebacks, they did nothing to disguise or alter the fundamental fact that bands that had begun by satirizing rock stars suddenly became rock stars.

One of the reasons for that irony is the music that influenced grunge. While most independent music up until that time ignored commercial hard rock (or at least pretended to), grunge reveled in it. Kurt Cobain said "we just accepted the fact that we liked the music we grew up on: Alice Cooper, the MC5, Kiss.... We're paying homage to all the music we loved as kids, and we haven't denied the punk-rock energy that inspired us as teenagers." But, with commercial success, many bands began to spend more time polishing their recordings in the studio. That effectively destroyed the "Seattle Sound," much of which came from producer Jack Endino, who used a simple four-track recorder to get a deliberately rough sound. Cobain himself admitted that he thought the production of *Nevermind* was a little too slick. Punk energy was often filtered out by producers looking to make a more palatable recording.

By 1994, many of the original grunge bands had cut their hair and begun to release more mainstream albums. Effectively, Grunge ended with the suicide of Kurt Cobain in the spring of 1994. Nonetheless, it had already forced an essential change in the recording industry; major labels became much more willing to sign new acts, even when they did not fit into a preconceived commercial formula.

—Bill Freind

FURTHER READING:

Azerrad, Michael. *Come As You Are: The Story of Nirvana.* New York, Bantam Doubleday Dell, 1993.

Humphrey, Clark. *Loser: The Real Seattle Music Story.* Portland, Feral House, 1995.

Grusin, Dave (1934—)

Combining classical music training, jazz virtuosity, and a popular culture sensibility, Dave Grusin has become one of the most prolific composers of the late twentieth century. Born and raised in Littleton, Colorado, Grusin was a classical piano major at the University of Colorado. But he had an affinity for jazz and played with such visiting artists as Art Pepper and singer Anita O'Day. After moving to New York to pursue an academic career, Grusin found a job touring behind Andy Williams. He became Williams' musical director and moved to Los Angeles to work on *The Andy Williams Show*. Grusin left the show in 1964 to score the Norman Lear/Bud Yorkin film, *Divorce American Style*. Since then, Grusin has been one of Hollywood's premier composers. Nominated for eight Academy Awards for his scores for such films as *Heaven Can Wait, On Golden Pond, Tootsie,* and *The Fabulous Baker Boys*, Grusin won an Oscar for *The Milagro Beanfield War*. His work is also familiar to television audiences—he wrote the theme songs for *Good Times, Maude, Baretta,* and *St. Elsewhere*. Despite his cinematic successes, Grusin has remained true to his jazz roots. Highly respected in the jazz community, his successful recording and performing career has spanned three decades and he has won ten Grammy Awards, making him a modern day musical Renaissance man.

—Victoria Price

FURTHER READING:

Carr, Ian, et al. *Jazz: The Rough Guide.* London, The Rough Guides, Ltd., 1995.

Guaraldi, Vince (1928-1976)

Vince Guaraldi was one of the finest jazz pianists of the 1950s and 1960s. Eventually the leader of his own group, his resume also included time with jazz greats Cal Tjader and Duke Ellington. In 1963 he won a Grammy for his song "Cast Your Fate to the Wind," and although Guaraldi recorded many successful albums and had a thriving concert career, he will forever be known as the composer for the Charlie Brown television specials. His music for *A Boy Named Charlie Brown* and *A Charlie Brown Christmas* became irrevocably linked to the Peanuts franchise, and several of his songs, including "Linus and Lucy," "Red Baron," and "Great Pumpkin Waltz," became standard music for all Peanuts specials. Guaraldi's music introduced children to jazz, and his upbeat, bouncy style seemed a perfect fit to the characters created by Charles Schultz. Although Guaraldi died unexpectedly in 1976, performers from Wynton Marsalis to David Benoit continue to play his compositions and his albums continue to sell.

—Geoff Peterson

FURTHER READING:

Gioia, T. *West Coast Jazz: Modern Jazz In California, 1945-1960.* New York, Oxford University Press, 1992.

Hamlin, J. "Guaraldi's 'Peanuts' Legacy Lives On: Late Pianist's Music Still Makes Money." *San Francisco Chronicle.* February 11, 1997, E1.

Sullivan, J. "Peanuts' Composer's Legacy." *San Francisco Chronicle.* October 18, 1998, 44.

The Guardian Angels

Founded by Curtis Sliwa in 1979, the Guardian Angels are a volunteer organization dedicated to protecting law-abiding citizens from violent crime on the New York subway. The organization subsequently spread throughout the United States, and 'chapters' were established in cities in Canada, South America, Australia, and Europe. The members, who wear a uniform of red berets and white sweatshirts, carry no weapons, but undergo training in martial arts, first aid, and instruction in citizen's arrest laws. In 1993, revelations that Sliwa had staged some of the Angels' much-publicized successes caused the decline of many chapters. However, while law enforcement agencies have tended to skepticism about the Angels' effectiveness in crime prevention, their presence has frequently shamed authorities into improving policing on subway systems.

—Chris Routledge

FURTHER READING:

Haskins, James. *The Guardian Angels.* Hillside, New Jersey, Enslow Publishers, 1983.

Sliwa, Curtis, and Murray Schwartz. *Street Smart: The Guardian Angel Guide to Safe Living.* Reading, Massachusetts, Addison Wesley Publishing, 1982.

Gucci

The history of the Gucci brand illustrates the precariousness of luxury brand names. Guccio Gucci founded his leather business in Florence in 1906, having been inspired by the beautiful leather luggage of guests at the Ritz Hotel in London where he had worked in the kitchen. After World War II when leather was scarce, Gucci printed his company's interlocked-G's logo on canvas luggage and accessories in bright red and green. This phenomenal success in placing high prices on what was inherently less expensive to produce fueled the imagination of the second-generation Guccis. Interlocked G's were licensed shamelessly and any number of products enjoyed Gucci cachet, despite degenerating quality. In the 1970s, Gucci leather loafers with a gilt horse-snaffle were an expensive favorite of the nouveau riche. By the 1980s, the luxury brand had become a bad joke. In the 1990s, some selectivity was restored, Tom Ford was garnering hype for vulgar but media-generating clothes, and Gucci seemed a business reborn.

—Richard Martin

FURTHER READING:

McKnight, Gerald. *Gucci: A House Divided.* New York, Donald I. Fine, 1987.

Guiding Light

The longest running soap opera in broadcast history, Procter & Gamble's (P&G's) *The Guiding Light,* premiered on radio in 1937. Although recognized as one of the many soaps developed by the legendary Irna Phillips, a 1946 lawsuit ruled that a former writer, Emmons Carlson, share credit for its creation. The veteran soap's logo, a rotating lighthouse beacon, was an apt metaphor for its significance as a guidepost in the cultural lives of generations of fans and for the genre itself. Over the decades, *Guiding Light* evolved into a paradigm model for the melodramatic excesses of soap opera, both influencing, and being influenced by, its imitators and successors. Within the liberating parameters of its world, it was frequently a ground-breaker, daring to dramatize previously taboo topics, and through its sheer longevity, has permeated American popular culture.

Reverend John Ruthledge (Arthur Peterson) served as the program's central character for many years, counseling not only family and flock in the fictional hamlet of Five Points, but the nation's radio audiences, comforting them through economic depression and war, and preaching against such evils as racism. When the show moved production from Chicago to Los Angeles, Peterson resigned, Ruthledge was killed off, and Five Points was transformed into the town of Selby Flats, California. The original thrust of the program was left far behind, and a new set of characters, the Bauers, became the core family in *Guiding Light*'s new incarnation. The ratings suffered and, with Hollywood thought to be the culprit, the production migrated once again, this time eastward to New York.

The Guiding Light premiered on CBS television in 1952, and ran parallel with continuing radio broadcasts for the next four years. Meta Bauer (Jone Allison, later Ellen Demming), who would maintain a presence for four decades, emerged as a popular young heroine at this juncture. When Phillips exited the show in 1958, she eliminated Meta's stepdaughter by having her crippled and then killed in a traffic accident, eliciting a howl of protest from viewers. The proprietorial involvement of soap opera fans thus made its existence known to the creators.

The 1960s saw *The Light*'s setting shift once again, this time to the Midwestern town of Springfield. Agnes Nixon, future creator of *All My Children*, took over the reins as head writer and proceeded to afflict matriarch Bertha Bauer (Charita Bauer) with cervical cancer, a trend-setting idea that had both P&G and CBS worried about negative fallout. However, the only consequence was to educate female viewers about the need for a yearly Pap smear. Nixon was also instrumental in bringing racial integration to Springfield, with Billy Dee Williams and Cicely Tyson, and later James Earl Jones and Ruby Dee, inhabiting the roles of Dr. Jim and Martha Frazier, a professional, African-American couple. This new strand happily failed to validate the misgivings of executives who thought ratings might suffer; rather, it influenced other soaps to strive for racial diversity. In the 1970s, the husband-and-wife writing team of Jerome and Bridget Dobson offered a timely marital rape story based on the real-life Rideout case. The installment, involving nefarious Roger Thorpe (Michael Zaslow) and his wife Holly Lindsey (Maureen Garrett), was imitated by such programs as *Days of Our Lives* and *Another World*. In 1978 the series title was simplified to just *Guiding Light*.

The writing turnover continued in the 1980s. *General Hospital* had recently set the standard for appealing to Baby Boomers and *Light* was now duty-bound to follow its lead. When writer Douglas Marland left *General Hospital* due to creative differences, *Guiding Light* snapped him up. After listening to his own teenage niece's romantic fantasies, Marland paired teen Morgan Richards (Kristin Vigard, later Jennifer Cooke) with much older medical student Kelly Nelson (John Wesley Shipp) and added a jealous golddigger, Nola Reardon (Lisa Brown). Morgan and Kelly slept together while she was still a minor, but CBS balked, albeit briefly, at allowing them to marry. The story turned the coupling of innocent teenage girls with experienced older men into a soap opera staple.

The newly introduced Reardons provided a working-class presence, and after Nola manipulated Kelly into believing he had fathered her unborn child while in a drunken stupor, and as she contemplated abortion, a series of vignettes in which she imagined herself the heroine of such classic films as *Dark Victory* and *Casablanca* delighted fans and prompted mimicry on other programs. In 1982, Marland's tenure with the show ended when he challenged the dismissal of a favorite actor. During this period, scholar Michael Intintoli had ventured behind the scenes at *Guiding Light,* generating a published study entitled *Taking Soaps Seriously.* Among other things, Intintoli chronicled the creators' concerns about targeting youthful demographics.

Various writers tried their hand in Marland's wake, continuing to highlight tangled teen romances. The Lewis oil dynasty and the upper-crust Spauldings had been added to the cast of characters in the early 1980s, with the Spauldings, especially, slowly displacing the Bauers at *Guiding Light*'s core. But it was brazen Reva Shayne (Kim Zimmer) who emerged as the program's vixen-turned-heroine by marrying her former father-in-law, Lewis patriarch H.B. (Larry Gates), and finally settling on her former brother-in-law Josh Lewis (Robert Newman) for an on-again, off-again, "super couple" turn.

The 1990s began at a cracking pace with the resurrection of villain Roger Thorpe and the death of Reva, and quickened further under executive producer Jill Farren Phelps. A blackout story produced new and intriguing character links. Later, soaps such as *All My Children* and *Sunset Beach* attempted similar shakeups with their own disaster scenarios. Phelps angered fans by killing off matriarch Maureen Bauer (Ellen Parker) in response to focus group data, but the working-class Coopers, led by Vietnam veteran Buzz (Justin Deas), gained a foothold. The super-coupling of Buzz's daughter Harley (Beth Ehlers) and her fellow police officer encouraged replication a few years later on *Another World*. A planned love story between Buzz's other daughter, virginal Lucy (Sonia Satra), and drifter Matt Reardon (Kurt McKinney) did not materialize after Matt's affair with forty-something divorcée Vanessa Chamberlain (Maeve Kincead). Fans enthralled with the May/September romance wanted more, and writers obligingly shepherded the pair into matrimony and parenthood. Lucy was eventually raped by a cross-dressing psychopath in a story line that had Internet fans fuming about women's victimization and creeping sensationalism.

Guiding Light's top-tier ratings of the 1950s and 1960s had dipped downward with the Baby Boom influx. Caught lagging behind in its attempts to lure this generation and younger viewers, the show failed to recoup its losses during the next two decades. The 1990s saw a parade of personnel, including Phelps and several older actors, axed, while Reva was brought back, first as a spirit and, later, fully embodied—an absurdity that actually gave the show a boost. However, when producer Paul Rauch went further and tried to ape the fantasy-oriented NBC soap *Days of Our Lives* by cloning Reva, Internet fans, who named the clone "Cleva," bristled. Still, as the millennium drew near, the show had become such a comforting fixture in its continuity, trend-setting social relevance, and comparative verisimilitude throughout the better part of six decades, that many of these sometimes disgruntled viewers have remained faithful and "keep turning on the *Light*."

—Christine Scodari

FURTHER READING:

Allen, Robert. *Speaking of Soap Operas.* Chapel Hill, University of North Carolina Press, 1985.

Intintoli, Michael. *Taking Soaps Seriously: The World of "Guiding Light."* New York, Praeger, 1984.

Matelski, Marilyn. *The Soap Opera Evolution: America's Enduring Romance with Daytime Drama.* Jefferson, North Carolina, McFarland, 1988.

Museum of Television and Radio, editors. *Worlds Without End: The Art and History of the Soap Opera.* New York, Harry N. Abrams, Inc., 1997.

Poll, Julie, and Caelie Haines. *"Guiding Light": The Complete Family Album—Anniversary Edition.* New York, General Publishing Group, 1998.

Scodari, Christine. "'No Politics Here': Age and Gender in Soap Opera 'Cyberfandom.'" *Women's Studies in Communication.* Fall 1998, 168-87.

Waggett, Gerard. *Soap Opera Encyclopedia.* New York, Harper Paperbacks, 1997.

Gulf War

In the early nineties, the Gulf War marked a new dawn for American hegemony. Former adversaries of American militarism—the Communists, the Arabs, and the American left—were held in check, as the United States armed forces were able to quickly expel an Iraqi invasion of Kuwait. With her Soviet, Chinese, and Arab rivals needing American economic support, the United States obtained the consent of many governments for a war in the Persian Gulf. New techniques in public relations extended this consent to a vast majority of American citizens, making it the most popular war since World War II.

On August 2, 1990, Iraq invaded the kingdom of Kuwait. President Saddam Hussein of Iraq contended that the attack was justified because Kuwait's royals were plundering a commonly held oil field. Within hours, the large army of Iraq overwhelmed puny defenses and occupied Kuwait. The next day, a majority of Arab states called on Hussein to withdraw. On August 6, the United Nations Security Council imposed a total trade embargo against Iraq. By August 31, Operation Desert Shield had deployed over 60,000 United States troops in Saudi Arabia. In September, the Soviet Union gave support to armed intervention, and on November 29 the United Nations Security Council voted, for the first time since 1950, to use force.

In the Gulf, the new might or New World Order of the United States was unveiled. The unprecedented consent of Communist and Arab states showed how completely the United States dominated politics. With little opposition, Americans acted to preserve the lifeblood of Western economies: the steady flow of cheap oil. On January 17, 1991 military operation Desert Storm, an attack plan to free Kuwait, was unleashed. The United States Air Force flew 1,300 sorties, while the Navy fired hundreds of cruise missiles; almost immediately air supremacy was established and heavy casualties were inflicted on the ground. On February 24, ground forces began their attack. Within 100 hours they were deep inside of Iraq. Six weeks after it had begun, the Gulf War was essentially won.

Satellite transmissions for the first time televised war instantly. With televisions now in nearly every home in America, the war was

General Colin Powell visiting troops in the field during the Gulf War.

broadcast widely and played to high Nielson ratings. American newsmedia, now global corporations vying for market share, sought to outdo one another in a heated competition for the large viewing audience. Live updates, exclusive Pentagon interviews, and dazzling graphics captured the public's attention. Detailed discussions of American military technology helped to explain America's superior machinery of war. As daily reports of United States victories came home, President George Bush's approval rating soared to a presidential record 90 percent. Bush pronounced, "We've licked the Vietnam syndrome!"

At home, some critics accused journalists of anti-Arab and anti-Muslim bias in reporting, but pro-war propaganda mostly avoided the tradition of racializing the enemy. Nor, as in times past, was the invaded country a featured victim. Kuwait's brutal monarchy did not invite a great deal of sympathy. In a highly publicized testimony before the United States Congress, however, a young Kuwaiti aristocrat sobbed as she testified that Iraqi troops had torn babies from hospital incubators and skewered them on their bayonets. The testimony, which was later exposed as a fabrication, helped arouse both public and political sentiment against the purported barbarism of Iraqis.

Most pro-war propaganda targeted Saddam Hussein, whose name became synonymous with evil. From President Bush to the editorials of major newspapers, "Saddam" was the entire focal point for American bombs. Saddam was said to have stockpiles of chemical and biological weapons, a budding nuclear weapons program, and designs on conquering Israel and Saudi Arabia.

Perhaps the most startling Gulf War legacy left to American popular culture was the transformed nature of mass-mediated information. Unlike the Vietnam War, journalists were denied access to the front and could report only on the Pentagon's tightly controlled press releases. Moreover, a great deal of the information and military photography provided to journalists was falsified to augment the image of American military and technological prowess. Reports of Patriot missiles intercepting enemy SCUD missiles later proved to be completely untrue. Dramatic footage of a smart or guided missile entering the shaft of an Iraqi building was discovered to be a hoax. Scenes of death from friendly fire, Iraqi civilian casualties and other carnage were censored by the Pentagon. As it turned out, the much lauded surgical strike, the clean precision of American smart bombs, was actually the neat appendectomy of objective journalism. In the made-for-television coverage of the war, only the most optimistic scenes reached the viewing audience.

Critical opinions of the war had limited space in the newsmedia. The accusation that the United States fought only to restore the flow of cheap oil from Kuwait's dictatorship went unheard. On the home front, massive antiwar rallies in San Francisco and Washington D.C. and at universities and elsewhere received little coverage in the news, and were often balanced with scenes of small gatherings of people displaying yellow ribbons. Yellow ribbons, the symbol of support for the war, adorned schools, shopfronts, citizens, and were included in corporate advertising. Many members of the newsmedia used a graphic of the yellow ribbon in their broadcasts of the war. New advances in the crafting of political spin, military public relations, and television computer graphics collaborated to make a collage of smooth triumph. The soundbite, the live satellite broadcast, and other recent innovations were utilized in the journalistic arena as never before. A picture of national solidarity blanketed the nation. Not since the World War II had such journalistic unity or common opinion been realized.

Despite overwhelming public approval for the war, President Bush and General Colin Powell feared that a prolonged war would generate dissent. Declaring Kuwait liberated and Saddam's might curtailed, Bush terminated the war and declared victory. In the war's aftermath, Bush's popularity fell with an economic recession and with the continued bellicose posturing of Saddam Hussein. Hussein held power through widespread famine and disease resulting from a continuous embargo of Iraq, and remained the single most demonized figure on the political landscape of the 1990s.

—Dylan Clark

FURTHER READING:

Bates, Greg, editor. *Mobilizing Democracy: Changing the U.S. Role in the Middle East.* Monroe, Maine, Common Courage, 1991.

Graubard, Stephen R. *Mr. Bush's War: Adventures in the Politics of Illusion.* New York, Hill and Wang, 1992.

Leslie, Paul, editor. *The Gulf War as Popular Entertainment: An Analysis of the Military-Industrial Media Complex.* Lewiston, New York, E. Mellon Press, 1997.

Yant, Martin. *Desert Mirage: The True Story of the Gulf War.* New York, Prometheus, 1991.

Gunsmoke

In a 1993 *TV Guide* article, *Gunsmoke,* the longest running Western drama, as well as the longest running prime-time show with continuing characters in history (from 1955 to 1975), was named one of the "All-Time-Best TV Programs." The magazine was succinct: "No contest, this was THE TV Western." The series marked a revolutionary approach to a familiar Westerns formula, and its popularity, which led to extensive merchandising that included Matt Dillon dolls, *Gunsmoke* trading cards, and comic books, precipitated a rash of TV Westerns—so much so, that at one point there were approximately 30 prime time contributions to the genre.

Originating as the vanguard of the "adult Western," the show had its genesis as a CBS radio drama that began in 1952, and endeavored to bring realism—and considerable violence—to standard heroics, claiming in its opening narration to be "the story of the violence that moved west and the man that moved with it." The premise involved the denizens of Dodge City, Kansas, circa 1873, who were protected by Marshal Matt Dillon (William Conrad), a tough but fair lawman, who often struggled to reconcile the differences between the law and his personal feelings. Dillon was assisted by the crusty but soft-hearted "Doc" Adams (Howard McNear), and loved by Kitty Russell (Georgia Ellis), the owner of the Long Branch Saloon.

Praised as being better acted and scripted than other radio Westerns, the show enjoyed immense popularity, and its twice-weekly broadcasts were transmitted to U.S. forces abroad during the Korean War. The recipient of several broadcasting awards, *Gunsmoke* had been extensively researched by its writers, who injected such a sense of veracity into the scripts that the head of the Chamber of Commerce of Dodge City is said to have written the producers inquiring as to what years Matt Dillon served as sheriff.

While the radio version continued to run until 1961, the television version of the show debuted as a half-hour drama on September

10, 1955, introduced by John Wayne as ''a new kind of Western.'' And so it proved. The opening episode, entitled ''Matt Gets It,'' had its leading character getting shot and, as one critic described it, ''left lying in the dusty streets of Dodge, ministered to by a cheap dance hall girl and a seedy looking doctor, while his crippled deputy stood by.'' This was a gritty and realistic departure from the formula wherein the heroes of other popular shows such as *The Lone Ranger* and Hopalong Cassidy were always larger than life and escaped such indignity.

The television incarnation also featured different actors. While the radio actors had been considered, the producers felt that the visual medium made strongly attractive physical attributes a major requirement, particularly for the role of Matt Dillon. Among the several replacements considered, who were either rejected, or who themselves turned down the offer because TV was still viewed by some as an unworthy medium, were Raymond Burr, Richard Boone, and Robert Stack. While the rumor that John Wayne was approached to play Dillon was without foundation, the big screen's most famous Western star did suggest a young actor that he'd worked with named James Arness. Beyond bit parts, Arness' claim to fame was playing the title character in Howard Hawks' sci-fi classic, *The Thing* (1950). However, his commanding six-foot-seven-inch frame and strong, silent demeanor secured him the role. Feature film veteran Milburn Stone was cast as Doc Adams, and Amanda Blake inherited the role of Kitty, both of them staying with the show for most of its run. Prior to his feature film career and TV star turn in *McCloud,* Dennis Weaver played Dillon's first deputy, Chester Goode. He was replaced in 1964 by Ken Curtis, a former singer with the Tommy Dorsey band who played scruffy hillbilly deputy Festus Haggen. Also of note was Burt Reynolds' pre-superstar turn as half-breed blacksmith Quint Asper from 1962 to 1965, during which time many opportunities were found to feature him without his shirt. After Reynolds' departure, Roger Ewing joined the show as the young novice, followed by Buck Taylor (son of actor Dub Taylor) who arrived in 1967 to play the humble gunsmith Newly O'Brian.

Debuting opposite the popular *George Gobel Show,* television's *Gunsmoke* was not an immediate hit, but its popularity rose steadily, taking it to number eight in the ratings in its second season. By its third season (1957/58), it displaced the ever-popular *I Love Lucy* to become number one, and remained there for the next four seasons. The series and its cast were all nominated for Emmys that year, with the show winning for Best Dramatic Series. (Dennis Weaver later won in 1959, and Milburn Stone in 1968.)

While the majority of the *Gunsmoke* radio episodes conveniently served as fodder for the teleplays, their brutality had to be toned down for the small screen. While William Conrad's Matt Dillon was a hardened, abrasive, and often pessimistic loner who could make tragic mistakes, Arness rendered the television Matt as a man of few words, vulnerable, often restraining his personal feelings in order to do the right thing, and never making a mistake. Likewise, while Georgia Ellis' Kitty was portrayed as a toughened whore and barfly who was nevertheless Matt's confidante, Amanda Blake became ''Miss'' Kitty, the owner of the Long Branch saloon who, as Blake contended, ''had to walk a very narrow line between schoolmarm sweet and saloon hall tough.'' Owing to the restraint of the writing, many have speculated over the Matt-Kitty ''friendship,'' but the chemistry between them, and the many plot lines requiring their sacrifices for each other, indicated deep and abiding love. That they never married is easily explained: as long as he remained a lawman Matt would not want to risk leaving Kitty a widow. Finally, while

Howard McNear's Doc could be guilty of greed and cynicism on radio, Milburn Stone transformed the television character into an irreproachable ideal of the dedicated, kindly, and wise country doctor.

Like the radio show before it, the substance of *Gunsmoke* lay in its morality, which pitted the good people of Dodge City against the ugly forces of lawlessness. However, in remaining true to a realistic approach, the scripts not only avoided sentimentality and pat endings, but the writers made sure that, just as in life, the evildoers were not always brought to justice. Then, too, in response to the anti-violence movement of the 1960s, the show's emphasis shifted from physical confrontation and gunplay to dramatic situations that were more character and issue-driven. *Gunsmoke* began dealing with race, religion, and other social conflicts, and evolved into a sort of dramatic anthology series with the interaction between the regular characters taking a back seat to conflicts faced by characters (often played by guest stars) who were passing through Dodge.

Despite these changes, the central characters and setting of *Gunsmoke* took on a mythic status in America's collective consciousness. This lofty position was confirmed by events in the late 1960s. Despite its expansion to an hour, and the transition to color by 1966, the show so declined in ratings that CBS decided to cancel it at the end of the 1966/67 season, the producers claiming it to be the victim of ''program fatigue.'' Public response, however, was immediate and vehement. Letter-writing campaigns were mounted, and CBS affiliates in the Midwest threatened to boycott all of the network's programs unless *Gunsmoke* returned. Senator Byrd even went so far as to criticize the network's decision from the floor of Congress. The end result was that CBS president William Paley interceded, and in a last-ditch effort, switched the show to Monday nights when it miraculously zoomed into the top ten until its run finally ended in 1975. It was the last prime time Western series on television.

After its initial run, *Gunsmoke* was revived in a succession of TV movies, beginning with *Gunsmoke: Return to Dodge* in 1987, which up to that date was the most expensive made-for-TV movie of all time. Costing $3.5 million, it featured James Arness, Amanda Blake, and Buck Taylor. The story had Kitty, who had left Dodge a year before the series' cancellation, back in her hometown, New Orleans. Matt Dillon has retired from the law to become a trapper, and Newly O'Brian is the new sheriff. The TV movie's popularity led to four further sequels in the early 1990s. In *Gunsmoke: The Last Apache* (1990), Matt learns that he had sired a daughter by Mike (Michael Learned), the woman he had become romantically involved with while suffering from amnesia in an earlier episode of the series, and sets out to look for the girl, who has been taken by an Indian tribe. The movie was dedicated to Amanda Blake, who, sadly, had recently died from AIDS. *Gunsmoke: To the Last Man* (1991) concerned feuding in the Pleasant Valley Wars of the 1880s and the death of Mike. *Gunsmoke: The Long Ride* was broadcast in 1992, while the last, *Gunsmoke: One Man's Justice* (1993) found Matt Dillon owning his own ranch. It also revealed details of Matt's background, and the fact that he had been motivated to become a lawman because his father, a Texas Ranger, had been shot in the back and killed.

Gunsmoke retained an extensive supporting cast of townspeople, and supplied many character actors with the opportunity to play a variety of roles over the years. Victor French, later of *Little House on the Prairie* and *Highway to Heaven* fame, played 19 different characters in the course of the run, and directed five episodes. Morgan Woodward, Jack Elam, Denver Pyle, Jim Davis, Claude Akins, Strother Martin, and Lane Bradbury appeared in ten or more roles, while one of Jeanette Nolan's nine roles—as itinerant "Dirty Sally"—resulted in a short-lived spin-off series in 1974. (Interestingly having been rejected for the television series, William Conrad went on to star in *Cannon, Nero Wolfe,* and *Jake and the Fat Man* on TV, while Howard McNear was Floyd the Barber in TV's *The Andy Griffith Show*).

Gunsmoke was in television's top ten most watched programs for 13 seasons and was named in first or second place as Best Western Series by the *Motion Picture Daily* annual television poll throughout its run. A 1966 episode entitled, "The Jailer," starring Bette Davis, was ranked 27th by TV Guide's 100 Greatest (Television) Episodes of All Time. All of the leading actors were inducted into the National Cowboy Hall of Fame, while James Arness received an International Broadcasting Award as Man of the Year in 1973, and in 1989 was voted the number six television star of all time by *People* magazine. The series also won several awards for writing and technical achievement in the course of its long run.

—Rick Moody

FURTHER READING:

Barabas, SuzAnne, and Gabor Barabas. *Gunsmoke.* Jefferson, North Carolina, McFarland, 1990.

Guthrie, Arlo (1947—)

Folksinger Arlo Guthrie has preserved the musical and political heritage he learned from his father, Woody Guthrie. He debuted at the 1967 Newport Folk Festival, where he introduced the talking blues composition "Alice's Restaurant Massacre." This 18-minute anti-war song became a favorite among draft resistors and provided the title for both his first album and a feature film (1969). His popularity soared with his appearance at Woodstock in 1968, and peaked with the release of the single, "City of New Orleans" (1972). By the mid-1970s, Guthrie had re-embraced his folk roots, releasing albums of folk standards and, in 1984, hosting a documentary about his father. In 1991, he opened a community center for HIV/AIDS patients at the Stockbridge, Massachusetts, church in which much of *Alice's Restaurant* was filmed. After landing a role in Steven Bochco's short-lived television series, *Byrds of Paradise* (1994), Guthrie released *Mystic Journey* (1996) on his own label, Rising Son Records. Throughout the 1990s, he wrote books for children, and has toured and performed with his own son, Abe.

—Bryan Garman

Guthrie, Woody (1912-1967)

Folk singer, composer, writer and homegrown radical, Woody Guthrie became the self-appointed folk spokesman for the Dust Bowl migrants and agricultural workers during the Great Depression. His pro-labor/anti-capitalist stance attracted many radical and left-leaning liberals during the 1930s and 1940s, but his lasting fame came from his influence on the folk revival of the 1960s, especially on Bob Dylan. Best known for ballads such as "This Land is Your Land,"

Woody Guthrie

"This Train is Bound for Glory," and "Union Maid," Guthrie's music extended beyond the bounds of radical protest to become American folk classics.

Born in Okemah, Oklahoma, and named in honor of the presidential nominee, Woodrow Wilson Guthrie spent his childhood in several different households in various parts of Oklahoma and Texas. His mother suffered from Huntington's Chorea (the same disease that Guthrie himself later struggled with for 15 years before finally succumbing to it in 1967), and he was often left to his own devices. In 1933, at the age of 21, he married his best friend's sister, but a necessary search for work, coupled with a restless nature, took him on the road, traveling along with many other "Okies" and "Arkies"—displaced farmers and others—who headed to California in search of work. In Los Angeles, Guthrie found work with his cousin Jack "Oklahoma" Guthrie, the singing cowboy, and together they presented the *Oklahoma and Woody Show* on KFVD. Woody's popularity grew as he attracted an audience of transplanted southwesterners who enjoyed his traditional songs and "cornpone philosophy." He also became politically educated at KFVD, encouraged by station owner Frank Burke, who also produced the radical newspaper *The Light,* for which Guthrie occasionally wrote.

Guthrie's national notoriety developed when he wrote and performed songs about the influx of Dust Bowl migrants into California, and contributed to the communist newspaper *People's World.* In 1940, he released his first album, *Dust Bowl Ballads.* The album included "I Ain't Got No Home in This World Anymore," a parody of a traditional Baptist hymn; "Vigilante Man," describing the vigilante tactics of farm labor employers; "Pretty Boy Floyd," about the exploits of the Oklahoma outlaw; "Goin' Down This Road Feelin' Bad," a song used in the film version of *The Grapes of Wrath* (1940), and "Tom Joad," a song about that film's hero figure that Guthrie wrote after seeing it.

His reputation as a spokesman for the down and out was reinforced through his association with folklorist Alan Lomax of the Library of Congress and singer Pete Seeger. With Lomax, Guthrie recorded songs and stories for the Library of Congress and, with Seeger, he joined the Almanac Singers, a folk-oriented protest group. Lomax, Guthrie and Seeger collaborated on a collection of folk songs published as *Hard Hitting Songs for Hard Hit People* (1967). Guthrie also appeared on numerous radio programs, including *Pipe Smoking Time* and *Cavalcade of America*. Hired for one month by the Bonneville Power Administration in 1941, he composed 26 songs about the hydro-electric construction projects of the Pacific northwest, including "Roll On Columbia," "The Grand Coulee Dam," and "Pastures of Plenty." In 1943, he published the autobiographical *Bound for Glory* (made into a 1976 film by Hal Ashby, starring David Carradine as Guthrie). Throughout the late 1940s and early 1950s, he continued to write protest songs such as "1913 Massacre" about a strike in Calumet, Michigan, and "Deportee" (a.k.a. "Plane Wreck at Los Gatos") about a plane crash of Mexican deportees. He also began writing songs for children, such as "Take Me for a Ride in the Car-Car," and "Put Your Finger in the Air." Guthrie's *People's World* columns were collected in *Woody Sez* (1975), and a second literary work, *Seeds of Man,* appeared in 1976. A volume of previously unpublished writings, *Pastures of Plenty: A Self-Portrait,* was published in 1990.

Throughout his writings, Guthrie expressed his belief in justice and his faith that it could be brought to prevail through action. For him personally, action took the form of singing and writing, best exemplified by the slogan proudly displayed on his guitar: "This Machine Kills Fascists." His sense of the role of a folksinger as crusader for the less fortunate and as a critic of society's oppressors and manipulators had greater influence on the course of American popular music than his style of singing or any one composition. His philosophy—that "a folk song is what's wrong and how to fix it"—permeates the protest music of the late twentieth century, from anti-Vietnam War songs of the 1960s to songs of victimization in the 1990s.

From the late 1950s onwards, Woody Guthrie's influence on a successive crop of folksingers was evident. It began with "Ramblin'" Jack Elliot (who often claimed to be his son), The Weavers, who had a national hit with the Guthrie song "So Long, It's been Good to Know Ya," and Bob Dylan, who arrived at his fascination for Guthrie through Elliot. Dylan visited the dying Guthrie in New York in 1961 and composed "Song for Woody," a tribute using the melody of Guthrie's "1913 Massacre." Guthrie's influence on Dylan is most readily seen in Dylan's early albums such as *Bob Dylan* (1962), *The Freewheelin' Bob Dylan* (1963) and *The Times They Are A-Changin'* (1964), and even in the style of the monochrome cover photograph of *The Times They Are A-Changin'*. Protest music of the 1960s owed much to this remarkable individual, whose compositions were revived by new folk groups such as Peter, Paul and Mary, while Phil Ochs and Barry McGuire adopted his style in their own original songs. Woody's son, Arlo Guthrie, began performing in the 1960s, presenting his father's work, as well as his own songs such as "Alice's Restaurant Massacre" (1967).

Reverence for Guthrie continued into the late 1980s and 1990s, with performers such as Bruce Springsteen and John Mellencamp attributing their own development to his influence in a documentary tribute recording titled *A Vision Shared: A Tribute to Woody Guthrie and Leadbelly* (1988). Springsteen credited Guthrie with the development of his own social consciousness: "To me, Woody Guthrie was that sense of idealism along with a sense of realism that said maybe you can't save the world, but you can change the world." Guthrie's influence on Springsteen is best demonstrated in *Nebraska* (1982), and the Dust Bowl-inspired *The Ghost of Tom Joad* (1995). Mellencamp, believing that later contributions to protest music pale in comparison to Guthrie's, said, "None of us are ever going to make the impact that Woody made." Mellencamp's pro-family farmer songs on *Scarecrow* (1987) illustrate Guthrie's impact, and Mellencamp even sports a Guthriesque anti-fascist statement on his guitar in the music video, "Your Life is Now" (1998). *A Vision Shared* also features, among others, Emmylou Harris, Arlo Guthrie, Pete Seeger, and the Irish rock band U2, whose lead singer Bono states that "the thing Woody Guthrie left behind to me was a sense of the poetry of ordinary lives . . . I see Woody Guthrie as a poet."

In 1998 a new collection of Guthrie songs, *Mermaid Avenue,* unveiled lyrics written in the late 1940s and early 1950s, with music composed by British singer/songwriter Billy Bragg and American neo-country rock band Wilco. Augmented with performances by Natalie Merchant, the album is the result of a collaboration between the musicians and Woody's daughter, Nora, who initiated the project and opened up the Guthrie archives to them. The result introduced his music to yet another generation of listeners.

—Charles J. Shindo

FURTHER READING:

Greenway, John. "Woody Guthrie: The Land, the Man, the Understanding." *American West*. Vol. 3, No. 4, 1966, 25-30, 74-78.

Guthrie, Marjorie, and Harold Leventhal, editors. *The Woody Guthrie Songbook*. New York, Grosset and Dunlap, 1976.

Klein, Joe. *Woody Guthrie: A Life*. New York, Alfred A. Knopf, 1980.

Miller, Terry E. *Folk Music in America: A Reference Guide*. New York, Garland, 1986.

Reuss, Richard A. "Woody Guthrie and His Folk Tradition." *Journal of American Folklore*. Vol. 83, No. 329, 1970, 273-303.

Seeger, Pete, editor. *Woody Guthrie Folk Songs*. New York, Ludlow Music, 1963.

Yurchenco, Henrietta. *A Mighty Hard Road*. New York, McGraw-Hill, 1970.

Guy, Buddy (1936—)

Perhaps the greatest showman to ever play blues guitar, Buddy Guy was a crucial link between blues and rock 'n' roll. Virtually unknown to the general public for most of his career, Guy was universally hailed by rock musicians from America and Britain. Guitarists Stevie Ray Vaughan and Jimi Hendrix cited him as a prime influence, and Eric Clapton stated in *Musician Magazine* in 1986 that Buddy Guy "is by far and without a doubt the best guitar player alive."

The reason for such praise stemmed not just from Guy's technical skill, but also from his astounding and often unpredictable antics

Buddy Guy

on stage. Guy held nothing back in performance, torturing his guitar into sonic oblivion and singing himself into a frenzy. Although others have been known to play with their teeth and parade through audiences, Guy was one of the first to do so. Before Guy came to Chicago, blues was played sitting down.

Born on July 30, 1936 in Lettsworth, Louisiana, into a family of sharecroppers, George "Buddy" Guy spent much of his spare time during childhood listening to Muddy Waters, Howlin' Wolf, and Sonny Boy Williamson on the radio. As Guy grew older, he began hanging out at the Temple Roof Garden, a 300-seat club in Baton Rouge where he would see B. B. King, Bobby Bland, and his biggest inspiration, Guitar Slim.

Guitar Slim (Eddie Jones) had a Number 1 R&B single with "The Things (That) I Used to Do" in 1954 and was the top draw of the southern "Chitlin' Circuit" of black clubs. Slim was a wild man on stage, wearing outlandish costumes with matching wigs, swinging from the rafters and dancing through crowds on a 150-foot guitar cable. "When I saw him . . . I'd made up my mind," Guy said in Donald E. Wilcox's biography, *Damn Right I've Got the Blues*. "I wanted to play like B. B. but act like Guitar Slim." Around this time, an uncle bought Guy his first real guitar for $52.50.

By the mid 1950s, he was playing around Louisiana behind local musicians "Big Poppa" John Tilley and Raful Neal. In 1957, Guy recorded a demo tape at radio station WXOK in Baton Rouge and decided to try to make it big in Chicago. Guy brought his tape to Chess Records, the top label in town, but got nowhere. After six months of struggling, Guy finally got to sit in with Otis Rush. He began to play regular gigs around town, and his frantic stage show soon set him apart from the crowd.

"Buddy's act was not premeditated or contrived," Wilcox said in his biography of Guy. "His style was merely a natural by-product of being self-taught, having a compulsion to play, and being insecure enough to feel that if he didn't dazzle and hypnotize his audience with the flamboyant techniques he'd seen work for Guitar Slim, he'd be buried by competition from guitarists who were better technicians."

Word of the crazy kid from Louisiana spread and Chess producer and songwriter Willie Dixon soon recognized Guy's talent. Dixon brought Guy in and immediately put him to work as a session musician with Muddy Waters, Howlin' Wolf, Sonny Boy Williamson, and Koko Taylor.

Chess tried recording Guy as a solo artist, but failed to find the right niche. R&B ballads, jazz instrumentals, soul, and novelty dance tunes were all recorded during the early 1960s, but none were released as singles. Guy wanted to record a set similar to his live shows, boosting his guitar's volume and cutting loose, but Chess wouldn't take the chance. Meanwhile, Guy's reputation spread to Great Britain, where young rockers like Clapton and the Rolling Stones were seeking out Chess singles and learning about Guy. His tour of England in 1965 brought exposure to a generation of musicians eager to soak it up, repackage it, and turn around and sell it to Americans as the hip new thing. "[Chess founder] Leonard Chess would eventually realize his mistake in not recognizing Buddy's appeal in the clubs, or that much of the appeal of the British rock bands was based on the kind of 'noise' that Buddy was producing live," Wilcox noted in his biography of Guy. "Still, Chess had not yet released a single album by Buddy Guy. What saved Buddy at Chess was his versatility."

Guy was invited to play with harmonica player Junior Wells on his Delmark album *Hoodoo Man Blues* in 1965. Delmark, a small jazz label, wasn't interested in producing singles, and encouraged the band to play as if it were a live show. The result was the first recording of a Chicago blues band in its natural environment and the album became the best-selling record in the label's history. On the first pressing, Guy was listed only as "Friendly Chap" due to his contract with Chess.

After leaving Chess in frustration in the late 1960s, Guy recorded for Vanguard Records and continued to play with Wells. In 1972, Eric Clapton convinced Atlantic Records to record Guy and Wells and *Buddy Guy and Junior Wells Play the Blues* was the result. The album should have been Guy's breakthrough, but Clapton's work as producer was hampered by his heroin addiction. The album wasn't completed for two years and was virtually ignored.

Guy continued to record on various small labels, often in Europe, through the 1970s and 1980s, and he bought the Checkerboard Lounge on Chicago's South Side. He later opened Buddy Guy's Legends just south of Chicago's Loop, which soon became the city's premier club.

Guy often jammed with prominent guitarists like Clapton, Vaughan, and Robert Cray and his higher profile helped him land a contract with England's Silvertone Records, which released *Damn Right, I've Got the Blues* in 1990. With guests like Clapton and fellow Brit Jeff Beck, the album was criticized by purists as leaning too far towards rock. Still, it won a Grammy Award as best contemporary blues album and he collected five W. C. Handy awards in 1992. Guy recorded four more albums for Silvertone through 1998, influencing a new generation of young guitarists, including Jonny Lang and Kenny Wayne Shepherd.

—Jon Klinkowitz

FURTHER READING:

DeCurtis, Anthony. "Living Legends." *Rolling Stone*. September 21, 1989, 89-99.

Murray, Charles Shaar. "Strat Cats" (Interview with Guy and Jeff Beck). *Guitar World,* July 1991, 80ff.

Obrecht, Jas, editor. *Blues Guitar: The Men Who Made the Music*. San Francisco, GPI Books, 1990.

Whiteis, David. "Buddy Guy: 50 Million Riff Thieves Can't Be Wrong." *Down Beat*. October 1991, 22-23.

Wilcox, Donald E. *Damn Right I've Got the Blues: Buddy Guy and the Blues Roots of Rock-and-Roll.* San Francisco, Woodford Press, 1993.

Gymnastics

Once an exercise for warriors preparing for battle, gymnastics has evolved into one of the most avidly followed Olympic events and a popular conditioning activity for all ages. Though male gymnasts are admired for their strength and skill, it is largely women's gymnastics that captivates audiences and inspires thousands of children to take up the sport.

Derived from the Greek word *gymnos,* which means naked, the combination of acrobatics and tumbling that we call gymnastics was devised by the Greeks as an exercise to balance the mind and body and learn skills useful in battle. Other ancient cultures, notably the Chinese, Indians, and Persians, performed similar conditioning exercises. It was in the early nineteenth century that the benefits of gymnastics were popularized in Europe when Friedrich Jahn established *Turnvereins,* or gymnastics clubs, all over Germany. American clubs in the style of Jahn's clubs were opened in Cincinnati in 1848 and in St. Louis in 1865.

By 1881 the European Gymnastics Federation was established in Belgium (renamed International Gymnastics Federation or FIG in 1921), and gymnastics became an Olympic event in 1896. Women's Olympic gymnastics began in 1928. Olympic events involve performing athletic feats of leaping, swinging, and tumbling on a variety of apparatus, judged on the basis of the Code of Points, established and regularly updated by the FIG. For men, there are six types of official apparatus: the floor exercise, the pommel horse, the still rings,

Legendary gymnastics coach Bela Karolyi spots for 14-year-old Domique Moceanu during the 1996 U.S. Olympic Gymnastic Team Trials.

the vault, the horizontal bar, and the parallel bars. Women do the floor exercise as well, along with the vault, the uneven parallel bars, and the balance beam.

Gymnastics underwent an enormous leap in popularity in the early 1970s. In the 1972 Olympics, Soviet gymnast Olga Korbut dazzled both judges and spectators around the world with her athletic and aggressive style, performing a back flip on the balance beam for the first time ever. In 1976, Romanian Nadia Comaneci became the first person in history to earn perfect scores for her gymnastic routines.

The dramatic performances of these skilled athletes and many others created a shift in perspective for women's gymnastics. No longer a demonstration of graceful motion juxtaposed with the male gymnast's display of power and strength, women's gymnastics became a powerful sport in its own right. With the new respect for women gymnasts came a surge in the popularity of gymnastics in the general population. In 1972, fifteen thousand amateur athletes learned acrobatics and tumbling at gymnastics clubs in the United States. A decade later there are one hundred fifty thousand, and the number continues to increase considerably after each summer Olympics. Whether it is Olympic hopefuls training to compete or children learning to tumble at the local community center, gymnastics has taken its place in American society.

With this new popularity comes a certain amount of worry. Competitive gymnastics can be a grueling sport, causing injuries to muscle, bone, and ligament. A 1990 study of Swedish male gymnasts found they had as many degenerated disks in their spines as the average sixty-five-year-old man. While male gymnasts reach their peak of performance in their late teens and early twenties, female gymnasts peak while they are still children of thirteen to sixteen, before bones and other bodily structures are fully formed. Some concerned trainers and parents refer to the "female athlete triad" of eating disorders, delayed onset of menstruation, and premature osteoporosis, which endanger female athletes who begin their careers at increasingly younger ages. It is not uncommon for young gymnasts to begin their training at age five and to work out for five hours a day by the time they are teenagers. Such demanding schedules combined with super-competitive coaching have pushed young gymnasts to injury and beyond. Small slips while practicing flips and leaps have resulted in several cases of paralysis, the most famous being Sang Lan of China, who fell in a practice session during the 1998 Olympics, breaking her neck.

In response to concerns about the physical and emotional effects of competition on very young girls, the Olympic Committee has changed its rules, making sixteen the minimum age for Olympic teams. Parents and many coaches have also tried to refocus the sport on fun and personal accomplishment and away from the intense competition that drives athletes to risk injury and permanent damage.

Gymnastics continues to grow more popular, especially among young girls, who find needed role models in the strong young women who fly so gracefully through the air at the Olympics. The parameters of the sport keep expanding. When Olga Korbut performed her back somersault on the balance beam in 1972, the move was revolutionary. In less than three decades, ten year olds could do it in gymnastics class, and elite gymnasts in competition perform three back flips in a row. Perhaps that is the real romance of such athletic displays: the ability of a vulnerable young girl to increase the limits of human physical achievement.

—Tina Gianoulis

FURTHER READING:

Kauffman, Helen, and Matthew Smith. "Well, Doc, Ya Ain't No Nadia Comaneci . . . (Gymnastics Is the Latest White-Collar Rage)." *Los Angeles Magazine.* Vol. 25, May 1980, 115.

Silverstein, Herma. *Mary Lou Retton and the New Gymnasts.* New York, F. Watts, 1985.

Smither, Graham Buxton. *Behind the Scenes of Gymnastics.* London, New York, Proteus Press, 1980.

H

Hackett, Buddy (1924—)

Though primarily known in the 1990s for his nightclub comedy, Buddy Hackett is a versatile performer whose career spans more than half of the twentieth century. He has performed in films, television and cable specials, and has written a book of poetry. He was offered, and refused, the opportunity to replace Curly in *The Three Stooges,* preferring to remain a solo act. Hackett frequently makes himself—his short stature, his rotund build, and his Jewishness—the subject of his humor. His stand-up is risque in an old-fashioned way; little of the anger and social commentary of Lenny Bruce, Richard Pryor, or Chris Rock is to be found. His cherubic face, twinkling eyes, and gentle self-mockery take off much of the sting from his profane language.

Buddy Hackett was born Leonard Hacker on August 31, 1924, in Brooklyn, New York. After serving in the United States Army he tried his luck as an upholsterer (like his father) and a waiter. Comedy, though, was his calling. He honed his craft at the resorts of the Catskill Mountains, 100 miles northwest of New York City, in the area known as "The Borscht Belt." Many American Jews came there to vacation in an atmosphere where Jewish culture was celebrated and Jewish humor brought distraction from the troubles of the city. Hackett made his reputation in Catskill venues like the Concord Resort Hotel.

Buddy Hackett (center), Dean Jones, and Michele Lee in a scene from the film *The Love Bug.*

Television was enjoying its first "Golden Age" when Buddy Hackett made his premiere appearance. His night club style fit perfectly with the Dumont series *School House.* The premise came straight from vaudeville: a teacher character (Kenny Delmar) played host to a variety of unruly "students," actually comedians doing their shtick. Buddy Hackett was among the ever-changing cast, which also included Wally Cox and Arnold Stang. *School House* aired only from January through April of 1949. Hackett remained a presence on early television, however, appearing on *The Tonight Show, The Jack Paar Show,* and *The Jackie Gleason Show.*

As the 1950s progressed the television situation comedy developed into the medium's dominant form. From September 1956 to March 1957, Hackett starred in NBC's live sitcom *Stanley.* He played Stanley Peck, a newsstand owner who constantly gets in trouble trying to help other people. Future variety series star Carol Burnett played Stanley's girlfriend, Celia; the voice of imperious hotel owner Horace Fenton was provided by comedian Paul Lynde. The show was not a success. A bigger misstep was CBS' attempt the next fall to pair Hackett with comedian Jackie Gleason in a revival of the latter's comedy-variety program. Audiences refused to accept Hackett in Art Carney's role as Gleason's sidekick; the series lasted only three months.

Buddy Hackett made a number of memorable film appearances throughout the 1960s, including *The Music Man* (1962), *The Wonderful World of the Brothers Grimm* (1962), and the teen comedy *Pajama Party.* His manic performance in Stanley Kramer's *It's A Mad, Mad, Mad, Mad World* (1963) stood out among the film's overcrowded cast.

The greatest showcase of his acting ability came on television in 1979. NBC's *Bud and Lou* was a made-for-television biography of the comedy duo of Bud Abbott and Lou Costello. Hackett shined as Costello opposite Harvey Korman's Abbott. Though the film recreated many of the team's classic bits, it was the portrayal of their often strained relationship and the sadness of Costello's later life which allowed Hackett to show the world he could embody a complex dramatic character.

Stand-up comedy remained the backbone of Buddy Hackett's career. He frequently played casinos in Las Vegas and Atlantic City. In 1983, a new generation discovered his Catskills roots with the Home Box Office (HBO) special *Buddy Hackett—Live and Uncensored.* New fans learned that the funny little guy from Walt Disney's *The Love Bug* (1969) could swear and speak graphically, and hilariously, about his bodily functions. The program was so successful that in 1986, HBO's live comedy series *On Location* featured the episode "Buddy Hackett II—On Stage at Caesar's Atlantic City."

Hackett has lent his distinct raspy voice to several animated productions, most notably Disney's *The Little Mermaid* (1989). His character, a seagull named Scuttle, was patterned after him. Scuttle shares Buddy's hefty build and habit of talking out of the side of his mouth. Much less successful was CBS' *Fish Police,* a failed attempt to cash in on the success of Fox's *The Simpsons,* which ran for only a few weeks in 1992.

Buddy Hackett is a comedy legend. In 1997 he appeared in the PBS (Public Broadcasting Station) *Great Performances* special "The College of Comedy with Alan King." Fellow Catskills veteran King moderated a discussion of comedy with Hackett, Tim Conway, Paul Rodriguez, and Judy Gold. Hackett showed off his willingness to joke about politically incorrect subjects like Alzheimer's Disease and disability. As always, his high spirits and self-deprecation kept the humor from being insulting. Hackett earned a mark of pop culture distinction when, in 1995, he was the subject of a gag on *The Simpsons*. It comes in the episode "Lisa's Wedding," which is set in the year 2010. In a joke so fast it can only be seen if viewed frame-by-frame, a television newscast announces the search for a series of outlaw celebrities, including "The Artist Formerly Known as Buddy Hackett." The real Buddy Hackett can be found entertaining night club and talk show audiences with simple, bawdy humor which transcends fashion and generations.

—David L. Hixson

FURTHER READING:

Frommer, Myrna Katz, and Harvey Frommer. *It Happened in the Catskills: An Oral History in the Words of Busboys, Bellhops, Guests, Proprietors, Comedians, Agents and Others Who Lived It.* New York, Harcourt & Brace, 1986.

Hackett, Buddy. *The Naked Mind of Buddy Hackett.* Los Angeles, Nash Publications, 1974.

———. *The Truth About Golf and Other Lies.* Los Angeles, Nash Publications, 1968.

Kanfer, Stefan. *A Summer World: The Attempt to Build a Jewish Eden in the Catskills from the Days of the Ghetto to the Rise of the Borscht Belt.* New York, Farrar, Straus & Giroux, 1989.

Richman, Irwin. *Borscht Belt Bungalows: Memories of Catskill Summers.* Philadelphia, Temple University Press, 1998.

Hackman, Gene (1930—)

Gene Hackman quickly gained critical recognition and Academy Award nominations for his roles in *Bonnie and Clyde* (1967), *I Never Sang for My Father* (1970), and *The French Connection* (1971). Hackman demonstrated considerable range, from the mousy surveillance expert involved in a murder in *The Conversation* (1974) to the delightfully overplayed Lex Luthor in *Superman: The Movie* (1978). Playing an inspirational basketball coach in *Hoosiers* (1986) revived his career from a slight slump. In the 1990s, Hackman found considerable success playing psychologically complex antagonists in movies such as *Unforgiven* (1992), *Crimson Tide* (1995), and *Extreme Measures* (1996). Even when he plays the villain, Hackman retains an amiable integrity that makes his performances compelling.

—Christian L. Pyle

FURTHER READING:

Hunter, Allan. *Gene Hackman.* New York, St. Martin's Press, 1987.

Munn, Michael. *Gene Hackman.* London, Robert Hale & Co., 1997.

Haggard, Merle (1937—)

Country singer, songwriter and guitarist Merle Haggard was among the founders of the popular and distinctive "Bakersfield

Merle Haggard

sound." While Nashville was, and is, the undisputed capital of country music, Bakersfield, California, often called the "second Nashville," emerged as its rival, noted for an element of western swing that produced a more up-tempo style than the "Nashville sound." Haggard, with Buck Owens, Tommy Collins, Red Simpson, and Billy Mize, was the core of this western headquarters of country music, and Haggard and Owens rode the sound to stardom over the next two decades. After helping to establish this new "honky-tonk" music, known for its harder edge and barroom themes, Haggard branched out into other styles of music and, by the 1970s, had joined the ranks of country's crossover artists. His career represents a combination of change and tradition: despite the diversity of his music, he always tried to maintain his ties to traditional country music, which earned him a reputation as contemporary country's music-historian. Haggard's unique blending of tradition and change proved to be a recipe for overwhelming success.

While Haggard showed an interest in music from a very early age, his early life was anything but indicative of future success. He was born into poverty in Oakdale, California in 1937, his parents having migrated westward from Oklahoma during the Dust Bowl to seek work as itinerant farmers. His father died when Merle was very young, and the boy lived a rough and reckless childhood. As a teenager he alternated between odd jobs and reform school, and as a young man spent time in jail for various petty crimes. An arrest for burglary finally landed him in San Quentin Penitentiary for three years, an experience that gave him the resolve to change his life. After being paroled in 1960 (Governor Ronald Reagan granted him a full pardon in 1973), he went to Bakersfield and worked a series of odd jobs, mostly manual labor, while moonlighting as a guitarist in the raucous nightclubs and bars in the "beer can hill" area. Over time, his troubled youth became one of his greatest assets, as he churned out hit after hit revolving around themes of barrooms, prisons, and life on the margins of society.

Haggard landed a job as guitarist for a band led by singer Wynn Stewart, and eventually signed his first recording contract with Tally Records. His first hit was "Sing a Sad Song" (1963), followed by a Top Ten single ("My Friends Are Gonna Be) Strangers." The success of this tune brought a deal with Capitol Records, and by the mid-1960s Haggard was becoming a country music sensation with his songs of drinking, cheating, and breaking the law. During these years he married Bonnie Owens, a musician also under contract with Tally, and assembled a band, the Strangers. Soon Merle Haggard and the Strangers were producing a string of hits, including "Swingin' Doors" and "The Bottle Let Me Down," both recorded in 1966, and, that same year, his first number one single, "I'm A Lonesome Fugitive." Several more of his songs reached the top of the charts in the late 1960s, among them "Branded Man" (1967) and "Mama Tried" (1968). These successes earned him his first Top Male Vocalist of the Year award from the Academy of Country Music. His outlaw image set a trend in the industry—several artists emerged during these years who sought popularity by cultivating a reputation of lawlessness.

Yet, just as he had risen to fame as an outlaw, Haggard soon became a patriotic hero to a large and different sector of the nation. He attracted national attention and caused controversy with the release of "Okie From Muskogee," in 1969, a song that centered on life in a small Oklahoma town and championed the attitudes of the "silent majority" during the social tumult wrought by the Vietnam War. The song, which declared "we don't burn our draft cards down on main street," and "we don't smoke marijuana in Muskogee," became an anthem for those Americans who had tired of social unrest and viewed protest against the nation's policies in Southeast Asia, or American society generally, as a lack of patriotism. Haggard later claimed to be somewhat surprised by the attention the song received, asserting that it had been written as a satire. Nevertheless, in 1970 he recorded "The Fightin' Side of Me," also based on the theme of patriotism.

By the early 1970s, the country music industry was undergoing great change as audiences responded to new styles that combined country with elements of other musical genres. Nashville, alert to the trend, introduced a wave of "crossover" artists who could sell records on multiple charts, while more traditional musicians were given correspondingly less play time. Haggard responded well to these changes, revealing perhaps his greatest talent: his ability to maintain his reputation as a traditional country musician and survive the seemingly constant changes in audience taste. His enormously successful single "If We Make It Through December" (1973) established him as one of the industry's crossover artists by reaching the pop charts; yet he complemented this success with tribute albums to earlier country music icons. The first of these was *Same Train, A Different Time* (1969), dedicated to the music of the "singing brakeman," Jimmie Rodgers, followed by an album recognizing Bob Wills' contributions to country music, *A Tribute to the Best Damn Fiddle Player in the World* (1970). It was not long after that Haggard branched out into areas far removed from the honky-tonk style of his early career. His concept albums were well-received: *Land of Many Churches* (1973), a double album focusing on gospel recordings, and *I Love Dixie Blues* (1974), recorded in New Orleans. These brought him recognition and respect both from fans and his peers in the industry for his versatility. By the late 1970s, he was a fixture of the country music scene, making numerous television appearances and even a cameo appearance in the Clint Eastwood movie *Bronco Billy* (1980).

These years brought increased recording success and national popularity. In 1977 Haggard signed with MCA Records, where he produced even more number one hits, including "Think I'll Just Stay Here and Drink" and "Rainbow Stew," bringing his number of chart-making recordings to over fifty. He also made celebrated duet albums with George Jones and Willie Nelson, both of which generated hits: "Yesterday's Wine" with Jones and "Pancho and Lefty" with Nelson. The album *Pancho and Lefty* earned Haggard and Nelson the Country Music Association's Best Album of the Year Award.

In 1990 Merle Haggard signed with Curb Records, and was still continuing to compose, record and tour at the end of the decade. His album *Merle Haggard 1996* represents a musical overview of his entire career, offering a wide variety of styles, and duets with country stars young and old. "The Hag," as his fans came to call him over the years, received almost every major award offered by the country music establishment; and his band, the Strangers, has shared in the fame, garnering numerous accolades from the country music industry, including several Touring Band of the Year awards.

—Jeffrey W. Coker

FURTHER READING:

Byworth, Terry. *The History of Country & Western Music*. New York, Bison Books, 1984.

Haggard, Merle, with Peggy Russell. *Sing Me Back Home: My Story*. New York, Times Books, 1981.

Malone, Bill C. *Country Music U.S.A.* Revised edition. Austin, University of Texas Press, 1985.

Hagler, Marvelous Marvin (1954—)

Known outside of boxing circles for his bald head, goatee, menacing stare, and muscular physique, a ring announcer once told Marvin Hagler that if he wanted to be announced as "Marvelous Marvin," he should go change his name. So Hagler did just that, legally changing his name to "Marvelous Marvin Hagler." During the 1980s, when athletes' incomes skyrocketed and attitudes towards athletes in the media changed from idolatry to suspicion and scorn, Hagler came to symbolize the throwback fighter of yesteryear. Where his nemesis Sugar Ray Leonard fought his first professional fight in 1976 on national television for a five figure purse, Hagler began his professional career in obscurity, fighting for very little money. Hagler and Leonard fought for their first world titles on the same card but not against each other; Hagler fought the preliminary bout against middleweight champion Vito Antefermo for $40,000 and failed to gain the middleweight title when he was awarded a draw in a fight most observers felt he won, while Leonard fought the main event for $1,000,000 and won the welterweight title with a 15th round knockout against Wilfred Benitez. Leonard was the media darling whose career was carefully orchestrated, Hagler was the blue collar champion who earned everything he ever received.

As a struggling middleweight contender unable to get a title shot, Hagler was once told that he had three things going against him—he was black, he was left-handed, and he was good. In fact that statement was only partly true. Hagler is in fact African American, but while he could fight southpaw, he could also fight right-handed, and he was not just good, he was great. As a result of his being better than just good, he was able to rise above the obscurity to which most talented, black left-handers have been relegated throughout boxing history.

Marvelous Marvin Hagler

When Sugar Ray Leonard retired in 1982 due to a detached retina, Hagler, who was by then the undisputed middleweight champion of the world, took Leonard's place as the biggest star in boxing. Wins in highly publicized bouts against fellow Hall of Famers Roberto Duran and Thomas Hearns lead to endorsement deals, most notably for Right Guard deodorant. Right Guard used Hagler's instantly recognizable face, and the association of his face with brutality, and made an ironic, comic television commercial in which Hagler, perched atop a horse and dressed in equestrian attire, declares that anything less than Right Guard would be "uncivilized." Marvelous Marvin Hagler, the everyman champion, had finally reached the superstar plateau that Sugar Ray Leonard had occupied in his own heyday.

When Leonard eventually returned to the ring in 1987, he and Hagler met in one of the most anticipated fights in the history of boxing. During negotiations for the bout, Hagler insisted on more money than Leonard. Leonard complied, and Hagler received $14,000,000 to Leonard's $12,000,000, instead of a $13,000,000 apiece split. In exchange for the million dollars, Hagler agreed to a 12 round rather than a 15 round distance. The shorter distance theoretically benefitted Leonard, the naturally smaller fighter who would have to expend more energy than Hagler in order to remain competitive in the bout. As it turned out, Leonard started the fight quickly and Hagler came on strong later. Marvelous Marvin's late rounds rally

was not enough, and Leonard won the split decision, taking Hagler's middleweight title. Unlike almost all other former champions, Hagler never made a comeback. Instead he moved to Italy, where this blue collar throwback fighter became, of all things, a popular and successful Italian action-movie star.

—Max Kellerman

FURTHER READING:

Gloecker, Carolyn. *Marvin Hagler*. Mankato, Minnesota, Crestwood House, 1985.

Haight-Ashbury

There are few crossroads with the name recognition of the San Francisco intersection of Haight and Ashbury. A seemingly enchanted place, the Haight-Ashbury district begins at the top of a rise that gradually makes its way west to the beach. The fog drifts up past Golden Gate Park with ritual regularity, settling over the gingerbread Victorians and the Monterey Pines. In the space of a little under five years, the Haight traced an arc from a quaint if somewhat dilapidated working-class neighborhood to the Mecca of the psychedelic counter-culture and back again. By the early 1970s, there was no longer any indication that the street had once hosted a vibrant alternative society. It had collapsed utterly under the weight of its own inner contradictions.

Comprised of a nine-block stretch of Haight Street ending at Golden Gate Park to the west, Haight-Ashbury, or The Hashbury as it was affectionately dubbed, was the result of a mixture of happenstance and proximity, and the peculiar tolerance of San Francisco, a city well known for a certain moral lassitude left over from the Gold Rush era when it was a lascivious rough-and-tumble city of dubious morality, heralded as the Babylon of the west. The city's reputation made it an attractive spot for bohemians; waves of disaffected artists made habitual migrations to the City by the Bay throughout its history—most notably the Beats of the 1950s, who made it a prime destination in the world-wide Beatnik circuit, along with Paris, Tangiers, New York, and Los Angeles.

In 1963, Beatniks were fleeing North Beach to take advantage of the cheap rents and available storefronts of the Haight. But a sea change took place between the scruffy existential Beats and the earliest denizens of the Haight: LSD. Haight-Ashbury was the site of a remarkable syncretism, an admixture of influences that coalesced over time into the psychedelic eddy that Haight Street became. Like the collection of thrift-store finery and period costumes the original hippies fancied, their philosophy was fashioned from Eastern mysticism, comic books, science fiction, and the Beat writers who acted as a filtering agent through which the younger poets picked and chose their reading. Similarly, acid-rock emerged out of a grab-bag of styles: Be-bop Jazz improvisation, folk and bluegrass modalities, dabbed on a heavy *impasto* of garage-rock primitivism. For the hippies, LSD was their communion, and rock music their liturgy.

At first the scene was remarkably self-supporting, with small venues catering to a local group of cognoscenti. In 1965, there were an estimated 800 hippies in residence. By 1966, new arrivals had flooded the Haight, with an estimated 15,000 hippies in residence. A more disturbing statistic, but at this point hardly a blip on the radar were the 1,200 runaway teens who flocked to the Haight as if guided by some special teen-alienation magnet. Shops, boutiques, restaurants, and clubs sprang up to cater to the new arrivals, and an activist collective, the Diggers, provided for the needs of the more indigent among them with a soup kitchen, crash pads, and later, a free store.

The year 1967 started off optimistically enough with the first ''Be-In,'' a massive free concert and showcase of the local musicians.

A hippie parade in the Haight-Ashbury district, 1967.

It was by all accounts a magical event. The next logical phase, or so it seemed to the movers-and-shakers of the community, was to invite the youth of America to the Haight for the summer. They envisioned a kind of hippie training: the youth would come, get turned on, and return from whence they came with the blueprint for a new culture. It didn't quite turn out that way. Young people did arrive for the summer, but they were not the beautiful people the Haight habitués anticipated. "They had bad teeth and acne scars and it was easy to see why they hadn't been voted homecoming king or queen back in Oshkosh or Biloxi or wherever they'd come from," wrote Jay Stevens. "These kids were rejects; they'd come here because they were losers, and while they had a certain Christian appropriateness, it was not what the Council for the Summer of Love had expected."

By summer's end, the dream of a self-sufficient urban conclave of tripping Luddites had dissolved in a miasma of hard drugs, runaways, and incipient neglect. The fragile social infrastructure the counterculture had built was overcome by the onslaught. Tour buses and sight-seers flooded the district, as did reporters. Their dispatches only added to the throng of destitute, addled kids. The indiscriminate use of every variety of drug was legion, as were drug busts, hence informing and informers. "The language was Love," writes Hunter S. Thompson, "but the style was paranoia." That October, the Diggers held a mock burial of the "Hippie, son of Media" in Golden Gate Park. It was a pointed bit of street theater, but it was after the fact. The wave had surged and broken, leaving human jetsam in its wake. By then, the Haight-Ashbury pioneers had already fled to higher ground.

By 1971 Haight Street was once again a depressed commercial district with a couple of struggling mom-and-pop enterprises which predated the hippies. Then came the lean years, the urban blight and street violence, but through the district's darkest hour, tour buses continued to visit the neighborhood, offering a glimpse of what had been. By the mid 1980s, boutiques, used clothing stores and coffee shops lined the street. Bookstores, head-shops, and galleries peddled sixties nostalgia to the new generation of adherents—college students and European tourists who looked on the street as a holy relic. And with the new-found prosperity, old problems reasserted themselves. Homeless celebrants ranged through the park and panhandled on the street corners, their ranks swelled by a second wave of runaway kids: teenage adherents of the Grateful Dead, punk rockers, racist skinheads. Predictably, street violence and drug abuse were not short in following.

Haight Street now lives on marketing the allure of that brief, heady period. There is no longer a pretense that Haight-Ashbury is anything but what it appears to be. Ironically, this new business cycle has thrived longer than the cultural moment on which its products are based. Without its idealistic communitarian ethos, the Haight-Ashbury is certainly more resilient, but what was at one time disturbing, or thrilling, is now little more than a titillation, a pleasant way to spend an afternoon.

—Michael Baers

FURTHER READING:

Didion, Joan. *Slouching Towards Bethlehem*. New York, Farrar, Straus, & Giroux, 1968.

Hoskyns, Barney. *Beneath the Diamond Sky*. New York, Simon & Schuster, 1997.

Perry, Charles. *The Haight-Ashbury*. New York, Rolling Stone Press, 1984.

Stevens, Jay. *Storming Heaven, LSD and the American Dream*. New York, Grove Press, 1987.

Von Hoffman, Nicholas. *We Are the People Our Parents Warned Us Against*. New York, Quadrangle Books, 1967.

Wolfe, Tom. *The Electric Kool-Aid Acid Test*. New York, Bantam, 1981.

Hair

A new milestone in Broadway history was set in 1968 when *Hair,* the first rock musical, opened to mass popularity. Tackling controversial and explosive issues of the era in a theatrically innovative fashion, the brash and exciting musical sustained a five year run at New York's Biltmore Theater. The show eventually spawned a total of fourteen national companies and produced eleven cast albums in different languages worldwide. A concept musical reflecting the anti-establishment energy of 1960s American "hippie" youth culture, *Hair* was seen by over four million people in its first two years of production, and the show ultimately grossed over $22,000,000 in revenue. The revolutionary musical generated several hit radio singles and brought to public attention a number of talented performers. The enormous success of *Hair* paved the way for a series of ambitious rock musicals, including *Jesus Christ Superstar* in the 1970s and *Rent* in the mid-1990s.

The project that eventually came to be known as *Hair* evolved in 1965 from the creative minds of Broadway performers Gerome Ragni and James Rado. Although they had never formally written a musical project before, the two co-authors were fascinated by the as yet untapped theatrical potential of 1960s youth culture and began to do field research in New York City. Ragni and Rado interviewed and documented the lifestyles of hippies who had rejected dominant social mores and values, choosing instead to fight for abstract principles like freedom, justice, and liberty. Celebrating the newly arriving "Age of Aquarius," these youth held decided opposition to American military involvement in Vietnam, carried a fondness for marijuana and other experimental drugs, cherished a newfound sense of sexual freedom, and positioned themselves firmly against environmental destruction, racial segregation, and religious dogma.

Ragni and Rado were also enticed by the opportunity to breathe new life into the musical theater scene. Daring musicals like *Cabaret, West Side Story,* and *Fiddler on the Roof* had already begun to experiment with form, relying less on text and placing more emphasis on music and dance. In 1968, *Hair* would come to alter the formal possibilities for musicals by explicitly drawing on both experimental theatrical techniques, including those pioneered by visionaries such as Antonin Artuad and Jerzy Grotowski, and on the energy of the avant-garde downtown New York theater scene. In contrast to *Oklahoma,* which had revolutionized Broadway theaters in the 1940s, *Hair* was less concerned with character and plot, and instead focused on thematic content and the depiction of lifestyle.

After completing the bulk of their field research, Ragni and Rado decided to collaborate with Canadian composer Galt McDermot, who wrote the amiable and infectious rock tunes that would bring *Hair* to public endearment. The nearly incoherent plot centered on Claude, a young man who had been drafted to service in Vietnam; his friend Berger who had "dropped out" from society; and their friend Sheila, an anti-war student at New York University. Joseph Papp of the New

A scene from the stageplay *Hair*.

York Shakespeare Festival took an interest in the experimental script and decided to produce it at his Public Theater in downtown New York. Papp's off-Broadway run of *Hair: An American Tribal Love Rock Musical* at the Public Theater was only a modest success, however. Ragni and Rado came into frequent conflict with director Gerald Freedman, who chose to concentrate on the book of the musical and to polish its look rather than attempt to convey the "authenticity" of the youth counterculture on to the stage.

Upon the completion of the run of *Hair* at the Public Theater, Michael Butler, a young wealthy political with a pressing concern for the welfare of Native Americans, took an interest in producing the experimental musical. Butler financially backed the show at the Cheetah, a popular dance hall discotheque in Manhattan. The unsuccessful run proved that the show needed to be overhauled before being brought to Broadway. Tom O'Horgan, a director who had honed an impressive amount of experience in his work at the avant-garde New York theater LaMama, was hired to revamp the show; while Robin Wagner, Jules Fisher, and Nancy Potts were respectively hired to redesign the scenic design, lighting design, and costume design.

O'Horgan virtually wiped the show clean of its narrative and concentrated more intently on the concept. Thirteen songs were added to enhance the show's pro-love, pro-sex, pro-drugs, and racial harmony message.

In its new form, the show fearlessly broke certain taboos of the theater. Headed by the two authors in the leading roles, the young and talented cast demolished the "fourth wall" of the theater by entering through the audience to arrive on stage. The cast often switched roles interchangeably. For the first time on the mainstream stage, audiences witnessed drug use, explicit language, an openly gay character, and drag queens. During the infamous "Be-In" scene, the cast stripped nude under blinking strobe lights to the shock and surprise of the spectators. The show's popularity was enormous; and in April of 1968, the members of the original cast performed a free, jam-packed show in Central Park.

For all its experimental bravery, *Hair* was met with derision by distinguished theatrical critics and lost the Best Musical Tony Award to a more traditional musical, *1776*. Nonetheless, the musical brought to attention a series of gifted performers like Ben Vereen, Diane

Keaton, Melba Moore, and Nell Carter, each of whom went on to greater success in areas of film, television, and music. The musical also spawned a series of spin-off albums like *Disinhairted* that consisted largely of outtake material that had been excised on the show's path to Broadway. As performed by groups like the Fifth Dimension and the Cowsills, infectious songs like "Let the Sunshine In," "Good Morning Sunshine," and "Aquarius" soon topped the American pop charts.

After generating an impressive number of road shows, *Hair* closed on Broadway in 1972. The show was revived in 1977, but by then, the material no longer seemed as topical and original as it had in 1968. In 1978, the musical became reworked as a critically acclaimed film directed by Milos Forman, and in 1988 some of the original cast members rejoined at the United Nations to celebrate the musical's twentieth anniversary reunion concert. A European tour of the musical continued to prove successful into the 1990s; and in 1998, an off-Broadway revival of *Hair* briefly played to commendable reviews. Yet, as evidenced by the success of the rock musical *Rent* in 1995, the impact of Hair has been long lasting. A document of a profoundly turbulent and explosive era in American history, *Hair* forever changed not only the look and the sound of the Broadway musical, but also its very possibilities.

—Jason King

FURTHER READING:

Davis, Lorrie, and Rachel Gallagher. *Letting Down My Hair*. New York, Arthur Fields, 1973.

Horn, Barbara Lee. *The Age of Hair: Evolution and Impact of Broadway's First Rock Musical*. New York, Greenwood Press, 1991.

Hairstyles

Human beings have styled and adorned their hair since the beginning of recorded history. This styling has different and often contradictory purposes. As an intrinsic, yet malleable part of the body, the hair and its styling can serve as an intimate form of self-expression. Yet hair is also a public and very visible part of personal presentation, and, as such, hairstyle becomes a public, even a political statement. As part of the physical body, hair has a role in sexuality, and it is often one of the first things noticed in a prospective sexual partner. Hair is also a major component of fashion, the way that society dictates its members should look. Because of its many interpretations, hairstyle can serve as a medium of conformity or rebellion, it can lure or rebuff prospective mates, and it can be a constant source of frustrating labor for the individual who cannot get it to behave.

Though hairstyles have constantly changed, and those changes have often been seen as radical innovations, most styles have come and gone many times. The straight hairstyle that has become popular for women in the late 1990s and was *de rigueur* in the late 1960s and early 1970s is basically the same style that was considered appropriate for unmarried girls in medieval Europe. Though hairstyles are constantly changing, there are usually strictly enforced cultural norms, beyond which it is forbidden to deviate. These norms are enforced by rules in schools and on the job as well as by social pressure.

Throughout history, hair has been shaped and decorated to announce its wearer's place in society. In ancient Egypt, nobility was denoted by a bald, shaved head which was then covered by thick, black wigs made of wool, palm fibers, or human hair, braided and decorated. Ancient Romans made marble wigs for their statues in order to update them as hairstyles changed. They changed often, according to one Roman writer: "It would be easier to count the acorns on an oak tree . . . than to count the number of new hairstyles that appear every day."

In fifteenth-century Europe, a high forehead was prized, and Elizabethan women plucked their hair out to the very tops of their heads. Queen Elizabeth herself had more than eighty red wigs to make sure that her hairstyle was always in perfect condition. Louis XIV brought wigs into fashion in early eighteenth-century France when he wore them to conceal his balding head. In the late 1700s, Madame de Pompadour, mistress of Louis XV, led French fashion with the elaborate hairstyle that was named for her. Women of the day wore flowers, feathers, jewels, and even model ships in hair that was piled high and held in place with beef fat. This pomade often attracted insects, and folklore of bugs and even mice living in the depths of elaborately styled hair persisted right up to the beehives of the 1950s.

Up until World War I, respectable American women wore their hair primly up on their heads, but by the 1920s, women were entering a freer era, as documented in F. Scott Fitzgerald's story "Bernice Bobs Her Hair." Men often express a preference for long, flowing hair on women, and a by-product of both twentieth-century waves of feminism has been the popularity of short hairstyles, announcing a new independence from men. The short bobs of the Roaring Twenties were appropriate for the breezy informality of the times as well as being a sort of feminist statement, freeing suffragists and their sisters from the time-consuming triviality of hair care.

The 1930s and 1940s marked a return to glamour, with cascading tresses. These were reined in somewhat during World War II by a severe, all-business style that reflected women's role working on the home front. In the 1950s and early 1960s, big hair was back, with beehives and stiffly lacquered curls. Many women teased their hair to get the desired volume or wore "rats," balls of hair or netting that were placed underneath to increase hair height. As the hippie counter-culture rose at the end of the 1960s, the natural look came into vogue, and women who had once tortured their hair into tight curls began to iron it or roll it on beer cans and toilet paper rolls to achieve the lank straightness prized both on fashion runways and at university sit-ins. Men, too, began to wear their hair long in the late 1960s, and long, straight hair became a symbol of the youthful culture of protest and revolution. The Broadway musical that claimed to define the generation was called, simply, *Hair*.

With the punk movement of the 1980s, hair fashion exploded beyond any modern precedent. Expressing the nihilistic angst of youth rebelling against complacency, punks made themselves look freakishly dramatic. Both women and men dyed their hair bright blues, purples, and oranges, using gel or dramatic cuts to create sculpted spikes of hair. Some wore their hair in "mohawks," imitating the traditional hairstyle of an American Indian tribe who shaved the sides of the scalp, leaving a sheaf of hair standing in the middle. Though conservative society despaired, the punk rockers did much to liberate the boundaries of fashion.

Though women are usually considered the primary slaves to fashion, men are also quite attentive to their hair, and men's hairstyles have often been the focus of media scrutiny. Whether it was the slicked-back duck tails of the 1950s, the revolutionary shaggy bangs

Several examples of male hairstyles, 1955.

of the early 1960s Beatles' haircut, or the defiantly shoulder- and waist-length tresses of the hippies of the late 1960s and 1970s, men have frequently used hairstyle as rebellion and self-expression. Sometimes male hair experimentation has drawn more dramatic reactions than women's changing styles. Perhaps because women are expected to follow fashion, even to look ridiculous in its name, women are allowed more flexibility in hairstyle. A man who deviates from the narrow range of conservative hairstyles permitted for men faces

An example of several women's hairstyles, 1970.

derision and worse. Long-haired hippies of the 1970s were mocked, threatened, even beaten because of the length of their hair. Schools and businesses have also been slow to permit men freedom to wear their hair in unconventional styles.

Male pattern baldness, and the desire to conceal it, has long been a motivating factor in the hairstyles of older men. Some men try drugs or hair transplants to fight hair loss, while others attempt the often-ridiculed approach of growing one side long and combing it over the top of the head to cover bald spots (a method called a "comb over"). Male baby-boomers now entrenched in middle age have brought into fashion a neat ponytail, often acceptable in the modern business world, which, even paired with a balding pate, makes a discreet statement about its wearer's "hipness."

Almost all modern American hair fashion is predicated on the fairly straight or wavy European hair type. Those whose hair is by nature very different from that model, such as African Americans, some Jews, and others, are hard put to force their hair into the prescribed styles. For African Americans especially, hair has been an intensely political issue. Because all things black have been long stigmatized by white American culture, blacks tried for decades with chemicals, machines, and intensive labor to change their hair, even calling natural, tightly curled black hair "bad" hair and straighter hair "good" hair. In the late 1960s, with the rise of the civil rights movement, a notion of "black pride" took hold, and many blacks began to grow their hair out in Afros or "naturals," which sometimes stood several inches out from the head. In the 1970s and 1980s, inspired by the politics and culture of the Jamaican Rastafarians, some blacks began to let their hair grow long and gather naturally into dreadlocks, soft ropes of hair that retain their shape as they grow.

Many whites find both Afros and dreadlocks on blacks to be threatening, perhaps both because they often go along with radical anti-racist politics and because they represent a new positive black-identified culture that might challenge the dominion of white culture. One reaction of white culture to this challenge has been to repress such expressions of ethnic identity, such as forbidding certain hairstyles in the workplace, but another reaction has been to appropriate them. Many blacks were outraged in 1979 when actress Bo Derek appeared in the film *10* wearing her hair in "cornrows," or many small braids close to the head. Cornrow braids had long been a traditional African-American hairstyle, but the media and much of the white public greeted Derek's style as an innovation. Though cornrows enjoyed a brief popularity among whites, few credited the black community as its source. Similarly, in the 1980s and 1990s, some young countercul-ture whites, seeking a rebellious political statement, or identifying with black struggles, trained their hair to grow in an approximation of dreadlocks. While some blacks may find this imitation to be a kind of support, many consider it to be insulting and ignorant.

If European styles were historically shaped by kings and courte-sans, American styles have been most consistently influenced by our own form of nobility—film and television stars. Dynamic actress Louise Brooks led the way to the boyish bobs of the 1920s, while "blonde bombshell" Jean Harlow and redhead Rita Hayworth made flowing curls a fashion favorite. Veronica Lake popularized her trademark look by letting her blond hair cascade in front of one eye. In more recent years, Farrah Fawcett's shaggy "disco mane" became the most imitated style of the 1970s, and in the early 1990s women flocked to hairdressers requesting the "Rachel" worn by Jennifer Aniston's character on the television series *Friends*. Men, too, imitate the hairstyles popularized in the media, whether Michael Jackson's 1980s "Jeri curls" or the slicked-back retro look of "gangster chic"

returning to the 1990s. Even lack of hair became a fashion as some shaved their heads after seeing the style on Irish singer Sinead O'Connor and actress Sigourney Weaver in *Aliens*.

Hairstyle is not only a personal choice, a fashion statement, or even political action, it is also a multimillion dollar industry. As people struggle to coax their hair into the latest style, the popular color, or the perfect statement of their own values, they purchase a variety of hair products and fashion magazines, and spend hundreds of dollars a year on hairdressers. There is even computer software that allows a user to view her/himself in various hairstyles before making the crucial decision. The hair care industry often relies on a culturally induced insecurity about looks, particularly among women, as well as the notion that a different "look" will bring happiness and fulfill-ment. The media feeds this insecurity with its ads ("Is it true blondes have more fun?"), talk-show makeovers, and slavish reportage of celebrity fashion. As more images bombard us, it becomes harder and harder to find the personal element of style. However, whether it is African Americans reclaiming a cultural heritage, 1970s lesbians recognizing each other by their close-cropped hair, or punk rockers throwing a purple spiky head in the face of convention, there always seems to be room for genuine identity to peek through the rigidity of fashion.

—Tina Gianoulis

FURTHER READING:

Astley, Amy. "The Politics of Hair." *Vogue*. Vol. 184, No. 12, December 1994, 229.

Cooper, Wendy. *Hair, Sex, Society, and Symbolism*. New York, Stein and Day, 1971.

McCracken, Grant David. *Big Hair: A Journey into the Transforma-tion of Self*. Woodstock, New York, Overlook Press, 1996.

Halas, George "Papa Bear" (1895-1983)

George Stanley Halas was "Papa Bear" to almost anyone familiar with the Chicago Bears football team . . . and rightly so. For 61 years Halas was affiliated with the Bears in one capacity or another—he named the Bears, played for the Bears, coached the Bears, and owned the Bears. At the time of his retirement as a coach in 1968, he had compiled the best coaching record in the history of professional football, with 326 wins, 150 losses, and 31 ties. Halas's teams became known as the "Monsters of the Midway," winning 11 championships, primarily for their physical brand of football. His greatest moment probably came in the 1940 championship game when his underdog Bears crushed the Washington Redskins, 73-0. From 1970 until his death, Halas served as the first president of the National Football Conference.

—Lloyd Chiasson, Jr.

FURTHER READING:

Carroll, Bob. *Total Football: The Official Encyclopedia of the National Football League*. New York, HarperCollins, 1997.

Mausser, Wayne. *Chicago Bears, Facts and Trivia*. Wautoma, Wis-consin, E. B. Houchin, 1995.

Vass, George. *George Halas and the Chicago Bears.* Chicago, Regnery Press, 1971.

Whittingham, Richard. *Bears: A Seventy-Five-Year Celebration.* Rochester, Minnesota, Taylor Publishing, 1994.

———. *The Bears in Their Own Words: Chicago Bear Greats Talk About the Team, the Game, the Coaches, and the Times of Their Lives.* Chicago, Contemporary Books, 1991.

———. *The Chicago Bears: An Illustrated History.* Chicago, Rand McNally, 1979.

Haley, Alex (1921-1992)

In 1976, author Alex Haley did something no black person had been able to do before: he got Americans to view history from a black perspective. The vehicle he used was *Roots: The Saga of an American Family,* his 688-page fictional interpretation of the genealogy of his family beginning with a kidnapped African boy brought to the United States as a slave in the mid-1700s. It was not the first time Haley had successfully shown readers life from the black perspective. Before he wrote *Roots,* he wrote *The Autobiography of Malcolm X,* a story about the transformation of Malcolm Little from a street-savvy hustler to Malcolm X, a Black Muslim who went from hating whites to becoming an advocate of integration just before he was assassinated by fellow Black Muslims. When Alex Haley died, one creative writing professor, referring to *Roots* and *Malcolm X,* said that Haley had produced two classics in his lifetime. That was not bad for a college dropout who began his career in the Coast Guard as a messboy waiting on white officers.

Haley embarked upon his writing career while still in the Coast Guard. He began by composing love letters for shipmates who did not feel up to the task and then produced articles for magazines. One of his articles, "Hope Springs Eternal," appeared in *Atlantic* in June 1954. While it focused on one of his great aunts, the article mentioned his grandmother's having "a paper tracing her family back to a freed slave," a hint of the phenomenal family saga Haley would interpret a decade later in *Roots.*

About halfway through Haley's 20-year Coast Guard career, the admiral he served as a steward was so impressed by one of Haley's articles that he successfully petitioned the Coast Guard to create the rating of journalist for Haley. After retiring from the Coast Guard in 1959, Haley became a freelance writer, eventually conducting the first *Playboy* interview (with Miles Davis) and several others, including Martin Luther King, Jr., Cassius Clay (later to become Muhammad Ali), Sammy Davis, Jr., Johnny Carson, and George Lincoln Rockwell, a racist and anti-Semitic neo-Nazi.

Just as a modest article about a great aunt became *Roots,* Haley's interview with Malcolm X and an earlier article about the Nation of Islam for *Reader's Digest* led to Haley's collaborating with Malcolm X to write *The Autobiography of Malcolm X.* The book was in type when Malcolm X was assassinated on February 24, 1965, and Haley immediately wrote a lengthy epilogue explaining how he and Malcolm X had collaborated on it. *The Autobiography of Malcolm X* became a bestseller and was adopted in college literature courses around the country. The book was published at a time of growing racial divisions in the United States and rising interest in African-American leaders. Malcolm X, for example, was routinely written

about in the mainstream press and his pronouncements were well publicized. His assassination increased interest in his life, although the book, because it tells the story of redemption and transformation, transcends that tragedy. Spike Lee based his movie *Malcolm X* on Haley's book.

When *Roots* appeared in 1976, it too became an immediate bestseller. News accounts tell of Haley appearing at an autograph session expecting to find hundreds of people, only to be swamped by thousands. He had given African-Americans their sense of identity; he had given them a history. The book appeared during the nation's bicentennial year and Haley dedicated it "as a birthday offering to my country within which most of *Roots* happened." It is worth repeating the subtitle of the book, *The Saga of an American Family,* for it demonstrates that Haley was trying to make a broad statement about everyone's roots, not just those of African Americans, and no doubt he struck a chord. It was as if the entire country was having an identity crisis and readers of any race could better understand their own lives through the multigenerational saga Haley had written.

Roots consumed Haley both in researching and writing, and also after it was published. He spent about 12 years doing research, even traveling in the hold of a ship to get a feel for how slaves must have felt when they were being transported in chains from Africa to the United States. He became even more popular after *Roots* appeared as a six-night 12-hour miniseries on television, a show watched by 130 million people. Haley was overwhelmed with speaking engagements and requests he could never satisfy. He gave the world two classics in his lifetime and that is what he will be remembered for.

—R. Thomas Berner

FURTHER READING:

Berner, R. Thomas. *The Literature of Journalism: Text and Context.* State College, Pennsylvania, Strata Publishing, 1999.

Fisher, Murray, editor. *The Playboy Interviews.* New York, Ballantine, 1993.

Haley, Alex. *The Autobiography of Malcolm X.* New York, Grove Press, 1965.

———. *Roots: The Saga of an American Family.* Garden City, New York, Doubleday, 1976.

Kern-Foxworth, Marilyn. "Alex Haley." In *Dictionary of Literary Biography.* Vol. 38. *African-American Writers After 1955.* Detroit, Gale Research, 1985.

Haley, Bill (1925-1981)

Often referred to as the founding father of rock 'n' roll, Bill Haley was the first performer to become famous in association with the new genre. William John Clifton Haley was born near Detroit, but raised in rural Pennsylvania. He left school in 1940, having completed the eighth grade. Coming of age during World War II, Haley was spared military service by a blind left eye. He had become interested in country and western music as a child, and during the war he began to perform on a semiprofessional basis.

Bill Haley and His Comets

By late 1943 Haley was a regular member of a country band, and for the next several years he sang, yodeled, and played rhythm guitar in bands like the Down Homers. In 1946 he struck out on his own with a group he called the Range Drifters. Like the other bands with which Haley was associated before 1952, the Range Drifters wore "drug store" cowboy outfits, like Roy Rogers. After a year of unprofitable touring, the Range Drifters broke up and Haley found work of a different kind. He spent the next few years as a disc jockey in various parts of New England and Pennsylvania. On one station, he was able to indulge his growing appreciation of "race music" or R&B, when the station owner began a daring policy of mixing genres—playing country, pop, and R&B shows during the course of any given day.

Bill Haley capitalized on his growing popularity in Pennsylvania and surrounding states by forming a new band, the Four Aces of Western Swing. As the name indicates, the band attempted to bring musical genres together. It was regionally successful and even recorded a few singles in 1948 and 1949. Along with occasional personnel changes over the years, the band also changed its name. By 1950 it was Bill Haley and His Saddlemen and was recording actively on a variety of labels. Increasingly Haley's repertoire included covers of R&B hits, like the popular "Rocket 88" that the Saddlemen released in 1951. The following year Haley moved to the Essex label and changed the band's name for the last time. Bill Haley and His Comets was a much better name for a band that by then sought to minimize its Western influences and to shoot for pop stardom.

The Comets had their first real hit, "Crazy Man, Crazy," in 1953. The next year the band released several records, including "Rock Around the Clock," which were met with only tepid response. It was in the summer of 1955 that the song finally became a national hit. Its innovative use as theme music in *The Blackboard Jungle*, a powerful motion picture about juvenile delinquency in a New York high school, brought the song (and Bill Haley) to the attention of millions of theater-goers in a few weeks' time. Decca, Haley's label,

quickly rereleased "Rock Around the Clock" and it raced to the number-one position on the *Billboard* singles charts in July 1955.

Some commentators find the beginning of the rock 'n' roll era in the moment when "Rock Around the Clock" became the number-one pop single in America, ostensibly the first rock 'n' roll hit on the pop charts. However, Haley himself could take credit for the first rock hit with "Crazy Man, Crazy" in 1953, as well as a major hit with "Shake, Rattle and Roll" in 1954. The first number-one pop hit that would later be acknowledged as a rock 'n' roll song was probably the Crew Cuts' summer 1954 cover of "Sh-Boom," originally by the Chords. ("Rock Around the Clock" had its dismal first release at about the same time that "Sh-Boom" was rising to number one.)

Bill Haley and His Comets enjoyed some indisputable firsts, however. They were the first rock 'n' roll band to achieve stardom due to exposure in a movie, *The Blackboard Jungle*. In 1956 they became the first band to star in rock 'n' roll exploitation films: Alan Freed's *Rock Around the Clock* and *Don't Knock the Rock*. Haley's success in the pop music business was inseparable from his stature as a media star, a correlation that would come to be routine for music giants like Elvis Presley, the Beatles, and many more.

Unfortunately for Bill Haley, rock 'n' roll changed rapidly during the late 1950s, while he and the Comets were left behind. After "Shake, Rattle and Roll" and the rerelease of "Rock Around the Clock," Haley had only two more major hits. "Burn That Candle" came out in November 1955, and "See You Later, Alligator" was released two months later. Aside from a few minor songs to follow, the group was essentially washed up in the United States before the end of 1956. The Comets' careers as worldbeaters were over in well under two years.

Haley's problems were just starting. His business manager took the band into bankruptcy shortly thereafter, and his world tour of 1958 resulted in teenage riots and anti-rock editorials in more than one nation. Haley continued to record singles and albums at a furious pace and sold a large number of them around the world without making the Top 40 again. Finally he fled the country, spending most of the 1960s in Latin America in fear of the Internal Revenue Service. In Mexico and elsewhere in Latin America he made and sold many Spanish- and English-language records. On occasion he would tour Europe and South America, places where his popularity had not diminished.

After settling his income tax problems in 1971, Haley returned to live in the United States. His touring continued, however, with longer periods of retirement in between. In 1979 he played for Queen Elizabeth II in a Royal Command Performance, a high point of his career.

For many fans of rock 'n' roll, Haley remained one of the most important and influential musicians of his generation. For others, he was an obscure curiosity, unable to change with the times. It is beyond dispute that popular music was heavily influenced by his innovation of mixing country instruments and vocal styles with R&B; the full development of this trend was left to the much younger and more charismatic Elvis Presley, who sprang to stardom only six months after Haley. On February 9, 1981, Bill Haley died in his home in Harlingen, Texas, of a heart attack. He was 55.

—David Lonergan

FURTHER READING:

Haley, John W., and John von Hoelle. *Sound and Glory*. Wilmington, Delaware, Dyne-American Publishing, 1989.

Nite, Norm N. *Rock On Almanac.* 2nd edition. New York, Harper Collins, 1992.

Swenson, John. *Bill Haley: The Daddy of Rock and Roll.* New York, Stein and Day, 1983.

Hall and Oates

Comprised of singer Daryl Hall and guitarist/vocalist John Oates, the middle-of-the-road, Philadelphia-based pop duo Hall and Oates rose to fame in the mid-1970s with emotive ballads like "Sarah Smile" and "She's Gone." Initially dubbed "blue-eyed soul" by some critics, stressing that the twosome was a white act singing "black music," Hall and Oates veered towards a more rock oriented sound at the end of the 1970s, resulting in a slew of platinum singles and albums such as *Private Eyes* and *H20.* By 1984, their sales had made them the biggest selling duo in history, replacing the 1960s folk act the Everly Brothers. Despite such success, Hall and Oates parted ways after the phenomenally successful 1984 effort *Big Bam Boom.* After the breakup, most of the duo's backing musicians went on to form the house band for television's *Saturday Night Live,* while Hall embarked on a mildly successful solo career, and the thickly mustached Oates remained in relative obscurity until a Hall and Oates reunion in the 1990s.

—Shaun Frentner

FURTHER READING:

Gooch, Brad. *Hall and Oates.* New York, Ballantine, 1984.

Tosches, Nick. *Hall and Oates: Suburban Contemporary: An Authorized Biography.* New York, St. Martin's Press, 1984.

Hallmark Hall of Fame

The *Hallmark Hall of Fame* specials are among the high points of each television season. The dramas, usually movie-length, bring to the viewers fine actors in quality adaptations of recent Broadway shows or older classic plays, as well as screenplays based on popular books. The presentations are shown during holiday seasons, which are peak card-giving periods, and times that the sponsor, Hallmark Cards, wants to get its name before the public. While the programs are praised for their quality, by industry standards they are not always big hits in terms of ratings. Yet, Hallmark has been steadfast in their support because the quality of the programs enhances the corporate reputation for quality.

The first special was presented on December 24, 1951 as a "thank you" to the consumers who had sent Hallmark Cards over the holidays. The host, Sarah Churchill, briefly thanked the viewers for their support of Hallmark Cards, then Gian Carlo Menotti's Christmas opera, *Amahl and the Night Visitors* was shown without further interruption. It was the first opera to be shown on television.

Each succeeding year Hallmark has presented some of the most acclaimed programs of any given season. The first specials were often

Jason Robards as Abraham Lincoln in a scene from the *Hallmark Hall of Fame* production *Abe Lincoln in Illinois.*

Shakespearean plays such as *Hamlet* (1953 with Maurice Evans and restaged in 1970 with Richard Chamberlain), *MacBeth* (1954), and *Taming of the Shrew* (1956), but the first programs also included nonclassical plays such as *Alice in Wonderland* (1955), *Born Yesterday* (1956), and *Victoria Regina* (1961). The series has been responsible for bringing to television viewers such exceptional plays as *Anastasia* (1967), *Winter of Our Discontent* (1983), *The Secret Garden* (1987), *Stones for Ibarra* (1988), *April Morning* (1988), and *Sarah, Tall and Plain* (1991) which was the highest rated movie of the season—two years later the sequel, *Skylark,* was aired (1993). Also presented in 1993 was *To Dance with the White Dog* which was the top-rated movie for the 1993-1994 season.

Hallmark Hall of Fame has also showcased other plays by Shakespeare, including *Richard II* and *The Tempest,* as well as six plays by George Bernard Shaw, including *Pygmalion, Saint Joan,* and *Caesar and Cleopatra.* More current works have included Rod Serling's *A Storm in Summer,* James Costigan's *Little Moon of Alban,* John Nuefeld's *Lisa Bright and Dark,* and Sherman Yellen's *Beauty and the Beast.*

In addition to critical acclamations, some of the presentations have won praise for their depiction of current social problems. Two such acclaimed specials were *Promise* (1986) which concerned the difficulties faced by a man caring for his mentally ill brother, and *My Name is Bill W* (1989) which chronicled the life of the founder of Alcoholics Anonymous. Both specials starred James Garner and James Woods.

Often cited as epitomizing the company slogan, "when you care to send the very best," *Hallmark Hall of Fame* received a Peabody in 1964 and Joyce Hall, president of Hallmark Cards, was inducted into the Television Hall of Fame in 1985.

—Denise Lowe

Halloween

Nothing less than a horror-film renaissance was spawned with the release of director John Carpenter's *Halloween* in 1978. *Halloween* also gave independent film producers something to scream about. With a budget of around $300,000 and no major studio behind them, executive producers Irwin Yablans and Moustapha Akkad backed the film, which Carpenter co-wrote with Debra Hill (who also served as producer). The film went on to earn an estimated $55 million, siring several not-so-memorable sequels as well as some worthy and unworthy imitators in the early 1980s.

The plot of *Halloween* is a deceptively simple one. The film begins in the sleepy town of Haddonfield, Illinois, on Halloween night, 1963. Little six-year-old Michael Myers has just murdered his sister with a butcher knife. Cut to fifteen years later. Michael has reached the age of twenty-one within the walls of a mental hospital, under the care of Dr. Loomis (played with fidgety obsessiveness by Donald Pleasence). Loomis describes Myers as a monster who must never be released or allowed to escape. Of course, he escapes on the day before Halloween and returns to Haddonfield to finish what he started. With Loomis giving chase, Myers (described as "the Shape" in the credits, played by Nick Castle) returns home. Myers' modus operandi is consistent: he goes after high-school girls, including Laurie Strode (played by Jamie Lee Curtis in her first and most recognizable screen role).

With a lean budget and only one star, Carpenter had to depend upon skill and luck to author a film with a tone that is as eerie as it is unprecedented in horror. His musical score is the sparsest imaginable, but the tinkling piano keys above the menacing drone of electronically produced strings and brass set a terrifying mood. Thanks to cinematographer Dean Cundey, *Halloween*'s bright, but somehow claustrophobic daylight exterior shots make even the quiet neighborhoods of Haddonfield seem ominous. The shadowy interiors of Haddonfield's houses only half reveal the terror within them, making that threat seem even greater.

By locating the threat within a mundane, middle-class suburb, *Halloween* creates the giddy unease of an urban legend. The chants of trick-or-treat rhymes at the beginning of the film, the sexual precocity of the teenaged characters, the babysitting nightmare, the legendary murder fifteen years before—all recall the themes of urban legends, evoking similar campfire-ghost-story responses without exploiting them as mere plot devices. Carpenter's greatest innovation, as well as his most copied, is the use of the point of view of the monster/stalker. Audiences used to the syntax of horror films—the empty dark space over the heroine's shoulder, the fake-terror-relief-then-real-terror economy in classic horror films by William Castle and Roger Corman—were introduced to a new phenomenon. By offering the point of view of the Monster, audience instincts for fight or flight were frustrated

and tension in the audience soared. Finally, the monster himself: created by production designer Tommy Lee Wallace simply by painting a two-dollar William Shatner mask white, this false face became the most uncanny of monsters, a blank slate that could hold infinite horrors in the imagination of the audience.

In 1978, audiences consisted mainly of kids the same age as the teenagers being murdered and mutilated in the film. These audiences responded enthusiastically to the psychosexual themes in *Halloween*. Like the many imitators and their sequels that followed—*Friday the Thirteenth, Prom Night,* etc.—*Halloween* consisted of teenagers being maimed and slaughtered before, during, or after intercourse. Sex precedes death in these films. Coitus became the foreplay for the climax(es) of the film, the murders of promiscuous (and mainly female) teenagers. Despite the apparent Puritanism and sexism of *Halloween* and its cousins, California-Berkeley Professor Carol Clover finds an almost feminist formula in them. Clover points out that it is, after all, Laurie Strode who survives *Halloween:* "The image of the distressed female most likely to linger in memory is the image of the one who did not die: the survivor, or Final Girl. She is the one who encounters the mutilated bodies of her friends and perceives the full extent of the preceding horror and of her own peril; who is chased, cornered, wounded; whom we see scream, stagger, fall, rise and scream again. . . . She alone looks death in the face, but she alone also finds the strength either to stay the killer long enough to be rescued (ending A) or to kill him herself (ending B). But in either case, from 1974 on, the survivor has been female."

—Tim Arnold

FURTHER READING:

Clover, Carol. *Men, Women, and Chainsaws: Gender in the Modern Horror Film.* Princeton, Princeton University Press, 1992.

Waller, Gregory A., editor. *American Horrors: Essays on the Modern American Horror Film.* Urbana, University of Illinois Press, 1987.

Halston

Halston's (Roy Halston Frowick, 1932-1990) first fame was the simple and much-imitated pill-box hat Jacqueline Kennedy wore at the 1961 Presidential Inauguration. His success continued in the 1970s. Within the maelstrom of Paris fashions, youthquake, minis, and maxis, Halston reasserted the unadorned cut and practicality of American sportswear: easy, simple, and eternal. In 1972, his plain Ultrasuede shirtwaist sold 60,000 copies. Halston's flowing movement and versatile layers allowed women of all sizes and shapes to find him their perfect designer and Halston came to claim that he would design for every woman in America, to say nothing of custom-order clients Liza Minnelli, Martha Graham, and Elizabeth Taylor. In 1983, he initiated Halston III for J. C. Penney and was dropped from stores who would not permit him to design for their elite clientele and for everyone. Brilliant and charismatic, Halston could make and market anything, except genuine democracy in American fashion.

—Richard Martin

FURTHER READING:

Gaines, Steven. *Simply Halston: The Untold Story.* New York, Putnam, 1991.

Minnelli, Liza, and Polly Mellen, ''Halston, 1932-1990.'' *Vogue.* July 1990.

Hamburger

In the mid-twentieth century, the hamburger emerged as a symbol of American democracy and prosperity. As fast food became dominant on the American landscape, the hamburger provided to millions of people an inexpensive serving of meat. To consume a hamburger was, in a sense, to fulfill the promise of democracy, and to enact one's Americanness.

The hamburger or ''burger,'' minimally defined as a cooked ground beef patty between two pieces of bread, was born in America sometime around 1890. Loosely based on the ground-beef steak popular in the German town of Hamburg, the hamburger gained national repute at the 1904 St. Louis World's Fair. In the 1920s the White Castle chain of restaurants helped popularize the hamburger, which was beginning to become a common food in many regions. In the 1930s and 1940s, the Great Depression and World War II severely impacted the ability of most Americans to purchase meat, but after the war, America's economy began to boom, and the hamburger rode the crest of a wave of new prosperity. Simple to prepare and available in every corner of America, the hamburger made meat cheaply available to a nation familiar with hunger and rationing. The hamburger celebrated the end of the war, the democratization of wealth, and America's robust economy.

By 1954, when Ray Kroc bought McDonald's, the hamburger was becoming popular nationwide at diners and roadside stands. With the rapid diffusion of McDonald's franchises in the 1960s, and later with a national advertising campaign for the Big Mac, the hamburger began to take on increased cultural importance. Because of its popularity, its standardization, and its heavy representation on television, the hamburger came to be identified as the most American food. It appeared alongside celebrities and the stars-and-stripes, and it was heralded in television drama, movies, and rock and roll.

The hamburger's surge in importance collaborated with widespread ownership of automobiles. Together, the burger and the car appealed to and reinforced American affinities for speed and convenience. Drive-in and drive-through restaurants proliferated, buoyed by their staple food, the hamburger. The burger could be prepared

The hamburger's popular culture influence is apparent in this sign advertising the Bun Boy fast food restaurant in Indiana, 1989.

rapidly, eaten without utensils, and eaten on the run. In the new culture of fast food, the hamburger could be eaten alone, breaking many ethnic traditions of social dining.

As the quintessential American food, the hamburger was the main way Americans ingested beef, and, in the same bite, the mythologies of beef. In addition to prosperity, beef was linked to manliness and patriarchy, to domination over nature, to physical strength, to athletic prowess, and to being a "red-blooded" or an authentic American. The low cost and widespread availability of hamburgers ensured that all citizens could symbolically—and democratically—impart these national ideals.

Beef's popularity peaked in 1976, when each American ate 127 pounds of it a year, with the hamburger patty as its most popular shape. In the late 1970s, new consciousness about dietary fat markedly reduced the hamburger's popularity. By the 1980s red-meat consumption, including hamburgers, was considerably reduced, and many medical studies were linking red meat consumption to cancer and heart disease. While the cattle industry responded with a multimillion dollar ad campaign: "Beef: Real Food for Real People," fast-food restaurants began to diversify their offerings. While the beef hamburger remained the bedrock of fast food, salads, chicken, fish, and burritos made inroads into the market.

Down from prior levels, Americans in 1995 still consumed twenty-nine billion hamburgers a year: an average of 120 per capita. Together, fast-food chains and cattle ranching made one of the largest industries in America, impacting ecosystems, water resources, and land ownership of large parts of America in its push for a large supply of inexpensive beef—the key to success for the fast-food hamburger. By converting much of the Western wilderness into ranch land, and by securing water rights and government subsidies, cattle ranchers could profitably sell beef at less than a dollar per pound. Powered by the popularity of hamburgers, an enormous cattle industry transformed millions of acres of wilderness. Barbed wire fences, cattle manure, grazing, and drought caused by the diversion of water sources radically altered land from Texas to Oregon. From the 1960s onward, parts of Latin-American rain forests were cleared to raise beef for American fast-food burgers.

By the close of the century, the traditional hamburger was in decline. Environmentalists alleged that the hamburger was a major threat to ecosystems, and health advocates warned Americans to reduce intake of red meat. The small but growing popularity of vegetarianism also challenged the hamburger, and even though most Americans did not disavow meat altogether, many reduced their intake. But while the beef burger was waning in popularity, other versions of the burger were ascendant: the "hamburger" was being reinterpreted. "Burgers" were being made with fish, chicken, turkey, soy beans, or grains. In the 1990s, the "veggie burger," a grain-based burger, rapidly increased in popularity.

—Dylan Clark

FURTHER READING:

Levi-Strauss, Claude. *The Raw and the Cooked.* Translated from French by John and Doreen Weightman. New York, Harper and Row, 1969.

McDonald, Ronald L. *The Complete Hamburger: The History of America's Favorite Sandwich.* Secaucus, New Jersey, Carol, 1997.

Rifkin, Jeremy. *Beyond Beef: The Rise and Fall of the Cattle Culture.* New York, Dutton, 1992.

Robbins, John. *Diet for a New America.* Walpole, New Hampshire, Stillpoint, 1987.

Trager, James. *The Food Chronology.* New York, Henry Holt, 1995.

Hamill, Dorothy (1956—)

Easily recognizable for the pixie haircut that is her trademark, Dorothy Hamill created one of the first true media frenzies surrounding a figure skater. Hamill reigned as a National, World, and Olympic Champion in the 1970s and helped develop the popularity of professional ice skating shows. During the 1976 Olympics, girls all over the world copied her hairstyle, which led to Hamill becoming a spokesperson for hair care products.

Born in Riverside, Connecticut, to Chalmers and Carol Hamill, Dorothy became interested in skating at the age of eight. She began taking lessons with former Czech champion, Otto Gold, in 1965. Almost immediately, the Hamill family decided that their talented daughter should train seriously, with the idea of competing at the national level. Dorothy passed her first Preliminary Test to compete

Dorothy Hamill

in 1965. By 1967 she had switched coaches to train with Swiss coach, Gustav Lussi. She later studied with former U.S. Champion, Sonya Klopfer Dunfield.

Hamill became the U.S. National Ladies Novice Champion in 1969, at the age of 12, and continued to move up the skating ranks. Another coaching change was soon made, and the teenager began studying with Carlo Fassi, who had also coached champion Peggy Fleming. Hamill soon moved up to the Senior Ladies Division. In her first National Championship in 1971, she placed a very respectable 5th place. By 1973 she had matured so much that she barely lost to the National Championship to Janet Lynn. That same year, Dorothy came in 4th in the World Championships.

In 1974 Hamill won the National Championship and went on to represent the United States at the World Championships, which were held in Munich, Germany. During the competition an incident occurred, which will long be remembered by the skating fans who witnessed it. The audience for the long program, upset by low scores given to local skater, Gerti Schrandel, began booing as Hamill prepared to skate. Although they were not booing her, Hamill became so upset she left the ice in tears. A few moments later she again took the ice, having declined the opportunity to compose herself and skate later in the competition. Showing the determination that had already gotten her so far, Hamill skated almost flawlessly and finished with the silver medal behind Christine Erath of East Germany.

During the 1975 season, Hamill defended her National Championship and again finished second at the World Championships, this time to Diane deLeeuw of the Netherlands. Things continued to heat up throughout the season before the 1976 Olympic Games in Austria. Hamill and World Champions deLeeuw and Erath remained neck in neck, with no clear favorite for the Olympic Gold medal. In the media frenzy before the games, however, it became clear that Hamill was the press and audience favorite. Her parents and coach, Carlo Fassi, tried to insulate Hamill from the spotlight as she continued to train for the Olympics. When the games were over, Hamill was crowned the new Olympic Champion. Shortly thereafter, she captured the World Championship, and the interest in Hamill and her professional and private life grew. She became a commercial spokesperson for Short & Sassy hair care products, which capitalized on her famous haircut.

After she turned professional, skating with the Ice Capades, Hamill continued to command the spotlight, although not to the extent she had during the Olympics. She starred in ice shows and popular television specials, such as *Romeo and Juliet On Ice*. It was Hamill who really brought worldwide interest to professional ice shows.

When her first marriage to actor Dean Paul Martin broke up, she married sports-medicine specialist, Dr. Kenneth Forsythe. In 1993, after she had skated with the Ice Capades for several years, Hamill, her husband, and businessman Ben C. Tinsdale, purchased the show. Her first production as part owner was *Cinderella . . . Frozen in Time*. Although the show was a success, the company did not prosper as hoped and, in 1994, a conglomerate acquired it.

Dorothy Hamill helped increase interest in figure skating, both on the amateur and professional levels. She became one of the first real superstars of figure skating. Along the way she also became an icon to young girls all over the world.

—Jill A. Gregg

FURTHER READING:

Dolan, Edward F., Jr., and Richard B. Lytle. *Dorothy Hamill: Olympic Skating Champion*. New York, Doubleday, 1979.

Malone, John. *The Encyclopedia of Figure Skating*. New York, Facts on File, 1998.

Milton, Steve. *Skate: 100 Years of Figure Skating*. Vermont, Trafalgar Square Publishing, 1996.

Hammerstein, Oscar, II

See Rodgers and Hammerstein

Hammett, Dashiell (1894-1961)

For a writer who turned out only five novels, Dashiell Hammett made a strong and lasting impression on the twentieth century and is considered one of the founding fathers of the hard-boiled school of detective fiction, a tough, unsentimental style of American crime writing. In *The Maltese Falcon* he introduced Sam Spade; in *The Thin Man* it was Nick and Nora Charles. Four decades after his death all his novels remain in print along with many of the short stories and novelettes he wrote for the *Black Mask* detective pulp magazine. The Bogart film version of *The Maltese Falcon* (1941) can still be seen regularly on television or video. All six of the Thin Man films,

Dashiell Hammett

starring the memorable team of William Powell and Myrna Loy, are also easily accessible.

Born in Maryland, Samuel Dashiell Hammett dropped out of school while in his early teens, later worked as an operative for the Pinkerton Detective Agency in Baltimore, and served as a driver in the Ambulance Corps during World War I. In the early 1920s, married and living in San Francisco, he began submitting stories to magazines and soon became a regular contributor to *Black Mask*. Using a restrained yet tough vernacular first-person style, he wrote a series about a plump, middle-aged operative anonymously known as the Continental Op who worked for the Continental Detective Agency in Frisco. Based in part on his own experiences as a Pinkerton, the stories offered considerable action, gunplay, romance, and melodrama. When Joseph T. Shaw took over as *Black Mask* editor in 1926, he quickly decided that Hammett was the best man he had; he promoted Hammett to star contributor and worked to persuade other writers to follow in his footsteps.

Of the several dozen stories Hammett wrote for the pulp, nearly thirty were about the Continental Op, and the fat private eye also figured in his first two novels. After being serialized in *Black Mask,* both *Red Harvest* and *The Dain Curse* were published by Alfred A. Knopf in 1929. *The Maltese Falcon* began that same year as a serial and was published as a book by Knopf in 1930, followed by *The Glass Key* in 1931. Hammett's final novel, *The Thin Man,* first appeared in *Redbook* in 1933 and as a book, with a few allegedly risqué lines restored, in 1934.

Both critics and readers were enthusiastic about the Hammett books, and his reputation soon spread beyond the pulpwood and mystery novel ghettos. *The Maltese Falcon* was early added to the Modern Library list and the little remaining fiction Hammett wrote was found in such glossy paper, and high-paying, magazines as *Collier's.* More important to Hammett's future and his finances was the fact that Hollywood took notice of him. The year after *The Maltese Falcon* was published, Sam Spade took his first step into another medium. The initial Warner Brothers version starred former Latin lover of the silents Ricardo Cortez as Spade, and the second, titled *Satan Met a Lady* and ineptly played as a comedy, featured Warren William as the sleuth. Finally in 1941 John Huston persuaded the studio to let him write and direct a new version that stuck closely to the Hammett original. That *Maltese Falcon* became the definitive one, gave Humphrey Bogart the role that helped rejuvenate his career, and helped establish the film noir genre. Hammett, who sold all motion picture rights to his book back in 1931, didn't profit directly from the later two adaptations.

The earliest radio Sam Spade was Edward G. Robinson, who played the role in a 1943 broadcast of the *Lux Radio Theatre.* Bogart himself repeated his role in an early 1946 half-hour version for a short-lived show called *Academy Award.* That same year *The Adventures of Sam Spade* became a regular weekly show. While this latest Spade was not exactly Hammett's Spade, he was a tough, whimsical, and appealing operative; and the show was a hit. Produced by William Spier, it was written for the most part by Gil Doud and Bob Tallman. Howard Duff, who hadn't yet begun his movie career, was cast as Spade. He had a distinctive radio voice and could sound hard-boiled and still get the most out of the gag lines that showed up often in this less gloomy recreation of Hammett's world. The show remained on the air until 1950, when Hammett's political troubles made sponsors and networks wary of him. *The Adventures of the Thin Man* radio show, which had been broadcast fairly regularly from 1941 to 1950, also fell victim to the greylisting of the era. A third Hammett radio

show, *The Fat Man,* was heard from early 1946 to early 1951. Besides allowing his name to be tacked on the program and the nickname of the villain from *The Maltese Falcon* to be used as the nickname for a fat private eye, Hammett had nothing to do with the production. It, too, fell when the other shows did.

Hammett went to Hollywood in 1930 and remained there throughout the decade. According to one of his biographers, "during this period he was credited with one screenplay and contributed original screen stories on at least six credited productions." Some of those original screen stories were contributed to the Thin Man movies that followed the initial one. His other avocations were drinking and Lillian Hellman, neither of which contributed significantly to his well-being, although Hellman was supposedly the inspiration for Nora in the Thin Man series.

Hammett's literary reputation slipped during the 1930s and early 1940s, despite the branching out of his characters into movies and radio. But in the early 1940s Frederic Dannay, the literary half of Ellery Queen, began reprinting Hammett's old pulp stories in the new *Ellery Queen's Mystery Magazine.* That was followed by a series of several paperback reprint collections. These did a good deal to bolster Hammett's standing and gain a new audience for his written work.

Long suspected of being too liberal, Hammett was caught by a subpoena in 1951. As a bail bond trustee for an organization called the Civil Rights Congress, he was asked to provide the names of contributors to the fund. The questioning had to do with four suspected Communists who had jumped bail and vanished. Hammett, although he reportedly didn't know any, nevertheless refused to name names. Convicted for contempt, he spent nearly six months in a federal prison. After suffering from tuberculoses for much of his life, Hammett died in New York in 1961.

—Ron Goulart

FURTHER READING:

DeAndrea, William L. *Encyclopedia Mysteriosa.* New York, Prentice Hall, 1994.

Goulart, Ron. *The Dime Detectives.* New York, Mysterious Press, 1988.

Nolan, William F. *Dashiell Hammett: A Casebook.* Santa Barbara, McNally & Loftin, 1969.

Hancock, Herbie (1940—)

Herbie Hancock has forged a career that has pushed the envelope of jazz music and, in doing so, has reached a wider audience than any other jazz musician ever has. His 1973 album, *Head Hunters,* is the biggest selling jazz record in history. This Chicago native is easily among the most eclectic musicians of any genre. Hancock has worked within the field of jazz playing free, bebop, and fusion styles, and outside performing world music, hip-hop, funk, and dance music. Along with Miles Davis, he helped create the style known as jazz fusion in the late 1960s and, as a solo artist during the early 1970s, Hancock was one of the first to pioneer the use of synthesizers within jazz. And on his 1983 hit single, "Rockit," he introduced the mainstream pop world to turntable scratching, an element of hip-hop music that uses a turntable and an album as a musical instrument by manually manipulating the sounds it makes. Throughout his long

Herbie Hancock

career, Herbie Hancock has continually evolved and challenged genre boundaries in all forms of music.

A child prodigy, Hancock studied music in school and, at age 11, performed with the Chicago Symphony Orchestra at a young people's concert. He later formed a high school jazz group, played with the likes of Donald Byrd and Coleman Hawkins at local Chicago jazz clubs, and then left for New York City in 1960 to join and record with Donald Byrd's combo. Soon after working with Byrd, Hancock was offered a solo contract with the jazz label Blue Note, which released his 1962 debut, *Takin' Off.* The album spawned the hit and soon-to-be jazz standard "Watermelon Man," positioning Hancock as an important jazz band composer. During the 1960s, Hancock wrote such classics as "Maiden Voyage," "Dolphin Dance," and "I Have a Dream" (a tribute to Martin Luther King, Jr.).

After an extended stint in Miles Davis' second legendary quintet (which also included Wayne Shorter, Ron Carter, and Tony Williams), Hancock released a number of solo albums. He then formed his first important group, Mwandishi, which included Joe Henderson, Johnny Coles, Garnett Brown, Albert "Tootie" Heath, Buster Williams, and, of course, Hancock. From 1969 to 1972, the Mwandishi band explored funk and rock fusion, and was one of the first jazz groups to use a synthesizer, specifically the Moog. Displeased with the poor commercial reception of the records this group produced,

Hancock disbanded Mwandishi, but not before he released *Sextant,* a landmark album that heavily incorporated the synthesizer into the band's laid-back funk vamps.

Hancock then formed the Headhunters, an instrumental jazz/ pop/rock/funk combo (featuring Hancock, Bennie Maupin, Paul Jackson, Harvey Mason, and Bill Summers), that became hugely popular. That group's 1973 album, *Head Hunters,* sold more records than any jazz record had ever sold before, beginning a steady stream of success for Hancock that included 17 albums charting from 1973 to 1984. Due to his widespread popularity, many charges of "selling out" were leveled against him—charged which he dismissed them as merely being "elitist." His popularity culminated with the release of 1983's "Rockit," an electro-funk breakdancing staple that featured the turntable wizardry of Grandmaster D.S.T., marking the first time the art of the hip-hop DJ was heard by a mainstream audience. This song has been cited as a major inspiration for a generation of hip-hop DJs and artists which followed.

During the rest of the 1980s and 1990s, Hancock released a handful of modestly-selling albums, which included the world music fusion of *Ids Is DA Drum* and, in 1998, an album by the re-formed Headhunters.

—Kembrew McLeod

FURTHER READING:

Porter, Lewis, and Michael Ullman, with Edward Hazell. *Jazz: From Its Origins to the Present.* Englewood Cliffs, Prentice Hall, 1992.

Vincent, Rickey. *Funk: The Music, the People, and the Rhythm of the One.* New York, St. Martin's Griffin, 1996.

Handy, W. C. (1873-1958)

Though he never would have called himself a blues musician, W. C. Handy is often hailed as the "Father of the Blues." Handy grew up immersed in the folk music of the African American people, a music nurtured by slavery and with roots in the various African cultures from which slaves were torn. A trained musician, Handy translated this "primitive" music into compositions that revealed the richness and diversity of the black musical tradition. His "Memphis Blues" was the first published blues tune, and he left a legacy of musical compositions to which much of the modern blues can trace its roots.

William Christopher Handy was born on November 16, 1873, in either Florence or Muscle Shoals, Alabama. Both his father and grandfather were clergymen and were eager for young Handy to follow in their shoes, but Handy developed an early love for music. He recalled in his autobiography, *Father of the Blues*, that his father stated that he would rather follow his son's hearse than have him become a musician. Still, Handy persevered, taking vocal lessons

W. C. Handy

from a church singer and secretly buying a cornet and taking lessons from its former owner. By the time he was a teenager, Handy had amassed a good deal of training in music and, at age 15, he joined a travelling minstrel show that began a tour of the South. The tour soon fell apart, however, and Handy returned home to start a normal life.

In 1892, Handy graduated from the Huntsville Teachers Agricultural and Mechanical College and began working as a teacher—until he found out that he could make more working for a pipeworks factory in Bessemer, Alabama. When wages there were cut, Handy left the factory to follow his first love, music. He organized a group called the Lauzette Quartet and left to play the Chicago World's Fair—only to find that they had arrived in Chicago a year early. Dejected, Handy travelled to St. Louis, Missouri, where he eked out a living playing his cornet and soaked up the downscale ambiance of the city's impoverished black population.

Shortly thereafter, Handy, whose reputation as a talented horn player was spreading, had the good fortune to be hired to play for wealthy Southerners in Henderson, Kentucky. "I had my change that day in Henderson," Handy wrote in his autobiography. "My change was from a hobo and a member of a road gang to a professional musician." Handy also found an opportunity to study with a local music teacher, who taught him more about music in a few short months than he had yet learned in a lifetime.

In 1896, a minstrel group known as W. A. Mahara's Minstrels asked Handy to join them, and he traveled extensively with the group from 1896 to 1900 and from 1902 to 1904. On his travels, the group played to an Alabama audience that included Handy's father. "Sonny," his father told him, "I haven't been in a show since I professed religion. I enjoyed it. I am very proud of you and forgive you for becoming a musician." During this time, Handy's band played for white and black audiences. The story is that a white audience asked him to play some of his own music; Handy failed to meet their request and the audience protested. Handy's band was replaced by a group of three local black musicians who played a type of early blues on string instruments. Handy decided that in spite of his musical erudition, he had missed an important lesson. He decided to look into the blues.

Handy put that lesson to good use in 1909 when he was asked to write a campaign song for Edward H. "Boss" Crump of Memphis, Tennessee. The song was soon adapted to include the following lyrics:

Mr. Crump won't 'low no easy riders here.
We doan care what Mr. Crump don't 'low,
We gon'to bar'l-house anyhow.
Mr. Crump can go and catch hisself some air.

This tune, with new words, soon became famous as "The Memphis Blues." It was the first written composition to use the flatted thirds and sevenths, the "blue notes." The great jazz bandleader Noble Sissle claimed that "The Memphis Blues" was the inspiration for the fox trot. Vernon and Irene Castle heard their musical director, James Reese Europe, use the "Memphis Blues" as a cooling off piece during intermissions. The Castles loved the rhythm and developed a slow dance to it, called first the Bunny Hug and then the Fox Trot.

Following the success of this song, Handy decided to specialize in a type of music that was little known outside the South, the blues. Handy had a great musical memory, coupled with a well-developed musical knowledge. He freely acknowledged the roots of his blues being in black folk songs.

Each one of my blues is based on some old Negro song of the South. . . . Something that sticks in my mind, that I hum to myself when I'm not thinking about it. Some old song that is a part of the memories of my childhood and of my race. I can tell you the exact song I used as a basis for any one of my blues.

At the time, the blues had not yet taken on the classical form in which they are known today. This 12 or 16 bar form in which the I-IV-V chords are used in a set pattern, open to variations, was basically established by Handy as he wrote down the music he heard on his band tours. Handy's blues are more polished than the "primitive" blues that preceded him and were played well into the century by musicians such as John Lee Hooker.

In 1912, Handy, after much struggle, published his first song, "Memphis Blues." Others soon followed, including "St. Louis Blues" (1914), "Beale Street Blues" (1917), and 1921's "Loveless Love," a favorite of Louis Armstrong. The difficulty that Handy experienced in publishing his first song led him to found his own publishing house, but he still had a hard time getting his music distributed. In his autobiography he remembered an encounter with a retailer:

At the time I approached him his windows were displaying "At The Ball" by J. Lubrie Hill, a colored composer who had gone to New York from Memphis some time earlier. Around it were grouped copies of recent successes by such Negro composers as Cole and Johnson, Scott Joplin, and the Williams and Walker musical comedies. So when he suggested that his trade wouldn't stand for his selling my work, I pointed out as tactfully as I could that the majority of his musical hits of the moment had come from the Gotham-Attucks Co., a firm of Negro publishers in New York. I'll never forget his smile. "Yes," he said pleasantly. "I know that—but my customers don't."

Despite such difficulties, Handy continued to publish his works, selling many of them from his own music company, the still-existing Handy Brothers Music Company of Manhattan.

Handy's "St. Louis Blues" is the most recorded song in musical history. At his death in 1958 it was still earning him $25,000 per year. It was the King of England's favorite song and became the Ethiopian fight song against Mussolini. Bessie Smith, with Louis Armstrong on cornet, immortalized the work. Armstrong later recorded the tune a number of times, even playing it as a tango.

In 1917 Handy moved to New York City where he recorded with his Memphis Orchestra. He began his own recording company in 1922, though it soon failed. Handy's written output faltered, as a result of his increasing eye problems, but he continued playing cornet and recorded with a number of top jazz musicians, including Henry "Red" Allen and Jelly Roll Morton.

In 1928 Handy became the first black performer to play in New York's Carnegie Hall. That concert was one of the only elements of Handy's life that was recreated accurately in his film biography *St. Louis Blues* (1958), which starred Nat King Cole as Handy. While largely inaccurate, the film served to spark rerecordings of many of Handy's tunes. Shortly before Handy's death, Louis Armstrong and the All Stars recorded an album of Handy tunes and Handy was recorded reflecting on his career and on Armstrong. The album, *Louis*

Armstrong Plays W.C. Handy (1954), was a fine corrective to the movie.

Handy's autobiography, *Father of the Blues* (1941), relates his story and struggles in establishing his work. The fact that the blues were so identifiably black in origin and so different from the usual Tin Pan Alley tunes eventually worked in his favor. Anyone could put the word blues in a song, but not everyone could write an authentic sounding blues tune. Handy could and did. The blues became part of jazz and the basis of rock 'n' roll. Handy's music is inseparable from twentieth-century world music, a fact recognized by the city of Memphis, in which Handy is a legend. There is a park named in his honor, and a statue of Handy stands prominently. Handy is in the Alabama Music Hall of Fame, has had a postage stamp named after him, and is recognized as a major contributor to American music.

—Frank A. Salamone

FURTHER READING:

Handy, W. C. *Father of the Blues,* edited by Arna Bontemps. New York, Macmillan, 1941, New York: Da Capo, 1991.

Lee, George Washington. *Beale Street: Where the Blues Began,* introduction by W. C. Handy. New York, R. O. Ballou, 1934.

Montgomery, Elizabeth Rider. *William C. Handy: Father of the Blues.* Champaign, Illinois, Garrard Publishing, 1968.

Hanks, Tom (1956—)

One of only two men to ever win back-to-back Academy Awards for Best Actor, Tom Hanks has proven that he is one of the most talented and versatile actors of the twentieth century. From his early days as cross-dressing Kip in the television show *Bosom Buddies,* Hanks went on to win Oscars for two vastly diverse roles. First, he won Best Actor for 1993's *Philadelphia,* in which he played Andrew Beckett, a gay lawyer dismissed from his law firm after being diagnosed with AIDS. In 1994, Hanks brought home a second statue for his portrayal of the title character in *Forrest Gump,* an amiable Southerner with questionable intelligence and the good fortune to be present at a number of important historical events. For his role as Andrew Beckett, Hanks lost so much weight that he lent grim reality to the deteriorating physical condition of the gay lawyer. In *Forrest Gump,* Hanks developed a slow drawl that perfectly presented Gump's drawn-out mental processes and childish naivete. Not one to be satisfied with making history, Hanks followed up the two wins with an Oscar-worthy performance that allowed him to bring a life-long dream close to reality by playing astronaut Jim Lowell in *Apollo 13* (1995). Hanks was also nominated for his performance in 1998's *Saving Private Ryan,* Steven Spielberg's gripping World War II drama.

Tom Hanks was born July 9, 1956, in Concord, California. When he was only five years old, his parents divorced. Hanks and his older siblings lived with his father, while the youngest child remained with his mother. The divorce was followed by multiple sets of step-parents and frequent moves. As the perennial new kid on the block, Hanks learned that people liked him when he made them laugh, so he became

Tom Hanks (left), Matt Damon (center), and Ed Burns in a scene from the film *Saving Private Ryan*.

a clown. In 1978 he married Samantha Lewes, with whom he has two children, son Colin and daughter Elizabeth. They divorced in 1985. In 1985, while filming the comedy *Volunteers,* Hanks met Rita Wilson and they were married in 1988. Hanks and Wilson have two sons, Chester and Truman. While accepting the Academy Award for *Forrest Gump* in 1994, Hanks brought tears to many eyes with his acknowledgement of their mutual love and respect.

The years between *Bosom Buddies* (1980-82) and his two Academy awards were full of both successes and failures for Hanks. Director Ron Howard gave Hanks his first shot at superstardom by casting him opposite mermaid Darryl Hannah in *Splash* (1984). He followed these movies with comedies, such as *The Man with One Red Shoe* (1985) and *The Money Pit* (1986), that endeared him to fans but which were panned by critics. However, in 1988 Hanks won over the critics with the role of Josh Baskin in Penny Marshall's *Big*. This story of a young boy who gets his wish to grow up overnight was the perfect vehicle for Hanks because it allowed him to combine his youthful appeal with a mature performance, garnering a Best Actor nomination. Unfortunately, Hanks followed up his success in *Big* with less successful roles in *Punchline* (1988), *Turner and Hooch* (1989), and *The Bonfire of the Vanities* and *Joe Versus the Volcano* (both 1990). His return to critical acclaim came in 1992 with the role of Jimmy Dugan in Penny Marshall's *A League of Their Own*. While

the female stars were the focus in this tale of a women's baseball team, Hanks more than held his own as the bitter, tobacco-chewing, has-been manager of the team.

Hanks' versatility is the key to his success as an actor. The physically and mentally draining role of the gay lawyer in *Philadelphia* was immediately followed by a love story that was to become a classic: *Sleepless in Seattle* (1993). *Sleepless* drew on the earlier classic love story of *An Affair to Remember* (1957) for its plot. Instead of star-crossed lovers, Hanks and Meg Ryan play potential lovers who never get together until the final scene, which takes place at the Empire State Building in New York City. The phenomenal success of *Forrest Gump* was followed by the Disney favorite *Toy Story* (1995). Hanks lent his voice to Woody, a computer-generated cowboy puppet displaced in his boy's affections by spaceman Buzz Lightyear (the voice of Tim Allen). Even in this children's tale, Hanks presents a character to whom his audience can relate and offers friendship as a moral lesson and proof of character development.

Adding producer, writer, and director to his list of accomplishments, Tom Hanks created his own movie with *That Thing You Do* (1996), a charming, simple story of a one-hit 1960's rock band. *From the Earth to the Moon,* a 1998 mini-series, proved to be even more ambitious. In several installments, the mini-series followed the entire history of the space program.

Tom Hanks has frequently been compared to Jimmy Stewart, an actor who was so well loved that the Los Angeles airport was renamed to honor him after his death in 1997. Hanks and Stewart are, indeed, similar in their appeal to both men and women and in their versatility. It is likely that Tom Hanks will go down in history as the most popular and the most critically acclaimed actor of the latter half of the twentieth century.

—Elizabeth Purdy

FURTHER READING:

Nikart, Ray. *Tom Hanks.* New York, St. Martin's Press, 1987.

Passero, Kathy. "That Thing He Does: The Perpetual Appeal of Tom Hanks." *Biography.* July 1998, 30-37.

Pfeiffer, Lee, and Michael Lewis. *The Films of Tom Hanks.* Secaucus, New Jersey, Carol Publishing, 1996.

Quinlan, David. *Tom Hanks: A Career in Orbit.* London, B. T. Botsford, Ltd., 1998.

Trakin, Roy. *Tom Hanks: Journey to Stardom.* New York, St. Martin's, 1995.

Hanna-Barbera

William Hanna and Joseph Barbera, both through their own creativity and that of their studio, were second only to Walt Disney in the number of memorable, durable, and famous characters they introduced to the art of American animation. Known and loved throughout the world, the Hanna-Barbera cartoons differed from those of Disney in exclusively mining contemporary American life for their ideas, permeating the popular culture with images that reflected it in cartoon form. Their output was prodigious and many of their creations famous, but they will forever be synonymous with the world's most popular cat-and-mouse duo, Tom and Jerry, whose inspired an hilarious adversarial relationship, serviced over 100 cartoon shorts, and won Academy Awards for seven of them, of which *Johann Mouse* (1952) is perhaps the most outstanding of all.

Born in 1910 in Melrose, New Mexico, Hanna began his professional career at age 20, working as a story editor, lyricist, and composer for an independent studio; Barbera, born in New York City in 1911, was an accountant and a freelance magazine cartoonist. The two men met at MGM in 1937, the year they both joined the studio and, with Fred Quimby, created Tom and Jerry. The imaginative narrative line of the cartoons, in which Jerry Mouse emerged the victor of the battles, pushed the frontiers of animated entertainment and risked using more sadistic imagery than was then usual in the genre. Jerry had the distinction of being taught to dance "The Worry Song" by Gene Kelly in a stunning sequence, combining live action and animation, in MGM's *Anchors Aweigh* (1945). And for Kelly's *Invitation to the Dance* (1956), Hanna, Barbera and Quimby directed the third segment of the film, in which cartoon characters and Kelly danced to Rimsky-Korsakov's "Scheherezade."

In 1957 MGM closed its cartoon division, whereupon William Hanna and Joseph Barbera set up their own production company,

Hanna-Barbera, and launched themselves into a new medium—television. They created the first cartoons for television at a time when many people thought it couldn't be done, partly because the expense of the animation process only seemed feasible for feature films. Hanna and Barbera, however, devised a less expensive technique by reducing the size of the storyboards, and if the results lacked the detail and background of animated features, they were nonetheless highly successful. *The Ruff and Reddy Show* premiered on NBC in 1957, paving the way for several decades of Hanna-Barbera cartoons and Saturday morning viewing rituals, and creating characters who became entrenched in American popular culture, recurring in syndication and cartoons for decades. Among the best known were Yogi ("smarter than the average bear") Bear and his sidekick Boo Boo Bear, Augie Doggie and Doggie Daddy, Huckleberry Hound, Quickdraw McGraw, and Snagglepuss. Perhaps their most famous and durable creation was *The Flintstones*. When it aired in 1960, it was the first animated half-hour prime time sitcom on television. Modeled after *The Honeymooners*, *The Flintstones* earned Hanna-Barbera a permanent place in American television history. As the first animated cartoon featuring human characters, the series laid the ground for such later shows as *The Simpsons* and *King of the Hill*.

Besides the lovable and goofy characters of its early years, Hanna-Barbera productions created action and super-hero cartoons in the 1960s. One of the first of these was *The Adventures of Johnny Quest*. Johnny went on adventures with his scientist father and companions Hadji and Race Bannon. First appearing in 1964, the show was revamped in the 1990s with a focus on computer animation. Other heroes of the time were Space Ghost, the Herculoids, Birdman, the Mighty Mightor, and animated versions of the comic-book super team, The Fantastic Four. However, parents' groups eventually objected to the violence and Hanna-Barbera returned to making more humorous cartoons.

The company turned out product at an extraordinary rate and embraced computerized systems. Of their later cartoon characters, Scooby-Doo (named after lyrics from a Frank Sinatra song), was the most popular. A cowardly and often ravenous Great Dane, Scooby-Doo starred in *Scooby-Doo, Where Are You?* (1969) with four teenage co-stars. They traveled around in a psychedelic van called the Mystery Machine, solving mysteries that usually had a supernatural slant. Scooby and the gang enjoyed several incarnations over the next several decades. Also popular in the 1970s were *Josie and the Pussycats*, the *Hair Bear Bunch*, *Penelope Pittstop*, and the villains *Dastardly and Muttley*, while Hanna-Barbera's biggest success of the 1980s was *The Smurfs*, small blue creatures whose names (Handy and Vanity, for example) matched their dominant traits. Led by the red-clad Papa Smurf, the Smurfs constantly fought against the evil Gargamel. Besides the Smurfs, Hanna-Barbera did animated versions of nationally popular live action shows. Cartoon versions of *Happy Days*, *Laverne and Shirley*, *Mork and Mindy*, and *The Dukes of Hazzard* appeared on Saturday mornings courtesy of Hanna-Barbera. Some shows, such as *Josie and the Pussycats* and *Pebbles and Bamm Bamm*, incorporated contemporary rock music into their shows. Though not as memorable as the Disney classics, the songs keyed into the tastes of their audiences at the time, especially the pre-teen audience.

Also during the 1960s, Hanna-Barbera expanded their activities to make a handful of feature films, beginning with *Hey, There, It's Yogi Bear* (1964), and ending with *Jetsons: The Movie* (1990),

William Hanna (left) and Joseph Barbera

featuring the characters from their TV series of the same name. If individual Hanna-Barbera characters did not reach quite the icon status of Mickey Mouse, they were more typically American and of this world than Disney's famous creations. The Jetsons, for example, were space age counterparts to the Flinstones, all of them archetypal American families. The shows exploited the conflicts that typically occur in American homes, while adding gags appropriate to the period. The contemporaneous approach was what probably made these two cartoon families the most famous and memorable of the Hanna-Barbera stable.

Hanna and Barbera won many awards. In addition to their Oscars, there were Emmys, and, in 1988, 50 years after they met, they received the Governor's Award from the National Academy of Television Arts and Sciences. That year, too, the company was absorbed into the Great American Broadcasting company, with Joseph Barbera as president. But perhaps their greatest honor is the impact they had on the American public. Their TV cartoon series were significant in the lives of countless, who entered adulthood still able to sing part, if not all, of the theme songs, and reciting such catch phrases as "Yabba dabba do," "Smarter than the average bear," "Jane, stop this crazy thing!," and "Heavens to Murgatroyd," which had their origins in Hanna-Barbera's cartoons.

—P. Andrew Miller

FURTHER READING:

Sennett, Ted. *The Art of Hanna-Barbera.* New York, Viking Studio Books, 1989.

Hansberry, Lorraine (1930-1965)

A black American playwright who produced only two plays before her death from cancer at 34, Lorraine Hansberry nonetheless made a tremendous contribution to the American stage and to African American culture. Her first and best known play, *A Raisin in the Sun* (1959), winner of the New York Drama Critics Circle Award, is now considered a landmark of American drama. The story of the struggling Younger family, who aspire to a better life, *A Raisin in the Sun* was the first Broadway production by a black woman, and its commercial success opened the stage doors to other black writers. *The Sign in Sidney Brustein's Window,* Hansberry's challenging but commercially disappointing second play, followed in 1964. Posthumously produced plays *To Be Young, Black, and Gifted* (1969), *Les Blancs* (1970), and *What Use Are Flowers?* (1972), adapted by her ex-husband and literary executor Robert Nemiroff, confirm Hansberry's great ability to combine artistic integrity and skill with commitment to social reform.

—Barbara Tepa Lupack

FURTHER READING:

Carter, Steven R. *Hansberry's Drama: Commitment amid Complexity.* Urbana, University of Illinois Press, 1991.

Cheney, Anne. *Lorraine Hansberry.* Boston, Twayne, 1984.

Leeson, Richard M. *Lorraine Hansberry: A Research and Production Sourcebook.* Westport, Connecticut Greenwood, 1997.

Scheader, Catherine. *They Found a Way: Lorraine Hansberry.* Chicago, Children's Press, 1978.

Happy Days

For ten years, from 1974 to 1984, a fictional image of suburban Milwaukee brought the 1950s back to America through ABC's *Happy Days.* The picture of the world that was painted by this television comedy shaped a whole generation's image of the 1950s. It was world of drive-ins and leather jackets, of cars and girls, but mostly of hanging out and solving day to day problems. It was noticeably *not* the 1950s of McCarthy and Korea. In the first seasons of the show, a number of episodes focused on specific 1950s topics: electioneering for Adlai Stevenson, Beatniks, rock 'n' roll shows, gangs; but after that, *Happy Days* settled into its stride to present a more general backdrop of the period, against which the Cunninghams and Fonzie developed as characters.

In addition to *Laverne and Shirley* and *Joanie Loves Chachi,* *Happy Days* spawned a Saturday-morning cartoon show, *The Fonz and the Happy Days Gang.* Also, the much-loved 1978 sitcom *Mork & Mindy* was based on an episode of *Happy Days.* Indeed, the series was influential in setting the standard for popular comedies during the later 1970s and through the 1980s.

Happy Days was created by Garry Marshall, a veteran comedy writer who had worked on the *Dick Van Dyke Show* and who had produced *The Odd Couple.* Marshall produced a pilot for ABC in 1971, titled *New Family in Town.* The network was not interested, and the pilot later surfaced as a segment of *Love, American Style.* Aired on February 25, 1972, it was titled "Love and the Happy Day," and featured Ron Howard, Marion Ross, Harold Gould, and Susan Neher as a 1950s family acquiring their first TV set. In the meantime, however, film director George Lucas had seen the pilot, and used it as the inspiration for his tremendously popular movie *American Graffiti* (1973), with Ron Howard as a 1950s "Everyteen." The success of the movie rekindled ABC's interest in Garry Marshall's original pilot.

Over its lifetime, *Happy Days* was really at least three shows. In the first two seasons, it focused on the life of Richie Cunningham (Ron Howard) and his family, which consisted of Dad (Tom Bosley), a hardware storeowner, Mom (Marion Ross), and little sister Joanie (Erin Moran). Early on, there was also a basketball-wielding, mono-syllabic older brother, Chuck, but he left the collective memory along with the actor when cast changes were made after the second season. Outside of the family home, Richie's social life was lived primarily at Arnold's Drive-in, where he hung out with his friends Potsie Weber (Anson Williams) and Ralph Malph (Donny Most), and consulted with his leather-jacketed mentor, Fonzie (Henry Winkler). This early

incarnation was much like the 1950s comedies it emulated, offering a basic and likable story. Then they discovered Fonzie.

By the third season, things on *Happy Days* had changed. The show went to the top of the ratings and became the foundation for ABC's rise as the powerhouse of television in the 1970s. No longer just a show about the antics of high school kids, the series began to focus on the relationship of Fonzie and Richie, their mutual admiration and dependency, and the growth and development of Fonzie.

Eventually, both the fictional Richie Cunningham and actor Ron Howard grew up and left the show, leaving it to feature a younger generation of characters and an adult Fonzie in its final years. While attention was transferred to Joanie and her friends in high school, but within the basic format, the dynamic of the show changed as Fonzie's transformation from rebellious youth to mentor and folk hero became complete.

Two things were true at the outset of this show. Before Ron Howard would accept a role as another television youth (after practically growing up on the *Andy Griffith Show*), he made Marshall promise that his character would be allowed to age each year through high school into college. Fonzie had originally been envisioned by Marshall—and portrayed by Winkler—as a brooding, rebellious dropout. In one of those great bits of television folklore, the ABC network had decreed that Fonzie should wear a cloth jacket rather than the "threatening" leather one. Marshall suggested a compromise, permitting Fonzie to wear the leather jacket when he rode or worked on his motorcycle. So, in the beginning, Fonzie was not seen without his motorcycle. Eventually, however, Fonzie rode his motorcycle less and less, but continued to wear his leather jacket.

Fonzie was originally intended as a minor character, but proved to be extremely popular with the audience and they decided to emphasize the role. To take advantage of Fonzie's popularity, he was moved into an apartment above the Cunningham's garage in 1975. The move enabled Fonzie to maintain his independence, but allowed the scriptwriters to involve him in the Cunninghams' domestic life. The Chuck character was no longer necessary, since Fonzie would fill the role as big brother to Richie.

As *Happy Days* moved into its second and third years, Fonzie received ever more attention. He made *Happy Days* unique and distanced the show from the middle-class family. In many ways, the middle years of this show seemed simultaneously anti-authority, yet accepting of it. Fonzie epitomized all that the middle-class 1950s were supposed to fear. He is cool, he is a drop out, and he gets all the women. Fonzie was the working class character, and the leader of the youth pack around Arnold's Drive-in, the youth Mecca in *Happy Days'* Milwaukee. When Fonzie first came to the forefront, he was the prototypical "hood," whose menace served as a counterpoint to the goodness of Richie and his friends.

This new Fonzie was a more human Fonzie, one who can show his feelings and vulnerability without sacrificing the essential toughness of his character. In this permutation, he became a combination of father confessor and guru to Richie's pals. Fonzie is the epitome of cool (almost to the point of caricature), he is the one who can dispense advice, settle disputes, and serve as role model. This was all a far cry from the standard 1950s sitcom, where only parents could dispense wisdom to children, and working class, non-educated teens were perceived as a threat rather than a role model.

This new dynamic powered the show to its huge success. The rest of the characters, too, were pulled up with Fonzie, but over time it got to be too much—too much formula, not enough pizzazz. So much

The stars of *Happy Days* (from left) Don Most, Henry Winkler, Anson Williams, and Ron Howard.

so, that several years of episodes would feature a trip (to a dude ranch, to Hollywood) where Fonzie can save the day by riding a bull or water skiing over a shark. He became one of the family, and was thus diluted into a stereotype, a ''good'' role model, as the character was gradually stripped of most of his threatening qualities.

This was not all bad, and the interaction between Richie and Fonzie provided the opportunity to broaden the show's topics, while Ralph and Potsie were relegated to comic relief. In the fall of 1977, Richie, Potsie, and Ralph began college at the University of Wisconsin in Milwaukee. Joining the cast that season were Scott Baio as Fonzie's enterprising young cousin, Charles ''Chachi'' Arcola, who became Joanie's boyfriend, and Lynda Goodfriend as Richie's girlfriend, Lori Beth Allen.

Ron Howard and Donny Most left the series in 1980, written out by having Richie and Ralph leave to join the army; in May of 1981 Richie married Lori Beth by proxy, and their baby, Richie, Jr., was born in the fall of 1981. Meanwhile, Fonzie had become a teacher of auto shop at good old Jefferson High. Joining the cast were Ted McGinley as Marion's nephew Roger, who became Jefferson's new basketball coach and English teacher, and Cathy Silvers (1980 to 1983) as Joanie's boy-crazy girlfriend, Jenny Piccalo. In the fall of 1982 Fonzie found himself falling in love with a divorcée named Ashley (played by Linda Purl). Ashley's daughter was played by Heather O'Rourke. In addition Crystal Bernard joined the show as Howard's niece, K.C., who lived with the Cunninghams. One reason for this addition was that Joanie was not at home, having moved to her own (short-lived and unsuccessful) spin-off, *Joanie Loves Chachi*. By the fall of 1983, in what would be *Happy Days'* final season, Fonzie had become the dean of boys at George S. Patton Vocational High. Joanie and Chachi, whose spin-off had flopped, came back to Milwaukee, and plans were made for their wedding. Also returning were Richie and Ralph, who showed up in a special two-part episode.

Increasingly, over its ten-year run, the life of the show took on a more 1970s feel in clothes, in language, and, occasionally, in storyline. It retained the music and basic settings. but seemed to stop caring about the period that was its inspiration. Though Fonzie rose to prominence, it was always Richie who provided the focus and balance for the show. When he left, it was never the same again, and many would say it never recovered, although it went on for four more seasons.

Though it appeared at the same time as reality-based comedies like *All in the Family* and *M*A*S*H*, *Happy Days* opted for lighter humor and interaction. Due primarily to Fonzie, who became such a cultural icon that his leather jacket is part of the Smithsonian collections, this show became a part of social consciousness. For the generation of Vietnam and Watergate, it represented a perfect combination: a nostalgic reflection on an earlier time when life seemed less difficult, with a strong character that can solve the problems and who, while allowing us to see his failings, can retain that strength. Last but not least, *Happy Days* reflected the problems of everyday life, placed at a safe remove and tempered by humor.

—Frank E. Clark

FURTHER READING:

Castleman, Harry, and Walter J. Podrazik. *Harry and Wally's Favorite Shows: A Fact-filled Opinionated Guide to the Best and Worst on TV.* New York, Prentice Hall Press, 1989.

Marc, David, and Robert J. Thompson. *Prime Time, Prime Movers: From I Love Lucy to L. A. Law—America's Greatest TV Shows and the People Who Created Them.* Boston, Little Brown, 1992.

McNeil, Alex. *Total Television: A Comprehensive Guide to Programming from 1948 to the Present.* 3rd ed. New York, Penguin Books, 1991.

Putterman, Barry. *On Television and Comedy: Essays on Style, Theme, Performer and Writer.* Jefferson, North Carolina, McFarland, 1995.

Happy Hour

Happy hour is the two-hour period before dinner when bars offer discounted alcoholic beverages. In the 1920s, "happy hour" was Navy slang for the scheduled period of entertainment on-ship. After the passage of the Volstead Act, civilians held "cocktail hours" at speakeasies, and in their own homes, to fortify themselves before dinner. Post-prohibition cocktail lounges continued the custom of pre-dinner cocktails. "Happy hour" became a common term around 1960; it appeared in a 1959 *Saturday Evening Post* article on military life. Owing its name to the word "happy" as meaning "slightly drunk," happy hour became known more as an after-work ritual, instead of a prelude to the evening. In the 1980s, bars offered complimentary hors d'oeuvres for happy hour, in response to the heightened enforcement of anti-drunk-driving laws. The military reflected these changes too, when in 1984, General John A. Wickham, Jr. abolished happy hours at United States military base clubs.

—Daryl Umberger

FURTHER READING:

Abel, Ernest L. *Alcohol Wordlore and Folklore.* Buffalo, Prometheus Books, 1987.

Cassidy, Frederick, editor. "Happy." *Dictionary of American Regional English.* Cambridge, Harvard University Press, 1985.

"Happy Hour." *Random House Historical Dictionary of American Slang.* New York, Random House, 1994.

Kirby, David. "Not-So-Happy-Hour: Industry Hit Hard by Drunk Driving Proposals." *Restaurant Business.* April 1, 1998, 16.

Mariani, John. "Happy Hour." *The Dictionary of American Food and Drink.* New York, Hearst Books, 1994.

Hard-Boiled Detective Fiction

Hard-boiled detective fiction is often defined in terms of what it is not. It is not set in an English village; the solution is not reached by analyzing clues. To paraphrase Raymond Chandler, one of its most famous writers, it is not about dukes and Venetian vases, or handwrought duelling pistols or curare or tropical fish. Hard-boiled detective fiction emerged in 1920s America as an antidote to such things. It exploits familiar urban and industrial settings; its heroes, and now heroines, are ordinary people, working alone.

Hard-boiled detective fiction can be recognized by four main elements: the language, the setting, the detective, and the detection. The first of these is what links hard-boiled detective fiction with other literature of the period. Hard-boiled language describes things rather than ideas; adjectives are kept to a minimum; it reports what happened and what was said, not how it felt. Perhaps the most famous writer of non-detective fiction in this style is Ernest Hemingway, and many writers of hard-boiled detective fiction have said that they began by imitating him.

This style was also affected by financial concerns. Hard-boiled detective fiction first appeared in the "pulp" magazines and novelettes that were popular during the 1920s; the writers for these magazines were paid by the word, and editors were keen to eliminate unnecessary description that would cost them money. Some "pulp" writers, such as Horace McCoy and Dashiell Hammett continued to use this pared-down style in their later novels, while others, such as Raymond Chandler, thought that readers would actually enjoy description if it were done well. His language still reports only what happened and what was said, but settings and people are described in a poetic and often complex way. Since the 1980s, some hard-boiled writers, such as James Ellroy, have tried to eliminate the single narrative voice altogether; Ellroy presents his readers with transcripts of newspaper and radio reports about the investigation, heightening the illusion of realism and objectivity.

The setting for hard-boiled detective fiction is almost always urban. Perhaps because of its origins in the period of Prohibition and the Depression of the 1920s, the cities it describes tend to be dark, dangerous places run by corrupt politicians and gangster syndicates. Early writers of hard-boiled detective fiction considered themselves to be describing city life in a new, realistic way. The sort of crime that takes place in their stories also could be read about in newspapers. The people in the stories were like people the readers knew or had heard about; they seemed to speak as people really spoke. As Raymond Chandler puts it, the world they describe is "not a very fragrant world, but it is the world you live in."

The hero of hard-boiled detective stories is most often, though not always, a private detective. It is generally thought that he first appeared in *Black Mask* magazine in 1922 in the form of Carroll John Daly's Race Williams. Sara Paretsky, who began her V. I. Warshawski series in the 1980s, was among the first to create a hard-boiled detective heroine. Before then he was always a man, and the audience for the stories he appeared in was almost exclusively male. The origins of the hard-boiled detective hero are in the frontier heroes of the nineteenth century, and it could be argued that both types of hero bring order to the lives of the people they choose to help. Where they differ is that the frontier hero assists in establishing new settlements and a new civilization, while the hard-boiled detective only patches up an old and corrupt one. Despite the efforts of writers like Paretsky, since the mid 1970s the police procedural has been the dominant detective fiction form. While the language and action of these novels often owes much to the hard-boiled style, the emphasis on the police implies that the lone hard-boiled private detective is no longer a convincing defense against society's many ills.

The fourth defining characteristic of hard-boiled detective fiction is the method of detection itself. In keeping with origins in Western and romance stories, the hard-boiled detective is usually presented as being on a quest, and it is the quest itself, rather than its solution that forms the main source of interest for readers. Even in the best examples of the genre, the solution to the mystery is often unsatisfactory or contrived, but rather than wanting to know what has already happened, readers want to find out what will happen next. More particularly, they want to know how the detective will deal with physical and moral difficulties encountered along the way.

From Race Williams to V. I. Warshawski, hard-boiled detective fiction reassures us that individuals can succeed where government law enforcement has failed. Hard-boiled detectives are ordinary people who take extraordinary risks for the sake of what they see as right. They suggest to their fans that however mundane their lives may seem, and however dangerous the world appears, they too have a little of what it takes to be heroic.

—Chris Routledge

FURTHER READING:

Cawelti, John G. *Adventure, Mystery, and Romance: Formula Stories as Art and Popular Culture.* Chicago, University of Chicago Press, 1976.

Chandler, Raymond. "The Simple Art of Murder." (1950). In *Pearls Are a Nuisance.* London, Pan Books, 1980. 173-90.

Geherin, David. *The American Private Eye: The Image in Fiction.* New York, Ungar, 1985.

Messent, Peter, editor. *Criminal Proceedings: The Contemporary American Crime Novel.* London, Pluto, 1997.

Harding, Tonya (1970—)

Tonya Harding, considered one of the greatest athletes in women's figure skating in the 1990s, has always been a hard-luck case in that glamorous sport. According to sportswriter Joan Ryan, "Harding's unforgivable sin in the skating community was not that she had no class or taste but that she refused to allow anybody to give her some." National Champion in 1991, Harding's career veered wildly between success and disaster, and was finally ended by her participation in a plot that disabled Nancy Kerrigan on the eve of the 1993 Nationals, which Harding went on to win. The much-hyped "duel" between Kerrigan and Harding at the Olympics fizzled when Harding performed poorly. Capitalizing on the public fascination with the rivalry, a television film, *Tonya and Nancy,* appeared in 1994.

She avoided imprisonment, but was barred from amateur competition and stripped of her National title, and has since struggled to return to skating.

—Mary Hess

FURTHER READING:

Baughman, Cynthia, editor. *Women on Ice: Feminist Essays on the Tonya Harding/Nancy Kerrigan Spectacle.* New York, Routledge, 1995.

Brennan, Christie. *Inside Edge: A Revealing Journey into the Secret World of Figure Skating.* New York, Anchor Books, 1996.

Frey, Jennifer. "Harding, Kerrigan: Another Sad Performance." *Washington Post.* February 8, 1998.

Ryan, Joan. *Little Girls in Pretty Boxes: The Making and Breaking of Elite Gymnasts and Figure Skaters.* New York, Doubleday, 1995.

The Hardy Boys

The Hardy Boys Mystery Stories debuted in 1927 as the first series of mysteries written for children, and eventually became the longest-enduring series of boys' fiction in American history. The Hardys' influence on juvenile fiction and television has been pervasive, while their unequaled longevity has made them icons of nostalgia A product of the Stratemeyer Syndicate, the company that produced Tom Swift and the Bobbsey Twins, the Hardy Boys first took shape when Edward Stratemeyer pitched the series to his publishers at Grosset & Dunlap in 1926. Expressing the belief that "detective stories are as interesting to boys as grown folks," he outlined a series of adventures that would center on two teenage brothers, whose "work as amateur detectives would furnish plenty of incident, exciting but clean." With those few words, Stratemeyer set the tone that would propel the Hardy Boys from a humble idea to a national phenomenon, encompassing multiple forms of popular media.

Stratemeyer tapped one of his ghostwriters, Leslie McFarlane, to launch the series. As McFarlane later explained in his autobiography, *Ghost of the Hardy Boys,* he welcomed the opportunity to originate a series, rather than merely add to a pre-existing one. "It seemed to me that the Hardy boys deserved something better than the slapdash treatment [prior assignments] had been getting. It was still hack work, no doubt, but did the new series have to be all that hack? There was, after all, the chance to contribute a little style... I opted for Quality." Under the pseudonym Franklin W. Dixon, McFarlane continued as the Hardys' primary ghost for twenty years before retiring. By then the series was well established and well loved, and easily survived the transition to different (and often less able) writers.

Educators, however, were not fans of the books, and mounted a strong opposition. Even before the birth of the Hardys, products of the Stratemeyer Syndicate were shunned by librarians and teachers for their sensationalism, flatly formulaic structure and minimal literary value. Despite the truth of these observations, children embraced the books and made them bestsellers.

The popular Hardy formula drew much inspiration from preceding series. Like Stratemeyer's earlier brother-protagonists, the Rover Boys, Joe and Frank Hardy traveled in a pack of three, with their chum Chet Morton (other friends appeared frequently, too) and enjoyed unfettered mobility. On motorcycles, in their boat the *Sleuth,* in planes, trains and automobiles, the Hardys could go anywhere their cases led them. Early volumes mostly kept them in or near their hometown of Bayport, a fictional city on the Eastern seaboard, but as the years passed their travels increasingly took them to foreign countries. The books also offered their readers the vicarious thrill of gadgetry; the Hardys had a laboratory where they used microscopes, fingerprinting kits and other tools of the trade to analyze clues. They could fix anything, could pilot any type of vehicle, and kept abreast of whatever technological innovations were available at the time—from short-wave radios in the 1940s to voice-printing techniques in the 1970s.

The major factor in the Hardy Boys' success, however, was the ingredient that Stratemeyer had believed would make the series unique: its adaptation of the mystery genre for a pre-teen audience. Scholar Carol Billman, calling the Hardys "soft-boiled" detectives, notes that they were launched in the same period that saw the increasing growth of adult detective fiction. What Dashiell Hammett and Raymond Chandler did for mature audiences, "Franklin W. Dixon" did for children. The Hardy Boys, as Billman observed, provided "the novel lure of the detective mystery [fused] with the earlier adventure tale tradition," a combination that accounted for their wide appeal both at home and abroad. (The books have been translated into more than a dozen languages.)

Unlike Chandler's sinister Los Angeles, the Hardys' milieu had to be "exciting but clean," as dictated by Stratemeyer. Bayport is full of criminals, yet remains a fundamentally safe community. The crimes committed are wicked but not gruesome; Frank and Joe can fight the villains with their fists, they never shoot or stab them. The heroes never smoke, drink, or discover the joys of sex. Although Stratemeyer provided the brothers with "girlfriends," the relationships were kept innocent and superficial; indeed, the action is decidedly gender-exclusive, with women and girls barely registering but for the more substantial character of the bossy but lovable Aunt Gertrude. The Hardys live in a male-oriented, protected and self-referential world, rich in preposterous adventure yet devoid of any real threats to a child's peace of mind. The narrowly observed gender distinctions of the Hardy Boys' universe insulate its young readers from insecurity.

Inevitably, the Hardy Boys' steadfast purity over the decades gradually reduced them to objects of ridicule as the century grew more knowing and sophisticated, and its youth precocious. After the 1960s, parodies in print and on stage showed the boys in narcotic and sexual situations, including homosexual spoofs that called them the "Hardly Boys." But the books' spirit of eternal youth and innocence, so absurd to cynical adults, has been a crucial element of their success with children. Their existence outside social anxieties make them especially appealing to the age group most wracked by those problems. Indeed, the Hardys' innocence surpasses even that of other Stratemeyer characters. Noting that early Syndicate blockbusters the Rover Boys and Tom Swift lost their popularity after marrying and having children, Stratemeyer's heir, Harriet Adams, decreed that the Hardy Boys would not suffer the tragedy of maturing. They aged early on in the series, from their mid-teens to their late teens, but thereafter dwelled in a state of arrested development.

Two significant events altered the tone and direction of the *Hardy Boys Mysteries*. A massive revision project was begun in 1959 to modernize the books and erase the most egregious racial stereotyping. Ranging from simple "cut-downs" to completely rewritten stories, the revisions scrubbed away the original narrative flavor, along with the automats, running boards, and ghastly depictions of non-WASPs. The second significant change accompanied Simon & Schuster's acquisition of the title after Harriet Adams' death. The publishers revitalized the series, adding new dimensions to plots, locales, and characterizations. The changes influenced the age group the publisher targeted. Between the 1920s and 1950s, Grosset and Dunlap had targeted the series to 10 to 15 year-olds. Simon and Schuster pitched the series to 8 through 11 year-olds. They also extended the franchise, introducing several spin-off series. *The Hardy Boys Case Files,* conceived in 1987 for older readers, increased the levels of danger and violence. The boys' cases now included murders, while they demonstrated a heightened awareness of the opposite sex (but still no sexual activity). The Nancy Drew and Hardy Boys *Supermysteries*, begun in 1988, featured collaborations between Frank and Joe, and their popular girl-detective counterpart, and another collaboration was attempted in 1992 when the publishers briefly paired the Hardys with Tom Swift. The Clues Brothers, starring grammar-school versions of Frank and Joe, debuted in 1997 for younger children. While these ancillary series were appearing, the core Hardy Boys continued to expand.

Television has adapted the Hardys many times, with varying degrees of success. In 1956 they appeared under the auspices of the Disney juggernaut, starring in two serials on *The Mickey Mouse Club*. The boys, played by Tommy Kirk and Tim Considine, were portrayed as roughly 12 and 13 years old, far younger than their book-ages of 17 and 18. A decade later, Twentieth Century-Fox produced a pilot for an hour-long series starring a young Tim Matheson as Joe and newcomer Rick Gates as Frank. Though slightly older than Kirk and Considine, these actors were still only about 15, proving that America's popular imagination definitely saw the Hardys as "boys," not as young men, no matter what the books implied. In 1969 the Hardys re-emerged as the stars of a Saturday morning cartoon on ABC, characterized as leaders of a "rock" group that solves mysteries between gigs. Reflecting the social inclusivity of the era, the show added a girl and an African-American boy to the Hardys' band, along with old friend Chet Morton (renamed "Chubby"). Perhaps because the tone of the books had been too compromised, the animated Hardy Boys were a failure, lasting only one season. Among the surprising amount of merchandise inspired by this short-lived program were two record albums of the group's sugary pop music.

Not until 1977 did the Hardys truly succeed in a television market. Universal Studios' *The Hardy Boys/Nancy Drew Mysteries* was a prime-time series that alternated episodes of the Hardys' adventures with those of Nancy Drew in an hour-long format. Shaun Cassidy and Parker Stevenson, clearly young men rather than boys, achieved fame as teen-idols for their roles as Joe and Frank. The series lasted nearly three seasons, each of which took the Hardys progressively further away from the insularity of the books. By the end of its run, *The Hardy Boys Mysteries* (renamed after the cancellation of the Nancy Drew episodes) had the brothers working for the U.S. Justice Department, and routinely involved in romance as well as mystery. In 1995, Nelvana/New Line television produced a half-hour series which aired in syndication, again with a companion Nancy Drew series. After a search that included casting calls over the Internet, Paul Popowich and Colin Gray were chosen to play the brothers. The series received lukewarm reviews, and its popularity was further hindered by its floating status in syndication. Without a prime-time slot or heavy promotion, the show died quickly.

At the same time, the success of the Hardy Boys books began to wane as young readers increasingly turned to more sensational fare. R. L. Stine's *Goosebumps*, and other series flavored with science fiction or horror, routinely outperformed the classic Stratemeyer Syndicate books. That the Hardy Boys were eclipsed in popularity could be put down to their success in revolutionizing their field—a success largely responsible for the continuing tradition of serial adventures for children, featuring numerous imitators. Ironically, just as the Hardys began to falter with their primary audience, they became increasingly popular with adults. The outpouring of merchandise (toys, puzzles, games), from the multiple television series, as well as the ever-evolving changes in the books' formats, created a healthy market of adult collectors. The Hardy Boys retains a formidable status as the best-loved American series of boys' books of the twentieth century.

—Ilana Nash

FURTHER READING:

Billman, Carol. *The Secret of the Stratemeyer Syndicate: Nancy Drew, the Hardy Boys, and the Million Dollar Fiction Factory.* New York, The Ungar Publishing Company, 1986.

Kismaric, Carole, and Marvin Heiferman. *The Mysterious Case of Nancy Drew & The Hardy Boys.* New York, Simon & Schuster, 1998.

McFarlane, Leslie. *Ghost of the Hardy Boys.* Toronto, Methuen/Two Continents, 1976.

Prager, Arthur. *Rascals at Large, or, the Clue in the Old Nostalgia.* Garden City, New Jersey, Doubleday & Company, Inc., 1971.

Hare Krishna

Of the colorful and exotic features of the American urban landscape during the hippie era in the late 1960s and 1970s, none, perhaps, was so striking as the small bands of men with shaved heads and saffron robes and women in saris gathering at love-ins or on street corners. Together they danced to the sound of Indian drums as they recited their mantra—"Hare Krishna, hare Krishna, Krishna Krishna, hare hare; hare Rama, hare Rama, Rama Rama, hare hare"—and solicited alms.

The worldwide Krishna movement was founded by one elderly man from India who came to America with a vision, determination, and hardly a penny to his name. Born in 1896, Abhay Charan De had already studied economics and English at the University of Calcutta when he became a disciple and the eventual successor of Bhaktisiddhanta Sarasvati Swami, the tenth in a line of gurus beginning in the late fifteenth century with Lord Chaitanya Mahaprabhu, who had founded a religious system within Hinduism particularly devoted to the god Krishna.

A divinity with many of the attributes of the trickster archetype, Krishna appears in India's epic poem the *Mahabharata* as charioteer to his friend Arjuna. A great battle has begun in which, Arjuna realizes, he will have friends and relatives on both sides. He asks

A group of Hare Krishnas involved in public chanting.

Krishna whether he ought to fight or not, and Krishna explains why he should do so, in a classic discourse about reality and illusion (the source of Ralph Waldo Emerson's lines "If the red slayer thinks he slays / And the slain thinks he is slain"). This interlude on the eve of the battle is also the setting for the *Bhagavad-Gita,* or "Song of God," a central text in Hindu religious literature.

Chaitanya and his successors revered Krishna as the essential manifestation of God and prescribed a way of life which eschewed earthly sensory pleasures in favor of meditative practice, study of the *Bhagavad-Gita* and other holy books, and the chanting of the "Hare Krishna" mantra. As such, the followers of Krishna might have been simply one of many Indian sects within Hinduism. The crucial difference came when Abhay Charan De, now called Bhaktivedanta Swami Prabhuda, brought his teaching to America, arriving in New York on a freighter in 1965.

Starting with evening lectures on the *Bhagavad-Gita,* Bhaktivedanta Swami soon attracted a small but enthusiastic band of followers who became the International Society for Krishna Consciousness (ISKCON) in 1966; two years later the group acquired a farm in West Virginia which they dubbed New Vrindavana (after the town in India which was believed to be Krishna's birthplace) and which later grew to 1,000 acres. In 1972, to educate the increasing number of Hare Krishna children, ISKCON started the Gurukula School and its enrollment grew to 150 over the next three years. By the time of Bhaktivedanta Swami's death in 1977, the Krishna movement boasted 10,000 full-time members worldwide, 5,000 of them in America alone, and could claim several million others who came to worship at ISKCON temples.

Those who joined the communities were expected to abstain from drugs, including alcohol, tobacco, coffee, and tea. Sexual relations were permitted only for couples married by an ordained minister in Krishna Consciousness; there was to be no courtship or dating as such, either within the community or with outsiders. Also forbidden were gambling and "frivolous games and sports"; children, however, were encouraged to play games such as a Krishna version of hopscotch called "Hopping to the Spiritual World," "I Love Krishna," and "The Hanuman Hop." For adults, the everyday routine included six temple ceremonies, several hours of classes, work within the temple compound for three hours in the morning, and *sankirtana*—public chanting, preaching, and solicitation of alms—for another three hours each afternoon.

Many devotees saw in the Krishna communities a welcome refuge from a prior life of adolescent turmoil, insecurity, and drug use. But relatives and friends of converts, alarmed by the strictures of the temple regimen and the apparently hypnotic effect of chanting the Hare Krishna mantra 108 times a day, sometimes brought accusations of brainwashing and coercion, particularly when children were involved. The grandparents of one boy whose mother had joined the movement spent 16 months finding him and restoring him to his father, ultimately resorting to counter-demonstrations at Chicago's O'Hare airport, a favorite *sankirtana* site.

Such clashes of worldviews raised troublesome civil liberties issues for the courts and generated adverse publicity for the movement. The public backlash made it harder to raise money openly for Krishna Consciousness, so that sales of books and incense on the street came to be divorced from preaching (some males donned toupees to cover their shaved heads), seeming to defeat the purpose of *sankirtana.*

Anticipating his death, Bhaktivedanta Swami had designated 11 gurus to preside over districts within the worldwide organization, as well as a Governing Body Council (GBC), which was to be ISKCON's central administrative committee. A crisis of conflicting authority soon erupted between the GBC and several of the regional gurus, four of whom resigned during the next decade. There was also bad press from a California police raid which turned up a large cache of firearms on a ranch owned by the movement, and from the murder of a former member, turned vocal critic, at the New Vrindavana compound.

Nevertheless, ISKCON survived, making changes to accommodate members unable or unwilling to join the temple communities (including outreach to expatriate Indians), and broadening its product line to include vegetarian specialty foods and restaurants. A new generation has found the Krishna-Conscious lifestyle an appealing alternative to what one convert, a former heavy-metal musician, described as "fashion, cliques, sex, drugs, and loud music." As sociologist E. Burke Rochford put it, "ISKCON's ability to adapt to what have often been the most adverse circumstances points to the flexibility and ultimate resiliency of the movement. It is these qualities, combined with the deep faith and commitment of the devotees themselves, which will be the Krishna movement's greatest assets as it approaches the twenty-first century."

—Nick Humez

FURTHER READING:

Bhaktivedanta Swami Prabhuda, A. C. *Krsna Consciousness: The Topmost Yoga System.* Boston, ISKCON Press, 1970.

———, editor. *The Bhagavad-gita As It Is.* New York, Macmillan, 1972.

Bhaktivedanta Swami Prabhuda, A. C., and John Lennon. *Search for Liberation.* Los Angeles, Bhaktivedanta Book Trust, 1981.

Daner, Francine Jeanne. *The American Children of Krsna: A Study of the Hare Krsna Movement.* New York, Holt, Rinehart and Winston, 1976.

Hiltebeitel, Alf. *The Ritual of Battle: Krishna in the Mahabharata.* Ithaca, Cornell University Press, 1976.

Hubner, John, and Lindsey Gruson *Monkey on a Stick: Murder, Madness and the Hare krishnas* San Diego, Harcourt Brace Jovanovich, 1988.

Muster, Nori J. *Betrayal of the Spirit: My Life Behind the Headlines of the Hare Krishna Movement.* Urbana, University of Illinois Press, 1997.

Rochford, E. Burke. *Hare Krishna in America.* New Brunswick, Rutgers University Press, 1985.

Yanoff, Morris. *Where Is Joey?: Lost among the Hare Krishnas.* Chicago, Swallow Press, 1981.

Haring, Keith (1958-1990)

Among the most popular and frequently reproduced graphic images to have emerged from the 1980s are the broad cartoonish outlines of a baby on all fours, a boxlike barking dog, and a series of identical funny little men striking a variety of energetic poses. These figures—featureless yet evocative through outline alone—had their genesis in the spontaneous ink drawings Keith Haring began making in 1980, drawings out of which, the artist told his biographer John

Gruen, his "entire future vocabulary was born." Seeking the incompatible goals of immediate acceptance with the masses and critical recognition from the art establishment, Haring lived fast, painted furiously, and died tragically young.

Growing up in Kutztown, Pennsylvania, where as a young child he drew pictures with his father, Haring was obsessed with the art of Walt Disney, Dr. Seuss, and Charles Schulz's earliest Charlie Brown comics. Television cartoons and the cartoonish sitcoms of the 1960s fascinated him, and he started a local Monkees fan club. In junior high school he won an award for a drawing on adding-machine tape which pitted the hippies against the police—a sign, perhaps, of his budding rebelliousness. After high school, Haring briefly attended the Ivy School of Professional Art in Pittsburgh and worked at the Pittsburgh Arts and Crafts Center. During this period he was influenced profoundly by Robert Henri's book *The Art Spirit,* which echoed Haring's own artistic musings, and by a 1977 retrospective of Pierre Alechinsky, whose work, said Haring, "was the closest thing I had ever seen to what I was doing with these self-generative little shapes."

In 1978 Haring moved to New York City to attend the School for Visual Arts, where his introduction to semiotics, or the study of signs, made a deep impression. He was fascinated by the graffiti in the New York streets and subways and was by 1980 making graffiti himself, eventually collaborating with and promoting other graffiti artists. In the early 1980s he became well-known for a series of surreptitious drawings he made in the New York subway stations on the empty black panels placed there to cover up old advertisements; the barking dog, the "Radiant Baby," and the active little men which became fixtures in much of his later work were all present here. The opening of his big show at New York's Shafrazi Gallery in 1982 was a sensation, attended by famous painters and graffiti artists alike.

Haring often created the art for his gallery shows on-site a few days before their opening. Onlookers were amazed at his ability to complete huge projects quickly with nary a false brush stroke, whether on paper, tarpaulins, canvas, or building facades. Large-scale projects ranged from a section of the Berlin Wall to the walls of museums, hospitals, and churches, generally with the blessing of property owners and often for socially conscious causes. His collaborators included Andy Warhol and William S. Burroughs, both of whom he considered mentors, and armies of neighborhood children. Haring dabbled in body painting and designed sculpture. Commercial projects included painting a car for BMW, ads for Absolut Vodka, and watch faces for Swatch. In 1986 Haring, wanting as usual to communicate to a wide audience, opened the Pop Shop in New York City to sell inflatable babies, toy radios, buttons, embroidered patches, and T-shirts bearing his and others' designs; a similar venture in Tokyo failed. Haring's work was extremely popular in Europe and Japan and as early as 1983 the artist had noticed imitations of his work "springing up all over the world." Throughout much of the late 1970s and 1980s Haring was immersed in recreational drugs and sex, the New York club scene, and friendships with celebrities including Madonna, Brooke Shields, Andy Warhol, and Timothy Leary. Haring died from AIDS in 1990 at the age of 31.

At the close of the twentieth century, Keith Haring's artistic legacy is still being debated. Calvin Tomkins, writing in the *New Yorker,* described Haring's natural gift as "the ability to cover and animate a surface with strong, simple, cartoon-style images that had an iconic resonance." Kurt Andersen, writing in the same publication, found Haring's work unpretentious and unimportant and saw in Haring all the salient artistic features of the 1980s: "a return to figurative style, the disappearance of distinctions between high and low, and the rise of full-bore marketing and of the overnight sensation.'' A major retrospective at New York's Whitney Museum of American Art in 1997 revealed Haring to be a more versatile and, often, sexually provocative artist than his mass-produced images would suggest. Certainly he was a master of line drawing, a tireless worker, and an adept self-promoter. While antecedents from Fernand Léger to R. Crumb may be cited, Haring's immediately recognizable work bears his own unique imprint.

—Craig Bunch

FURTHER READING:

Andersen, Kurt. ''The Culture Industry.'' *The New Yorker.* July 7, 1997, 23-24.

Gruen, John. *Keith Haring: The Authorized Biography.* New York, Prentice Hall Press, 1991.

Haring, Keith. *Art in Transit: Subway Drawings by Keith Haring.* New York, Harmony Books, 1984.

———. *Keith Haring Journals.* New York, Viking, 1996.

Sussman, Elisabeth. *Keith Haring.* New York, Whitney Museum of American Art, 1997.

Tomkins, Calvin. ''The Time of His Life.'' *The New Yorker.* July 8, 1996, 66-67.

The Harlem Globetrotters

Since 1927, the Harlem Globetrotters have toured continually showcasing the skills of African American basketball players and developing an entertaining blend of athletics and comedy. In the process they have helped to introduce basketball throughout the world, inspired athletes of all races, and laid the ground work for the freewheeling ''showtime'' style of basketball that has contributed to the growth of basketball's popularity since the early 1970s. The Globetrotters' style of basketball, and particularly their style of comedy, were products of American racial segregation and discrimination. Their fancy dribbling, flamboyant passing, and spectacular leaping, which they pioneered, were seminal expressions of an African American athletic style. Their comedic routines (called ''reems'' by the Globetrotters), drew upon older minstrel show traditions and Sambo stereotypes of African Americans as childish clowns. Both of these dimensions of the Globetrotter—one forward looking and celebratory of African American creativity and excellence; the other looking backward and reinforcing racist images—have contributed to their success.

On their early tours, the Globetrotters and owner/booking agent/coach Abe Saperstein (a Jewish immigrant of Polish parentage), crammed into a small coupe and drove throughout the upper Midwest, taking on town teams for a percentage of the gate. They rarely had money for hotels, and when they did, they often found themselves barred because of their race. The same was true for restaurants. In some locales, the Globetrotters were treated as an anthropological exhibit by people who had never met anyone of African ancestry. Unlike other African Americans who had to endure these indignities, the Globetrotters could also enjoy the subversive pleasure of getting paid to consistently beat white teams on the court. Although the

origins of the Globetrotters' move into comedy have been shrouded by Saperstein's myth-making, it is clear that the primary motivation was to increase the likelihood of a return engagement by not running up the score against inferior competition, and providing extra entertainment for fans who were bored by lopsided contests. By the late 1930s, basketball tricks and comedy were an integral part of most performances by the Globetrotters.

The lead clowns—such as Reece ''Goose'' Tatum and Meadow ''Meadowlark'' Lemon—enjoyed the laughter, attention, and extra money that their comedic talents brought them. Rather then complaining about assaults to their dignity, they seized opportunities to expand upon the traditional reems. Despite the fact that their humor could easily be interpreted as reinforcing negative racial stereotypes, few Globetrotters have publicly expressed misgivings. One notable exception is Connie Hawkins, a basketball hall-of-famer who spent four years in the 1960s with the Globetrotters. In a 1972 biography, *Foul,* by David Wolf, Hawkins complained that the Globetrotters were ''acting like Uncle Toms. Grinnin and smilin and dancin around—that's the way they told us to act, and that's the way a lot of white people like to think we really are.'' Hawkins' observations help explain how the Globetrotter's humor contributed to the team's success by undercutting the racial implications of their superiority as basketball players.

The formula has been very successful. First, in the 1930s and 1940s their tours expanded to encompass the entire North American Continent. In 1950, they undertook their first European visit, and the following year embarked on an around-the-world tour. The State Department found that the Globetrotters' happy-go-lucky style was an effective counter to communist propaganda about American race relations, and, along with the armed forces, provided logistical support for their overseas trips during the Cold War. The demand for the Globetrotters was so great in the 1950s, that the team fielded three separate units in the United States, and an all star international squad. Since 1954, the Globetrotters have made numerous television appearances and have starred in their own cartoon series (1970-1973), and a variety show (1974). Although their cultural import has diminished, the Globetrotters continue to tour, make appearances on television and in advertisements, and recently have secured lucrative corporate sponsorships.

As straight basketball players, the Globetrotters were once formidable and influential. Prior to the integration of the National Basketball Association (NBA) in 1950 (a move that Saperstein resisted), playing for the Globetrotters was nearly the only way that an African American could make a living from basketball. Their victory in the 1940 World Tournament of Basketball, demonstrated that they were among the best professional teams in the United States. Wins over the National Basketball League champion Minneapolis Lakers in 1948 and 1949 further enhanced their reputation, and struck a blow for racial equality. Even after the integration of the NBA, the Globetrotters had to be taken seriously as a straight basketball team. From 1950 to 1962 they played an annual series against teams of college all-stars, winning 162 games, and losing only 44. Since the conclusion of this series, the Globetrotters have all but abandoned straight basketball in favor of comedy and entertainment.

More important than their ability to beat top teams was the Globetrotters' style of play. Against real competition, they generally dropped the reems, but retained the rest of their repertoire. Where most of the white teams in the first half of the century played a stilted, regimented game, the Globetrotters freelanced and had fun. In recent years, the no-look and behind the back passes, thrilling dunks, flashy

The original Harlem Globetrotters, 1941.

dribbling, and gambling help-out defense that they developed and displayed during years of barnstorming, have entered mainstream basketball as key elements of an African American athletic aesthetic. Perhaps their greatest impact has been in demonstrating how basketball skills could be a form of entertainment. NBA stars like Ervin "Magic" Johnson often cite the Globetrotters, particularly master dribbler Marques Haynes, as an inspiration. Much of basketball's growth in popularity since the 1970s has been due to casual fans who savor those moments that most resemble the Globetrotters at their best. Players who induce smiles and laughter, not with comedic set pieces, but with a surprising pass, a crossover dribble, or an acrobatic shot in the heat of competition are an important part of the Globetrotters' legacy.

—Thomas J. Mertz

FURTHER READING:

Lemon, Meadowlark, with Jerry B. Jenkins. *Meadowlark.* Nashville, Thomas Nelson Publishers, 1987.

Nelson, George. *Elevating the Game: Black Men and Basketball.* New York, Harper Collins Publishers, 1992.

Wilker, Josh. *The Harlem Globetrotters.* Philadelphia, Chelsea House Publishers, 1996.

Wolf, David. *Foul: The Connie Hawkins Story.* New York, Holt, Rinehart and Winston, 1972.

Harlem Renaissance

Post-World War I Harlem was the undisputed center of a complex cultural movement out of which emerged a proliferation of black intellectuals, writers, musicians, actors, and visual artists. Variously called the Harlem Renaissance, the Negro Renaissance, and the New Negro Movement, it was an artistic flowering that coincided with socio-political expressions of black pride—the rise of the "New Negro" and Garveyism—in much the same way as the

Black Arts and Black Power Movements emerged simultaneously in the 1960s. Although scholars posit differing views on when it began and ended, most agree that the movement was at its height between the dawning of the Jazz Age in 1919 and the stock market crash in 1929.

Harlem, the area James Weldon Johnson dubbed the Black "culture capital," was appropriately the center of this outpouring of black creativity, in part because it held one of the largest settlements of blacks in any area outside the south and, in part, because of the prevailing *zeitgeist* of racial affirmation. Intellectuals such as Johnson and Alain Locke saw Harlem as a place of great opportunity where blacks could, according to Locke, shed the "chrysalis of the Negro problem." Locke's 1925 landmark essay "The New Negro" announced the demise of the "Old Negro" and became a kind of cultural manifesto for artists then and for, at least, the next generation.

The creation of a "Negro" Harlem was indeed remarkable, a curious admixture of affluence and poverty, of black creativity and black exploitation. On the one hand, music, literature, plays, and paintings depicting black life flourished; black entrepreneurship thrived; on the political front, the National Association for the Advancement of Colored People (1909) continued its work as the largest civil rights organization in the United States, alongside the National Urban League (1911) and the more controversial politics of Marcus Garvey, who was laying the groundwork for his project of African colonization. On the other hand, even well-intentioned white patrons helped to perpetuate stereotypes of black life that resulted in the paradoxical "Negro vogue" of the 1920s when white spectators went "slumming" in Harlem to see blacks perform in Jim Crow night clubs. They patronized small bars and cabarets formerly frequented only by blacks and, according to Langston Hughes in his autobiography *The Big Sea,* were given "ringside tables to sit and stare at the Negro customers—like amusing animals in the zoo."

Yet these very contradictions helped to make Harlem the exciting city within a city that it was then and the cultural icon it has since become, in terms of both the place itself and the artists associated with it. It was a place and a time of burgeoning African American music—notably the blues and jazz—and a long list of black performers were recording their own compositions and appearing in black musicals, in concerts, and on radio programs. Classic jazz composers and performers all over the United States were increasingly drawn to New York as the nation's music center. Articles and books devoted exclusively to jazz were being published, and recording companies specializing in jazz were established. Black female blues and jazz singers, while held in high regard by their fans, were often considered "unrespectable" and their music "low culture" by some members of the black bourgeoisie. The blues revivals of the 1960s and 1980s reflected a major shift in that thinking. Both popular and lesser-known performers of the 1920s were rediscovered through new releases of their recordings that reached broader audiences. Angela Davis, in *Blues Legacies and Black Feminism,* notes that "with the globalization of music distribution . . . the scope of black music and its historically broad cultural implications can no longer be confined to African American communities." Indeed, in 1987, Congress passed a resolution declaring jazz "a rare and valuable national treasure."

Writers such as Hughes, Claude McKay, Nella Larsen, Jessie Fauset, Countee Cullen, Zora Neale Hurston, and Jean Toomer appeared on the literary scene, forming a kind of literati that they themselves jokingly referred to as the "Niggerati." Publishers clamored for anything "Negro," as Nella Larsen observed, and white patrons such as Carl Van Vechten and Charlotte Osgood Mason (self-proclaimed the "Godmother" because of her financial support of

artists) saw to it that they got what they wanted. Indeed, the overwhelming popularity of Van Vechten's own controversial novel *Nigger Heaven* (1926), depicting a seamy side of black life in Harlem, epitomized what publishers believed "Negro" actually meant. Similarly, early productions of work by white playwrights Eugene O'Neill and Frederick Ridgely Torrence were instrumental in creating interest in the plays of black writers, and also in bringing talented young black actors, singers, and dancers to the stage. Eubie Blake and Noble Sissle's 1921 musical comedy *Shuffle Along* was the first black Broadway show of the decade, and Hughes cites it as the show that gave a "scintillating send-off to the Negro vogue." At various points during its first run, it showcased the talents of Paul Robeson, Florence Mills, and the exotic, controversial entertainer Josephine Baker. Aaron Douglas designed posters advertising the work of various writers and entertainers but is best known for his contributions to major periodicals, including *The Crisis* and *Opportunity*, official publications of the NAACP and The National Urban League, respectively. The simultaneity of art and politics is vividly represented in the use of these two magazines, devoted in part to socio-political reporting of black experience but also to the artistic endeavors of the young black literati.

Clearly, a black cultural flowering was taking place in other major cities at the same time. However, despite the ongoing debates about whether or not the Harlem Renaissance is a misnomer, whether or not it was a successful movement or any kind of movement at all, black Harlem of the 1920s has become a symbolic "figure" that resonates across time and space, as well as across gender, racial, and cultural boundaries. According to James De Jongh, in the epilogue of *Vicious Modernisms: Black Harlem and the Literary Imagination*, "many writers of European and Asian as well as African descent have found the idea of Harlem to be relevant to their preoccupations and employed the figure of black Harlem in significant ways." Striking examples are the "blaxploitation" films of the 1970s where Harlem is seen as a haven for drug dealing and other illicit operations, teeming with violence. Black filmmakers of the 1980s and 1990s, especially males, have modeled their notions of the "Hood"—any black poor and working-class urban community—on a symbolic figuration of Harlem. Some of the most popular films, although not necessarily set in Harlem, for example *Boyz N the Hood* (1991), attempt to reinterpret the concept of the black urban environment promulgated by earlier popular movies such as *Shaft* (1971) and *Superfly* (1972) with images of racially self-aware men who are connected to, rather than alienated from, family and community. Harlem, reinterpreted, provides the actual setting for one of Spike Lee's major films, *Jungle Fever* (1991); and the opening of *She's Gotta Have It* (1986) pays homage to Zora Neale Hurston, a writer rediscovered, indeed reclaimed, by black feminists and co-opted by a host of academicians in a wide range of disciplines. Similarly, novels and short stories set in Harlem continued to be published into the 1990s, and *The Music of Black Americans: A History* cites Quincy Jones' *Back on the Block* as the album that "took his listeners back to the old inner-city neighborhood" to learn the history of black music.

In many ways, this idea of Harlem has shaped later generations' views of individual Renaissance artists, thereby determining who emerges as most representative of the place and the period. At the time, however, the issue of representation was hotly debated. Many of the black intelligentsia believed that the cultural arts were a means to correct the distorted images of blacks and to advance their political agendas. Charles S. Johnson, editor of *Opportunity*, set strict guidelines for literary submissions to the magazine. Marcus Garvey was critical of those he believed ''prostituted'' their intelligence and art by succumbing to the demands of white audiences. W. E. B. Du Bois espoused the idea that ''all Art is propaganda and ever must be.'' While some tried in various ways to escape the stigma of ''blackness,'' others, such as Langston Hughes, one of the chief poets of the period, turned to the folk as a source of material for their work. Hughes proclaimed that the younger black artists were determined to portray their ''dark-skinned selves without fear or shame'' regardless of what audiences, black or white, thought. This is the attitude that has had the most profound effect on a hip-hop generation of youths who have both reclaimed and reinvented black cultural traditions in their language, music, and dress.

With the stock market crash came the end of an era and, as Hughes put it, the end of the gay times. By then, some of its most enthusiastic proponents were growing disillusioned with the concept of the ''New Negro.'' Some had simply moved on to take up their careers elsewhere. Garvey had been convicted of mail fraud, spent two years in an Atlanta prison, and been deported in 1927. However, though the ''Negro vogue'' ended, art and activism did not. Renewed interest in the Harlem Renaissance and in individual artists has prompted a plethora of scholarship, biographies, docu-dramas, plays, and personal sojourns into the past, such as Alice Walker's search for Zora Neale Hurston's resting place. Black American music has helped to lessen the gap between ''high'' and ''low'' culture. A shift in views about paintings depicting black life might best be exemplified by the current respect for Palmer Hayden, whose work was dismissed during his own day as simplistic and naive, but who notable black artists such as Romare Bearden later extolled as the ''leading folklorist'' among them. This revival of interest focuses on the Renaissance as a pivotal period in African American culture that intersects with a rich cultural past and a promising future. Through their music, drama, art, and literature, blacks in Harlem's heyday confronted blackness head-on in a profound desire for self-discovery and, in so doing, left Harlem its most enduring cultural legacy.

—Jacquelyn Y. McLendon

FURTHER READING:

Bearden, Romare and Harry Henderson. *A History of African-American Artists From 1792 to the Present*. New York, Pantheon Books, 1993.

Davis, Angela. *Blues Legacies and Black Feminism: Gertrude ''Ma'' Rainey, Bessie Smith, and Billie Holiday*. New York, Pantheon Books, 1998.

De Jongh, James. *Vicious Modernisms: Black Harlem and the Literary Imagination*. New York, Cambridge University Press, 1990.

Dyson, Michael Eric. *Reflecting Black: African American Cultural Criticism*. Minneapolis, University of Minnesota Press, 1993.

Hughes, Langston. *The Big Sea*. New York, Hill and Wang, 1940.

Southern, Eileen. *The Music of Black Americans: A History*, 3rd edition. New York, W. W. Norton & Company, 1997.

Harlequin Romances

In a market where 60 percent of all households in the United States do not purchase even one book per year, romance novel readers spend an average of 1,200 dollars a year on their addiction, whether for escape or titillation. Though the compilers of ''bestseller'' lists scorn to include romance novels, the genre accounts for over 40 percent of all paperback sales in North America and is spreading in popularity to a surprising number of countries around the world. Employing strictly formulaic guidelines and innovative marketing, Canadian publisher Harlequin Enterprises controls 85 percent of the romance market worldwide. Any supermarket or variety store customer will recognize the mildly lurid cover with a title like *Savage Promise* or *Fierce Encounter* on sale by the checkout stand as a romance novel, and almost all will be familiar with the name that is almost synonymous with the romance novel, Harlequin Romance.

Harlequin Enterprises began as a small reprint house in Winnipeg, Manitoba, in 1949 under the leadership of Richard and Mary Bonnycastle. The Bonnycastles bought reprint rights to a variety of out-of-print books in the United States and Great Britain and republished them for Canadian audiences. When Mary Bonnycastle noticed the popularity of their reprints of the romance novels of British publisher Mills and Boon, she suggested that Harlequin focus on romances alone. Her idea was so successful that by 1971 Harlequin had bought Mills and Boon and begun to amass its own stable of writers to churn out romances.

In the 1970s, Larry Heisey, a marketing specialist who had previously worked at Proctor and Gamble, created Harlequin's most innovative and most successful marketing strategy. Reasoning that almost the entire readership of the romance novel was comprised of women, Heisey figured that the same techniques that sold cleaning products to women could sell them novels—a clearly recognizable brand name and convenient one-stop availability. He developed the Harlequin Presents series with uniform trademark covers, differing only by the particular title, author, and racy cover art. Further, he marketed the books in the places where women already shopped: the grocery store, the drug store, and the variety store. Using these skillful marketing practices, Harlequin's profits began to rise. In 1975, the company was bought by publishing giant Torstar, which also owns the *Toronto Star* newspaper. In 1985, troubled by competition from Silhouette Books, Simon and Schuster's new romance division, Harlequin slid around anti-trust laws in the United States to gobble up Silhouette, thus gaining the power to claim a huge share of the romance market which many claimed was on the verge of dying.

In the years following the start of the women's liberation movement, social critics had predicted the death of the pulp romance novel. Women, they said, would no longer be hypnotized by the gauzy fantasy romances that had allowed them escape in more repressive times. The critics turned out to be wrong. Spurred by its acquisition of Silhouette and its expansion abroad, Harlequin continued to grow. By the 1990s, it had become the world's largest publisher of romance fiction, releasing over 60 new titles per month and selling over 165 million books per year, in 23 languages and in over 100 countries.

Employing around 2,000 writers and cover artists, Harlequin Enterprises has created a system that turns the writing of romance novels into a kind of science. With strict guidelines as to length (exactly 192 pages for Harlequin Presents novels), and content (plots ''should not be too grounded in harsh realities''; writers should avoid such topics as drugs, terrorism, politics, sports, and alcoholic heroes), Harlequin does not allow much room for pesky creativity that could lead to failure. Traditional romance novels all loosely follow the same general formula: a young and beautiful heroine with a romantic name such as Selena, Storm, or Ariana, meets a rakishly handsome man, often older, often darkly brooding, with a romantic name such as Bolt, Colt, or Holt. They encounter difficulties—perhaps she is unsure for most of the novel whether the man is hero or villain—but by the end of the novel they are passionately reconciled. Happy endings are an absolute requirement for the Harlequin Romance.

Company research shows that the average Harlequin Romance reader is a 39-year-old woman with a household income of 40,000 dollars a year. Forty-five percent of romance readers are college graduates and 50 percent work outside the home. With an ever sharp eye on the consumer market, Harlequin continues to branch out within its chosen genre, offering several different series of novels, with differing guidelines, to appeal to different readers. The Romance line guidelines for authors recommend avoiding "explicit sexual description," while the Temptation line suggests, "love scenes should be highly erotic, realistic, and fun." The Superromance and American Romance lines offer longer, more sophisticated novels, while the Love Inspired line consists of Christian romances where faith is featured as prominently as passion. The Golden Eagle adventure line and the Worldwide Mystery line represent Harlequin's more successful attempts to reach out to the male reader.

Even in foreign countries, the Harlequin formula seems to work. In 1992, the romances sold in Hungary at the astounding rate of 17,000 per day. Even in cultures that are very different from the Western European culture reflected in the novels, such as Japan and the Philippines, Harlequin Romances are welcomed with very little change apart from translation. Indeed, with Caucasian couples in rapt embrace on the cover, the books sell as rapidly in Asia as in Canada. In North America as well, even though heroes and heroines are almost universally white, the books are consumed ravenously by whites and people of color alike, perhaps proving the power of fantasy.

It is perhaps the mostly female writers of the novels who are left with the fewest illusions about the world of the Harlequin Romance. Signed to restrictive contracts, writers are required to choose pen names, also often romantic, such as Desiree or Jasmine, which Harlequin insists add to the fanciful image of their books. There is, however, a very practical side to the pen-name requirement. If an author leaves Harlequin to go to another publishing house, her pen-name remains the property of Harlequin Enterprises, who will probably use it on the work of another writer. This effectively prevents the author from retaining any following she may have gained under the pen name. Another conflict between publisher and author has arisen over the issue of the reversion of rights. It is common practice with most publishers to allow copyright on out of print works to return to the author, so that the author can make use of writing that is no longer being used by the publisher. Harlequin Enterprises has frequently not been willing to return rights to authors, often citing its ownership of the pen name as reason.

Though writers and agents have attempted to reason or force Harlequin into a position more favorable to author's rights, the publisher has not only refused but often retaliated by refusal to assign more books to recalcitrant writers, and by threatening to convert its contracts to "work for hire." Under a traditional author's contract, Harlequin writers are paid an advance fee for a novel (2,000 to 3,000 dollars for beginners, as much as 15,000 for a veteran). After the book is published, authors are paid royalties, or a percentage of sales. A hot seller can bring an author as much as 40,000 dollars in royalties. Under a "work for hire" contract, a publisher buys an author's work outright, with no further compensation no matter how high the sales.

In spite of such threats, organizations like the Author's Guild and Novelists, Inc. continue to investigate Harlequin's questionable policies, including the legality of its 1985 acquisition of Silhouette.

Notwithstanding the drama unfolding around its own corporate policies, Harlequin Enterprises continues to crank out volumes of lushly improbable escape for readers mired down in "harsh realities." While men might find their escape in sports or action movies, women have tended to seek an exotic world, where women are surrounded by adventure with a passionate reward at the end. Somewhat like magazine serials and somewhat like television soap operas, these romances are not meant to be taken seriously; they are meant to provide a temporary reality far removed from mundane modern concerns. Their popularity is merely an indication of just how much this alternate reality continues to be needed in modern society.

—Tina Gianoulis

FURTHER READING:

"Harlequin Enterprises Limited." http://www.harlequin-enterprises.com. June 1999.

Linden, Dave Wechler and Matt Rees. "I'm Hungry, But Not for Food." *Forbes*. Vol. 150, No. 1, July 6, 1992, 70.

Mallet, Gina. "The Greatest Romance on Earth." *Canadian Business*. Vol. 66, No. 8, August 1993, 18.

Pollack, Richard. "Romance Slaves of Harlequin." *The Nation*. Vol. 254, No. 10, March 16, 1992, 33.

Harley-Davidson

There are few material objects that hold the degree of mystique that envelops the Harley-Davidson motorcycle. The very name conjures a warehouse of connotations: the loud rumble of a Harley engine; black leather riding apparel; and, of course, the Hell's Angels and other stereotypically unsavory, grizzled, bearded, beer-swilling, tattoo-covered biker gangs. Over the years, the "hog," as the bike is affectionately known by its riders, developed a reputation as the preferred transportation of outlaws; a gritty subculture grew up around the motorcycle and established it as an iconic badge in America and abroad. Though remaining the ride of choice for hard core bikers, by the end of the 1990s the Harley—once feared and despised by law-abiding middle and upper-class Americans—had been gradually transformed into well-polished, sporty recreational vehicles for "weekend warriors." Ironically, possession of a Harley—with its rich history and lore—was becoming a status symbol.

Harley-Davidson motorcycles neither set out to target the fringe element of the market, nor consciously to create the wild image that developed around their products. Soon after the dawning of the twentieth century, draftsman William Harley and his pattern-maker friend Arthur Davidson, set out simply to design and manufacture a motorized bicycle that would eliminate the need for pedals. They were helped along by Ole Evinrude, a German draftsman who later became known for his superior outboard boat motors. Evinrude had worked in a French factory and provided the duo with De Dion engine drawings to get them started. Davidson made the patterns for a small air-cooled engine while Harley designed the bicycle. In need of an

A Harley-Davidson motorcycle, c.1911.

experienced mechanic, they called upon Davidson's brother Walter, a machinist for a Kansas railroad, to come home to Milwaukee, Wisconsin. Another brother, William, later joined the operation as well.

The Davidsons' father, a cabinet maker named William C. Davidson, assisted the entrepreneurs by fixing up a ten-by-fifteen-foot shed in the backyard as the first factory with ''Harley-Davidson Motor Company'' painted on the door. The ''factory'' was officially opened in Milwaukee in 1903, and the Harley-Davidson Motor Company was incorporated in 1907. The Harley-Davidson company web site (http://www.harley-davidson.com) proposes two reasons why Harley's name comes first: because he built the actual bicycle, or, perhaps, thanks to a gentlemanly gesture by the Davidsons, who outnumbered Harley three to one. Harley became the company's chief engineer and treasurer, while Arthur Davidson was secretary and general sales manager. Walter Davidson was appointed company president, and William Davidson held the position of works manager.

Nicknamed the ''Silent Gray Fellow,'' the original Harley-Davidson motorcycle was a far cry from the thundering, macho vehicle it later became. Initially, the company installed large mufflers to subdue the noise, and tried to sell the bikes as practical family transportation, provided a sidecar was purchased. The product, however, instead caught on with fun-loving sportsmen.

Into regular production of their bikes by 1905, the Harley-Davidson firm moved their factory to Chestnut Street, now called Juneau Avenue, in Milwaukee, where the corporate offices still stand. Their uncle, James McLay, a beekeeper, loaned them money to build the 2,380-square-foot shop. In 1907, they produced 150 motorcycles, and in 1909, the number had increased to 1,149. By 1912, Harley-Davidson cranked out over 9,500 vehicles in one year. The company's sales and their reputation were growing due to the rugged strength and reliability of the bikes, but the firm really started to make its mark in racing competitions. By mid-1910s Harley-Davidson was

the third largest motorcycle manufacturer in the country, and by 1920 held the number one position, with dealers in 67 countries.

With Arthur Davidson concentrating on sales strategy and Bill Harley focusing on testing and development, the company ensured its staying power. By 1953, when its main competitor, Indian, closed its doors, Harley-Davidson became the sole remaining American motorcycle company, and by 1995 it boasted a production of over 105,000 bikes, with demand continuing to grow. Its legendary Sportster model was first released in 1957. Part of Harley-Davidson's success was due to Davidson's initiative in setting up a network of dealers that would sell only Harley-Davidson motorcycles, with an accompanying dedication to those dealers that their profits would come first. In addition, the company boasted a strong product guarantee. Harley-Davidson even survived during difficult economic times, thanks to its foreign sales, and the fact that it supplied the U.S. Postal Service and police departments.

In both World War I and II, Harley-Davidsons were used to run dispatch on the front lines; in fact, nearly all of the company's output during the World War II went to support the Allied forces. At that time, soldiers began the practice of chopping off parts—including headlights and fenders—to make the machine go faster. Thus, the word ''chopper'' came to refer to an altered Harley. Eventually it was expected that ''hog'' owners would personalize their bikes, not only by making them into choppers, but also with custom paint jobs or fenders and other unique touches. A couple of theories have evolved as to why Harleys were also dubbed ''hogs.'' One story notes that a Harley racing enthusiast around 1920 used to do his victory laps with his pet pig accompanying him on the bike; the Harley-Davidson web site claims the term is an acronym for the Harley Owner's Group, the company-sponsored club that was formed in 1983.

In 1947, the image of the outlaw biker gained full momentum when an article in *Life* magazine detailed the horrors of a rebel motorcycle gang who terrorized a town in California. No longer seen as simply sporting enthusiasts, most riders were now lumped with those known as Hell's Angels, a group of criminal-element bikers who took their name from a 1930s Howard Hughes film about flying men. This was bad publicity for Harley-Davidson, but grist to the media mill, which continued to beef up the stereotype, with films like Marlon Brando's *The Wild One* (1954) portraying the biker subculture. Unfortunately, the stories surrounding biker gangs—rape, robbery, beatings, looting—were often more truth than fiction. In the 1960s, journalist Hunter S. Thompson infiltrated the ranks of the Hell's Angels, posing as a member, and wrote a full-length book on his experiences called *Hell's Angels: The Strange and Terrible Saga of the Outlaw Motorcycle Gang.* After his exposé was published, he was mercilessly beaten up by a group of members.

During the 1960s and 1970s, the preferred vehicle for a mainstream motorcycle enthusiast was usually a lower-priced Japanese model, derogatorily nicknamed a "rice burner" and denounced by Harley riders as watered-down imitations of "true" motorcycles. However, foreign bikes were more accepted in polite society because they were free of the stigma of the Harley, which had come to symbolize low-class, dirty deviants. Magazines like *Easy Rider,* featuring half-naked cover models, contributed to the bike's sleazy connotations. However, during the 1980s the image of the Harley rider began to change again. Though the leather-clad anti-social bike gang members still existed, more and more "yuppie" bikers began to take to the open road. In addition to the appeal of Harleys as well-made American vehicles, a new class of men was undoubtedly also intrigued by the outlaw image.

Harley-Davidsons soon became a recreational vehicle for successful businessmen, much like a boat or Jet-Ski. The bikes could be seen lined up outside hip nightspots in major cities on weekends, and streaming down highways headed out of town. Harley accessory boutiques mushroomed in upscale shopping districts around the country. The company set up a slick web site, and appropriated events like Daytona Bike Week in Florida and the annual motorcycle rally and races in Sturgis, South Dakota, for generating corporate publicity. In 1994 Turner Original Productions produced a television special titled *Harley-Davidson: The American Motorcycle,* narrated by actor James Caan and featuring celebrities such as David Crosby, Peter Fonda, Wynonna Judd, and a leather-clad Larry Hagman touting their love of the bike and its accompanying aura. *The Tonight Show* host Jay Leno became another well-known aficionado. As the Harley-Davidson approached its hundredth anniversary, it seemed to be regaining its originally intended use as a vehicle for genteel sportsmen and women, while its continuing popularity remains a tribute to American entrepreneurship and hard work.

—Geri Speace

FURTHER READING:

Bolfert, Thomas C. *The Big Book of Harley Davidson: Official Publication.* Milwaukee, Wisconsin, Harley Davidson, Inc., 1991.

"Harley-Davidson Motor Company." http://www.harley-davidson.com. March 1999.

Johnson, David. "Family Affair: Four Men, One Dream." *Cycle World.* September 1993, 60.

Leffingwell, Randy. *Harley-Davidson: Myth & Mystique.* Osceola, Wisconsin, Motorbooks Publishers & Wholesalers, 1995.

Norris, Martin. *Rolling Thunder: The Harley-Davidson Legend.* London, Quintet Publishing, Ltd., 1992.

Thompson, Hunter S. *Hell's Angels: The Strange and Terrible Saga of the Outlaw Motorcycle Gangs.* New York, Ballantine Books, 1966.

Wagner, Herbert. *Harley-Davidson 1930-1941: Revolutionary Motorcycles & Those Who Rode Them.* Atglen, Pennsylvania, Schiffer Publishing Ltd., 1996.

Harlow, Jean (1911-1937)

Known for her platinum blonde hair, low-cut gowns, and buxom figure, Jean Harlow was Hollywood's original "blonde bombshell." Harlow's bold sexuality—she refused to wear undergarments, for example—made her both a box-office hit and an icon of modern sexual freedom. But it was not only Harlow's starring roles—in such films as *Platinum Blonde* (1931), *Red Dust* (1932), and *China Seas* (1936)—that made news. The unexplained suicide of her husband, MGM executive Paul Bern, and her own mysterious death from uremia at age 26, made Harlow a tragic symbol of the fleeting pleasures of Hollywood stardom.

—Samantha Barbas

FURTHER READING:

Shulman, Irving. *Harlow: An Intimate Biography.* New York, Dell, 1964.

Stenn, David. *Bombshell: The Life and Death of Jean Harlow.* New York, Doubleday, 1993.

Harmonica Bands

Although harmonica bands and orchestras have generally been forgotten, the harmonica was one of the most popular musical instruments from the 1920s through the 1940s. Its cheapness made it an ideal instrument for teaching music to children during the Depression, and the harmonica youth orchestras were influential in instilling discipline. In the years between the two world wars—a period called the "the golden age of the mouth organ in America"—sales of the tiny, inexpensive instrument increased dramatically. Bands of harmonica players became famous on the vaudeville circuit, on radio, and in Hollywood films; whole orchestras of harmonica-playing youth were organized in cities all over the United States, and public schools offered harmonica instruction courses. The craze finally hit its peak in 1947 when the Harmonicats' rendition of "Peg O' My Heart" became the number one hit of that year.

It all began during the Boy Council of Philadelphia's 1923 "Boy Week" celebration when philanthropist Albert Hoxie began organizing successful harmonica contests. Hohner Company, a German manufacturer of harmonicas, began sending experts to public schools that year to teach children how to play the instrument. In 1924, over ten thousand children participated in the contest, and in the following years harmonica youth bands began forming, including one led by Hoxie himself: the Philadelphia Harmonica Band. Hoxie's band, consisting of about 60 young men, was modeled on military lines—the musicians wore marching-band uniforms, were given ranks, and ended each show with "Stars and Stripes Forever." The band lasted until 1936, traveling around the country and playing for presidents, royalty, and visiting dignitaries, and at events such as the Philadelphia celebration of Charles Lindbergh's transatlantic flight, the heavyweight championship fight between Jack Dempsey and Gene Tunney, and Franklin D. Roosevelt's inaugural parade.

Hoxie also sent harmonica assistants to schools to encourage children to play the affordable instrument during the Depression years. His efforts paid off. By the end of the 1930s over 150 harmonica youth orchestras existed in Chicago alone; 1,200 public school children learned to play it in Dayton, Ohio, and in Los Angeles 115,127 children were enrolled in the harmonica band program from 1927 to 1937. Boy Scouts could earn merit badges for harmonica playing, and over two thousand harmonica bands were formed in the United States during the Depression.

Albert Hoxie's efforts were not the only factor responsible for the appeal of harmonica bands in the schools. Up until the 1920s the harmonica was based on the diatonic scale and each instrument was limited to the notes found in the key to which it was tuned. However, in the mid-1920s, Hohner Company developed the polyphonia, bass, chord, and chromatic models, which expanded the range of the instrument and the overall sound of the bands. Vaudeville acts using the new instruments began to appear as early as 1927, when the Harmonica Rascals combined music and slapstick comedy onstage. Other bands soon followed, making the instrument even more popular as fans were inspired to try it themselves.

The Harmonica Rascals, formed by Borrah Minevitch, were like "the Three Stooges with mouth organs" and audiences loved them. Their image was based on the ragamuffin/tramp motif and their act centered on Johnny Puelo, a four-foot-one-inch midget who played the largest harmonica available, the polyphonia, for comic effect. The Harmonica Rascals were so successful that Minevitch simultaneously ran three separate bands by that name—each with its own midget—in different regions of the country until the end of World War II. Besides appearing on vaudeville, the Harmonica Rascals had a weekly radio program, and appeared in nine movies between 1935 and 1943. Other 1930s bands, inspired by the Harmonica Rascals, included the Harmonica Scamps, a vaudeville band that featured an African-American midget, and the Harmonicuties, an all-girl band boasting a female midget. The Harmonica Harlequins, whose members dressed in clown outfits, formed in 1934 as a competitor to the Harmonica Rascals and worked the vaudeville circuit, played on the radio, and recorded. Other bands from the 1930s include the Cappy Barra Harmonica Ensemble and the Philharmonicas, both of whom specialized in big band arrangements; the Harlemonicats, a jazz trio; the Three Harpers, the Stagg McMann Trio, the Harmonica Hi-Hats and the Harmonica Lads.

World War II ended the golden age of the harmonica. A ban on German goods prohibited the importation of harmonicas from Germany, where the highest-quality instruments were made; youth orchestras disbanded and schools halted their instruction programs; and large harmonica bands pared down to smaller units, usually trios. The most famous trio materialized when former Harmonica Rascals Jerry Murad and Don Les teamed up with Al Fiore to form the Harmonicats in the mid-1940s. Their 1947 version of "Peg O' My Heart"—recorded as a B-side filler—stayed at number one on the *Billboard* chart for 26 weeks. The record subsequently sold over 20 million copies to become the second-most popular 78 rpm of all time, surpassed only by Bing Crosby's "White Christmas." The record's success even convinced the Musician's Union to accept the harmonica as a legitimate instrument and allow harmonica players to join.

The Harmonicats went on to record 36 albums, and Murad kept the trio alive (Les retired in 1972, Fiore in 1982) until his death in 1996. Other harmonica bands also performed after World War II, but none equaled the success of "Peg O' My Heart." The Don Henry trio had a minor hit in the 1950s with their version of "The Saber Dance." Johnny Puelo, the original midget from the Harmonica Rascals, formed the Harmonica Gang, which appeared on television with Milton Berle, Dean Martin and Perry Como in the 1950s, played live at the Latin Quarter in New York and the Stardust in Las Vegas, and recorded seven albums until Puelo's retirement in 1973; and Dave Doucette had some success with his quintet The Stereomonics in 1968, and with the Big Harp in 1975.

The size and versatility of the harmonica—in all of its forms—allowed entertainers to combine music with comedy on the vaudeville stage, which proved to be the inspiration and/or the training ground for many future American harmonica soloists and session players such as Richard Hayman, Pete Pedersen, Mike Chimes, Leo Diamond, Alan Shackner, Charles Newman, and the world-famous soloist Larry Adler, who elevated the tiny instrument to near-classical status in the concert hall.

—Richard Levine

FURTHER READING:

Field, Kim. *Harmonicas, Harps, and Heavy Breathers*. New York, Simon and Schuster, 1993.

Krampert, Peter. *The Encyclopedia of the Harmonica*. Illinois, Tatanka, 1998.

Harper, Valerie (1940—)

Valerie Harper was a little-known actress-dancer when she was cast as Rhoda Morgenstern, neighbor and best buddy of Mary Richards, on CBS's landmark 1970s TV sitcom *The Mary Tyler Moore Show*. Harper emerged as one of television history's most beloved second bananas. The Jewish, Bronx-accented Rhoda was a true New York neurotic: obsessed by her weight and her looks; uncomfortably single and ever-anxious in her relationships with men; and a perfect wisecracking comic contrast to Mary, the more subdued, always perfectly-coifed Midwesterner.

Harper won three Comic Supporting Actress Emmy Awards for playing Rhoda. In 1974, she left the series to star in *Rhoda*, a *Mary Tyler Moore Show* spin-off. Here, Rhoda Morgenstern was relocated to New York, and her character was far more attractive and assertive. Early in the show's first season—in one of the all-time top-rated TV sitcom episodes—Rhoda married Joe Gerard (David Groh). Meanwhile, Rhoda's sister and neighbor Brenda (Julie Kavner) became the homelier, insecure second banana. *Rhoda* lasted four seasons, during which she and Joe separated—and Harper added another Emmy to her mantle, this one as Outstanding Series Comic Actress.

—Rob Edelman

FURTHER READING:

Alley, Robert S., and Irby Brown. *Love Is All Around: The Making of The Mary Tyler Moore Show.* New York, Delta, 1989.

Harper's

Harper's magazine, one of America's most culturally significant periodicals, was founded in 1850 under the name *Harper's New Monthly* magazine by the New York-based Harper & Brothers, the largest publishing company in nineteenth-century America. Initially conceived as a miscellany—a collection of reprints from other publications—consisting mostly of fiction, *Harper's* gained a broad middle-class audience by positioning itself as the Victorian reader's gateway to refinement and respectability. In the twentieth century, *Harper's* transformed itself into the magazine of choice for an elite, well-educated readership whose opinions and tastes have helped shape the nation's political debates and social trends.

With an antebellum circulation of two hundred thousand, *Harper's* was easily the best-read and most influential magazine of its time; its list of nineteenth-century contributors reads like a roll call of some of the era's finest British and American fiction writers. But in spite of its long record of prosperity, by the end of World War I, *Harper's* was in financial trouble, its circulation down to seventy-five thousand. Over the course of the first few decades of the twentieth century, the genteel, culturally ambitious, middle-class readership upon which *Harper's* had based its success had fragmented. A number of forces, including a widening income gap between rich and poor, increasing cultural diversity through immigration, the rise of the suburbs, and the impact of emerging technologies such as film and radio, split the relatively unified nineteenth-century reading public into lowbrow, middlebrow, and highbrow audiences. Those periodicals which were able to maintain a mass national circulation, such as *Ladies' Home Journal* or the *Saturday Evening Post,* did so by cutting prices and simplifying article content in order to appeal to the largest possible audience, while relying on extensive advertising to compensate for lost subscription revenue.

Rather than follow the lead of the mass-market magazines to try to regain its position as market leader, *Harper's* decided to redefine itself as the journal for the well-educated and well-read, seeking serious, though not scholarly, discussion of the issues of the day. In 1925, editor Thomas Wells redesigned the magazine, slimming it down and removing most of the elaborate artwork. The new *Harper's* assumed a distinctly progressive—never radical—political tone. Most significantly, the amount of fiction, long the magazine's hallmark, was reduced and replaced by nonfiction articles debating major social and political issues to satisfy its readership.

As its mid-century editor, Frederick Lewis Allen, noted, the types of issues discussed in the magazine's pages evolved with the changing interests of its audience. In the 1920s, *Harper's* was full of articles on the social upheaval of the modern era. Numerous articles voiced concerns about the role of the newly enfranchised and emancipated woman and her impact on family life. Other writers like James Truslow Adams in "Is Science a Blind Alley?" expressed fears about the decline of religion in the face of rapid technological change. By the 1930s, moved by the Great Depression and the specter of war in Europe, *Harper's* turned toward political and economic issues, such as the rise of German and Japanese power abroad and the possibility of social unrest among the unemployed at home.

The entrance of the United States into World War II solidified the magazine's increasingly global focus. *Harper's* wholeheartedly supported the war effort; Henry L. Stimson defended the bombings of Hiroshima and Nagasaki in its pages. Editor Lewis H. Lapham has noted that through the 1950s and the 1960s *Harper's* was a significant forum for America's cold-war intellectuals, including Arthur Schlesinger Jr., Van Wyck Brooks, Richard Hofstadter, and Henry Steele Commager. Later, as the role of the public intellectual waned, and as public cynicism waxed in the Vietnam and Watergate eras, *Harper's* responded again by changing to a more journalistic, exposé-oriented style.

In 1965 *Harper's* magazine was acquired by the Minneapolis Star and Tribune Company, which was buying up Harper & Row (the successor of Harper & Brothers) stock. By 1980 the magazine was once again in debt. When the new owners considered terminating *Harper's,* the John D. and Catherine T. MacArthur Foundation and the Atlantic Richfield Company provided funds to set up the *Harper's* Magazine Foundation, headed by John R. MacArthur, to publish the magazine independent of its parent and make it less reliant on subscription and advertising revenue.

In 1984, under the leadership of editor Lapham, *Harper's* was again redesigned. In a pair of editorials, Lapham invoked the nineteenth-century origins of the magazine, comparing the situation of Americans of the 1850s facing a new national industrial economy to that of his own readers as the country became integrated into a new global economic order, and vowed to continue to provide a national forum for debate on issues of social and political importance. Interestingly, Lapham also reaffirmed *Harper's* original mission as a miscellany, but with a difference. While the editors of 1850 had offered their readers what they felt was the best in entertaining and useful information, Lapham announced new departments which would offer representative statistics, or small excerpts from significant publications or public documents in a context often designed to startle the reader and to demystify or even mock the offered text. That change alone, from a tone of Victorian earnestness to one of postmodern irony, speaks volumes about the altered self-image of the writer-intellectual—from ardent educator to alienated commentator—over the course of more than a century. Lapham also promised to continue what he suggested the magazine had tried to do since its inception, to steer a middle course between the banalities of mass-market journalism and the jargon of highly specialized publications.

The magazine's major goal at the end of the twentieth century—to provide a national forum for debate on those forces and trends with global origins and impact to an elite readership—is perhaps problematic. There is some difficulty inherent in identifying national interests as being those of this comparatively small group of readers. As of 1998, Harper's had a circulation of 216,630, a healthy and respectable number, to be sure, but hardly comparable to the million-plus circulations of mass-market periodicals, and only slightly more than the magazine's highest circulation in the nineteenth century. Whether *Harper's* magazine's fiercely loyal readers continue to represent, under rapidly changing conditions, what editor Lapham has called the nation's "general interest" is a question only the twenty-first century can answer.

—Anne Sheehan

FURTHER READING:

Charvat, William. *The Profession of Authorship in America, 1800-1870.* Edited by Matthew J. Bruccoli. Columbus, Ohio State University Press, 1968.

Exman, Eugene. *The Brothers Harper.* New York, Harper & Row, 1965.

————. *The House of Harper: One Hundred and Fifty Years of Publishing.* New York, Harper & Row, 1967.

Harper, J. Henry. *The House of Harper: A Century of Publishing in Franklin Square.* New York, Harper & Brothers Publishers, 1912.

Lapham, Lewis H. "In the American Grain." *Harper's.* Vol. 268, No. 1605, February 1984, 6-8, 10.

————. "Letter to the Reader." *Harper's.* Vol. 268, No. 1604, January 1984, 10, 12.

Mott, Frank Luther. *A History of American Magazines, 1850-1865.* Cambridge, Harvard University Press, 1938.

Nourie, Alan, and Barbara Nourie, eds. *American Mass-Market Magazines.* New York, Greenwood Press, 1990.

Peter, Theodore. *Magazines in the Twentieth Century.* Urbana, University of Illinois Press, 1964.

Tebbel, John. *A History of Book Publishing in the United States.* 4 vols. New York, R. R. Bowker, 1975-81.

Hart, Lorenz

See Rodgers and Hart

Hate Crimes

Crimes of violence motivated by hatred based on race, religion, ethnicity, gender, or sexual orientation have always been a part of the American political landscape. At various times legislative efforts have been made to address the problem, such as laws passed in the late 1960s making it a federal crime to interfere violently with black Americans exercising their legal civil rights. In the 1980s, an American society trying to assimilate the changes wrought by the various liberation movements of the 1960s and 1970s began to look for stronger ways to show its intolerance for bias-motivated crimes. Defining these crimes as "hate crimes," some groups began to lobby for them to be treated as more heinous than crimes not motivated by the perpetrator's prejudice and to be punished more severely.

Political organizations such as the Southern Poverty Law Center and the New York City Lesbian and Gay Anti-Violence Project began to keep records of the occurrence of bias-motivated crimes. Pressured by such groups and by the victims of hate crimes, the federal government passed the Hate Crimes Statistics Act. Passed in 1990, and later extended at least through 2002, the act requires the Federal Bureau of Investigation to monitor and keep reliable statistics on crimes motivated by prejudice based on race, religion, ethnic or national origin, disability, or sexual orientation. In 1996, these statistics showed that 8,759 hate crimes were reported, the majority of them racially motivated.

More than forty states have enacted hate crimes statutes requiring stiffer penalties for a crime if it is categorized as a hate crime. These laws are controversial for many reasons. Conservatives minimize the occurrence of hate crimes, accusing interested groups of inflating the figures. They ridicule the laws as "identity politics," insisting that "thought police" will be required to prove motivation. Even some liberals express concern that the laws potentially interfere with free speech. Racial bias, homophobia, and other prejudices are cultural problems, they say, and must be solved by education rather than legislation. Supporters of hate crime legislation argue that hate crimes deserve greater penalties because they have more serious implications for society than crimes which are not motivated by bias. They cite the fear engendered in targeted groups as a whole by the crimes of intimidation against them, and point to Nazi attempts at the genocide of Jews, Gypsies, gays, and other groups as an example of what can occur in a society that tolerates hate crimes.

Another element of controversy is the inclusion of sexual minorities as a protected group. Of the states that do have hate crime laws, only about half include sexual orientation in their wording. While right-wing groups and politicians resist any sort of legitimization of gay lifestyles, many gay and lesbian groups continue to fight for state and federal hate crime laws that will include crimes against them.

Part of the problem of enacting hate crime legislation lies in attempting to define hate crimes. While beatings, murders, and firebombings of churches, synagogues, or community centers are clear examples of criminal activity, some actions are less obvious. Some states have included cross burnings and swastika displays under their hate crime laws only to be challenged in court for limiting free speech. Many groups, especially colleges and universities, have instituted codes of speech in an effort to outlaw racial epithets and slurs but many argue that the abridgment of free speech is not the answer. Many feminists have lobbied to have rape and domestic violence included as crimes of hate against women. That definition was included in the 1993 Violence Against Women Act, but the hate-crime wording was eliminated in the final version. Though hate-crime legislation was primarily introduced in the hopes of curbing the cross-burnings, synagogue-bombings, and beatings associated with racism, anti-Semitism, and homophobia, it also covers any bias-related crime. Ironically, one of the first supreme court decisions supporting hate-crime laws dealt with an African-American perpetrator in a crime against whites.

Though the debate goes on over the best way to deal with hate crimes, it seems to be clear from statistics that bias-motivated crime continues to be a global problem. Whether the perpetrators are angry, often disenfranchised, individuals or members of an organized hate group such as the Aryan Nation or the Ku Klux Klan, perhaps the debate itself is an important step in eliminating these crimes. The light of exposure robs them of their most frightening and powerful aspect—the secret complicity of society.

—Tina Gianoulis

FURTHER READING:

Bowling, Benjamin. *Violent Racism: Victimization, Policing and Social Context.* Oxford, New York, Clarendon Press, 1998.

Jost, Kenneth. "Background: Violence and Prejudice." *C. Q. Researcher.* Vol. 3, No. 1, January 8, 1993, 7.

Kelley, Robert J., and Jess Maghan, eds. *Hate Crime: The Global Politics of Polarization.* Carbondale, Illinois, Southern Illinois University Press, 1998.

Lawrence, Frederick M. *Punishing Hate: Bias Crimes under American Law.* Cambridge, Massachusetts, Harvard University Press, 1999.

Havlicek, John (1940—)

While the National Basketball Association's Boston Celtics have had a history of illustrious players, perhaps none is as closely associated with a single moment in the team's history as John Havlicek. Few Celtics fans cannot imitate long-time Celtics' announcer Johnny Most's raspy yell, "Havlicek Stole the Ball, Havlicek Stole the Ball," describing the player's crucial steal as time ran out in the seventh and deciding game of the 1965 Eastern Division Finals against perennial Boston rival Philadelphia, which preserved a narrow one-point win for Boston and opened the way for another Boston championship.

Perhaps it is ironic that Havlicek is so famed for a single play, for his career was marked by a longevity and consistency which few players in NBA history have been able to match. Havlicek's steal came early in a distinguished career, during which he played on eight NBA Championship teams and appeared in 13 All-Star games, among his many honors. His hallmark was an almost supernatural endurance, as Havlicek remained in perpetual motion on both offense and defense throughout entire games. At 6 feet, 5 inches, Havlicek was able to play both guard and forward, using his size and strength to overpower smaller guards and his quickness to beat larger, slower forwards with drives to the basket and quick passes. In addition to his

John Havlicek

physical stamina, Havlicek also was an avid student of the game. Longtime Boston sportswriter Bob Ryan notes in *The Boston Celtics* that Havlicek's "physical abilities were exceeded by his extraordinary basketball mind. If he saw his opponents run a play, he made a note of the hand signal or verbal call that initiated it. Thereafter he always got the jump on it. He couldn't understand why other players didn't retain basketball knowledge equally well."

A three-sport star in high school, Havlicek initially played both baseball and basketball at Ohio State University, although he cut short his baseball career at OSU to concentrate on basketball. Nonetheless, Havlicek's versatility and athletic ability was so great that he was drafted by both the National Football League's Cleveland Browns in the seventh round of the NFL draft and the Celtics in the first round of the NBA draft following his graduation from OSU in 1962. Havlicek was the last player cut by the Browns, where he tried out as a wide receiver, which allowed him from that point on to devote himself solely to basketball.

Havlicek joined the Celtics in the midst of the team's run of eight consecutive championships between 1959 and 1966. For his first four seasons, a time when the Celtics were rich with veteran players, Havlicek enjoyed the role of "Sixth Man," coming off the bench late in the first quarter of games to provide instant scoring at a time when other players were putting their weaker reserve players in the game. While Havlicek played this vital reserve role on the Celtics championship teams of the early and mid 1960s, he became an even more central figure in the teams' 1968 and 1969 championship seasons, as older veterans gradually became less effective. In 1968, for example, Havlicek scored 40 of Boston's 100 points in a hard-fought seventh game victory over Philadelphia in the Eastern Division Finals, which put the Celtics into the NBA Finals.

The early 1970s were a more difficult period for the Celtics following the retirement of Bill Russell in 1969, although Havlicek raised his level of play to a new high, enjoying his best scoring seasons in 1970-71 and 1971-72 and leading the league in minutes played in both seasons. In 1972-73, the Celtics had their best-ever regular season record, 68-14, but lost in the Eastern Conference Finals against the New York Knicks, hampered by a shoulder injury that Havlicek suffered in the third game of the series.

Havlicek, or "Hondo," as he came to be known by Celtics fans in an homage to the John Wayne movie of the same name, concluded his career as a leader and elder statesman for a younger generation of Celtics during championship campaigns in 1974 and 1976, both of which offered a number of memorable moments. In the 1974 NBA Finals, the Celtics defeated the Milwaukee Bucks in a seven-game series that included one overtime and one double-overtime game. Havlicek was named the Most Valuable Player in that series. In the 1976 NBA Finals, the Celtics faced the Phoenix Suns, who played the Celtics in the first four games of the series for a 2-2 tie. Boston won Game Five by a score of 128-126 in three overtimes in one of the greatest games in NBA history, due in no small part to several key baskets by Havlicek, and returned to Phoenix to close out the series in six games.

Following the 1976 season, the Celtics nucleus of the past two championships began to disperse for various reasons. Havlicek retired following the 1977-78 season, one of the worst in Boston history, at age 37, as the sixth-leading scorer in NBA history, scoring an impressive 29 points in his final game at Boston Garden. Havlicek's all-around play and consistency is reflected in his career statistics. Havlicek holds Boston records for most games played, most minutes played, and most points scored, and he ranks second in team history in assists and third in rebounds. He was elected to the Naismith Memorial Basketball Hall of Fame in 1983 and named one of the NBA's 50 greatest players in 1996.

—Jason George

FURTHER READING:

Fitzgerald, Joe. *That Championship Feeling: The Story of the Boston Celtics.* New York, Charles Scribner's Sons, 1975.

"John Havlicek" (online biography) http://www.nba.com/history/ havlicek_bio.html. January 1999.

Ryan, Bob. *The Boston Celtics: The History, Legends, and Images of America's Most Celebrated Team.* Reading, Massachusetts, Addison-Wesley Publishing Company, 1989.

Hawaii Five-O

By the time the final episode aired on April 4, 1980, *Hawaii Five-O* was the longest continuously running police drama in the history of television. The show premiered in September of 1968 and retained loyal viewers for most of its 278 episodes. Producer Leonard Freeman, the main creative force behind the show, brought together the elements that made the show a hit: a well chosen cast that went virtually unchanged for ten years, dynamic music, and the lush scenery of Hawaii.

The main appeal of the show was the main character, the tough, no-nonsense Steve McGarrett, who was the head of the Five-O. McGarrett's elite special investigating unit dealt with crimes that were too big for conventional police forces, and he answered only to "the Governor and God." Freeman's original title for the series was *The Man,* and every criminal in the Aloha State knew that McGarrett was the man. And when the wrong element came to the Hawaiian shores from elsewhere, McGarrett was quick to let them know "you're on my rock now." In the pilot, recurring nemesis Wo Fat described McGarrett as "the proverbial character you would not want to meet in a dark alley."

Jack Lord played the role of McGarrett with intensity. Lord was a driven perfectionist and dedicated himself to the show. Lord's McGarrett was a larger-than-life character who struck fear into the hearts of the islands' criminal element and inspired fierce loyalty from the men and women he commanded. After Freeman's death in 1974, Lord became the guiding force behind the show.

McGarrett's right-hand man was Danny "Danno" Williams, played by James MacArthur. In the pilot, the part of Danno had been

Jack Lord on the beach filming an episode of *Hawaii Five-O.*

played by Tim O'Kelly, but when he did not get a favorable rating from a test audience in New York Freeman replaced him with MacArthur before the regular series began filming. MacArthur proved to be a crucial ingredient in the successful chemistry of the show. The best remembered and most often repeated line from *Hawaii Five-O* was McGarrett's clipped command of "Book 'em Danno." For eleven seasons, Danny Williams was a loyal and stolid sidekick to McGarrett. MacArthur tired of the role and left the show at the end of the 1978-79 season. The successful formula was lost, and the series could only limp along for one additional year.

While the network required that the two lead characters be played by haoles (Caucasians from the mainland), the other members of the Five-O team were played by local actors. Kam Fong Chun (credited as Kam Fong), who had served on the Honolulu Police Department for eighteen years before turning to acting, played Chin Ho Kelly for ten seasons. For the first five years of the series, local musician and stand-up comic Gilbert "Zoulou" Kauhi (credited as Zulu) played Kono Kalakaua. After Zulu's departure two new characters were introduced: Ben Kokua, played by Al Harrington, and Duke Lukela, played by Herman Wedemeyer.

In addition to dealing justice to murderers and mobsters, Hawaii Five-O was occasionally called on to save the free world from Communism. McGarrett fought his own cold war against red Chinese spy Wo Fat, played by Khigh Dhiegh. Wo Fat matched wits with McGarrett in the series pilot, "Cocoon," and in ten episodes of the series. In the final episode of the series, titled "Woe to Wo Fat," their conflict came to a resolution when McGarrett personally locked Wo Fat behind bars.

Perhaps the most memorable element of *Hawaii Five-O* was Morton Stevens's driving theme music. Stevens won Emmys for his scores to the episodes "Hookman" and "A Thousand Pardons, You're Dead."

The cast played out their dramas in the midst of the photogenic scenery of the Hawaiian Islands. Producer Freeman insisted that the series be filmed entirely on location in Hawaii. Some members of the Hawaiian tourism industry initially were concerned that the weekly portrayals of murder and corruption would make the islands seem too dangerous. However, the small screen visions of palm trees and blue skies enticed many viewers to take a firsthand look. As *Hawaii Five-O* became a hit, tourism soared.

—Randy Duncan

FURTHER READING:

Rhodes, Karen. *Booking "Hawaii Five-O": An Episode Guide and Critical History of the 1968-1980 Television Detective Series.* Jefferson, North Carolina, McFarland & Company, 1997.

Hawkins, Coleman (1904-1969)

The first jazzman to win fame as a tenor saxophonist, Coleman Hawkins joined Fletcher Henderson's band in 1923 and was already its star when young Louis Armstrong was added a year later. Unmatched on his instrument—once ignored by jazzmen—Hawkins brought his distinctive warm tone to slow ballads like "Body and Soul" and a surging profusion of notes to fast numbers. In the 1930s he worked for five years in Europe, enhancing his international

reputation. When bebop appeared on the scene in the 1940s, the innovative Hawkins recorded this new jazz form with Charlie Parker and Dizzy Gillespie. His primary interest remained conventional swing, working often with his favorite trumpet man, Roy Eldridge, in both Europe and America.

—Benjamin Griffith

FURTHER READING:

Atkins, Ronald, editor. *All That Jazz.* London, Carlton, 1996.

Balliett, Whitney. *American Musicians.* New York, Oxford Press, 1986.

Hentoff, Nat, and Albert J. McCarthy, editors. *Jazz.* New York, Da Capo Press, 1974.

Hawks, Howard (1896-1977)

Considered one of the great film auteurs of the Hollywood Studio era, Howard Hawks directed forty-six films and has the distinction of being one of the few directors to work in every major genre, including the gangster film (*Scarface,* 1932); the war film (*The Road to Glory,* 1936, and *Air Force,* 1943); the screwball comedy, (*Bringing Up Baby,* 1938); the biopic (*Sergeant York,* 1941); the Western (*Red River,* 1948, and *Rio Bravo,* 1959); science fiction (*The Thing,* 1951); film noir (*The Big Sleep,* 1946); and the musical

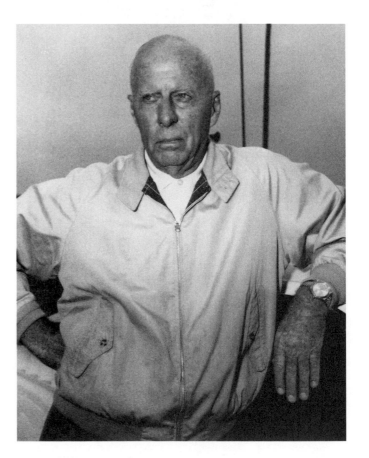

Howard Hawks

(*Gentleman Prefer Blondes,* 1953). His films are among the most popular still shown on U.S. television.

Hawks started in film as a prop man for the Mary Pickford Company in 1919. Within six years, he had risen to editor, scriptwriter, and assistant director. He directed his first feature film in 1926. His first all-talking film was produced four years later, a First National release entitled *The Dawn Patrol.* Arguably, his most important film as a director during his early years was *Scarface,* starring Paul Muni and Ann Dvorak. Though finished in 1930, the film was not released until 1932 because the producer, Howard Hughes, fought over censorship issues with the Hays Office, the administrative body which oversaw the industry's Production Code, which found the film too violent and amoral. Upon release, it was a critical and popular success, and was instrumental in establishing the gangster genre.

Other films for which Hawks is praised include *Only Angels Have Wings* (1939), *His Girl Friday* (1940), and *To Have and Have Not* (1944). As with most auteurs, artists of the cinema who have managed to transcend the studio system and "imprint" on their oeuvre thematic motifs and a formal style unique to their use of film as personal expression, Hawks is noted for his visual style and recurring character types and themes. The "Hawksian vision," as described by film scholar Peter Wollen, consists of a high value placed on the camaraderie of exclusive all-male groups with women as threat to the all-male community, professionalism of the protagonists; and in comedy, regression to childhood and the reversal of gender roles.

In 1975, the Academy of Motion Picture Arts and Sciences presented Hawks with an Honorary Award, for a master American filmmaker whose creative efforts hold a distinguished place in world cinema.

—Frances Gateward

FURTHER READING:

Hillier, Jim, and Peter Wollen, eds. *Howard Hawks, American Artist.* London, BFI Publishing, 1996.

McCarthy, Todd. *Howard Hawks: The Grey Fox of Hollywood.* New York, Grove Press, 1997.

Wollen, Peter. *Signs and Meaning in the Cinema.* Bloomington, Indiana University Press, 1972.

Wood, Robin. *Howard Hawks.* London, BFI Publishing, 1981.

Hayward, Susan (1918-1975)

After some years of apprenticeship, stardom and the first of five Oscar nominations came to former photographer's model Susan Hayward with *Smash-Up—The Story of a Woman* (1947). From then on the gifted, husky-voiced, and ravishing redhead, despite playing a range of parts that included sultry temptresses, rich bitches, and intrepid heroines, became uniquely identified with suffering, both harrowing and poignant but always gutsy. A huge box-office draw during the 1950s, she won hearts portraying singer Jane Froman who was crippled in an air crash, was superb as singer Lilian Roth suffering from alcoholism in *I'll Cry Tomorrow* (1956), won her Academy Award for *I Want to Live* (1958) in which she went to the gas chamber, and was the natural choice to star in the remakes of *Back Street* (1961) and *Dark Victory* (retitled *Stolen Hours,* 1963). Born

Edythe Marrener in Brooklyn, New York, she suffered much off-screen, too—a stormy marriage, custody battles, and a suicide attempt before dying of a brain tumor at the age of 56.

—Robyn Karney

FURTHER READING:

Linet, Beverly. *Portrait of a Survivor: Susan Hayward.* New York, Atheneum, 1980.

Shipman, David. *The Great Movie Stars: The International Years.* London, Angus & Robertson, 1980.

Hayworth, Rita (1918-1987)

The most glamorous Hollywood screen idol of the 1940s, it was Rita Hayworth for whom the press coined the phrase "love goddess." Expertly packaged and produced by various different men throughout her career, Rita Hayworth was transformed from a half-Spanish dancing girl into an "American classic" and the favorite pin-up to thousands of GIs. Best known for her role as the *femme fatale* Gilda in Charles Vidor's 1946 film of the same name, she embodied a dangerous brand of femininity.

She was born Margarita Carmen Cansino in Queens, New York, to an Irish mother and Spanish father. The Cansinos were a family of professional dancers. "They had me dancing almost as soon as I could walk," Hayworth later recalled. As a voluptuous thirteen-year-old Hayworth became her father's co-star and began captivating audiences with her sensual stage presence. It was in 1933 that Hayworth was spotted by executives from the Fox Studios and was given her first break as a dancer in the epic *Dante's Inferno.* After a string of second-rate movies, her contract at Fox was terminated when

Rita Hayworth

her mentor Winfield Sheehan was fired and she was subsequently dropped. She then met the middle-aged Edward Judson, a shrewd businessman who saw her as a marketable product. They married in 1937. Judson negotiated her contract at Columbia, where she was to work for the next twenty years for the tyrannical Harry Cohn, who treated her as a "combination daughter, slave and financial investment." Between them, Judson and Cohn created her new image, removing all traces of Latiness: her surname was changed to the Anglo "Hayworth," a new spelling of her mother's maiden name, her low hairline was lifted by electrolysis and her hair dyed auburn. These flowing auburn locks became Hayworth's trademark; directors would urge her to "act with her hair" which she does unforgettably on her entrance in *Gilda*.

At Columbia, Hayworth's break as a serious actress came with the film *Only Angels Have Wings* (1938) with Cary Grant. Her success in this picture and a subsequent photo shoot for *Life* magazine turned her into a real star. She starred in a couple of musicals with Fred Astaire, *You'll Never Get Rich* (1941) and *You Were Never Lovelier* (1944), and the couple caught the public's imagination. Astaire allegedly named her as his favorite dancing partner. Hayworth had her biggest success with the movie *Cover Girl* (1944) with Gene Kelly. Divorced from Judson since 1942, Hayworth announced she had married noted director and wunderkind Orson Welles during the shooting of *Cover Girl*.

Gossip columnists were puzzled by this match between Beauty and Brains, but the couple were famously smitten by each other. In 1944 Hayworth gave birth to a baby girl, Rebecca, but by 1946 the marriage had ended. That same year Hayworth starred in *Gilda*. The ad line announced, "There never was a woman like Gilda"; Hayworth was soon to learn that there was never a *role* like Gilda either. The film is a tale of a destructive love triangle, in the words of the leading man Glenn Ford, about "how hate can be as exciting an emotion as love." Hayworth's mesmerizing dance routine to the song "Put the Blame on Mame," in which she performs a partial strip tease, removing two long black satin gloves and throwing them to the crowd, is highly erotically charged. In a concession to the film censors, the script later reveals Gilda's virtue, she had only pretended to be a tramp to incense her lover. The film was a box-office smash.

In 1948 Harry Cohn assigned Hayworth to work with her estranged husband Orson Welles on *The Lady from Shanghai*. Hayworth played the "preying mantis" Elsa, a twisted version of Gilda upon whose fame Welles was hoping to cash in. Welles, in a characteristically maverick move, had Hayworth's hair cropped short and bleached blonde for the part. Hayworth's new hair was not a success with her fans nor with her boss at Columbia and the film flopped. Cohn rushed through Hayworth's next movie *The Loves of Carmen* for release that same year to soften the blow.

Later that year Hayworth went on a trip to Europe, where she met and fell in love with the international playboy Prince Aly Khan. Their subsequent marriage made Hayworth a princess. Aly had been entranced by the film *Gilda,* as was often the case with the men in her life. Hayworth remarked sadly to a friend, "Every man I've known has fallen in love with Gilda and woken up with me."

Hayworth's comeback movie *Affair in Trinidad* (1952), in which she starred with Glenn Ford again, was the last time she played the central sex symbol. Hayworth continued to work consistently throughout the 1950s while her personal life continued in its disastrous vein, with two more marriages that both ended in divorce. She began to suffer from alcoholism and later on from Alzheimer's; after a

long struggle with the disease she died in 1987. Her last film was *The Wrath of God* at MGM in 1972.

Hayworth was a typical product of Hollywood, transformed from Margarita Cansino and relentlessly promoted by husbands, directors, and studio bosses. Adored by men but also admired by women, she was the symbol of American glamor and beauty of the time. Although she played a catalog of siren roles, including the legendary Carmen and Salome, in reality she was the exact reverse: unassuming, reserved, and eager to please. Ultimately Rita Hayworth was the hardest role for the reserved Margarita Cansino and playing it took its toll upon her life.

—Candida Taylor

FURTHER READING:

Friedrich, Otto. *City of Nets: A Portrait of Hollywood in the 1940s.* London, Headline, 1987.

Kobal, John. *Rita Hayworth: The Time, the Place and the Woman.* London, W. H. Allen, 1977.

Leaming, Barbara. *If This Was Happiness: The Life of Rita Hayworth.* London, Weidenfeld and Nicolson, 1989.

Morella, Joe, and Edward, Z. Epstein. *Rita: The Life of Rita Hayworth.* New York, Delacorte Press, 1983.

Ringgold, Gene. *The Films of Rita Hayworth—The Legend and Career of a Love Goddess.* New York, Citadel Press, 1974.

Hearst, Patty (1954—)

The granddaughter of newspaper publisher William Randolph Hearst, 19-year-old heiress Patty Hearst was abducted from her Berkeley college residence in February 1974, sparking the biggest manhunt since the Lindbergh kidnapping. Surprisingly, Hearst was next spotted in bank surveillance footage, brandishing automatic weapons during robberies. She released statements stating she had sided with her captors, members of the revolutionary Symbionese Liberation Army, and renounced her family. Los Angeles police had a televised shootout with SLA members, but Hearst, who now called herself "Tania," fled. She was apprehended in September of 1975. At her trial, famed defense attorney F. Lee Bailey maintained that Hearst had been brainwashed by SLA leaders through psychological torture, and was thus not responsible for her crime spree. Hearst was nonetheless convicted and sentenced to prison in 1977. Two years later, her sentence was commuted by President Jimmy Carter. The Hearst episode was sensationalized in the media of the day. She married her prison guard and retired to life as a middle-class homemaker. By the 1990s, however, she was resigned to her notoriety and began writing mystery novels and acting in outré movies, including bad-taste auteur John Waters' *Pecker* (1998).

—Andrew Milner

FURTHER READING:

Alexander, Shana. *Anyone's Daughter: The Times and Trials of Patty Hearst.* New York, Viking, 1979.

Boulton, David. *The Making of Tania Hearst.* London, New English Library, 1975.

Hearst, Patricia. *Murder at San Simeon.* New York, Pocket Books, 1996.

Hearst, Patricia, with Alvin Moscow. *Every Secret Thing.* New York, Doubleday, 1982.

Reeves, Kenneth J. *The Trial of Patty Hearst* (trial transcript). San Francisco, Great Fidelity Press, 1976.

Weed, Steven, with Scott Swanton. *My Search for Patty Hearst.* New York, Crown, 1976.

Hearst, William Randolph (1863-1951)

Larger-than-life American publisher William Randolph Hearst acquired his first newspaper, the *San Francisco Examiner,* in 1886. Over the next two decades, he built a media empire which revolutionized journalism. His dictatorial style and sensational approach to the news generated a fortune as well as controversy. Hearst's seemingly limitless ambition led him to campaign for social reforms, serve in Congress, run for the presidency, famously ignite the Spanish-American war, and become, according to recent biographer Ben Proctor, "arguably the best-known American, not just in the United States but around the world."

In the eyes of many, Hearst personified the American dream. Born to Phoebe Apperson, a Missouri school teacher, and George

William Randolph Hearst

Hearst, a self-made millionaire miner and rancher, William Randolph Hearst parlayed family support, fierce independence, and a sense for drama into enormous wealth and power. In 1880 his father acquired the *Examiner* as payment for a gambling debt. "I am convinced," Hearst wrote to his father from Harvard six years later, "that I could run a newspaper successfully. Now, if you should make over to me the *Examiner*—with enough money to carry out my schemes—I'll tell you what I would do. . . ."

At its height, Hearst's empire published twenty-eight newspapers and nine magazines. His motto was simply "Get Results." Within a year he doubled the *Examiner*'s circulation. He modeled it after Joseph Pulitzer's newspapers, emphasizing human interest, crusading for worthy causes, and making up news stories if there were none to be found. His newspapers were among the first to offer obituaries and to regularly cover weather and women's issues. Hearst also made it a policy to pay for talent. He invested in stars like Thomas Nast, Stephen Crane, Mark Twain, and the great "sob sister" investigator Annie Laurie.

In 1895 he bought the *New York Journal* and entered into a circulation war with Pulitzer. Within a year the *Journal*'s circulation tripled. Not even the comics pages escaped the competitive frenzy. Pulitzer ran the popular strip "The Yellow Kid." Hearst hired the cartoonist away. When Pulitzer hired a new cartoonist, the two newspapers' advertising departments plastered the city with yellow promotional flyers. The campaign gave rise to the term "yellow journalism," which subsequently became a derisive reference to the sort of sensational excesses in news coverage that characterized the Hearst-Pulitzer circulation war.

A legendary anecdote, perhaps apocryphal, describes the excessive competition between the two men, the increasing power of the press, and Hearst's reckless force of will. From roughly 1895 until the end of the Spanish-American war in 1898, Hearst and Pulitzer attempted to attract readers with trumped-up anti-Spanish atrocity stories from Cuba. Although Spain had consented to U.S. demands with respect to Cuban politics, Hearst sent artist Frederick Remington to the island. Remington cabled Hearst to say "[e]verything is quiet. There is no trouble here. There will be no war. Wish to return." Hearst replied: "Please remain. You furnish the pictures, I'll furnish the war."

Hearst's newspapers were distinguished largely by their style. They were among the first to use striking photographs and illustrations. They specialized in flashy headlines and sensational reports of topics like fires, crime, sex, and sports. Hearst encouraged his editors to conduct endless streams of lotteries, giveaways, and serials. He formed a "murder squad" of writers who chased criminals and a "detective corps" of investigative reporters paid to keep check on people in positions of power. Hearst also demanded his newspapers serve the masses. They ran stories calling for improved police and fire protection, better roads, sewers, schools, and hospitals. They promoted the eight-hour workday and public assistance after the 1906 San Francisco earthquake.

Overt political stances taken by Hearst publications eventually provoked accusations of opportunism. Critics maintained that Hearst abused his First Amendment rights. They accused him of recklessness and insatiable greed, suggesting that he sparked the Spanish-American War just to sell his newspapers. Readers also grew wary of Hearst's tactics, boycotting his newspapers in the wake of the assassination of President McKinley in 1901 because they believed that relentlessly inflammatory articles and editorials endorsed by Hearst inspired the assassin.

Although he was often denounced for his nationalist politics, Hearst publications helped construct an American national identity, especially within burgeoning early-twentieth-century immigrant communities. In his efforts to reach the widest possible audience, Hearst directed his editors to seize upon the human element in the news, to encourage writers to craft stories which emphasized similarities among Americans by underlining universal fears and desires.

By the time he entered into politics at the turn of the century, Hearst was well practiced at using his media outlets to fuel his political interests. Although many believed he orchestrated both Theodore and Franklin D. Roosevelt's successful presidential campaigns, he largely failed to realize his own political ambitions. He served two terms as a U.S. representative, but lost bids to become governor of New York and mayor of New York City.

Despite his unsuccessful foray into formal politics, Hearst and his movie-star mistress Marion Davies often entertained world leaders and celebrities at his California estate, San Simeon, a museum-like place many referred to simply as Hearst Castle. People accepted invitations to visit San Simeon out of friendship, curiosity, and fear. Hearst reveled in his role as eccentric kingmaker, unabashedly using his media power to promote his friends and ruin his enemies. In the end, however, he seemed to consider more people enemies than friends. He gained a reputation as a xenophobe, a red-baiter, and a fascist. He vehemently opposed anything or anyone who interfered with his profits, forbidding his employees to unionize, fighting against taxation, and demonizing hemp growers with a famous ''reefer madness'' campaign because they posed a threat to the profits he made supplying timber to the paper-making industry.

Hearst's life inspired the 1941 Orson Welles film *Citizen Kane*, a stirring portrait of a media tycoon ruined by his own excesses. After a Hollywood preview, Hearst launched a full-scale campaign against the movie and its director, effectively blocking the film's distribution by threatening lawsuits, running venomous reviews, and yanking advertising.

Even into his eighties, Hearst maintained firm control over his newspapers, regularly sending out memos to editors across the country. His print-media companies were among the first to enter radio and television broadcasting. He also produced movie newsreels and is widely credited with creating the comic strip syndication business. Hearst's King Features Syndicate became the largest distributer of comics and text features in the world. Threatening, inspiring, domineering, William Randolph Hearst was a genius entrepreneur with an appreciation for the value of information that was ahead of his time.

—Adrienne Russell

FURTHER READING:

Hearst, William Randolph Jr., and Jack Casserly. *The Hearsts: Father and Son.* Toronto, Key Porter Book, 1991.

Proctor, Ben. *William Randolph Hearst: The Early Years 1863-1910.* New York, Oxford University Press, 1998.

Swanberg, W. A. *Citizen Hearst.* New York, Scribner, 1961.

Heavy Metal

Heavy metal, a genre of rock music that was hugely popular in the United States and much of the world during the 1980s, not only left an influence on successive trends in rock music, but affected the cultural tastes and style of its many fans. The heavy metal sound was characterized by loud and distorted guitars and vocals; its image by aggressive male posturing and a preoccupation with sexuality, identity, and the corrosion of traditional social institutions. While sometimes causing controversy, even outrage among the establishment for its perceived negative influence on youth, heavy metal expanded the range of recognized images and sounds in rock 'n' roll, developing a formula that combined musical virtuosity with social rebellion. While the groups achieved little Top 40 success even at the height of the genre's popularity, their albums and concerts outsold all their contemporaries, and outlasted them in influence.

Historically, the term ''heavy metal'' refers to radioactive elements or powerful artillery units. While heavy metal music was not directly named to signify either of these traditions, the bands have always welcomed the associated imagery. Rock critics first began applying the label in the late 1960s, referring primarily to the British bands Deep Purple, Led Zeppelin, and Black Sabbath. These three are considered to have laid the framework for the genre. Deep Purple brought classical influences, Led Zeppelin adapted and applied the African-American blues hook, and Black Sabbath lent an air of dark mysticism to their work. Each stressed the importance of distorted guitar sound and long guitar solos.

Axl Rose of the heavy metal band Guns N' Roses.

Heavy metal might never have reached beyond a fanatical cult following if not for a reintroduction of the genre's principles by British and American chart-friendly bands at the beginning of the 1980s. From overseas came Def Leppard, Judas Priest, Iron Maiden, and Ozzy Osbourne (the original vocalist of Black Sabbath). Homegrown American metal of this era included KISS, Van Halen, and Mötley Crüe. This second generation of heavy metal artists was better groomed and less gloomy than their predecessors, and their heavy metal was about lifestyle as well as music. Their songs were played on MTV as often as on the radio and, for the first time, heavy metal records found a market among women and minorities. However, the music never lost its core following of white, teenage suburban males. Record sales remained more stable than any other genre of the 1980s, and bands from the expanding array of heavy metal groups often dominated the top five album spots. Pop and rap acts incorporated guitar solos, a revived blues tradition, and power chords. MTV premiered *Headbanger's Ball* in 1986, and the show quickly became their top-rated offering. Throughout the decade, heavy metal dominated summer tour attractions such as the ''Monsters of Rock'' and ''US Festival.''

With so much commercial success, heavy metal was bound to splinter. Bands who toned down their anger, and the volume on their guitars, came to be referred to as ''glam metal'' or ''pretty metal.'' Groups such as Bon Jovi, Warrant, and Poison sold albums on their hairsprayed, long locks and sexually risque lyrics. Bon Jovi produced the third-best-selling album of the decade in 1986 with *Slippery When Wet*. By contrast, bands like Metallica and Megadeth were intent on preserving a rawer, purer form of heavy metal, and gained the mainstream in the late 1980s. Termed ''speed metal'' or ''thrash'' because of their blistering drum beats, these bands infused an animal, Punk-rock sensibility into heavy metal, playing loud and hard, growling or screaming, and delving into the psychological and pathological. Crunching along amid the mainstream were the gloomy ''dark metal'' bands, a subgenre of throwbacks to the early days—led by Judas Priest and Iron Maiden—who employed visual and lyrical images of fantastic worlds, monsters, and heroes.

The heyday of heavy metal appeared to coincide with a period of cultural mistrust in America. The divorce rate was increasing and an American president had resigned. While disco and lite rock dominated the airwaves, heavy metal, like punk rock, built a following around tearing down discredited social institutions. The thrill of a heavy metal concert or a punk show lies at least partially in the bold flaunting of as many rules of decency as possible. While punk called for a rebellious stance against conformity and a simplicity in its attack on social mores, heavy metal insisted on musicianship and even virtuosity. Guitar heroes of the heavy metal age needed to display stage presence, pure speed, and a thorough knowledge of blues and classical music. Heavy metal publicized their heroes through extravagant concert productions and live videos.

The enormous negative reaction of mainstream America to heavy metal music indicates just how influential it was. Tipper Gore, wife of then-senator Al Gore, formed the Parental Music Resource Center in the early 1980s to examine the effects of modern music lyrics on American youth. The PMRC took Ozzy Osbourne to court for ''Suicide Solution,'' a song they claimed encouraged and glorified suicide (Ozzy maintained that it warns of the dangers of drink). Their next target was Judas Priest—the PMRC claimed that when they played Judas Priest's 1978 album *Stained Class* backwards they found satanic messages on it. Though each case was resolved in the

musicians' favor, critics continued to connect heavy metal to Satanism, violence, and drug use. Black Sabbath's use of symbols such as the inverted cross, and Iron Maiden's album, *Number of the Beast,* seem to invite such attacks. The bands almost always pointed to the ultimately positive message of their work—while, for example, they openly dabbled in the occult, the good guy always won.

The graphic imagery of heavy metal's most lasting offspring, speed metal, horrifies many casual listeners. ''Landmine has taken my head/has taken my arms/has taken my legs . . .'' shouts Metallica in 1998's ''One.'' Again, a closer examination of the song reveals an anti-war theme. Heavy metal artists have never denied that they lead a life laced with sex and drugs—Van Halen's 1978 debut single ''Running With The Devil,'' long considered a prototype of the genre, celebrates a life led with no regard for social convention or restriction. ''We're not like this because we're in a rock band,'' said Van Halen's David Lee Roth in one interview, ''we're in a rock band because we're like this.''

Whether or not one gives any credence to the supposed sociological or psychological messages claimed by its adherents, heavy metal indubitably advanced rock 'n' roll by breaking through visual and lyrical taboos. Though eventually commercially successful in their own right, heavy metal bands climbed to that success through the ranks of the counterculture, and proved that there was much more to the American popular music scene than reaching the Top 40. Its hardcore, purist nature would demand ''authenticity'' from the next generation of musicians. The guitar heroes of heavy metal upped the ante for rock stars of their era by insisting on classical training and technical prowess, while their feral, sexual lead singers reminded fans and singers that the essence of rock 'n' roll lay in excess.

—Colby Vargas

FURTHER READING:

Arnett, Jeffrey Jensen. *Metalheads: Heavy Metal Music and Adolescent Alienation.* Boulder, Colorado, Westview Press, 1996.

Bangs, Lester. ''Heavy Metal.'' *The Rolling Stone Illustrated History of Rock and Roll.* New York, Random House, 1980.

Bashe, Phillip. *Heavy Metal Thunder.* Garden City, New York, Doubleday, 1985.

Walser, Robert. *Running With the Devil: Power, Gender, and Madness in Heavy Metal Music.* Hanover, Wesleyan University Press, 1993.

Hee Haw

This long-running (1969-92) television series kept the comedy-variety genre alive into the 1990s with its mix of down-home humor and musical performances from top country and western acts. *Hee Haw* was one of the first shows to draw a southern rural audience to network television. Sketches set in fictional ''Kornfield Kounty'' affectionately parodied the lives of farmers, moonshiners, and small town dwellers. Hosts Roy Clark and Buck Owens were established country stars who brought musical credibility to the comedic proceedings. The series garnered consistently high ratings, both during its CBS run and as one of the pioneer successes in first-run syndication.

Willard Scott (left) and Roy Clark on the television show *Hee Haw*.

Hee Haw had the longest run of original syndicated episodes of any television series.

This quintessential show of the South was actually the product of three Canadians and a New York City-born Italian-American. In 1967 producer Sam Lovullo (the New Yorker) was working on CBS' *The Jonathan Winters Show* when writers John Aylesworth and Frank Peppiatt were brought on board. *The Jonathan Winters Show* was a comedy-variety series with an audience composed mostly of urban northeasterners. Lovullo noticed that ratings, particularly in the South, rose significantly when the musical guests were country and western stars like Roy Clark and Jimmy Dean. At the same time, CBS was seeing ratings success with rural situation comedies like *The Beverly Hillbillies* and *Green Acres*. A rural variety show seemed a logical move for the network. Aylesworth and Peppiatt created the concept. Their personal manager and fellow Canadian Bernie Brillstein came up with the name *Hee Haw*. When CBS canceled *The Jonathan Winters Show* after the 1968-69 season they sent Lovullo, Aylesworth, and Peppiatt to Nashville, Tennessee, to produce the new show in the country music capital of America.

Hosts Clark and Owens were natural choices. Roy Clark was a virtuoso on guitar and banjo. His amiable comedic personality had been previously showcased on *The Jonathan Winters Show* and *The Beverly Hillbillies*. Buck Owens was one of Nashville's premiere songwriter-performers. At the time of *Hee Haw*'s creation he was hosting a regionally syndicated television variety series and looking for a vehicle with which to reach the national audience. He too had appeared on *The Jonathan Winters Show*. Owens and Clark's wide-ranging abilities helped blend together the series' mix of country music and broad sketches.

The cast included a number of comedians and musicians with a country background and style. Writer-actor Archie Campbell, twins Jim and Jon Hager, Louis "Grandpa" Jones, Lulu Roman, David "Stringbean" Akeman, and former real-life moonshiner Junior Samples were among the original group to populate sketches like "The

General Store" and "The Kornfield." In 1970 the show acquired perhaps its most prized catch: comedienne Minnie Pearl. Her trademark gingham dresses, hat with price tag attached, and gently humorous anecdotes on rural life became staples of the show. In later years, George "Goober" Lindsay (of *The Andy Griffith Show)*, Misty Rowe, actor Slim Pickens, and even Jonathan Winters would spend time in *Hee Haw*'s ensemble.

The show debuted June 15, 1969. It was an instant ratings success. The traditional music and "down-home" humor struck a chord with audiences weary of social unrest and uninterested in seeing television taboos shattered by comedians like the Smothers Brothers. Though originally a summer replacement series, *Hee Haw* was added to CBS' prime time line-up in December 1969. Its impact was already clear. Earlier that year, on the weekend of August 15-17, half a million rock fans, hippies, and war protesters made Woodstock the counterculture event of the twentieth century; the rest of America made *Hee Haw* the number one show of the weekend.

During its run *Hee Haw*'s guest list was a virtual who's who of country music in the 1960s, 1970s, and 1980s. Merle Haggard, George Jones, Tammy Wynette, Ray Charles, Waylon Jennings, Charlie Rich, Ronnie Milsap, Johnny Cash, and Boxcar Willie all graced the *Hee Haw* stage. Singers like Garth Brooks, Randy Travis, and Vince Gill, who would see great success in the country music boom of the 1990s, made some of their first national television appearances on *Hee Haw*. Even non-country performers visited the Korn field: pop vocalists Sammy Davis, Jr. and Phil Harris, baseball legends Mickey Mantle, Johnny Bench, and Roger Marris, and actors Ernest Borgnine, Leslie Nielsen, and John Ritter all made appearances.

CBS canceled *Hee Haw* after the 1971-72 season. The network had tired of its rural image; also axed that year were *The Beverly Hillbillies; Green Acres; Gomer Pyle, USMC;* and *Mayberry RFD*. The producers wasted no time in finding a new home for the show. *Hee Haw* debuted in first-run syndication September 18, 1971. Most markets aired it Saturdays at 7:00 p.m., a time slot ceded to local stations as a result of the Federal Communications Commission's Prime Time Access Rule, which forbade off-network reruns on affiliates from 6:00-8:00 p.m. These stations needed programming, and *Hee Haw* was a pre-packaged, proven hit.

Hee Haw was so popular it spawned a spin-off in the fall of 1978. *Hee Haw Honeys* starred regulars Misty Rowe, Gailard Sartain, Lulu Roman, and Kenny Price, and young actress Kathie Lee Johnson, who would become better known by her married name, Kathie Lee Gifford. Their characters—Misty, Willie Billie, Lulu, Kenny, and Kathie Honey—are a Nashville family who own a country nightclub. Like its parent show *Hee Haw Honeys* featured musical guests and cornpone humor. It failed to match the older show's success, lasting only 26 episodes.

Hee Haw remained relatively unchanged until 1991. Slipping ratings inspired Gaylord Entertainment, the owners of the show, to revamp the format. Much of the cast was replaced. The old "Korn field" set was gone, and a new bright, modern stage appeared. The look was reminiscent of the 1980s pop music series *Solid Gold*. Longtime viewers felt angry and betrayed. Ratings fell precipitously, and the series was canceled. The last original *Hee Haw* aired May 30, 1992.

Though production ended, the series was far from gone. Reruns of the classic episodes began airing on the Nashville Network. *Hee Haw* quickly became one of the cable network's most popular offerings. A live stage version at the Grand Ole Opry in Nashville brought the Korn field briefly back to life. *Hee Haw* is still treasured by fans of traditional country music and down-home, simple good times.

—David Hixson

FURTHER READING:

Beck, Ken. "Hee Haw Is Back—Packaged for the 90s." *The Courier-Journal.* January 9, 1997.

Bessman, Jim. "Hee Haw Returns on TV, Video, and in New Book." *Billboard.* November 23, 1996.

Lovullo, Sam, and Marc Eliot. *Life in the Kornfield: My 25 Years at Hee Haw.* New York, Boulevard Books, 1996.

Moses, Edward. "*Hee Haw* Gives Boot to Hillbilly Look: TV Show Faces 90s, Aging Market; Slow Sales Force Format Updating." *Billboard.* August 31, 1991.

Wohland, Chris. "*Hee Haw* Goes to Town: In Its 24th Season, the Country Variety Show Is Shucking the Cornfield for a New Suburban Image." *The Atlanta Journal & Constitution.* June 5, 1992.

Hefner, Hugh (1926—)

If America experienced a sexual revolution in the latter half of the twentieth century, then one of the first shots surely was fired by Hugh Marston Hefner in 1953, the year that he introduced *Playboy* magazine to the world. The first issue of the magazine featured a centerfold of a nude Marilyn Monroe (who had posed for it years earlier, before attaining the stardom she enjoyed in 1953), and it sold well enough to guarantee that other issues would follow in the months to come.

The "shocking" new magazine was based in Chicago, the city where Hefner, the older of two sons, had grown up in a typical middle-class household. After army service and college, Hefner married and then tried to earn a living as a free-lance cartoonist. In this he was unsuccessful, but he did land a low-level job with *Esquire* magazine, the most prestigious "men's magazine" of the day, which featured articles and photo layouts on elegant clothing, sports cars, and other "male" interests. Nude photos in American periodicals in the early 1950s were limited to a few "nudist" and "art photography" magazines that skirted the edge of the law and were sold "under the counter" at newsstands when they were available at all.

Within a year after *Playboy*'s premiere, Hefner's life had undergone significant changes. He was devoting all of his time to the magazine, except for the attention he gave to the beautiful and sexually available young women who worked for, or posed for, the magazine. The Hefners separated in 1955, with divorce to follow in 1959. Mrs. Hefner retained custody of the couple's two children. As the magazine's circulation continued to grow, Hefner began to adopt the lifestyle epitomized by his publication's title. He *became* a playboy, and he had the business sense to realize that being a public embodiment of what the magazine was all about could attract even more readers. For *Playboy* was, from the beginning, more than just a "skin magazine." There were the nude pictorials, of course—generally three per issue, including the centerfold "Playmate of the Month"; but like *Esquire* before it, *Playboy* featured articles about luxury cars, fine food, wine, stereo equipment—in short, everything the modern "playboy" would want to own. And if, as was likely, the

Hugh Hefner

reader's income was insufficient to support the described lifestyle—well, he could always dream, and *Playboy* would be there to provide the material for his fantasies.

Hefner's playboy image shifted into high gear in 1959 with his purchase of a seventy-room mansion on Chicago's Gold Coast. After extensive remodeling (including installation of a revolving, circular bed, eight feet in diameter, in the master bedroom), the Playboy Mansion was open for business, and its business was pleasure—pleasure for its sole permanent resident and for his many and frequent guests. A brass plate on the mansion's front door had engraved on it the Latin phrase "Si non oscillas, noli tintinnare," which the host loosely translated to mean "If you don't swing, don't ring."

Beginning in 1962, the magazine's articles on the good life began to be accompanied by a dose of philosophy—*Playboy* style. The December issue of that year included the first installment of Hefner's "Playboy Philosophy." There would be twenty-five installments in all (amounting to about 150,000 words) before the series ended in 1966. In these columns, Hefner defended his magazine's content and values, assailed his critics, and espoused positions on social issues—he was in favor of increased sex education, legalized abortion, and freedom of expression; and opposed to censorship, prudery, and archaic sex laws. In addition to decrying the sexual puritanism of American life, Hefner was also an early and vocal advocate of civil rights for minorities. The magazine's editorial content reflected this view, as did Hefner's policy for booking entertainers at the mansion, the chain of Playboy Clubs that began in 1959, and two syndicated television shows (*Playboy's Penthouse,* 1959-61, and *Playboy after Dark,* 1968-70). Hefner brought in black entertainers (such as Sammy Davis Jr., Dick Gregory, and Nancy Wilson) at a time when having ''black'' acts in a predominantly ''white'' venue just was not done.

Hefner's empire went through some tough times in the late 1970s and 1980s. Circulation of the magazine declined, partly due to competition from publications like *Penthouse* and *Hustler,* both of which were often more sexually graphic than Hefner wanted *Playboy* to be. Further, the close relationship existing between the Reagan administration (which came into office in 1981) and fundamentalist Christian groups like the Rev. Jerry Falwell's Moral Majority made for a political climate that was inhospitable to sexual liberationists like Hefner.

Hefner unloaded the Chicago Playboy Mansion in the early 1980s and moved full-time into Playboy Mansion West, an estate he had purchased in Los Angeles. After suffering a mild stroke in 1985, Hefner began turning over day-to-day operation of his empire to his daughter Christie, whom he had brought into the business eight years earlier. In the late 1990s, Christie Hefner worked as chairman and CEO of Playboy Enterprises, Inc., although her father remained listed as editor-in-chief of the magazine.

Hugh Hefner was married a second time in 1989, to former Playmate of the Year Kimberly Conrad. The union produced two children, but the couple separated in January of 1998, allowing Hefner to return once again to his ''playboy'' lifestyle.

—Justin Gustainis

FURTHER READING:

Brady, Frank. *Hefner.* New York, Macmillan, 1974.

Byer, Stephen. *Hefner's Gonna Kill Me When He Reads This.* Chicago, Allen-Bennett Publishers, 1972.

General Publishing Group. *The Playboy Book: Forty Years.* Santa Monica, California, General Publishing Group, 1998.

Hellman, Lillian (1906-1984)

One of the most daring and inventive playwrights of her generation, Lillian Hellman's own life was the stuff of drama. As Carl Rollyson has written, ''The key to Lillian Hellman's character, to what made her a legend in her own time, was her sense of herself as a grande dame.'' Indeed, Hellman is not only remembered for her work—award-winning plays such as *The Children's Hour, The Little Foxes,* and *Watch on the Rhine*—but for her audacious persona. A tough-talking, cigarette-smoking Jewish woman from New Orleans, Lillian Hellman loved attention. She got it through her plays, through her difficult relationship with the brilliant writer Dashiell Hammett, and through her left-wing politics. When called before the House Un-American Activities Committee, Hellman refused to be a friendly witness, uttering her most famous line: ''I cannot and will not cut my conscience to fit this year's fashions.'' In her advancing years, Hellman wrote three extraordinary memoirs, making her very public life even more so. When a story from one of them was made into a major motion picture, *Julia* (1976), starring Jane Fonda and Vanessa Redgrave, Hellman became a heroine to a new generation of women. Lillian Hellman liked money; she also liked fame. She got both, and became, in the process, a one-of-a kind American icon.

—Victoria Price

FURTHER READING:

Hellman, Lillian. *An Unfinished Woman.* Boston, Little, Brown and Company, 1969.

———. *Pentimento: A Book of Portraits.* Boston, Little, Brown and Company, 1973.

———. *Scoundrel Time.* Boston, Little, Brown and Company, 1976.

Rollyson, Carl. *Lillian Hellman: Her Legend and Her Legacy.* New York, St. Martin's Press, 1988.

Wright, William C. *Lillian Hellman: The Image, The Woman.* New York, Simon and Schuster, 1986.

Hello, Dolly!

Hello, Dolly! occupies an enduring place in popular American culture. Not only has it become one of the most popular Broadway musicals since its opening in 1964, but it is a musical adaptation of playwright Thornton Wilder's *The Matchmaker.* The original production furnished Carol Channing with one of her trademark roles as turn-of-the-century New York widowed matchmaker and ''fixer'' for all occasions, Dolly Gallagher Levi. Dolly's second-act entrance at the Harmonia Gardens Restaurant, where she sings the title song as she descends a red-carpeted staircase into the company of her admirers for a show-stopping production number, has become one of the classic scenes of the musical theater.

With music and lyrics by Jerry Herman, book by Michael Stewart, and choreography and direction by Gower Champion, *Hello, Dolly!* played 2,844 performances in its initial New York run. The show won a myriad Tony Awards, including best musical, book, score, actress (Channing), and director-choreographer. Channing's co-stars in the original cast included David Burns, Eileen Brennan, and Charles Nelson Reilly. The 1969 film version, which Herman considers definitive, starred Barbra Streisand and Walter Matthau, was directed by Gene Kelly, and marked the last of the big Hollywood musicals. It is oft-revived all over the world and on Broadway.

—William A. Everett

FURTHER READING:

Hirshberg, Jack. *Hello, Dolly! Journal.* Twentieth Century-Fox Film Corporation, 1969.

Suskin, Steven. *Opening Night on Broadway: A Critical Quotebook of the Golden Era of the Musical Theatre, Oklahoma! (1943) to Fiddler on the Roof (1964).* New York, Schirmer Books, 1990.

Hell's Angels

During the height of their notoriety, the motorcycle gang Hell's Angels made headlines from coast to coast, with stories appearing in the *New York Times, Newsweek, Time, True,* the *Nation,* and a host of other publications. With their death's-head emblem, outré habits, and the mystique of modern-day Quantrill's raiders, the Angels were tantalizing to the press. In fact, their seedy allure was heightened by the press to such a degree that it spawned a national—and then

Barbra Streisand and Louis Armstrong from the film *Hello, Dolly!*

international—fascination with outlaw motorcyclists. From magazines and books, the Angels' story spread inexorably to movie theaters, and biker movies became so popular that they inspired a rash of films based on the Angels' true-life exploits. Predictably, the fictional amplification of their misdeeds bore only a faint resemblance to the real-life models, increasing their fascination, so much so that the Angels now have charters throughout Europe and beyond.

It all started in California after World War II "when most ex-GIs wanted to get back to an orderly pattern: college, marriage, a job, children—all the peaceful extras that come with a sense of security," wrote Hunter S. Thompson, whose book is perhaps the definitive work on the Angels. But not everybody felt that way: "There were thousands of veterans in 1945 who flatly rejected the idea of going back to their prewar pattern. They wanted more action, and one of the ways to look for it was on a big motorcycle." In California, where the weather is clement year-round and a premium is placed on mobility of all kinds, these young men congregated in groups—adopting names like the Booze Fighters or the Market Street Commandos—regularly making runs to resort towns throughout the state—trips that were always tinged by menace. These were the culprits who tore up the agricultural town of Hollister, California, in 1947, the first motorcycle riot, coverage of which inspired producer Stanley Kramer and actor Marlon Brando to make *The Wild One* in 1954.

In Fontana, California, a steel town east of Los Angeles, the original Hell's Angels emerged out of the wreckage of an earlier club, the Booze Fighters. They were blue-collar types, scornful of normalcy, and among motorcycle outlaws, the Angels were soon known as the toughest, most obdurate of the motorcycle outlaws—kings of violence and depravity. For fifteen years the San Bernardino Angels were the de facto leaders, bestowing new charters at their whim. But the Berdoo Angels, as they were called, who had a reputation for inspired depravity, persisted in their folly a might too long. They became the victims of massive police harassment—much deserved no doubt—and soon the chapter had been decimated by an exodus to Oakland, known as the promised land to Angels, and by the early 1960s a large concentration of Angels had gathered in the Bay Area.

For all their colorful ways, it took until the mid-1960s for them to come to the attention of the state law enforcement apparatus. The occasion was a Labor Day Run to Monterey which had resulted in allegations of rape, and although the defendants were eventually acquitted, the state attorney general's office was alarmed enough to launch a six-month investigation. Much of the report was unfounded or so prejudiced as to be beyond credulity, and the Angels might have faded back into obscurity were it not for a sole *New York Times* correspondent in Los Angeles who filed a lurid dispatch. Appearing in the *Times* gave the bikers credibility. *Newsweek* and *Time* weighed

Two members of the Hell's Angels.

in with their own alarums. Other publications followed, and soon the bikers had grown accustomed to the media's presence and were earnestly trying to capitalize on their new-found fame.

The heightened publicity had benefits and drawbacks. The Angels truly enjoyed seeing themselves in print, and their presence acquired a certain amount of hip cachet in bohemian circles throughout the Bay; but police harassment had increased exponentially, and many of the outlaws were summarily dismissed by their employers as a result of the ensuing hysteria. Many of the Angels grew restive over the fact that they had failed to profit from the storm of controversy that had swept over them. And they had become self-conscious. Oakland President Sonny Barger, having grown accustomed to giving well-attended press conferences, took himself seriously enough to attack a peace march in Oakland, the first time the Angels had shown even the faintest interest in politics. The attack and its subsequent notoriety heralded a drop in media interest, but Hollywood was just catching on.

From the philosophical 1969 *Easy Rider* (not so much a biker film as a paean to the myth of the outlaw biker), arguably the best of the lot, to the outlandish *Werewolves on Wheels*, the myth of the nefarious yet noble biker was worked through all its possible permutations to varying degrees of success and/or profit. First of the group was *The Wild Angels* (1966), starring Peter Fonda and Nancy Sinatra. Director Roger Corman, always quickest to the draw, had cobbled together a story from elements of the Lynch Report; and in its story of paying tribute to a fallen comrade (based on the death of a Sacramento Angel that January), *The Wild Angels* came closest to portraying the Angels in their natural state. Yet, the film had an equivocal tone, part denunciation, part hero worship, and it set the standard for the rash of biker films that would follow. *The Born Losers,* released the following year, concentrated on the Angels' reputation for gang rape, and so was a slightly less sympathetic account. After the Angels' participation in the havoc at Altamont, the Angels' screen persona degenerated further. By the early 1970s, the genre was commonly linked with the occult or Satanism.

Since the coverage of the Hollister motorcycle riot in 1947, the relationship between the media and the bikers has always been symbiotic. The Angels' appeal was archetypal—the vanishing outlaw beset on all sides by an increasingly regimented society. It is arguable that had not the national news media, and then Hollywood, exploited the Angels' very existence, they would have remained a local phenomenon. As it was, Hell's Angels clubs sprang up in Great Britain, Germany, the Scandinavian countries, even in the Soviet Union where Angels rode World War II-era army surplus machines when they rode anything. In 1994, the Angels made news when a rival gang blew up the Swedish Hell's Angels clubhouse near Oslo with hand-launched rockets stolen from a Swedish military base. The Hell's Angels phenomenon was truly international in scope.

As for the California Angels, they persisted at the fringes of society, often making headlines for their role in various drug-smuggling conspiracies, but the threat and the allure were gone. They seemed more like picturesque anachronisms than voracious, threatening marauders. As of the late 1990s, there are magazines devoted to outlaw motorcyclists, and an annual run to Sturgis, North Dakota, is a well-organized, fairly tame event, drawing participants from around the world. But still, when a big Harley piloted by an Angel in cutoff jeans jacket and the ubiquitous death's-head patch pulls past on the freeway, the frisson is palpable, and one can imagine the fear and trepidation such a sight would have inspired back in the summer of 1965.

—Michael Baers

FURTHER READING:

Lavingne, Yves. *Hell's Angels: Into the Abyss.* Toronto, Harper, Collins, 1996.

———. *Hell's Angels: Taking Care of Business.* Toronto, Deneau & Wayne, 1987.

———. *Three Can Keep a Secret If Two Are Dead.* Toronto, Harper, Collins, 1990.

McClure, Michael. *Freewheeling Frank, Secretary of the Angels As Told to Michael McClure.* New York, Grove Press, 1967.

Morgan, Raymond C. *The Angels Do Not Forget.* San Diego, Law and Justice Publishers, 1979.

Thompson, Hunter S. *Hell's Angels, A Strange and Terrible Saga.* New York, Ballantine, 1966.

Hemingway, Ernest (1899-1961)

At the height of his popularity, Ernest Hemingway was hailed as the greatest writer of American literature, a hero of several wars, a world-class sportsman in the fields of bullfighting, boxing, hunting, and fishing, and a connoisseur of food, wine, writing, and painting. He was viewed as a colossus who strode all fields of action, excelling in all the manly pursuits. At his worst, Hemingway was derided as a writer who specialized in evasion and repression; an illiterate, inarticulate ox who avoided literary circles to disguise his own limitations; a bully, misogynist, and homophobe with the world's most famous castration anxiety; a self-aggrandizing egotist and poseur who

Ernest Hemingway

shamelessly promoted the legend of his exploits in popular magazines; a belligerent and jealous writer who betrayed and publicly insulted all the authors who helped his career; an overpaid, glorified journalist who sold his talent to feed his ego, ending up as a rich, decadent alcoholic who succumbed to dementia in later years, and who finally took his own life when he realized that he could not write anymore.

Born Ernest Miller Hemingway in Oak Park, Illinois, on July 21, 1899, Hemingway developed his terse style by writing for the *Kansas City Star* in 1917. In 1918 he volunteered as a Red Cross ambulance driver in Italy, where he was badly wounded attempting to save a soldier's life. Hemingway's war experiences and his severe injuries seem to have carved a deep scar in the young man's psyche, and he suffered from insomnia and a fear of sleeping in the dark. All his early writing reveals a preoccupation with violence and wounds, and a terror of death. The honesty with which Hemingway wrote about naked emotions in the 1920s—which contrasts sharply with the bloated legend of himself that he promoted in the 1930s and beyond—was immediately greeted as a major innovation in modern writing. His rapid development and swift rise to acclaim derived from his willingness to learn from older writers: while living in Paris among the expatriates he sought, and followed, the advice of Gertrude Stein, James Joyce, Ezra Pound, Ford Madox Ford, and F. Scott Fitzgerald.

Though most famous for his terse, stark narrative style and realistic dialogue, Hemingway was certainly not the first to write plainly and simply; he did not singlehandedly overthrow the decadent conventions of the Victorian novel. Many predecessors, including Mark Twain, Gertrude Stein, and Sherwood Anderson, had cleared

the prolix path that Hemingway strode more boldly. He did however drive verbal terseness and austerity to its limit, setting an unsurpassable standard, while avoiding Stein's and Anderson's eccentricities. Hemingway's early prose was taut and brittle, achieving its effects through extremely subtle suggestion while refusing to be "literary." He jettisoned the worn accouterments of alliteration, assonance, simile, and metaphor to look directly at life and report only what he saw, unencumbered by literary conventions. This does not mean, however, that Hemingway's fiction was stripped of emotion, as it may seem to a careless reader. Hemingway refrained from describing emotion, avoiding phrases like "he felt," or "he thought," and discarding adverbs and adjectives, but he suggested the characters' emotions by reporting what they saw, noticed, or did. For instance, in the short story "Big Two-Hearted River," Hemingway conveys the anxiety of a veteran, Nick Adams, returning home from the war and trying to repress his painful memories. But the author does this not by telling us that Nick is trying to repress his thoughts, but rather by meticulously reporting Nick's concentration on mundane but consoling activities such as fishing and making lunch. Such indirect and subtle effects were quite powerful when done well, but could result in long passages of pointlessness when done badly, as in some of his later work.

Also notable in his early writing is a willingness to portray what his characters really felt rather than what they were supposed to feel. He did not care to write edifying stories; if his character felt empty and hollow after an event that was supposed to make a respectable man feel sad, the story gained power through its honest realism. The most successful specimens of Hemingway's method were his short stories. His first novel, *The Sun Also Rises* (1926), also managed to sustain the dramatic tension and power of the shorter works. Hemingway made extensive revisions at Fitzgerald's suggestion, and the book revealed remarkable parallels with Fitzgerald's *The Great Gatsby* (1925). But ironically Hemingway soon displaced Fitzgerald as the major new author of the postwar generation. Fitzgerald had been feted as the author of the Jazz Age, and appealed to collegiate readers stateside. Hemingway became known as the author of the "Lost Generation" (though the phrase, made famous by Gertrude Stein, referred cynically to the same generation as Fitzgerald's Jazz Age). Hemingway made a stronger impression among war veterans, and *The Sun Also Rises* became the most significant work of the growing genre of postwar novels about world-weary veterans. The book was amazingly influential: young women began talking like the flippant heroine, Brett Ashley, and young men started acting like Jake Barnes or Hemingway's other male characters, muttering tough-sounding understatements and donning the repressive sackcloth of machismo. Hemingway's portrayal of the wounded, taciturn hero resounded among men who might not ordinarily read "serious literature," and validated an archetype in popular culture which survived for several generations in icons such as John Wayne, Charles Bronson, and Clint Eastwood.

Hemingway's next novel, *A Farewell to Arms* (1929), returned to the theme of the wounded soldier, and the pastoral charms of escape and a "separate peace." It was a bestseller, as all of Hemingway's subsequent books would be, and secured his reputation as a major author. Unfortunately, *A Farewell to Arms* marked the end of Hemingway's rapid development and uncompromised artistic integrity. In 1932, he published *Death in the Afternoon*, a handbook on the art of bullfighting. Treating bullfighting as a tragic ritual, the book provides many insights into Hemingway's views on death, performance, courage, and art—all important themes in his fiction. Although the book has interesting digressions on literature, it also has entire chapters devoted to specific bullfighting techniques or appraisals of long-dead bullfighters which make for very tedious reading.

But the real subject of the book was not bullfighting; it was Hemingway. In *Fame Became of Him,* John Raeburn identifies nine personae that Hemingway projected in *Death in the Afternoon* and in later autobiographical works: world traveler, arbiter of taste, bon vivant, heroic artist, exposer of sham, initiated insider, battle-scarred stoic, sportsman, and manly man. Three of these—arbiter of taste, world traveler, and bon vivant—form a cluster of roles typical of the literary gentleman. Writers can often be counted on to offer tips on wine, dining, arts, and travel. In these roles Hemingway was similar to the effete, foppish dilettantes whom he usually detested, such as Ford Madox Ford or Henry James. To a lesser extent, the roles of heroic artist, exposer of sham, and initiated insider are also common among writers. The heroic artist who suffers for his muse was a familiar pose of the Romantics (particularly Byron), and the exposer of sham has a long pedigree in satirical writing. The battle-scarred stoic had become a common, though resonant, figure in post-war writing. The initiated insider was partly related to the veteran figure, but initiation into a select fraternity of like-minded fellows became quintessentially Hemingway. He pretended to follow a code of conduct which was all the more dignified for being unspoken, above defense, and inscrutable to outsiders.

But the uniqueness and popularity of Hemingway's public personality lay in joining these highbrow roles with those of sportsman and manly man. Readers knew of his interest in fishing, hunting, and bullfighting from his early fiction, where these sports were embraced as pastoral pleasures of escape for the physically or mentally wounded, solitary pastimes for taciturn men. But when described as Hemingway's own hobbies in his non-fiction, they lost the therapeutic element—presumably because Hemingway was loath to admit any psychological wounds—and became games of competition, obligatory tasks of masculinity, demonstrations of "cojones," or balls. Indeed, Hemingway seemed to devote the rest of his life from the 1930s onward to proving his cojones, perhaps embarrassed by theories that Jake Barnes, the protagonist of *The Sun Also Rises* whose penis was shot off in the war, was an autobiographical character. In later works Hemingway seemed to dissociate himself from such vulnerable characters, and also alienated himself from writers—an unmanly lot—by quarreling with, defaming, and even threatening almost every major writer of his generation. He derided homosexuals in *Death in the Afternoon,* dismissing the artistry of Gertrude Stein, Oscar Wilde, Andre Gide, Walt Whitman, and Francisco Goya on the theory that they were inherently flawed and therefore disqualified as artists.

Such masculine posturing proved enormously popular, and soon after *Death in the Afternoon* Hemingway began a series of essays for the newly founded men's magazine, *Esquire,* which was marketed toward a sophisticated, though not intellectual, audience. He wrote 36 *Esquire* essays on topics such as fishing, hunting, and wine. He even wrote beer ads disguised as essays. Whereas *Death in the Afternoon* had a professed artistic impetus in Hemingway's desire to view death in order to write "truly" about the experience, the *Esquire* articles lacked any artistic purpose and were pointedly non-literary. Hemingway was beginning to fashion a new character, whose name was Ernest Hemingway. He continued this farce in another book of nonfiction, *Green Hills of Africa* (1935). A personal account of Hemingway's safari adventure, *Green Hills of Africa* reads more like a novel than *Death in the Afternoon,* sporting vivid descriptions of action and dialogue. But Hemingway's style of writing "truly" faltered the

more he wrote about himself: the book simply promoted the virile Hemingway legend without revealing anything intimate about the author. The *Esquire* experience and his swelling fame distorted his self-awareness and blurred his ability to distinguish fact and fiction. His self-aggrandizing grew more frequent as the burgeoning medium of photojournalism got bigger and flashier. Hemingway's striking demeanor and handsome, husky appearance made him a favorite of glossy magazines such as *Life* and *Look,* which wedded big colorful photos to the trenchant aphorisms Hemingway was happy to provide.

Another product of Hemingway's African adventure was the short story, "The Snows of Kilimanjaro," which told of a writer who, dying of gangrene while hunting in Africa, realizes too late that he has squandered his talent. The protagonist laments "poor Scott Fitzgerald" as a writer ruined by his fascination with the rich. Hemingway thus deflected suspicion that the ruined writer of the story might represent himself by this slanderous jab at Fitzgerald. Whether or not he needed this decoy to write with his old frankness, he wrought a rich and complex story. However, most critics recognized that the declining writer was Hemingway himself, and soon it would be obvious to everyone.

When Hemingway finally returned to novel writing in 1937 with *To Have and Have Not* he was a very different writer from the artistic innovator of the 1920s. Whereas his earlier fiction masterfully portrayed vulnerable characters through extremely subtle prose which seemed to mirror the repressed nature of the character himself, in *To Have and Have Not* repression triumphs over revelation. Masking his own vulnerabilities, Hemingway also masked those of his characters, stripping them of human interest. His latest protagonist, Harry Morgan, a tough-talking weapons smuggler in trouble with the mafia and the government, betrayed no weakness and awoke no pathos. After losing his arm in an accident, he stoically responds, "[If] you lose an arm, you lose an arm." The novel was barely distinguishable from pulp fiction. Hemingway's half-hearted attempts at political significance made the work more embarrassing than redeeming. During the Depression, critics of the New Left favored novels of social relevance, like those of John Steinbeck or Sinclair Lewis. Many writers of the 1920s, such as Fitzgerald and Thornton Wilder, had fallen out of critical favor for their indifference to politics. Hemingway, who seemed to appeal to the common man because of his simple prose and simple pleasures, was urged by some critics to write more socially relevant stories. He capitulated with *To Have and Have Not,* and found favor with the more naive members of the Left, but most critics recognized the novel as politically simplistic. Although the novel was a bestseller, and Hemingway was more popular than ever, his critical reputation sunk to its lowest.

Whereas William Faulkner had spent the 1930s producing one masterpiece after another in the most astonishing series of achievements in American literature since Henry James, Hemingway had churned out a preponderance of facile nonfiction, mostly in slick popular magazines. Always jealously competitive, Hemingway responded to the challenge of Faulkner's achievement and set out to regain the championship he had held in the 1920s. The result was *For Whom the Bell Tolls* (1940), his longest and most ambitious work. The novel seems to have been intended as his masterpiece, embracing a wider range of themes than any of his previous novels. However, Hemingway's carefully crafted style was ill-suited for such a broad canvas, and the novel's sheer bulk diluted the potency of his prose. The novel was almost as politically simplistic as *To Have and Have Not.* Although Hemingway strove to weave grand themes of nature, technology, and the unity of mankind, his truer, deeper preoccupations were still with the solitary man proving his mettle and facing death alone. The hero, Robert Jordan, was cut from the same cloth as earlier Hemingway heroes, solitary, glum, absinthe-drinking men. Robert Jordan was a professor of Spanish, but the intellectual side of the character was sketchy, unconvincing, and incongruent with his more familiar Hemingwayesque traits. The intended effect of the novel was unachieved. Hemingway failed to unify his themes and symbols, all the more ironic since the unity of mankind was the overarching theme. Nevertheless, the novel was extraordinarily successful, selling 360,000 copies and generating a movie.

Hemingway continued to make money by writing for *Collier's* magazine as a war correspondent in Europe during World War II. The 1940s were highly profitable for Hemingway, and brought him fame as a war hero (although the extent of his military participation is disputed). He did not return to novel writing until 1950. At the pinnacle of fame and arrogance, Hemingway consented to an interview with Lilian Ross, in which he boasted about his forthcoming work and his enduring position as "champ" in American fiction. This memorable character sketch, entitled "How Do You Like It, Now, Gentlemen?," was very different from the usual adulating articles honoring Hemingway as a champion sportsman and manly man. Although affectionate, the sketch revealed Hemingway's eccentricities and egotism. He called himself Papa, posing as the wise, grizzled old man of American letters. He claimed that he had once lived with a bear in Montana, where they drank and slept together. But what proved to be most embarrassing to Hemingway was his boast that his forthcoming novel would be his best ever. When *Across the River and into the Trees* appeared four months later, it was almost unanimously regarded as the worst novel of his career. It was an abysmal work, so poorly written that it seemed a parody of his own style, riddled with his pet words "good," "true," "well," and so on. Though not without redeeming qualities, it is best enjoyed as a parody of the famous Hemingway style from the master's own pen.

The contrast between Hemingway's published boastfulness and the critics' sudden disfavor became even more painful when Faulkner won the Nobel Prize that same year. Five years earlier Faulkner had been a well-kept secret, and Hemingway (in his role as initiated insider and arbiter of taste) had been able to confide to Jean-Paul Sartre and others that Faulkner was a better writer than himself. Once Faulkner won the Nobel Prize, and myriad belated accolades tumbled his way, Hemingway could no longer regard himself as the champ of American letters, as he had boasted in the Ross interview, and he turned on Faulkner, declaring that no one ever wrote a decent novel after winning the Nobel Prize. Meanwhile, Hemingway labored over a long autobiographical novel, *Islands in the Stream*. The novel was disjointed, tedious, and uninspired. Aging, alcoholic, and unhealthy, Hemingway seemed to be losing his talent. However, he salvaged the last part of the novel and published it as an independent work in *Life* in 1952 as *The Old Man and the Sea*. A painfully poignant tale of an aged fisherman who catches the biggest marlin of his life and loses it to sharks, the story was told in a beautifully simple, chaste style that surpassed anything Hemingway had written since the 1920s. Struggling with artistic and physical decline, Hemingway had made one final effort to write truly, and succeeded by reaching inside himself to wrench out the painful theme of failure. "Man was not made for defeat. A man can be destroyed but not defeated." The *Life* issue sold five million copies, and the story was instantly hailed as a masterpiece. In 1954, Hemingway won the Nobel Prize, largely on the achievement of *The Old Man and the Sea*.

Throughout the 1950s Hemingway worked on a novel, *The Garden of Eden*, but remained unhappy with it and withheld publication. He also discovered a cache of memoirs he had begun in the 1920s, and proceeded to revise and expand them into a book called *A Moveable Feast*. The rediscovered writings reminded Hemingway of his youth, when he was establishing his reputation as a bold new artist of uncompromising integrity, and made it painfully clear that the aging writer had squandered his talent for the gratifications of fame. Although he had accused Fitzgerald and Faulkner of ruining their talent on stories for the *Saturday Evening Post* and movies for Hollywood, Hemingway had compromised his talent even more grotesquely by creating an absurd fabrication of himself. His public persona was his own worst character and had infected most of the characters he had created since the 1920s. Realizing that he could no longer write, nor maintain his own egotistical standards, Hemingway shot himself on July 2, 1961.

The adulation continued years after his death, and posthumous novels, stories, and nonfiction continued to appear well into the 1990s. But biographies also appeared, and emerging evidence gradually revealed Hemingway to be a despicable man motivated by egotism, jealousy, and a sexual insecurity that led him to ridicule others and prove his own manhood ad absurdum. Such macho posturing already seemed out of place in the 1960s, and utterly ridiculous by the 1990s, though academic interest in Hemingway continued to thrive under deconstructive and feminist approaches to literature. By the turn of the century it seemed unlikely that Hemingway would ever regain the swollen stature of his middle period. However, his influence over American literature is immense and ubiquitous. As one of the major prose stylists of the English language, he has bred more imitators than any other American writer. But few authors were able to attain the suggestive power and subtlety of Hemingway's finest work. Faulkner captured it in his stark, brittle potboiler, *Sanctuary*, and Fitzgerald employed a certain Hemingwayesque subtlety amid the softly echoing motifs of *Tender Is the Night*. But more often one found mere verbal imitation by inferior authors such as Erskine Caldwell, who simply borrowed the outward trappings of conscientious monosyllables and tough dialogue for their otherwise conventional narrative and perfunctory symbolism. Hemingway's best fiction set a standard that few could attain, not even the later Hemingway.

—Douglas Cooke

FURTHER READING:

Baker, Carlos. *Ernest Hemingway: A Life Story*. New York, Scribner's, 1969.

Burgess, Anthony. *Ernest Hemingway and His World*. New York, Scribner's, 1978.

Larson, Kelli A. *Ernest Hemingway: A Reference Guide, 1974-1989*. Boston, G. K. Hall, 1990.

Raeburn, John. *Fame Became of Him: Hemingway as Public Writer*. Bloomington, Indiana University Press, 1984.

Wagner-Martin, Linda. *Ernest Hemingway: A Reference Guide*. Boston, G. K. Hall, 1977.

Weeks, Robert P., editor. *Hemingway: A Collection of Critical Essays*. Englewood Cliffs, Prentice Hall, 1962.

Hemlines

Hemlines have been equated with both fashion and culture, defining particular decades, generations, economies, media, and gendered ideologies, thereby working as imagistic markers within systems of popular culture. Couture culture's system of design traditionally has fed the contents of fashion magazines with fantasy imagery fabricating a "look," color, or hemline for readers. Such is the case with Christian Dior's New Look of 1947, the essential feature of which was the full skirt fish-tailing from cinched waist to mid-calf. This shape and length were adapted for department-store and catalogue sales and for home-sewing patterns, thus becoming part of popular fashion.

Hollywood's studio system of the 1930s and 1940s established a primary place for designers, whose costumes glamorized the female star, made her a screen icon, and typified the genre character she played, especially in melodrama and film noir. Two films released in 1957, *Designing Woman* (Minnelli) and *Funny Face* (Donen), parodied the arbitrariness of the fashion system and its fixation on the viewable woman.

Television sitcoms of the 1950s and 1960s conventionalized the look of the well turned-out wife and mom, dressing her in the essential style and hemline seen in the costuming of Gracie Allen (*The George Burns and Gracie Allen Show*), Lucille Ball (*I Love Lucy*), Harriet Nelson (*The Adventures of Ozzie and Harriet*), and June Cleaver (*Leave It to Beaver*). Weekly, these original sitcom women performed their domestic roles wearing variations of the New Look's vertical line, most commonly the shirtmaker dress of trim bodice and sleeves, tailored collar, buttoned front, and mid-calf skirt flaring out from a defined waist. The full skirt was often underpinned by a crinoline. But, whether flaring or straight, their dresses often were accessorized by that symbol of the proper woman, a neat strand of cultured pearls. The middlebrow American homemaker represented in these sitcoms was a picture of postwar comfort, consumerism, and suburbia. She was also a trickster who juggled her husband's money to maintain her image by shopping for fashionable clothes.

British designer Mary Quant's radical miniskirt of the 1960s, emerging out of a "swinging" London of Carnaby Street and boutique-store culture, countered the Americanized femininity of Lucy and her sitcom generation.

Boutique culture's eclecticism prevailed into the 1970s, displacing the long-or-short hemline dilemma with fashionable options, notably the "maxi," which fell to the ankle or below. Mid-calf lengths, given the term "midi," were reincarnated in looser styles and fabrics. By the 1980s, the long-or-short hemline dilemma had become passe, though still part of fashion rhetoric in style magazines and department store flyers promoting "seasons," "the new" or "the latest" in ready-to-wear labels and commercial brands.

Asymmetrical hemlines in variation (a short front with dipping back, or a side-to-side diagonal) signalled the compromise of designers in the 1980s and early 1990s. Similarly, the flash effect of vertical off-side slits, found on every skirt length from maxi to mini, made one leg visible and emphasized the thigh. Manufactured in office wear as well as evening garb, this style allowed for greater mobility but also a loss of skirt-control when the wearer sat down. The ladylike posture of crossed legs became an instinctive defence against exposure. The vertical side-slit was less about utility than about projecting a feminine essence—reminiscent of the New Look, if more sexualized.

In the late 1990s the hemline debate has been given timely twists and fell victim to self-conscious parody in the popular television series *Ally McBeal*. Ally's short skirts (the micro-mini in tailored form) are a feminine tool to test, sometimes to arrest, the sexist patriarchal structures of the legal system and courtroom. Anne Hollander argues in *Sex and Suits,* ". . . the first [1960s] function of small, short modern skirts was to put women's clothed bodies into a complete physical correspondence with men's . . . visual assumption of public equality for men and women." Ally McBeal's ultra short skirts bring forward this struggle for the contemporary young woman within American culture who presumably strives to be taken seriously as a professional and to be desirable to men. Ally's short hemlines and sputtering naive persona externalize the cultural tentativeness that followed a long line of fashionable sitcom figures, from Lucy and Gracie as maneuvering wives in the 1950s to Mary Tyler Moore's single woman negotiating with male newsroom colleagues and boyfriends in the 1970s.

Ally McBeal's character is popular culture's good girl reincarnated, whose short skirts do not render her sexually secure or successful. At the same time, Ally's quirkiness exudes what the cool if neurotic bad girl of 1950s "B" movies had to suppress. The "bad but beautiful" movie genre persona of actress Ida Lupino in *Women's Prison* (Seiler, 1950) is embodied by her simple, sophisticated costuming. In her pencil-slim, mid-calf dark skirt and crisp white blouses, Lupino's mean prison warden metes out a professional woman's control. Unable to handle power, in this tale of morality she is not only asexual but must die. It is the decent women prisoners, garbed in striped shirtmaker dresses, midi-length, who are domesticated and make sacrifices in order to survive. In the moment of her destruction, the warden's clean blouse and midi skirt give way to a straightjacket, her cold femininity and existence erased.

American film, television, and magazines can be charted historically through fashion and hemlines for shifts and slippage in the popular imagery and ideologies of femininity. One slippage is the persistence of retro hemlines and looks. In late 1998 *Vogue Patterns,* a magazine for home sewers, launched a Vintage Vogue Collection of their patterns from the late 1930s to mid-1940s, a service said by the editor to be based on contemporary readers' "wishes" and "needs." Pleated, straight, and A-line skirts all fall below the knee or to mid-calf in these designs, perhaps a conservative reordering in the face of Ally McBeal's minis and the trendy knit maxi skirt of the 1990s.

—Joan Nicks

FURTHER READING:

Breward, Christopher. *The Culture of Fashion.* Manchester University Press, 1995.

Gaines, Jane, and Charlotte Herzog, editors. *Fabrications: Costume and the Female Body.* New York, Routledge, 1990.

Hollander, Anne. *Sex and Suits.* New York, Alfred A. Knopf, 1994.

Henderson, Fletcher (1898-1952)

As a bandleader, composer, and arranger, Fletcher Henderson was one of the definers and shapers of jazz music in the swing era of the 1940s and 1950s. After graduating from Atlanta University with majors in chemistry and math, Henderson moved to New York in

1920 for post-graduate study. There he accepted a part-time job as a pianist with W. C. Handy, and his career goals changed. In 1923 he assembled a band widely recognized as the first large jazz orchestra, one that included such celebrated sidemen as Louis Armstrong, Coleman Hawkins, and Benny Carter. His most lasting work came in the swing era as an arranger for the Dorsey brothers and Benny Goodman. His style of big band jazz featured the reeds pitted against the brass section as well as highly rhythmic passages of ensemble chords by the entire band. Typical Henderson arrangements can be heard on recordings of ''King Porter Stomp'' and ''Sometimes I'm Happy'' by the Goodman band.

—Benjamin Griffith

FURTHER READING:

Atkins, Ronald, editor. *All That Jazz.* New York, Carlton, 1996.

Collier, James Lincoln. *Benny Goodman and the Swing Era.* New York, Oxford, 1989.

Simon, George T. *The Big Bands.* New York, MacMillan, 1974.

Hendrix, Jimi (1942-1970)

Jimi Hendrix was the quintessential 1960s rock star. A black superstar in what was by then predominantly a white industry and an American who first found success in Great Britain, Hendrix embodied many of the contradictions of the late 1960s music scene. As a guitar player, he single-handedly redefined the genre's most important instrument and remains widely considered the best ever to have played it. As a performer, he combined showmanship and musicianship in equal parts, and played the best remembered sets of the two best remembered music festivals of the period. His death at age 27 from an overdose of drugs (albeit prescription) completed the picture of what became a cultural archetype of the late twentieth century: that of the enormously talented, misunderstood rock star whose meteoric rise to fame is matched by a tragic fall and early death.

Johnny Allen Hendrix was born in Seattle on November 7, 1942, to 17-year-old Lucille Hendrix while his father, Al, was in the army. His early childhood was one of nonstop confusion, as he lodged with a variety of family members in houses and hotels as far away as Texas, California, and Vancouver. In 1946 Al changed his son's name to James Marshall. Lucille died in 1958 when Jimmy was 15, the same year he got his first guitar. He began playing in the high school band until he dropped out in 1960. Arrested for riding in a stolen car, Hendrix received a suspended sentence by promising to sign up with the military. He became a parachutist in the 101st Airborne in 1961. He soon tired of the military life, though, and was discharged after breaking his ankle in 1962. At this point he became a professional musician, setting up his own group in Nashville with army buddy Billy Cox, and backing up a variety of rhythm-and-blues artists who came through town. In the spring of 1963, Hendrix left Nashville as part of "Gorgeous" George Odell's band.

For the next three years, Hendrix backed up many of the biggest names in R & B—the Isley Brothers, Little Richard, Ike and Tina Turner, King Curtis, Sam and Dave—though he made no significant recordings. Anxious to make his own music, he settled in New York City in 1965 and by early 1966 was focusing his efforts on his own band, Jimmy James and the Blue Flames. They performed in the

Jimi Hendrix

Greenwich Village folk-rock club Café Wha? for a pittance in front of a scant audience, but his astonishing command of blues, soul and rock guitar styles greatly impressed fellow musicians like Mike Bloomfield, John Hammond Jr., and a small group of cognoscenti. In September of 1966, Animals bassist Chas. Chandler, who was looking to make his mark as a manager and producer, signed Hendrix and took him to England.

London was in the midst of a blues craze, led by John Mayall, the Rolling Stones, and Eric Clapton. It was immediately apparent that Hendrix was head and shoulders above the top local guitarists: Clapton, Jeff Beck, and Pete Townshend all made a point of seeing Hendrix wherever he was playing, before he had a recording contract or even a band. After sitting in at London's hippest clubs, Hendrix formed the Jimi Hendrix Experience with two young white Englishmen, bassist Noel Redding and drummer Mitch Mitchell. At Chandler's insistence, the group's first single was a cover, "Hey Joe," but the gifted guitarist soon demonstrated his skill as a composer and came up with the next single, "Purple Haze"—probably his best known composition. Though there is no evidence that Hendrix had taken LSD at that point, his generous use of guitar effects—unusual intervals like flatted fifths and sharp ninths, and bizarre lyrical themes—perfectly suited him to lead the psychedelic movement which was starting to sweep through rock 'n' roll.

Released in the spring of 1967, the first Experience album, *Are You Experienced?* was a tour de force, replete with complex guitar sounds that had never been heard before. By then, following the Beatles' lead, every British band that counted was scrambling to pile up as many weird sounds and special effects as they could, but none had Hendrix's touch for making consistent musical sense with them. Like Stevie Wonder a few years later, Hendrix humanized electronic effects, using the rapidly advancing technology of the late 1960s to communicate timeless emotions. And when it suited the material, he could create perfectly beautiful music without any effects at all (as in "The Wind Cries Mary," the third Experience single). The album also contained his first protest song, "I Don't Live Today," which he often dedicated in concert "to the American Indian." And he wasn't above exploiting the stereotype of the macho black male, as in "Fire."

The U.S. release of the album was supplemented with the "A" sides of the first three singles; two blues numbers were excised, helping create the myth of Hendrix as an ahistorical, purely intuitive talent. A highly anticipated performance at the Monterey Pop Festival in June 1967 marked the Experience's American debut, complete with guitar-burning theatrics, and cemented Hendrix's reputation as an international star, though his wild appearance and demeanor tended to be promoted at the expense of his musicianship. A second album, *Axis: Bold As Love*, followed close behind the first; it contained his most-covered composition, "Little Wing," the individualist anthem "If 6 Was 9," and an experimental tape collage, "EXP," plus innovative use of effects like wah-wah and phasing.

By the end of 1967 Hendrix's relationship with Chas. Chandler had deteriorated, and he took over the production reins himself for his next album, *Electric Ladyland*, at the same time keeping to a heavy touring schedule. Released as a double LP in October 1968, the set's sprawl offended some critics, and the UK cover, featuring photos of 21 nude women, caused some controversy, but it went to the top of the charts (the only No.1 album Hendrix ever had in the United States) thanks to hard rock classics including "Voodoo Chile (Slight Return)" and the Bob Dylan cover "All Along the Watchtower." Despite their commercial success the Experience was having problems. Hendrix was arrested in Sweden in January 1968 after smashing up his hotel room, a lawsuit by unscrupulous producer Ed Chalpin was holding up the band's royalties, and Noel Redding was more interested in his side project, Fat Mattress. The Experience broke up in June 1969 after abortive attempts at a fourth album, and Hendrix went into seclusion in upstate New York while he tried to figure out his next move.

Even without a steady band, Hendrix's mystique was enough to earn him headliner status at the Woodstock Music and Arts Festival. Unfortunately, being the final act at a chaotic three-day show meant that he and his barely rehearsed rag-tag group finally went on stage at eight o'clock on Monday morning when most of the crowd had already left. If not for the sound and film crews on hand, Hendrix's performance might have gone virtually unnoticed. As it was, his ear-splitting rendition of "The Star Spangled Banner" became the symbol of the peace-and-love counterculture celebration. Offstage, however, Hendrix was overwhelmed by problems. He was busted for bringing drugs into Canada; his Band of Gypsys group with Buddy Miles and Billy Cox fell apart shortly after forming; nearly every dollar he made touring was sunk into the building of his own state-of-the-art recording studio, Electric Lady Studios. Several more attempts at recording went sour, even though a new band stabilized around Cox and Mitchell, and it wasn't until mid-1970, after the studio was completed, that Hendrix was able to make a serious push to finish a new

album, tentatively titled *First Rays of the New Rising Sun*. Recording was complicated by a judgment awarding Ed Chalpin rights to one album's worth of Hendrix material. The award was based on a 1965 contract Hendrix had signed with Chalpin that Chandler had inadvertently failed to buy out—not a bad return on a one dollar investment—and several songs intended for *First Rays* wound up on a hastily assembled live recording, *Band of Gypsys*, released in April 1970. Though seriously flawed, the album did include "Machine Gun," an anti-war number with a lengthy, breathtaking guitar solo. *Band of Gypsys* was the last album Hendrix would live to see released.

In August 1970, Hendrix reluctantly left New York, where the new album was nearing completion, for a European tour. He played in front of his largest audience yet at the Isle of Wight Festival, but the tour fell apart a few days later after a bad LSD trip sent Cox into paranoid delusions. On September 18, after spending several days visiting friends, Hendrix took several prescription sleeping pills belonging to girlfriend Monica Dannemann, fell asleep and never woke up—he choked to death in the ambulance en route to the hospital. Though Rolling Stone Brian Jones had died prematurely in 1969, Hendrix was the first well-known rock star to die of a drug overdose. What seemed a tragic isolated accident at the time soon became just another cliché surrounding the fast-paced rock 'n' roll lifestyle: Janis Joplin died of a heroin overdose two weeks later, and Jim Morrison followed in less than a year, giving anti-hippie pundits plenty of ammunition to attack rock music as hedonistic and self-destructive.

But Jimi Hendrix's three complete albums (dozens more, mostly of abominable quality, followed after his death) and countless live appearances had changed popular music more than any superficial moralizing could undo. Beyond his direct imitators—Stevie Ray Vaughan, Ernie Isley, Robin Trower, Funkadelic's Eddie Hazel and Mike Hampton—Hendrix's influence extended directly and indirectly to all pre-punk guitar players; Led Zeppelin and a horde of hard rock and heavy metal bands made their careers exploring areas Hendrix had opened up. In rock 'n' roll, almost any black man with a guitar was compared with Jimi Hendrix, including musicians as dissimilar as Vernon Reid and Prince; while Chuck Berry and Little Richard are remembered as musical founders but not as continuing sources of inspiration. Criticism is necessarily reductive: a white rock band will often be compared to the Beatles, the Stones or the Velvet Underground; a white male solo artist to Bob Dylan, Jim Morrison or Bruce Springsteen; a female singer to Janis Joplin or Joni Mitchell. But for black men in rock, Jimi Hendrix is the only archetype available.

—David B. Wilson

FURTHER READING:

Henderson, David. *'Scuse Me While I Kiss The Sky: The Life of Jimi Hendrix*. New York, Doubleday, 1978.

Shapiro, Harry, and Caesar Glebbeek. *Jimi Hendrix Electric Gypsy*. New York, St. Martin's Press, 1991.

Henry Aldrich

The quintessential teenager of the 1940s, Henry Alrich was born on the Broadway stage in 1937. He reached his widest audience through radio, a string of "B" movies, and a television series. Henry Aldrich, who was likable, clean-cut, and monumentally prone to mishap, influenced a whole generation of teen characters on the radio, in movies, and even in comic books.

While college youths had become popular culture stereotypes in the 1920s, high school kids didn't really get that much notice until a decade later. Swing music and the jitterbug craze helped put them on the map. Writer Clifford Goldsmith introduced Henry Aldrich in his play *What A Life!* According to radio historian John Dunning, Goldsmith "was virtually penniless and making his living on the high school lecture circuit when he wrote the play." In 1938, the then immensely popular crooner Rudy Vallee invited Goldsmith to write some skits about the Aldrich Family for his weekly radio variety show. Next came a similar invitation from Kate Smith's variety show, and by the autumn of 1939 *The Aldrich Family* was a regular weekly radio program, sponsored by Jell-O on NBC.

The family lived in a typical small town and consisted of Henry, his parents, and his older sister Mary. His high school pal Homer was underfoot virtually all of the time. The opening of the show became one of the best known, and most quoted, in radio. Henry's long-suffering mom would call him—"Henry, Henry Aldrich!"—and he'd reply, in his harried adolescent croak, "Coming, Mother!" Ezra Stone, who had created the role on the stage, was the first radio Henry, with Jackie Kelk as Homer. House Jameson, who also played the radio detective known as the Crime Doctor, was the head of the household.

The show, though it touched on real family situations, was played for rather broad comedy. Preoccupied with girls, cars, and school, Henry saw no reason why he shouldn't have all the rights and perks of the adult he felt he'd be any day now. His anxious and elaborate schemes and his frequent dreams of glory led him into all sorts of unforeseen complications. His parents, of course, rarely understood him, and often acted as though he might have contracted some rare disease that caused him to run amok on occasion, or behaved as if he might even be an alien invader masquerading as their son.

Paramount Pictures turned Goldsmith's play into a movie in 1939, casting Jackie Cooper as Henry. The script was by Charles Brackett and writer-director Billy Wilder, whose several brilliant creations included the same year's *Ninotchka* for Garbo. Cooper appeared in the second film in the series in 1941, with Eddie Bracken as his sidekick, and then turned the role over to Jimmy Lydon. Less handsome and gawkier than Cooper, Lydon made nine Henry Aldrich films. John Litel, who'd also been girl detective Nancy Drew's screen father, was Sam Aldrich, and Olive Blakeney was Henry's mom. She later became Lydon's off-screen mother-in-law.

Henry and his kin were early arrivals on television, with *The Aldrich Family* premiering on NBC on October 2, 1949. An actor named Robert Casey was the first of five juveniles who took turns enacting the role of Henry Aldrich. Jackie Kelk moved from radio to TV to play Homer, and House Jameson returned to repeat Sam Aldrich. Three actresses portrayed Mrs. Aldrich: Lois Wilson (1949, 1951), Nancy Carroll (1950-51), and Barbara Robbins (1952-53). Jean Muir, a movie actress in the 1930s and 1940s, had been scheduled to take over the part in 1950, but because of her liberal sympathies she found herself listed in *Red Channels,* the right-wing publication dedicated to rooting out alleged Communist sympathizers from the entertainment business. Muir was blacklisted by the sponsor and the network and never got the chance to say, "Henry, Henry Aldrich!"

The Aldrich Family remained on radio and television until 1953, when Henry stepped aside to make way for a new breed of teenage stereotypes.

—Ron Goulart

FURTHER READING:

Dunning, John. *Tune In Yesterday.* Englewood Cliffs, Prentice-Hall, 1976.

Eames, John Douglas. *The Paramount Story.* New York, Crown Publishers, 1985.

Halliwell, Leslie. *Halliwell's Film Guide.* New York, Charles Scribner's Sons, 1987.

Henson, Jim (1936-1990)

Puppeteer and filmmaker/director Jim Henson was the genius behind the world famous puppet creations known as Muppets. By the end of the twentieth century, Henson's name was synonymous with modern puppetry, children's television programming, and family based entertainment. With his talented team of artists, he revolutionized the ancient art of puppetry by fusing it with twentieth century technology—first through his television shows *Sesame Street* (1969) and *The Muppet Show* (1976), then through films and computer animation. Yet Henson was not famous solely for his technical innovations. His work expressed a strong moral vision—humorous, uplifting, full of tolerance, and love—that viewed all individuals as worthy of respect. It was this vision, expressed through his life-like puppets, that transcended lines of age and culture (Henson's work has been seen in 120 countries), and brought Jim Henson praise as his century's greatest entertainer-educator.

—Brian Granger

FURTHER READING:

Finch, Christopher. *Jim Henson: The Works.* New York, Random House, 1993.

———. *Of Muppets and Men: The Making of the Muppet Show.* New York, Muppet Press/Alfred A. Knopf, 1981.

Henson, Jim

See also Muppets, The

Hep Cats

An important term in the history of African American slang, a "hep cat" was a jazz aficionado in the marijuana-using urban subculture of the 1940s and 1950s. A hep cat's essential qualities included a free-spirited rejection of societal convention, intense creativity, and an unflagging rejection of all things "square." First entering the language in the late 1930s, the term was an amalgam of "hep," an older term meaning "smart" or "aware," and "cat," slang for "man." Its roots stretch back to the Wolof language of Africa where "hepi" meant "to see," and "hipi" meant "to open one's eyes," while "hipicat" translated as "wise" or "informed." As hep cat was appropriated by white beatniks in the 1950s, African Americans turned to using fresher terminology like "hip" and "hipster." Continuing to evolve with stylistic changes in American musical and drug-related subcultures, its roots survive in terms like hippie and hip-hop.

—Steve Burnett

FURTHER READING:

Jonnes, Jill. *Hep-Cats, Narcs, and Pipe Dreams: A History of America's Romance with Illegal Drugs.* New York, Scribner, 1996.

Major, Clarence, editor. *Juba to Jive: A Dictionary of African-American Slang.* New York, Penguin, 1994.

Thorne, Tony. *The Dictionary of Contemporary Slang.* New York, Pantheon, 1990.

Hepburn, Audrey (1929-1993)

From her first starring role as a princess in *Roman Holiday* (1953), Audrey Hepburn, the daughter of an Anglo-Irish banker and a Dutch aristocrat, was lauded for bringing a stately "European" elegance to Hollywood. Her director in 1954's *Sabrina*, Billy Wilder, declared: "After so many drive-in waitresses in movies, here is class." Hepburn's androgynous looks and waifish physique—photographer Cecil Beaton called her "the gamine, the urchin, the lost Barnardo boy"—challenged and redefined the dominant popular image of femininity in the fifties, the curvaceous, all-American bombshell typified by Marilyn Monroe. Hepburn often played royalty (*Roman Holiday; War and Peace,* 1956) or a poor, modest girl who achieves a fairy-tale rise to high society (*Sabrina; Funny Face,* 1957; *My Fair Lady,* 1964). Though cast somewhat against type as a scandalous socialite in *Breakfast at Tiffany's* (1961), Hepburn's Holly Golightly, as Robyn Karney observes, "passed into the iconography of the 1960s."

—Martyn Bone

FURTHER READING:

Karney, Robyn. *A Star Danced: The Life of Audrey Hepburn.* London, Bloomsbury, 1993.

Hepburn, Katharine (1909—)

Always a role model for female independence, self-determination, and integrity, actress Katharine Hepburn is thought by many to be one of the most monumental and enduring of all of Hollywood's stars. At the end of the twentieth century, Hepburn holds the record for Oscar wins (four) and nominations (twelve).

Hepburn spent her early years in Hartford, Connecticut, where her parents were liberal intellectuals who did not raise their children along traditional sex roles, but encouraged them to excel at all their endeavors and expand their boundaries. Her father was a successful physician and her mother an active suffragette, which gave Hepburn an expanded view of woman's role from an early age.

Audrey Hepburn

Hepburn was drawn to acting early and participated in local productions before going to Bryn Mawr and appearing in college theatricals. She graduated in 1928 and made her Broadway debut in *The Warrior's Husband* (1932) for which she garnered critical praise. She was then approached by Hollywood, but thinking Hollywood was not "legitimate," she demanded an extremely high salary, which, to her amazement, RKO accepted. Hepburn made her screen debut in 1932 in *Bill of Divorcement* starring John Barrymore, which was both a critical and box-office success. Upon her arrival in Hollywood Hepburn refused to conform to the standard starlet mold. She preferred to wear slacks to revealing dresses, avoided publicity, and closely guarded her private life. She shunned the party crowd of Hollywood and demanded to be dealt with respectfully.

She won her first Oscar for her third film, *Morning Glory* (1933), in which she played the aspiring actress/understudy who, after many manipulations, becomes an overnight success when the veteran actress has a breakdown that necessitates the understudy taking her place. The same year she appeared as Jo in *Little Women,* a role that she found personally rewarding. One of her next projects was the screwball comedy *Bringing Up Baby* (1938), which ranks as one of the best examples of the genre. Hepburn portrayed the madcap heiress

Susan Vance, who falls in love with an absentminded paleontologist (Cary Grant) and enlists his aid in caring for a tame leopard named Baby to keep him from marrying his staid assistant. Later that same year Hepburn appeared in *Holiday,* again with Grant.

For some reason, film exhibitors branded her "box office poison" despite her many successes, and Hepburn left Hollywood for Broadway, where she appeared in *The Philadelphia Story,* forgoing a salary in favor of a percentage of the profits and screen rights. It was a huge hit and enabled Hepburn to return to Hollywood with the upper hand. She sold the screen rights to MGM but maintained creative control, which allowed her to choose the director and her costars (Cary Grant and James Stewart). The film broke attendance records and won Hepburn the New York Film Critics Award as well as her third Oscar nomination.

Her next film, *Woman of the Year* (1942), paired her for the first time with Spencer Tracy and began a twenty-five-year-long relationship that ended only with Tracy's death. On-screen they were a remarkable team that made eight more films together: *Keeper of the Flame* (1942), *Without Love* (1945), *The Sea of Grass* (1947), *State of the Union* (1948), *Adam's Rib* (1949), *Pat and Mike* (1952), *Desk Set* (1957), and their final film, *Guess Who's Coming to Dinner?* (1967). Offscreen they remained devoted to one another and were seldom seen apart. Hepburn did appear in several films without Tracy during this period. In *African Queen* (1952) she portrayed an uptight spinster who falls in love with Humphrey Bogart's reprobate supply-boat "captain." She also appeared in *Summertime* (1955); *The Rainmaker* (1956); *Suddenly, Last Summer* (1959); and *Long Day's Journey into Night* (1962).

She retired from the screen for several years as Tracy became more ill but both returned in 1967 to appear in their last picture together, *Guess Who's Coming to Dinner?,* for which she won her second Oscar. She won her third Oscar for *The Lion in Winter* (1968) in which she portrayed Eleanor of Aquitaine, and her fourth for *On Golden Pond* (1981), for which she also won the British Academy Award.

While her work on television has not been as extensive, her performances have been of consistent quality. She received Emmy nominations for her performances in *The Glass Menagerie* (1973) and *The Corn Is Green* (1979), and won an Emmy for her portrayal of an elderly woman who finds *Love among the Ruins* (1975). She has also starred in several television movies including *Mrs. Delafield Wants to Marry* (1986), *Laura Lansing Slept Here* (1988), *The Man Upstairs* (1992), and *This Can't Be Love* (1994).

—Denise Lowe

FURTHER READING:

Felder, Deborah G. *The 100 Most Influential Women of All Time.* New York, Citadel Press, 1996.

Hepburn, Katharine. *Me.* New York, Alfred A. Knopf, 1991.

Martin, Jean, ed. *Who's Who of Women in the Twentieth Century.* New York, Crescent Books, 1995.

McHenry, Robert, ed. *Famous American Women.* New York, Dover Publications, 1980.

Herbert, Frank (1920-1986)

Science fiction writer Frank Herbert is ranked among such well-respected authors of imaginary worlds as J. R. R. Tolkien, C. S. Lewis, and Isaac Asimov. Though he wrote more than twenty novels and several short stories, his fame is linked to his "Dune Chronicles." His first book in the series, *Dune* (1965), won the first-ever Nebula award and shared a Hugo award for best novel. Although initially rejected by twenty publishers, the book became the best-selling science fiction book in history, with more than twelve million copies sold. By the end of the twentieth century the book had not yet gone out of print. Intended as the beginning of a trilogy, *Dune* instead spawned five sequels, with a sixth left unfinished at the time of Herbert's death in 1986. *Dune* was made into a major motion picture in 1984. The series, set on the planet of Arrakis, or Dune, follows the history of the Atreides family over thousands of years. The "Dune" saga is considered one of the greatest science fiction stories ever written.

Born in Tacoma, Washington, in 1920, Frank Patrick Herbert possessed a wide-ranging mind. He attended the University of Washington for a year in 1946 before becoming a reporter. He worked as a reporter and editor of west coast newspapers, including the *Glendale Star* (California), the *Oregon Statesman,* the *Seattle Star,* and the *San Francisco Examiner,* between 1939 and 1969, and later an educational writer for the *Seattle Post-Intelligencer* from 1969 to 1972. With the success of *Dune* in 1965, however, Herbert was able devote his attention to his novel writing. But he did continue to lecture and act as a social and ecological consultant.

A strong believer in self-reliance and ecological harmony, Herbert generated his own energy on his small farm with solar heating, methane gas from chicken dung, and wind power (from an

Katharine Hepburn

improved windmill design for which he was awarded a U.S. patent). Herbert wove many of his ecological ideas into all his novels. Throughout his work Herbert provides his readers with complex adventure plots and probing questions about the cosmos, human nature, and society.

Dune is a work of extraordinary complexity, telling the story of the desert planet Arrakis and its inhabitants. Set 25 centuries in the future, the novel introduces a universe that is controlled by two opposing political powers, the Imperium and the Great Houses. The interstellar civilization is a precarious balance between the political, military, and economic forces of the largest powers as well as the disruptive smaller independent organizations, including the Spacing Guild (which has a monopoly on interplanetary travel), the Bene Gesserit order, the massive CHOAM trading company, and the Bene Tleilax. The story is a remarkable metaphor of late twentieth-century American society with the blending and balancing of political, economic forces with religious, cultural, and business interests—and of course the ever present, but largely ignored, ecological phenomena. *Dune* successfully created the most complete and detailed imaginary world ever before written.

The success of *Dune* was a turning point in science fiction publishing. The book's popularity broadened the audience of science fiction. It also "paved the way for large advances, bigger printings, best-seller status, and heavy subsidiary sales for many other writers," according to Willis E. McNelly. The ecological thinking examined in *Dune* made it a college campus cult classic, in fashion with J. R. R. Tolkien's *Lord of the Rings* or the original *Star Trek* series. The attention directed toward *Dune* in the 1970s and 1980s was in many ways the predecessor of the type of fandom that sprang up around *The X-Files* in the 1990s. Many young people strived to become more ecologically minded, patterning themselves after Herbert's character Liet Kynes, the planetary ecologist, who was aware of and concerned with the consequences of human actions on the environment. The novel also attracted those interested in the effects of drugs on behavior. The book discussed a substance called spice, which increased awareness and cerebral functions and allowed Mentats (human computers) to pursue their vocation in a world that has banned thinking machines. Users of controlled substances claimed many of the same effects as those discussed in *Dune*. Although illegal, hallucinogens called "smart drugs" were used in areas of California to aid complex problem solving and another street drug, named "ecstasy," reportedly improved sexual awareness and pleasure.

Despite the intense interest in turning *Dune* into a movie, a script written by David Lynch, and a 40- to 50-million dollar budget, the resultant film flopped in 1984. But the disappointing film did not damage the cult-like interest in Herbert's original material. By the late 1990s, New Amsterdam Entertainment (NAE) announced that, in cooperation with ABC and The Sci-Fi Channel, it would produce a six-hour miniseries adaptation of *Dune* (although the future of this series is uncertain).

Herbert's "Dune Chronicles" inspired several popular musicians. Iron Maiden, a heavy metal band, performed what they called a Dune song, "To Tame a Land," on their 1983 *Piece of Mind* album. The Blind Guardian released a Dune inspired song, "Traveler in Time," from *Tales From the Twilight World* in 1991. A German techno band called itself Dune. The band's electronic instrumentals were popular in American techno dance clubs in the mid-1990s where the oft repeated refrain of "the spice must flow" could be heard.

Some of the jargon found in *Dune* has infiltrated popular speech. Many analogies have been made between the *Dune* storyline, with its

obsession over the spice melange, and the Middle Eastern oil reserves and their influence on the global economy. "The spice must flow," a quote from a third grade guild navigator, is referred to quite often in its modern version "the oil must flow." In addition, statements such as "long live the fighters," "the gom jabbar," and "fear is the mind killer" are as ingrained in popular jargon as "may the force be with you" from *Star Wars* and "Grokking" and "Sharing Water" from *Stranger in a Strange Land* by Robert Heinlein.

The Dune story has been adapted into several games. In 1979, Avalon Hill created a board game called "Dune the Board Game" based on the novel. Five years later, Parker Brothers developed a board game titled "Dune," which was based on the movie. Computer versions of the Dune saga soon appeared on the market. In 1992, the first computer Dune game combined both strategy and adventure. A sequel, titled "Dune II: The Builders of Dynasty," followed in 1993. An improvement over the first, Dune II became an even bigger hit. It was awarded the 1993 Strategy Game of the Year Award. The continuing success of Dune II led to the introduction of "Dune 2000," released in 1998. "Dune 2000" is a real-time strategy game that can be played singly on CD-rom, over the Internet, or over local area networks. The game is focused on military strategy and political intrigue with Fremen warriors battling legions of Sardaukar and House Harkonnen plotting against House Atreides while the Emperor, the Guild Navigators, and the Bene Gesserit reek havoc where they can. Five Ring Publishing produced "Dune: The Eye of the Storm," a customizable card game, which was very popular in the 1990s. Though the games follow much of the Dune saga, none have incorporated any serious consideration of ecology, which was one of Herbert's central ideas in the series.

Herbert had considered *Dune* a "training manual for consciousness." Others agreed and the Dune Chronicles have been used in architecture, literature, and philosophy, among other courses at universities across the country. Herbert attributed the popularity of *Dune* in college classrooms to the genre of science fiction, which he noted "lends itself to that because we're dealing with ideas a great deal of the time." Indeed, Herbert's greatest contribution lies in his imaginative ideas.

—Craig T. Cobane

FURTHER READING:

DiTommaso, Lorenzo. "History and Historical Effects in Frank Herbert's *Dune.*" *Science-Fiction Studies.* Vol. 19, No. 3, 1992, 311-325.

Ellis, R. J. "Frank Herbert's *Dune* and the Discourse of Apocalyptic Ecologism in the United States." In *Science Fiction Roots and Branches: Contemporary Critical Approaches.* Edited by Rhys Garnett and R. J. Ellis. New York, St. Martin's, 1990.

Levack, Daniel J. H., and Mark Willard. *Dune Master: A Frank Herbert Bibliography.* Westport, Connecticut, Meckler, 1988.

Liddell, Elisabeth, and Michael Liddell. "*Dune*: A Tale of Two Texts." In *Cinema and Fiction: New Modes of Adapting 1950-90,* edited by John Orr and Colin Nicholson. Edinburgh, Edinburgh University Press, 1992.

McNelly, Willis E. *The Dune Encyclopedia.* New York, Putnam, 1984.

Miller, David M. *Frank Herbert.* San Bernardine, California, The Borgo Press, 1980.

Minowitz, Peter. "Prince versus Prophet: Machiavellianism in Frank Herbert's *Dune* Epic." In *Political Science Fiction,* edited by Donald M. Hassler and Clyde Wilcox. Columbia, University of South Carolina Press, 1997.

O'Reilly, Timothy. *Frank Herbert.* New York, Frederick Ungar Publishing, 1981.

Touponce, William. *Frank Herbert.* Boston, Twayne Publishers, 1988.

Hercules: The Legendary Journeys

Initially starting out in 1993 as a made-for-TV movie, *Hercules: The Legendary Journeys* became a syndicated television series in the 1995-96 television season. Starring Kevin Sorbo as the half-god Hercules, the series combined action, special effects, and camp to create one of the most popular syndicated shows of the 1990s, rivaling the *Star Trek* franchise and *Baywatch* for ratings. In fact, the show spawned a number of spin-offs and imitators.

The show's executive producers, Sam Raimi (the writer and director of cult favorite movie *The Evil Dead*) and Ron Tapert, combined unlikely elements to make the show a success. The show deviated from previous incarnations of the Greek hero played by such musclemen as Steve Reeves and Lou Ferrigno. Sorbo, while lean and muscular, was not just a muscle bound hero. Though he usually beat up villains and groups of bad guys in highly choreographed and often farcical fights, he was chiefly portrayed as a hero with heart. The show's title narration told the story: It was a time when the gods were cruel and played with mortals. Hercules, the son of Zeus and the mortal Alcmene, stood up for the common man against his family, the gods.

But just portraying Hercules as champion of the people didn't account for the show's popularity. Many reviewers gave credit to the fact that the show used pop culture references and a healthy dose of camp to entertain a broad spectrum of the television audience. For instance, the show didn't care about historical or mythological accuracy. It went instead for hipness and, at times, silliness. In one episode titled "Porkules," Hercules was transformed into a super-strong pig. Ares, the god of war, was always dressed in leather as was the goddess Discord. Their choice of attire was the source of many double entendres about their possibly kinky preferences. Apollo, the sun god, was portrayed as riding a type of golden snowboard and talking like a late-twentieth-century adolescent.

The show offered plenty of action. Almost every episode featured Hercules and Iolaus, or one of the other heroes, battling a group of armed men. These scenes feature Hercules and his cohorts butting

Kevin Sorbo in a scene from the television series *Hercules: The Legendary Journeys*.

heads, throwing men through the air, doing flips, and throwing old fashioned punches. While violent, most shows had no deaths. Occasionally though, a battle scene was just that, a battle with fatalities. Hercules also faced off against special effects monsters, such as Echidna.

The show also displayed wit and imagination. The producers did a post-modern episode that featured the cast looking for Kevin Sorbo, the actor. Another episode was a retelling of the movie *Some Like It Hot.* The producers and writers of the show weren't afraid to take chances.

Besides Hercules, the show had a cast of regular characters. Hercules's constant sidekick throughout the first five seasons was Iolaus, played by Michael Hurt. Ares, played by Kevin Smith; Autolycus, the King of Thieves, played by Bruce Campbell; and Salmoneus, played by Robert Trebor, were also regulars. On some occasions, the show never even featured Hercules but focused on the supporting characters.

One of the characters to appear on the series was Xena, Warrior Princess. Xena's character was spun off into its own series, and actually became more popular than *Hercules.* The two shared supporting casts and occasionally crossed over from one show to the other. The characters were also the co-stars of an animated movie. A second spin-off of the show was *Young Hercules,* a show broadcast on Saturday mornings on the Fox network. The show featured the adventures of the juvenile Hercules and Iolaus.

After *Hercules* scored big in the ratings, other companies brought out mythic figures to try to cash in on the show's success. However, such shows as *Sinbad* and *Tarzan* didn't have the popular appeal of *Hercules.* Besides television, Hercules and Xena found a large home on the Internet with many fan pages devoted to both shows. Computer games and multi-player on-line games featured the characters as well.

—P. Andrew Miller

FURTHER READING:

Freeman, Michael. "Mything in Action." *MEDIAWEEK.* April 29, 1996.

Gliatto, Tom, and Kirsten Warner. "Sorbo the Greek: As TV's New Hercules, Minnesota's Kevin Sorbo Gives the Mythic Muscleman a Sensitive Spin." *People Weekly.* July 3, 1995.

Herman, Woody (1913-1987)

Along with Benny Goodman and Artie Shaw, Woody Herman was one of a triumvirate of clarinet-playing band leaders in the big band era. Playing a high-pitched instrument that could cut through the sound of the ensemble in those days of poor amplification, Herman for more than fifty years headed one of the most popular and innovative of the bands in the swing era. His greatest contributions to jazz history came from his ability to organize and sustain a talented big band that was wholly dedicated to the cutting edge of jazz during the severe economic trials of the Great Depression. His band, Herman's Herd, spawned a number of great jazz soloists as well as writers and arrangers of major importance.

Born Woodrow Charles Thomas Herrmann of German parents in Milwaukee in 1913, Herman seemed destined for the spotlight from the age of nine. He toured the state of Wisconsin for eight weeks as one of a troupe of actors who played a live prologue to the

Woody Herman

screening of silent films. That same year Herman began studying the alto sax and clarinet. His teacher, Herman recalled, was Art Beuch, "an old German fellow who would take nothing but hard work." His advice to the budding jazzman was: "Practice until you turn blue and your lip is numb and your teeth hurt and you may accomplish something."

When Herman began playing in local dance bands in high school, he became dedicated to the life of a jazzman. He left home at seventeen with a band led by Tom Gerun, playing in a reed section that included Tony Martin, who later gained fame as a singer and film star. After unsuccessfully trying to form his own band, Herman joined the Isham Jones orchestra in 1934 and was featured on tenor sax, clarinet, and vocals on the band's Decca records. When the band folded two years later, the 23-year-old persuaded key sidemen to join a band he was organizing on his own. In that year—the depth of the Great Depression—Herman ran his band on a cooperative, share-the-profit basis. Featuring the blues as well as some pop songs in their repertoire, the band slowly gained fame, soon to be enhanced in 1939 by their biggest hit, the upbeat blues piece "Woodchopper's Ball," which ultimately was to reach the five million mark in sales.

Still overshadowed by the Basie, Ellington, and Goodman bands, Woody Herman's Herd had begun to attract national attention. Dave Dexter, writing in *Downbeat* in January 1940, suggested that a part of the band's problem in finding major bookings was the delay caused by the band members (as shareholders) voting on each booking proposition.

In 1941 the band filmed a musical short for Warner Brothers in Brooklyn, and later that year they went to Los Angeles to be featured in a Universal picture called *What's Cookin'?*. The Andrews Sisters and Donald O'Connor also appeared in this "typical wartime musical," as Herman called it.

When the band began a new recording contract with Columbia in 1945, it was coming under the strong influence of the new bebop style of jazz played by Charlie Parker and Dizzy Gillespie. Joining the band at this time were three devout boppers: Neal Hefti, Shorty Rogers, and Pete Candoli, and Herman's First Herd was soon widely known as one of the most advanced and innovative bands of its era. Davey Tough, the perfect drummer for the new Herd, received belated acclaim when he raised the band to new heights in 1944-45 on a series of nationwide radio programs. His unique style can be heard on such Columbia record hits as "Apple Honey," "Laura," and "I Wonder."

In 1946 the great Russian composer Igor Stravinsky composed *Ebony Concerto* expressly for the Herman band, adding to the band's prestige after a sold-out performance in Carnegie Hall. That year the band won the *Downbeat, Metronome, Billboard,* and *Esquire* polls. Gunther Schuller, in his book *The Swing Era,* attributed this great success to the highly original arrangements by Ralph Burns and Neal Hefti and to the band's playing "night after night with an infectious exuberance, an almost physically palpable excitement and a never-say-die energy."

In 1986, still active at age 73 after fifty years as bandleader, Herman led his band on a jazz cruise aboard the *SS Norway*, and after spending time in the hospital with heart problems, led the Herd in November at the Kennedy Center awards ceremony in Washington. He died in October of the following year.

—Benjamin Griffith

FURTHER READING:

Lees, Gene. *Leader of the Band: The Life of Woody Herman.* New York, Oxford Press, 1995.

Schuller, Gunther. *The Swing Era.* New York, Oxford Press, 1989.

Simon, George T. *The Big Bands.* New York, MacMillan, 1974.

Troup, Stewart, and Woody Herman. *The Woodchopper's Ball.* New York, Dutton, 1989.

Voce, Steve. *Woody Herman.* London, Apollo Press, 1986.

Herpes

The Herpes simplex virus I (oral) and II (genital) are persistent, embarrassing, and often devastating sexually transmitted diseases. Symptoms can include small painful blisters or lesions around the lips, nose, mouth (cold sores), or genitals; fever; headaches; swollen lymph glands; and feelings of isolation and depression. Herpes spreads through direct contact with infected areas, and is only detectable with a blood test as the virus can remain dormant indefinitely. After an initial outbreak, herpes can disappear for months, only to recur during periods of stress or a weakened immune system. Between 50 and 80 per cent of the American adult population is infected with a form of herpes, yet only one third of these carriers ever experience symptoms. There is no known cure for herpes, but it is not life threatening, and advances in treatment have made living with herpes more manageable and less stigmatizing.

—Tony Brewer

FURTHER READING:

Ebel, Charles. *Managing Herpes: How to Live and Love with a Chronic STD.* North Carolina, American Social Health Association, 1998.

Hersey, John (1914-1993)

Born in China to missionaries, John Hersey began his journalism career as a correspondent for *Time* and went on to cover cover World War II for that magazine and *Life.* He had already won a Pulitzer Prize for a World War II novel he had written—*A Bell for Adano* (1944)—when in 1946 *The New Yorker* published in a single issue his most famous and enduring work, titled simply *Hiroshima.* The 31,147 word nonfiction story described the experiences of six survivors of the atomic bombing by the United States of the Japanese city. The bomb killed 78,150 people, injured 37,425, and left 13,983 missing. Forty years after *Hiroshima* appeared, Hersey updated the story with an epilogue telling how the lives of the six survivors had progressed. Overall, he published 25 books during his career.

—R. Thomas Berner

FURTHER READING:

Hersey, John. *Hiroshima.* New York, Random House, 1989.

Sanders, David. *John Hersey Revisited.* Boston, Twayne Publishers, 1991.

Hess, Joan (1949—)

Joan Hess has infused her mystery writing with her knowledge of her home state of Arkansas and its regional culture. She has two important mystery series—the first features Claire Malloy, a book store proprietor who is the widow of an English professor, and the second is set in Maggody and features Arly Hanks, who returns to Maggody after an unsuccessful marriage, as its central character. Both series are set in Arkansas and are marked by a kind of off-center humor that enlivens the action and rounds out the characters. Among the books in the two series are *Strangler Prose, The Murder at the Mimosa Inn, Dear Miss Demeanor, A Diet to Die For, A Holly Jolly Murder* (all Claire Malloy), *Malice in Maggody, Mischief in Maggody, Maggody in Manhattan, O Little Town of Maggody,* and *The Maggody Militia* (all Arly Hanks). In addition, Hess has another series featuring Theo Bloomer, written under the name Joan Hadley. Hess has won the American Mystery Award, among others, and is president of the American Crime Writers League.

—Frank A. Salamone, Ph.D.

Heston, Charlton (1924—)

"'Hard' is what I do best," Charlton Heston once told a photographer. "I don't do 'nice.'" Strange words, perhaps, coming from an actor who has specialized in playing symbols of rectitude such as Moses, Judah Ben-Hur, and even Jehovah Himself. Yet this steely-eyed, jut-jawed performer has excelled at infusing his heroic portrayals with an almost fearsome iconic power. He has brought a comparable flintiness to his civic life as a firearms activist and itinerant right-wing gadfly.

A speech and drama graduate of Northwestern University, Heston was a stolid if unspectacular presence in Westerns and war pictures of the 1950s. He made his big (Red Sea) splash playing Moses in the 1956 epic *The Ten Commandments*. That Biblical classic started him on a long string of historical parts, including the title roles in *Ben-Hur* (1959), for which he earned a Best Actor Oscar, and *El Cid* (1961). He also played a muscular Michelangelo in *The Agony and the Ecstasy* (1965).

In 1968, Heston made *Planet of the Apes*, a film *Entertainment Weekly* called "the *Citizen Kane* of guilty pleasures." As George Taylor, an astronaut stranded on a world ruled by simians, Heston chews the scenery with the voracity of a starving dog attacking a T-bone steak. Glowering, grimacing, and barking at his ape captors through clenched teeth, Heston is the apotheosis of Nixonian macho. "Damn you! God damn you all to hell!" he rails into the empty sky at the film's climax—and we feel like lining up obediently to face the brimstone.

Planet of the Apes proved a career turning point for Heston—the precise moment he made the transformation from respected leading man to endearing camp figure. He solidified that newfound status with two early 1970s science-fiction films, *The Omega Man* in 1971 and *Soylent Green* two years later. Both pictures traded on his macho man persona, affording him copious amounts of screen time with his shirt off and an automatic weapon in his hand. The reactionary subtext was unmistakable. In the first film, he fights off an army of hippie zombies; in the second he vainly tries to save the planet from government-sponsored euthanasia (those damned liberals!). In both movies he ends up prostrate ("Soylent Green is PEE-pullll!!!"), sacrificing his own life for humanity, in a crucifixion pose. Perhaps Heston wished to end his career by playing every possible permutation of the godhead.

There were other prominent roles for Heston in the 1970s. He did a string of disaster movies, most notably *Earthquake* (1974), but turned down the lead in *Jaws* when he had tired of them. After growing too old to carry a picture by himself, he settled comfortably into character actor status. He was used, effectively, by Kenneth Branagh as the Player King in the British auteur's 1997 production of *Hamlet*.

For the most part, however, Heston concentrated on political endeavors. He spoke out often and endlessly on right-wing causes, from family values to "white pride." "I'm pissed off when Indians say they're Native Americans," he railed to *Time* in 1998. "*I'm* a Native American, for Chrissakes!" Especially dear to Heston's heart was the right to gun ownership. In 1997, "Moses," as his critics invariably derided him, was elected first vice president of the National Rifle Association (NRA). The next year the actor ascended to the presidency itself, ousting a candidate who was deemed "too conservative" by the NRA rank and file. While liberals may have shuddered at the thought of Charlton Heston being considered a moderate alternative, the actor continued to provide them with red meat for their fundraising letters. In speeches, he publicly called for the return of a society where one could "love without being kinky . . . be white without feeling guilty" and other back-to-the-future nostrums.

—Robert E. Schnakenberg

FURTHER READING:

Heston, Charlton. *In the Arena*. New York, Simon & Schuster, 1995.

Mulrine, Anna. "Moses Fights for Gun Rights." *U.S. News & World Report*. May 19, 1997.

Schilling, Mary-Kaye. "Charlton Heston: Treasured Chest." *Entertainment Weekly*. September 5, 1997.

Higginson, Major Henry Lee (1834-1919)

A Boston Brahmin who had been a major in the Civil War, Higginson was the sole founder of the Boston Symphony Orchestra in 1881. He set the example for other businessmen to establish a tradition of noblesse oblige in the performing arts that in Europe had initially been the province of landed aristocracy.

Higginson approached the task with a unique blend of "boosterism," sound business principles, and overtones of evangelical Christianity and patriotism. He would not tolerate any deviance from the high musical and operational standards he set by the professionals he engaged. Higginson believed firmly that men who had survived the Civil War (he himself had been wounded) had a moral obligation to make America a better country, which meant creating better cultural institutions. It also meant a willingness for an aristocracy—in America it would be comprised of businessmen—to step forward and take responsibility for those developments.

—Milton Goldin

FURTHER READING:

Goldin, Milton. *The Music Merchants*. New York, Macmillan, 1969.

Johnson, H. Earle. *Symphony Hall, Boston*. Boston, Little, Brown, 1950.

High Noon

Director Fred Zinnemann's film *High Noon* was made during the McCarthy era. Consequently, it has been invested with political significance way beyond the striking simplicity of its plot. The allegorical claims that are made for it originated with its screenwriter Carl Foreman, a victim of the McCarthy witchhunt in Hollywood, who professed to see his script as an allegory of his own situation. Fred Zinnemann denied this interpretation, considering it the story of a man driven to act in accordance with his own conscience, while conceding that the town in which the action takes place is "a symbol of democracy gone soft." The nature of the film's message continues to challenge the film scholars, historians and critics who examine and analyze it, but in the annals of popular culture it remains a classic Western, one of the best of all time. To legions of ordinary moviegoers, *High Noon* conjures the lasting image of Gary Cooper's weary and reluctant hero, the young Grace Kelly's ice-maiden beauty, Dmitri Tompkin's haunting theme song, "Do Not Forsake Me, O My Darling," and Floyd Crosby's atmospheric black and white photography.

Carl Foreman based his screenplay on "The Tin Star," a two-page magazine story. Played out in "real time"—the 90 minutes in which the incidents take place correspond to the 90-minute running-time of the film—denoted by Zinnemann's artful use of a clock as a

Gary Cooper as Sheriff Will Kane in the film *High Noon*.

marker that contributes to the tension, the story begins 10:40 a.m. on a Sunday morning in the fictional frontier town of Hadleyville. Sheriff Will Kane (Gary Cooper), is at his own wedding reception, prior to retiring and leaving town to start life afresh with his young quaker bride, Amy (Grace Kelly). During the festivities, however, Kane is warned that Frank Miller (Ian MacDonald), a murderer whom he had helped to convict, has been released from the penitentiary. Miller is heading for Hadleyville to exact revenge by killing Kane and will arrive on the 12:00 noon train. Three of Miller's old cohorts are already waiting at the otherwise deserted train depot to escort him into town for the fatal shoot-out.

Amy implores her new husband to leave town immediately but, determined to face out Miller and rid the town of the killer's malign influence, he ignores her pleadings, and those of others, including Helen Ramirez (Katy Jurado), his former lover, who urges him to take his new bride and escape to safety. For an hour, between 10:45 a.m. and 11:45 a.m., Kane attempts to drum up support from among the townspeople, but nobody is willing to stand by him. A number of people begin to throw their belongings into wagons, preparing to leave town temporarily before the trouble starts at noon; even Kane's deputy, resentful at having been passed over for the job in favor of a

stranger, deserts him. Amy, too, prepares to leave—on the same train that is bringing Miller to town—and, while waiting at the hotel, learns from the clerk that many inhabitants of Hadleyville would like to see Miller kill her husband because they want a return to the kind of town where saloons and gambling are allowed to flourish.

The noon train arrives on time. Frightened and alone, but wedded irrevocably to his own moral code, Kane makes out his will and prepares to face the gunmen, who ride into town. He ambushes one, and kills a second in a shoot-out. Hearing the gunfire, Amy rushes to her husband's aid, shoots another of Miller's henchmen in the back, but is seized by Miller himself as a hostage. During the struggle that ensues in her trying to free herself, Kane is able to shoot Miller dead. He throws his badge in the dust and rides out of the deserted town with his wife.

When *High Noon* was released it was not an immediate hit. In the strained climate of the times, that gesture of Kane's—throwing away his badge—was interpreted by some as an insult to Federal authority and led to accusations of subversion. As Zinnemann interpreted it, Kane's action was simply intended as "a gesture of contempt for a craven community." The film captured the public imagination only gradually, but its excellence was recognized in the winning of four Academy Awards (music score, title song, editing, and best actor) and three nominations (picture, screenplay, and director), and over the years it came to gross several million dollars of profit.

While widely viewed as a "classic" Western, several commentators consider *High Noon* a realist Western, providing a documentary depiction of a place and its people that was undoubtedly representative of a hundred towns across the frontier during the 1870s. It can also be read as a commentary on the genre itself, one that observes the classical unities of time and action. Some have even credited the film with inaugurating a new subgenre, the "adult western," in its mature treatment of its otherwise familiar "good vs. evil" theme. What cannot be denied, however, is that *High Noon* changed the Western genre by both streamlining and rethinking it as both an extension and a commentary upon the classic tradition.

As opposed to the ultimate redemption of townspeople in such later films as *The Magnificent Seven,* the citizens of Hadleyville are craven to the end. This is, of course, in direct opposition to the mythology of the West, in which the venality of the common man is redeemed by a folk hero whose bravery in the face of overwhelming odds inspires them to rise above themselves for the common good. On the other hand, the contradictory currents running through the town (development vs. frontier lawlessness) and the ambivalence of the citizens who, each for their own reasons, refuse to side with Kane can be taken to represent the currents of the American political climate in the 1950s. This interpretation is underpinned by the deliberate vagueness of the town's location and the film's exact historical time period. Thus, on an allegorical level, Hadleyville could be any town at any point in history, where the common man falls prey to cowardice and fear, and the high moral courage of the few is severely tested. The chronological symmetry of the film and the relentless progress of the ever-present clock not only helps create and maintain tension, but counterpoints Kane's agonizingly slow progress in trying to recruit help and decide his course of action.

In its characterizations, the film offers an anti-mythological touch that sets it apart from most examples of the Western genre. Will Kane does not conform to the usual heroic figure that audiences of the 1950s had come to expect. Both the character and the man who portrayed him are somewhat past their prime. Cooper, who was not in the best of health, appeared haggard and drawn, and conveyed an air of world weariness—precisely the quality that director Zinneman had in mind. The female characters also depart from the female stereotype found in most Westerns. Though both Helen and Amy are emotionally involved with Will and are diametrically opposed (Helen is a fiery Hispanic businesswoman, Amy a Nordically cool and devout Quaker pacifist), both are highly principled and intelligent and cannot be pigeonholed. They are allowed to move the action forward by their principled stands, and are able to bond across racial lines while respecting their differences. Both survive the action and give strong evidence of strength and independence. This was not only rare in traditional bound Westerns, but flew in the face of 1950s American social convention when women had not yet assumed positions of power.

In the opinion of many, *High Noon* has continued to stand head and shoulders above most frontier Westerns in its depiction of ethical conflicts and ideas that cannot be confined to one particular genre, place, or time, but which always seem to manifest themselves in their most elemental form in the Western. The film has been credited as a significant influence on later Westerns, inspiring such thoughtful and revisionist films as *Pat Garrett and Billy the Kid* (1973), *Butch Cassidy and the Sundance Kid* (1969), *The Wild Bunch* (1969), *High Plains Drifter* (1973), *The Shootist* (1976), *and Unforgiven* (1992), all of which dealt with the ending of the Western way of life and the death of the "six-gun mentality."

—Steve Hanson

Further Reading:

Bodeen, Dewitt. "High Noon." In *Magill's Survey of Cinema*. New Jersey, Salem Press, 1980.

Combs, Richard. "When the Big Hand Is on the Twelve . . . or Seven Ambiguities of Time." *Monthly Film Bulletin*. June 1986, 188.

Foster, G. "The Women in *High Noon*: a Metanarrative of Difference." *Film Criticism*. Spring 1994, 72-81.

Prince, Stephen. "Historical Perspective and the Realist Aesthetic in *High Noon*." *Film Criticism*. Spring 1994, 57-71.

Reynolds, D. J. "Taking Care of Things: Evolution in the Treatment of a Western Theme, 1947-1957." *Literature/Film Quarterly*. July 1990, 202-208.

Zinnemann, Fred. *A Life in the Movies*. New York, Charles Scribner's Sons, 1992.

Highway System

In the mid-1950s, at a time when Detroit automobile manufacturers sold 7.92 million cars in one year and 70 percent of American families owned automobiles, the American road system was still noted for its inadequacies. No four-lane highways existed, except for the eastern toll roads, and expressways were to be found only in the nation's cities. President Dwight Eisenhower, who once made the trip from coast to coast along the nation's roads, was well aware of the problems and became the originator of the interstate highway system. Building a national highway system was more expensive and elaborate than most New Deal programs. In addition, the highway system shifted economic power to the Sunbelt, bypassing the main streets and roadside towns that had been travel waystations, and homogenizing

American roadside culture. By making longer commutes possible, the highways changed how many of us worked.

Americans have had a long fascination with transcontinental travel and with linking both coasts by roads. The first continental crossing by automobile was made in 1903 by physician H. Nelson Jackson, who drove from San Francisco to New York in 65 days. As early as 1911, legislation was introduced in Congress calling for seven national highways, one of which was to be transcontinental.

Traveled Americans at this time were often more familiar with Europe than with their own country. New York socialite Emily Post's 1915 cross-country automobile trip illustrates how little faith Americans had in the transcontinental road system. When Post asked a well-traveled friend the best road to take across the country, she replied, "the Union Pacific (Railroad)." Her friend greeted Post's intentions with incredulity:

> Once you get beyond the Mississippi the roads are trails of mud and sand. . . . Tell me, where do you think you are going to stop? These are not towns; they are only names on a map, or at best two shacks and a saloon! This place North Platte why, you couldn't stay in a place like that!

Post's friend might seem to be the quintessential ethnocentric Manhattanite, but her concern was not misplaced. Most of the improved roads early in the century were centered around cities. Often, "improvement" merely meant that the road was graded; there was no asphalt or concrete, and brick and gravel roads were scarce. If the rain did not make roads impassable for motorists, a trip during dry weather was bumpy and dusty.

After the formation of the Lincoln Highway Association in 1913, the first coast-to-coast highway was completed by 1915, running from San Francisco to New York, at a cost of $10 million. Sensing the commercial importance of a continuous route, towns and cities in between the coasts competed to have the highway run through their towns. Known as "America's Main Street," the Lincoln Highway "was the last, great nineteenth-century trail," Lyell Henry, Iowa City historian and Mount Mercy College professor, told writer Dave Rasdal. "In the early days, automobile routes were called trails. The Lincoln does overlap a considerable amount of the Oregon Trail." Now, a sixty to ninety day transcontinental automobile trip had been cut to twenty to thirty days. Despite the improvements, the two-lane routes, with their low speed limits and stop-start traffic, hampered the trucking industry.

By the 1930s, road travel was further eased by the completion of long-span bridges like the San Francisco Bay Bridge, the Golden Gate Bridge, and the Mark Twain Bridge which spanned the Mississippi at Hannibal, Missouri. Popular tourist attractions, like the Henry Ford Museum and Greenfield Village, accelerated tourism in the late 1920s.

Before the 43,000 mile interstate system was created, the toll roads had been the first major development in the highway system. The Pennsylvania Turnpike, the nation's first toll road, was "the first long-distance, high-speed, limited-access, four-lane divided road—the direct conceptual predecessor of the interstate system," writes Dan Cupper in *American Heritage*. The Lincoln Highway (U.S. Route 30) and the William Penn Highway (Route 22), may have provided continuous routes, but such narrow two-lane roads were a nightmare to drive, especially in rough terrain like the Allegheny Mountains of western Pennsylvania. During winter, the narrow roads' sharp curves and steep grades made travel so treacherous that trucking

Typical freeway traffic, c. 1960s.

companies rerouted their shipping hundreds of miles to avoid trouble spots.

When the Pennsylvania Turnpike opened in 1940, only 11,070 out of 3 million miles of roadway were wider than two lanes. But turnpike engineer Charles M. Noble wrote in *Civil Engineering* in 1940 that the days when roadways were challenges to be surmounted by motorists were coming to an end:

> Every effort has been directed towards securing uniform and consistent operating conditions for the motorist. . . . [T]he design was attacked from the viewpoint of motor-car operation and the human frailty of the driver, rather than from the difficulty of the terrain and methods of construction.

On opening day, a sunny October 6, 1940, motorists waited up to four hours to enter the turnpike and join the new accessible automotive experience.

After decades of false starts by Congress on the issue of highway development, Eisenhower began the first moves towards a national highway system in 1954. Like many other Americans who fought in Europe during World War II, Eisenhower was impressed by Hitler's autobahns, Germany's modern and broad four-lane highway system.

In addition, Eisenhower sought a national transport system that could facilitate military movement or evacuation from the cold war threat of nuclear attack. This need was underscored by the Formosa Straits crisis of 1955, in which tensions rose between the U.S. and China over the perceived threat to Taiwan by the mainland communists. More than any real danger of military conflict with China, the incident raised concerns about America's ability to evacuate cities like Washington, D.C.

Eisenhower knew the hardships of road travel from personal experience. In 1919, as a lieutenant-colonel, Eisenhower joined an army truck convoy on a cross-country trip to test Army vehicles. Traveling mostly along the Lincoln Highway, from Washington, D.C., to San Francisco, the convoy contained almost 300 men and took 56 days. Eisenhower's biographer, Stephen Ambrose, describes Eisenhower's experience as "a lark. He camped out for the entire summer . . . went hunting and fishing, played practical jokes and poker, and thoroughly enjoyed himself." However, the trip also impressed upon the future president just how "miserable the American road network was—the convoy hardly averaged five miles per hour."

Eisenhower's goal to improve the nation's roads faced many of the same obstructions as road builders of the prior two decades. One of the constant factors had been federal/state disputes over who pays for construction. As Phil Patton, the author of *Open Road: A Celebration of the American Highway,* argues, "the whole phylogeny of federal-state relations is recapitulated in the ontogeny of every interstate." Once the project was underway, Eisenhower soon discovered that it would not be easy to realize his vision. The high price of urban land acquisition drove costs higher, and construction stalled as funding methods were debated. Eisenhower, writes Ambrose, "envisioned a road network that would link all U.S. cities with populations of 50,000 or more with defense installations." He also felt that the main part of the system would be composed of farm-to-city routes, with highways that traveled around the cities, rather than through them. In order to sway Congressional votes for the 1956 Interstate Highway Bill, the administration negotiated a large share of expenditures for big cities which largely opposed the bill. Foreseeing how "very wasteful (it is) to have an average of just over one man per $3,000 car driving into the central area and taking all the space required to park the car," Eisenhower once considered a tax on city-bound automobiles, but soon abandoned the idea. Another aspect of the president's vision failed to materialize: he did not want to see billboards along the new highways.

Regardless of the obstacles and imperfections, the effects of the new highway system were enormous. Economic power shifted away from the small towns that the old routes passed through as new sectors of the economy grew around the beltways. City freeways changed the patterns of urban life as entire neighborhoods were sacrificed, and highways facilitated the spread of the suburbs that created a middle-class exodus from the city limits. The era of building the system ended around 1969 as a backlash emerged against tearing down entire city neighborhoods for highways. Money was diverted towards mass transit, and Congress slowed funds for maintaining the highway system.

The man who shared Eisenhower's vision, Francis Turner, the secretary to the committee that was charged with implementing the highway system, found himself caught in the backlash just as he became the head of the Federal Highway Administration. Turner had shared Eisenhower's vision of the farm-to-city routes. "Having conquered mountain ranges, rivers, and swamps," writes Patton, "they were being stopped by human forces. Soon no mayor could support a downtown interstate." Turner derided mass transit, commonly referred to as "rapid transit"; Turner called it "rabbit transit." "If you like waiting for elevators," Patton quotes Turner as saying, "you'll love rabbit transit."

If the Eisenhower administration was unconcerned with the project's social effects, others, argues *American Heritage* contributor Lawrence Block, decried the changes in roadside culture, citing the highway system as a homogenizing factor:

> When you drove across the country in 1954, bouncing along on bad roads, risking ptomaine in dubious diners, holing up nights in roadside cabins and tourist courts, you were rewarded with a constant change of scene that amounted to more than a change of landscape. There were no chain restaurants, no franchised muffler-repair shops, and even brands of beer and gasoline were apt to change when you crossed a couple of state lines.

Once the national highway system was built, writes Drake Hokanson in *The Lincoln Highway,* it became possible to "cross the entire state of Wyoming and never smell sagebrush," instead to enjoy a "great franchised monoculture that extends from sea to sea."

These lamentations for the changes along the road might be labelled as mere nostalgia, if it were not for the overwhelming role that the road and road travel has played within American culture. As early as the nineteenth century, Alexis de Tocqueville in *Democracy in America* recognized the restlessness in our national character:

> If at the end of the year of unremitting labor [the American] finds he has a few day's vacation, his eager curiosity whirls him over the vast extent of the United States, and he will travel fifteen hundred miles in a few days to shake off his happiness.

"O public road," serenaded Walt Whitman in 1856, "You express me better than I can express myself." John Steinbeck portrayed the road as symbolic of the Okie's search for prosperity during the depression-era migration to California in *The Grapes of Wrath* (1939). The modern myth of the road is contained in the works of Jack Kerouac, especially *On the Road* (1957), as a place to find the real America as well as a forum for self-discovery.

The sense of adventure afforded by the new roadways was popularized in the media by productions like the television show *Route 66* (1960-1964). Named after the highway that ran through the American southwest, *Route 66* featured two young drifters who traveled the road in their Corvette. True to the myth of hitting the road to discover America, the TV heroes traveled through small towns and cities, encountering outcasts and dreamers in an existential drama. Kerouac's beatnik vision was converted for mainstream palatability, putting a stamp of approval upon "the search for America."

Of course, not all Americans lamented the passing of the highway system of old. On the new highways, long-haul truckers and travellers now found it possible to drive from one coast the other in less than a week. Many regarded the new roadways as technological marvels. Cloverleaf intersections, in which two highways interchange through a series of entrance and exit ramps that resembled the shape of a four-leaf clover, were one such marvel. In the era of the Sputnik launch, even highways were associated with the Space Age by being called "roads to the future." Early postcards of highways depicting tunnels and cloverleaves, with the legend "America's Super Highway," portray the sort of regard for highways that would seem inconceivable in later years.

The changes to American life and the benefits provided by the interstates are now so largely taken for granted that they exist below the level of consciousness. Because the highways have become so much a part of the landscape, these changes were seldom felt, although they can be easily measured. In 1994, for instance, the average motorist traveled about 3,000 miles a year on the interstate system. The number of accidents per year remained more or less constant prior to, and after, the construction of the interstates; however, the number of vehicles tripled between the 1950s and 1990s.

The mythic qualities of the road are connected to regaining the sense of discovery embodied by the pioneers. Several car models were named after explorers: DeSoto, Cadillac, Hudson. The frontier sense of car travel did not seek to compare itself to the hardships felt by the pioneers, but to the sense of adventure one gained in discovering one's own land. These qualities were manifested by strange people, places, and food, the threat of speed traps, wrong turns, or the backwoods sheriff who could turn a minor road violation into a night in jail. In this analogy, the highways acted as the settlement, and fears of the unknown were mitigated by roadside tourist attractions, familiar brand-name advertising, and restaurant and hotel chains. In a decade that many Americans look back upon as dull and sterile, the "frontier" was being tamed for a second time.

—Daryl Umberger

FURTHER READING:

Ambrose, Stephen E. *Eisenhower: Soldier, General of the Army, President-Elect, 1890-1952.* Vol. 1. New York, Simon & Schuster, 1983.

———. *Eisenhower: The President.* Vol. 2. New York, Simon & Schuster, 1984.

Block, Lawrence. "How Have We Changed?" *American Heritage.* December 1994, 62.

Cupper, Dan. "The Road to the Future." *American Heritage.* May/June 1990, 102-11.

Hokanson, Drake. *The Lincoln Highway: Main Street Across America.* Iowa City, Iowa University Press, 1988.

Kammen, Michael G. *Mystic Chords of Memory: The Transformation of Tradition in American Culture.* New York, Alfred A. Knopf, 1991.

Lockridge, Deborah, and Jack Roberts. "How We Got Our Highway System." *Overdrive.* July 1996, 54-7.

Patton, Phil. "Agents of Change." *American Heritage.* December 1994, 88-109.

———. *Open Road: A Celebration of the American Highway.* New York, Simon & Schuster, 1986.

Radal, Dave. "Trail Lore Connects Decades: Lincoln Highway's Reputation Outlasts the Original Pavement." http://www.gazetteonline.com/special/lincoln/linc001.htm. June 1999.

Rose, Mark H. *Interstate: Express Highway Politics, 1941-1956.* Lawrence, Kansas, Regents Press of Kansas, 1979.

Tocqueville, Alexis de. *Democracy in America.* 1835; New York, Colonial Press, 1996.

Hijuelos, Oscar (1951—)

New Yorker Oscar Hijuelos' bestselling novels are epic family sagas of the twentieth-century Cuban-American experience. His debut, *Our House in the Last World* (1983), charts the cultural identity crisis of two brothers and their Cuban-born parents in New York during the years after World War II. Pulitzer Prize-winning *The Mambo Kings Play Songs of Love* (1989) flamboyantly depicts 1950s New York as a musical, multicultural melting pot. The Irish-Cuban protagonist of *The Fourteen Sisters of Emilio Montez O'Brien* (1993) is torn between fulfilling the mainstream American Dream of movie stardom and the doting, redeeming love of his all-female family. All of Hijuelos' novels, including even the more understated and contemplative *Mr. Ives' Christmas* (1995), exhibit a troubled fascination with the cultural hegemony of Hollywood. It is therefore appropriately ironic that the 1992 Warner Brothers production, *The Mambo Kings*, brought Hijuelos' work to a wider, moviegoing public.

—Martyn Bone

Hiking

As views of nature in America have changed during the twentieth century, so too has the recreational practice of hiking. Throughout the twentieth century hiking was linked to a love of the outdoors, and was a means by which to express a connection to the land. But as the meaning of the American landscape for Americans changed with time, so too did the popular meaning of hiking.

The idea of hiking for amusement would not gain widespread attention until the presidency of Theodore Roosevelt (1901-09). With the ear of the nation, Roosevelt became the greatest proponent of outdoor appreciation. Where earlier politicians had urged Americans to exploit natural resources, farm, and conquer wilderness, Roosevelt often called for preservation of nature. Deeply influenced by the British Imperial fashion of making one's manhood by entering and besting nature, Roosevelt traveled to many wild places. In the Dakotas, Michigan, and other parts of America, Roosevelt "roughed it" camping and hunting. He helped to popularize a masculinity based not on comfort and cultivation, but upon strength and the ability to tolerate hardship. By entering nature, one could prove one's "rugged individualism."

Roosevelt's regard for nature and individualism coincided with and helped forge America's emerging sense of itself as a new kind of nation. United States democratic ideals clashed with popular concepts of the limp-wristed privilege and elitism of European aristocracy. Fearing European "flabbiness" and "slothful ease," Roosevelt and others promoted contact with nature so as to cultivate in Americans a "vigorous manliness" and a "life of strenuous endeavor."

America also came to view itself as a growing industrial giant, reaping seemingly limitless resources from a great expanse. To hike was to enter nature to appreciate the stuff of which America was made. America was coming to see itself as a nation favored by God, and its land was part of God's gift to the nation. Roosevelt, and "naturalists" such as John Muir and Aldo Leopold, were also concerned to preserve the stunning beauty of America. Europe had annihilated much of its wilderness, and Americans had already plundered millions of acres. The still popular writings of Henry David Thoreau and John Muir, the paintings of Thomas Moran, and later the photography of Ansel Adams, revealed new ways of seeing the natural world. A powerful American "wilderness cult" became the vanguard of a movement to protect millions of acres of wilderness. This movement somewhat slowed resource extraction and greatly accelerated forest recreation. Out of all of these ideas "hiking" came into being.

Ironically, it was the popularity of the automobile which gave hiking its greatest boost. As the twentieth century aged, the proliferation of cars brought millions of Americans to their forests and parks. In the 1950s, widespread car ownership, new parks, and new ideas about recreation in nature resulted in an explosion in visits to wilderness preserves. At this time, "hiking" was typically a short jaunt from the car, followed by a picnic. Though adventurous, hiking was closely affiliated with the prevailing notion that leisure was to be relaxing and peaceful.

People often see wilderness as the antithesis of civilization. As such, hiking in the wilderness offers salvation from a variety of social ills. For example, urbanites throughout the twentieth century sometimes went hiking to have contact with a natural world which they seldom saw. Overdeveloped suburbs and "concrete jungles" of urban blight left some people alienated from the natural world. Hiking could "renew the spirit." In the 1970s, the fitness movement and the environmental movement changed the practice of hiking. Better and lighter equipment—the external frame backpack, the down sweater, and the lighter hiking boots—helped to increase enjoyment of overnight adventures.

In the 1970s and 1980s, hiking grew exponentially. As the nation sought to move beyond the pain of the Vietnam War and as environmentalism grew in popularity, communing with nature was a way of living simply and finding harmony with the Earth. By being in the woods, many hikers were enacting their environmental beliefs and "getting back to nature." Groups such as the Sierra Club not only lobbied government to preserve wilderness, but recruited hikers as part of their preservation strategy. Hikers were easily converted to conservation, and hikers helped to change the way wilderness was used. In the later quarter of the twentieth century, hiking was extended to all parts of the continent, as places once looked upon as "wastelands" were seen and experienced as sites of stark, arid beauty. In a sense, these areas were symbolically reclaimed for nature through the act of hiking. Land once considered "useless" for anything but resource extraction could be transformed by hiking—hiking literally made use of the land.

—Dylan Clark

FURTHER READING:

Devall, Bill, and George Sessions. *Deep Ecology.* Salt Lake City, Peregrine Smith Books, 1985.

Gruen, Lori and, Dale Jamieson, editors. *Reflecting on Nature: Readings in Environmental Philosophy.* New York, Oxford University Press, 1994.

Nash, Roderick. *Wilderness and the American Mind.* New Haven, Yale University Press, 1982.

Thoreau, Henry David. *The Portable Thoreau,* edited by Carl Bode. New York, Viking, 1964.

Hill, Anita
See Anita Hill-Clarence Thomas Senate Hearings

Hill Street Blues

First airing on January 15, 1981 and ending its broadcast television run on May 12, 1987, *Hill Street Blues* broke new ground to become one of the most critically acclaimed television dramas ever, and won 26 Emmy Awards for NBC. Police dramas had been a staple, if not a cliché, since the beginning of prime time television broadcasting, with shows such as *California Highway Patrol* and *Dragnet* setting the standard from the 1950s onwards. These series featured straight-laced, tight-lipped cops upholding the law in a black-and-white world where every crime was solved within 30 minutes. The focus changed radically when NBC President Fred Silverman, his network mired in third place, gave Steven Bochco free rein to create and produce a show that would reinvent television police drama. As Robert J. Thompson, Director of the Center for the study of Popular Television at Syracuse University summarized it, "What Bochco

The cast of *Hill Street Blues*.

did in 1981 was change the television cop show by making it more realistic."

Steven Bochco had chosen television over work in film, and both he and the medium benefited. After graduating from Carnegie Tech, Bochco had a film script produced at Universal Studios in 1971. By the time *Silent Running* (a knockoff of *2001: A Space Odyssey,* starring Bruce Dern) was released, he had decided to leave film for television. Bochco told British ITV's distinguished *South Bank Show* presenter Melvyn Bragg, "In a week and a half I wrote a script. . . . It was a shocking experience for me. It was so devalued by the actors involved, and . . . it made me determine somehow to get more control over the things I wrote." Seeking that control in television, Bochco wrote several scripts for NBC's Sunday Mystery Movie, *Columbo* (also produced at Universal Studios), between 1971 and 1973 and, with these writing credits to back him up, he created or produced several television pilots and series for NBC, including *The Invisible Man* (1975), *Delvecchio* (1976), and *Paris* (1979). With his television apprenticeship behind him and NBC's Nielsen ratings in the doldrums in the late 1970s and early 1980s, Bochco got his opportunity. The result was *Hill Street Blues.*

Much of the show's style derived from police documentary films, particularly Susan and Alan Raymond's *Police Tapes* (1977) and Frederick Wiseman's *Law and Order* (1969). The *cinema verite* style adopted for *Hill Street Blues* had previously been seen on television only in the news, and it lent a startling immediacy and realism to prime time drama. *Hill Street* employed shaky, hand-held cameras and grainy film stock that appeared to be the result of pre-exposing, or "flashing," the stock. The result was a low-contrast, shadowy, and claustrophobic world, well suited to the characters and story lines. Interior shots were particularly tight, busy with supporting cast members and extras going about police business in the background while close shots of the main characters filled the foreground. This heightened realism had a profound influence on the genre, and altered the style of successive series, which were quick to apply the new gritty, hard-edged approach of *Hill Street.*

In addition to its landmark style, *Hill Street*'s plot lines and subject matter were also new to prime time network dramas. Law and order was negotiated in interrogation rooms and courtrooms, and the lines between criminal and cop were often blurred. The serial nature of *Hill Street* was also critical to this more naturalistic treatment of the criminal justice system. While prime time soap operas like *Dallas* had serial plots, the impulse of most police dramas was to present a self-contained story in a closed 30-minute format or, as Bochco had learned with *Columbo,* a two-hour movie slot. But the plots and the characters that filled *Hill Street* were too complex for quick resolution.

The characters, too, were innovative, exhibiting human dimensions of weakness as well as strength that came to dictate character-driven cop series such as the contemporaneous *Cagney and Lacey* and, notably, of course, Bochco's later *NYPD Blue.* Bochco, rather curiously, described his characters in a 1997 *New York Times* interview as "broad-brushed, almost comedic. . . ." Foremost among the ensemble cast was Precinct Captain Frank Furillo, played by Daniel J. Travanti. Furillo is an unwaveringly ethical leader, a recovering alcoholic (as was Travanti) married to sane and professional Public Defender Joyce Davenport, played by Veronica Hamel. Other characters are more idiosyncratic: Frank's shrill ex-wife (played by Bochco's wife Barbara Bosson) is arrested for marijuana possession in one episode; Sergeant Phil Esterhaus (Michael Conrad) died of a heart attack *in medias coitus*; and Detective Mick Belker (Bruce Weitz) was not above biting suspects to subdue them. Other cast members included Charles Haid, Michael Warren, Taurean Blacque, Kiel Martin, Ed Marinaro, Joe Spano, Rene Enriquez, James B. Sikking, and Dennis Franz as Detective Norman Buntz. Franz's relationship with Bochco crossed over into *NYPD Blue.*

Hill Street Blues, along with the sitcom *Cheers,* made NBC's Thursday lineup unbeatable and helped the network climb back into the Nielsen ratings race by the mid-1980s. Mike Post's theme music became a hit on radio, just as his theme for *The Rockford Files* had done in the 1970s. By the end of the decade *Hill Street* had spawned innumerable imitators, including *St. Elsewhere* (often called "*Hill Street* in a hospital") by Bochco protégé David E. Kelley. Bochco continued experimenting with the form, creating a show about minor league ball players called *Bay City Blues,* but he was not infallible. The 1990 musical drama *Cop Rock,* in which characters launched into song in the middle of an arrest or a court proceeding, was a bizarre and unfortunate mistake. *NYPD Blue,* Bochco's series for ABC, first aired in October of 1994 and continued to push the envelope where content was concerned, airing mild nudity that caused some affiliates to cancel or pre-empt the show. The furor died down after the first season, and *NYPD Blue* became a huge and ongoing critical and ratings success. Bochco then broke new ground yet again with *Murder One* (1995), a one-season serial that followed one murder trial to its conclusion, and carried unmistakable resonances of the O. J. Simpson case.

In a 1995 interview in the *New York Times,* Bochco, referring to *Murder One,* clarified his vision for television drama. "What we're trying to do," he said, "is create a long term impact. One which requires its viewership to defer gratification for a while, to control that

impulse in anticipation of a more complex and fully satisfying closure down the road. It's the same commitment you make when you open up to the first page of a novel." And Daniel J. Travanti reminisced in a 1997 interview in *The Washington Post,* "It's nice to know that in a minor key, we are legendary." Unlike most such legends, however, *Hill Street Blues* indubitably impacted on American cultural expectations of the genre, and the successful series that have followed in its wake stand on its shoulders.

—Tim Arnold

FURTHER READING:

Thompson, Robert J. *Television's Second Golden Age: From Hill Street Blues to ER.* Syracuse, Syracuse University Press, 1996.

Hillerman, Tony (1925—)

Since 1970, writer Tony Hillerman has developed the detective fiction genre with his highly regarded series of detective novels set on Navajo customs and culture. His two Native American detectives, Joe Leaphorn and Jim Chee, pursue their investigations in and around the Navajo reservation that covers parts of Arizona, New Mexico, and Utah. Hillerman's major innovation to detective fiction has been to transplant an essentially European American method of detection into the Native American cultural context. The effect is to reveal the method's shortcomings and address Native American concerns by showing that a detective must have intimate knowledge of the specific culture in which a crime takes place. Without that knowledge of cultural difference, the so-called analytical method of detection cannot be used successfully to solve a mystery. For a white writer even to consider entering such a difficult cultural arena as this is remarkable in itself, but criticism of Hillerman's work suggests he has done so with great sensitivity, subtlety, and no little success.

Hillerman was born and brought up in a small farming settlement near Konawa, Oklahoma. His father and uncle ran a farm and a general store during the 1930s, and Hillerman attributes his skill as a storyteller to the social gatherings on the front porch of the store; he describes his mother in particular as a great storyteller. He escaped dust-bowl-struck Pottawatomie County first by attending Oklahoma State University and later, having dropped out of his chemical engineering degree to help on the farm, by enlisting in the army and going to fight in Europe.

Extracts from his wartime letters home were published as a story by a journalist with the *Daily Oklahoman,* and it is this that pushed Hillerman toward writing as a career. After the war he returned to the University of Oklahoma where he gained a bachelor of arts degree in journalism. Suitably qualified, he found work as a journalist for newspapers and news bureaus in Oklahoma, Texas, and New Mexico. His decision to begin writing fiction coincided with his return to academic study, and after completing a master of arts degree in 1965, he became a faculty member at the University of New Mexico in Albuquerque, where he eventually became chair of the Department of Journalism.

Only one of Hillerman's fourteen published detective novels does not have a Native American setting or theme. In 1995 he departed a second time from the Navajo theme, and also from detective fiction, to write a novel, *Finding Moon,* based in Asia at the time of the fall of Saigon. He has written detective short stories and nonfiction essays and books on subjects such as the southwestern states, Navajo culture, and the process of writing. He has also written a children's book, edited various collections of essays about the West, and (with Rosemary Herbert) is the editor of a collection of American detective stories.

For a man who grew up in relative poverty and cultural isolation, Hillerman has achieved remarkable success, both in his career on the faculty of the University of New Mexico, but especially as a writer of detective fiction. Critical responses to his fiction have been almost universally good, and his books have sold well. Among the several awards he has won are the prestigious Mystery Writers of America Edgar Allan Poe Award for *Dance Hall of the Dead* (1973) and the Mystery Writers of America Grandmaster Award (1989).

—Chris Routledge

FURTHER READING:

Erisman, Fred. "Tony Hillerman." *Western Writers Series*. No. 87. Boise, Idaho, Boise State University, 1989.

Herbert, Rosemary. "Tony Hillerman." *The Fatal Art of Entertainment: Interviews with Mystery Writers*. New York, G. K. Hall, 1994, 85-111.

Murray, David. "Reading the Signs: Detection and Anthropology in the Work of Tony Hillerman." In *Criminal Proceedings: The Contemporary American Crime Novel*. Edited by Peter Messent. London, Pluto Press, 1997, 127-149.

Reilly, John M. *Tony Hillerman: A Critical Companion*. Westport Connecticut, Greenwood Press, 1996.

Himes, Chester (1909-1984)

College dropout, pimp, bootlegger, and convicted armed-robber, Chester Himes began writing his acclaimed "Harlem Cycle" of crime novels in Paris in 1957. His most famous creations, the black detectives Coffin Ed Johnson and Gravedigger Jones work as a team and deal with transgressors in a ruthless, violent way, brandishing and using huge guns to settle disputes. The absurdity of the level of violence the two detectives both mete out and suffer is presented as representative of the wider absurdity of the lives of African Americans, and perhaps the absurdities of Himes's own life. Whatever Coffin Ed and Gravedigger do, they cannot end the cycle of crime and violence that grips black city life, just as, in Himes's view, whatever African Americans do, they cannot escape the cycle of racism that controls their lives.

The "Harlem Cycle" crime thrillers describe life among the struggling poor of Harlem in such vivid detail as can only come from experience, but Himes was born into a respectable, middle-class family in Jefferson City, Missouri. His father was a college professor who was head of the mechanical department of the Lincoln Institute in Jefferson and later worked at Alcorn College in Mississippi. His mother was a descendent of wealthy southern whites and made a point of declaring the family's superiority whenever she could, often criticizing her husband for his dark skin. This contrast between his father's dark skin and his mother's pride in her pale almost-whiteness reappears in Himes's novels as a dynamic of good and evil; evil

characters in his work tend to have light-colored skin. After his father lost his job at Alcorn, the Himes family moved to St. Louis and later to Cleveland, Ohio, where the relationship between his parents deteriorated. Himes graduated from high school in Ohio and, after recovering from falling down an elevator shaft, began studying at Ohio State University.

Himes's university career did not last long. In his own way he began to resist the discrimination he experienced even among young African Americans by rejecting what he called the "light-bright-and-damn-near-white" social clique at the university in favor of friends he made among gamblers, pimps, and prostitutes in the ghetto. As a result he was forced to resign his college place, and began a short but formative career as a criminal, selling bootleg whiskey during Prohibition and taking part in robberies. After his parents' divorce, and his father's decline into menial, low-paid jobs, Himes was eventually involved in an armed robbery, for which he was given a twenty-year prison sentence. With encouragement from his devoted mother, he began to write in prison, and published stories in magazines such as *Abbott's Monthly,* owned by and marketed to African Americans. He also managed to sell occasional stories to the more lucrative *Esquire* magazine, from which he concealed his racial origins.

Himes served seven and a half years in prison and, when he was paroled in 1936, began trying to earn a living from his writing. He continued to write for the magazines, but when he and his first wife, Jean, moved to California during the war, he worked in the shipyards and began to write his first novel, *If He Hollers Let Him Go,* which he completed in 1945. Himes had a difficult time with the autobiographical protest novels he wrote in the following seven years, all of which struggled to find publishers. His parents died, his marriage to Jean failed, and his various affairs with white women, most notably with Vandi Haygood, ended in disaster. In 1953, with money from the advance on *Cast the First Stone,* he bought a ticket to France. He lived briefly in London and Mallorca, co-wrote a novel with a woman he had met on the ship from New York, and finally moved to Paris.

In 1957, he met Marcel Duhamel of the publishing house Gallimard, which published American hard-boiled novels under the famous imprint, "La Série Noire," and was recruited to write detective stories. The first of these, published in America as *For Love of Imabelle* (1957), and now known as *A Rage in Harlem,* won the "Grand Prix de la littérature policière" in France and made him famous overnight. He wrote a total of ten detective novels, nine involving Gravedigger and Coffin Ed, one of which, *Plan B,* was published posthumously in 1993. The "Harlem Cycle," as these novels have become known, allowed him to address the themes of racism and violence that had made his earlier novels unpopular. As Stephen F. Soitos states, in Himes, racism is present among both blacks and whites, and as such his novels represent the growing awareness among African Americans in the 1950s of race and class, though his attitude towards women is far from progressive. His detectives are only too aware of the absurdity of their real task. They must protect whites and white society from black criminals and the latent chaos of Harlem so that they do not become too afraid to go there. If that should happen, black criminals and con artists would be deprived of their income.

Although his Harlem crime novels won awards and sold well from the start, it is only since the 1980s that they have been given the critical attention they deserve. Like James Baldwin, another African American writing in France about life in New York, Himes looked back at America with the clarity of an exile's eye. His elaborate hierarchies of good and evil characters, signaled by their skin color, and his experiments with nonlinear time and simultaneous plot events in his novels have informed the work of later novelists such as Ishmael Reed. Although they were written for commercial reasons, Himes's crime novels are an angry continuation of his early challenges to America, and a significant contribution to the development of American detective fiction.

—Chris Routledge

FURTHER READING:

Muller, Gilbert H. *Chester Himes.* Boston, Massachusetts, Twayne, 1986.

Skinner, Robert E. *Two Guns from Harlem: The Detective Fiction of Chester Himes.* Bowling Green, Ohio, Bowling Green State University Popular Press, 1989.

Soitos, Stephen F. *The Blues Detective: A Study of African American Detective Fiction.* Amherst, University of Massachusetts Press, 1996.

The *Hindenburg*

The May 1937 explosion of the German airship *Hindenburg* is one of the most memorable disasters of the twentieth century, outshining other more serious and costly catastrophes. Of the ninety-seven passengers and crew on board, thirty-six lost their lives in the conflagration. Images of its fiery denouement would make their way through the pop culture pantheon, onto T-shirts and album covers (most famously, the eponymous debut of Led Zeppelin), while the mystery of the *Hindenburg*'s final flight would inspire a feature film (1975) and numerous documentaries. Various theories on the cause of the explosion blame a hydrogen leak, electrostatic discharges in the air igniting the ship's highly flammable fabric covering, or an anti-Nazi act of sabotage. A NASA scientist claimed to have resolved the dispute in favor of the flammable covering thesis in 1997, but doubters remained. "For reasons which are not clear to me even now, however," wrote Michael Mooney in his history of the flight, "the *Hindenburg* disaster seemed to sear the memory of everyone even remotely connected to it." Perhaps it was a conjunction of the times, the fragile peace preceding World War II, and the spectacular manner of the airship's end.

Perhaps it was because the *Hindenburg* was destroyed in direct view of the assembled press, with cameras clicking and newsreel film rolling and radio announcers squawking excitedly into their microphones, their coverage competing with the screams of the dying. "Here it comes, ladies and gentlemen, and what a sight it is, a thrilling one, a marvelous sight," exclaimed radio announcer Herb Morrison for the benefit of his listeners in Chicago as the *Hindenburg* prepared to dock over a Lakehurst, New Jersey, airfield. Only moments later his tenor changed abruptly from enthusiasm to abject terror. "It's burst into flames," cried the horror-stricken reporter, "It is burning, bursting into flames and is falling . . . Oh! This is one of the worst . . . Oh! It's a terrific sight . . . Oh! . . . and all the humanity!" Morrison broke down, finding himself unable to continue.

Spectators on the ground claimed they saw a small explosion toward the stern followed by an enormous secondary burst. The lighter-than-air *Hindenburg* plummeted toward earth, passengers leaping from the observation platform as it descended. Others managed to flee from the wreckage once it came to rest on the airfield—some parting the white-hot aluminum superstructure with bare hands. The unlucky were trapped in the burning superstructure or were mortally wounded in escaping.

Zeppelin travel had attracted those who disliked sea travel, those for whom time was of the essence, and a great many who were attracted by the sheer novelty of airships. Thus far, zeppelins had provided safe, fast transport between the Americas and Germany for close to twenty years. (Only Germany had managed to master the art of the zeppelin, with French and English efforts ending in failure.) Having served a year of regular flights between Germany and New York, the *Hindenburg,* 804 feet long with a cruising speed of 78 miles per hour, was the largest and most advanced of the airships, providing comfortable, luxurious passage in a fraction of the time it would take the fastest steamer to traverse the Atlantic.

According to the dramatic sabotage legend, a letter had arrived at the German Embassy in Washington, D.C., the day before the flight warning of a saboteur among the paying passengers. As a result, security was unusually thorough, and Captain Ernst Lehmann, the newly appointed director of the Zeppelin Company (his predecessor having resigned in disgrace), and two SS officials scrutinized the passengers. By journey's end, Captain Lehmann was convinced the letter was a figment of SS paranoia. Nothing of import had transpired. He did not know that Erich Spehl, a young rigger on the ship whose job it was to tend to the bags of highly flammable hydrogen within the aluminum superstructure, had surreptitiously planted a bomb within Gas Cell IV long before the ship had left its hangar. It was left to Spehl to rip open the gas bag shortly before landing and set the timer on his rudimentary bomb. It was not Spehl's intention to kill anyone: the innocent farm lad was motivated to perform his "act of genius" by his older, sophisticated girlfriend under whose tutelage Spehl had grown violently opposed to the Nazi regime. As the *Hindenburg* circled to position itself for landing, Erich Spehl slit the gas cell and set the bomb's timer for two hours, long after the passengers and crew should have disembarked. Unfortunately, the timer malfunctioned, or in his haste, he set it wrong. The *Hindenburg* was just preparing to dock when the bomb exploded, burning the silk bag and allowing air to rush in and mix with the highly flammable hydrogen.

Whether the explosion was caused by such a saboteur or not, a more dramatic black eye for the Nazi regime could scarcely have been planned. The disaster was featured in newsreels within the week, and it made a phenomenal spectacle, the bright white flames leaping into the dark sky as the silhouetted bulk of the zeppelin descended gracefully toward the earth. The German government, hoping to avoid an international incident, ascribed the disaster to "an act of God." A binational commission was convened, but the Germans had been expressly warned not to find any evidence of sabotage. The FBI, in turn, played along, but the commission met nightly, and convictions were aired off the record. The decision to sweep the mess under the rug abruptly brought any further experiments with passenger airships to an end.

—Michael Baers

FURTHER READING:

As Reported by The New York Times: Great Moments of the Century: Catastrophes. New York, Arno Press, 1976.

The *Hindenburg* explosion, May 1937.

Greystone Communications. *The Hindenburg* (video). New York, A & E Home Video, 1996.

Hoehling, A. A. *Who Destroyed the Hindenburg?* Boston, Little, Brown and Company, 1962.

Mooney, Michael M. *The Hindenburg.* New York, Dodd, Mead & Company, 1972.

Stacey, Thomas. *The Hindenburg.* San Diego, Lucent Books, 1990.

Hip-Hop
See Rap/Hip-Hop

Hippies

The post war "baby boom generation" was something of an anomaly both to parents and to the children they would eventually

raise. Growing up amid the contradictory conditions of prosperity and paranoia that prevailed during the 1950s, as they grew into adults this young generation tired of abundance and yearned for a more "authentic" life. Their quest initiated outlandish fashions and tastes, broke taboos, and, together with an eager television and music business, monopolized the culture industry, saturating public discourse with hedonistic and sentimental idioms. With the objective of a new classless society of sincerity and trust, some of these young people adopted the term "hip" from beatnik slang and donned the flowery, flamboyant posture of "hippies."

By the mid-1960s, hippies began to appear in high schools, colleges, and enclaves around the country. Their unique combination of hedonism and morality depended on the spin they placed on the "generation gap" that separated them from their elders: in high moral gear, hippies projected every conceivable social and ethical defect of society onto their parents—the generation who, having survived depression and war, clung to middle-class prosperity and values like drowning sailors to a life vest. From the perspective of the young, this "materialism" was evidence of the bleak life of "straight" society, and of the moral bankruptcy that spawned war, environmental damage, racism, and sexual persecution.

Starting around 1964 and increasing steadily into the early 1970s, hippies began gathering in lower income, inner city neighborhoods (the same areas their parents had worked so hard to escape) such as New York's East Village and, particularly, San Francisco's Haight–Ashbury, and later formed communes and settlements in the countryside. Largely white, middle class, and educated, hippies whipped up their own philosophy of natural living, easy sexual and social relations, sincerity, and hedonism through a blend of Eastern mysticism, left-wing social critique, and Beatnik appropriations of African-American slang. To the hippies, ''squares'' were ''uptight,'' out of touch with their feelings and with each other, and it was this isolation from human feeling which had made them such aggressive, authoritarian, and often brutal people. The hippie lifestyle, on the other hand, was not only more fun, it was morally superior.

Drugs played a special part in this hedonistic moral rebirth. By ''blowing one's mind,'' drugs allowed one to see through the fake values of middle-class materialism and into the profound layers of one's innermost being. The hippie political outlook was just as fanciful. Hippies imagined the older generation working together in a massive authoritarian conspiracy called ''the Establishment,'' or ''the Man.'' They believed the main objective of the recognized social order was to restrain and control the innocent love of life, nature, and happiness that defined hippie life. The Vietnam war provided a ready target for hippie opposition and rebellion: the words ''peace'' and ''love'' became symbolically loaded terms, lumping together a call for military withdrawal from Vietnam, an attitude of

A Hippie couple.

mutual acceptance and trust between people, and a sense of personal awareness and happiness. The famous photograph of a hippie protester inserting flowers into the rifle barrels of a line of National Guard troops demonstrates the unique style of hippie morality, which connected personal feeling with political intent.

It is possible to bracket a viable and active hippie counter culture between the years 1965 and 1973. Over this period, a few important dates stand out: in 1966, the Beatles, having already made long hair an important emblem of youth culture, released *Sergeant Pepper's Lonely Hearts Club Band,* rock's first concept album. The jacket featured the band in lavish, mock Napoleonic military garb, a look that coined much early hippie camp and whimsy. One song in particular, ''A Day in the Life,'' crystallized the hallucinatory drug-induced sense of the absurd which was to become known as ''psychedelic.'' The song wove together two quite different sounds; one, sung by Paul McCartney, took an everyday, commonsensical tone, ''woke up, got out of bed, dragged a comb across my head. . . ,'' while the other, sung by John Lennon, interrupted McCartney's narrative to coo dreamily, ''Ahhhhhhh. . . I'd love to turn. . . you. . . on. . . .'' The song seemed to split reality into two, the mundane and the fantastic, the square and the hip. And, along with another track on the record, ''Lucy in the Sky with Diamonds,'' *Sergeant Pepper* was thought to advocate psychedelic drug use as the necessary bridge from the drab world of old straights to the lush and expressive world of the young and the free.

In 1967, the Monterey Pop Festival provided the first in a series of major outdoor rock concerts, and in 1969, the Woodstock Music and Arts Festival provided the movement's thrilling climax. Hundreds of thousands of hippies clogged the region around the concert trying to get in, and, after airlifts of food, water, and flowers from state troopers, the event subsided without incident, a testimony to the solidarity and mutual goodwill of a counterculture guided by feelings of love and peace. However, over time, the climate of the counterculture changed: hippie urban frolicking turned into serious homelessness and poverty, and the drug culture grew into an organized and dangerous underworld. Petty criminals, drifters, and profiteers overran many of the hippie hangouts and communes. The Manson murders and a violent outbreak of violence and murder at a concert at Altamont, California, in 1969 brought to the fore a growing tension within hippie culture between middle class and idealistic hippies and a growing criminal drug culture with no idealistic pretensions to speak of.

But more than the criminal underclass, the hippie movement faced a far greater challenge from the same force that had brought it into existence: the mainstream media, which commercialized hippie culture and dulled its radical edge. By 1970, psychedelic styles were a common feature of advertising, bell-bottom pants were marketed to children, and even conservatives were seen to sport sideburns and long hair. When Lyndon B. Johnson was photographed in retirement on his farm with hair down to his shoulders, it was clear that the counterculture had become mainstream culture.

—Sam Binkley

FURTHER READING:

Bisbort, Alan, and Parke Puterbaugh. *Groovy, Man: Tripping through the Psychedelic Years.* Los Angeles, General Publishing Group, 1998.

Gitlin, Todd. *The Sixties: Years of Hope, Days of Rage.* New York, Bantam Books, 1993.

Miller, Timothy. *The Hippies and American Values.* Knoxville, University of Tennessee Press, 1991.

Willis, Ellen. *Beginning to See the Light: Pieces of a Decade.* New York, Random House, 1981.

Wolfe, Tom. *The Electric Kool-Aid Acid Test.* New York, Farrar, Straus, and Giroux, 1968.

Hirschfeld, Albert (1903—)

Since 1927 Al Hirschfeld's instantly recognizable pen-and-ink drawings for the *New York Times* have chronicled the worlds of theater, film, television (when it came along), and indeed virtually every area of performance based artistry in the last three-quarters of the twentieth century. His mastery of the sinuous line to reveal the essence of a performer or role remains undiminished. Calling himself not a caricaturist but a "characterist," Hirschfeld has relied on wit and humor, never malice, to bring life to his subjects and a smile to the faces of those who read the *New York Times.* Since the birth of his daughter Nina in 1945, Hirschfeld has regularly hidden her name in the folds of clothing or elsewhere, prompting many admirers to an even closer reading of his eloquent drawings. Energy unabated, he produced in 1991 the designs for a set of United States postage stamps honoring great American humorists, while in its final 1997-1998 season he drew a set of *TV Guide* covers featuring the stars of *Seinfeld.*

—Craig Bunch

FURTHER READING:

Hirschfeld, Al. *Hirschfeld: Art and Recollections from Eight Decades.* New York, Charles Scribner's Sons, 1991.

Hispanic Magazine

A "Latino version of *People*" at the time of its 1988 debut, *Hispanic* was one of the first general interest magazines for Hispanic Americans to be printed in English and nationally distributed. Launched in Washington, D.C. by Cuban native Fred Estrada, with former New Mexico governor Jerry Apodaca as his publisher, *Hispanic* initially revolved around celebrity photo spreads and articles that were roundly dismissed as "fluff." The debut issue featured Raquel Welch "of all people" on its cover, as Estrada's son Alfredo would later lament. After a dismal first year of receipts, *Hispanic* underwent extensive reformatting. Becoming far more career and professional-oriented, the magazine's new focus was on the achievements of Hispanic business leaders and politicians such as Secretary of Housing and Urban Development Henry Cisneros, with regular articles on corporate America and its relationship to Hispanics.

The shift was successful. Almost immediately, ad pages increased by more than 200 percent and, by its third year, *Hispanic* was turning a profit. Reformatting was so successful, in fact, that *Hispanic* continues to be confused with its competitor, the California-based *Hispanic Business* (founded in 1979), which threatened a copyright infringement lawsuit in 1993.

While many print periodicals faced increasing difficulty in an era of expanding media technology, *Hispanic* remained solvent throughout the 1990s, largely due to the rapidly increasing demographic of Hispanic Americans, whose numbers were growing at five times the rate of the general population. It was a trend that advertisers had taken over two decades to grasp. Whereas in 1977, the total national ad expenditures in all Hispanic print media were only about $800,000, by 1997 that figure had skyrocketed to $492 million. As Alfredo Estrada noted, referring to the "lean" early years, "the idea that Hispanics spoke English was heresy [in those days] . . . even now, some advertising agencies remain wedded to the idea that the only effective way to reach Hispanics is in Spanish." Indeed, as recently as 1992, *Hispanic* challenged *Forbes* magazine for its claim that the Hispanic market was practically non-existent. Why then, asked a Hispanic writer, had 70 of the Fortune 500 companies invested in it?

Early pioneering Latino magazines such as *Nuestro* (published from 1975 to 1981) and *Latina* (1982-1983) may not have survived long enough to witness the exponential growth in advertising revenue, but the fact that they existed at all certainly paved the way for publications like *Hispanic.* In turn, the hard work of the Estrada family broke down barriers for later competitors, some of whom were based in large entertainment and publishing conglomerates, such as *People en Español,* launched by Time Warner in 1996, and *Latina,* which was first published by African American-owned Essence Communications in 1996.

In the 1990s, *Hispanic* saw several changes in operation strategies and long-term goals, which seemed both to expand and focus its efforts at once. The publication instituted, for example, the "Latina Excellence Awards," in an effort to "honor Hispanic American women who have made significant contributions in their chosen field of endeavor," as well as the "Schools of Excellence Awards," to pay tribute to secondary-school principals with unique academic and enrichment programs for Hispanic students.

Other changes included relocating its family-owned publishing headquarters, in 1994, from Washington, D.C. to Austin, Texas. The consortium (which now owned Florida-based *Vista* as well), also joined the new wave of publishers offering titles for Latinas; its quarterly supplement, *Moderna,* became a stand-alone publication in 1996.

In 1999 *Hispanic*'s circulation was a solid 250,000. Estrada remained chairman and founder, while Alfredo , a former lawyer and graduate of Harvard University, served as editor and publisher. When the elder Estrada heard one advertiser note that the flood of new publications for Latinos had finally "brought credibility to Hispanic print," he asked, incredulous, "What am I, chopped chorizo?" By the year 2050, Hispanics will comprise nearly 25 percent of the American population. Over a decade ago, *Hispanic* was one of the first to offer them a publication that honored their dreams and triumphs.

—Kristal Brent Zook

FURTHER READING:

Estrada, Alfredo J. "The Decade of *Hispanic.*" *Hispanic.* December 1997, 70.

Kanellos, Nicolás, editor. *The Hispanic American Almanac: A Reference Work on Hispanics in the United States.* 2nd edition. Detroit, Gale Publishing, 1997.

Manley, Lorne. "Mixing Business with Pleasure." *Folio.* November 15, 1998, 56.

Hiss, Alger (1904-1996)

Alger Hiss's life up to 1948 seemed, on the surface, to be an American success story. He attended Johns Hopkins and Harvard Law School and was a stellar student at both institutions. As he pursued his law career and joined the State Department in Washington, D.C., his road to success was soon blocked by accusations that he was a Soviet spy. Hiss would work relentlessly to clear his name, but to no avail. He died haunted by the specter of accusations brought against him during a period in America marked by political infighting and mass hysteria.

At Harvard, Hiss met a professor named Felix Frankfurter—a future Supreme Court justice. He served a term as a law clerk to Justice Oliver Wendell Holmes, continuing what he thought was his pursuit of a successful career in law. This was followed by private law practice in Boston and New York. The election of Franklin Roosevelt, however, brought Hiss to Washington to work on the New Deal. He worked at the Agricultural Adjustment Administration and was also a lawyer for the Nye Committee, a committee of Congress which was investigating the arms industry. In 1936, Hiss joined the State Department.

In 1939, a man named Whittaker Chambers paid a visit to Assistant Secretary of State Adolf Berle. Chambers claimed to be a former Communist who knew of the existence of "fellow travelers" in the federal government. Chambers made similar claims in follow-up interviews with the Federal Bureau of Investigation (FBI). Alger Hiss was one of the persons fingered by Chambers, but the allegations were not acted on at the time.

Hiss took part in the 1944 Dumbarton Oaks Conference, which tried to lay the framework for a postwar United Nations Organization and an international economic order. Hiss also accompanied President Roosevelt to the historic 1945 conference of the major Allied leaders in Yalta. In 1947, he became president of the Carnegie

Alger Hiss

Endowment for International Peace after being recruited by John Foster Dulles, a New York lawyer who later became President Eisenhower's hard-line anti-Communist Secretary of State.

In 1948, the Hiss Case began when Chambers gave testimony to the House Committee on Un-American Activities (HUAC). Chambers alleged that he had known Hiss in the 1930s, and that both of them had been Communists. Hiss was allegedly part of a Communist underground which existed in the federal government during Roosevelt's administration and which tried to turn federal policy in directions desired by the Communists. Chambers denied, however, that he had been involved in any spying.

Hiss demanded, and got, an opportunity to appear before HUAC. He denied the charges of Communism, and he denied having known Chambers. Hiss gave an impressive performance, but one member of HUAC, a freshman Republican congressman named Richard Nixon, wanted to look deeper into the matter. HUAC agreed that Nixon could continue with the investigation in order to find out if Chambers and Hiss had actually known each other.

Chambers was then summoned to give testimony in executive session, where he gave details (some accurate, some not) about Hiss and his wife from the period when Chambers claimed to have known Hiss. There was then a secret session at which Hiss was examined by HUAC members. Hiss backtracked on his earlier denial of having met Chambers. He had met a man called George Crosley who might have been Chambers. But Hiss denied knowing "Crosley" as a Communist. In a later face-to-face confrontation, Hiss confirmed that Chambers was the George Crosley he had known in the 1930s. Hiss also challenged Chambers to repeat his allegations outside the context of a congressional hearing so that Hiss could file a defamation lawsuit.

Chambers did indeed repeat outside of Congress his charge that Hiss was a Communist. Hiss, as promised, sued Chambers for defamation. Then, during the pretrial discovery phase of the lawsuit, Chambers made new accusations. Reversing his earlier testimony, Chambers said that Hiss had spied for the Soviet Union, using Chambers as a courier. To back up his dramatic accusation, Chambers produced various documents, including what he said were papers typed by Hiss—allegedly copies of government (mostly State Department) documents which Hiss had made, and then turned over to Chambers for use by the Soviets. Chambers also produced some allegedly incriminating microfilm representing State Department documents which Hiss had desired to send the Soviets. The microfilm had been hidden in a hollowed-out pumpkin on Chambers's farm until he felt able to turn them over to HUAC.

Chambers's espionage allegations were serious, and federal prosecutors believed them, but the statute of limitations on espionage had expired in Hiss' case. He was, however, indicted by a New York grand jury for allegedly committing perjury about espionage and his relationship with Chambers.

In Hiss' two trials, the prosecution backed up Chambers' story by trying to show that the Hiss typewriter had been used to write some of the documents in Chambers's possession. Hiss countered by attacking Chambers's credibility and by using character witnesses. And the list of character witnesses was impressive. Felix Frankfurter (Hiss's former teacher, now on the Supreme Court), Justice Stanley Reed, and Illinois governor Adlai Stevenson all appeared to vouch for Hiss's character. His first trial in 1949 ended with a hung jury (the vote was eight to four for conviction). At a second trial, Hiss was convicted, and he subsequently served forty-four months in prison.

For the remainder of his life, Hiss denied having spied for the Soviets. He wrote two books defending his innocence, and he had many supporters among those who thought that the Hiss prosecution was simply a politically motivated effort by conservatives to smear the New Deal and the Democrats by making up stories about Communists in the government. According to the pro-Hiss view, the Hiss prosecution was a product of the anti-Communist hysteria of the times. When Richard Nixon resigned from the Presidency as a result of the Watergate scandal, Hiss supporters argued that if Nixon was capable of the ''dirty tricks'' of the Watergate period, he was certainly capable of fabricating a case against Hiss. In the post-Soviet era, a Soviet general in charge of certain secret archives announced that there was no evidence in the archives that Hiss had been a spy, although he later added that such evidence might have been over-looked or destroyed.

Hiss's opponents cite Soviet documents which seem to confirm Chambers' account of a 1930s spy ring in Washington. Hiss's enemies also point to recently declassified United States translations of secret Soviet communications. One of the communications de-scribes an agent who is described in such a way as to fit only four people, including Hiss. Historians and others continue to debate the veracity of Chambers's claims as part of the continuing reassessment of events during the Cold War.

—Eric Longley

FURTHER READING:

Chambers, Whittaker. *Witness.* Chicago, Henry Regnery, 1969.

Gay, James Thomas. ''The Alger Hiss Spy Case.'' *American History.* Vol. 33, No. 2, 1998, 26 ff.

Hiss, Alger. *In the Court of Public Opinion.* New York, A. A. Knopf, 1957.

———. *Recollections of a Life.* New York, Seaver Books, 1988.

Klehr, Harvey, et al. *The Secret World of American Communism.* Trans. by Timothy D. Sergay. New Haven, Yale University Press, 1995.

Tanenhaus, Sam. *Whittaker Chambers: A Biography.* New York, Random House, 1997.

Weinstein, Allen. *Perjury: The Hiss-Chambers Case.* New York, Alfred A. Knopf, 1978.

Hitchcock, Alfred (1899-1980)

Universally acknowledged as ''The Master of Suspense,'' the British-born film director Alfred Hitchcock reached the zenith of his accomplishments within the American film industry, with a series of now classic psychological thrillers that remain a constant presence in the cultural landscape of the moviegoer. Regarded as one of the major artists of Hollywood's Golden Age, Hitchcock created and perfected his own genre of thriller, one which was by turns romantic, comedic, and macabre, and his unique gift for creating suspense has given the adjective ''Hitchcockian'' to the language. A supreme cinematic stylist, it was said of him that he filmed murder scenes as if they were love scenes and love scenes as if they were murder scenes. Thanks to his hosting of *Alfred Hitchcock Presents* during the 1950s, he became probably the only film director whose face was recognizable to the general public, although, master showman that he was, he made a fleeting trademark appearance in virtually every one of his films,

Alfred Hitchcock

giving audiences the added *frisson* of trying to spot him on the screen. His mastery of film technique, refined in the silent era, combined with his ability to, as he put it, ''play the audience like an organ,'' made his films extremely popular—so popular, in fact, that the respect of his critics and peers was not immediately forthcoming. Today, however, his place in the cinematic pantheon is secure, and his work continues to exert an overwhelming influence on upcoming generations of film-makers. For better or worse, Hitchcock's most lasting impact may prove to have been the floodgate of still-escalating violence which he unleashed on screen in his 1960 masterpiece, *Psycho.*

Alfred Joseph Hitchcock was born in suburban London on August 13, 1899. Raised in a Catholic household by an emotionally repressed father, he was a painfully shy child. Years later, he would often repeat the story of how his father had instructed the local police to place the boy in a cell for a short time in order to demonstrate what happens to bad little boys who misbehave. A recurring theme of his films is a fear of the police. Young Hitchcock developed an interest in art, but his first job was as a technical clerk in a telegraph company. In 1919, he joined the Islington branch of the Famous Players Lasky film company as a designer of title-cards. He was hired as an assistant director for the production company run by Michael Balcon and Victor Saville in 1923, where he met Alma Reville, a petite film editor whom he married three years later. Reville would remain Hitchcock's collaborator and confidante for the remainder of his life. After starting to write scripts, Hitchcock was sent to work on a German-British co-production at the UFA studios, famous home of the German Expres-sionist cinema, which would eventually reveal its influence in his own work.

By 1925, he had worked on half-a-dozen British silents in various capacities as assistant director, art director, editor, and co-scriptwriter. That year he directed his first solo feature, *The Pleasure Garden,* but it was his third, *The Lodger* (1926), that began to earn him his early reputation. Starring the British composer of "Ruritanian" musical romances and matinee idol of the musical stage, Ivor Novello, the tale concerned a mysterious stranger wrongly thought to be Jack the Ripper. Many years later, Hitchcock said of the film, "It was the first time I exercised my style . . . you might almost say it was my first picture." He only returned to the thriller form six pictures and three years later with *Blackmail,* the first British talkie or, more accurately, part-talkie (it had begun shooting as a silent). Alternating thrillers with "straight" pictures for a time, Hitchcock truly hit his stride in 1934 with *The Man Who Knew Too Much,* a fast-paced story of kidnapping and espionage, filled with memorable set-pieces such as the assassination attempt during a concert at Albert Hall. He remade it in 1956 starring James Stewart, Doris Day, Vistavision and the song "Que Sera Sera", but despite its massive box-office success, critics continue to agree that the early version was the more refined and effective.

The Man Who Knew Too Much launched what is now referred to as Hitchcock's "British period," in which he turned out one successful thriller after another, notably *The Thirty-Nine Steps* (1935) and one of the most famous of British films, *The Lady Vanishes* (1938). The former, one of several screen versions of John Buchan's novel, starred Robert Donat and Madeleine Carroll, and set the tone for many Hitchcock classics to follow, in its combination of comedy, action, and romance, and its theme of an innocent man hounded by the police as well as the arch-villains. Though it would take a generation for the more intellectual film critics to catch up with the public which made these movies hits, Hitchcock's films were remarkable for the craft with which they so skillfully hooked audiences and kept them in suspense for an hour and a half. The director paid immaculate attention to working out every detail, and often claimed that, with the script and storyboard complete, the actual filming itself was an anti-climax. He called upon the fullest vocabulary of cinema, from casting and camera-work to editing and sound, to tell his stories, and was a great believer in the power of montage, which he employed masterfully.

Inevitably, Hollywood beckoned, and Hitchcock signed a contract with producer David O. Selznick. Their first collaboration, *Rebecca* (1940), from the novel by Daphne Du Maurier and starring Joan Fontaine and Laurence Olivier, was largely British in flavor, but won Hitchcock the first of his five Academy nominations for Best Director, seven additional nominations (including one for Judith Anderson's immortal Mrs. Danvers) and carried off the Best Picture and Cinematography Oscars. *Rebecca* was an unqualified triumph, but Hitchcock chafed under the oppressively hands-on methods of his producer, and yearned for artistic independence. Meanwhile (sometimes on loan-out to other studios), he directed American films that continued his cycle of spy-chase thrillers but, in keeping with the World War II years, cunningly carried anti-Nazi propaganda messages as in *Foreign Correspondent* (1940, with Joel McCrea in the title role as an American war correspondent tangling with Nazi thugs), *Saboteur* (1942, with Robert Cummings tangling with Fifth Columnists), *Lifeboat* (1944, with Tallulah Bankhead and others surviving a German torpedo and seeking safety), and *Notorious* (1946), the second of three with Ingrid Bergman and four with Cary Grant, who infiltrate a group of Nazi conspirators in South America in one of the director's most stylish thriller-romances.

Sometimes cited by Hitchcock as his personal favorite, *Shadow of a Doubt* (1943), which starred Joseph Cotten as a killer escaping detection by "visiting" his adoring relatives, brilliantly dramatized the terrors that can lurk in the shadows of a seemingly normal small town. It was this penchant for perceiving the disturbance underneath the surface of things that helped Hitchcock's movies to resonate so powerfully. Perhaps the most famous demonstration of this disjunction would come in *North by Northwest* (1959), where Cary Grant, seemingly safe on a sunny day, surrounded by miles of empty farm fields, suddenly finds himself attacked by a machine-gunning airplane. Before the rich collection of war years thrillers, there was a beguiling and polished foray into domestic comedy drama with *Mr. and Mrs. Smith* (1940, with Carole Lombard and Robert Montgomery) and the romantic and sophisticated suspense tale *Suspicion* (1941, Grant and Fontaine), which pointed the way toward Hitchcock's fertile 1950s period.

The postwar decade kicked off with the adaptation of Patricia Highsmith's novel *Strangers on a Train* (1950), in which Farley Granger and Robert Walker swap murders. The film climaxed with one of Hitchcock's most famous and memorable visual set pieces, a chase in a fairground. It was filmed in black and white, as was *I Confess* (1952, with Montgomery Clift as a priest who receives an unwelcome confession). To date, the Master of Suspense had only ventured into color twice (*Rope,* 1948, and, one of his rare failures, *Under Capricorn,* 1949). Now, he capitulated to color for the remainder of his career, with the well-judged exceptions of the Henry Fonda vehicle, *The Wrong Man* (1956), and his most famous film, *Psycho.* Along with color, his taste for blonde leading ladies took on an almost obsessional aura and led, during the 1950s, to films with Grace Kelly, Doris Day, Eva-Marie Saint, Kim Novak, Janet Leigh, Julie Andrews, and, famously in *The Birds* (1963) and then in *Marnie* (1964), the previously unknown Tippi Hedren (whose career swiftly petered out thereafter).

His professional reputation secure, Hitchcock gained his artistic independence and entered a high period in which he turned out success after success, some better than others, but all of them entertaining. However, along with *North by Northwest,* which saw out the 1950s, the two masterpieces of the decade emerged from his three-picture collaboration with James Stewart, and marked a new dimension of interior psychological darkness that, in each case, infused every frame of an absorbing plot line. The films were, of course, *Rear Window* (1954) and *Vertigo* (1958), both of which dealt with obsession under the deceptive guise of a straightforward thriller. The first, with Stewart laid up with a broken leg and witnessing a murder across the way as a result of spying on his neighbors by way of a pastime, hinted at voyeurism; the second, in which he turns the lookalike of an illicit dead love into an exact copy of her predecessor (both played by Kim Novak), deals in guilt and sick delusion. *Vertigo,* for sheer artistic expertise, combined with Stewart's grim, haunted performance and the disturbing undertones of the piece, is quite possibly the most substantial of the postwar Hitchcock *oeuvre,* but the public impact of his first for the new decade capped all of his recent accomplishments.

The director's first excursion into unabashed horror, *Psycho* (1960) sent shock waves which continue to reverberate through the genre. The murder of Janet Leigh in the shower has been imitated, suggested, and ripped off in countless films since, and has become part of the cinema's iconography. In certain cases, such as *Dressed to Kill* (1980), Brian De Palma made no secret of the fact that he was drawing on the association in open homage to Hitchcock. *Psycho* (which drew on the Ed Gein multiple murder case for its inspiration) caused much controversy on its release, and has since been analyzed endlessly by film historians and academics. When a shot-by-shot color remake by Gus Van Sant, made ostensibly as the highest form of compliment to the original, emerged late in 1998, a rash of fresh argument was unleashed as many bemoaned the pointlessness of the exercise or, indeed, the travesty that many considered it to be. The original is generally considered as Hitchcock's last great film, attracting additional reverence for the contribution of his frequent collaborators Bernard Herrmann (who composed the pulsating score) and Saul Bass, the great designer of opening titles. Several of the Hitchcock masterpieces owe a debt to these two creative artists, and the Bass titles for *Vertigo* remain a work of art in their own right.

The follow-up to *Psycho, The Birds* (1963) was less highly regarded, but is a durable and complex experiment in terror, and a monument to technical expertise. In the late 1990s it, too, became the subject for renewed examination and analysis, notably by the controversial feminist academic Camille Paglia, who admired it greatly. There were only five more after *The Birds*—a varied quintet that signaled a decline in the director's prodigious powers—and he bowed out, somewhat disappointingly it has to be said (but he was, after all, 77 years old), with *Family Plot* in 1976. By then, however, thanks to TV's *Alfred Hitchcock Presents,* he had cemented his image in the public consciousness as the endearingly roly-poly master of dryly witty gallows humor. In his later years, Hitchcock had the pleasure of being lionized by the newer generations of film-makers, and the wistful experience of attaining honors which long earlier should have been his. Although, inexplicably, he never won an Oscar for directing, the Academy did ultimately honor him with the Irving Thalberg Award in recognition of his work, and he was also made the recipient of the American Film Institute Lifetime Achievement award.

Knighted by Queen Elizabeth II, he died Sir Alfred Hitchcock a few months later, at his Bel Air home in 1980. Almost two decades after his death, and almost 40 years after his last great film, Hitchcock remains a symbol of a certain kind of entertainment and excitement in a darkened movie theater. He is still one of the most admired and most emulated of movie-makers, but his many imitators have never remotely replicated his consummate artistry or penetrated the personal and private obsessions that drew him to stories of innocence accused, double identities, morbid romance, and the other themes and undercurrents now recognized as Hitchcockian. If the mid-twentieth century has rightly been called "The Age of Anxiety," then Hitchcock was the quintessential artist of his time.

—Preston Neal Jones

FURTHER READING:

Bogdanovich, Peter. *Who the Devil Made It?* New York, Ballantine, 1998.

Freeman, David. *The Last Days of Alfred Hitchcock.* Woodstock New York, Overlook Press, 1984.

Gottlieb, Sidney, ed. *Hitchcock on Hitchcock.* Berkeley, University of California Press, 1997.

Leff, Leonard J. *Hitchcock and Selznick: The Rich and Strange Collaboration of Alfred Hitchcock and David O. Selznick in Hollywood.* New York, Weidenfeld & Nicholson, 1987.

Smith, Steven C. *A Heart at Fire's Center: The Life and Music of Bernard Herrmann.* Berkeley, University of California Press, 1991.

Spoto, Donald. *The Dark Side of Genius: The Life of Alfred Hitchcock.* Boston, Little Brown, 1983.

Taylor, John Russell. *Hitch: The Life and Times of Alfred Hitchcock.* New York, Pantheon (Random House), 1978.

Truffaut, Francois. *Hitchcock.* New York, Simon and Schuster, 1984.

Hite, Shere (1942—)

Shere Hite burst upon the American scene in 1976 with the publication of her first book, *The Hite Report: A Nationwide Study on Female Sexuality.* Since then, she has authored a number of other best-selling books on sex and relationships—delighting her publishers, intriguing her public, and frustrating many social scientists, who consider her research to be seriously flawed.

Born Shirley Diana Gregory in St. Joseph, Missouri, Hite spent her childhood being shuttled between parents, grandparents, and other relatives. She earned bachelor's and master's degrees in history from the University of Florida. She then moved to New York City, where she dropped out of a doctoral program at Columbia, worked as a model, and eventually joined the National Organization for Women (NOW). Feminism led her to the realization that female sexuality had rarely been studied scientifically, and the determination to change that fact set Hite on the path that ultimately led to the writing and publication of *The Hite Report.*

The method that Hite used to gather data for her first book was also employed in most of the succeeding volumes. Hite pays to have surveys printed in a number of national publications, and invites readers to answer the questions (all requiring mini-essays) and mail in the surveys. For *The Hite Report,* she placed her surveys in such publications as *Ms. Magazine,* the *Village Voice,* and *Modern Bride.*

It is this method of research which has brought Hite so much criticism from those versed in the techniques of survey administration. Her approach to data gathering involves what is referred to in social science as a "self-selecting sample"—that is, the only people included in the "sample" (the pool of respondents) are those who choose to participate by answering and returning the questionnaire. Such respondents are likely to be both few in number and extreme in their views on the subject of the survey, since only those with the strongest opinions will usually take the trouble to fill out and mail the survey.

This approach to gathering data may explain the results that Hite reported in her books. She found that 70 percent of her responding women who had been married more than five years reported having an affair, and 76 percent of them claimed not to have feelings of guilt about their infidelity. More than 95 percent of women surveyed for Hite's third book claimed to have suffered "emotional and psychological harassment" from their men, and 98 percent replied that they desired "basic changes" in their relationships with husbands or lovers.

These, and similar results, which Hite freely generalizes to all American women, are usually at odds with other surveys using more traditional methods. For example, Hite's statistic about a 70 percent infidelity rate is in sharp contrast to a survey funded by *Playboy* that found 34 percent of married women reporting infidelity, and another study, sponsored by *Redbook* magazine, which reported the figure to be 29 percent.

Undeterred by her critics, Hite continued to produce books using similar survey methods, several of which were best-sellers. In the 1980s, she moved to Paris and her books began to take on more of a ''self-help'' aspect, such as her 1989 work, *Good Guys, Bad Guys: The Hite Guide to Smart Choices.* In the 1990s, she published her first novel, *The Divine Comedy of Ariadne and Jupiter,* and also set up an internet site, through which she offered her services as either a ''business consultant'' or ''personal consultant,'' and where she posted an exhibition of her art works.

—Justin Gustainis

FURTHER READING:

Hite, Shere. *The Hite Report: A Nationwide Study on Female Sexuality.* 1976.

———. *The Hite Report on Male Sexuality.* 1981.

Wallis, Claudia. ''Back Off, Buddy: A New Hite Report Stirs Up a Furor over Sex and Love in the '80s.'' *Time.* October 12, 1987, 68.

Hobo

See Tramps

Hockey

North American hockey is a fast and violent game, played on ice, which began in Canada in the mid-nineteenth century. The six-member teams, wearing skates and heavy pads, use sticks with which to propel a flat rubber disk known as the puck. It is thought that hockey derives its name from the French word for a shepherd's crook, in reference to the shape of the sticks with their curved playing end. The origins of ice hockey are much debated, and have been sought in several other sports such as hurly, shinty, bandy, field hockey (played with a small, hard ball) or the Native American Mic Mac game; but there seems to be general agreement that the earliest match that can be identified with any certainty as hockey was played in 1855 on a frozen harbor by soldiers of the Royal Canadian Regiment in Kingston, Ontario. It remained an outdoor game for the next 20 years, played by nine-man teams, and—influenced by the rules of rugby—no forward passing.

Students at Montreal's McGill University played the first indoor game in 1875, and developed the first hockey league in 1877. In 1883, the McGill team won the first game to be termed a ''world championship'' and, ten years later, teams were competing for the Stanley Cup, donated by Canada's governor-general, Lord Stanley, in a national championship. By then, the game had spread across the border to Yale and Johns Hopkins universities in the United States, and to Europe.

In the spirit of most sport during the Victorian era, when competing for financial gain was considered ungentlemanly and socially unacceptable, hockey flowered as an amateur game. This changed in the first decade of the twentieth century, which saw the advent of professional hockey. The world's first professional team, the Portage Lakers of Houghton, Michigan, was American, albeit using imported Canadian players. It was organized in 1903 by J. L. Gibson, a dentist, who, in 1904, established the first professional circuit, the International Pro Hockey League. Other leagues soon sprang up in Canada: the Ontario Professional League, the Pacific Coast Hockey Association, and the National Hockey Association. By this time most teams were using only seven players a side, but the

NHA, for reasons of economy, dropped yet another man from the ice, and six a side eventually became the standard team composition.

The most innovative of the leagues was the PCHA formed by the wealthy Patrick family. They led the way in building arenas for indoor hockey played on artificial ice. They also pioneered rules that allowed the goalie to move about, permitted forward passing, and credited with an ''assist'' those players setting up a goal-scorer. The league expanded to the American northwest and in 1917 the Seattle Metropolitans became the first U.S. team to win the Stanley Cup.

In 1917 the NHA gave way to the National Hockey League, which was to become the dominant professional league in the world. The NHL had teams in Toronto, Montreal, Hamilton and Ottawa, and after 1926, when it shrewdly bought out the Pacific Coast League and acquired all its players for $250,000, it had no rival. It began to admit American franchises, of which the first was the Boston Bruins in 1924, followed by short-lived teams such as the Pittsburgh Pirates, Philadelphia Quakers, St. Louis Eagles, and the New York (later Brooklyn) Americans. American teams that endured included three that entered in 1926: the New York Rangers, the Detroit Cougars (later the Falcons, later the Red Wings), and the Chicago Blackhawks. Canadian franchises that flourished for a time, only to disappear, included the Ottawa Senators (which had won four cups during the 1920s), Hamilton Tigers, Montreal Wanderers, Montreal Maroons, and Quebec Bulldogs.

When World War II ended, only six teams remained in the NHL but many consider the period between 1945 and 1967 to have been the golden age of hockey. It was certainly the era of elegant skaters and scorers such as Maurice ''Rocket'' Richard and Jean Beliveau of the Montreal Canadiens, Frank Mahovlich of the Toronto Maple Leafs, and Andy Bathgate of the Rangers; and of powerful forwards such as Johnny ''The Beast'' Bucyk of the Bruins, and Gordie Howe and ''Terrible'' Ted Lindsay of the Red Wings. There has never been a trio of goaltenders to match Chicago's Glen Hall, Montreal's Jacques Plante (inventor of the goalie mask), and Detroit's Terry Sawchuk. Rock-hard defensemen like Doug Harvey and Elmer ''Moose'' Vasko contended with players who had perfected the slap-shot which could propel the puck over 100 mph—shooters such as ''The Golden Jet'' Bobby Hull and Bernie ''Boom Boom'' Geoffrion.

The expansion of the NHL to six more American cities in 1968 and the appearance in 1971 of 12 more teams in the rival World Hockey Association diluted the quality of the sport. Players of exceptional talent, however, such as the magical Bobby Orr, could still shine. Orr revolutionized his position when he became the first defenseman to win the scoring trophy. The bidding wars for players that ensued during the 1970s drove up salaries and costs, thus causing many franchises to go under during the decade, and the frenzy stopped only in 1979 when the WHA folded and its four remaining teams were accepted into the NHL. One of the players who came in to the NHL from the WHA was Wayne Gretzky of the Edmonton Oilers, who went on to set innumerable scoring records in the 1980s and 1990s before retiring amid fanfare in 1999.

Up until the 1980s the overwhelming majority of professional players were Canadian, but developments in world hockey soon began to change that. An amateur team from the United States had caused an upset in the 1960 Winter Olympics when they returned with the gold medal, but that victory did not have nearly the impact of the 1980 ''Miracle On Ice'' when an under-dog American squad, amid Cold War tensions, defeated the seemingly unstoppable Soviets to reach the Olympic finals where they beat Finland for the gold. A number of players on this team went on to the NHL and their example

A physical altercation develops between the Philadelphia Flyers and the Boston Bruins during the 1974 Stanley Cup Finals.

encouraged many more young Americans to take up the game and do well at it. These new recruits to the big league were joined by a flood of highly skilled players from newly democratized countries in Eastern Europe seeking employment in North America.

There was plenty of work for the newcomers. The NHL was committed to a relentless policy of expansion, targeted particularly in the American west and sun belts, with the expectation that, by 2001, there would be 30 teams in the league, 24 of them in the United States. The aim was to penetrate large media markets that would provide the kind of giant television contracts that American networks were handing to professional baseball, basketball, and football leagues. The NHL had not yet hit television paydirt by 1999 (largely because Americans still preferred watching televised bowling and stock car races to seeing hockey on the small screen), while spiraling costs had caused the demise of small-market clubs in Canada and stretched the resources of many franchises in America.

As the millennium approached, the fate of hockey looked uncertain. College hockey in the United States, and women's hockey throughout the world, seemed set for more success; in Russia, however, once mighty teams were in a state of poverty-stricken post-communist collapse. Canada seemed destined to breed great players, while being unable to afford to watch them play in person. In the United States, the question was whether the National Hockey League

could afford to continue relying largely on gate revenues, with so little financial assistance from television. Faster than football, more violent than pro wrestling, at once graceful and crude, hockey had yet to completely win over the American sports fan.

—Gerry Bowler

FURTHER READING:

Coffey, Wayne R. *1980 U.S. Hockey Team.* Woodbridge, Connecticut, Blackbirch Press, 1993.

Dryden, Ken, and Roy MacGregor. *Home Game.* Toronto, McClelland and Stewart, 1991.

Farrington, S. Kip, Jr. *Skates, Sticks, and Men: The Story of Amateur Hockey in the United States.* New York, McKay, 1971.

Hockey's Heritage. Dubuque, Iowa, Kendall/Hunt, 1982.

Hubbard, Kevin, and Stan Fischler. *Hockey America.* Indianapolis, Masters Press, 1997.

McFarlane, Brian. *One Hundred Years of Hockey.* Toronto, Ontario, Deneau, 1989.

McKinley, Michael, Derik Murray, Ken Koo, and Ken Dryden. *Hockey Hall of Fame Legends: The Official Book.* 1995.

Potvin, Denis, with Stan Fischler. *Power on Ice.* New York, Harper & Row, 1977.

Powers, John, and Arthur C. Kaminsky. *One Goal: A Chronicle of the 1980 U.S. Olympic Hockey Team.* New York, Harper & Row, 1984.

Rockwell, Bart. *World's Strangest Hockey Stories.* Mahwah, New Jersey, Watermill Press, 1993.

Wendel, Tim. *Going for the Gold: How the U.S. Won at Lake Placid.* Westport, Connecticut, L. Hill, 1980.

Whitehead, Eric. *The Patricks, Hockey's Royal Family.* Garden City, New York, Doubleday, 1980.

Hoffman, Abbie (1936-1989)

One of the most colorful figures to emerge from the social turmoil of the 1960s, Abbie Hoffman put his personal stamp on the activism of the decade with his insistence that radical politics find expression in personal attitudes as well as political positions. Linking the spirited hedonism of the hippies with the politics of the Civil Rights movement, the New Left and the anti-war movement, Hoffman's attitude was pure hippie—*Revolution for the Hell of It* was the title of his first and most influential book. His doctrine of absurdity and wit, combined with an unmatched media savvy, marked him for the elite ranks of the counter-culture. A founding Yippie, and a hippie, activist, visionary and knave, he left an enduring legacy of influence and controversy.

Born in Worcester, Massachusetts, in 1936, Abbie Hoffman's life was an extraordinary patchwork of triumphs, calamities, and accidents. After fighting the Ku Klux Klan in Mississippi, he moved to New York where he joined the hippie counter-culture and undertook a series of flamboyant public stunts designed to infuse the growing hippie mob with political purpose. After organizing protests at the Democratic National Convention in 1968 he went underground in 1973, reappeared in 1980 to resume his activist work, and committed suicide in 1989.

Abbie Hoffman

In 1967, Hoffman left the Deep South for Manhattan's Lower East Side, where he joined the "diggers," a group of hippie community pranksters and activists, and opened a store to sell craft products produced in Mississippi homesteads. Together with Jerry Rubin, Hoffman formed the "Yippies" ("Youth International Party" was offered as the formal name only when pressed by reporters), and began a campaign of high-profile stunts meant to focus media attention on the movement. He understood what the media wanted and he set out to give it to them, aiming to swell the ranks of the movement with new conscripts through publicity. His actions, promoted with press releases and high-level media contacts to ensure maximum hype, emphasized the whimsy and humor characteristic of hippies. In one incident, bags of dollar bills were dumped from the visitors' gallery onto the floor of the New York Stock Exchange, causing mayhem as investors squabbled over the cash. In another, soot bombs were sent to Con Edison to protest pollution standards, and over 3,000 marijuana cigarettes were mailed to people randomly selected from the phone book, one of who turned out to be a prominent journalist. A celebration of the Spring Equinox at Grand Central drew over 6,000 hippies to a midnight gathering at the cavernous station, where police in riot gear waited nervously outside as hippies ran wild, tearing the hands off clocks, dancing, and squealing "Yippeee!!" Hoffman's "Exorcism of the Pentagon" was another landmark event, drawing 50,000 hippies to the nation's capital in an effort to levitate the entire Pentagon complex through magical means. The hippies joined hands, forming a human chain around the building as television crews soaked up the colorful event.

However, the tone of Yippie activism changed at the 1968 Democratic National Convention in Chicago. Yippies gathered there to offer a "festival of life" to counter what they called the "convention of death," but their innocence and prankishness turned into ugly riot as the demonstration was consumed in police violence. Outside the convention, where Hubert Humphrey was clinching the Democratic nomination for president, hippies, anti-war activists, and others massed, chanted, and sang, and when Chicago Mayor Richard Daley ordered police to disperse the throng, widespread panic and bloodshed resulted, lending credibility to the conservative call for law and order then being touted by Republican presidential candidate Richard Nixon. Hoffman and seven others stood trial as "the Chicago Eight" for conspiring to incite the riot, though after Black Panther Bobby Seale was remanded for separate trial by Judge Julius Hoffman, the Chicago Seven (which included Rubin and other Yippies and anti-war activists) achieved nationwide notoriety. Though Judge Hoffman issued 175 contempt citations during the trial, the seven were ultimately found innocent and other charges of "crossing State lines to incite a riot" were dropped on appeal in 1973.

By the early 1970s, however, Abbie Hoffman had other problems. Faced with accusations of egoism and showmanship from the organized left, and charged with chauvinism and authoritarianism from feminists, hippies, and other cultural factions, he now found himself standing at the center of a splintering movement. His response was to "resign" in an open letter addressed to the movement in 1971, and in 1974, fearing a lifetime jail term on a cocaine possession charge, he went into hiding, where he would remain for six years. Even underground, however, Hoffman retained his media "smarts," granting a well-publicized interview to *Playboy* magazine, in which he pledged to maintain his resistance and organize an underground movement aimed at toppling the government of the United States. After undergoing plastic surgery and taking up a prominent role incognito as a community environmental activist in Canada, Hoffman came out of hiding in 1980 to face charges. He served only a short term before he was once again free to resume his activism until his death. Hoffman's public stunts secured his lasting reputation as a spirited activist, cemented by the wide circulation of his books. *Revolution for the Hell of It, Steal This Book,* and *Woodstock Nation* were, and continue to be, staple reading for activists and latter-day hippies. His later titles included *Steal This Urine Test,* a commentary on the drug testing craze of the 1980s, and *Square Dancing in the Ice Age.*

—Sam Binkley

FURTHER READING:

Becker, Ted. *Live This Book; Abbie Hoffman's Philosophy for a Free and Green America.* New York, Nobel Press, 1991.

Hoffman, Abbie. *Revolution for the Hell of It.* Chicago, Dial Press, 1968.

———. *Steal This Book.* New York, Pirate Editions Inc., 1969.

Hoffman, Abbie, and Daniel Simon. *The Best of Abbie Hoffman.* New York, Four Walls Eight Windows, 1989.

Hoffman, Jack, and Daniel Simon. *Run Run Run: The Lives of Abbie Hoffman.* New York, Putnam's, 1994.

Jezer, Marty. *Abbie Hoffman: American Rebel.* New Brunswick, New Jersey, Rutgers University Press, 1992.

Raskin, Jonah. *For the Hell of It: The Life and Times of Abbie Hoffman.* Berkeley, University of California Press, 1996.

Sloman, Larry. *Steal This Dream: Abbie Hoffman and the Countercultural Revolution in America.* New York, Doubleday, 1998.

Hoffman, Dustin (1937—)

Beginning in the late 1960s, Dustin Hoffman established himself as one of his generation's finest film actors and helped usher method acting into the American cinema mainstream. From his first screen success as Benjamin Braddock in *The Graduate* (1967), Hoffman appeared in a series of diverse films that showcased his great range and indicated the rise of the character actor as superstar. He and actors such as Gene Hackman, Jack Nicholson, and Robert De Niro symbolized a new breed of movie star that was known more for fully inhabiting their characters than for their perfect profiles. Hoffman was, at times, criticized for being "difficult" to work with, but none could criticize his ability to employ the teachings of the method tradition that stressed the performer's ability to temporarily "become" his character.

Born on August 8, 1937, in Los Angeles, California, this son of a Columbia Pictures set decorator and an aspiring actress was named after silent screen cowboy star Dustin Farnum. He developed an early interest in performing, and his acting career began at age 12, when, as the shortest boy in John Burroughs High School, he was recruited to play Tiny Tim in a production of *A Christmas Carol.* He was an accomplished pianist and enrolled in the Los Angeles Conservatory of Music to study classical and jazz piano. By 1957, he began to devote less time to his music and increasingly concentrated on acting. He studied at the famed Pasadena Playhouse and later moved to New York. He entered The Actor's Studio, where he developed his craft alongside his roommates, future film stars Robert Duvall and Gene

Dustin Hoffman

Hackman. Under the direction of noted acting teacher Lee Strasberg, Hoffman was taught the method's performance goal of becoming rather than acting. To support himself he took on a series of jobs, such as janitor, waiter, and weaver of Hawaiian leis. He even worked as a hospital attendant in a psychiatric ward, where he observed the patients' behaviors in the hopes of improving his dramatic technique. Hoffman established himself as a respected New York theater actor in the early 1960s by appearing in acclaimed works like *The Journey of the Fifth Horse* and the British comedy *Eh?* However, Hoffman's ultimate goal was to become a film star.

After years of honing his craft, Hoffman became an "overnight" sensation in 1967 with the release of director Mike Nichols's *The Graduate*. The film concerned an innocent college graduate who is seduced by an older woman. Although Charles Webb's novel, upon which the film was based, described the character of Benjamin Braddock as a handsome, well-bred, surfer-type, Nichols gave the role to the short, dark Hoffman. Furthermore, at age 30, Hoffman was a decade older than the character. Hoffman's performance as the confused and depressed college graduate who begins an affair with a friend of his parents, the infamous Mrs. Robinson, captured the mood of the American youth of the late 1960s who had grown disenchanted with their parents' generation. Author Jeff Lenburg quoted a letter to *The New York Times* written by a university student shortly after the film's release to demonstrate the impact it had upon the youth culture. The student wrote: "I identified with Ben . . . I thought of him as a spiritual brother. He was confused about his future and about his place in the world, as I am. It's a film one digs, rather than understands intellectually." The baby boomer generation's uncertainty of the

future was best captured in the film's final scene where Ben and Elaine (Mrs. Robinson's daughter) flee her wedding and mother only to realize the uncertainty of their final destination. Hoffman was nominated for an Academy Award for his portrayal of the embodiment of 1960s youth angst.

Following his early success in *The Graduate* Hoffman appeared in a number of landmark films. In 1969, he starred as the tubercular small-time street hustler Ratso Rizzo in *Midnight Cowboy*. The controversial film about male prostitution was an enormous hit and the first x-rated film to win the Academy Award for best picture. For *Little Big Man* (1970), Hoffman aged on screen from a teen to the age of 121 to play Jack Crabb, a witness to U.S. mistreatment of the American Indians. He portrayed the doomed comedian Lenny Bruce in *Lenny* (1974) and starred as *Washington Post* reporter Carl Bernstein in the Watergate drama *All the President's Men* (1976). He was named best actor in 1979 for his performance as a divorced father facing a child-custody battle in *Kramer vs. Kramer*. In 1984, he returned to the stage for a widely praised performance as Willy Loman in *Death of a Salesman*. His ability to play both straight drama and broad comedy is seen in his most acclaimed roles. In *Tootsie* (1982) Hoffman mocked his reputation as a difficult actor by playing a man who disguises himself in drag to get a job on a soap opera. For *Rainman* (1988) he masterfully depicted an autistic savant. He earned a second Oscar for this classic performance. Hoffman remained a popular performer into the 1990s and scored another hit as a Hollywood producer attempting to cover up a presidential sex scandal in *Wag the Dog* (1998). Hoffman's filmography also contains one of Hollywood's most notorious disasters—the comedic misfire *Ishtar* (1987).

Dustin Hoffman has remained a star after more than 30 years in film because he invests all his portrayals with sensitivity and realism. He commented on his technique by stating: "All I know is I try to be as personal as I can in my work, by being personal, to be able to bring to it a truth in what I observe and what I feel." Through his method acting skills and non-flashy, realistic appearance he opened mainstream American film to a style of performance that had seldom been achieved before on screen.

—Charles Coletta

FURTHER READING:

Anderson, Christopher. *The New Book of People*. New York, G. P. Putnam's Sons, 1986.

Brode, Douglas. *The Films of Dustin Hoffman*. Secaucus, Citadel Press, 1983.

Lenburg, Jeff. *Dustin Hoffman: Hollywood's Anti-Hero*. New York, St. Martin's Press, 1983.

Hogan, Ben (1912-1997)

With his perfect swing, golfer Ben Hogan achieved a kind of mythic stature in the collective mind of the American public. During his career, Hogan won sixty-three tournaments, including nine major championships. He was the PGA tour's leading money-winner five times, won the Vardon Trophy for lowest scoring average five times, and was one of the first inductees into the World Golf Hall of Fame in 1974. As awesome as that record is, the folklore concerning Hogan's

Ben Hogan

arduous rise to the top of his profession and his famed comeback after a near-fatal auto accident nearly transcends it.

Perhaps the most famous photograph of Hogan (collected in *The Hogan Mystique,* 1994) captures much of the essence of the mystique: a shot of Hogan's flawless swing taken at its height and from the golfer's back, it extends outward to feature an attentive gallery on two sides of a tree-lined fairway. Thus, Hogan's face is not shown; his personal identity is subordinated to a frozen image of the mechanical perfection of his golfing prowess. Throughout his career, Hogan was notoriously aloof from competitors, the press, and even his public. In addition, the peak years of his achievement preceded the wide coverage of golf by television; thus he was not captured repeatedly in widely distributed images as were Arnold Palmer, Jack Nicklaus, Gary Player, and Lee Trevino. Hogan became, though, something of an icon to these later figures, and what they admired was "Hogan's game" and the story of the literally painful way in which it had been developed.

The son of a blacksmith, Hogan was born in small-town Dublin, Texas, in 1912 and moved with his family to Fort Worth in 1921. His father, who had suffered from depression and alcoholism, committed suicide the following year, and Hogan's family was immediately plunged into poverty. In order to help out financially, young Ben became a caddie at Glen Garden Country Club, thus discovering the

sport that would change his life. At Glen Garden, he met a fellow caddie, Byron Nelson, with whom he quickly became a fierce competitor.

Hogan turned professional in 1930 but would achieve success only after years of relative obscurity. Throughout this early period, his status on the PGA tour was always subordinate to that of Nelson. Hogan was not in effect a natural golfer and only realized his famous swing by regularly practicing until his hands literally bled. Perfection resulting from a puritan work ethic, long a central ingredient in American mythology, would become an essential element of the Hogan mystique. This grim self-creation was also a key factor in his legendary aloofness; always struggling to improve, he never felt that he had time for, nor did he see any point in, small talk with his playing partners or courting tournament galleries.

Hogan did not win his first tournament on the tour until 1940, when he won four. He followed that with five victories in 1941, but his new success was interrupted when he was drafted into the U.S. Army in 1943. It was in the immediate postwar period that Hogan began to dominate the PGA tour and his legend started to take form. He won his first major title, the PGA tournament, in 1946. In 1948, he repeated his success in the PGA and, in a rare exhibition of golfing perfection, won his first of four U.S. Open championships. Just as he seemed finally to have reached the peak of his success and his career, he was nearly killed in an automobile accident in February of 1949. His doctors were not certain first that he would live, then that he would walk again, and then that he would play competitive golf again. Hogan did all three, returning to the tour in January of 1950. In that year, he won his second U.S. Open: the often recounted "Hogan comeback" was under way, and the final ingredient was added to the Hogan mystique, that of the courageous underdog who survived extreme adversity.

The story would prove so compelling that Hollywood would have to film it, even if inadequately. *Follow the Sun,* supposedly the story of Hogan's life and climaxing with his comeback, was released in 1951. Its script was cliched; and Glenn Ford, as Hogan, was badly miscast. In the words of Hogan biographer Curt Sampson: "Ford, an unathletic man whose hobby was gardening, held the club as if it were a trowel and swung it like a rake."

In 1953, Hogan reached the pinnacle of his golfing career when he won the U.S. Open, his second Masters tournament, and his first British Open, thus sweeping three of professional golf's four major events (he did not enter the PGA tournament that year). The British Open win in Carnoustie, Scotland, especially contributed to the Hogan myth. Already known as "Bantam Ben," he was nicknamed "The Wee Ice Mon" by Scottish fans who were simultaneously paying tribute to his determined concentration and his triumph over physical adversity. (Hogan was, in fact, of average height). In July of that year, he was treated to a ticker tape parade down Broadway in New York City.

Hogan wrote a popular five-part series on the basic elements of the correct golf swing for *Sports Illustrated* beginning March 11, 1957. After retiring from competitive golf in 1971, Hogan fittingly devoted his time to manufacturing and selling golf clubs until his death on July 25, 1997.

—James R. Giles

FURTHER READING:

Campbell, Malcolm, and J. M. Fox. *The Random House International Encyclopedia of Golf.* New York, Random House, 1991.

Davis, Martin, et. al. *The Hogan Mystique: Classic Photographs of the Great Ben Hogan by Jules Alexander.* New York, Broadway Books, 1994.

Diaz, Jaime. "One of a Kind." *Sports Illustrated.* August 4, 1997, G6-G10.

Matuz, Roger. *Inside Sports Magazine Golf: Your Ultimate Tour Guide.* Detroit, Visible Ink, 1997.

Nelson, Byron. "The Mystique Lives On." *Sports Illustrated.* August 4, 1997, 26-29.

Sampson, Curt. *Hogan.* New York, Broadway Books, 1996.

Hogan, Hulk (1953—)

While limited in his talent as an in-ring performer, Hulk Hogan's physique, interviews, and incredible personal charisma made him the undisputed star of a professional wrestling boom that began in 1984 and remains, with the exception of a few years, stronger than ever in the late 1990s. Throughout this time, Hogan has been the most recognizable personality to nonprofessional wrestling fans. To promoters, Hogan has been a marketable presence, headlining live events, selling merchandise, performing on television, and appearing in the main event for the majority of Pay-per-View (PPV) shows. Hogan has parlayed his wrestling fame into roles in movies, television, and commercials. Simply, he is the greatest drawing card in the history of professional wrestling.

Hulk Hogan

Born Terry Bollea, Hogan began weightlifting as a teenager while living in Tampa, Florida. After studying business administration and music at the University of South Florida, he was discovered by two professional wrestlers when he was playing bass in a rock band. Hogan started wrestling in the southern United States under names such as Terry "the Hulk" Boulder and Sterling Golden. Hogan first hit the big time with the World Wrestling Federation (WWF) in the early 1980s. With "heel" manager Classie Freddie Blassie at his side, Hogan played the muscular, egotistical blond villain. As was then a common occurrence, Hogan left one wrestling territory and moved to the next: the Minneapolis-based American Wrestling Association (AWA).

Though Hogan had appeared in both the WWF and AWA, it was his trips to Japan which created the phenomenon known as "Hulkamania." Japanese wrestling fans immediately took to Hogan, and he became a superstar. Upon his returned to the United States, he was booked back in the AWA as a "heel." But the fans rejected that role for Hogan and, instead, cheered him. He was turned "baby face" and quickly set attendance records across the Midwest. Hogan extended his success in the ring with a small but very noticeable part in *Rocky II*; playing "Thunder Lips" he was paired with Rocky in a charity boxer vs. wrestler match. By 1983, Hulk Hogan was the biggest name in professional wrestling, but this was only the beginning.

Vince McMahon, Jr. lured Hogan from the AWA and made him the star of his nationally expanding WWF promotion. In 1984, Hogan defeated the evil Iron Sheik in less than ten-minutes at New York's Madison Square Garden to become the WWF champion. Hogan began starring in wrestling shows across the country as the WWF became nationally syndicated and featured on cable programs. Hogan's feud with Roddy Piper in 1984 led first to the "brawl to settle it all" broadcast live on MTV, and then a few months later to "Wrestlemania," the first wrestling event broadcast on closed-circuit TV nationally. Hogan teamed with TV actor Mr. T in the main event. Taking advantage of a late cancellation, Hogan and Mr. T were able to host *Saturday Night Live* the evening before "WrestleMania." The success of "WrestleMania" soon won it a monthly show on NBC, and Hogan bolstered the show's popularity. He was featured on the cover of *Sports Illustrated* and in *Time*. Hogan's image was everywhere: on T-shirts, on the cover of a record album, in wrestling videos and TV guest appearances. After a hugely successful match against Andre the Giant at the Pontiac Silverdome—which drew over 80,000 people plus another million or so watching on closed circuit TV and the very young PPV industry—NBC moved wrestling to prime time in February 1988.

But by the early 1990s, Hogan encountered his most serious challenge in wrestling, when a doctor affiliated with the WWF was arrested for dealing illegal steroids. The case expanded to include WWF owner Vince McMahon, with Hogan as a witness for the government. Hogan went on the *Arsenio Hall Show* and denied being a steroid user or abuser, confessing only to a limited use of steroids for medical purposes. Although at the trial he confessed to more use. The prosecutor mocked Hogan's catch phrase extolling children to "say your prayers and eat your vitamins" while "all the while [the WWF was] pumping him with steroids." After Hogan won the main event at "WrestleMania XIII," he disappeared from wrestling as the steroid scandal intensified. A short comeback proved to be a flop as Hogan's physique had shrunk, and with it, seemingly, his popularity. After losing the WWF title in June 1993, which he had won again at "WrestleMania XIV," Hogan severed his relationship with the WWF.

After some movie and television work, including a short-lived show called *Thunder in Paradise,* Hogan returned to the U.S. wrestling scene in the summer of 1994 just as the verdict of "not guilty" came down in the WWF steroid case. Hogan went to work for Ted Turner's World Championship Wrestling (WCW) and had an immediate impact, as ratings and PPV revenue increased. But Hogan's act had played too long. Even though he was still a "good guy," Hogan was booed at arenas.

After failing to toughen up his image, Hogan finally "turned" on the fans in 1996 and adopted the persona of Hollywood Hogan, forming, along with other wrestlers, a group called the New World Order (NWO). The NWO soon became the hottest gimmick in wrestling and Hogan was the focus of the promotion: always in the main event, always in the key part of the television programs. Behind the scenes, Hogan was acting as the de facto "head booker" deciding which wrestlers got TV time, wins, and championship belts. Hogan also demonstrated his star power, drawing celebrities such as NBA players Dennis Rodman and Karl Malone into the ring. One of the most memorable of these celebrity fights was between Hogan and *Tonight Show* host Jay Leno in the "Hog Wild" PPV in August 1998. Hulk Hogan's flamboyance and theatrics has come to epitomize the appeal of professional wrestling.

—Patrick Jones

FURTHER READING:

Corliss, Richard. "Hype! Hell Raising! Hulk Hogan!" *Time*. April 15, 1985, 104.

Lentz, Harris M. *Biographical Dictionary of Professional Wrestling.* Jefferson, North Carolina, McFarland & Company, 1997.

Morton, Gerald, and George M. O'Brien. *Wrestling to Rasslin': Ancient Sport to American Spectacle.* Bowling Green, Ohio, Bowling Green State University Press, 1985.

Newman, Bruce. "Who's Kidding Whom?" *Sports Illustrated.* April 29, 1985, 28-34.

Hogan's Heroes

Depending upon whom one asks, *Hogan's Heroes* was either a cutting edge situation comedy or a testament to how desensitized to human suffering American television viewers had become in the 1960s. The basic plot of the popular television show centered around American Col. Robert Hogan, played by Bob Crane, and a band of other prisoners of war, who had established a secret complex within and below the grounds of Stalag 13, a Nazi concentration camp. From there they engaged in sabotage and rescue operations against the Third Reich. Every bed was a passageway, every coffee pot a radio. For six seasons on CBS, Hogan and his group used a stash of supplies, that would have made the Third Army envious, to confound Hitler's hapless forces in and around Dusseldorf.

Hogan's Heroes was loosely based on the play *Stalag 17,* triggering a lawsuit by the producers of the play, but also contained elements of the 1963 hit movie *The Great Escape.* Hogan's team was composed of demolition expert Andrew Carter (Larry Hovis), radio

operator Ivan Kinchlow (Ivan Dixon), all-around procurer Peter Newkirk (Richard Dawson), and chef Louis LeBeau (Robert Clary). Their primary nemesis was Wilhelm Klink (Werner Klemperer), a pompous colonel who sought promotion to general by constantly reminding his superiors that "No one has ever escaped from Stalag 13!" He was aided by Sgt. Major Hans Schultz (John Banner), who regularly stumbled across Hogan's escapades but, unable to fathom the consequences of his perceptions, managed to ignore them by chanting the mantra "I see nothing!" Among Klink's regular superiors were General Albert Burkhalter (Leon Askin) and Gestapo Major Wolfgang Hochstetter (Howard Cain). The show never actually featured Adolf Hitler as a character, but he was impersonated twice— once on radio and once in person—to great comic effect.

While *Hogan's Heroes* was a popular show, it was also a lightning rod for controversy. In 1965, when the program first aired, organized reaction to America's involvement in Vietnam was intensifying. It did not help matters much that corporate America was making huge amounts of money and the "silent majority" was settling back once a week to revel in the lighthearted high jinks, as a fun-loving bunch of POWs confounded their dumb-but-lovable Nazi tormentors. This was not new territory. *McHale's Navy*, which debuted in 1962, featured Ernest Borgnine as the Commander of an American PT boat crewed by a load of drunks and petty thieves and catered to by an escaped Japanese POW named Fuji, who they hid from their dumbfounded commanding officer Admiral Binghamton (Joe Flynn). But the members of *McHale's Navy* rarely fought the enemy face-to-face. By comparison, a whole concentration camp of prisoners, who could have left at any time and chose not to, policed by representatives of a system of imbecility that appeared to stretch all the way to the top of the chain of command, was more than many people, particularly those less than a generation removed from the war, could stand.

The show's defenders countered that it was meant to be nothing more than slapstick entertainment. Indeed, the action of the show was extremely unrealistic—in one episode they smuggled a whole German army tank into camp, in another Hogan convinced Klink and Burkhalter that the war was over. They also pointed out that Clary had spent most of his early life in a concentration camp and thought ridicule a more than appropriate treatment of the Nazis. But those defenses mattered little to the show's critics, and *Hogan's Heroes* was regularly attacked throughout its run.

—Barry Morris

FURTHER READING:

Royce, Brenda Scott. *Hogan's Heroes: Behind the Scenes at Stalag 13.* Los Angeles, Renaissance, 1998.

Shive, Nathan. *The Official "Hogan's Heroes" Companion.* New York, Macmillan, 1995.

Holbrook, Hal (1925—)

On April 6, 1959, a thirty-four-year-old actor named Hal Holbrook literally became the seventy-two-year-old Mark Twain and made theatrical history as the creator of a new genre. From his hair to his shoes, from his voice to his movements, Holbrook was, from that night on, a living version of the icon of American literature. What was

Werner Klemperer (left) and Bob Crane in a scene from the television show *Hogan's Heroes*.

so extraordinary and historical about this innovative dramatic event was that no actor had ever done a one-person show for two hours not merely reciting, but acting out a character. Holbrook's feat was a masterpiece of creativity; his acting was electrifying, and he received standing ovations every night. Holbrook thus initiated the one-actor play based on an historical, political, or literary figure.

For more than forty years Holbrook has advanced the public's knowledge of Samuel Clemens's writings. Prior to that momentous evening, the young actor had invested years of research in a scholarly study of Twain to create *Mark Twain, Tonight!,* which he has played more than two thousand times in forty-eight states, Canada, Eastern and Western Europe, and Scandinavia. In recognition of his unique contribution to the humanities, Holbrook received an honorary degree from Ohio State University in 1979; since that time many other institutions have awarded him similar honors. He has also received an Outer Critics Circle Award, a Drama Desk Vernon Rice Award, a Tony, and a special OBIE Award for *Mark Twain, Tonight!*

Along with his stage work in *Twain* and other plays including *King Lear* and *Death of a Salesman,* Holbrook has been a well-respected television and film actor since the 1950s. He is the recipient of five Emmy awards: for *Mark Twain, Tonight!* (1966, CBS); for his

portrayal of Lincoln in *Sandberg's Lincoln* (1973), for his Kennedy-like senator in *The Senator* (1971), and two for his performance as Commander Bucher on the ill-fated *Pueblo* (1973); and for his part as the informational host of *Portrait of America: Alaska* (1989). He also accepted the challenge to be cast in the very first television drama dealing with homosexuals in the critically acclaimed *That Certain Summer* (1972). Holbrook portrayed Abraham Lincoln in the *North and South* TV miniseries in 1985 and 1986; Reese Watson in *Designing Women* (with third wife, Dixie Carter) from 1986 to 1990; and "Wild Bill" McKenzie in several *Perry Mason Mystery* episodes in the 1990s. Holbrook has acted in numerous motion pictures, most of which were not worthy of his exceptional talent with the notable exception of his portrayal of "Deep Throat" in the award-winning *All the President's Men.*

Holbrook was born in Cleveland but was raised by his grandfather in Hartford, Connecticut. He attended Culver Military Academy and Denison University where he majored in acting. After his graduation, he and his first wife, actress Ruby Holbrook, toured the southwestern United States, playing Shakespeare to small-town high schools. These road shows ceased after two children arrived, and Holbrook returned to New York to act in the CBS television day series

The Brighter Day from 1954 to 1959. At this time, Holbrook was encouraged and backed financially by his former drama teacher at Denison and others to take his one-man Twain to Broadway.

—Toby Irene Cohen

Holden, William (1918-1982)

From his discovery in the late 1930s actor William Holden rose to be one of the most dependable and most likeable leading men of 1950s Hollywood, appearing to personify the mild-mannered charm of the Eisenhower era while, at his best, suggesting that the period's integrity and feeling went deeper than its relatively bland, conformist tendencies sometimes suggested. During more than forty years Holden had seventy roles where, for the most part, he met his fate with varying mixtures of wryness, cynicism, and good humor that was always believable and often attractive, but particularly successful in the mid-1950s.

Holden revealed a homely and good-natured appeal in a number of features including *Golden Boy* (1939) and *Our Town* (1940) before joining the wartime air force. On his return, following a number of forgettable Westerns, he got an important break in Billy Wilder's *Sunset Boulevard* (1950) as a late replacement for Montgomery Clift. Here, Holden showed a seedier version of where his good looks might lead him playing a failed Hollywood scriptwriter turned gigolo.

William Holden

Though the film was not a popular success, roles in *Born Yesterday* (1950) and his Oscar-winning performance in the prison camp comedy *Stalag 17* (1953) brought a much higher profile. The lovable rogue of *Stalag 17* is archetypal of Holden's best roles: relatively mild-mannered but opportunistic, brave if necessary, but preferring to avoid confrontation. A series of roles as cads, lovers, and occasional reluctant heroes followed—*The Moon Is Blue* (1953), *Sabrina* (1954), *The Country Girl* (1954), *The Bridges at Toko-Ri* (1954), *Love Is a Many Splendored Thing* (1955), *Picnic* (1955), *Bridge on the River Kwai* (1957)—most of which were highly successful. One of the top ten box-office stars from 1954 to 1956, Holden was able to arrange a deal for *Bridge on the River Kwai* bringing him 10 percent of the film's gross. However, as his looks began to fade and as audiences sought younger, more overt rebels, Holden was no longer a box office certainty (in 1968 he made *Variety*'s list of overpaid stars). As an increasingly grizzled figure, marked by the alcoholism that would kill him in his 1960s, he was still capable of outstanding performances: most notably in *The Wild Bunch* (1969) as a sadistic and psychopathic cowboy, and as the fading anchorman in *Network* (1976), clinging wearily, grimly, to job and wife.

Holden was a reliable and consistent, rather than dazzling, performer whose films could be depended on to succeed in an uncertain period in Hollywood for many actors. Like John Wayne or Robert Mitchum, Holden appeared most successful where he did not need to "act," but merely characterize a certain form of masculinity which appeared particularly attractive to 1950s audiences. Not as attached to the uncompromising code of the Wild West as Wayne or as superhumanly laid back as Mitchum, his masculinity had a broad appeal. Holden's good nature is tempered by a skepticism and suspicion that gives an edginess to his heroism and sees his moral choices made with his self-preservation very much in mind. In a sense, he reflected the experiences of a generation of men who had been at war and knew the dangers of moral absolutes and strict codes of behavior that do not allow for circumstances (essentially the subject of *Bridge on the River Kwai*). Also, the stability and the prosperity of the 1950s carried fears of both failure and the banality of conformity. Holden offered a believable, but attractive, male lead with choices to do good or bad who swung convincingly between the two before making the right decision (allowing Bogart to get Hepburn in *Sabrina,* not taking Grace Kelly from Bing Crosby in *The Country Girl.*

Holden flourished in the space between the bad guy heroes of the 1930s and 1940s gangster movies and the increasingly youth-oriented anti-heroes of the 1960s. He was an understated representation of male hopes and fears in the 1950s, of the anxiety that individualism is impossible in an increasingly rationalized world and any attempt to be different might bring failure down on the precariously placed wage slave. Holden is a hero of this period exactly because in so many of his roles his actions are in spite of his skepticism of heroics, in spite of his quite palpable sense of self-preservation.

—Kyle Smith

FURTHER READING:

Parrish, James, and John Stanke. *The All-Americans.* New York, Arlington House, 1977.

Thomas, Bob. *Golden Boy: The Untold Story of William Holden.* London, Weidenfeld & Nicholson, 1983.

Holiday, Billie (1915-1959)

Billie Holiday, certainly one of the foremost American song stylists and often called the greatest American jazz singer, was born Eleanora Harris on April 7, 1915 in Philadelphia. After her birth to Sadie Harris, the facts about Billie are often in dispute, due in large part to Billie's own tendency to spin tales about her life that have small kernels of truth but cannot be accepted wholesale as fact. The truth about her life is as interesting, if not more so, than her invention—recent biographers benefitted from extensive oral interviews done for a projected biography by Linda Kuehl (who died before completing it).

Listening to her recordings is a parallel version of her tumultuous and heartfelt life, one that expresses her beauty and soulfulness—however, as writer Hetty Jones warns, ''Sometimes you are afraid to listen to this lady.'' Her short life was consumed by trouble: the wrong men, alcohol, heroin, racism, and just plain hard times, yet her personality was so winning that it shone through her vocals and she was well loved by her friends. What is certain is that the singer gave as good as she got; alternately tough-minded and intensely vulnerable, she helped create the mystique of Lady Day and nurtured it throughout her career.

Her ''autobiography,'' *Lady Sings the Blues* (written by *New York Post* writer William Dufty), is the prime source for the Billie Holiday mythology; she bragged that she had never even read it, yet enough of her salty humor and dramatic timing made it into the book to capture an audience that was more than ready to accept it. What was

Billie Holiday

painful to Billie was often transformed in the narrative; the circumstances of her birth being a good example. Her mother, Sadie, told Billie her father was Clarence Holiday, a talented guitarist best known for his work with Fletcher Henderson's band, and Billie states in the book that ''my mother and father were just a couple of kids when they got married.'' They were never married nor lived together; Clarence Holiday acknowledged Eleanora, though their relationship was strained and awkward as he was married to another woman and disliked having his daughter around as evidence of his past.

Growing up in Fell's Point, a tough waterfront neighborhood in Baltimore, Eleanora experienced a brief, brutal childhood—her mother, forced to take work in New York as a maid, left her daughter in the care of abusive relatives. Only her great-grandmother (who she recalls with special fondness in *Lady*) was a source of solace to the little girl. Picked up for truancy, she was sent to the House of Good Shepherd for Colored Girls, a Catholic residential facility, where she was baptized and found some stability after a succession of ''stepfathers'' and being shunted around. Her recollections of Good Shepherd were mixed; she was glad to escape the harsh institution. Sadie wasn't able to handle her daughter, having enough problems of her own, and the breaking point came when the eleven-year-old girl was raped by a neighbor. She was returned to Good Shepherd, but stayed only a short while before returning home to Sadie.

The seminal event of young Eleanora's life was the discovery of jazz—she absorbed her first musical education listening to her lifelong idol, Louis Armstrong, on a Victrola in a neighborhood brothel. ''I heard a record by, as we call him, Pops, and it was called 'West End Blues' and . . . he sang 'Ooh be doo,' and I would wonder why he didn't sing any words and he had the most beautiful feeling.'' She always credited Louis Armstrong as her major influence as a singer, although she was certainly influenced by Bessie Smith and others; Billie loved Armstrong and performed with him on a number of occasions.

Now fifteen, Eleanora became a prostitute in madam Alice Dean's house, and soon was declared ''out of control'' by her guardian. Her exodus from Baltimore marked a turning point in her life when she made her way to New York to join her mother, who was employed as a maid. She was picked up in a Harlem vice raid along with Sadie, charged with prostitution and spent a short time in a workhouse. After her discharge she found could make a good living as a singer in clubs, and in juke joints she perfected her craft. At this time she adopted her father's surname and chose ''Billie'' after silent film actress Billie Dove. She loved the life, and she also took to marijuana, a commonplace in the music world—aficionados were called ''vipers'' and ''sticks'' were cheap and easy to find. Billie had a prodigious tolerance for all substances: alcohol, marijuana, and finally, heroin. It would be a mistake to focus on Billie Holiday as a singer ruined by addictions, yet there is no doubt her appetites shortened her life and harmed her voice. She was part of a culture that accepted drugs easily—one critic called them ''an occupational hazard.''

The discovery of Billie Holiday has been claimed by more than one person, and she herself told a story about auditioning as a dancer at ''Pod and Jerry's'' and being hired as a singer which was more fancy than fact. What is true is that white jazz writer and producer John Hammond did hear her sing in early 1933 and was astonished by what he heard, but it wasn't until November of that year that he was finally able to schedule a recording session and later signed her for Columbia Records. The next year she met saxophonist Lester Young, her soul mate musically and personally: their friendship was one of Billie's deepest and most enduring relationships. It was Young who named her "Lady Day" (the "Day" from Holiday) and christened Sadie, "Duchess" when he lived with them after he first came to New York. Billie called him "Prez" (short for "President" since he was "the greatest" in her opinion) and their careers would intertwine over the years with memorable recordings to prove it. Billie liked and supported other female singers: she and Ella Fitzgerald admired each other; she also befriended the young Lena Horne.

Billie may have sung the blues, but she was primarily a jazz singer and one of the best interpreters of pop music ever. She disliked the title of her autobiography for that reason (the publisher chose it). In the words of the musicians who almost universally admired her: "She had ears," meaning she understood the music thoroughly, earning the respect of Count Basie, Artie Shaw, and many others. Duke Ellington said Billie was the "coolest." Her signature song, "Strange Fruit" is indescribably wrenching; an indictment of lynching so potent it silenced audiences whenever she performed it—with "Strange Fruit" her artistry confronted the fashionable jazz world of Cafe Society with the brutal reality of racism that black musicians knew first hand. Lillian Smith told Billie the song inspired her to write her novel of the same name. Touring the South with Artie Shaw's band, Billie felt the force of Jim Crow. In her autobiography she stated, "It got to the point where I hardly ever ate, slept, or went to the bathroom without having a major NAACP-type production."

A song Billie Holiday made her own, "The Man I Love," along with "T'ain't Nobody's Business If I Do," and especially, "My Man" have been often held up as an example of how Lady Day felt about the men in her life. Billie was often exploited and abused by many people she trusted, but her choices reflected her deep ambivalence about love, and a measure of masochism. Musicians who worked with her loved her and deplored her boyfriends. One, Bobby Tucker, a favorite accompanist, called them "pimps," because they "lived off her," particularly the brutal John Levy and husband Louis McKay, who managed the singer by facilitating her drug habit and draining her financial resources. Hospitalized several times and jailed at Alderson Federal Reformatory in 1947, Holiday was penalized for her high-profile troubles—she lost her New York City Cabaret license, which paradoxically opened up venues like Carnegie Hall (where she performed several legendary concerts in 1948) but severely restricted her ability to make her living.

The 1972 film *Lady Sings the Blues,* a showcase for singer Diana Ross crafted for her by Berry Gordy as a new venue for Motown, distorted Billie Holiday's life story and created a love story from Louis McKay's viewpoint (he served as a technical advisor on the picture). Despite Ross's strong performance, the film failed to create a convincing portrait and was critically panned. It did generate new interest in Billie Holiday and her recordings, which translated into such diverse appreciations of Holiday such as Alice Adams's novel *Listening to Billie* and an Australian film, *Billy's Holiday* (a fantasy wherein a male fan discovers he can sing like his favorite singer). Images of Holiday are ubiquitous on such items as t-shirts and posters: the "Lady with the Gardenia" (the flower she often wore in her hair), dressed to kill in elegant gowns, is an icon that has not only endured but has become ever more popular, much as Marilyn Monroe or Elvis has. In her discography, the Verve recordings (beginning in 1946) are often touted as her greatest, with her voice at its mature best and her spirit radiant in songs she made standards: "All of Me," "Autumn in New York," "Don't Explain" and the song she co-authored, "God Bless the Child," best reflects Billie's essential personality—an artist, first and foremost. A last recording, the

controversial "Lady in Satin" shows the singer diminished but still innovating, working with a lush orchestral accompaniment.

Her death on July 17, 1959 followed a long, sad decline precipitated by the death of Sadie and accelerated by her addiction. Hospitalized in New York in May, 1959, she was arrested for possession of narcotics in her hospital bed, a last indignity. In a 1956 interview, Billie told Mike Wallace why she thought jazz greats die young: "we try to live a hundred days in one day, and we try to please so many people. Like myself, I want to bend this note, bend that note, sing this way, sing that way, and get all the feeling, eat all the good foods, and travel all over in one day, and you can't do it."

A legendary stylist, Frank Sinatra, stated: "Billie Holiday was, and still remains, the greatest single musical influence on me." Her friend, writer Leonard Feather, said of Billie that "her voice was the voice of living intensity, of soul in the true sense of that greatly abused word. As a human being, she was sweet, sour, kind, mean, generous, profane, lovable, and impossible, and nobody who knew her expects to see anyone quite like her ever again."

—Mary Hess

FURTHER READING:

Baraka, Imiri. *Black Music.* New York, William Morrow, 1968.

Chilton, John. *Billie's Blues: The True Story of the Immortal Billie Holiday.* London, Quartet Books, 1975.

Clarke, Donald. *Wishing on the Moon: The Life and Times of Billie Holiday.* New York, Viking Press, 1994.

Davis, Angela. *Blues Legacies & Black Feminism: Gertrude "Ma" Rainey, Bessie Smith & Billie Holiday.* New York, Pantheon, 1998.

De Veaux, Alexis. *Don't Explain: A Song of Billie Holiday.* New York, Harper and Row, 1990.

Gourse, Leslie. *The Billie Holiday Companion: Seven Decades of Commentary.* New York, Schirmer Books, 1997.

———. *Louis' Children: American Jazz Singers.* New York, Quill, 1984.

Holiday, Billie, with William Dufty. *Lady Sings the Blues.* New York, Doubleday, 1956.

James, Burnett. *Billie Holiday.* New York, Hippocrene, 1984.

Jones, Hetty. *Big Star Fallin' Mama: Five Women in Black Music.* New York, Viking Press, 1997.

Nicholson, Stuart. *Billie Holiday.* Boston, Northeastern University Press, 1995.

O'Meally, Robert. *Lady Day: The Many Faces of Billie Holiday.* New York, Little Brown, 1991.

Vail, Ken. *Lady Day's Diary: The Life of Billie Holiday 1937-1959.* Chessington, United Kingdom, Castle Communications, 1996.

White, John. *Billie Holiday.* New York, Universe Books, 1987.

Holiday Inns

Kemmons Wilson transformed roadside accommodations by building or franchising look-alike motels known as Holiday Inns. In 1952, entrepreneur Wilson, a high school dropout and home builder, opened the first Holiday Inn in Memphis, Tennessee, after returning from a road trip to Washington, D.C., with his wife and five children, disappointed with the typical motel or roadside cabin of the day—overpriced, cramped units charging $2 extra for each child. Wilson's first motel, opened at the start of the postwar auto travel boom, was the prototype for the thousands of Holiday Inns that later formed a global giant much imitated by newer hotel-motel chains. Wilson retired in 1978, and 18 years later Holiday Inns Inc. was acquired for more than $2.2 billion by the British firm Bass PLC., which, by century's end, operated or franchised more than 2,700 Holiday Inns and other hotels in 90 countries. Holiday Inns caught the public's fancy by offering uniformly family-friendly, unsurprising, and moderately priced accommodations, with each motel easily recognized by a large green and white sign.

—Michael Posner

FURTHER READING:

Walton, William B., with Mel Lorentzen. *Innkeeper.* Wheaton, Illinois, Tyndale House, 1987.

Wilson, Kemmons, with Robert Kerr. *Half Luck and Half Brains: The Kemmons Wilson, Holiday Inn Story.* Nashville, Tennessee, Hambleton-Hill, 1996.

Holliday, Judy (1921-1965)

Judy Holliday, in her relatively limited career, elevated the stock character of the dumb blonde from a movie stereotype to a complex combination of naiveté, common sense, intelligence, and vulnerability in a handful of memorable roles on stage and screen.

Born Judith Tuvim in New York City on June 21, 1921, Judy Holliday began her career in 1938 as a telephone operator for Orson Welles's Mercury theater company. This led to friendships with Betty Comden, Adolph Green, and others, who formed a cabaret act, called ''The Revuers.'' From Greenwich Village night clubs, the act moved to posh New York clubs and, eventually, to a 16-week radio show on NBC and an extended run at Radio City Music Hall. ''The Revuers'' headed for Hollywood in 1944, but failed to gain important notice.

Holliday, however, performed supporting roles in three films at Fox, but her contract was not renewed. She headed back to New York, where she was cast in the 1945 play, *Kiss Them for Me,* playing the part of Alice, a dumb blonde. Judy was praised for rendering her character's sensitivity and vulnerability. Audiences loved her, but the play lasted only 14 weeks.

In 1946, Holliday replaced Jean Arthur in *Born Yesterday* when Arthur left the play in Philadelphia. She learned the part of Billie Dawn in three days, and the play was a sensation when it opened on Broadway at the Belasco Theater on February 4, 1946. This led to the part of Doris Attinger in the film *Adam's Rib* (1949) with Spencer Tracy and Katharine Hepburn at MGM. According to Hollywood legend, this role was really Holliday's screen test for Harry Cohn, the tyrannical boss at Columbia Pictures. Following this first success, Holliday starred as Billie Dawn in the film version of *Born Yesterday* (1950), which was released in December 1950. Holliday won an Academy Award as best actress for the role, beating out Bette Davis, Gloria Swanson, Celeste Holm, and Anne Bancroft.

In 1952 Holliday was accused of communist leanings by the McCarran Committee. The accusation kept her out of films briefly, but she performed in a series of roles in *The Marrying Kind* (1952), *It*

Should Happen to You (1954), *Phffft* (1954), and *Solid Gold Cadillac* (1956). In 1956 she was back on Broadway, cast as the lonely telephone operator in *Bells Are Ringing,* a Comden and Green, Jule Styne musical. The show had a three-year run, which led to her assignment by MGM to repeat the role in the 1960 film version opposite Dean Martin. It would be her last film. In 1963 she was diagnosed with breast cancer, and following a valiant two-year struggle, she died on June 7, 1965, two weeks before her 44th birthday.

—James R. Belpedio

FURTHER READING:

Thomson, David. *A Biographical Dictionary of Film.* 3rd edition. New York, Alfred A. Knopf, 1998.

Holly, Buddy (1936-1959)

As a songwriter, performer, and musician, Buddy Holly remains one of the most influential rock 'n' roll entertainers of all time. Artists such as the Beatles, the Rolling Stones, Bob Dylan, the Byrds, Eric

Buddy Holly

Clapton, Pete Townshend, Elton John, and Bruce Springsteen have all acknowledged Holly's influence on their music. His career was painfully short, lasting from September 1957—when "That'll Be the Day" became a chart-topping hit—to February 3, 1959—when Holly died in a tragic plane crash in Iowa. But, as Holly biographer Philip Norman has pointed out, in that short period of time, "he created a blueprint for enlightened rock stardom that every modern newcomer with any pretense at self-respect still aspires to follow."

Holly's musical legend is replete with many firsts. He was the first rock performer to insist on artistic control over his material. He was the first to write his own songs, and the first to arrange them and supervise his own studio sessions. He was the first to master the technical aspects of the recording business, achieving effects with echo, double-tracking, and overdubbing. He was the first rocker to eschew the "pretty boy" looks of most performers of the 1950s, adopting a more bookwormish look complete with black horn-rim glasses. In addition, he was the first rock performer capable of attracting a faithful male audience as much as a female one. Holly was only twenty-two years old when he died, but he left behind a legacy of songs that have steadily grown in stature and influence, making him one of the genuine legends of popular music.

Born on September 7, 1936, in Lubbock, Texas, Holly's musical influences included country and western music and rhythm and blues. At age five, Holly made his first appearance on stage, joining his brothers Larry and Travis in a talent contest that won them five dollars. During his childhood, Holly took lessons to play the guitar, violin, and piano, and taught himself boogie-woogie rhythms on the piano. At age twelve, he entertained friends with Hank Williams' songs, and in 1949 formed the Buddy and Bob bluegrass duo, with friend Bob Montgomery. During this period, Holly learned to play the banjo and the mandolin, and in 1949 he made his first recording—a song titled "My Two Timin' Woman"—on a home tape recorder. By 1952, Buddy and Bob had become a sensation in Lubbock, and they recorded two songs in Holly's home that year and another in 1953. Also in 1953, they performed on KDAV radio, added Larry Welborn on bass, and were given their own program, *The Buddy and Bob Show*. KDAV disc jockey "Hipockets" Duncan became the trio's manager, landing them shows in the West Texas area. The trio added fiddler Sonny Curtis and steel guitarist Don Guess to the group in 1954, and together they made recordings in the Lubbock and Wichita Falls studios. That year the group added drummer Jerry Allison and opened Texas concerts for Bill Haley and his Comets and Elvis Presley. Holly was intrigued by Presley's rock 'n' roll style, but continued to play country music.

Holly's group landed its first recording contract in December 1955 with Decca records. The band, now minus Montgomery, recorded four songs in a Nashville studio on January 26, 1956. From that session, Decca released "Blue Days, Black Nights," backed with "Love Me," under the name of Buddy Holly and the Three Tunes. However, by September 1956, Holly left Decca because of the label's insistence that he continue playing country music, and due to the loss of his band members because of differences with Decca's session men. In late 1956, Holly, Allison, and Welborn traveled to Clovis, New Mexico, where they recorded two songs at a local studio. After returning to Lubbock, Holly formed the Crickets with Allison and Wiki Sullivan, who played rhythm guitar. On February 25, 1957, they returned to Clovis and recorded the classic "That'll Be the Day," trading their country stylings for a definitive rock 'n' roll sound. Numerous record companies rejected the song until it was released by

Brunswick Records in May 1957. With Clovis studio owner Norman Petty now their manager and Joe B. Mauldin having joined the group as bassist, "That'll Be the Day" received heavy promotion and reached number one by September 1957.

On the heels of the release of "That'll Be the Day," Buddy Holly and the Crickets spent three months touring the United States, playing such venues as the Apollo Theater in New York and Howard Theater in Washington, D.C. Holly's band recorded an impressive body of work in 1957, including such classics as "Words of Love," "Maybe Baby," "Not Fade Away," "Everybody," "Oh Boy," and the legendary "Peggy Sue." Holly was very experimental in the studio, and used a variety of new production techniques, including overdubbing vocals and double-tracking guitar parts. "Peggy Sue" reached number three on the charts in the United States and "Oh Boy" number ten during 1957. The group closed out this watershed year by appearing on the *Ed Sullivan Show*, an appearance they repeated in January 1958.

That same month, the Crickets recorded "Rave On" in New York and toured Australia for six days, then recorded "Well . . . All Right" on February 1958. Then, in early March of that year, Holly's group toured England, where their songs were topping the charts. Upon their return to America, the Crickets joined a tour assembled by disc jockey Alan Freed that included Jerry Lee Lewis and Chuck Berry. Also in 1958, Holly married Maria Elena Santiago, recorded "Heartbeat," "Wishing," and "Love's Made a Fool of You," and held recording sessions that included extra musicians, including Waylon Jennings, Phil Everly, and King Curtis.

By the time Holly's group toured the Northeast and Canada in October 1958, tension was growing between Holly and manager Petty, and there was friction among band members because of their lead singer's expressed desire to become a solo artist. During the tour, Holly left his manager, with the Crickets leaving Holly to stay with Petty. On October 21, 1958, Holly, working with producer Dick Jacobs and studio musicians, recorded "True Love Ways," "It Doesn't Matter Anymore," "Raining in My Heart," and "Moondreams." In January 1959, Holly assembled a new band, also to be called the Crickets, to take on the "Winter Dance Party" tour of the Midwest. Included in the tour were Ritchie Valens, the Big Bopper, and Dion and the Belmonts. The tour began on January 23, 1959, in Milwaukee, Wisconsin, and the evening show on February 1 was canceled due to bad weather. The tour then played Clear Lake, Iowa, on February 2. Following this fateful show, Holly, Valens, and the Big Bopper chartered a small place to take them to the next date in Moorhead, Minnesota. The idea was to avoid taking the tour bus, which had previously broken down and had a defective heater. Shortly after takeoff, the plane crashed in a cornfield about five miles north of Clear Lake, killing Holly, Valens, the Big Bopper, and their pilot. Don McLean later memorialized the date as "the day the music died" in his song "American Pie."

Holly's popularity skyrocketed after his death, with his influence still impacting the contemporary music scene. Even as late as the 1980s, unreleased Holly material was still being issued. During the 1970s, Paul McCartney purchased the Holly song catalogue, and he began sponsoring annual Buddy Holly Week celebrations. Holly fan clubs, magazines, books, and Web sites flourish, and movies and musicals have been based on his life. A statue of him stands in Lubbock, and two memorials to Holly have been placed in Clear Lake, Iowa. One memorial is a large, grey stone located at the Surf Ballroom, where Holly performed his last show. The other is a guitar and three records fashioned out of stainless steel placed at the crash site.

—Dennis Russell

FURTHER READING:

Amburn, Ellis. *Buddy Holly: A Biography.* New York, St. Martin's Press, 1995.

Goldrosen, John, and John Beecher. *Remembering Buddy: The Definitive Biography.* New York, Penguin, 1987.

Norman, Philip. *Rave On: The Biography of Buddy Holly.* New York, Simon and Schuster, 1996.

Tobler, John. *The Buddy Holly Story.* New York, Beaufort Books, 1979.

Hollywood

In America, Hollywood is the promised land—a sun-kissed Mediterranean playground with the weather of a modern-day Eden. For much of its history, Hollywood was the place where the old rules no longer applied. If one was beautiful enough, or talented enough, or simply talked a good game, one could cast off the Protestant work ethic like a ratty winter coat and join the gilded throngs of a new American aristocracy. Hollywood was enticement personified; anything and everything could be bought, nothing was out of reach. Money flowed like water from its jeweled grottoes, and sex was in all around, as palpable as the scent of eucalyptus wafting down through Benedict Canyon. Through the twists and turns of its history, the California town named Hollywood has remained America's capital of glamour *non pareil* (even after downtown Hollywood had become a

sleazy mixture of tourist attractions and dilapidated office buildings, the legendary stars imbedded on Hollywood Boulevard covered in grime, and frequently, obscured by the bodies of the homeless). In its Golden Age, Hollywood was a glamour factory, a metropolis of illusion. Enormous film studios lined its side streets, talent agencies occupied its office buildings, swank restaurants and nightclubs occupied its busy thoroughfares. It was the home of the stars, who built monuments to their image high above in the Hollywood hills, hard by the famous Hollywood sign, beckoning through the smog like a red dot on a map signifying, you are here.

But where exactly was "here?" How did this remote backwater change so suddenly from citrus groves and barley fields into the headquarters of the eleventh largest industry in the United States? In part it had to do with the early economics of the film industry, in part with the weather. In 1887, long before the film industry was a reality in Hollywood, let alone a going concern, a Kansas real estate tycoon named Horace Henderson Wilcox began mapping out the streets of a town built especially for stolid Midwesterners, sick of ice and snow. Being pious Midwesterners themselves, they banned saloons and offered land gratis to any church willing to locate there. The Wilcoxes' embryonic community was nestled at the foot of a ridge of gentle hills which sheltered the farms from the brutal desert winds, twelve miles from the Pacific Ocean. It was an idyllic setting, and fittingly, Wilcox's homesick wife named the nascent settlement Hollywood after the country place of a family friend.

Hollywood was not exactly an overnight success. In 1903, future *Los Angeles Times* publisher Harry Chandler and railroad tycoon General Moses Hazeltine Sherman formed a syndicate that managed to get the still vacant fields incorporated as an independent municipality—a prime example of the land speculation so typical of Los Angeles history up to the present day. They built a trolley line from downtown (the population at the time was a mere 500 people) and a

The Hollywood sign overlooking the city of Los Angeles, California.

thirty-three room Spanish-style hotel on as-yet-unpaved Hollywood Boulevard. To stimulate sales, Chandler and Co. liberally posted signs reading SOLD among the lots, perhaps the first in a long line of Hollywood subterfuges. In order to attract what they considered as solid citizens (Midwestern farmers) they continued in the pious tradition of the Wilcoxes: beside outlawing saloons, in 1910 the Hollywood Board of Trustees officially banned movie theaters, at which time there was not a one.

The film industry came to Los Angeles in 1907 as the result of a fluke. Winter storms prompted William Selig of the Chicago-based Selig Studios to send his leading man west in search of an alternate location. The filming of *The Count of Monte Cristo* (1908), the first film shot in California, was completed in Laguna Beach not long after, and Selig was so taken by the area that he returned the following year, setting up shop in a converted Chinese laundry east of downtown. Soon film companies were flocking to Los Angeles. There were both financial and legal reasons for the move. Outdoor shoots could occur year round, and the Los Angeles basin afforded a wealth of natural scenery. "It was all rather pristine and primeval," writes Otto Friedrich. "Cops and robbers chased each other through the streets and directors improvised their stories as they went along. The official histories explain this first flowering as a happy combination of sunshine, open spaces, and diverse settings: the Sahara, the Alps, and the South Seas could all be simulated within Los Angeles' city limits." A further incentive lay in Los Angeles' remote location. Independent film producers were then at war with the Edison syndicate, who, by enforcing patents on film and projection equipment, were set on milking the industry ad infinitum. In remote Los Angeles, collecting royalties would be no easy endeavor for the Edison bund.

At first, the majority of studios settled in Edendale, a hilly and somewhat congested area just west of downtown. It wasn't until 1910 that the first film studio, the Nestor Film Company, established itself in Hollywood proper. (By a happy coincidence, the city of Los Angeles had subsumed Hollywood, rendering the prohibition against movie theaters null and void.) By the 1920s, film production was wholly centered in Hollywood, with a scattering of studios established to the north, in Burbank, or southwest in Culver City. The stars had also staked their claim to the geographic high-ground, moving from the downtown—the adjacent Silver Lake was the neighborhood of choice for the earliest silent stars—to the Hollywood Hills and just west to the lush canyons of Beverly Hills.

By some accounts (most notably, Kenneth Anger's lurid, sensationalistic bio-dissection, *Hollywood Babylon*), the silent era was a never-ending party of dope, booze, and aggressive promiscuity. In this innocent time, drugs were an acceptable subject for pictures. In 1916, for instance, Douglas Fairbanks starred in *The Mystery of the Leaping Fish,* appearing as Coke Ennyday, a somewhat besotted detective who availed himself liberally of "joy powder." It was a free and easy time, and the stars, by wallowing in their licentiousness, appeared to be testing the limits of public opinion. And push they did, with tragic results. In 1920, popular starlet Olive Thomas committed suicide in Paris, occasioned by her failure to procure heroin; in 1921, comedian Fatty Arbuckle was arrested for the death of aspiring starlet Virginia Rappe during "rough sex." The following year director William Desmond Taylor was murdered in his home, and once again the studio publicists worked overtime at damage control. But the hemorrhaging had gone too far. In the wake of public outrage, the Hollywood production heads reluctantly appointed William H. Hays, a Republican functionary, to act as arbiter of the public morality. Into the 1940s, the notorious Hays Commission would pass judgment on

all Hollywood product. Hays declared that the movies needed purifying, both in content and cast. To aid in the latter, he released a notorious black-list, the kiss of death for many a screen idol. Wallace Reid, one of Paramount's biggest stars, made the list (he died in a sanitarium the following year), as did Juanita Hansen and Alma Rubens, both popular leading ladies, and both soon to be deceased.

At the time, the 1920s were considered a Golden Age in Hollywood, but in fact they were merely a holding pattern, killing time until the next big thing—sound—came along. In short order talkies separated the wheat from the chaff. Actors who had succeeded on their looks, but were not trained in elocution (or who had unfortunate speaking voices, or thick regional accents) became also-rans, as irrelevant as yesterday's newspaper. Clara Bow, born and raised in Brooklyn, found her career effectively ended when she blew out the microphones on her first sound scene. One of Hollywood's most successful leading men, John Gilbert, found his career ruined after sound technicians neutered his tenor voice, and Marie Prevost's career was ruined by her thick Bronx accent; each had succumbed to alcoholism by the mid-1930s.

With the advent of sound, the movies—and Hollywood itself—entered into maturity. No longer a curiosity, movies, and moviemakers, were the unwitting producers of dreams, miners of the American unconscious. Apart from a few fallow periods—the early 1960s, for instance—what the astute student of film lore observes is the complex inter-relationship between entertainment and the values of a people. And like the compartmentalized functions of the brain itself, the different studios each specialized in a particular sub-myth; Warner Brothers specialized in gangster films, (the reptilian rear-brain); Universal made its living off of horror films (the unconscious); MGM, rigorously wholesome light-hearted fare (shades of the super-ego); Columbia, wise-cracking screwball comedies (the ego) and Frank Capra pictures (another example of the socializing super-ego). Moviegoers could take their pick from a smorgasbord of the unconscious, and the relationship was reciprocal only insofar as a film that failed to tap into deep-seated archetypes was apt to sink from view in a matter of weeks.

As the instrument of our unconscious desires, film stars took on a preternatural significance. They were demi-gods and goddesses, archetypes, and by the same token, repositories of innately American virtues and vices. And Hollywood itself was their charmed playland, the center of a galaxy of restaurants, bars, and nightclubs like a neon-lit Mount Olympus come to life (in fact, a Hollywood housing development of the 1960s was named Mount Olympus). For a time, the places where film people staged their debauches became as well known as the stars that patronized them. Chasen's, Musso & Frank's, The Brown Derby, and The Montmarte—these names evoke an era where film deals were made over three martini lunches and stars relaxed after a tough day of shooting at one of several exclusive watering holes. Celebritydom was enjoyed in public, movie stars less cloistered than they are today. At lunch time, crowds would gather around Hollywood eateries in the hopes of catching a glimpse of a Cary Grant or a Marlene Dietrich. While the rest of the country struggled through the Depression, Hollywood wallowed in abundance, and far from taking umbrage with their antics, the public took their high-living as a reassuring sign that better times lay ahead. "Around the globe Hollywood became Tinseltown, a land of dreams and luxury," writes Ronald L. Davis. "For the American public, raised on an ethic that emphasized success, material wealth, and social mobility, Hollywood embodied a national ideal."

Similarly, the nation's movie palaces acted as an extension of this mythology. If the studios were in the business of selling dreams, then the theaters with their slavish attention to detail augmented that feeling. The gilded, air-conditioned temples were calculated to awe, and for many, the very act of going to the movies was a panacea, where for thirty cents one could temporarily shut out the overwhelming tide of misery around them. Although Hollywood was not alone in its luxurious theaters, those that lined Hollywood Boulevard became world famous, especially for the red-carpeted premieres they so frequently hosted. Graumann's Chinese Theater became something of a national landmark, for its premieres as well as the foot and hand prints embedded in fresh concrete around the box office. While over the course of time, the Chinese Theater's neighbors—the El Capitan, the Egyptian—have fared poorly (until very recently), Mann's has remained a virtual institution, along with Musso & Frank's, the last vestige of Hollywood's glamour years.

Even as Hollywood wallowed in its good fortune, its destruction was at hand. 1939 had been a good year for Hollywood. The movie industry was the nation's eleventh largest industry, grossing $700 million that year, attracting more than fifty million Americans to the nation's theaters every week. Within a decade, this illusion of omnipotence would prove to be just that, illusory. After two decades of staving off Justice Department anti-trust lawsuits, the moguls had relented and divested themselves of their theater holdings and ended their unreasonable, but lucrative, booking practices (in effect, theater owners were forced to buy films in blocks, accepting many duds in order to book the one film they wanted). In addition, the star-system the moguls had pinned their fortunes on had backfired with disastrous results. Enormous salaries were one thing, but when the stars began packaging their own deals, in effect usurping the role of the studios, the moguls could only watch in horror as the power they had so carefully nurtured slipped through their fingers. Now it was the actors, agents, and managers who called the shots.

Television was a contributing factor to the demise of the studio system. The big studios ignored the threat, and only marginal companies like RKO realized a profit, hiring their facilities out to the upstart medium. Through the 1950s and early 1960s, the studios watched their profits evaporate as they grew further out of touch with the post-war audience. Even then, Hollywood generated a kind of anti-alchemy with Film Noir, one of film's most enduring and symbolically rich genres, so perfectly in step with the mood of paranoia and desperation sweeping over the land. But Film Noir's richness was unintentional; for the most part, the genre consisted of "B" movies and programmers, not the kinds of epic, sweeping dramas that studios took pride in.

Ironically, it was these same "B" movie actors and directors, more attuned to the changing times, who saved the majors, ushering in the New Hollywood, what was for many the last Golden Age of American movie-making. By the early 1960s, Hollywood profits had withered on the vine. Film production companies were being snapped up by oil and insurance companies (like Gulf & Western's acquisition of Paramount), which looked upon the film industry as an opportunity to diversify their investments. Desperately casting about for a white knight to rescue them from the financial doldrums, executives began to take chances. First there was Mike Nichols' *The Graduate* (1967), a film that not only redefined the parameters of what could be shown, but in casting Dustin Hoffman in the lead opened up the way for ethnic actors such as Robert De Niro and Al Pacino to be treated as legitimate leading men. There was no one true breach that destroyed the dam of Hollywood's old system, it was more like many small

ruptures in a dike. *The Graduate* was followed by *Bonnie and Clyde* (1967), *Easy Rider* (1969; producer and star Peter Fonda joked that before the film was finished, the executives shook their heads in incomprehension, and afterwards, nodded their heads in bewilderment), then *Midnight Cowboy* (1969), all films that would have been unthinkable ten years before. The executives, who were as scornful of this new generations' politics as they were of their artistic influences, could finally do nothing more than let the floodwaters inundate them.

It would not last long. The 1970s were a time of great artistic ferment in Hollywood, a changing of the guard in which the director, who had long been considered no more than a glorified technician by the studios, was now a hero. With their newfound power, directors explored territory that only a decade earlier would have been strictly forbidden. As director Robert Altman put it, "Suddenly there was a moment when it seemed as if the pictures you wanted to make, they wanted to make." This was the decade when Martin Scorsese, Francis Ford Coppola, William Friedkin, Hal Ashby, and Peter Bogdanovich burst into prominence, making edgy, uncompromising films. The dark side of the auteur equation, however, was that as the decade edged towards its conclusion, the film budgets grew more outrageous; directors, fueled by a combination of drugs and hubris, grew more stunning in their arrogance; and when the inevitable shift in the cultural winds hit, it was the studio executives, nursing a decade of bruised egos, who had the upper hand.

Hollywood operates by a complex logarithm that is by nature amoral. In the Glamour Years, Hollywood produced and the audience bought tickets—a simple equation—but with the advent of marketing, sneak previews, and audience polling, the situation had come full circle. America spoke with its dollars, and Hollywood had become very attentive. But what really spelled the death knell of the New Hollywood was the success of two films: *Star Wars* (1977) and *Jaws* (1975). What a nation weary from over a decade of war and civil unrest wanted was entertainment; not the sort of entertainment television could provide, but spectacle. America wanted to be wowed, and that is exactly these films did. Within a few years, a man named Don Simpson would turn spectacle into a science, producing a string of mindless, but entertaining hits, simple films that could be summed up in twenty-five words or less. His first hit, *Flashdance* (1983), could be summed up thus: blue collar dancer yearns to be ballerina. Naturally film critics decried Simpson's films—*Top Gun, Beverly Hill Cop, Days of Thunder*—but the high concept film was now king. And through the 1980s and 1990s, it was the event film, the summer blockbuster, that was Hollywood's bread and butter, an all-American spectacle of excess: sex, violence, and mind-boggling special effects. In effect, these films were simply glorified genre films.

Of course, Hollywood has always been a business, as one of its nicknames, the Glamour Factory, makes abundantly clear. What it sells is glamour, sex, violence, physical beauty, and extravagance, while convincing the public it is buying virtue and art. From the moment Chandler and company set out their faked "SOLD" signs on the vacant lots, the modus operandi of Hollywood—deception—was firmly entrenched. And while Hollywood Boulevard molders, with only a few relics of the glory years remaining amongst the cheap tourist gift shops, the homeless people, and Scientology buildings, its legend is still repackaged and sold to a naïve public. Hollywood will always be a valuable commodity. While the locus of power in the entertainment industry has moved elsewhere, down-at-the-heels Hollywood remains its most visible symbol.

But while the shifting dynamics of the industry have made Hollywood-the-place obsolete, it still remains a powerful symbol.

More than can ever be measured, Hollywood created the dreams of America in the twentieth century, allowing generations access to a symbolic tapestry in the darkened hush of the movie theater. It is a paradox that while Hollywood can be defined and measured in square mileage, the map of its streets is but a dim shadow of the much more complex and ineffable map of the American psyche. Hollywood exists and yet it is entirely ephemeral, a locked room in the collective unconscious. In 1949, David O. Selznick was wandering the empty streets of Hollywood late one night when he turned to his companions, saying, "Hollywood's like Egypt. Full of crumbling pyramids. It'll never come back. It'll just keep on crumbling until finally the wind blows the last studio prop across the sand." He was right and he was wrong. The myth of the place has become an archetype, and even while multinational corporations own every major studio outright, there has never been any question that Hollywood remains the center of film production both in spirit and in substance.

—Michael Baers

FURTHER READING:

Anger, Kenneth. *Hollywood Babylon*. New York, Dell Publishing, 1975.

Biskind, Peter. *Easy Riders, Raging Bulls: How the Sex, Drugs, and Rock-n-Roll Generation Saved Hollywood*. New York, Simon and Schuster, 1998.

Davis, Ronald L. *The Glamour Factory*. Dallas, Southern Methodist University Press, 1993.

Fleming, Charles. *High Concept: Don Simpson and the Hollywood Culture of Excess*. New York, Doubleday, 1998.

Friedrich, Otto. *City of Nets*. New York, Harper & Row, 1986.

Gabler, Neil. *An Empire of Their Own: How the Jews Invented Hollywood*. New York, Crown Publishers, 1988.

Schatz, Thomas. *The Genius of the System: Hollywood Filmmaking in the Studio Era*. New York, Pantheon Books, 1988.

Sommer, Robin Langley. *Hollywood: The Glamour Years (1919-1941)*. New York, Gallery Books, 1987.

Hollywood Squares

One of television's most popular game shows during its 15 year run from 1966 to 1981, *Hollywood Squares* combined high camp, humor, and a modicum of intellect to become an audience favorite. As described in *Entertainment Weekly*'s "The Best Game Shows of All Time," "Nine celebs sat inside a three-story ticktacktoe board and parried questions with wacky ad-libs (which turned out to be scripted)." Hosted by the good-natured Peter Marshall, the squares were occupied by A- and B-list stars from film, television, and music. The center square, however, was the hub of the show. First occupied by Ernest Borgnine, the center square came to be the domain of the acerbically witty and very camp Paul Lynde, and was later taken over by the inimitable Joan Rivers. A hip new *Hollywood Squares* debuted in 1998 with Whoopi Goldberg in the coveted center square, proving that pop culture always has a place for amiable schlock.

—Victoria Price

FURTHER READING:

"The Best Game Shows of All Time." *Entertainment Weekly's The 100 Greatest TV Shows of All Time* (special issue). 1998, 70-1.

Holms, John Pynchon, et al. *The TV Game Show Almanac*. New York, Chilton Book Co., 1995.

Shaw, Jessica. "Question: What Campy Celebrity-Studded Game Show Is Making Whoopi with a $25 Million Face-Lift? Answer: You Need to Ask?" *Entertainment Weekly*. September 18, 1998.

Watson, Bret. "When It Was Hip to Be Square." *Entertainment Weekly*. October 18, 1996.

The Hollywood Ten

In the fall of 1947, a group of ten prominent artists working in film who were to enter American history as the Hollywood Ten, were subpoenaed by the House Un-American Activities Committee (HUAC) as part of investigations into "the extent of Communist infiltration in the Hollywood motion picture industry." Taking the First Amendment, the Hollywood Ten denied HUAC's constitutional legitimacy as well as its right to inquire into an individual's personal and political beliefs, and refused to answer any of the Committee's questions. In their prepared statements, they went so far as to compare the activities of the Committee to those of Nazi Germany and stated that HUAC heralded the onset of a new fascism within American life. The Ten's refusal to co-operate in admitting to their political affiliations resulted in their being tried at the Washington, D.C., Federal court in April, 1948. Found guilty of contempt, writer-producer Herbert Biberman, director Edward Dmytryk, producer-writer Adrian Scott, and screenwriters Alvah Bessie, Lester Cole, Ring Lardner, Jr., John Howard Lawson, Albert Maltz, Samuel Ornitz, and Dalton Trumbo were each sentenced to one year in jail and a thousand-dollar fine. They were blacklisted by the film industry, and for many years were able to work only by living abroad or under cover of a pseudonym. (Robert Rich, for example, who won an Oscar for *The Brave One* in 1956, was actually Trumbo).

The Hollywood Ten became a benchmark for resistance against the investigative powers of the congressional committees during the Cold War, but their treatment left a shameful blot on the community that ostracized them. It was an omen for a much wider process that expanded to all sectors of American society and eventually all but destroyed the liberal left in America. The cultural consequences of their indictment and the subsequent blacklisting of many of their distinguished peers were serious—Hollywood was deprived of many of its finest and most intelligent creative talents, and the climate of fear that came to prevail led to blandness, even sterility, of artistic expression and new ideas for fully a decade.

Matters grew worse when Edward Dmytryk recanted his position and agreed to co-operate with the HUAC. He was released early from jail, admitted past membership of the Communist Party, and took himself to England. Ironically, Dmytryk is admired for the socially conscious, humane stance of some of his best work, including the anti-fascist drama *Hitler's Children* (1943) and *Crossfire* (1947), a serious attempt to address anti-Semitism. He returned from exile in 1951, stood as a witness in the HUAC's second round of hearings into Hollywood and named names. He was not alone. Altogether over this dark period in Hollywood's history, some 300 "witnesses" confessed to their own past Communist affiliations, and many also

The set for the 1970s game show *Hollywood Squares*.

incriminated their fellows. Among the more celebrated who failed to take the First Amendment were writers Clifford Odets, Isabel Lennart and Budd Schulberg, actors Sterling Hayden and Larry Parks, and, famously, the great director Elia Kazan, whose appearance to receive a special Oscar at the 1999 Academy Awards ceremony opened old wounds and provoked furious controversy.

The fate of the Hollywood Ten exemplified that of anyone who refused to cooperate with the HUAC. The refusal of any individual to name names before the Committee was interpreted as evidence of Communist or fellow-traveling sympathies, and the fate of the Ten instigated an ignominious cycle of cowardice and betrayal in the Hollywood community. The FBI put many creative artists under surveillance, and at least two victims of the hearings committed suicide. The roll call of those either ''named'' by their peers or blacklisted on suspicion is long, shocking, and substantial. Among the many who suffered the harsh artistic, economic, and social consequences of blacklisting were writers Ben Barzman, Waldo Salt, Dashiell Hammett, Lillian Hellman, documentarist Joris Ivens, director Joseph Losey, writer-directors Carl Foreman, Jules Dassin, and Abraham Polonsky, actors Anne Revere and Gale Sondergaard, satirist Dorothy Parker, and Paula Miller (Mrs. Lee Strasberg). Foreman, Dassin, and Losey in particular continued to forge careers in Europe; the more fortunate actors found work on the stage, while

others were forced into retirement. Actor John Garfield died in 1952, aged 40, from a heart attack said to have been caused by the strain of the investigations.

Blacklisting began to fade in the late 1950s, along with the rest of the McCarthyite hysteria that had for so many years held Americans under threat. Many of the previously blacklisted writers and directors were able to return openly to Hollywood, where their achievements were a salutary lesson in the loss that films had suffered by their absence. Thanks to the insistence of Kirk Douglas and Otto Preminger respectively, Dalton Trumbo was the first screenwriter to re-emerge under his own name on the credits of *Spartacus* and *Exodus* (both 1960). Robert Rossen added *The Hustler* (1961) to his distinguished body of work pre-1951. Abraham Polonsky, whose career had been completely ruined by the hearings and his subsequent exile, came back to make only his second of three films, the highly regarded Western, *Tell Them Willie Boy is Here* (1970), and Ring Lardner, Jr. wrote the Academy Award-winning screenplay for *M*A*S*H* (1970). Carl Foreman, who had just completed the screenplay for *High Noon* (1952) when he was blacklisted, never returned from Britain, but was posthumously acknowledged in 1985 for his previously uncredited Oscar-winning work on *The Bridge on the River Kwai*. Waldo Salt received the Oscar for *Midnight Cowboy* (1969), shared it for *Coming Home* (1978), and was nominated for *Serpico* (1973).

The unwavering courage of the Hollywood Ten and others continues to stand as a historic reproach to the movie moguls who caved in to McCarthyite demands to "clean up" their industry.

—Nathan Abrams

FURTHER READING:

Bentley, Eric, editor. *Thirty Years of Treason: Excerpts from Hearings before the House Committee on Un-American Activities, 1938-1968.* New York, Viking, 1971.

Ceplair, Larry, and Steven Englund. *The Inquisition in Hollywood: Politics in the Film Community 1930-1960.* New York, Anchor/Doubleday, 1980.

Kahn, Gordon. *Hollywood on Trial: The Story of the Ten Who Were Indicted.* New York, Boni & Gaer, 1948.

Navasky, Victor S. *Naming Names.* New York, Viking, 1980.

Holocaust

Over the span of four nights, between April 16 and 19, 1978, approximately 120 million Americans watched at least some of an NBC miniseries that graphically portrayed the genocide of six million Jews during the Nazi era. Commercial prime-time television may have seemed an unlikely venue for this kind of subject matter, but *Holocaust* appeared during a moment in American network history when more serious subject matter threatened to get a toehold in prime time. The phenomenal and unprecedented success the year before of the miniseries *Roots* paved the way for *Holocaust.* In fact, NBC gave the production its go-ahead during the week that *Roots* aired. That series' record-breaking Nielsen numbers apparently gave the network confidence that if American viewers were willing to sit through night after night of brutal, realistic depictions of slavery in America, then those same viewers might also brave the images of genocide.

Producer Herbert Bodkin, director Marvin Chomsky (who had directed an episode of *Roots*), and writer Gerald Green did not want to just produce a Jewish *Roots,* however. They managed to avoid some of the production issues that were problematical in *Roots.* While *Roots* was shot entirely on the Hollywood back lot, *Holocaust* was filmed in Europe. The Matthausen concentration camp in Germany stood in for Auschwitz, thus giving camp scenes a chilling sense of verisimilitude. Also eery were some responses to the project during its production. In Gemany and Austria, many local technicians declined to work on the shoot. Swastikas occasionally appeared on sets. Officials in Hungary, Czechoslovakia, and Yugoslavia refused permission to film in their countries, arguing that the script contained "Zionist" elements.

Holocaust also differed from *Roots* in that it avoided filling its cast with highly recognizable stars. The producers didn't want viewers to be distracted by the star power of performers, but rather to accept the actors as the characters they played. *Holocaust*'s cast included then little-known players as Meryl Streep, James Woods, and Michael Moriarty.

Like *Roots, Holocaust* used the family melodrama genre to tell its sweeping tale of human misery and survival. The series focused on two German families: the Weisses, who were thoroughly assimilated German-Jews; and the Dorfs. Most of the Weisses are sent to concentration camps. The artist son (James Woods) finds himself in Tereisen, the Nazis' "model" camp for high profile Jews, especially those with artistic talent. The narrative focuses on the utter squalor and horror of the place and the attempt by artists to document their experience there. The Weisses' daughter (Blanche Baker) is raped and then put into a hospital for the mentally ill, where the Nazi policies toward "mental defectives" ensure that she is quickly killed. Mr. and Mrs. Weiss, along with their Catholic daughter-in-law (Meryl Streep), end up in Auschwitz. A particularly graphic scene portrays the supposed "showers" the women were to have; the audience views a portrayal of them being gassed. Only the youngest son (Timothy Bottoms) survives. He escapes a concentration camp and joins Jewish partisans fighting the Germans. The Dorf family includes Erik (Michael Moriarty), an unemployed lawyer, and his ambitious wife, who persuades him to take a job with the Nazi security forces. Dorf rises quickly through Nazi ranks, becoming an aide to top architect of the Final Solution, Heinrich Heydrich (David Warner).

The miniseries received many of the same criticisms heaped on *Roots.* It took one of history's greatest human horrors and turned it into a soap opera. It made the unimaginable too easily accessible. It gave audiences only abject Jewish passivity on the one hand and heroic, active Jewish resistance on the other hand. Other critics praised the production for not flinching from brutality. There was no turning away from scenes of mass murder, torture, and death camp ovens. The realism proved too much for some midwestern NBC affiliates, who found scenes of naked women driven to the gas chambers too graphic and asked NBC to delete the offending scenes in their markets. Critics also complimented the series for not portraying the Nazis as boot-clicking, saluting caricatures. Instead, the actors played their characters as ordinary people who too easily followed the instructions of a fascist regime. Notably, the actors did not attempt German accents.

While *Holocaust* was a success in North America, it became a phenomenon of historic proportions when broadcast in West Germany in January 1979. Nearly half of the population watched at least some of the series, the vast majority responding to it positively. Germans had been exposed to relatively little information about the Nazi period or the Holocaust since the end of the war. The broadcast of *Holocaust* may have broken that silence. The miniseries was preceded by the showing of documentaries and followed by television debates and phone-in programs. Almost overnight, Germans, especially younger ones, demanded discussion of Germany's Nazi past. In the political arena, the showing of *Holocaust* may have also been instrumental in influencing the Bundestag to vote to discontinue a policy of statute of limitations for Nazi war crimes.

In North America, *Holocaust* demonstrated that network television could tackle weighty issues of human tragedy. In Germany, the miniseries might have caused an entire nation to reflect seriously on its historical demons.

—Aniko Bodroghkozy

Holyfield, Evander (1962—)

The only fighter besides Muhammad Ali to become a three-time heavyweight boxing champion, Evander Holyfield might unfortunately be remembered not for his achievements, but as the boxer whose ear Mike Tyson bit off in June 1997. In the 1990s, Holyfield and Tyson portrayed the diametrically opposing images of professional boxers. Holyfield rejected the snarling pitbull image projected by Tyson and so many boxers and instead presented the calm, reasoned demeanor of a serious professional.

Holyfield, raised in Atlanta, Georgia was the youngest of eight children. A scrawny child who sat on the bench during most of his sophomore football season because he was so small (five feet four inches tall, 115 pounds), Holyfield grew to 6 feet 2 inches and trained hard to reach about 212 pounds. Nevertheless, Holyfield was still considered little in the world of heavyweight boxing, where opponents weighing 230 pounds regularly entered the ring. Undaunted by his many doubters, who thought his lighter weight meant he wasn't as powerful as his opponents, Holyfield steadily rose through the heavyweight ranks to become the undisputed heavyweight champion in 1990. Losing his title in 1992, he reclaimed it from Riddick Bowe in 1993. Having lost his title a second time in 1994 to Michael Moorer, Holyfield discovered that he had a heart problem and was forced to retire.

A devout Christian, Holyfield had always given much of the credit for his success in the ring to God and to his spiritual upbringing. Relying on his faith and continuing his rigorous training schedule, he made it back to the ring. Holyfield was poised to win the heavyweight title in 1997 from Mike Tyson, who had recently reentered the ring after his stint in prison for a rape conviction. When Tyson bit off a portion of Holyfield's ear, the fight was stopped. Holyfield won a rematch later that year and remained a top contender in the heavyweight ranks at the turn of the century.

—D. Byron Painter

FURTHER READING:

"Evander Holyfield Credits God, Wife, and Family for Championship." *Jet.* December 9, 1996, 46-51.

Holyfield, Evander and Bernard Holyfield. *Holyfield: The Humble Warrior.* Nashville, Tennessee. T. Nelson Publishers, 1996.

Ryan, Jeff. "Holy Revival." *Sport.* December 1997, 34-39.

Home Improvement

The ABC network sitcom *Home Improvement* first aired on September 17, 1991 and ran for eight seasons, through May 1999. During only its second season, the show was renewed for three additional seasons, an unusual decision in the television industry. Based on the stand-up comedy routine of its star, Tim Allen (born Timothy Allen Dick in 1953), *Home Improvement* initially reflected Allen's love of power tools, cars, and Sears department stores, as well as mirroring his own family situation. Allen portrayed Tim Taylor, the host of cable TV's "Tool Time." His wife, Jill, was portrayed by Patricia Richardson. More than just comedy, though, *Home Improvement* epitomized the concerns of the largest generation in history, the baby boomers.

The Taylors were a representation of the average American family of the 1990s, and their struggles, although treated with lighthearted humor, reflected the struggles of the show's demographic. In the main, three fundamental concerns of the boomer generation were examined on a weekly basis—relationships, family, and the search for spirituality.

One trend that *Home Improvement* influenced was a return to more defined gender roles. While women in the 1960s and 1970s discarded their bras and retained their own last names within marriage, while men grew their hair long and explored the sensitive side of their natures, couples in the 1990s rediscovered the fundamental differences between the sexes. *Home Improvement* gave propulsion to such bestselling pop psychology books as John Gray's *Men Are From Mars, Women Are From Venus* (1992), with its, at times, stereotypical gender roles. On "Tool Time," buxom tool-girl Heidi (Debbe Dunning) seemed more like window-dressing than a flesh-and-blood character. In the Taylor household, Tim grunted, worked on cars, was obsessed with "more power," and didn't read unless a book had the word "illustrated" in the title. He was into sports and often didn't listen to his wife. Jill, on the other hand, didn't understand cars and called tools "thing-a-ma-jigs." An example of Mars/Venus stereotyping was seen in the episode "Shooting Three to Make Tutu," where Jill wanted Tim to take one of their sons to the ballet, but he had plans to take him to a basketball game instead. In this episode, and others like it, real men don't like ballet (or opera), and women don't like sports.

The series, however, wasn't content merely to stereotype male/female relationships, and in stretching itself, made the characters search for an identity beyond roles. Jill Taylor lost a job, found another, struggled with how to keep family and job together ("Abandoned Family"), and decided to go back to college. Tim Taylor dealt with the death of a mentor ("Arriverderci, Binford") and the arrival of a new boss; he dealt with work rivalries and an inferiority complex with Bob Villa ("What About Bob"). In other episodes, *Home Improvement* broke the stereotype of the dumb male that it had helped to perpetuate. The formula that had always put Tim in the wrong was overthrown as Jill realized her own shortcomings (e.g., "Heavy Meddle" and "Slip Sleddin' Away"). Their three boys (Zachary Ty Bryan, Taran Noah Smith, Jonathan Taylor Thomas) grew older and dealt with issues of their own: identity, dating, sex, drugs, and pulling away from Mom and Dad. Al Borland (Richard Karn), originally cast as a foil to Tim, became even more sensitive—the man every woman wants, the representative of the 1990s Iron John manhood movement (see "Reel Men" for Al's yearning for male bonding). Heidi was given more to do as she juggled work with a new baby.

As Tim Taylor was fond of saying on "Tool Time," "It's not just about home improvement, it's about male improvement," and *Home Improvement* could be said to be about marriage improvement. Episodes didn't shy away from tough topics that boomers were having to confront in their own marriages, such as sexual temptation on both sides ("Eye on Tim" and "Jill's Passion"), legal separation of friends and family members ("He Ain't Heavy, He's Just Irresponsible"), marriage counseling, lack of intimacy, and taking each other for granted ("Taking Jill for Granite").

Home Improvement reflected the concerns of an aging baby boomer population. It resisted a sitcom staple that infuses life into dying ratings: an impending pregnancy. Instead, it went in the opposite direction and began pulling in extended family. Boomers became increasingly aware of aging parents, and so the series introduced Tim's mother and brothers, Jill's parents and sisters. In "Taps," the audience vicariously experienced the death of a parent as Jill lost her father. In "No Place Like Home," Tim dealt with his mother selling the home in which he grew up. In the final season, Jill faced an emergency hysterectomy ("Love's Labor Lost"), forcing her into menopause, a condition with which female audiences could readily identify.

During the 1990s, the baby boomers were frantically searching for who they were and where they fit into the cosmos. The idealistic 1960s had faded, along with their bell-bottom jeans, leaving many to wonder where their ideals had gone. Their search for spiritual values was found in Wilson (Earl Hindman), the Taylors' over-the-fence neighbor. He regularly gave out spiritual platitudes with as much profundity as a fortune cookie, but Wilson developed along with the show and audiences saw more of his family, heard the story of his dead wife ("My Dinner with Wilson"), and watched romance bloom in his life. Wilson's wisdom, like spirituality in the latter 1990s, drew on many wells: Buddha, Jesus Christ, Mark Twain, Shakespeare, Gandhi, Galileo. A running gag, and a technical challenge to the crew, was Wilson's partially obscured face, reflective of the boomers' belief that spirituality has many faces and none are clearly illumined.

Home Improvement won many awards, including Emmys, People's Choice, and TV Guide Reader's Poll, as did its two central stars, Allen and Richardson. Tim Allen won the People's Choice Award for "Favorite Male Performer in a Television Series" for the eight years of *Home Improvement*'s run. He won the Golden Globe Award for "Funniest Actor in a Television Series" in 1997 and was nominated again in 1998. Patricia Richardson was nominated four times for an Emmy as "Outstanding Lead Actress in a Comedy Series" and twice for the Golden Globe Award. The show held a mirror up to the baby boom generation, and the baby boom generation made sure that the Taylors knew they were America's Family.

—Cheryl A. Smith

FURTHER READING:

Allen, Tim. *Don't Stand Too Close to a Naked Man.* New York, Warner, 1994.

———. *I'm Not Really Here.* New York, Hyperion, 1996.

Arkush, Michael. *Tim Allen Laid Bare: Unauthorized.* New York, Avon Books, 1995.

Lichter, Robert S., Linda Lichter, and Stanley Rothman. *Prime Time: How TV Portrays American Culture.* Washington, D.C., Regnery Publications, 1995.

Home Shopping Network/QVC

Home Shopping Network (HSN) and Quality, Value, Convenience (QVC) were responsible for a historic change in American consumer habits, and have become as much a feature of television as religious channels. These two cable television channels feature live broadcasts of themed sales presentations, 24 hours per day, during which viewers can call a toll-free telephone number, speak with the presenters live on the air, and order the products.

Home Shopping Network got its start in 1977 when a Clearwater, Florida, radio station agreed to accept an advertiser's merchandise in lieu of payment of an overdue bill. Saddled with 112 electric can openers, the station manager offered them for sale on the air. When they sold out instantly and callers clamored for other products, he established a regularly scheduled radio show called *Suncoast Bargaineers.* In 1981, the show moved to a local access cable channel in a Tampa Bay area and was given a new name: Home Shopping Channel. In 1985, it was renamed Home Shopping Network (HSN) and transmitted 24 hours per day through cable and broadcast

television to a national audience, becoming a publicly quoted company on the American Stock Exchange in 1986.

In 1990, HSN stock became available on the New York Stock Exchange, and in 1995 Barry Diller, former Chairman of the Board and CEO of Paramount Pictures and Fox, was welcomed as Chairman of the Board of HSN. James Held, Senior Vice-President of Bloomingdale's department store was named President and CEO. In 1997, HSN's parent company (HSN, Inc.) acquired a controlling interest in Ticketmaster, the world's largest special events ticketing company. In 1998, after purchasing the majority of Universal Studios Inc.'s television assets, HSN, Inc. changed its name to USA Networks, Inc., and purchased the remainder of Ticketmaster. That year also saw the premiere of a Home Shopping Channel in Spanish, the result of a partnership with Univision. With 4,000 employees and more than five million active customers, by 1998 HSN had become an electronic retailing giant rivaled only by one other conglomerate: QVC.

HSN faced its first major competition in the electronic retailing forum in 1986. Quality, Value, Convenience (QVC), Inc., was founded in West Chester, Pennsylvania, by Joseph Segel, founder of the Franklin Mint. With revenues of over $112 million, QVC broke the American record for first full-fiscal-year sales by a new public company and, like HSN, QVC broadcast live 24 hours per day. By 1993, QVC boasted access to 80 percent of all U.S. cable-subscribing households. Reaching 64 million cable households and three million satellite dishes in the United States alone, QVC made more than two billion dollars in sales in 1997 as the result of 84 million phone calls and 56 million orders. QVC, through a 1997 joint venture with BSkyB in the U.K. and Ireland, reached an additional 6.6 million households, broadcasting live 17 hours per day. QVC became best known for its jewelry sales, which accounted for 35 percent of its programming time, and made it one of the world's largest purveyors of 14-carat gold and sterling silver jewelry. At times derogatorily referred to as QVCZ, the channel brought cubic zirconium to the forefront of the shopping public's consciousness with its sales of Diamonique, a low-cost alternative to diamonds.

Home shopping evolved from the world of impulse buying to become a relevant, meaningful form of shopping by the late 1990s. The customer base of HSN and QVC spans all socioeconomic groups, who share two common characteristics: cable subscription and above-average disposable income. The products offered on the channels vary from hour to hour because of the varying demographics of viewers at any given time. Because the channels offer unconditional, money-back guarantees on their products, consumers are able to shop with confidence. Many Americans now prefer to shop from home for the sake of convenience, but for bedridden or other homebound individuals, QVC and HSN offer a viable link to the outside world. Instead of relying solely on caregivers for their shopping needs, homebound people have access to a significant means to independence. The regular hosts of home shopping programs came to provide viewers with a sense of companionship because, unlike ordinary news or talk show hosts, the electronic retailers take calls directly from the viewing audience and, indeed, consider it their job to chat with the callers and not always push a hard sell. Many viewers avidly follow the hairstyles of the hosts, and what few personal details they can glean about them, speculating about their off-screen lives with the fervor of soap-opera fans.

Critics of home shopping held that it was tantamount to the downfall of Western civilization because it gave already television-dependent people yet another excuse to avoid the outside world. They found fault with the hyper-enthusiasm of the product-selling hosts, claiming that viewers were not even permitted to formulate their own emotional responses to the products because the hosts, like deadpan singers in a Greek chorus, force-feed reactions to the audience. However, the elimination of any room for (mis)interpretation is precisely what has appealed to so many consumers. Since every feature of a given product is described in detail, and the sometimes skeptical questions of callers answered candidly, live on the air, viewers feel secure in their understanding of the benefits and drawbacks of the product. Home shopping television may have helped internet shopping in its infancy. By the time retailers began to offer their wares on the world-wide web in the mid-1990s, channels like QVC and HSN had acclimated Americans to the concept of remote shopping. Consumers were thus less leery of giving their credit card numbers to a disembodied voice (in the case of home shopping channels) or to a faceless computer screen.

—Tilney Marsh

FURTHER READING:

Home Shopping Network homepage. http://www.hsn.com. June 1999.

Levine, Kathy, with Jane Scovell. *It's Better to Laugh . . . Life, Good Luck, Bad Hair Days, and QVC.* New York, Pocket Books, 1995.

McCauley, Stephen. "Selling Anything, Enthusiastically, at 3 A.M." *New York Times,* July 26, 1998, 27.

QVC homepage. http://www.qvc.com. June 1999.

The Honeymooners

The Honeymooners is one of television's best-remembered and most imitated comedies in the history of television. Although the series ran for only one year in prime time (during the 1955-1956 season on CBS), it has succeeded remarkably in syndication and on videocassette. Generations of viewers have identified with Jackie Gleason's portrayal of Ralph Kramden, the aggravated bus driver from Brooklyn, whose dreams of advancement were continually upended.

The Honeymooners was among the last of the urban, working-class comedies on 1950s television. As the nation experienced postwar prosperity, so did the families on television. The Nelsons on *The Adventures of Ozzie and Harriett,* the Andersons on *Father Knows Best,* and the Cleavers on *Leave It to Beaver* all lived in the tree-lined, secure suburbs. By 1955, even the prototypical proletariat family, the Goldbergs, had moved out of the city. The Kramdens, however, were the exception. Ralph and his exasperated wife, Alice (Audrey Meadows) were stuck in the urban chaos—a cold-water apartment above a noisy, New York street, without any creature comforts of Eisenhower conformity. Their main possessions were a plain dining table and a depression icebox. They shared their lower-class frustrations with the upstairs neighbors, the Nortons. Slow-witted Ed (Art Carney) worked in the sewers, while his wife Trixie (Joyce Randolph) commiserated with Alice about their common hardships. Unlike the suburban couples on television, the Kramdens and the Nortons were childless, just trying to keep themselves above water.

Much of the comedy revolved around the couples' schemes to get rich quick. In the classic episode, "Better Living Through Television," Ed and Ralph appear in a television commercial to sell

Happy Housewife Helpers. The yearning to get out of near poverty reflected Gleason's own boyhood: he had grown up in the same Brooklyn environment as Ralph. Gleason wanted his show to be based in reality so he instructed his writers to "make it the way people live. If it isn't credible, nobody's going to laugh."

Gleason introduced Ralph and Alice (first played by Pert Kelton) on his DuMont variety series, *Calvacade of Stars.* Gleason's original writers, Joe Bigelow and Harry Crane, wanted to call the sketch "The Beast," but Gleason understood underneath Ralph's blustery exterior was a tremendous need for affection. In the opening monologue of this October 5, 1951 telecast, he saluted another Ralph, Ralph Branca of the Brooklyn Dodgers, who served the infamous homerun pitch to Bobby Thomson during the 1951 playoff game against the New York Giants. Like his namesake Branca, Kramden would suffer the blows of fate; but no matter what, his love for Alice endured. From the beginning, Ralph proclaimed to her, "Baby, you're the Greatest!" The six-minute live sketch, also featuring Art Carney as a policeman, proved so popular that Gleason and company created new struggles for the couple. Soon afterwards, the physically agile Carney joined the regular cast with actress Elaine Stritch as the first Trixie.

A year later, William Paley of CBS stole Gleason and his staff from the downtrodden DuMont network. Gleason was given a much larger budget to produce a weekly live extravaganza on Saturday nights. A younger actress, Audrey Meadows, was hired to replace Kelton, who suffered from heart difficulties and political accusations. Gleason had created many memorable characters—Joe, the Bartender, the Poor Soul, and Reginald Van Gleason, III—but the audiences wanted more of the Kramdens. During the first three years, *The Honeymooner* sketches grew from ten minutes to over 30.

In 1955 the Buick Motor Company offered Gleason six million dollars to produce *The Honeymooners* as a weekly situation comedy for two years. The corpulent comedian formed his own production company and used a new film technology, the Electronican process, to record the series live on film. The program was shot two times a week before an audience of 1,100 people. During the first season Gleason was disturbed by the amount of rehearsal time and felt that these recorded episodes lacked the spontaneity and originality of the live sketches. He discontinued the series after 39 programs and decided to return to the live, variety format. He sold the films and syndication rights to CBS for a million and half dollars.

The Honeymooners remained a prominent part of Gleason's succeeding variety series with the writers trying to do something unusual with the trusted material. During the 1956-1957 season of *The Jackie Gleason Show,* the Kramdens and the Nortons took a live musical trip to Europe. At the end of the season, Carney left the series, and Gleason did not revive the sketch until his 1960s extravaganza, *The American Scene Magazine.* When Carney was available, Gleason revived the sketch on videotape, often with new cast members. Sue Ane Langdon and Sheila MacRae played Alice, while Patricia Wilson and Jean Kean were recruited for Trixie. Despite the changes, the familiar catchphrases remained: "One of these days . . . Pow! Right in the kisser!"; and "Bang! Zoom," Ralph's stock phrases to Alice as well as Ed's greeting to Kramden, "Hiya there, Ralphie boy."

After his variety series ended in 1970, Gleason produced four more *Honeymooner* specials with Carney and the returning Meadows. But Ralph Kramden remained fixed in the popular imagination because the 39 episodes of *The Honeymooners* were a perennial success in syndication. For over 20 years a local station in Manhattan played them every night. There was great celebration among fans when The Museum of Broadcasting and Jackie Gleason unearthed the

The cast members of *The Honeymooners*, (l-r) Jackie Gleason, Art Carney, Audrey Meadows, and Joyce Randolph.

live sketches during the mid-1980s. Those "lost" episodes found another life on cable television and the home video market.

Whether as a recorded situation comedy or a live sketch, *The Honeymooners* is a comic reflection of urban, postwar America. America is a land of opportunity for dreamers like Ralph Kramden, even though success remains elusive. The search for the American Dream turned Arthur Miller's salesman, Willy Loman, into a tragic hero; the same quest made Gleason's bus driver a comic archetype. His bravado and anxieties can be felt in all subsequent, working-class underdogs on television—Fred Flintstone, Archie Bunker, Roseanne, and Homer Simpson.

—Ron Simon

FURTHER READING:

Bacon, James. *The Jackie Gleason Story*. New York, St. Martin's, 1985.

Cresenti, Peter, and Bob Columbe. *The Official Honeymooners Treasury*. New York, Perigee Books, 1985.

Henry, William. *The Great One: The Life and Legend of Jackie Gleason*. New York, Doubleday, 1992.

McCrohan, Donna. *The Honeymooners' Companion*. New York, Workman, 1978.

McCrohan, Donna, and Peter Cresenti. *The Honeymooners Lost Episodes*. New York, Workman, 1986.

Meadows, Audrey. *Love, Alice My Life as a Honeymooner*. New York, Crown, 1994.

Waldron, Vince. *Classic Sitcoms*. New York, Macmillan, 1987.

Hooker, John Lee (1917—)

The undisputed "King of the Boogie," John Lee Hooker has not only achieved commercial success—a rare feat among blues singers—but he has maintained it for over five decades. His one-chord, droning grooves lend themselves, as Robert Palmer writes, to "building up a cumulative, trancelike effect." Although he has attempted to redefine himself in recent years, much to the detriment of the legendary style and talent that made him famous, Hooker is still an original whose contributions to music in the twentieth century remain in a category of their own.

Born near Clarksdale, Mississippi, on August 22, 1917, Hooker's primary influence was his stepfather, Will Moore, a Louisiana-born guitarist who played in a style very different from that of other Delta players. Occasional visits by legendary bluesmen like Blind Lemon Jefferson, Charley Patton, and Blind Blake (who all knew Moore) certainly influenced young John Lee's style as well, especially his singing.

Leaving home at 14, Hooker settled in Memphis, where he worked as an usher in a Beale Street movie theater while moonlighting as an entertainer at neighborhood house parties. After a seven-year stint working for a cesspool draining company in Cincinnati, he relocated to Detroit in 1943. With the city's factories operating at peak wartime production, jobs were not hard to find and Hooker continued to limit his musical forays to occasional sit-ins and weekend gigs at various Hastings Street clubs.

One night, a black record-store owner heard Hooker playing in a friend's living room and took him to see Bernie Bessman, a local record distributor. Bessman helped to record Hooker's first single, the seminal "Boogie Chillen," a primitive effort featuring only guitar and vocals. Issued by Modern Records in 1948, "the thing caught afire," as Hooker later remembered. "When it come out, every jukebox you went to, every place you went to, every drugstore you went, everywhere you went, department stores, they were playin' it in there. And I was workin' in Detroit in a factory there for a while. Then I quit my job. I said, 'No, I ain't workin' no more!'" With the success of follow-up efforts like "Hobo Blues," "Hoogie Boogie," and

"Crawling King Snake Blues" over the next year, Hooker never came to regret his decision.

Although contractually bound to Modern Records during this period, Hooker recorded for many other labels using a variety of pseudonyms including "Texas Slim," "Delta John," "Johnny Lee," "Johnny Williams," and even "Little Pork Chops." He finally reached an exclusive agreement with Vee-Jay Records in 1955, recording from then on under his own name. The format of his music, however, changed dramatically with the addition of a backing band, often including the superb duo of guitarist Eddie Taylor and harmonica player Jimmy Reed. While most of Hooker's Vee-Jay material lacked the spark of his initial recordings, he did re-enter the charts in 1958 with "I Love You Honey," in 1960 with "No Shoes," and finally in 1962 with "Boom Boom."

After cranking out "Big Legs, Tight Skirt," his last hit for Vee-Jay, in 1964, Hooker underwent another round of label-hopping, recording for Verve, Chess, and BluesWay, among others. His 1960s recordings presented him in a variety of contexts—folk bluesman, old-time boogie master, or quasi-rock-and-roll artist—always in an attempt to appeal to the changing blues-rock audience. Hooker became a major figure in both the British blues invasion (with two major groups, the Yardbirds and the Animals, both tackling "Boom Boom") and the American folk-blues revival, with acoustic recordings and frequent coffeehouse appearances. In 1970, he teamed up with rock artists Canned Heat for the hit album *Hooker 'n' Heat;* unfortunately, many of his subsequent recordings were blatant attempts to recapture the album's popularity and redefine Hooker as a rock-and-roller.

Bandmate and slide guitarist extraordinaire Roy Rogers organized a 1989 recording session which eventually became *The Healer,* a major comeback album for Hooker. Once again, he returned to the spotlight, though in this case more due to the superstar guests who

John Lee Hooker

appeared on the album, including Bonnie Raitt, Keith Richards, Carlos Santana, Robert Cray, and Los Lobos. The disc won a Grammy Award as best traditional blues recording, and set the stage for another all-star session, *Mr. Lucky* (1991), which featured guitarists Albert Collins and Johnny Winter, among others. Hooker went into semi-retirement after the album's release, enjoying his newfound wealth and fame. He continued, however, to record and tour when inspired, even appearing in television commercials for Pepsi-Cola. He now stands as one of the few remaining links to the Delta blues tradition; a living legend and a true original.

—Marc R. Sykes

FURTHER READING:

Oakley, Giles. *The Devil's Music: A History of the Blues.* London, Da Capo Press, 1983.

Palmer, Robert. *Deep Blues.* New York, Viking, 1981.

Hoosiers

Basketball in many parts of the country is like religion, and *Hoosiers,* a 1986 film written by Angelo Pizzo and directed by David Anspaugh, is a clear homage to that sentiment. Set against an idyllic rural Indiana backdrop, *Hoosiers* traces the training of the team at the tiny Hickory High School for the state basketball championship. The film looks at first glance like the classic David versus Goliath sports movie, with a predictably familiar ending but, in this case, predictability neither lessens the impact of the drama, nor detracts from audience response to the emotions and feelings that are revealed on the screen.

Some very prominent actors were drawn to this small-budget production. Gene Hackman portrays Norman Dale, a former college coach who was fired for striking a player in a moment of rage. The troubled Dale, now head coach of the Hickory Huskers, has come to Indiana as his last chance to work at the game he loves. The always excellent Hackman gives a convincing portrayal of a man who, throughout the action of the film, attempts to contain his competitive nature and learn to trust others. Barbara Hershey plays Myra Fleener, a teacher who tries to draw the town phenomenon, Jimmy Chipwood, away from basketball and into the classroom. A relationship develops between Coach Dale and the teacher Fleener, despite their differences on the future of Chipwood. Dennis Hopper tackles the role of Shooter, the town drunk who constantly recounts the glory days of his high school basketball career. The relationship between Dale and Shooter that develops illustrates Dale's attempts to give somebody a second chance—something that he himself had been denied years before. Hopper's performance earned him an Oscar nomination.

Hoosiers was based on the true story of little Milan High School, which shocked the Indiana basketball world by winning the state championship in 1954 on a last second shot. True to form, the Hickory Huskers also make the improbable charge through the series, defeating larger schools and better teams. Star player Jimmy Chipwood, played by Maris Valainis, makes the winning shot with time running to immortalize himself and his team in the town of Hickory and all of Indiana.

Though no surprises appear in this familiar underdog story, *Hoosiers* is still able to maintain the tension and excitement needed to entertain audiences. The film provides an accurate depiction of life in rural Indiana in the 1950s, with several high school students forced by necessity to work on the farm instead of playing basketball. The all-white Huskers battle a city team made up of largely black players and a black coach in the championship game, another accurate portrayal of social life in the Midwest in the 1950s. *Hoosiers* also clearly demonstrates the importance of high school athletics to small, rural communities. Almost the entire town would caravan to every away game and to each step of the state tournament. The community meeting held to determine the fate of Coach Dale midway through his season, and the Saturday morning discussions at the barber shop illustrate just how important the team is and how much civic pride athletics can create.

—Jay Parrent

FURTHER READING:

Harris, Ann. "Hoosiers" in *Magill's Cinema Annual.* Englewood Cliffs, New Jersey, Salem Press, 1987.

Kauffmann, Stanley. "Hoosiers" (movie review). *The New Republic,* April 6, 1987, 26-27.

Hoover Dam

The Colorado River bobs and jukes through the crisp sandstone of the western high plains. Earliest explorers saw it as a defining characteristic of Arizona and much of the semi-arid western United States. Today, the river is a monument to American riverine technology, as aqueducts and hydroelectric dams use the Colorado to make the American West a hydraulic society. The first of the incursions into the river is also the most famous: Hoover Dam.

Opened in 1935, Hoover Dam stands as a larger-than-life symbol of fluctuating meaning for generations of Americans. Even without such symbolic significance, the dam remains among the nation's most impressive engineering achievements.

A major part of the dam's significance derives from the structure itself. The dam, which has long-since repaid the $165 million cost for construction, is a National Historic Landmark and has been rated by the American Society of Civil Engineers as one of America's Seven Modern Civil Engineering Wonders. The structure contains over 4 million cubic yards of concrete, which if placed in a monument 100 feet square would reach 2.5 miles high—higher than the Empire State Building.

As proposed in 1910, the mammoth Boulder Dam (as it was first referred to) served as the linchpin of a western land-use policy known as reclamation. After policymakers and developers finally conceded that a serious lack of rainfall stood in the way of their dreams of the "garden of the West," they sought a way to turn their adversity into opportunity. Reclamation grew out of the impulse to "reclaim" these dry, barren regions by applying human ingenuity to the few existing waterways, including the Colorado. In 1912, five western states agreed on the Colorado Compact, which parceled up the great river's flow among the signees—including at least two states that never made contact with the river. Most of the flow, including the electricity made at Hoover Dam, would be managed by the Six Companies contractors

Hoover Dam

to power development over 300 miles away in southern California. By the late 1990s, the majority of Hoover Dam's power is passed over wires to Los Angeles.

The symbolic significance of this immense structure became obvious immediately, which led developers to name it after President Herbert Hoover (an engineer who had been a great supporter of the project). Upon its completion in 1935, Hoover Dam became a symbol of America's technological prowess, firmly placing the United States with the great civilizations in world history. One observer described it as the "Great Pyramid of the American Desert, the Ninth Symphony of our day" and "a visual symphony written in steel and concrete. . . . magnificently original, strong, simple, and majestic as the greatest works of art of all time and all peoples, and as eloquently expressive of our own as anything ever achieved." Particularly during the Great Depression, Hoover Dam's restoration of national confidence led to its appearance throughout popular culture, including advertisements, Coca-Cola serving trays, and numerous collectible mementos.

Hoover Dam remains a symbol in contemporary America; however, the changing attitude of river-management technology has altered its image. In the 1990s, many observers saw Hoover Dam as the symbol of all the development that has prohibited the Colorado from reaching the ocean for over twenty years. As the great dams begin to clog with silt, many observers suggest that Hoover and the other dams may have only a limited life. Marc Reisner noted that "we set out to tame the rivers and ended up killing them." He suggested that Hoover and others might eventually be viewed as "uniquely productive, creative vandalism."

In terms of structural design, though, Hoover Dam will always serve as a symbol of the modern era. For many Americans, achievements such as this sleek yet powerful dam led the way to a century of innovation and development.

—Brian Black

FURTHER READING:

Jackson, Donald C. *Building the Ultimate Dam.* Lawrence, University of Kansas Press, 1995.

Reisner, Marc. *Cadillac Desert.* New York, Penguin, 1986.

Stevens, Joseph E. *Hoover Dam.* Norman, University of Oklahoma Press, 1988.

Hoover, J. Edgar (1895-1972)

When J. Edgar Hoover died in 1972, the *New York Times* wrote of him, "For nearly a half century, J. Edgar Hoover and the FBI were indistinguishable. That was at once his strength and its weakness." Hoover was a strong personality, fiercely patriotic, and highly organized and controlling. Head of the Federal Bureau of Investigation (FBI) from the presidency of Calvin Coolidge until the presidency of Richard Nixon, he transformed the face of the United States Justice Department and became the definition of law enforcement in America, for better or worse.

John Edgar Hoover was born into a solidly middle class neighborhood in Washington, D.C. His father was in the Coast Guard and later worked as a low-level employee of the federal government. Brought up to the exacting standards of his strict mother, Hoover determined he would surpass his unambitious father. He remained

J. Edgar Hoover

devoted to his mother, living with her in the house in which he was born until her death in 1937.

Hoover received both a bachelors and a masters of law at George Washington University, and went to work for the government. He worked at the Library of Congress until the advent of World War I. In 1917, seeking to avoid the draft, which would force him to leave his aging parents, he obtained a clerical job at the Department of Justice, from which he moved up quickly. An extremely moralistic man, Hoover was virulently anti-Communist and anti-radical, and he gained prestige in the Justice Department by overseeing its wartime campaign against American radicals. In 1924, he took over as head of the Bureau of Investigation of the Justice Department (renamed Federal Bureau of Investigation in 1935).

When Hoover took over as director, the Bureau was a slack organization, largely made up of political appointees and "hacks," who were not law enforcement professionals. Hoover immediately began to revamp the organization, first firing much of the staff and retraining those who remained. He eliminated the seniority system of promotions and instituted a merit system, with regular performance reviews. Over the course of his almost 50-year directorship, he succeeded in turning the FBI into one of the world's most efficient crime fighting organizations, with a state-of-the-art criminal lab, an ingenious fingerprint filing system designed by Hoover himself, and a prestigious training school for law enforcement agents.

Hoover is perhaps most famous for his success against the gangsters of the prohibition era, arresting renowned crime figures such as Al Capone and John Dillinger, and for his post-World War II activity against the Communist Party and against the Ku Klux Klan. He also grew infamous for abusing the power of his agency and exceeding its jurisdiction. If he turned the FBI into a crack crime-fighting force, he also turned it into an internal secret surveillance tool. Hoover's FBI employed tactics of infiltration, provocation, illegal wiretapping, and even burglary to amass volumes of damaging information about both public figures and private citizens. Even presidents and their families were not exempt from FBI scrutiny. This information was kept by the director in secret files that were allegedly used to control the activities of government officials, influence the outcome of elections, and quash public dissent. In the 1960s, with the support of President Lyndon Johnson, Hoover created counterintelligence programs (COINTELPROs) to infiltrate and disrupt the activities of many leftist organizations, the Black Panthers and Students for a Democratic Society among them.

Hoover and his G-men were hailed as heroes during the gangster-fighting days of prohibition. Although they garnered much popular support during the anti-Communist 1950s, with the rise of the New Left in the 1960s more people began to question the authority of the FBI. On March 8, 1971, a small group calling themselves "Citizens' Commission to Investigate the FBI" broke into the agency's offices in the town of Media, Pennsylvania. They found and publicized files proving the illegal activities involved in the FBI's COINTELPROs, changing the public image of Hoover's Bureau from dashing G-men to secret police.

J. Edgar Hoover died suddenly in 1972 of undiagnosed heart disease. He had been a religious man, an unbending moralist, obsessed with details and with eradicating any threats to the American way of life as he defined it. Though Hoover had used his agency to enforce Lyndon Johnson's civil rights legislation and to root out the Ku Klux Klan, he was personally a racial bigot and the FBI had a poor record of hiring minorities. Throughout his life he was followed by rumors of homosexuality. He was a dandified dresser who was never

romantically associated with women, but who did form intimate attachments with men, notably Clyde Tolson, his second in command at the FBI, with whom he had a long, close friendship which some compared to marriage. Hoover violently denied any allegations that he had sexual relations with men, and his strict moral code would certainly forbid either the relations themselves or the acknowledgment of them. It is the type of information one might expect to find in a confidential folder in a secret file at the Federal Bureau of Investigation.

—Tina Gianoulis

FURTHER READING:

DeLoach, Cartha. *Hoover's FBI: The Inside Story by Hoover's Trusted Lieutenant.* Washington, D.C., Regnery Publications, 1995.

Demaris, Ovid. *J. Edgar Hoover: As They Knew Him.* New York, Carrol & Graf, 1994.

Gentry, Curt. *J. Edgar Hoover: The Man and the Secrets.* New York, Plume, 1991.

Keller, William W. *The Liberals and J. Edgar Hoover: Rise and Fall of a Domestic Intelligence State.* Princeton, New Jersey, Princeton University Press, 1989.

O'Reilly, Kenneth. *Black Americans: The FBI Files.* New York, Carroll and Graf, 1994.

———. *Hoover and the Un-Americans: The FBI, HUAC, and the Red Menace.* Philadelphia, Temple University Press, 1983.

Potter, Claire Bond. *War on Crime: Bandits, G-men and the Politics of Mass Culture.* New Brunswick, New Jersey, Rutgers University Press, 1998.

Powers, Richard. *G-men: Hoover's FBI in American Pop Culture.* Carbondale, Southern Illinois University Press, 1983.

Theoharis, Athan G., and John Stuart. *The Boss: J. Edgar Hoover and the Great American Inquisition.* Philadelphia, Temple University Press, 1988.

Hopalong Cassidy

A multimedia cowboy hero, Hopalong Cassidy first appeared in a series of magazine stories that were published in 1905 and 1906. Clarence E. Mulford, who was residing in Brooklyn at the time and had never been West, was the author. His Cassidy was a tough, tobacco-chewing redhead, who bossed the hands at the Bar-20 Ranch and got his nickname from the fact that a gunshot wound in his leg had left him with a permanent limp. The more familiar image of this popular American fictional hero, however, is the one personified in movies and on television by silver-haired actor William Boyd. Boyd's Hopalong Cassidy was a dapper, soft-spoken cowboy, who almost always wore black, and was taken into the hearts of millions of kids. In his later television incarnation, Hopalong products became one of the first merchandising sensations inspired by television.

Mulford, who worked for over 20 years in a civil service job, sold his earliest Hopalong Cassidy stories to a travel monthly called *Outing Magazine.* The first collection of those stories in book form was titled *Bar 20* and came out in 1907. All told, Mulford wrote over two dozen novels and story collections about his limping, hard-bitten cowhand between then and 1941. Much of the material appeared

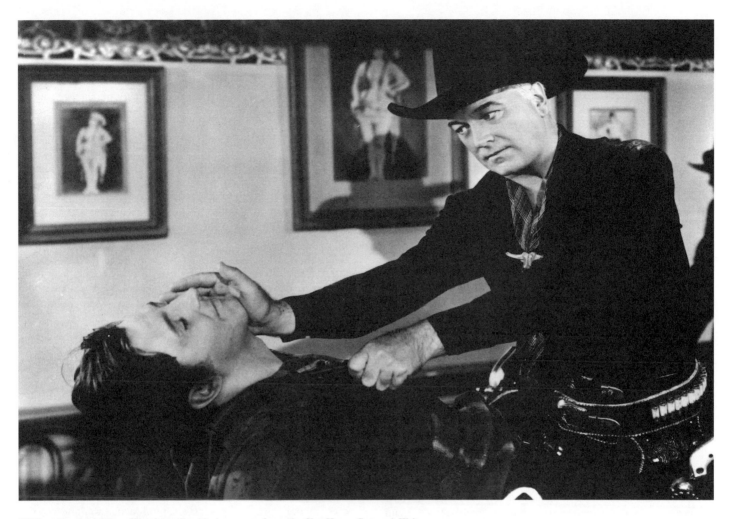

William Boyd (right) as Hopalong Cassidy in a scene from the film *Hoppy Serves A Writ*.

initially in such pulp fiction magazines as *Argosy* and *Short Stories*. A dedicated researcher and collector of Western lore, Mulford did eventually travel extensively in the Western states but, despite the popularity of his books, he is remembered today chiefly as the man who coined the name that others used to create an almost entirely different hero.

As Francis M. Nevins pointed out, "the man ultimately responsible for Hoppy's transformation into a screen hero was Harry Sherman." An entrepreneur since silent movie days, and one of those who helped finance *The Birth of A Nation,* Sherman bought the screen rights to the Mulford books and then put together a movie production outfit to make the films, which were distributed by Paramount. The actor Sherman chose to play Cassidy was also a veteran of the silents. A protégé of Cecil B. DeMille, William Boyd became a star in the 1920s in such films as *The Volga Boatman* and *The Yankee Clipper,* but by the mid-1930s he'd slipped some and was appearing in lower budget action films. The first movie in Sherman's cowboy series was *Hop-A-Long Cassidy,* released in 1935. In this film, the prematurely grey Boyd actually did limp, but in later outings he lost the limp, and the hyphens.

A formula was established from the start. Hoppy always had two sidekicks—one young and handsome (played originally by James Ellison), the other, crusty and humorous (first portrayed by Gabby Hayes). Known as a hellraiser in real life, Boyd reformed as the series progressed and Hopalong, who soon acquired the black outfit that was to become his trademark, also underwent changes. As a movie hero, he never drank, smoked or swore, and his relations with women were almost always nothing more than avuncular. A hit from the first, the Hoppy series eventually stretched to 66 titles. As one film historian noted, the pictures, "long on human interest, short on violence, were especially popular with family audiences."

Hopalong first moved into comic books at the end of 1942, as a back up feature in Fawcett's *Master Comics*. The following year, Fawcett started a *Hopalong Cassidy* comic book, which they kept going until 1954. In the late 1940s, Boyd took over the production of the Hoppy films and also bought the rights to all of the earlier Sherman productions. This proved to be an especially wise move. In 1949, NBC started showing the movies nationally, every Friday night from eight to nine p.m. and, as the number of American households with television sets grew, so did Hoppy's popularity. "The show became a hit very quickly," wrote Richard O'Brien, "and almost as quickly a wide variety of manufacturers leaped aboard Hopalong's bandwagon. There were Hopalong Cassidy costumes, tin windups, toy soldiers, binoculars, dart boards, knives, badges, shooting galleries, and of course a wide variety of guns and holsters." A comic strip began in 1949, drawn by Dan Spiegle and distributed by King Features.

In 1951, Boyd, who had last played Hoppy in 1948, produced and starred in a *Hopalong Cassidy* television series. It ran on NBC until the end of 1952, with movie veteran Edgar Buchanan as the hero's crusty sidekick. A radio show had been put together in 1948, but it wasn't until the character became a craze through TV that it showed up on national radio—first on Mutual and then on CBS. Andy Clyde, the resident old coot sidekick from the later movies, repeated his role as California Carlson on the radio networks. The show was last heard late in 1952. During the heyday of Hoppy, Boyd became a national celebrity and his personal appearances drew enormous crowds of dedicated kids. Hoppy gradually faded away, although the comic book, taken over by DC, continued until 1959. By the time he retired, Boyd, who controlled all the merchandising on the character, was a multimillionaire. He died in 1972.

—Ron Goulart

FURTHER READING:

Keltner, Howard. *Golden Age Comic Books Index.* Gainesville, Keltner, 1998.

Nevins, Francis M. *The Films of Hopalong Cassidy.* Waynesville, The World of Yesterday, 1988.

O'Brien, Richard. *The Story of American Toys.* New York, Artabras, 1990.

Sampson, Robert. *Yesterday's Faces,* Vol. 1. Bowling Green, Bowling Green University Popular Press, 1983.

Hope, Bob (1903—)

Entertainer Bob Hope is unquestionably an American show-business icon and the facts surrounding his multi-decade, multi-generational success sustain the myth. Hope's entertainment persona has been evident in every decade of the twentieth century, from his 70 movies to celebrating an unprecedented 56 year-contract with NBC in 1993. He entertained American troops in both war and peace time and was hailed as "America's most prized ambassador of goodwill throughout the world" when presented with the Congressional Gold Medal by President Kennedy.

The fifth of seven sons, he was born Leslie Townes Hope in Eltham, England, on May 29, 1903. His father, William Henry Hope, was a stonemason who decided on an impulse to migrate with his family to Cleveland, Ohio. His Welsh mother, Avis Townes Hope, who had been a concert singer, instilled in him a love for music and entertaining. Hope would later claim that he first warmed to an audience laughing at him when his voice cracked while singing at a backyard family reunion. In 1920, by virtue of his father's naturalization, "Bob"—the name by which the world would later know him—and his brothers also became U.S. citizens.

After high school, Hope took dancing lessons from African American entertainer King Rastus Brown and from vaudeville hoofer Johnny Root. A natural, he soon began teaching classes. He also worked briefly as a newspaper reporter and tried amateur boxing under the name of Packy East. At 18, Hope persuaded his girlfriend, Mildred Rosequist, to become his dance partner. Appearing at nearby vaudeville houses they worked their way to the generous wages of $8 an night. But the partnership would not last long: when Rosequist's mother finally saw their act she thought it was just too risqué for her

daughter. Hope then teamed up with a friend, Lloyd Durbin. After developing their act in local bookings they were hired by the Bandbox Theater in Cleveland as a "cheap act" for the Fatty Arbuckle Show. Arbuckle, who headlined the touring revue, loved Hope and Durbin's comedy/dancing act and helped the boys get better bookings. Following the accidental death of Durbin, Hope took on another partner, George Byrne, with whom he developed a blackface act.

After several career reversals, Hope and Byrne were almost ready to give it all up when they were hired to emcee Marshall Walker's Whiz Bang review in New Castle, Pennsylvania. Hope went out on stage alone and entertained the audience with his ad-libbed wisecracks. He was using for the first time a technique that would prove good enough to last through seven decades: not only parrying and jousting with anything an audience member or fellow comic could throw at him, but also being brave enough to wait on stage in front of the toughest audience until everyone had gotten his jokes.

In 1929, Hope went to New York and was given a movie screen test, but was told his "ski nose" had killed his possibilities. With material from legendary gagster Al Boasberg, Hope continued his career on stage, appearing in *The Antics* of 1931. His performance impressed the audiences and led to an even better theatrical gig — *The Ballyhoo* of 1932—in which Hope was encouraged to ad-lib to his heart's content. But his first major recognition, by critics and the public, came in 1933 for his wise-cracking role as Huckleberry Haines in the highly successful Broadway musical, *Roberta*. Not only Hope's professional life would change from then on: one of his co-performers in the musical, George Murphy, introduced him to a young singer, Dolores Reade. After a brief courtship, Dolores and Bob got married in February 1934. They went on to have four children and four grandchildren.

With his vaudeville show at New York's Capitol Theater came along his first radio appearance, on the "Capitol Family Hour," hosted by Major Edward J. Bows, which originated from the theater every morning. After guest spots and semi-regular work on a couple of shows, Bob was signed on by Pepsodent toothpaste for his own show on NBC. He went on to become a huge radio star and a Tuesday-night regular for the next 15 years.

On his half-hour program, Hope opened with a monologue which fired off barbs about current news events and usually set the tone for the rest of the show. Every time a news story broke, everybody would look forward to hearing what Hope was going to say about it on his next show. With his "and I wanna tell you" catch phrase, he inaugurated a comedy style in which no joke, whether resulting in irrepressible laughs or a just a smile, was any more important than the next one coming up.

In 1937 Hope traveled to Hollywood to film *The Big Broadcast of 1938*, in which he sang the Oscar-winning song "Thanks for the Memories" as a duet with Shirley Ross. The song has been his signature theme ever since. Between 1934 and 1936 he had appeared in eight comedy shorts, all filmed in New York, but his first screen hit would come only in 1939 with *The Cat and the Canary*. In the next year he struck it big with *Road to Singapore* (1940), the first of seven successful "Road" pictures he was to make over the years with Bing Crosby and Dorothy Lamour, highly praised for featuring in-jokes about Bob and Bing's private lives.

Relying heavily on rapid quips and topical wisecracks, Hope built his own style of screen comedy which would reach a peak in the western parody *The Paleface* (1948). His films of the 1950s were a mixed bag and were less and less profitable. Writer/directors Norman Panama and Melvin Frank suggested that Hope should start playing straight dramatic roles. The advice resulted in Hope playing Eddie Foy Sr. in *The Seven Little Foys* (1955), a character which gave him the chance to combine drama and humor. Hope's last dramatic role was as New York City Mayor Jimmy Walker in *Beau James* (1957). In the same year, Hope started working as his own producer and brought forward successes like *Alias Jesse James* (1959) and *The Facts of Life* (1960), with Lucille Ball as his co-star.

In the 1960s, however, the public began to find Hope's films increasingly less entertaining. With *Boy, Did I Get a Wrong Number* (1966) and *The Private Navy of Sgt. O'Farrell* (1968), he dissatisfied even his most loyal fans. Besides, Hope's conservative political ideas were at odds with the general frame of mind concerning the Vietnam War. At that point, Hope was criticized severely for not being able to separate his stage persona from his political beliefs. When traveling to entertain the troops, he found for the first time a welcome that was less than enthusiastic and his overall career was never quite the same from then on.

Television came calling as early as the 1930s, but Hope was not at all convinced the ''new'' entertainment medium would succeed. He participated in an experimental show for CBS; in the first commercial television broadcast on the West Coast in 1947; and as a surprise guest on Ed Sullivan's ''Taste of the Town'' in 1949. But his formal debut on NBC television would only happen on Easter Sunday in 1950. Douglas Fairbanks, Jr., Beatrice Lillie, and Dinah Shore were Bob's guest stars in the special *Star Spangled Revue*, sponsored by Frigidaire. His annual trips overseas to entertain the U.S. troops—which had started full bore during World War II and lasted through Korea and Vietnam, to the Persian Gulf conflict of 1990/91—soon became a regular Christmas television event. For 60 consecutive years Hope aired his specials with NBC-TV stars. But his jokes were gradually becoming outdated and predictable, his style getting more and more insipid. In 1996 something that everybody was already expecting happened: NBC announced the end of their contract with Bob Hope. That year's *Bob Hope Salutes the Presidents* was his final Christmas special.

Hope's work with NBC guaranteed him a place in the Guinness Book of Records as the entertainer with the longest-term television contract. He is also in Guinness as the most honored entertainer in the world, for he has more than two thousand awards and citations for humanitarian and professional efforts, including 54 honorary doctorates. Although he never received an Oscar for his for his acting, Hope frequently emceed the ceremonies and he himself won special Academy Awards five times (1940, 1944, 1952, 1959, 1965), for humanitarian action and contribution to the industry. In July 1976, by order of Her Majesty Queen Elizabeth, Hope was made an Honorary Commander of the Order of the British Empire (CBE) for his services to British troops around the world during World War II and his lifetime professional achievements were acknowledged by Kennedy Center honors in 1985.

Hope has also been an avid golfer and his name became associated with the *Bob Hope Desert Classic*, an annual event that produced millions of dollars for charity. The extensive list of his golfing buddies includes presidents Dwight D. Eisenhower, Richard Nixon, Gerald Ford, Ronald Reagan, George Bush, and Bill Clinton.

Hope, who over the years assumed the stature of a national institution, authored several humorous books about his career and travels. He has been honored and befriended by presidents of the United States since Roosevelt. President Johnson honored Bob with the Medal of Freedom and President and Mrs. Carter hosted a White House reception in celebration of his 75th birthday. Harry Truman

played the piano for him and Bill Clinton bestowed on him a Medal of the Arts. In his nineties and nearing total blindness, Hope is likely find consolation in knowing his long years dedicated to the entertainment industry were extremely profitable: with his fortune estimated at hundreds of millions, mostly in real estate, securities, oil and gas wells, thoroughbred horses, a broadcasting company, and at one point the Cleveland Indians baseball team, he is one of the richest performers ever.

—Bianca Freire-Medeiros

FURTHER READING:

Mielke, Randall G. *Road to Box Office: The Seven Film Comedies of Bing Crosby, Bob Hope, and Dorothy Lamour, 1940-1962*. Jefferson, North Carolina, McFarland & Co., 1997.

Morella, Joe. *The Amazing Careers of Bob Hope; From Gags to Riches*. New York, W. H. Allen, 1974.

Quirk, Lawrence J. *Bob Hope: The Road Well-Traveled*. Applause Theatre Book Publications, 1998.

Hopkins, Sam ''Lightnin''' (1912-1982)

Blues guitarist Sam ''Lightnin''' Hopkins enjoyed a six-decade career that took him from the streets of Houston to festival stages around the world. As a youngster, Hopkins worked with guitarist Blind Lemon Jefferson as a ''guide boy'' before striking out on his own in 1946. For the next several years, he had a string of national rhythm and blues hits for the Aladdin, Modern, and Mercury labels, including ''Katie May,'' ''Shotgun Blues,'' and ''Lightnin's Boogie.'' As musical styles changed, however, Hopkins found himself out of vogue, and eventually landed back in Houston.

''Rediscovered'' in the early 1960s and repackaged as a folk-blues artist, Hopkins found a role in the forefront of the blues revival, starring at university coffeehouses, on television programs, and on European tours. He continued to record for a variety of labels including Vee-Jay, Arhoolie, and Verve. In 1967, filmmaker Les Blank captured Hopkins' eccentric lifestyle in the documentary *The Blues Accordin' to Lightnin' Hopkins*. Hopkins died in Houston in 1982.

—Marc R. Sykes

FURTHER READING:

Oakley, Giles. *The Devil's Music: A History of the Blues*. New York, Da Capo Press, 1983.

Palmer, Robert. *Deep Blues*. New York, Viking, 1981.

Hopper, Dennis (1936—)

From young Hollywood rebel, to counter-cultural icon, to dropped-out druggie, to acclaimed character actor, Dennis Hopper's art has often mimicked his life. In the process, however, he came to exert a profound cultural influence on Hollywood, opening the way for the new, independent, youth-oriented cinema that took hold in the 1970s.

Dennis Hopper

As a starstruck boy born and raised on a farm in Kansas, Hopper dreamed of becoming a Hollywood actor. When his family moved to San Diego, California, 14-year-old Dennis fell in with a drug-using party crowd. But he also found an outlet for his acting ambitions by working at the Old Globe Theatre and the La Jolla Playhouse, where he was cast in his first professional role. At 18, Hopper was signed to a seven-year contract with Warner Brothers. There, he appeared in a small role in *Rebel Without a Cause* (1955) and became a close friend of James Dean and Natalie Wood.

Hopper's breakthrough film was *Giant* (1956), starring Dean, Rock Hudson, and Elizabeth Taylor, and for most of the next 10 years he was known as a rebellious but gifted and successful young actor. It wasn't, however, until he tried his hand at directing that he became a Hollywood icon. In 1969, Hopper and his good friends Peter Fonda and Jack Nicholson made *Easy Rider*, a film that reflected the attitudes of nearly a decade of the counter-culture from which it sprang. *Easy Rider* captured the imagination of a generation, shone the spotlight on future megastar Nicholson and, significantly, caused convulsive changes in the thinking of the established movie industry. He used his heightened success and new influence to direct *The Last Movie* (1971) on location in Peru, but the result was a muddled drama and a commercial and critical disaster. Hopper then dropped out for almost 15 years, doing drugs in New Mexico and making foreign films.

He returned to Hollywood respectability with an astonishingly brilliant portrait of psychologically disturbed brutality in David Lynch's indie favorite, *Blue Velvet*, in 1986. That same year he made *Hoosiers*, another independent film, which earned him an Oscar nomination. His comeback was complete, and in 1988 he directed the decently crafted *Colors*. Actor, director, writer, photographer, and art collector, Dennis Hopper continued to work in a varied and variable mix of movies throughout the 1990s, by which time he had become Hollywood's favorite iconoclast and a pop culture institution.

—Victoria Price

FURTHER READING:

Hoberman, J. *Dennis Hopper: From Method to Madness.* Minneapolis, Minnesota, Walker Art Center, 1988.

Monaco, James, and the Editors of Baseline. *Encyclopedia of Film.* New York, Perigee, 1991.

Rodriguez, Elena. *Dennis Hopper: A Madness to His Method.* New York, St. Martin's Press, 1998.

Thomson, David. *A Biographical Dictionary of Film.* New York, Alfred A. Knopf, 1994.

Hopper, Edward (1882-1967)

Born in 1882 in Nyack, New York, Edward Hopper developed a style of realist painting that art critic Rolf Günter Renner suggests revealed the limits that humanity and nature impose on each other. This tension is put into sharp relief in one of Hopper's best known paintings, *Gas, 1940,* which shows a lone attendant checking the pumps at a Mobil gas station bordered by woods. Hopper is perhaps most widely recognized for his *Nighthawks* (1942), a painting of two men and a woman late at night in a diner, which entered the popular realm as a poster, "Boulevard of Broken Dreams," with the men transformed to James Dean and Humphrey Bogart, the counterman to Elvis Presley, and the woman to Marilyn Monroe. Hopper's figures in this and other paintings displayed an edginess and detachment from the moment, possibly in search of something grander. The poster commodified this alienation through the figures of tragic, troubled movie stars.

Hopper studied illustration at a commercial art school for two years before switching to the New York School of Art in 1901. There, he worked most closely with Robert Henri, a member of the Ashcan School. Hopper's studies of people seem to build on the urban gaze of Ashcan School painter John Sloan, whose etchings hovered between reportage and voyeurism. Hopper travelled to Europe three times between 1906 and 1910. Thereafter, he settled in New York City and summered at South Truro near Cape Cod with his wife Josephine (Jo) Verstille Nivison, whom he married in 1924.

Until the mid-1920s Hopper worked as a commercial artist. In 1925 he painted *House by the Railroad.* The painting captured Hopper's themes of loneliness, detachment, and alienation. Hopper said his goal was "to achieve the best possible realization of my most intimate impressions of my surroundings." According to Gail Levin, Hopper's biographer, the eerie mood of this painting led to it being used as a model for the house in Alfred Hitchcock's 1960 film *Psycho.*

The German filmmaker Wolfgang Hastert has suggested that Hopper's paintings are like storyboards for films. In a short film on the painter he drew comparisons to Hopper's work and films such as *Paris, Texas,* by Wim Wenders, and *Blue Velvet* by David Lynch. The brooding nature of Hopper's work lends itself to such comparisons and his use of light and shadow could be compared to the technical dimensions of film noir. One reason Hopper's work draws such analogies is that much of it deals self-consciously with the process of looking. In many of Hopper's paintings, the field of sight is clearly from the outside looking in or the inside looking out. For instance, in *Office in a Small City* (1953), Hopper lets us look from the outside at a man at work, and simultaneously, at the vision before that man from his office window.

Edward Hopper

Hopper's wife Jo was a constant presence in his life and paintings. The photographer Arnold Newman has suggested that his 1960 photograph of Hopper at South Truro, in which Jo dances in the distant background while Hopper grimaces at the camera, is indicative of their relationship, with Jo always in the background. But Jo was a constant figure in Hopper's paintings and Renner suggests paintings such as *Girlie Show* (1941), *New York Movie* (1939), *Summertime* (1943), and *Western Motel* (1957)—all of which feature a woman similar in appearance to Jo—reveal a sexual tension, perhaps unfulfilled desire, in Hopper's work. Renner further suggests that *New York Office* (1962), in which a woman is framed in light through a large office window, shows Hopper finally realizing sexual fantasies by dominating the female figure through the act of painting.

The initial attraction of Hopper's paintings for many might well be a surface appeal to an idealized American past. The paintings, however, retain their allure because they stretch the imagination beyond their initial appeal into often forgotten realms of American life.

—Ian Gordon

FURTHER READING:

Goodrich, Lloyd. *Edward Hopper.* New York, H. N. Abrams, 1971.

Hastert, Wolfgang. *Edward Hopper: The Silent Witness* (film). West Long Branch, New Jersey, Kultur International Films, 1994.

Levin, Gail. *Edward Hopper: An Intimate Biography.* New York, Knopf, 1995.

Renner, Rolf Günter. *Edward Hopper, 1882-1967: Transformation of the Real.* Cologne, Taschen, 1993.

Hopscotch

Children in Europe and in North, Central, and South America, as well as in Russia, China, and India, play the same hopping game, with only minor variations, and variously called hopscotch, potsy, paradise, heaven and hell, airplane, and hop-round. The game is played on a pattern chalked on a sidewalk or traced in dirt. The pattern consists of several single and occasional side-by-side squares or circles, which are often sequentially numbered. Play begins when a player tosses an object (usually a rock) into the pattern, then hops into the pattern, careful to skip the square containing the rock and to land without touching the lines in all the empty squares. Scholars believe the game may be as much as a thousand years old, suggesting that the pattern derives from the figure of the labyrinth, a motif found as far back as the iron age, and through which youth were required to walk during an initiation ceremony.

—Dorothy Jane Mills

FURTHER READING:

Bancroft, Jesse H. *Games.* New York, Macmillan, 1937.

Lankford, Mary D. *Hopscotch around the World.* New York, Morrow, 1992.

Sutton-Smith, Brian. *The Folkgames of Children.* Austin, University of Texas, 1972.

Horne, Lena (1917—)

The career of singer and entertainer Lena Horne has both evolved with and mirrored the times. From the Jim Crow years in the South, to the 1950s McCarthy blacklists, to the Mississippi marches for Civil Rights, Lena was there as a performer and a sympathizer, despite the fact that her career often suffered according to the extent of her involvement. From her beginnings—at the age of 16—as a chorus girl at Harlem's whites-only Cotton Club in the 1930s, Horne developed a reputation as a moderately talented singer with a tendency to coast on beauty and charm. But Horne was troubled by the fact that her celebrity image did not seem to match her personal beliefs. It seemed that every decision she faced about roles to take or songs to sing resonated with symbolic reference to race. Too refined (and "too white") to be taken seriously as a blues singer, she honed her image as a cabaret artist, only to be criticized for a perceived lack of warmth in her vocal delivery that was itself partly based on the "down and dirty" stereotype she could not fulfill. Her marriage to a white man, music arranger Lennie Hayton, also contributed to her reputation, as her African American fans were offended by her perceived betrayal of faith. Horne's autobiography, *Lena*, written in 1965, captures all these experiences in memorable detail, reading like a textbook on the combined effects of race and class in American cultural life during the twentieth century.

As a movie actress under contract to Metro-Goldwyn-Mayer in the 1940s and 1950s, Horne's light skin held her back from playing

Lena Horne

African America roles, for which she wasn't "black" enough, and from white roles, for which she was too "colored." When she tried using dark make-up on her fair skin, she felt it looked like the blackface used in a minstrel show. Max Factor was called in to create a special foundation color for Horne called "light Egyptian," later used for white actresses playing mulattos. One option Horne did not especially like was to play Latin parts, though she did so in the otherwise forgettable film *Panama Hattie* (1942). In fulfillment of her contract with MGM, she was frequently asked to perform "guest numbers" as a chanteuse, elegantly gowned and leaning against a pillar. These sequences would then be edited out of the films for showings to white audiences in the South. Horne found greater satisfaction in all-black films like the fanciful religious fable *Cabin in the Sky* (1943) and *Stormy Weather* (1946), for which she was leant to Twentieth Century Fox. Based on the life of dancer Bill "Bojangles" Robinson, the title song to *Stormy Weather* became Horne's theme song in the years to come.

Over the next thirty years, Horne stayed busy performing in posh clubs in New York, Hollywood, and Las Vegas; making television appearances on the popular shows of the day, including those of Ed Sullivan and Perry Como; and taking part in numerous political

benefits. One goal she seemed unable to fulfill was finding the right part in a Broadway show. Although she enjoyed singing the songs of Harold Arlen and Yip Harburg in the musical *Jamaica,* which opened in 1957, she hated her part; that of a silly island woman in love with American consumer goods. It took another two decades and several personal tragedies (Horne lost her father, her son, and her husband to fatal illnesses within a few short months in 1967-68) for Horne to find the right role.

In 1981, at age 64, when other performers might have been ready to retire, she opened in *Lena Horne: The Lady and Her Music,* which was to become the longest-running one-woman show in Broadway history. She held the audience's rapt attention from the opening phrase of her first song—Cole Porter's aptly titled "From This Moment On." The public was re-introduced to a woman they never really knew, who evinced a bold sense of humor and the ability to laugh at herself. After her Broadway success, Horne's recording career also blossomed, with releases like *We'll Be Together Again* (1994) and *Being Myself* (1998), which she produced at the age of 81. Horne's renditions of old standards like "My Buddy" and "Willow Weep for Me" mix poignancy with wit, echoing the experiences of a full and courageous life.

—Sue Russell

FURTHER READING:

Haskins, James, with Kathleen Benson. *Lena: A Personal and Professional Biography of Lena Horne.* New York, Stein and Day, 1984.

Horne, Lena, and Richard Schickel. *Lena.* London, Andre Deutsch, 1965.

Horror Movies

No popular genre has proven more reflective of America's unpredictable cultural mood swings than the horror movie. At the same time, no popular genre has proven more conducive to the expression of idiosyncratic nightmare visions than the horror movie. If these claims seem contradictory, even vaguely paradoxical, that is hardly surprising. For the horror genre consists of a group of texts as diverse as they are numerous, as controversial as they are popular, as conservative (or progressive) in their overt messages as they are progressive (or conservative) in their subtler implications. But although the horror genre may be lacking in firm boundaries or essential features, its rich and storied history, which spans the entire twentieth century, exhibits a remarkable degree of coherence. There are at least three reasons why this is so. For one thing, what appear at first to be utterly dissimilar entries often turn out upon closer inspection to conform in crucial ways, whether formally, stylistically, or thematically. For another thing, as is typically the case with pop cultural phenomena, market forces have dictated that the most commercially successful entries would each spawn a host of unimaginative imitators. This in turn has led to a fairly reliable boom-and-bust periodization of the genre. But most importantly, what all horror movies have in common is the intention to transform, through metaphor, symbol, and code, real-life fears—whether historically specific or psychologically universal—into terrifying narratives, uncanny images, and, above all, cinematic representations of monstrosity. Not all horror movies succeed in realizing this intention (many of them fail), but it is the fact that they try that makes them horror movies.

The horror film genre has its roots in the English gothic novels of the eighteenth and nineteenth centuries. After the Selig Polyscope Company produced a brief adaptation of *Dr. Jekyll and Mr. Hyde* in 1908, the stage was set for Robert Weine's masterpiece of German Expressionist cinema, *The Cabinet of Dr. Caligari* (1919). *Nosferatu* (1922), F. W. Murnau's silent magnum opus starring an emaciated Max Schreck as the decidedly unglamorous, unromantic undead Count, soon followed. Universal Pictures, heavily influenced by the dark, shadowy German style, imported a number of that country's most gifted film technicians in an effort to stave off bankruptcy. It worked—in just a few years, Universal became king of the sound horror movie. Classic versions of *Phantom of the Opera* (1925), *Dracula* (1931), and *Frankenstein* (1931) made household names out of their larger-than-life monster-stars, Lon Chaney, Bela Lugosi, and Boris Karloff. These pictures were exceedingly popular not least because audiences of the time were desperate for entertaining diversions as the Great Depression loomed. Although sober admonitions were issued against such human foibles as avarice, impetuosity, and, especially, scientific hubris, the source of threat in these films was nearly always supernatural. And, to reassure viewers that things would turn out all right, the monster was always soundly defeated in the end.

Universal's reign ended towards the beginning of the Second World War, and the studio eventually stooped to the level of self-parody with such entries as *Frankenstein Meets the Wolf Man* (1946) and *Abbott and Costello Meet Frankenstein* (1948). During this period, RKO producer Val Lewton wisely encouraged his directors to avoid the straightforward depiction of violence, and attempt instead to make viewers conjure up images of horror by means of suggestion and innuendo. Jacques Tourneur's *Cat People* (1942) is without a doubt the most highly acclaimed Lewton production, but the influence of Lewton's cinematic approach and techniques extended all the way into the 1960s, as evidenced by Robert Wise's masterful *The Haunting* (1963).

America's Cold War anxieties, coupled with advancements in special effects technology, gave rise to a cycle of highly successful science-fiction horror movies in the middle of the century. Some of these films, most notably *The Thing from Another World* (1951) and *The Invasion of the Body Snatchers* (1956), focus on man's brave (i.e. ''patriotic'') battle against a hostile alien threat. Others, such as *Them!* (1954), reflect American fears of atomic explosion and radioactive fallout. But it was a return to traditional horror film iconography that proved most responsible for the genre's huge popularity boom in the late 1950s. A small British studio, Hammer Films, took advantage of the industry's greater permissiveness with respect to the depiction of violence and sexual activities; starting with *The Curse of Frankenstein* in 1957, Hammer released a string of highly colorful, gruesomely detailed versions of the Universal classics. American International Pictures quickly followed suit, churning out its own series of campy horror-comedies, starting with *I Was A Teen-age Werewolf* (1957). AIP also acted as distributor for Mario Bava's atmospheric Italian masterpiece, *Black Sunday* (1960), as well as for Roger Corman's cycle of Edgar Allen Poe adaptations, most of which starred Vincent Price as a mentally unstable aristocrat. In these color gothics, lavish set designs and extravagant costumes served to reflect the decadence of Poe's characters. Price also starred in William Castle's best-known gimmick horror film, *The Tingler* (1959), which made use of ''Percepto'' technology—really just theater seats equipped with electric buzzers—to shock audience members during key scenes.

In 1960, two films—Alfred Hitchcock's *Psycho* and Michael Powell's *Peeping Tom*—effectively initiated a whole new era in the history of horror cinema by making their monsters not just human, but psychologically realistic. The killers in these movies—both male, both normal enough on the surface—are driven by instinctual drives and irresistible compulsions to commit murder against sexually transgressive women. Making disturbing connections between male-upon-female voyeurism and the objectification of women, between gender confusion and murder as substitute for sex, these two films suggest in the most vehement of terms that monstrosity is as likely to be located within (at least if you are a male) as without.

The majority of horror movies to come out in the 1960s and 1970s—though by no means all of them—followed the lead of *Psycho* and *Peeping Tom,* and audiences were treated to a not-always-so-impressive array of deranged psychotics, demented schizophrenics, homicidal maniacs, and general, all-purpose, knife/machete/chainsaw-wielding madmen. And the occasional madwoman. *What Ever Happened to Baby Jane?* (1962) was the first in a series of ''menopausal murder stories'' starring aging actresses whose characters are driven to perform grotesque acts of violence in the best Grand Guignol spirit. In *Halloween* (1978), John Carpenter's phenomenally successful slasher (or, more precisely, stalker) movie exemplar, the *Psycho/ Peeping Tom* elements, though still operative, are finally overshadowed by an intense, life-or-death game of terror waged between the (now masked, now superhuman) psycho killer and the film's only surviving female. Partly to create space for sequels, partly to exploit the insecurity and paranoia of modern viewers, open-ended narratives soon became the order of the day. Following directly on the heels of *Halloween* came the outer-space slasher *Alien* (1980), the campier, bloodier, and just as popular *Friday the 13th* (1980), and a host of progressively less original and less successful slasher variants.

Although Hitchcock, ''master of suspense'' that he was, typically eschewed focus on bloody spectacle in favor of tension building sequences and the occasional shock effect, another director of horror movies working in the 1960s, Herschell Gordon Lewis, took precisely the opposite approach. His low-budget, independently-produced ''splatter films''—given such transparent names as *Blood Feast* (1963) and *Color Me Blood Red* (1965)—promised to make up for their lack of narrative suspense with an abundance of gory close-ups. Although Lewis' films appealed only to a small number of hard-core horror fans, they achieved a kind of cult status, and, whether directly or indirectly, have exerted a powerful influence on the genre. Tobe Hooper's much-discussed *Texas Chainsaw Massacre* (1974), in which a male family of unemployed slaughter house workers set their sights on a group of vapid teenagers, can be seen as (among other things) a slasher/splatter hybrid; the film's tagline, for example, reads ''Who will survive, and what will be left of them?'' Canadian writer-director David Cronenberg, whose disturbing and highly-original works include *Scanners* (1980), *Videodrome* (1983), *The Fly* (1986), and *Dead Ringers* (1988), has been highly praised *and* harshly criticized for raising ''body horror'' to an art form. Few if any would say this about Sam Raimi, whose ''splatstick'' cult faves *The Evil Dead* (1982) and *Evil Dead II* (1987) somehow manage to find the humor in gore. And in Italy, legendary horror film directors Mario Bava, Dario Argento, and Lucio Fulci made successful contributions of their own to the splatter subgenre with such entries as *Bay of Blood* (1971), *Deep Red* (1975), and *Zombie* (1979), respectively.

Because of their emphasis on male-against-female violence and the heinous nature of the crimes they depict, the slasher and splatter

Max Von Sydow in a scene from the horror film *The Exorcist*.

subgenres (to the extent that these are distinguishable) have repeatedly been accused of exploitation, misogyny, even sadism. Wes Craven's *Last House on the Left* (1972), Meir Zarche's *I Spit On Your Grave* (1978), and Abel Ferrara's *Driller Killer* (1979) were all banned in England under the controversial ''video nasties'' bill that passed through Parliament in 1984. Brian De Palma's *Dressed To Kill* (1980) raised the ire of feminists by featuring a male transvestite who murders (punishes?) women for their promiscuity and/or sex appeal. And John McNaughton's *Henry: Portrait of a Serial Killer* (1990), denied an R rating by the MPAA in spite of favorable reviews by such prominent critics as Roger Ebert, was finally released (unrated) four years after sitting on a distributor's shelf. That there are misogynist messages in many of these films is undeniable; recently, however, attention has been drawn to the fact that, in a number of slashers/ splatters, female ingenuity and the employment of self-defense are actually championed. Nowhere is this more apparent than in the rape-revenge cycle of horror movies that appeared in the late 1970s-early 1980s.

Backing up a bit, for those who choose to downplay the revolutionary significance of *Psycho* and *Peeping Tom,* 1968 inevitably marks the birth of the modern horror movie. *Rosemary's Baby,*

Roman Polanski's paranoid urban gothic, stars Mia Farrow as an ingenuous young newlywed who moves into a Manhattan apartment building only to discover that her kind old neighbors are really devil-worshipping witches. Conspiring with Rosemary's husband and obstetrician (among others), they have effected a diabolical plan to make Rosemary the mother of Satan's child. Based on the best-selling novel by Ira Levin, *Rosemary's Baby* effectively taps into fears and anxieties surrounding pregnancy and childbirth. Because the film is shot almost entirely from Rosemary's point of view, it succeeds in conveying her growing sense of alienation and despair as she struggles to find someone she can trust in a huge, unfriendly city.

Also appearing in 1968 was George Romero's *Night of the Living Dead,* widely considered to be among the most distressing horror movies of all time. Made for only $114,000 (in stark contrast to the big-budgeted *Rosemary's Baby*), and unrated at the time of its release, this no-frills black-and-white film centers on a small group of isolated individuals who try, with little success, to stave off the murderous advances of an ever increasing army of flesh-eating zombies. Although notable for its excessive gore and apocalyptic overtones, *Night of the Living Dead* is effective primarily because it conveys so well the claustrophobia and hysteria of the trapped party, and because it vividly portrays the horror of seeing members of one's own family turned into monsters before one's very eyes. Not without socio-political implications, Romero's film also serves to register the dissatisfaction of America's "silent majority," and illustrates the breakdown of patriarchal order under highly-stressful conditions.

Rosemary's Baby and *Night of the Living Dead* were followed by a slew of movies which locate the source of horror within the nuclear family. If *Psycho* and *Peeping Tom* made the monstrous human, these films brought the monstrous home, making it not so much human as familiar. More than ever before, generic horror conventions were now being put to use, especially by auteur directors, in the service of social statement. One finds in this period movies such as *Deathdream* (1972), Bob Clark's tale of a young solider, killed in combat at Vietnam, who is temporarily brought back to life—unfortunately as a vampiric zombie—by his mother's passionate prayers. Larry Cohen's *It's Alive!* (1974) re-presents the Frankenstein legend in distinctly modern terms, giving the role of ambivalent creator to the father of a grotesquely deformed baby-on-a-rampage. Not all of these films were low budget, independently-produced affairs. In his eagerly anticipated 1980 adaptation of Stephen King's *The Shining,* for example, Stanley Kubrick uses haunted house conventions primarily as a means of exploring the real-life horrors of alcoholism, child abuse, and domestic violence. Even the plethora of "revenge of nature" films that came out in the late 1970s after the massive success of Steven Spielberg's PG-rated *Jaws* (1975), were most of them family horror movies at heart. Participating in a tradition that goes at least as far back as Hitchcock's *The Birds* (1963), and, arguably, all the way back to James Whale's *Frankenstein* (1931), these pictures—*Squirm* (1976), *Piranha* (1978), and *Alligator* (1982), to name a few— externalize the manifest source of horror, all the while insinuating that what should be most feared is something lying within the individual, the family, or the community at large.

By far the most acclaimed and talked about family horror movie of the 1970s and 1980s was William Friedkin's *The Exorcist* (1973). Winner of two Academy Awards and nominated for eight others, this film was the subject of intense media scrutiny from the time of its initial release. Loosely based on a reported real life exorcism, the film chronicles the efforts of a disenchanted priest to save the life of a young girl who has been possessed by demonic forces. The display of Christian iconography in the presence of foul sexual language, nauseating special effects, and graphic exhibitions of self-mutilation outraged many religious groups. But stripped of its demonic-possession theme, *The Exorcist* provides a moving commentary on, among other things, the uselessness of modern medicine when confronted with unknown illnesses, the crises of guilt and responsibility faced by single mothers, and, in general, the difficulty parents have comprehending and responding to their often aggressive, hormonal children. Although inspired by *The Exorcist,* and highly successful in its own right, Richard Donner's own "satanic child" film, *The Omen* (1976) lacked its predecessor's underlying concern with domestic issues. Instead, it terrified viewers with threats of the apocalypse, and, what ultimately amounts to the same thing, the infiltration of evil agents into the political sphere.

Although the proportion of horror movies within the overall film population continued to increase well into the 1980s, by the end of the decade it was obvious that a staleness had set in. *Halloween* was up to its fourth sequel in 1989, *Friday the 13th* its seventh, and the overuse of narrative and technical conventions was (not surprisingly) accompanied by a decline in viewer interest. But with Jonathan Demme's Academy Award-winning *The Silence of the Lambs* (1991) selling the

mystique of the serial killer to mainstream audiences, the horror-thriller-suspense hybrid received a massive boost in popularity. In the mid-1990s, glossy, big-budgeted, star-powered films such as *Copycat* (1995), *Se7en* (1995), and *Kiss the Girls* (1997) focused on the gruesome handiwork of charismatic, creative serial killers and reflected public fascination with those who commit mass murder on principle (or so they would have us believe), not merely because of some underlying psychosexual disorder.

Other, more conventional horror movies of this period sought to supernaturalize the serial killer. Inspired by Wes Craven's modern classic *A Nightmare on Elm Street* (1984), in which a once-human child murderer takes revenge on those who lynched him by invading the dreams of their offspring, films such as *Child's Play* (1988), *The Exorcist III* (1990), *The Frighteners* (1996), and *Fallen* (1997) either give supernatural powers to a serial killer or else give serial killer characteristics to a supernatural being. Another Wes Craven movie, *Scream,* was a sleeper hit in 1996, and became the first in a slew of neo-stalkers. These highly self-reflexive works, which include *Scream 2* (1997), *Halloween H20* (1998), and *Urban Legend* (1998), contrive to satirize stalker film conventions while still providing genuine scares; they succeed in this task only insofar as they are able to avoid too heavy a reliance on the very conventions they are mocking. Despite the fact that almost all of the neo-stalkers to come out in the late 1990s have done quite well at the box office, many critics view the ever-increasing emphasis on parody, intertextuality, and pastiche as signs that the genre has exhausted itself, and that a dark age in horror cinema is imminent.

In spite of such gloomy predictions, judging from the horror movie revivals of the late 1950s, early 1970s, and mid-1990s, it seems safe to declare that no matter how grim things may look at times, the genre's eventual return from the deadness resulting from excess, imitation, and oversaturation is inevitable. At least as inevitable as the next wave of young people desperate to consume accessible texts in which their ambivalent attitudes towards society, family, and self receive imaginative—and so relatively safe—communal expression. Unless, of course, America's self-proclaimed moral guardians finally succeed in having laws enacted which would place strict limitations on the freedom of horror movie writers and directors to (re-)present our collective nightmares in the bloodiest of hues. Even then there would be no real cause for alarm; for the most committed of the lot would in that case surely go back to the Lewton-Tourneur-Wise school of "fear by suggestion," and rediscover ways of horrifying viewers that do not depend on the so-called "spectacle of death."

—Steven Schneider

Further Reading:

Grant, Barry K., editor. *Planks of Reason: Essays on the Horror Film.* Metuchen, New Jersey, Scarecrow Press, 1984.

Jancovich, Mark. *Horror.* London, B. T. Batsford, 1992.

Kellner, Douglas, and Michael Ryan. "Horror Films." *Camera Politica: The Politics and Ideology of Contemporary Hollywood Film.* Bloomington, Indiana University Press, 1988, 168-193.

Prawer, S. S. *Caligari's Children: The Film as Tale of Terror.* New York, Oxford University Press, 1980.

Schneider, Steven. "Monsters as (Uncanny) Metaphors: Freud, Lakoff, and the Representation of Monstrosity in Cinematic Horror." *Other Voices: A Journal of Critical Thought.* Vol. 1, No. 3,

1999, http://dept.english.upenn.edu/~ov/1.3/sschneider/monsters.html. March 1999.

Skal, David J. *The Monster Show: A Cultural History of Horror.* New York, Norton, 1993.

Tudor, Andrew. *Monsters and Mad Scientists: A Cultural History of the Horror Movie.* Oxford, Basil Blackwell, 1989.

Waller, Gregory, editor. *American Horrors: Essays on the Modern American Horror Film.* Urbana, University of Illinois Press, 1987.

Williams, Tony. *Hearths of Darkness: The Family in the American Horror Film.* Madison, Farleigh Dickinson University Press, 1996.

Wood, Robin. *Hollywood from Vietnam to Reagan.* New York, Columbia University Press, 1986.

Hot Dogs

Long a staple of sports arenas and backyard cookouts, the unpretentious hot dog is one of America's favorite sandwiches. More than 20 billion of them are consumed in the United States each year.

Allegedly married to the ubiquitous bun when Harry Stevens, who sold ice cream at New York Polo Grounds, instructed his crew to sell frankfurters on rolls, the hot dog did not become famous until it came to Coney Island, New York. Though the hot dog had been served at Feltman's 7,000 seat restaurant for years, Nathan Handwerker, once an employee at Feltman's, sparked interest in the hot dog when he sold his dogs for a nickel (half the price of Feltman's) at his hot dog stand just steps away from the subway stop on Coney Island. Interest in hot dogs was so great that Oscar Meyer began marketing hot dogs in supermarkets in the 1930s. Not only was Oscar Meyer the first to sell hot dogs through supermarkets, it was also the first to specifically target children as consumers of the food. From 1936 Oscar Meyer's

A fashion advertisement for hot pants.

Weinermobile began driving across the country promoting its hot dogs to children.

In its simplest iteration a hot dog consists of a frankfurter in an oblong-shaped bun with any of various toppings including mustard, ketchup, pickle relish, cheese, sauerkraut, and beans. Legend has it the hot sausage sandwiches were given their descriptive moniker by sports cartoonist T. A. "Tad" Dorgan, who caricatured the wieners as dachshund dogs at the turn of the century. The term "hot dog" first appeared in print in the *Oxford English Dictionary* in 1900. Traditional hot dogs are made of beef, pork, veal, chicken, or turkey, with or without skins. Regular hot dogs are about six inches long, although they are also available in two-inch "cocktail" and foot-long varieties.

—Robert E. Schnakenberg

FURTHER READING:

Herbst, Sharon Taylor. *The New Food Lover's Companion.* New York, Barron's Educational Series, 1995.

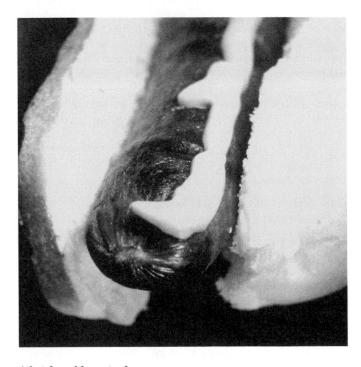

A hot dog with mustard.

Hot Pants

Hot pants were a short-lived fashion of the early 1970s that evoked the unconventional attitudes of the youth that had burgeoned in the 1960s. An adaptation of the 1960s mini skirt, hot pants offered the wearer a measure of modesty that the mini could not provide. For those who wished their panties to be revealed, the stylish solution lay in short, tight, sometimes cuffed, hot pants. Designed to be worn either as an item of clothing in its own right, or as the revealed undergarment of maxi-length outfits, hot pants looked smartest when worn with tights (fishnets, opaques) and platform boots. The open fronts and side slits of maxi outfits permitted legs and hot pants to be visible, effecting a mod look and attitude that signified the trendiness of the wearer in that period.

—Joan Nicks

Hot Rods

Americans love speed. It suffuses our culture, coloring every aspect of it from food to mail service. It should come as no surprise, therefore, that the automobile holds a hallowed space in the American myth. Nowhere is this more evident than in the culture of the hot rod, a rich substrata in popular culture dedicated to the car. The popularity of the hot rod ties in with this American preoccupation with youth, speed, and individualism, and the artists who pioneered the hot rod have after years of ignominious labor become recognized as master artists outside of this very specific milieu. Over 50 years after its invention, the hot rod is still omnipresent on the road and off, dedicated to the pursuit of speed and style, or rather, speed in style.

Hot-rod culture first emerged in the early 1940s—the war years—particularly in Los Angeles, where, as Tom Wolfe writes of the period, "Family life was dislocated, as the phrase goes, but the money was pouring in, and the kids began to work up their own style of life—as they've been doing ever since." In these early years, aesthetics and necessity joined to create a new form of car. Owing to war rationing, cars and car parts were scarce, and under-age car enthusiasts resorted to junkyard salvaging, creating hybridized cars with primitively hopped-up engines.

The aggressively declassé activities of these youngsters, who engaged in illegal drag race competitions and ostentatiously public congregations at drive-in restaurants, created an atmosphere of public alarm, not unlike that which accompanied the Hell's Angels two decades later. Part of the public opprobrium had to do with appearances. Hot-rodders cultivated a distinctly sinister look, chopping (lowering the top of the car) and channeling (lowering the body itself down between the wheels) their cars, which gave them a sinister appearance. The '32 Ford Roadster, one of the most popular objects of customizing of all time, in the hands of the hot-rodder was reduced to little more than a streamlined square, brightly painted and wedded to 30 inch tires and an enormous chrome engine. Nor did frequent contretemps between police and illicit road-racers improve the hot-rodders' reputation. A whole hot rod culture had emerged around the rituals of customizing, cruising, and drag racing. In Los Angeles, drag racing took place on a deserted stretch of road in Culver City nicknamed "Thunder Alley," and large-scale police raids were a not uncommon occurrence.

The public might have viewed hot-rodders with distaste, but a middling movie writer named Robert Petersen was fascinated by the religious fervor with which teenagers were pouring money into their cars. In the late 1940s Petersen started *Hot Rod Magazine,* which eventually ballooned into Petersen Publishing, a magazine empire devoted to automotive speed and beauty. By the early 1960s, there existed not only Petersen's conspicuous empire, but models, T-shirts, toy cars, stickers, music groups, and movies; in short, any product

Two men working on their hot rod, 1953.

tangentially associated with hot-rodding was produced and rapidly consumed. But even after the point where hot-rodding had been "rationalized," as Wolfe puts it, subjected to capitalism's "efficient exploitation," the hot rod's anti-social qualities remained central to their allure.

This brazen nose-thumbing quality was best expressed by Ed "Big Daddy" Roth, a customizer who specialized in a baroque, grotesque creations, exemplified in automobiles with names like the Beatnik Bandit and Mysterion, and T-shirts with brand names like Weirdo and Monster (harkening back to the pieced-together Frankenstein quality of early hot rods) that featured grotesque hot-rodding creatures (Wolfe calls them "*Mad* magazine Bosch") alongside slogans such as "Mother is wrong" or "Born to Lose. Writes Wolf:

> Roth pointed out that the kids have a revealing vocabulary. They use the words "rotten," "bad," and "tough" in a very fey, ironic way. Often a particularly baroque and sleek custom car will be called a "big, bad Merc" (for Mercury) or something like that. In this case "bad" means "good," but it also retains some of the original meaning of "bad." The kids know that to adults, like their own parents, this car is going to look sinister and somehow like an assault on their style of life.

The first act in the narrative of the avant-garde artist begins with the rebellious artist struggling, ignored and unrecognized, with his work. Then comes recognition, then absorption into the mainstream, where the artists ideas are assimilated and become commonplace. So it was that the superstars of customizing—Roth, Daryl Starbird, George Barris—started their careers as pariahs and ended with Detroit car makers wooing them as highly valued consultants. In fact, Detroit had been assiduously following their careers for some time. Barris, who claimed to have had more than twenty designs lifted from him by Detroit, recounted for Tom Wolfe that Detroit stylists knew all about cars he had customized as far back as 1945, way back in the early days of customizing. Stylistic innovations such as tailfins, bubbletops, frenched headlights, and concealed headlights all derived from the customizers. The early era of muscle cars—Rivieras, Sting Rays, Barracudas, and Chargers—all drew freely upon hot rod aesthetics.

By the late 1990s hot-rods were a recognized art form, with Roth and his peers exhibiting their work in museums and galleries. A entire magazine empire is engineered around hot rods, and ever since the Robert Petersen put on the first hot rod car show back in 1948, such shows have been a perennially popular attraction. Hot rod clubs continue to flourish, nourished by each new generation of teenage boys who become obsessed with customizing. And so the tradition continues in unbroken lineage from the original World War II era kids to today's customizers of Japanese imports, affectionately known as ''rice-rockets.'' It is a tradition, and as such, it is more about craft than rebellion, but the outlaw implications of hot-rodding still hold true. A custom car is by its very nature a menace, and in this menace lies the allure.

—Michael Baers

FURTHER READING:

Blair, John. *The Illustrated Discography of Hot Rod Music.* Ann Arbor, Popular Culture, 1990.

Felsen, Henry Gregor. *Street Rod.* New York, Random House, 1953.

Genat, Robert, and Robin Benat. *Hot Rod Nights: Boulevard Cruisin' in the USA.* Osceola, Motorbooks International, 1998.

Gifford, Barry. *H-o-t R-o-d.* San Francisco, Chronicle Books, 1997.

Roth, Ed, and Howie ''Pyro'' Kusten. *Confessions of a Rat Fink: The Life and Times of Ed ''Big Daddy'' Roth.* New York, Pharos Books, 1992.

Roth, Ed, and Tony Thacker. *Hot Rods.* Osceola, Motorbooks International, 1995.

Smith, Tex. *Hot Rod History: Tracing America's Most Popular Automotive Hobby.* North Branch, Car Tech, Inc., 1994.

Wolfe, Tom. *The Kandy-Kolored Tangerine Flake Streamline Baby.* New York, Farrar, Strauss and Giroux, 1963

———. *The Pump House Gang.* New York, Farrar, Strauss and Giroux, 1968.

Houdini, Harry (1874-1926)

Before there was a Doug Henning, a David Copperfield, or a Siegfried and Roy, Harry Houdini was the celebrity magician without peer. A worldwide celebrity thanks to his relentless touring, he was the first entertainer to take full advantage of the emergent mass media, engaging in death-defying public stunts that cannily made use of newspapers, radio, and film. Had Houdini simply been another skilled magician, he might have been forgotten along with the generation of

Harry Houdini

vaudevillians from which he sprang, but the magnitude of his exploits, combined with his tormented personality and unexpected demise, have left an allure that has hardly dimmed over the passing decades. Houdini was a figure out of Greek tragedy: the indestructible warrior with an Achilles Heel, and his legend, like all archetypal figures, has only increased with time.

Born Erich Weiss in Budapest, Hungary, Houdini was the son of a rabbinical scholar of somewhat dubious credentials who moved his family to America in 1878 after securing a position as rabbi for a small synagogue in Appleton, Wisconsin. Ultimately, Mayer Weiss was not to the liking of his small-town flock. Perhaps it was his advanced age, or his European conceits or his habit of conducting services in German, but for whatever reason the congregation cut him loose, and the Weiss family, now numbering seven, moved to Milwaukee, barely scraping by on Mayer's earnings as a freelance minister. Young Erich felt the family's poverty keenly, and was hurt by his father's humiliation; in his later years he would take pains to ennoble the hapless rabbi. When the family had finally settled in Manhattan, Erich found work as a tie-cutter at the age of eleven. His ailing father—who soon was laboring alongside Erich in the tie factory—and the rest of the family joined him in short order. It was with a measure of relief that Erich and his family witnessed the passing of the ill and unhappy head of the household in 1892.

Houdini possessed a meager education, but he retained as part of his father's legacy a deep respect for learning, and it was a book that changed his life. While reading *The Conjurers Unveiled*, French magician Robert-Houdin's autobiography, 17-year-old Erich discovered not only a fascination with all things illusory, but a template on which to build his own fictionalized autobiography. Robert-Houdin appears to have replaced the unsuccessful Rabbi Weiss as the young man's father figure, and Erich excised vast chunks of his tome to fill in the holes of his own shabby biography, even borrowing the dead magician's moniker to replace his own name.

With his father dead, Erich was no longer constrained in his career choices by filial piety, and embarked on his career as a professional magician as one half of the Houdini Brothers. Harry (possibly a version of his nickname, Eiri) with his young wife, Bess Rahner, acting as assistant, plied the length and breadth of the country playing dime museums, burlesque shows, traveling carnivals, and medicine shows. One trick in particular, a bait and switch act, was a favorite with audiences, and the astute Houdini was soon specializing in escape tricks of a myriad variety, which had the added advantage of familiarity in their resemblance to the stunts of many spiritualist mediums. The escape tricks were especially well suited to Houdini, a small, compact man with a lifetime enthusiasm for sports, for they demanded strenuous exertion, muscular control, and prodigious endurance. For seven years he labored in obscurity and was in the midst of rethinking his career options when he was offered a position on a vaudeville circuit by theater impresario Martin Beck.

At the turn of the century, vaudeville was the height of mass-entertainment, and theater chains, in stiff competition for audiences, were building palatial theaters to house their acts. For an entertainer such as Houdini, accustomed to making $25 a week, vaudeville was a quantum leap in remuneration and prestige. Under the management of Beck, Houdini was soon gaining nationwide notoriety and commanding a substantial salary. To promote his act, he had begun making a practice of escaping from jails and police stations, miraculously freeing himself from manacles and cells alike. Houdini was always anxious to keep one step ahead of the competition: as a refinement, he began to perform his escapes in the nude or dressed only in a loincloth, flabbergasting the police and inflaming the public's curiosity with each successive news story.

When he sailed for England in the summer of 1900, Houdini had established himself as the "Handcuff King," adept at unshackling himself under a variety of conditions. He was not long in creating a sensation in Great Britain and on the Continent. Europe embraced his act with such enthusiasm that he stayed a full five years. He continued his habit of escaping from jail cells and offering a prize to anyone who could produce a lock he could not pick. This practice almost led to public humiliation in Birmingham, when a local judo expert and teacher of physiognomy devised a system of shackles that left the magician nearly immobilized. For a torturous hour and a half he struggled with his bonds, finally freeing himself, but not without casting a pall of suspicion over the escape with the suspicious filing marks he produced in his efforts.

Returning to the United States in 1905, Houdini was alarmed by the legion of shameless imitators that had sprung up in his absence. He forsook handcuffs, leaving them to the copycats, and concentrated on new escapes, ideas for which flowed out of him in a constant stream. He had always known the importance of remaining in the public eye, and he began to perform high-visibility stunts, escaping from straitjackets, bags, crates—whatever could be thrown off a bridge. He toured for the next ten years, constantly refining his act, innovating, and pushing his body to the limits of endurance. This period saw the introduction of the milk-can escape, the Chinese Water Torture (perhaps the best remembered of his escapes and the most frequently performed today), the Vanishing Elephant and, for outdoor performances, an aerial straitjacket act. In this last, with his ankles secured by heavy rope, he was hauled to the top of a skyscraper and, suspended above the crowd, was left to wriggle free. In terms of cinematic potential the aerial straitjacket escape improved on his previous publicity stunts a hundred-fold.

With the advent of film, Houdini realized that vaudeville's days were numbered. By 1918, he was hard at work on his first film. Until his death in 1926, he would for the most part forsake live performances for film acting, and moved to Los Angeles, where he starred in his first short, *The Grim Game*. Not content simply to star in movies, he started his own production company, which lost money at an alarming rate. But while Houdini the movie star carried on with his work in a desultory fashion, Houdini the whistle-blower was waging a fierce battle against the forces of hokum. Besides being a possessor of tremendous energy, he had a streak of the pedant in him. He had met the author Arthur Conan Doyle, the creator of Sherlock Holmes and a believer in spiritualism. Houdini, who had made his living artfully faking his way out of impossible situations, was skeptical of such beliefs. He had made a parlor game out of unmasking mediums and now directed his towering scorn at one Mina Crandon—better known as Margery—a society woman who, with the aid of her deceased brother, Walter, had impressed *Scientific American* as a legitimate medium. Houdini would have none of it, and in a series of seances where he deduced one trick after another, finally reduced Margery to fuming impotence and irrevocably splintered the *Scientific American* panel.

In December of 1925 Houdini launched his two-and-a-half-hour extravaganza, *Magic*, on Broadway. It was his first big tour in a number of years, and started with a first act consisting of nothing but magic tricks—he even went so far as to pull a rabbit out of a hat to prove he was a magician—followed by an expose of spiritualism, and then an escape act. For the status conscious Houdini, *Magic* was a step up. This was a theater, not a vaudeville house, and when the show opened, it placed Houdini in direct competition with the lions of Broadway. The show ran through the spring, with time out for Houdini to take his anti-spiritualist campaign to Washington where he testified for Congress. During this break, he had a chance to unmask another fraud, a fakir named Rahman Bey, who allowed himself to be submerged in a coffin for an hour, claiming he had put himself in a trance. Houdini would have none of it. He trained himself to ration oxygen, and in a glass-fronted coffin he remained underwater for an hour and a half. It was to be his last unmasking.

When the tour resumed in the fall, Houdini seemed rundown. If the testimony of his friends can be believed, he had also become convinced of his imminent death, and tearfully bade goodbye to several of his acquaintances. In Albany, he broke his ankle while being hoisted into the Chinese Water Torture apparatus and continued the tour on crutches. When he arrived in Detroit, he had a temperature of 102. Persevering through the night's performance despite his condition, he collapsed backstage immediately after, and was soon hospitalized with a ruptured appendix. After surgery, peritonitis set in and the master escapologist died six days later, on October 31, 1926. Houdini lore contends that the ruptured appendix resulted from a hit in the stomach. Houdini took great pride in his physical condition and often asked men to punch him to prove the strength of his abdomen muscles. In Detroit a man asked him if his muscles were indeed that strong and Houdini said they were. The man punched him, but Houdini was not expecting it and therefore was not prepared. It is inclear if this incident did in reality take place, but it does add to the eeriness surrounding his death.

Harry Houdini was a transitional figure in the cultural pantheon, marking the end of the Victorian era and the beginning of the modern one. A complex man, he was a textbook case of repressed neurosis in which Freud would have delighted. For a man whose very livelihood depended on nerves of steel, he was notoriously emotional. Vain and egotistical, he left a trail of broken friendships and hurt feelings in his wake. An immigrant of humble origins, he was obsessed by status, once buying a dress commissioned by the recently deceased Queen Victoria in order that his mother might wear it while entertaining her old-world relatives. Yet, despite his mother-love, his status-consciousness, his Victorianisms, Houdini was quick to embrace the expanding technical universe. A lover of gadgetry, Houdini filled his house with a surfeit of modern appliances. A masterful manipulator of the mass media, he did not allow the thrust of progress to leave him stranded as it had so many of his confederates in vaudeville. In the archetypal pattern of a tragic hero, Harry Houdini had been struck down by his own blind ambition, but it is for his extraordinary feats of endurance that his legend lives on.

—Michael Baers

FURTHER READING:

Kellock, Jarold. *Houdini: The Life Story.* New York, Blue Ribbon Books, 1928.

Meyer, Bernard. *Houdini: A Mind in Chains.* New York, E. P. Dutton & Company, 1976.

Milbourne, Christopher. *Houdini, The Untold Story.* New York, The Thomas Y. Crowell Co., 1969.

Silverman, Kenneth. *Houdini!!! The Career of Erich Weiss.* HarperCollins, 1996.

Houston, Whitney (1963—)

Singer Whitney Houston, an African American beauty with a clear soprano voice, became a megastar in the 1980s. She was born (in East Orange, New Jersey) the daughter of gospel singer Cissy Houston and a cousin to singing star Dionne Warwick, and began singing herself at age 11 with the New Hope Baptist Choir. In her teens she sang backup for Chaka Khan and Lou Rawls, but at 18 became a successful model and appeared in television comedies, while pursuing her singing career. This took off when she was signed exclusively by Clive Davis of Arista Records. Under his careful management, she launched her first album, *Whitney Houston,* in 1984. It sold 14 million copies, setting a debut album record. She became a household name and, by the late 1990s, she was the recipient of five Grammy Awards, 21 American Music Awards, and numerous Gold and Platinum discs. In 1982, Houston married singer Bobby Brown, and embarked on a screen career, starring opposite

Kevin Costner in *The Bodyguard.* She acted on screen again in *Waiting to Exhale* (1985), directed by actor Forest Whitaker with an all-female African American cast, and in *The Preacher's Wife* (1996) with Denzel Washington. All three movies yielded massive hit songs, most notably ''I Will Always Love You.'' Houston's commanding, multi-octave range has allowed her to sing a wide range of material— gospel, R&B, pop, rock, and, most popularly, love ballads. By the late 1990s, despite commercial competition from performers such as Mariah Carey, Whitney Houston was still a favorite among female American vocalists, both at home and in Britain.

—Brian Granger

FURTHER READING:

Whitburn, Joel. *The Billboard Book of Top 40 Hits.* New York, Billboard Publication, Inc. 1996.

How the West Was Won

Featuring narration by Spencer Tracy, individual segments directed by Henry Hathaway, John Ford, and George Marshall, a gigantic all-star cast (including Henry Fonda, Karl Malden, Gregory Peck, George Peppard, Debbie Reynolds, Jimmy Stewart, Eli Wallach, John Wayne, Richard Widmark, and Walter Brennan), and an engaging story and thrilling action sequences, MGM's *How the West Was*

James Stewart in a scene from the film *How the West Was Won.*

Won (1962) is widely considered one of Hollywood's greatest epics. The film episodically tells the story of three generations of the Prescott family, who migrate Westward over a fifty year period during the 19th century. This was the first theatrical release featuring Cinerama, a filming technique which employs three cameras sharing a single shutter in order to replicate the scope of the human eye. The process is far less impressive on TV or video cassette. In theaters, however, the film, much of which was shot on location in various spots throughout the American West, is spectacular. Despite Cinerama's initial popularity, after *How the West Was Won* few films successfully utilized the process, which ultimately resulted in its demise. Nevertheless, *How the West Was Won* remains a classic example of big-budget Hollywood filmmaking at its best.

—Robert C. Sickels

FURTHER READING:

Darby, William. *John Ford's Westerns: A Thematic Analysis, with Filmography.* Jefferson, McFarland & Co. Inc., 1996.

Hall, Sheldon. "*How the West Was Won*: History, Spectacle, and the American Mountains." In *The Book of Westerns,* edited by Ian Cameron and Douglas Pye. New York, Continuum, 1996.

The Howdy Doody Show

Howdy Doody was the name of a 27-inch, big-eared, freckle-faced, wooden puppet. Howdy appeared in a starring capacity on an immensely popular children's television show of the same name that ran on NBC from 1947 to 1960. It was broadcast live from 30 Rockefeller Plaza in New York City.

The Howdy Doody Show was the creation of Robert E. Smith (1917-1998), a former radio personality, who appeared along with his wooden counterpart at first on a weekly basis and later five days a week from Monday through Friday, starting at 5:30 in the afternoon. Howdy, clad in a red bandanna, dungarees, and a checkered shirt, would exchange banter with Smith, whose on-screen persona was that of Buffalo Bob Smith, and interact with the colorful denizens of Doodyville, among whom were the following: Phineas T. Bluster, the crusty mayor of Doodyville; Flub-a-Dub, a zoological pastiche comprised of eight different animals allegedly caught by Buffalo Bob himself in a South American jungle; Princess Summerfall Winterspring, a puppet at first but later a real person played by Judy Tyler; Clarabell the Clown (first played by Bob Keeshan, also known as Captain Kangaroo), a virtual mute who engaged in Harpo Marx-like antics and frequently brandished a seltzer bottle with which he would squirt Bob; and miscellaneous others. Hallmarks of the show were the Peanut Gallery, a kiddy audience between the ages of three and eight; the call and response between Bob and the Peanut Gallery, which had the former shouting "Say, kids, what time is it?" to which the galvanized Gallery would respond, "It's Howdy Doody time"; and the Howdy Doody theme song, the music of which was borrowed from "Ta-ra-ra-boom-de-ay."

The Howdy Doody Show holds a number of records. It was, for example, the first daily show on NBC to feature live music and the first to be broadcast in color. When it placed Buffalo Bob in New York and Howdy in Chicago for a special broadcast to celebrate

Buffalo Bob Smith and Howdy Doody, 1952.

NBC's having become a transcontinental network, it became the first show to employ the split-screen technique. And as Smith himself put it, "We were the first show on every day in quite a few markets. . . . There was no daytime television, just a test pattern until 5:30. We were the first show to reach 1,000 shows, then 2,000."

The importance of *The Howdy Doody Show* is not confined to record-breaking firsts, however. Howdy, Buffalo Bob, and the rest of the cast made an indelible impression on their baby-boomer fans. In 1970 Smith received a call from a graduate student at the University of Pennsylvania who asked him to come to the campus to do a show. At first, he thought it was a hoax, but the student was serious. Smith agreed and a *Howdy Doody* revival was born. Columnist Bob Greene wrote in 1987 that the show "may have been the most important cultural landmark for my generation."

Howdy Doody resides at Robert Smith's former home in Flat Rock, North Carolina. A replica, known as Double Doody, now resides at the Smithsonian Institution.

—William F. O'Connor

FURTHER READING:

Davis, Stephen. *Say Kids, What Time Is It?: Notes from the Peanut Gallery.* Boston, Little, Brown, 1987.

"Howdy Doody Host Delighted a Generation." *The Ottawa Citizen.* July 31, 1998, B-5.

Smith, Buffalo Bob, and Donna McCrohan. *Howdy and Me: Buffalo Bob's Own Story.* New York, Plume, 1990.

Williams, Scott. "Happy Birthday, Howdy Doody." *Pittsburgh Post-Gazette.* December 27, 1997, C-7.

Howe, Gordie (1928—)

In the world of professional hockey, Gordie Howe gained legendary status as a record-setter and as an all-around athlete. Known for his longevity, Howe played into his fifties in a demanding sport in which professionals typically retire in their early thirties. His prowess, on and off the ice, led to his honorary title of "Mr. Hockey." Outside the world of professional hockey, Howe's name and awards served to generate interest in a professional sport that has received little recognition compared to football, basketball, and baseball.

In 1946, at the age of 18, Howe began his professional career as a right wing forward with the Detroit Red Wings of the National Hockey League (NHL). After 25 years with the Red Wings and five decades as a professional, he retired in 1980 at the age of 52. It was his second retirement.

Gordie Howe was born on March 31, 1928, in Floral, Saskatchewan, Canada, the fourth of nine children. He played amateur hockey and had one year in the minors before joining the NHL. Howe's first three years with Detroit were less than stellar, but by 1949 he was the highest scorer in the NHL playoffs. By the early 1950s, he had become the first player to win three consecutive scoring titles. His other records included becoming the League's top scorer

Gordie Howe

six times, and being named six times as the League's Most Valuable Player. When he retired from the Red Wings, he had set NHL records for playing in 1,687 games, for scoring 1,809 points on 786 goals and 1,023 assists, and for serving 1,643 penalty minutes.

His numerous "most" records are detailed in his official biography at the National Hockey League Hall of Fame. They include most seasons played, most regular-season games, most career goals in regular season play, most winning goals, most career assists by a right winger, most career points by a right winger, and most selections to the NHL All-Star team. He also set several All-Star Game records.

Ambidextrous and known for his incredible strength, Howe's playing style has been described as a combination of effortless and deceptively fast skating and outstanding stick-handling. When he first started as a professional, his father said he worried that his son might kill someone if he happened to get into a fight because of his strength and his ability to use both hands. As a young man, Gordie had impressed his father with his strength when he had worked summers on construction crews and could easily heft 90 pound cement sacks with either hand.

Howe was also known for his astonishing staying power. After a two-year retirement (1970-1972), he returned to professional hockey at age 45. The physician who gave him his team physical described Howe's pulse rate as comparable to that of a man half his age. His dedication as a player is revealed in a story about the 1950 Stanley Cup semi-final series when he slammed his head into a sideboard. The blow knocked him unconscious and he had to be transported to the hospital for immediate brain surgery. As he was wheeled into the operating room, he apologized to the team manager for being unable to help the team more that night.

Despite seeming laconic, Gordie Howe was never considered introverted on the ice, practicing what he called "religious hockey"—a philosophy in which he considered it better to give than to receive. His NHL penalty record of 1,643 penalty minutes and his career record of 2,421 penalty minutes attest to this. According to *Fischler's Ice Hockey Encyclopedia,* former Red Wings teammate Carl Brewer once called Howe the "dirtiest player who ever lived. A great player, but also the dirtiest. He'd gouge your eye out if you gave him a chance, carve you up. He's both big and tough and used his size to intimidate guys."

In 1971, at age 43, Howe retired from the NHL and was elected to the NHL Hall of Fame in in 1972. Two years later he made a remarkable comeback, joining the World Hockey Association (WHA) to play for the Houston Aeros with his sons Mark and Marty. The three Howes led the Aeros, winning the AVCO Cup and WHA titles in both 1974 and 1975. At age 47, Howe was awarded the Most Valuable Player in the 1975 playoffs. In 1977, he again left professional hockey, but in 1979, aged 51, he returned once more, this time to play with the Hartford Whalers. Howe finished his pro career in the 1979/80 season at the unprecedented age of 52.

In celebration of his fiftieth year in hockey and to set a record as the only professional hockey player to play in six consecutive decades, Howe briefly came out of retirement in October of 1997, at age 69, adding to his professional longevity record by playing an opening shift with the Detroit Vipers of the International Hockey League.

During the 1950s and 1960s when Gordie Howe was at his career peak, hockey great Dave Keon, former captain of the Toronto Mapleleafs (quoted in *Fischler's Ice Hockey Encyclopedia*), observed there were "two weak teams in the NHL and four strong ones—and the strong ones were Toronto, Montreal, Chicago, and Gordie Howe.''

—Mary Lou Nemanic

FURTHER READING:

Fischler, Shirley, and Stan Fischler. *Fischler's Ice Hockey Encyclopedia.* New York, Thomas Y. Cromwell Co., 1979, 272-275.

Hollander, Zander, editor. *The Complete Encyclopedia of Hockey.* Detroit, Visible Ink Press, 1993.

Libby, Bill. *Great Stanley Cup Playoffs.* New York, Random House, 1972.

Swift, E. M. ''On and On and On and . . . .'' *Sports Illustrated.* January 17, 1994, 40-43. (Reprinted from *Sports Illustrated,* January, 1980.)

Howlin' Wolf (1910-1976)

Standing six-foot-three and weighing almost 300 pounds, Chester Burnett, popularly known as ''Howlin' Wolf,'' was, in the words of Giles Oakley, ''one of the most menacingly forceful singers of his time.'' A farmer until his eighteenth birthday, Wolf's life was dramatically altered by a chance meeting with Delta legend Charley Patton. The marriage of his half-sister Mary to harmonica player Sonny Boy Williamson further shaped Wolf's musical style.

Howlin' Wolf

Howlin' Wolf's 1950s sides for Chess Records stand as some of the finest blues records ever produced. Hits like ''I Ain't Superstitious,'' ''Little Red Rooster,'' and ''Spoonful'' became even more popular when covered by British rock bands. In 1970, Chess attempted to capitalize on Wolf's newfound popularity with a white audience by teaming him with a British ''supergroup'' including Eric Clapton and members of the Rolling Stones. Howlin' Wolf died of heart failure in 1976; 15 years later, he was inducted into the Rock 'n' Roll Hall of Fame.

—Marc R. Sykes

FURTHER READING:

Oakley, Giles. *The Devil's Music: A History of the Blues.* New York, Da Capo Press, 1983.

Palmer, Robert. *Deep Blues.* New York, Viking, 1981.

Hubbard, L. Ron (1911-1986)

Founder of the Church of Scientology in the second half of the twentieth century, La Fayette Ron Hubbard was known chiefly in literary circles as a talented and prolific author of pulp fiction from the time of his first sale in 1934 until the early 1950s. In those penny-a-word days, if survival was to be maintained, being prolific was just one of the job requirements, and Hubbard more than met it. His stories appeared in magazines devoted to high adventure and mystery, as well as science fiction. Perhaps his two most famous stories in that genre were *Fear* and *Typewriter in the Sky.* Because of his skills at weaving the fantastic into plausible narratives, Hubbard was among such authors as Robert Heinlein and Isaac Asimov whom editor John Campbell relied on to fill the pages of *Astounding Science Fiction,* the leading periodical in its field.

Yet, it was ultimately not a story but an essay in *Astounding* which marked the turning point for Hubbard and eventually thrust him into the international arena. Campbell was so taken with Hubbard's new ideas for developing human potential that he printed Hubbard's 1600-word article, ''Dianetics,'' in the May 1950 issue of *Astounding.* Hubbard's thesis traced all human misery and misunderstanding to the distorted and confused signals received by the fetus in the womb. Further, it was Hubbard's contention that a person could ''clear'' himself of these misapprehensions and inhibitions by submitting to an ''auditing'' process of questions-and-answers conducted by a practitioner of Dianetics. (According to Scientology literature, the term Dianetics is a combination of the Greek words *dia* ''through'' and *nous* ''soul.'')

Although widely ridiculed by medical professionals (especially psychiatrists, who could claim with some justification that Hubbard's new science had appropriated certain psychological tenets for its own purposes), the ''Dianetics'' article created sufficient stir that Hubbard soon expanded it into a full-length book, *Dianetics: The Modern Science of Mental Health.* The book, in turn, sold well (it is still in print) and created interest in many individuals to invest in ''becoming clear.'' Author Hubbard was now in the Dianetics business, training auditors and charging fees for their services. By 1954, in a move considered by some to be an attempt to gain mainstream respectability (and circumvent prosecution for quackery), Dianetics had evolved into an official religion, dubbed with the new name Scientology. Healing has been a long-time tradition in many religions, and in the

L. Ron Hubbard

early 1950s, faith-healers (such as Oral Roberts) were as prevalent on television as professional wrestlers. Significantly, those who claim to heal under the auspices of a given religion are not customarily held to the same rigorous standards of accountability as are medical professionals.

For years, a possibly apocryphal story has circulated in science-fiction circles that at a gathering of his fellow writers, the young Hubbard had declared that the way to become rich would be to found a new religion. (Some state that Hubbard was indeed at the discussion in question but that it was another man who made the infamous pronouncement.) The fact remains that Hubbard prospered. By the end of the twentieth century, there were hundreds of Scientology churches around the world. Almost as long as it has been in existence, Scientology has been an object of controversy, accused of everything from cultic brainwashing to tax evasion. Yet despite these attacks, including government investigations, Scientology has always defended itself rigorously in court and in the public media, and weathered each storm largely unscathed. And, despite many books and periodical articles (including a 1991 cover story in *Time* magazine) which have attempted to debunk Scientology's precepts and reveal unscrupulous practices, the Church of Scientology seems in the 1990s to be thriving more than ever. As a religion born in the twentieth century, Scientology has proven itself a most media-savvy church, taking full advantage of modern methods, from television to cyberspace, to promote its methodology, attack what it views as the evil of psychiatry, and engage in positive public relations. The Scientologists' claims for Hubbard's teachings include techniques to improve education and combat drug addiction, although mainstream acceptance of

these ideas, particularly when it would mean forming an alliance with the controversial Church of Scientology, has not been forthcoming.

Hubbard eventually went into seclusion, remaining the subject of rumors and speculation until his death was announced in 1986. But Scientology goes on. This twentieth-century church may or may not be a cult, but it certainly believes in the power of "the cult of celebrity." To bolster its claims, an army of publicists continually point to prominent men and women in the arts who feel that Scientology has been of immeasurable benefit in their personal and professional lives. Among these accomplished citizens are film stars John Travolta and Kelly Preston (Travolta's wife), Tom Cruise and Nicole Kidman (Cruise's wife), jazz musician Chick Corea, and composer Mark Isham. The church is populated by many people who feel they have gotten their money's worth from following its precepts. As long as Scientology is recognized as a religion in the United States, its adherents are free to place their faith in it, as are those of any other religions, whether their roots can be traced back for many centuries or to the more recent outcropping of "New Age" spirituality.

FURTHER READING:

Atack, Jon. *A Piece of Blue Sky: Scientology, Dianetics and L. Ron Hubbard Exposed.* New York, Carol Publications, 1990.

Behar, Richard. "The Thriving Cult of Greed and Power." *Time.* May 6, 1991, 50.

Corydon, Bent. *L. Ron Hubbard: Messiah or Madman?* Fort Lee, Barricade Books, 1996.

Hubbard, L. Ron. *Dianetics: The Modern Science of Mental Health.* Los Angeles, Bridge Publications, 1992.

———. *Fear.* New York, Gnome Press, 1951.

———. *Scientology, a New Slant on Life.* Los Angeles, Bridge Publications, 1997.

———. *Typewriter in the Sky.* New York, Gnome Press, 1951.

———. *What Is Scientology? The Comprehensive Reference on the World's Fastest Growing Religion.* Edited by the Staff of the Church of Scientology, International. Los Angeles, Bridge Publications, 1992.

Hudson, Rock (1925-1985)

Actor Rock Hudson's unmistakable masculinity made him a screen idol of the 1950s and 1960s. Hudson was a traditionally handsome figure and a romantic hero when such types were becoming rare. He was brought into film as the heir to Clark Gable and Gary Cooper. His broad shouldered, six-foot frame and dark brooding eyes gave him an enormous screen presence. He was twice voted the nation's top box office draw and was the recipient of numerous national and international awards. He also earned the respect of critics, in particular for his fine performances in *Magnificent Obsession* (1954) and *Giant* (1956).

Born Roy Scherer, Jr., on November 17, 1925, in Winnetka, Illinois, Hudson was a member of a blue-collar family. His father was an automobile mechanic and his mother a telephone operator. Hudson's years at New Trier High School were ordinary: he sang in the

Rock Hudson

school's glee club, and residents of the city remember him as a shy boy who delivered newspapers, ran errands, and worked as a golf caddy. The 1937 movie *The Hurricane* captivated and inspired Hudson to an acting career.

In 1943 Hudson was drafted into the Navy. After a military discharge in 1946, he briefly returned to Winnetka and worked as a piano mover. After doing poorly as a salesman in his father's appliance shop he took on a job as a truck driver with a food company. He moved to Los Angeles to pursue an acting career and applied to the University of Southern California's dramatics program, but was rejected due to poor grades. Pursuing his dream of becoming a film star, Hudson sent out numerous resumes and photographs to movie studios. He received only one response, from talent scout Henry Wilson, a representative for David O. Selznick.

Wilson renamed the ruggedly handsome young man "Rock Hudson"—Rock for the Rock of Gibraltar, and Hudson for the famous New York river. Hudson was introduced to the Hollywood studios, but did not make a lasting impression due to his shyness. His screen test for Twentieth Century-Fox studios was so bad that it was shown to beginning classes as a classic example of poor acting.

Hudson landed his first acting job in a one-line bit part in Raoul Walsh's *Fighter Squadron* (1948). According to Hollywood legend, Hudson needed 38 takes to get his line ("Pretty soon you're going to have to write smaller numbers") correct. But Hudson learned to act on the job, and within six years he had appeared in 28 pictures. The roles were primarily characters lacking depth.

Hudson soon came under the wing of Universal Studios tutor Sophie Rosenstein, who helped him in his bit parts and supporting

roles. During the 1950s he was cast in longer parts in a series of adventure and "B" pictures. After the release of *Magnificent Obsession,* Hudson's career took off. In 1954 *Modern Screen* magazine cited Hudson as the most popular actor of the year, and in 1955 *Look* magazine named him as the top male movie star. He was wed to Phyllis Gates in 1955; the marriage lasted three years, and Hudson did not remarry.

Hudson's acting career proceeded in a new direction as a sustaining figure in women's pictures. Under the professional direction of George Stevens, Hudson was able to give real depth to the characterization of Texas rancher Bick Benedict in *Giant* (1956). After Richard Brooks's notable *Something of Value,* and a moving performance in *A Farewell to Arms* (1957), the actor moved into comedy roles, usually paired with Doris Day. While the films varied in quality, they allowed Hudson the opportunity to explore his comedic talents. Utilizing innuendo, the films bridged the gap between humor and permissiveness. From 1959 to 1965 he portrayed humorous characters in *Pillow Talk* (1959); *Come September* (1961); *Lover Come Back* (1961); *Send Me No Flowers* (1964); *Man's Favorite Sport* (1964); and *Strange Bedfellows* (1964). Hudson afterward appeared in a number of unsuccessful and mediocre films.

By age 55 Hudson was faced with a dilemma: whether to pursue a fading film career or take roles in television. Initially Hudson was not interested in a small-screen career, but the series *McMillan and Wife* (1971), in which he starred as the police commissioner of San Francisco, proved to be a hit. He made few worthwhile films afterward, and he appeared in two television miniseries, *The Martian Chronicles* (1980) and *The Star Maker* (1981). He also was cast in the poorly conceived *Devlin Connection* (1982). His last recurring television role was in *Dynasty* (beginning in 1981).

Hudson made his final screen appearance in the 1984 television film *The Las Vegas Strip Wars.* The following year, while in Paris seeking medical treatment for an undisclosed illness, Hudson collapsed. The news broke that Hudson had been diagnosed with AIDS. Friends stated he had discovered that he had the disease in mid-1984, but chose to continue acting on *Dynasty* while secretly undergoing treatment. For years Hudson, his managers, and the studios had avoided the issue of his homosexuality. His illness, however, brought it into the open. Author Armistead Maupin stated he met with Hudson in 1976 and urged him to reveal his homosexuality. Acquaintances often described Hudson as gay, but he refused to publicly comment on or acknowledge the reports. Rock Hudson became the first major public figure to declare he had AIDS.

His last appearance at a benefit hosted by former leading lady Doris Day revealed the horrifying truth of AIDS in vivid and unflinching detail. Before his death Hudson stated, "I am not happy that I am sick. I am not happy that I have AIDS. But if that is helping others, I can at least know that my own misfortune has had some positive worth." Rock Hudson passed away at his home in Beverly Hills, California, on October 2, 1985.

—Michael A. Lutes

FURTHER READING:

Bego, Mark. *Rock Hudson: Public and Private: An Unauthorized Biography.* New York, New American Library, 1986.

Clark, Tom, and Dick Kleiner. *Rock Hudson: Friend of Mine.* New York, Pharos Books, 1989.

Gates, Phyllis, and Bob Thomas. *My Husband Rock Hudson: The Real Story of Rock Hudson's Marriage to Phyllis Gates.* New York, Doubleday Books, 1987.

Oppenheimer, Jerry, and Jack Vitek. *Idol, Rock Hudson: The True Story of an American Film Hero.* New York, Villard Books, 1986.

Royce, Brenda Scott. *Rock Hudson: A Bio-Bibliography.* Westport, Connecticut, Greenwood Press, 1995.

Hughes, Howard (1905-1976)

When he passed away on August 16, 1976, billionaire financier Howard Hughes was considered the world's most mysterious man. Rumors abounded about the strange way he looked, his eccentricities, and the odd way he lived. But before he became a man on the run, moving from continent to continent with his cadre of Mormon aides, Hughes was the embodiment of the Jazz Age wealthy playboy, the 1930s-era aviation hero, the 1940s and 1950s millionaire-as-super-star, and the 1960s Las Vegas casino mogul. Along the way, he also

Howard Hughes

riled censors and packed movie houses with several milestone films that pushed the boundaries of sex and violence.

Born in Houston on Christmas Eve, 1905, Howard Robard Hughes Jr. was the son of an oilman who had developed a drill bit that revolutionized oil drilling the world over. The Hughes rock bit, or rollerbit, was the foundation of the family fortune that Hughes Jr. inherited at age eighteen. That fortune financed Hughes's earliest Hollywood ventures, which began in 1926 and climaxed with the monumental World War I aviation epic *Hell's Angels* in 1930. Because its production spanned the silent and talkie eras, the early sound movie required reshoots and a new leading lady. Hughes chose the unknown starlet Jean Harlow. He also took over as director. By the time of its lavish premiere, ''Hughes's Folly,'' as it was called, was the costliest movie of its time. With its dazzling aviation sequences and Harlow's presence, it also proved a crowd-pleaser, establishing Hughes as a major filmmaking force. But after producing several significant films of the early 1930s, including *The Front Page* and the violent *Scarface,* he turned his attention to the skies.

His love of aviation had begun at age fourteen with a five dollar flight in a Curtiss flying boat. An astute flight student, he made headlines in 1932 when he was discovered working under an alias for American Airlines as a baggage handler. With Hughes Aircraft Company, he developed and built the planes in which he made various speed records. Those efforts led to the development of the first retractable landing gear, flushed rivets, streamlined airplane designs, and advances in high-altitude flying. His July 1938 flight around the world, in three days, nineteen hours, enshrined him as a ticker-tape hero and the country's most famous aviator since Charles Lindbergh. Hughes's romances with Ginger Rogers, Katharine Hepburn, and others gave the matinee-idol-handsome Hughes a reputation as a ladies' man.

His interest in women, and the female figure, was evident when he returned to filmmaking with the audacious western *The Outlaw.* Producer-director Hughes was so determined to glorify his leading lady's bustline that he once stopped production in order to design a better brassiere for newcomer Jane Russell. He spent two years editing the movie and battling censors, and finally opened *The Outlaw* in 1943. Inexplicably, he pulled it from distribution after eight record-breaking weeks. Rereleased in later years, the film, which remains noteworthy for its early depiction of cleavage, denoted Hughes's obsessive nature and eccentricities.

The 1940s saw Hughes wielding his power and wealth to romance a ''Who's Who'' of Hollywood luminaries, including Bette Davis, Ava Gardner, Rita Hayworth, and Lana Turner. Expanding his empire, he became principal shareholder of TWA Airlines in 1947. That same year he also defiantly faced a Senate subcommittee hearing involving the HK-1, Hercules. Popularly known as the Spruce Goose, the government-funded, eight-story plane had not been completed in time to ferry soldiers over the ocean during World War II. When government sources doubted it would fly at all, Hughes personally proved them wrong. Though the flight of November 2, 1947, lasted less than one minute, it was a benchmark in aviation history.

Yet Hughes was already on a dark, downward spiral, as symbolized by his July 1946 crash while test piloting an XF-11 photo reconnaissance plane. Obsessive-Compulsive Disorder had not yet been diagnosed, but Hughes has since been identified as a classic OCD sufferer. This biologically based condition led to his dependence on drugs, which were first given to him following the 1946 crash.

Hughes ventured back into filmmaking in 1948, purchasing a controlling interest in RKO Pictures. The studio legacy included such revered titles as *King Kong, Citizen Kane,* and the Fred Astaire-Ginger Rogers musicals. Under Hughes, filmmakers were dismayed to learn that they had to cast Hughes's assorted girlfriends, including Terry Moore. But during his tenure, Hughes personally salvaged a career that became legendary: following a notorious September 1948 marijuana arrest, Robert Mitchum thought his career was over, but Hughes stood by the actor and went on to cast him in a string of enjoyable crime thrillers. Hughes, who never did set foot on the studio lot, eventually became sole owner of RKO, which he sold in 1955. Shortly afterward, he became so reclusive that when he and actress Jean Peters secretly married in 1957, both used assumed names.

In the 1960s, as his companies pioneered space and satellite ventures, Hughes lived behind the blackened windows of the Desert Inn penthouse suite, amassing a then-unsurpassed Las Vegas desert kingdom of casinos and hotels. He left the city in the dead of night in November 1970 and thereafter was a man on the run. Pursued by various government agencies, attorneys, process-servers, and the media, he was so isolated that the publishing world fell for an elaborate hoax perpetrated by writer Clifford Irving, who claimed he was working with Hughes on his autobiography.

Following Hughes's death and the ensuing battle for his money, revelations detailed his germ phobia, food fetishes, and drug usage. That the once dashing, adventurous Hughes had died weighing just ninety three pounds, with broken hypodermic needles imbedded in his arms, was proof that money does not buy happiness. Meanwhile, the hoaxes continued, most notably that of the "Mormon will." The fraudulent document left money to gas station attendant Melvin Dummar, whose saga was the impetus for the 1980 film *Melvin and Howard.*

—Pat H. Broeske

FURTHER READING:

Bartlett, Donald L., and James B. Steele. *Empire: The Life, Legend and Madness of Howard Hughes.* New York, W.W. Norton, 1979.

Brown, Peter Harry, and Pat H. Broeske. *Howard Hughes: The Untold Story.* New York, Dutton, 1996.

Dietrich, Noah, and Bob Thomas. *Howard: The Amazing Mr. Hughes.* Greenwich, Connecticut, Fawcett, 1972.

Phelan, James. *Howard Hughes: The Hidden Years.* New York, Random House, 1976.

Hughes, Langston (1902-1967)

With his essay "The Negro Artist and the Racial Mountain" (1926), writer Langston Hughes helped to define the spirit that motivated the Harlem Renaissance, a black cultural movement of the 1920s. In the essay, he argues against blacks seeking integration at the expense of race pride and proclaims that instead "we younger artists who create now intend to express our individual dark-skinned selves without fear or shame," a bold statement for those racially unsettling times that were marked by lynchings and riots. Perhaps his determination to affirm, indeed revel in, black culture had something to do with his father's hatred of black people, a sentiment that affected the son profoundly. Hughes wrote in his autobiography *The Big Sea* (1940) that "my father hated Negroes. I think he hated himself, too, for being

a Negro." Unlike his father, early in life Hughes had been seduced by the *joie de vivre* of a people who simply could have been bitter because their lives were filled with injustice. In nearly everything he wrote, and he wrote more than fifty books in every conceivable genre, he sought to capture the complexities of, and pay homage to such people, especially those who were poor or of modest means. He believed that they "had as much in their lives to put into books as did those more fortunate." Thus, the black folk idiom, the rhythm and tones of its language and music, was the only choice for Hughes, and he became the poet laureate of the people for one simple reason—he spoke their language.

Hughes himself had very humble beginnings, and it may well have been his memory of those beginnings that fed his desire to be in touch with the masses. He was born James Langston Hughes on February 1, 1902, in Joplin, Missouri, to James Nathaniel and Carrie Mercer Langston Hughes, who separated soon after his birth. He lived on and off with his mother, but primarily lived with his grandmother for the first twelve years of his life. After his grandmother's death, he lived with friends of hers whom he referred to as Auntie and Uncle Reed, then went to live again with his mother, who had remarried and given birth to another son. In the loneliness of such a childhood, Hughes turned to books. Even living as modestly, often quite poorly, as they did, his mother took him to see plays and introduced him to literature. His grandmother had been a great storyteller, and although her staunch pride sometimes prevented their having enough to eat, the stories she told about heroic blacks seemed to instill a similar pride in Hughes that would later manifest itself in his deep affection for his people and in the stories he eventually would tell.

His early poems were in imitation of Paul Laurence Dunbar and Carl Sandburg until he began to find his own voice, drawing on his observations of the people and culture that so fascinated him. For example, the inspiration for "When Sue Wears Red," extolling the majestic beauty of African American women, was a "little brownskin girl" from the South whom he had met at a high school dance. At age seventeen, he wrote one of his best-loved and most enduring poems, "The Negro Speaks of Rivers," published in *Crisis* in 1921, the first of his poems to appear in a national publication. It was later set to music by composer Howard Swanson, and Marian Anderson performed it at Carnegie Hall. His collection of blues and jazz poems, *The Weary Blues* (1926), was an unprecedented use of those particular cultural forms, winning him first prize in *Opportunity* magazine's literary contest and establishing him as an influential writer whose art was deeply rooted in racial pride. Hughes's biographer, Arnold Rampersad, commented that poems such as "The Negro Speaks of Rivers," "Mother to Son," and "Harlem" are "virtual anthems of black America."

Hughes's participation in the Harlem Renaissance, major though it was, constitutes only a small part of his literary career. His influence has been far-reaching, extending beyond the black American community. His appointment by President Lyndon Johnson as the American representative to the First World Festival of Negro Arts, held in Dakar, Senegal, in April of 1966, attests to his having achieved a widespread international reputation. Senegal's poet-president Léopold Sédar Senghor considered Hughes important to the concept of négritude, saying that "we considered Langston to be the greatest black American poet because it was Langston Hughes who best answered our definition," according to Rampersad in *The Life of Langston Hughes.* Senghor believed Hughes to be a "model . . . for the world." Also,

The hula hoop in action.

according to Rampersad, the *New York Times* reported that while Hughes was attending the festival "young writers from all over Africa followed him about the city and haunted his hotel the way American youngsters dog favorite baseball players."

The impact of Hughes's work did not diminish with his death in 1967. Many scholars have come to see him as black America's most original poet; long before the Black Arts Movement of the 1960s, Hughes's poetry reflected the idea that black music is essential to the artistic creation of an authentic "black" voice. Further, the kind of fusion of black music and literary forms that has come to be associated with his poetry is reflected in much of the black popular music of the 1970s, 1980s, and 1990s. His poem "Afro-American Fragments" inspired the title of a music CD made in 1995 by Ensemble Sans Frontiére, which pays tribute to Hughes and musicians Dizzy Gillespie, Charles Mingus, and Miles Davis. Perhaps the blues revival of the 1980s and Congress's resolution declaring jazz a "rare and valuable national treasure" has helped to secure Hughes's acceptance by mainstream literary audiences, for he is the only African American to be included in the "Voices and Visions" series that explores the lives and works of thirteen famous American poets.

The last line of *The Big Sea* reads, "Literature is a big sea full of many fish. I let down my nets and pulled. I'm still pulling." One has only to look at his legacy of poetry, drama, musicals, libretti, fiction,

and nonfiction to know that even now the poet of the people is "still pulling."

—Jacquelyn Y. McLendon

FURTHER READING:

Hughes, Langston. *The Big Sea: An Autobiography.* New York, Hill and Wang, 1940.

Rampersad, Arnold. *The Life of Langston Hughes.* Vols. I, II. New York, Oxford University Press, 1986.

Rampersad, Arnold, and David Roessel, eds. *The Collected Poems of Langston Hughes.* New York, Vintage Classics, 1995.

Hula Hoop

One of the simplest concepts in toy design, the hula hoop deserves the title of the most popular, mid-twentieth century fad. In 1958, children and fun-loving adults were reeling and wiggling, trying to spin the four-foot, plastic hoops around their waists. Marketed by the toy manufacturer Wham-O, the hula hoop was introduced to the public in California and quickly became popular throughout America. The craze crossed both oceans; within a year hula hoops were a mania in Europe, the Middle East, and Japan. Approximately one-hundred million hoops were sold in the first year of the toy's production.

When two young chemists working for Phillips Petroleum discovered a durable, heat-resistant, and inexpensive plastic (Marlex), the material turned out to be perfect for the production of the kind of hoops that were used in exercise gyms. American children loved the fun of gyrating like a hula dancer to keep the colored, lightweight plastic rings aloft. The hula hoop craze introduced the public to the plastics industry that would produce everything from baby toys to automobile parts as the twentieth century progressed.

—Sharon Brown

FURTHER READING:

Asakawa, Gil, and Leland Rucker. *The Toy Book.* New York, Knopf, 1992.

Hull, Bobby (1939—)

To become a legend, a hockey player needs something special in addition to great playing abilities. In the case of Bobby Hull, the Chicago Black Hawks famous #9, his speed and the incredible force of his slapshots have contributed to give ''The Golden Jet'' a unique profile. One of the finest hockey players ever to take to the ice, he became a three-time NHL point-scoring champion, and two-time MVP while playing left wing for the Black Hawks. He is still considered the best left-winger in the history of hockey.

Born Robert Marvin Hull on January 3, 1939, in Pointe Anne, Ontario, he progressed quickly through the minor league hockey ranks. At age 10, he was already considered a potential NHL player. He played junior hockey in Hespeler and Woodstock, Ontario, and with the St. Catharines Tee Pees, where he was coached by Rudy Pilous, his future Black Hawks coach.

The blond player earned the nickname ''The Golden Jet'' because of his speed, power, and charisma. He joined the Chicago Black Hawks for the 1957-1958 season, and played left wing for them from 1957 to 1972. (His brother, Dennis, also played for the Hawks from 1964 to 1977). Although his first two seasons were not particularly brilliant (with only 31 goals, 13 in the first year, 18 in the second), he used them to perfect his speed and his unique slapshot. He was considered the NHL's fastest skater, clocked at 28.3 mph with the puck, 29.7 without it. His powerful, booming slapshot—clocked once at 118.3 mph, some 35 mph above the league average—was thought to be the league's hardest. That ''high-velocity piece of lead,'' according to goalie Jacques Plante, could easily thrust a goalie backward into the net—along with the puck.

Gradually, Bobby Hull became a top player for his team. With 39 goals in his 3rd season, 31 in his 4th, he led Chicago to their first Stanley Cup in 23 years in 1960-61. The following year, he matched the NHL's 50-goal scoring record, before raising it for the first time ever to 54 in 1965-1966 and to 58 in 1968-1969, even while playing

Bobby Hull

part of the season with his mouth wired shut because of a broken jaw. In 16 NHL seasons, Hull scored 610 goals and added 560 assists (for a total of 1,170 points) in regular season play, plus 129 points (62 goals and 67 assists) during the Stanley Cup playoffs. He led the NHL in goals scored in seven different seasons.

Bobby Hull displayed all the skills of some of the game's best players: he perfected Boom-Boom Geoffrion's slapshot; he had the speed of Howie Morenz, the goal-scoring abilities of Maurice ''Rocket'' Richard, and the strength and control of Gordie Howe. Not surprisingly, he was voted hockey's Player-of-the-Decade in a 1970 Associated Press poll of writers and sportscasters. He won the Ross Trophy three times, the Lady Byng once, the Hart twice, and the Patrick Trophy in 1969 for the outstanding contribution he made to hockey in the United States. He was a regular choice in All-Star selections, named ten times to the First NHL All-Star Team and twice to the Second Team.

In 1972, a contract dispute with the Hawks management caused a major surprise when Hull jumped to the Winnipeg Jets of the upstart World Hockey Association. Hull's contract made him hockey's first millionaire, as the Jets were offering high salaries to attract stars to their team. For the Black Hawks, it was a major setback: his departure may have cost the organization close to $1 billion over ten years due to drops in attendance. The NHL tried legal action to block the move,

a black woman's quest for self-identity is interspersed with folk-tales, which Hurston had collected during a research trip supervised by noted anthropologist Franz Boas. In 1943, her autobiography *Dust Tracks on a Road* (1942) won *The Saturday Review*'s Anisfield Award for the best book on race relations. Although this award made her a well known public figure, she always refused the role of spokesperson for the African American community. She also held controversial views on race, which led her to write an article against school desegregation in 1955. In the years following her death, notably in the 1980s and 1990s, Hurston's work has achieved a prominent position in the American literary canon.

—Luca Prono

FURTHER READING:

Bloom, Harold, editor. *Zora Neale Hurston-Modern Critical Views.* New York, Chelsea House Publishers, 1986.

Gates, Henry Louis, Jr. *The Signifying Monkey-A Theory of Afro-American Literary Criticism.* New York, Oxford University Press, 1988.

Hemenway, Robert E. *Zora Neale Hurston-A Literary Biography.* Urbana, University of Illinois Press, 1977.

Walker, Alice. *In Search of Our Mothers' Gardens.* New York, Harcourt Brace, 1983.

Hustler

As the twentieth century drew to a close, pornography was a $10 billion-a-year business in America. About $1 billion of that cash flow was generated by magazine sales. One of the most provocative and controversial of the so-called "men's magazines" was Larry Flynt's *Hustler.* The raunchy periodical, founded on its publisher's oft-stated desire to cater to the "erotic imaginations of real people," helped redefine the "mainstream" of porn and wielded an influence far beyond the cloistered realm of XXX literature.

In its essence, the *Hustler* story is inseparable from that of its founder, Larry Flynt. A child bootlegger from the mountains of Kentucky, Flynt escaped the torpor of Appalachia at age 15 by joining the United States Army. Upon leaving the service, and surviving a failed first marriage, he established a profitable chain of go-go bars. In 1972, he moved into publishing, starting up an eponymous newsletter for his Hustler club. The new periodical, later expanded into a glossy magazine, became notorious for its explicit depiction of the female genitalia. Whereas the other men's magazines of the time, like *Playboy* and *Penthouse,* bathed their nude models in a gauzy glow that obstructed the view of their "naughty bits," Flynt's *Hustler* examined every nook and cranny of the distaff form with an almost gynecological zeal. The approach shocked many in the beginning— no doubt a part of Flynt's plan all along—but had soon resulted in expanded parameters for what could and could not be shown in a newsstand periodical.

A host of imitators cropped up in the wake of *Hustler*'s initial success. Often they bore titles that aped *Hustler*'s pornoscenti cachet, titles like *Swank, Gent,* and *High Society.* But few of these publications could match Flynt's élan or his flair for generating publicity. In 1975, Flynt created a furor by running telephoto pictures of a naked

***Hustler* publisher Larry Flynt.**

Jackie Onassis sunbathing in Greece. Amid howls from the world's opinion elites, Flynt gleefully cashed his checks. The scandalous photo spread helped attract 1.3 million readers to *Hustler*—and allowed a former strip club owner from Appalachia to rake in more than $30 million a year.

Not surprisingly, Flynt's ability to reach a mass audience made him a ripe target for all manner of detractors. Foremost among these were American feminists, to whom Flynt gave plenty of ammunition. *Hustler*'s visual features repeatedly portrayed sex as ugly and dirty, with women depicted in rape fantasies, smeared with excrement, or likened to pieces of meat. One infamous cover showed a woman being fed into a meat grinder. The backlash to such content was swift and visceral. In an op-ed piece for the *New York Times,* Gloria Steinem compared *Hustler* to a Ku Klux Klan publication and derided Flynt for printing images of women being "beaten, tortured and raped" and "subject to degradations from bestiality to sexual slavery."

African Americans and other minority groups also heaped scorn on *Hustler,* for its monthly parade of cartoons and features that were blatantly racist, bigoted, or putridly scatological. Even fellow pornographers had little tolerance for this type of material. "I think [Flynt's] dangerous and demented," opined *Penthouse* publisher Bob

Guccione. ''I don't believe he's normal by any stretch of the imagination. He's very sick and disoriented.'' To all of these critics a defiant Flynt had the same answer: ''We're an equal opportunity offender,'' he declared repeatedly, adopting the rhetoric of civil rights law to defend his cause. ''Every month we try to figure out who we haven't offended yet.''

Hustler has not lacked for high-profile defenders. One of Flynt's most ardent apologists has been the outspoken author and academic Camille Paglia, who lauded the maverick publisher as ''a hero'' who ''forces people to confront their own buried snobbery about the South and working-class culture.'' Paglia went on to laud *Hustler* for ''being totally frank, playing no more games, laying it out for everyone to see. It's the kind of explicitness you'll see in tribal cultures.''

Nevertheless, such ''explicitness'' has cost *Hustler* dearly among mainstream advertisers, almost all of whom have shunned the magazine despite having no qualms about gracing the pages of *Playboy* and *Penthouse*. Even more damaging, Flynt has found himself hauled into court on numerous occasions to defend the magazine against indecency charges. The legal cost of defending *Hustler* over the years has been estimated at $50 million. It was during one such trial, in 1978, that *Hustler*'s publisher nearly paid the ultimate price for his commitment to pornography. Joseph Paul Franklin shot Flynt twice from close range with a high-powered rifle outside a courthouse where he was being prosecuted for obscenity. Flynt survived the attack, but lost the use of his legs permanently.

The after-effects of the assassination attempt nearly sank *Hustler,* as a devastated Flynt briefly found religion under the tutelage of President Jimmy Carter's evangelical sister, Ruth Carter Stapleton. The bizarre life change found its way onto the pages of the magazine, which suffered a drop in circulation. Flynt's subsequent addiction to painkilling drugs, with the attendant high spending, resulted in a severe money crunch.

In the 1980s, Flynt reconsidered his spiritual awakening and opted to return *Hustler* to its raunchy roots. He placed advertisements in the Hollywood trade press offering $1 million to any top television or film actress who would pose nude in the pages of the magazine. Spurred by the advent of videocassette recorders, he started producing porno videotapes under the *Hustler* imprimatur. The first entry depicted an 18-year-old medically certified virgin being deflowered in front of the cameras. ''She was holding out for the right man,'' Flynt crowed, ''but the right price won out.''

Hustler's ability to keep publishing such sordid material was nearly compromised during the Reagan era, when Moral Majority leader Jerry Falwell sued Flynt for libel over a scatological ad parody depicting the preacher in an outhouse having sex with his mother. After a lower court ruled in Falwell's favor, the United States Supreme Court in 1988 reversed the decision and upheld Flynt's right to satirize a public figure. Some First Amendment advocates began hailing Flynt as a poster child for free speech, though many other civil libertarians felt uncomfortable with the association.

Flynt's defenders were plainly cheered by the appearance in 1996 of a reverential biopic, *The People vs. Larry Flynt,* directed by Academy Award winner Milos Forman and starring *Cheers* hayseed Woody Harrelson as the eponymous pornographer. The film sugarcoated many of the more tawdry facts of Flynt's life, while avoiding the issues of *Hustler*'s racism and misogyny entirely. Though dismissed as a tendentious mess by some critics, and savaged by feminists as a whitewash, the feature nonetheless proved a major hit and gave the bumptious publisher a brief ripple of renewed popularity.

Flynt used his newfound status as a media darling to his own advantage in 1998, injecting himself into the debate over the Impeachment of President Bill Clinton. In the October issue of *Hustler,* he offered up to $1 million to anyone willing to admit to having an affair with a member of Congress. His target, he claimed, was the ''hypocrisy'' of conservatives who were pursuing Clinton for lying about sex, while leading less-than-pure lives themselves. By December, Flynt had bagged his first victim, when Representative Robert Livingston, the Republicans' choice to be Speaker of the House, resigned after investigators hired by *Hustler* determined that he had been unfaithful to his wife. With Flynt promising more damaging revelations for the future, Americans of all political persuasions briefly recoiled at the thought that such a figure could effectively alter the course of history.

—Robert E. Schnakenberg

FURTHER READING:

Flynt, Larry. *An Unseemly Man: My Life as a Pornographer, Pundit, and Social Outcast.* New York, Dove Books, 1997.

Smolla, Rodney A. *Jerry Falwell v. Larry Flynt: The First Amendment on Trial.* New York, St. Martin's, 1988.

Huston, John (1906-1987)

The multi-faceted John Huston entered modern cinema history in 1941 when he wrote the screenplay for *The Maltese Falcon,* also making his directorial debut. The film established his reputation, began a significant working relationship with Humphrey Bogart, and pointed to his preference for mining literary sources for his material—in this case, Dashiell Hammett. In the course of a long and decidedly erratic career, Huston dealt memorably with human greed in *The Treasure of the Sierra Madre* (1947), winning Oscars for his screenplay and direction, and *Key Largo* (1948); plaudits greeted *The Asphalt Jungle* (1950), often considered his best film, and he entranced audiences by pairing Katharine Hepburn's missionary and Humphrey Bogart's booze-drenched river trader as companions in adversity in *The African Queen* (1952)—an idea beguilingly echoed by Deborah Kerr's nun marooned on a wartime Pacific island with Robert Mitchum's marine in *Heaven Knows, Mr. Allison* (1957). (*The African Queen* was voted one of the 100 best American films of the century by the AFI in 1998.) Huston acted frequently from the 1960s on, and, while many look fondly on his genial Noah in *The Bible,* which he directed in 1966, it is his tycoon in Polanski's *Chinatown* (1974), oozing cruelty and corruption, that is burnt in the collective memory.

As a director, Huston's films reflected his wide interests and, like the man, often present a rough exterior beneath which hovers tenderness, or even romantic idealism. Most of his heroes are either fiercely independent or social misfits, or both: the artist Toulouse-Lautrec, played by Jose Ferrer in *Moulin Rouge* (1953), Gregory Peck's Captain Ahab (*Moby Dick,* 1956), the eponymous *Freud* (a tortured and miscast Montgomery Clift, 1962), Stacy Keach's disintegrating prizefighter in *Fat City* (1971, one of Huston's quality films in a period of failures). His best work reflects a sense of irony and a sharp attention to character, focused in a decisive narrative style, as in *The Man Who Would be King* (1975), adapted from Kipling and one of his last real successes. Some of the films are off-beat and tend to

John Huston

misfire, though the imagery of elephants and the accompanying doom-laden message of *Roots of Heaven* (1958) is interesting, and while comedy barely features in his *oeuvre,* he ventured successfully into parody with the spoof adventure-thriller *Beat the Devil* (1954, Bogart again).

Although a five-times married womanizer in life, with a handful of exceptions, women are largely peripheral to Huston's heavily masculine on-screen world. As David Thomson accurately observes, "There is no real female challenge to the smoke-room atmosphere of the films. But there is a list of female onlookers as wan and powerless as Jacqueline Bisset in *Under the Volcano,* Elizabeth Taylor in *Reflections in a Golden Eye* and Dominique Sanda in *The Mackintosh Man.*" One might add a dozen others, but the casting of his daughter Anjelica in *Prizzi's Honor* (1987), one of his last and most entertaining films, helped her to an Oscar.

Huston's failures, ranging from the pretentiously arty such as *Under the Volcano* (1984) through the tedious, the slapdash and the irredeemably dreadful (e.g. *The List of Adrian Messenger,* 1963) are numerous, and seriously tarnish his reputation. In truth, it is almost impossible to define the particular gift, characteristic, or achievement that led to his enduring position as a Hollywood—indeed, an American—legend, and perhaps it is to the man himself that history must look for the answer. It was not only his huge frame and powerfully craggy face that made him larger than life, but his hell-raising extroversion and colorful exploits, coupled with courage and an adventurous nature (as well as a mean streak). He was born in Nevada, Missouri, on August 5, 1906, the son of the distinguished actor Walter Huston, and later himself fathered sons, Tony and Danny, who

became a screenwriter and a film director, respectively. He had a peripatetic childhood, traveling the vaudeville circuit with his father and the horse-racing circuit with his mother (they divorced when John was seven), left school at 14 to become a boxer and, at 19, embarked on a short-lived career as a stage actor in New York, also marrying the first of his wives.

For the next 12 years or so, Huston led an unsettled life that embraced a period as an officer with the Mexican cavalry, small parts in a few films, and reporting for the New York *Graphic.* A fruitless stint as a contract scriptwriter in Hollywood followed before he took off for a nomadic and often poverty-stricken existence in London and Paris, where he studied painting. Back in Hollywood by 1937, he settled in as a writer at Warner Bros., applying himself seriously to his work, which included collaborations on such films as *Jezebel* (1938), *Dr. Ehrlich's Magic Bullet* (1940), *High Sierra,* and *Sergeant York* (both 1941).

Professionally, the sheer length, breadth, and range of Huston's filmography astonishes: in a career that began in 1929 with an acting role in *The Shakedown,* and ended with his directing of *The Dead* in 1987, he accrued almost 90 credits in his various capacities as screenwriter, director, and/or actor. He joined the army in 1942 and made three of the most acclaimed documentaries ever to emerge from the conflict of World War II. The most searing of these, *Let There Be Light* (1945), dealing with the treatment and rehabilitation of shell-shocked soldiers, was banned by the War Department because of its sensitive subject, and was first shown publicly in 1980.

In 1947, along with William Wyler and others, Huston formed the Committee for the First Amendment to counteract the HUAC Hollywood witchhunt. The following year, with the expiration of his Warners contract, he formed Horizon Pictures with independent producer Sam Spiegel, and in 1952, unable any longer to tolerate the McCarthyite atmosphere, he bought a vast country estate in Ireland. He resided there for 20 years with his family, living the hunting-shooting-fishing life of a squire between films. In 1972, he moved to Mexico, married and divorced for the last time, and made nine more films, including his only musical, *Annie* (1982).

In 1987, increasingly ill with emphysema and keeping himself alive with an oxygen tank and sheer will, John Huston directed *The Dead.* Adapted from James Joyce by his son Tony and starring his daughter Anjelica, this delicate and elegiac piece marked the exit of one of American cinema's great warriors.

—Robyn Karney

FURTHER READING:

Finler, Joel W. *The Movie Directors Story.* New York, Crescent Books, 1986.

Grobel, Lawrence. *The Hustons.* New York, Charles Scribner's Sons, 1989.

Huston, John. *An Open Book.* New York, Alfred A. Knopf, 1980.

Thomson, David. *A Biographical Dictionary of Film.* New York, Alfred A. Knopf Inc., 1994.

Hutton, Ina Ray (1916-1984)

A pioneer in bringing women musicians onto the jazz scene, svelte Ina Ray Hutton, "The Blonde Bombshell of Rhythm," led an all-girl swing band, the Melodears, from 1935-39 and again in a television series in 1956. Although her idea was ahead of its time, when the Melodears opened a set with their theme song, "Gotta Have Your Love," few would dispute critic George Simon's claim that "Without a doubt, the sexiest of all big bandleaders was Ina Ray Hutton."

At age fourteen, Chicago-born Ina Ray, the younger sister of June Hutton (who sang with Tommy Dorsey's Pied Pipers) was already in show business, singing and tap dancing with Gus Edwards's vaudeville revues at the Palace Theater in New York City. Four years later she was in the chorus line of the Ziegfield Follies and George White's Scandals. Her background in dance prepared her for her special style of leading a band, more choreography than conducting.

Changing mind-sets in that era was difficult, and Simon, reviewing an appearance by Hutton's Melodears, wrote: "Only God can make a tree, and only men can play good jazz." Fans of the Melodears praised the band's soloists: Betty Sattley on tenor sax; Alyse Wells, who played several instruments; and Betty Roudebush on piano. Another musician in the band, Ruth Lowe, went on to write two great Frank Sinatra hits: "I'll Never Smile Again" and "Put Your Dreams Away."

After the Melodears folded in 1939, Hutton fronted a band of male musicians in the 1940s, one critic describing her technique as "waving her long baton in a languorous, seductive sort of way." If Hutton's beauty had attracted the crowds, the critic added, good dance music by the band held them there. By 1943, as the band continued to find a wider audience, it took on an international flavor with the addition of the Kim Loo sisters. Stuart Foster was a popular soloist in the band. One of the leading musicians in the band, tenor saxophonist and arranger George Paxton, went on to form his own orchestra in 1944, but his greatest success came in heading one of New York's most successful music publishing businesses as well as being head of a recording company.

In the early 1950s Hutton returned to her original concept, leading a jazz orchestra of female musicians. Aired nationally on NBC beginning in July 1956, her half-hour variety show had no male regulars or guests. The musicians included Mickey Anderson, clarinet; Deedie Ball, piano; Harriet Blackburn and Lois Cronin, trombones; Janie Davis, Peggy Fairbanks, and Helen Hammond, trumpets; Evie Howeth and Margaret Rinker, drums; and Helen Smith, Judy Van Ever, Zoe Ann Willey, and Helen Wooley, reed section. The show ended in September 1956.

—Benjamin Griffith

FURTHER READING:

Esposito, Tony, ed. *Golden Era of the Big Bands*. New York, Warner, 1995.

Simon, George T. *The Big Bands*. New York, MacMillan, 1974.

I Dream of Jeannie

NBC's *I Dream of Jeannie* popped onto the NBC airwaves from 1965-1970, debuting with a handsome young Air Force astronaut, forced to abort a mission, parachuting down onto a deserted island. While waiting for the rescue team, he finds a groovy purple bottle and uncorks it. In a puff of smoke, a curvaceous genie in a harem outfit appears, calls him Master and instantly falls in love with him. Coming hot on the heels of *Bewitched* (and instigating the age-old "Jeannie or Samantha" debate among guys), *Jeannie* featured another magical blonde who was denied use of her powers by the misguided man in her life. The difference was, Jeannie called her roommate (and the man she loved) "Master," although one could argue that Jeannie was really the one in charge of that relationship.

Barbara Eden, who played Jeannie (and occasionally, her naughty sister) told *Entertainment Weekly,* "'Master' didn't mean she was a slave. 'Master' was the master because he got the bottle." Nevertheless, Jeannie did stop calling him Master once they got married, which was toward the end of the series run. The long-suffering character's name was actually Anthony Nelson played by Larry Hagman.

The only other character who knew of Jeannie's existence at first was Tony's girl-crazy best friend and fellow astronaut, Roger Healey, played by Bill Daily. The supporting characters included Dr. Bellows,

the base psychiatrist and perpetually dour straight man (Hayden Rorke), his overbearing wife Amanda (Emmaline Henry), and an assortment of commanding officers. The first year it was General Stone (Philip Ober), to whose daughter Melissa Tony was engaged, but jealous Jeannie made short work of that. By the second season father and daughter were both gone, the series went to color, and General Peterson (Barton MacLane) came in as the authority figure for most of the series after that, replaced only in the last season by General Schaeffer (Vinton Hayworth). Originally captains, Nelson and Healey became majors during the course of the series.

When Captain Nelson was first rescued, he tried to tell everyone about his magic discovery, but no one believed him, least of all Dr. Bellows who diagnosed him as delusional. Adding to that was the fact that Jeannie would disappear if anyone but Tony and Roger were around, often leaving them holding the bag. And therein lay the rub week after week: well-meaning, mischievous Jeannie would "blink" Tony into trouble, leaving him to find a way to explain it to Dr. Bellows. Sometimes Roger added to the mix, putting Tony into situations that made Jeannie jealous; her favorite punishment was "blinking" someone into the tenuous position of hanging by a rope over a pit of alligators. The show's magical element gave the writers carte blanche with historical figures and situations; Tony was either "blinked" back in time, or they were "blinked" to him. Viewers also got to learn some unsubstantiated history of the Fertile Crescent—after all, Jeannie, like Spock and Data from the *Star Trek* universe, never, ever used contractions and was originally from Baghdad.

I Dream of Jeannie could only have existed where and when it did, on the cusp of the women's movement. Notwithstanding the whole master-slave issue, the arc of the show from beginning to end could also be interpreted as a metaphor for an old-fashioned view of the "power" that women have over men. She knows she'll land him, she uses her "magic" on him; he tries to deny the power and remain a bachelor, but finally succumbs. It's interesting to note that in subsequent attempts at featuring genies in sitcoms (all of them awful), the genies have been male. (In one especially misguided 1983 attempt called *Just Our Luck,* the genie was an African American male . . . with a white "master.")

The show also captured the mid-to-late 1960s fascination with the post-Kennedy space program. After all, the genie could just as well have been found by a tire salesman, but Nelson was an astronaut, frequently sent off on missions. The moon landing seemed as magical as Jeannie's powers back then. It was somehow fitting that the series ended soon after the actual moon landing and as the more jaded 1970s began.

Nineteen seventy-three brought an animated *Jeannie* to Saturday mornings. This Jeannie wasn't discovered by an astronaut, but by a high school student named Corey Anders. In 1985, the dream heroine returned to television in the unimaginatively titled TV movie *I Dream of Jeannie Fifteen Years Later.* Barbara Eden and Bill Daily came back with it, but Larry Hagman, by then again a household name as the ruthless J.R. Ewing on *Dallas,* would have seemed quite out of place and Wayne Rogers (Trapper from TV's *M*A*S*H**) signed on as Tony Nelson. This movie had a special significance: viewers were finally treated to the sight of Jeannie's belly button. Although Eden had spent much of the original series in a low-cut harem outfit, the pants were high-waisted enough to cover her navel, by order of NBC

Barbara Eden in a scene from the television show *I Dream of Jeannie.*

(they didn't seem to have a problem with cleavage). Another network rule the series had to follow was that Jeannie's bottle could never be seen in Tony's bedroom.

Eden and Daily reunited again in the TV movie *I Still Dream of Jeannie* in 1991. The original series, created by bestselling schlock novelist Sidney Sheldon and presumably named after the old Stephen Foster tune, enjoyed rerun success on "Nick at Nite" in the 1990s. "It's timeless," said Barbara Eden in *Entertainment Weekly.* "A genie is always in a costume, and the guys in the show are in uniform, so it doesn't become dated."

—Karen Lurie

FURTHER READING:

Baldwin, Kristen. "Dream Team." *Entertainment Weekly.* January 24, 1997, 11.

Brooks, Tim, and Earle Marsh. *The Complete Directory to Prime Time Network and Cable TV Shows 1946-present.* New York, Ballantine Books, 1995.

McNeil, Alex. *Total Television.* New York, Penguin, 1996.

Mukherjee, Tiarra. "Still Dreaming of 'Jeannie.'" *Entertainment Weekly.* September 20, 1996, 91.

I Love a Mystery

The Golden Age of Radio produced many successful adventure series, but none is recalled with quite the same mixture of devotion and awe as Carlton E. Morse's *I Love a Mystery.* Radio historian John Dunning says that the program "weaves a spell over its fans that is all but inexplicable"; Gerald Nachman notes that it "was the most respected show of its type"; and Jim Harmon brands it simply as "the greatest radio program of all time." While nostalgia often filters the static of creaky plots and wheezing gags characteristic of much old-time radio, the few extant recordings of *ILAM* prove it to be worthy of its extravagant reputation and have made it the "most-sought of all radio shows," according to Dunning. *ILAM* is to the world of radio mystery what *Amos 'n' Andy* is to radio comedy and *One Man's Family* is to radio soap opera—the peak achievement of its particular form. The bizarre adventures of the trio forming the A-1 Detective Agency ("No job too tough, no mystery too baffling") may have been too outrageous to be especially influential in the world of popular entertainment, and the series was not successful in its few forays into books and movies (although Indiana Jones would have fit right in as a fourth partner), but the program still bears examination for the way in which it exhibits, and yet transcends, many of the qualities which defined the classic era of radio drama.

ILAM's opening train whistle, followed by the haunting strains of Sibelius's "Valse Triste" and the eerie chiming of a clock, first sounded in 1939, heralding an initial string of 15-minute and half-hour serial adventures which would come to the end of its line in 1944. Reappearing in 1948 in a curiously muted form as *I Love Adventure*, the series finally got back on track in 1949, with a new cast reprising the scripts from the initial run, until the last chime sounded in 1952. Regardless of the format, Carlton Morse wrote the series at a feverish pitch, with a globe right next to him to help locate the next

exotic setting to which he would zip his peripatetic heroes and rapt listeners. Whether holed up in a gloomy mansion with "The Thing That Cries in the Night" or facing down the mad Holy Joe on "The Island of Skulls," *ILAM*'s intrepid trio would be certain to encounter enough baffling mysteries, beautiful women, and howling terrors to outrage parents and delight their offspring.

Jack Packard was the leader of the group, a tough-talking rationalist who could find a logical explanation for anything he couldn't punch, but never found a dame he could trust. Texas cowboy Doc Long was Jack's loyal assistant ("Honest to my Grandma!") and spent most of his time making certain that the many damsels in distress rejected by Jack were well taken care of. The trio was rounded out occasionally by spunky secretary Jerri Booker but most famously by British Reggie Yorke, who was voiced by a young Tony Randall in the show's later years and could be counted on to lend a more gentlemanly air to the proceedings. Plunging headlong into whatever harebrained escapade Morse could conjure up, the three comrades lived a life so outlandish as to make *The Shadow* or *The Green Hornet* seem positively sedate in comparison.

While the series was most notable for its creative exaggeration of adventure genre trappings, it was innovative in at least three other ways as well. Although Jack, Doc, and Reggie encountered only the most remarkable mysteries and terrible villains, the three men themselves were satisfyingly ordinary. Lacking any special abilities beyond their love of a good scrap and grim determination, they were often puzzled, incorrect, or just plain scared out of their wits, lending to the otherwise fantastical goings-on a realism that listeners could identify with and share. The prosaic nature of the program's heroes was another key ingredient in *ILAM*'s unique formula, which combined elements from the private eye and adventure genres to create a new form capable of encompassing both traditional "whodunits" and blood-and-thunder terrors. Listeners could never know, from one case to the next, which would get a greater workout, thinking caps or fists. Finally, Morse was innovative in his storytelling style. While most radio dramas switched settings several times an episode, Morse liked to open and close each installment in the same location and to approximate "real time" as closely as possible. Such adherence to Aristotelian unity not only bolstered the show's verisimilitude, but also heightened the suspense and allowed Morse to give each of his varied settings a powerful and individual atmosphere.

While the crazed characters and bizarre plots made the most immediate impact, it is the peculiar mood associated with each adventure that remains in the memory—the sound of a phantom baby crying before each murder in Grandma Martin's gloomy mansion, for example, or the howling winds of the Western ghost town with the unlikely name of Bury Your Dead, Arizona, or the "roar with lights and shades in it" which conjured the image of the giant waterfall hiding the magical "Stairway to the Sun." It is, finally, this almost dreamlike evocation of an other-worldly reality that enables *I Love a Mystery* to haunt listeners long after the final train whistle vanished in the distance.

—Kevin Lause

FURTHER READING:

Dunning, John. *On the Air: The Encyclopedia of Old-Time Radio.* New York, Oxford University Press, 1994.

Harmon, Jim. *The Great Radio Heroes.* New York, Doubleday and Co., 1967.

————. *Radio Mystery and Adventure and Its Appearances in Film, Television and Other Media.* Jefferson, North Carolina, McFarland and Co., 1992.

Maltin, Leonard. *The Great American Broadcast: A Celebration of Radio's Golden Age.* New York, Dutton, 1997.

Nachman, Gerald. *Raised on Radio.* New York, Pantheon, 1998.

I Love Lucy

I Love Lucy is, without question, the most popular and influential television comedy of all time. Since it's debut on CBS on October 15, 1951, the show has been translated into almost every language in the world and has run continuously in international syndication in over 100 U.S. markets and virtually every country in the world for almost half a century. When the show first began to rerun episodes in 1959, its ratings outperformed most of CBS's new programming that year. Such is the continuing popularity of the show that each episode is also available in Spanish, Japanese, Italian, Portuguese, and French. The program has also become a popular culture phenomenon inspiring worldwide fan clubs, web sites, retrospective screenings, and memorabilia for avid collectors. Post cards featuring classic scenes from the show, CDs of music from the show, dolls, lunch boxes, T-shirts, pajamas, aprons, and videotapes of the show continue to sell at a phenomenal rate.

A scene from the television show *I Love Lucy*.

In 1983, a Los Angeles television station honored Lucille Ball on her 72nd birthday by airing a 13 hour *I Love Lucy* marathon running from nine o'clock in the morning until ten o'clock at night. The station vaulted to number one in the ratings and stayed there for the entire day with each half hour winning its time period. The show has also been honored by the Academy of Television Arts and Sciences and by the Museum of Television and Radio.

The secret of the show's continuing popularity beyond the fact that it was incredibly funny and unceasingly creative is that it held up a mirror to every married couple in America and although the mirror was more of the fun house than the cosmetic type, it was still unstintingly honest in its depiction. "We just took ordinary situations and exaggerated them," Ball admitted.

Additionally, the unpretentious family oriented sitcom virtually revolutionized the production and distribution of television shows, setting the standard for all of the TV shows to follow. The show was one of the first comedies performed before a live audience. It also originated the concept of producing a program on film instead of broadcasting it live. Shot with three cameras, the show could be fully edited before it was shown. Using film permitted the rebroadcast of high quality prints of the show at a time when most of its competitors were rerunning their programming on poor quality kinescopes of live shows photographed off of the TV screen. The use of film hastened the move of the television industry from New York to Los Angeles which, during the 1950s, became the hub of filmed programming. It also popularized the concept of reruns, and proved that recycled programming could have renewed life on local stations once its network prime-time days had ended.

Despite the later success of *I Love Lucy,* the show was viewed by many as a long shot when it began. In the late 1940s Lucille Ball had been playing opposite actor Richard Denning on a popular radio show *My Favorite Husband.* CBS-TV became impressed with the show and wanted to bring it to television, but Ball would only agree if her real husband Desi Arnaz could play opposite her in the Denning role. According to a number of sources, this demand was a ploy on her part to save her marriage, which had been gradually deteriorating. Although Ball and Arnaz had been married since 1940, they had been separated by the demands of their work with him touring with his band while she was confined to Hollywood making films. According to Ball, if both stayed in one place and did a television show, the process of working together would help their relationship. Unfortunately, CBS executives and the program's potential advertisers didn't buy the idea, feeling that casting a thick-accented Latino as the husband of a typical American wife would not sit well with U.S. viewers.

To convince them otherwise, the two performers formed Desilu Productions, put together a 20-minute skit and took it on a cross-country barnstorming tour. When the TV show did not immediately materialize, however, Lucy went back to radio and Desi returned to his band. By the end of 1950, CBS relented somewhat, agreeing to let them do a pilot of the proposed show but declined to finance its production or the air time. Undeterred, Ball and Arnaz raised the money themselves and came up with a script about a successful bandleader and his movie star wife. Yet, the show could not find a sponsor willing to put the show on the air. The basic problem was that the pilot was too vaudeville-esque with an over-emphasis on rapid repartee and one liners.

At this point, composer Oscar Hammerstein, Jr., who had toured with Arnaz, stepped in and suggested that the show be re-written. He lobbied to keep the comedic sense of the show but to shed the movie star trappings and to make the characters appear more like an ordinary couple. Arnaz remained a band leader but, would be a struggling one, like many Americans, he would occupy his time trying to get his big break. When the show began, his character was earning $150 a week leading the house band at New York's Tropicana night club. Ball's character would be an ordinary housewife harboring visions of breaking into show business that she would act upon almost weekly with inevitably comic results.

Another stumbling point for the show was the title. Arnaz was an unknown quantity, while Ball had a popular following from her motion pictures and radio work, so CBS wanted to call the program *The Lucille Ball Show.* Ball objected because Arnaz's name was not in the title so an advertising agency executive working on the show suggested the "off the wall" title *I Love Lucy.* Since the *I* stood for Arnaz, Ball quickly agreed feeling that the almost equal billing would help her marriage. Not only was her husband's name in the title but with this format he was actually listed first.

The show's production location became yet another source of contention. CBS wanted to broadcast from New York City, the center of the fledgling television industry in 1950 but the Arnazes were reluctant to leave Los Angeles and their show business connections in case the show failed. CBS objected because broadcasting from Los Angeles would mean that the rest of the country would be able to view the show only through the use of kinescopes. Arnaz suggested that if the show were shot on 35 millimeter film as motion pictures were, CBS could distribute high quality prints to network affiliates throughout the country in a manner similar to the distribution systems employed by most movie studios. The production costs would be higher but the overall product would be much better.

The network agreed but was still faced with the never-before-attempted problem of actually filming a 30-minute TV show. To overcome this hurdle, CBS hired Oscar-winning cinematographer Karl Freund (*The Good Earth,* 1937) who collaborated with Ball and Arnaz on treating the show like a stage play and filming it before a live audience, a rare occurrence in 1950. It was also decided to film with three cameras, each shooting from a different angle, and then edit the best shots into the finished product. Director Marc Daniels, one of very few directors to have experience with three cameras, was hired to direct the show. Daniels also had a background in the theater working with live audiences.

To provide counterpoint for Ball and Arnaz's married couple, another couple who lived upstairs joined the cast of characters. After a number of actors and actresses were considered, the parts went to Vivian Vance and William Frawley. However, both were considered risky choices at the time. Vance was coming off a string of stage successes but was not nationally known (in fact, the Arnazes had never heard of her when her name was proposed); Frawley was rumored to be an alcoholic and unreliable. But, the producers took a chance on both.

The show's four lead characters of Lucy and Ricky Ricardo; Fred and Ethel Mertz (Frawley and Vance) related to each other amazingly well. The combination of the younger, more affluent Ricardos and the older, fixed-income Mertz's gave the show's writers a number of opportunities to take the show in different directions without beating the same themes to death week after week. One episode might find Lucy and Ethel involving themselves in a crazy scheme with Ricky and Fred attempting to teach them a lesson. The next might feature the two men planning a secret outing with the women attempting to crash the party. The Mertzes provided a mainstream older couple to offset the always volatile mixed marriage of the Ricardos.

The Ricardos portrayed a recognizable American family. Together, they explored the dynamics of their relationship in a manner that was new to television sitcoms. They were able to convey the fact that while they were adversaries in many of Lucy's "break into show business" shenanigans, they were also deeply in love with each other at the same time. Though bonded as a couple, each character maintained his own unique individuality.

Lucy, with her natural clown-like features reflected a combination of Yankee bravura with a touching vulnerability. Although, true to the times, she was cast as a housewife, she displayed a striking independence and was unafraid to speak her mind to her macho Latin husband. For his part, Ricky Ricardo represented a spectrum of familiar characters. Beginning with the macho hubris of a Latin lover, his expressive face and brown eyes ran the gamut from childlike vulnerability to fiery Latin anger that expressed itself through an hilarious accent that mangled the English language beyond repair.

Lucy, was a stage-struck schemer, possessed with a hyperactive imagination. The character relied on an arsenal of visual and vocal tricks in her effort to execute her wild schemes to crash the world of show business or to outsmart her husband when she got caught. The first was her tendency to drop her jaw in an open-mouthed stance to express her disbelief at what was occurring. If this didn't work, she would hold both arms straight out in front of her and then drop her forearms to indicate that something had gone wrong. Vocally, she would adopt a high pitched voice that erupted in a shriek when she was caught in an embarrassing moment. Then came the cry, monumental in nature, which would rise from her gut and then slowly wail its way up the register to the pitch of a police siren. This would be followed by a blubbering whimper that would constitute her final plea for sympathy and understanding. If her adversary happened to be Ricky, as was most often the case, she would then throw his mangled English language back at him as he attempted to read her the riot act.

The writers used the characters' differing ethnic backgrounds to great comedic effect. Ricky Ricardo's accent and nationality formed the nucleus of some of the show's more popular running gags. In addition to his mispronunciation of words, which was a very real occurrence for Arnaz as well as his character Ricky, the Cuban actor also erupted in a string of Latin epithets whenever he got mad. As Arnaz admitted in an interview, he had to walk a fine line in his use of the language to make sure that it came across as humor instead of rage. "It was the most difficult problem I faced while playing Ricky," he said. "It helped to overemphasize the Latin use of hands and arms when I was excited. Most of all, the rat-tat-tat parade of Spanish words helped me tread that thin line between funny-mad and mad-mad." He augmented this with an ability to pop out his eyes in an inimitable expression of incredulity in reaction to Lucy's antics.

The Mertzes, on the other hand, provided a calmer counterpart to the fiery Ricardos. Ethel and Fred were, first and foremost, older than their downstairs neighbors and somewhat more passive. The Vivian Vance character provided a "girlfriend" for Lucy and a partner in crime. Fred was a pal of Ricky's and someone who helped him in his schemes to thwart Lucy. He also provided one of the series' recurring gags with many jokes and episodes being built on his tightness with a buck. He simply did not like to spend money—a fact that would send the other three characters into a tizzy.

The show premier won unanimous critical approval. It achieved the 16th position in the ratings within eight weeks and climbed to number three by the end of the season with an average of 29 million viewers watching the show each week. The premise was established in the pilot show when Lucy disguised herself as a clown to sneak into Ricky's nightclub act. Throughout the rest of the season, she continued to rebel against the confines of her life as a housewife and the unfair restrictions of a male-dominated society that seemingly conspired to thwart her dreams of breaking into show business. Each of her attempts to enter into the entertainment world ended in a spectacular mess and she is inevitably forced to backtrack into the shackles of home and hearth.

The show was so popular that department stores, doctors, and dentists canceled their Monday night hours because viewers would not leave their TV sets. During the presidential elections, candidate Adlai Stevenson's office was flooded with hate mail when he cut in on *I Love Lucy* for a five-minute campaign spiel. This mistake was not repeated a decade later when CBS was tempted to pre-empt morning reruns of the show to televise the Senate Vietnam War hearings but backed away due to fears that viewers would be outraged.

In succeeding seasons the show continued to build on the basic premise as their on-screen married life evolved. In the second and third seasons the show centered on the birth of Little Ricky, which was the most popular episode in television history for many years (interestingly, more people watched the birth of Little Ricky than watched the inauguration of Dwight D. Eisenhower as 34th President of the United States and the coronation of Queen Elizabeth of England, all in 1953). Predictably, the biggest adjustment for Lucy lay in the impact of motherhood on her dreams of crashing into show business. The fourth season found Ricky landing a screen test with a Hollywood studio and devoted a number of episodes to a cross country trip from New York to Hollywood where Lucy became involved in a number of adventures with celebrity guest stars including a now famous encounter with William Holden in a comedy of mistaken identities.

The fifth season found the family returning to New York but quickly taking off on a laugh-filled adventure tour of Europe. The final season revolved around the exploits of now five-year old Little Ricky and the couple's move to the suburbs. Ricky purchased the Tropicana and renamed it the Club Babalu and the family grew in affluence and began to tackle a variety of family issues.

One of the prime secrets of the show's success in addition to the chemistry among the four regulars was that the production team stayed relatively intact over the full run of the show. The writer/producer Jess Oppenheimer and the two regular writers Madelyn Pugh and Bob Carroll, Jr. came over with Ball from the *My Favorite Husband* radio show and only three directors were employed during the show's original production: Marc Daniels (1951-52), William Asher (1952-56), and James V. Kern (1955-56).

By 1957, however, Ball and Arnaz had grown tired of the weekly grind of series TV and ceased production of the program. But that was not the end of the characters. The characters were featured over the next three years, a series of 13 one-hour episodes airing as specials and as episodes of the *Westinghouse-Desilu Playhouse* which ran from 1958 to 1960. Their production company, Desilu, which was started primarily to produce *I Love Lucy,* grew from 12 employees in 1951 to 800 in 1957 and branched out into producing a number of well-regarded programs including *The Danny Thomas Show* for other networks and producers. In 1958, the company purchased the old RKO Studios and continued to be one of the most influential producers of the 1950s and 1960s.

The Arnazes divorced in 1960 and Ball went to New York to appear in a Broadway show *Wildcat.* She married comedian Gary

Morton and returned to network TV in 1962 with *The Lucy Show,* which also featured Vivian Vance and Gale Gordon. The show ran until 1968 when it was retitled *Here's Lucy* and featured Ball's real life children Lucie and Desi, Jr. Vance made only sporadic appearances between 1968 and 1971 but the show continued until 1974 as part of the CBS Monday night comedy block that dominated the ratings for the entire period that Ball's show ran.

—Steve Hanson and Sandra Garcia-Myers

FURTHER READING:

Andrews, Bart. *The I Love Lucy Book.* Garden City, New York, Doubleday, 1985.

Brooks, Tim, and Earle Marsh. *The Complete Directory to Prime Time Network and Cable TV Shows 1946 - Present.* New York, Ballantine Books, 1995.

Hill, Tom. *Nick at Night's Classic TV Companion.* New York, Simon and Schuster, 1966.

Horowitz, Susan. *Queens of Comedy.* Australia, Gordon and Breach Publishers, 1997.

Krohn, Katherine E. *Lucille Ball: Pioneer of Comedy.* Minneapolis, Lerner Publications, 1992.

McClay, Michael. *I Love Lucy: The Complete Picture History of the Most Popular TV Show Ever.* New York, Warner Books, 1995.

Mitz, Rick. *The Great TV Sitcom Book.* New York, A Perigee Book, 1983.

Oppenheimer, Jess. *Laughs, Luck and Lucy: How I Came to Create the Most Popular Sitcom of All Time.* New York, Syracuse University Press, 1996.

Waldron, Vince. *Classic Sitcoms.* New York, Macmillan Publishing, 1987.

Warner Bros. *Warner Bros. Presents Television Favorites.* Miami, Warner Bros. 1995.

I Spy

The popular NBC network program, *I Spy* ran for three years from 1965 to 1968. Arriving in the wake of the James Bond phenomenon in the mid-1960s, it was one of several American television series of the period whose fantastic plots revolved around matters of espionage. It was the alchemical starring partnership of Robert Culp and Bill Cosby, however, that elevated *I Spy* to the pantheon of well-loved and well-remembered escapist entertainment, although the duo was supported by scripts that were consistently witty. The stars played secret agents, who roamed the world masquerading as a professional tennis player (Culp) and his manager/trainer (Cosby). Cosby thus became the first black actor in American television to star in prime-time drama as a hero-character on an equal footing with his white fellow actors. Noteworthy, too, for its foreign locations, *I Spy* was filmed almost entirely outside the United States, frequently in Mexico, in the Mediterranean areas of Europe, and in Asia.

—David Lonergan

FURTHER READING:

Brooks, Tim, and Earle Marsh. *The Complete Directory to Prime Time Network TV Shows,* 5th edition. New York, Ballantine Books, 1992.

I Was a Teenage Werewolf

I Was a Teenage Werewolf is generally considered the first of a genre of horror films targeting teenage audiences. The birth of this genre can be attributed to television, drive-in theaters, and the rise of suburbia. Because adults in the 1950s were content to stay home and watch television, teenagers became the marketing targets of the motion picture industry. The film was the brainchild of 29-year-old producer, Herman Cohen. American International Pictures (AIP) released the film to much notoriety. In this very conservative and frightened era, parents and even the federal government felt the delinquency depicted in the film would promote the same type of behavior offscreen—there were government investigations which attempted to prove this. All this negative publicity brought teenagers to see the film in droves—it became AIP's biggest money maker of 1957 and spawned a series of films putting a different spin on the original title.

—Jill A. Gregg

FURTHER READING:

Arkoff, Samuel. *Flying Through Hollywood by the Seat of My Pants: From the Man Who Brought You I Was a Teenage Werewolf and Muscle Beach Party.* New Jersey, Carol Publishing Group, 1992.

McGee, Mark Thomas. *Fast and Furious: The Story of American International Pictures.* North Carolina, McFarland, 1984.

Iacocca, Lee (1924—)

Lee Iacocca grew up as a blunt-spoken, patriotic son of immigrants, and rose to become president of the Ford Motor Company and later, chief executive officer of the Chrysler Corporation.

Born Lido Anthony Iacocca in Allentown, Pennsylvania, in 1924, Iacocca earned an engineering degree from Lehigh University and a masters degree from Princeton University before joining Ford Motor Company as a student engineer in 1946. After less than a year he talked his way into a sales job and, at the age of thirty-three, became the head of all national car marketing at the company's Detroit headquarters. He became vice president and general manager of the Ford Division in 1960.

In his new position, Iacocca recognized the growing power of the youth market and organized a team to design a car for it. Iacocca repackaged the engine and platform from the moderately successful Ford Falcon and placed it within a European-inspired, stylish shell. The result was the Mustang, a small car that sat four people and weighed less than most cars on the road. At $2,300 each, Ford sold more than four hundred thousand Mustangs in 1964, its first model year. The car's styling captured the excitement of youth. The average age of car buyers was thirty-one. Soon Mustang clubs sprang up around the country, and Mustang paraphernalia such as key chains

Lee Iacocca

and hats were suddenly available everywhere. A picture of the Mustang ran simultaneously on the covers of both *Time* and *Newsweek,* and Lee Iacocca also appeared in it.

In 1970, Iacocca was named president of Ford, second in the company only to Chairman Henry Ford II. Iacocca soon brought out another successful car, the Cougar, as well as a large failure, the Pinto. When Iacocca's aggressive ambition and showboating drew the ire of Ford, a power struggle developed between the two men. As each attempted to outmaneuver the other, Ford installed other executives above his former number-two man. In 1978, Iacocca was fired. Ford Motor Company had earned profits of $1.8 billion in each of the previous two years.

Iacocca soon accepted the position of CEO at the unprofitable and debt-ridden Chrysler Corporation across town. He was famous when working at Ford, but at Chrysler, Iacocca built himself into a celebrity. The car industry in America traditionally represented the best successes of American capitalism. But, by the 1970s, it had come to signify inefficiency and the abdication of America's economic leadership role to international, or "foreign," competition. When Iacocca took over Chrysler, it was the smallest of the "big three" American automakers and was rapidly losing money and market share.

Iacocca made a number of radical, public steps to turn the company around. He did what was then unthinkable and lobbied the American government to bail Chrysler out of its financial problems. After a protracted public debate in the media and on Capitol Hill, both houses of Congress approved $1.5 billion dollars of loan guarantees for the company. Iacocca won discounts from his suppliers, wage concessions from his workers, and loan payment reschedulings from Chrysler's creditors. These actions were unprecedented. The auto industry had traditionally fought government interference and proudly recalled the day Henry Ford shocked the country by doubling his workers' wages. Its executives had boasted of how America's prosperity was tied to its successful auto industry.

As part of his aggressive salvage effort, Iacocca put a face on America's tenth largest corporation, appending his signature to Chrysler print ads, and personally appearing in its television ads. He played the role of the blunt, tough-talking, honest businessman by challenging the public, ''If you can find a better car—buy it!'' He not only personalized the fight to save Chrysler as *his* fight but represented it as America's fight to save itself. In Chrysler's television ads he appeared surrounded by red, white, and blue, entreating viewers, ''Let's make America mean something again.'' Iacocca's public persona was the right image at the right time. Under Ronald Reagan, a wave of patriotism swept the country, and the American carmaker's challenge to be proud of America and its products was met with a warm response.

In 1980, Chrysler released its line of utilitarian K-cars, similar in build to Iacocca's beloved Mustang but its polar opposite in terms of character and style. The K-cars were boxy, plain, and functional. They were spare, restrained cars for a time of diminished economic expectations. Iacocca, ever the patriot, boasted that, though they were small and light, they were still ''big enough to hold six Americans.'' His next move was to introduce the nation's first minivan. It was wildly successful, and other automakers soon released their own versions.

By 1984, the Chrysler Corporation had paid back its loans seven years early and was a remarkable success story by any measure. Iacocca was treated as a national hero and was considered a possible presidential candidate. In the mid-1980s, he published a best-selling autobiography and served as chairman of the commission that renovated the Statue of Liberty.

Iacocca retired from Chrysler in 1992. After his departure, he publicly criticized the new management's efforts to improve quality and, in 1996, joined an investment group seeking to acquire the automaker. The effort failed and, ironically, earned him such enmity from within Chrysler that it canceled plans to name its new headquarters after him.

As the father of the Mustang, Iacocca considered himself a ''car man'' who disdained the ''bean counters'' at Ford and understood what made automobiles magical and exhilarating to Americans. Though he depended on the government, his workers, his creditors, and his suppliers to help Chrysler out of trouble, his unabashed challenge to be proud of America and its products won him the image of a self-reliant patriot out to redeem the country. Throughout, Iacocca was a master creator of products, profits, and his own image.

—Steven Kotok

FURTHER READING:

Collier, Peter, and Chris Horowitz. *The Fords: An American Epic.* New York, Summit Books, 1987.

Iacocca, Lee, and William Novak. *Iacocca: An Autobiography.* New York, Bantam Books, 1984.

Ingrassia, Paul J., and Joseph B. White. *Comeback: The Rise and Fall of the American Automobile Industry.* New York, Simon & Schuster, 1994.

Levin, Doron P. *Behind the Wheel at Chrysler: The Iacocca Legacy.* New York, Harcourt Brace, 1995.

IBM (International Business Machines)

According to the *Washington Post,* ''IBM didn't invent the computer . . . it invented the computer industry.'' Eventually expanding to become the largest company in the world, International Business Machines (IBM) came to represent, at different points in its history, the best and the worst of big business and American corporate culture.

Charles Ranlegh Flint, the ''Father of Trusts,'' founded the Computing-Tabulating-Recording Company in 1911 upon the acquisition and merger of three manufacturers of such products as shopkeepers' scales, punch clocks, and large tabulating machines used by the census bureau. Flint hired Thomas J. Watson, Sr. to run his new company.

Watson was a star salesman and business executive at National Cash Register before joining what would become IBM. Upon his arrival, he implemented a system of territories, quotas, and commissions for his salesmen. The motto ''T-H-I-N-K'' was posted in all branch offices and salesmen were required to dress in sharp blue suits and white shirts. Those who met their quota joined the One Hundred Percent Club. The methods were successful, and by 1920, the company had tripled its revenues to $15.9 million. Watson renamed the firm International Business Machines in 1924. The sales focus and buttoned-up image Watson honed during the company's early days came to define IBM through the remainder of the twentieth century.

But beyond his sales focus, Thomas Watson was evangelical in his company pride and instilled his brand of optimism in his employees. He offered perks such as company sports teams, bands, and family outings. In the 1930s, IBM became one of the first companies to offer life insurance, survivor benefits, and paid vacations to its staff, and during World War II, it used profits from manufacture of weapons for the government to start a fund for widows and orphans of IBM war casualties.

From its origins as a manufacturer of tabulating machines, hawked by impeccably-dressed salesmen, IBM came to dominate the computer mainframe market in the 1950s, 1960s, and 1970s, earning the moniker, ''Big Blue.'' Fueled by the personal computer boom of the early 1980s, the company became the largest and most profitable corporation the world had yet known. Ranked as America's most admired company year after year in surveys of U.S. businesses, IBM astonished the business community and consumers alike with its consistent growth and profitability, its lifetime employment policy, famed management methods, crack sales force, and technological leadership. It represented to many the ideal of what American corporate culture and big business could achieve.

By the early 1990s, however, IBM had come to represent just the opposite. In a very public fall from grace, it recorded the largest ever loss in corporate history, abandoned its lifetime employment guarantee, and shed tens of thousands of workers. The company, it seemed, had become the epitome of an overgrown, anonymous, monopolistic,

An IBM computer and printer c. 1980s.

bureaucratic monster—outmatched in marketing and technology by swifter, nimbler competitors; too big to change, it appeared destined to collapse under its own ungainly weight. By the end of the twentieth century, though, IBM staged a turnaround, and reemerged as a profitable corporate giant once more.

From the beginning, IBM grew rapidly. Through the 1920s and 1930s, the company profited by renting electric punched-card accounting machines to large companies. During the Great Depression, famously holding to its optimism and faith that the economy would improve, the company continued production at full capacity, even as sales declined. By 1936, IBM held 85 percent of the office machine market, with sales of $26 million. New Deal programs, such as the Social Security Act of 1935, required businesses and government alike to keep more records, thus increasing the demand for IBM's punched-card tabulating systems. By 1940, IBM had revenues of $46 million and a workforce of nearly 13,000 employees. Wrote *Fortune* that same year, "The International Business Machines Corp. has beheld no past so golden as the present. The face of Providence is shining upon it . . . it has skirted the slough of the Great Depression . . . its growth has been strong and steady."

It was the mainframe computer business that propelled IBM's explosive growth in the post-war era. After World War II, Watson Sr. greatly increased the firm's research and development budget, and his son, Thomas Watson, Jr., championed computer development. In 1948, IBM installed one of its first computers, a-buzz with thousands of neon lamps, relays, switches, tape readers, and punches on the ground floor of its New York headquarters for passersby to gawk at through a window. By 1960, there were 5,000 computers in the United States, most of them made by IBM, whose annual revenues had ballooned to $1.6 billion.

During this period, IBM was legendary as a fair and generous employer. Watson, Sr. had not resorted to mass layoffs during the Depression, and continued to pay salaries to absent employees serving in World War II. The firm generously paid moving expenses for transferred employees, guaranteeing a minimum resale price for their homes and retraining spouses for jobs in their new cities. Most famous of all was IBM's guarantee of lifetime employment for all workers.

Through its introduction of what became large-scale public goods, the company became an institution. IBM created FORTRAN in 1957, the world's first widely accepted computer language. In 1964, it implemented the largest civilian computerization task ever undertaken, the revolutionary SABRE reservation system used by American Airlines, and proceeded to implement similar systems for the other major airlines. In 1973, IBM created and implemented the ubiquitous Universal Product Code and bar code systems used in supermarkets.

But IBM's core business was mainframe computers, and in this area, it held a 70 percent market share through the 1960s. Its competitors, left to split up the remainder of the industry, were often referred to in the business press as the "seven dwarfs." IBM's investment in research and development was unmatched. In the 1960s, the company undertook the largest ever development project up to that point, a five-billion-dollar effort to create the next generation of mainframe computers, an effort larger than the Manhattan Project.

As technology advanced, computing power became less concentrated in large mainframes and, by the mid-1970s, personal computers were possible in the home, each as powerful as the early mainframes of decades before. IBM's next challenge was to sell these types of computers, not directly to other businesses via its sales network as in the past, but to consumers through the retail market. In the early 1980s, the company unveiled its line of personal computers, which propelled its growth ever higher, even as new competitors such as

Apple Computer and Microsoft began to stake out claims in the growing market with their own rapid growth.

Dubbed by *Barron's,* "America's most beloved stock" and by *The Washington Post,* "long the bluest of the blue-chip performers," the reliability and size of IBM stock and dividend growth was renowned. Said *Barron's,* "just about everyone and his dog owns IBM." Watson, Jr. was labeled by *Fortune* Magazine, "the greatest capitalist in history." IBM was highlighted in the 1982 business book *In Search of Excellence.* It grew to be the most valuable company in the world in 1984, worth $72 billion and earning the largest profit ever to that point, $6.6 billion.

But as IBM's reputation was growing as a fair, wildly successful and innovative company, it was coming to represent something else, too. In 1969, the government began a 13-year, ultimately unsuccessful, anti-trust case against the accused monopolist. In 1975, IBM pulled the plug on its five-year Future Systems development project for the next generation of mainframe computers, effectively wasting over $100 million and many millions of staff hours. The impression was spreading that IBM was just too big and involved in too many businesses; too bureaucratic to execute or innovate, as a monopoly it just didn't have to try.

In 1984, the year of IBM's record profits and valuation, a comparatively small upstart, Apple Computer, ran a historic television advertisement during the Super Bowl. In the ad, an endless regiment of identical gray drones stared at a large screen, listening to a speech by an authoritarian leader—only to be freed by a colorful interloper who shatters the screen. This portrayal of "Big Blue" as "Big Brother" was an explicit reference to George Orwell's dystopic totalitarian vision in his novel *1984.*

The final blows came in the early 1990s, when the company suffered its first loss in history and its stock market value fell by more than half. In 1993, the company took a loss of $8.5 billion. Said *Barron's* in late 1992, "The old saw that IBM is always a safe stock pick, handed down through the generations . . . finally bit the dust last week." Also in 1992, *Fortune* wrote about IBM's "bulging, lethargic bureaucracy," and said, "employee morale is in the dumps," labeling the company a "humbled American corporate behemoth" with an "inward-looking culture" that had "lost touch with consumers." According to *The Wall Street Journal* in 1993, the company had "unraveled." IBM ran nearly one hundred different voluntary buyout and early retirement programs to reduce staff while trying to maintain its no-layoff policy.

By the late 1990s, IBM had largely recovered. By hiring its first ever CEO from outside the company, acquiring other firms, and selling off some of its businesses, it was able to regain profitability, but not its unquestioned dominance in what had become a much larger industry.

For many Americans, IBM—strong, paternalistic, and rapidly growing—was emblematic of the triumph of American corporate culture for most of the twentieth century. Indeed, their methods and image were similarly regarded internationally. This made its dramatic failures in the early 1990s all the more astonishing, as observers watched the company rapidly became a symbol for all that was wrong, not right, with corporate America. Its reemergence in the late 1990s saved the company, but not the rarefied ideal that large, benevolent corporations could represent the best of an ingenious, industrious, and compassionate American business culture. An American myth that IBM helped to create, it now helped to dispel.

—Steven Kotok

FURTHER READING:

Campbell-Kelly, Martin, and William Aspray. *Computer: A History of the Information Machine.* New York, HarperCollins, 1997.

Carrol, Paul. *Big Blues: The Unmaking of IBM.* New York, Crown Publishers, 1993.

Mills, Daniel Quinn, and G. Bruce Friesen. *Broken Promises: An Unconventional View of What Went Wrong at IBM.* Boston, Harvard Business School Press, 1996.

Pugh, Emerson W. *Building IBM: Shaping an Industry and Its Technology.* Boston, MIT Press, 1995.

Rodgers, William H. *Think; A Biography of the Watsons and IBM.* New York, Stein and Day, 1969.

Watson, Thomas J., and Peter Petre. *Father, Son and Co.* New York, Bantam Books, 1990.

Ice Cream Cone

The ice cream cone is a familiar feature of the American leisure landscape, carrying with it associations of fairgrounds, ice cream parlors, drugstore soda fountains, and all-American kids (and adults) enjoying a sunshine treat. Since its invention early in the twentieth century, the cone has spread to become a common confection all over the developed world. Ice cream itself was a popular confection in America as early as the 1800s, but was only placed in an edible

A triple scoop vanilla ice cream cone.

container 100 years later. The first patent for an ice cream cone maker was granted to New York City ice cream vendor Italo Marchiony in 1903, but aficionados continue to debate the true inventor of the cone. The popularity of the ice cream cone dates to the 1904 St. Louis Exposition, when Ernest Hamwi, a Syrian who sold waffles next to an ice cream concessionaire, thought to combine the two treats, creating the "World's Fair Cornucopia"—a portable way to eat ice cream.

During the 1920s and 1930s, new cone designs came out almost every year, resembling real or fanciful objects such as skyscrapers and rocket ships, but by the 1940s, two main types dominated the cone market—the flat-bottomed "waffle" cone cast from batter, and the pointed "sugar" cone, made from a large waffle-patterned wafer. Along with the rise of specialist ice cream shops like Ben & Jerry's in the 1980s came a new interest in homemade cones. Sometimes costing as much as the ice cream itself, the new waffle cones, hand-baked and hand-rolled, are offered in a variety of flavors, including chocolate, chocolate chip, oat bran, and honey.

—Wendy Woloson

FURTHER READING:

Damerov, Gail. *Ice Cream! The Whole Scoop.* Lakewood, Colorado, Glenbridge Publishing Ltd., 1995.

Dickson, Paul. *The Great American Ice Cream Book.* New York, Atheneum, 1972.

Funderburg, Anne. *Vanilla, Chocolate, and Strawberry: A History of American Ice Cream.* Bowling Green, Ohio, Bowling Green State University Popular Press, 1995.

Gustaitis, John. "Who Invented the Ice Cream Cone?" *American History Illustrated.* Vol. XXII, No. IV, 1988, 42-44.

Ice Shows

No sport grew as phenomenally during the last two decades of the twentieth century as figure skating. Having been a favorite sport among women, its popularity was bolstered by Olympic gold medal winners Peggy Fleming (1968), Janet Lynn (1972), Dorothy Hamill (1976), Scott Hamilton (1984), Brian Boitano (1988), and Kristi Yamaguchi (1992). While diehard fans followed the sport through various ice shows, competitions, and television performances, it was the bumbling fiasco of the attack on Nancy Kerrigan in 1994 by the cohorts of a jealous Tonya Harding that propelled figure skating into the news headlines. By the end of the twentieth century, it ranked second behind pro football in television ratings. It is particularly significant that the sport came so far after suffering the devastating loss of its entire roster of top skaters and coaches in an airplane crash on the way to the World Championships in Lyon, France, on February 5, 1961.

Though ice shows benefitted greatly from a new surge in popularity with increased exposure and million-dollar incomes for top skaters, ice shows had been an American tradition since the early twentieth century. The first show was held at the Hippodrome in New York City in 1915. It was followed by an ice ballet imported from Berlin, *Flirting in St. Moritz,* which ran for an unprecedented 300 days and inspired the movie *The Frozen Warning* in 1916. The Ice Follies began in 1936 and continued to entertain audiences for 30 years. Ice skating had its super stars even in its early days. Norwegian

skating sensation Sonja Henie enticed fans to ice shows by the thousands and eventually skated her way into Hollywood films.

The Ice Capades was the most venerable of ice shows. Beginning on February 14, 1940, in Hershey, Pennsylvania, it featured some of the greatest names in ice skating: Dick Button, Scott Hamilton, Jane Torvil, Christopher Dean, and Dorothy Hamill, who bought the show in 1991. Hamill believed that the focus of the show should be on telling a story rather than on the disjointed vaudevillian skits of the past. *Cinderella Frozen in Time,* for example, turned the classic fairy tale into a skating spectacular. Unfortunately, the Ice Capades foundered under her stewardship.

In 1986, after Scott Hamilton won the 1984 gold medal for men's figure skating, he determined that skaters should have more opportunity for participating in the sport they loved. The result was Stars on Ice, sponsored chiefly by Discover Stars of America. Each year, roughly a dozen top skaters spend December through April touring the country, providing fans with performances that are elegant, breathtaking, or funny. A number of other ice shows, including Campbell's Tour of World Champions and Disney's World on Ice, have followed suit. Before the establishment of these modern ice shows, skaters often performed in ten to twelve shows a week, a grueling schedule that sapped both their energies and their talents. While the shows appear glamorous, they require hard work from skaters who spend much of the year traveling from city to city and rarely staying long enough to enjoy the local sights. They frequently spend holidays away from their families and friends, and members of the professional skating world often fall victim to broken relationships that cannot survive the strain.

For fans, though, ice shows are memorable events. No other sport offers the diversity of so much talent. Whether it be the spectacular jumps of Brian Boitano, the crazy antics of Scott Hamilton, the sheer beauty of Kristi Yamaguchi, the elegance of Ekaterina Gordeeva, the awesomeness of Isabelle Brasseur and Lloyd Eisler, the innovativeness of Jane Torvil and Christopher Dean, the athleticism of Surya Bonaly, or the unexpectedness of Gary Beacom, ice shows are sheer magic.

In addition to the traveling shows, television has become a smorgasbord of skating talent. Virtually every major skater has had at least one television show devoted to his or her talents. In 1988 Brian Boitano became the first male athlete to have his own television special with *Canvas on Ice.* In addition, his *Skating Romance* specials were featured annually on American television. In December 1998, the USA network aired *Skate against Hate,* one of a number of theme-related shows with Boitano as both producer and star. Peggy Fleming, a frequent star of skating specials after bringing home the gold in 1968, joined co-host Dick Button in serving as commentator for ice skating competitions. Scott Hamilton frequently joins them, along with appearing in specials of his own, such as *Disney's Scott Hamilton Upside Down.* Both Nancy Kerrigan and Kristi Yamaguchi also became regular hosts for skating events. Canadian Elvis Stojko appeared in *Elvis on Ice.* Russian skater Ekaterina Gordeeva starred in the Christmas specials featuring Snowden the snowman. Boitano joined Russian skaters Oksana Baiul and Viktor Petrenko in an ice show version of *The Nutcracker Suite.*

With its phenomenal success, ice skating has become a gold mine for skaters and promoters alike. Kristi Yamaguchi reportedly earned three to four million dollars a year in the late 1990s. Other millionaire skaters include Brian Boitano, Scott Hamilton, Nancy Kerrigan, and Oksana Baiul. Michelle Kwan and Tara Lipinski, who won the Olympic silver and gold respectively in the 1998 Olympics, were well on the way to joining that elite group by the end of the century. Paul Wylie, 1992 silver medalist, chose to continue skating over entering Harvard Law School, declaring that he would be foolish to give up the income of a high profile professional skater. Given their enormous popularity and ability to rake in huge revenues, ice shows will continue to entertain a besotted American public and inspire young skaters to reach for the gold.

—Elizabeth Purdy

FURTHER READING:

Boitano, Brian, and Suzanne Harper. *Boitano's Edge: Inside the Real World of Figure Skating.* New York, Simon and Schuster, 1997.

Brennan, Christine. *Edge of Glory: The Inside Story of the Quest for Figure Skating's Olympic Gold Medals.* New York, Penguin, 1999.

———. *Inside Edge: A Revealing Journey into the Secret World of Figure Skating.* New York, Anchor, 1997.

Gordeeva, Ekaterina, with E.M. Swift. *My Sergei: A Love Story.* New York, Werner Books, 1996.

Torvil, Jane, and Christopher Dean, with John Man. *The Autobiography of Ice Dancing's Greatest Stars.* Secaucus, New Jersey, Birch Lane Press Books, 1996.

Ice-T (1958—)

Releasing his first track, "The Coldest Rapper," in 1983, Ice-T became Los Angeles's first rap artist. He has since become one of America's most outspoken rappers, boasting a violent past in which he claims to have been shot twice. Indeed, his name was inspired by

Ice-T

former pimp and best-selling author Iceberg Slim. Ice-T recalled in his book *The Ice-T Opinion,* "He would talk in rhyme—hustler-like stuff—and I would memorize lines. People in school would always ask me to recite them." Ice-T's experiences as a gang member provided the material for four albums in three years. Although the first rapper to have warning stickers placed on his album sleeves, Ice-T emerged as a voice for dispossessed black youth. He went on to become an institution on the West Coast, running his own record company, Rhythm Syndicate.

Ice-T was born Tracy Marrow in Newark, New Jersey. Following his parents' death he moved to Los Angeles and attended Crenshaw High School in South Central L.A. His journey to the big time was anything but smooth. He made several records and appeared in three hip-hop films, *Rappin'* (1985), *Breakin'* (1984), and *Breakin' II,* without any notable success. It wasn't until a few years later that he signed a record deal with Sire Records, releasing his debut album *Rhyme Pays* in 1987. While most of the album's tracks dealt with the familiar topics of sex and women (for example, "I Love Ladies" and "Sex"), two stood out in particular: "6 in the Morning" and "Squeeze the Trigger." These tracks were to define the subject matter of Ice-T's later hardcore rapping: living in the ghetto, street violence, criminal activity, and survival. He stated, "I try to walk the edge. I'm going to tell you what you need to hear, not what you want to hear." Indeed, it was the latter track that inspired actor/director Dennis Hopper to ask Ice-T to contribute the title song to his movie *Colors* (1988), a brutal depiction of gang culture in L.A.

Following the success of the track "Colors," Ice-T released his second album *Power* (1988). The record depicts an L.A. cityscape that would not be out of place on the set of a blaxploitation movie: pimps, hookers, hit men, cars, and drugs. This was backed up by wah-wah guitar riffs and samples borrowed from Curtis Mayfield giving the album the sound of 1970s funk. On "I'm Your Pusherman," Ice-T lifted a track wholesale from Mayfield's *Superfly.*

Ice-T's third album, *Freedom of Speech* (1989), seemed to demarcate a shift to an even more militant stance. The track "Lethal Weapon" recalls Public Enemy's "Miuzi Weighs a Ton," adopting a violent persona with lines such as "I'm a nigger on the trigger/ Madder than a pit bull." Ice-T still had not discarded his earlier pimp/player image, which is evidenced in his fourth album *Original Gangster (O.G.)* (1991). The title of the album coined a new phrase that entered the rap lexicon, and the album as a whole was placed alongside some of rap's best recordings.

Ice-T recorded two more albums, *Home Invasion* (1993) and *Born Dead* (1994), as a solo artist and appeared in several films, the most notable being his part as a cop in *New Jack City* (1991). In addition to his solo performances, Ice-T also formed a spinoff metal/hardcore band called *Body Count* that released an eponymous album in 1992. The inclusion of the notorious track "Cop Killer" ensured further headlines and earned Ice-T the number-two slot on the FBI National Threat list.

As Ice-T continued to appear in films and on television throughout the 1990s, the controversy he incited receded. His gangster persona was copied and perfected by many other West Coast "gangsta" rappers such as Snoop Doggy Dogg and Dr. Dre. Nonetheless, it could be argued that without Ice-T these rappers would not have become a part of popular culture in America, for he was the first West-Coast rapper to gain respect in rap's birthplace, New York City.

—Nathan Abrams

FURTHER READING:

Fernando, Jr., S.H. *The New Beats: Exploring the Music Culture and Attitudes of Hip-Hop.* Edinburgh, Payback Press, 1995.

Ice-T. *The Ice Opinion: Who Gives a Fuck?* New York, St. Martin's Press, 1994.

Nelson, Havelock, and Michael A. Gonzales. *Bring the Noise: A Guide to Rap Music and Hip-Hop Culture.* New York, Harmony Books, 1991.

In Living Color

Airing on Fox Television from 1990-1994, the series *In Living Color* was the first sketch comedy to feature a majority African American cast. Keenan Ivory Wayans was the creative force behind the show, which included his brother, Damon Wayans, and a smattering of other comic actors such as David Alan Grier, Tommy Davidson, Chris Rock, and Jim Carrey. *In Living Color* brought to the screen lasting characters like Homey the Clown, gay film critics Blaine and Antoine in "Men on Film" (with their ratings system of "two snaps up"), and the oblivious Fire Marshal Bill, in addition to a troupe of well-choreographed female dancers ("Fly Girls") that appeared after skits. Though the show was sometimes criticized for its stereotypes and objectionable material, it was nevertheless respected for being the first to address urban themes in such a context.

—Geri Speace

FURTHER READING:

Brumley, Al. "'In Living Color' Brightens with Age." *The Dallas Morning News.* October 7, 1997, 1C.

Justin, Neal. "The Wonderful World of 'Color.'" *Star Tribune.* August 26, 1997, 1E.

The Incredible Hulk

The Incredible Hulk is one of Marvel Comics' most popular superheroes. Created in 1962 by Stan Lee and Jack Kirby, the Hulk is a green-skinned brute with enormous physical strength, dull wits, and a hot temper. He is the alter-ego of Dr. Bruce Banner, a nuclear physicist accidentally exposed to gamma radiation. Banner transforms into the Hulk during times of stress.

Along with Spider-Man, the Hulk established Marvel's definitive formula of troubled superheroes alienated from the society that they fight to protect. Constantly misunderstood by the public and persecuted by the authorities, the Hulk became a natural favorite among young people during the 1960s and 1970s who identified themselves with anti-establishment trends.

The Hulk's popularity peaked in the late 1970s when his comic book was adapted into a successful prime-time CBS TV series. Despite frequent revisions in the Hulk's appearance and character during the 1980s and 1990s, he remains one of the most recognizable superheroes ever produced by the comic-book industry.

—Bradford Wright

FURTHER READING:

Daniels, Les. *Marvel: Five Fabulous Decades of the World's Greatest Comics.* New York, Harry N. Abrams, 1991.

Lee, Stan. *Origins of Marvel Comics.* New York, Simon and Schuster, 1974.

Independence Day

Directed by Roland Emmerich, *Independence Day* was an epic film about an apocalyptic invasion of the Earth by extraterrestrials. The film opened in July of 1996 to enormous box-office profits. It benefitted from a canny advertising campaign featuring as its centerpiece a shot of the destruction of the White House and set a record by collecting $100 million in six days. *Independence Day* went on to earn $306 million, putting it among the top ten highest grossing films ever. Most critics were less kind to the film, pointing to its stereotypical ethnic characters, an implausible *deus ex machina* ending, and a rather nationalistic subtext disingenuously cloaked behind its multicultural pretensions. Others pointed to the extremely derivative nature of the film, including not-so-subtle science fiction borrowings from *The War of the Worlds, The Day the Earth Stood Still, Alien, Star Wars, Close Encounters of the Third Kind, V,* and *The X Files.* Nevertheless, audiences flocked to *Independence Day,* making it the cinematic success story of 1996.

Set in the month of July during a year in the early twenty-first century, the film opens ominously, with a shot of a gigantic shadow, accompanied by rumbles and tremors, passing over the site of mankind's first lunar landing. Scientific and military organizations alike quickly detect that an immense object one-fourth the size of the moon, apparently under intelligent control, is taking up a position in near-Earth orbit. The object, which turns out to be a mother ship, releases 15 smaller, but still miles across, disc-shaped craft that enter the Earth's atmosphere in clouds of fire to hover silently over major world cities. The film then introduces its major characters, all of whom will transcend personal failure to become heroes in the upcoming battle: the politically embattled U.S. President and veteran Gulf War pilot, Thomas Whitmore; Steven Hiller, an F-16 pilot and failed NASA applicant; Jasmine Dubrow, Hiller's exotic-dancer girlfriend; David Levinson, a New York cable-television scientist who has failed at his marriage and his career; Constance Spano, Levinson's ex-wife and aide to President Whitmore; and Russell Casse, an alcoholic cropduster and Vietnam War veteran pilot. As a panicked civilization becomes increasingly destabilized, Levinson discovers that the discs are using Earth's satellites to synchronize a countdown to a simultaneous worldwide attack. Accompanied by his father, Levinson convinces Constance to tell the president about the imminent attack. Though the news comes too late for any effective evacuation, the president, some of his staff, and the Levinsons are able to escape Washington just as the discs, acting in concert, fire their primary weapons to create firestorms that engulf and utterly destroy the world's major cities, including New York and Los Angeles.

The second part of the film focuses on mankind's counterattack against the alien invaders. The president, who has lost his wife in the invasion, personally commands the national, and eventually worldwide, effort. Hiller not only survives a massive but futile F-16 attack on one of the discs and its hordes of fighters, but also manages to shoot down and capture alive one of the aliens. During the counteroffensive, Whitmore learns to his anger that a covert branch of the government, kept secret even from the president, has been studying an alien fighter, captured in the late 1950s, at the infamous Area 51 in the Nevada desert. Through close inspection of the captured ship, Levinson finds that he will be able to introduce a disabling computer virus into the alien computer network, provided someone can dock the smaller fighter with the mother ship. Hiller volunteers to fly the alien fighter. Meanwhile, the president and Russell Casse, among other volunteers, suit up to fly a coordinated F-16 attack against all of the discs the second the virus paralyzes the alien craft and lowers their shields. Whitmore delivers an inspirational speech to the amassed volunteers shortly before the attack. Even with the virus successfully introduced and the shields down, however, the discs prove too hardy for missiles until Casse's suicide plunge into a disc's primary weapon shows the other pilots how to bring the discs down. Hiller and Levinson, barely escaping the destruction of the mother ship, fly back to Earth to find that the smaller discs have all been destroyed as well. The victory, which takes place on July 4, ensures that Independence Day will no longer be only an American holiday.

German born Roland Emmerich and American Dean Devlin, the creative duo behind *Independence Day,* first teamed up in the United States for 1992's *Universal Soldier,* which starred Jean Claude Van Damme. Emmerich and Devlin achieved name-recognition status and modest commercial success with 1994's *Stargate,* a film about aliens, time travel, the modern military, and ancient Egypt. For *Stargate,* Emmerich directed, co-wrote, and co-produced and Devlin co-wrote and co-produced, as would be the case with their next project. According to its creators, *Independence Day* was conceived to be an homage to war and adventure movies, specifically the 1970s epic-scale and multi-character disaster movies. The chairman of Twentieth Century-Fox, Peter Chernin, agreed to back Emmerich and Devlin's project. Solid, recognizable actors such as Will Smith (Steve Hiller), Bill Pullman (President Whitmore), Jeff Goldblum (David Levinson), Randy Quaid (Russell Casse), Mary McDonnell (the First Lady), Judd Hirsch (doting Jewish father Julius Levinson), Harvey Fierstein (David's boss Marty Gilbert), and Brent Spiner (in a brief but unforgettable cameo as the outlandish Dr. Brakkish Okun, scientific leader at the Area 51 research facility) were cast. Location shooting began in 1995. Manhattan provided an urban background for crowd reaction shots to the awe-inspiring arrival of the interstellar visitors. The Bonneville Salt Flats in Utah served as a panoramic backdrop for the scene where Hiller leads an enormous caravan of refugees to the Area 51 facility. The hangars of the old Hughes aircraft facility in Los Angeles housed the special effects facilities involving the film's extensive pyrotechnic and miniatures (aircraft, cities, alien ships) work. In postproduction, dozens of computer-generated images were combined with existing special effects shots to create an intricately layered, visually spectacular depiction of the alien invasion. (The special effects won the 1996 Academy Award in that category.) The film ultimately cost $71 million, which was not an extravagant amount by 1990s cinematic budgetary standards. The resultant financial success of *Independence Day* placed enormous pressure on Emmerich and Devlin to produce a film of similar spectacle and profitability as a follow-up. However, their 1998 film *Godzilla,* while profitable, was considered to be one of 1998's big-budget flops. Also released in 1998, the laser disc edition of *Independence Day* is eight minutes longer than the already lengthy theatrical release, primarily because of additional dialogue between the principal characters and

one scene involving Dr. Okun's inspection of the interior of the alien fighter.

—Philip L. Simpson

FURTHER READING:

Aberly, Rachel, and Volker Engel. *The Making of Independence Day.* New York, HarperCollins, 1997.

Rogin, Michael. *Independence Day.* Bloomington, Indiana University Press, 1998.

The Indian

Numerous tribes of Indian people populated the Americas for thousands of years before the arrival of Europeans. As Jack Weatherford writes in his book, *Indian Givers,* these peoples created great architectural monuments, made intelligent use of natural resources, created new plant species through selective breeding, made great discoveries in mathematical and astronomical knowledge, and reshaped the physical landscape. But as impressive as the achievements of Indian peoples have been, the *image* of "the Indian"—in literature, in the visual arts, in advertising, in entertainment, and elsewhere—has cast a far longer shadow upon the consciousness of the Euro-American society than the living individuals themselves. This has been true since the earliest days of European contact.

One of the earliest outlets for disseminating the image of "the Indian" was the outpouring of "Indian captivity narratives," which began in the early eighteenth century. These popular writings recorded hair-raising tales—both true and fictional—of settlers captured by Indians. Bearing titles such as *The Redeemed Captive Returning to Zion* (1707) by Massachusetts minister John Williams, they followed a rather predictable formula. In it, a white hero or heroine was abducted, underwent sufferings and even torture, was initiated into Indian society, but was finally and miraculously delivered once again to his or her own people, through the grace of God. The Indian which emerged out of these narratives was typically a *savage beast*: primitive, sadistic, cunning, filthy, villainous, and altogether terrifying. Especially in the Puritan era, he was often shown as a direct tool of Satan, and he shrank not even from such vile acts as human mutilation, dismemberment, and cannibalism.

The captivity narratives were more than just a well-loved form of American entertainment, although they were certainly that: virtually no first edition copies of captivity narratives exist today because people actually read them until the pages disintegrated. But besides diverting their audience, the captivity narratives also instructed. Their wide circulation made them a very influential source of information about Indians in both America and Europe, and one which allowed the Puritans to think through their place and mission in the "New World." In them, America became the new, biblical "Promised Land" to be given over to them, the children of God, after the occupying hordes of pagans, the children of Satan, had been driven out.

It is hardly the case, however, that all the images of the Indian in America have been negative. To stand alongside the "bad Indian" of the captivity narratives, Americans also invented a "good Indian" or "noble savage." The good Indian was handsome, strong, gentle, kind, brave, intelligent, and unfettered by the artificiality and various corruptions of "civilized" life. One powerful version of the "good Indian" appeared in the early nineteenth century. This was the image of the Indian as *wise healer*. By this time, Euro-Americans had discovered that American Indians had a sophisticated knowledge of a great many medical procedures and preparations (including bone setting, febrifuges, and painkillers). Whereas the "bad Indian" had been ideologically useful to the dominant society, the Indian healer turned out to be commercially useful. White purveyors of patent medicine began capitalizing on widespread respect for Indian medical knowledge by associating their products with Indians, and traveling medicine shows such as the Kiowa Indian Medicine and Vaudeville Company often featured Indian performers. Unfortunately, however, the main ingredients in patent medicines commonly consisted of alcohol, cocaine, or opium, rather than any of the more useful therapeutic substances known to Indian physicians. The increasing sensationalization of medicine shows, along with the professionalization and increasing social power of white physicians, eventually caused "Indian medicine" to fall into disrepute.

Nevertheless, "the Indian" did not disappear from public consciousness with the eclipse of the "healer" image. In 1883, William F. ("Buffalo Bill") Cody introduced a new kind of traveling entertainment, the wild West show, which also featured Indian performers. Here, however, these performers appeared as ferocious *warriors*. In staged battles, they assaulted wagon trains, fired off volleys of arrows, and displayed impressive equestrian skills. Many Indian people—including even the great Sioux chief Sitting Bull—acted in these shows. The same warrior image had been featured in the cheap paperbacks of the mid-nineteenth century known as "dime novels," and it was eventually transferred with little alteration into Western movies, the first and most famous of which was *The Great Train Robbery*. Like the captivity narratives which were their literary forebears, the Western movies frequently thematized the savage horrors which awaited whites who fell into Indian hands. "Save the last bullet for yourself" was Hollywood's oft-repeated advice to anyone fending off an Indian attack.

The Western shows, books, and movies defined the war-bonneted Plains tribesman as *the* prototypical or "real" Indian. This image has remained the standard against which Indian-ness was commonly measured even into the closing years of the twentieth century. Yet those years have also introduced some new roles for this standardized Indian to play. One of the more important is the role of the *gentle ecologist*. American boys' and girls' clubs such as the Scouts, Woodcraft Indians, and Campfire Girls played a significant role in the dissemination of this, another "good Indian" image, ever since the early years of the twentieth century. The clubs packed young people off to summer camps with Indian-sounding names where they were to enjoy outdoor sports and natural living after the supposed fashion of native peoples, who were imagined as innocent children of nature with a deep knowledge of its secrets. American youths progressed within the hierarchy of the clubs by acquiring knowledge of such things as woodsmanship, nature lore, and the production of rustically imagined Indian crafts such as "buckskin" clothing and birchbark models.

Commercial advertising has also made free use of the ecologist image, and its best-known representative was the late Iron Eyes Cody, an actor who starred in an educational campaign for the nonprofit organization, Keep America Beautiful, in the 1970s. The television

advertisement in which Cody rode a horse down a beach polluted with garbage, silently surveyed the desecration of the land, and finally allowed a single tear to slip down his weathered cheek, burned itself into the minds of an entire generation of Americans. The advertisement is interesting for at least two reasons. For one thing, it reveals a great deal about how Americans conceptualize "the Indian." Its remarkable symbolic efficacy both depends upon and illustrates some of the most powerful modern racial stereotypes: that Indians are typically stoic and unemotional (what depth of suffering can move an *Indian* to tears!) and that they are bound to the natural world in a romanticized and inexpressible union. For another thing, although Iron Eyes Cody is still one of the most recognized "Indian" figures in America, he was *not* of Indian ancestry. Rather, he was the son of two Italian immigrants. In this, Cody is a typical Hollywood figure. Whereas many of the performers in the early wild West shows were, in fact, Indians, many of the best known actors who later played them in films and on television have not been.

If Americans in the 1970s used the imagery of the Indian to address developing ecological values and concerns, they had other uses for it as well. This was a period in which the hopefulness with which the post-World War II generation had once viewed science and technology had begun to fade, and in which Americans had become increasingly discontented with the visions for human fulfillment which these held out. People expressed a renewed interest in spirituality, but many of them found the faiths of their parents unsatisfying. They turned, accordingly, to non-Western traditions, including those of American Indians. Out of this burgeoning spiritual discontent was born the image of the *mystical ceremonialist*. Americans were widely introduced to this impressive personage by anthropologist Carlos Castaneda. In his long series of fictionalized books, starting with *Journey to Ixtlan* (once considered to be accurate ethnography), Castaneda relates the story of his supposed tutelage by "Don Juan," a Yaqui *brujo,* or possessor of traditional Indian sacred knowledge. The articulation of Castaneda's immensely popular works with the counterculture's interest in the use of mind-altering drugs to expand ordinary consciousness is evident; he describes in detail the many revelatory experiences that he had while under the influence of peyote (a substance officially classified in the United States as a hallucinogenic drug, but which some tribal peoples use, under carefully controlled ceremonial conditions, as a sacrament).

The mystical ceremonialist did not disappear when other preoccupations of the counterculture fell by the wayside. Instead, he was reinvented in the 1980s and 1990s by adherents of that loose association of movements collected together under the rubric of "New Age" spirituality. The "New Age" includes religious believers who may call themselves Wiccans, goddess worshippers, Druids, eco-feminists, and many other names. Its followers have replaced their predecessors' preoccupation with drugs with an equally intense interest in a variety of esoteric subjects such as reincarnation, crystals, alternative healing, astral projection, extra-sensory perception, and the like. Accompanying all these various fascinations is a frequent attraction to (more or less accurately reproduced) versions of traditional, American Indian ceremonial practices. The New Age faithful ravenously consume "how-to" manuals penned by Indian "shamans" (often self-proclaimed and fraudulent), who purport to reveal everything from the sacred beliefs and rituals of Indian medicine people to their secret sexual practices. Inquirers also crowd seminars, workshops, and "spiritual retreats" claiming to offer the experience of Indian rituals and they flock to reservations and sacred sites to participate in Indian ceremonies. Some non-Indians have associated themselves so closely with this recent image of the mystical Indian as to assert that they were "Indian in a past life," even though they currently exist in a non-Indian body.

The upsurge of interest in Indian sacred rituals created by the image of the mystical Indian has created a great deal of tension in Indian communities. As Cherokee scholar Andy Smith writes in her ironic essay, "For All Those Who Were Indian in a Former Life," "nowadays anyone can be Indian if he or she wants to. All that is required is that one be Indian in a former life, or take part in a sweat lodge, or be mentored by a 'medicine woman,' or read a how-to book. . . . This furthers the goals of white supremacists to abrogate treaty rights and take away what little we [Indians] have left. When everyone becomes an 'Indian,' then it is easy to lose sight of the specificity of oppression faced by those who are Indian in *this* life."

Of all the many images of Indians which have remained with Americans into the last years of the twentieth century, perhaps the most vulgarly stereotyped appears in the sports mascot. Professional and college teams include the Kansas City Chiefs, the Atlanta Braves, and the Florida State Seminoles. Innumerable high schools similarly name themselves the "Indians," "Injuns," and "Savages." Indian mascots range from the Cleveland Indians' clownishly grinning "Chief Wahoo" to the Washington Redskins' dignified silhouette of a warrior. Fans for all these teams frequently sport feathers and "war paint" at games, give "war whoops," beat "tom-toms" and perform the "tomahawk chop," a slicing gesture intended to encourage the players to "scalp" the other team.

Non-Indian (and some Indian) commentators contend that sports mascots are intended to honor American Indians and their historic record of bravery in battle. However, many others, including representatives of the American Indian Movement and the American Indian Education Commission, have protested. They complain that the use of Indian names and imagery suggests a blind spot where this specific racial group is concerned. Brian Barnard, in "Would You Cheer for the Denver Darkies?," wonders if anyone would fail to see the offensive implications of a team which "honored" African Americans by christening itself as the title of his piece suggests. And what if the same team sponsored half-time shows featuring mascots in blackface and Afro wigs, who danced around grunting their own version of supposed African chants?

Some Indian leaders have brought lawsuits against particular sports teams, alleging racial discrimination or human rights violations. So far, these suits have not succeeded, but protests against mascots have made some headway. For instance, in 1994, the University of Iowa announced that it would no longer play non-conference athletic events against teams which employed Indian names or symbols. Several universities have banned from their campuses the buffoonish Chief Illiniwek, a white University of Illinois student dressed as an Indian, who performs at half-time. And some newspapers (including the *Minneapolis Star Tribune* and the Portland *Oregonian*) have decided not to print the names of specific teams with Indian names or mascots. Instead, they simply refer to "the Washington team," "the Atlanta team," and so on. Teams themselves have sometimes opened discussions on the question of whether they should change their names or their mascots, but the suggestions are frequently met with angry resistance from fans. Avis Little Eagle reports in a 1994 *Indian Country Today* article, that

students at the University of Illinois recently responded to such a proposal with the slogan, "save the chief, kill the Indian people."

American popular culture has played host to a diversity of images of "the Indian" over a period of several hundred years. Through all the changes, however, certain things have remained fairly constant. One is the tendency of the Indian to function as a magnifying mirror of Euro-American values and concerns. Non-Indians have persistently made and remade their ideas about Indians to serve the social goals of every historic period. Indians have functioned sometimes as a vehicle for social criticism, as in the ecology movement's exploitation of associations between Indians and nature which reproved American irresponsibility toward the land. They have served, at other times, as a foil against which non-Indians have displayed all that is right with America and the European settlement thereof. This is nowhere more evident than in the wild west shows which boldly dramatized the juggernaut of conquest: the inevitable and laudable progress of "civilization" over all that was savage, primitive, untamed.

A second constant in popular imagery of Indians is the assumption that their cultures and peoples are "vanishing"—that they have died out, or will soon do so. James Fenimore Cooper's much-loved, nineteenth-century novel, *The Last of the Mohicans*, and a great many romanticized, popular artworks of a related theme, depend for their poignant appeal upon this motif. See, for instance, Frederick Remington's easily recognized bronze, "The End of the Trail," which Remington described as depicting the hapless, homeless, and helpless Indian, discovering himself driven to the final, Western rim of the American continent by European expansion. A corollary of the vanishing Indian theme is the belief that there are no more "real" Indians: that those who may *claim* an Indian identity today have lost the culture which once distinguished them from other Americans, and their racial "authenticity" along with it.

Finally, throughout American popular culture runs a constant and pronounced fascination with the idea that non-Indians can "become" Indians. The fantasy is tirelessly replayed all the way from the earliest captivity narratives through modern movies (including such blockbusters as *Little Big Man* and the more recent *Dances with Wolves*), which frequently feature protagonists who somehow traverse the great racial divide between red and white. The New Age sensibility, which allows the overburdened, modern executive briefly to exchange his or her Fortune 500 responsibilities for a weekend spent "crying for a vision" (with the able assistance of a shaman-for-hire), is a final (and often extremely capital-intensive) culmination of this journey of the non-Indian imagination.

Clearly, the use of "the Indian" in popular culture betrays complex psychological dynamics which have manifested themselves on a national scale. No doubt the ability of "the Indian" to serve as a projection screen against which the dominant society has played out both its greatest aspirations and anxieties—whatever those implied at the moment—derives in large part from the essential *emptiness* of the image. As Robert Berkhofer suggested in his book, *The White Man's Indian*, at no time has the Indian in popular culture ever been developed into an actual person. Instead, he is invariably bereft of complexity, motive, personality, or other individualizing features. The result is an infinite possibility, a metaphor which can be employed to give substance to the most starkly diverse ideas. Because "the Indian" is simply a container to be filled with the purposes of the speaker, he can be used interchangeably as, for instance, the symbol of savagery *and* as the symbol of primal innocence.

The persistent themes of the vanishing Indian and of the non-Indian who becomes an Indian are a bit harder to explain than America's ability to use "the Indian" as a vehicle for exploring and communicating an enormous range of its own concerns and interests. Jack Forbes addresses this problem in his essay, "The Manipulation of Race, Caste, and Identity: Classifying AfroAmericans, Native Americans and Red-Black People." He suggests that the aforementioned themes originate in Americans' persisting knowledge of themselves as aliens in a "New World" wrested from its first inhabitants only through unspeakable violence. From the beginning of the European occupation of America, he writes, Indians "had to vanish because they were a threat or an impediment to the colonial settlers. That is, the colonial settlers could not truly become 'native' until the real natives were gone. . . . " Moreover, Forbes continues, "[t]his is the most compelling reason why 'Indians' must still vanish. Their continued existence as a separate population is a constant reminder of the foreignness" of American immigrants. This theory addresses not only the enduring American fascination with the vanishing Indian, but also with the idea of "becoming" Indian. Changing one's racial identification is a way to complete the symbolic journey from conqueror to conquered and to achieve vindication for the national sins of the past.

Nevertheless, with Indian people as with humorist Mark Twain, "reports of their death have been greatly exaggerated." The last decades of the twentieth century have seen many important contributions to popular culture which speak in the voice of individuals who have most certainly *not* "vanished." These works honestly express and address the concerns and values common to Indian people themselves, rather than those of the larger society, and they have no need to explore the notion of "becoming Indian" because their authors have been Indian all along. Into this category, one might place, for instance, novels such as M. Scott Momaday's *House Made of Dawn,* a familial and tribal recollection of Kiowa migration, Louise Erdrich's *Tracks,* the story of an Ojibwe family struggling to retain its tribal allotment, and Leslie Marmon Silko's *Ceremony,* a poetic and profound excursion into the tormented world of a Vietnam veteran who returns to his childhood home in Laguna Pueblo. That these sophisticated works, with their carefully-elaborated themes and characters, have proven popular with audiences of both Indians and non-Indians suggests that America at the dawn of the twenty-first century may be ready to encounter Indian people in their individual and tribal particularity and real-life complexity. It has taken 500 years, but perhaps America is finally becoming willing to think about Indian people as more than a series of interchangeable representatives of the generic category of "the Indian."

—Eva Marie Garroutte

FURTHER READING:

Barnard, Brian. "Would You Cheer for the Denver Darkies?" *Indian Country Today.* August 17, 1994, A5.

Berkhofer, Robert, Jr. *The White Man's Indian: Images of the American Indian from Columbus to the Present.* New York, Vintage, 1979.

Castaneda, Carlos. *Journey to Ixtlan: The Lessons of Don Juan.* Simon and Schuster, 1972.

Cooper, James Fenimore. *The Last of the Mohicans.* Oxford, Oxford University Press, 1998.

Deloria, Philip J. *Playing Indian.* New Haven, Yale University Press, 1998.

Derounian-Stodola, Kathryn. *The Indian Captivity Narrative, 1550-1900.* New York, Twayne, 1993.

Forbes, Jack D. "The Manipulation of Race, Caste, and Identity: Classifying AfroAmericans, Native Americans and Red-Black People." *Journal of Ethnic Studies.* Vol. 17, No. 4, 1990, 1-51.

Little Eagle, Avis. "University of Illinois Staff, Students Say Chief Illiniwek Violates Civil Rights." *Indian Country Today.* April 13, 1994, A1.

Smith, Andy. "For All Those Who Were Indian in a Former Life." *Ms.* November/December 1991, 44-45.

Van Der Beets, Richard. "The Indian Captivity Narrative as Ritual." *American Literature.* Vol. 43, 1972, 548-62.

Weatherford, Jack. *Indian Givers: How the Indians of the Americas Transformed the World.* New York, Ballantine, 1988.

Williams, John. *The Redeemed Captive Returning to Zion; or a Faithful History of Remarkable Occurrences in the Captivity and Deliverance of Mr. John Williams.* Ann Arbor, University Microfilms, 1966.

Indianapolis 500

For most of the twentieth century, the Borg-Warner trophy, awarded to the winner of the Indianapolis 500 Motor Speedway race, has been the most coveted prize in auto racing. Known as "the greatest spectacle in racing," the Memorial Day event—which since the late 1960s has actually been run on the Sunday before Memorial Day to permit the scheduling of a rain delay—has featured the best drivers and the fastest speeds in the sport.

The Indianapolis 500 consists of 200 laps around the Indianapolis Motor Speedway's two-and-a-half-mile oval. The first race, in 1911, lasted most of the day; the 1997 race was won by Arie Luyendyk in less than three-and-a-half hours. The first race averaged a then staggering 74.5 miles per hour but, by the end of the century, the course speed record was held by Rick Mears, who won the 1991 race with an average speed of over 176 miles per hour. One other difference is notable: Ray Haroun took home a hefty $10,000 for winning the first Indianapolis 500, while 1998 winner Eddie Cheever pocketed over $1.4 million.

Like most non-team sports, the history of auto racing is chronicled in the personalities who defined its various eras. Other than one notable exception, NASCAR's Richard Petty, racing's dominant personalities gravitated to Indianapolis. In the early years, when the Speedway was paved with over three million bricks (a 36-inch strip of which is still visible at the finish line), it was the home of barnstormers like Haroun, Ralph DePalma, and Howdy Wilcox. In those days, drivers would carry mechanics in the car with them, and repairs would be undertaken on the track.

The next great Indianapolis legend was Wilbur Shaw, who won the race three times in four years (1937 to 1940). In 1946,

The 1996 Indianapolis 500.

Shaw convinced Anton "Tony" Hulman to buy the Speedway from an ownership group that included the legendary Captain Eddie Rickenbacker; Shaw became its president. It was under the guidance of Shaw (who died in a plane crash in 1954) and Hulman that the Indianapolis 500 became the premier auto-racing event in the world. The 1950s and 1960s saw Indianapolis become the unofficial home of racing greats such as Maury Rose, Bill Vukovich, Johnnie Parsons, and Parnelli Jones, who drove the first turbine-powered race car to within six laps of a win before gearbox failure cost him the race.

The personality that most defines the Indianapolis 500, though, is A.J. Foyt, Jr. Foyt first raced in Indianapolis in 1958 and continued to be an integral part of the facility's lore for the next 40 years. His records include most career starts (35), most consecutive starts (35), most competitive miles during a career (12,273), and most races led (13). Foyt's record of four wins is matched only by his contemporary Al Unser. Another reason why Foyt has cast such a long shadow over Indy racing is that he stands as a nostalgic contrast to the reality that championship racing has now become the province of only the best-financed teams. The names of drivers like Rutherford, Andretti, and Clark have been overshadowed by the names of owners like Penske and Newman/Haas. Because so much money is now at stake in championship Indy-car racing, the complexion of the sport is changing, and the pre-eminence of the Indianapolis 500 is in danger. In 1994, Speedway president Tony George inaugurated the Indianapolis Racing League, a circuit meant to compete with the Championship Auto Racing Teams League established by Roger Penske. The friction between the rivals has caused many of the sport's most

popular drivers to skip the Indianapolis 500 in order to boost CART's leverage in the marketplace. The outcome of this controversy will go a long way toward determining for how long, or if, the Indianapolis 500 will remain "the greatest spectacle in racing."

—Barry Morris

FURTHER READING:

Binford, Tom. *A Checkered Past: My Twenty Years as Indy 500 Chief Steward.* Chicago, Cornerstone, 1998.

Taylor, Rich. *Indy: 75 Years of Auto Racing's Greatest Spectacle.* New York, St. Martin's Press, 1991.

Industrial Design

The "American system" of mass production, successfully implemented during the mid-1800s, was characterized by the large-scale manufacture of standardized products with interchangeable parts. Much different than the individualized hand craftsmanship which preceded it, this method of production required artificially-powered machine tools and simplified operations, endowing products made from machine production with a certain aesthetic—an industrial design. At first used for the manufacture of revolvers, clocks, pocket watches, and agricultural machinery, the American system eventually produced most consumer goods.

Sewing machines and typewriters were the first products consciously designed with different contexts of use in mind—an early implementation of industrial design. In order to sell his sewing machines, Isaac Singer believed that they should be ornamented when in the home in order to fit into the more decorative aesthetic of the domestic sphere; likewise, they should be plain black when found in a factory setting. Early typewriters shared the same aesthetic variations as their sewing machine counterparts, and these were two of the earliest manufactured objects influenced by the machine ethic that produced them.

A few decades later, in 1908, Henry Ford improved upon assembly line production by making an automobile, the Model T, specifically for a mass market. Ford believed in the design philosophy called "functionalism," a system also touted by architect Louis Sullivan (1856-1924). Functionalism, one of the first self-conscious modern design movements, stressed that an "honest" design did not hide what an object did, a belief summed up most eloquently by Sullivan's famous phrase, "form follows function." As historian Gregory Votolato wrote, "Sullivan and Ford approached design as a means of addressing social, technical and commercial problems specific to the time and place. In its early years of development, the automobile, like the skyscraper, called for a design which would tap a huge, potential demand and which would make the most efficient use of the available technology in its production and construction." Frank Lloyd Wright (1869-1959) was a well-known proponent of the functionalist aesthetic, but designed only for an exclusive clientele. It was not until the rise of business in the 1910s and 1920s, which required the mass manufacture of office equipment and furniture, that functionalism was brought to the masses.

During the 1910s, the fine arts, especially from Europe, still remained influential in popular design, overshadowing the sheer power of machinery and industry that would prevail in the following decades. Art Nouveau, expressed most clearly in the work of Belgian designer Henry van de Velde, was based on organic forms and the insistence that production occur in small craft workshops—a reaction against the forces of machine-driven mass production. Although meant for the elite, his designs were easily and readily appropriated for the mass market. Dadaist Marcel Duchamp celebrated prosaic utilitarian objects as works of art, promoting the idea that ordinary objects should be works of art. Le Corbusier expounded Purist theories, believing that man was merely another functional object like a machine, and that objects should be made as extensions of the human body. Piet Mondrian and Gerrit Rietveld expressed the ideals of De Stijl, a movement founded in Holland in 1917. De Stijl condensed things down to their fundamental elements—basic shapes, right angles, and primary colors which could be applied as easily to furniture or paintings. Although these schools all enjoyed many followers and influenced to various degrees the design of consumer goods, the most influential on American industrial design was the Bauhaus movement, founded in Germany in 1919. Walter Gropius, Marcel Breuer, and Mies van der Rohe, among others, believed that art and technology could be unified and used to produce objects of good design and integrity.

It was not until the crash of 1929, however, that industrial design in America became professionalized and considered a valid pursuit in its own right. Many designers who were previously involved in the theater or in advertising were put into service during the Depression to find viable and useful product designs in a small yet very competitive market. These American designers were highly influenced by the Modernist aesthetic of the Bauhaus, which celebrated industrial materials, like metal and elevated machines, to works of art. In addition, they brought industrial design into the home, applying Modernist principles to appliances, furniture, and even architecture.

Walter Dorwin Teague (1883-1960) started out as a graphic designer, and began applying his skills to the three-dimensional realm during the mid-1920s. Throughout his career he designed cameras for Kodak, and became well known for improving on the designs of heavy machinery and office equipment. Raymond Loewy (1893-1986), a Frenchman who emigrated to America, became well known in the field after he redesigned the Gestetner duplicating machine, making it more functional and better looking. In 1935, Loewy improved upon the design of the Coldspot refrigerator for Sears, enclosing the cooling unit with white enameled steel, giving it chrome hardware, and adding features with the needs of the user in mind: it could accommodate different-sized containers, had a semi-automatic defroster, and came with instant-release ice cube trays.

Henry Dreyfuss (1904-1972) was originally a stage designer who opened up an interior design business in 1929. In 1937, he redesigned the telephone for Bell, giving it a low profile and combining the receiver and earpiece into one handset. It was a simple design—easy to use, easy to clean, and easy to manufacture. Dreyfuss was particularly interested in the interaction between humans and the objects around them. He spent much of his time studying the human body and was the first true proponent of ergonomics, best expressed in his books, *Designing for People* (1955) and *The Measure of Man* (1961).

Norman Bel Geddes (1893-1958), yet another stage designer, put his talents to work designing more substantial objects like airplanes. Although he did not invent streamlining, he did democratize it. Popular between 1927 and the beginning of World War II, streamlining was characterized by smooth metal surfaces, long, sweeping, horizontal curves, rounded edges, and the elimination of extraneous detail. It was based on scientific principles and produced shapes with the least resistance in water and air. Streamlining was a wildly popular design aesthetic that appeared in objects from railroads and camping trailers to toasters and juicers and symbolized speed, efficiency, and a forward-looking mentality that was much needed during the Depression years. Examples of streamlining included the Boeing 247 of 1933, the Douglas DC1 (an all metal structure with an aluminum skin), and Carl Breer's 1934 Chrysler ''Airflow.''

Industrial design styles did not change much during the decades immediately following World War II. Sullivan's ''form follows function'' credo had become the accepted canon in the design world. The exceptions to the functionalist design aesthetic appeared in the automobile industry. The Cadillacs and Buicks of the 1950s and early 1960s were known for their outlandish colors—pink, turquoise, yellow—and for their exuberant body styles, complete with jutting ''tailfins'' that resembled something from outer space.

As an outgrowth of the celebration of post-War material abundance and American primacy in the world, most American homes were filled with products of American design. By the mid-1960s, this began to change—the liberal culture was becoming more tolerant of design variations, and other countries began to contribute their taste cultures to the American public. Slim-line Bang and Olufsen stereos, from Denmark, and the more militaristic Japanese versions began appearing in the dens of American audiophiles. Italian Olivetti typewriters appeared alongside IBM (International Business Machines) Selectrics in the corporate office. Braun coffee makers from Germany showed up in progressive kitchens.

By the late 1970s and early 1980s, technology put toward the miniaturization of electronic equipment radically changed Americans' material universe. While Dreyfuss, Teague, Bel Geddes, and the other modernists could place functional objects in attractive packages, they could not get rid of their bulk. The impact of computers was revolutionary, both in terms of how people communicated and in the nature of design itself. Computers used on the production line allowed for more flexibility, shorter production runs, and therefore more differentiation in design—a return to the nature of production 100 years earlier. In addition, smaller parts like microchips allowed the products themselves to become smaller, more portable, and more personal, symbolizing the increasing interpersonal disconnectedness and self-interest pervading the culture at the end of the twentieth century. Watches with LED (Liquid Electronic Display) crystals threatened to make analogue time-telling obsolete; it did not, but did create a new meaning for analogue faces which hearkened back to a nostalgic past. Microcomponents also meant that electronic gadgets became very toy-like: the ''mouse'' used with the Macintosh computer was only one example. Indeed, the triumph of microprocessing made machines both personalized and intimate—people often wore them on their bodies. The Sony Walkman was a portable stereo that one strapped on one's belt or wore around the neck; similarly, people carried pocket calculators, beepers, cellular telephones, and even laptop computers. The influence of microcomputers on design, what historian Peter Dormer called "the electronic technologist's great gift to designers" was "the means to create working icons of personal freedom through greatly enhanced power and portability."

At the same time microprocessing was allowing objects to become smaller, thinner, and more portable, postmodern design also changed the outward appearance of industrially-produced objects. Architect Robert Venturi (1925—) became one of the first American proponents of postmodern design with his 1972 book *Learning From Las Vegas.* Formally established in Italy in 1981 and called "Memphis," the school of postmodernism embraced exuberant styles and colors. Memphis, referring to both Elvis and Egypt, reacted against the cultural supremacy assumed by modern design, which its proponents saw as a constant restatement of the power of technology and the triumph of large American corporations. In contrast, postmodern design attempted to be more egalitarian, incorporating stylistic elements from both high and low art—from marble to formica, from Greek columns to polka dots. Michael Graves (1934—) was another American architect and designer who embraced the postmodern aesthetic, and began designing toasters, picture frames, and other housewares for a middlebrow department store chain near the end of the 1990s, indicating a "trending downward" of taste, and selling what had formerly been high style to the masses. The appearance of postmodernism to some, however, marked the triumph of surface over substance. Influenced more by the information than the industrial age, postmodernism perhaps signaled the end of the reign of industrial design and the beginning of a new design ethic based on and in the hyperreality of cyberspace rather than the materiality of tangible objects.

—Wendy Woloson

FURTHER READING:

Bayley, Stephen, et. al. *Twentieth-Century Style and Design.* New York, Van Nostrand Reinhold Co., 1986.

Bush, Donald J. *The Streamlined Decade.* New York, George Braziller, 1975.

Dormer, Peter. *Design Since 1945.* New York, Thames and Hudson, 1993.

Forty, Adrian. *Objects of Desire: Design and Society Since 1750.* New York, Thames and Hudson, 1986.

Heskett, John. *Industrial Design.* New York, Thames and Hudson, 1987.

Horn, Richard. *Memphis: Objects, Furniture, and Patterns.* Philadelphia, Running Press, 1985.

Lupton, Ellen. *Mechanical Brides: Women and Machines from Home to Office.* New York, Princeton Architectural Press and Cooper-Hewitt National Museum of Design, 1993.

Pulos, Arthur J. *American Design Ethic: A History of Industrial Design to 1940.* Cambridge, The MIT Press, 1983.

Sexton, Richard. *American Style: Classic Product Design from Airstream to Zippo.* San Francisco, Chronicle Books, 1987.

Votolato, Gregory. *American Design in the Twentieth Century: Personality and Performance.* Manchester and New York, Manchester University Press, 1998.

Wilson, Richard Guy, et. al. *The Machine Age in America, 1918-1941.* New York, Harry N. Abrams and the Brooklyn Museum, 1986.

The Ink Spots

With their wistful, plangent, sentimental love songs, the Ink Spots are redolent of the 1940s, when their music provided a romantic backdrop to lovers throughout the years of World War II and beyond. They had their first and greatest hit, the million-seller "If I Didn't Care" in 1939, while among the best and most enduring of the many that followed were "My Prayer"; "I Don't Want to Set the World on Fire"; "To Each His Own"; "Maybe"; "Java Jive"; "Prisoner of Love"; "It's a Sin to Tell a Lie"; and "I'll Never Smile Again."

The group was formed in Indianapolis in 1932, initially calling themselves the Riff Brothers, then the Percolating Puppies. The original members were tenor and lead vocalist Jerry Daniels; Ivory Watson, baritone vocals and guitar; Charles Fuqua, tenor vocals, guitar and ukulele; and Orville "Hoppy" Jones, bass vocals and guitar. In 1934, the quartet settled on calling themselves the Ink Spots, and Bill Kenny eventually replaced Jerry Daniels. It was Jones who conjured up their trademark "talking chorus" in which the lead singer speaks, rather than sings, for added dramatic effect. Across the decades, the Ink Spots underwent numerous personnel changes. Perhaps the most significant came in 1945, when Bill Kenny was replaced by Jim Nabbie, who led the group until his death in 1992.

All the popular black vocal "doo-wop" groups of the early rock 'n' roll years owed a supreme debt to the Ink Spots. Their soft, smooth, group harmonizing, backing the steady, silky-throated vocalizing of their lead singers, inspired a generation of adolescents who started out singing on urban street corners in the early 1950s, some of whom went on to score some of rock 'n' roll's earliest hits. Nobody, however, quite succeeded in emulating the unique sound of the Ink Spots, whose high delicate tenors seemed almost to have originated from classical music's counter-tenor tradition. The Ink Spots were inducted into the Rock and Roll Hall of Fame in 1989 and, extraordinarily, although they had long been superseded in the charts, and their original members were no more, the Ink Spots were still touring the country in the 1990s, a nostalgic throwback to a gentler past.

—Rob Edelman

FURTHER READING:

Goldberg, Marv. *More Than Words Can Say: The Ink Spots and Their Music.* Lanham, Maryland, Scarecrow Press, 1998.

Watson, Deek, with Lee Stephenson. *The Story of the "Ink Spots."* New York, Vantage Press, 1967.

Inner Sanctum Mysteries

During a period from 1941 to 1952, which spanned the golden era of classic radio, this macabre anthology series invited listeners each week to pass through its famous opening creaking door into a world which provided a unique mixture of horror with the darkest of comedy. In its own era, *Inner Sanctum* was perhaps the quintessential radio program, using sound to produce effects which wove a spell unique to the medium. In a larger sense, the show's peculiar combination of chills and chuckles has influenced the American horror genre ever since and has found expression in everything from EC Comics in the 1950s to the self-referential works of Stephen King and Wes Craven in the 1990s. A listener today who has the nerve to step through the *Inner Sanctum* doorway (being careful not to bump into that corpse "just hanging around over there") will discover a world both historically distant and entertainingly familiar.

There were three principal ways in which *Inner Sanctum* used sound to horrify and amuse its listeners. First among these was, of course, the famous creaking door, an effect which radio historian John Dunning has said "may have been the greatest opening signature device ever achieved." The door was the brainchild of the program's creator Himan Brown, who once claimed that it was one of only two sounds in all of radio to be trademarked—the other being the NBC chimes. Regardless of its legal status, however, there is no doubt that the ominous squeak of the *Inner Sanctum* portal takes its place right along with Fibber McGee's overcrowded closet, the menacing chuckle of the Shadow, and the sputtering of Jack Benny's car as the most well-remembered sounds of old-time radio—causing Stephen King to recall years later that "nothing could have looked as horrible as that door *sounded.*" Brown's second achievement in sound was *Inner Sanctum*'s innovative use of the organ. While other suspense programs used the instrument in its musical guise, Jim Harmon reports that Brown "warned his organist never to play a recognizable song . . . or even an original snatch of melody." The man at the somber Hammond organ was to play sharp "stings"—a high musical note struck to emphasize an important piece of dialogue and "doom chords" designed to produce a sense of unease and foreboding in listeners. Dunning goes so far as to claim that "the organ became one of the star players . . . brooding, ever-present, worrying, fretting . . . the epitome of radio melodrama." Finally, Brown was grimly innovative in his creation of realistic sound effects to lend the outlandish goings-on the necessary believability to render them truly terrifying. Only on *Inner Sanctum,* for example, would the soft thunk of a man's skull being crushed be so deliciously captured in the sound of a small metal hammer striking a melon, a Brown favorite.

Presiding over this dark world of sound was the show's famous host, Raymond. Played most notably by Raymond Edward Johnson (1941-1945), Raymond was the source of much of the program's black humor as he ushered listeners in and out of the creaking door with a series of ghoulish puns ("Quiet now—no 'coffin.' We have 'grave' matters to uncover") and doubtful morals ("Careful the next time you ask your wife to 'pass' the knife. She may do it—right through you. Good Niiiiiight!") The tradition of the sardonic host to horror would find equally memorable expression years later in American popular culture in figures such as the Cryptkeeper in EC Comics and Rod Serling in television's *The Twilight Zone,* but the stories introduced by Raymond were unique in their ability to arouse and exploit audience fears of the supernatural before ultimately providing a "realistic" explanation. As otherworldly as the universe of the *Inner Sanctum* sometimes seemed for most of the tale, events were always finally shown to be the result of a very human combination of folly and foible—of greed, ambition, and just plain bad luck.

The show's self-imposed need to create situations which were as outlandish as possible and yet capable of such "rational" explanation in the final moments led to some of the most wildly improbable twists and turns imaginable, and it is this element which makes the series both memorable and campish simultaneously. It is also for this reason that the creative peak of the program is usually regarded as the early series of episodes performed by Boris Karloff and Peter Lorre and based upon classic works by Poe and Maupassant, skilled practitioners of the peculiar art of "realistic horror."

In its unique mixture of horror and humor, classics and camp, the supernatural with the everyday, *Inner Sanctum* helped shape the face of popular horror in all media—even in its own time promoting a whole set of *Inner Sanctum* novels and occasional movies. And yet the series can also be fondly recalled today as a program which exploited the basic elements of radio perhaps more than any other show, taking an entire generation of listeners deep into the "inner sanctums" of their own imaginations.

—Kevin Lause

FURTHER READING:

Dunning, John. *On the Air: The Encyclopedia of Old-Time Radio.* New York, Oxford University Press, 1998.

Harmon, Jim. *The Great Radio Heroes.* Garden City, Kansas, Doubleday, 1967.

Nachman, Gerald. *Raised on Radio.* New York, Random House, 1998.

International Business Machines
See IBM (International Business Machines)

International Exhibition of Modern Art
See Armory Show, The

The International Male Catalog

With its bold, off-beat fashions, and its subtly suggestive, all-male photography layouts, International Male has gained a certain popularity and renown among trendy twenty- and thirtysomethings looking for clothes that are unique and stylish. The company's focus on colorful and daring styles from around the world, including pants in bright prints, mesh shirts, and an vast selection of unique men's underwear, gives it a special appeal to gay men. Lesbians too, have been drawn to the mail-order company by clothes that often transcend gender with kaleidoscopic élan. Part of Hanover, Pennsylvania-based Brawn of California, International Male has its corporate offices in San Diego. One of the originators of the mail order boom, the company has been in business since the early 1970s and each year serves over eight million customers around the world.

—Tina Gianoulis

FURTHER READING:

Brubech, Holly. "Mail Order America." *The New York Times Magazine.* November, 21, 1993, 54.

International Male Web Site. http://www.internationalmale.com April 1999.

The Internet

The term didn't appear in a major American newspaper until 1988, but the Internet has become the most powerful individual electronic communications network in the world's history. From high-pressure advertising to a brief message from a political prisoner, Internet e-mail and World Wide Web sites make it possible for anyone with a computer, software, and an appropriate connection to speak to the world at the speed of light with the touch of a keypad. In the process, the Internet has added a host of new phrases and words, such as information superhighway, spam, hyperlink, chat rooms, flames, and dotcom, into the English language and revolutionized the culture. It has also led to serious concerns about the ready access it provides to pornography, violence, and hate literature, the loss of personal privacy it has occasioned, the spread of mis- and disinformation, and the future of books, newspapers, and magazines. Yet, efforts were underway at the end of the twentieth century to increase the transmission speed of Internet connections still further, and to create a second Internet, both of which would provide computerized copies of entire feature films and books in seconds and make possible the first practical mix of moving images, sound, and the printed word.

The telegraph, or the Victorian Internet, as historian Tom Standage has called it, was the antecedent of the Internet. The earliest scheme for using electricity to send messages appeared in a British magazine in 1753, and two French brothers transmitted the first electronic message in 1791, but it was American inventor Samuel F. B. Morse who gave the United States Congress an opportunity to buy outright his patent to the telegraph technology in 1844. The government failed to see the advantage of a single, standardized electronic communications network, however, and thousands of privately owned telegraph companies resulted before they were gradually purchased or put out of business by the telegraph monopoly, Western Union. In turn, the monopoly provided everything from the first professional National League baseball scores in 1876 to breaking the news of the bombing of Pearl Harbor in 1941 and the sending of love messages, all at a low, nearly universal cost. The American Telephone and Telegraph (AT&T) system, developed in the wake of Alexander Graham Bell's patent of the telephone in 1876, became the standardized telephone monopoly, controlling long and most short distance communication for radio and television networks and interpersonal information consumers.

One factor common to the telegraph and telephone was that neither could work without interconnection. A telephone without someone to call is useless. Even the first cumbersome, room-sized electronic computer, however, developed by Iowa State University physicist John V. Atanasoff between 1939 and 1942, could function alone. As a result, it took longer for people to recognize the advantages of computer networks. In 1964, a group of scientists at the

RAND Corporation conceived of a configuration of computers interconnected by pathways similar to telephone lines as a means for military personnel to communicate following a nuclear war. Such an occurrence would have disrupted standard military communication channels, preventing surviving military personnel from coordinating a response. Such a network would not have a central station and thus could continue operating even if major portions were destroyed.

In 1969, Advanced Research Projects Agency Network (ARPANET) was created as a system of 20 individual computer stations, or nodes, located at various distances from one another. Each node used a common language, or control protocol, that allowed it to communicate electronically, and a transmission protocol that made all nodes equal rather than a central station hierarchy. By using special connections between the nodes, messages could be sent from one place to another on a number of pathways. Even if several nodes were destroyed in an attack, messages could still be transmitted as long as there was at least one remaining pathway. Both AT&T and Western Union had developed multiple contingency plans for their systems, but they required block-long manual switchboards in central locations vulnerable to attack. ARPANET, however, could re-route critical messages between nodes and around interruptions instantaneously, without any human intervention.

Three years later, 46 university and research organization networks were added to the system and ARPANET began to grow, as the Internet would, by chance rather than design. Perhaps one of its strongest appeals was that no one could predict accurately its future. UNIX was developed as a common operating system language in 1972. Branches with names such as Bitnet and Usenet were developed, attracting new users. Rapid communication characteristics allowed the first computerized electronic mail—e-mail—as researchers corresponded with each other. Group e-mails could be sent simultaneously at the touch of a key, eliminating the age-old need for duplicate messages to be created. Discussion areas, called news groups, allowed users to meet with others interested in specifically designated topics. The decentralized Jeffersonian democracy of the Internet held appeal for Americans in the 1970s and 1980s, the decades of individualism and corporate downsizing. The decline of Western Union and the court-ordered breakup of AT&T in 1982 only added to the attraction of a communications system without a central station or control. There were 500 host computers on the Internet, as some people were calling it, by 1984.

In spite of its wider advantages, the growth of the Internet was tightly controlled by the military during its first years. The Department of Defense did permit university nodes to share supercomputing resources, reducing the need for physical travel. That allowed researchers to perform complicated computerized research at a fraction of the otherwise expensive cost of main-frame computing machines. However, the news groups and university research-oriented networks such as CSNET (Computer Science Network) and NSFNET (National Science Foundation Network) soon began to overtax the system in the 1980s, dictating a new addressing system that allowed users to distinguish between government or educationally-endorsed content and content generated by individuals or groups without sanction or authority. The new addressing system allowed the Internet to evolve from a medium for simple back-and-forth messages such as the telegraph and telephone to one capable of providing a more complex mass audience content, similar to small-scale publishing or broadcasting. The glut of the new network traffic inspired the military to develop a new network for itself and the use of the ARPANET declined until it ceased to exist in June 1990. But the military left a deep impression on the Internet before it left. Beyond the Internet's decentralized structure and the teaching of three generations of computer scientists in the difficult art of computer networking, the military helped spawn startup computer network companies such as 3Com and the manufacturer of Ethernet.

Meanwhile, major developments were taking place in computer hardware and software that would broaden the appeal of the Internet. Marcian Hoff, Jr. of Intel Corporation combined several integrated electronic circuits into a tiny piece of electronics called a microprocessor in 1972. The new chips performed arithmetic and logic functions and could be programmed just like traditional, more expensive wired circuits. The availability of the new Intel microprocessor attracted the attention of computer hobbyists and home experimenters such as Stephen Wozniak and Steven Jobs, who began marketing the Apple I in Wozniak's garage in 1976 and created the Apple Macintosh in 1980. Mainframe computer manufacturer IBM unveiled its own "micro" computer in 1981, employing an operating system provided by Harvard University dropout Bill Gates. Within a few years, Apple and IBM had created a market for a previously unknown product, the personal computer. Other manufacturers, including Dell, Hyundai, and Gateway, joined the fad, selling inexpensive "clones" of the IBM PC, and software writers developed thousands of programs to use on the new machines, from computerized spreadsheets and word processors to a wide variety of mind-boggling games. But until the Internet, one of the greatest strengths of personal computers, communication, remained largely untapped. In fact, software baron Gates actively opposed the Internet until 1995.

As the military backed away from the Internet in the 1980s, the content evolved from serious, often computer-related topics to material more representative of popular American culture. Not surprisingly, the first three alternative news groups, known as alt. groups, were alt.sex, alt.drugs, and alt.rock and roll. The High Performance Computing Act of 1991, sponsored by then U.S. Senator Albert Gore, opened the Internet to elementary and high schools and community colleges. The telephonic backbone of the Internet enabled it to spread from the United States to other countries that had existing systems coupled with political systems that allowed at least a limited form of free speech, and the Internet became truly global by the late 1980s. The growing Internet audience attracted new application developers, people whose aspirations went beyond data processing to providing uses such as education, reference, and entertainment. Businesses also began logging onto the Net, as it was being called, to conduct research and share information. The National Science Foundation accepted the task of managing the Net's backbone in 1987, but its task was just that—to manage, rather than control, the growth. The speed at which the quantity and variety of information became available was so dramatic that published directories could not keep up with it. Computerized organizational systems such as Archie, named not after the comic-book character but as a version of the word "archive," Wide Area Information Servers or WAIS, and Gopher, named after its creator University of Minnesota's mascot, became the first "search engines," providing databases of various Internet resources broken down by categories, subjects, and locations.

By the end of the 1980s, the Internet had most of the hardware technology it needed, but it lacked visual appeal or any demonstrable superiority other than speed over print. Screens were limited to two colors, crude illustrations often created by alphabetic letters, and unattractive computer-style typeface. One solution was the introduction of the World Wide Web (WWW) in 1989, in which vast amounts of information, including graphics and print-style type faces, could be delivered. Another was the advent of hypertext markup languages (HTML) in 1991. The term "hypertext" was coined by Theodor A. Nelson in 1972 and meant information referencing. For centuries, print authors had used internal text references or footnotes to direct readers to related or supportive information, but the process of finding those materials could take days, months, or even years. Clicking with a mouse on a hyperlink, a highlighted or underlined passage in a Web text, could speed a reader to related information instantaneously. The process was manipulative in that the links were chosen by an author, and often confusing since there was no predictable, logical basis for the order of documents consulted. Nonetheless, readers had never before been able to check the veracity or gain a more detailed explanation of information presented to them so quickly and effortlessly. The process of hyper-linking between all of the files and directories of the Internet, as if it were one large computer, was simplified in 1992 when the National Center for Supercomputing at the University of Illinois wrote and released the first Web "browser" Mosaic, software that allowed Web users to switch between Web sites more easily. The Illinois program evolved into the Netscape Corporation in 1994.

The proliferation of personal computers and modems, electronic devices that allowed differing types of computers to communicate with each other over telephone lines, accelerated the growth of the Internet. The number of host computers on the Net rose from 80,000 in 1989 to 1.3 million in 1993, 2.2 million in 1994, 10 million in 1996, and perhaps 50 million by the end of the century. The first movie, *Wax: Or the Discovery of Television Among the Bees*, was "Netcast" in May 1992. Presidents had complained about a lack of access to the American electorate since George Washington, but Bill Clinton became the first to provide a daily perspective on his administration on a mass basis via a White House Web site in 1993. Congress followed suit a year later along with thousands of federal, state, and local agencies, and politicians. The first "Wanted" poster was posted on June 24, 1994, the same year the first computer radio station went on-line, and the first music concert (the Rolling Stones from Dallas' Cotton Bowl) was shown live. Libraries began offering Web versions of books, and newspapers and magazines, the last bastion of print culture, began putting their contents on line for free. The latter practice helped stimulate advertising on the Internet, first made possible in 1991. Internet ads were an anathema to traditionalists but the only practical means of supporting expensive commercial ventures such as news-gathering organizations. Even by the end of the twentieth century, subscription fees for services other than expensive, large-scale databases were few and far between on the Web. The *Wall Street Journal* was the only major newspaper or magazine to be profitable, charging an up-front subscription fee for its Web site. The growing commercial character of the Internet was acknowledged in 1995 when the National Science Foundation backbone became commercially supported. An Internet Activities Board (IAB) guides the evolution of the Internet, the Internet Address Network Authority (IANA) assigns network numbers, and a hired private company, Network Solutions, Inc., registers Web site names.

Like the personal computer and software industries, the Internet created new dynasties of American wealth. When tax preparation firm H & R Block purchased CompuServe in 1980, no one expected that the unknown computer time-sharing company would one day account for one-third of its parent company's profits. CompuServe was joined in the national on-line computer bulletin board industry, made possible by improvements in personal computer modems, by a specialized bulletin board service for Commodore users, an early PC competitor of the Apple, that had developed a graphical rather than letterset user interface in 1985. The firm evolved into an Apple and Windows bulletin board server known as America Online (AOL) by 1993. Both CompuServe and AOL began offering Web access and by 1996, AOL accounted for 55 percent of all household usage of the Web or proprietary consumer services. AOL bought CompuServe in 1998 and purchased Netscape the following year, generating tremendous proceeds each time. The profit turnaround was even quicker for the founder of Netscape, Jim Clark, who became an instant billionaire in 1995 when his company went public. Two Stanford University students, Jerry Yang and David Filo, made $65 million dollars each in one day when their Internet search engine company, Yahoo! went public in April 1996. The stock of online auction house eBay, one of a growing number of Internet companies known as dotcoms, increased 2,000 percent in value in less than a year when it went public in 1998, and the stock of other new Internet companies frequently doubled or trebled in price overnight upon going public. Not to be outdone altogether, the public jumped on the Internet financial bandwagon at the turn of the century by buying and selling securities through economical on-line brokerage firms offering margin loans. Unfortunately, trades still had to be transacted by human brokers, raising concerns among the Securities and Exchange Commission that orders were not being acted upon as quickly as they could or that traders would inadvertently plunge themselves into debt. And new Internet companies such as Amazon.com promised, but have not always delivered, massive profits in the brave new world of e-commerce.

With the advantages of the Internet have come numerous societal concerns. The FBI and police added computer specialists to their ranks to deal with on-line paedophiles and stalkers and established special centers to handle Internet fraud cases. Historically, pornography has often been one of the first areas to be exploited by a new mass communication technology and the Internet has been no exception. The pervasiveness of sexually explicit images induced Congress and President Clinton to approve the Communications Decency Act of 1996, which prohibited indecency on the Internet to persons under 18. The Supreme Court declared most of the law unconstitutional the following year. Ironically, the House of Representatives was considering a replacement act in September 1998, at the same time that the explicit Kenneth Starr Report on President Clinton's sexual indiscretions was released to the general public on the Internet by Congress. The shooting deaths of 12 Colorado high school students in 1999 took on an additionally tragic aspect when it was discovered that one of the student murderers had an AOL Web site critical of athletes and African Americans and laden with information on anarchism and bomb construction.

From their first widespread instance in 1988, viruses became a scourge to computer users as they were spread exponentially via the Internet. Virus-protection software became a necessity that fueled a new industry as professionals sought to keep up with amateur virus

creators. Chat rooms and other forms of "cyber"-conversation renewed concerns about how people were spending their time. More than 50 million people sent e-mails in 1996, but the seductive genie of computer messaging has encouraged stream-of-consciousness bursts that often involved inadvertent shedding of inhibitions. Software billionaire Bill Gates saw a series of blunt e-mails between his executives become a smoking gun in an anti-trust case against Microsoft. All of these concerns were made more difficult to regulate or censor due to the decentralized nature of the Internet. Efforts by the Federal government and microprocessor manufacturer Intel to provide discrete identification of Internet users met with resistance from privacy advocates.

With the Internet still a relatively new medium of communication at the dawn of the twenty-first century, there were many grandiose predictions for its future. Part of the American economic expansion of the 1990s was based on the prospects of Internet-related companies such as Yahoo!, Netscape, AOL, Amazon.com, and eBay, but critics warned of an Internet bubble that could lead to a general economic downturn much like earlier technology booms such as electricity and defense spending. Cable and telephone companies positioned themselves to provide so-called broadband and DSL Internet service, persistent 24-hour lines that allow instant Internet access without the necessity of individual modem connections, at speeds fast enough to allow downloading of full-length movies, books, and other large files. WebTV and other new companies were banking on an Internet-television hybrid. An initiative started by 34 universities in 1996, Internet2 will be a high-bandwidth computer network allowing real-time video streaming and 24-hour user access. The Internet is a story of luck and hard work by many, but it recognizes and plugs into a basic human need: as an unknown e-mailer paraphrased French philosopher Rene Descartes, "I post, therefore I am."

—Richard Digby-Junger

FURTHER READING:

Kiesler, Sara. *Culture of the Internet.* Mahwah, New Jersey, Lawrence Erlbaum Associates, 1997.

Oslin, George P. *The Story of Telecommunications.* Macon, Georgia, Mercer University Press, 1992.

Porter, David, editor. *Internet Culture.* New York, Routledge, 1997.

Randall, Neil. *The Soul of the Internet.* London, International Thompson Computer Press, 1997.

Rensberger, Boyce. "Networks Are Conduits for the 'Infection': 50,000 Terminals Affected by Outbreak." *Washington Post.* November 4, 1988, A4.

Segaller, Stephen. *Nerds 2.0.1: A Brief History of the Internet.* New York, Harper-Collins, 1998.

Standage, Tom. *The Victorian Internet.* New York, Walker and Co., 1998.

Surratt, Carla G. *Netlife: Internet Citizens and Their Communities.* Commack, New York, Nova Science Publishers, Inc., 1998.

Swartz, Jon. "Boys' Web Site Illustrates How Hate Is Finding a Voice Online." *San Francisco Chronicle.* April 23, 1999, A7.

Wright, Robert. "Journey Through Cyberspace: As a Place to Eavesdrop, the Internet Is Without Peer in Human History." *Ottawa Citizen,* September 18, 1993, p. B4.

Zimmerman, Andrew B. "The Evolution of the Internet; Internet/Web/Online Service Information." *Telecommunications.* June, 1997, 39-44.

Intolerance

Intolerance (1916) is one of the first great American epic films. Over three-and-one-half hours long, it has a complex narrative which consists of four separate melodramatic plots. Each is set in a different era, and all four are intercut to create a complicated historical critique of injustice and intolerance throughout the ages. Three of the stories concentrate upon the effects of historical events upon ordinary people.

D.W. Griffith, who has been called the father of the American Cinema, was America's first great movie showman, and the first director who saw moviemaking not merely as entertainment but as an important art form. Stung by charges of racism leveled at him by the critics for his first important feature, *Birth of a Nation* (1915), Griffith responded by making *Intolerance,* a film of a complexity and scale never seen before this time—a film so grand in its conception that the original rough cut was, according to film historian David Cook, eight hours long. Although it was a critical success and is considered a masterpiece of the silent cinema, the rather preachy *Intolerance* was not a success at the box office.

—Jeannette Sloniowski

FURTHER READING:

Cook, David. *A History of Narrative Film.* New York, W.W. Norton and Company, 1990.

Drew, William. M. *D.W. Griffith's Intolerance: Its Genesis and Its Vision.* Jefferson, North Carolina, McFarland & Company, 1986.

Simon, Scott. *The Films of D.W. Griffith.* New York, Cambridge University Press, 1993.

Invisible Man

First published in 1952, Ralph Ellison's (1914-1994) *Invisible Man* revolutionized the literary and cultural world by examining the near-total lack of awareness of African Americans that pervaded mainstream society. One of the most widely read novels in American literature, *Invisible Man* has been translated into at least 15 languages and has undergone numerous printings and special editions. It has been called the *Moby Dick* of the twentieth century—epic in scope, mythic in subject, and classic in structure. Part of its appeal lies in its quintessentially American theme: the quest for identity. What distinguishes Ellison's treatment of this theme is his bold creation of a central character who is black and unnamed, everyman and no one.

Foregrounding black identity while universalizing the central character on his quest for self-realization, the text expands the horizons of the American hero to include racial difference. By naming the invisible condition of his central character, Ellison broke barriers of silence and challenged traditional representations of African Americans, anticipating the movement for racial equality of the 1960s.

The book's central metaphor of the "invisible man," however, raises many questions, as Susan Parr and Pancho Savery point out. Particularly important is the question of how best to view the novel: should it "be valued primarily as a work with universal implications, as an example of the best that the American literary tradition offers, or as a representative of black American fiction?" To what extent do the social and political issues represented in the text contribute to its power? Given the nonfictional parameters of these social issues, should the novel be judged by aesthetic or sociological terms? That this novel has opened up these questions points to its importance in helping to shape a continually evolving American identity.

Built on a classical three-part structure consisting of a prologue, a 25-chapter narrative, and an epilogue, the book is narrated in first person by an unnamed narrator and follows a circular rather than linear trajectory. The prologue begins with the narrator's announcement of the book's major interrelated themes of identity and race, innocence and experience, and rebirth and transformation. "I am an invisible man," he says, and the reader enters into the world of the narrator after the series of events about to be told have already taken place. Elaborating on his condition of invisibility, the narrator goes on to say "That invisibility to which I refer occurs because of a peculiar disposition of the eyes of those with whom I come in contact. A matter of the construction of their inner eyes, those eyes with which they look through their physical eyes upon reality." Thus stated, Ellison's narrator brings to light unspoken tensions generated by divisions of race and class.

Much like a bildungsroman, the novel traces the development of the narrator as a young man who believes in the possibility that hard work will reward him with success, through a number of painfully illuminating episodes. Although he retains his innocence through disillusioning experiences, he does mature and undergoes rebirth. From his Southern hometown of Greenwood, he travels to Harlem, and passes through a series of initiations into adulthood. These adventures are often represented as surreal and dream-like, narrated in an energetic and intense voice, often punctuated with humor as he makes observations about white culture and learns more about black history.

Among his most pivotal early experiences is the death of his grandfather, who first opens the young boy's eyes to the fact that appearances do not always represent reality. Following this are his humiliating experiences at a "battle royal" and public speaking contest, which results in an award which sends him to college. Ultimately expelled, he finds his way to Harlem, where he works in a paint factory that blows up, joins "The Brotherhood" of the Communist Party, and eventually returns to the basement where the reader first met him in the prologue. Pondering his condition, he is matter-of-fact: "So, there you have all of it that's important," he says, "Or at least you almost have it. I'm an invisible man and it placed me in a hole—or showed me the hole I was in." Devoid of anger or self pity, the narrator remains philosophical, recognizing that "the world is just as concrete, ornery, vile and sublimely wonderful as before, only now I better understand my relation to it and it to me."

Invisible Man is thick with allusions to other texts, literary, philosophical, political, and psychological. Ellison draws from sources as diverse as classical European texts, major American works of literature, African American literature and folklore, Native American mythology, children's games, sermons, blues and gospel music, as well as his own experience. Music plays a major role illuminating some of the book's major themes. Ellison himself identified five works as essential background reading to *Invisible Man:* Melville's *Moby Dick,* Malraux's *Man's Fate,* Stendhal's *Red and the Black,* Twain's *Huckleberry Finn,* and Doestoevsky's *Brothers Karamazov.* In short, as Mark Busby writes, ''Ellison uses everything he knows, not to prove anything to anybody but to exploit as fully as possible the artistic materials he is conjuring—to render Harlem with enough accuracy that Harlemites who read the book would recognize the place. . . .''

Ellison was awarded the National Book Award for *Invisible Man* (his only novel) in 1952. His other work includes two collections of essays, *Shadow and Arts* (1964) and *Going to the Territory* (1986), which were republished posthumously in 1995 under one title, *The Collected Essays of Ralph Ellison.* A collection of short stories, *Flying Home and Other Stories,* was also published posthumously in 1996.

—Lolly Ockerstrom

FURTHER READING:

Busby, Mark. *Ralph Ellison.* Boston, Twayne, 1991.

Ellison, Ralph. *Invisible Man.* New York, Random House, 1952.

———. *The Collected Essays of Ralph Ellison.* New York, Modern Library, 1995.

———. *Flying Home and Other Stories.* New York, Random House, 1996.

Graham, Maryemma, and Amritjit Singh, editors. *Conversations with Ralph Ellison.* Jackson, University of Mississippi, 1995.

O'Meally, Robert, editor. *New Essays on Invisible Man.* Cambridge, Cambridge University Press, 1988.

Parr, Susan Resneck, and Pancho Savery, editors. *Approaches to Teaching Ellison's Invisible Man.* New York, Modern Language Association, 1989.

Reilly, John M., editor. *Invisible Man: A Collection of Critical Essays.* Englewood Cliffs, New Jersey, Prentice-Hall, 1970.

Sundquist, Eric J., editor. *Cultural Contexts for Ralph Ellison's Invisible Man.* Boston, Bedford Books of St. Martin's Press, 1995.

Iran Contra

No other scandal in American history has had such far-reaching complexities with so few consequences as the Iran-Contra scandal that plagued presidents Ronald Reagan and George Bush in the 1980s.

During the presidency of Ulysses S. Grant, corruption was the order of the day, and cabinet members and federal judges were forced to resign to avoid impeachment. Grant prudently decided not to seek a third term. Warren G. Harding, considered by most scholars to be the worst president of all time, was spared removal from office only by

his death. His wife then burned his papers to spare what was left of his reputation. Richard Nixon was not so fortunate. Once he was ordered to release tapes of conversations conducted in the Oval Office that revealed a coverup of the Watergate hotel break-in, Nixon reluctantly resigned. Bill Clinton was dogged by opponents from the point that he became the frontrunner in the 1992 presidential campaign. While he survived the Whitewater scandal, in 1998 he became only the second president to be impeached when he was accused of lying under oath about having an affair with a White House intern. Both Ronald Reagan and George Bush, however, survived their presidencies with few scars. Unlike the Watergate defendants, the Iran-Contra defendants escaped prison terms.

On the surface, Iran Contra was an arms-for-hostage exchange. Upon closer examination, it was much more. President Ronald Reagan and his advisors chose to sell arms to Iran, a designated enemy of the United States, in order to finance the activities of the anticommunist insurgents known as the Contras in Nicaragua. While noted scholar Theodore Draper wrote in his extensive study of the Iran Contra affair that ''selling arms to Iran and funding the Contras was two separate operations carried out by the same Reagan errand boys,'' they were inherently connected because the Reagan administration could not have financed the Contras without the proceeds from the arms sale.

In November of 1986, a Beirut magazine broke the story that the United States had sold arms to Iran despite an embargo against such activities that had been in effect since 1979. The American public later learned that after arms were shipped to Iran through Israel, American hostages were released. While still reeling from the repercussions of this story, the Reagan administration was forced to admit that it had used from 10 to 30 million dollars of the money from the arms sale to finance the Contras' battle against the Sandinista-led government in Nicaragua, even though both groups had been charged by international groups with human rights violations. Later Reagan wrote in his memoirs that he believed that dealing with the moderates in Iran would open up channels of communication. Critics argued that the action took place simply because it was a pet project of the president's; and when Congress refused to appropriate the money, Reagan looked elsewhere for funds.

Other than Ronald Reagan and Vice President George Bush, the chief players in the Iran-Contra scandal were Bud McFarlane and John Poindexter, both national security advisors, and Oliver North, a mid-level member of the National Security Council staff. A subsequent congressional investigation determined that the three were the ''ringleaders of a cabal of zealots who were headquartered in the National Security Council (NSC).'' The common consensus was that the three believed higher-ups who told them that selling arms to Iran was a way of easing existing hostilities. While North and Poindexter took advantage of the Fifth Amendment's protection from self-incrimination during the investigations, McFarlane talked to members of Congress. He later attempted suicide when faced with the repercussions of the scandal. Oliver North, who was considered by many to be a fall guy for the entire affair, became a cult hero and escaped prison when a federal judge handed down his judgment: three suspended sentences, two year's probation, $150,000 in fines, and 1200 hours of community service. In 1992 Admiral John Poindexter was found guilty on five separate charges, and Caspar Weinberger was indicted on charges of perjury and making false statements

Oliver North being sworn in during the Iran Contra Hearings.

during the inquiry. Nevertheless, in 1992 outgoing president George Bush quietly pardoned McFarlane and the others who had been found guilty on Iran-Contra charges. Both the Tower Commission appointed by Ronald Reagan and a subsequent investigation by Special Prosecutor Lawrence Walsh revealed serious misconduct throughout Iran-Contra activities.

In his autobiography, Oliver North admitted that Ronald Reagan knew everything that was going on from the beginning. Whether Richard Nixon had known what was going on from the beginning had been instrumental in his eventual resignation. Robert Timberg argued that there were inherent similarities with the Watergate scandal: abuses of authority existed in both; a bunker mentality was prevalent in both; presidential coverups followed the unveiling of the facts in both; Oval Office tapes proved involvement and coverups in both; televised hearings were held in both; and world-class irresponsibility permeated both. Nixon, he wrote, was smart but paranoid. Reagan was not nearly so smart; yet he was charming and made a slicker getaway. Whatever his reasons for engaging in the activities of the Iranian hostage deal and funding the Nicaraguan Contras, Ronald Reagan admittedly did both. Later investigations revealed that George Bush had been privy to the activities from the beginning. Both finished their terms while retaining the respect of the American people. It will be left to future scholars with the benefit of hindsight to understand why.

—Elizabeth Purdy

FURTHER READING:

Draper, Theodore. *A Very Thin Line: The Iran-Contra Affairs.* New York, Hill and Way, 1991.

North, Oliver. *Under Fire: An American Story.* New York, Harper Collins, 1991.

Reagan, Ronald. *An American Life.* New York, Simon and Schuster, 1990.

Timberg, Robert. *The Nightingale's Song.* New York, Simon and Schuster, 1995.

Iron Maiden

Perhaps the quintessential heavy metal band, Iron Maiden has sold more than forty-five million records worldwide, remaining the object of a faithful international fan base since the early 1980s. Numerous hit singles and platinum albums have also attested to the consistency of the listening habits of metal fans long after the much-maligned genre had ceased to make headlines in the music press. Ditching the more bluesy grooves of hard rock bands from the 1970s such as Deep Purple and UFO, Iron Maiden came up with a faster, riff-laden, yet melodious song structure which set the standards for what most listeners came to understand to be heavy metal. A marked preference for lyrics grounded on horror, mythology, wars, and history became another of the genre's key reference points, not to mention Gargantuan onstage production values and globe-trotting concert tours.

Iron Maiden was formed in London in 1976 by bassist Steve Harris. At the height of the so-called "punk revolution" spearheaded by Sex Pistols and The Clash, Harris persisted with heavy metal through constant lineup changes and difficulties in finding performing venues. By the time both punk and disco were on the decline, however, Harris had managed to recruit more reliable group members, including singer Paul Di'Anno and lead guitarist Dave Murray. After playing the club circuit, the band began to generate some minor attention in the press, and produced an independent three song record in 1979. The single pressing of three thousand copies sold out so quickly that EMI offered them an album deal.

The early 1980s marked what the British press dubbed the "New Wave of British Heavy Metal": Iron Maiden, Def Leppard, Saxon, and other bands began to storm into the domestic charts and soon enjoyed international success. Heralded by the hit single "Running Free," from *Iron Maiden* (1980), their self-titled debut album, reached an impressive fourth place in the UK charts. This allowed the band to enlist the services of producer Martin Birch for their second album, *Killers* (1981). Birch had been at the helm of some classic Deep Purple albums in the 1970s and proved himself capable of bringing out the best in the band. Elaborate introductions and solos and an overall "cleanness" of sound became trademarks which countless musicians soon attempted to emulate. Harris always remained at the creative center, writing most of the songs, but the lineup now also featured a second lead guitarist, Murray's longtime friend Adrian Smith, who would write and co-write some of the band's greatest hits such as "Wasted Years" and "2 Minutes to Midnight." Early on, Maiden began to be identified with its fictitious mascot, "Eddie," a mummified zombie designed by artist Derek Riggs and featured on all their album covers. The band began playing larger venues in Europe and the United States, touring in support of Kiss and Judas Priest, and discovered the fanatical enthusiasm of their Japanese fans after a number of headline appearances in Japan. Surprisingly, at the end of the tour, Di'Anno departed, citing stress and exhaustion.

Former Samson singer Bruce Dickinson joined the band in 1981. The energetic and charismatic frontman became an immediate favorite with fans and indelibly embodied Iron Maiden's mainstream success in the 1980s. An accomplished songwriter with powerful, semi-operatic vocal skills and manic stage antics, Dickinson is also one of rock's most imitated singers. *The Number of the Beast* topped the UK charts in 1982, and the album's Satanic-themed cover and title song generated considerable outrage among conservative groups in numerous countries. Iron Maiden soon became a household name, alongside those of Black Sabbath, Ozzy Osbourne, and AC/DC whenever the supposedly harmful influence of heavy metal on young listeners became an issue of heated debates.

The album *Powerslave* (1984) probably saw the band at its peak in the studio, with exemplary instrumental passages that culminated in the thirteen-minute epic "The Rime of the Ancient Mariner," based on the Samuel Taylor Coleridge poem. *Powerslave* led to a mammoth-scale, year-long world tour—ambitiously labeled the "World Slavery Tour"—and sell-out crowds on four continents. A tradition of sorts was also inaugurated in 1984 when Maiden played a pioneering tour of Poland at a time when, among renewed international heights of nuclear fear, virtually no other Western artists ventured beyond the Iron Curtain. Over the years, the band would constantly

Members of the band *Iron Maiden* (l-r) Adrian Smith, Bruce Dickinson, Dave Murray, Nicko McBain, and Steve Harris.

make an effort to "brave" new territories previously ignored by other bands, such as Moscow, Istanbul, and even war-torn Sarajevo. Another high point of their 1984-85 tour was an appearance at the megalomaniac "Rock in Rio" festival in Brazil, in front of an estimated crowd of two hundred thousand people.

After five consecutive platinum albums in the United States, Iron Maiden saw local musical tastes shift toward the more commercial sounds and glamorized looks of groups like Bon Jovi and Cinderella. The band's popularity dwindled in North America during the late 1980s and early 1990s, but its international following remained strong, as evidenced by two headline appearances at the annual "Monsters of Rock" festival in Donington, England, in 1989 and 1992 in front of one-hundred-thousand-plus crowds. In 1993, Dickinson announced his departure after eleven successful years, leaving for a more low-profile solo career. The search for his replacement began through an international contest sponsored by the band, resulting in thousands of tapes being sent in by would-be rock stars. Blaze Bayley, formerly with Wolfsbane, was ultimately announced as the new singer. With the retirement of Martin Birch, Harris himself was now at the helm producing the band's records and videos.

Apart from Birch, another backstage personality who played a key role in the lasting success of Iron Maiden was manager Rod Smallwood, the man who, from the beginning, ran the band's financial and commercial arm, Sanctuary Music. In the late 1990s, Sanctuary was also managing a number of other bands—whose records were sometimes produced by Harris—and even entered London's stock market in an ambitious (and successful) move. Maiden also proved to be multimedia-savvy with the creation of a state-of-the-art video game featuring Eddie and by re-releasing all of its albums in enhanced CDs containing the band's music videos.

—Alex Medeiros

FURTHER READING:

Arnett, Jeffrey Jensen. *Metalheads: Heavy Metal Music and Adolescent Alienation.* Boulder, Westview Press, 1996.

Harris, Steve, and Rod Smallwood, compilers. *Visions of the Beast: A Pictorial History of Iron Maiden—And Eddie 1979-1997.* London, Omnibus Press, 1999.

Wall, Mick. *Iron Maiden: Run to the Hills: The Official Biography.* London, Omnibus Press, 1998.

Walser, Robert. *Running with the Devil: Power, Gender, and Madness in Heavy Metal Music.* Hanover, University Press of New England, 1993.

Weinstein, Deena. *Heavy Metal: A Cultural Sociology.* Lexington, Lexington Books, 1991.

Ironman Triathlon

The Ironman Triathlon, arguably the world's toughest endurance competition, has come a long way from very humble origins. In 1977, a group of recreational athletes and naval officers in an Oahu bar got into a dispute over who was the better athlete—the runner, the swimmer, or the cyclist. Trying to resolve the argument, Naval Commander John Collins jokingly proposed a race combining the 2.4 mile "Waikiki Roughwater Swim," the 122 mile "Cycle around Oahu," and the Honolulu Marathon. A year later, 15 bold adventurers gathered on a Waikiki beach to attempt the first Ironman Triathlon, unaware they were to become a part of history. By the early 1990s, the annual Hawaii Ironman had become an internationally-televised professional competition, and the Holy Grail for hundreds of thousands of triathletes worldwide. It had also helped transform the world of exercise, inspiring the entire concept of cross-training and countless other multi-sport events.

Triathlons first gained recognition in 1979, when *Sports Illustrated* published an article on the second annual Hawaii Ironman. The next year, a highlight package was aired on ABC's *Wide World of Sports*. Although the Ironman was presented as an obscure competition for only the most obsessed athletes, the telecast still helped

Natascha Badmann wins the women's division of the 1998 Hawaiian Ironman Triathlon.

launch hundreds of other multi-sport challenges. In 1981, the Hawaii competition was moved from Waikiki to the Kailua-Kona on the Big Island, to take advantage of the spectacular backdrop of open shores and lava fields. But it was the telecast of the dramatic 1982 Hawaii Ironman that truly placed triathlons in the public conscience. Just two miles from the finish line, women's leader Julie Moss collapsed, in severe glycogen debt, but refused to accept any medical attention. She staggered over the final two miles, literally crawling to the finish line as Kathleen McCartney passed for the victory. Viewers around the world watched in awe, wondering not only whether she would finish the race, but whether she would survive. The next year, the field of competitors doubled and over 12 million people tuned in for the live telecast. The popularity of triathlons skyrocketed through the 1980s, resulting in the establishment of other major Ironman races, a World Cup Circuit of shorter races, and thousands of multi-sport events for more recreational athletes. The multi-sport craze swept the world, inspiring other "extreme" adventure races, like the multi-day Eco-Challenge and the Raid Gauloises, combining trail running, cycling, mountaineering, paddling, and sometimes even sky-diving.

By the late 1980s, triathlons had become both a professional competition, where full-time athletes competed for prize money and sponsorship, and the ultimate challenge for the amateur athletes. The Hawaii race, with its mumuku headwinds and searing temperatures, often reaching into triple digits along the lava flats, remained the main event; just to enter, competitors had to either qualify at a national competition or hope for one of the coveted lottery spots. As the competition grew, being a triathlete came to require more than a large lung capacity and a large threshold for pain; it required a large wallet. A week in Hawaii plus all the equipment—including titanium bicycles, wetsuits, shoes, accessories like heart-rate monitors, and enough food to replace the 5000 calories a triathlete might burn in a day of training—could cost thousands of dollars. The Ironman slowly became a sport for the rich, a status symbol for business executives and athletes in other disciplines.

The competitive men's field was dominated by six-time winners Dave Scott and Mark Allen throughout the 1980s and early 1990s. In the dramatic 1989 Hawaii Ironman, Allen narrowly edged Scott after racing side-by-side for nearly eight hours. Scott made a miraculous comeback in 1994, returning at the age of 40, after a two and half year retirement, to place second. The competition increased throughout the 1990s, and the winning time dropped substantially. Luc Van Lierdes' record 8:04 hour time set in 1996 is over three hours faster than Gordon Haller's 1978 winning time. The improvement over the years in the women's field was even more remarkable. In 1992, eight-time winner Paula Newby-Fraser finished in just under nine hours, an astonishing four hours faster than Lyn Lemair, the first female winner in 1979.

In 1998, the Hawaii Ironman celebrated its twentieth anniversary. In just two decades, it evolved into the world's most recognized endurance race, with 1,500 competitors, including 140 professional triathletes, competing for pride and $250,000 in prize money. During its 20 years, the multi-sport race has completely transformed the world of exercise, spawning the entire concept of cross-training and capturing the imagination of both recreational and professional athletes around the world. The simple bar bet also received its ultimate compliment, when a shorter version of the competition became an official medal sport for the 2000 Olympics in Sydney, Australia.

—Simon Donner

FURTHER READING:

Cook, Jeff S. *The Triathletes*. New York, St. Martin's Press, 1992.

Edwards, Sally. *Triathlon: A Triple Fitness Sport*. Chicago, Contemporary Books, 1983.

Levin, Dan. "Gall Divided into Three Parts." *Sports Illustrated*. October 10, 1983, 86-91.

Moore Kenny. "Big Splash in Hawaii." *Sports Illustrated*. May, 1997, 63-69.

Scott, Dave. *Dave Scott's Triathlon Training Guide*. New York, Simon and Schuster, 1986.

Irving, John (1942—)

The novels of John Irving have been regular bestsellers ever since *The World According to Garp* won international acclaim in 1978. Irving's first novel, *Setting Free the Bears* (1968), established many of the fictional characteristics that would earn him critical and popular favor in works that include *The Hotel New Hampshire* (1981), *The Cider House Rules* (1985), *A Prayer for Owen Meany* (1988), and *A Son of the Circus* (1994). Believing that "exquisitely developed characters and heartbreaking stories were the obligations of any novel worth remembering," Irving is a comic novelist whose books are distinguished by engaging heroes and detailed plots. Thematically, many have returned to issues of parenthood, children, the relationships between men and women, and the entanglements of sex. Irving's novels have sold in their millions and both *The World According to Garp* and *The Hotel New Hampshire* have been made into films.

—Paul Grainge

FURTHER READING:

Freeland, Alison. "A Conversation with John Irving." New England Review. Vol. 18, No. 2, 1997, 135-142.

Reilly, Edward C. *Understanding John Irving*. Columbia, University of South Carolina Press, 1991.

It Happened One Night

A spoiled and willful young heiress, cocooned from reality by bodyguards and her father's trillions, jumps ship off the Florida coast when her father wishes to have her recent unconsummated marriage to a gold-digging roue annulled. Her worried father hires detectives to comb the land for his runaway daughter, offers a hefty reward for news of her, and has headlines blazon her disappearance while she sets off to reach New York by cross-country bus—her first foray into the real world of ordinary people. She runs into difficulties and a broke, straight-talking journalist who has just been fired. He recognizes her, spots a scoop, and escorts her through a series of adventures to the obligatory climax of temporary misunderstandings and true love.

Such are the bones of *Night Bus,* a short story by Samuel Hopkins Adams that, retitled *It Happened One Night,* became not only one of the most successful, enduring, and best-loved romantic comedies of all time but—as written for the screen by the accomplished Robert Riskin, directed by Frank Capra with a sure sense of its characters, its comedy, and its humanity, and played with irresistible charm and polish by Clark Gable and Claudette Colbert—was arguably the most influential contribution to screwball comedy.

Screwball was a genre born of the troubled times of the Depression to provide a perfect escape from the humdrum into a celluloid world teeming with glamor, wealth, romance, and laughter. Curmudgeonly or eccentric, but never dangerous, characters supplied a thread of reality. The films satirized the rich in an era of poverty, but did so with affection, often creating a happy alliance between the idle rich and the ordinary working person. Heroines were spirited, independent-minded women, a liberating departure from the sweet-natured and compliant wives or girlfriends, hard-bitten molls, or fallen women who were the staple characters of pre-1930s cinema, and the "feel-good" plot resolutions were always arrived at via comedy, often so screwy as to give the genre its name, but constructed, in the best of them, with infallible logic and sincere conviction.

It Happened One Night conformed gloriously to the rules, and did so with seamless panache. Gable's middle-class journalist, virile, opportunistic, and commanding, gets more than he bargains for from Colbert's heiress, whom he addresses as "Brat" throughout but who turns out to have unexpected wit and intelligence. In a series of inspired sequences that have become justly famous anthology pieces, the pair constantly turn the tables on each other. The best known of these are the "walls of Jericho" and hitchhiking scenes. In the first, he turns the tables on her apprehensive suspicions by lending her his pajamas and stringing a blanket between two beds in a room they're forced to share (Gable's removal of his shirt to reveal a bare chest famously sent the sales of undershirts plummeting); in the second, she triumphs, seductively hitching her skirts to get them a ride after his self-proclaimed expertise with his thumb has failed to stop a succession of vehicles.

The chemistry between Gable and Colbert is potent, a battle of the sexes in which acid insults give way to warm wisecracking and then to a beguiling sweetness and vulnerability in both of them. Aside from the major set-pieces, the film offers a cornucopia of treasurable lunacies—Alan Hale's singing crackpot who gives them a ride; Colbert's unsuitable suitor clad in top hat and tails piloting himself to their wedding in a gyroplane; Gable and Colbert fooling detectives by faking a blue-collar marital row, to mention but three. Amidst the comedy Capra, always a devoted chronicler of the common man, introduces an episode on the bus when a group of passengers play and sing popular songs. Colbert's childlike glee and amazement as she listens to "That Daring Young Man on the Flying Trapeze" serves to highlight with some poignancy her previously cosseted isolation—a moment of truth in the fantasy.

Arguably the first, and certainly the greatest, of the screwball comedies of the 1930s, the tale of *It Happened One Night*'s success is a tale of alchemy: all the right ingredients combined and perfectly controlled to create a concoction of pure magic. It is also, like so many Hollywood success stories, a tale of happy accidents. In 1934 little Columbia, run on a relative shoestring by the foul-mouthed autocratic Harry Cohn, was considered a Poverty Row studio, and struggled to

Clark Gable and Claudette Colbert in a scene from the film *It Happened One Night*.

compete with giants such as MGM. One of its few assets was Frank Capra who, having fallen on hard times after his first early successes with silent comedy, accepted a contract with Columbia in the late 1920s which later proved to have been the turning point in the fortunes of both studio and director.

Capra read *Night Bus* in *Cosmopolitan* magazine and persuaded an unenthusiastic Cohn to buy it for $5000. Capra wanted MGM's Robert Montgomery for the role of journalist Peter Warne, but Louis B. Mayer refused to loan him out. He proved amenable, however, to the idea of lending Clark Gable to Columbia, viewing a spell on Poverty Row as suitable punishment for his rising star who, in a rebellion against his tough-guy typecasting, had checked himself into a hospital on grounds of overwork. Several actresses having rejected the role of heiress Ellen Andrews, Columbia turned to Claudette Colbert. (Her debut film, *For the Love of Mike* [1927], directed by Capra, had been a failure.) By now desperate to fill the role, Columbia agreed to Colbert's punishing demands: double her contract salary at Paramount and a shooting schedule guaranteed not to exceed four weeks. The auguries were not of the best.

At the 1935 Academy Awards, *It Happened One Night* made a grand slam, winning the Oscars for best picture, director, screenplay adaptation, actor, and actress, an unprecedented feat not equaled until *One Flew Over the Cuckoo's Nest* forty-one years later. Its success elevated Capra's status, made Colbert a star, brought Gable superstardom and his desired freedom of choice, and transformed Columbia into a major studio.

The film set the tone for a certain style of romantic comedy officially defined as Capraesque over sixty years later and, like all true works of art, defied time to give pleasure to successive generations of viewers.

—Robyn Karney

FURTHER READING:

Carney, Raymond. *American Vision: The Films of Frank Capra.* Cambridge, Cambridge University Press, 1987.

McBride, Joseph. *Frank Capra: The Catastrophe of Success.* New York, Simon and Schuster, 1992.

Pogue, Leland A. *The Cinema of Frank Capra: An Approach to Film Comedy.* New Jersey, A. S. Barnes, 1973.

It's a Wonderful Life

Although a box office failure in 1946, Frank Capra's *It's a Wonderful Life* today is a well-loved Christmas classic for many Americans. Combining sentimental nostalgia and tough realism to deliver a popular message of faith in God and faith in basic human decency, the film tells the story of everyman George Bailey (James Stewart), and his desire to escape what he considers the everyday boredom of his hometown, Bedford Falls. Despite his efforts, events conspire against him, forcing him to give up his dreams of travel he stays home to run the family Building and Loan. In the meantime, without realizing it, George becomes a pillar of his community, helping to protect the people of Bedford Falls from Mr. Potter (Lionel Barrymore), a mean, frustrated millionaire. Finally, on Christmas Eve 1946, Potter threatens George with financial ruin. George considers suicide but is rescued by an elderly angel, Clarence Oddbody (Henry Travers). Clarence shows George how much poorer the world would

be without him, teaching him that each life touches another, and that no one is a failure as long as one has a friend. The film ends on an exhilarating note as grateful friends bring George all the cash they can scrape together and help him defeat Potter.

It's a Wonderful Life began life as "The Greatest Gift," a short story by Philip Van Doren Stern. Stern had sent it as a Christmas card to his friends, and the story was later published in *Good Housekeeping.* Charles Koerner, head of production at RKO, purchased the rights to "The Greatest Gift" and hired three writers—Dalton Trumbo, Marc Connelly, and Clifford Odets—to make it into a screenplay. However, they were unable to produce a solid script. Odets's main contribution, it seemed, was to name one of George's children "Zuzu." Knowing that Capra (just out of the army and trying to establish his own production company, Liberty Films) was looking for good material for his first postwar film, Koerner offered it to him. Delighted with the story, Capra bought the film rights and developed a script with writers Frances Goodrich and Albert Hackett (Jo Swerling and Dorothy Parker also contributed, although they received no screen credit).

The film Capra crafted from this final script is an artful mixture of nostalgia, light sentimentality, and film noir. Capra makes clear links between George's personal life and national events (for example, the influenza epidemic of 1919, the Roaring Twenties, the Great

James Stewart (center) in a scene from the film *It's a Wonderful Life*.

Depression, and World War II) that would profoundly and nostalgically resonate with his audience. Although many of these milestones were moments of great trial for the country, he sentimentalized them by depicting his small-town characters as facing these difficulties with courage, pluck, and warmth. For example, during the Depression, we see George and his new bride, Mary (Donna Reed), successfully fend off Potter's attempted takeover of the Building and Loan. In a remarkable example of American virtue, the couple sacrificed their own honeymoon money, loaning it to their worried customers. Later that night, in a warm and endearing scene, Mary arranges a simple, homespun honeymoon complete with a roaring fire, a homemade dinner, and local townspeople crooning ''I Love You Truly'' outside. By contrast, Capra depicts the world without George as a dark, cold, and pitiless place. Borrowing shooting techniques from the popular film noir genre, he used deep shadows and uncomfortably odd close-ups and camera angles to produce the paranoia, distrust, and heartlessness that reigns in a George-less Pottersville.

Considering the film's immense popularity today, it may be hard to believe that it was not a hit with the audiences or critics of 1946, who were not quite ready to accept a dark Christmas story. Furthermore, it was simply too naive in the wake of the Second World War. The film's heartwarming conclusion could not expunge the dark cruelties of Pottersville. Although it was nominated for a Best Picture Academy Award (with Capra and Stewart also receiving nominations), it could not draw enough box office to cover its production costs. Liberty Films went under, and the rights to *It's a Wonderful Life* reverted to Capra's distributor, RKO. Capra went on to make other films, including *State of the Union* (1948) and *A Pocketful of Miracles* (1961), but his career never recovered.

Eventually, RKO sold *It's a Wonderful Life* to television, where it began to develop a following each Christmas season. By the late 1980s, the film was enormously popular among holiday audiences. With the advent of cable, it could be seen on various networks for practically twenty-four hours a day, generating thousands of dollars in advertising revenue. (Ironically, however, Capra received no royalties, having lost them to RKO with the collapse of Liberty. The situation was later rectified when grateful broadcasters paid him a large sum of money.)

Capra himself called *It's a Wonderful Life* his favorite of all his films. Most critics also have come to recognize the film as Capra's best and most typical work, although not always without reservations. The *New Yorker,* for example, grudgingly admitted that ''in its own icky, bittersweet way, it's terribly effective.''

—Scott W. Hoffman

FURTHER READING:

Bassinger, Jeanine. *The It's a Wonderful Life Book.* London, Pavilion, 1986.

Schickel, Richard. *The Men Who Made the Movies.* New York, Athenum, 1975.

Umphlett, Wiley Lee. *Mythmakers of the American Dream: The Nostalgic Vision in Popular Culture.* Lewisburg, Pennsylvania, Bucknell University Press, and New York, Cornwall Books, 1983.

Willis, Donald C. *The Films of Frank Capra.* Metuchen, New Jersey, The Scarecrow Press, 1974.

It's Garry Shandling's Show

It's Garry Shandling's Show was the beginning of comedian and sometime 1980s *Tonight Show* guest host Garry Shandling's ongoing exploration of lives led in front of the camera, while parodying the world of television; his magnum opus, the fruits of these years, is *The Larry Sanders Show.*

Shandling, with former *Saturday Night Live* writer Alan Zweibel, created *It's Garry Shandling's Show,* which was on Showtime from 1986 to 1988, and Fox from 1988 to 1990. The gimmick of the show was inspired by a device that hadn't often been used since the 1958 end of *Burns and Allen*'s run: breaking the fourth wall. Shandling played himself, a neurotic comedian, and regularly talked to the camera, making observations, updating the plot, or interjecting a joke. The difference was that everyone else in the cast knew they were on television, too; sometimes other characters criticized Shandling for paying too much attention to the camera or to his appearance, or complained about not being featured in an episode. And, of course, the live audience was in on it, too. If Shandling were leaving, he'd tell the audience they could use his living room while he was gone, and they would. He would also go into the audience to get reactions, or ''take a call from a viewer.''

The sitcom took place in Shandling's Sherman Oaks condominium. The supporting cast included Garry's platonic friend Nancy (Molly Cheek), his mother Ruth (Barbara Cason), his married friend Pete (Michael Tucci), Pete's wife Jackie (Bernadette Birkett), their intellectual son Grant (Scott Nemes), and nosy condo manager Leonard (Paul Wilson). In 1989-1990 season, both Garry and Nancy acquired steady love interests: Nancy's was Ian (soap opera actor Ian Buchanan) and Garry's was Phoebe (Jessica Harper), whom he married before the show ended.

The format and premise allowed guest stars to drop by and play themselves, among them Tom Petty, Zsa Zsa Gabor, and the late Gilda Radner in one of her last television appearances. There was also a 1988 election special with *Soul Train*'s Don Cornelius providing political analysis. Garry's ''wedding'' was attended by Bert Convy, Connie Stevens, and Ned Beatty. Besides covering Shandling's trials and tribulations with girlfriends, his mom, and his friends, *It's Garry Shandling's Show* lovingly spoofed television conventions and sitcom ''rules'' with parodies of *Lassie* and *The Fugitive.* Even the show's theme song winked at tradition: ''This is the theme to Garry's show, the opening theme to Garry's show, Garry called me up and asked if I would write his theme song. . . .''

The idea for the show originated in a sketch on NBC's *Michael Nesmith in Television Parts* that featured Shandling narrating a date with Miss Maryland to the camera. The sitcom was pitched to the three networks, all three of which turned it down. Showtime, for whom Shandling had done two successful comedy specials, *Garry Shandling: Alone in Vegas* (1984) and *The Garry Shandling Show 25th Anniversary Special* (1986), picked it up. Though other shows (such as *Moonlighting* and *Saved By the Bell*), came to break the fourth wall occasionally during the 1980s, *It's Garry Shandling's Show*'s use of the device was fresh and innovative, providing the creators with an effective outlet to skewer their own industry.

—Karen Lurie

FURTHER READING:

Brooks, Tim, and Marsh, Earle. *The Complete Directory to Prime Time Network and Cable TV Shows 1946-present*. New York, Ballantine Books, 1995.

Jarvis, Jeff. "It's Garry Shandling's Show." *People Weekly*. September 15, 1986, 21.

McNeil, Alex. *Total Television*. New York, Penguin, 1996.

Ives, Burl (1909-1995)

Perhaps the most versatile entertainer America has produced in the twentieth century, Burl Ives did it all. He sang; acted on stage, screen, and television; wrote songs and prose; compiled books of traditional music—which he often arranged—and taught music in a series of popular guitar manuals. Once dubbed by Carl Sandburg as "the mightiest ballad singer of any century," throughout his life Ives remained quintessentially American. A man of strong populist leanings (as evidenced by his 1949 autobiography *The Wayfaring Stranger*), Ives always saw himself as a grassroots folksinger. It is Ives's musical legacy that remains his most significant contribution, preserving for

Burl Ives

future generations an enormous wealth of material, a musical portrait of the America he had known.

Born to a farm family of modest means in Jasper County, Illinois, Ives was raised on music. His whole family sang. His maternal grandmother taught him the ballads of her Scotch-Irish-English forefathers. By the time he was four, Ives was performing in public as a child entertainer and evangelical singer. Pressured to pursue a more conventional career than minstrel, in 1927 he entered Illinois State Teachers College with a mind toward becoming a football coach, but he left a year shy of attaining a degree, preferring to live the life of a vagabond to the static life of a teacher. Recalling his college career, Ives said, "I never did take to studies."

But Ives had several innate talents which kept him afloat during his early professional years, and they eventually would prove his most distinctive features as an entertainer. He was a friendly man, of abundant natural charm, with an innate gift for storytelling. He was also a singer who labored for years to perfect his voice. And at a time when folk music was looked down on as a musical form, Ives's faith in the ballads he had learned at his grandmother's knee—and while traversing the country—preserved him through the lean years prior to his meteoric rise to fame.

While wandering throughout forty-six of the forty-eight states, Ives supported himself by playing music in bars or doing odd jobs, sleeping rough, and hitchhiking from town to town. In 1931 he was living at the International House in Manhattan, a cheap hotel catering to foreign students, working in its cafeteria while he continued the formal musical training he had begun in Terre Haute, Indiana. An avid music student, Ives absorbed the classical canon, finding work singing in churches and in madrigal groups. But his ambitions were hampered by a sinus problem which affected his voice as well as his lingering doubts about singing classical music. At heart he was still a folk balladeer. He credits one Ella Toedt, a well-known voice instructor of the day, with curing his sinus problem—enduring a year of falsetto exercises before he was rid of the blockage—and with encouraging his folk music. Soon Ives was singing ballads at charity events and parties, sharing his vast repertoire of folk songs with appreciative audiences that often included some of the leading lights of New York's leftist intelligentsia.

He was encouraged by his show business friends to try a hand at acting. Ives won a small part in an out-of-town production, then charmed his way into a nonsinging part in the Rodgers and Hart musical *The Boys from Syracuse* (1938). The duo then cast him in a traveling production of *I Married an Angel,* which Ives followed with a four-month engagement at the Village Vanguard. By 1940 he had his own radio show, *The Wayfaring Stranger,* on which he sang and told stories from his years of traveling. Suddenly, folk songs were in vogue.

By 1945 Ives was starring in *Sing Out Sweet Land,* a musical revue based on the folk songs he had popularized on his radio broadcasts, and the next year he made his film debut, playing a singing cowboy in *Smoky.* He went on to appear in numerous Broadway productions, in films, and began a recording career that would eventually number more than one hundred releases. His visibility was further enhanced by his appearance as Big Daddy in the 1958 film *Cat on a Hot Tin Roof,* a role he already had popularized on Broadway. That year he won an Oscar for his performance opposite Gregory Peck in *The Big Country.*

Throughout the 1960s, 1970s, and 1980s, Ives continued to appear in theater, film, and television productions, such as the *Roots* TV miniseries (1977), and portrayed a mean-spirited racist in noted filmmaker Samuel Fuller's last film, *White Dog* (1982). He also kept abreast of the times, expanding his repertoire to include standards like "Little Green Apples," and going so far as to cover Bob Dylan's "The Times They Are A-Changing," although his fling with the counterculture was brief.

By the time of his death in 1995, Ives was best remembered as a singer of children's songs; a narrator of animated Christmas specials for television; the kindly, avuncular man with the hefty girth.

—Michael J. Baers

FURTHER READING:

Ives, Burl. *Tales of America.* Cleveland, World Publishing Co., 1964.

———. *Wayfaring Stranger.* New York, Whittelsey House, 1948.

———. *A Wayfaring Stranger's Notebook.* Indianapolis, Bobbs-Merrill, 1962.

Locher, Frances C., ed. *Contemporary Authors.* Vol. 103. Detroit, Gale Research, 1982.

Ivy League

The term "Ivy League" is informally used to describe eight East Coast universities—Brown, Cornell, Columbia, Dartmouth, Harvard, Princeton, the University of Pennsylvania, and Yale—which are acknowledged as among the most prestigious postsecondary schools in the United States. The ivy image derives from the fact that these institutions are also among the oldest in the country, with stately buildings and beautiful historic campuses. Because of highly selective admissions criteria, an "Ivy League" degree represents the near-guarantee that a graduate will rise to the top of his—or, only since the 1970s, her—profession (the Ivy League colleges were originally all-male institutions). As educational writer Joseph Thelin wrote, the mystique of the Ivy League describes "the process by which the collegiate ideal has been . . . associated with trade marks, and brand-name imagery."

The term itself did not originally connote academic excellence: it was coined in the late 1930s by Cas Adams, a *New York Herald-Tribune* reporter, who bestowed the name on the schools because he noticed that buildings on all eight campuses were covered in vines. Before the 1880s, as Thelin wrote, "contacts between these institutions were few" until intercollegiate athletic teams began to develop.

A view of the Ivy League's Yale University.

Walter Camp, a Yale student in the 1870s, had all but invented college football and, by the turn of the century, the eight universities were dominating the sport.

With applications to most Ivy League universities topping 20,000 a year by the 1990s, and acceptance rates hovering between 10 and 15 percent, it is not hard to see how the Ivy League sets the benchmark of exclusivity against which other postsecondary institutions are measured. Many high school seniors and their parents invest so much in acceptances—from SAT preparation classes to costly counselors—that they overlook colleges that do not have such recognizable brand names. Loren Pope, author of the college-application handbook *Looking beyond the Ivy League,* is one of many authors who try to dispel myths of an Ivy League education as making or breaking one's future success. The first myth on Pope's agenda is

"An Ivy . . . College Will Absolutely Guarantee the Rich, Full, and Successful Life." More often than not, however, efforts to dispel these myths serve only to perpetuate them.

—Daryna M. McKeand

FURTHER READING:

Goldstein, Richard. *Ivy League Autumns.* New York, St. Martin's Press, 1996.

Pope, Loren. *Looking beyond the Ivy League.* New York, Penguin, 1995.

Thelin, John. *The Cultivation of Ivy: A Saga of the College in America.* Cambridge, Massachusetts, Schenkman Publishing, 1976.

J

J. Walter Thompson

Number one in industry billings from 1922 to 1972, the J. Walter Thompson agency redefined the advertising industry and transformed the business of media in America. Founded in New York City as Carlton and Smith in 1864, the agency was originally a broker of advertising space in religious journals. The agency hired its namesake, James Walter Thompson, in 1868. Thompson purchased the agency from William James Carlton in 1877, renamed it after himself, and rapidly positioned it as the exclusive seller of advertising space in many leading American magazines.

Most large magazines had existed on subscription and newsstand revenue alone. To create a market for ad space, Thompson persuaded reluctant publishers—who feared advertisements would tarnish their images—to accept advertising in their pages. Thereafter, America's largest magazines relied on advertising as their largest source of revenue, increasing the import of the composition of a publication's readership, and its appeal to advertisers.

Stanley Resor joined the company in 1908, and soon hired copywriter Helen Lansdowne. He purchased the agency in 1916 and the two were married the next year. Together they remade the agency and developed it from a mere broker of space into a full service shop that conceived and executed major national advertising campaigns.

Print advertising of the previous era emphasized brand identity, iconic images, and simple slogans. J. Walter Thompson pioneered a new strategy aimed at delivering a "hard-sell" print ad, known as the "reason-why" approach. These advertisements typically captured the reader's attention with a bold, capitalized statement accompanied by an artistic or arresting image. The ad copy methodically outlined each selling point of the product and ended with a free or reduced-price product offer.

Women made most household purchasing decisions at this time and Helen Lansdowne Resor, in her words, "added the feminine point of view" to advertising to ensure that it was "effective for women." Her wing of the offices was known as the Women's Copy Group. Among the most famous advertisements produced under Helen Lansdowne Resor were campaigns for Lux soap, Maxwell House coffee, and Crisco shortening. Her infamous "A skin you love to touch" ad for Woodbury's Facial Soap featured a man seductively caressing a woman's arm and kissing her hand. The overt sexuality caused a number of *Ladies' Home Journal* readers to cancel their subscriptions but launched one of the most successful selling techniques of all time.

In 1912, Stanley Resor commissioned the market research study, "Population and Its Distribution." The study detailed both the composition of the American population and the distribution of retail and wholesale stores across the cities and rural areas. In 1915 Resor was the first to open a research department, inaugurating the massive efforts of corporate America to determine consumer desires.

As part of this effort, Resor hired John Hopkins University behavioral psychologist John B. Watson in 1920. Watson theorized that humans are capable of only three basic emotions—love, fear, and rage—and sought to tap these feelings with advertising. Watson's application of psychology to advertising anticipated the later use of psychological and subliminal selling techniques.

Watson's hiring coincided with the trend toward "whisper" advertising that sowed insecurity in the reader. One such J. Walter Thompson ad, for Odorono deodorant in 1919, read in part, "It is a physiological fact that persons troubled by underarm odor seldom detect it themselves." The use of testimonials from stars, such as Joan Crawford's 1927 endorsement of Lux Soap, was another of the agency's firsts.

The J. Walter Thompson agency first led the industry in billings for 1922, and held that position for the next 50 years, its revenues growing from $10 million to nearly $1 billion during this period. By 1938, national radio advertising surpassed that in magazines. As with magazine publishers, early radio operators initially resisted commercial advertising. But by 1933, J. Walter Thompson's clients sponsored nine weekly shows including *Kraft Music Hall* and the *Fleischmann Yeast Hour*. Products were promoted in short "spots" that lasted from 15 seconds to a couple of minutes and were often live mini-dramas in their own right complete with original jingles. Television advertising adopted the same model in the 1940s and 1950s.

As a result of J. Walter Thompson's innovations, most media depend upon advertising as their primary source of revenue. Advertising is so culturally ubiquitous and established that advertisements themselves are considered an art form worthy of serious critique. Numerous awards annually honor outstanding work.

Americans are bombarded with thousands of advertising messages each year and most can recite slogans and jingles from their most, or least, favorite advertisements. "Where's the beef?"—a line from a Wendy's restaurants television spot of the 1980s—was embraced so eagerly by the public that Walter Mondale used it as a rejoinder in a presidential debate. The Nixon Administration's machinations and untruths once led Ralph Nader to label it a "J. Walter Thompson production" and, in fact, five of Nixon's top aides were former employees. The creative pressure and client dependency that is the recognizable perpetual state of agencies was captured in television programs such as *Bewitched* in the 1960s and *thirtysomething* in the 1980s.

In the 1950s, J. Walter Thompson was one of the first agencies to aggressively expand internationally, eventually growing into a global corporation. It finally lost its number one billings ranking in the 1970s when smaller "hot shops" emerged as creative boutiques more in tune with the era's cultural shifts and other large global agencies grew to comparable size and reach. In 1980 it became a subsidiary of JWT Group Inc., a Delaware-based holding company that was in turn purchased by the British marketing firm WPP Group in 1987.

The J. Walter Thompson agency's influence on the multi-billion dollar advertising industry and the media it supports was profound. Informative, persuasive, seductive, and intrusive, advertising became omnipresent in the national media and the national consciousness. As the industry leader for decades, both creatively and financially, J. Walter Thompson defined the advertising agency to a public inundated with its product.

—Steven Kotok

FURTHER READING:

Fox, Stephen R. *The Mirror Makers: A History of American Advertising and Its Creators.* New York, Morrow, 1997.

Meyers, William. *The Image Makers: Power and Persuasion on Madison Avenue.* New York, Times Books, 1984.

Sivulka, Juliann. *Soap, Sex, and Cigarettes: A Cultural History of American Advertising.* Belmont, California, Wadsworth Publishing Company, 1998.

Strasser, Susan. *Satisfaction Guaranteed: The Making of the American Mass Market.* New York, Pantheon Books, 1989.

Jack Armstrong

In perhaps the longest high school career on record, Jack Armstrong remained an All-American Boy for close to two decades. For the greater part of its radio life, *Jack Armstrong, the All-American Boy* was a 15-minute-a-day children's serial. The show began in the summer of 1933 and didn't leave the air until the summer of 1951—although it was considerably modified by then. The sponsor for all those years was Wheaties, the Breakfast of Champions. The show originated in Chicago, long the center for soap operas and the adventure serials that filled the 5-6 pm children's hour on radio. The producer of the Jack Armstrong show was an advertising agency headed by Frank Hummert—who with his wife Anne would later produce such long-lasting programs as *Ma Perkins, Just Plain Bill, Our Gal Sunday,* and *Mr. Keen, Tracer of Lost Persons.* The writer who developed the idea and turned out the initial scripts was Robert Hardy Andrews, a prolific and supremely self-confident man, and the first actor to portray the clean-cut and adventure-prone Jack was Jim Ameche.

Jack, who attended high school in the Midwestern town of Hudson, excelled as both an athlete and a student. He was clearly inspired by the dime novel hero Frank Merriwell. While every show opened with a vocal quintet singing the school fight song—"Wave the flag for Hudson High, boys, show them how we stand"—Jack spent relatively little time behind a desk or even on the gym floor. Instead, accompanied by his teen friends Billy and Betty Fairfield, he traveled to the four corners of the world and got entangled in an endless series of intriguing adventures. During the early years of the program Jack, Betty, and Billy journeyed to the Northwest to work with the Royal Canadian Mounted Police, found a lost tribe of Eskimos in the Arctic, outwitted cattle rustlers in Arizona, hunted for a lost city in the jungles of Brazil, and returned to Hudson to round up a gang of counterfeiters. A character named Captain Hughes served as a mentor and adult companion on many of the adventures. Don Ameche, Jim's brother, was the first actor to play that role.

In the spring of 1936 Talbot Mundy, who'd written such successful adventure novels as *King of the Khyber Rifles, Jimgrim,* and *Tros of Samothrace,* was having money problems. So he accepted the job of writing *Jack Armstrong,* and stayed with it until his death in 1940. He took Jack and his companions to such locations as Egypt, Easter Island, India, Africa, and Tibet. Most of those spots had been favored settings for Mundy's novels and stories in the 1920s and 1930s. According to Jim Harmon, it was Mundy who introduced a new mentor in the person of Uncle Jim to the show in the fall of 1936. The uncle of Billy and Betty Fairfield was an industrialist and an inventor. Actor James Goss had a distinctive radio voice that fit "the

commanding but warm father figure" he played. Uncle Jim traveled with the young trio on their adventures, many of which stretched across several months. Mundy was able to recycle not just settings but plots from his novels. In an early 1937 story, for instance, Jack and the gang end up in Africa hunting for the ivory treasure to be found in the Elephants' Graveyard. The plot, with considerable changes, was earlier used in Mundy's 1919 novel *The Ivory Trail.*

The program was a great promoter of premiums. Whenever a portable gadget was introduced into a continuity, listeners could be certain that it would eventually be offered for sale. But first its utility and desirability—emphasized in many instances by the fact that the current villains would do almost anything to get hold of the object in question—were usually romanced for several weeks. All kids usually had to do to get their copy of the gadget was to send a Wheaties box top and a dime. There were dozens of premiums from 1933 to 1948. Among them a Torpedo Flashlight, a Pedometer, an Explorer Telescope, a Secret Bombsight, a Dragon's Eye Ring, a Rocket Chute, an Egyptian Whistling Ring, and Tru-Flite model planes. The more popular items sold in the millions.

The only outside merchandising in the 1930s involved two Big Little Books issued by the Whitman Publishing Co. Both *Jack Armstrong and the Ivory Treasure* (1937), which once again used the Elephants' Graveyard story line, and *Jack Armstrong and the Mystery of the Iron Key* (1939) were based on Mundy scripts. These small, fat illustrated novels had pictures by the gifted Henry E. Vallely. His Jack was a handsome fellow in polo shirt, jodhpurs, and riding boots, who looked to be in his early twenties. The Jack Armstrong property didn't seriously branch out into other media again until after World War II. The year 1947 was when several things happened—not only a movie serial but also the start of a comic strip and a comic book. Columbia Pictures produced the 15-chapter serial with John Hart, later to play the Lone Ranger on television for two seasons, as a somewhat older Jack. In the spring of that year, the Register and Tribune Syndicate introduced a *Jack Armstrong* newspaper strip. Bob Schoenke was the artist and, as one comics historian has pointed out, his "Jack was nowhere near as dashing as Vallely's and looked more like the sort of youth who'd spend much of his time on the bench." The strip was dropped in 1949. The *Parents' Magazine* outfit started a comic book late in 1947. Like their *True Comics,* it was rather dull and polite, never capturing the fun and gee-whiz spirit of the radio show. It, too, folded in 1949, after just 13 issues.

Charles Flynn had inherited the role of Jack in 1939 and, except for a year out for military service, he stayed with it to the end. In 1947, with the popularity of daily serials waning, Wheaties transformed *Jack Armstrong* into a half-hour program heard two or three times a week. Then in 1950 the title was changed to *Armstrong of the SBI.* Jack had started working for the Scientific Bureau of Investigation some years early and also had acquired a new mentor, Vic Hardy, a reformed crook, who headed up the SBI. Uncle Jim had long since been phased out, Billy went next, and only Betty remained of the old gang in the final days; through all those adventurous years she and Jack had never been more than just good friends.

—Ron Goulart

FURTHER READING:

Dunning, John. *On The Air.* New York, Oxford University Press, 1998.

Goulart, Ron, editor. *The Encyclopedia of American Comics.* New York, Facts On File, 1990.

Harmon, Jim. *Radio Mystery and Adventure*. Jefferson, McFarland & Company, 1992.

The Jackson Five

When Motown recording artists, the Jackson Five, burst upon the music scene in 1969, this group of five brothers followed an extremely successful career trajectory that launched the youngest brother, Michael Jackson, into superstardom. But as a group, the Jackson Five was more than the sum of its parts, or even the sum total of Michael Jackson's charisma: all of the brothers were talented singers and songwriters in their own right. During the 1970s, they enjoyed a lengthy string of hit singles, becoming the most popular black soul vocal group of all time.

The Jackson Five were comprised of Jackie Jackson (born May 4, 1951), Tito Jackson (born Oct. 15, 1953), Marlon Jackson (born Mar. 12, 1957), Jermaine Jackson (born Dec. 11, 1954) and Michael Jackson (born Aug. 29, 1958)—all of whom sang. The five brothers were born into a very large family run by authoritative patriarch,

Joseph Jackson, an aspiring amateur musician who occasionally played around their hometown of Gary, Indiana. In addition to those five brothers, there were three sisters (Rebbie, La Toya and Janet) and one brother, Randy Jackson, who joined the group when they moved to Columbia Records and were re-dubbed the Jacksons.

The Jacksons were a musical family. Joseph and his wife Katherine often led the brothers in singing harmony-rich songs in the family's living room during their childhood. As the result of constant practice overseen by Joseph, the boys—soon dubbed the Jackson Five—evolved into a popular regional act that eventually came to the attention of Motown president and founder Berry Gordy. In 1969 Motown signed the group, and their first single, "I Want You Back," went to number one on the *Billboard* Pop charts in January of 1970.

This began a string of thirteen top-twenty pop singles, including "ABC," "I'll Be There," "Never Can Say Goodbye," "Mama's Pearl," and "Dancing Machine," among others. The Jackson Five were among the last groups to produce hits following Motown's tradition of using in-house songwriting and recording teams, a practice that had become increasingly infrequent once Motown artists Marvin Gaye and Stevie Wonder had begun to break out on their own. And soon, the assembly line Motown production techniques began to

The Jackson Five: (from left) Tito, Marlon, Michael, Jackie, and Jermaine.

Mahalia Jackson

the Baptist religion, absorbing the church music that would prove the major influence on her life and her music. At the age of 16, she moved to Chicago to stay with an aunt, and supported herself in a variety of humble domestic jobs while, at the same time, joining the Greater Salem Baptist Church and singing with the Johnson Singers, a quintet that toured local churches. She turned down an offer from Earl Hines, but met Tommy Dorsey, with whom she forged a mutually beneficial relationship. (Some of Dorsey's songs were dedicated to Jackson). By 1938, Jackson had married, opened a beauty and floral shop, and acquired real estate. Her early performances in Chicago were in diverse venues. Not accepted in the established black churches, she had to perform at storefronts and in basement halls, and it was Studs Terkel, author and radio host, who first presented her to his largely white radio audience.

Few of Jackson's early performances were recorded but she signed with Decca, for whom she recorded "God Shall Wipe Away All Tears" (1934) and "God's Gonna Separate the Wheat . . ." (1937). These early recordings were artistically but not commercially successful, and her refusal to record blues music led Decca to drop her. In 1948, she signed with Apollo records and recorded her million-plus bestseller, the Rev. W. Herbert Brewster's composition, "Move On Up a Little Higher," and cut a long-playing album, *No Matter How You Pray*. Her early recording repertoire is mixed and the artistic quality variable—the Apollo recordings suffer from technical problems and undistinguished accompaniment, but her voice is in fine form. By 1952, her relationship with Apollo had reached an impasse and she signed with Columbia records in 1954. The Columbia sessions, consisting of early compositions previously recorded on

Apollo as well as new material, generally excelled in both technical and artistic quality, and she made several albums for the label. By the 1950s, she had engaged Mildred Falls, a gem of a gospel pianist, who received neither the recognition nor the remuneration that she deserved, and organist Ralph Jones, as her accompanists. The duo was called the Falls-Jones Ensemble.

When in her finest form, Jackson's contralto swoops, dives, and easily vacillates from high declamatory shouts to low lyrical melodies, couched in the style of black preachers and executed within a single breath. She confounded musicologists by breaking all the rules while holding her audiences spellbound. Jackson and her pianist Mildred Falls also made liberal use of blues phrasing, together with the rhythmic vitality of the sanctified church. Notable and memorable recordings in her repertoire of congregational style chants, hymns, and African-American spirituals include "Amazing Grace," "Nobody Knows the Trouble I've Seen," "Didn't It Rain," and "Deep River," as well as Dorsey compositions such as "Precious Lord." She recorded a small number of secular songs such as "I Believe." Jackson frequently sang parts of a song without meter and preferred songs heavily infused with the scale, chords, and modified structure of blues. "Walk Over God's Heaven," "Move On Up a Little Higher," "Jesus Met the Woman at the Well," and "I'm Going to Live the Life I Sing About" fall into this category.

Jackson performed at the Newport Jazz Festival in 1958, and is featured singing "The Lord's Prayer" at the end of the film *Jazz on a Summer's Day*. She sang, too, with Duke Ellington's band, both at the Festival and in the studio, explaining away her participation by saying that she considered Ellington's band "a sacred institution." The same year she appeared in the film *St. Louis Blues*, the biopic of W.C. Handy that starred Nat "King" Cole, and then provided the emotional climax to Douglas Sirk's remake of *Imitation of Life* (1959), singing "Trouble of the World" at the tear-sodden funeral of Lana Turner's black maid (Juanita Moore). By then, Jackson had given many international concert tours and was world famous. During the 1950s and 1960s she appeared frequently on television and sang at John F. Kennedy's inauguration.

By the late 1960s she commanded mostly large, white audiences in Europe and America, but by then her voice and her health were in decline. Her favorite pastime was cooking and she continued to consume the rich soul food of her home, New Orleans, including red beans, rice, and ham hocks. She weighed as much as 250 pounds at one time. Her grueling touring schedule, her entrepreneurial ventures, two failed marriages, and other personal problems had exacted a heavy toll on her health. Mahalia Jackson suffered heart failure and died in Chicago at the age of 60. Her body lay in state as thousands of mourners filed past to pay their respects to this unique performer. At her funeral, her good friend Aretha Franklin sang "Precious Lord," just as the great gospel singer herself had done at the funeral of Martin Luther King.

—Willie Collins

FURTHER READING:

Goreau, Laurraine. *Just Mahalia, Baby: The Mahalia Jackson Story*. Gretna, Louisiana, Pelican Publishing, 1984.

Jackson, Mahalia, with Evan McLeod Wylie. *Movin' On Up: Mahalia Jackson*. New York, Avon Books, 1966.

Schwerin, Jules. *Got to Tell It: Mahalia Jackson, Queen of Gospel*. New York, Oxford University Press. 1992.

Jackson, Michael (1958—)

The nucleus of his own mammoth pop sideshow, pop singer Michael Jackson absorbed the most affecting African American musical traditions with which he had grown up, infused them with his own musical eccentricity and the popular trends and technology of the moment, and created a popular explosion of nearly unprecedented proportions. Although perceived as the ultimate sexual, racial, and social "Other," between 1982 and 1984 Jackson helped sell over 40 million copies of the record album called, most appropriately, *Thriller.* In the late 1980s, Jackson again established new records with his album *Bad* and its accompanying worldwide concert tour. During the early 1990s, Jackson's inscrutable off-stage antics made him one of the best-known eccentrics in modern history.

By the time Jackson left on the notorious 1984 "Victory Tour" as lead singer of the Jacksons pop-soul singing group, he had already broken all the rules of popular success in the late-twentieth-century music industry. A teen idol without any apparent sexual interests of his own, he attracted a huge popular audience without compromising his black musical roots, and displayed eccentricities that constantly kept him in the headlines. An obviously unhappy man, Jackson revealed his social and personal discontent in his overwhelming, unavoidable, and disturbing strangeness. That strangeness reached disconcerting proportions in 1993, when a thirteen year old Beverly Hills boy made a criminal complaint against Jackson alleging sexual molestation—a claim Jackson repeatedly denied. After a thirteen month investigation—during which time Jackson settled a multi-million dollar lawsuit— the district attorneys in Los Angeles and Santa Barbara counties announced that they would not file charges unless and until a child witness agreed to testify against Jackson in open court. They also announced that the case would not close until the statute of limitations ran out in August of 1999.

Michael Jackson

Those allegations continued to disrupt Jackson's career well into the late 1990s. He suffered financial setbacks during this time and, while his albums still sold well in Europe, they did not fare as well in the United States. As of 1999, Jackson had not recorded an album of all new material since the early 1990s. Instead, he concentrated on arranging his personal financial matters, frequently announcing plans to fund theme parks in such places as Poland, Brazil, Japan, and Las Vegas.

Before the "madness" of *Thriller* and the subsequent publicity stunts and notorious allegations regarding his personal life, Michael Jackson was a member of a family singing group from Gary, Indiana, called the Jackson Five. In addition to Michael himself, the group originally included four of his five brothers. A child performing sensation from the age of five, Jackson was one of the nation's finest 1960s rhythm & blues vocalists long before his grade school graduation. An acolyte of James Brown and Jackie Wilson, the young Jackson was also a dancer of nearly unmatched ferocity and versatility. His singing skill far surpassed any other child recording artist; young Michael almost literally sang his heart out. The eleven-year-old boy sang of desire, joy, anguish, and loss with all the sophistication and embittered knowledge of a man in his 40s. His presence on the radio in the early 1970s stunned and impressed listeners. Very quickly, the group amassed a vast collection of gold records and was able to move to a California mansion.

Although clearly gifted, Michael did not come by his success "naturally"; he was trained by a fierce, brutal, and unforgiving group leader: his father. Joseph Jackson was a crane operator at a Gary steel mill who left a music career behind in the early 1950s to support his rapidly growing family. He put his guitar away in a closet as a "memory piece" and warned the children never to touch it. When nine-year-old Tito Jackson was caught playing the guitar in 1962, he was, by his own account, "torn up" by his father. This was the founding event of the Jackson Five; after the incident with Tito, Joseph began to organize the youngsters into a singing group. The group, at first, did not include three-and-a-half-year-old Michael; he made his entrance when his parents caught him imitating older brother Jermaine's singing. They were alarmed and delighted, and Michael was immediately installed as the group's tiny new front man.

Michael and his siblings have reported being beaten and terrorized by their father during their childhood. Joseph Jackson ran long daily rehearsal sessions armed with belts and switches, which he used with frequency and severity. Sister La Toya Jackson has said that the beatings the siblings endured were bloody and often involved the use of fists, while Michael reported in his autobiography that he fought back with his own small fists. "I would fight back and my father would kill me, just tear me up. Mother told me I'd fight back even when I was very little, but I don't remember that. I do remember running under tables to get away from him, and making him angrier." Joseph denied this charge to the Associated Press with telling succinctness: "Maybe I should've punched La Toya, like any other normal parent would do, but La Toya stayed quiet and never did get into any trouble or nothing." La Toya Jackson also made charges of sexual abuse against her father, which he has repeatedly denied. At the age of thirty-four, Michael said he was still frightened of his father and that on meeting him, he often "would get sick; I would start to regurgitate." Joseph responded to this, too. "If he regurgitated," Joseph told Michelle McQueen on ABC-TV's *Day One* program in 1993, "he regurgitated all the way to the bank."

Joseph kept a grueling rehearsal schedule and groomed his sons to be polished professionals in a very short time. By the age of nine,

Michael was singing in nightclubs, working side by side with strippers and drag queens, and getting an education in the process. "This one girl with gorgeous eyelashes and long hair came out and did her routine," he later wrote, "She put on a *great* performance. All of a sudden, at the end, she took off her wig, pulled a pair of big oranges out of her bra, and revealed that she was a hard-faced guy under all that make-up. That blew me away."

In late 1968, Michael and his brothers were on their way to New York for a taping of their first television appearance on *David Frost,* when they received a call from Motown Records. The group handily passed their audition for Berry Gordy, owner and founder of Motown, then the largest black-owned business in America. Gordy told the boys that they would have three number one records in a row, and become The Next Big Thing. The success engendered by Michael's singing and dancing prowess went beyond even Gordy's confident estimates. The young brothers became the first black teen idols and Michael made his first "teen dream" solo album at age twelve. Rock critic Vince Aletti expressed amazement at the ability of so young a boy to convey such subtle emotions as "anguish and doubt" with startling authenticity.

During the winter of 1972-73, Michael's voice broke, leaving both his career and that of the group in question. The music business has been generally unkind to former boy sopranos, and Berry Gordy seemed ready to move on to other projects. It looked as though Michael Jackson was destined to be a pubescent golden-oldie. The group began to think seriously of breaking their contract. According to his memoirs, it was fifteen-year-old Michael himself who presented Berry Gordy with the ultimatum: "Let us have creative control or we're gone." In 1974, the family held a press conference to announce that they would sign a new record contract with Epic Records, a division of the CBS Records conglomerate.

After two lukewarm CBS albums with the group, and one big success, Michael made good on CBS's plan for him to record a solo album, though he later remarked that he felt they were merely securing their investment. He had his own, more grandiose plans for a solo career. His first tentative step in this direction involved his acceptance of Gordy's offer to co-star in an all-African American version of *The Wizard of Oz,* renamed *The Wiz.* Oscar-winning producer Quincy Jones was the musical director of *The Wiz.* Jones got on well with Michael during the shoot, and when Jackson suggested that Jones produce his next solo album, he agreed. The collaboration worked both musically and artistically: the *Off The Wall* album turned out to be smooth as silk, with Jones applying sandpaper to Jackson's audible and exciting rough edges. The tracks conformed to a soft, cascading beat underneath the rich, erotic yearning of Jackson's voice. This new voice, full and mature with low moans and floating falsetto wails, was entirely unrecognizable. The child sensation was gone—in more ways than one.

It was during this period that Jackson began to display, for the first time, some of the odd personal characteristics for which he would later gain notoriety. During the filming of *The Wiz,* Jackson gave several promotional interviews. Timothy White of the rock magazine *Crawdaddy* was assigned to interview Jackson and found him quite amusing. He said Jackson appeared "to be in some sort of daze" as he ate food with his fingers at a glitzy French restaurant in Manhattan. During this transitional time, Jackson began to hone his skills as a songwriter. On the Jacksons' album *Triumph,* he unveiled the idiosyncratic and disquieting songwriting style that would drive the success of the *Thriller* album. One song, called "This Place Hotel," "came from a dream I had. I dream a lot," he told a reporter. "Live

and sin," the song begins, making the narrator's guilt an overwhelming and permanent condition. Set in a haunted hotel run by "wicked women" who appear suddenly in groups of two or three, the singer is trapped by "faces staring, glaring, tearing through me." Probably inspired by the unstable nature of public fame, Jackson's legendary paranoia makes its first appearance: "Every smile's a trial thought in beguile to hurt me." At one point, the singer declares bluntly, "hope is dead." The singing is pained, open-throated, and raw.

In 1982, Jackson was completing work on his second Quincy Jones collaboration. Determined that the new album must match or exceed *Off The Wall's* popularity, Jones and Jackson sought more powerful music. When Jackson brought in a tape of a new song, "Beat It," Jones began to realize that Jackson could become a powerful phenomenon—a crossover to the "white rock" market. Jackson's hard rocking song about backing away from a fight fit perfectly in the rock style. Jones brought in metal guitarist Eddie Van Halen to do a solo, and the pounding beat coupled with the song's accompanying visual representation of a rhythm & blues singer performing "white" rock began literally to change the face of the music industry.

As the album neared the end of production, Jones still needed one more solid hit and asked Jackson to write another song. For reasons that are unclear, Jackson wrote a fierce song denying paternity of a little boy whose "eyes were like mine." "Billie Jean" is now considered a rock classic. There are times during the song when it seems that the arrangement just cannot keep up with the singer's passion, and Jackson's frenzy seems barricaded by the cool, solid majesty of the arrangement, singing as if lives really did depend on listeners believing his story. The magic of the song is, of course, that the singer is not really sure if he believes himself.

The new album quickly jumped to number five on its release. This time, reluctantly, Jackson did a great number of promotional interviews. He spoke to reporters from *Ebony, Newsweek, Interview,* and *Rolling Stone* and filled out written questionnaires for other publications like *Creem.* He did television shots for *Entertainment Tonight, Ebony/Jet Showcase,* and *America's Top Ten.* The interview that everyone talked about, however, was the February 17, 1983 cover story for *Rolling Stone.*

"I'm the type of person who will tell it all, even though it's a secret. And I *know* that things should be kept private," Jackson explained to interviewer Gerri Hirshey, neatly encapsulating the "secret" of his success as well. Hirshey described him as extremely nervous and flighty; he suffered the interview as if he were getting stitches. He said he liked to watch cartoons and explained why: "It's like everything's all right. It's like the world is happening now in a faraway city. Everything's fine." Hirshey says the interview remained tense until Jackson relaxed when talking about his animals; he even forced Hirshey to play with his boa constrictor. Then, unbidden by Hirshey, he asked, "Know what I also love? Mannequins . . . I guess I want to bring them to life," he went on. "I like to imagine talking to them." It may have been with those lines that *Thriller* mania really began. It wasn't just that Michael Jackson sounded or even looked peculiar; he'd marked himself as irrefutably "Other," a stranger in a strange land.

By early spring of 1983, "Billie Jean" skyrocketed to number one on the *Billboard* charts, and remained there for seven weeks. This song was followed almost immediately by "Beat It" which stayed on top four weeks. *Thriller* also reached number one and stayed there. At one point in early 1983, Michael Jackson had an unprecedented number one record on four charts: pop singles and albums, and Black singles and albums. To promote ''Billie Jean,'' CBS had meanwhile financed an expensive '' music video,'' a little film set to the tune. The chief outlet for airing these videos was the cable channel founded in 1981 called Music Television or MTV. According to a September 22, 1986 *T.V. Guide* story, the cable channel refused to air the video because they said it was not ''rock and roll'' enough for their format. When CBS threatened to pull all its videos from the cable channel, ''Billie Jean'' became a rock 'n' roll song.

In 1983, Michael participated in the *Motown 25* televised reunion and stole the show with his innovative and breathtaking dancing. He unveiled his famous ''moonwalk'' for the first time, spun as if on ice skates, and perched precariously on his toes for the briefest moment. He pursued his dance in a sort of calamitous rage. Michael seemed to sense that this was his chance to escape the confines of mere stardom and become something quite different: not the ''star'' he'd been for years, but an iconic signifier on the order of Marilyn or Elvis. The show aired in May, with ''Beat It'' and *Thriller* already laying waste to the charts. After this, there was a buzz of excitement surrounding Jackson, as if each new gesture brought with it a revelation.

As time went on, the revelations his gestures brought were increasingly disturbing. The shadowy transformation revealed itself quickly; in 1984, Michael Jackson very reluctantly submitted to his father's pressure to go on a concert tour with the Jacksons. This ''Victory Tour'' turned into an unmitigated disaster; high ticket prices created a backlash, the tour was mismanaged, the infighting unmerciful. In the end, Michael himself decided to give away all his proceeds to charity.

After the tour, Michael Jackson ''went away'' for a while in an attempt to cope with an onslaught of unprecedented pop pressure. He severed many ties with his family, and finally moved out of the family home to a new ranch in Santa Barbara County that he called ''Neverland.'' When he did appear in public, he often wore a surgical mask over his face, which served to hide the cosmetic changes he was making to his appearance. His skin became lighter (due, he said later, to a skin disease), his nose thinned after several surgeries, and he added a cleft to his chin. During this time, Jackson engaged in a variety of eerie publicity stunts. His manager announced Jackson's wishes to sleep in a hyperbaric chamber and purchase the skeleton of Joseph Merrick, England's ''Elephant Man.'' By the time he returned to the popular music scene in 1987, Jackson was widely regarded as a freak. Although his music still sold alarmingly well (and was alarmingly good), and though he was perhaps more famous than ever, by 1993 Jackson was a figure of extreme curiosity, arousing as much pity as fascination.

That the denouement was troubling should not have been altogether surprising; Jackson's life since *Thriller* seemed to consist of a series of troubling crises. On August 17, 1993, a Los Angeles County child protective services caseworker took down a report alleging that Jackson had molested a young boy. (In November of that year, the underage son of one of Jackson's former employees also made a claim of impropriety to L.A. County's CPS.) After Jackson settled the civil case and the investigation closed, he resumed his career. First he married Elvis Presley's daughter Lisa Marie, and when that union ended after 18 months, he married and produced two children with Debbie Rowe, a Los Angeles nurse. By the late 1990s, Jackson seemed to simply revel in his role as a human oddity.

—Robin Markowitz

FURTHER READING:

Anderson, Christopher P. *Michael Jackson: Unauthorized.* New York, Simon and Schuster, 1994.

Campbell, Lisa D. *Michael Jackson: The King of Pop.* Boston, Branden Books, 1993.

George, Nelson. *The Michael Jackson Story.* New York, Dell, 1984.

Hirshey, Gerri. *Nowhere to Run: The Story of Soul Music.* New York, Times Books, 1984

Jackson, K., with Wiseman, R. *The Jacksons: My Family.* New York, St. Martin's Paperbacks, 1990.

Jackson, La Toya. *LA Toya: Growing Up in the Jackson Family.* New York, Dutton, 1991.

Jackson, Michael. *Moonwalk.* New York, Doubleday, 1988.

Matthews, Gordon R. *Michael Jackson.* New York, J. Messner, 1984.

Taraborrelli, J. Randy. *Michael Jackson: The Magic and the Madness.* New York, Birch Lane Press, 1991.

Jackson, Reggie (1946—)

Slugging outfielder Reggie Jackson was a larger-than-life figure who saved his best performances for baseball's biggest stage. Nicknamed ''Mr. October'' for his ability to shine in baseball's autumn post-season showcase, Jackson earned Hall of Fame status based

Reggie Jackson

largely on his prodigious World Series play. He was also the first baseball player to have a candy bar named after him, a powerful indicator of his impact on the popular imagination.

The native of Wyncote, Pennsylvania, was chosen second in the 1967 amateur draft by the Oakland Athletics. He quickly established himself as a powerful home-run hitter who struck balls out of the park at a near-record pace. He first grabbed national headlines when he swatted a home run over the roof at Tiger Stadium during the 1971 All-Star Game in Detroit, and the A's domination of the World Series from 1972 to 1974 kept him firmly planted in the public eye. Though a knee injury kept Jackson out of the Fall Classic in 1972, he returned the following season with a stellar campaign. The American League's Most Valuable Player with a .293 average and a league-leading 32 home runs, Jackson was named World Series MVP as well, establishing the post-season reputation he was to solidify in years to come. In June of 1974, *Time* magazine put Jackson on its cover. "Reginald Martinez Jackson is the best player on the best team in the sport," the periodical proclaimed.

Baseball's brave new world of free agency gave the rising superstar the chance to test his value on the open market. The New York Yankees responded with a lucrative five-year contract offer. Jackson leapt at the chance to play in the world's largest media market. The marriage of convenience between the swaggering Jackson and the club's dictatorial owner, Cleveland shipbuilder George M. Steinbrenner III, was to prove an eventful one.

Arriving in New York, Jackson almost immediately proclaimed himself "the straw who stirs the drink"—alienating the Yankees' team captain, Thurman Munson, along with almost everyone else in town. Sportswriters found Jackson made for great copy, but his manager, Billy Martin, couldn't stand him. Martin looked for every opportunity to humiliate his star slugger, benching him for no reason at one point and pulling him off the field mid-game at another. Their feud came perilously close to blows on more than one occasion. Nevertheless, the feudin' Yankees steamed over the American League on their way to the American League pennant.

The 1977 World Series proved to be the high point of Jackson's career. "Mr. October" became the first player ever to hit five home runs in one World Series. He clouted three in the sixth game alone, on three consecutive pitches, off three different Los Angeles Dodger pitchers. That feat, never accomplished before or since, helped earn Jackson Most Valuable Player honors as the Yankees took the championship four games to two.

That off-season, Jackson became the toast of New York. While still in Oakland, he had once boasted, "If I played in New York, they'd name a candy bar after me." Someone at Standard Brands Confectionery was obviously taking notes that day, because in 1978 Jackson got his candy bar. The *Reggie!* bar was a crumbly lump of chocolate, peanuts, and corn syrup sculpted to the approximate diameter of a major league baseball. It cost a quarter (quite a bargain in the age of inflation) and came packaged in an orange wrapper bearing the slugger's likeness.

Sportswriters had a field day with the unpalatable confection. One wag wrote that when you opened the wrapper on a *Reggie!* bar, it told you how good it was. Another derided it as the only candy bar that tasted like a hot dog. But the ultimate verdict came from Yankee fans, 44,667 of whom were given free samples on April 13, 1978, when the Yankees opened their home campaign against the Chicago White Sox.

In typical Jackson fashion, the slugger clouted a home run in his first at-bat, making it four "taters" in four swings at Yankee Stadium dating back to the sixth game of the 1977 Series. The raucous crowd

then showered the field with *Reggie!* bars as Jackson made his trip around the bases. Ugly orange wrappers quickly carpeted the green field. The only detractor from the prevailing air of absurdist resignation was White Sox manager Bob Lemon, who groused, "People starving all over the world and 30 billion calories are laying on the field."

Lemon was whistling a different tune that August when, after being fired by the White Sox, he took over for Billy Martin as Yankee manager. The volatile Martin had finally worn out his welcome with a drunken screed against Jackson and Steinbrenner in which he famously declared, "One's a born liar, the other's convicted"—an apparent reference to the imperious shipbuilder's rap sheet for making illegal contributions to Richard Nixon's presidential campaign. Undeterred, Lemon, Jackson, and the Yankees stormed to a second straight World Series championship.

Jackson wore out his own welcome with Steinbrenner in 1982, when the owner refused to renew his contract. He played a few seasons with the California Angels before returning to Oakland for his final season in 1987. In retirement, Jackson served as a coach with several teams before accepting a nebulous front office position with the Yankees in 1996. He was fired by Steinbrenner in 1998 for running up thousands of dollars in unapproved expenses on his team credit card. The merry-go-round, it seems, has not stopped for "Mr. October."

—Robert E. Schnakenberg

FURTHER READING:

Jackson, Reggie, with Mike Lupica. *Reggie: The Autobiography.* New York, Villard Books, 1984.

Shatzkin, Mike. *The Ballplayers: Baseball's Ultimate Biographical Reference.* New York, William Morrow, 1990.

Jackson, Shirley (1916-1965)

About her short story "The Lottery," Shirley Jackson wrote, "It was not my first published story, nor my last, but I have been assured over and over that if it had been the only story I ever wrote or published, there would be people who would not forget my name." First printed in the *New Yorker* in June of 1948, the chilling story of ritual violence generated more mail to the magazine than any piece of fiction before or since, and hundreds of shocked readers canceled their subscriptions. Since then, "The Lottery" has been translated into hundreds of languages and made into a radio play, two television plays, a ballet, and even an opera. It is ubiquitous in short story anthologies and part of the required curriculum of many high school English programs.

The story concerns a ceremonial custom in a small, unnamed town. With masterful strokes, Jackson builds a sense of trepidation and horror, describing a perfectly normal village making preparations for their annual lottery. Children gather piles of stones as the villagers arrive, excited and nervous, in the town square. The ritual is performed with the utmost seriousness and formality, with a few murmurs about other towns giving up their lotteries. Finally, Mrs. Hutchinson's name is chosen and the villagers stone her to death.

Jackson avoided graphic violence or gross-out horror at all times. Her no-words-wasted style is especially evident in the last line of ''The Lottery'': '''It isn't fair, it isn't right,' Mrs. Hutchinson screamed, and then they were upon her.'' The ugly flow of blood that must accompany her appalling end is left to the imagination of the reader.

The torrent of mail that descended on the *New Yorker* offices could broadly be divided into three categories. Some readers wrote to demand an explanation for the story; others wrote abusive letters, venting their spleen against Jackson for her ''sick'' surprise ending. The most bizarre and disturbing response came from those who inquired where these lotteries took place, and whether they could go and watch. Jackson generally refused to explain the meaning of the story, but suggested in private to at least one friend that anti-Semitism in North Bennington, Vermont was at its heart. (Her husband, literary critic Stanley Edgar Hyman, was Jewish.) On another occasion she told a journalist, ''I suppose I hoped, by setting a particularly brutal rite in the present and in my own village, to shock the readers with a graphic demonstration of the pointless violence and general inhumanity of their own lives [but] I gather that in some cases the mind just rebels. The number of people who expected Mrs. Hutchinson to win a Bendix washer at the end would amaze you.''

Shirley Jackson was born in San Francisco on December 14, 1916 (not 1919, as in some accounts), and grew up in California and in Rochester, New York. She graduated from Syracuse University in 1940 and married Stanley Edgar Hyman. They settled in North Bennington, Vermont, in 1945, where they owned an enormous library and hosted dinner parties for guests who included literary luminaries Bernard Malamud, Ralph Ellison, and Dylan Thomas. They also raised four children.

Dubbed ''the queen of the macabre,'' Jackson wrote dozens of short stories, most of which, like ''The Lottery,'' concerned gothic terrors lurking just beneath the surface of everyday life. In addition, she authored a series of darkly funny stories about her family's bustling home life, collected in *Life Among the Savages* (1953) and *Raising Demons* (1957). Unlike many horror writers, she had an elegant way with the English language. Famously, one critic wrote, ''Miss Jackson seemingly cannot write a poor sentence.''

Her novels *The Haunting of Hill House* (1959) and *We Have Always Lived in the Castle* (1962) are classics of the horror genre. Her understated yet intensely powerful brand of horror inspired even Stephen King, who dedicated his novel *Firestarter* ''In memory of Shirley Jackson, who never had to raise her voice.'' King also wrote that Eleanor Vance, the heroine of *The Haunting of Hill House*, ''is surely the finest character to come out of this new [identity-centered] American gothic tradition,'' and, coupling her with Henry James, asserted that this novel and *The Turn of the Screw* are ''the only two great novels of the supernatural in the last hundred years.'' In 1963, *The Haunting of Hill House* was made into a horror film, *The Haunting*. Directed in Britain by Robert Wise, it failed to live up to the standard of the book but, in keeping with Jackson's literary style, no violence is shown directly, and an aura of fear pervades the film from start to finish.

A sometime witch, Jackson claimed she could bring kitchen implements to the top of a drawer by ''calling'' them. She was an excessive smoker, drinker, and eater, and a workaholic writer prone to debilitating anxiety. After intense periods of productivity, she would endure periods of serious depression, and also suffered on and off from asthma. She died of heart failure in North Bennington on August 8, 1965.

—Jessy Randall

FURTHER READING:

Hall, Joan Wylie. *Shirley Jackson: A Study of the Short Fiction.* Twayne's Studies in Short Fiction, No. 42. New York, Twayne, 1993.

King, Stephen. *Danse Macabre.* New York, Everest House, 1981.

Oppenheimer, Judy. *Private Demons: The Life of Shirley Jackson.* New York, Putnam, 1988.

Jackson, ''Shoeless'' Joe (1887-1951)

''Shoeless'' Joe Jackson endures in baseball lore as the game's tragic hero, the naive country boy who became embroiled with big-time gamblers in the infamous ''Black Sox'' scandal of 1919 and who was subsequently banned for life from the sport, cutting short an otherwise brilliant career.

The illiterate son of a Southern miller, Jackson grew up near Greenville, South Carolina. He acquired his famous nickname while playing baseball with the local mill teams as a teenager. Having

''Shoeless'' Joe Jackson

bought a new pair of spikes, Jackson found himself with blistered feet. Desperate to play and unable to wear his old shoes due to the soreness, Jackson lumbered out to right field in stocking feet. The crowd picked up on Jackson's lack of footwear, and henceforth he became known as "Shoeless" Joe.

Jackson's stellar play in the mill leagues attracted scouts, and, in 1908, he signed with the Philadelphia Athletics. Frightened by big cities and wary of leaving his family behind, Jackson initially refused to report. In 1909, he made his debut with the Athletics, but endured intense taunting from teammates and fans for his alleged ignorance and naivete. A disheartened Jackson failed to live up to his promise with the Athletics, and manager Connie Mack shipped the young outfielder to the Cleveland Indians. In Cleveland, Jackson developed into a star. In 1911, his first full season, Jackson batted .408; the following year, he batted .395. His stellar defense in the outfield and fearless base running made Jackson a complete ballplayer and ticketed him for the baseball stratosphere.

Strapped for cash, the Indians sent Jackson to Chicago in 1915 in exchange for three undistinguished players and $31,500. Jackson hit an uncharacteristically low .301 for the championship-winning 1917 White Sox, but rebounded with a more typical .351 for the 1919 team, which lost that season's World Series to the Cincinnati Reds.

In September of 1920, in the midst of one of Jackson's greatest seasons, in which he was batting .392 with 121 RBI, a shocking revelation rocked the country: eight White Sox players, including Jackson, had conspired with gamblers to fix the 1919 World Series. Jackson admitted his complicity in the scheme shortly after journalists had uncovered the sordid tale. Emerging from a Chicago courtroom, where he and his teammates were standing trial for defrauding the public, Jackson, according to baseball lore, stumbled upon a teary-eyed youngster whose only words to Jackson were "Say it ain't so, Joe." The grand jury ultimately acquitted all the players, but new baseball commissioner Judge Kenesaw "Mountain" Landis subsequently banned them all from the sport for life. Jackson returned to his native South Carolina, where he started a dry-cleaning business and occasionally played in sandlot and outlaw games.

A groundswell of support for Jackson's reinstatement to baseball developed after his death in 1951. Alternately pointing to his naivete and to his .375 batting average in the World Series as evidence that he had not deliberately tanked the series, supporters of Jackson pushed for his reinstatement and his admission to the Hall of Fame. Writers romanticized Jackson's tragic tale; the Chicago outfielder was the subject of W. P. Kinsella's wistful *Shoeless Joe,* later turned into the major motion picture *Field of Dreams* (1989). The 1988 movie *Eight Men Out* also attempted to rescue Jackson and the others from their misdeeds, suggesting that the gambling fix represented the players' only escape from Chicago owner Charles Comiskey's penury. Still, as of the late 1990s, there appeared little chance that baseball's governors would absolve Jackson from his sins.

—Scott Tribble

FURTHER READING:

Asinof, Eliot. *Eight Men Out: The Black Sox and the 1919 World Series.* New York, Henry Holt and Company, 1963.

Gropman, Donald. *Say It Ain't So, Joe: The Story of Shoeless Joe Jackson.* Boston, Little, Brown, 1979.

Kinsella, W. P. *Shoeless Joe.* New York, Ballantine Books, 1982.

Rader, Benjamin. *Baseball: A History of America's Game.* Urbana, University of Illinois Press, 1992.

Shatzkin, Mike, editor. *The Ballplayers: Baseball's Ultimate Biographical Reference.* New York, Arbor House, 1990.

Jakes, John (1932—)

John Jakes was born in Chicago, Illinois, on March 31, 1932. His parents fostered a love of the library in him and his association with books has followed him throughout his life. Jakes has enjoyed a long and distinguished writing career but has worked hard for his success. He is the prolific author of over seventy books and over two hundred short stories in such diverse categories as mystery and suspense, science fiction, the western, and children's literature. He is, however, best known for his best-selling historical fiction and intergenerational family sagas. He was so prolific in the mid- to late twentieth century that one rumor stated that John Jakes was actually the pen name for a group of writers, historical researchers, and publishers. His works have sold millions of copies each and several have had the distinction of being on the *New York Times* Bestseller List. His historical novels have been so influential that he is often referred to as the "godfather of the historical novel" and "the people's author."

John Jakes's early plans to be an actor lasted until he sold his first short story and felt the exhilaration of publication. He graduated with a degree in creative writing from DePauw University and went on to earn a master's degree in American Literature from Ohio State

John Jakes

University. He also has been awarded several honorary degrees and has served as a writer-in-residence and research fellow at several universities. Such recognition shows his dedication to the historical accuracy of his works and his influence as a popular historian. Jakes worked at several advertising agencies as a copy writer after graduation while devoting his spare time to the pursuit of his writing career. Mary Ellen Jones quotes him as remarking that his inspiration came from "the swashbuckling adventure films of the 1930s and 1940s" that offered adventure and romance within a framework of loosely-based historical events. His most famous works include the eight-volume Kent Family Chronicles, the North and South trilogy, *California Gold, Homeland,* and its sequel, *American Dreams.* Six of his novels have been made into television miniseries, with the North and South saga being one of the highest rated miniseries of all times.

John Jakes has enjoyed a wide following as a writer of American historical fiction. Historical fiction and the historical romance novel have enjoyed widespread popularity in America since the career of popular author Sir Walter Scott in the early nineteenth century. John Jakes is best known for his works in this tradition of historical fiction that are set in America. Jakes traditionally places his fictional characters into a background of real historical events and personages based on extensive research. This attention to detail makes his works dominate in an important field of public history. Jakes adopts this work ethic because he is aware that he is often the reader's only source of history. He also understands that the author must entertain the reader in order to educate them. Jones characterizes his works as promoting "an optimistic affirmation of America and its principles." Jakes's popularity should assure him a lasting reputation as "America's History Teacher."

—Marcella Bush Treviño

FURTHER READING:

Budick, Emily Miller. *Fiction and Historical Consciousness: The American Romance Tradition.* New Haven, Yale University Press, 1989.

Jones, Mary Ellen. *John Jakes: A Critical Companion.* Westport, Greenwood, 1996.

James Bond Films

The James Bond films, concerning the adventures of the debonair British secret agent, are one of the most successful series of films in cinema history, with 18 official films released between 1962 and 1997. Collectively they are known for a number of elements, including spectacular stunts, outrageous villains, and beautiful women. The films have survived multiple changes in the actors playing Bond and changing times as well, to captivate the public imagination the way few other series have.

The roots of the Bond character begin with British author Ian Fleming, who served in World War II as a member of British Intelligence. In the early 1950s he began a career as a writer with the publication of *Casino Royale,* a hardboiled adventure about British Intelligence agent James Bond. The book contained many elements the character would eventually be renowned for: an exotic location (the casinos of Monaco), an outrageous villain (Soviet agent Le Chiffre), and a beautiful woman (the doomed Vesper Lynd).

Fleming's books were an instant sensation, with their mixture of high living, violence, and sex proving irresistible to readers. No less a public figure than President John F. Kennedy was a professed fan of Fleming's spy fiction. Inevitably, film and television producers courted Fleming for the rights to his creation, but found little success. One such failed deal, with Irish film producer Kevin McClory in 1959, would come back to haunt Fleming.

In 1961, Fleming closed a deal with producers Harry Saltzman and Albert "Cubby" Broccoli to make the first Bond film, *Dr. No.* While its pace and style may seem slow and old fashioned to contemporary audiences, the film's casual violence and even more casual sex shocked and excited the crowds of the 1960s. Scottish actor Sean Connery, who played Bond, became a star for his tough, ruthless portrayal of the secret agent. The image of the film's love interest, actress Ursula Andress, rising from the ocean in a white bikini with a knife strapped to her side, has become an indelible commentary on female sex appeal.

Ian Fleming would die in the early 1960s, but his most famous creation was already destined to outlive him. A second film was soon in production, and when *From Russia with Love* was released in 1963, it found more success than the first. It was not until the release of *Goldfinger* in 1964, however, that the films reached their highest pinnacle yet. The film, concerning Bond's efforts to stop a madman's attempt to detonate a nuclear warhead in the Fort Knox gold depository, became one of highest grossing films of its time. It captured the public's imagination with its fantastic imagery and set a standard future Bond films would have to work hard to match: the body of a nude woman covered in gold paint; production designer Ken Adam's spectacular stainless steel Fort Knox; Bond's Aston Martin DB-5, a classic automobile equipped with a number of deadly gadgets; the most famous Bond woman of all, Honor Blackman playing Pussy Galore; mad villain Auric Goldfinger and his lust for gold; and Goldfinger's lethal henchman Odd Job and his razor-edged bowler hat. Sean Connery was never more appealing to audiences. His blend of ruthlessness and humor defined the part of Bond for a generation.

Connery starred in the next two Bond films: *Thunderball* (1965) and *You Only Live Twice* (1967). *Thunderball* was the source of litigation from McClory, who accused Ian Fleming of using material they had developed together in 1959. McClory won the lawsuit and was involved in the 1965 production, which concerned the terrorist hijacking of a pair of nuclear warheads by Bond's arch enemies, the forces of SPECTRE. The Bond films reached fantastic heights in *You Only Live Twice,* with its gorgeous Japanese scenery and incredible technology of sleek space rockets and SPECTRE's glimmering headquarters in the heart of a dormant volcano. It also marked the first on-screen appearance of one of Bond's more sinister foils, Ernst Stavros Blofeld, played by Donald Pleasance. While the films' successes continued unabated, Connery had tired of the role and wanted to seek other challenges as an actor.

On Her Majesty's Secret Service (1969) was the first Bond film to feature an actor other than Connery in the role of the deadly agent. George Lazenby, an inexperienced actor, took over the role. While competent, he lacked Connery's appeal and conflicts with producers prevented him from taking the role again. The film is considered by some purists to be one of the better Bond films; it hews closely to its source novel and features former *Avengers* star Diana Rigg as Bond's doomed wife, Tracy. Box office results did not reach the heights they had under Connery, however, and he was coaxed back for a farewell performance in *Diamonds Are Forever.* The baton was finally passed for good when Roger Moore took over the part in *Live and Let Die*

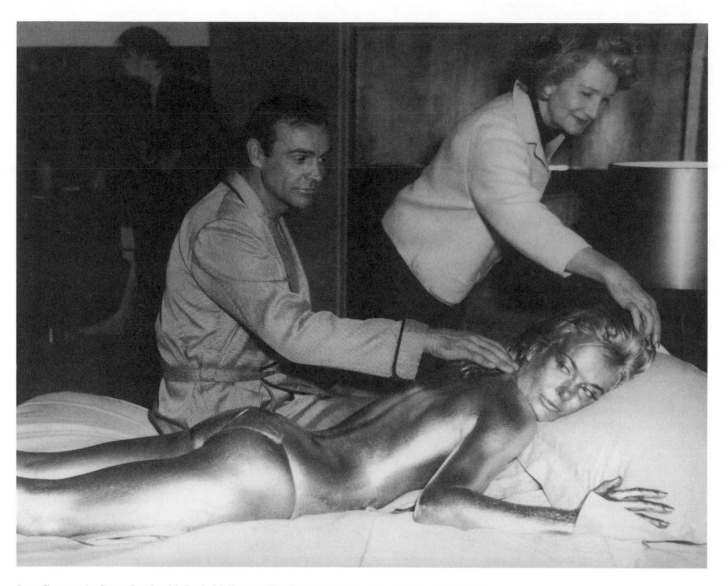

Sean Connery (as James Bond) with Tania Mallet (as "The Golden Girl") on the set of the film *Goldfinger*.

(1973). Moore's portrayal differed considerably from Connery's; Moore lacked Connery's sense of menace, but compensated with his own sophistication and sense of humor, creating a lighter kind of Bond film which was perfect for the jaded 1970s.

Moore would return in *The Man With the Golden Gun* to face off against Christopher Lee's villain, Scaramanga, but box office receipts were dropping. Broccoli bought out his partner Saltzman, and came back in 1977 with *The Spy Who Loved Me*, Moore's third as Bond and the most lavish to date. It found tremendous success with audiences. The film was laden with expensive sets and elaborate stunts, including a sleek sports car that transformed into a submersible. It also included the steel-toothed villain Jaws, played by the imposing Richard Kiel. Moore returned again in the successful *Moonraker* (1979), which took advantage of the late 1970s craze for science fiction spawned by the blockbuster *Star Wars*. It had Bond in an outer space adventure centered around the Moonraker space shuttle.

For Your Eyes Only (1981) marked a return to more realistic espionage adventure that would continue in Moore's next two efforts as Bond, *Octopussy* (1983) and *A View to a Kill* (1985). *A View to a*

Kill would be Moore's last film as Bond. His decision to retire from the part led to respected stage and film actor Timothy Dalton assuming the license to kill. His first outing, *The Living Daylights* (1987), was a moderate success. His next effort, however, *License to Kill* (1989) was poorly received by critics and fans alike. While a superb actor who stayed true to Fleming's characterization of Bond as a dark, driven man, Dalton's grim performances simply came as too much of a change after the lighthearted Moore. The Bond saga would now endure a six year hiatus, owing to protracted legal and financial troubles involving the films' producers and studio, Metro Goldwyn Mayer/United Artists. When Bond returned, however, it was with a bang.

Goldeneye (named for Ian Fleming's Jamaica estate) was released in 1995 to excellent reviews and the highest ticket sales in the series' history. Irish actor Pierce Brosnan assumed the role at last (after briefly having the part and then losing it to Dalton due to his commitment to the television series *Remington Steele*) to great acclaim. His mixture of Connery's toughness, Moore's humor, and his own good looks and skills as an actor made him perfect for the role. His next effort, *Tomorrow Never Dies* (1997) was another huge box office and critical success.

Certain unofficial Bond productions have seen the light of day through the years. Eon Productions did not obtain the rights to *Casino Royale* in 1961—they had already been sold for a black-and-white CBS television production starring American actor Barry Nelson as Bond. These rights were then bought for a late 1960s spoof of the Bond phenomenon starring David Niven, Orson Welles, and Woody Allen. Kevin McClory's *Thunderball* rights led to *Never Say Never Again* (1983), which featured one last encore by Sean Connery as Bond.

More than just a series of massively successful films, Bond has worked his way into the fabric of our culture. His name and certain other phrases—license to kill, Agent 007—have become synonymous with action, adventure, and a glamorous lifestyle. The Bond series has spawned uncounted spoofs and imitators, from the 1960s spy craze that included the Matt Helm films, the Flint movies, and the television series *Mission: Impossible, The Man from UNCLE, The Avengers,* and *The Wild, Wild West,* to such 1990s productions as the spectacular *True Lies* and the affectionate spoof, *Austin Powers: International Man of Mystery.* Bond theme songs frequently become Top 40 hits. Moreover, the Bond films have in large part set the bar for the action film genre with their incredible stunts and high production values.

Bond also reflects the changing times. The Bond of Connery—sexist, violent, and cruel—so popular in the 1960s changed with the changing attitudes of the times, especially concerning women, into the more gentle and funny Bond of Moore in the late 1970s and 1980s. As the Cold War ended, Dalton's Bond found himself facing a maniacal drug dealer in *License to Kill* and the AIDS crisis prompted a monogamous (!) Bond in *The Living Daylights.* In the new world order of the 1990s, Brosnan's Bond has faced ex-Soviet agents in *Goldeneye* and a crazed media baron in *Tomorrow Never Dies.* Through the years, Bond has even quit smoking.

Bond has lasted this long because of his appeal to our fantasies. Bond enjoys the exotic locales, expensive clothes, and fantastic technology that few people experience in their lives. Men envy his appeal to women, and women find actors portraying Bond attractive in their own right. Through him, both genders can live a life of danger, excitement, and heroism. He changes with the times in order to remain relevant. Where his contemporaries have largely vanished, Bond remains visible without compromising the heart of the character.

—Jay Parrent

FURTHER READING:

Pfeiffer, Lee, and Phillip Lisa. *The Incredible World of 007.* New York, Carol Publishing Group, 1992.

Rubin, Steven Jay. *The Complete James Bond Movie Encyclopedia.* Chicago, Contemporary Books, 1990.

Rye, Graham. *The James Bond Girls.* New York, Carol Publishing Group, 1996.

James, Elmore (1918-1963)

Undeniably the most influential electric slide guitarist of all time, Elmore James revolutionized the blues with his raw, sharp sound. Born in Canton, Mississippi, in 1918, James first learned to play on a homemade instrument fashioned from a broom handle and a lard can. James became an itinerant musician in his teens, frequently meeting up with other players including the legendary Robert Johnson and Howlin' Wolf. After serving in the Navy during World War II, James moved to Memphis and became a frequent "guest star" on local radio stations.

James' first solo recording, "Dust My Broom," became the largest rhythm and blues hit of 1951. Not long after the session, James moved to Chicago, assembling his all-star band the Broomdusters and recording for the Chess label. In the next ten years, he shuttled back and forth between Chicago and Mississippi before suffering a fatal heart attack in 1963. In 1980, Elmore James was elected to the Blues Foundation's Hall of Fame, and in 1992 he was inducted into the Rock 'n' Roll Hall of Fame.

—Marc R. Sykes

FURTHER READING:

Oakley, Giles. *The Devil's Music: A History of the Blues.* New York, Da Capo Press, 1983.

Palmer, Robert. *Deep Blues.* New York, Viking, 1981.

James, Harry (1916-1983)

Reared in a circus atmosphere by parents who toured with the Big Top, Harry James studied trumpet with his father and won the Texas State Championship with a solo at age 14. One of the star trumpet players of the swing era, 20-year-old James made his recording debut with the Ben Pollack Band in September 1936. Three months later he was a featured sideman with the Benny Goodman Band, a springboard to forming his own swinging, Basie-style band in January 1939. Ironically, James's biggest hits with his own band were *not* the upbeat numbers like "Two O'clock Jump," but the dulcet-tone, non-jazz solos like "You Made Me Love You." James continued to play in the style of his favorite horn men, Louis Armstrong and Muggsy Spanier, and the band remained widely popular into the late 1950s.

—Benjamin Griffith

FURTHER READING:

Balliett, Whitney. *American Musician.* New York, Oxford Press, 1986.

Collier, James Lincoln. *Benny Goodman and the Swing Era.* New York, Oxford Press, 1989.

Simon, George T. *The Big Bands.* New York, MacMillan,

Japanese American Internment Camps

Between February and November 1942, nearly 120,000 West Coast residents of Japanese descent were evacuated from their homes and sent to government War Relocation Authority camps in remote areas of the West, South, and Southwest. Many of these Japanese and Japanese Americans would spend the remainder of World War II in the camps, which were located in Gila River, Arizona; Granada, Colorado; Heart Mountain, Wyoming; Jerome, Arkansas; Manzanar,

California; Minidoka, Idaho; Poston, Arizona; Rohwer, Arkansas; Topaz, Utah; and Tule Lake, California. The largest camp, Tule Lake, housed nearly 19,000 internees, while Granada held about 7,000. The camps' residents lived in crudely built barracks, and ate, bathed, and washed clothes in communal facilities. Each camp was surrounded by barbed wire and guarded by armed soldiers. The first camp, Poston, opened in May, 1942. Nearly two years later the government began closing the camps starting with Jerome, in June, 1944, and ending with Tule Lake, in March, 1946.

The internment of the issei (first generation) and the Nisei (second generation, American-born) was authorized by President Franklin D. Roosevelt through Executive Order 9066 (February 19, 1942), which sanctioned the evacuation of any and all persons from "military zones" established along the coastline. Although the federal government also viewed persons of German and Italian descent with suspicion, only residents of Japanese ancestry were forced to leave their homes.

Executive Order 9066 was a response to Japan's attack on Pearl Harbor on December 7, 1941. Following the attack, government officials including U.S. attorney general Francis Biddle, Los Angeles congressman Leland Ford, and California attorney general Earl Warren called for securing the issei and Nisei population. They believed that West Coast Japanese helped plan the attack on Pearl Harbor and hoped the internment would prevent further acts of disloyalty. Studies indicate, however, that anti-Japanese sentiment, which had been building on the West Coast since the late nineteenth century, played a role in the forced evacuation. These studies point to the fact that only West Coast issei and Nisei were removed—not those living in Hawaii or on the East Coast—and that the residents calling for their removal were California nativists, laborers, and farmers, who had long viewed Japanese immigrants as social and economic threats. The 1982 report issued by the Commission on Wartime Relocation and Internment of Civilians concluded that the removal of the issei and Nisei was not a military necessity, but occurred because of racism, wartime hysteria, and poor political leadership.

Under the direction of Lieutenant General John L. DeWitt, the issei and Nisei were first evacuated to assembly centers at county fairgrounds and racetracks, and they were later moved to the permanent relocation camps. In some locations, such as Terminal Island in San Pedro, California, residents of Japanese descent were given as few as two days to dispose of, or store, their belongings before departing. In other areas, the evacuees had several weeks to prepare. Though the Federal Reserve Bank and the Farm Security Administration helped handle the property and belongings of the issei and Nisei, they lost hundreds of thousands of dollars through quick sales of their homes and land at below-market prices. While in camp the evacuees suffered additional losses through vandalism, arson, and neglect of the belongings that had been stored.

Life in the camps proved difficult. Internees had lost their jobs, social networks, and educational opportunities and were removed from "mainstream" life. Angered by the loss of their rights and freedom, and bitter towards the U.S. government, internees sometimes directed their hostility toward one another. In some camps riots broke out during clashes between pro-Japanese and pro-American factions. A loyalty test administered by the War Relocation Administration also helped to factionalize the evacuees. As a result of the turbulence, hundreds of young Nisei left the camps when the opportunity appeared. Colleges such as Oberlin in Ohio sponsored Nisei students, allowing them to relocate and resume their education. Christian churches arranged for Nisei to work in homes and offices

located in the South and Midwest. In addition, more than 1,000 men joined the U.S. military forces and served in the all-Nisei 442nd Regimental Combat Team.

Although many evacuees protested the removal, four individuals, Fred T. Korematsu, Mitsuye Endo, Minoru Yasui, and Gordon K. Hirabayashi, challenged the constitutionality of the relocation order through the courts. Initially all four petitions were denied. But in December of 1944 the U.S. Supreme Court decided that Endo's detention in the camps violated her civil rights. Following this decision, in January of 1945, the War Department rescinded the evacuation orders and arranged for the internees to leave the camps.

It was not until the 1970s that branches of the U.S. government acknowledged any wrongdoing. In 1976, President Gerald R. Ford proclaimed that the evacuation was wrong. The 1982 commission report and its condemnation of the relocation sent an even stronger message. In 1983 Fred Korematsu, Gordon Hirabayashi, and Minoru Yasui, refiled their petitions, which the court granted. The change in political tenor encouraged the Nisei and Sansei (third generation) to seek redress and reparations for the forced relocation. Their organizing efforts culminated in September of 1987, when the U.S. House of Representatives formally apologized to the former evacuees and provided $1.2 billion as compensation.

—Midori Takagi

FURTHER READING:

Commission on Wartime Relocation and Internment of Civilians. *Personal Justice Denied.* Washington, Government Printing Office, 1982.

Daniels, Roger, Sandra C. Taylor, and Harry H.L. Kitano, editors. *Japanese Americans from Relocation to Redress.* Seattle, University of Washington Press, 1986, 1991.

Girdner, Audrie, and Anne Loftis. *The Great Betrayal: The Evacuation of the Japanese-Americans During World War II.* Toronto, The Macmillan Company, 1969.

Irons, H. Peter. *Justice at War.* Berkeley, University of California Press, 1993.

Jaws

Steven Spielberg's *Jaws* (1975) is a significant cultural landmark in the Hollywood cinema of the late twentieth-century. In addition to the unprecedented box-office gross, which made it the first film in history to top $100 million on its initial release, it established its relatively unknown 27-year-old director as a powerful creative force. Spielberg went on to achieve major financial and critical success in the "new Hollywood" with a string of memorable films that confirmed him as Hollywood's pre-eminent storyteller. This supreme gift was unveiled in *Jaws,* a fundamentally very simple tale that seamlessly combined elements from the action adventure, thriller, and horror genres. Exciting, engrossing, and scary, *Jaws* is also, in the final analysis, fun, as were the then fashionable "disaster" movies such as *The Towering Inferno* (1974), which it far outstripped in providing well-characterized protagonists in a setting designed to strike a chord with Americans of all ages.

One of the earliest examples of the now familiar Hollywood staple, the "summer blockbuster," *Jaws* was released to an eager

Robert Shaw (left) and Richard Dreyfuss under siege in a scene from the film *Jaws*.

public in June of 1975. The film's plot centered on a series of fatal shark attacks at the beaches of a New England resort town, and the efforts of an ill-matched trio of men to kill the 25-foot great white shark responsible for the deaths. Promoted through a massive advertising campaign and given unprecedentedly widespread distribution by Universal studios, *Jaws* lived up to the expectation it generated. With its rousing adventure and horror elements and its crowd-pleasing finale, it became a worldwide phenomenon, and for at least one summer made millions of people very nervous about swimming in the ocean.

If the success of the film was nothing short of remarkable, the novel upon which it was based had proved a commercial phenomenon in its own right. In January 1973, author Peter Benchley submitted to the New York publishing house of Doubleday the final draft of a novel inspired by his memory of a monstrous great white shark caught off the coast of Montauk in 1964. In a documentary accompanying the laser-disc release of the film, Benchley recalls how several titles (such as "Stillness in the Water" for example) were considered and rejected for the novel before the simple, visceral *Jaws* was chosen. Very quickly, Bantam paid for paperback rights to the novel, and Hollywood producers David Brown and Richard Zanuck bought not only the film rights, but also the services of author Benchley for a first-draft screenplay. This early interest in the novel, combined with

book-club deals and an aggressive promotional strategy by Doubleday and Bantam, ensured the novel's climb to the top of the *New York Times* bestseller list, where it stayed for months.

Benchley's book is divided into three sections. The first opens with a nighttime shark attack upon a skinny-dipping young woman, whose mutilated body is discovered on the Amity town beach the next morning, leading the chief of police to urge the mayor to close the beaches for a few days. The request is refused, and the shark strikes again, killing a six-year-old boy and an elderly man in two separate attacks in full view of horrified onlookers. Now forced to close the beaches, the authorities hire Ben Gardner, a local fisherman, to catch the shark, but he disappears at sea, another victim. Part one ends with the arrival of Matt Hooper, an ichthyologist there at the invitation of the editor of Amity's newspaper.

Part Two focuses on the domestic tensions between chief of police Brody and his wife Ellen, whose discontent with her marriage leads her into a brief affair with the handsome and rich Hooper. Brody suspects the affair just as his battle to keep the beaches closed during the lucrative Fourth of July weekend reaches its highest pitch, and he learns that the mayor is fighting so hard to re-open the beaches because he is in debt to the New England Mafia. Brody reluctantly opens the beaches again, the shark almost kills a teenage boy, and the town hires another shark fisherman named Quint to tackle the problem. Out of duty and a sense of guilt, Brody accompanies Quint and Hooper on Quint's boat, the *Orca,* to search for the man-eating fish.

The shark hunt occupies the final third of the novel. Blue-collar fisherman Quint takes an immediate dislike to the collegial Hooper, and the hostility between Hooper and Quint and Hooper and Brody acts as a human counterpoint to the ensuing struggle between man and fish. The shark proves to be larger and fiercer than anticipated, and Quint's repeated failure to harpoon their quarry compels Hooper to descend beneath the surface, in a shark cage, in an effort to kill it. The shark tears the cage apart and devours Hooper. On the last day of the hunt, Quint manages to harpoon the shark, but the weight of the fish sinks the boat and Quint is drowned. Brody is unexpectedly saved when the shark succumbs to the harpoon wounds and dies.

The Academy Award-nominated film that grew out of this narrative kept the main characters and the basic three-act structure but radically changed the characterizations and deleted the Hooper/Ellen subplot. Also gone were the mayor's links to the Mafia, while Brody was transformed from a local man to a New York outsider, facing his first summer as police chief of Amity where, ironically, he has come in order to escape urban violence. Hooper became a much more humorous and sympathetic character, to the extent that later drafts of the script spared him from the fatal jaws of the shark. While retaining Quint as a blue-collar antagonist for the preppie Hooper, thus providing an extra focus for tension aboard the somewhat ramshackle *Orca,* the fisherman's mania for shark hunting was explained as a result of his having survived a shark feeding frenzy following the sinking of a cruiser during World War II. Instead of drowning as in the novel, Quint is eaten during the shark's final wild assault upon the *Orca.*

All of these changes were beneficial to the screenplay, giving it a more straightforward line and lending it veracity. Spielberg and Benchley reportedly argued over many of the changes, including Spielberg's suggested new ending. Spielberg wanted a much more cathartic resolution and came up with the idea that one of Hooper's oxygen cylinders should explode in the shark's mouth. Benchley scoffed at the idea, insisting that no one would believe it. Spielberg's vision prevailed, and the author subsequently admitted that the filmmaker was right. Aside from Benchley, and Spielberg himself, screenwriters John Milius, Howard Sackler, (both uncredited) and Carl Gottlieb (credited) contributed to the script at different stages in its development and throughout the location shooting. By all accounts, the actors and/or crew improvised much of the dialogue and many of the most memorable moments, but unlike countless other films where too many cooks invariably spoil the broth, *Jaws* finally achieved a convincing coherency of plot and character.

Production difficulties were foreshadowed by the early script problems and initial casting choices that fell through before the three crucial leading roles went to Roy Scheider (Brody), Robert Shaw (Quint) and Richard Dreyfuss (Hooper), all three of whom turned in convincing and compelling performances. After an extensive scouting expedition, production designer Joe Alves selected Martha's Vineyard as the location for the fictional Amity and Robert Mattey built three full-size mechanical sharks at a cost of $150,000 each. The producers hoped that the mechanical sharks, when inter-cut with second-unit footage of real great white sharks shot off the coast of Australia by famed underwater team Ron and Valerie Taylor, would prove convincing enough to scare audiences, which they triumphantly did. During the production, however, the mechanical sharks caused

much anguish (one sank during a test, and the complex hydraulic system exploded during another test run). The recalcitrance of the models prevented Spielberg from showing them on screen as completely as he had intended, and may actually have helped the film's suspense by keeping the killer shark's appearances brief and startling. Other troubles, such as changing weather conditions, shifting ocean currents, and labor disputes were serious impediments, and worried studio executives even considered abandoning the production. All of these combined difficulties extended the original 52-day shooting schedule into over 150 days, and the $3.5 million initial budget quickly ballooned into $12 million.

In the end, what saved *Jaws* from anticipated disaster was the brilliance of Spielberg's unifying vision, which somehow managed to impose order on the chaotic shoot, John Williams' Oscar-winning score with its now famous four-note motif for the shark scenes, and the director's close collaboration with film editor Verna Fields. In post-production, the two managed the near impossible by matching several scenes that had been shot months apart in completely different weather and ocean conditions. Fields won the editing Oscar, yet screenings of the rough cut had brought a lukewarm response from studio executives. Finally, in March of 1975, a sneak preview for the public was scheduled in Dallas. By all accounts, the audience loved the film, screaming loudest when the shark surprises Brody as he ladles chum off the stern of the *Orca.* Eager to get one more terrified shriek out of future audiences, Spielberg re-shot the scene where Hooper discovers the body of fisherman Ben Gardner in a swimming pool, and the film was ready for more sneak previews and exhibitor screenings. Stars Roy Scheider and Richard Dreyfuss were mobbed as heroes after one New York preview and favorable word of mouth spread rapidly. By the time *Jaws* was released to 490 theaters in June, the stage was set for it to become the most financially successful motion picture of all time until the summer of 1977, when George Lucas's *Star Wars* broke its record. Nearly every summer since 1975 has seen the major Hollywood studios competing to gross as many hundreds of millions of dollars as possible. Though many films have since surpassed *Jaws'* box-office success and three inferior sequels have somewhat diluted the impact of the original, the movie about a man-eating shark is often praised (or blamed) as the beginning of a Hollywood revival. By 1999, it was still holding its own in Hollywood history as the eleventh highest grossing film of the twentieth century.

—Philip Simpson

FURTHER READING:

Benchley, Peter. *Jaws.* Garden City, New York, Doubleday, 1974.

Blake, Edith. *On Location on Martha's Vineyard: The Making of the Movie Jaws.* New York, Ballantine, 1975.

Brode, Douglas. *The Films of Steven Spielberg.* New York, Citadel Press, 1995.

Gottlieb, Carl. *The Jaws Log.* New York, Dell, 1975.

Mott, Donald R., and Cheryl McAllister Saunders. *Steven Spielberg.* Boston, Twayne, 1986.

Taylor, Philip M. *Steven Spielberg: The Man, His Movies, and Their Meaning.* New York, Continuum, 1992.

Jazz

Of all the great American musical forms—blues, rock 'n' roll, country, and jazz—jazz has proven to be the most subtle, the most flexible, the most capable of growth and change, the one which has developed from folk art and popular art to fine art. Due partly to the extraordinary talents and innovators who have dotted the history of jazz, the wide range of artistic possibilities available to jazz are inherent in the form itself: a music which is structured enough to permit intricate compositions for ensemble play, but loose enough to allow for individual improvisation, individual style and voicing, and considerable virtuosity.

Jazz developed around the turn of the twentieth century in the South and Southwest, particularly New Orleans. It built on a number of earlier African American musical forms, including blues and ragtime, and European-influenced popular music and dances. The first great New Orleans jazz innovators, such as Buddy Bolden (who never recorded), Louis Armstrong, Bunk Johnson, Jelly Roll Morton, Freddie Keppard, King Oliver, and Sidney Bechet, added a number of key African American musical techniques to conventional popular and dance music styles. The two most important were the blue note, a microtonal variation on conventional pitch, and the complex rhythmic variations developed from the polyrhythmic heritage of African drumming. These additions gave jazz the rhythmic flexibility that came to be called "swing"—an almost indefinable quality which has been summed up best in the Duke Ellington song, "It Don't Mean a Thing If It Ain't Got That Swing."

Although there are reports of jazz being played in the first few years of the twentieth century, the early musicians were not recorded. The first recorded jazz album came in 1917 when a white group, the Original Dixieland Jazz Band, recorded for both Columbia and RCA Victor, with million-selling results. It took longer for record companies to take a chance on black jazz musicians. Mamie Smith's

Jazz musician Al Jarreau.

recording of "Crazy Blues," in 1920, began a blues craze, and many of the early appearances on record by the great African American jazz masters, like Armstrong, were as accompanists to blues singers.

Meanwhile, as the recording industry grew throughout the 1920s, the post-World War I generation found itself restless, dissatisfied, and looking for expressions of his own identity. The era was called the Jazz Age, but the Jazz Age was basically a white, middle-class phenomenon, and the music which became popular was mostly by white groups like the Original Dixieland Jazz Band. Some of them were excellent musicians—in particular Iowa-born cornetist Bix Beiderbecke.

The African American musicians of New Orleans continued to be the artistic vanguard of jazz, although the scene had shifted. King Oliver was one of many who moved to Chicago. Arriving in 1918, he formed his first band in 1920, and was joined by Louis Armstrong in 1922. Oliver's New Orleans-style ensemble jazz influenced many musicians, both black and white, but it was Armstrong who became jazz's seminal influence. He left Oliver in 1924 to join Fletcher Henderson's orchestra in New York, then returned to Chicago to record with his own groups, the Hot Five and the Hot Seven. Armstrong's extraordinary technique and his artistic intensity and innovation dominated jazz, and as a result, the role of the soloist became predominant. Armstrong in the 1920s not only created one of the greatest artistic legacies of any American artist, he also established the importance of individual creativity in jazz.

During this same era, however, ensemble jazz was developing into orchestral jazz—the big bands, featuring section arrangements and tight organization. Armstrong, through his work with Henderson, was important here too, in integrating the concept of fiery, original jazz solo work into the large ensemble framework. Equally important in Henderson's band was the work of Coleman Hawkins, a great soloist who, more than any other musician, introduced the tenor saxophone as an important jazz solo instrument.

Just as jazz experienced its first great wave of popularity in the 1920s, the era of the phonograph record, Prohibition, and the speakeasy, big-band jazz was also a product of its time. As newly-legal nightclubs closed and musical groups disbanded due to the hardships incurred by the Great Depression, jazz continued to find audiences in major supper clubs, such as the Cotton Club (located in New York's Harlem, but open only to white audiences), and ventured into the increasingly important medium of radio. With fewer venues, the bigger, richer sound of big-band jazz become more popular. At the same time, the glut on the market of talented musicians drove salaries down, and made it cheaper for a successful bandleader to hire a large group.

The single most successful band of the big band, or Swing Era, was led by Benny Goodman. Goodman's success was due to his brilliant musicianship and his organizational and promotional skills, but it was also due to the fact that he was white. Goodman used his preeminence to advance the mainstream acceptance of black jazz musicians. He not only hired Fletcher Henderson as an arranger, which was a behind-the-scenes job, he integrated his band, hiring great black musicians like Teddy Wilson (piano), Lionel Hampton, and Charlie Christian. There had been a few other integrated jazz groups before, but none as successful as Goodman's group.

Artistically, the Duke Ellington and Count Basie bands represented the pinnacle of the big-band style. Ellington, who began as a bandleader in the mid-1920s, and continued to lead a band far beyond the Swing Era, until his death in 1974, may have been the first jazz musician to gain an international reputation as a serious artist—the first to draw attention to jazz as a serious art form, although this battle was not to be won for a long time. By the end of the 1970s, jazz was being taught in universities, and major grants and awards were going to jazz musicians and composers. But in 1965, Ellington was passed over for the Pulitzer Prize for music because of a stubborn insistence by older conservatives on the committee that jazz was not really art.

Count Basie, who came from the Kansas City tradition of blues-influenced jazz, was arguably the most important figure in developing the concept of ''swing'' in the big-band idiom. J. Bradford Robinson, in *The New Grove Dictionary of Jazz,* says that his rhythm section ''altered the ideal of jazz accompaniment, making it more supple and responsive to the wind instruments.'' Basie's approach to rhythm, and the musical innovations of his leading soloists, particularly tenor saxophonist Lester Young, provided an important basis for the revolutionary changes that were to come.

Throughout the 1930s, jazz was primarily popular music. Goodman, Ellington, and Basie played for dances, just like the ''sweet'' big bands led by Sammy Kaye, the Dorsey Brothers, and others. But in the 1940s, jazz enjoyed the fruits of the steady growth of the previous decade. After the end of Prohibition, a new generation of jazz clubs had begun to grow throughout the 1930s. They tended to be small, which meant they created a demand for small group jazz, generally a rhythm section and two lead instruments. The most important of these clubs were on 52nd Street, in New York, making New York more than ever before the center of jazz creativity.

New jazz musicians, primarily black, gravitated to New York, where they represented an urban, sophisticated generation. Impatient with what they perceived as the ''Uncle Tom'' image of many black showmen, like Armstrong and Cab Calloway, they presented themselves as cool, cerebral, and introspective. They were artists, more than entertainers.

These new musicians investigated the possibilities of improvisational music, trying more complex rhythms and harmonies and improvisations built on melodic and chordal substitutions which went way beyond conventional melodies. The two most important figures in the modern jazz, or bebop, movement were alto saxophonist Charlie Parker and trumpeter Dizzy Gillespie. Their experiments galvanized an entire generation of musicians, who began to hear music in a whole new way. Experimentation became the new wave of jazz. In 1941 Minton's, a small club in Harlem, became the center for a series of after-hours jam sessions which soon attracted all the best players who were interested in the new music.

Modern jazz attracted a fiercely dedicated audience, though it was never as large as the audience for the big bands. It created a style: the hipster, who wore a beret, sunglasses, and a goatee, and listened to unintelligible music and spoke in an unintelligible slang. Jazz, and the jazz subculture, filled an important role in the post-World War II era, as mainstream America plunged headlong into the conformity of prosperity, and a small vanguard was left to search for more elusive artistic and social values.

The artistic legacy of the bebop and cool jazz years, the 1940s and 1950s, is extraordinary. Besides Parker and Gillespie, other important figures include Thelonious Monk, Max Roach, Gerry Mulligan, the Modern Jazz Quartet, Sonny Rollins, Dave Brubeck, and Miles Davis, who was to play an increasingly important role in the next decades of jazz.

In addition to the achievements of individual musicians, the modern jazz era also drew attention to the aesthetic importance of jazz. It began to be described, for the first time, as ''America's classical music.'' Widespread acceptance of jazz as an art form was slow in coming to America, however; European intellectuals embraced it much more quickly.

During the 1950s, the jazz audience became more communal. The 1940s prototype had been the night-owl, club-hopping hipster; in the 1950s, the jazz festival became a fixture. The first jazz festival was held in Nice, France, in 1948; the first in America was the Newport (Rhode Island) Jazz Festival in 1954. By the 1990s, there were estimated to be close to 1000 significant jazz festivals held annually around the world.

As the experimental sounds of modern jazz entered the mainstream, and became accepted by mass audiences (TV shows like *Peter Gunn* used jazz soundtracks), young jazz musicians were finding a new avant-garde. An historic 1959 engagement at New York's Five Spot Cafe by alto saxophonist Ornette Coleman was a milestone in the emergence of free jazz. While bebop had explored unusual possibilities and inversions in conventional chord and harmonic structures, free jazz virtually dispensed with them.

Coleman, Don Cherry, and Cecil Taylor were among the young iconoclasts who pioneered free jazz. At first rejected by the 1950s jazzmen, they proved impossible to ignore, and soon major jazz figures like John Coltrane, Eric Dolphy, and even Miles Davis were exploring its possibilities.

Free jazz was the artistic vanguard of the anti-establishment 1960s. Like bebop before it, it made previous styles sound tired and a little formulaic. Unlike bebop, though, it never established itself beyond a small, avant-garde audience. Nevertheless, it remained an important alternative musical direction.

The indigenous music of the 1960s was rock, and by the end of the decade, some jazz musicians were becoming intrigued by the artistic possibilities of this phenomenally popular form—most importantly, Miles Davis. Davis had been listening to Jimi Hendrix and other rock innovators, and he realized there was musical promise in a fusion between the improvisational freedom of jazz and the simple beat of rock. At the same time, rock musicians like John McLaughlin and Jack Bruce were being drawn to the creative possibilities of jazz.

Purists refused to accept jazz-rock fusion as real jazz. Its rhythmic regularity deadened the swing of jazz. But many noted jazz musicians, particularly Davis alumni Herbie Hancock and Chick Corea, embraced the new form. A number of young musicians, like the members of the group Spiro Gyra, made their entire careers playing fusion. None of them were very good.

Fusion was essentially an artistic dead end. The next generation of jazz musicians was not much interested in pursuing its leads. Jazz in the late 1970s, 1980s and 1990s became in many ways a retro music. With no new dominant style, many young musicians looked to the past—all eras of the past. The most dominant young musician of the 1980s and 1990s, trumpeter Wynton Marsalis, showed on his early albums that he could play in all styles, from the free jazz of Ornette Coleman to the classic jazz of Louis Armstrong.

A salient symbol of this era is the jazz repertory company, a jazz orchestra made up of young musicians, devoted to playing the jazz classics. The National Jazz Ensemble, founded by bassist Chuck Israels, was the first of these, and the Lincoln Center Jazz Orchestra, led by Marsalis, was probably the best known. This was the era during which jazz studies courses entered the universities, when the Smithsonian Institution issued its Classic Jazz collection, when grants for jazz studies, composition, and performance burgeoned in both the government and private sectors. Equally important to this period was the CD explosion, which created a new listener interest in the jazz of all periods.

The 1980s and 1990s, even without developing a new sound, have their own importance in the history of jazz for precisely this recombinant quality. Jazz developed so fast—no other art form in human history has moved from folk to popular to fine art in such a short amount of time—that its revolutionary vanguard frequently eclipsed earlier styles. Players not in the vanguard were too often dismissed as ''moldy figs,'' in the slang of the beboppers. That changed in the 1980s and 1990s. The artistry—and the modernity and innovation—of artists like Armstrong, Hawkins, and Basie became fully recognized.

Jazz will probably never again be the popular music it was in the 1930s. But it remains something other than an art music to be put alongside classical music in the concert halls and the academy. It retains that mystique of something hip, something adventurous, a music for the vanguard of young audiences to graduate to, after rock begins to lose its immediate appeal.

—Tad Richards

FURTHER READING:

Bailliett, Whitney. *American Musicians: 56 Portraits in Jazz.* New York, Oxford University Press, 1986.

Blesh, Rudi, and Harriet Janis. *They All Played Ragtime.* New York, Knopf, 1950.

Collier, James Lincoln. *The Making of Jazz: A Comprehensive History.* New York, Houghton Mifflin, 1978.

Giddins, Gary. *Rhythm-A-Ning.* New York, Oxford University Press, 1986.

———. *Riding on a Blue Note.* New York, Oxford University Press, 1981.

———. *Visions of Jazz.* New York, Oxford University Press, 1998.

Gioia, Ted. *The History of Jazz.* New York, Oxford University Press, 1986.

———. *The Imperfect Art: Reflections on Jazz and Modern Culture.* New York, Oxford University Press, 1988.

Gitler, Ira. *Jazz Masters of the Forties.* New York, Macmillan and Co., 1966.

Hentoff, Nat, and Nat Shapiro. *Hear Me Talkin' to Ya: An Oral History of Jazz.* New York, Dover, 1966.

Hodeir, Andre. *Jazz: Its Evolution and Essence.* New York, Grove Press, 1956.

Kernfeld, Barry, ed. *The New Grove Dictionary of Jazz.* New York, St. Martin's Press, 1988.

Sales, Grover. *Jazz: America's Classical Music.* Englewood Cliffs, New Jersey, Prentice-Hall, 1984.

Williams, Martin. *The Jazz Tradition.* New York, Oxford University Press, 1983.

The Jazz Singer

Produced in 1927, *The Jazz Singer* brought sound film to Hollywood. Directed by Alan Crosland and starring Al Jolson, the film was based on the 1922 short story ''The Day of Atonement'' by Samson Raphaelson. This story of Jewish assimilation to American culture through popular music has been adapted as a Broadway play (starring George Jessel in 1925), two radio plays (both starring Al Jolson in 1936 and 1947), a televised production (starring Jerry Lewis in 1959), and two subsequent film versions (starring Danny Thomas in 1953 and Neil Diamond in 1980). *The Jazz Singer* not only illustrates the emergent sound technology of the 1920s, but also illustrates the mainstream acceptance of jazz music and comments on the acculturation process of immigrants to America.

The Jazz Singer recounts the story of Jakie Rabinowitz, the son of immigrant parents in New York, who is expected to succeed his father, as well as many ancestors, as the cantor in their synagogue. But young Jakie has ambitions of fame and fortune as a jazz singer, expressing himself in American popular music instead of Jewish religious music. Jakie's intentions of singing popular music leads to his father's denunciation and sends Jakie (now Jack Robin) to a career on the vaudeville circuit. As Jack's career progresses he falls in love with Mary Dale, a star dancer and gentile. Jack's two worlds collide when he accepts a part in a Broadway revue (starring Mary) and returns to New York upon his father's sixtieth birthday. Jack's father has still not accepted his son, but seeing him results in his father falling ill. In the film's climatic scene, Jack must decide between the show's opening on Broadway or filling in for his dying father at the synagogue singing ''Kol Nidre'' for *Yom Kippur,* the day of atonement. Jack fulfills his father's dying wish, and still manages to make it big on Broadway, bringing a sense of balance between his parents' old-world immigrant ways and his new Americanized life.

The Jazz Singer is often referred to as the first sound film, yet this is only partially true. The idea of synchronized sound and motion picture is as old as the movies themselves, but it was not until the early 1920s that a workable method of recording both image and sound came into use. Warner Brothers studio was the first to undertake sound film production, primarily as a last ditch effort to battle the larger studios who had, by the 1920s, solidified their hold on the movie industry. Warner's first efforts at sound film were variety programs with talking shorts, musical numbers, and staged productions using a sound-on-disc recording technology. Fox studios also entered the sound film market with its Movietone newsreels which presented news stories with a sound-on-film technology. Different studios could utilize different sound formats since each studio primarily exhibited at their own theaters. Warner's *The Jazz Singer,* however, was the first feature film to integrate the use of sound, both music and dialogue, into the story itself. The film is primarily a silent film with a musical soundtrack, but in several scenes, synchronized singing and dialogue are presented, most notably in the scene where Jack sings to his mother and after finishing one song says to her ''You ain't heard nothin' yet.''

The film's significance goes beyond its historical role in film technology to illustrate the mainstream acceptance of jazz music as an American art form. Even though the music in the film is not, strictly speaking, jazz music, its does contain elements of jazz style, such as increased syncopation and a blues tonality. More importantly, the film expresses the belief that jazz music is an Americanizing force since it is a uniquely American form of music. The original author of the story, Samson Raphaelson, wrote in the introduction to the published stage play that ''in seeking a symbol of the vital chaos of America's soul, I find no more adequate one than jazz.'' Ironically, in order to perform jazz music onstage Jack Robin dons the costume of a minstrel performer, including blackface. Jack ''becomes'' black in order to become an American, and in the process reinforces nineteenth-century stereotypes of African Americans in popular culture.

Al Jolson in a scene from the film *The Jazz Singer*.

The film promotes both acculturation and the maintenance of ethnic identity as significant parts of economic prosperity and success, the American dream.

—Charles J. Shindo

FURTHER READING:

Carringer, Robert L., editor. *The Jazz Singer*. Madison, University of Wisconsin Press, 1979.

Raphaelson, Samson. *The Jazz Singer*. New York, Brentano's, 1925.

Jeans

Jeans, or more commonly blue jeans, comprise the range of casual or work trousers made most often of indigo blue cotton denim with reinforced stitching at the seams and metal rivets placed at stress points. Though introduced as durable work clothing, jeans have become an almost universal part of modern culture, and are worn by people all over the world as both work and fashionable attire. Blue jeans, originally associated with the hard-working spirit of miners during the California Goldrush, were most directly descended from the "waist overalls" developed by Levi Strauss and Jacob Davis in 1873. Featured in American movie Westerns as early as the 1930s and 1940s, jeans began to attain cult status through their association with pop icons. Military servicemen during World War II wore jeans regularly while engaging in leisure activities, but it was their children growing up during the 1950s who embraced blue jeans as a symbol of their generation. Banned from many public schools, hard-to-get in stores outside of the United States, and worn by rebellious characters of movies of the 1950s, jeans became a symbol of power for the restless youth of the 1960s. Eventually jeans became popular worldwide through the influence of U.S. servicemen stationed overseas, through the popular influence of the cinema, and distribution of mass marketing media. Levi's blue jeans were first sold in Europe in 1959; by the end of the twentieth century denim blue jeans could be found in virtually every country on the globe. The manufacture of jeans had become a worldwide industry, supporting a wide variety of styles, colors, designers, fashions, and accessories, as the notion of jeans as a symbol of comfort, leisure, and youthful status replaced that of jeans as durable work wear.

Jean fabric, originally a tough, long-lasting, blended twill fabric, can be traced to twelfth century Genoa, Italy. The term ''jeans'' has been applied generally to describe the working man's outer wear in Europe since the seventeenth century. The modern blue jean, however, is most often manufactured not from jean fabric but from denim. The name ''denim,'' from ''serge de Nimes,'' refers to a finer grade serge fabric, also a twill, which appears to have originated in Nimes, France. Denim was originally a woven blend of wool and silk, but U.S. textile mills began using cotton as a substitute for the more expensive imported wools and linens and as a means of gaining independence from foreign suppliers as early as the mid-nineteenth century. The popular favor this trend gained resulted in the continuing use of cotton in both denim and jean fabrics. Denim tends to wear better, becoming softer with each successive wash, as opposed to jean fabric. One popular myth of the nineteenth century claimed that any worker who once wore denim would never go back to wearing jeans; at any rate denim fabric eventually became the preferred material for the manufacture of work jeans.

The modern connotation of jeans is usually of a line of denim trousers developed by dry goods manufacturer Levi Strauss in San Francisco in the 1870s. Popular myth ascribes Levi Strauss with the invention of blue jeans, imagined somewhat romantically as a figure rising to the occasion of hardship and innovation during the California Goldrush by the creation of much-needed overalls for miners using surplus tent canvas and surplus indigo for dye. In actuality, company archives of Levi Strauss & Co. attribute the invention of modern jeans to Jacob Davis, a Latvian tailor who immigrated to Reno, Nevada. According to company records, Davis invented a process whereby copper rivets were added to stress points in the seams which greatly enhanced their durability. Davis' overalls were an immediate success among the miners. Wanting to establish a patent for his process of rivetting overalls but not having the funds to do so, Davis reportedly approached Strauss, a successful dry goods merchant in San Francisco, and offered to share the proceeds with Strauss if he would put up the money for the patent. Strauss agreed, and a patent was issued in 1873. Trousers made using this process were known as ''waist overalls'' until 1960, when the common term ''jeans'' was inserted into Levi Strauss & Co. company advertising and literature.

Western stars of the 1940s and early 1950s such as John Wayne started the popular association of jeans with the hero myth of rugged individuals who braved harsh elements and savage attacks and helped build the American West. Later in the 1950s stars such as Marlon Brando and James Dean, portraying desperate men on the fringe of society gave jeans an association of rebelliousness. The clothing worn in these movies was espoused by impressionable youth as a symbol of the carefree lifestyle they wished to emulate. In truth, jeans had been commonly worn by U.S. military servicemen during World War II as leisure wear. After the war, veterans continued to wear jeans for recreation, and children born during this era naturally associated the wearing of blue jeans with leisure activities.

Jeans gained notoriety in American schools in part because of the popular association with rebelliousness, itself a derivation of

simple leisure. Leisure wear was considered to give students the wrong impression of the importance of school activities throughout the 1950s and 1960s. In actuality, the original complaint against the wearing of waist overalls in schoolrooms seems to have stemmed from the fact that the copper rivets damaged wooden desks and chairs. Nonetheless, jeans were banned from many schools until as late as the early 1980s. The outlaw notion has only added to the popularity of wearing jeans among youth looking for status and peer acceptance.

Whatever the case, jeans gained notoriety and became a highly integrated symbol of the anti-establishment movement during the 1960s. This association has persisted through the end of the 1990s, when other popular youth forms including ''gansta rap'' music, skate-boarding, and baggy clothing have influenced the wearing of jeans by the incorporation of styles symbolizing yet another disenfranchised generation. In the 1960s, styles changed dramatically to accommodate the needs of wearers to associate with the societal fringe. Ironically, a pair of blue jeans became part of the permanent collection of the Smithsonian Institution in Washington, D.C. in 1964. Jeans were elevated to the level of art in this era, as blue jeans were decorated, modified, painted, and displayed as one of the most defining American icons. The first jeans developed exclusively for women were introduced on the market in this decade. Later, during the 1980s, jeans fashions returned to the cultural mainstream with the advent of designer jeans, denim trousers distributed by famous designer labels such as Calvin Klein, Jordache, and Guess. Almost as a closure to the vast cycle of development of jeans fashions, a trend toward ''vintage jeans'' grew out of the 1990s, when many aging members of the original ''blue jeans generation'' sought to inculcate the earlier, uncomplicated days of leisure during their childhood. Also by the end of the twentieth century, corporations enforced increasingly relaxed standards of work attire, and instituted ''casual days'' and the ''dress-down Friday'' in the American workplace. Many workers choose to wear jeans on these days as an acceptable choice for casual work wear.

—Ethan Hay

FURTHER READING:

Downey, Lynn. ''The Invention of Levi's 501 Jeans.'' *All about Levi Strauss & Co.* http://www.levistrauss.com/about/invention.html. April 1999.

Owens, Richard, and Tony Lane. *American Denim: A New Folk Art.* New York, Harry N. Abrams, 1975.

Levi Strauss & Co. *501: This Is a Pair of Levi's Jeans: The Official History of the Levi Brand.* San Francisco, Levi Strauss & Co., 1995

Weidt, Maryann N. *Mr. Blue Jeans: A Story about Levi Strauss.* Minnesota, Carolrhoda Books, 1990.

Jeep

The Jeep is a multipurpose light motor vehicle developed by the U.S. Army Quartermaster Corps for Allied military forces in World War II. Designed by Colonel Arthur William Sidney Herrington

(1891-1970) at the Marmon Motor Corporation in Indianapolis, one million jeeps were manufactured by the Willys-Overland Motors Company in Toledo and under license by American Bantam Car Company and the Ford Motor Company from 1941 to 1945.

The small, sturdy, versatile Jeep had the ruggedness of a truck and the maneuverability of an automobile. It carried four passengers or one-quarter ton of cargo over difficult terrain at speeds up to 65 mph. The origin of its name is unclear. It may derive from its military nomenclature, general purpose vehicle (g.p.), or come from Eugene the Jeep, a 1936 Popeye comic strip character drawn by E. C. Edgar. In any case, American newspapers were using the name Jeep by 1941. The fast, lightweight, all-terrain reconnaissance vehicle was used in World War II by all U.S. military forces as well as the British, French, Russian, Australian, and New Zealand armed forces. The war correspondent Ernie Pyle recalled the Army jeep was "as faithful as a dog, as strong as a mule and as agile as a goat." The United States military continued to use M38A1 jeeps for various purposes at the end of the twentieth century.

Army surplus jeeps were used in a variety of agricultural, construction, and commercial purposes by American veterans familiar with the jeep's practicality. By 1945 Willys-Overland designed the CJ-2A jeep, the first model intended for civilian use, an all-steel sedan or station wagon used as a two-wheel drive seven passenger or delivery vehicle. By 1949 a four-wheel drive, six-cylinder jeep was produced for the growing number of drivers who used it for fishing, hunting, skiing, and other recreational off-road activities.

In 1953 the Kaiser-Frazer Company acquired the Willys-Overland Company and produced the larger, wider CJ-5 Willys Jeep Station Wagon, a functional four-wheel drive utility vehicle. This civilian jeep, based on the Army M38A1 jeep used in the Korean war, became a milestone in postwar American automotive history, was manufactured for 30 years in 30 countries, and sold in 150 nations. By 1963 the new Jeep Wagoneer marked the end of the classic Willys Wagon which ceased production in 1965. The Wagoneer was the first sport utility vehicle (SUV), and by 1970 it tripled annual jeep production and was imitated by Ford, Chevrolet, and Chrysler.

In 1970 the American Motors Corporation took over the Kaiser-Jeep Corporation, thus gaining the Wagoneer's expanding baby boomer market. Throughout the 1970s more comfortable models derived from the jeep were seen on highways around the world as Plymouth, Toyota, and Isuzu introduced similar off-road vehicles (ORV). In the 1980s, when fuel conservation was no longer the concern it had been in the 1970s, larger, heavier, more expensive SUV models became popular with suburban motorists. Although not replacing the jeep, the most popular SUV models, with names evocative of the outdoors and the Western frontier (such as the Navigator, Explorer, Renegade, Blazer, Mountaineer, Trooper, Rodeo, Wrangler, Comanche, Cherokee, and Pathfinder), combined the rough and tough jeep reputation with the appealing features of the station or ranch wagon and the pick-up truck.

When Chrysler absorbed AMC in 1987, it was largely to gain the jeep's increasing share of the market. A right-hand drive Jeep Cherokee model was produced for the U.S. Post Office and in Britain, Australia, and Japan, and the Grand Cherokee replaced the Wagoneer in 1993. Chrysler, having merged in 1998 with the Daimler Benz Company, continued to produce a variety of Daimler Chrysler jeep models for civilian, military, and government drivers.

Since World War II, when soldiers drove the American jeep around the world, it has proven to be a ubiquitous war-horse, workhorse and the most popular vehicle ever manufactured. One indication of the jeep's popularity with the G.I.s was Glenn Miller's Army Air Force Band recording of "Jeep Jockey Jump" in 1943 and Fats Waller's song "Little Bo Peep Has Lost Her Jeep." The 1944 movie *Four Jills in a Jeep* recreated a USO troupe entertaining soldiers during the war. Television featured the jeep in two popular programs: *The Roy Rogers Show* (NBC, 1951-57) had a jeep named Nelliebelle, and *The Rat Patrol* (ABC, 1966-68) showed a U.S. Army jeep squad harassing Rommel's Afrika Korps during the war.

Perhaps the most unusual legacy of the jeep may be the Manila jeepney. These brightly colored, elaborately decorated jeep taxis carry one-third of the city's commuter and tourist traffic daily. Many other tourist and resort centers used jeeps for off-road recreation at the end of the twentieth century, as did millions of dedicated jeep motorists around the world.

—Peter C. Holloran

FURTHER READING:

Cattanach, John. *The Jeep Track.* London, Regency Press, 1990.

Fetherston, David. *Jeep: Warhorse, Workhorse and Boulevard Cruiser.* Osceola, Wisconsin, Motorbooks International, 1995.

Guttmacher, Peter. *Jeep.* New York, Crestwood House, 1994.

Torres, Emmanuel. *Jeepney.* Manila, GCF Books, 1979.

Jefferson Airplane/Starship

Formed in 1965, Jefferson Airplane was the most commercially successful band to come out of San Francisco in the mid- to late 1960s. Along with contemporaries like the Grateful Dead, they pioneered a blend of folk, blues, and psychedelia to play what became known as West Coast Rock. Their presence at some of the 1960s' defining cultural moments attests to their status as one of the key bands of this era.

While Jefferson Airplane's eclectic sound could be traced to folk music and the blues, it also signaled significant departures from such generic origins, with its distorted, extended guitar improvisations and lyrics which referred to altered states of consciousness and countercultural concerns. As *Time* pointed out in June 1967, what became known as the San Francisco sound "encompasses everything from blue-grass to Indian ragas, from Bach to jug-band music—often within the framework of a single song."

Bay Area artists like Jefferson Airplane only could have flourished in historically tolerant San Francisco and in close proximity to the University of California campus at Berkeley. Living communally in the hippie epicenter of Haight-Ashbury, the band drew much of its support and attitude from this politically active and culturally experimental milieu. Sharing in their audience's background, values, and choice of chemical stimulants, the symbiosis between the group and their fans was typical of an initially democratic musical scene. As Airplane guitarist Paul Kantner himself acknowledged, "it was like a

The Jefferson Airplane: (from left) Spencer Dryden, Marty Balin, Jorma Kaukonen, Grace Slick, Paul Kantner, and Jack Casady.

party. The audience often far overshadowed any of the bands, and the distance between the two was not that great. Grace [Slick] used to say that the stage was just the least crowded place to stand.''

Jefferson Airplane was the first of the San Francisco bands to sign for a major record label. Their debut album, *Jefferson Airplane Takes Off* (1966) was moderately successful. However, it was not until original vocalist Signe Anderson departed and was replaced by Grace Slick that the band achieved wider acclaim and commercial success. Slick left rival band The Great Society to join the Airplane, and significantly brought two of their songs with her—the anti-romantic love song ''Somebody to Love'' and the trippy ''White Rabbit.'' These tracks subsequently became the first of the group's top ten hits and featured on the breakthrough album *Surrealistic Pillow* (1967), which stayed in the Billboard top ten for most of what became known as the ''Summer of Love.''

The counterculture was built around rock music, which expressed its values and acted as a powerful recruiting vehicle for the movement. In January 1967, Jefferson Airplane had played at a counter-cultural gathering christened the ''Human Be In'' alongside the poets Allen Ginsberg and Gary Snyder in San Francisco's Golden Gate Park. Later in the same year they appeared at the nation's first national rock festival in Monterey, which drew an audience in excess of 200,000. While this event also was billed as a counter-cultural

happening—''three days of music, love, and flowers''—it was also undeniably a shop-window for profit-making talent. As Jon Landau wrote, Monterey witnessed an ''underground culture at [the] point of transformation into mass culture.''

Subsequent late 1960s recordings consolidated the band's commercial appeal. In 1969, they appeared at Woodstock, an event which confirmed that rock music was now big business and that any counter-cultural politics it might espouse had taken a backseat to hippie chic. In December of that same year Jefferson Airplane performed at Altamont—an event mythologized as symbolic of the death of the decade's youthful optimism. While the Rolling Stones played ''Sympathy for the Devil,'' a number of Hells Angels murdered a black spectator, Meredith Hunter, and later attacked Airplane member Marty Balin when he tried to help another black youth. For Jon Landau, ''Altamont showed that something had been lost that could not be regained.''

In recognition of this shift in mood, the band released the angrier, more explicitly political album *Volunteers* (1969). Its lyrical and musical aggression channeled the frustration and outbursts of violence that characterized the tail end of the 1960s. In ''We Can Be Together'' the group called on listeners to unite and overthrow the ''dangerous, dirty and dumb'' policies of the Establishment, and screamed ''Up against the wall, motherfuckers.'' *Volunteers* was a powerful statement about post-Chicago 1968, Vietnam-embroiled America.

By the early 1970s any lingering idealism in both the Bay Area music scene and the counter-cultural movement that it fed and served had evaporated. During this period, founder member Marty Balin left and the band released two more studio albums and a live set, the last release to bear the Jefferson Airplane name.

The 1970s and 1980s were marked by personnel changes and shifts in musical style. Under the creative control of Kantner and Slick the band evolved into Jefferson Starship. Balin's return in 1975 coincided with a revival in the band's commercial fortunes. However, both Slick and Balin (again) left in 1978, and 1979's album *Freedom from Point Zero* saw the band move towards a hard rock formula suited to the lucrative stadium market. Detoxed and dried-out, Grace Slick returned to the lineup in the early 1980s, and a now Kantner-less Starship emerged with a series of MTV-friendly hits such as the self-mythologizing "We Built This City" and the anodyne "Nothing's Gonna Stop Us Now." Things turned full circle in 1989, when Grace Slick left Starship and joined up with the rest of the original lineup to resurrect Jefferson Airplane.

It has become impossible to separate West Coast Rock from the counter-culture. This was ably demonstrated when "White Rabbit" was memorably featured in Oliver Stone's Vietnam movie *Platoon* (1986), in which it functioned as audio shorthand for a specific cultural moment. As rock critic Robert Palmer has pointed out, "behind the media-friendly facade of peace, love, and flowers, the sixties were a period of violence, conflict, and paranoia." The story of Jefferson Airplane demonstrates this tension.

—Simon Philo

FURTHER READING:

Friedlander, Paul. *Rock and Roll: A Social History.* Boulder, Westview, 1996.

Gillett, Charlie. *The Sound of the City: The Rise of Rock and Roll,* London, Souvenir Press, 1983.

Gleason, Ralph. *The Jefferson Airplane and the San Francisco Sound.* New York, Ballantine, 1969.

Landau, Jon. "It's Too Late to Stop Now." *The Penguin Book of Rock and Roll Writing,* edited by Clinton Heylin. London, Penguin, 1993.

Palmer, Robert. *Dancing in the Street: A Rock and Roll History.* London, BBC Books, 1996.

Storey, John. "Rockin' Hegemony: West Coast Rock and Amerika's War in Vietnam." *Tell Me Lies about Vietnam,* edited by Jeffrey Walsh and Alf Louvre. Open University Press, 1988.

The Jeffersons

In 1971, independent producer Norman Lear introduced the most controversial sitcom in television's brief history. That show was the groundbreaking CBS program, *All in the Family* . One particular occasional character was Archie Bunker's irascible black neighbor, George Jefferson (originally played by Mel Stewart). Jefferson never backed down from a fight, sparring successfully with the bigoted Bunker and generally winning the argument. In 1973 the role was assumed by veteran actor Sherman Hemsley . This character was such a hit with viewers that Helmsley was soon cast in the spin-off series, *The Jeffersons,* which first aired on CBS Television in January of 1975 and was, like *All in the Family,* the brainchild of writer-director and independent producer Norman Lear.

The Jeffersons focused on the lives of George and his wife Louise Jefferson—a nouveau riche African American couple. The show's gospel-toned opening musical theme, "Movin' on Up!" played while George and Louise moved into "their dee-luxe apartment in the sky." George was a successful businessman, millionaire, and the owner of seven dry-cleaning stores. Louise (played by Isabel Sanford) was a former maid attempting to adjust to the life of a woman of means. Together they lived in a ritzy penthouse apartment on Manhattan's fashionable and moneyed East Side with their son, Lionel (played at various times by Damon Evans and Mike Evans). Their home was filled expensive furnishings, and they even had their own black housekeeper, a wise-cracking maid named Florence (played by Marla Gibbs).

A unique supporting cast included an eccentric Englishman neighbor named Harry Bentley (Paul Benedict), the ever-obsequious Ralph the Doorman (Ned Wetimer), and most significantly, Helen and Tom Willis, (Roxie Roker, Franklin Cover) an interracial couple with two adult children—one Black, one White—the first such scenario on prime time television. George's elderly mother, the quietly cantankerous "Mother Jefferson," played by Zara Cully, made occasional appearances until the actress's death in 1978.

George Jefferson was rude and headstrong and referred to white people as "honkies." An article in *Ebony* magazine described him as "bombastic, frenetic, boastful, ill-mannered, prejudiced, and scheming." Louise, referred to by George as "Wheezy" spent most of her time apologizing for him. Some of the funniest moments came with the repartee between George and Florence the maid, who contributed to the humor with her continuous putdowns of George. She referred to him as "Shorty" and never missed a chance to put him in his place, fully contemptuous of the expected etiquette between employee and employer.

George, though a millionaire businessman, was often positioned as a buffoon or the butt of everyone's joke. As the *Ebony* article noted, "He was often the victim of his own acts: a put-down that backfires, a contrivance that goes astray, an ego-filled balloon suddenly deflated." No one, not even his maid took him seriously. Some blacks questioned whether audiences were laughing *with* George and his contempt of convention, or *at* George as he made a fool of himself? As with *Amos 'n' Andy* some twenty years prior, America's black community remained divided in their assessment of the program—even as the conservatism of the Reagan years brought a slight change in the tone of the program.

The Jeffersons was an enormously popular and highly rated program that lasted ten years on prime time television. Along with two other Lear products (*Good Times* and *Sanford & Son)* it featured a mostly African-American cast, the first such programming since the cancellation of the infamous *Amos 'n' Andy Show* in 1953. With its sometimes biting humor and daring scenarios it helped set a new tone

Sherman Hemsley (left) and Isabel Sanford celebrate the 200th episode of *The Jeffersons* with series creator Norman Lear (center).

in prime time television, while proving that programming with black casts could be successful and profitable, earning it a significant place in the history of 1970s television.

—Pamala S. Deane

FURTHER READING:

Barnow, Eric, *Tube of Plenty*. Oxford University Press, 1982.

Brooks, Tim and Earle Marsh. *The Complete Directory of Prime Time Network TV Shows, 1946-Present*. New York, Ballantine Books, 1985.

MacDonald, J. Fred, *Blacks and White TV: Afro-Americans in Television Since 1948*. Chicago, Nelson-Hall Publishers, 1983.

Marc, David, and Robert J. Thompson. *Prime Time, Prime Movers: From I Love Lucy to L.A. Law, America's Greatest TV Shows and the People Who Created Them*. Boston, Little, Brown, 1992.

Robinson, Louis. "The Jeffersons: A Look at Life on Black America's New 'Striver's Row.'" *Ebony*, January 1976.

Taylor, Ella. *Prime Time Families: Television Culture in Postwar America*. Berkeley, University of California Press, 1989.

Jell-O

Once given its trademarked name, Jell-O quickly became "America's Most Famous Dessert" with more than one million boxes sold every day by the late 1990s. Even more than apple pie or hot dogs, Jell-O epitomizes not just American cuisine, but America itself and has been one of its most enduring icons. Powdered gelatin, invented in 1845 by Peter Cooper, was one of the first convenience foods in America, making the arduous task of preparing gelatin from scratch—boiling calf's hoofs for hours—merely a matter of adding water to powder and leaving in a cool place to set. Not until the end of the century, however, did the concept of granulated gelatin catch on. In 1897, Pearl B. Wait invented a fruit-flavored gelatin, named Jell-O by his wife. Because of low sales, he sold the patent to Orator Francis

Woodward in 1899 for $450. Woodward began his first advertising campaign in 1902, making Jell-O, manufactured by the Genesee Pure Food Company of Leroy, New York, a worthy contender with Knox, Cox, Plymouth Rock, and other instant gelatins on the market at the time.

Although gelatin was an important ingredient in aspics and desserts, its rigorous preparation requirements meant that before the turn of the century it only graced the tables of the wealthy, who had the time, money, equipment, and paid labor to make such dishes. Preparations like powdered gelatins democratized desserts in America. Jell-O, the most popular, was inexpensive, initially selling for ten cents a box, and simple to make. Further, Jell-O instituted a premium system that allowed one to send away for free "melon" molds with the purchase of so many boxes of Jell-O products. Even in its early years, Jell-O came in a variety of flavors that allowed women to create many bright, fanciful dishes; strawberry, raspberry, orange, and lemon were the first flavors and continued to be the most popular. Jell-O also offered an Ice Cream Powder which, something like a frozen pudding, brought a variation of the frozen confection to the homes of the masses. In addition to these, the Genesee began producing D-Zerta, the first sugar-free gelatin, in 1923. Later that same year, the company changed its name to the Jell-O Company, and was then acquired by the Postum Company in 1925, forming the foundation for what would become General Foods. Rounding out its product line, the Jell-O Company introduced its pudding powder in 1929, eventually making 51 different flavors.

Advertising played a key role in Jell-O's popularity over other gelatins and made it the quintessential "American" dessert. From the beginning, brightly colored promotional recipe booklets touted the Jell-O product line and also educated women about how to use this new foodstuff. The Jell-O Girl appeared in 1903 as the personification of Jell-O's purity and ease of preparation. In later years the talents of well-known people were instituted to promote Jell-O. Rose O'Neil, creator of Kewpie dolls, refashioned the Jell-O Girl in 1908. In the 1920s, such familiar artists as Norman Rockwell and Maxfield Parrish illustrated its print material. Even L. Frank Baum, author of the Oz series, published a set of his books in conjunction with Jell-O.

In later years, as advertising media expanded, so did Jell-O's use of popular talents, including famous celebrities. Jack Benny and Mary Livingston promoted it on radio, coming up with the catchy "J-E-L-L-O" tune. Kate Smith sang the praises of Jell-O in magazine advertisements during World War II. In the 1950s, such luminaries as Roy Rogers, Andy Griffith, and Ethel Barrymore became spokespeople. From the 1970s through the 1990s, beloved actor and comedian Bill Cosby was the chief spokesperson for Jell-O and Jell-O Pudding.

As a food, Jell-O has recorded transformations in eating patterns and ethnic and regional variations in American foodways. Jane and Michael Stern have said that "More than any other food, Jell-O symbolizes how America really eats . . . Jell-O is Americana in a mold." At the beginning of the twentieth century, Jell-O proved to be an affordable and accessible version of a previously upper-class food, hence its great appeal. In later years it reflected events in American history and changes in food fads. During World War I, Jell-O still sold for ten cents a box and appealed to a woman's need to live within her budget during the expensive war years. During World War II, Jell-O answered the needs brought on by food rationing, as it could make low-sugar desserts and main dish salads.

Because Jell-O by nature is a colorful and moldable substance, the things made from it have embodied America's aesthetic sensibilities of the time, from daring dishes like Egg Slices en Gelée in the

roaring 1920s to modern one-crust instant pudding pies in the convenience-driven 1950s to postmodern creations like Pistachio Almond Delight—also known as Watergate Salad—in the 1980s. Jell-O not only manifested adult preoccupations but also appealed to the younger set. Ever since the days of the Jell-O Girl, Jell-O was associated with children, who have comprised a large group of Jell-O's consumers. Bill Cosby's 1970s "Kids Love Pudding" campaign was followed by the advent of multi-colored, multi-shaped Jell-O Jigglers for children of the 1980s, and increased the popularity of gelatin-based candies like Gummy Bears in the 1980s and Gummy Worms in the 1990s.

Jell-O's versatility has been a large factor in its enduring nature as an icon in American culture during the twentieth century. It has frequently appeared as a palliative dessert on hospital meal trays, accompanied families to potluck dinners as a side dish, and shown up in the lunch boxes of school children. It has also been used in ways not officially approved of by the General Foods Corporation. Jell-O "shooters," popular in the 1980s and 1990s, were college novelty cocktails that mixed Jell-O powder with vodka or grain alcohol and, once congealed, were eaten with spoons out of cups or by the cube from trays. Novelty wrestling, a popular bar entertainment during the 1980s, involved body-to-body combat of typically scantily-clad women; when not wrestling in mud, they wrestled in Jell-O, with lime being the most popular color/flavor.

—Wendy Woloson

FURTHER READING:

Publications International. *Celebrating One Hundred Years of Jell-O.* Lincolnwood, Illinois, Publications International, Ltd., 1997.

Stern, Jane, and Michael Stern. *The Encyclopedia of Bad Taste.* New York, HarperCollins, 1990.

Jennings, Peter (1938—)

The man who would eventually help to usher in the age of the super-anchor, veteran journalist Peter Jennings, got an early start to his broadcast career. At age nine he was the host of *Peter's People,* a short-lived Saturday morning children's radio show on the Canadian Broadcasting Corporation. For the precocious Jennings, journalism qualified as a family business. When the Canadian Broadcasting Corporation was established in the mid-1930s, his father Charles Jennings became its first voice, and was known as the "Edward R. Murrow of Canada."

Jennings was born in Toronto. A high school drop-out, he never finished tenth grade. Initially discouraged by his father from choosing journalism as a career, Jennings worked as a bank teller for three years before joining a small private radio station in Brockville, Ontario. In 1961 Jennings made the transition to television, joining one of Canada's first private television stations. There his duties included everything from reporting news to hosting a Canadian version of *American Bandstand.* When his television station became part of CTV, Canada's first national private chain, Jennings was appointed co-anchor of the national newscast. His work in this role caught the attention of ABC (American Broadcasting Corporation) news executives in New York.

Hired by ABC's *World News Tonight* in 1964, Jennings and his first wife, Canadian Valerie Godsoe, moved to New York City.

Peter Jennings

Within a year, the twenty-six year-old Jennings became America's youngest national network anchor ever, an appointment that failed because Jennings lacked journalistic experience and in-depth knowledge of the United States. After three years of miserable ratings Jennings resigned and was replaced by Frank Reynolds. The network made Jennings a traveling correspondent, and he quickly headed overseas. In 1969 he opened a permanent ABC bureau in Beirut, Lebanon, the first time an American-based television reporter had a full-time post in the Arab world. Jennings spent seven years in Lebanon as Beirut bureau chief, during which time he also met and married his second wife, Anouchka.

In 1975, Jennings returned to Washington, D.C., to anchor *A.M. America,* the predecessor to *Good Morning America.* Disliking both the job and the city, however, he arranged a transfer to London by 1977. In 1978, while still posted in London, Jennings was named co-anchor of the ABC evening news as part of an innovative three-anchor system that included Frank Reynolds in Washington and Max Robinson in Chicago. Referring to his time in London as his "dream job," because the triumvirate system gave him both the flexibility to travel and the status to cover major news stories, he stayed in the position for six years. While in London he met and married his third wife, Kati

Marton, in 1979. By 1982, the couple had two children, Elizabeth and Christopher.

In 1983 one of the anchoring triumvirate, Frank Reynolds, became ill with cancer, and Jennings reluctantly returned to the United States to fill in during his illness. In an interview he explained his problem with being sole anchor: "Anchor people are slaves to the daily broadcast. Very high-priced slaves I grant you. But slaves." Instead, Jennings prefers field reporting, and has been known to speak with a "little regret about not being in the trenches covering stories." When Reynolds died, however, Jennings was re-appointed to the sole anchor position he had held sixteen years earlier.

Jennings and his peers Dan Rather and Tom Brokaw have transformed the role of network news anchor into superstar journalist. In their book *Anchors,* authors Robert and Gerald Goldberg explain that while Walter Cronkite was "the original 800-pound gorilla," Jennings, Rather, and Brokaw have "acquired a different order of magnitude." These super-anchors command huge salaries, and have their trustworthiness figures measured just like the president. Acting as the "living logos" of the network news divisions, they provide news to more Americans than any other source.

FURTHER READING:

McNeil, Alex. *Total Television: A Comprehensive Guide to Programming from 1948 to the Present.* 4th ed. New York, Penguin, 1996.

Jessel, George (1898-1981)

George Jessel lived his life in show business, and he toiled with boundless energy to adapt to the changing modes of the entertainment world. His professional career spanned three-quarters of a century, from 1907 to just before his death. Primarily, he was a live-audience entertainer, with his show business persona evolving from the cocky-but-lovable Jewish-American immigrant boy, to the middle-aged professional emcee and purveyor of nostalgia, to the pompous, self-proclaimed Toastmaster General pose of his last twenty years.

With an unfailingly brash personality, semitic good looks, a nasal voice, and quick-tongued wit, Jessel began performing in musical-comedy "kid acts" at the age of nine, shortly after the death of his father. Before long he was a featured performer with other youthful talents such as Eddie Cantor and Walter Winchell in vaudeville acts produced and written by Gus Edwards. By the time he reached his twenties, Jessel had developed into a successful vaudeville monologist, with a specialty routine of speaking on the telephone to his immigrant Jewish "Momma." Each of his dozens of comical

George Jessel

telephone routines similarly began, "Hello, Operator! Fentingtrass 3522. Hello, Momma? Georgie!"

In spite of his prosperity in vaudeville, Jessel strived to conquer New York's legitimate stage. He received his break in 1925 when he was awarded the role of Jack Robin/Jake Rabinowitz in Samson Raphaelson's *The Jazz Singer*, a melodrama about a young man torn between the confining world of his Jewish roots and the exhilarating American culture of the Jazz Age. Jessel successfully performed the role in New York and around the country for two years and was negotiating with Warner Brothers to star in the film version. Yet the role was not to be his, due in part to his extraordinary demands for remuneration, and the fact that Al Jolson (who had been Raphaelson's inspiration for writing *The Jazz Singer*) had become interested in playing the screen role. Jessel may have been a headliner in vaudeville and a success in the play, but Jolson was the king of their profession, a nationally known top draw who would garner a much larger audience. Jessel never forgave Jolson for usurping the role, and publicly griped about the circumstances of the loss for decades.

Jessel's own career as a film star was quite short-lived, in part because his ethnicity limited his opportunities for lead roles. Also, the few feature films he made in the late 1920s demonstrated that his guileless acting style was more suited to the stage than to the close scrutiny of the motion picture camera. He fared better in radio, and on stage as a nightclub and variety show emcee/singer/joke teller.

By 1945, as American soldiers were returning home from World War II, Twentieth Century-Fox recognized a desire among moviegoers to look backwards with longing to the lifestyle of the early years of the century. Acknowledging in the middle-aged Jessel an expertise in selling nostalgia to audiences, Fox signed him to produce musicals which featured warm memories of show business and home life. Among the charming and heartwarming films he produced in the immediate post-war years are *The Dolly Sisters* (1945), *When My Baby Smiles at Me* (1948) and *Oh, You Beautiful Doll* (1949). Yet Jessel's personal life was fraught with scandal. He was married four times, claimed numerous love affairs, and was involved in a $200,000 paternity suit.

As Jessel aged, he became more effusive in his on-stage monologues. As a popular emcee, he made elaborate after-dinner speeches at testimonials to leading performers. This style of monologue evolved into Jessel's becoming the self-proclaimed "Toastmaster General of the United States." By the Vietnam War years, he had become an aging self-parody as he appeared on television talk shows in military regalia. Here, he endlessly pontificated on the state of the world and shamelessly name-dropped as he cited his association with politicians and royalty. As more years passed and many of his colleagues and friends died, he put his talent for speech-making to work as a eulogizer at many celebrity funerals.

Even when his own health was fading, Jessel refused to quit show business. Blind and arthritic, he continued to work. Although his audience had dwindled and he was considered—by those who remembered him at all—the ghost of vaudeville past, Jessel still performed, telling jokes in restaurants and obtaining an occasional club date.

—Audrey E. Kupferberg

FURTHER READING:

Jessel, George. *"Hello, Momma."* Cleveland and New York, World Publishing Company, 1946.

————. *This Way Miss.* New York, Henry Holt and Company, 1955.

————. *Elegy in Manhattan.* New York, Holt, Rinehart and Winston, 1961.

————. *The World I Lived In.* New York, Henry Regnery Company, 1975.

Jesus Christ Superstar

Few musical forms have fallen into such low repute as the rock opera. Through the bombastic efforts of a handful of well-meaning composers, the whole enterprise has become almost synonymous with egotism in the minds of pop music consumers. Yet the form continues to have its adherents. A stage revival of The Who's trailblazing *Tommy* opened to packed houses on Broadway in 1995. And *Jesus Christ Superstar,* the mind-blowing 1970 rock opera about the last days of Christ, continues to work its magic on theatergoers the world over in countless touring company and summer stock productions.

Originally conceived as a stage musical, *Jesus Christ Superstar* was the brainchild of two enterprising English whiz kids, composer Andrew Lloyd Webber, who was twenty-three, and lyricist Tim Rice, who was twenty-six. The pair's 1968 collaboration, *Joseph and the Amazing Technicolor Dreamcoat,* had set the Old Testament story of Jacob's feuding sons to a throbbing backbeat, to the consternation of many in the rabbinate. With *Superstar,* the composers took the even more audacious step of setting the sufferings of Jesus to music. Not surprisingly, they had difficulty finding financial support for such a venture. Eventually they were forced to give up their stage plans and settle instead for a double-sided record set. Dubbed a ''concept album'' in the hipster parlance of the times, the LP was released in late 1970 with a drab brown cover featuring almost no religious iconography. But such precautions did little to stave off the inevitable ecclesiastical backlash.

The question of blasphemy aside, few could dispute the quality of the recording itself. A tight backing band provided muscular support for vocalists Murray Head, Ian Gillian, and Yvonne Elliman. The LP's 24 songs chronicled the final days of Jesus, from his entry

A scene from the film *Jesus Christ Superstar.*

into Jerusalem through his trial and crucifixion by the Roman authorities. A number of songs were cast in the form of dialogues, with various New Testament figures hurling accusation and invective at one another. The balladeering chores were assigned to the Hawaiian-born Elliman, whose mellifluous renditions of "Everything's Alright" and "I Don't Know How to Love Him" became FM radio staples.

Not surprisingly, a mass market rock 'n' roll composition on so hallowed a subject could not pass public scrutiny without generating some religious controversy. But negative reaction to *Superstar* was muted and with good reason. While hardly the stuff of a theological dissertation, *Superstar* in the final analysis was no less scripturally sound than the average Catholic missal. Other than the arguably tasteless references to Christ as "J.C.," there was little here to offend Christian traditionalists. The issue of Jesus's resurrection was by-passed entirely, consistent with the entire "opera's" depiction of Jesus as an imperfect mortal struggling with a divine commission he could not fully understand. "If you knew the path we're riding," wailed "Jesus" Gillian in one typical number, "you'd understand it less than I." Perhaps most galling to strict spiritual constructions, however, was the central role afforded to Judas Iscariot, voiced with quivering urgency by Murray Head. Questioning both the political message and personal behavior of his master in such songs as "Heaven on Their Minds," this Judas is no treacherous asp but rather a conflicted, doubting Thomas.

Jesus Christ Superstar sold more than 2 million copies in 12 months and became 1971's number-one-selling album. In July of that year, 13,000 *Superstar* fans packed Pittsburgh's Civic Arena to see the opera performed in concert. That performance was just the runner-up to a full-blown Broadway production—the realization of Rice and Lloyd Webber's original dream—that opened at the Mark Hellinger Theater in New York on October 12, 1971. Newcomer Jeff Fenholt assumed the role of Jesus, while a youthful Ben Vereen essayed the part of Judas. Surprisingly, Andrew Lloyd Webber would later renounce this production, which lasted just 20 months on the Great White Way.

More to the composer's liking was the 1973 film version, directed by Norman Jewison. Today the film seems dated, with its army of scraggly hippies disembarking from a psychedelic bus. But it benefits from a number of strong performances. Black actor Carl Anderson makes a dynamic Judas, while Texas rock drummer Ted Neeley, an understudy in the Broadway production, brings a wild-eyed passion to the title role. Derided by some as "the screaming Jesus" for his piercing tremolo, Neeley got the part only after Ian Gillian turned it down because he could make more money touring with his band Deep Purple. Neeley has since turned playing Jesus Christ into a career, calling himself "a palette on which people project the Jesus they came to see."

Spurred on by a wave of 1970s nostalgia, *Superstar* has been revived in the 1990s. A 25-month, 116-city anniversary tour, starring Styx's Dennis DeYoung, was mounted in 1994. It is estimated that musical theater productions of the show have grossed in excess of $150 million worldwide. Certainly it launched its co-composers into celebrity status. Since ending their professional relationship in 1978, Rice has gone on to co-write the songs for Disney's *Lion King;* Lloyd Webber created *Cats* and *Phantom of the Opera,* which would amass a fortune of some $1.15 billion.

Jesus Christ Superstar continues to meet with some localized pockets of resistance from those who disagree with its portrayal of a flawed, all-too-human Jesus. But its greatest defenders remain its legions of devoted fans who were acknowledged in a comment by one-time Judas Ben Vereen: "What the people up in arms failed to look at is that as long as people were rockin' to Jesus, everything was gonna be all right for humanity."

—Robert E. Schnakenberg

FURTHER READING:

Daly, Steve. "A Hit of Biblical Proportions." *Entertainment Weekly.* July 19, 1996, 88.

Kelly, Christina. "A Superstar Is Reborn." *Entertainment Weekly.* December 23, 1994, 65.

Sella, Marshall. "Is God Ted?" *New York.* January 23, 1995, 46.

Jet

On the heels of his success with *Ebony,* the African American version of *Life,* Chicago magazine publisher John H. Johnson was looking to start a new publication in 1951. Magazine trends that year pointed away from the large-format publications such as *Life, Look,* and *Ebony* to pocket-sized digests, fast information for busy readers. Johnson envisioned a black version of *Quick,* a short-lived mainstream news digest, providing a weekly synopsis of important news and events for African Americans. *Jet* magazine, introduced on November 1, 1951, quickly gained acceptance among blacks for providing understandable, accurate information, and they came to view it as the definitive word on current events, the so-called "Negro's bible." In the process of achieving that fame, *Jet* was also the first national publication to print the photograph of the corpse of a fourteen-year-old boy lynched for whistling at a white woman in Mississippi in 1955. That picture alerted African Americans, especially those in the press, to the building civil rights movement in the South a full year before the Montgomery, Alabama, bus boycott.

Quick, a vest pocket-sized magazine featuring capsulized news that Americans could read "on the bus or in the beauty parlor," was introduced by Gardner Cowles, Jr., the publisher of *Look,* in 1949. It represented a problem for advertisers because its small size, four by six inches, required special advertising copy, and Cowles discontinued the publication in 1953 due to a lack of advertising. John H. Johnson, the Chicago magazine publisher who had started his business with a $500 loan from his mother in 1942, planned to use the profits of *Ebony* to support his new pocket-sized publication until advertisers could adjust. The word "jet" was tailor-made for his purposes, meaning dark velvet-black on one level, fast on another. "In the world today, everything is moving along at a faster clip," Johnson wrote in the first issue. "Each week will bring you complete news coverage on happenings among Negroes all over the U.S.—in entertainment, politics, sports, social events as well as features on personalities, places and events." The first issue of *Jet* sold out and garnered a circulation of 300,000 within six months, making it the largest black news magazine in the world.

Jet was still a new publication during the tempestuous 1950s but lynching was an old problem in the South, dating back to slavery. The U.S. Supreme Court's 1954 *Brown v. Board of Education* school desegregation case had made the South a dangerous place for blacks again, a fact that visiting Northern blacks did not always recognize. When fourteen-year-old Emmett Till, a Chicago boy visiting relatives in Money, Mississippi, allegedly whistled at a white woman in August 1955, he was lynched and his corpse mutilated. His mother asked photographers to shoot pictures of his mangled body when it was returned to Chicago for burial. Johnson and his editors agonized over the gruesome photographs but published them in the September 15, 1955, *Jet*, providing the first national coverage of the murder. The issue sold out, traumatizing African Americans and preparing "the way for the Freedom Movement of the sixties," as Johnson recalled. An interracial team of *Jet* and *Ebony* reporters and photographers covered the resulting trial in Mississippi, alerting other Northern journalists to the deteriorating situation in the South. The Montgomery, Alabama bus boycott, begun by Rosa Parks and led by the Rev. Dr. Martin Luther King, was born a year later, on December 1, 1955.

Jet went on to cover the civil rights movement, along with other business, education, religion, health, medicine, journalism, politics, labor, and crime news of the day. In the 1990s its contents were set: "Census" was a weekly digest of births and deaths. "Ticker Tape" was a Walter Winchell style feature discussing news and news personalities written by Washington D.C. bureau chief Simon Booker. "This Week in Black History" provided a recap of traditional and more recent historical events. "People are Talking About" offered gossip about personalities. "Sports" provided an overview of black athletes and predominantly black teams and "Jet Beauty of the Week" showed a traditional bathing beauty. The magazine also listed the top 20 Black singles and albums along with television highlights and a weekly photo. *Jet* offers no editorial comment, although the stories and images of African Americans are positive and upbeat, reflecting Johnson's conservative beliefs in free markets and working within the system. Its circulation at the end of the twentieth century was around 900,000.

—Richard Digby-Junger

FURTHER READING:

Dates, Jannette L., and William Barlow. *Split Image: African Americans in the Mass Media.* Washington, D.C., Howard University Press, 1990, 374.

Johnson, John H., and Lerone Bennett, Jr. *Succeeding against the Odds.* New York, Warner Books, 1989.

Pride, Armistead S., and Clint C. Walker. *A History of the Black Press.* Washington, D.C., Howard University Press, 1997.

Walker, Daniel C. *Black Journals of the United States.* Westport, Connecticut, Greenwood Press, 1982, 213-14.

Wolseley, Roland E. *The Black Press, U.S.A.* 2nd edition. Ames, Iowa, Iowa State University Press, 1990, 88, 144-46.

Jet Skis

In 1974, Kawasaki introduced the Jetski, a revolutionary jet-propelled, single-person watercraft capable of speeds up to 40 mph. Based on the concept of a motorized waterski, the original Jetski required the rider to stand and use considerable strength and balance for control. It was not until 1986, when Yamaha introduced the Waverunner, a more manageable sit-down version, that "personal watercraft" gained widespread appeal. Within ten years, it blossomed into a $300 million a year industry with annual sales over 200,000 in the United States alone, and led to the creation of two competitive

Jetski racing circuits. But in the late 1990s, increased complaints about safety, fuel emissions, and noise resulted in a public backlash. Several states enforced mandatory driver's education and minimum age restrictions, and some areas, including Lake Tahoe, the San Juan Islands, and the majority of the National Parks, banned the craft outright. Industry experts agreed that the continued popularity of personal watercraft would depend on improved driver education and cleaner, quieter engines.

—Simon Donner

Jewish Defense League

In 1968, Rabbi Meir Kahane started the Jewish Defense League (JDL) in the Orthodox Jewish neighborhoods of Brooklyn, New York. The JDL was initially a vigilante organization dedicated to the protection of Jews but, fueled by the fanaticism of its founder, it swiftly grew to become one of America's most high profile terrorist organizations. Between 1968 and 1987, members of the JDL committed 50 terrorist acts directed at the Palestine Liberation Organization, Soviet officials, and one Nazi war criminal. The organization forged close links to the conservative extremist Kach party in Israel. Rabbi Kahane was murdered by an Egyptian fundamentalist on November 5, 1990, and on February 24, 1995, Baruch Goldstein, a former JDL member, opened fire on Palestinians at prayer, killing 35 people. This massacre resulted in the banning of the Kach party by the Israeli government.

—S. Naomi Finkelstein

FURTHER READING:

Dolgin, Janet *Jewish Identity and the JDL.* Princeton, New Jersey, Princeton University Press, 1977.

Kahane, Meir, *The Story of the Jewish Defense League.* Radnor, Pennsylvania, Chilton Book Co., 1975.

JFK (The Movie)

Upon its release in 1991, director Oliver Stone's controversial film *JFK* elicited cries from citizens who insisted that the U.S. government make public confidential Warren Commission files pertaining to the 1963 assassination of President John F. Kennedy. That the government made public some (but not all) of the files following the film's popular success not only reflects the power of Stone's film but also the overall power of film as a pop culture medium.

With *JFK*, Stone challenged the government by providing an alternative theory to the one reached by the Warren Commission. Stone not only consulted texts by popular historians (Jim Garrison and Jim Marrs) and historical records, but he also posited his own interpretation of events concerning JFK's assassination. Furthermore, although many individuals and groups have challenged the Warren Commission Report since its release, for the most part the mass public had not responded to the report with a collective fervor until Stone presented his film. Following the film's release, acting in response

A jet skier jumping a wake.

to—among other things—*JFK* viewer outcry, President George Bush "signed into law the President John F. Kennedy Assassination Records Collection Act of 1992. [T]he bill provided for the establishment of an independent commission charged with releasing all government records related to Kennedy's assassination except those that clearly jeopardized personal privacy or national security."

Stone's film chronicles the events propelled into motion by New Orleans District Attorney Jim Garrison in 1969, when Garrison brought New Orleans businessman Clay Shaw to trial, accusing him of conspiring to assassinate JFK. In the film, Stone presents myriad characters—some actual, some hypothetical, and some composites. The technical achievements of *JFK* add a dimension of realism to the film, but this realism gives audience members (particularly historians) a potential problem in distinguishing fact from fabrication. For example, Stone blends actual Zapruder film footage with his fabricated footage, editing them together in a seamless fashion. Finally, in *JFK*, viewers learn about Stone's theory in which the American government, the military, the Mafia, Cuban nationalists, the military-industrial complex, then Vice-President Lyndon Johnson, and, of course, Clay Shaw and Lee Harvey Oswald all conspired to assassinate JFK.

The overall response to *JFK* by both the general public and the media was both positive and negative. Positive responses mostly came from those viewers whom Stone enlightened, such as younger citizens out of touch with the assassination. The negative responses to the film came (and still come) from those whom Stone attacks, mainly the press, the government, and historians. Interestingly, to promote further reading on the topic and to appease his harshest critics, Stone released a fully-documented screenplay to the film, replete with some ninety critical articles dealing with the film as well as the assassination itself and actual historical records.

Stone included the phrase "The Story That Won't Go Away" in his title for *JFK*. If overall response to the film provides any indication, this story certainly has not gone away. If anything, Stone brought it back into the public consciousness with *JFK*—a film whose power relies not upon its accuracy in portraying certain events but on its ability to reopen one of the darkest chapters in American history.

—Jason T. McEntee

FURTHER READING/VIEWING:

Garrison, Jim. *On the Trail of the Assassins.* New York, Warner Books, 1988.

JFK. (film). Warner Brothers, 1991.

Mackey-Kallis, Susan. *Oliver Stone's America: Dreaming the Myth Outward.* Boulder, Westview Press, 1996.

Marrs, Jim. *Crossfire: The Plot That Killed Kennedy.* New York, Carroll & Graf Publishers, 1989.

Stone, Oliver, and Zachary Sklar. *JFK: The Book of the Film, a Documented Screenplay.* New York, Applause Books, 1992.

Jimenez, Jose

See Dana, Bill

Jogging

If there was a physical activity that caught on during the last few decades of the twentieth century, it was jogging. Running and sprinting had been around since time immemorial and were associated with competitive running. Jogging, on the other hand, achieved currency when individuals took up the deliberately paced trotting as part of fitness regimes. At some point, when the briskness or doggedness of noncompetitive jogging reached a certain level, the more impressive word "running" came to be more or less interchangeable with "jogging."

James (Jim) Fixx was an important figure on the cusp of the jogging boom. In 1977, Fixx triggered a revolution in physical activity with his book *The Complete Book of Running.* He made getting out of bed early to put on sweat clothes and sneakers the stylish thing to do. Panting and sweating became fashionable. Although Fixx popularized the movement, years earlier Dr. Kenneth Cooper had advocated jogging as a healthful activity in his book *Aerobics* in 1968. Others, such as runner Bill Rodgers, had promoted physical activity as good for one's health. But runners credited Fixx with universalizing the sport through his book, which sold almost a million copies in hardback over a few years. He got overweight people off couches and onto the roads of America. He advocated jogging or running as good for everything, from weight loss to better sex. He said joggers digested food better, felt better, and had more energy.

Would-be converts to running could identify with Fixx as an average guy, perhaps like them. In his book, he described how running changed his life. He was overweight and smoked two packs of cigarettes a day before hitting the road at age 32 in New York City,

Kevin Costner as District Attorney Jim Garrison in Oliver Stone's *JFK*.

Members of the National Jogging Association.

where he worked as a magazine editor in Manhattan. "One of the more pleasant duties was to entertain authors at lunches and dinners," he wrote of his editor's job in the foreword to his book. He noted that in high school he weighed 170 pounds but ballooned later to 214 pounds. His only activity was weekend tennis. Ironically, it was a pulled calf muscle from playing tennis that led to regular jogging. He started running slowly to strengthen the muscle and later became a running addict, competing eight times in the famed Boston Marathon.

Fitness experts urged people to get physical examinations before starting rigorous running programs. This included stress tests where the heart could be tested by cardiologists during a fast walk on a treadmill. The purpose of jogging was to improve the heart and lungs by improving the delivery of oxygen through the body. Speed was not the main goal, fitness experts said, but time spent performing an aerobic activity which strengthened muscles and overall cardiovascular system. Trainers suggested three or four runs a week, to give muscles that break down during exercise time to renew between runs. The experts said that during runs, an individual's pulse rate should rise to about 70 or 80 percent of his or her maximum rate. The rule of

thumb for calculating one's maximum rate was 220 minus one's age. Thus, a 40-year-old runner's rate should rise to a level somewhere between 125 and 145 beats a minute. To test the level of strain, runners were urged to take a talk test. If they could not talk easily while running, they were straining and should slow down.

Fixx stressed that running could lower cholesterol and blood pressure, thus improving the cardiovascular system and otherwise giving people better lives. Fixx himself, however, could not outrun his own genes. His father had suffered a heart attack at the age of 36 and died seven years later. While running on a country road in Vermont in 1984, Jim Fixx himself, fell and died of a heart attack, shocking American and the running world. As it turned out, Fixx had not paid enough attention to earlier signs of heart problems, including chest pains he experienced only weeks before he died. He was 52.

Fixx's death stunned runners but did not stop them. U.S. presidents had already taken up the jogging craze and others continued it. A famous picture of Jimmy Carter showed him exhausted after a jog. George Bush became the first well-known Republican jogger—other Republican presidents, such as Dwight Eisenhower and Gerald

Ford, were better known for golf. But Bush combined both a form of jogging and golf. He was known as a speed golfer who would dash through an 18-hole course as fast as he could. Democratic president Bill Clinton was an often photographed jogger who had run daily through the streets of Arkansas when he was governor. When he went to Washington as president, he caused a brief furor by having a jogging track built around part of the South Lawn of the White House to shield his running form from the prying lenses of photographers.

Senators, congressmen, and celebrities such as Madonna, the singer-actress, were runners as were ordinary housewives, businessmen, and students, all of whom were determined to get in their regular runs. Some runners ran into physical problems, however, including knee, leg, and muscle injuries. In 1994, Senator Slade Gorton of Washington suffered a mild heart attack while running in Boston. He was hospitalized and later recovered.

The influence of Fixx, Bill Rodgers (who won eight Boston and New York marathons between 1975 and 1980), and other advocates of a good workout spread. They pioneered a movement that led to an industry of exercise schools, aerobics programs, television shows, sports stores for runners, special clothing, public health campaigns aimed at combating inactivity and lowering cholesterol, and, above all, the ubiquitous running shoe. They changed the landscape of America and created a scene where city streets and country roads featured walkers, joggers, runners, and others out getting some exercise.

—Michael L. Posner

FURTHER READING:

Burfoot, Amby. "Like Father, Like Son. (John Fixx, Son of Jim Fixx)." *Runner's World.* Vol.29, August 1, 1994, p.45.

Fixx, James F. *The Complete Book of Running.* New York, Random House, 1977.

Glover, Bob, and Jack Shepherd. *The Runner's Handbook.* New York, Penguin, 1985.

John Birch Society

The death of Senator Joseph McCarthy in 1957 left a vacuum in the conspiracy-minded wing of the American conservative movement. In 1958, retired candy-manufacturer Robert Welch, who suspected that the Wisconsin Senator had been murdered by the Communist conspiracy, formed the John Birch Society to continue McCarthy's mission. The Society took its name from Captain John Birch, a young American soldier killed by Chinese Communists in 1945 and regarded by Welch as the first American martyr of the Cold War.

Like McCarthy, the Birch Society offered an ideology that combined anti-Communism with anti-liberalism and populism. For the Birch Society, Communism included not just the external threat of the Soviet Union, but also the more pernicious danger of internal subversion by the "creeping socialism" of the New Deal. Liberals and moderate conservatives are regarded by the Society as being either Communist agents or unwitting dupes. Especially dangerous are elitist liberal intellectuals, allegedly in control of the universities, the mass media, and the government. At various times, Welch estimated that between 60 to 80 percent of America was under Communist control.

In building up the Birch Society, Welch drew on his considerable managerial expertise as a successful businessman, but he also deliberately imitated what he perceived as the tactics of the communist enemy. Like Lenin, Welch created a tightly organized and well-disciplined movement with little room for debate. Not a political party but a political movement, the Birch Society sought to control the Republican Party at the grass-roots level. The Society also sought to influence public opinion by sponsoring a wide variety of magazines—*American Opinion, The New America*—and books—*Global Tyranny . . . Step by Step.*

As the Cold War heated up in the early 1960s, the Birch Society gained tens of thousands of members and was a powerful force in the Republican Party in states like California, Texas, and Indiana. The Society played an important role in securing the nomination of Barry Goldwater as the Republican candidate for president in 1964. In the early 1960s, the young George Bush actively invited Birch Society members to fill key Texas Republican party offices.

Yet, in its moment of greatest political influence, the Birch Society came under increasing scrutiny and criticism. The Anti-Defamation League denounced the extremism of the Society while cartoonist Walt Kelly mocked their paranoia in his comic strip *Pogo.* In 1961 Welch described former President Dwight Eisenhower as a "dedicated, conscious agent of the Communist conspiracy." In response, mainstream conservatives like William F. Buckley, Jr. felt that they had to distance themselves from the Birch Society. In the pages of *National Review* Buckley denounced "the drivel of Robert Welch." In 1965 Goldwater called upon all Republicans to "resign from the Society."

After the mid-1960s, the Society underwent a steep decline in membership and also changed its orientation. Unwilling to support the war in Vietnam, which he saw as being sabotaged by Communists in the American government, Welch turned his attention to domestic issues like the civil rights movement (opposed with the slogan "Impeach Earl Warren"). African Americans who fought for civil rights were seen by the Society as pawns of an anti-American conspiracy and described as "indigenous animals" and "gorillas."

Balanced against this focus on racial politics was a radical extension of the Birch Society's conspiracy theories. In 1966 Welch declared that "the Communist movement is only a tool of the total conspiracy" controlled by the "Bavarian Illuminati," which he believed had masterminded the French and Russian Revolutions, the two World Wars, the creation of the United Nations (U.N.), and many other world events. The U. N., as the supposed center of a world conspiracy, became a particular bete-noir for the Society, which adopted the slogan "U.S. out of the U.N.!"

Initially, Welch's elaborate conspiracy theories about the Bavarian Illuminati and the U.N. alienated members and further marginalized the Society. Yet even in its low point of the 1970s, the Society had some prominent and influential supporters, including Congressman Larry McDonald of Indiana. Further, with the death of Robert Welch in 1985 and the accession of G. Vance Smith to leadership, the Society began to re-vitalize itself.

In the conspiracy-minded 1990s, the era of the *X-Files,* the Birch Society has gained new prominence and popularity. In the post-Cold War world, many other right-wingers, especially those belonging to militia groups, share the Society's fear of the U.N. Among right-wing militias, the Birch society is respected as an organization of scholars who have uncovered the secret agenda of the U.N.—although, unlike some of the militias, the Birch Society does not advocate overthrowing the government by violence. "There is a plethora of newsletters, tabloids, magazines, and radio shows out there mimicking us,'' complained G. Vance Smith in 1996. Smith did take comfort in the fact that more respectable media organs were now spreading the Birch Society gospel to the unconverted. For example, Pat Buchanan, co-host of Cable News Network's (CNN) *Crossfire* and perennial Republican presidential candidate, has praised the Society's *New American* magazine for ''its advocacy, its insights, its information, [and] its unique point of view.'' A special issue of the *New American* devoted to conspiracies sold more than half a million copies in 1996.

Outside of politics, the Birch Society has also exerted remarkable influence on popular culture. Its ideas have been frequently parodied, notably in the movie *Dr. Strangelove* (1964), where the character General Jack D. Ripper mouths Birch Society conspiracy theories. *Mad* magazine mocked the Society along the same lines in 1965. In the 1996 movie *Conspiracy Theory,* the main character has a copy of the *New American* in his apartment. Despite its small numbers and eccentric ideas, the Birch Society has been a unique and potent force in American life for more than 40 years. In an age of conspiracy theories, the Birch Society has been at the forefront of American paranoia.

—Jeet Heer

FURTHER READING:

Hofstadter, Richard. *The Paranoid Style in American Politics and Other Essays.* New York, Knopf, 1965.

Judis, John B. *William F. Buckley, Jr.: Patron Saint of the Conservatives.* New York, Simon and Schuster, 1988.

Lipset, Seymour Martin, and Earl Raab. *The Politics of Unreason: Right-Wing Extremism in America, 1760-1977.* Chicago, University of Chicago Press, 1977.

John, Elton (1947—)

Pop music's most flamboyant superstar during the early 1970s, Elton John has become the music industry's most consistently successful artist, fielding a Top 40 single every year since 1970. John's penchant for outrageous costumes and zany eyeglasses made him one of rock 'n' roll's most recognizable icons during the 1970s. He is also a tremendously gifted songwriter, whose versatility and ability to churn out memorable melodies has guaranteed him longevity in a field where so many of his fellow performers quickly faded into obscurity.

Born Reginald Kenneth Dwight on March 25, 1947 in a London suburb, he showed prodigious talent as a pianist at a young age and, at eleven, won a scholarship to the prestigious Royal Academy of Music, where he attended classes for gifted children. Although classically trained, Reginald loved rock 'n' roll, particularly performers such as Buddy Holly, Chuck Berry, and Ray Charles. He joined his first band in 1961, Bluesology, a blues-soul-rock combo, which had moderate success opening for American acts throughout the 1960s. But as other bands rose to stardom, the teenage musician grew frustrated and quit the band. Changing his name to Elton John, he auditioned for lead singer in a number of bands before hooking up with lyricist Bernie Taupin in the late 1960s. The duo became one of the top songwriting teams in England before John won his first record contract.

Elton John

After the release of their moderately successful first album in 1969, Taupin and John collaborated on a lushly orchestrated eponymous second effort, which quickly climbed the charts in America and England on the strength of the Top Ten single, ''Your Song.'' Following up with three albums in less than two years—*Tumbleweed Connection, Madman across the Water,* and *Honky Chateau*—Elton John soon became one of the most prolific and popular rock 'n' roll musicians of the 1970s.

Although Taupin and John produced hit after hit throughout the decade, it was John's flamboyant onstage persona that made him a star. Taking his cue from the early 1970s Glam Rock movement in Britain, John was a peerless live performer, wearing anything from ostrich feathers to $5,000 eyeglasses that spelled out his name in lights to a Donald Duck costume. John's sartorial splendor became his trademark, as his singles such as ''Crocodile Rock,'' ''Daniel,'' and ''Bennie and the Jets'' became global top-ten hits.

In 1976, Elton John revealed his bisexuality in an interview with *Rolling Stone.* His confession was said to have put off many of his fans and his popularity gradually began to wane. In truth, though his sexual orientation may have deterred some of the American public from buying his records, it was more the case that John's prolific output of sixteen top-twenty singles in four years and fifteen LPs in seven years had left him exhausted. He took a hiatus from performing, cut back on his recording schedule, and even stopped working with Bernie Taupin.

In 1981, Elton John signed with Geffen Records and, throughout the decade he continued to produce gold albums, each of which contained at least one top-forty single. However, while his career remained successful, John's personal life was in a state of turmoil. He had become addicted to cocaine and alcohol and he struggled with substance abuse throughout the 1980s. After announcing his bisexuality in 1976, John was afraid to reveal his homosexuality and, in 1984, he married Renate Blauel. Four years later, he was divorced and, after a playing a record-breaking five nights at Madison Square Garden in 1988, Elton John auctioned off all of his costumes and memorabilia, effectively breaking with his past.

In 1991, Elton John announced his sobriety and his homosexuality, and also established the Elton John AIDS Foundation. As the first celebrity to befriend AIDS patient Ryan White, John has tirelessly given of his time and energy in contributing to the fight against AIDS. Since the early 1990s, John has continued to release successful albums and singles on a yearly basis, reestablishing himself as one of pop music's most consistent performers, even as he devoted more and more time to his philanthropic efforts.

In 1994, John collaborated with Tim Rice to create the music for Disney's *The Lion King,* which earned him an Academy Award for best original song. Three years later, Elton John once again came to global attention, with the deaths of two close friends in less than two months of each other. Shortly after attending the funeral for murdered fashion designer Gianni Versace with Princess Diana, John performed at the internationally televised memorial service for the princess herself, playing a revised version of his hit single, "Candle in the Wind." His recording of the single, with all proceeds going to charity, became the fastest-selling single of all time. Four months later, HRH Queen Elizabeth II named the fifty-year-old Elton John a Knight of the British Empire.

The subject of an unsparing 1997 documentary, *Tantrums and Tiaras,* made by his partner David Furnish, John has made peace with both himself and his persona, becoming a perfect role model for millennial pop culture. Flamboyant yet sober, the philanthropic celebrity continues a pop music phenomenon, even as he embraces his new spiritual ethos. The metamorphosis of John through the decades has seemed to mirror the popular mood, even as the talented singer continues to help define what the world likes to hear.

—Victoria Price

FURTHER READING:

Bernardin, Claude, and Tom Stanton. *Rocket Man: Elton John from A-Z.* New York, Praeger, 1996.

Cagle, Jess. "Elton John." *Entertainment Weekly.* December 26, 1997-January 2, 1998, 36-37.

Eden, Dawn. "Elton John." *Good Housekeeping.* Vol. 226, February 1998, 29-30.

Walters, Barry. "A Triumph of Love." *Advocate.* January 20, 1998, 95.

Johns, Jasper (1930—)

With only two years of formal art training from the University of South Carolina, Jasper Johns moved to New York City at the age of twenty-four. A southerner, Johns was born in Augusta, Georgia, and brought up in the Carolinas. He supported himself as a window decorator and a salesman in a Manhattan bookstore while painting during his spare time. Johns painted objects that were familiar to both

him and his audience. He once stated, "Using the design of the American flag took care of a great deal for me because I didn't have to design it. So I went on to similar things like targets—things the mind already knows. That gave me room to work on other levels." The innovative way that Johns approached common subjects attracted the attention of art dealer Leo Castelli. Castelli was visiting Johns's upstairs neighbor and friend, the artist Robert Rauschenberg, in 1957, when the art dealer asked for an introduction to Johns. Castelli, immediately taken with the paintings of flags and targets including *White Flag* (1955) and *Target with Plaster Casts* (1955), added Johns to his stable of gallery artists, beginning a relationship that has lasted more than thirty-five years. In 1958, Johns had his first solo exhibition at the Castelli gallery; it was an unqualified critical success for both artist and dealer, establishing both of their reputations. The show sold out and the Museum of Modern Art bought a total of five pieces, an unprecedented amount from an artist's first show.

Signaling the end of Abstract Expressionism, Jasper Johns's paintings, prints, and sculptures helped usher in the era of American Pop Art in the late 1950s; additionally, his artwork became instrumental to the tenets of minimalism and conceptual art. Beginning in the 1950s, Johns's appropriated images of flags, targets, maps, the alphabet, numbers, and text contrasted sharply with the abstracted, emotion filled paintings that exemplified Abstract Expressionism. His use of commonplace symbols focused the attention onto the surface of the canvas. His chosen media, encaustic, oil, or acrylic paints, were as important, if not more important than his subject matter. His artwork inspired several generations of artists and his adaptation of cultural icons and mass media signage have become almost as familiar as the images they mimic.

Johns's early work in the 1950s and 1960s reflected the influences of Marcel Duchamp and the found object; Johns collected items such as ceramic pieces, brooms, and rulers, and attached them to his canvases. Several actual sized, cast sculptures of everyday items such as beer cans, light bulbs, and flashlights along with Johns's painted repetition of flags, numbers, and letters became abstracted and ceased to exist as powerful objects; the representations become tools of the medium and exert their power only as an artwork. Johns's artwork challenges the line between art and reality. His concern was with questioning the basic nature of art, with the process as the significant core of the works. The process, to Johns, was of utmost importance and his images were often the result of chance or accident. Variations in letters and numbers were consequently a result of the types of stencils available. Decisions on placement did not necessarily stem from aesthetics, but from necessity; for example, the bronze cast elements of a light bulb, *Bronze* (1960-61), came back to Johns in pieces—the bulb, the socket, and the cord. Johns left them unassembled, feeling that the pieces issued a provocative statement in that form.

With the beginning of the 1970s, Johns's work became increasingly abstract. In the mid-1970s, he adopted a method of crosshatched painting as seen in *The Dutch Wives* (1975). The wide brush strokes covered the entire canvas, again focusing in on the process and technical aspects of his medium; Johns has remarked that he was "Trying to make paintings about painting." However, this abstract period soon gave way to a more representational era in the 1980s. Johns began to pay homage to his artistic inspirations, Pablo Picasso, Paul Cezanne, and Edvard Munch, in a body of work that embodied some of his most revealing personal and psychological matter. John's contemplation on the cycle of life and death in *The Seasons* (1986) incorporates a shadowy figure of Johns's body; this imagery refers to Picasso's *The Shadow* (1953).

The paintings, sculpture, prints, and drawings by Johns all contain either biographical elements or iconographical components from the second half of the twentieth century. Johns changed the direction of American painting with his adaptation of common icons and his emphasis on the technique of painting. His later works, filled with psychological dramatics, continue to have the impact of earlier works that redefined the common symbols and icons of American culture. Often reproduced, Johns's *Flags* and *Targets* have become popular greeting card and poster images, introducing new generations to his work.

—Jennifer Jankauskas

FURTHER READING:

Brundage, Susan, editor, with essay by Judith Goldman. *Jasper Johns—35 Years—Leo Castelli.* New York, Harry N. Abrams, Inc., 1993.

Crichton, Michael. *Jasper Johns.* New York, Harry N. Abrams, Inc., 1994.

Varnedoe, Kirk. *Jasper Johns: A Retrospective.* New York, Harry N. Abrams, 1996.

Varnedoe, Kirk, editor. *Jasper Johns: Writing, Sketchbook Notes, Interviews.* New York, Museum of Modern Art, 1996.

Johnson, Blind Willie (c.1900-1947)

Blind Willie Johnson was an itinerant Texas street singer who made his last record in 1930 and died in poverty. Yet such was the force and individuality of his guitar playing and singing that all thirty of the gospel songs he recorded during his brief professional career are easily available today. His versions of "If I Had My Way I'd Tear This Building Down," "Keep Your Lamp Trimmed and Burning," and "Bye and Bye I'm Going to See the King" are now considered classics and have attracted admirers in many fields of popular music.

Johnson dropped back into obscurity after his fifth and final recording session for Columbia Records in the spring of 1930 and for many years his strong, highly personal renditions of gospel songs could be heard only on bootleg records. But eventually, through the efforts of jazz historians like Samuel Charters, more and more people became aware of his work. Eventually Columbia reissued Johnson's entire output in both cassette and CD formats.

An intensely religious man, Johnson nevertheless utilized many of the techniques of the rowdy, secular blues in his performances. On most of his recordings he'd shift from his normal tenor to a gruff, growling bass and his slide guitar playing, done with the blade of a pocket knife, was harsh, intense, and impressive. "He had few equals as a slide guitarist," said Francis Davis in *The History of the Blues.* Although Johnson's faith underlies all of his performances, there's a grimness to many of his songs. Many are of such stark intensity that one can imagine his causing his sidewalk listeners' hair to stand on end.

Johnson was not born blind, but lost his sight as a child after his angry stepmother threw lye in his face. He eventually took to the streets of his native Marlin, Texas, and sang on corners, begging with a tin cup. He played in other Texas towns and eventually in neighboring states. It is uncertain who discovered him and persuaded him to record for Columbia. The company had a fairly ambitious program of

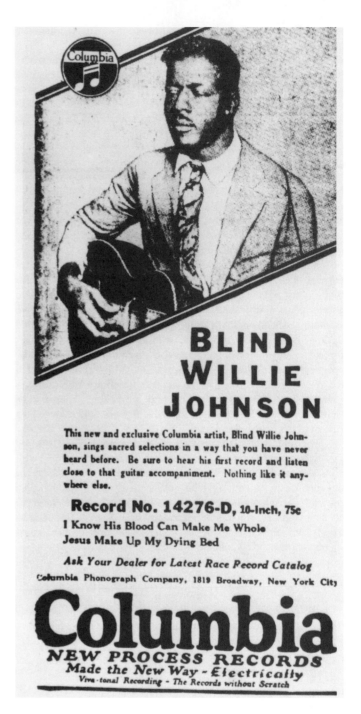

An ad for a new Blind Willie Johnson record.

issuing what were then called race records, employing scouts to work throughout the South. Blind Willie Johnson cut his first six 78-rpm sides in a makeshift studio in Dallas in early December of 1927. According to Charters, the first record, issued on Columbia's 140000 Race series, sold extremely well—over 15,000 copies, better than the popular Bessie Smith was doing—and Johnson from the start "was one of the strongest selling artists in the Columbia series."

Only one picture of Johnson is known to exist. It comes from a small ad that was run in black newspapers to promote the first record. "I Know His Blood Can Make Me Whole" appeared on one side, "Jesus Make Up My Dying Bed" on the other. The company assured potential buyers that Blind Willie Johnson ''sings sacred selections in a way that you have never heard before.''

In December of 1928 Johnson cut four more sides, again in Dallas. This time a woman named Willie B. Harris, whom Charters says was Johnson's first wife, recorded as a sort of backup singer. It was another year before Johnson, accompanied by a different woman singer, recorded again. These third and fourth sessions took place in New Orleans in a studio set up above Werlein's Music Store, on the French Quarter side of Canal Street. The last session was in Atlanta, where Blind Willie Johnson, again working with Harris, recorded ten songs.

The Depression ended his recording career, as it did that of many other folk artists. Johnson, with a new wife, continued his wanderings, singing and begging on street corners in Texas and Louisiana. They eventually settled in Beaumont, Texas, and he died there of pneumonia in 1947. He'd slept in their shack after a fire had gutted it and the dampness caused his sickness. Many years later Charters tracked down his widow and when he asked her if she'd brought her sick husband to a hospital, she answered that she had but ''they wouldn't accept him.''

—Ron Goulart

FURTHER READING:

Charters, Samuel. Liner notes for *The Complete Blind Willie Johnson.* New York, Sony Music Entertainment, 1993.

Davis, Francis. *The History of the Blues.* New York, Hyperion, 1995.

Johnson, Earvin "Magic" (1959—)

Earvin ''Magic'' Johnson was one of the marquee basketball players of his era. He began his National Basketball Association career in 1980. During the following decade, he and Larry Bird helped to elevate the popularity of professional basketball to previously unscaled heights. Johnson's wall-to-wall smile and ingratiating manner made him a favorite of hoop and non-hoop fans alike. Nonetheless, he will be remembered for much more than his exploits on the hardwood. On November 7, 1991, he shocked America—and the sporting world in particular—by announcing his retirement from basketball because he was HIV-positive. This admission, in such a public forum, forever altered the face of the AIDS plague. AIDS no longer could be ghettoized and trivialized as a disease whose sufferers were promiscuous gays and intravenous drug abusers, or lived far away on another continent.

Earvin Johnson, Jr., the sixth of ten children, grew up in Lansing, Michigan, and was dubbed ''Magic'' by a sportswriter after amassing some sterling statistics—36 points, 18 rebounds, and 16 assists—in a high school game. Wherever he played, Johnson helped to pilot a winner. For four straight years, he made the Michigan all-state high school team. In his senior year he tallied 28.8 points and 16.8 rebounds per game and led Lansing's Everett High School to a 27-1 record and the state championship. He attended Michigan State University, where as a freshman he guided the Spartans to a 25-5 record and their first Big Ten championship in 19 years. He capped

Earvin ''Magic'' Johnson

his college career in 1979, when he was a sophomore. That season, Michigan State won the NCAA title and Johnson, who averaged 17.1 points per game, was named the tournament's most outstanding player.

The 6' 9" point guard decided to turn pro after his second year at Michigan State and was selected by the Los Angeles Lakers as the first overall pick in the 1979 NBA draft. In his first year with the team, he maintained his status as a winner by helping the Lakers take the NBA title. He capped off his season by being the first rookie cited as MVP of the NBA finals. In the deciding game against the Philadelphia 76ers, he replaced an ailing Kareem Adbul-Jabbar at center and went on to score 42 points, adding 15 rebounds and seven assists in a 123-107 victory. However, Johnson lost Rookie of the Year honors to Larry Bird, who become one of his chief on-court adversaries during the 1980s.

In his 13 seasons with the Lakers, Johnson astounded fans and players alike with his no-look passes, clutch baskets, and ''showtime'' style of offense. He led the team to four additional NBA titles, with the Lakers' 1987 victory against Bird and the Boston Celtics especially sweet. In the deciding minutes of Game 4, with the Celts holding a one-point lead, Johnson won the contest with an Abdul-Jabbar-like sky hook. The Lakers went on to beat their rivals in six games.

In 1987, 1989, and 1990, Johnson was the league's MVP; he also earned two additional MVP citations for starring in the NBA finals.

Prior to his retirement he played in 11 All-Star Games, and in 1990 he was the contest's MVP. Between 1983 and 1991, he was first-team all-NBA. He led the NBA in assists on four occasions. During the 1990-91 season he broke the all-time NBA assists record and completed his career with 10,141.

Johnson came out of retirement to score 25 points and make nine assists in the 1992 NBA All-Star game, helping the West earn a 153-113 victory and winning a second All-Star MVP trophy. Near the end of the contest, he inspired the crowd by making successive three-point shots while being defended by Michael Jordan and Isaiah Thomas. Johnson joined Jordan, Bird and other NBA stars as a member of the U.S. Olympic Dream Team, which drubbed opponents by an average of 43.8 points per game, earned a Gold Medal at the 1992 Barcelona Olympics, and helped to escalate the sport's popularity across the globe. He then announced his pro comeback, but retired again prior to the beginning of the 1992-93 NBA season. In March, 1994, Johnson became head coach of the Lakers, but quit as the team completed the season with a 5-11 record. He also became a minority owner of the team and came out of retirement one last time during the 1995-96 season, in which he played in 32 Lakers games. Also in 1996, he was cited as one of the 50 Greatest Players in NBA History.

In his post-NBA career, "Magic" Johnson has been a frequent guest on TV talk shows. His own venture into late-night television, *The Magic Hour,* flopped soon after its 1998 premiere. More importantly, he is a celebrity who has eagerly donated his services to an array of charitable organizations. He has been active as a fundraiser for the Starlight Foundation, the American Heart Association, the Muscular Dystrophy Association, the American Cancer Society, the United Negro College Fund, and the Urban League. He has offered his name and his presence to a host of HIV/AIDs awareness programs. He established the Magic Johnson Foundation, which bestows grants to community-based, youth-oriented organizations.

He became chairman and chief executive officer of Magic Johnson Enterprises, whose projects include the Johnson Development Corporation, Magic Johnson All-Star Camps, and Magic Johnson Theaters. He believes that all business endeavors must benefit society and so his theater chain, developed in conjunction with Sony Entertainment, consists of state-of-the-art multiplex cinemas located in economically depressed urban neighborhoods. The first opened in Baldwin Hills, a run-down area of Los Angeles.

—Rob Edelman

FURTHER READING:

Gutman, Bill. *Magic, More Than a Legend.* New York, Harper Paperbacks, 1992.

Haskins, Jim. *"Magic": A Biography of Earvin Johnson.* Hillside, New Jersey, Enslow Publishers, 1981.

Johnson, Earvin, and Richard Levin. *Magic.* New York, Viking Press, 1983.

Johnson, Earvin, and Roy S. Johnson. *Magic's Touch.* Reading, Massachusetts, Addison-Wesley Publishing Company, 1989.

Johnson, Earvin, with William Novak. *My Life.* New York, Random House, 1992.

Pascarelli, Peter. *The Courage of Magic Johnson: From Boyhood Dreams to Superstar to His Toughest Challenge.* New York, Bantam Books, 1992.

Johnson, Jack (1878-1946)

Jack Johnson, the first modern African American heavyweight boxing champion of the world, served as a lightning rod for the racial turmoil of the early twentieth century. Johnson won the heavyweight title in 1906 and then defeated a series of "Great White Hopes," culminating in his epic match with ex-champion Jim Jeffries which was billed from the start as a battle between the "The Hope of the White Race vs. The Deliverer of The Negroes." The implications of Johnson's ensuing easy victory frightened many white Americans, inspired many black Americans, and upset the understood racial hierarchy of Victorian America.

One of six children, Arthur John Johnson was born in Galveston, Texas in 1878. Johnson lived a tough childhood and dropped out of school after receiving five or six years of elementary education. By the mid-1890s, Johnson earned a living by working a variety of jobs around the port of Galveston and by participating in battle royals. Organized by all-white athletic and social clubs for the entertainment of their members, battle royals featured groups of young black man fighting in a ring until only one man was left standing. These "exhibitions" had no rules, and the last fighter in the ring received a

Jack Johnson

small purse of a few dollars for his efforts. A frequent winner of these matches, Johnson gradually began to be matched one-on-one against the best local fighters, both black and white, in traditional boxing matches. By the turn of the century, Johnson had beaten all challengers in eastern Texas, and he took to the road to find new competition.

Over the next few years, Johnson traveled all over the country, from Philadelphia to Chicago to San Francisco, learning the "manly art" and slowly building a national reputation. By 1903, Johnson had beaten all the best black heavyweights in the country and had claimed the mythic "Negro Heavyweight Championship." A separate title for black boxers was necessary, because the white champion, Jim Jeffries, following a tradition established in the 1890s by America's first boxing superstar, John "The Boston Strongboy" Sullivan, refused to cross the color line and box against African American fighters.

In 1905, though, with only a lackluster group of white fighters to challenge him, Jeffries tired of the boxing game and retired without having been beaten. In the ensuing scramble for the now-vacated championship, a mediocre Canadian boxer named Tommy Burns claimed the title. Over three years of mounting disinterest, Burns defended his championship for smaller and smaller purses against an increasingly weak selection of white boxers. Finally in 1908, in order to generate interest (and a larger payday), Burns agreed to fight Johnson, still a leading contender for the championship. Although Burns was the heavy favorite of both the gambling community and the crowd—which showered Johnson with racial epithets throughout the fight—he was no match for the stronger and quicker black fighter. Johnson dominated the fight for 13 rounds, punching the overmatched white boxer at will until police stopped the match and saved the bloody and battered Burns the indignity of being knocked out.

After more than five years of fruitless challenges, Johnson had finally gotten his day in the ring and had proven himself against the best white boxer in the world. While white America struggled to come to grips with the fact that an African American had been crowned the heavyweight champion, Johnson returned to Chicago to celebrate his victory. Much to the chagrin of mainstream America, however, Johnson refused to play by the prevailing racial rules of the day. Instead of being humble and respectful as African Americans were expected to act, Johnson flaunted his newfound wealth, buying fast cars and throwing lavish parties. More threatening to many Americans, though, Johnson broke the ultimate taboo and publicly romanced white women.

In response to the new champion's behavior, Jack London, writing in the *New York Herald,* echoed the popular sentiment and appealed to the last great white champion: "But one thing now remains. Jim Jeffries must now emerge from his alfalfa farm and remove that golden smile from Jack Johnson's face. Jeff it's up to you. The White Man must be rescued." After Johnson defeated several mediocre white challengers, Jeffries bowed to the public pressure and, though overweight and out-of-shape, agreed to come out of retirement to fight for the title. Scheduled for July 4, 1910 in Reno, Nevada, the build-up to the fight was frenzied and front page news across the country. The conventional wisdom reasoned that, although the black boxer was emotional, strong, and violent, the smart, quick, and scientific Anglo-Saxon would easily win the match. Once again, however, the expectations of white America were shattered. The old and tired ex-champion was simply no match for Johnson. Again, the black fighter controlled the action in the ring, toying with his opponent and delivering a savage beating for 15 rounds, until Jeffries' corner men stopped the fight.

White America reacted with disbelief and anger after Johnson's victory. The nearly all-white crowd filed out of the arena in silence, as social critics wondered how an African American could be so successful. More ominously, white Americans began to take out their frustrations on their helpless black neighbors. In cities around the country, "race riots" broke out in response to the fight, as gangs of whites descended violently on innocent blacks to forcefully remind them of their position in society despite Johnson's victory.

Finally, the federal government undertook to do what no white boxers had been capable of, defeating Jack Johnson. In 1912 Johnson was arrested and convicted of violating the Mann Act. Known popularly as the White Slave Traffic Act, the Mann Act made it illegal to transport women across state lines "for the purpose of prostitution or debauchery, or for any other immoral purpose." The law was intended to target organized rings of prostitution, and, although Johnson was technically guilty for travelling around the country with several of his white girlfriends, he was one of only a handful of people ever tried under the Mann Act for anything over than participation in prostitution.

Before his sentencing, however, Johnson fled the country and remained abroad for the next seven years during which time he lost his title to a 6-6, 250-pound giant from Iowa named Jess Willard. Having lost his title and squandered his winnings, Johnson returned to the United States in 1920 and was sentenced to one year in jail. Although he would fight a few times in the 1920s, his serious boxing days were over, and Johnson drifted into the relative obscurity of an ex-champion. On June 10, 1946, outside of Raleigh, North Carolina, Johnson was killed in a car accident. Although eulogized as a good fighter, no representatives from the boxing community attended his funeral, and Johnson had become a shell of the person who 40 years earlier had terrified white Americans and upset the racial sensibilities of white America.

—Gregory Bond

FURTHER READING:

Batchelor, Denzil. *Jack Johnson and His Times.* London, Weidenfild and Nicolson, 1990.

Gilmore, Al-Tony. *Bad Nigger! The National Impact of Jack Johnson.* Washington, Kennikat Press, 1975.

Naison, Mark. "America Views Jack Johnson, Joe Louis, and Muhammad Ali." *Sport in America: New Historical Perspectives,* edited by Donald Spivey. Westport, Connecticut, Greenwood Press, 1985.

Roberts, Randy. *Papa Jack: Jack Johnson and the Era of Great White Hopes.* New York, The Free Press, 1983.

Johnson, James Weldon (1871-1938)

James Weldon Johnson enjoyed success as a novelist, poet, songwriter, educator, diplomat, lawyer, and as an official of the National Association for the Advancement of Colored People (NAACP). A celebrated writer and active leader, Johnson was a venerated figure of the Harlem Renaissance. He believed that artistic achievement was a key to racial uplift, and he urged fellow African American artists to assimilate black folk culture into their work. His novel *The Autobiography of an Ex-Colored Man* (1912) explores the dilemmas faced by a light-skinned black man who turns away from his cultural heritage and decides to "pass" for white. Johnson's ideas and themes had a marked influence on the African American literary tradition, as shown in works by Jean Toomer and Ralph Ellison. Johnson was also a talented musician and songwriter who penned the lyrics to "Lift Every Voice and Sing" (1900), which has become the official song of the NAACP and is widely known as the "Black National Anthem."

—Adam Golub

FURTHER READING:

Johnson, James Weldon. *Along This Way*. New York, Penguin, 1990.

———. *The Autobiography of an Ex-Colored Man*. New York, Penguin, 1990.

Oliver, Lawrence, and Kenneth Price, editors. *Critical Essays on James Weldon Johnson*. New York, GK Hall, 1997.

Johnson, Michael (1967—)

The unique convergence of spectacular achievement, special time and place, and creative image allows certain athletes to make indelible impressions on the popular mind. Michael Johnson exemplifies this phenomenon—his name evokes memories of an unprecedented accomplishment in track and field, the 1996 Olympic Summer Games at Atlanta, and golden running shoes. Few athletes have more consciously planned their moment of greatest triumph than did Johnson. Deprived of individual achievement in the 1992 Summer Olympics in Barcelona by illness and aware of the American public's relative disinterest in track and field, he relentlessly determined that he would make the Atlanta Olympics uniquely his own. He resolved to win both the 200 and the 400 meter races in Atlanta, something that had never been attempted in the Olympics, and to do so while wearing golden shoes. The pre-Olympic pressure on Johnson was enormous, with the media nominating him in advance as the star of the Atlanta games. Spectacularly fulfilling his own and others' expectations, he first won the 400 meters easily, literally running away from the rest of the field. Three days later, he won the 200 meters in the astonishing world-record time of 19.32 seconds. At the age of twenty-nine, Johnson was unquestionably the dominant figure in international track and field.

Even before Atlanta, he had established an impressive record as a sprinter. In the 1995 World Championship meet held in Goteborg, Sweden, he previewed his Atlanta performance by completing the 200-400 double and won a third gold medal by anchoring the winning United States 4 x 400 meter relay team. He had previously won three World Championship gold metals (individually the 200 meters in 1991 and the 400 meters in 1993 and as the anchor of the U.S. 4 x 400 meter relay team in 1993). Nevertheless in a sport that traditionally valorizes youth, Johnson had been something of a slow starter. A native of Dallas, he never won a Texas state high school running championship.

Born on September 13, 1967, Johnson is the son of a truck driver and an elementary school teacher. His father, Paul Johnson Sr., determined that his five children would obtain college degrees and

began teaching them early the virtues of planning and dedication. All five children did in fact earn degrees, and son Michael proved to be an especially receptive student of his father's lessons. As an adult, Michael leads a rigidly compartmentalized life and has been described by friends and rivals as being virtually inhuman in his concentration and dedication on immediate tasks and challenges. Michael attended Skyline High School in Dallas where, an obviously gifted athlete, he surprised people by participating in track rather than football. Upon graduation, he was recruited by Baylor University's track and field coach Clyde Hart, primarily to fill out Hart's successful relay teams. Under Hart's tutelage, Johnson's potential as a sprinter began to manifest itself quickly, though injuries kept him from recording the collegiate record that he might have (he did win the NCAA 200 meter championship in 1989 and 1990 and the NCAA outdoor 200 meter title in 1990).

After graduation from Baylor, Johnson's running achievements became more and more spectacular until they culminated in the Atlanta Olympics. In between though, there was Barcelona. Going into the 1992 Olympics, Johnson was viewed as the meet's most certain individual winner, but he contacted food poisoning and failed to qualify for the finals in either of his events. He did, however, win his first Olympic gold medal as a member of the U.S. 4 x 400 relay team. After Barcelona his determination began to pay off even before Atlanta. Between 1992 and 1996, he was virtually unbeatable; and between 1989 and 1997 he won an amazing fifty-eight consecutive 400 meter finals. Beginning in 1993, awards began to pour in for Johnson, climaxing in 1996 when he received the Sullivan Award as U.S. amateur athlete of the year and the Associated Press Male Athlete of the Year Award.

Since Atlanta, Johnson's career, because of recurring injuries, has been less than spectacular. The biggest damage to his golden image was truly unnecessary. Johnson agreed to an exhibition race on June 1, 1997 with Olympic 100 meter champion Donovan Bailey of Canada to determine the mythical title of "world's fastest human." From the beginning, the event took on a carnival atmosphere; and, with fifty meters left in the race, Johnson, who was trailing Bailey, pulled a muscle in his left thigh and dropped out. Afterward, Bailey ridiculed Johnson on Canadian television, calling him a "chicken" and a "coward." Responding to criticism, Bailey subsequently apologized for his harsh comments. The entire episode proved a black eye for track and field rather than the boost anticipated by the two competitors and their sponsors. Still plagued by the thigh injury, Johnson went on to have a mediocre 1997 season. Yet the golden touch had not entirely deserted him; and, when he could not otherwise qualify, Johnson was granted a waiver to compete in the World Championships in Athens, where he won the 400 meter finals. This win represented his seventh World Championship title, second only to Carl Lewis's eight.

In 1998, he won the 400 meter championship in the Goodwill Games at Uniondale, New York, and anchored the U.S. 4 x 400 medal relay team to victory in world record time. The Bailey race fiasco seems not to have seriously damaged Johnson's image. He will always be the man who achieved the "impossible double" and who ran the "astonishing" 19.32 in the 200 meters in the Atlanta Olympics while wearing his golden shoes. If he hasn't reawakened U.S. interest in track and field, he is a nationally and internationally admired athletic figure. At the age of thirty-one, he remains the golden boy of running.

—James R. Giles

Michael Johnson

FURTHER READING:

Griffith-Roberts, C. "The Road to Atlanta." *Southern Living,* May 31, 1996.

Miller, David. *Atlanta 1996: Official Commemorative Book of the Centennial Olympic Games.* San Francisco, Woodford Press, 1996.

Ribowsky, Mark. *Twice Golden: The Story of Michael Johnson and His Triumphs in Atlanta.* Secaucus, New Jersey, Carol Publishing, 1997.

Smith, G. "The Tortoise and the Hare." *Sports Illustrated Olympics Preview Issue.* July 27, 1996.

Sports Illustrated 1997 Sports Almanac. Boston, Little, Brown, 1997.

Johnson, Robert (1914?-1938)

Arguably the most influential figure in the history of the blues, Robert Leroy Johnson was at once a virtuoso guitarist, a gifted poet, and a skilled vocalist. Johnson, who emerged out of the Mississippi Delta in the early 1930s as one of the premier practitioners of the blues form, left a recorded legacy of just 41 songs. However, the tracks he laid down over two sessions in 1936 and 1937 became fundamental to the repertoires of other blues players and, after the "rediscovery" of the blues by white musicians in the 1960s, to blues-influenced rock artists everywhere. (Among the most covered and recorded Johnson compositions are "Crossroads Blues," "Sweet Home Chicago," and "Love in Vain.")

So prodigious were Johnson's skills on the six-string guitar, a legend (fostered by Johnson himself) grew up around him that he had sold his soul to the devil in exchange for this particular gift. Johnson's violent and untimely demise, allegedly at the hands of the jealous husband of one of his many lovers, combines with the romance of his shadowy, itinerant life to make him one of the most celebrated folk legends of the twentieth century. His enormous talent and the dark reputation he self-consciously promoted help explain his enduring place in the popular imagination. The fact that Johnson, unlike many other talented blues musicians of the early part of the century, was recorded has further cemented his reputation as one of the all-time greats of the genre.

Born in Hazelhurst, Mississippi, to Mary and Noah Johnson, "Little Robert" was fascinated with making music from an early age. As sharecroppers in the fertile but dirt-poor Yazoo basin, the Johnsons had neither the inclination nor the means to give Robert a formal musical education, and certain of his contemporaries have suggested that young Robert, while wildly enthusiastic about music, was not much of a musician. Eddie James "Son" House, Jr., one of the most respected blues performers of the generation before Johnson's, remembered the youngster as an eager apprentice, but one who did not at first show much promise. Johnson would show up at the juke joints and house parties, where House was a Saturday night fixture, and beg the older man to teach him to play. Rebuffed and mocked by the older musicians he worshipped, Johnson eventually took to the road in search of a willing mentor.

A reluctant maestro, Eddie "Son" House nevertheless made a large impression on the young Johnson. House's sometime traveling partner Willie Brown, later immortalized in a Johnson song, also affected the youngster profoundly. ("You can run, you can run," Johnson sings in the last verse of "Crossroads Blues," hinting at the cost of his infernal bargain, "Tell my friend poor Willie Brown. / Lord, I'm standing at the crossroads / I believe I'm sinking down.") Johnson's style, however startlingly unprecedented it seems in retrospect, was in fact fashioned from elements taken from such players as 1920s Texas great Blind Lemon Jefferson, Mississippi Delta legend Charlie Patton, and, of course, House.

Johnson's brand of the blues emphasizes an intricate interplay between guitar and voice. In many of his recordings, he highlights sung lines with rhythmic bursts of guitar playing, typically playing a bass line with his thumb while picking out chords and riffs with his fingers. A major innovator of slide-guitar technique—in which the player frets the instrument with a glass or metal object—Johnson routinely makes his guitar sound like a human voice, his voice like a guitar. On such numbers as "If I Had Possession Over Judgment Day," he creates a drum-like beat with slide fingerings. He pushes his plangent alto across the verses, often dropping into a speaking voice at the end of lines (e.g. "Stones in My Passway").

His early travels account in part for the mystery in which Johnson's life would always be shrouded. He traveled under both his father's and two stepfathers' names (Dodds and Spencer), but on returning to his home county was coy about where he had been. He further bolstered his mysterious reputation by bragging that he'd made a Faustian pact to become the best guitar player alive—a publicity strategy that had been used to great effect by older blues men such as Skip James, whose "Devil Got My Woman" Johnson refashioned as "Hellhound on My Trail." Johnson's wanderlust remained unsatisfied throughout his brief life, as evidenced by his two-year ramble with Johnny Shines and Walter Horton from 1933 to 1935. Two widely reproduced photographs of Johnson exist: one seems to have been taken in a coin-operated photo booth, the other, a studio portrait, features a giddy-looking Johnson in a new suit and hat. The obscure provenance and suggestive composition of the two pictures have fed the imaginations of scholars and fans alike, and have helped keep the Johnson legend alive.

More crucial to the continuation of the legend than the photographs, though, are the sound recordings Johnson cut. These were made during a boom period for so-called "race records"—78 rpm recordings of African American blues and jazz singers, aimed at the non-white market. Race records were a big business in the 1920s and 1930s, and music scouts from the white-owned record companies were commonly sent into the American south in search of new talent. Blind Lemon Jefferson, whose artistic influence on Johnson is noted above, was one of the top-selling artists of his day, and thus a model of both aesthetic and business success for Johnson. (Jefferson became so popular that Paramount, his record company, began issuing his sides with lemon-colored labels.) In 1936, Don Law, an American Recording Company (ARC) engineer tasked to find the next Blind Lemon, recorded Johnson in San Antonio, Texas. Law famously reported that Johnson suffered so badly from stage fright that the young singer recorded his songs facing the back wall of the hotel room in which the session was held.

Johnson's shyness has entered somewhat too easily into the historical record. The story of an enormously talented but bashful country boy overwhelmed and intimidated by the big city has, of course, a certain charm. But a convincing explanation for Johnson's apparently timid behavior in Law's improvised recording studio might be found in his reluctance in other contexts to show other musicians his riffs. He was, it seems, somewhat notorious among musicians in the south for his refusal to reveal his unconventional fingerings to potential competitors, and was known to conceal his hands from audiences as he played. This secrecy, of course, had the collateral advantage of enhancing his satanic reputation.

Whatever his motives for turning away from the team from ARC, Johnson managed to lay down a bona fide hit during the San Antonio session, the sly "Terraplane Blues." The song, which playfully confuses a complaint about a lover's infidelities with a car owner's frustration over a rough-running jalopy (anticipating by decades smashes such as Chuck Berry's "Mabeline" and Prince's "Little Red Corvette"), sold around 5,000 copies and established Johnson's reputation as a leading performer of the blues. Sings Johnson: "Now, you know the coils ain't even buzzin' / Little generator won't get the spark / Motor's in bad condition / You gotta have these batteries charged. / But I'm cryin' please, please don't do me wrong / Who been driving my Terraplane / Now for you since I been gone?"

Law recorded Johnson again in July of 1937, this time for Vocalion Records, in Dallas. In the second session, Johnson recorded what would become some of his best-loved, most enduring sides, "Dust My Broom" and "Love in Vain." Together with the first session, the second provided the 29 cuts which, much to the delight of blues and folk aficionados, Columbia brought out in 1961, nearly a quarter century after Johnson's death. Before the appearance of the Columbia LPs, Johnson's records were known to only a very select few—notwithstanding the 1930s juke box popularity of "Terraplane Blues." Johnson's entire recorded oeuvre, the 29 songs from the 1961 release plus 12 alternate takes, was at last released in 1991, again by Columbia.

Robert Johnson has the dubious distinction of being the only blues musician to have had a Ralph Macchio movie made about his legend (Crossroads, 1986). The film, with guitar playing taking the place of martial arts for "The Karate Kid," is significant in that it suggests the longevity and seemingly universal appeal of the Johnson legend. For better or worse, Johnson's songs have been recorded by such British rock heavyweights as Led Zeppelin, the Rolling Stones, and Cream, groups whose work continues to have a considerable influence on rock musicians on both sides of the Atlantic. The mysterious circumstances of Johnson's death—some say he was knifed, others claim that, like his hero Blind Lemon Jefferson, he drank poisoned coffee—have further enhanced the romance of his story. A particularly provocative rumor that has circulated about Johnson is that just prior to his death he had been in Chicago, where he put together an electric-guitar based combo. Whether Johnson was in Chicago or not, his influence there shines through clearly in the work of, among others, Muddy Waters, viewed by many critics as the next link in the chain connecting traditional country blues to electrified blues-based urban forms such as rhythm and blues, soul, and rock and roll.

—Matthew Mulligan Goldstein

FURTHER READING:

Guralnick, Peter. *Searching for Robert Johnson.* New York, Dutton, 1989.

Lomax, Alan. *The Land Where the Blues Began.* New York, Pantheon, 1993.

Welding, Pete and Toby Byron. *Bluesland: Portraits of Twelve Major American Blues Masters.* New York, Dutton, 1991.

Johnson, Virginia
See Masters and Johnson

Jolson, Al (1886-1950)

Al Jolson lived "The American Dream." Born in Lithuania, Jolson rose through the ranks of vaudeville as a comedian and a blackface "Mammy" singer. By 1920, he had become the biggest star on Broadway, but he is probably best remembered for his film career. He starred in *The Jazz Singer* (1927), the first talking movie ever made, and his legend was assured in 1946 with the release of the successful biography of his life called *The Jolson Story.* Jolson was the first openly Jewish man to become an entertainment star in America. His marginal status as a Jew informed his blackface portrayal of Southern blacks. Almost single-handedly, Jolson helped to introduce African-American musical innovations like jazz, ragtime, and the blues to white audiences. The brightest star of the first half of the twentieth century, Jolson was eternally grateful for the opportunities America had given him. He tirelessly entertained American troops in World War II and in the Korean War, and he contributed time and money to the March of Dimes and other philanthropic causes. While some of his colleagues in show business complained about his inflated ego, he certainly deserved his moniker: "The World's Greatest Entertainer."

Perhaps it should come as no surprise that the man who made his mark singing "My Mammy" in blackface was himself a "mamma's boy." Jolson was born Asa Yoelson in Seredzius, Lithuania, sometime between 1883 and 1886. He was the youngest of four children—the baby of the family and his mother Naomi's favorite. When Asa was four, his father, Rabbi Moshe Reuben Yoelson, left Lithuania to put down roots for the family in America. From age four to age eight, Asa was raised by his mother. She introduced him to the violin and told him that if he practiced hard he could become a star performer in America someday. When Asa was eight Rabbi Yeolson brought his family to Washington, D.C., where he had found work as a rabbi and a cantor at a Jewish congregation. Later that same year, Naomi died. Seeing his mother in her death throes traumatized young Asa, and he

Al Jolson

spent much of his life struggling with that trauma. After her death, he remained withdrawn for seven months until he met Al Reeves, who played the banjo, sang, and introduced him to show business. At age nine, Asa and his older brother Hirsch changed their names to Al and Harry, and by age 11 Al was singing in the streets for nickels and dimes that he used to buy tickets to shows at the National Theater.

After running away from home to New York City and doing a stint with a circus, Al joined his brother Harry on the vaudeville circuit. In 1904, the brothers teamed up with a disabled man named Joe Palmer to form a comedy troupe. A friend of Joe's wrote them a comedy skit, but Al was uncomfortable with it until he took James Dooley's advice to try performing it in blackface. Jolson remained in blackface for the rest of his stage and screen career. His blackface routine was a hit on the vaudeville circuit and he came to New York to perform it in 1906. His trademarks were a whistling trick that approximated a frenetic birdcall, a performance of vocal scales, and very dramatic facial expressions. He billed himself "The Blackface with the Grand Opera Voice." After his New York debut, he had success as a blackface comedian and singer in California. In 1911 he returned to New York to star in *La Belle Paree,* a vaudeville revue. There Jolson quickly established himself as the biggest star on Broadway.

Jolson's film career began inauspiciously with a short film for the Vitagraph Company in 1916. In 1923, he agreed to star in a film by D. W. Griffith, but backed out of his contract after filming had begun because Griffith had assigned an assistant to direct Jolson's scenes. In 1926, he made another short film for Warner Brothers, and in 1927, he was signed to star in a screen version of Samuel Raphelson's play *The*

Jazz Singer. This was the role that Jolson had waited his whole life to play. Based on Jolson's own life, it was the story of a Jewish boy named Jackie Rabinowitz who runs away from his father, who is a cantor from the old world, because Jackie wants to be in show business. Jackie returns home to chant the Kol Nidre service as his father lies on his deathbed. The film was incredibly popular because it combined old silent film technology (words printed on the screen) with four dramatically innovative vitaphone ''talking'' sequences. Jolson quickly became the first movie star in the modern sense. He went on to make *The Singing Fool* (1928), *Say it with Songs* (1929), *Mammy* (1930), and *Big Boy* (1930) before returning to Broadway in 1931. His star dimmed a bit in the late 1930s and early 1940s until the highly acclaimed biographical film *The Jolson Story,* starring Larry Parks, was released in 1946. Parks mouthed the songs which Al Jolson himself sang for the film, and the sound track of the film sold several million copies.

Al Jolson was to jazz, blues, and ragtime what Elvis Presley was to rock 'n' roll. Jolson had first heard African-American music in New Orleans in 1905, and he performed it for the rest of his life. Like Elvis, Jolson gyrated his lower body as he danced. In *The Jazz Singer,* white viewers saw Jolson moving his hips and waist in ways that they had never seen before. Historian and performer Stephen Hanan has written in *Tikkun* that Jolson's ''funky rhythm and below-the-waist gyrations (not seen again from any white male till the advent of Elvis) were harbingers of the sexual liberation of the new urban era. Jolson was a rock star before the dawn of rock music.'' Al Jolson paved the way for African-American performers like Louis Armstrong, Duke Ellington, Fats Waller, and Ethel Waters. It is remarkable that a Jewish mamma's boy from Lithuania could do so much to bridge the cultural gap between black and white America.

—Adam Max Cohen

FURTHER READING:

Freeland, Michael. *Jolie: The Story of Al Jolson.* New York, Stein and Day, 1972.

Goldman, Herbert. *Jolson: The Legend Comes to Life.* New York, Oxford University Press, 1988.

Hanan, Stephen Mo. ''Al Jolson: The Soul Beneath the Mask.'' *Tikkun.* Vol. 13, No. 5, 1998, 21-22.

Leonard, William Torbert. *Masquerade in Black.* Metuchen, New Jersey, Scarecrow Press, 1986.

Jones, Bobby (1902-1971)

Golf has changed over the years. Balls fly farther. Clubs are made of space-age materials like graphite and titanium. Courses are longer, more demanding, and come in more shapes and sizes with more grass types than ever before. But no one, not ever, dominated the game during any era like Bobby Jones did during his. No one has ever won so much in so short a time. From 1923 when he won his first major, the United States Open, to his retirement in 1930, Jones won the U.S. Amateur five times, the U.S. Open four times, the British Open three times, and the British Amateur once. In 1930, at age twenty-eight, he accomplished what no one else has done when he won the Grand Slam—the U.S. Open, the British Open, the U.S. Amateur, and the British Amateur—in the same year. After winning

Bobby Jones

his first major, Jones won 62 percent of the major championships he entered. There is little question that golf has had its share of greats: Harry Vardon, Walter Hagen, Gene Sarazen, Byron Nelson, Sam Snead, Ben Hogan, Arnold Palmer, Jack Nicklaus, Tiger Woods. But no one has come close to matching Jones's record. No one has dominated his contemporaries as completely. And Jones did it all for fun, for free, as an amateur.

Robert Tyre Jones, Jr., stood out in other ways. Of the top echelon players in golfing history, he was one of the most highly educated, with degrees in mechanical engineering (Georgia Tech), literature (Harvard), and law (Emory). Born in Atlanta in 1902, Jones was the son of attorney Robert Jones and his wife Clara. From an early age it was apparent that the youngster possessed a special talent. He began playing golf at age five; at age nine he won the junior championship at East Lake, his father's club; at age 14 he won the Georgia State Amateur; at age 15 he won the Southern Amateur; at age 17 he was runner-up in both the Canadian Open and the U.S. Amateur. Jones's early success was so great that public expectations may have hindered him in tournaments, since he won no major titles until 1923. However, it appears that during this time, Jones, a perfectionist prone to bursts of anger, learned to control his emotions so well that throughout the remainder of his career he would be known for his sportsmanship and decorum on the course.

Jones's retirement, however, did not mean he was finished with golf. Although uninterested in endorsements, he produced a series of movie shorts entitled "How I Play Golf," and even helped design a new standard of golf club for Spalding Company. However, no one accomplishment demonstrated Jones's remarkable versatility as clearly as his great masterpiece—the Augusta National Golf Club. Jones, who helped raise funds to purchase land in Augusta, Georgia, known as Fruitland, co-designed the course with Dr. Alister MacKenzie. In 1934 the first annual Invitational tournament was held. By 1938 it was being called the Masters, and it eventually came to be considered as one of the four major tournaments in the world.

In 1948, Jones contracted syringomyelia, a rare and crippling spinal disease. His condition worsened over the years until he was eventually confined to a wheelchair. His greatest tribute came in 1958, when he received the Freedom of the City Award at St. Andrews, Scotland, in what many have called one of the most moving ceremonies in the history of game.

—Lloyd Chiasson Jr.

FURTHER READING:

Barkow, Al. *Getting' to the Dance Floor: An Oral History of American Golf.* New York, Atheneum, 1986.

Davis, Martin. *The Greatest of Them All: The Legend of Bobby Jones.* Greenwich, Connecticut, American Golfer, 1996.

Grimsley, Will. *Golf: Its History, People and Events.* Englewood Cliffs, New Jersey, Prentice-Hall, 1966.

Miller, Dick. *Triumphant Journey: The Saga of Bobby Jones and the Grand Slam of Golf.* New York, Holt, Rinehart and Winston, 1980.

Rice, Grantland, from the writings of O. B. Keeler. *The Bobby Jones Story.* Atlanta, Tupper & Love, 1953.

Jones, George (1931—)

Despite the trends that transformed country music over the second half of the twentieth century, George Jones continued to thrill audiences with his traditional "honky-tonk" voice, which remained a steady force in the industry from the 1950s onward. Initially, Jones was an improbable star, offering a twangy voice reminiscent of earlier hillbilly music at a time when rock and roll was making inroads into country music, but with his emergence as a star in the late 1950s, he went on to become a country music icon—indeed, contemporary star Garth Brooks once commented that "anybody who has ever wanted to sing country music wants to sound like George Jones." Between 1951 and 1971, Jones placed at least one song on the country top ten charts each year, and has won every major industry award in existence, including Single of the Year, Artist of the Year, and Video of the Year. He has lived a tumultuous personal life, complete with battles with drug abuse, divorce, and arrest.

Jones's early life made him an unlikely candidate for stardom. He was born in Saratoga, a small town near Beaumont in the "big thicket" area of East Texas, tucked away in the deep pine woods. He was the youngest of seven children born to a poor family. His father worked as a pipe fitter and truck driver to support the family during the Depression, but young George was surrounded by music as a child. His mother played the piano at church, and the entire family

George Jones

listened to country music on the radio, especially the "Grand Ole Opry" broadcast from Nashville, and Jones came of age listening to musical heroes Floyd Tillman, Ernest Tubb, Roy Acuff, and Bill Monroe. In the years during and after World War II, an older Jones made his way to dance halls in towns such as Port Arthur and Orange, which were brimming with wartime industrial growth, and found the atmosphere intoxicating.

George began playing the guitar in high school, and from then on focused all of his energies on becoming a recording star. Attempting to sound like his heroes Roy Acuff and Hank Williams, he sought out venues such as local clubs and events such as school dances where he could hone his skills. He joined the marines during the Korean War, served for three years, then returned to Texas where, beset with doubts that he could ever break into show business, he found employment as a house painter. Nonetheless, he continued to sing and play guitar whenever he could, and over the next few years became a regular of the Texas honky-tonk circuit, performing in small towns throughout the area. Based on his local success, Jones then contacted producer Pappy Dailey at Starday Records, located in Beaumont, about making a record. The partnership proved a good one—Starday, as a local record company, was one of the few country music labels that was not moving into the rockabilly style then taking Nashville by storm.

The Starday label recorded and released Jones's first hit, "Why Baby Why" in 1955, but his first couple of years as a recording musician met with varied results. He was invited to join the Grand Ole Opry in 1956, a lifelong dream come true, and two years later left Starday for a deal with the more prestigious Mercury label. In 1959, his single "White Lightning" reached number one on the country charts, and by 1961 he was a country music celebrity, recording two number one hits, "Tender Years" and "She Thinks I Still Care." These prompted the Country Music Association to name him Male Vocalist of the Year in 1962 and 1963. Throughout the 1960s, Jones recorded hit after hit under a variety of labels, including United Artists, Musicor, and Epic. Singles that reached number one included "Window Up Above," "We Must Have Been Out of Our Minds," "Take Me," and "The Race is On." While dominating the country charts, he also toured ceaselessly, both nationally and internationally, seemingly without rest.

His celebrity status and the exhausting pace of his tours began to take a serious toll on George Jones. During the 1960s he began drinking heavily which, periodically, led to his cutting concerts short or canceling them altogether. He appeared drunk on stage regularly, and by the mid-1960s his career seemed to be on the verge of collapse. In 1967, however, it was rejuvenated when he began touring with singer Tammy Wynette, who had recently emerged as a new country music star. The combination was ideal, for both sang ballads in a traditional country style and both were known for their very distinctive voices. Fans were thrilled when Jones married Wynette in 1968—his third marriage—a relationship which proved to be more public than private. On stage, they sang both solos and duets, generally ending a concert with a song proclaiming their mutual devotion. The marriage proved lucrative, too, as the couple began recording together under the Epic label, churning out hit after hit in the early 1970s—including the 1974 number one, "We're Gonna Hold On." At the same time, Jones recorded solo hits such as "The Grand Tour" and "The Door," both of which reached number one in 1974.

Although the public image of his star-studded marriage to Wynette bolstered Jones's career, it was not long before he again began to experience hard times. He and Tammy lived in constant pursuit by reporters, and the resultant strain caused their relationship to grow turbulent and destructive. As the situation worsened, Jones again began to drink heavily. Their inevitable break-up added bizarrely to their public appeal and in 1976, the year they divorced, the couple recorded "Golden Ring" and "Near You," both of which became hits. In the years following the divorce, Jones's career once again seemed to be nearing the end. He missed several show dates, leading to numerous legal entanglements and an eventual declaration of bankruptcy, and the early 1980s found him more often in the news for his legal problems than his music. He was arrested on a number of occasions relating to his alcohol and drug abuse, and was sued by ex-wives and numerous creditors.

Yet Jones continued to perform and record, even during the darkest times. In 1980, he released what is perhaps his best known single, "He Stopped Loving Her Today," considered by some to be the best country music recording ever. A major hit, it won him Single of the Year from the Country Music Association in 1980 and 1981. Jones's personal problems never affected his popularity and he continued recording a string of hits throughout the 1980s. In 1986, he entered a new phase of his career by winning the Country Music

Association's Video of the Year award for his single "Who's Gonna Fill Their Shoes"; in 1991, he signed a new recording deal with MCA Records, and the following year he was selected as a member of the Country Music Hall of Fame. In the late 1990s, Jones enjoyed further success by incorporating rock and roll into his music with hits such as "I Don't Need Your Rockin' Chair" and the successful album *High-tech Redneck*.

While these new hits demonstrated the singer's versatility and his willingness to experiment with contemporary styles, he continued to thrive on the music that had first brought him success. His album *It Don't Get Any Better Than This* (1998) is very much in the traditional George Jones style, and he also recorded a reunion album with Tammy Wynette called *One* in 1995. In many respects, George Jones stands as a reflection of country music itself: open to innovation while rooted in tradition.

—Jeffrey W. Coker

FURTHER READING:

Allen, Bob. *George Jones: The Saga of An American Singer.* Garden City, New York, Doubleday & Co., 1984.

Jones, George, with Tom Cater. *I Lived to Tell It All.* New York, Villard Books, 1996.

Malone, Bill C. *Country Music U.S.A.* Revised edition. Austin, University of Texas Press, 1985.

Nash, Alanna. *Behind Closed Doors: Talking with the Legends of Country Music.* New York, Alfred Knopf, 1988.

Jones, Jennifer (1919—)

Actress Jennifer Jones's affair with the renowned producer David O. Selznick attracted a great deal of attention and launched her career. He signed her to a long-term contract, changed her name, and prepared her for stardom. Her first screen lead was in *Song of Bernadette* (1943), a film whose popularity earned her an Academy Award. She was nominated for Oscars as best supporting actress in *Since You Went Away* (1944), *Love Letters* (1945) and *Love Is a Many Splendored Thing* (1955). While Jones played a wide variety of characters, including the innocent and placid as well as the tempestuous and sensuous, she was not considered a formidable actress. But she undoubtedly captured a mood Americans longed for because, ultimately, she became one of the most popular melodramatic actresses of the 1940s.

—Liza Black

FURTHER READING:

Epstein, Edward Z. *Portrait of Jennifer: A Biography of Jennifer Jones.* New York, Simon & Schuster, 1995.

Jones, Leroi

See Baraka, Amiri

Jones, Tom (1940-)

Many comparisons have been drawn between Welsh singer Tom Jones and rock legend Elvis Presley . Both appropriated singing styles associated with black R&B music, both became infamous for their sexually charged dancing styles, and both were loved for over-the-top Las Vegas club performances in the 1960s and 1970s. Indeed, Jones and Presley maintained a well-documented admiration for each other and often performed cover versions of each others' songs. However, Jones' diversity and longevity far exceeded Presley's. Throughout the 1980s and 1990s, when many of his contemporaries had devolved into all-but-forgotten lounge lizards, Jones performed pop, rock, country, and dance tunes, often collaborating with a roster of acts half his age for the ears of equally young listeners.

Born Thomas Jones Woodward in Pontypridd, South Wales, on June 7, 1940, Jones grew up in the song-filled atmosphere of a coal-mining community, often putting on performances for his mother in the family living room. However, Jones' days of such youthful frolic were relatively short, and by age seventeen he was both a husband and father. Having no real training in a trade, Jones bounced between a number of odd jobs to support his growing family, including glove cutting and selling vacuums door-to-door. Nevertheless, Jones still

Tom Jones

found the time to sing at night in local dance halls, and after a number of years he had earned a sizable reputation fronting Tommy Scott and the Senators, a rock and soul outfit influenced by R&B singers Solomon Burke and Jackie Wilson, as well as Elvis Presley and Jerry Lee Lewis.

After being discovered by songwriter and manager Gordon Mills in 1963, Jones was able to sign with the Decca label. Jones' debut single was only mildly successful, but the follow-up, ''It's Not Unusual,'' became a giant international hit, as well as Jones' signature tune. However, the unbridled sexual delivery of Jones' singing, as well as his pelvis-thrusting dance moves, were considered too racy for conservative broadcast companies like the BBC. Moral squeamishness could not restrain public demand, and after ''It's Not Unusual'' was leaked out by an off-shore pirate radio station, Jones became a highly visible sex symbol. Throughout the 1960s, many of Jones' singles were major hits, notably the Burt Bacharach-penned ''What's New Pussycat,'' and he honed his stage performance touring with world-class acts like the Rolling Stones.

During the 1970s, Jones occasionally scored with singles like the uptempo dance cut ''She's a Lady,'' but his presence on Top 40 charts gradually declined, perhaps due to changing currents in pop music. However, his popularity as a live performer grew. Fully the master of his wide-ranging voice, Jones injected such raw passion into his stage shows that often adoring fans were moved to tossing their underwear at Jones' feet. He became an essential booking for the top clubs in the Las Vegas circuit, and was even given his own television variety show on the ABC network, *This Is Tom Jones.*

For years, Jones kept a relatively low profile, but in the late 1980s his career took on an expected new breath of life. Beginning with a remake of the Prince song ''Kiss'' in collaboration with the British electronic innovators the Art of Noise in 1988, Jones worked with many younger acts from diverse musical backgrounds, meeting with a high level of approval from all age groups. In 1992, for example, Jones masterminded a unique six-part series called *The Right Time* in which he gave tribute to a number of musical genres through intimate performances with acts as wide-ranging as Joe Cocker, Stevie Wonder, the dance groups EMF and Erasure, and pop warblers Shakespears' Sister. Continuing in this vein, in 1994 Jones signed to the Interscope label, a company devoted almost exclusively to edgy young acts like Nine Inch Nails and Snoop Doggy Dog. As with country legend Johnny Cash, it seemed that Jones was able to extend his legacy into the generation of the 1990s, largely without the element of irony or kitsch appreciation that tinged the later careers of other 1960s holdovers.

—Shaun Frentner

FURTHER READING:

Macfarlane, Colin. *Tom Jones: The Boy from Nowhere.* New York, St. Martin's Press, 1988.

Jonestown

Officially known as the People's Temple, this community of American religious zealots who lived and died in the small South

Dead bodies fill the Peoples Temple compound after mass suicide in Jonestown, Guyana.

American country of Guyana during the 1970s has become synonymous with fanatical cultism and mass suicide. The group had originated in northern California under the leadership of pastor Jim Jones. As Jones became increasingly megalomaniacal and unstable, he relocated his church and its followers to an isolated jungle compound, where he used brainwashing tactics to break their will and force them to comply with his demands. Government officials in the United States became concerned after hearing reports of church members being held against their will, and a delegation was sent to investigate. After a violent confrontation between cultists and the delegation, Jones ordered his followers to commit suicide by drinking a cyanide potion. Those who refused were shot. When United States officials entered the compound on November 18, 1978, they found 914 bodies, including that of Jones himself.

—Tony Brewer

FURTHER READING:

Kerns, Phil. *People's Temple, People's Tomb.* Plainfield, New Jersey, Logos International, 1979.

Kilduff, Marshall, and Ron Javers. *The Suicide Cult.* New York, Bantam Books, 1978.

Krause, Charles. *Guyana Massacre: The Eyewitness Account.* New York, Berkley Books, 1978.

Jong, Erica (1942—)

Erica Jong's first novel, *Fear of Flying* (1973), made her one of the central figures of the sexual revolution of the 1970s. Her frank and explicit depictions of women's sexual desire shocked the world and gained her the praise of everyone from *Playboy* editors to John Updike. But women have given her a more mixed reception. While her many works of fiction and poetry about women fulfilling their fantasies of sexual abandon played well among the newly liberated generation of women in the 1970s, feminists of the 1980s and 1990s have challenged her promotion of anonymous sex for its own sake and her claim to speak for baby-boomer women's sexual desires. Nonetheless, her fame rests on the fact that she brought the difficulties of women trying to balance love, sex, self-development, and creativity to the attention of a mass audience.

Jong grew up in an affluent Jewish family in New York and attended Barnard College. She was a Ph.D. candidate at Columbia, studying eighteenth-century British literature, when she began her career as a writer. She published two volumes of poetry, and when her *Fear of Flying* caught the attention of Henry Miller, who compared the book to his *Tropic of Cancer,* and John Updike, who compared it to Philip Roth's *Portnoy's Complaint* and J. D. Salinger's *Catcher in the Rye,* her name became a household word. She was repeatedly asked by reporters to help explain women's perspectives on sexual liberation, and her frank, sassy commentary provided good copy for *Playboy* and *Redbook* alike.

Fear of Flying, which opens with the then-shocking intimation that the heroine is not wearing a bra, captured a cultural moment when women were shedding propriety and clothing in an attempt to gain fulfillment and freedom, giving birth to feminism and the sexual revolution. It tells the story of Isadora Wing, a writer who accompanies her stiff, cold, psychiatrist husband to a conference in Zurich. There she meets an Englishman who seems to epitomize unrepressed, guiltless sexual fulfillment, which she calls the "zipless fuck," a phrase that became a catchword for her generation and has been forever associated with Jong's popular image. Isadora soon learns, though, that the man who has rescued her from her prosaic life is impotent, causing her to return to her husband. The book ends with Isadora convincing herself that her search for empty and meaningless orgasms was no substitute for true self-development.

Jong continued Isadora's story in *How to Save Your Own Life* (1977) and *Parachutes and Kisses* (1984). In the first book, Isadora becomes a successful author, leaves her husband, begins life over with a young screenwriter, and has a baby. In the final installment of the trilogy, Isadora finds herself deserted by the father of her baby and has to learn how to be a single mother. What has stood out for readers and critics, in all three books, and her many other novels, short stories, and poetry, is Jong's message that sexual freedom is paramount to self-discovery for women.

While her subsequent books never repeated the success of *Fear of Flying,* she has continued throughout the 1980s and 1990s to be a prominent voice on women's issues. She has been pitted against other feminists like Camille Paglia, Katie Roiphe, and Andrea Dworkin on talk shows and in popular magazines, accused of upholding the virtues of heterosexual experimentation for women in a time when date rape and violence against women are prominent concerns. Other feminists simply consider her recipe for liberation an inadequate one. Amy Virshup has argued that despite Jong's advocacy of self-empowerment, "it is always Mr. Right who leads [her heroines] onward and upward." And Anne Z. Mickelson has charged that her depictions of sex mirror those found in "girlie magazines" and that "by adopting the male language of sexuality, Jong is also fooling herself that she is preempting man's power." In her memoir *Fear of Fifty* (1994), Jong went on the counter-offensive, attacking the "puritan feminists" who she feels have tried to silence her for her positive portrayals of heterosexual sex and motherhood.

While Jong has longed for a permanent place in America's high literature, she has remained a popular icon. She has called the success of *Fear of Flying* a "curse," adding that it "typecast me in a way that I've been trying to get free of ever since. I'm enormously grateful to it, and yet very eager to be seen as a woman of letters and not just Erica 'Zipless' Jong." But even as she has attempted to solidify her reputation, even writing *The Devil at Large: Erica Jong on Henry Miller* (1993), in which she describes her literary relationship with this prominent writer, she has also remained tied to her historical moment. In *Fear of Fifty* and *What Do Women Want?: Bread, Roses, Sex, Power* (1998), she has portrayed herself as a spokesperson for baby-boomer women who wanted sexual fulfillment and empowerment

in the 1970s and who want to reinvent their relationships with men on the basis of love and mutual respect in the 1990s.

—Anne Boyd

FURTHER READING:

Jong, Erica. *Fear of Fifty.* New York, HarperCollins, 1994.

———. *What Do Women Want?: Bread, Roses, Sex. Power.* New York, HarperCollins, 1998.

Mickelson, Anne Z. *Reaching Out: Sensitivity and Order in Recent American Fiction.* Metuchen, New Jersey, Scarecrow Press, 1979.

Virshup, Amy. "For Mature Audiences Only." *New York.* July 18, 1994, 40-47.

Joplin, Janis (1943-1970)

Regarded as the greatest white female blues singer, Janis Joplin is also remembered as a hedonistic, hard-drinking, bra-disdaining, bisexual challenger of social conventions. She often is associated with Jimi Hendrix and Jim Morrison, a trio of dynamic performers

Janis Joplin

who all died within a year of each other between September 1970 and July 1971, and whose "live hard, die fast" philosophy not only epitomized the 1960s but also tolled the end of that spectacular, turbulent epoch.

The young Joplin was an intelligent, creative girl with many interests and talents. Born January 19, 1943, in Port Arthur, Texas, she was raised by liberal parents who encouraged her interests in music, art, and literature. Her favorite author was F. Scott Fitzgerald, and she identified with the glamorous, ruinous lives of Scott and Zelda Fitzgerald and her favorite singers, Billie Holiday and Bessie Smith. She learned to sing the blues, as well as play guitar, piano, and autoharp. But Joplin's main ambition was to become an artist: she drew and painted, and majored in art in college. Her interests drew her to the beatnik scene in San Francisco in 1964, where she met Robert Crumb and other artists. She sold paintings, sang with various blues bands, and developed an amphetamine addiction. In 1965 she returned to Texas to withdraw from the temptation of drugs, and she returned to college.

A year later she was invited back to San Francisco to sing with Big Brother and the Holding Company. She returned to find the beatnik scene succeeded by the hippie scene. She partied with the Grateful Dead, Country Joe and the Fish, and Jefferson Airplane. Joplin soon distinguished herself even among these luminaries with her booming, unbridled vocals and the raw, electric blues of Big Brother. They cut several singles, and their growing reputation took them to the Monterey International Pop Festival. Cashing in on Joplin's new popularity, Mainstream Records repackaged their singles as *Big Brother and the Holding Company, Featuring Janis Joplin* (1967). Released without the band's permission, it is an uneven album wavering between folk, psychedelic, and pop music. Their next album, *Cheap Thrills* (1968), revealed a band that had found its identity in raunchy electric blues. Joplin is at her best in the sultry, sizzling "Summertime" and "Piece of My Heart," which reveals the tortured combination of toughness and vulnerability that became her trademark.

Big Brother was never esteemed by the critics, and Joplin was persuaded to form a new band for her next album, *I Got Dem Ol' Kozmic Blues Again Mama!* (1969), but she never developed a rapport with the Kozmic Blues Band. With two sax players and a trumpeter, they had a brassy sound that smothered Joplin's vocals. Nor was there anything particularly cosmic about their blues style, which was more mainstream than Big Brother's. Joplin recognized the unsuitability of this group and formed the Full Tilt Boogie Band. The brassy sound of the Kozmic Blues Band was discarded, and the two keyboardists—rather than the two aggressive guitarists of Big Brother—allowed Joplin's vocals free rein.

Joplin wrote few of her own songs, but turned others' songs into her own through wrenching, probing performances. She chose her songs well, finding a medium through which she could express her soul in all its passion and insecurity. Prescriptive feminists are uncomfortable with the sexual desperation Joplin revealed in her recordings, but singing was her catharsis; she was not only rebelling against the double standards of the age but also exploring her soul more honestly than prescriptivism allows. Ellen Willis claims that Joplin was compelled to stay in show business because of the limited opportunities that would have awaited her as a woman. The truth is that Joplin sang because she loved and needed it, and she had plans to open a bar when her singing career ended. The *female=victim* equation shows little appreciation for the bold young woman who left her hometown for San Francisco in 1964, relying only on her talents

to make it on her own, and announced to the male-dominated rock world that "a woman can be tough."

Joplin's popularity was now at its zenith, and she felt pressured to live up to her hedonistic image, attempting to sustain the intensity of her stage performances in her daily life. She drank constantly and resorted to heroin. She lost contact with the sensitive woman she had been and started rumors that she was unpopular in school and had been estranged from her parents (although letters printed in *Love, Janis* reveal that she was always close to her family). This side of Joplin was exploited in the sensationalistic 1979 Bette Midler film *The Rose,* loosely based on Joplin's life.

On October 4, 1970, after a recording session with Full Tilt, Joplin died from a heroin overdose. "Buried Alive in Blues" was left as an instrumental, but *Pearl* (1971) is otherwise complete. It is Joplin's most polished album, containing the unforgettable "Me and Bobby McGee." It is difficult to listen to Joplin's music without a pang of regret for her tragically wasted talent, but she often said that she would rather live intensely than spend a long life in front of the TV. When friends warned her that she would lose her voice if she kept shrieking, she replied that she would rather give it her all and be a great singer while young, rather than be a mediocre singer with a long career. Joplin's excess was part of her artistry.

The enduring fascination Joplin commands is testified by many posthumous releases, including *Janis Joplin in Concert* (1972), *Janis Joplin's Greatest Hits* (1973), *Janis* (documentary and soundtrack, 1975), *A Farewell Song* (rarities, 1983), *Janis* (three-CD box set, 1988), *Janis Joplin: 18 Essential Songs* (selections from the box set, 1995), and *Janis Joplin with Big Brother and the Holding Company, Live at Winterland '68* (1998). Joplin was elected to the Rock and Roll Hall of Fame in 1995.

—Douglas Cooke

FURTHER READING:

Dalton, David. *Janis.* New York, Simon and Schuster, 1971.

Friedman, Myra. *Buried Alive: The Biography of Janis Joplin.* New York, William Morrow & Co., 1973.

Joplin, Laura. *Love, Janis.* New York, Villard Books, 1992.

Willis, Ellen. "Janis Joplin." *The Rolling Stone Illustrated History of Rock & Roll.* Rev. ed. New York, Random House, 1980.

Joplin, Scott (1868-1917)

As a pioneering African American composer of ragtime music, Scott Joplin took part in a musical revolution in America at the turn of the twentieth century and left an enduring mark on the musical culture of the country. Best known during his lifetime for *Maple Leaf Rag* (1899), Joplin wrote some two dozen compositions in the catchy, syncopated style that served as accompaniment to cakewalk dancing, to new forms of urban sporting life, and to a more generalized revolt against nineteenth-century gentility and restraint. He helped establish the conventional structure of ragtime compositions and successfully blended familiar genres of European music with African American rhythms and melodies into a genuine musical hybrid. After 1900, ragtime music emerged as the first nationally recognized American music, and Tin Pan Alley publishers flooded the popular sheet music market with thousands of snappy, syncopated songs and piano pieces.

Scott Joplin

Hiram K. Moderwell, one of Joplin's contemporaries, called ragtime the "folk music of the American city," and John Stark, the publisher of *Maple Leaf Rag,* dubbed Joplin the "King of Ragtime Writers."

Although he was unquestionably born with a musical gift, Joplin's genius must be attributed at least partly to childhood influences from the region of his birth. Born near Linden, Texas, in 1868, the second son of sharecroppers Jiles and Florence Joplin, the future composer grew up amid former slaves and their rich musical traditions. As a youngster he heard black work songs, spirituals, and ring shouts, as well as the European waltzes, schottishes, and marches that black musicians like his father performed at white parties and dances. When the Joplins moved to Texarkana, which had sprung into existence in the early 1870s at the junction of the Texas & Pacific and Cairo & Fulton Railroads, Scott not only attended school but also learned to play the piano belonging to a wealthy family whose house his mother cleaned. As his talent developed, he began studying with a German music teacher (thought most probably to be Julius Weiss) from whom he learned the basic elements of serious European compositions and the rhythms, melodies, and harmonies on which they depended. Joplin began performing as an adolescent, impressing those who heard him with the originality of his music. As one contemporary later recalled, "He did not have to play anybody else's music. He made up his own, and it was beautiful; he just got his music out of the air."

It is not known exactly when Scott Joplin left Texarkana, but sometime in the 1880s he set out to make his living as an itinerant musician. It also is not known where he worked and lived before he gained fame in Sedalia, Missouri, in the 1890s. Oral histories place

him at the World's Columbian Exposition in Chicago in 1893, where he tried out some of his arrangements with a newly formed band performing, no doubt, in the city's tenderloin district. He was convinced that his rhythmically daring music had a ready, eager audience. Ragtime's misplaced accents, its complex melodies that flowed from bass to treble and back, and the flurry of its notes invited toe-tapping, knee-slapping, head-bobbing movement from those who heard it; it was perfect for the flashy strutting of the popular cakewalk. Moreover, the 1890s economic depression, which affected the middle class as well as the underpaid or unemployed working class, sparked a nationwide questioning of the long-held American belief in self-denial and personal restraint. Joplin's music literally struck a chord with a generation ready to shake off the vestiges of nineteenth-century propriety by kicking up its heels to the exuberant strains of ragtime.

Following the World's Columbian Exposition, Joplin made his way to Sedalia, Missouri, an important railhead in the east-central part of the Show-Me State. More significantly, perhaps, for the black musician, Sedalia was the home of the George R. Smith College for Negroes. Joplin enrolled in music courses at the black institution and began performing in various settings in Sedalia along with other talented African American musicians, earning a reputation as a popular entertainer and composer of ragtime music. He performed with the Queen City Band, an all-black group that provided music for various public entertainments, and played in clubs, brothels, dance halls, and at private parties. He also mentored and collaborated with younger black musicians such as Arthur Marshall and Scott Hayden. Marshall remembered his teacher as "a quiet person with perfect manners who loved music and liked to talk about it." He was "a brother in kindness to all."

Undoubtedly the most important association Joplin formed in Sedalia was with a white publisher of sheet music, John Stark. By the time Stark published *Maple Leaf Rag* in 1899, Joplin had published four other compositions—two marches, a waltz, and *Original Rags.* Although skeptical of the marketability of Joplin's work—he viewed the composition as too difficult for local patrons—Stark admired *Maple Leaf Rag* and agreed to put out a limited printing. Very quickly, orders for Joplin's rag began to pour in, and Stark issued several new editions over the next few years. Stark moved his business to St. Louis in 1900 and continued to publish Joplin works—*Peacherine Rag* (1901), *Augustan Club Waltz* (1901), *A Breeze from Alabama* (1902), *Elite Syncopations* (1902), *The Entertainer* (1902), and *The Strenuous Life* (1902). Stark also promoted Joplin's career by declaring him the "King of Ragtime Writers," by aggressively marketing his latest works, and by regularly contributing advertising copy and articles about him to the nationally circulated *Christensen's Ragtime Review.* Stark's business sense no doubt contributed to Joplin's decision to write *The Cascades* (1904) as a tribute to the attraction of that name at the Louisiana Purchase Exposition in St. Louis in 1904. As Joplin's fame spread, he, too, moved to St. Louis, where he lived from 1901 to 1907. There he continued composing, performing, and mixing socially and professionally with such black musicians as Tom Turpin, Sam Patterson, and Joe Jordan.

While writers after his death remembered Joplin principally as the composer of dance-hall music, Joplin himself harbored grander ambitions for his art. Even as he relied on sheet music sales, teaching, and performance to make a living, he devoted much of his creative energy to the writing of serious music with syncopated rhythm. His first such effort, a ragtime ballet called *The Ragtime Dance,* featured current African American dance steps choreographed to vocal and piano accompaniment. Although he had composed several profitable rags for Stark in 1901 and 1902, the publisher only reluctantly agreed to publish *The Ragtime Dance* in 1902, but it never sold well. *The Guest of Honor*, a ragtime opera that unfortunately no longer exists, marked Joplin's second venture in the field of serious composition. In 1903, he formed the Scott Joplin Drama Company in St. Louis and recruited former students to perform in the ambitious work. The cast rehearsed and Joplin rented a theater, but only one dress rehearsal is known to have taken place because Joplin failed to find financial backing for the production. Despite these setbacks, the composer continued his endeavors toward the incorporation of African American and ragtime motifs into serious music and after 1907 worked feverishly on his second opera, *Treemonisha.*

Joplin spent the last decade of his life in New York, where he worked on *Treemonisha,* published more than 20 compositions, including such well-known pieces as *Gladiolus Rag* (1907), *Pine Apple Rag* (1908), and *Solace—A Mexican Serenade* (1909), gave private music lessons, and performed on the vaudeville stage. He was an early active member of the Colored Vaudevillian Benevolent Association, whose membership included many of the cultural leaders in black Harlem. His obsession with the seriousness of his work was reflected in *School of Ragtime—Six Exercises for Piano* (1908), which demanded "proper time" and "the supposition that each note will be played as it is written." "[T]he 'Joplin ragtime' is destroyed," he insisted, "by careless or imperfect rendering." He railed publicly against flashy performers who played his, and other, rags too fast and sloppily, and he decried the vulgar lyrics that accompanied many popular ragtime songs.

Most importantly, in 1911, Joplin finished his second opera and began searching diligently for financial backers and a suitable venue to stage a performance. The opera's main theme—the need for education in the African American community to combat the pernicious effects of ignorance and superstition—placed the work squarely in the middle of one of the most serious debates spawned by the "Race Question." Moreover, in a rare newspaper interview in 1911, Joplin defended *Treemonisha* as serious—not popular—art: "In most of the strains I have used syncopation (rhythm) peculiar to my race, but the music is not ragtime and the score is grand opera." The opera was performed only once during Joplin's lifetime, in 1915, and the production suffered from lack of props, costumes, and an orchestra. It was met by utter critical silence and quickly faded from collective memory.

The failure of Joplin's second opera coincided with the composer's personal decline. Although reasonably successful as a composer and performer, and widely recognized as the King of Ragtime, his adult life had not been happy. In 1900 he had married Belle Jones, who offered little support for his artistic endeavors and who either died or left him shortly after the death of their only child in 1906. A second marriage ended quickly and tragically with his wife's death. Lottie Stokes, Joplin's third wife, whom he married in New York, cared for her husband during his final battle against the debilitating symptoms of syphilis. Increasingly distracted, frequently unable to play the piano or compose, and grown unreliable as a private music teacher, Joplin spent the final two years of his life in the throes of the disease that eventually took his life on April 1, 1917.

More than 50 years after his death, Joplin became the focus of popular and scholarly attention when Vera Brodsky Lawrence recovered and republished his collected works, Joshua Rifkin recorded many of them, and the hit movie, *The Sting* (1973), featured his music. In the wake of this rediscovery, biographies of Joplin began to appear, and *Treemonisha* was revived by serious opera companies around the

country. In his own day, however, the musician faced numerous barriers to his success, only some of which he overcame. Race prejudice, of course, placed severe limits on the kinds of compositions that would garner financial support, while his lack of academic credentials hindered his acceptance as a serious composer among both blacks and whites. Despite these injustices, Scott Joplin was a vital contributor to the cultural shake-up that took place in the United States in the early 1900s, and his classic ragtime pieces helped propel the nation into the modern era.

—Susan Curtis

FURTHER READING:

Benson, Kathleen, and James Haskins. *Scott Joplin.* Garden City, New York, Doubleday, 1978.

Berlin, Edward. *The King of Ragtime: A Biography of Scott Joplin.* New York, Oxford University Press, 1994.

Curtis, Susan. *Dancing to a Black Man's Tune: A Life of Scott Joplin.* Columbia, University of Missouri Press, 1994.

Janis, Harriet, and Rudi Blesh. *They All Played Ragtime: The True Story of an American Music.* New York, Alfred Knopf, 1950.

Jordan, Louis (1908-1975)

One of America's most prominent musicians of the 1940s, Louis Jordan was a singer, a baritone and alto sax player, a clarinetist, and a bandleader. From 1942 to 1951, he had 18 number one hits on the R&B chart and was one of the biggest African-American box office draws in the country, besides being an important figure and role model in black popular entertainment. His music reflected his African-American roots while appealing to both black and white audiences. His combo, Louis Jordan and the Tympany Five helped to define the shuffle boogie rhythm as well as "jump," a term first used in jazz and later in rhythm and blues, that referred to the instrumentation of trumpet, alto and tenor sax, piano, bass, and drums. The innovative Jordan was the first jazz musician to make a short film based on one of his popular hit songs ("Caldonia"), an early precursor of the contemporary music video. His influence on rock and roll can be heard in the music of Bill Haley, Chuck Berry, Fats Domino, and James Brown, among others.

From his earliest years, Jordan was guided and motivated by a strong conviction and desire to become an entertainer. "I wanted to give my whole life to making people enjoy my music. Make them laugh and smile. So I didn't stick to what you'd call jazz. I have always stuck to entertainment," he once said. Jordan embodied a melding of visual showmanship, detached humor, impeccable musicianship, and a gratifying original and rhythmic vocal style.

Born Louis Thomas Jordan on July 8, 1908 in Brinkley, Arkansas, Louis Jordan was the son of James Jordan, a musical talent, and of a mother who died when he was young. James Jordan, his father was a multi-instrumentalist, organizer of the local Brinkley Brass Band, and a motivational figure in his life. As a boy, Jordan sang in the local Baptist church, mastered the clarinet and saxophone family of instruments, and during the summer, along with his father, toured with the Rabbit Foot Minstrels and Ma Rainey's TOBA Troupe. These early experiences developed in Jordan a passion for perfecting his music through disciplined rehearsals and an appreciation for showmanship.

Louis Jordan (center).

Jordan worked as a sideman with Ruby Williams's band in Hot Springs, Arkansas before moving on to Philadelphia.

Once in Philadelphia, professional opportunities presented themselves to Jordan. He met Ralph Cooper, bandleader and coordinator of the amateur night at the Apollo Theater in Harlem. who hired him as member of the Apollo house band. Jordan joined Chick Webb's band, playing at the Savoy Ballroom from 1936-1938. He left the Webb band confident enough to organize his own group, "The Louie Jordan Elks Rendezvous Band," (the "Louie" spelling was intentional since people often mispronounced his name as Lewis), which began its engagements at The Elks Club in Harlem. The band's name was later changed to Louis Jordan and His Tympany Five, which remained constant despite personnel changes. The word tympany was included for a period because drummer Walter Martin actually played that instrument in the group.

Louis Jordan and His Tympany Five became one of the most successful small bands in jazz history. Jordan signed a Decca contract that lasted from 1938-1955, recording many compositions in its "Race Series." His recording of "A Chicken Ain't Nothing but a Bird" signaled a pivotal point in the direction and kind of material Jordan would record. This song's novelty lyrics, shuffle and boogie rhythm, and the soloing of lead instrumentalists all proved to be a successful formula. The subsequent recording of "I'm Gonna Move

to the Outskirts of Town," a 12-bar blues, launched Jordan as a major recording star. Then followed a string of major hits posting in the top ten on the R&B chart, including "What's the Use of Getting Sober" (1942), "Five Guys Named Moe" (1943), "Ration Blues" (1943), "G.I. Jive" (1944), "Is You Is Or Is You Ain't (Ma' Baby)" (1944), "Mop Mop" (1945), "Caldonia," (1945), "Don't Let the Sun Catch You Cryin'" (1946), "Choo Choo Ch'Boogie" (1946), "Ain't That Just Like a Woman" (1946); "Ain't Nobody Here But Us Chickens" (1946), "Let the Good Times Roll" (1946), "Open the Door Richard" (1947), "Beans and Corn Bread" (1949), and "Saturday Night Fish Fry (Part I)" (1949), among others. Jordan's recording of "Caldonia" and the short film of the same name marked the first time that a film was based on a tune. This arrangement was a huge success with both white and black audiences. When rock and roll came into its own in the 1950s, Jordan's career began to decline and his contract with Decca ended. He signed with Mercury records and rerecorded old hits, including "Caldonia." Jordan moved to Los Angeles in the early 1960s and recorded one album with Ray Charles's Tangerine label. He formed Pzazz, his own record label in 1968.

A number of Jordan's recordings can be classified as blues, which Jordan sang with perfect diction in a sophisticated, cosmopolitan, smooth, and crooner style that attracted black and white audiences. For a number of his touring engagements, promoters booked his band to play two separate engagements in the same evening—one for a white and one for a black audience. He also led a big band from 1951-52.

Jordan was a competent jazz improviser, and his work on alto sax is memorable. His choice of songs as well as his own compositions were based on gospel, blues, jazz, and the vernacular of black speech and African-American folk culture. Jordan sang about the subjects of black folk, women (chicks and chickens), Saturday night fish frys, drinking, love, and partying—in sum the travails and pleasures of African-American experience in urban areas after their postwar migration. Jordan's music epitomized an era of good times, paving the way for rhythm and blues. He continued to tour until he collapsed and died of a heart attack on February 5, 1975 in Los Angeles. Since his death, there has been a gradual rebirth of interest in his work, with his music featured in various movie sound tracks such as *The Blues Brothers. Five Guys Named Moe,* a musical that featured Jordan's music, opened on Broadway in 1992 and captured a Tony Award nomination for best musical.

—Willie Collins

FURTHER READING:

Chilton, John. *Let the Good Times Roll: The Story of Louis Jordan and His Music.* Ann Arbor, The University of Michigan Press, 1994.

Jordan, Michael (1963—)

The most successful and skilled player in the history of professional basketball, Michael Jordan came into the public eye in the mid-1980s. He went on to win six NBA (National Basketball Association) scoring championships (1990/91, 1991/92, 1992/93, 1995/96, 1996/97, 1997/98) and five Most Valuable Player awards (1987/88, 1990/91, 1991/92, 1995/96, 1997/98). An international sports icon and a role model for youth and adults alike, Jordan helped redefine the male athlete as a figure of sublime grace, technical skill, and ferocious athleticism. His determination, diligence, and fiercely competitive attitude also enhanced the public perception of black masculinity during the 1980s and 1990s. Aside from his professional prowess, as a commercially valuable endorser and an entrepreneur, Michael Jordan became one of the highest paid sportsmen of his era and announced his final retirement from basketball in 1999 while at the top of his game.

Michael Jordan was born on February 17, 1963, in Brooklyn, New York. His father, James Jordan, was a General Electric employee, and his mother Delores worked as a supervisor at a local bank. Soon after Michael's birth, the family relocated to Wallace, North Carolina, and then to Wilmington, where the young Jordan was raised. In early childhood as well as adolescence, Michael showed exceptional skill in all areas of sports, including baseball and football. When he suffered a minor injury while playing football in high school, his parents encouraged him to pursue basketball. Jordan did not initially make the starting squad for his high school basketball team, but made the lineup in his junior year, having shot up to six-foot-three in height. (He would eventually reach his maximum height of six-foot-six-inches). Much of his early skill and training in basketball was derived from playing with his brother Larry in the backyard at home; in his formative years he also idolized and patterned himself

Michael Jordan

after the legendary Julius Erving (a.k.a. Dr. J.), one of the great players of the 1970s.

After high school, Jordan settled on attending the University of North Carolina at Chapel Hill, where he would play on the basketball team under coach Dean Smith. Although Smith by reputation rarely played his freshmen, Jordan's unique abilities guaranteed him time on the court. The young athlete quickly became known for his incredible agility and dexterity on the court, as well as for his ability to think instinctively and create innovative shots. For his efforts, Jordan was voted ACC (Atlantic Coast Conference) Rookie of the Year. After bringing his team to the NCAA (National Collegiate Athletic Association) championships, he won nearly every major individual award in college basketball, including the Wooden Award, the Naismith Award, and the Rupp Trophy. He was also voted College Basketball Player of the Year by *The Sporting News.* In 1984, at 21 years of age, Jordan made the United States Olympic Games basketball team under coach Bobby Knight. Averaging a remarkable 17 points a game, Jordan led the team to a gold medal in eight straight wins. The Olympic win brought Jordan to high visibility in basketball circles and made him a household name in America.

After announcing his decision to leave school early and enter the NBA draft in 1984, Jordan was selected by the Chicago Bulls in the first round (third pick overall). Wearing jersey No. 23 in his rookie professional season, he averaged 28.2 points a game, third highest in the league. With his outstanding leaping ability and uncanny grace in the air, Jordan seemed to defy the laws of gravity. His spectacular individual efforts were fodder for latenight sports highlight programs and quickly fed his growing legend. For the combination of his high scoring abilities and his stylish acrobatics, the handsome, soft-spoken player was voted Rookie of the Year and was rapidly becoming America's best-loved sports star. The (at that time struggling) Nike shoe company took advantage of Jordan's popularity and signed him to a lucrative endorsement deal that resulted in the Air Jordan shoe, which quickly became the most successful product in sports marketing history. The high sales of the product marked the beginning of a long and commercially rewarding relationship between Nike and Jordan.

Throughout his 1985/86 season, Jordan continued soaring to new heights. When he fractured his ankle early in the season, the dedicated star ignored doctors' orders and went back to regular play, despite the danger of doing more serious damage. By the end of the season, however, he had led his team to the playoffs against the Boston Celtics. On May 20, 1986, Jordan established a NBA Playoffs record by scoring 63 points in a single game against the Celtics. He continued his high scoring rate through the 1987/88 season and became the first player to win both the Defensive Player of the Year award and the NBA scoring title in the same year. He also took home the Most Valuable Player (MVP) award in the All-Star game. Although he again won the scoring title in the 1988/89 season, Jordan remained personally unsatisfied that he had not yet managed to lead the Bulls past Eastern Conference power (and hated rivals) Detroit and into the NBA finals.

In the 1990/91 season, his seventh in the NBA and under new coach Phil Jackson, Jordan received increased on-court support from his gifted teammate Scottie Pippen. As a result, the Bulls finally advanced past Detroit to an NBA finals showdown with the Los Angeles Lakers. In the much publicized on-court match-up between Jordan and the Lakers' legendary Magic Johnson, the Bulls finally prevailed, and Jordan received the title he had so long fought for. In the following 1991/92 season, he took home his third consecutive MVP award and his sixth straight NBA scoring title with a 30.1 point average per game. In the playoffs that year, the Bulls repeated as champions against the Portland Trailblazers by bouncing back from an 81-78 deficit in the final game. Jordan scored 12 of the Bulls' final 19 points to clinch a 97-93 victory.

The successes continued to rack up for Michael Jordan over the forthcoming seasons. In 1992, he once again joined the U.S. team for the Olympic Games. Supported by Magic Johnson, Larry Bird, and others, the American ''Dream Team'' won their games by an average of 44 points, securing the Gold Medal. In the 1992/1993 NBA season, Jordan took home his seventh straight scoring title and won the championship against Charles Barkley and the Phoenix Suns. Jordan averaged 41 points per game in the six-game final series.

By this time, Jordan's success had brought him international superstardom, yet his most important role was, perhaps, behind the scenes. In 1990, he had married Juanita Vanoy. Together, the couple would raise three children (Jeffrey, Marcus and Jasmine) in the Highland Park suburb of Illinois, and the sports star would eventually bring home $45 million a year from endorsement deals that ranged from breakfast cereal to his own line of cologne products. He also purchased a restaurant in Chicago, Michael Jordan's Steak House, which instantly became a popular tourist stop. His profile had risen to such an extent that he even hosted an episode of NBC television's *Saturday Night Live* in 1991.

Although Jordan, well-known for his charity work, was widely recognized as an admirable role model, there were persistent rumors that he had become addicted to gambling, and some began to criticize him for overly aggressive behavior on the court. In 1993, his father was shot to death in South Carolina by two local youths who were attempting to steal his automobile. On October 6th of the same year, in the midst of the tragedy surrounding his father, Jordan shocked the world by announcing his retirement from basketball. He was only 30 and at the peak of his game and popularity. Speculation persisted that Jordan's ''retirement'' was actually a league-ordered suspension of the NBA's brightest star amid substantiated stories that Jordan was wagering hundreds of thousands of dollars on golf games.

Again to the surprise of the public, Jordan took advantage of his retirement to pursue one of his long lost dreams: he signed with the Chicago White Sox to play minor league baseball, with the swaggering declaration that his ultimate goal was to make the major leagues. Although numerous onlookers took this new career move to be a publicity stunt or a way to stay competitively sharp during his ''suspension,'' many of his fans were intrigued by his daring. Jordan rode the team bus, shared small locker rooms, and received a pittance in comparison to his salary during his tenure with the Bulls. Unfortunately, in contrast to his performance on the basketball court, Jordan's abilities on the baseball field were limited even on a minor-league standard. Yet, his courage to try and his humility on the baseball field made the larger-than-life sports star seem more human and more vulnerable, further endearing him to his already loyal fans. In the meantime, the Chicago Bulls were suffering without their star player and were quickly eliminated from the playoffs. The NBA as a whole also suffered; sorely missing Jordan's star appeal, the playoffs in 1993 between the New York Knicks and the Houston Rockets drew an uncharacteristically low television audience.

Providence intervened for Jordan fans. On March 18, 1995, due to a baseball strike, Jordan returned from his 18-month hiatus from the court to rejoin the Bulls. In his return game—against the Indiana Pacers—Jordan posted 19 points, 6 rebounds, 6 assists, and 3 steals in 43 minutes of play. Eventually, however, the Bulls were defeated in the playoffs by the Orlando Magic, who were bolstered by the presence of young and versatile players like Shaquille O'Neal and Penny Hardaway. In the 1995/96 season, Jordan and the Bulls were joined by the outrageous Dennis Rodman, ironically their longtime nemesis from the Detroit Pistons' Bad Boys days.. Along with Rodman and Pippen, Jordan once again led the Bulls to the NBA title, their fourth in six years. The star also picked up his eighth scoring championship with a 30.4 points per game average, as well as another MVP award; that year he also claimed *Sport Magazine*'s award as the top athlete of the last half of the twentieth century. In 1996, Jordan made his film debut in the half-animation, half-live action star vehicle *Space Jam,* which was a box office hit.

In the 1997/98 season, Jordan was given a $30 million contract for one year's play, and also earned his fifth MVP Award. He became the first player in history to be selected to the NBA All Defensive First Team nine times, beating Bobby Jones's previous record of eight. Jordan was named MVP of the 1998 All-Star Game, and won his sixth NBA championship after leading the Bulls past the Utah Jazz in the playoffs.

On January 13, 1999, aged 35 and at the top of his game, Michael Jordan again announced his retirement, this time on the heels of a protracted labor dispute which saw the league lock-out the players over a dispute in their collective bargaining agreement. It seemed the proper time for perhaps the greatest player ever to step down. In just 14 years, Jordan had risen not only to a certain place in the basketball Hall of Fame, but also to the highest level of status and achievement in global popular sports culture. Throughout his professional career, he had been a shining symbol of the American Dream, expanding the very possibilities of human achievement in his field. In the June 1998 issue of *Hoop* magazine, one writer described Jordan professional career as the new "universal measuring device in appraising greatness."

—Jason King

FURTHER READING:

Halberstam, David. *Playing for Keeps: Michael Jordan and the World He Made.* New York, Random House, 1999.

Jordan, Michael. *For the Love of the Game: My Story.* New York, Crown Publishers, 1998.

Jordan, Michael. *Rare Air: Michael on Michael.* San Francisco, Collins Publishers.

Joy of Cooking

An eight-hundred page cookbook that begins with a quote from Goethe's *Faust* seems an unlikely candidate for a spot on a list of the best-selling books of the century, but Irma S. Rombauer's *Joy of Cooking* (first edition 1931), sold 14 million copies before 1997—a record that speaks for itself in terms of the enormous influence it has wielded in the development of social culture. In 1977 a revised edition was issued by its new publisher, Simon & Schuster, and despite the vast changes in the eating habits of American households over the decades, the detailed tome again landed on the best-seller lists. By the end of the twentieth century, it was the top-selling all-purpose cookbook in publishing history, deemed the bible of American culinary customs, from cocktails to custards.

Part of *Joy of Cooking*'s success lies in the way it presents the art of food preparation in simple, forthright terminology. Rombauer was a widowed St. Louis socialite of patrician German birth when she began assembling her wealth of recipes into book form in 1930, partly at the request of her two grown children. Married to a lawyer in 1899, she had had little experience in the kitchen as a young wife, and like other affluent women of the era, she relied on domestic staff to help plan and cook meals for family dinners and social events. Her husband was an avid outdoor man, however, and had instructed her in some of the basics of the camp stove. Over the next few decades Rombauer matured into an accomplished chef and renowned hostess. One of her aims in writing the book was to persuade American women that cooking was not a daily, labor-intensive, time-consuming chore, but rather a delight, indeed, a "joy." The book's title has something of an ironic tinge, because Rombauer's husband had suffered from depression for much of his adult life, and committed suicide in the family home in St. Louis a few months after the stock market crash of 1929. He left his wife and two children an estate of just 6000 dollars, and Rombauer used half of that sum to put her first edition into print.

The recipes that Irma Rombauer assembled for the first *Joy of Cooking: A Compilation of Reliable Recipes with a Casual Culinary Chat* (1931) provided new cooks with the basics. Illustrated by her artistic-minded daughter, Marion Rombauer Becker, the book sold 3,000 copies, literally out of Rombauer's St. Louis home. The stylized, art-deco cover depicted a gowned St. Martha of Bethany, the patron saint of cooks, slaying a dragon representing kitchen drudgery;

inside were to be found old European recipes, such as braised heart slices in a sour sauce, adapted for use with American ingredients and tools. There were several meat dishes that reflected traditional peasant economics, whereby when an animal was slaughtered almost no inch of it went to waste—neither brains nor tongue, intestine or feet. On a lighter note, Rombauer told readers about her cook, Marguerite, and Marguerite's culinary prowess. Her chatty style extended to explaining the mechanics of food preparation: she assumed, for example, that novices in the kitchen did not know how to separate egg whites when a recipe called for it, and so guided them through it; likewise, she instructed them in other fundamentals such as flour sifting and deboning chicken.

In 1936, Indianapolis publisher Bobbs-Merrill brought out a *Joy of Cooking* edition rewritten and enlarged by the author. This version displayed Rombauer's unique set-up for each recipe that became the book's most famously identifying feature. Ingredients were listed in bold type so that a recipe could be quickly scanned to determine whether the ingredients were on hand in the pantry or refrigerator; more importantly, just what to do with those ingredients was detailed in a step-by-step sequence. This edition was an immediate success, due in part to the fact that, with the Great Depression, many well-to-do households could no longer afford to keep servants, and numerous affluent American women had recently entered the kitchen full-time. They sorely needed Rombauer's instructions.

In 1939, Rombauer was far ahead of her time in recognizing the need for a cookbook designed to help working women prepare quick and easy meals. *Streamlined Cooking* was the result, and the relatively recent invention of the pressure cooker was a key element in many of the main-dish recipes. It was not as successful as her first volume, but when she merged the two into a 1943 edition of *Joy of Cooking,* she hit upon the perfect formula. Combining the easy recipes from *Streamlined* with the step-by-step instruction method of *Joy* produced an instant classic. Large numbers of women were working outside the home as a result of labor shortages created by World War II, and Rombauer's recipes took the countrywide wartime food rationing into consideration. When the third revision of the book appeared in 1951, household help had become a relic of a bygone era for all but the wealthiest of households. Census figures from between 1930 and 1960 tracked a decrease in the median age of men and women at the time of marriage, and the number of households, families, and married couples zoomed from 34.9 million in 1940 to 52.7 million in 1960. Though many women worked outside the home during this era, the image of the competent, attractive homemaker advanced by advertising and television programs was firmly entrenched by the postwar decade, and *Joy of Cooking* became the "how-to" guide to achieving domestic fulfillment for legions of American women.

By the 1960s *Joy* was a perennial best-seller, the standard bridal-shower gift, and a staple accessory of almost every middle-class household. "Its virtues were its compendiousness, its useful tables and explanations, its pragmatic, clear directions and a certain sprightly and encouraging tone," declared Diane Johnson in a 1997 assessment for the *New York Review of Books*. Johnson explained that later food critics of the 1970s and 1980s railed against some the book's more archaic elements and reliance on processed foods, especially after American culinary tastes grew more daring and gourmet cooking became all the rage. This trend was exemplified by Julia Child's's *Mastering the Art of French Cooking,* first published in 1961, which made the canned-soup recipes in the *Joy of Cooking* seem not only dated but somewhat pedestrian. By the 1962 edition, Marion Rombauer

Becker had taken over the project, though her mother's name remained on the cover, and this and successive editions were revised, with certain recipes discarded, to reflect America's increasing culinary sophistication. The quote from Goethe remained, however: "That which thy fathers have bequeathed to thee, earn it anew if thou wouldst possess it."

Irma Rombauer died in 1962, and her *New York Times* obituary noted that "the cookbook that brought her fame is considered one of the most lucid and accurate ever written. Mrs. Rombauer wrote charmingly and well about food." The paper also credited her with introducing elegant European recipes in accessible terminology "so they could be prepared with relative speed and ease by the average American housewife." A fifth edition of *Joy of Cooking* published in 1975 became the best-selling of all with an estimated 3.5 million copies sold in 20 years, and, despite editorial changes, still provided many delightful reminders of a bygone era. "Unless you choke your duck, pluck the down on its breast immediately afterward, and cook it within 24 hours, you cannot lay claim to having produced an authentic Rouen duck," begins the recipe for Duckling Rouennaise, a modified version of the genuine article. The recipe instructs readers to roast a five-pound bird on a spit or rotisserie, and then serve sliced in a chafing dish with a sauce prepared from its crushed liver, veal pate, onion, butter, and burgundy wine. Recipes for veal kidney, blood sausage, lamb head with a rosemary wine sauce, and pig's tails still abounded, and even a diagram for skinning a squirrel remained. *Stand Facing the Stove: The Story of the Women Who Gave America "The Joy of Cooking"* (1966) is a chronicle of the book and its successive revisions by food writer Anne Mendelson, who praised the 1975 edition for its flaws as well as its virtues. "It records," wrote Mendelson, "the sheer improbability of twentieth-century American cooking from the Great Depression to the Ford administration, a lawless melange of blueprints for progress, nostalgic hankerings, gourmet cults, timesaving expedients, media-inspired fads, and unexpected rebellions."

Rombauer's grandson, Ethan Becker, revised *Joy* for a 1997 edition, the first in over two decades. Expanded to an exhaustive 1100-plus pages, the latest release vaulted to the best-seller lists immediately. As always, it had changed with the times: leaner, low-fat recipes prevailed, and a range of new ethnic dishes such as Vietnamese pho were included. In 1998 publisher Scribner brought out a facsimile of the very first edition, complete with the dragon-slaying, St. Martha cover.

—Carol Brennan

FURTHER READING:

Johnson, Diane. "American Pie." *New York Review of Books.* December 18, 1997, 20-23.

Levenstein, Harvey. *Paradox of Plenty: A Social History of Eating in Modern America.* New York, Oxford University Press, 1993.

Mendelson, Anne. *Stand Facing the Stove: The Story of the Women Who Gave America "The Joy of Cooking."* New York, Henry Holt, 1996.

"No More Simmered Porcupine." *U.S. News & World Report.* May 19, 1997, 10.

Rombauer, Irma S., and Marion Becker Rombauer. *Joy of Cooking.* New York, Scribner, 1975.

The Joy of Sex

Published in 1972, during a period when the English-speaking world was experiencing a rapid relaxation of many of its Victorian-era taboos about the open discussion of sexuality, Dr. Alex Comfort's "lovemaking manual," *The Joy of Sex,* caused an immense stir for its frankly nonpuritanical and lighthearted approach to a subject previously shrouded in religious stricture and clinical seriousness. For readers eager to "swing" with the "sexual revolution," or just to perk up a drab marital bed, this volume, and its sequels and spinoffs over the next two decades, were the first mass-market books that offered graphic text and illustrations designed to help people guiltlessly expand their sexual horizons by experimenting with new techniques and positions. Although it was welcomed in many progressive circles, *The Joy of Sex* was roundly criticized for its gender and cultural bias that singularly described female organs with vulgar language; that relied on expressions like "exotic" and "oriental" to describe some unfamiliar techniques; and that dismissed same-sex relations as trivial and unfulfilling. Still, the book was considered a breakthrough for the way in which it brought sexuality to the arena of everyday conversation, paving the way for the more relaxed approach taken by later sexologists like Dr. Ruth Westheimer and Dr. Judy Kurlansky.

As published by Crown, *The Joy of Sex; A Gourmet Guide to Lovemaking* (also known in some editions as *The Joy of Sex: A Cordon Bleu Guide to Lovemaking*) was described in the jacket copy as "the first really happy and outstanding new lovemaking manual, a contemporary Western equal to the great Eastern classics of the *Kama Sutra* and the Pillow Books of China." Based on the "experience of happily married people and edited by Dr. Alex Comfort with the advice of doctors and professional counselors," the book offered more than one hundred line drawings and several pages of paintings in full color by Charles Raymond and Christopher Foss. Also included were sixteen pages of "oriental exotic art from Japan, India, and China." Although Comfort, a British gerontologist, social activist, and poet-novelist, was listed as the book's "editor," in reality he researched and wrote the entire manuscript, explaining later that he could not be identified as its author because of restrictions that then prohibited British physicians from writing "popular" books. Although the book claimed to be based "on the work of one couple," Comfort later confessed that he employed other "consultants" as source material. It was Comfort's original intention to illustrate *The Joy of Sex* with actual photographs of couples, but the photos never "caught the proper zest," as he later told Hugh Kenner. "There was always an expression that asked, 'Am I doing it right?' So two artists [Raymond and Foss] worked from the photographs to produce the illustrations you see. . . . But if the pictures help people turn on, that's part of what the book is for," he explained.

In his introduction, Comfort wrote that "one aim of this book is to cure the notion, born of non-discussion, that common sex needs are odd or weird." He added, "There are, after all, only two 'rules' in good sex, apart from the obvious one of not doing things which are silly, antisocial, or dangerous. One is 'don't do anything you don't really enjoy,' and the other is 'find out your partner's needs and don't balk them if you can help it.'" Comfort wanted couples to be willing to acknowledge a wide "range of human needs" that might include practices and fantasies—aggression and role-playing, for example—that "the last half-century's social mythology pretended weren't there."

Based on his premise that fine sex was analogous to a cook's finesse in blending ingredients and techniques to create a meal of both "culinary fantasies as well as staple diets" ("just as you can't cook without heat, you can't make love without feedback," he wrote), Comfort organized his menu-like table of contents into four sections: Starters, Main Courses, Sauces and Pickles, and Problems. Among the "sauces and pickles" were several dozen "dishes" that in a more puritanical age would have been called naughty or even perverse; the hodgepodge bill-of-fare included items both familiar and obscure: anal intercourse, bondage, "foursomes and moresomes," grope suits, harness, ice, motor cars, pompoir, railroads, rubber, vibrators, and viennese oyster. (Comfort later confessed to curious readers that the "grope suit," a purportedly Scandinavian gadget designed "to induce continuous female orgasm," was really a "joke" he invented.) Some of the items listed incurred the wrath of critics who objected to Comfort's cultural insensitivity in describing certain sexual techniques using Western-centric terms such as "chinese style," "indian style," "japanese style," and "south slav style." Other items, perhaps evocative of an earlier, Anglocentric bias when French postcards were considered the ultimate in naughtiness, were cast in terminology such as "feuille de rose," "pattes d'araigné" and "postillionage."

Besides the expected condemnations by conservative religious critics, *The Joy of Sex* came under fire from feminists who complained that Dr. Comfort used street-slang terms for women's body parts while describing male organs in clinical fashion, and from nonmainstream couples who found their lifestyles were demeaned or ignored in the book. In the 1972 edition, same-sex behaviors were relegated to the "problems" section, under the misleading heading of "bisexuality." Though Comfort generously admitted "all people are bisexual: that is to say they are able to respond sexually to some extent towards people of either sex," he made few friends in the gay and lesbian community when he declared that "Being homosexual isn't a matter of having this kind of response, but usually of having some kind of turn-off towards the opposite sex which makes our same-sex response more evident or predominant." Comfort concluded the section on "bisexuality" by declaring "Straight man-woman sex is the real thing for most people—others need something different but their scope is usually reduced, not widened, by such needs."

This heterosexist attitude inspired the publication, in 1977, of the gay-positive *The Joy of Gay Sex,* by Dr. Charles Silverstein and Edmund White, with illustrations by Michael Leonard, Ian Beck, and Julian Graddon. It was Dr. Silverstein who, in 1973, had successfully persuaded the American Psychiatric Association to remove homosexuality from its list of mental disorders. In his introduction, Silverstein wrote that *The Joy of Gay Sex* was "by gays, for gays, about the gay subculture that comes equipped with its own rituals, its own agonies and ecstasies, its own argot."

With the emergence of the AIDS crisis in the 1980s, both *The Joy of Sex* and *The Joy of Gay Sex* underwent revisions and new editions that promoted safer sex, a topic that had been thought relatively unimportant in the 1970s when, for example, Comfort could write that, between lovers, "Sex must be physically the safest of all human activities (leaving out social repercussions)" or when Silverstein could write "Gonorrhea (clap) is the most serious disease facing gay men." Safer-sex instruction, together with illustrations of models using condoms, were included in some of the sequels and spinoffs to both series, including Comfort's *The New Joy of Sex* (1992) and *The New Joy of Gay Sex* (1991), in which Silverstein

collaborated with Felice Picano, with illustrations by Deni Ponty and Ron Fowler.

—Edward Moran

FURTHER READING:

Comfort, Alex. *The Joy of Sex: A Cordon Bleu Guide to Lovemaking* (also known as *The Joy of Sex: A Gourmet Guide to Lovemaking*). New York, Crown, 1972.

Comfort, Alex. *More Joy of Sex.* New York, Crown, 1987.

———. *The New Joy of Sex,* edited by Julie Rubenstein. New York, Crown, 1992.

Comfort, Alex, and John Raynes (illustrator). *Sexual Foreplay.* New York, Crown, 1997.

Kenner, Hugh. "The Comfort behind the Joy of Sex." *New York Times Magazine.* Oct. 27, 1974, 18ff.

Silverstein, Dr. Charles, and Edmund White. *The Joy of Gay Sex.* New York, Crown, 1977.

Silverstein, Dr. Charles, and Felice Picano. *The New Joy of Gay Sex.* New York, HarperCollins, 1992.

Joyner, Florence Griffith (1959-1998)

One of the most beloved athletes of the late twentieth century, Olympic track and field star Florence Griffith Joyner, or more commonly "FloJo," inspired legions of young aspiring female athletes with her speed, her confidence, and her winning looks. Almost as famous for her muscular physique and her flamboyant style, particularly her six-inch-long, intricately patterned and polished fingernails, Joyner made the track and field establishment sit up

Florence Griffith Joyner

and take notice, and officials and fans alike mourned her sudden death, at 38, of an apparent heart seizure.

Blazing down the track in brightly colored outfits, including her one-legged tights, Joyner was hailed as the world's fastest woman runner at the peak of her career in the mid-1980s. A phenomenal sprinter holding records in the 100- and 200-meter dashes, she also won three gold medals and two silvers at the 1988 Summer Olympics in Seoul, Korea. While a planned comeback in 1996 failed to materialize due to an Achilles tendon injury, Joyner continued to be a presence in track and field events even after her Olympic sweep.

Born December 21, 1959, Joyner was raised in the projects of the Watts district of Los Angeles, the seventh of ten children of electronics technician Robert Griffith and his wife, after whom Florence would be named. Starting to run for sport at age seven, Joyner continued her hobby even after doctors found the teenaged runner had a heart murmur and advised her to quit. Under the tutelage and encouragement of coach Bobby Kersee, Joyner earned a sports scholarship to the University of California, Los Angeles. During her time at UCLA, she ranked as NCAA champion with a 22.39 time on the 200-meter dash before graduating in 1983 with a degree in psychology. After college, Joyner continued to develop her phenomenal speed, and went on to win the silver medal in the 200 meters during the 1984 Olympics in her home town of Los Angeles.

Retiring briefly from running after her Olympic victory to pursue work as a bank secretary and beautician, Joyner was encouraged to return to the track by Kersee. Her records in the 100- (10.49) and 200-meter (21.34) dashes in Seoul remained unbroken after her death. In October 1987 she married coach and Olympic gold medalist Al Joyner, the older brother of heptathlon world-recordholder Jackie Joyner-Kersee. The couple made their new home in Mission Viejo, California, and in 1988 Al Joyner took over coaching duties for his wife from Kersee. The couple's daughter, Mary, was born in 1991.

Retiring from her career as a sprinter in 1989, Joyner turned her enormous energies to designing sportswear and working toward getting her cosmetology license. Her determination and desire for perfection drove her in these areas as they had her running career. She also designed uniforms for the NBA team the Indiana Pacers, and co-chaired the President's Council on Physical Fitness as a means of further inspiring young athletes.

Joyner's untimely death at age 38 was noted by President Clinton, who told reporters that "We were dazzled by her speed, humbled by her talent, and captivated by her style. Though she rose to the pinnacle of the world of sports, she never forgot where she came from." While some in the media speculated that Joyner's rumored use of performance-enhancing drugs such as steroids may have contributed to her death, such rumors had consistently been disproved throughout her career: during the Olympics she was tested for drug use 11 times without problem. It was widely known that the athlete had suffered from a number of medical problems throughout her career and had been hospitalized on several occasions. She also experienced increased episodes of fatigue during 1997. An autopsy revealed that Joyner died in her sleep of asphyxiation, the result of an epileptic seizure. Left behind to mourn this energetic and inspiring athlete were her husband, her seven-year-old daughter Mary, and legions of fans who considered themselves fortunate to have witnessed the amazing performance of the fastest woman in the world.

—Pamela L. Shelton

FURTHER READING:

Moore, Kenny. "Very Fancy, Very Fast." *Sports Illustrated.* September 14, 1988.

Pellegrini, Frank. "FloJo, 1959-1988." *Time.* September 22, 1998.

Stewart, Mark. *Florence Griffith-Joyner.* New York, Children's Press, 1997.

Tresniowski, Alex, et al. "Like Lightning." *People.* October 5, 1998.

Joyner-Kersee, Jackie (1962—)

Born in East St. Louis, Illinois, and raised in a house she remembers as "little more than paper and sticks," Jackie Joyner-Kersee eventually became known throughout the world as one of the finest female athletes of all time. The winner of six Olympic medals, three of them gold, a record-holder in both the multi-event heptathlon (the female version of the decathlon) and the long jump, and a world-class basketball player, Joyner-Kersee stands as an example of how strength and determination can triumph over adversity. An African-American, she has battled racial discrimination and gender bias and triumphed in the male-dominated field of athletic competition, despite her personal battle with a debilitating medical condition.

Born on March 3, 1962, Joyner-Kersee was one of four children born to Al Joyner and his wife, Mary. Her brother, Al Joyner, is also an athlete who has achieved Olympic greatness, winning the gold in the triple jump in 1984; he would marry runner Florence "FloJo" Griffith in 1987. An active child, Joyner-Kersee joined the track team at East St. Louis's Lincoln High School, where she benefited from having some excellent coaches and excelled at the long jump. However, her performance on the basketball court was what got her noticed, and after graduating in 1980, Joyner-Kersee was able to attend the University of California, Los Angeles on a basketball scholarship.

At UCLA Joyner-Kersee first met Bob Kersee, a controversial coach who would have a great impact not only on her career but on her personal life as well. Her college years proved to be challenging as, under Kersee's direction, the young athlete perfected her skills and ultimately won the NCAA heptathlon two years in a row, as well as walking away with the 1982 USA championship. The injury that would dog Joyner-Kersee's career—a pulled hamstring—first made itself known as she prepared to compete in the 1983 World Championships in Helinski, Finland, and she was forced to withdraw. She was also diagnosed with an asthmatic condition requiring constant medication. However, Joyner-Kersee's medical setbacks were nothing compared to learning of the tragic death of her 37-year-old mother, Mary, who had been the young woman's inspiration. While Joyner-Kersee's grief momentarily threatened to derail her academic and athletic career, she rallied, as she had from each of her medical setbacks, and went on to pursue her dreams. Graduating with a major in history in the top ten percent of her class from UCLA, she was also named the school's athlete of the year in 1985, and won the Broderick Cup for being chosen the country's most outstanding female collegiate athlete.

Her first year out of college would prove to be a momentous year for Joyner-Kersee. She and her coach were married in January of

Jackie Joyner-Kersee

1986, and Kersee continued to coach his wife to a heptathlon victory at that year's Goodwill Games in Moscow. Setting the world record of 7,148 points for the event during the Games, Joyner-Kersee competed in other events across the country, winning the Jesse Owens Award for outstanding performance in track and field that same year.

Joyner-Kersee made outstanding performances in a number of events during 1987, including the Mobil Indoor Grand Prix (winner, women's overall), the Pan American Games (winner, long jump), and the World Championships, held in Rome, where she equalled the world record of 24 feet 5 1/2 inches in the long jump. She suffered her first major asthma attack after returning from the Rome Games, and doctors prescribed the short, periodic use of prednisone, a steroid banned in athletic competition, in addition to her regular medication. Because Joyner-Kersee resisted becoming reliant upon drugs and stopped taking any medications as soon as she felt better, her condition worsened over the coming years, and during 1993's spring games she would be forced to compete wearing an allergen-filtering mask. Meanwhile, the 1987 Jesse Owens Award would once again go to Joyner-Kersee for her outstanding track and field performance that year.

Joyner-Kersee continued to break records over the following decade. In 1988's Olympic Games she took the gold in both the heptathlon and long jump, and equaled the U.S. record for 100-meter

hurdles. Sidelined by a painful injury to her right hamstring during the heptathlon's 200-meter run at Tokyo's 1991 World Championships, a resolute Joyner-Kersee worked her way back into top form, taking the gold for the heptathlon and the bronze for the long jump at the following year's Olympic Games at Barcelona.

Joyner-Kersee set the U.S. record for indoor 50 hurdles before losing the heptathlon event at the Olympics for the first time in her career in 1996. Despite the recurrent hamstring injury that forced her to withdraw from the event, she still managed to win the Olympic bronze in the long jump while in Atlanta. She also renewed her love affair with basketball, joining the Richmond, Virginia, Rage and playing in the newly formed American Basketball League for women.

Her performance at the 1998 Goodwill Games held in New York City would signal Joyner-Kersee's retirement from athletic competition. And what a performance it was. Ending the two-day, seven-event heptathlon with an outstanding performance in the 800-meters, she took the title with 7,291 points, breaking her own world's record set in 1986. Her Goodwill victory was Joyner-Kersee's 25th win out of the 36 multi-event competitions she had entered during her career. Retiring after an amazing career, Joyner-Kersee had plans to build a youth center in her native East St. Louis, and to begin raising a family with her husband.

—Pamela L. Shelton

FURTHER READING:

Harrington, Geri. *Jackie Joyner-Kersee.* New York, Chelsea House, 1995.

Johnson, Lindsey. *A Woman's Place Is Everywhere: Inspirational Profiles of Female Leaders.* New York, Master Media, 1994.

Joyner-Kersee, Jackie. *A Kind of Grace: The Autobiography of the World's Greatest Female Athlete.* New York, Warner, 1997.

Judas Priest

Rock band Judas Priest, originally British, gained national recognition in the United States in the 1980s. They were one of the first such groups to be associated exclusively with the term ''Heavy Metal'' and their onstage theatrics included motorcycle rides, pyrotechnics, and the wearing of leather outfits with chain and spike accessories. Their music evoked a dark fantasy world where rugged heroes wandered in ruined landscapes and defeated evil forces. A decade of hard rock was shaped by the image and message of Judas Priest, and their influence permeated to new forms of rock in the 1990s.

The band was officially formed in 1969 when the original British Invasion of groups such as the Beatles, the Rolling Stones, and the Yardbirds slowed down and made way for American rockers. The original members of Judas Priest hailed from Birmingham in the industrial midlands of England, where Black Sabbath and many other

Rob Halford of Judas Priest.

British hard rock groups got their start. Judas Priest's first American record release, 1977's ''Sin after Sin,'' gained them only a cult following in the United States, and it was not until their album *British Steel,* released in 1980, that the band received significant air play with the singles ''Living After Midnight'' and ''Breaking the Law''—loud and simple party anthems that showcased vocalist Rob Halford's alternately growling and screaming voice. 1982's ''Screamin' for Vengeance'' featured Judas Priest's typical mix of machismo and futuristic doom and was their largest success to date, while their throaty tribute to pride and revenge, ''You Got Another Thing Comin','' entered the pop charts and was the band's first successful video.

In 1985, Judas Priest was cited in a suit filed by Tipper Gore's Parental Music Resource Center as being influential in several highly publicized suicide pacts. The secret messages found in their songs ''Let's Be Dead'' and ''Do It'' were presented as evidence, and although no direct link was ever established, the case attests to Judas Priest's stature as a figurehead for the genre of Heavy Metal. The band survived this legal onslaught and several lineup shifts during the 1990s, continuing to release new work 30 years after their inception. Younger Heavy Metal groups expanded, diversified, and absorbed enough mainstream norms to sell records, but Judas Priest remained loud and angry, true to their roots.

Priest's formula for success—aggressive presentation, operatic screams, extended guitar solos, allusions to mythology and apocalypse—would be adopted and adapted by many other acts over the next decade. Their guitarists K.K. Downing and Glenn Tipton had long bleached hair; Halford had impressive biceps to match his clenched teeth, and rode his Harley-Davidson on stage as the last encore for each elaborate concert. They tapped into a mysterious suburban longing—young record-buying white males seemed particularly attuned to Judas Priest's territorial posing and violent fantasies. Judas Priest was one of the first Heavy Metal bands to expand successfully beyond the comfortable realm of mammoth concerts and album sales; they cracked the MTV market in an age where pop and new wave dominated the channel, and managed somehow to maintain a reputation as purists and outsiders even at the height of their commercial success. Grunge musicians of the next generation often mentioned Judas Priest as a primary influence, and ''Breakin' the Law'' found new cult life when MTV's *Beavis and Butthead* air-guitared regularly to the song in the 1990s. Rarely has a musical act so consistently and unabashedly typified a late twentieth-century style of musical expression.

—Colby Vargas

FURTHER READING:

Gett, Steve. *Judas Priest, Heavy Duty: The Official Biography.* Port Chester, New York, Cherry Lane Books, 1984.

''The Judas Priest Homepage.'' http:\www.judaspriest.com. April 1999.

Weinstein, Deena. *Heavy Metal: A Cultural Sociology.* Lexington, Lexington Books, 1991.

Judge

A flourishing weekly American humor magazine for close to sixty years, *Judge* was renowned during the 1920s for bringing a new generation of sophisticated humor writers and cartoonists to the attention of American readers, including S. J. Perelman, Theodor Seuss Geisel ("Dr. Seuss"), Ralph Barton, Johnny Gruelle, Ernie Bushmiller, and Harold Ross.

Judge was founded in New York City in 1881 and survived until 1939 in its initial run, offering a mix of jokes, short humor pieces, reviews, and gag cartoons. The humor magazines of the nineteenth century, unlike late twentieth-century publications such as *Mad* and *Cracked,* were aimed at grown-up readers and included topical and political observations as well as broad comedy and ethnic jokes. *Judge* was founded just five years after the appearance of one of its chief competitors, *Puck,* which, as one historian has pointed out, soon "shed its crude image—with jokes about minorities, slapstick humor, and puns—and became a sophisticated humor magazine with longer articles and more society and suburban subjects." Similar to *Puck* in form and content, *Judge* also owed something to Britain's well-established *Punch.* A key figure in the early development of *Judge* was cartoonist James Albert Wales, who left *Puck* to put together the group that launched the new magazine.

The next major humor weekly to come along was *Life,* which debuted in 1883. *Puck* folded in 1918, but *Judge* and *Life* remained rivals well into the 1930s. Though never quite as slick or sophisticated as *Life, Judge* managed to hold its own against its competitor, and by 1925 proclaimed "Larger circulation than any other humorous weekly in the world" on its covers. The man credited with boosting *Judge's* circulation over 100,000 was Norman Anthony, who became editor in 1923. He promoted the single-caption cartoon—as opposed to the traditional he-she type of earlier years-and with coming up with theme issues devoted to a specific topic, such as the Advertising Number, Celebrities Number, Radio Number, and College Number. Among the new contributors Anthony recruited for these issues were S. J. Perelman, "Dr. Seuss," and cartoonist Jefferson Machamer. Initially a cartoonist as well as a writer, Perelman contributed somewhat surreal cartoons as well as humor pieces and magazine parodies; his cartoons were always accompanied by a block of copy in the style that would later show up in his *New Yorker* pieces and in the nonsense dialogue he contributed to the Marx Brothers movies. Harold Ross, who later founded the *The New Yorker,* worked for Anthony briefly, and other eventual *New Yorker* contributors, such as Chon Day, Charles Addams, Gardner Rea, and Whitney Darrow, Jr., all did work for *Judge.* Other contributors included Milt Gross, Don Herold, William Gropper, Bill Holman (creator of *Smokey Stover*), Vernon Grant, and Ernie Bushmiller (creator of *Nancy*). *Judge's* theater critic in the 1920s and early 1930s was the formidable George Jean Nathan, and movie reviews were provided by Pare Lorentz, an acclaimed documentary filmmaker.

Anthony was lured away to *Life* in 1929 and was replaced as editor by John Shuttleworth. In 1931, Anthony created *Ballyhoo,* a much more raucous magazine that satirized advertising and many other icons of popular culture. *Life,* a monthly by that time and trying unsuccessfully to mimic *The New Yorker,* ended its run in 1936, selling its title to Henry Luce for his new picture weekly. By this time, *Judge* itself was a monthly, and for a time ran a cover line: "Including the humorous tradition and features of *Life.*" The magazine held on until 1939 before folding; it was revived twice, but never regained its earlier popularity.

—Ron Goulart

FURTHER READING:

Horn, Maurice, editor. *The World Encyclopedia of Cartoons.* New York, Chelsea House Publications, 1980.

Trachtenberg, Stanley, editor. *American Humorists, 1800-1950.* Detroit, Gale Research Company, 1982.

Judson, Arthur (1881-1975)

Between 1930 and 1950, Arthur Judson exerted unprecedented influence in the field of classical music in the United States, acting as unofficial chief advisor to the country's major symphony orchestras. The engagement of both conductors and soloists for symphony concerts depended, to an extraordinary degree, on his recommendations. Officially, Judson held dual positions as president of Columbia Concerts Corporation, the country's leading artists' management agency—which came to be known as "the Judson Empire"—and simultaneously managed the New York Philharmonic and Philadelphia orchestras. However, it was not only his powerful status that won the trust of orchestra boards, but his knowledge of music and his impeccable judgment of quality. To these virtues were added shrewd business sense, and an instinct for what would draw audiences. As artists' manager, he was known to represent only the finest musicians and, accordingly, won their confidence and loyalty. No one person since has taken control of classical music to the same extent as Arthur Judson.

—Milton Goldin

FURTHER READING:

Smith, Cecil. *Worlds of Music.* New York, Lippincott, 1952.

Judy Bolton

Judy Bolton was the protagonist of a popular girls mystery series. Unlike contemporary series produced by syndicates and ghost-writers using pseudonyms, the Judy Bolton series was created and written entirely by Margaret Sutton. Grosset & Dunlap initially published four volumes in 1932, then printed one per year through 1967 for a total of 38 volumes. Many of the stories were based on real events, sites, and Sutton's or her acquaintances' experiences. The books appealed to readers because Judy Bolton was more realistic than other series sleuths. Four million copies of Judy Bolton books sold before the series was canceled.

Sutton wrote her first books before the Nancy Drew series was published, but Grosset & Dunlap was not interested in her idea. Sutton was told how syndicate books were written, and she declined to write formulaic plots. Because of Nancy Drew's popularity, girl detective stories became marketable, and an editor at Grosset & Dunlap contacted Sutton about publishing the Judy Bolton tales. In 1932 *The Vanishing Shadow, The Haunted Attic, The Invisible Chimes,* and *Seven Strange Clues* were issued. More interested in literary craft than commercial success, Sutton's writing did not resemble the contents of mass marketed books sold in other series. Judy Bolton differed from other detective heroines in girls series books because she realistically grew up and was not frozen at a specific age. She was also concerned about social issues and sensitive to members of other socioeconomic classes and cultures. Judy chose her friends and cases because she was interested in those people and wanted to improve their living conditions. Although she was not as popular as Nancy Drew, she provided a stronger role model for readers.

In the first book, Judy, a doctor's daughter, was a red-haired, 15 year-old high school student living in northwestern Pennsylvania during the 1930s. Judy wanted to be a detective, explore the world, and solve problems, but her life remained ordinary, sometimes disappointing, and not spectacular like Nancy Drew's. In the series, Judy aged to 22 years old, graduated from high school and college, worked, married, and accepted adult responsibilities. This maturation did not limit her adventures or inquisitiveness and reinforced the reality of her stories unlike other series in which characters were static and artificial. Judy traveled and met new people, establishing relationships beyond her family. She confronted social issues and displayed tolerance and acceptance of others. Judy Bolton was also depicted as sometimes being outspoken, temperamental, and capable of making mistakes, causing her to appear more human to readers, who could identify with Judy more than with flawless detectives such as Nancy Drew. Judy relied on her intellect, not her appearance, and used her ability to surmount obstacles instead of counting on material goods or family connections like Nancy Drew. Judy persistently sought the truth with the help of her cat Blackberry, brother Horace, friend Honey, or romantic partner Peter Dobbs, a Federal Bureau of Investigation (FBI) agent who considered Judy his equal. They liked to solve mysteries together.

The Judy Bolton series successfully endured for three decades. Grosset & Dunlap canceled the series after number 38, *The Secret of the Sand Castle,* was published in 1967. Sutton believed that Grosset & Dunlap capitulated to pressure from the Stratemeyer Syndicate because Judy Bolton ranked second to Nancy Drew in sales. The monopolistic syndicate disliked competitors and discouraged Grosset & Dunlap from advertising and distributing series books. Sutton also claimed that the syndicate had stolen plots and titles from her books for their series. She had planned a thirty-ninth book, *The Strange Likeness,* set in the Panama Canal Zone where Judy gave birth to twins Peter and Pam.

Scholars have scrutinized the Judy Bolton books for themes and symbolism, praising the sound plots, thrilling pace, realism, and social commentary. Some critics have labeled Judy as a feminist who was an independent thinker; a confident, capable person who resented restrictions based on gender. They have identified such recurrent series themes as the problems of urbanization and the search for identity. Scholars stressed that Judy's encounters with stereotypes about ethnic and religious groups and awareness of class consciousness addressed timeless issues that would impact readers of all generations. Judy challenged prejudices and attempted to understand circumstances so that she could change them. The books provided commentary about child labor, unsafe work conditions, unemployment, and elitism. For example, Judy cleverly hosted a costume party so that members of different social classes did not know the identity of each other and mingled. Although the books never mentioned the Depression during which they were created, many of the mysteries were connected to economic conditions, situations, and motivations.

The Judy Bolton books were nostalgic collectibles for adult women. Marcia Muller, pioneering author of hard-boiled detective novels featuring the savvy female protagonist Sharon McCone, revealed that Judy Bolton was her favorite teenage girl detective because Judy seemed real and could speak for herself. Muller also

stated that the Judy Bolton mysteries were interesting and not improbable like other series. In 1985, author Kate Emberg and a group of collectors formed the Judy Bolton Society which published the *Judy Bolton Society Newsletter.* This group became the Society of Phantom Friends, named for the thirtieth volume in the series, and its newsletter, *The Whispered Watchword,* discussed Judy Bolton and other series books. Every summer the Margaret Sutton Weekend enabled fans to visit book sites. The Phantom Friends developed a friendship with Sutton and presented her their Life Achievement Award. Emberg wrote and published a new Judy Bolton, *The Whispering Belltower,* with Sutton's permission, and *The Talking Snowman* was co-written by Sutton and Linda Joy Singleton. Phantom Friends Melanie Knight, Rosemarie DiCristo, and Linda Tracy compiled the *Guide to Judy Bolton Country,* a comprehensive reference manual about all aspects, major and trivial, of the Judy Bolton books. Judy Bolton fans have also created internet sites about the popular character and the local school in Sutton's hometown painted a mural of Judy Bolton for an art and history project. Because the Judy Bolton series was out of print, Applewood Books and Aeonian Press published facsimile reprints in the 1990s. Avid collectors, including Sutton, continue to search for original volumes in used bookstores.

—Elizabeth D. Schafer

FURTHER READING:

Mason, Bobbie Ann. *The Girl Sleuth: A Feminist Guide.* Old Westbury, New York, The Feminist Press, 1975.

Juke Boxes

Automatic record players activated by putting a coin in them were one of the earliest methods of making money from Thomas Edison's phonograph invention. The juke box really came of age in the 1930s and 1940s when the Great Depression almost eliminated the sale of records to individuals and made the coin-slot record player an important source of musical entertainment. These machines brought specific kinds of music to the public and played a part in the ascent of swing and rock 'n' roll as mass movements of popular culture.

The failure to develop a long-playing record in the first half of the twentieth century put a premium on technology which could automate the process of playing several records one after the other. The first automatic record changer was patented in 1921, and it was followed by many different devices that could pick and play discs; some could even play both sides of a record.

The first coin-slot machine with electronic amplification and a multi-record changer was produced in 1927 by the Automatic Music Instrument Company. AMI was joined by J. P. Seeburg, Rudolph Wurlitzer, and the Rockola Manufacturing Company in devising coin-slot machines with advanced record-changing mechanisms that could select from 20 or 24 discs.

At the end of the 1920s, only around 50,000 of these machines were in use, but the repeal of Prohibition in 1933 brought about a dramatic change in social life as Americans flooded back to bars and clubs. No popular drinking establishment was without one. The name

An old-fashioned juke box.

juke box originated from the lingo of the South, where dancing or "jooking" to records was a popular pastime. Small drinking establishments with only recorded sound as their musical entertainment were called "juke joints." Here patrons would dance to blues or country music that they selected from the discs stored in the juke box. In the hedonistic atmosphere of these bars, loud dance music, comedy routines, and raunchy songs about sex were popular choices on the juke box. Dancing was a very important part of social life, and swing records on a juke box were the next best thing to attending (and paying for) a live concert. The juke box made the most of the technological development of amplification and loud speakers. It could project sound to every corner of a bar or soda fountain. The very loud volume of the playback made it possible to hear and dance to the music above the noise of a crowded bar. For listeners during the 1930s, juke boxes gave them the highest volume of sound reproduction outside the movie theater.

The Great Depression drastically cut back the sale of records, which many considered to be a luxury good. Radio became a major source of music in the home, but listeners still wanted to pick the music they wanted when they wanted to hear it. Instead of buying a record for a dollar they paid a nickel to hear it on a juke box. During the 1930s the number of juke boxes in use rose to a high of 500,000, and they could be found in taverns, pool halls, restaurants, hotels,

cafes, bus stations, and even beauty parlors. More than half of the nation's juke boxes were in the South. The store of records in the nation's juke boxes required changing every week, and by 1936 over half of all record production in the United States was destined for them. The demand for records for juke boxes provided valuable work for musicians during the Depression, especially for jazz and blues musicians, whose livelihoods were most threatened by the bad economic times. Many of the classic jazz and blues records of the 1930s were made for juke boxes.

The customers' choices of recordings provided valuable information in the marketing of recordings, and juke boxes were fitted with indicators that displayed to the operator which of the discs were the most popular. Returns from juke boxes were an important indicator of the growing popularity of rhythm and blues records in the 1940s and then rock 'n' roll in the 1950s. Independent record companies often had to resort to bribery to get juke box operators to use their records, and there were allegations made that this lucrative business was often in the hands of organized crime. In the postwar years juke boxes became larger and more ornate; the modernistic designs of Wurlitzer made the coin-slot machine stand out in a bar or restaurant. But the days of the juke box were numbered as a booming economy allowed consumers to buy their own records. Attempts to produce video juke boxes in the 1960s and 1970s were technically successful but could not return this machine to the dominant place in public entertainment it enjoyed in the 1930s and 1940s.

—Andre Millard

FURTHER READING:

Chapple, Steve, and Garofalo, Rebe. *Rock 'n' Roll Is Here to Pay.* Chicago, Nelson Hall, 1977.

Millard, Andre. *America on Record: A History of Recorded Sound.* New York, Cambridge University Press, 1995.

Sanjek, Russell. *American Popular Music and Its Business.* New York, Oxford University Press, 1988.

Julia

Debuting on NBC in September, 1968 *Julia* was the first network television series to star an African American in the leading role since *Amos 'n' Andy* and *Beulah* left the air in 1953. The gentle situation comedy featured Diahann Carroll as Julia Baker, a widowed black nurse with a six year-old son, Corey, living a thoroughly integrated lifestyle in a Los Angeles apartment building. Surrounded by whites, the Bakers encountered only the most innocuous instances of prejudice. The series reached the airwaves during a particularly incendiary moment in American race relations—the aftermath of Martin Luther King's assassination; a "long hot summer" of riots and burning in inner city ghettos, and rising Black Power militancy. Inevitably, the series, which ignored all these issues, stirred controversy. Julia was dismissed by some as a "white Negro" and the series was considered irrelevant, if not dangerous, especially because it featured no African American male characters of authority or narrative importance. On the other hand, the series was praised for opening doors to subsequent African American sitcoms and for demonstrating that American audiences, black and white, could enjoy non-stereotyped black characters on prime-time. After a successful three year run, *Julia* left the air in 1971.

—Aniko Bodroghkozy

FURTHER READING:

Bodroghkozy, Aniko. "'Is This What You Mean By Color TV?': Race, Gender, and Contested Meanings in *Julia.*" In *Private Screenings: Television and the Female Consumer,* edited by Lynn Spigel and Denise Mann. Minneapolis, University of Minnesota Press, 1992, 143-67.

Juliá, Raúl (1940-1994)

Raúl Juliá was a beloved stage and screen actor who was admired for his work on and off the screen. Due to his fine training and technique, he was one of the few Hispanic actors successful in transcending cultural stereotypes to win a diverse and interesting series of roles in Hollywood and abroad. Juliá broke onto the stage in New York in Hispanic community plays and through Joseph Papp's innovative casting in the New York Shakespeare Festival's production of *Macbeth* in 1966. He continued to appear in Shakespeare

Raúl Juliá

Festival productions, and made his Broadway debut in 1968. In the early 1970s, Juliá broke into film, the medium that led to his greatest popularity.

Born Raúl Carlos Juliá y Acelay in San Juan, Puerto Rico, on March 9, 1940, into a relatively well-off family, Juliá began acting in school plays and, while studying law at the University of Puerto Rico, continued devoting much time to amateur productions. Juliá moved to New York to study acting in 1964 and shortly thereafter made his stage debut in a Spanish-language production of Calderón de la Barca's classic *La vida es sueño (Life Is a Dream).* Soon, Juliá was performing in the Hispanic neighborhoods of the city in small theaters and in the open air.

In 1966, famed producer Joseph Papp gave Juliá his first break, disregarding Juliá's ethnicity and casting him in *Macbeth.* Juliá subsequently performed in a number of Papp plays, including Shakespeare's *Hamlet,* and Hispanic community theater in the late 1960s and early 1970s. Juliá went on to be cast in Broadway roles, to receive rave reviews and four Tony nominations for work in *The Two Gentlemen of Verona, Where's Charley, Threepenny Opera,* and *Nine.* His debut on Broadway was as the servant Chan in Jack Gelber's 1968 production of *The Cuban Thing.* A milestone in his career was the success of Papp's *Two Gentlemen of Verona* and Juliá's Tony-nominated portrayal of Porteus in this musical adaptation; the play moved from Central Park's Delacorte Theater to Broadway's St. James Theater.

During the 1980s and early 1990s, Juliá created a distinguished career as a film actor, playing a wide variety of roles from romantic detectives to evil villains. One of his most highly acclaimed parts was that of a revolutionary in the Academy Award-nominated *Kiss of the Spiderwoman* in 1985. Juliá also played some very popular offbeat roles in such highly commercial films as *The Addams Family* (1991) and its sequel, *Addams Family Values* (1993). Among his other noteworthy films are *The Eyes of Laura Mars* (1978), *One from the Heart* (1982), *Compromising Positions* (1985), *Tequila Sunrise* (1988), *Moon over Parador* (1988), *Tango Bar* (1988), *Romero* (1989), *The Rookie* (1990), and *Havana* (1990).

When not acting on stage or screen, Juliá made frequent appearances on *Sesame Street,* and donated his services to the Hunger Project, an international organization whose goal it is to eradicate hunger by the year 2000. Juliá also worked with Hispanic community organizations, most notably the Hispanic Organization of Actors (HOLA). He died of a massive stroke on October 24, 1994.

—Nicolás Kanellos

FURTHER READING:

Mortiz, Charles, editor. *Current Biography Yearbook.* New York, Wilson, 1982.

Stefoff, Rebecca. *Raul Julia.* New York, Chelsea House, 1994.

Tardiff, Joseph T., and L. Mpho Mabunda, editors. *Dictionary of Hispanic Biography.* Detroit, Gale, 1996.

Jurassic Park

Jurassic Park is the title of Michael Crichton's best-selling novel (1990) and its popular film adaptation by Steven Spielberg

A Tyrannosaurus Rex attacks in a scene from the film *Jurassic Park*.

(1993). In the story Jurassic Park is the name of the theme park placed on a tropical island where millionaire John Hammond plans to exhibit live dinosaurs created out of fossilized DNA. Following the technophobic discourse originally enunciated by Mary Shelley's novel *Frankenstein* (1818), Crichton and Spielberg narrate how, inevitably, the supposedly safe environment of the park collapses under the pressure of the dinosaurs' instincts. The attack of the dinosaurs turns an enjoyable inaugural tour of Jurassic Park into a nightmare for Hammonds' team, his family, and his guests, including prestigious scientists. *Jurassic Park* was followed by a less successful sequel, *The Lost World* (novel by Crichton, 1995; film by Spielberg, 1997). The plot focuses here on another island where the species of the park breed unchecked and on the efforts of another group led by Dr. Malcolm, a victimized guest in *Jurassic Park,* to stop the dinosaurs and the men who want to capture them for commercial purposes. *The Lost World* is, incidentally, a title that relates Crichton's and Spielberg's work to the fiction that originated the vogue for dinosaurs: Arthur Conan Doyle's novel *The Lost World* (1920) and its silent film adaptation by Willis O'Brien (1925).

Like *Frankenstein, Jurassic Park* examines the ethical dilemmas involved in using technoscience to create life out of dead matter. The targets of Crichton's criticism are the frivolous use that business may make of biotechnology and the lack of a proper control on

laboratories working with human and animal DNA. But Crichton is also concerned by the dependence of scientific research on business interests. This is shown in the relationship between the paleontologist Alan Grant, the main character in *Jurassic Park,* and Hammond. Hammond's funding of Grant's research places the principled scientist at the same level of dependence as his unprincipled colleagues. Ambitious young scientists and unscrupulous businessmen like John Hammond may form a lethal alliance leading to dangerous ventures like Jurassic Park and even to the extinction of human life on Earth. Dr. Malcolm, Crichton's spokesman in the novel, emphasizes the technophobic message when he protests that "there is no humility before nature. There is only a get-rich-quick, make-a-name-for-yourself-fast philosophy. Cheat, lie, falsify—it doesn't matter." In the novel version, the dinosaurs eventually kill both Hammond and Malcolm. Hammond's death is presented as an act of poetic justice. Malcolm's somehow unjust death proves the accuracy of his use of chaos theory, but also of Crichton's apocalyptic vision.

In Spielberg's *Jurassic Park,* Hammond and Malcolm survive, whereas the dinosaurs are destroyed. The grim moralizing of Crichton's cautionary tale and his introduction of chaos theory are thus significantly modified to make way for hope. Spielberg's happier ending even forced Crichton to ignore the death of Dr. Malcolm to make him reappear as the accidental hero of *The Lost World.* But beyond its hope for the future—and for a future sequel—Spielberg's film differs from Crichton's novel in an important aspect. The technophobic message of Crichton's novel has to compete for the spectators' attention with Spielberg's skilful use of special effects. The film's appeal is based on the celebration of the technology behind the animatronics (electronic puppetry designed by Stan Winston) and infographics (computer simulations developed by ILM) employed to represent the dinosaurs. By endorsing Spielberg's films, Crichton undermines his own message. The association of technology and business appears to have at least a positive outlet in the world of entertainment: film. But this is an ambiguous message. Spielberg's and Crichton's Midas' touch suggests that, should they decide to open the real Jurassic Park, people would flock to meet the dinosaurs—hopefully not to be devoured by them—thanks to, rather than despite, the novels and films. People do go, indeed, to the Universal Studios theme parks, where the fake dinosaurs of *Jurassic Park* can be seen.

Feminist writers like Marina Warner have criticized a problematic aspect of *Jurassic Park* (film and novel): the sex of the dinosaurs. They are all created female, so as to ensure that no natural reproduction takes place on the island, and also because, since all embryos are initially female, ''from a bioengineering standpoint, females are easier to breed,'' as Dr. Wu notes. The scientists refer, though, to giants like the Tyrannosaurus Rex as male. The irony that was not lost on feminist commentators is that the scientists of Jurassic Park also believe that females are easier to control. As the plot develops, this is proved radically wrong. After wreaking havoc on the island, some female dinosaurs mutate into males capable of starting sexual reproduction. This is presented by Crichton in ambiguous terms, as a symbol of life's unstoppable drive towards reproduction. The controversial theme of the female monster that threatens human life with uncontrolled reproduction is also the focus of films like *Aliens* (1986) and *Species* (1995). Godzilla, though, turns out to be a hermaphrodite in the eponymous 1998 film.

Dinosaurs are always popular with audiences of all ages, which helped *Jurassic Park* (novel and film) become an enormous hit. The popularity of these creatures is based on their unique status as monsters: they are threatening monsters of nightmare because of their enormous size, but also the fragile victims of a mysterious turn in the path of evolution. Dinosaurs send a clear Darwinian message to adult readers and spectators, inviting them to consider the thin threads on which human life depends. In *Jurassic Park* genetic engineering, rather than a freak of evolution, transforms the dinosaurs from relics of the prehistoric past into a threat for the future, akin to that of other monsters of science fiction, often extraterrestrial. Dinosaurs also make wonderful toys for children, as Spielberg and Universal Studios know well. But the true measure of *Jurassic Park*'s success can only be assessed by a glimpse into the future that lets us see whether the real Jurassic Park will ever open.

—Sara Martin

FURTHER READING:

Blanco, Adolfo. *Cinesaurios*. Barcelona, Royal Books, 1993.

Brode, Douglas. *The Films of Steven Spielberg*. New York, Citadel Press, 1995.

Cohen, Daniel. *Hollywood Dinosaur*. New York, Pocket Books, 1997.

Kinnard, Roy. *Beasts and Behemoths: Prehistoric Creatures in the Movies*. Metuchen, New Jersey, The Scarecrow Press, 1988.

Perry, George. *Steven Spielberg: Close Up; A Making of His Movies*. Thunder's Mouth Press, 1998

Warner, Marina. ''Monstrous Mothers: Women over the Top.'' *Managing Monsters: Six Myths of Our Time*. London, Vintage, 1994, 1-16.

Juvenile Delinquency

This term refers to lawbreaking by minors, including status offenses such as truancy, homelessness, and being unsupervised by a suitable adult guardian. The term appeared first after the Civil War when criminologists and social reformers called attention to the poverty, disease, crime, and inadequate home life in urban, often immigrant, communities. Jane Addams, Robert Woods, Florence Kelley, and other settlement house leaders in the 1890s lobbied state legislators and private and public charities to eliminate juvenile delinquency by eradicating these social problems. They proposed new school attendance, public health and safety laws to protect children. Activists concerned with assisting troubled youth founded recreational organizations (such as the Boy Scouts and Girl Scouts), team sports, sunday schools, juvenile courts, pediatric medical clinics, and the field of child psychology during the early twentieth century.

Sociologists and criminologists, many from the University of Chicago, argued that delinquents were a byproduct of poverty, since statistics seemed to indicate that the incidence of crime increased with unemployment. Later studies attributed delinquency to a wide range of environmental conditions associated with poverty: overcrowded, slum-like dwellings, a low level sanitation, and inadequate recreation. By the 1920s the Harvard Law School Crime Survey supported this view, particularly according to research conducted by Sheldon and Eleanor Glueck. They used an interdisciplinary approach for a multiple-factor theory of juvenile delinquency. The evidence they gathered pointed to the quality of a child's family life as the most important factor criminal behavior. Recidivism rates were high among juvenile delinquents despite professional intervention. However, after 1950 most sociologists blamed delinquency on individual or family dysfunction rather than low social or economic class.

Adolescent gang wars, although not unheard of in the nineteenth century, became a national concern after World War I and more so after World War II. Many urban streets and parks were unsafe. Despite greater police patrols and an expansion of state reform schools for delinquents, juvenile delinquents continued to avoid school and loiter and make trouble in public spaces. Churches and social workers developed summer camps and other recreation programs to control the problem. They also initiated foster home services. American psychologist G. Stanley Hall, who coined the term adolescence in 1901, advocated the scientific study of juvenile delinquency. The British-American psychiatrist William Healy, the first child psychiatrist in the United States, pioneered diagnosis of emotionally disturbed children in Chicago (1900) and Boston (1917). He and his wife, Augusta Fox Bronner, trained a new generation of social workers, psychologists, and probation officers to treat young offenders.

During the Great Depression, Hollywood recognized juvenile delinquency as an important urban problem that rendered great material for movie plots. Some of the films that grew out of this recognition were as *Angels With Dirty Faces* (1938), *Boys Town* (1938), *Crime School* (1938), and *They Made Me A Criminal* (1939). *Rebel Without a Cause* (1955) was centered around alienation felt by middleclass, suburban teenagers. *West Side Story* (1961), a film adaptation of the landmark Broadway musical by Leonard Bernstein, was a modern revision of Shakespeare's Romeo and Juliet, featuring gangs in New York City in the 1950s in lieu of the two feuding families. *Blackboard Jungle* (1955), the first film to feature rock 'n' roll music, showed the harrowing experience public school teachers encountered in a New York City high school in the 1950s. The treatment of rebellious middleclass adolescents in modern psychiatric centers was depicted in *Born Innocent* (1974). In contrast, *Boyz N the Hood* (1991) portrayed senseless violence and drug abuse in South Central Los Angeles black teenage gangs.

Juvenile delinquency remained a serious social and legal problem into the late twentieth century. Many conservative activists and scholars proposed that is was exacerbated by the 1960s sexual revolution and excessive drug use. Some criminologists reported that most criminal behavior was perpetrated by unemployed young male, and later included female, delinquents. By the close of the twentieth century youthful criminal offenders continued to frustrate the population, particularly law enforcement and educational professionals and the victims of juvenile criminal conduct.

—Peter C. Holloran

FURTHER READING:

Bartollas, Clemens. *Juvenile Delinquency.* New York, Wiley, 1985.

Glueck, Sheldon, and Eleanor T. Glueck. *One Thousand Juvenile Delinquents.* Cambridge, Harvard University Press, 1934.

Hawes, Joseph. *Children in Urban Society.* New York, Oxford University Press, 1971.

Holloran, Peter C. *Boston's Wayward Children: Social Services for Homeless Children, 1830-1930.* Boston, Northeastern University Press, 1984.

Sandhu, Harjit S. *Juvenile Delinquency: Causes, Control, and Prevention.* New York, McGraw-Hill, 1977.